D0593417

84th Congress, 2nd Session - - - - - House Document No. 477, Vol. XVIII

Foreign Relations of the United States, 1955–1957

Volume XVIII

Africa

Editor in Chief John P. Glennon

Editor Stanley Shaloff

United States Government Printing Office
Washington
1989

DEPARTMENT OF STATE PUBLICATION 9683

Office of the Historian

Bureau of Public Affairs

For sale by the Superintendent of Documents, U.S. Government Printing Office
Washington, D.C. 20402

Preface

The publication *Foreign Relations of the United States* constitutes the official record of the foreign policy of the United States. The volumes in the series include, subject to necessary security considerations, all documents needed to give a comprehensive record of the major foreign policy decisions of the United States together with appropriate materials concerning the facts which contributed to the formulation of policies. Documents in the files of the Department of State are supplemented by papers from other government agencies involved in the formulation of foreign policy.

The basic documentary diplomatic record printed in the volumes of the series *Foreign Relations of the United States* is edited by the Office of the Historian, Bureau of Public Affairs, Department of State. The editing is guided by the principles of historical objectivity and in accordance with the following official guidance first promulgated by Secretary of State Frank B. Kellogg on March 26, 1925.

There may be no alteration of the text, no deletions without indicating where in the text the deletion is made, and no omission of facts which were of major importance in reaching a decision. Nothing may be omitted for the purpose of concealing or glossing over what might be regarded by some as a defect of policy. However, certain omissions of documents are permissible for the following reasons:

a. To avoid publication of matters which would tend to impede current diplomatic negotiations or other business.

b. To condense the record and avoid repetition of needless details.

c. To preserve the confidence reposed in the Department by individuals and by foreign governments.

d. To avoid giving needless offense to other nationalities or individuals.

e. To eliminate personal opinions presented in despatches and not acted upon by the Department. To this consideration there is one qualification—in connection with major decisions it is desirable, where possible, to show the alternative presented to the Department before the decision was made.

Documents selected for publication in the *Foreign Relations* volumes are referred to the Department of State Classification/ Declassification Center for declassification clearance. The Center reviews the documents, makes declassification decisions, and obtains the clearance of geographic and functional bureaus of the Department of State, as well as of other appropriate agencies of the government.

The Center, in coordination with geographic bureaus of the Department of State, conducts communications with foreign governments regarding documents or information of those governments proposed for inclusion in *Foreign Relations* volumes.

Stanley Shaloff compiled this volume under the supervision of M. Paul Claussen. John P. Glennon directed final preparation of the volume with the assistance of Harriet D. Schwar. Rita M. Baker performed the technical editing. Max Franke prepared the index.

William Z. Slany
The Historian
Bureau of Public Affairs

Contents

List of Unpublished Sources

Department of State

1. *Indexed Central Files.* Papers in the indexed central files of the Department for the years 1955–1957 are indicated by a decimal file number in the first footnote. The following are among the most useful of these files: 032, 033.1100, 033.45J11, 110.11–DU, 120.1580, 122.536H2, 122.536H3, 320, 350, 511.55A3, 611.51, 611.51S, 611.70, 645K.60, 645K.61, 661.76, 670.901, 711.56371, 711.56371A, 711.5855A, 745K.00, 745K.02, 751S.00, 770.00, 771.00, 772.56, 773.5–MSP, 775.11, 775.5–MSP, 775.5622, 776.11, 811.05145J, 845J.00–TA, 845J.411, 855A.453, 870.00.

2. *Lot Files.* Documents from the central files have been supplemented by lot files of the Department, which are decentralized files created by operating areas. A list of the lot files used in or consulted for this volume follows:

AF Files: Lot 58 D 562

Files on South Africa, British East Africa, the Central African Federation, and Mozambique for the years 1943–1955, as maintained by the Office of African Affairs.

AF Files: Lot 58 D 627

General subject files on Africa and British East Africa for the years 1948–1956, as maintained by the Office of African Affairs.

AF/AFE Files: Lot 62 D 417

Subject files for the Union of South Africa for the period 1956–1957, as maintained by the Office of African Affairs and later by the Office of Southern Africa Affairs.

AF/AFE Files: Lot 64 D 358

Political subject files on South Africa and South West Africa for the years 1958–1959, as maintained by the Office of African Affairs and later by the Office of Southern Africa Affairs.

AF/AFI Files: Lot 62 D 406

Political/military files for the years 1951–1960, as maintained by the Politico-Military Adviser of the Office of African Affairs, later the Bureau of African Affairs.

AF/AFN Files: Lot 60 D 577

Moroccan Desk files for the years 1941–1957, as maintained by the Office of African Affairs and later by the Office of Northern Africa Affairs.

AF/AFN Files: Lot 63 D 250

Subject files on Morocco for the years 1956–1962, as maintained by the Office of Northern Africa Affairs.

AF/AFNE Files: Lot 67 D 226

Political and defense files on Ethiopia for the years 1950–1962, as maintained by the Officer in Charge of Northeast African Affairs.

AF/AFS Files: Lot 59 D 293

Regional and technical assistance files for the years 1955–1957, as maintained by the Officer in Charge of Economic Affairs in the Office of African Affairs, later the Office of Southern Africa Affairs.

AF/AFS Files: Lot 60 D 37

Memoranda and correspondence on Central and Southern Africa for the year 1957, as maintained by the Office of Southern Africa Affairs.

Conference Files: Lot 59 D 95

Collection of documentation on official visits by ranking foreign officials, and on major international conferences attended by the Secretary of State, for the years 1949–1955, as maintained by the Executive Secretariat.

Conference Files: Lot 60 D 627

Collection of documentation on visits to the United States by ranking foreign officials, and on major international conferences attended by the Secretary of State for the years 1953–1955, as maintained by the Executive Secretariat.

Conference Files: Lot 62 D 181

Collection of documentation on visits to the United States by ranking foreign officials, and on major conferences attended by the Secretary of State for the years 1956–1958, as maintained by the Executive Secretariat.

Conference Files: Lot 63 D 123

Collection of documentation on visits to the United States by ranking foreign officials and on major international conferences attended by the Secretary of State for the years 1955–1958, as maintained by the Executive Secretariat.

INR–NIE Files

Files retained by the Bureau of Intelligence and Research.

IO Files: Lot 60 D 113

Files of the Assistant Secretary of State for International Organizations Affairs for the years 1955–1957.

IO/ODA Files: Lot 62 D 225

Master subject and country files of the Office of Dependent Area Affairs for the years 1953–1959.

NEA Files: Lot 57 D 616

Files of the Richards Mission to the Middle East, including general country and subject files, briefing books, and reports to the President and Congress, for the period November 1956–August 1957, as maintained by the Office of Near Eastern, South Asian, and African Affairs.

OCB Files: Lot 62 D 430

Master files of the Operations Coordinating Board for the years 1953–1960, as maintained by the Executive Secretariat.

PPS Files: Lot 66 D 70

Policy Planning Staff subject, country, and chronological files for the year 1955.

PPS Files: Lot 66 D 487

Policy Planning Staff subject, country, and chronological files for the year 1956.

PPS Files: Lot 67 D 548

Policy Planning Staff subject, country, and chronological files for the years 1957–1961.

Presidential Correspondence: Lot 64 D 174

Correspondence between President Eisenhower and heads of foreign governments for the years 1953–1960, as maintained by the Executive Secretariat.

Presidential Correspondence: Lot 66 D 204

Exchanges of correspondence between the President and heads of foreign governments for the years 1953–1964, as maintained by the Executive Secretariat.

Secretary's Memoranda of Conversation: Lot 64 D 199

Chronological collection of the Secretary of State's memoranda of conversation for the years 1953–1960, as maintained by the Executive Secretariat.

S/P–NSC Files: Lot 62 D 1

Serial and subject master file of National Security Council documents and correspondence for the years 1948–1961, as maintained by the Policy Planning Staff.

S/S–NSC Files: Lot 63 D 351

Serial master file of National Security Council documents and correspondence, and related Department of State memoranda for the years 1947–1961, as maintained by the Executive Secretariat.

S/S–NSC (Miscellaneous) Files: Lot 66 D 95

Administrative and miscellaneous National Security Council documentation, including NSC Records of Action, for the years 1947–1963, as maintained by the Executive Secretariat.

WE Files: Lot 58 D 90

Political files on French domestic politics and colonial affairs for the years 1943–1957, as maintained by the Office of Western European Affairs.

Dwight D. Eisenhower Library, Abilene, Kansas

Dulles Papers

Records of John Foster Dulles, 1952–1959.

Whitman File

Papers of Dwight D. Eisenhower as President of the United States, 1953–1961, maintained by his personal secretary, Ann C. Whitman. The Whitman File includes the following elements: the Name Series, the Dulles–Herter Series, Eisenhower (DDE) Diaries, Ann Whitman (ACW) Diaries, National Security Council Records, Miscellaneous Records, Cabinet Papers, Legislative Meetings, International Meetings, the Administration Series, and the International File.

National Archives and Records Administration, Washington, D.C.

JCS Records

National Archives Record Group 218, Records of the Joint Chiefs of Staff and the Chairman of the Joint Chiefs of Staff.

Washington National Records Center, Suitland, Maryland

ICA Director's File: FRC 61 A 32

ICA Director's subject file containing correspondence, memoranda, reports, messages, and other material for the years 1955–1958.

ICA Message Files: FRC 57 A 248

Telegrams and airgrams to and from all field missions from July 1, 1955, to June 30, 1956, as maintained by ICA headquarters in Washington.

List of Abbreviations

AA, Administering Authority
ABAKs, Alliance des Bakings
ACLU, Arab Confederation of Labor Unions
AC&W, Aircraft Control and Warning System
ADCC, Air Defense Control Center
AEC, Atomic Energy Commission
AF, Office of African Affairs, Department of State
AFN, Office of Northern Africa Affairs, Department of State
AFS, Office of Southern Africa Affairs, Department of State
AFIS, Amministrazione Fiduciaria Italiana della Somalia
AFL–CIO, American Federation of Labor–Congress of Industrial Organizations
AFP, Agence France Presse
AID, Agency for International Development
AmEmb, American Embassy
ANC, African National Congress
AOF, Afrique Occidentale Française
ARA, Bureau of Inter–American Affairs, Department of State
AvGas, Aviation Gas
B.C.A. Fed, British Central African Federation
BNA, Office of British Commonwealth and Northern European Affairs, Department of State
BP, Baghdad Pact
C, Counselor of the Department of State
CA, Office of Chinese Affairs, Department of State; Constituent Assembly; circular airgram
CARE, Cooperative for American Remittances to Everywhere
CCTA, Consultative Committee for Technical Assistance in Africa
CFEP, Council on Foreign Economic Policy
CGT, Confédération Générale du Travail
ChiCom, Chinese Communist
CIA, Central Intelligence Agency
C.I.D., Criminal Investigation Department
CINCEUR, Commander in Chief, United States Forces, Europe
CINCNELM, Commander in Chief, United States Naval Forces, Eastern Atlantic and Mediterranean
CINCSOUTH, Commander in Chief, Allied Forces, Southern Europe
CINCUSAFE, Commander in Chief, United States, Air Force, Europe
CIO, Congress of Industrial Organizations
cirtel, circular telegram
Cominform, Communist Information Bureau
CNO, Chief of Naval Operations
CO, Commanding Officer
Comdr, Commander
COMNAVACTS, Commander of Naval Activities
ConGen, Consulate General
CP, Communist Party
CPAO, Chief Public Affairs Officer
CPI, Communist Party of India
CPP, Convention People's Party (Gold Coast)
CRO, Commonwealth Relations Office
CRS, Compagnie républicaines de sécurité
DCM, Deputy Chief of Mission
DEF/ISA, Office of the Assistant Secretary of Defense for International Security Affairs

Delga, series indictor for telegrams from the United States delegation to the United Nations General Assembly
Depcirtel, Department of State circular telegram
Deptel, Department of State telegram
desp, despatch
DFS, Direct Forces Support
DLF, Development Loan Fund
DNI, Director of Naval Intelligence
DOD, Department of Defense
DOT's, Dependent Overseas Territories
DRN, Division of Research for the Near East, South Asia, and Africa, Department of State
DS, Defense Support
Dulte, series indicator for personal telegrams from Secretary of State Dulles while away from Washington
E, Bureau of Economic Affairs, Department of State
ECA, Economic Cooperation Administration
ED, Economic Development Division, Bureau of Economic Affairs, Department of State
EDAC, Economic Defense Advisory Committee
EDC, European Defense Community
EE, Ofice of Eastern European Affairs, Department of State
Embdes, Embassy despatch
Embdesp, Embassy despatch
Embtel, Embassy telegram
ESS, Egypt, Saudi, Syria Pact
E.S.T., Eastern Standard Time
ETA, estimated time of arrival
EUCOM, European Command
EUR, Bureau of European Affairs, Department of State
EUR/WE, Office of Western European Affairs, Department of State
Euratom, European Atomic Energy Community
EXIM, Export–Import Bank of Washington
Eximbank, Export–Import Bank of Washington
FAMA, Foundation for Mutual Assistance in Africa
FBI, Federal Bureau of Investigation
FBO, Office of Foreign Buildings, Department of State
FCN, Treaty of Friendship, Commerce, and Navigation
FE, Bureau of Far Eastern Affairs, Department of State
FEA, French Equatorial Africa
FLN, Front de Libération Nationale
FOA, Foreign Operations Administration
FOA/W, Foreign Operations Administration/Washington
FonMin, Foreign Minister, Ministry
FonOff, Foreign Office
FonSec, Foreign Secretary
FWA, French West Africa
FY, Fiscal Year
FYI, for your information
G, Office of the Deputy Under Secretary of State
GA, United Nations General Assembly
Gadel, series indicator for telegrams to the United States delegation to the United Nations General Assembly
GARIOA, Government and Relief in Occupied Areas
GG, Governor General
GOA, Government of Afghanistan
GOC, Government of Ceylon
GOF, Government of France
GOI, Government of India
GOI, Government of Italy
GOL, Government of Liberia
GOL, Government of Libya
GOM, Government of Morocco
GOP, Government of Pakistan
GOT, Government of Tunisia
GRC, Government of the Republic of China
H, Assistant Secretary of State for Congressional Relations
H. Con. Res., House of Representatives concurrent resolution
HICOM, High Commission, Commissioner
H.J. Res., House of Representatives Joint Resolution
HM, His (Her) Majesty
HMG, His (Her) Majesty's Government
HQ, Headquarters
HVA, Helmand Valley Authority
IAC, Intelligence Advisory Committee
IBRD, International Bank for Reconstruction and Development
ICA, International Cooperation Administration

ICA/W, International Cooperation Administration, Washington
Icato, series indicator for telegrams from the International Cooperation Administration in Washington to the missions abroad
ICFTU, International Confederaton of Free Trade Unions
ICJ, International Court of Justice
ICS, Indian Civil Service
ICU, Industrial and Commercial Workers Union
IEG, Imperial Ethiopian Government
IES, International Educational Exchange Service
ILO, International Labor Organiztion
IMF, International Monetary Fund
INR, Bureau of Intelligence and Research, Department of State
instr, instruction
IO, Bureau of International Organization Affairs, Department of State
IPU, Inter-Parliamentary Union
IRBM, intermediate-range ballistic missile
IRR, Institute of Race Relations
ISA, Office of the Assistant Secretary of Defense for International Security Affairs
JAS, Joint Administration Service
JCS, Joint Chiefs of Staff
K.C.M.G., Knight Commander of the Order of Saint Michael and Saint George
L, Office of the Legal Adviser, Department of State
L/E, Assistant Legal Adviser for Economic Affairs, Department of State
L/EUR, Assistant Legal Adviser for European Affairs, Department of State
L/MSA, Assistant Legal Adviser for Mutual Security Affairs, Depatment of State
L/SFP, Assistant Legal Adviser for Special Functional Problems, Department of State
L/UNA, Assistant Legal Adviser for United Nations Affairs, Department of State
LA, Latin America
LAJAS, Libyan-American Joint Service
LARC, Libyan-American Reconstruction Commission
LPDSA, Libyan Public Development and Stabilization Agency
MA, Military Attaché
MAAG, Military Assistance Advisory Group
MAP, Military Assistance Program
MATS, Military Air Transport Service
MDA, Mutual Defense Assistance
MDAP, Mutual Defense Assistance Program
MDS, Mutual Defense Security (Act)
ME, Middle East
MEA, Ministry of External Affairs
MEDO, Middle East Defense Organization
memcon, memorandum of conversation
MEP, Mahajana Eksath Peramuna Coalition, Ceylon
MKA, Morrison-Knudsen Corporation, Afghanistan
MNA, Mouvement National Algérien
MS, Mutual Security
MSA, Mutual Security Agency/Act/Agreement
msg, message
msn, mission
MSP, Mutual Security Program
MTLD, Triumph of Democratic Liberties Party (Mouvement pour le Triomphe des Libertés Démocratiques)
mytel, my telegram
NAC, National Advisory Council on International Monetary and Financial Problems; North Atlantic Council
NATO, North Atlantic Treaty Organization
NCNC, National Council of Nigeria and the Cameroons
NE, Near East; Office of Near Eastern Affairs, Department of State
NEA, Bureau of Near Eastern, South Asian, and African Affairs, Department of State
NEA/EX, Office of the Executive Director of the Bureau of Near Eastern, South Asian, and African Affairs, Department of State
NEA/P, Public Affairs Adviser, Bureau of Near Eastern, South Asian, and African Affairs, Department of State
NESA, Office of Near Eastern, South Asian, and African Affairs, Office of the Assistant Secretary of Defense for International Security Affairs

niact, night action, communications indicator requiring attention by the recipient at any hour of the day or night
NIE, National Intelligence Estimate
NSC, National Security Council
NSGT's, Non-Self-Governing Territories
NUP, National Unionist Party
NWC, National War College
NWFP, North West Frontier Province of Pakistan
NYT, *New York Times*
OASD/ISA, Office of the Assistant Secretary of Defense for International Security Affairs
OCB, Operations Coordinating Board
ODA, Office of Dependent Area Affairs, Department of State
OFD, Office of International Financial and Development Affairs, Bureau of Economic Affairs, Department of State
OIR, Office of Intelligence Research, Department of State
OSD, Office of the Secretary of Defense
OSP, offshore procurement
PAA, Pan American Airlines
PAF, Pakistani Air Force
Pak, Pakistan
PAO, Public Affairs Officer
PDP, Peoples Democratic Party
PF, Pakistani Forces
P.L., Public Law
PM, Prime Minister
POL, petroleum, oil, lubricants
PolAd, Political Adviser
PRC, People's Republic of China
PSA, Office of Philippines and Southeast Asian Affairs, Department of State
PTP, Togolese Progress Party (Parti Togolais du progrès)
PTT, post, telegraph, and telephone
R, Office of the Special Assistant for Intelligence, Department of State
RA, Office of European Regional Affairs, Department of State
RCA, Radio Corporation of America
RDA, Rassemblement Démocratique Africain
REA, Office of Inter-American Regional Economic Affairs, Bureau of Inter-American Affairs, Department of State
refdesp, reference despatch
reftel, reference telegram
RGA, Royal Government of Afghanistan
RILU, Reformed Industrial and Commercial Workers' Union
S/AE, Special Assistant to the Secretary of State for Atomic Energy Affairs
S/MSA, Special Assistant to the Secretary of State for Mutual Security Affairs
S/P, Policy Planning Staff, Department of State
S/S, Executive Secretariat, Department of State
S/S-RO, Reports and Operational Staff, Executive Secretariat, Department of State
SA, South Africa
SABC, South African Broadcasting Corporation
SABRA, South Arican Bureau for Racial Affairs
SAC, Strategic Air Command
SACEUR, Supreme Allied Commander, Europe
SAS, Sections Administratives Specialisées
SC, United Nations Security Council
SEA, Southeast Asia
SEATO, Southeast Asian Treaty Organization
SecDef, Secretary of Defense
Secto, series indicator for telegrams to the Department of State from the Secretary of State (or his delegation) at international conferences
SFIO, Section Française de l'Internationale Ouvrière
SHAPE, Supreme Headquarters, Allied Powers, Europe
SNIE, Special National Intelligence Estimate
SOA, Office of South Asian Affairs, Department of State
SOF, status of forces
S.Res., Senate resolution
SYG, United Nations Secretary-General
SYL, Somali Youth League
TA, technical assistance
TAA, Tanganyikan African Association
TAC, Tactical Air Command
TANU, Tanganyika African National Union
TC, Trusteeship Council; technical cooperation

TCA, Technical Cooperation Administration
TCM, Technical Cooperation Mission
Tedul, series indicator for personal telegrams to Secretary of State Dulles while away from Washington
TIAS, Treaties and Other International Acts Series
Toica, series indicator for telegrams to the International Cooperation Administration in Washington from its missions abroad
Tosec, series indicator for telegrams from the Department of State to the Secretary of State (or his delegation) at international conferences
TS, Top Secret
TUC, Trade Union Congress
TWA, Trans World Airlines, Inc.
U, Office of the Under Secretary of State
U/MSA, Special Assistant for Mutual Security Affairs, Office of the Under Secretary of State
UDMA, Union Démocratique du Manifeste Algérien
UGTA, Union Générale des Travailleurs Algériens
UK, United Kingdom
UMT, Union Morocaine du Travail
UN, United Nations
UNCIP, United Nations Commission for India and Pakistan
UNGA, United Nations General Assembly
UNICEF, United Nations International Children's Emergency Fund
unn, unnumbered
UNO, United Nations Organization
UNP, Office of United Nations Political and Security Affairs, Department of State
UNSC, United Nations Security Council
UP, United Press
UPC, Union des Populations Camerounaises
UPNA, Uniao das Populacoes de Norte de Angola
urtel, your telegram
USA, United States Army
USAF, United States Air Force
USAFE, United States Air Force, Europe
USBA, Union Syndical des Bases Americains
USCINCEUR, United States Commander in Chief, Europe
USDel, United States Delegation
USDelUN, United States Delegation to the United Nations
Usfoto, series indicator for telegrams and airgrams from the Foreign Operations Administration to its missions abroad
USG, United States Government
USIA, United States Information Agency
USIS, United States Information Service
USLO, United States Liaison Office
USN, United States Navy
USOM, United States Operations Mission
USOM/L, United States Operations Mission, London
USSR, Union of Soviet Socialist Republics
UST, *United States Treaties and Other International Agreements*
USTA, Union Syndicale des Travailleurs Algériens
USUN, United States Mission at the United Nations
VOA, Voice of America
VP, Vice President
WAAC, West African Airways Corporation
WE, Office of Western European Affairs, Department of State
Weeka, weekly interagency summary analysis from United States diplomatic missions
WFTU, World Federation of Trade Unions

List of Persons

Achilles, Theodore C., Minister at the Embassy in France to May 1956; Ambassador to Peru from July 1956

Aklilou Abte Wolde. *See* Habtewold.

Aldrich, Winthrop W., Ambassador to the United Kingdom to February 1957

Alger, Frederick M., Jr., Ambassador to Belgium to March 1957

Allen, George V., Assistant Secretary of State for Near Eastern, South Asian, and African Affairs, January 1955–August 1956; Ambassador to Greece, October 1956–November 1957; Director of the U.S. Information Agency from November 1957

Alphand, Hervé, French Representative at the United Nations, June 1955–September 1956; thereafter Ambassador to the United States

Ammar, Tahar Ben, Tunisian Prime Minister to April 1956

Balafrej, Ahmed, Moroccan Foreign Minister from May 1956

Barco, James W., Senior Adviser on Political and Security Council Affairs at the Mission at the United Nations to June 1955; thereafter Counselor of the Mission

Barnes, Robert G., Director of the Executive Secretariat, Department of State, August 1955–May 1956; thereafter Special Assistant to the Under Secretary of State for Mutual Security Affairs

Bliss, Don C., Ambassador to Ethiopia from June 1957

Bourgès-Maunoury, Maurice, French Minister of the Armed Forces, January–February 1955; Minister of the Interior, February 1955–January 1956; Defense Minister, January 1956–June 1957; Prime Minister, June–October 1957; thereafter Minister of the Interior

Bourguiba, Habib, Tunisian Prime Minister, from April 1956; President from July 1957

Brundage, Percival F., Deputy Director of the Bureau of the Budget to April 1956; thereafter Director

Bulganin, Nikolai Aleksandrovich, Chairman of the Council of Ministers and Member of the Presidium of the Communist Party of the Soviet Union from February 1955

Byroade, Henry A., Assistant Secretary of State for Near Eastern, South Asian, and African Affairs to January 1955; Ambassador to Egypt, March 1955–September 1956; Ambassador to South Africa from October 1956

Cabell, Lieutenant General Charles P., USAF, Deputy Director of Central Intelligence

Caccia, Sir Harold A., British Deputy Under Secretary of State for Foreign Affairs to November 1956; thereafter Ambassador to the United States

Cannon, Cavendish W., Ambassador to Greece to July 1956; Ambassador to Morocco from October 1956

Clark, Lewis, Consul General at Algiers
Couve de Murville, Maurice, French Ambassador to the United States to July 1956; thereafter Ambassador to the Federal Republic of Germany
Cutler, Robert L., Special Assistant to President Eisenhower for National Security Affairs to April 1955 and from January 1957
Cyr, Leo G., Deputy Director of the Office of African Affairs to February 1955; Director, February 1955–October 1956; Director of the Office of Northern Africa Affairs, October 1956–June 1957; Consul at Tangier, June–August 1957; thereafter Consul General

de Margerie. *See* Jacquin de Margerie
Deressa, Yilma, Ethiopian Ambassador to the United States; Foreign Minister from April 1957
Dillon, C. Douglas, Ambassador to France to January 1957; Deputy Under Secretary of State for Economic Affairs from March 1957
Dulles, Allen W., Director of Central Intelligence
Dulles, John Foster, Secretary of State

Eden, Sir Anthony, British Secretary of State for Foreign Affairs to April 1955; Prime Minister, April 1955–January 1957
Eisenhower, Dwight D., President of the United States
Elbrick, C. Burke, General Deputy Assistant Secretary of State for European Affairs to February 1957; thereafter Assistant Secretary of State for European Affairs
Ely, General Paul H.R., French Commissioner–General and Commander of the French Forces in Indochina to May 1955; thereafter Chief of the Army General Staff

Faure, Edgar Jean, French Foreign Minister, January–February 1955; Prime Minister, February 1955–January 1956
Faure, Maurice, French Secretary of State for Foreign Affairs from January 1956; also Secretary of State for Moroccan and Tunisian Affairs, November 1956–June 1957
Ferguson, C. Vaughan, Jr., Consul General at Dakar to October 1955; Consul General at Tangier, October 1955–May 1957; thereafter Director of the Office of Southern Africa Affairs, Department of State
Flake, Wilson C., Counselor of Embassy in South Africa to July 1955; Counselor of Embassy in Italy, August 1955–May 1957; Ambassador to Ghana from June 1957

Gaillard, Felix, French Minister of Finance, June 1957–November 1957; thereafter Prime Minister
Gerig, O. Benjamin, Deputy Representative to the United Nations Trusteeship Council; Director of the Office of Dependent Area Affairs
Gleason, S. Everett, Deputy Executive Secretary of the National Security Council
Goodpaster, Colonel Andrew J. (Brigadier General from January 1957), Staff Secretary to President Eisenhower
Gray, Gordon, Assistant Secretary of Defense for International Security Affairs, July 1955–February 1957; thereafter Director of the Office of Defense Mobilization
Gruenther, General Alfred M., Supreme Allied Commander in Europe to November 1956

Habtewold, Aklilou, Ethiopian Deputy Prime Minister and, to April 1957, Foreign Minister
Hadsel, Fred L., Special Assistant in the Bureau of Near Eastern, South Asian, and African Affairs, 1955; Deputy Director of the Office of African Affairs, 1955–October 1956; Director of the Office of Southern Africa Affairs, October

1956–April 1957; First Secretary of the Embassy in the United Kingdom from April 1957

Haile Selassie I, Emperor of Ethiopia

Halim, Sayyid Mustafa Ben, Libyan Prime Minister to May 1957

Hammarskjöld, Dag, Secretary–General of the United Nations

Herter, Christian A., Consultant to the Secretary of State from January–February 1957; thereafter Under Secretary of State and Chairman of the Operations Coordinating Board

Hollister, John B., Director of the International Cooperation Administration, July 1955–July 1957

Holmes, Julius C., Special Assistant to the Assistant Secretary of State for European Affairs to May 1955; Diplomatic Agent and Consul General at Tangier, May 1955–July 1956; thereafter Special Assistant to the Secretary of State

Hoover, Herbert, Jr., Under Secretary of State and Chairman of the Operations Coordinating Board to February 1957

Houghton, Amory, Ambassador to France from April 1957

Howe, Fisher, Deputy Special Assistant for Intelligence, Department of State, to March 1956; thereafter Director of the Executive Secretariat

Humphrey, George M., Secretary of the Treasury to July 1957

Idris I, King of Libya

Jacquin de Margerie, Roland, Assistant Director General of Political and Economic Affairs, French Foreign Ministry, to June 1955; Director General, June 1955–July 1956

Jebb, Sir Hubert Miles Gladwyn, British Ambassador to France

Jernegan, John D., Deputy Assistant Secretary of State for Near Eastern, South Asian, and African Affairs to October 1955; Minister-Counselor of the Embassy in Italy from October 1955

Jones, G. Lewis, Ambassador to Tunisia from October 1956

Jones, John W., Director of the Office of Western European Affairs, Department of State, to February 1957; thereafter Deputy Assistant Secretary of State for European Affairs

Jones, Richard Lee, Director of the Foreign Operations Mission in Liberia to June 1955; thereafter Ambassador to Liberia

July, Pierre, French Minister for Moroccan and Tunisian Affairs, February–October 1955

Key, David McK., Assistant Secretary of State for International Organization Affairs to July 1955

Khrushchev, Nikita Sergeevich, First Secretary of the Central Committee of the Communist Party of the Soviet Union

Ku'bar, Abd al-Majid, Libyan Deputy Prime Minister and Foreign Minister, March–May 1957; thereafter Prime Minister

Lacoste, Robert, French Minister Resident in Algeria and Governor–General of Algeria from February 1956

Ladgham, Bahi, Tunisian Deputy Prime Minister, April 1956–July 1957; thereafter Acting Vice President and Secretary of State for Coordination and Defense

LaMont, George D., Consul General at Casablanca to December 1956; thereafter Deputy Director of the Office of Southern Africa Affairs

Lay, James S., Jr., Executive Secretary of the National Security Council

Lloyd, Selwyn, British Minister of Supply to April 1955; Minister of Defence, April 1955–December 1955; thereafter Secretary of State for Foreign Affairs

Lodge, Henry Cabot, Representative at the United Nations
Louw, Eric H., South African Minister of External Affairs; to July 1956, also Finance Minister
Lucet, Charles, Minister in the French Embassy in the United States from October 1955

MacArthur, Douglas, II, Counselor of the Department of State to December 1956
Macmillan, Harold, British Minister of Defence to April 1955; Secretary of State for Foreign Affairs, April–December 1955; Chancellor of the Exchequer, December 1955–January 1957; thereafter Prime Minister and First Lord of the Treasury
Makins, Sir Roger M., British Ambassador to the United States to October 1956; thereafter Joint Permanent Secretary of the Treasury
Margerie. *See* Jacquin de Margerie
Massigli, René, Secretary–General of Foreign Affairs, French Foreign Ministry, to July 1956
McElroy, Neil H., Secretary of Defense from October 1957
Merchant, Livingston T., Assistant Secretary of State for European Affairs to May 1956; Ambassador to Canada from May 1956
Mohamed V (Mohamed ben Youssef), Sultan of Morocco (deposed August 1953; reinstated November 1955) to August 1957, when he assumed title of King
Mokaddem, Sadok, Tunisian Secretary of State for Foreign Affairs from July 1957
Mollet, Guy, French Prime Minister, February 1956–June 1957
Murphy, Robert D., Deputy Under Secretary of State for Political Affairs

Nixon, Richard M., Vice President of the United States
Nkrumah, Kwame, Prime Minister of the Gold Coast to March 1957; thereafter President of Ghana

O'Connor, Roderic L., Special Assistant to the Secretary of State to December 1955; Deputy Assistant Secretary of State for Congressional Relations from December 1955

Padmore, George A., Liberian Ambassador to the United States from April 1956
Palmer, Joseph, II, Deputy Director of the Office of European Regional Affairs, Department of State, to September 1955; Acting Director, September 1955–September 1956; thereafter Deputy Assistant Secretary of State for African Affairs
Phleger, Herman, Legal Adviser of the Department of State to April 1957
Pinay, Antoine, French Foreign Minister, February 1955–January 1956
Pineau, Christian R., French Foreign Minister from February 1956
Pinkerton, Lowell C., Ambassador to Sudan, May 1956–August 1957
Porter, William J., Consul General at Rabat to August 1956; Counselor of Embassy in Morocco, August 1956–August 1957; thereafter Director of the Office of Northern Africa Affairs

Radford, Admiral Arthur W., Chairman of the Joint Chiefs of Staff to August 1957
Reinhardt, G. Frederick, Counselor of the Department of State from March 1957
Richards, James P., Representative from South Carolina and Chairman of the House Foreign Affairs Committee to January 1957; Special Assistant to the President from January 1957
Robertson, Reuben B., Jr., Deputy Secretary of Defense, August 1955–April 1957
Rountree, William M., Deputy Assistant Secretary of State for Near Eastern, South Asian, and African Affairs from August 1956

Savary, Alain, French Secretary of State for Moroccan and Tunisian Affairs, February–October 1956

Sears, Mason, Representative to the United Nations Trusteeship Council

Seydoux de Clausonne, Roger, French Deputy Minister of the Residence General in Tunisia to September 1955; High Commissioner in Tunisia, September 1955–June 1956; French Ambassador to Tunisia, June–August 1956

Shuckburgh, Charles Arthur Evelyn, British Assistant Under Secretary of State for Foreign Affairs to June 1956

Simonson, Joseph, Ambassador to Ethiopia to May 1957

Simpson, Clarence Lorenzo, Liberian Ambassador to the United States to June 1956

Slim, Mongi, Tunisian Minister of State to September 1955 and April–August 1956; Minister of the Interior, September 1955–April 1956; Ambassador to the United States from September 1956 and Representative at the United Nations from November 1956

Soustelle, Jacques, Governor–General of Algeria, January 1955–January 1956

Spaak, Paul–Henri, Belgian Minister of Foreign Affairs to May 1957; thereafter Secretary General of NATO

Stassen, Harold E., Director of the Foreign Operations Administration to June 1955; Special Assistant on Disarmament to President Eisenhower from March 1955 and Deputy Representative to the United Nations Disarmament Commission and Sub-Committee from August 1955

Strijdom, Johannes Gerhardus, South African Prime Minister

Tappin, John L., Ambassador to Libya

Taylor, General Maxwell, USA, Chief of Staff, U.S. Army, from June 1955

Timmons, Benson E.L., III, First Secretary of the Embassy in France and Director of the Foreign Operations Mission to July 1955; Minister for Economic Affairs, July–September 1955; thereafter Director of the Office of European Regional Affairs, Department of State

Tolbert, William R., Jr., Vice President of Liberia

Tubman, William V.S., President of Liberia

Twining, General Nathan F., Chief of Staff of the Air Force to July 1957; thereafter Chairman of the Joint Chiefs of Staff

Tyler, William R., Deputy Director of the Office of Western European Affairs, Department of State, July 1955–February 1957; thereafter Director

Vimont, Jacques, Minister–Counselor of the French Embassy in the United States to August 1957

Wailes, Edward T., Ambassador to South Africa to August 1956

Walmsley, Walter N., Jr., Minister–Counselor of the Embassy in the Soviet Union to October 1956; thereafter Deputy Assistant Secretary of State for International Organization Affairs

Welensky, Sir Roy, Minister of Transport and Communications in the Federation of Rhodesia and Nyasaland to November 1956; thereafter Prime Minister and Minister of External Affairs

Whitney, John Hay, Ambassador to the United Kingdom from February 1957

Wilcox, Francis O., Assistant Secretary of State for International Organization Affairs from September 1955

Wilson, Charles E., Secretary of Defense to October 1957

Yost, Charles W., Minister–Counselor of the Embassy in France, July 1956–December 1957

GENERAL UNITED STATES POLICIES TOWARD AFRICA [1]

1. Memorandum of a Conversation, Department of State, Washington, February 1, 1955 [2]

SUBJECT

Participation of African States in Afro–Asian Conference [3]

PARTICIPANTS

Mr. John D. Jernegan, Deputy Assistant Secretary, NEA
M. Jacques Vimont, Minister, French Embassy
Mr. J. Jefferson Jones, III, SOA

M. Vimont, referring to his conversations with Mr. Utter regarding the attendance of African states at the Asian–African Conference, asked if the Department had reached a final decision as to whether it would discourage African states from attending the Conference.

Mr. Jernegan replied in the affirmative stating that we thought there should be a distinction made between the Asian and African states in so far as attendance at the Conference was concerned. However, we perhaps did not make so great a distinction as did the British or the French. We were happy with the British position of discouraging discreetly the Gold Coast and Central African Federation from attending. It was too dangerous in our opinion to discourage the attendance of Liberia and Ethiopia. The Department had sent telegraphic instructions to our missions in these two countries requesting them to maintain a hands off position; however, if the two states should decide to attend, it was recommended that they send the ablest possible representation. [4]

---

[1] For previous documentation on this subject, see *Foreign Relations*, 1952–1954, vol. XI, Part 1, pp. 1 ff.

[2] Source: Department of State, Central Files, 670.901/2-155. Secret. Drafted by Jones.

[3] The Afro–Asian Conference was attended by 29 nations in April 1955 at Bandung, Indonesia.

[4] These instructions were conveyed in telegrams 91 to Monrovia and 205 to Addis Ababa, January 28. (Department of State, Central Files, 670.901/1–2855) At an earlier meeting on January 21, the Secretary of State and the Director of Central Intelligence,

Mr. Jernegan continued that on balance we believed that it was in our interest to encourage friendly non-communist invitees to go to the Conference. We intended to point out, however, to these friendly countries that the communists would attempt to dominate the Conference. However, if the non-communist invitees were represented by capable delegates, and the delegates cooperated, they should be able to block communist maneuvers and perhaps introduce constructive resolutions.

The Department was engaged in studying what influence we could exert in appropriate manners in connection with the Conference. We would appreciate the benefit of any thoughts on this subject which the French might have.

M. Vimont expressed his appreciation for the information furnished him by Mr. Jernegan and said that the French position was more or less the same. However, the French Government had hoped that the US would use its influence in order to prevail upon Liberia and Ethiopia not to send representatives to the Conference.

Allen Dulles, expressed their apprehension that Bandung portended a new Communist drive in Africa. (Memorandum of conversation by McAuliffe, January 21; *ibid.*, 670.901/1–2155) At a subsequent discussion on January 27, Jernegan indicated that one of his objectives was to preclude the establishment of a precedent whereby Africans and Asians dealt with outside powers as a bloc. (Memorandum of conversation by Selby, January 27; *ibid.*, 670.901/1–2755) Eugene Vincent McAuliffe and Richard Roy Selby, Jr. were both on the Reports and Operations Staff of the Executive Secretariat.

---

2. Letter From the Secretary of State to the Representative at the United Nations (Lodge) [1]

Washington, February 9, 1955.

DEAR CABOT: We are confronted by the problem of determining the United States position in regard to certain parts of the Reports of the Trusteeship Council's 1954 Visiting Mission to the Trust Territories of Tanganyika, Ruanda-Urundi and Somaliland under Italian administration. [2] These Reports are permeated with the principle of

---

[1] Source: Department of State, Central Files, 350/2–955. Confidential. Drafted by Robbins, ODA, and cleared in draft with EUR and NEA, the Departments of the Interior, Defense, and Navy, and in final form with IO.

[2] Reference is to reports on Tanganyika (U.N. docs. T/1142 and 1169), Ruanda-Urundi (T/1141 and 1168), and Somaliland (T/1143).

establishing hypothetical time limits for the attainment of various stages of self-government.

In the past the United States, as a general rule, has not supported the establishment of timetables for the achievement of self-government, and is unwilling to do so in the present instances. Our immediate problem arises from the fact that the United States Representative in the Trusteeship Council and member of the four-man Visiting Mission to the East African Trust Territories, Mr. Mason Sears, has endorsed the three Reports without reservation. [3]

As a member of the Visiting Mission which operated as an agency of the United Nations, Mr. Sears served in his individual capacity. Therefore the question of his right to express his own views is not an issue, nor does the Department fail to recognize in this situation that there is ample room for honest differences among individuals. On the other hand, all members of the Visiting Mission are officials of their respective Governments and nominated by them. As such it might be expected in some quarters that they would reflect their Government's views.

Our general policy in the colonial field was restated by me before the CIO Convention in Cleveland on November 18, 1953 when I said that the "orderly transition from colonial to self-governing status should be carried resolutely to a completion (but that) the development of genuine independence is a task of infinite difficulty and delicacy, (and) zeal needs to be balanced by patience." [4] This basis for our policy regarding trust and other non-self-governing territories has been stated repeatedly by United States spokesmen including Mrs. Frances P. Bolton and Mr. C. D. Jackson at the Eighth and Ninth General Assemblies, respectively. [5]

We have been approached by Sir Robert Scott, Minister of the British Embassy, who was instructed by his Government to express its concern over the position taken by the United States Representative on the Visiting Mission. [6] We are advised by our Embassy in Brussels that the Belgians will be taking this matter up with us

[3] Sears joined with Delegates from El Salvador and India in supporting recommendations to which Belgium and the United Kingdom objected. The fourth Mission member, New Zealand, entered a minority opinion.

[4] For text of the speech, see Department of State *Bulletin*, November 30, 1953, pp. 741–744.

[5] For previous documentation on this matter, see *Foreign Relations*, 1952–1954, vol. III, pp. 1075 ff. Frances P. Bolton and C. D. Jackson were members of the U.S. Delegations to the Eighth and Ninth Sessions of the U.N. General Assembly, respectively.

[6] The British indicated their objections to timetables and adult suffrage, as recommended for Tanganyika by U.N. doc. T/1142, in an approach to the Department of State on January 25, the same day the Visiting Mission report was made public. Scott indicated that, although the members might have acted in their individual (Continued)

shortly, [7] when their Representative in the Trusteeship Council, Governor General Pierre Ryckmans, comes to Washington within a few days in his capacity as Head of the Belgian Atomic Energy Program to discuss matters pertaining to uranium.

You are aware of the frequent need we have to rely upon our friends in the United Nations for support in obtaining positions to which we attach importance. This, however, is not the sole reason why we must not alienate unnecessarily our NATO allies and some of our staunchest supporters in the United Nations. We have problems of our own in the dependent areas field regarding which we require sympathetic understanding and support of the largest possible majority of United Nations Members. For example, if we should endorse a general 20–25 year timetable for the attainment of self-government in Ruanda-Urundi or Tanganyika, the Belgians, British, or any other United Nations Member could argue cogently that self-government for the widely scattered islands of our Trust Territory should be envisaged in a much shorter time because their peoples generally are more advanced and have had considerable experience through contacts with the outside world. This could be quite embarrassing for us since we are on record against the establishment of a timetable for the Trust Territory of the Pacific Islands. As recently as the Fourteenth Session of the Trusteeship Council, High Commissioner Midkiff stressed the importance we attach to the principle of not imposing an arbitrary rate of development. [8] It is precisely because we attach importance to the sound development of self-government that our policy emphasizes economic, social and educational advancement, a policy which finds full expression in the trusteeship provisions of the Charter. Thus in the Trusteeship Council and Committees of the General Assembly we should continue to stress balanced developments leading to effective and enduring self-government rather than giving the impression that we favor a hasty imposition of "western" political patterns.

I appreciate how carefully you have striven to maintain the delicate balance that is incumbent upon us in United Nations

---

(Continued)
capacities, his government was disturbed by the association of the United States with the report. (Memorandum of conversation by Withers, January 26; Department of State, Central Files, 778.00/1–2655)

[7] At a luncheon at the Belgian Embassy on February 15, Ambassador Silvercruys informally advised Deputy Under Secretary of State Robert Murphy of his nation's displeasure. That same day the Counselor of the Embassy, Georges Carlier, pursued the matter officially at the Department of State. He regretted that Sears supported the Indian position on timetables which was a departure from previous policy as indicated by U.S. abstention from voting on Resolutions 558(VI), 752(VII), and 858(IX). (Memoranda of conversations by Allen, February 15; *ibid.*, 350/2–1555)

[8] Frank Elbert Midkiff's statement had been made July 7, 1954 in the course of the 550th meeting of the Trusteeship Council. (U.N. doc. T/SR.550)

activities regarding dependent area matters which have occupied the attention of political committees in recent General Assemblies. In the Trusteeship Council and elsewhere in the United Nations we certainly do not wish to impair our independent position by aligning ourselves automatically with other administering powers or allowing them to think that they can always count on our support. It is, however, reasonable for them to want to know where we stand and whether we have changed our position.

The 1954 Visiting Mission's Reports are regarded by various Offices in the Government where they have been studied as unnecessarily controversial and tendentious. It is felt that criticisms of administrations are not balanced by a proper amount of credit for accomplishments and appreciation of the magnitude of the problems. The Department, after consultations with the Departments of Interior, Defense and the Navy, believes that the United States Representative in the Trusteeship Council cannot support action which would endorse the principle of establishing hypothetical timetables. In case the Council is asked to endorse other conclusions contained in these Reports, the United States Representative should use as guides our past positions and general statements to which I have referred along with the current position papers.

I am sure that you share our appreciation of the gravity of colonial problems wherever they arise in the United Nations, and our need to speak with one voice in regard to them, particularly in view of the tight-rope we are continually obliged to walk in relation to those matters.[9]

There is enclosed an additional copy of this letter which you may wish to pass to Mr. Sears.

Sincerely yours,

John Foster Dulles[10]

---

[9] In his reply, February 15, Lodge stressed Sears' adherence to official policy and indicated that Sears was willing to make a statement distinguishing between his own and his government's views. Moreover, Lodge explained that Sears had signed the reports so as not to polarize the Mission. In addition, according to Lodge, Sears had thought it would strengthen the U.S. position on the Council to be on India's side on one issue. (Department of State, Central Files, 350/2–1555) Replying for the Secretary on February 18, David McK. Key emphasized the need for a prompt and strong statement by Sears so as to assuage the British and Belgians and to erase any incorrect expectations on the part of the nonadministering members. (*Ibid.*, IO/ODA Files: Lot 62 D 225, U.S. Representative in Trusteeship Council)

[10] Printed from a copy that bears this stamped signature.

3. Memorandum From the Assistant Secretary of State for International Organization Affairs (Key) to the Deputy Under Secretary of State (Murphy) [1]

Washington, April 20, 1955.

SUBJECT

Meeting in your office with Mr. Mason Sears, U.S. Representative on the Trusteeship Council and on the Committee on Information from Non-Self-Governing Territories, April 29, at three-thirty

As you know, the United States positions on many colonial and trusteeship questions are the result of compromises reached by Interior, Defense and State, and therefore reflect what is practical, what is safe, and what is right and diplomatically expedient. The goals are generally agreed on, both internally and among our Allies, but the timing and methods of attaining them entail many differences of view.

The Department's line was defined by the Secretary in November 1953, when he warned against both too much delay and too premature action. His summary statement was as follows:

"There is no slightest wavering in our conviction that the orderly transition from colonial to self-governing status should be carried resolutely to a completion."

Mr. Sears has not always been too happy with Departmental guidance and tends to believe that we are frequently too solicitous of British, French and Belgian views. As a member of a recent United Nations Visiting Mission to East Africa he associated himself [in an individual capacity] [2] with a number of recommendations which the British and Belgian Governments flatly rejected and on which they made strong representations to the Department, particularly on the time-table concept for attaining self-government which he had endorsed. He was instructed to state in the Trusteeship Council that his Government did not believe it was realistic or practical to apply it now to Tanganyika or Ruandi–Urundi. [3]

The approach of the Department and that of Mr. Sears can perhaps be summarized in a nutshell as follows: Sears believes that

[1] Source: Department of State, IO/ODA Files: Lot 62 D 225, U.S. Representative in Trusteeship Council. Official Use Only. Drafted by Gerig.

[2] Brackets in the source text.

[3] On February 25, Sears informed the Trusteeship Council that his views differed somewhat from those of the U.S. Government. He indicated that the United States was opposed to the timetable principle in the case of Tanganyika. See *Official Records of the Fifteenth Session of the Trusteeship Council*, 585th Meeting, February 25, 1955, p. 175 and Press Release No. 2121 of the U.S. Mission to the United Nations, February 24, 1955. (Department of State, IO Files)

we should "make friends with the Africans, even if we alienate or irritate our European Allies." The Department agrees that we should make friends with the Africans, but without alienating our Allies. The second proposition is, of course, difficult and requires the greatest tact and diplomacy.

The purpose of the meeting in your office would be to get acquainted with Mr. Sears, hear his general views, and to explain how the Department's views are reached and how they often appear to be unsatisfactory to some of us.

It is proposed that the Assistant Secretaries or their Deputies from the geographic Bureaus principally concerned should be there to participate in the discussion. Later in the day I suggest that Mr. Gerig take Mr. Sears around to see Mr. Orme Lewis, at Interior, and the officials in Defense who are concerned with these questions as they affect our territories.[4]

I think you should allow a half- to three-quarters hour for this meeting in your office if possible.[5]

---

[4] No record of a meeting between Sears and Murphy has been found in Department of State files. However, there is a record of the conversations of Sears on that date with Captain Monroe B. Duffill, Director, Administration and Plans Division, Office of the Chief of Naval Operations, and with Assistant Secretary of the Interior Orme Lewis. Whereas the first discussion was general in nature, in the second Sears and Lewis entered into more substantive talks. Sears indicated that he considered it ridiculous to assume that if he advocated timetables, others on the Trusteeship Council would apply the principle to the Pacific Islands. (Memorandum of conversation by Robbins, April 29; *ibid.*, IO/ODA Files, Lot 62 D 225, U.S. Representative in Trusteeship Council)

[5] Murphy initialed his approval.

---

4. Editorial Note

Congressman John McCormack of Massachusetts introduced H. Con. Res. 149 in the 1st Session of the 84th Congress on May 31. It was debated and passed by the House on June 23 by a vote of 367 to 0, with 67 members not voting. The Senate followed suit on July 14 with 88 in favor, 1 opposed (Fulbright), and 7 not voting. The House accepted the Senate amendments and the Resolution was passed on July 18. The operative paragraph reads as follows:

"*Resolved by the House of Representatives* (*the Senate concurring*), that it is the sense of the Congress that the United States should administer its foreign policies and programs and exercise its influence so as to support other peoples in their efforts to achieve self-determination or independence under circumstances which will enable them to assume and maintain an equal station among the free nations of the world."

Assistant Secretary of State for Congressional Relations Thruston B. Morton, in a letter to Congressman James P. Richards on June 20, described the resolution as basically in conformity with the views of the administration. There was some concern as to the matter of timing, however, for it was feared that premature independence might result in a weak government which the Communists could take advantage of. The issues raised by this resolution and the administration response, as indicated in part by the Morton letter, are discussed in an "Outline of U.S. Approach to Colonial Questions in the United Nations" which Gerig submitted to Francis O. Wilcox, Assistant Secretary of State for International Organization Affairs, on September 14. (Department of State, IO/ODA Files: Lot 62 D 225, Colonial Policy)

---

5. Editorial Note

Upon his assumption of the Presidency of the Trusteeship Council on June 8, Sears offered some brief and general remarks. He noted that "For the first time the Council would have to deal with the transition of a Territory to self-government." He added that the Council would increasingly play a "useful role in the progress of Trust Territories towards self-government." See U.N. doc. T/SR.611, page 2.

In telegram 52, June 13, to the United States Information Agency, John Alfred Noon, Regional Public Affairs Officer at Nairobi, expressed his concern that Sears had not qualified his references to self-government. Noon assumed that Sears had stated his personal views and wondered to what extent these reflected official policy. (Department of State, IO/ODA Files: Lot 62 D 225, U.S. Representative in Trusteeship Council) Consul John R. Barrow at Nairobi followed Noon's lead in telegram 144, June 24, in which he criticized Sears' statement for antagonizing local officials and raising false hopes on the part of the Africans. Like Noon, he stressed how difficult it was to explain United States policy when divergencies occurred between the Department's and Sears' statements. (*Ibid.*, Central Files, 745P.02/6–2455)

The Director of USIA, Theodore C. Streibert, however, found Sears' comments consistent with United States policy. (Telegram 26 to Nairobi, June 23; *ibid.*, IO/ODA Files: Lot 62 D 225) The response of the United Nations Delegation was similar.

William O. Hall informed the Department on June 30 that Sears' comments had not constituted a statement of official policy. (Telegram 928 from USUN; *ibid.*, Central Files, 350/6–3055) Thereafter Nairobi was assured by a joint message from the Department and USIA that Sears' statements would be "guided" by established policy. (Circular telegram 12, July 7; *ibid.*, 350/7–755)

Sears wrote to Barrow on July 18 that the consular reaction resulted from an inaccurate perception of what he had said. He emphasized adherence to the policy defined by the Secretary, requested the basis of Noon's and Barrow's reaction to his Trusteeship Council statement, and questioned why they thought he had been out of step with United States policy. (*Ibid.*, IO/ODA Files: Lot 62 D 225)

---

6. Letter From the Consul at Nairobi (Barrow) to the Representative at the Trusteeship Council (Sears)[1]

Nairobi, July 28, 1955.

DEAR MR. SEARS: Thank you for your letter of July 18 regarding our telegrams about your opening remarks as President of the Trusteeship Council. Although I did not instigate the action, I did concur generally in Dr. Noon's telegram and sent a supporting telegram of my own when the Department of State requested clarification.

In retrospect, I believe Dr. Noon and I—in the interests of telegraphic economy—may both have been guilty of the very thing of which we complained, namely, partial exposition of our point of view which may have been misleading. I therefore welcome this opportunity to elaborate in a little more detail the causes of our concern.

[1] Source: Department of State, IO/ODA Files: Lot 62 D 225, U.S. Representative in Trusteeship Council. Official Use Only; Official–Informal. Enclosure to despatch 21 from Nairobi, July 28. (*Ibid.*, Central Files, 350/7–2855) Barrow requested the Department to forward the letter to Sears. There is no indication whether the Department did so.

Taken by itself—and as far as it goes—we find nothing exceptionable about your statement. It was what the statement did *not* say that concerned us. Moreover, statements of this kind are read not only in terms of their specific content but also in terms of what you and other important Americans have said before and since on the twin problems of colonialism and self-determination. It is thus not so much this statement or that statement, but the *total quantity* of them, that is causing us difficulty. The most recent expression of American opinion, for example, was the McCormack Resolution which was supported unanimously by 367 American Congressmen and 88 American Senators.

Unfortunately these statements as they are repeated and reemphasized give the over-all impression here that Americans see only one side of the problem. There is, we must admit, an emphasis in them on admonition to colonial powers to give ground to "self-determination", "self-government", or "independence", whereas rarely does one see in these statements any equivalent admonition to backward peoples to try to improve themselves to the point where self-determination would not likely result in self-destruction. Improving themselves in turn requires that they cooperate to a degree with colonial or other powers who are trying to help them.

Is self-determination a right that is axiomatic, automatic and divinely bestowed? Or is it a right that one must earn? Most of our American public statements seem to leave this clouded in doubt. People here have the impression we believe in the former. But I think that upon reflection nearly all of us would agree that the latter is closer to the truth. Does a child have an "inalienable right" to self-determination? Does even an adult have that right unless he is able to live up to his community responsibilities? Could an all-African government in East Africa, the Belgian Congo or French Equatorial Africa, presently meet its international obligations?

Whether one calls it "colonialism" or "paternalism" or what have you, some form of foreign protection to the African territories is likely to be necessary for quite some time to come, and while it remains necessary it would be strange to call such protection a "denial of inalienable rights of man" (to borrow a phrase from the McCormack Resolution).

There is another aspect which troubles us greatly. By repeated public mention of such clichés as "self-determination", "achievement of self-government", "progress to independence", et cetera, we Americans seem to be promising more to the African than we are—in most areas—actually able to deliver. In so doing there is grave danger of creating disillusionment. One may well wish to talk of these things in the Gold Coast or Nigeria where they are on the point of fulfillment, but elsewhere we feel our public expressions and opinion should be geared to what we, as Americans, are actually in a position to accomplish or to persuade others to accomplish.

In East Africa, for instance, we have advocated an all-out economic, social and educational campaign designed to raise the level of the African in these fields as a prelude to political advance. We are trying to help the British in this respect through technical assistance and educational exchange. Once we get our programs going we will have something we can safely talk about which will have concrete meaning to the people. In short, these will be promises on which we are actually delivering. But if we prematurely indulge in highly controversial public theorizing about the prospects of the people of this area for self-determination or self-government or independence, it seems to me we are going considerably beyond ourselves.

We are inclined to believe genuine political self-determination, as opposed to economic and social advance, is not a thing that can be unnaturally *forced* either forward or backward in time. It is a thing that evolves out of events and circumstances. When or how it will evolve here we do not at this time know. All we and the colonial power can do is work little by little in an effort to keep things moving on the right track, hoping for the best, and keeping controversies over vaguely conceived "isms" and "principles" to a minimum.

Our classified despatch No. 17 of July 20 [2] on reaction to the McCormack Resolution, as well as our classified despatch No. 1 of July 5 [3] commenting on the ideological program of the OCB discusses these same questions from the standpoint of the practical consequences to American interests. I assume these classified reports can be made available to you. I would also recommend your having a glance at the second paragraph of the Department's CA–7584 of May 4 [4] pointing out the danger of riding the colonial power too hard. We believe this is a point well taken. Where we have a colonial power that is working in the right direction, and is indeed enlisting our help in this work, we believe it is best to "take it easy" on applying pressures or giving unwanted advice. Otherwise the terrain may be closed to us as quickly as it opened.

Whereas I shall not be in charge here in October–December, I will certainly look forward to joining Consul General Dorsz and Dr. Noon in fuller discussions with you, as I believe we will all benefit greatly from having your point of view on these matters. I quite

---

[2] In despatch 17, Barrow recommended against publicizing the resolution since it would offend the Europeans without pleasing the Africans. (*Ibid.*, 511.00/7–2055)

[3] Not printed.

[4] Document 48.

realize that in much in what we have said we are on dangerous ground. We seem to be in some disagreement on method, though not on principle, with the unanimous opinion of 455 distinguished Congressmen and Senators aside from others. We nevertheless feel we would be doing less than our duty if we did not report frankly on how things look to us from here, and we hope that what we say will be looked upon in that light.

Sincerely yours,

John R. Barrow [5]

[5] Printed from a copy that bears this typed signature.

---

7. Memorandum From the Assistant Secretary of State for Near Eastern, South Asian, and African Affairs (Allen) to the Secretary of State [1]

Washington, August 12, 1955.

SUBJECT

United States Policy towards Africa South of the Sahara

It is my conviction that within the next ten years we shall face in Africa South of the Sahara the same acute dilemma of colonialism that we are presently facing in Asia and North Africa. I believe we should, therefore, begin planning our policy now with respect to this area.

I should like to bring to your attention a paper recently prepared in the Office of African Affairs which seeks to lay down guidelines for our policy in Africa South of the Sahara for the next decade (Tab B). [2] A summary of its observations is also attached (Tab A). [3] A draft of the full paper was circulated in S/P, and suggestions made there have been taken into consideration.

This paper is, in my opinion, only the first step. We need to clarify our policy with respect to the various regions within Africa.

[1] Source: Department of State, Central Files, 611.70/7–2055. Confidential. Drafted by Hadsel; sent through Robert G. Barnes, Robert Murphy, and Loy W. Henderson.

[2] In the wake of the Bandung Conference, a Principal Officers Conference in Africa South of the Sahara had been planned which Allen would have attended. Budgetary cuts forced the postponement of the conference. Hadsel's paper had been prepared for that gathering.

[3] Not printed.

We also need to face up to what this policy means in our relations with the Colonial powers and in terms of money, personnel, and housing.

If you approve of the general direction which this paper takes, we would like your authorization to proceed with detailed examination of the problems.[4]

[Tab B]

Memorandum Prepared in the Office of African Affairs[5]

Washington, August 4, 1955.

THE UNITED STATES IN AFRICA SOUTH OF THE SAHARA

The Point of Departure

There runs as a theme throughout any consideration of American policy toward Africa South of the Sahara the probability that in this area, as in Asia, the Middle East and North Africa, we will face in an acute form the dilemma of colonialism. This dilemma may arise from the tendency of the Metropolitan powers to become more sensitive in their attitude and more rigid in their policies, while the Africans meanwhile increase their demands for political and economic power. As a result, the United States may be constantly pressed to endorse either the European or African point of view, and we may find ourselves in a situation similar to that which currently confronts us in North Africa and elsewhere. Many of the elements of this conflict are now present in Africa below the Sahara. They have not reached the proportions of a major crisis for the United States, partly because of the nature of the situation itself and partly because we have so far had relatively little interest in much of the area. These two conditions, however, are rapidly disappearing. The potentials of conflict are becoming realities. Absence of interest is no longer feasible.

If there is any prospect of extricating ourselves from this dilemma, it lies in the development of a more independent policy in

[4] According to Roderic L. O'Connor, Dulles read the paper but was not willing "to be pinned down" as yet. He considered it too general to warrant his specific approval though he was prepared to authorize more detailed studies. Henderson advised the Secretary that unless more funds were obtained than were presently available it would not be possible to open new posts and assign more officers without curtailing operations elsewhere. (Memoranda by Henderson, August 23, and from O'Connor to Allen, August 30, attached to the source text)

[5] Confidential. Drafted by Hadsel.

Africa. Such an evolution provides, as a minimum, the means to avoid being caught in an unenviable position. It would, as an optimum, entail a greater ability to influence the course of events in Africa than we now possess, in order to assure attainment of our goals in this area. Attainment of this independent posture, however, will most certainly be difficult. We cannot adopt courses of action which will directly undermine the Metropolitan powers, for not only would this action ignore the constructive work they are doing, but it would arouse such resentment on their part as to weaken our general position. At the same time, we cannot afford to ignore the aspirations of the Africans, since our silence would be construed as opposition.

The construction of an independent policy is not a question of producing a revolutionary new program, for to a considerable extent it is a matter of accelerating what has already begun. Neither would such a policy reverse the ever-growing inter-dependence of the countries and territories of the world, for our action cannot ignore this trend. Instead, this effort would seek to create a greater sphere of activity which is identifiably American. To some extent, it would be a matter of creating policy where none has ever existed. It also would mean shedding outworn views of what Africa is and can be. It would require reviewing our present relationships with both the colonial powers and the dependent peoples. And it would mean bringing order into policies which hitherto have been adopted in a fit of absentmindedness.

One of the difficulties of shaping an intelligent policy towards Africa South of the Sahara is the simple matter of determining the geographic scope of such a policy. The southern half of the Continent is so diverse that policy designed to include the entire area may poorly fit the requirements of a particular locale. It is hard, moreover, to divide this area into two or three regional groupings, since these units will also contain many different conditions, peoples and problems. At the same time if one takes as a basis each of the score or more political territories of the area, a statement of policy would be broken into so many fragments as to be meaningless.

Because of these difficulties, it is probably best to consider U.S. policy from three points of view. Certain goals and courses of action can be dealt with on a sub-continental basis. Others must be considered on a regional basis. And finally, certain courses of action can only make sense when considered in connection with a particular territory. This paper treats only the general goals and courses of action, and seeks to establish a framework for later consideration of American policy on a regional or individual basis.

American policy must also take into account the fact that the African Continent is changing rapidly. Not only is this change taking place faster than we often think, but the tempo is hard to determine. We can point to the incredible economic development in the Copper Belt during the past five years, the transformation of large parts of the Congo during the past half century and the remarkable political evolution of the Gold Coast. Our knowledge, however, of the Continent is so limited that our techniques for measuring these changes are imperfect. One thing seems certain. Our future interests in Africa are bound to be far greater than they are today. Our policy must be based as much on the potentials of Africa as its present condition. Thus estimates of the future more than analysis of the present should be the major determinants of our policy.

The American Stake in Africa

In searching out a policy which the United States could hope to follow in Africa South of the Sahara during the coming decade, one should, as a preliminary, seek to define the present American stake in this Continent. This interest can best be summed up as *real* but *limited.*

The American stake in Africa is easy to identify in the economic field. We obtain a wide variety of resources from this Continent: chrome, rubber, uranium, diamonds, cobalt, manganese, palm oil, and a number of lesser known minerals which are essential to our industrial output. Our trade with Africa is expanding. Our markets in Africa are increasing. In addition to this direct role which Africa plays in our economy, the Continent provides important support to the economy of our allies in Europe.

The American military stake in Africa South of the Sahara is far smaller than it is in North Africa. Nevertheless, the Air Force continues to have a general interest in Roberts Field, Liberia; we have a military mission in Ethiopia; we have an interest in the Belgian defense of the Copper Belt; and we have at least a potential concern over the availability of a supply route through this Continent in times of crises.

The political stake of the United States in Africa is less easy to define. Yet in the broad balance of world power, this Continent is an extremely important area. The long-term attitude of the 120 million people living South of the Sahara is of very real significance in our general world position. The present Western orientation of the bulk of the Africans and practically all of the Europeans in Africa is an important factor in the evolution of this Continent. At the very least, this attitude gives us time to affect the evolution of the Continent and opens up the possibility of securing an orientation basically sympathetic to our own interests and aspirations.

Our cultural stake is perhaps the most indefinite of all our interests in Africa. We should not, however, discount either the historical influence of the missionary movement in Africa nor ignore its potentialities. American missionaries in Africa number some four to five thousand; while their influence can easily be exaggerated, they, nevertheless, make themselves felt in areas where otherwise the United States would be entirely unknown and American influence would be non-existent.

Despite the importance of these factors in America's relationship with Africa South of the Sahara, we should recognize that our present stake in this Continent is sharply limited. In a short-term crisis we could make do without the resources of the African subsoil. Our trade, though increasing, is only 3.5 percent of our total commerce.

From a military standpoint, there is a marked lack of interest in the Pentagon in strategic planning concerning Africa. We have no significant military mission or any active airbase in this part of the Continent. The trained white troops on a standing basis number less than 50,000. The African reserve is largely untrained. Thus, any effort to make out of Africa either a base of operations or an arsenal of men and ammunition would require tremendous effort on our part and a great deal of time.

Even in the political field, our ties are limited. We have no alliances or other commitments to this area, except through the Metropolitan powers. We have little affinity from the standpoint of political heritage with the Europeans in Africa. We have even less in common with the vast bulk of the population, those of African origin.

In the realm of cultural or moral influence, the missionary effort appears to be on the decline. The confidence of the American public in any special "civilizing mission" on its part is far less than that of the Europeans directly engaged in colonial activities. We are, moreover, constantly subject to the dilemma of sympathizing with our European allies on the one hand, and of feeling an emotional opposition to colonialism on the other. Right or wrong, this schizophrenia makes for a peculiar combination of uncertainty, guilt complex, and emotionalism on our part when we consider our role in this part of Africa.

Factors of Major Significance During the Next Decade

The fact that the present American stake in this part of Africa is real but limited is significant, but it is less important than the omnipresent indications that our interests are bound to increase.

While it is difficult to define the degree of change which the next decade will witness, it is still possible to identify the major factors which will affect this transformation. These factors will also be particularly important in considering the long-range aspects of American policy towards Africa South of the Sahara:

(1) The four Metropolitan Powers, Great Britain, France, Belgium, and Portugal, will continue to dominate the African scene. At the same time, these Powers are going to encounter varying degrees of difficulty in maintaining their present position. In the broad, the next decade will probably witness a decline in their influence. This fact will probably pose a number of difficulties for American policy, since the Metropolitan Powers may tend to become more suspicious of outside influences, less confident that they can manage the situation, and hence less flexible in their policy towards the dependent territory.

(2) Since the colonial powers will continue to play a significant role in Africa, it follows that our relationships with the Continent must necessarily be of a triangular nature. We shall have to take into account not only our own needs and interests but also the policies of the Metropolitan country and the aspirations and attitudes of the Africans involved.

In this relationship the United States will continue to face the dilemma of modern colonialism in varying degrees. Our ability to pursue a course of action with respect to the African area concerned will always be affected by the requirements of our policy towards the Metropolitan Powers. Assuming that the situation in Europe will not change radically during the next decade, we will not have a wide arc of maneuverability with respect to this part of Africa. By and large, if a showdown occurs between the needs of our European policy and those of our African policy, we shall have to recognize the superior demands of our alliance system in Europe.

(3) The means available to the United States during the next decade to influence events in Africa are likely to continue to be relatively limited. To date our aid program in Africa has been minuscule. Given the present trends of American economic assistance programs, our aid to Africa is not likely to expand greatly. We will, therefore, acquire little leverage through use of economic assistance funds. While the number and strength of our missions in Africa will undoubtedly increase, we do not anticipate a radical shift in our representation in the area. In the absence of war or a revolution in alliances, moreover, it is doubtful if there will be a major change in the military appreciation of Africa. As a result of this situation, we can assume that whatever the goals of United States policy may be with respect to this part of the Continent, our means to achieve these goals will be inadequate.

(4) The social and political ferment which is presently visible in most of Africa has only begun to make itself felt. As the standards of living go up, as the tribal organization breaks down further, as education becomes more widespread, and as parts of Africa become free, this ferment will increase both in pace and scope.

(5) One consequence of this change will be the rise in "African consciousness" on the part of the native population. Whether this consciousness will be local, regional, or continental in scope, it is at present most difficult to determine. Whatever its exact nature, however, it will have the characteristics of young nationalism. It will be emotional, irresponsible, exaggerated and xenophobic. It will undoubtedly have these and other traits found in the nationalism of the Middle East and South Asia. It may, in fact, have fewer restraints, since the new nationalism of many parts of the Middle East and South Asia has the underpinning of an old and somewhat stable civilization. In Africa the change will be so fundamental that the older way of life will provide no balance wheel to this new movement.

(6) Certain areas of Africa South of the Sahara will undoubtedly be the scene of tension and even conflict. In spite of the fact that the military phase of the Mau Mau movement appears to be drawing to an end, Kenya will be a country of tension and bitterness for many years to come. In South Africa the serious strain among social groups, and the apartheid policy of the nationalist government is not going to relax this tension. This friction may well spread elsewhere in the Continent, notably to the Rhodesias.

(7) The Communists may be expected to increase their efforts in Africa. One approach they will undoubtedly follow is that of continuing to identify the Soviet Union (which has the advantage of being remote) with "the oppressed colonial peoples of the world." They may try to substitute color for class in an African version of their dialectical materialism. Whatever the particular tactic, the tempo of their activity will undoubtedly increase.

(8) At the same time, we may also anticipate expansion of Islam especially in those portions of Africa just below the Sahara Desert. This expansion may tend to make progress in the Western sense more difficult, because the Koranic education is ill-adapted to meet the practical needs of the African for technical education. The growth of Islam may also provide a vehicle for greater Egyptian influence in Africa, since such guidance as exists in the Islamic movement comes as much from Cairo as from any other place. Since the variety of Islam which is expanding in Africa South of the Sahara has such a large ingredient of local fetish religion, it will not have the capacity to resist Communist infiltration which is normally ascribed to devout Moslem communities.

(9) The "Indian" problem of East and South Africa will continue to be extremely difficult. Even though immigration is restricted, those groups with their origin in the Indian sub-continent will continue to increase in numbers and economic influence. Although there is little prospect of these people acting cohesively except under extreme pressure, they will bulk large as an economic and political factor in all of East and South Africa.

(10) As important as these factors will be during the next decade of African affairs, none will probably be as significant as the economic revolution now taking place. This revolution will at the same time intensify Africa's basic problems and hold forth opportunities for coping with them.

Goals of United States Policy

Taking Africa South of the Sahara as a whole, the general goals of American policy may be summarized in the following manner:

(1) That the Continent remain free from inimical foreign influences, whether Communist, Indian or Arab;
(2) That the political, economic and social evolution of this Continent be in a manner friendly to the United States;
(3) That the United States obtain, on the most favorable possible terms, access to the economic resources of the area;
(4) That the United States increase its commercial, industrial and agricultural activities in the Continent;
(5) That the United States consolidate its cultural and moral position with respect to the Africans; and
(6) That American strategic needs with respect to the Continent be fully safeguarded.

Courses of Action

1. *Change the Tone of American Policy:* In part, the evolution of an independent policy towards Africa South of the Sahara will be the result of many courses of action. At the same time, there is a broad political element in such a policy that needs to be identified from the beginning, and which helps set the tone for the rest. In its initial phase, such action may be little more than the avoidance of a monotonous "me too" attitude with respect to the colonial powers. It may also consist of a conscious attempt to develop parallel courses of conduct—courses which neither directly contest the admitted role of the colonial powers nor automatically support the desires of the Africans. Whatever the form this attitude may take, it should be viewed as a state of mind in which every action is examined critically in order to determine its place in a pattern of policy directed towards achieving our goals. Without this point of view, we cannot expect to evolve a truly independent policy in Africa.

2. *Increase the Productivity of Africa:* One need not be an economic determinist to be convinced that only through a massive increase of the productivity of Africa and the Africans can long-term progress be made in the necessary transformation of the Continent. Such a transformation in the way of life of this Continent is a multiple necessity. Only in this way can the African meet his still elemental requirements of food, shelter and education. Only through such a change can the governments obtain the financial resources so necessary if the roads, dams, schools, and other requirements of a modern society are to be constructed. And only through providing a satisfactory response to these needs of the country can the present governmental structure evolve in such a manner as to head off implacable tension between racial groups.

Even though the United States will not assume in the near future a dominant role in increasing the productivity of Africa, there are at least four ways in which we can contribute to this end:

(a) We should encourage the investment of private capital in Africa. This program should not be merely one of providing governmental statistics. It should include public information, political support, diplomatic intervention if necessary to ensure favorable conditions for investment, and establishment of a small staff of officers experienced in securing new investors;
(b) We should support economic development loans wherever possible;
(c) We should expand steadily, but probably not dramatically, our technical cooperation program in the area; and
(d) We should develop this relationship with the area itself, not through the Metropolitan capital.

3. *Multi-racialism:* We should set ourselves the task of supporting a multi-racial approach to the problems of Africa South of the Sahara. Any other course of action would, in the long run, meet with such domestic opposition within the United States that it would be next to impossible to carry out. Moreover, there appears to be no other course of action which holds out real prospect for harmonizing the various elements of the situation in the Continent with our general policies. Unless one assumes that the present situation—whether that of the colonial powers or the Union of South Africa—can continue indefinitely, there is no other policy except multi-racialism which can hope to produce a compromise between white or black domination.

4. *Information and Education:* In no part of the world is the thirst for knowledge greater than in Africa. Perhaps this attitude is in part the product of the century of missionary activity, which though limited in scope, has penetrated into most of the hinterland of the Continent. Perhaps this desire comes from a very practical ambition on the part of the Africans to possess the means of a better life.

Whatever the source, the demand is so great that whoever brings the African education has the power to influence him in a basic fashion. While recognizing that in primitive communities there is a point beyond which a program of this kind cannot go at any given time, we should nevertheless expand our activities in three major directions:

(a) Increase our general information program, including libraries, press information, etc.;
(b) Expand our exchange of persons programs;
(c) Move to assist local education, especially in the vocational and medical fields. In view of the inevitable maladjustment of the foreign trained student, this local effort may well be the major one on our part.

5. *Private Organizations:* We should encourage private organizations in their activities in Africa. Not only are there many problems which they can work on in a better fashion than the Department, but they can reach into areas far removed from our American posts. We should especially assist the foundations in their efforts in Africa, with a view to identifying their efforts with the long-term interests of the United States.

6. *United States Representation in Africa:* The United States is presently handicapped in its policy in Africa by the small and scattered nature of its missions, the limitations on physical facilities, and certain morale problems somewhat peculiar to the area.

We should embark on a long-range, constant, but not revolutionary expansion of the staff of our missions in the area. In terms of officer personnel, such a program might not be larger than a five-year program of adding some half-dozen officers to the established posts each fiscal year. In addition, however, there should be a program of expansion in the number of posts, with the officer strength required for this expansion being over and above that needed for existing posts. During the coming five years, we should probably plan to open at least five new consulates, in order to keep abreast of developments in French West Africa, the Cameroons, Nigeria, Uganda, Somaliland, to say nothing of northern and eastern Nigeria, northern Gold Coast, central Africa (whether the Congo, the Federation, or elsewhere), and Madagascar.

We should make a special point of providing adequate accommodations and other living requirements for this staff, since the hazards of living in tropical Africa are unusually great and the impediments to effective work unusually large.

Finally, since we have the opportunity of building from relatively small types of establishments we should make every effort to secure well-integrated American missions. We should not establish autonomous, or semi-autonomous operations but see to it that all representatives are placed firmly under the principal officer. Our voice in Africa will not in any case be strong; it would be most unwise to reduce it to impotence through confusion of tongues.

Conclusion

The adoption of these proposals is obviously only the first step toward the independent policy which we require in Africa.

From the standpoint of policy, we should proceed to the extremely difficult task of applying these principles to the problems we face on a regional or country basis. Completion of this process should give us a pattern of action which would fit into our general decisions yet meet our needs in the individual territories.

At the same time, we should examine these policies to see what financial support is necessary in order to carry them out. This is not only a matter of funds for personnel and buildings, but it is even more a problem of economic assistance.

Both of these tasks will take considerable time. But if we wait for the African problems to reach a crisis stage before we set ourselves to solve them, we shall be too late to do anything effective. In Africa we still have the opportunity; it would be a putting off of our responsibilities if we fail to begin our efforts now.

---

8. Memorandum From the Assistant Secretary of State for Near Eastern, South Asian, and African Affairs (Allen) to the Secretary of State [1]

Washington, December 28, 1955.

SUBJECT

Technical Assistance for Dependent Overseas Territories

Southern Rhodesia wants us to start a modest technical assistance program in that country. It would cost about $500,000 to carry out a few specific projects, such as magnetometer survey of the Colony for minerals and materials, and technical and vocational training for Africans.

[1] Source: Department of State, Central Files, 745C.5–MSP/12–2855. Confidential. The source text bears no indication of the Secretary's approval or disapproval.

Mr. Todd, the Prime Minister of Southern Rhodesia, visited Washington in August 1955,[2] and left with the impression that the United States Government had no objection, in principle, to giving him some technical help. A considerable amount of discussion has taken place since that time and we now need a basic decision.

Mr. Hollister has been inclined to oppose our giving technical help to any Dependent Overseas Territories (DOT's) in either Africa or the Caribbean area, on the grounds that the responsibility for their welfare should rest with the governing country.

I feel strongly that we *should* have a modest program in those territories where the local authorities want us and the governing power does not object. The future of United States relations with the tremendously important continent of Africa is involved. If we do not gradually ease into the picture there, a rising nationalistic sentiment among the peoples south of the Sahara will look elsewhere for help and sympathy. It is a most fertile field for future (and not so distant future) Soviet activity. Moreover, American Negroes are beginning to look on Africa south of the Sahara with somewhat the same kind of sympathy and interest as American Zionists look on Israel. We should capitalize on this sentiment, utilizing it to work towards evolution rather than revolution in Africa. American Negroes, who are our best hope of keeping Africa oriented towards the United States, are anxious for the Department to help in the improvement of economic conditions in Africa and would be very much upset by a decision against any technical assistance programs there.

I understand that Mr. Hollister is putting the matter up to you for policy decision. I hope very much you will favor the DOT programs.

I have discussed the subject with Mr. Merchant and Mr. Holland, who are in general agreement.

[Here follow comments by the Assistant Secretaries of State for European and Inter-American Affairs relating exclusively to the Caribbean.]

---

[2] R.S. Garfield Todd met briefly with Dulles on August 10. (Memorandum of conversation by Hadsel, August 10; *ibid.*, 033.45C11/8–1055)

9. Memorandum by the Consul General at Leopoldville (McGregor)[1]

Leopoldville, December 28, 1955.

The paper on Africa south of the Sahara included with Department's CA–1535 of August 23, 1955, treats only "general goals and courses of action." Within this limitation there is imbedded an admission which if it indeed frames the thinking of our policy-making arm presents a very sorry picture indeed. I refer to the sentence "as a result of this situation" (it is doubtful if there will be a major change in the military appreciation of Africa) "we *can assume* that whatever the goals of U.S. policy may be with respect to this part of the continent, our means to achieve these goals will be inadequate."[2] In other words, what we are saying is that our goals can only be reached if the area becomes of first rate military significance. If this is indeed the case then we certainly need to change our thinking, planning and action. We should set goals that are American, realistic, realizable and ones that do not depend upon military action for their accomplishment.

The paper admits that "our techniques for measuring change in Africa are imperfect because our knowledge is limited." It also states that "our policy must be based on potentials of Africa and future more than present estimates should be the major determinant of U.S. policy."

In spite of these serious and crippling limitations, the paper strikes an optimistic note which appears to this observer as little short of wishful thinking. Speaking of the present "Western orientation of the bulk of Africans" the paper goes on to say that "at the very least this attitude gives us time to affect the evolution of the continent and opens up the possibility of securing an orientation basically sympathetic to our own interests and aspirations."

If we have no policy and can only hammer one out as our techniques for perfecting our knowledge are designed, surely we are only deluding ourselves by pretending that time is on our side. The impending tragedy of Africa is that in its present state it is potentially the prey to anyone with a policy or perhaps it is better put—

[1] Source: Department of State, Central Files, 611.70/12–2855. Confidential. Enclosure to despatch 220 from Leopoldville, December 28. It responded to circular instruction CA–1535, August 23, which forwarded Tab B of Document 7 and invited comments from Accra, Brussels, Dakar, Dar-es-Salaam, Elisabethville, Lagos, Leopoldville, Lisbon, London, Lourenco Marques, Luanda, Monrovia, Nairobi, Paris, Pretoria, Salisbury, and the Mission to the United Nations. (Department of State, Cental Files, 120.1470/8–2355)

[2] Despite the use of quotation marks, the references to the Hadsel paper are not exact; see Document 7.

to anyone whose policy is one of direct action. Isn't this what happened in Egypt with the Soviet arms deal?

I would rather see our *policy* based on present day realities rather than future potentialities; I would rather that this policy be of short range but flexible enough to adapt both to the gradual evolution of the African as well as to the perfection of our knowledge and improvement in our techniques.

The paper attempts to estimate what lies ahead of the area in the next decade: "continued Metropolitan domination of the scene albeit under conditions of declining influence resulting in greater inflexibility, more suspicions of outside influences and less sure of themselves." So if we accept the reasoning in the Hadsel paper (i.e. "we shall have to recognize the superior demands of our alliance system in Europe"), the United States, being tied to the Metropolitan powers, will in ten years be devoid of a policy that will appeal to an emerging and awakened indigenous population in Africa.

There is, however, some evidence in the paper that the author has covered considerable ground and would like to stand for a moment, assess the situation and come up with a policy.

It is my belief that we must do so. The paper suggests that we should be more "independent" in our policy toward Africa—which is taken to mean independent of the Metropolitan powers with African territories. This, I believe, is the first step toward a sound and up-to-date short-range reorientation of thinking on Africa. If we can divest ourselves of the a priori thought that we need be tied to a first consideration of our alliances with Metropolitan powers, we can bring African problems more directly into focus.

Of course, it will be very difficult to make up our mind regarding the best approach to the formulation of U.S. policy vis-à-vis present day Africa. A profound knowledge of the continent, its people, resources, history and external influences is prerequisite to all considerations of policy. Mr Hadsel admits our deficiency in this regard, and since I must also admit to such deficiency perhaps much of my difficulty is thereby explained.

Over and above this fundamental factor, however, it seems to me that we are caught in the middle of the jaws of a vice of our own design and fabrication: Until we can free ourselves from this restraint we have no ability to maneuver. On the one hand are our commitments to the European powers—who are also the Colonial powers; on the other is our traditional espousal of the principle of self-determination and independence for all peoples. As in operating a vice, a turn of the handle operates both jaws at once tightening the grip. So the harder we think about the problem of U.S. policy versus Central Africa, the faster we find ourselves gripped in the vice.

We may think because our motives are honest that the African knows we favor his obtaining independence. Actually the African understands no such thing. He knows we support indifferently whatever colonial power is administering an African territory. This means we support the Portuguese in Angola and Mozambique to the same political extent as the Belgians in the Congo, the French in A.O.F., F.E.A., and the British in their territories. Although there are many differences between the treatment of peoples in the Soviet satellite countries and in the colonies of Africa, we are seen to tolerate or overlook conditions in one area (Angola, South Africa, for example) that we castigate in another (Hungary, Rumania). We leave the impression that our stand on colonialism would remain static if it were not for the pressures of Soviet aggressiveness. This increases the "nuisance" value of the Soviet and makes them look even more like the champions of freedom and independence.

We are only too familiar with the bland manner in which the Soviet leaders espouse the cause of freedom only to enslave; we have seen in India and Burma recently how the Soviets easily reap the harvest that we who have sown should be harvesting. We are not succeeding in getting across to the masses the truth that the "new imperialism" of the Soviets is a greater menace—far greater than the vestigious evils of latter day European colonialism. Part of our failure is due to the techniques of Soviet propaganda which we cannot accept for our own without destroying the very ground we stand on. It is incredible to us that India, for example, should spend tens of thousands of pounds preparing popular receptions for the Soviet leaders in order to afford them a unique opportunity to sow sedition and lies, embarrass the Indian Government and castigate the West. [3] The Soviets, dealing as they have with their own masses for the past forty years and schooled in the technique of mass propaganda, are skillfully playing on the emotions of those who do not think. We have yet to develop a technique that is successful with the same audience. We do not even seem to have an antidote.

If we could devise a propaganda campaign that would effectively destroy the myth that the Soviet is the champion of democracy and freedom, we might be able to continue our present African policy. But we are being attacked as "imperialists" and there is just enough substance and truth in the assertions to render us self-conscious and to others suspicious. For example, we are well aware of the oppressive and medieval practices of the Portuguese in Angola. Many Angolan Africans in the Belgian Congo are naive enough to believe that the United States, once aware of conditions in Angola, will do something about them. We who deal with these

[3] Khrushchev and Bulganin began their official visit to India November 18.

people on the spot are sympathetic and attentive, all the while knowing that our relationships with the Portuguese in Europe preclude our doing anything. Can we not see, however, that we are in effect driving these well-meaning and sincere Africans toward the Communists who will raise the cry and at least point the finger at injustice?

Now that the issue of "colonialism" is being moved front and center by the Soviets, the essential thing it seems to me is that we free ourselves from the vice—adopt an American policy versus African colonialism and use our ingenuity to get that policy across to the masses in a constructive and positive manner.

The United States should stand for freedom from all forms of oppression, for self-government, and for independence based upon self-determination. It is true that Africans are not ready to make a success of self-government. But we who threw off the colonial yoke—did we think at that time whether we were ready to assume the responsibilities of self-government? Does any oppressed people count the cost of freedom? Does it make sense then for us to say to the African that he is really not ready for independence? The more we attempt to ram this down his throat the more we open his ears to the Communist slogan—"Wake up and break the shackles of Colonialism."

That "man does not live by bread alone" is proved by the ingratitude of the millions for the billions we give in economic and military aid. It is generally believed that we are repaid for these our gifts by some political quid-pro-quo, and our protestations to the contrary fall on deaf ears. The Soviets, whose material assistance to foreign countries is minimal, come along and "offer" the hand of fellowship in a struggle to throw off the yoke of imperialism and are everywhere welcomed and believed. So it is in Asia and so it will be in Africa unless we try a new technique or find a new policy.

Now our policy need not be novel just because it is new to us. It must be bold in the sense that we must free ourselves from the claws of the vice that has hindered our freedom of action. We should stop wooing the colonial powers (our N.A.T.O. partners) and instead let them seek us. Do we really fear that if we openly criticize proven injustices and basically espouse the cause of self-determination in Africa that we will sacrifice the cooperation and good will of those N.A.T.O. members who are also colonial powers? Does this barrier not exist really in our own minds? Is it not in fact born of our ignorance of Africa itself? The Belgian or the Frenchman who knows Africa will readily admit that the days of colonialism are numbered. Those who are liberal among them will say that the United States should bring pressures on the colonial powers; that these powers in their own interests should promptly divest themselves of the trappings of colonialism. In this connection I cite Brussels Embassy Despatch No. 430 of October 14, 1955,[4] indicating that responsible Belgians have matured to the point where they are receptive to constructive criticism of their colonial endeavors. The word "colonial" itself is outmoded and serves simply as a convenient mechanism for Communist propaganda. What would Belgium lose, for example, by a constitutional reform that would read the word "colony" out of its political lexicon? And why should it resent a suggestion in this regard?

Therefore it seems to me that the United States should go to all appropriate lengths to ascertain the facts in a given area in Africa. If the facts prove injustices, they should be laid bare, if after quiet talks with the administering power no effort is made to correct the abuse. I am thinking specifically of present conditions in Angola. This suggestion is not so much one of policy as of technique. It is designed to sow seeds ourselves in ground that is presently bare and fertile for the Communists.

Policy-wise we should get away if we can from thinking of French Africa, Belgian Africa, British Africa, Portuguese Africa, etc. In so doing, we shall first of all prepare ourselves to think of policies that apply to all of Central Africa. If possible, we might seek to arrest the trend toward nationalism in Central Africa. Such nationalism is superficial and ephemeral at best in this vast area where primary loyalty is still to the tribe and where there are literally hundreds of tribes. Pride is more of race and religion. Why not seek to build cooperatively a Union of Central Africa? We should not start this in a political sense or even from political motives. Just as in 1947 we conceived the Marshall Plan and saw this grow into a many hydra headed thing, so an African policy devoted to raising living standards, education, economic development can lead to political inter-cooperation even among European colonial powers themselves.

Is it too late to draw up a blueprint for economic development in Africa that disregards or transcends where necessary the geographical division of the continent? There is something very challenging in a bold attempt to redress the economic imbalance of Africa. (Researchers could have reference to the Berlin Conference of 1885 that blueprinted Central Africa for fifty years.) If we of the Western World can organize for defense, why cannot we also get together and organize for development? When the heat was on we found it easy because it was imperative that we and the British aid

[4] Despatch 430 indicated that Belgian Foreign Minister Paul-Henri Spaak had been criticized by some of his fellow socialists for his defense of France's Algerian policy. (*Ibid.*, 320/10–1455)

Egypt in the Aswan Dam project.[5] How long must we await decisions on other projects wherein we of the West have mutual interests in Africa?

It is heartening to note that the N.A.T.O. powers agreed at their last meeting to cooperate in the sense of Article 2 of the Treaty. Is this the framework within which to think out quietly and then implement publicly a "new deal" for Africa? All are agreed that Africa is vital to the defense of Europe and that the loss of its land-mass to the Soviets would imperil our own security. Then why not while so much of Africa is in the hands of N.A.T.O. powers bring it within the N.A.T.O. orbit. But not only for military reasons.

Instead of an information program that is uniquely U.S., why not combine with the French, British, Belgian and Portuguese to present bi-lateral programs designed to sell the African on the idea that his welfare and future depend upon Western ideas, culture and political systems. From what I have seen in the Congo, we are not reaching the masses with our USIS material. As long as we operate alone we cannot do so. But in conjunction with the colonial powers we can reach them not with the idea of preaching America but selling ideals we hold in common with those nations from whose midst we Americans have sprung.

Perhaps, since opinions as to what to do are so honestly divided, there might be merit in the suggestion that another "Mr. X" article be prepared for publication in the quarterly "Foreign Affairs". In it we could describe the dilemma. The writer could press heavily for a "new deal" in Africa—the last great land mass where modern techniques can be tried. If the article was properly tempered (as was the Kennan article in 1947),[6] it would be read and bring forth some very useful observations. Then in some quiet way we could serve notice on the Metropolitan powers that we are going to move into the forefront in espousing the cause of self-government for dependent peoples; that we will use all prudent means to press for progress in this field; that we will use our vote in the U.N. in favor of such a policy and that we are doing so in the interests of the Metropolitan powers themselves; that not to do so exposes Central African territories to the undermining influences of Soviet propaganda and the Bandung powers. The dike in Africa cannot be held against the combined assaults of Asia and the Soviets without a "Marshall Plan" for the continent. In the meantime, we should so maneuver as to cut

---

[5] The U.S. offer to assist Egypt in financing the Aswan Dam was withdrawn on July 19, 1956.

[6] George F. Kennan's article "The Sources of Soviet Conduct" appeared in the July 1947 issue of *Foreign Affairs*, pp. 566–582.

the ground out from under the "newer" by abolishing the vestiges of the "older" imperialism.

---

10. Memorandum From the Representative at the Trusteeship Council (Sears) to the Secretary of State [1]

New York, February 15, 1956.

SUBJECT

Future U.S. Policy in Africa

The attached report covers travels which I made under State Department orders during the autumn and early winter to Ethiopia, Kenya, Uganda, Tanganyika, Southern Rhodesia, South Africa, the Gold Coast, British Togoland and Nigeria. Its purpose was to collect information concerning various African problems bearing upon my duties as U.S. Representative on the Trusteeship Council and on the Committee on Information from Non-Self-Governing Territories.

Union of South Africa

This report begins with South Africa, where, thanks to our Embassy and Consulates, it was made possible for me to listen to many people, Europeans and non-Europeans, about the race question—whether it could be solved without going through a period of violence, and what were the long and short term prospects. Most of those with whom I talked did not anticipate any serious crisis for the next few years. Business men in particular were optimistic about the future. Industry is booming and they believed that an ever-expanding need for African labor would provide an orderly solution for all race problems. But, except for the Afrikaner (white Boer) Nationalists, they were alone in their confidence.

The Africans (negroes), Coloreds (half-castes) and Indians, although generally moderate in talk, were bitter about the extreme measures which the Strijdom Government is enacting in order to

[1] Source: Department of State, IO/ODA Files: Lot 62 D 225, U.S. Representative in the Trusteeship Council. Confidential. Enclosure to a letter from Lodge to Dulles, February 15, in which Lodge wrote: "Mason Sears may have irritated a few of the hard-shelled colonialists (although he is on very good terms with the actual administrators), but he certainly has made a lot of friends for us with the natives, who have the future in front of them and where it means something to the United States for the long pull."

apply an apartheid form of racial segregation. If present race supremacy policies, such as restricted education, no political rights, depressed wages, segregation, pass laws, and race hatreds persist, all of them spoke of the probability of being forced eventually into some form of peaceful resistance, such as strikes and boycotts. Strikes, if large enough, could break the national economy, but not without bloodshed, at least for so long as the present government remains in power—and most people believe that they will stay in power for a long time to come. [2]

It might be different if South Africa were a normal democratic community where governments can be voted in and out of office. But it is not. By packing the Senate, [3] the Afrikaner (Boer) nationalists have the votes to re-write the constitution at will and have already begun to create a police state. Furthermore, they are not a political party so much as the embodiment of resurgent anti-British Afrikanerdom. More than that, they are inspired by a religious belief in their racial superiority over the Africans. Put nationalism and religion together and add a universal fear of ultimately losing their racial identity in a sea of Africans and you have a party which is well nigh impossible to defeat by peaceful methods. This leaves a most uncertain prospect for South Africa.

But even if racial segregation is doomed to fail, as all but the fanatics agree, the important question is one of time. How long will it be before there is a first-rate blow-up? An important clue to this question is contained in the still confidential Tomlinson Report [4] which has been in the government's hands for two years. According to reliable information, this report concludes that if urgently needed soil preservation measures are not taken at once (which appears most

---

[2] Sears met with Harry Oppenheimer, Deputy Chairman of the Anglo-American Corporation and Member of Parliament for Kimberley; S.G. Menell, Chairman of the Board of the Anglo-Transvaal Consolidated Investment Company, Ltd.; and Dr. H.J. van Eck, Chairman of the Industrial Development Corporation of South Africa. On December 6, in the company of Ambassador Edward T. Wailes, Sears called on South African Prime Minister Johannes Gerhardus Strijdom. Sears reportedly saw as well: Dr. William Nkomo, Rev. S.S. Tema, Dr. A.B. Xuma, A.S. Tela, L.D. Newanca, B.B. Ramjee, F. Landman, and D. Brutus representing various segments of the non-white community. Information on these meetings is in despatch 168 from Pretoria, December 13 (*ibid.,* Central Files, 350/12–1355) and telegrams 129 from Johannesburg, December 7, and 194 from Pretoria, January 5, 1956 (*ibid.,* 350/12–755 and 350/1–556).

[3] To secure enough votes to pass a constitutional amendment to remove the Coloured from the common roll in the Cape Province, the Senate Bill was introduced on May 11, and passed on June 20, 1955. The Senate was increased from 48 to 89 seats of which the Nationalists gained 77 compared to 30 previously. This made possible the passage on February 13 of the South Africa Act Amendment Bill, 1956.

[4] The report of the Commission chaired by Professor F.R. Tomlinson of Pretoria University was submitted to the government on October 1, 1954. A 213-page summary of the nearly 4,000-page document was printed in March. (*Commission for the Socio-Economic Development of the Bantu Areas.* Summary of the Report (Pretoria, Government Printer, 1956))

unlikely), it will be too late to do much to save the productivity of the "native reserves". These are similar to our Indian reservations and are the cornerstone of apartheid, because it is planned that they will support the great bulk of the African population. Estimates are that if nothing is done, the food-growing capacity of the reserves will be largely exhausted within the short period of 15–20 years.

This is an important conclusion, because it defines quite precisely the critical 15–20 year period during which several millions of Africans will be forced off the reserves into city slums in search of work and food.

This means that the developing race crisis in South Africa—with all its implications for the other "white settler" areas of the continent—principally the Rhodesias and Kenya—could come to a head in 15 years and premonitory symptoms are before us now.

Rhodesias and Nyasaland

In the Federation of Rhodesia and Nyasaland, race relations are as important as they are in South Africa on its southern border. This new semi-self-governing federation is directly exposed to the contagious influence of racism in South Africa. Although Europeans amount to only 3% of the population, it is the second largest "white settler" area in Africa south of the Sahara. At present it looks as if its future would depend importantly upon how fast its European leaders can prove to the Africans that the official goal of race partnership is a sincere purpose. But it will not be easy to persuade the segregation-minded whites to reverse their long-standing customs of racial aloofness.

Prime Minister Todd of Southern Rhodesia, with whom I had a number of conversations, believes that the Federation has about ten years in which to make a success—to insulate itself from South African racism and to become a workable democracy. He feels that Nyasaland, which is almost 100% black African, is the central problem because it was forced into the Federation over the opposition of its entire population to any form of association with the "white settlers" of Southern Rhodesia.

A "white settler" district is not an easy district for a liberal man like Mr. Todd to represent. His constituency contains some 600 voters—nearly all white. He estimates that one-third of them are "poor whites". They are segregationist and anti-African—and a political road block to race partnership. One third are liberal and favor fast progress toward partnership. The middle third are easily frightened and sway from side to side. His problem is to bridge the gap between African and European thinking without losing his majority vote. If he fails he would be replaced by a less progressive representative, which would slow down the rate of progress toward "partnership". That is the problem in all white settler districts, wherever they are. Their progress is conditioned by the reactions of the most unprogressive—and the danger is that this may prove too slow to keep up with African evolution.

Another leader who has to face a "white settler" electorate is Sir Roy Welensky, who is slated to become Prime Minister of the Federation in the near future.[5] As one of the principal instigators of the new Federation, he is committed to race partnership, although his political life is dependent on the votes of the white miners of Northern Rhodesia (many of whom are South African Afrikaners) whose high pay is protected by the existence of an industrial color bar, which is the very opposite of race partnership. He told me that he could not deny that Africans would one day have complete control over the affairs of the Federal Government, and he spoke of the necessity of developing the Rhodesias as a buffer state, dedicated to race partnership, which could block Afrikaner race conflict from spreading north. But while these strictly private views may sound realistic and liberal, it is difficult to see how he can provide the necessary progressive leadership with the millstone of the white miners' union around his neck.

The hard core, conservative side of "white settler" politics is found in the views of Mr. Van Eeden[6]—new leader of the opposition in the Federal Assembly. His recent election to the Federal Assembly was won on a pure white state-apartheid issue. Mr. Van Eeden describes apartheid in South Africa—and his adaptation of it to the Rhodesias—as a "military movement" to protect the white man from the imminent danger of being swamped in a sea of Africans. His political success illustrates the difficulty which "white settlerism" poses for Messrs. Todd and Welensky, whose leadership depends entirely on their ability to win "white" votes.

Altogether the political situation in the Federation does not hold much prospect for the early assumption of sovereign self-government. Too many white people will have to revise radically their thinking about their status in Africa—and it is not going to be easy for them. In the meantime, it is unthinkable that the British Parliament will confer sovereignty upon the Federation and make it

[5] Sears met with Welensky, who succeeded Sir Godfrey M. Huggins as Federal Prime Minister in 1956, and with Todd. According to Consul General Loyd V. Steere, the meeting went well and Sears made a good impression, managing to conceal his impatience with the pace of African political advancement. (Letter from Steere to Cyr, December 1; Department of State, AF Files: Lot 58 D 562, Correspondence 1955 B.C.A.–Fed.)

[6] Guillaume François Marais Van Eeden left the United Federal Party and became a founder and leader of the right-wing Dominion Party in 1955.

eligible for membership in the British Commonwealth, until a majority of the Africans (negroes), particularly in Nyasaland, have changed their minds and expressed a desire to be included in the new nation. But the way things are shaping up, it is unlikely that race partnership can be brought about in time to create an effective barrier against the possible spread of South African racism, which was the original hope of the Federation founders.

Kenya

The only remaining "white settler" area of importance south of the Sahara is Kenya, whose white population, numbering less than 1% of the rapidly expanding African population, owns a vastly disproportionate share of the arable land. Here, as in the Rhodesias, the "white settlers" are divided between a minority of "white supremacists" and those who are less race-minded, or who would favor the rapid acceptance of Africans into the political and social life of the community. The leading "white settler" in public life is Mr. Michael Blundell, a very forward-looking, dynamic individual, who would go far in politics in whatever country he lived. His problem, as he describes it, is not the evolving African but the European. The difficulty, he says, is how to persuade the conservative wing of the "settler" group to think of themselves as cooperationists with the Africans rather than dominationists. He believes, however, that the Europeans, as a whole, have begun to take a new and a more understanding interest in African affairs.

This interest has been accelerated by the Mau Mau insurrection which I was reliably informed on all sides is nearly at an end. As of November last, there was said to be, all told, approximately 3,000 gangsters still at large. But their weekly losses at the hands of the forest tracker teams were such that the gangs would probably be broken up entirely within twelve months. Although large-scale rehabilitation and de-oathing of the Mau Mau captives is underway, it is an enormous task; and even when the gangs are no more, the anti-European aspect of the movement is expected to go underground, where it is hoped it will no longer be influenced by Mau Mau, with its fearful oath ceremonies.

In the meantime, progress toward self-government is slowly moving ahead with promise of faster progress in the future. In this regard Sir Frederick Crawford, the Deputy Governor told me that self-government could possibly be achieved considerably sooner than within the next generation. [7]

[7] This conversation is summarized in despatch 126 from Nairobi, October 20, 1955. (Department of State, Central Files, 350/10–2055)

The development of self-government in the Gold Coast, Nigeria, and Uganda will, of course, have a great impact on affairs in Kenya. There is also the effect of the 1955 report of a British Royal Commission on East Africa.[8] This will be interesting to watch as its comments and recommendations went much further and were fundamentally more revolutionary in their pro-African approach than the conclusions contained in the report of the 1954 Visiting Mission of the United Nations with respect to Tanganyika.

There is a brand of thinking in Kenya that the country could have a most interesting future—if it is given time, and if "white settlerism" and its segregationist ideas can moderate quickly enough. There is tribal rivalry and dislike between the Africans. There are also deep divisions among the Asians, as between Hindu and Moslem, Ishmaili, Sikh and Arab. Owing to this, some people think that when the electorate has become dominantly African, a European running for public office—where he would be obliged to be sensitive to the needs and wants of the African majority—might well become a successful and an effective, cohesive force in the future evolution of the territory, even after self-government. But that depends on the ability of the local Europeans to transfer power to the Africans fast enough to keep pace with African demands to possess it.

"White Settlerism" in General

I will not go into the subject of "white settlerism" or "white supremacy" in French North Africa, except to say that it gives every evidence of going the way it did in Indochina, only much faster. It is also clearly evident that "white settlerism" in Africa is the only real obstacle that stands in the way of finally eliminating not only the colonial issue (in its western sense) but also the even more dangerous racist issues upon all of which the Soviets thrive. But it must not be forgotten that these European nationals live where they do by constitutional right. They have made their homes in far-away lands. Furthermore, many of them have contributed greatly to their communities. Yet there must be somewhere an answer to the perplexing question of how to persuade or perhaps to force the obdurate, right wingers among the "settlers" to become cooperative with the Africans. In a continent of 200 million people it is out of all proportion that a handful of perhaps less than 20,000 white diehards in colonial territories and say 2,000,000 split between the "colons" of North Africa and the Afrikaner (Boers) of South Africa can provide the flame to spark an international colonial-race issue which has become damaging in the extreme to the leading powers of

[8] *Cmd.* 9475.

the free world, including the United States. But since they have, it becomes essential to recognize the implications of the Mau Mau insurrection in Kenya and the organized terrorism of the Moslems in North Africa. These violent movements resulted when the cleavage between the African "have nots" and the European "haves" became too prolonged and too pronounced for orderly settlement. Almost more disturbing has been the reaction of the white mobs to any solution of the race troubles in Algeria, Tunis and Morocco other than continued suppression by military means. It may be a small scale preview of where South Africa is heading.

West Africa

The place furthest removed from "white settlerism" is West Africa, where the evolution of the Imperial System of Great Britain into a modern and strong British Commonwealth will find its first African tests in the Gold Coast and Nigeria—and I also would include Uganda, which is being developed like these other two as a purely African state. Whereas progress toward self-government in East and Central Africa is being held back by "white settler" die-hards, the progress in British West Africa goes on at a pace which the Africans are finding it difficult to keep up with.

By far the most important and the most interesting political developments are in the Gold Coast, which already enjoys complete internal self-government and is expected to become entirely independent sometime in 1957. In fact, the Gold Coast is so much in charge of its own affairs that the British Governor is placed in the embarrassing position of having responsibility without authority. For this reason the British Government is extremely anxious to withdraw entirely from the Gold Coast at the earliest possible date. In the meantime, Prime Minister Nkrumah's timetable for the actual assumption of independence has been somewhat delayed by his political opponents in Ashanti (in the center of the country) and in the northern territories. This means that Mr. Nkrumah needs to exhibit a high degree of statesmanship in order to reconcile various conflicting political interests within his country. In fact, the ability of Africans to reconcile their tribal differences when they come to the brink of nationhood is being severely tested. If the Gold Coast fails to solve its current problems and the British are obliged to prolong their presence, the cause of African self-government throughout the continent will be thrown back for several years.

On the other hand, the Trust Territory of British Togoland will hold a United Nations supervised plebiscite in May. If the vote goes heavily for unification with the Gold Coast, as it probably will, it will be a great victory for Nkrumah and will help him to solve his problems in Ashanti.

Then there is also the fact that the forthcoming plebiscite in British Territory has already made it most difficult for the French Government to delay long in agreeing to a plebiscite on self-government for the adjoining territory of French Togoland.

In any event, the appearance of a number of sovereign African nations in West Africa will almost certainly have a disturbing influence upon race relations in South Africa, in the Central African Federation and in East Africa. In fact, it is bound to hasten the day of decision in those parts of Africa when the white settler will be forced to decide one way or another about his role in African affairs.

The whole African picture is further complicated by the Communist problem. With the inevitable growth of trade unionism and its possibilities for Communist penetration which has already occurred in Lebanon and Syria, and with the increasing Communist opportunities to encourage racism in white settler Africa, the whole question of whether Africa can be kept on the side of the free world becomes a matter of supreme importance. At all events, developments which will not be to our advantage, such as racial conflict, industrial unrest, and the political instability which is natural in new governments are about to take shape in the near future so that it would be too bad if our preoccupation with the more immediate and the more urgent problems of Europe and Asia should obscure the growing importance of Africa to our future.

In conclusion, it is one thing to describe the approaching difficulties which are certain to face the United States in its relationship with Africa, but is is quite another thing to suggest what to do about it. Political and economic evolution in Africa is still in such a formative stage that a "play it by ear" policy is about all we can pursue—for the moment. There are, however, several recommendations which I hope the State Department will see fit to consider.

Recommendations

1. My first recommendation concerns the Fourth of July, when our Embassies and Consulates all over the world hold large receptions in honor of our Declaration of Independence—and yet Africans are entirely excluded from American soil on this day in South Africa, and to a large extent in Southern Rhodesia, and in Kenya, where perhaps a few get by the bar, but not many. To me it seems a little off color that the fear of displeasing a tiny handful of anti-African Europeans should in any way restrain the representatives of the United States from publicly celebrating American tradition. The inclusion of Africans at these American receptions would be a very

little thing to do and would have a very happy effect upon millions of Africans all over the continent. I believe that this is a matter which should not be left to the discretion of our representatives on the spot. It should come as a clear and specific order from the Secretary of State, especially considering the recent disgraceful race riots in Alabama. It would please many citizens of the United States, and a careful program should be worked out to see to it that American opinion be informed of this decision.[9]

2. Another recommendation concerns the problem of the French Union and the necessity for it to become a strong and truly voluntary association of sovereign nations like the British Commonwealth, in which membership carries with it not only international representation but the right to resign. As it stands today, the French Union is fundamentally an imperial or colonial association in which the main source of political power is retained in Paris. This means that no French African overseas territory is going to be content to remain in the French Union so long as final authority over its most vital affairs remains in Paris and in the hands of French-born Frenchmen.

While each territory has technical representation in the French Parliament, they do not enjoy anywhere near equal representation with the citizens of metropolitan France. The French are in the process of being thrown out of North Africa, which some Frenchmen think may be a prelude to the ultimate loss of their position in the rest of Africa. This would be a great blow to the free world, because the stability of each emerging African nation can depend much upon its opportunity to affiliate with some strong free world international organization which has become a going concern. The French Union has not. For this reason, I believe that the United States should press and keep on pressing the French Government, whenever this can be done effectively, to reform their present Union, especially with respect to the status of its overseas territories, so that it may become a more attractive federation of equals, each with its own right of self-government and especially the right to resign. Nothing short of this will make it an organization which the French African territories would be glad to join.

3. The real problem of Africa, however, is the Union of South Africa, where I fear that little can be done. There is one aspect about the Union which worries me particularly. To be realistic, I would suppose that between the United Kingdom and the United States we are to a great extent—through our South African trade—helping to support and prolong the exploitation of African labor with its deliberately depressed wages, its segregation, and all the other evils

[9] See the editorial note, *infra.*

that arise out of the South African race problem. While I do not know what our position is with respect to our purchase of gold and nuclear materials, I suppose that the time will come when the purchase of one ounce of these materials will be of less value to us than a corresponding ounce of good will from the Asiatic-African peoples which would be ours if we were to apply some degree of trade sanctions in order to force South African racial reforms. I am not for one moment proposing that we adopt such a policy now, but I do suppose that between the United States and the United Kingdom we could—if we wanted to and dared to—impose some sort of trade restrictions on the Union of South Africa which would bring the Nationalist Government to its knees over night. But that is merely an observation—something to think about and to study for the future.

---

11. Editorial Note

In his February 15 letter to Secretary Dulles cited in footnote 1, *supra,* Ambassador Lodge expressed his concern about the domestic political repercussions of the segregated celebrations described by Sears in his first paragraph of recommendations. Lodge indicated that the Democrats "would certainly jump on the Fourth of July business if they knew about it. Per contra, we could get some credit at home if we ended this practice. I can't help wondering whether our people are pushing the issue as hard as the traffic will bear, or merely following the line of least resistance."

When Lodge raised the issue again with the Secretary on March 23, Dulles responded on April 3 that he entirely agreed "that invitations should not be issued on a basis of caste, color or creed at any of our public functions, either here or abroad. This is a good American principle that should guide all of us, all the time. As regards the applicability of this principle to specific posts abroad, I believe our people should apply it to the extent the traffic will bear. The equally American characteristic of good common horse sense should also apply." (Department of State, AF/AFE Files, Lot 62 D 417, Mason Sears Report: Union of S. Africa–2)

Subsequently, on June 7, Sears met with Officer in Charge of Southern Africa Affairs Donald Dumont, and a number of desk officers. Sears expressed his desire that Dulles issue an order mandating integrated July 4th celebrations in South Africa. He maintained that it would prove beneficial throughout Africa and not redound negatively against the United States in the Union. If Ambassador Wailes was declared persona non grata then Sears considered that a small sacrifice to pay for the many advantages to be gained. In rebuttal, Sears was told that this indeed would be a serious loss without comparable benefits and without consideration of the issues of defense and strategic materials. United States officials were alleged to have gone farther than most in developing contacts with non-Whites who were not even invited to Egyptian diplomatic functions. Were the United States to provoke the Union Government then it was likely that all access to non-Whites would be cut off. Moreover, Strijdom's government was described as having demonstrated, since September 1955, "a strong and dramatic desire to accommodate itself to the emergence of new African states to the north." Foreign Service officers in the Union had as their principal objective the perpetuation of stable, orderly development which included, Sears was informed, "whenever possible and practicable, the persuasion of responsible South African Whites to moderate their restrictive racial policies." (Memorandum of conversation by Johnson, June 7; *ibid.*, Central Files, 811.424/6–756) As a result of this meeting, Sears called Dumont the next day to indicate that he had abandoned his plan to pursue the matter with the Secretary. He indicated that he had been convinced that what he proposed was not in the best interest of the United States. (Memorandum of conversation by Dumont, June 8; *ibid.*, 811.424/6–856)

---

12. Letter From the Representative at the Trusteeship Council (Sears) to the Assistant Secretary of State for International Organization Affairs (Wilcox)[1]

New York, April 3, 1956.

DEAR FRANCIS: Yesterday in the Trusteeship Council the United States Delegation took a position in favor of requesting the British and Belgian Governments to consider the practicability of adopting programs of planned development in Tanganyika and Ruanda Urundi respectively, in the form of *intermediate targets* and dates in certain political, economic, social and educational fields. Our point of view was almost angrily opposed by the British Representative

[1] Source: Department of State, IO Files: Lot 60 D 113. Limited Official Use.

and less so by the Representative of Belgium. As a result, I have a hunch that the British and Belgian Embassies in Washington may make some sort of protest to the State Department and so I wished to give you a little background.[2]

First of all, I think it is right to tell you that the course which we took in the Council was initiated and strongly urged by me from the very start. However, its actual presentation was made with great skill by Ben Gerig, who is serving as the United States Representative during the period while I am serving as President.

Secondly, our position was taken from Section 9 of this year's position book in which we were under virtual instructions from the Department to favor the establishment of intermediate target dates. The position book stated that "If the question of timetables should come up, either in the Drafting Committees or in the Council itself, the Delegation *should support* a recommendation for the establishment of target dates for the achievement of intermediate goals in the fields of *political,* economic, social, and educational advancement in the territories where such target dates are realistic."[3]

Furthermore, in presenting our position yesterday with respect to Tanganyika, Ben Gerig made what I consider to be a remarkable speech in which he went no further than to invite the British merely to consider the practicability of adopting intermediate target dates for political, economic and social development, and he recommended that such programs might be considered in connection with the widening of suffrage, the increasing of legislative and executive powers, or in the building of representative institutions based increasingly on the consent of the governed. He also observed that such programs should be kept flexible enough so that they could be changed during the course of their operation. In brief, all that our Delegation did was to bring to the attention of the British authorities in Tanganyika the kind of idea which would call for the consideration of adding, let us say at the end of three years, perhaps three or more Africans to the Legislative Council. That was the type of thing we had in mind—nothing big—nothing startling, and nothing that could not be changed in mid-stream. And again, this is completely in line with Department recommendations, particularly

---

[2] On April 2, the Trusteeship Council approved reports on the trust territories of Tanganyika and Ruanda Urundi, including recommendations for intermediate target dates which the United Kingdom and Belgium opposed. The report on Tanganyika was drafted by a committee chaired by Gerig. For the record of the meeting and the texts of the reports, see U.N. documents T/SR.697, T/L.657, and T/L.653, respectively. The Council's recommendations were included in the appropriate chapters in its annual report to the General Assembly (U.N. document A/3170).

[3] Reference is to position paper SD/T/295, February 1, prepared for the delegation to the Seventeenth Session of the Trusteeship Council. (Department of State, IO Files: Lot 60 D 113)

those to be found on Page 2 of Section 9 of the Position Book for last year. This recommendation stated that "The Delegation might also support (the kind of) recommendation which would urge the further development . . . of executive and legislative organs . . . [4] the provision of increased opportunities for indigenous participation in government" and so on. I cannot imagine a more reasonable suggestion and I am confident that if it is adopted, it will have really beneficial effects in both Tanganyika and Ruanda Urundi. It will also be very well received by all literate Africans throughout Tanganyika.

Let me also add that East Africa is one area in the continent where the United States can well afford to pay more attention to its relations with the African people themselves.

If the British by chance should come to see you in order to protest against the United States position in the Council, I hope you will privately agree with me that it is a little unbecoming for a nation which is doing so much for self-government all over the world to take objection because the United States joined other nations in asking them merely to consider a course of action—even though it had to do in a most limited way with what to their Colonial Office is the sacrosanct subject of timetables. [5]

I send you my best regards and hope that you are enjoying your responsibilities in Washington.

Yours sincerely,

Mason Sears

P.S.—I am enclosing a copy of the speeches made by Mr. Gerig and Sir Alan Burns. [5]

[4] Ellipses in the source text.

[5] Not printed.

13. Editorial Note

Note No. 347 of May 25 from the British Ambassador to the Secretary of State protested United States support for the April 2 Trusteeship Council report on Tanganyika (cited in footnote 2, *supra*), which had included the recommendation that the British Government should indicate target dates for steps in the political, economic, social, and educational fields which would create conditions for Tanganyika's attainment of self-government or independence. (Department of State, Central Files, 350/5–2556)

A note of July 2 from the Secretary of State to the Ambassador stated that the United States continued to agree with the British concerning the "impractibility" of long-range timetables for the attainment of self-government or independence but defended United States support for the principle of intermediate targets. The note concludes:

"It is the belief of the United States Government that the establishment of intermediate targets and dates is not only a basically different concept but represents sound planning and will be advantageous to the United Kingdom in Tanganyika and to both Governments in the United Nations, particularly since, as was stated by the Deputy United States Representative in the Council, 'it is for the Administering Authority in every case to decide how far and how fast such programs can be carried out'.

"For the reasons elaborated above, the United States Government considers the principle of intermediate targets to be practicable and sound. The British Government, moreover, will appreciate that the United States Government cannot disregard opinion in the United States which is particularly sensitive regarding colonialism, even in its most enlightened form. Consequently, impatience tends to develop if the United States Government does nothing more than voice its opposition to proposals for long-range timetables looking toward the ending of the admittedly temporary colonial relationship.

"The United States Government, therefore, feels impelled, in rejecting impracticable proposals for final time limits, to support the constructive counterproposal for intermediate targets and dates. It is the hope of the United States Government that the British Government, upon closer study, will find itself able to apply the recommendation without in any way damaging its vital interests." (*Ibid.*)

The United Kingdom and United States Delegations met in Washington, October 10–11, for the third in a series of discussions on colonial matters. (Informal Summary Record of the U.S.–U.K. Colonial Talks, October 10–11; *ibid.*, IO/ODA Files: Lot 62 D 182, US–UK Colonial Talks) The British subsequently placed on the record their understanding of what transpired. (Note 49 to the Department of State, January 28, 1957; *ibid.*, Central Files, 320/1-2357) The United States position was principally stated by Christopher H. Phillips, Deputy Assistant Secretary of State for International Organization Affairs. Emphasizing that the United States should not be stereotyped as defender of colonialism, he assured the British that the United States had no intention of supplanting any colonial power, but in deference to nationalism was obliged to assume a more liberal and independent position. The United States, Sears added, could not "stop being the United States" and would therefore continue on its course except where security interests intruded. The Position Papers prepared in the Department of State for the use of the Delegation to the Eleventh Session of the General Assembly (*Attainment by the Trust Territories of the Objective of Self-Government or Independence*) called for continued support for intermediate target dates "primarily because it is practicable and right in itself, and incidentally because it would help to defeat unrealistic long-range timetable proposals." (SD/A/C.4/159, October 30; *ibid.*, IO Files)

On February 26, 1957, the General Assembly adopted Resolution 1064 (XI), which recommended that the administering authorities of the trust territories of Tanganyika, the Cameroons, Togoland, and Ruanda-Urundi take the necessary measures to ensure that those territories achieved self-government or independence at an early date. It also invited all administering powers to estimate the period of time required for this in their trust territories. The United States voted against the resolution. For text, see *American Foreign Policy: Current Documents, 1956*, pages 159–160.

14. National Intelligence Estimate [1]

NIE 72–56 *Washington, August 14, 1956.*

CONDITIONS AND TRENDS IN TROPICAL AFRICA [2]

The Problem

To identify the major trends and problems in the area and to estimate probable developments and their potential consequences for the Free World. [3]

Conclusions

1. Within the next decade, the accelerating trends in Tropical Africa toward self-government and hostility to European tutelage almost certainly will transform in varying degrees and ways the relationships between most of the remaining colonial territories and the powers that control them. The peoples of Africa will make increasing demands for self-government with little regard for wide differences in their degrees of development. (Para. 70)

2. Particularly in the areas under British control, and to a lesser degree in French Africa, the result is likely to be an increasingly rapid emergence of new native states. In the Belgian and Portuguese areas, self-government will come more slowly. (Paras. 71, 73)

3. Throughout Tropical Africa, regardless of how political demands are handled, interracial tensions between Africans and Euro-

---

[1] Source: Department of State, INR–NIE Files. Secret. National Intelligence Estimates (NIEs) were high-level interdepartmental reports presenting authoritative appraisals of vital foreign policy problems. NIEs were drafted by officers from those agencies represented on the Intelligence Advisory Committee (IAC), discussed and revised by interdepartmental working groups coordinated by the Office of National Estimates of the Central Intelligence Agency (CIA), approved by the IAC, and circulated under the aegis of the CIA to the President, appropriate officers of cabinet level, and the National Security Council. The Department of State provided all political and some economic sections of NIEs. The files are retained by the Directorate for Regional Research, Bureau of Intelligence and Research.

According to a note on the cover sheet, "The following intelligence organizations participated in the preparation of this estimate: the Central Intelligence Agency and the intelligence organizations of the Departments of State, the Army, the Navy, the Air Force, and the Joint Staff. Concurred in by the Intelligence Advisory Committee on 14 August 1956. . . . The Atomic Energy Commission Representative to the IAC, and the Assistant Director, Federal Bureau of Investigation, abstained, the subject being outside of their jurisdiction."

[2] This estimate supersedes NIE 83, "Conditions and Trends in Tropical Africa," published December 30, 1953. [Footnote in the source text. NIE 83 is printed in *Foreign Relations*, 1952–1954, vol. XI, Part 1, p. 71.]

[3] This estimate deals generally with all African territories south of the Sahara except for the Sudan and the Union of South Africa; the latter was covered in NIE 72, published 20 October 1952. [Footnote in the source text. NIE 72 is printed *ibid.*, p. 953.]

pean settlers, and between natives and Asians, especially Indians, in East Africa, will almost certainly increase. Such demands and tensions are likely to result in sporadic and even sustained violence, particularly in areas of heavy white settlement. (Para. 74)

The European powers may still have sufficient time to exert a moderating influence through the implementation of liberal colonial policies, which possibly might avert major hostilities. Should major violence occur, we believe that the European powers will retain the military strength to maintain their position for at least the next five years in the most troubled areas. However, the degree of control over the affairs of their territories exercised by metropolitan and colonial governments will continue to decline. (Para. 75)

5. Where self-government is achieved, there will remain formidable political and economic problems. The instability of the transition period of slackening European control probably will be followed by an instability arising from the contest for power between new states which themselves still lack strong internal cohesion. In their relationships with the present colonial powers, new native states are likely to be difficult to deal with. (Paras. 76–78)

6. Meanwhile, the Communists and the Arab-Asian states will be competing with the West for power and influence. Egypt will continue to encourage and support native nationalism and the spread of Islam as part of its effort to become a leader in Africa, particularly at the expense of the colonial powers. India will also continue to give support to African and other movements for independence in a bid for leadership of the Afro-Asian countries. (Paras. 79–80)

7. Despite the present weakness of the Communists, their influence and numerical strength will increase. Recent aid offers and various other moves by the USSR to extend its influence are almost certainly a prelude to more extensive efforts. With growing political unrest, some Africans will be disposed to accept assistance from any quarter. Moreover, native governments will become vulnerable to offers of economic assistance and of favorable trading arrangements. (Paras. 34–36, 81–82)

8. During the conflict between the metropoles and their territories which are demanding self-rule, the US will be bombarded by both sides with demands for diplomatic and moral support. Where new African states are established, the US will be increasingly pressed to extend political and economic support. Moreover, the US increasingly will be pressed by rival African states to favor their competing causes. Those which fail to enlist such support would be likely to seek aid from the Arab-Asian countries or from the Soviet Bloc. However, it is unlikely that most Africans will identify themselves closely with either side in the East-West struggle. Very few of the new African states are likely to be prepared to ally themselves

formally with the West; in general, new states will seek to avoid any type of agreement that appears to involve any commitment to either side. (Para. 83)

9. Notwithstanding prospective political changes, Western access to strategic and essential raw materials will generally be preserved. Tropical African exports of such materials will increase in the short run, but disorder and unrest may impair production and transport over the longer run. Of the important producing areas, the Belgian Congo probably will be one of the most stable, while British West Africa and probably the Federation of Rhodesia and Nyasaland may become less dependable sources of supply. (Para. 84)

10. In the event of another war, Tropical Africa could have substantial military importance. In particular, it could provide essential facilities to support Western lines of communication if the West were denied North African or Near Eastern operating bases or the Mediterranean-Suez line of communication. It could also provide operational staging and supply bases for Western operations elsewhere. The emergence of new native states tending toward a neutral position may result in a denial to the West of present or potential military facilities in their areas. Moreover, growing unrest and disorder would probably hamper, although it would not prevent, Western use of those military facilities available in the event of war. (Paras. 17, 85)

[Here follow sections entitled: "Introduction," "Over-All Problems and Trends," "Selected Regional Problems and Prospects," and "The Outlook for Western Interests."]

---

15. Editorial Note

Effective September 10, the Department of State established the new position of Deputy Assistant Secretary of State for African Affairs in the Bureau of Near Eastern, South Asian, and African Affairs. The existing Office of African Affairs was divided into the Office of Northern Africa Affairs and the Office of Southern Africa Affairs. The former had primary responsibility for the conduct of United States relations with Ethiopia, Libya, Morocco, Tunisia, British and French Somalilands and Somalia, and the Spanish Sahara. The latter was concerned with United States relations with the Union of South Africa, Liberia, Angola, Basutoland, Bechuanaland, the Belgian Congo, the Cameroons (British and French), French

Equatorial Africa, French West Africa, the Gold Coast, Spanish and Portuguese Guinea, Kenya, Madagascar, Mozambique, Nigeria, the Federation of Rhodesia and Nyasaland, Ruanda-Urundi, Sierra Leone, South-West Africa, Swaziland, Tanganyika, French Togoland, Uganda, Zanzibar, and various British and French Indian Ocean islands.

---

16. Memorandum From the Officer in Charge of Southern Africa Economic Affairs (Longanecker) to the Director of the Office of Southern Africa Affairs (Hadsel)[1]

Washington, October 31, 1956.

PRINCIPAL ECONOMIC PROBLEMS

Dakar

Our Consulate General at Dakar has no special economic problems relating to French West Africa. There are no U.S. assistance programs in French West Africa owing to the fact that the French Government has not been receptive to aid involving American technicians in its overseas territories. The French Government has been agreeable to accepting strictly financial aid but ICA has taken the position that in view of the French Government's rather negative attitude with respect to U.S. aid and to the evolution of its territories to self-government, U.S. aid should not be made available. We are interested, of course, in the political and economic development of French West Africa and in the development programs which the French Government is planning and carrying out there.

Monrovia

The major economic concern of our Embassy at Monrovia relates to our aid program in Liberia. The program goes back to World War II days when the FEA established economic and health missions in Liberia in connection with construction of the Port of Monrovia and its use by the United States military. The program was taken over by the Technical Cooperation Administration and is considered one of the more successful U.S. assistance activities

---

[1] Source: Department of State, AF/AFS Files: Lot 59 D 293, Regional Economic Reports 1956. Written in response to a memorandum from Hadsel of October 26 to Longanecker, Donald Dumont, and James J. Durnan. (*Ibid.*)

abroad. It has been popular with the Liberian Government and people until recently when the Government began to (1) manifest dissatisfaction with the amount of our aid in Liberia compared with other countries and (2) put out feelers for economic assistance as well. American private capital and enterprise, principally in rubber and mining industries, are contributing to a steady expansion of the Liberian economy and the revenues of the Government. This has encouraged the Government to draw up ambitious development plans which have reached the point where they are now taxing its financial, including loan servicing, capacity. Instead of tailoring the development plans to fit the country's financial capacity, the Government is endeavoring to build up a case for additional U.S. aid in the form of development assistance.

Accra

Our principal economic concern in the Gold Coast is whether this newly emerging self-governing territory will be able to plan and finance a rate of social and economic development which will insure sound and orderly progress and continued orientation to the West. The Gold Coast is primarily a one crop (cocoa) economy. Because of the very high prices which have prevailed for cocoa in the last three or four years the Government has been able to plan and implement a large and expanding development program. The revenues and expenditures of the Government, both for the ordinary services of government as well as for extraordinary development purposes, have multiplied in recent years. The approval of development projects, for which the necessary funds have been set aside, has been at an annual level which considerably exceeds the capacity of the country to carry out except over a period of years. There is consequently a several years backlog of approved and financed development work.

Within the past 12 months or so cocoa prices have dropped sharply from the peak reached in 1955. The price level is still high enough to return satisfactory profits, but the Government's revenues available from this source have dropped sharply necessitating a retrenchment in both ordinary and extraordinary budget expenditures. Sterling holdings of the Government are substantial and the Cocoa Marketing Board established some years ago to stabilize cocoa prices and the income of producers has an appreciable reserve fund.

The major project of interest to the Gold Coast Government at this time is the Volta River Scheme. This project involves a hydroelectric dam installation on the Volta River in combination with bauxite and aluminum production to be financed by a combination of loan capital from the British Government, private capital from Aluminium, Limited, of Canada and, contributions from the Gold

Coast Government. The project has been under study and discussion for several years and while the Gold Coast Government has already set aside an initial allocation of funds for it, the interest of both the British Government and Aluminium, Ltd., has declined appreciably during 1956. It is now in a decidedly uncertain status.

Various Gold Coast officials have visited the United States in the past year or so to discuss technical cooperation assistance. Several projects have been agreed on, the major one involving assistance in expanding the Gold Coast's community development activity. [2]

Lagos

Nigeria is also headed for independence in the relatively near future. Like the Gold Coast, the economy has been prosperous in recent years and there has been a steady expansion of government revenues and expenditures. Various Nigerian officials have visited the United States in the last year or so in connection with their interest in obtaining technical cooperation assistance. Several small projects have been agreed on in principle and it is likely that such cooperation between the two countries will grow. Particular emphasis has been expressed in assistance in the fields of education and community development. [3]

Yaoundé

Our principal economic concern in the French Cameroons is with general economic conditions and progress of the territory, and the need for U.S. assistance.

Leopoldville

We have no particular economic problems in the Belgian Congo. The economy of the Congo is prosperous and flourishing and it is difficult to justify U.S. assistance even if the Belgian Government should ask for it. Our major economic interest is in maintaining access to the Congo market and investment possibilities for American business and private capital, the continued development of the country's rich resources, and the availability to the American market of those Congo products we need.

---

[2] The Ghanaian Minister of Finance, K.A. Gbedemah, visited Washington on more than one occasion.

[3] Among the Nigerian officials who came to Washington were: Obafemi Awolowo, Premier of the Western Region; Nnamdi Azikiwe, Premier and Minister of Internal Affairs of the Eastern Region; the Federal Minister of Transport, Abubakar Tafawa Balewa; the Federal Minister of Communication, K.O. Mbadiwe; C.D. Akran, the Minister of Development of the Western Region; and I.U. Akpabio, Minister of Education of the Eastern Region.

Our particular interest at this time is the Inga Hydroelectric-Industrial complex development project on the lower Congo now being studied by representatives of the Belgian Government and Belgian industry. This is a very large project estimated to cost well over a half billion dollars. There is a growing disposition on the part of the Belgian Government to consider American private capital participation in this project. It remains to be seen, however, whether the long time nationalistic disposition of the Belgian Government and Belgian business and financial interests to pre-empt the commercial and economic potentials in the Congo will give way to the point of accepting any appreciable participation of American capital and enterprise in the Ingo project if it is undertaken.

Johannesburg, Pretoria

There are no special economic problems confronting our Embassy in the Union of South Africa as this is one of the two countries in Africa in which American capital and business enterprise have been welcome and have not had any particular difficulties with exchange or profit remittance regulations. The Union is not interested in U.S. aid and our economic interest is in the continued growth of South African economy and maintenance of the very satisfactory economic relations between the two countries.

Salisbury

We are very much interested in the success of the Federation of Rhodesia and Nyasaland. The economy is prosperous and flourishing and undergoing a rapid rate of economic development. The Government is trying to accelerate its already substantial social and economic development program in order to establish and maintain a progressive and democratic economy consistent with the objectives of the Federation. The Federation has a very favorable balance of trade and of payments with the United States and is therefore a large net earner of dollars. Its capital expenditures for equipment and supplies needed for both the government development program and private industrial expansions are a heavy drain on the country's foreign exchange earnings. With the beginning recently of the large expenditures for the Kariba Gorge project, the Government is heavily committed credit wise and may well have to slow down or restrict its development expenditures in other fields. We are very much interested in the success of the Federation and are examining ways and means in which we might demonstrate our sympathetic interest in the success of the Federation and its multi-racial objectives, by providing some assistance especially in those fields concerned with improvement of the native peoples, i.e., irrigation and resettlement projects, vocational training, etc.

Nairobi, Kampala

U.S. aid was extended for several small projects in British East Africa a few years ago. The Mau Mau situation together with the lack of progress in the territories toward self-government, however, have resulted in a disposition on the part of ICA not to extend further aid to these territories. U.S. technical cooperation could be useful in meeting some of these territories' problems but there are no prospects for such assistance at this time.

---

17. Editorial Note

Before a Joint Session of Congress on January 5, 1957, the President enunciated what came to be known as the Eisenhower Doctrine, intended to bolster the economic strength, defensive capacity, and independence of Middle East nations and to provide, upon request, military assistance to nations imperiled by Communist armed aggression. On March 9, the Congress authorized the implementation of a program of economic and military aid (Public Law 85–7, 71 Stat. 5). The President charged Ambassador James P. Richards with the responsibility of conveying United States proposals and explaining United States policies to the concerned nations. In the course of his mission between March 12 and May 8, Ambassador Richards visited Lebanon, Libya, Turkey, Iran, Pakistan, Afghanistan, Greece, Tunisia, Morocco, Iraq, Saudi Arabia, Yemen, Ethiopia, Israel, and the Sudan. Regarding Richards' talks in North and North East Africa, see Documents 118–120, 167, 213, 237, and 250–251.

18. Memorandum of a Conversation, Mid-Ocean Club Conference Room, Bermuda, March 23, 1957, 10:30 a.m.[1]

USDel/MC/8

PARTICIPANTS

United States
The Secretary
Sen. George
Amb. Whitney
Mr. Quarles
Mr. Murphy
Mr. Rountree
Mr. Elbrick
Mr. Hagerty
Gen. Goodpaster
Mr. Macomber
Mr. Phleger
Mr. Wilkins

United Kingdom
Mr. Selwyn Lloyd
Sir Frederick Hoyer Millar
Mr. P.H. Dean
Mr. Harold Beeley
Sir Harold Caccia

SUBJECTS

1. Communist Influence in Africa
2. Baghdad Pact
3. Tripartite Declaration of 1950
4. Question of Arms Supply to the Near East—Resolutions of the General Assembly
5. Agreed Positions, including Guarantees re Pipelines, Palestine, Suez, Oil Study, Aqaba and Libya
6. Germany
7. Communiqué

1. *Communist Influence in Africa.* Selwyn Lloyd referred to the paper entitled "Communist Influence in Africa"[2] and noted that the United Kingdom and the United States had reached an agreed position. He said he thought this subject was important because he believed that the battle for the next ten years would lie on the continent of Africa. He also said that recent Communist activities in Africa had rather taken the UK by surprise.

The Secretary said that we were in agreement with the UK regarding the importance of Africa and observed that we would be in serious trouble if Africa were lost to the Free World. As evidence of the importance which we attached to the future of Africa, the Department of State had recently requested the American Congress

[1] Source: Department of State, Conference Files: Lot 62 D 181, CF 861, Bermuda 1957 Memos of Con. (MP). Secret. Drafted by Wilkins on March 25.

[2] BEM D–5/1a, March 13, was approved in whole by NEA and BNA and in substance by EE. (*Ibid.*, CF 856, Bermuda Meetings—Briefing and Position Papers, Volume II)

to create a separate Bureau of African Affairs, to be headed by an Assistant Secretary.[3] We also were somewhat concerned regarding recent Communist activities in Africa and, to take a concrete case, we were a little disturbed to note a report that the new state of Ghana planned to establish diplomatic relations with the USSR, including a mission and staff. This development would, of course, provide the Soviet Union with a perfect opportunity to move into the West Coast of Africa. The Secretary asked Selwyn Lloyd if there was any way in which the establishment of diplomatic relations between Ghana and the Soviet Union could be stopped.

. . . British information indicated that when this matter had arisen for consideration within the Government of Ghana, there had been a sharp division on the subject, and that it was not as yet quite certain that a decision had been reached to establish diplomatic relations.

Selwyn Lloyd, in response to the Secretary's statement re the establishment of a separate American Bureau of African Affairs, commented that in England they had three government departments handling British foreign affairs. These were the British Foreign Office, the British Colonial Office, and the Commonwealth Relations Office. It was therefore necessary for Selwyn Lloyd to express his views with care.

Selwyn Lloyd said that the UK considered it important to maintain friendly relations with Ethiopia. The UK was endeavoring to reconcile the Ethiopians and the Somalis. If an independent state of Somalia should be created it would be weak and would probably fall under the influence of Egypt. A weak Somalia would be unfortunate because of the strategic importance of that area.

The Secretary said that when he had last seen the Ethiopian Foreign Minister[4] in London, the latter had expressed apprehension that the UK was trying to slice off a part of Ethiopia.

Selwyn Lloyd said that the British Foreign Office had recently given detailed examination to this question. They felt that first priority should be given to bringing about a reconciliation between the Ethiopians and the Somalis. . . . Selwyn Lloyd also observed that Italian control of Italian Somaliland was scheduled to end in 1960 and that the UK had urged Italy to make arrangements to remain.

The Secretary said that he thought the terminal date of 1960 for Italian Somaliland would be impractical. He added that the United

[3] Congressional approval was delayed and the Bureau was not established until August 1958.

[4] Ato Akilou Abte Wold.

States had tried to be forthcoming in its assistance programs in this area.

Selwyn Lloyd referred to the West Coast of Africa and said that steady progress was being made toward independent states [*status*?]. Nigeria would follow the model of Ghana. Three racial groups [5] were involved in Nigeria which complicated the problem. On the East Coast of Africa a different situation existed because of the mixed communities there which made it desirable to move more slowly. He noted that white elements in the Central African Federation were anxious for independence, whereas black elements in Nyasaland were not so interested. If independence were pushed it might have dangerous effects and be detrimental to the interests of South Africa and Rhodesia. He said that no constitutional review would arise before 1960 and hoped that colored elements would not be encouraged to press for swifter action. He said that Uganda was important because it contained the head waters of the Nile.

Selwyn Lloyd said he was interested to learn the Department planned a new Bureau of African Affairs and that the UK would work closely with it.

Selwyn Lloyd concluded that he thought the African paper on which agreement had already been reached between the United States and United Kingdom fully summarized the present situation in Africa.

The Secretary said that he wished to make a few additional comments. The UK should not feel that the United States was exerting pressure on various areas of Africa which would result in premature independence. If at any time the British thought that we were making statements or taking steps which would have this result, he hoped he could be informed. The Secretary said that he thought that there should be an evolutionary trend toward independence but that attainment of it should be qualified by the ability of the people of an area to sustain the responsibility. As the President had said, we hoped that in some cases these countries would not want to become independent and would retain their relationships with the mother countries. In some cases it was possible that independence might be followed by a Communist takeover. Relationships between the United States and the Philippines which had terminated in Philippine independence had required a period of 50 years. They had recently lost a great leader in Magsaysay [6] but seemed to be handling this tragic development in a responsible way. The Secretary said that he realized there was a tendency among

[5] Reference is probably to the Ibo of the Eastern Region, the Yoruba of the Western Region, and the Hausa and Fulani of the Northern Region.

[6] President Ramón Magsaysay died in a plane crash on March 17.

some groups in the United States to advocate the principle of independence and to press for its immediate application. He thought that this approach to such questions might cause unnecessary activity among some of the peoples of Africa and might raise false hopes among them. The United States for its part did not wish to embarrass the United Kingdom or other countries who had relations with the countries of Africa, but there were steps taken by some which were beyond our control and we could not prevent. We were aware that a grant of independence under present conditions was an important move because it would undoubtedly be followed by Communist efforts to take over the new country. Stalin's statements on nationality problems clearly indicated his technique of amalgamating all dependent areas by breaking them loose from the countries with which they were associated and thereafter amalgamating them within the Soviet Union.

Selwyn Lloyd said that in Africa we should not seem to be at cross purposes as perhaps had been the case in the Middle East. He noted that one of the Nigerian leaders had told him that all Africans had followed the course of British action in Ghana carefully and had been much impressed that the British had carried out their promises of independence . . . . All Nigerians know this and . . . confidence in the British to carry through on their promises has increased. Selwyn Lloyd concluded that if the US and UK would work together there would be an opportunity of keeping the Communists out of Africa.

[Here follows discussion of items 2 through 7.]

19. Report by the Vice President [1]

Washington, April 5, 1957.

REPORT TO THE PRESIDENT ON THE VICE PRESIDENT'S VISIT TO AFRICA

(*February 28–March 21, 1957*)

Detailed Conclusions and Recommendations

I. French Relations with North Africa.

French prestige and influence in North Africa are decreasing at an alarming rate. This is due to a number of causes:

A. The perpetuation of the Algerian war which is poisoning the atmosphere of all of North Africa from Morocco to Libya and is now beginning to reach down into Mauretania in French West Africa.

B. French failure to behave in their relations with Morocco and Tunisia in accordance with the requirements of the independence of those countries. Thus the French still maintain large military forces in Morocco and Tunisia in an uncertainly defined status and to deploy them with little if any regard for the sovereignty of those countries. At the same time, the French exploit the financial dependence of these countries on France in an effort to force compliance with French policies and actions with respect to Algeria. However understandable French attitudes on these questions may be, such tactics are bound to exacerbate relations and, in the long term, run the real risk of the loss of the French position in Morocco and Tunisia.

C. The growing belief of many in North Africa that France cannot over a long period marshall sufficient strength to win a military victory in North Africa and that they can therefore afford to hold out for a solution of the Algerian problem which will assure either immediate independence or independence within the foreseeable future. Thus, the more time that passes, the more intransigent the North Africans are likely to become.

[1] Source: Department of State, S/P–NSC Files: Lot 62 D 1, North Africa (Tunisia, Algeria, Morocco, NSC 5614, 5614/1). Secret. Enclosure to a memorandum for the National Security Council by Acting Executive Secretary S. Everett Gleason, dated April 22. For an unclassified version of the Nixon Report, see Department of State *Bulletin*, April 22, 1957, pp. 635–640. The Vice President was in Africa to lead the U.S. Delegation to the ceremonies marking the independence of Ghana, to demonstrate U.S. interest in Africa, and to gain a better understanding of the continent. (Circular airgram 6945, February 27; *ibid.*, Central Files, 511.00/2–2757)

Recommendations:

A. That the United States Government urgently consider a plan of action, which, while recognizing French interests and sensitivities, is calculated to awaken France to the extreme dangers which she faces and to which she is exposing the entire West in North Africa. We should make it clear that we have no desire to supplant France and, on the contrary, are concerned that she maintain a position of influence and assistance in this area. [2]

B. That the United States Government move as rapidly as possible to assure the continued pro-Western orientation and moderate nature of the Governments of North Africa by cementing our own relations with those countries. To this end, the United States should:

1. Invite the Sultan of Morocco to visit the United States this year. (I attach the greatest importance to this, having assured the Sultan of our desire to receive him as soon as arrangements can be worked out.) [3]
2. Avoid any identification with repressive features of French policies in Algeria and make clear as necessary that we expect France to respect the sovereignty of Tunisia and Morocco.
3. Proceed as rapidly as possible to implement our aid programs with Morocco and Tunisia. While the programs this year may be acceptable in size, we should anticipate increasing needs and demands for larger programs next year. [4]
4. Conclude as quickly as possible an agreement with Morocco to adapt our base rights arrangements with France to the new fact of Moroccan sovereignty. [5] The present absence of a direct understanding with Morocco stands in danger of affecting the whole range of our relations with that country.
5. Undertake a confidential study of how the stability and pro-Western orientation of Morocco and Tunisia could be assured in the event a rupture should result in the denial of the annual French subsidies of $80 million to Morocco and $50 million to Tunisia.

II. Relations of African States with Egypt.

Nasser's influence on the masses of the people in North Africa, the Sudan and the Moslem portions of Ethiopia remains high al-

[2] On April 28, the President wrote British Prime Minister Harold Macmillan that Nixon maintained that the United States, in its own interest, had to bring about a better relationship between France and "some of the North African regions" without hurting either side. Eisenhower suggested that it meant "walking a tight rope," but he thought it could be done. (Eisenhower Library, Whitman File, DDE Diaries)

[3] Muhammad V arrived in Washington November 25.

[4] Survey teams were sent to study the aid requirements of both countries. It was determined that $20 million in development assistance would be provided to Morocco in FY 1957 and Tunisia would receive $5 million together with technical cooperation projects as negotiated.

[5] The negotiating process began on May 6.

though probably less so than before his defeat by the Israelis. On the other hand, the Governments of those countries see in Nasser a threat to their independence and are therefore cautious in their attitudes towards him. In many cases, they have courageously opposed him. Libya, Tunisia and Morocco are now tending to look toward close cooperation among themselves to enhance their combined capability to resist Nasserism. Ethiopia and the Sudan also seem to be taking the first cautious steps for cooperation among themselves toward the same end.

Egyptian propaganda, particularly radio broadcasts, is highly effective among the Moslem populations of the countries we visited. This contrasts with the ineffectiveness of our own propaganda efforts. I believe that Egyptian efforts can be combatted effectively only by building up the indigenous broadcasting capabilities of the states of the area. Thus a Radio Morocco, Radio Tunisia, etc. would be much more effective than an expansion of VOA facilities in this area.

Recommendation:

That while avoiding any appearance of isolating Egypt, we quietly encourage and assist these states, both individually and collectively, to resist the efforts of Egypt to dominate them.

That funds which might otherwise be used for the expansion of VOA facilities in this area be utilized by USIA to strengthen the signal of potentially friendly indigenous radio stations in these countries.

III. Attitudes Towards Israel.

In the Arab countries which I visited, I made a point of talking to their leaders about the danger of the Middle Eastern situation and of eliciting their views about an Arab-Israel settlement. I found that almost without exception the leaders were realistic in privately recognizing that the Arabs must adjust themselves to the fact of Israel's existence. At the same time, they emphasized that the major obstacle which in their view stands in the way of a more open acceptance of Israel is the Arab refugee problem. They urged that close attention be given to the settlement of this problem both because of the moral and human issues involved and because of the contribution it would make to Middle East peace and stability.

Recommendation:

That we give new and careful attention to the Arab refugee problem with a view towards evolving a plan which at the appropriate time could form the basis for an equitable settlement.

IV. Ghana.

Ghana has many growing pains. It has great assets in terms of functioning institutions, responsible leadership and enthusiasm, but it also has liabilities in terms of the constitutional dispute now going on between the proponents of a strong central government and those who desire a large degree of regional autonomy for the native states. Moreover, the economy of Ghana is extremely vulnerable to the extent that it is largely based on cocoa, which has fluctuated widely in price over the period of the last few years. The Government of Ghana is anxious to diversify the economy and is particularly interested in the Volta River scheme for hydro-electric and irrigation development. The realization of this project would permit the production of large quantities of aluminum from the extensive bauxite deposits which are found within the country. The cost of the project is formidable—about $1 billion.

The Prime Minister [6] and other responsible leaders of Ghana emphasized to us their desire for strong United States representation in Ghana. They want an experienced officer capable of giving them the best possible advice during the difficult period ahead.

Recommendations:

1. That we assign our ambassadors to Ghana on the basis of merit, experience and absence of prejudice. I understand that we are about to assign an experienced Foreign Service Officer as Ambassador. He should arrive as soon as possible. [7]

2. That we follow most closely the evolution of this state, realizing that its success or failure is going to have profound effect upon the future of this part of Africa.

3. That we show ourselves sympathetic to assisting Ghana through technical cooperation, economic aid, etc., during the difficult period ahead. This assistance should be regarded as supplementary to any assistance the British provide. We should particularly follow closely the Volta River scheme with a view toward ascertaining whether it is a well-conceived and practical project which we should support in the IBRD and perhaps aid to a limited extent ourselves. [8]

---

[6] Kwame Nkrumah.

[7] Wilson C. Flake was appointed on May 20 and presented his credentials on June 19.

[8] The United States signed a technical cooperation agreement with Ghana on June 3, and obligated more than $700,000 for contract services to implement projects in agricultural extension and community development and to fund the technical library the United States had given as an independence gift. (TIAS 3838; 8 UST 793)

V. Liberia.

I was deeply concerned by conditions in Liberia. Contrasted with Ghana, Liberia is politically, economically and socially far less developed. The governmental structure corresponds closely to that of a Latin American type dictatorship, with a strong, although comparatively enlightened man, exercising virtually dictatorial powers. There is no opposition party and, so far as I could see, no potential leaders of the calibre of President Tubman.

It is perhaps too easy to excuse Liberia's deficiencies. The country has not had the same advantages as the Gold Coast, where a foreign power has provided extensive funds and assistance in the development of the country. Although Liberia has historically been a responsibility of the United States for over a century, it was not until 1944 that we began to assist the country to develop economically and socially. Private enterprise is now starting to play an increasingly important role in the development of the country and economic conditions should improve as more rubber acreage is brought into cultivation and as the country's considerable mineral resources are exploited. Some additional United States technical and economic assistance will undoubtedly be required, particularly with respect to education, the road program and agricultural development.

Liberia's greatest need, however, is for strong and patient advice in developing the political and social bases of the nation so as to bring about effective representation of all elements of the population in the national life.

Recommendations:

1. We must find ways and means of strengthening our ability to give the Liberians the advice and assistance which they require to broaden the base of the nation. This will often be advice which they do not wish to hear and any program of this kind will require careful consideration in order to get the essential points across without offending Liberian sensibilities and becoming counter-productive.

2. We should stand ready to increase in moderate amounts our grant and loan assistance to Liberia to assist in the development of the country.

VI. Ethiopia.

Ethiopia is ruled by a highly sophisticated and cultured minority—the Amharas. The large Moslem minority plays little role in the political life of the country. The Ethiopians are currently concerned about the potential for subversion which Colonel Nasser has among the Moslem populations. The first general elections in the history of the country are due to be held in the Fall, but it remains to be seen to what extent these will give effective representation in the Parliament to the minority groups. One has the impression that Ethiopia is looking more to maintaining the status quo by strengthening its armed forces than it is to a program of political, economic and social reform which, in the long run, will probably be more effective in assuring the loyalty of its populations and the stability of the area.

There have been in recent years a series of misunderstandings between the United States and Ethiopia. The Ethiopians maintain, for whatever motives, that we are not living up to the impressions they received regarding our plans and intentions at the time of the base agreement in 1953 and the Emperor's visit to Washington in 1955 with regard to assisting Ethiopia to build up its armed forces.[9] The Emperor made this case very forcibly to me and emphasized the need for a re-examination of relations between our two countries. I am assured that there has been no failure on our part to live up to our promises and I believe that many of the difficulties which have arisen are the result of misunderstandings which must be set straight as rapidly as possible.

Recommendations:

1. That our new Ambassador arrive in Addis Ababa as quickly as possible[10] and that his first task should be a thorough exploration of the whole range of United States-Ethiopian relations with a view toward identifying precise points at issue and taking corrective action.

2. That the Department of Defense review its attitude toward the Ethiopian armed forces with a view to deciding whether, in the light of Ethiopia's contribution to the UN action in Korea and its general attachment to the principles of collective security, it would not be in our military interest to encourage the building of an efficient fighting force in Ethiopia.

3. That in order to reassure the Ethiopians of our good intentions and our desire to assist them, we increase moderately the size of our military and economic programs. I believe this will be necessary in any event if we are to secure the additional base facilities we are now seeking. This should be done this year if possible, but, in any event, next year.

4. That the Department of Defense review our current military programs in Ethiopia with a view toward speeding up their imple-

---

[9] For documentation concerning the Emperor's 1954 visit to the United States and military understandings with Ethiopia, see *Foreign Relations,* 1952–1954, vol. XI, Part 1, pp. 418 ff.

[10] Don C. Bliss was appointed May 20 and presented his credentials on June 22.

mentation and assuring that Ethiopia receives the most serviceable equipment possible.

5. That ICA similarly speed up the implementation of our economic programs.

VII. Sudan.

The Sudan appears to be suffering at the present time from internal political dissension. The Prime Minister [11] gives the impression of a strong man who is pro-Western and anti-Communist and who is making a bid to consolidate his power. The Foreign Minister, [12] who appears to be powerful, is much less well-disposed toward the United States. I believe that we should be wary of him and stand ready to throw our support to the Prime Minister as appropriate opportunities arrive.

I believe that the Sudan will at least tacitly support the American Doctrine for the Middle East. In any event, it desires United States assistance.

The Sudan has ties both with the Middle East (particularly Egypt) and with Africa. I believe it to be in our interest to try to orient that country towards Africa and away from embroilment in Middle Eastern politics.

Recommendations:

1. That we support the Prime Minister, who appears inclined to be pro-American and anti-Communist.

2. That we proceed as rapidly as possible with a program of economic and technical assistance for the Sudan.

3. That in order to facilitate efforts to orient the Sudan towards Africa, it be included in the jurisdiction of the new Bureau of African Affairs when the latter is set up.

VIII. Libya.

Libya is a deficit economy. The position and intentions of the British are increasingly uncertain. The country occupies a key strategic position with respect to North Africa and the flank of NATO. We cannot afford to lose Libya. I understand that the British are presently contemplating a substantial withdrawal of forces and a cut-back in their budgetary support. I do not believe that we can afford to let a vacuum develop in Libya. This matter assumes greater importance when one considers the $100 million investment we have in strategic facilities as well as the additional requirements which we

---

[11] Abdullah Khalil.

[12] Muhammed Ahmad Mahjub.

may have in that country. The present government is well-disposed toward the United States. It deserves our support.

Recommendations:

1. That we stand ready to support the Libyan Government financially at such time as the British withdraw their financial support.
2. That we assist the Libyan Government to decrease its heavy dependence upon Egyptian personnel.
3. That we continue to increase moderately our program of economic assistance.
4. That we give sympathetic consideration to the building of a Libyan Army which would help to unify the country and fill the internal security vacuum which will be created by British withdrawal.

IX. North African University.

Libya is presently engaged in building a national university. Both Morocco and Tunisia are greatly interested in assistance in expanding their existing institutions of higher education. None of these countries (with the possible exception of Morocco) has the individual resources or capability of creating a first-class university. I believe that they would be receptive to the idea of combining their resources, with some assistance from us, to build a university which would meet their common needs. Because of sectional differences among the various states of North Africa, it would probably be desirable to establish such a university with various branches located in the different countries in a manner analogous to the state university system in California. Thus, an agricultural faculty might be located in one country, and law, medicine, engineering, etc., in another.

Recommendation:

That in view of the great importance of increasing higher education in North Africa, the interested agencies of the United States Government give high priority to exploring the possibility of assisting the North African countries to build a North African University with appropriate United States private and/or Governmental assistance.

X. General.

Recommendations:

1. That the Department of Defense and the ICA give higher priority than in the past to their programs and operations in the African area.

2. That the Department of State take immediate steps to strengthen its representation in Africa, both quantitatively and qualitatively. To the extent that this requires increased personnel, the opening of new posts and the granting of additional funds to ameliorate the conditions of service of our officers in the field, the Administration should give urgent consideration to requesting the necessary funds from the Congress. [13]

3. Assignments of United States representatives in the African area should be made on the basis of merit, experience and stability. We must assure that our African posts are staffed by our most highly qualified people if we are to meet the high standards of competition presently set by the Russians, Egyptians and others.

4. We should be sensitive to the fact that new states will be emerging from among the present dependent territories in Africa. We should begin to lay our plans for conducting direct relations with those states and for assuring that when they emerge into independent status, we have laid the best possible foundation for a close relationship with the United States. To the extent that this may require moderate amounts of technical and economic assistance to the dependent territories, we should be prepared to extend such aid. An immediate survey should be made to determine to what extent such programs would further the foreign policy objectives of the United States.

5. I believe that we often dissipate much of the political goodwill which our aid programs should engender by too much insistence on detail in our agreements with and programs in recipient countries, by slowness in implementing programs and by falsely raising expectations by engaging in too much planning for projects which have little, if any, hope of realization. These aspects of our aid programs should be carefully reviewed in an effort to assure the maximum political impact. In the new programs which we shall be implementing in Africa, we should make every effort to avoid the pitfalls we have encountered in other parts of the world.

---

[13] In Fiscal Year 1957, Consulates were opened in Kampala, Uganda; Yaoundé, French Cameroon; Abidjan, Ivory Coast; and Mogadiscio, Somalia. In Fiscal Year 1958, it was hoped that funds would be available to establish Consulates at Kaduna, Nigeria; Tananarive, Madagascar; and Brazzaville, Middle Congo, French Equatorial Africa.

6. We must look most carefully at our information output which, I suspect, is by no means as effective as that being disseminated by the Communists. In several places I was told by responsible African leaders that our points of view were not getting across. I believe it vital that we find out why and take corrective action.

There are attached copies of memoranda of the major talks I had with leaders of the countries which I visited.[14]

[14] See Documents 114–116, 129, 140, 166, 207, 227, 236, and 248.

---

20. Memorandum From the Director of the Office of Dependent Area Affairs (Gerig) to the Assistant Secretary of State for International Organization Affairs (Wilcox)[1]

Washington, May 9, 1957.

SUBJECT

Afro-Asian or Asian-African concept and its use by U.S. officials

As you suggested at our lunch a few days ago, I am putting down on paper this brief comment on the Afro-Asian concept and its use by American officials.

Ever since the Bandung Conference, and particularly at last year's General Assembly and in the discussions at the Trusteeship Council, it has become clearly evident that India is making a desperate bid to assert its influence, and even its leadership, throughout Africa. Part of this assertion is seen in the way India is attempting to get a so-called Afro-Asian concept accepted for voting purposes on many general questions, and particularly on the colonial question. The basis on which India is attempting to associate African peoples and States with Asia is, inter alia, (1) the colonial question, and (2) the race or color question.

I believe it is accepted Departmental policy that this development is not in the interest of the United States or of the Western World. Indeed, it is to the interest of the Western World to keep African orientation westward rather than eastward. If for historical reasons it should be difficult to continue the close ties which have associated much of Africa with Europe and with the United States, it

[1] Source: Department of State, IO/ODA Files: Lot 62 D 225, Afro-Asian Bloc. Confidential.

should certainly be to Western interests to have African peoples and nations develop on an independent basis rather than to be oriented eastward toward Asia. In particular, the associations of the northern and western half of Africa have been northward toward Europe and westward toward the United States; and if the color and race problems were to be handled properly this association, which is also soundly based on economic interests, should be continued. The projected Eurafrica and the common market are evidences of this natural and close relationship.

India, on the other hand, has presumed to assert her influence throughout Africa, including West Africa, and on a number of questions, large and small, in the United Nations has shown clearly what her intentions are. The U.S. Delegation, however, has been able in certain instances to lead an effective opposition to the Indian approach to Africa, and one illustration of a plenary vote will indicate our success in defeating the Indian plan by breaking up the so-called voting bloc, including African and Asian Members of the United Nations. India and the United States led two rival resolutions in connection with the future of French Togo. When the issue came to a vote on January 23, 1957, the U.S.-sponsored resolution resulted in a vote of 53 in favor, 16 against, and 7 abstentions. [2] Six of the so-called Afro-Asian group voted in favor of the U.S.-sponsored resolution: Laos, Liberia, Pakistan, Thailand, Cambodia, and Ceylon; 8 voted against: Libya, Sudan, Saudi Arabia, Syria, Yemen, Egypt, Iran, and Iraq; and 7 abstained: Lebanon, Morocco, Nepal, Afghanistan, Burma, India, and Indonesia. The break-up of the group which India aspires to lead caused her much anxiety. It should be a deliberate and studied objective of the United States Delegation to repeat this performance whenever possible.

If it is agreed that it is not in the United States interest to encourage or abet India's attempt to include the whole of Africa in the Asiatic bloc, then it seems evident that United States delegates and officials should avoid falling in with the use of the concept "Afro-Asian" or "Asian-African" since such usage would seem to admit a fait accompli which is not only far from being true, but which should not be admitted by us as being in any sense desirable or inevitable.

It may not always be possible to avoid this usage but if it is necessary to identify such a group it might be called by alternative terms, such as the "Bandung group" or "Arab-Asian group". In no case should we go farther than to speak of the "so-called Afro-Asian group". Often in statements, speeches, or Departmental documents

---

[2] Resolution 1046 (XI).

we could convey our ideas as well or better by speaking of "the African group" and "the Asian group".

The purpose of this memorandum, however, goes farther. It is to show that United States policy in this connection is soundly based on political as well as economic grounds. Emerging political institutions of Africa are largely based on Western political and constitutional philosophy. Moreover, it is the Western World that can bring economic aid and support for the development of African nations, not the East. Further, even in those areas of North and Middle Africa where Islam has penetrated, such peoples have no reason to be sympathetic with Eastern or communist philosophies.

This paper merely outlines some of the potentials of the question and does not in this brief space undertake to make any thoroughgoing evaluation. Its purpose will be served if it correctly identifies Asiatic, particularly Indian, objectives in Africa, and suggests some ways of keeping Africa either oriented westward or independent in its outlook.

---

21. Circular Instruction From the Department of State to Certain Diplomatic Missions and Consular Offices [1]

CA–308 *Washington, July 10, 1957.*

SUBJECT

Pan African Conference

1. For your guidance, the Department believes that the holding of a conference of independent African states is a natural development which should not be discouraged even though it may be premature and will in all probability be turned into a forum for the denunciation of colonialism and all its works.

2. The Department hopes that, as the occasion may arise, posts in participant countries will express the view that while the Department welcomes all new developments in the field of international cooperation, it hopes that controversial issues involving friendly

---

[1] Source: Department of State, Central Files, 770.00/7–1057. Confidential. Sent to Abidjan, Accra, Addis Ababa, Algiers, Brussels, Cairo, Capetown, Casablanca, Dakar, Dar Es Salaam, Durban, Elisabethville, Johannesburg, Kampala, Khartoum, Lagos, Leopoldville, Lisbon, London, Lourenco Marques, Luanda, Madrid, Monrovia, Nairobi, Paris, Port Elizabeth, Pretoria, Rabat, Salisbury, Tangier, Tripoli, Tunis, Yaounde, Mogadiscio, Asmara, and Rome.

countries not participating in the conference can be minimized. In particular, we would question the value of raising the Algerian and Suez questions in such a conference.

3. A conference of the eight independent states in Africa [2] in exclusion of the dependent areas (which comprise 87% of the population and 70% of the land in Africa South of the Sahara) cannot hope to come to grips with the enormous economic and social problems confronting the continent as a whole, and the United States would like to hope that future conferences of this nature could include representatives of the dependent areas [3] and the metropolitan states concerned. We do not, of course, believe it desirable to put forward this position publicly at this time, but it may be useful in informal discussions of the subject.

4. The Department would appreciate information as it becomes available regarding:

a) The reaction of the invited states to Nkrumah's proposed agenda.
b) What, if any, observers will be invited.
c) The role Egypt will play.
d) Whether Algerian nationalists will be invited either as participants or observers.
e) The composition of the various delegations.
f) The views of the metropolitan powers (UK excepted—their views are known).
g) The views of the indigenous leaders in the dependent areas.

5. The Department attaches considerable importance to this matter and would welcome the views of the addressee posts on the role the United States should or should not play. [4] The Department also wishes to be kept informed of all developments on a continuing basis.

Dulles

---

[2] The First Conference of Independent African States was held in Accra April 15–22, 1958. In addition to the host country, Ethiopia, Liberia, Libya, Morocco, Tunisia, the Sudan, and the United Arab Republic (Egypt) were represented.

[3] Nkrumah also sponsored the All-African People's Conference in Accra December 8–13, 1958, which drew delegates from 28 countries and observers from a number of other nations. It came almost one year after the Afro-Asian People's Solidarity Conference which Nasser hosted in the last week of 1957.

[4] Despatch 49 from Lisbon, July 30, reported that any encouragement of such a conference would damage relations with Portugal and make more difficult the use of Portuguese territories by U.S. armed forces. (Department of State, Central Files, 770.00/7–3057)

22. Memorandum From the Assistant Secretary of State for Near Eastern, South Asian, and African Affairs (Rountree) to the Secretary of State[1]

Washington, August 16, 1957.

SUBJECT

Request for Approval of a United States Policy of Cooperation with other Governments in Organizing a Colombo Plan[2] for Africa

Discussion:

The British Foreign Office has requested through the British Embassy in Washington the Department's views on a proposed Colombo Plan for Africa.[3] NEA has discussed the proposal with other interested offices of the Department and it is generally agreed that a Colombo-type plan of technical cooperation for Africa would be consistent with and contribute to United States foreign policy objectives. It was the consensus also that the United States should cooperate in developing the plan. The social, economic, and political ferment in Africa is undermining the influence of the Metropoles in guiding the evolution of the African peoples along sound and orderly lines. The situation calls for a cooperative and sustained effort in Africa by not only the Metropoles but other developed nations of the west. A Colombo-type plan of technical cooperation for Africa would:

1. Encourage (a) the Colonial Powers to continue to assist both their territories and former territories, (b) the African peoples involved to continue to collaborate with and look primarily to the Metropoles for assistance, and (c) continuation of the mutual interdependence so vital to them;
2. Increase the number of developed western nations participating in meeting Africa's development needs and the volume and types of technical assistance available to Africa;

---

[1] Source: Department of State, AF/AFS Files: Lot 59 D 293, Regional CCTA. Confidential. Drafted by Longanecker.

[2] The Colombo Plan for Cooperative Economic Development in South and Southeast Asia went into effect July 1, 1951. Intended to spur long-term development, it included as members: Australia, Burma, Cambodia, Ceylon, India, Indonesia, Japan, Laos, Malaya, Nepal, New Zealand, Pakistan, Philippines, Thailand, the United Kingdom (Singapore and British Borneo), the United States, and Vietnam.

[3] The Consultative Committee for Technical Assistance in Africa (CCTA) produced a modest "Colombo Plan" proposal which the British asked the United States to consider. (Memorandum of conversation by LaMont, June 3, and memorandum of conversation by Longanecker, August 13; Department of State, Central Files, 870.00/6–357 and 870.00/8–1357) CCTA was composed of Belgium, France, Portugal, the United Kingdom, the Union of South Africa, and the Central African Federation. It was set up in 1950, but not formalized until January 18, 1954. Ghana became a member in 1957 and Liberia in 1958.

3. Relieve the growing pressure on the United States to assume a major and expanding role in meeting Africa's need for external aid as our ability to do so is likely to be limited by the growing Congressional sentiment for reducing aid programs;

4. Encourage the African peoples to focus their attention on Africa instead of joining blocs with other parts of the world;

5. Provide a multilateral planning and consultative organization in which the dependent territories and independent countries in Africa (a) would be able to discuss their development needs and programs with the Metropoles and other western nations and (b) would have a wider choice of sources of aid.

Recommendation:

That you authorize the Department's representatives to inform the United Kingdom that the proposal for a Colombo-type plan of technical cooperation for Africa appears to have considerable merit and to be worthy of further consideration but that we would first wish to know the views of the other Metropoles before giving our final position. [4]

[4] When the British requested a reply on August 23, LaMont acknowledged that the plan had some merit, but indicated that since it was still in the formulative stage it was too early for the United States to make a judgment. (Memorandum of conversation by LaMont; *ibid.*, 870.00/8–2357)

---

23. Memorandum of Discussion at the 335th Meeting of the National Security Council, Washington, August 22, 1957 [1]

Present at the 335th Council meeting were the President of the United States, presiding; the Vice President of the United States; Christian A. Herter for the Secretary of State; the Secretary of Defense; and the Director, Office of Defense Mobilization. Also present were the Secretary of the Treasury; the Acting Attorney General (participating in Items 1, 2 and 3); the Director, Bureau of the Budget; the Chairman, Atomic Energy Commission (participating in Item 3); the Federal Civil Defense Administrator (participating in Item 3); the Acting Director, U.S. Information Agency; the Chairman, Council of Economic Advisers (participating in Item 3); the Director, International Cooperation Administration; the Acting Chairman, Interdepartmental Intelligence Conference, and the Chair-

[1] Source: Eisenhower Library, Whitman File, NSC Records. Top Secret; Eyes Only. Drafted by Gleason on August 23.

man, Interdepartmental Committee on Internal Security (attending for Items 1 and 2); the Deputy Secretary of Defense; William Leonhart, Department of State; the Chairman, Joint Chiefs of Staff; the Acting Director of Central Intelligence; the Deputy Assistant to the President; Special Assistants to the President Cutler and Dearborn; the White House Staff Secretary; the NSC Representative on Internal Security (attending for Items 1 and 2); the Executive Secretary, NSC; and the Deputy Executive Secretary, NSC.

[Here follows discussion of items 1–4.]

5. U.S. Policy Toward Africa South of the Sahara Prior to Calendar Year 1960 (NIE 72-56;[2] Memo for NSC from Executive Secretary, subject: "Report to the President on the Vice President's Visit to Africa", dated April 22, 1957;[3] NSC 5719;[4] Memo for NSC from Executive Secretary, same subject, dated August 20, 1957[5])

Mr. Cutler briefed the Council in very considerable detail on the highlights of NSC 5719. He noted that the Joint Chiefs of Staff had concurred in the draft statement of policy, and that the report contained no split views. He then asked the Vice President, as the "father" of this new policy on Africa, to make any comments he wished.

[Here follows discussion of the usefulness of an ongoing intelligence study: "Africa in Transition".]

The Director of the International Cooperation Administration asked at this point if he might make an observation. Mr. Hollister pointed out that on the economic side, one of the biggest problems confronting the U.S. Government was how to provide effective aid to those areas which were not likely in the near future to emerge from their present colonial status. He expressed the view that it was wasteful for the United States to try, for example, to do much in the Belgian Congo, and recommended that we concentrate our assistance either on the independent countries of Africa or on areas which were emerging into independence.

The Vice President then said that he had no objection to the proposed study on "Africa in Transition" if it was understood that it

[2] Document 14.

[3] Document 19.

[4] NSC 5719, July 31, was the first NSC paper on Sub-Saharan Africa. The text was the same as NSC 5719/1, *infra*, except for the change noted in NSC Action No. 1778, below. (Department of State, S/S–NSC Files: Lot 63 D 351, NSC 5719 Series)

[5] It conveyed a memorandum by the Chairman of the Joint Chiefs of Staff, General Nathan F. Twining, for the Secretary of Defense, August 16, recommending concurrence in the adoption of NSC 5719. (*Ibid.*)

was not being made to provide the basis for determining specific courses of U.S. political action in this area.

The Vice President then indicated that he had another point to make. He believed that he detected a tendency in the present report (NSC 5719) to underestimate the seriousness of the Communist threat in Africa. After all, we do not have to count only card-bearing Communists as a measure of the Communist threat. In Africa, the Vice President predicted, the Communists will clothe themselves in Islamic, racist, anti-racist, or nationalist clothing. The potential danger of Communist penetration he believed to be very great, because the Communists were always in a position to support and take advantage of extremist elements, where the United States could not do so. The Vice President indicated that he did not mean that his warning required a change in NSC 5719.

Secretary Herter said that he was very glad that the Vice President had brought up this point about the Communist danger, because it was a point which he himself wished to speak of along the same lines.[6] Secretary Herter continued by saying that he believed that the statement in paragraph 17 on page 12 of NSC 5719 was too optimistic, and he therefore suggested the addition of language which would indicate that the potential Communist threat to Africa was greater than the actual threat at the present time.[7]

In support of Secretary Herter's views, the Vice President cited various instances in different parts of Africa where the Communists had been effective in securing the support of various elements of the population. He went on to speak of the matter of Egyptian influence in Africa South of the Sahara. The Vice President believed that the Egyptians had already acquired tremendous influence in the Sudan and would from that point carry their influence further south. Much the same was true of the widespread Indian influence in Black Africa. Neither the Egyptian nor the Indian influence should be overlooked, because both might be used effectively by the Communists.

The President said he should have thought that the influence of Islam in general would be anti-Communist rather than pro-Communist. General Cabell replied that the President was correct, but that

---

[6] Dulles called Herter on August 21 to indicate that the paper needed stiffening in that it was overly optimistic regarding the lack of Communist activities. (Eisenhower Library, Dulles Papers, White House Telephone Conversations)

[7] At a meeting in Herter's office on the evening of August 21, attended by George LaMont of NEA, it was suggested, in regard to paragraph 17, that the words: "but its potential influence is a matter of growing concern" be added to the opening sentence: "By and large, Communism has not been a major problem in Africa South of the Sahara up to the present." (Memorandum from Rountree to Herter, August 22; Department of State, S/S–NSC Files: Lot 63 D 351)

the influence of Islam could be manipulated in favor of Communism, as, for example, in Egypt today.

General Twining indicated that the Joint Chiefs of Staff were inclined to the view that the statement of the military and strategic value of Africa South of the Sahara, as set forth in paragraphs 19 and 20 on page 13, played down somewhat the strategic importance of the area, although the Joint Chiefs were not recommending any precise change in the language of these paragraphs. Mr. Cutler replied by pointing out that the estimate in paragraphs 19 and 20 was a short-range estimate which could be changed in the future. He indicated that the Record of Action might well take note of the views of the Joint Chiefs of Staff on these paragraphs.

The National Security Council: [8]

a. Discussed the draft statement of policy on the subject contained in NSC 5719, in the light of the views of the Joint Chiefs of Staff thereon transmitted by the reference memorandum of August 20, 1957, and the comments by the Vice President at the meeting.

b. Adopted the statement of policy in NSC 5719, subject to the following amendment:

> *Page 12, paragraph 17, 1st sentence*: Add, at the end of the sentence, the words, "but its potential influence is a matter of growing concern."

c. Noted the statement by the Chairman, Joint Chiefs of Staff, relative to paragraphs 19 and 20 on page 13, affirming the desirability of periodically surveying the strategic importance of Africa South of the Sahara.

Note: NSC 5719, as amended, subsequently approved by the President and circulated as NSC 5719/1 for implementation by all appropriate Executive departments and agencies of the U.S. Government, and referred to the Operations Coordinating Board as the coordinating agency designated by the President.

[Here follows discussion of item 6.]

S. Everett Gleason

---

[8] The following paragraphs and Note constitute NSC Action No. 1778. The original language of paragraphs 19 and 20 in NSC 5719 was retained. (*Ibid.*, S/S–NSC (Miscellaneous) Files: Lot 66 D 95)

24. National Security Council Report [1]

NSC 5719/1 *Washington, August 23, 1957.*

NOTE BY THE EXECUTIVE SECRETARY TO THE NATIONAL SECURITY COUNCIL ON U.S. POLICY TOWARD AFRICA SOUTH OF THE SAHARA PRIOR TO CALENDAR YEAR 1960

REFERENCES

A. NIE 72–56 [2]
B. Memo for NSC from Acting Executive Secretary, subject: "Report to the President on the Vice President's Visit to Africa", dated April 22, 1957
C. NSC 5719 [3]
D. NSC Action No. 1778 [4]

The National Security Council, the Secretary of the Treasury, and the Director, Bureau of the Budget, at the 335th Council meeting on August 22, 1957, adopted the statement of policy on the subject contained in NSC 5719, subject to the amendment thereto which is set forth in NSC Action No. 1778–b.

The President has this date approved the statement of policy in NSC 5719, as amended and adopted by the Council and enclosed herewith as NSC 5719/1; directs its implementation by all appropriate Executive departments and agencies of the U.S. Government; and designates the Operations Coordinating Board as the coordinating agency.

Also enclosed, for the information of the Council, are Annex A ("Areas Included in Africa South of the Sahara"), Annex B ("United States Exports to and Imports from Africa, by Country"), Annex C ("Gold and Foreign Exchange Holdings of African Territories and Countries South of the Sahara as of December 31, 1956"), and a Financial Appendix. [5]

At the 335th meeting the Council also (NSC Action No. 1778–c):

Noted the statement by the Chairman, Joint Chiefs of Staff, relative to paragraphs 19 and 20 on page 13, affirming the desirabil-

---

[1] Source: Department of State, S/S–NSC Files: Lot 63 D 351, NSC 5719 Series. Secret.

[2] Document 14.

[3] See footnote 4, *supra.*

[4] See footnote 8, *supra.*

[5] Neither Annex B, Annex C, nor the Financial Appendix is printed.

ity of periodically surveying the strategic importance of Africa South of the Sahara.

James S. Lay, Jr. [6]

[Enclosure]

STATEMENT OF U.S. POLICY TOWARD AFRICA SOUTH OF THE SAHARA PRIOR TO CALENDAR YEAR 1960

Prefatory Note

1. Many of the problems of Africa South of the Sahara are long-range in nature. Appreciable progress toward their resolution will in some instances require a generation or more. The policy guidance contained in this paper is addressed to those actions which the United States can usefully take in the immediate future. Moreover, the projection of specific policies beyond this period is not feasible because of the marked political changes probable in the area after 1960.

The Nature of U.S. Interests

General

2. There is a growing awareness in the world that Africa is emerging as an area which will have an increasingly important influence on the course of world events and that the political alignment of the present and future independent nations of the continent will be deeply affected by the policies which Western nations, including the United States, pursue in the future.

3. The United States is concerned that Africa South of the Sahara develop in an orderly manner towards self-government and independence in cooperation with the European powers now in control of large areas of the continent. We hope that this transition will take place in a manner which will preserve the essential ties which bind Europe and Africa—which are fundamentally complementary areas. Africa depends on Europe not only as a source of the normal imports of undeveloped countries but also as the major supplier of investment, both public and private. Europe in turn needs the African market, as well as Africa's minerals and agricultural products. The United States, therefore, believes it to be generally desirable that close and mutually advantageous economic relation-

[6] Printed from a copy that bears this typed signature.

ships between the European powers and Africa should continue after the colonial period has passed.

4. We wish to avoid in Africa a situation where thwarted nationalist and self-determinist aspirations are turned to the advantage of extremist elements, particularly Communists. We also wish to avoid the deprivation of African markets and sources of supply to Western Europe, and the economic dislocations that could result from the termination of the social and economic development programs of the metropolitan governments in the dependent areas (which currently average $300 million annually in excess of ordinary budget expenditures).

Specific

5. *Economic.* American economic interests in Africa are important although not to be compared with other areas. Total American investment in Africa South of the Sahara is now about $500 million, the majority in the Union of South Africa. The area is a predominant source for the United States of such strategic materials as asbestos, cobalt, columbite, corundum, industrial diamonds, tantalum ore, palm kernel oil, and chemical chromite. The United States also imports many other agricultural and mineral products (including uranium) from the area. Our exports to the area, although limited in almost all parts of the area by governmental restrictions which discriminate in favor of the metropolitan powers, are important to the countries concerned. Total U.S. trade with Africa South of the Sahara now equals more than $1 billion annually. It is in our interest to promote and support as appropriate the sound economic development of the area, both as an end in itself and as an important factor contributing to democratic political evolution.

6. *Strategic.* The strategic value of Africa South of the Sahara, which is limited at present, stems principally from the area's geographic location athwart alternate air and sea routes to the Far East, and from its strategic materials. In the event of war or loss of Western access to the Mediterranean, control of the area's air and sea communications could be of considerable importance. Under present conditions, our primary strategic interest is to deny the area to Communist control. From bases in certain areas of Africa South of the Sahara, the Communists could pose a serious threat to communications in the Atlantic, the Indian Ocean, and the Red Sea, as well as to our important North African strategic facilities, the Mediterranean littoral, and the flank of NATO. Denial of the area to Communist control is also important in order to prevent both economic dislocations to Western Europe and Communist access to strategic materials.

7. *Political.* Despite the remoteness of this area from the Soviet periphery, its political stability is important to the United States. Many African leaders look to us to support indigenous desires for self-government, and the colonial powers look to us to support their varying policies. Should serious disorders develop in the area, there might be a further military and economic drain on some of the more important NATO powers, such as has been the case in Algeria. Furthermore, our major European allies would be adversely affected both economically and strategically by the denial to them of Africa South of the Sahara. We have, therefore, a very real interest in orderly political evolution in Africa South of the Sahara.

8. *Social and Humanitarian.* The United States has a long record of humanitarian work in Africa through missionary and similar organizations. Much of the good reputation we enjoy results from this type of activity.

Broad Lines of Present Policy

9. Our present policies, which must by the size of the area and the differences in people and forms of government vary considerably from place to place, are designed to encourage an orderly development of the whole area based on a mutually advantageous accommodation between the forces of nationalism and the metropolitan powers. This policy manifestly has its limitations, but for the foreseeable future it will remain the only logical and correct course of action to follow. The United States has, of course, a very great interest in promoting, wherever possible, the development and maintenance of the closest possible mutually-beneficial political and economic relationships between the emerging African peoples and the peoples of Western Europe.

10. Within this framework, we are attempting to bring our influence to bear through:

a. Welcoming and extending political support to new states, such as Ghana, as they emerge.

b. Technical and economic assistance.

c. Working directly with the metropolitan powers, through loans to them for specific projects in their African areas, participation in international conferences called by the powers in question, and informal exchanges of views.

d. Working through the United Nations, particularly where the Trust and other non-self-governing territories are concerned.

e. Supporting and encouraging constructive nationalism and reform movements in colonial areas in Africa, when convinced they are likely to become powerful and grow in influence; while publicly acknowledging steps taken by Western European powers toward indigenous self-government. Such support and encouragement can take the form of public statements by senior American officials, visits of prominent Americans to the area, an exchange of persons program, and general public and private sympathy in the United States for the desires of dependent peoples for a greater degree of self-government.

f. Opening new diplomatic and consular posts, strengthening the staffs of existing posts, and increasing leadership, educational exchange, informational and cultural programs.

11. Our future policy must be guided by the fact that in the long run the orientation of Africa South of the Sahara will depend on where the leaders and the peoples feel their best interests lie. To a considerable extent, the African is still immature and unsophisticated with respect to his attitudes towards the issues that divide the world today. The African's mind is not made up and he is being subjected to a number of contradictory forces. This pressure will increase in the future. The African is a target for the advocation of Communism, old-fashioned colonialism, xenophobic nationalism, and Egyptian "Islamic" propaganda, as well as for the proponents of an orderly development of the various political entities in the area in question, closely tied to the West. The eventual political orientation of the emerging African states will probably be determined by what the leaders and peoples conceive best serves their own interests, measured primarily in terms of "independence" and of "equality" with the white man. Our policies therefore must be designed to convince the African that by association with the West he can best achieve his goals in a manner which in the long run will be most to his advantage. These policies cannot be effective if the African feels he is merely a pawn in a power struggle.

Major Problems and Issues

Nationalism vs. Colonialism

12. Nationalism vs. colonialism is the great issue in Africa today. At the moment, all others, no matter how important, are subordinate to it. Our policies in any field will be of little or no value if we ignore this issue. The problem is enormously complicated and no pat answers are possible. The colonial powers follow different policies, from the Portuguese to the British (in West Africa) extremes. Furthermore, the peoples themselves now under colonial direction are different in culture, history, race and degrees of development. But sentiment and pressures for self-government are everywhere increasing at an accelerated rate. Premature independence would be as harmful to our interests in Africa as would be a continuation of nineteenth century colonialism, and we must tailor our policies to the capabilities and needs of each particular area as well as to our over-all relations with the metropolitan power con-

cerned. It should be noted that all of the metropolitan powers are associated with us in the NATO alliance or in military base agreements.

13. *Policy Guidance:*

a. Support the principle of self-determination (self-government or independence) consistently and in such a way as to assure that evolution toward this objective will be orderly; making clear, however, that self-government and independence impose important responsibilities which the peoples concerned must be ready and able to discharge.

b. Encourage those policies and actions of the metropolitan powers which lead the dependent peoples toward responsible self-government or independence.

c. Avoid U.S. identification with those policies of the metropolitan powers which are stagnant or repressive and, to the extent practicable, seek effective means of influencing the metropolitan powers to abandon or modify such policies.

d. As appropriate, cooperate with the metropolitan powers in the development programs of their dependent territories, making it clear that we are not trying to supplant the metropoles.

e. Emphasize through all appropriate media the colonial policies of the Soviet Union and particularly the fact that the Soviet colonial empire has continued to expand throughout the period when Western colonialism has been contracting.

Racialism

14. Racialism is, of course, closely allied to the colonial question but is most acute in the Union of South Africa[7] and, to a lesser extent, in Central and East Africa.

15. U.S. influence is restricted by the extremely distorted picture Africans have been given concerning the race problem in the United States.

16. *Policy Guidance:*

a. Emphasize U.S. progress in the field of race relations through all available media.

b. Encourage, where practicable, a more liberal approach in the areas where extremism is now the order of the day.

c. Point out on appropriate occasions the inevitability of violence as the result of rigid racial policies.

d. Seek to influence any consideration in the UN along constructive lines.

---

[7] There was some feeling in the Office of Dependent Area Affairs (ODA) that this paper offered insufficient guidance in respect to policy toward South Africa. While there was general accord that continued pressure was required, ODA was predisposed to work through the United Nations whereas the Office of Southern Africa Affairs (AF/S) preferred to concentrate on bilateral talks. (Memoranda from McGregor to Walmsley, August 22; Department of State, IO/ODA Files: Lot 62 D 225, Africa—General)

The Communist Threat

17. By and large, Communism has not been a major problem in Africa South of the Sahara up to the present, but its potential influence is a matter of growing concern. There is a discernible Communist influence in African and Indian political groups in the Union of South Africa and penetration of labor unions in West Africa. African students in Europe, furthermore, are assiduously cultivated by local Communists and many have been subverted. Soviet pretensions to being anti-colonial and non-European tend to be effective in Liberia and Ghana, and these governments are flattered by Soviet attempts to cultivate them.

18. *Policy Guidance:*

a. Cooperate locally with security organizations to combat Communist subversive activities to the extent that this can be done without assisting in the repression of responsible non-Communist nationalist movements.

b. Seek to prevent or at least curtail formal representation of Sino-Soviet Bloc countries in Africa.

c. Seek to provide constructive alternatives to Soviet blandishments but avoid trying to compete with every Soviet offer.

d. Give general support to constructive non-Communist, nationalist, and reform movements, balancing the nature and degree of such support, however, with consideration of our relations with our NATO allies.

e. In areas where trade unionism develops, guide it toward Western models by working with the International Confederation of Free Trade Unions, by direct advice and assistance, and by an exchange of persons program.

Military and Strategic Value

19. The limited military and strategic value of the area arises from its geographic location and strategic materials.

20. *Policy Guidance:* No immediate action appears called for. The area should be kept under periodic survey to determine any changes in our strategic requirements.

Economic Potential of the Independent States

21. The economic potential of the Union of South Africa is great and its development is steadily increasing. Ghana is prosperous but depends on a one-crop economy. Liberia, with which U.S. prestige is historically associated, requires external capital for its further economic development. Other states as they become independent may require investment capital and technical aid—in amounts varying with their several needs—which the metropolitan powers may no longer be either willing or able to provide. Successful U.S. programs in such countries can demonstrate to Africa the sincerity of our

friendship and help to prevent them from falling under Communist influence.

22. *Policy Guidance:*

a. Continue and expand U.S. technical assistance to Ghana. Be prepared to extend to Ghana development project loans which are consistent with relevant policy considerations, and to support proposals by international lending agencies for similar loans.

b. Provide such amounts of technical and economic assistance to Liberia as may be necessary to assist in the maintenance of a reasonable degree of economic stability and as are within its capacity to absorb.

Economic Potential of the Dependent Areas and the Capabilities of the Metropolitan Powers

23. There is wide variation in the economic potential of the dependent areas and in the capability of the metropoles for contributing to their economic development. The Belgians appear in the best position to continue the economic development of their dependent area, the Congo—a rich area in its own right. British and French capabilities are limited by their internal financial difficulties. Both countries have invested large amounts in economic, social and educational programs in their dependent areas in Africa South of the Sahara. The extent to which they can or will continue similar investments in the future, and the possibility of investment and assistance by other powers, requires thorough study. A number of the British territories have substantial foreign exchange holdings. The European Common Market plan, which offers an investment program for certain dependent African territories, may be of considerable help in the future. [8] Furthermore, the possibilities of a Colombo-type plan for Africa, which is already under discussion by the metropolitan powers, merit consideration. [9]

24. The prospect of adequate economic development support from the metropolitan powers will of course be heavily influenced by factors other than their financial capabilities. One very important factor will necessarily be a metropolitan power's appraisal of the likelihood that it will be able to maintain close political and economic ties with a particular colonial territory, either through an exten-

---

[8] The European Common Market plan calls for investment over a 5-year period of the sum of $581,250,000 in French, Belgian, Italian, and Dutch dependent areas in various parts of the world. It will come into effect in the near future following ratification by the signatory powers.

Of the territories covered by this paper, French West Africa, French Equatorial Africa, French Togoland, Madagascar, the Belgian Congo and Ruanda Urundi will benefit under this program to the extent of approximately $530,000,000. [Footnote in the source text.]

[9] See Document 22.

sion of the colonial relationship itself or through the development of a mutually-satisfactory new relationship, which could include continuation of trade discrimination in favor of the metropolitan powers. Should one or the other relationship fail to develop, the incentives of the metropolitan powers to provide financial or economic support, either through public or private investment, are likely to suffer rapid deterioration. Thus our success in attaining the previously-stated U.S. objective of preserving the essential ties between Europe and Africa, will probably have an important impact upon the rate of Africa's economic progress, while lessening Africa's reliance on U.S. assistance.

25. *Policy Guidance:*

a. Continue present policies as set forth in paragraphs 10–b and –c above, avoiding an impression in presently dependent areas that the United States is prepared to underwrite their eventual independence.

b. Support the European Common Market plan for investment in dependent African areas if, when operative, it is consistent with the U.S. interests set forth above.

c. Examine any joint plans for coordinated assistance to Africa South of the Sahara to see whether the United States should participate.

d. Attempt, as appropriate, to have removed discriminatory laws which discourage private American investment.

e. Undertake a long-range study, with respect both to the independent states and the emerging colonial areas, to determine:

(1) The mobilizable resources of the African areas.

(2) The prospects for continued investment by the metropolitan countries.

(3) The factors controlling the rate of economic development.

(4) The possibilities of international arrangements, such as the European Common Market or a Colombo-type organization, to contribute to beneficial interdependence between Europe and Africa.

(5) The role which the United States should assume in promoting economic growth in Africa.

Education and Training

26. Education is a crying need of the African and one of his most sought-for goals. American opportunities for assistance vary with the policies of the metropolitan powers concerned and the resources of the independent countries. Without increased educational opportunities it is impossible to expect any early advancement of most African peoples to the point where they are capable of running their own affairs.

27. *Policy Guidance:*

a. Encourage private American institutions and foundations to interest themselves in the fields of health, education and public administration in Africa South of the Sahara.

b. Assist the educational institutions in the area with teachers, books, visual aid media and, as resources are available, funds.

c. Promote and assist surveys of the educational requirements of the area.

d. Where existing facilities are inadequate for training both Americans for work in Africa and potential African leaders for increasing responsibility, consider the steps available to the U.S. Government to expand or improve them.

Detribalization

28. Although detribalization remains one of the major problems of the area, little positive action by the United States is possible. The tribal and family traditions of the people in question are such that they remain, despite the many advances that are currently being made, extremely primitive in many of their social outlooks. These traditions, while breaking up at an accelerated pace, remain strong, and even the urban African looks for a source of authority to replace the head of the tribe or family. Until some new loyalty is provided, the detribalized African will be an easy target for elements eager to exploit his traditional need for leadership and guidance.

29. *Policy Guidance:* No immediate tangible action seems possible. In general, support the work of Western-oriented labor organizations, educational institutions and, in some cases, government leaders in a position to influence the African looking for a new source of allegiance.

Cooperation Within the Area and With the Metropolitan Powers

30. The Balkanization of Africa is undesirable even though full consideration must be given to the vast differences found in the area. Neither the metropolitan powers nor the independent states have shown any great desire to work together. The issuance of invitations by the Government of Ghana to the other independent African states, including those of North Africa, to attend a future conference may be a beginning.[10] Periodic secret conversations between the metropolitan powers take place from time to time and are increasing in frequency, although no tangible achievements are yet visible.

---

[10] See Document 21.

31. *Policy Guidance:*

a. Encourage intra-area cooperation among all concerned in the economic, scientific and cultural fields. If inter-area conferences are held, consider what role the United States should play in connection with such conferences.

b. As an antidote to the blandishments of Egypt and the Soviets, encourage the North African states to exert influence in the area, without engaging in irresponsible irredentism, if practicable in the light of our relations with France.

c. Coordinate our technical assistance programs with any effective and satisfactory regional technical cooperation entity which may be established in the area.

Islam

32. Islam is spreading rapidly in Africa, although there is resistance to it in those areas where all Moslems are considered Arabs and all Arabs slavers. Up to the present, it has been reasonably free of anti-Western overtones, but its use by the Egyptians cannot be overlooked. Islam is more attractive to pagan Africans than Christianity since it is more adaptable to their traditional customs (e.g., polygamy) and way of life.

33. *Policy Guidance:*

a. No immediate action seems warranted. Islam is not necessarily hostile to the United States. On the contrary, in many areas it has proved to be a strong barrier to Communism. Unless its proselytizing forces are captured by hostile elements, no action by the United States would seem to be called for.

b. As noted above, encourage the Moslems of North Africa to exert an influence in the area as a counter-weight to the Egyptians.

Annex A [11]

AREAS INCLUDED IN AFRICA SOUTH OF THE SAHARA
(For purposes of this paper)

Independent Countries

Liberia
Ghana
Union of South Africa

UN Trust Territories

Cameroons (British)
Cameroons (French)
Togoland (French)

[11] Confidential.

Ruanda Urundi (Belgian)
Tanganyika (British)
South West Africa (South African Mandate)

British Possessions, Protectorates, etc.

Federation of Rhodesia and Nyasaland
Nigeria
Sierra Leone
High Commission territories in South Africa (Swaziland, Basutoland and Bechuanaland)
Zanzibar
Kenya
Uganda
Gambia

French Overseas Territories

French West Africa
French Equatorial Africa
Madagascar

Other European Dependencies

Belgian Congo
Angola (Portuguese)
Mozambique (Portuguese)
Rio Muni (Spanish)
Portuguese Guinea
Various insular dependencies of all the European powers

The following countries and territories are excluded:

Sudan
Ethiopia
The Somalilands (including the trust territory of Somalia and British and French Somalilands)

All three of these countries have common borders and common problems (notably Nile waters in the cases of Sudan and Ethiopia) with the area covered by this paper. They all have sizeable Negro minorities which give them a certain affinity with the area.

At the same time, these countries tend in their political, cultural and economic outlooks to be oriented much more towards North Africa and the Middle East (and towards each other) than they are toward tropical Africa. Thus the Moslem populations of Sudan and the Somali area look primarily towards their coreligionists in the other Arab states, while Christian Ethiopia looks to its religious ties with the Coptic Church in Egypt and the Orthodox churches elsewhere. All are highly dependent on the Red Sea waterways. All are concerned about Egypt's ambitions in the area. These and other considerations tend to give these countries a potential cohesiveness among themselves and to direct their attentions and energies northwards instead of to the south. We have, in fact, recognized this officially by including Ethiopia and Sudan in the general area of the Middle East for the purposes of the American doctrine.

In short, all of these countries exert an influence on—and are themselves influenced by—events to the south. For the foreseeable future, however, they will continue to be oriented towards North Africa and the Middle East, and our policy consideration should take that fact into account.

The Union of South Africa is included in the paper in view of its preponderant African population and the fact that racial problems are endemic in all of South and East Africa. Moreover, the South African approach to the problem of its African majority is basically colonialist in the worst sense of the word. Finally, events in South Africa are likely to have profound effect on the stability of the areas to the north and vice versa.

UNITED STATES POLICIES REGARDING FRENCH NORTH AFRICA [1]

25. Operations Coordinating Board Report [2]

Washington, June 1, 1955.

PROGRESS REPORT ON NSC 5436/1 [3]

UNITED STATES POLICY ON FRENCH NORTH AFRICA (TUNISIA, MOROCCO, ALGERIA)

(Policy Approved by the President, October 16, 1954)

(Period Covered October 17, 1954–June 1, 1955)

A. Summary of Major Actions

1. *Efforts to Bring About Political Progress.* Secretary Dulles expressed to Premier Mendes-France, during talks in Washington last November, U.S. concern over the need for rapid progress in French-Tunisian negotiations and for French steps to create conditions of confidence that would allow French-Moroccan negotiations. [4] The Paris Embassy and Department of State officials have reiterated these views to responsible French officials.

2. In efforts to facilitate negotiations, the Department of State and its representatives urged Egyptian and other Arab leaders and

---

[1] For previous documentation on this subject, see *Foreign Relations,* 1952–1954, vol. XI, Part 1, pp. 127 ff. See also Documents 58–100, 182–223, and 239–300.

[2] Source: Department of State, OCB Files: Lot 62 D 430, Horn of Africa. Top Secret. No drafting information is given on the source text. Enclosure to a memorandum for the OCB by Elmer B. Staats, dated July 18. The Progress Report, approved for transmission to the National Security Council on June 1, was noted by that body on July 14 in NSC Action No. 1423. At that meeting, Acting Secretary Hoover summarized the impact of events since June 1 and concluded that the correctness of following a middle-of-the-road policy had been confirmed by recent developments. He endorsed the wisdom of seeking to induce the French to adopt a more liberal and enlightened program in dealing with the Arab nationalists. (Memorandum of discussion by Gleason, July 15; Eisenhower Library, Whitman File)

[3] For text of NSC 5436/1, dated October 18, 1954, see *Foreign Relations,* 1952–1954, vol. XI, Part 1, p. 170.

[4] The substance of this conversation was summarized in telegram 1876 to Paris, November 22, 1954, *ibid.,* p. 181.

Spanish officials to moderate their broadcasts beamed to French North Africa. At the U.N., the U.S. voted against the original Arab-Asian resolution on Morocco and in favor of resolutions postponing further consideration of the Moroccan and Tunisian items "for the time being".

3. *Maintenance and Expansion of Military Facilities.* The Air Force and Navy are making use of their Moroccan bases but Air Force operations are seriously hampered by lack of French agreement on several points. French Government agreement was obtained for the rotation of USAFE units into Morocco for gunnery training and for the conduct of short periodic air maneuvers by elements of the Strategic Air Command. The French Government has not agreed to desired increased ceilings for military and civilian personnel and further increases in unit ceilings. Agreements between representatives of the American and French Air Forces concerning joint operations of the Moroccan Air Defense Control Center have been reached but they may require confirmation at the government level. Precise and satisfactory agreements are yet to be reached to provide for adequate air defense of the area.

4. There are a series of interrelated problems connected with the bases. They involve (a) the French insistence that it is required by prior agreements that Atlas Constructors, the American prime contractor in Morocco, start phasing out within the near future, (b) conclusion of agreements on tax relief and status of U.S. forces. In addition, there are the problems of (a) the French desire to utilize the airfield at Nouasseur for commercial traffic; (b) the French proposal that certain facilities for French use in Algeria and Tunisia be financed under NATO infrastructure; (c) the settlement of claims of reimbursement of cost of French contractors; (d) French inspection of construction; and (e) the shortage of on-base dependent housing. The French have not replied to requests for new facilities in Algeria and Tunisia, designed both to bolster air defense of the Moroccan bases and to implement NATO naval planning; recent discussions indicate French opposition to the peacetime stationing of U.S. troops in either Algeria or Tunisia.

5. On April 28, Generals Twining, Cook, Le May and Everest discussed most of these problems with Defense Minister Koenig[5] who, in the interests of obtaining an early settlement of these outstanding issues, proposed that he, Foreign Minister Pinay and Vice-Premier Palewski meet with Ambassador Dillon and U.S. military representatives at an early date; it is expected that such a meeting will take place shortly.

---

[5] The substance of the meeting with Pierre Koenig was summarized in telegram 4737 from Paris, April 29. (Department of State, Central Files, 711.56371A/4–2955)

6. *Deployment of French Troops and MDAP Equipment.* The increased violence and unrest has caused the French to deploy considerably larger forces to North Africa to the detriment of their military contribution to European NATO forces. Much of the equipment with these forces is of U.S. origin, largely MDAP financed, and consequently the North African nationalists tend to associate the United States with the painful repressions imposed upon them by these French troops. The Departments of State and Defense are seeking to prevent the use of this equipment for such purposes and to urge the return of MDAP equipped forces to the European theater.

7. *Moroccan Treaty Rights.* The French have been making it more difficult for us to exercise our treaty rights, primarily in the field of "economic liberty without any inequality" and we have formally protested the imposition of import quotas on certain items. At the same time, in response to French suggestions, we have expressed a willingness to consider any French proposals for negotiating a clarification of economic aspects of the Moroccan treaties though it appears unlikely that we could modernize our commercial relationship with Morocco without surrendering any of our present legal rights.

8. *Continuing Economic Aid Projects*

a. *Tunisia.* In an October 1954 agreement with the French Government, grants of $256,000 in technical assistance and 560 million French francs ($1,600,000) in development assistance are being made to France for the acceleration and expansion of agricultural development in the Medjerdah Valley.

b. *Morocco* and *Algeria.* A Basic Materials loan was made to the French Government in June 1953 totalling 2,638 million francs ($7,537,000) to help finance extension and improvement of the Port of Nemours, modernization of the Moroccan railroad system, and hydroelectric development and construction of high tension transmission system. Physical completion of the projects is not expected before the end of 1955.

9. *Information Activities.* USIA activities currently are limited to factual news reporting, and publicizing American cultural activities by means of the information centers, TV, radio and films.

B. Evaluation of Progress in Implementing NSC Policies and Objectives

10. *Summary.* French North Africa has been and will continue to be one of the world's key trouble spots. Arab nationalism clashes there with France's determinations to retain its control over the area. Solutions are made more difficult by the pressures of selfish French interests, the intransigence of important French political forces and the weakness of successive French governments. Reverberations of

the North African problem affect both NATO solidarity and our relations with the Arab-Asian world. Our policy is to steer a middle course and does not assure long term success in carrying out U.S. policies and objectives in that area. However, it is succeeding in limiting friction between the U.S. and France, on the one hand, and the U.S. and the Arab States on the other. Any alternative courses of action visible at this time would seriously undermine our relations with one or the other.

11. The most immediate objective of U.S. policy is to ensure effective use of our military bases in Morocco, which entails both satisfactory conditions in Morocco and military rights and bases in Tunisia and Algeria. Some progress has been made by the French and Tunisians in resolving their conflict, although the successful outcome is by no means assured. The French have made no real progress in allaying dissatisfaction in Morocco and Algeria. But the U.S. can do relatively little in a direct way to advance solutions of North African political problems without a major change in our policy.

12. The political situation obviously bears close watching so that North Africa will not develop into another "Indochina." Any disturbed, confused political situation such as this is a fertile fiêld that can easily be exploited by Communists. It is also obvious that if one of our most vital policy objectives—to take care of our military requirements—is to be achieved, substantial progress in our negotiations with the French must be realized in the near future. For the present, however, as indicated in paragraph 5 above and in parts of the discussion below, there are grounds for expectation that present policy objectives in North Africa may be further realized. Consequently the OCB does not at the present time recommend change or revision of U.S. policy set forth in NSC 5436/1 six months ago.

13. *Political Progress in the Area.* On April 21, after nearly nine months of negotiations, French and Tunisian negotiators signed a protocol which provides for limited autonomy which should go far to ease tensions in Tunisia. If the protocol is developed into a full agreement that is ratified by the French parliament during the next month or two—and this is by no means assured, a new era, favorable to U.S. objectives, would be opened in Franco-Tunisian relations.

14. In Morocco, the nationalists refuse to negotiate so long as the throne is occupied by the present Sultan, who replaced the nationalist-minded Sidi Mohammed ben Youssef in August 1953. Mendès-France was expected to seek answers to the more complicated Moroccan problems once Tunisian autonomy had been negotiated but he was voted out of office (ostensibly because of his North African policies) and the successor, Faure, government has only

attempted to repress the violence that resulted in the killing or wounding of roughly a thousand persons during the past year. It has failed to restore confidence although there are indications that the French are coming to recognize that a solution of the dynastic problem is a prerequisite to progress.

15. Unrest has also spread to Algeria, and so far French efforts have been primarily repressive with no indications of needed reforms in sight.

16. *Effectiveness of, and Limitations on, U.S. Actions.* There are severe limitations on the scope, and consequently, the effectiveness of U.S. actions. U.S. actions have encouraged the recent favorable Franco-Tunisian developments, but is was essentially French and Tunisian actions that brought them about. Similarly, the Moroccan and Algerian situations are such that the U.S. cannot effectively influence them short of direct intervention. Solutions depend as much on internal French politics as they do upon the actions or reactions of the native nationalists. The U.S. can urge moderation and compromise but attempts to press specific suggestions or proposals for solutions to these highly complicated and emotionally charged situations would not in most cases be effective or advantageous and might, in fact, react adversely upon our military program.

17. The French are suspicious of U.S. intentions with regard to North Africa and their suspicions are largely responsible for the limitations they place on the scope of our military program there. If we were to go too far in pressing the French toward North African reforms, our present fairly successful utilization of the bases in Morocco could be jeopardized. On the other hand, we cannot give the French the support they desire for their North African policies without incurring the enmity of the native populations and antagonizing the Arab-Asian nations, who at Bandung were united in attacking French policies in North Africa. Even our present middle-of-the-road position is criticized as being, in fact, in support of the French and has led to resentment of U.S. policy by North Africans, particularly in Morocco. At the same time, attitudes and interests of colonial powers must be recognized or we are liable to eventually alienate many of our European Allies.

18. The French do not like to see an American label on any economic aid extended to North Africa—it makes them fear that the Arabs will think that France is unable to provide for their basic needs and their economic development. Since last October there have been no new requests from the French Government for U.S. technical or development assistance for projects in Morocco or Tunisia nor is there reason to believe any such requests will be forthcoming in the near future. Although in the past few months emergency situations have arisen both in Morocco (locust invasions)

and in Tunisia (severe drought, local food shortages and locust invasions) which have been closely followed by FOA, State and Agriculture, the French have not indicated any need for outside assistance in meeting these emergencies.

19. As a result of French sensitivities toward any outside influence on the native population and toward foreign comment on what they consider their domestic affairs, the information program is necessarily limited.

20. *Alternatives to Present Policies.* We are conducting what in effect is a holding operation which is the best that can be done inasmuch as any alternative policies would be more prejudicial to overall U.S. interests. In the final analysis North Africa, though an international problem, is a French responsibility and we depend on the French for our strategic requirements in the Area. The importance of France in Europe and in the NATO Alliance, as well as the strategic and monetary value of the bases in Morocco, makes extremely difficult a shift of our policy towards more support of the nationalists against France. Such a move could easily lead to even more bloodshed than is caused by the present terrorist campaign of the nationalists and, certainly, the French would not allow themselves to be peaceably ejected from the area. Recent developments in Europe, such as French approval of German rearmament, or in Indochina do not give the U.S. any substantially freer scope of possible action with regard to North African problems so long as we wish to obtain maximum utilization of our bases in North Africa and to build strength in Western Europe, an area in which France geographically and politically occupies a central position.

C. Emerging Problems and Future Actions

21. Solutions are being sought for the problems set forth in paragraphs 3 through 7. It may be necessary to reach certain compromises to resolve these problems.

22. *Re-Examining Military Requirements.* Because of the French attitude described above and because of the questionable outcome of the conflict between the French and the native nationalists it may be necessary for the Department of Defense to re-examine its requirements for additional facilities to determine (a) whether they could be obtained in an alternate location, (b) if they cannot be re-located, whether they should be pursued further in spite of the difficulties involved. It should be noted that the larger our stake in French North African bases, the greater is the need to work with the French in the area.

23. *Political Progress.* The future implementation of our policy will depend to a great extent on the course of events over which the U.S.

will have limited influence. We shall continue to urge, to the extent possible, bilateral negotiations of necessary reforms in Morocco and Tunisia. We should seek to influence, to the limited extent possible, favorable evolutionary developments in Algeria.

24. *UNGA Consideration.* If the almost unanimous expressions of confidence contained in the 1954 UNGA resolutions are not realized, which is likely, many members at the next UNGA may demand that the UN investigate or intervene. Such developments would greatly complicate the problem of what the U.S. could or should do and consideration may have to be given to the course of action prescribed in paragraph 21 of NSC 5436/1 concerning making use of UN procedure if the French and nationalists are unable to reach bilateral agreement.

25. *French Efforts to Obtain Support.* Pursuant to a French Government statement just prior to final ratification of the Paris agreements, the Government may increase its efforts to obtain broad U.S. support for French North African policy under the guise of NATO solidarity on political issues.

26. *Information Activities.* The U.S. Information Agency has weighed the advisability of maintaining its posts in French North Africa where the program is restricted to factual news reporting and cultural activities. The decision to continue the operation is based on the fact that the general populations of Morocco, Tunisia and Algeria are being reached by press releases and are utilizing the library facilities and are participating in the cultural activities. The withdrawal of the U.S. Information Services would be interpreted by the non-French population as a withdrawal of our interest in their welfare. It would also give comfort to the French Administration which desires to eliminate all influence but its own. U.S. objectives are not identical with those of the French. Therefore, USIA is faced with the problem of continuing its activities in French North Africa in order to advance those long-range U.S. objectives with which the French are not identified.

27. *Economic Activities.* It has become apparent that the French Government's interest in possible U.S. assistance to French North African projects is restricted primarily to financial assistance. The French will accept technical assistance only as part of larger development assistance projects (only exception to this being a relatively minor interest in FOA-financed study in the U.S. for French colonial technicians). U.S. aid available in FY '55 for French African DOT's (including Morocco and Tunisia) has been limited to technical cooperation funds. The French Government has expressed no interest in availing itself of this aid for Morocco or Tunisia.

26. Telegram From the Embassy in France to the Department of State [1]

Paris, June 5, 1955—2 p.m.

5487. I am concerned over North African situation in itself, and at extent to which it has become both France's number one problem and number one sore spot in Franco-American relations which can affect relations in all fields. There are widespread indications that North Africa is far more in minds of both official and unofficial Frenchmen than any other external problem and there is little understanding or confidence in U.S. policy of support for French presence. There is increasing tendency here to seek to blame U.S. for French troubles there. In separate message [2] we are giving our evaluation of current French policy with respect to each of three North African areas.

France lost Indochina because of inability (1) to maintain its position by force or (2) to grant sufficient concessions in time to obtain native loyalty. U.S. policy suffered from a corresponding dualism. One school of thought was that we should do everything possible to assist French forcefully to suppress Communist-inspired rebellion. The other was that we should force French to grant the country independence and pull out as quickly as possible. The constant compromises between the two served gravely to handicap French efforts to secure a solution by military means without succeeding in bringing about independence except by steps which were substantially too little and too late.

History could easily repeat itself with respect to North Africa. I am not sure that French Government will succeed in holding North Africa by military means nor that it will have the foresight (or find it possible from domestic political point of view) to win true Nationalist friendship and support. Nevertheless I hope we will avoid insidious compromises in this case and make determined effort to obtain best rather than worst of both worlds.

Despite obvious differences in situation (absence of land frontier with Communism, probable inability of anti-French elements to mount more than guerrilla operations, greater French maneuverability, etc.), same problem does exist of French control over dependent peoples in area where maintenance Western control vital both to position of France as an ally and in our own strategic interest. Obviously our policy of (1) supporting French presence in North Africa combined with (2) encouragement of French progress

[1] Source: Department of State, Central Files, 7515.00/6–555. Secret.

[2] Not further identified.

in satisfying Nationalist aspirations is sound. Problem is for U.S. to avoid being caught in similar dualism (i.e. permitting points (1) and (2) above to pull in opposite directions) which proved fatal in Indochina. Without at this time expanding on possible considerations in U.S. policy towards North Africa it is apparent two points above must somehow be combined into single effective course of action. Convincing French of our sincere support of their continued presence in North Africa is prerequisite to successful pursuit point (2) above. Only on that basis can we hope to influence French toward major reforms in Morocco and later in Algeria.

In considering North Africa we must keep in mind that its retention represents last hope France has of maintaining anything approaching its present world status and particularly that Algerian departments of France are considered part of Metropolitan France. This makes fundamental difference, certainly in French eyes, between Algerian problem and that of protectorates of Tunisia and Morocco. Solution in protectorates presumably lies in increased autonomy. Algerian problem, at least as French see it, lies in (1) maintenance of internal order and (2) political and economic integration of French and Moslem populations on mutually satisfactory basis. Whether this will in effect provide permanent solution remains to be seen but we could not realistically hope to force French to adopt any other approach within foreseeable future. One major difficulty in applying our North African policy has been that all our efforts, whatever they might be worth in any event, to persuade French to adopt a more liberal policy have been handicapped by suspicion that we were basically working against them, a suspicion fostered by mere extent of U.S. presence in Morocco. Only exception to this was period after the Secretary made very clear to Bidault in 1953 our support for French presence. If our views are to have any weight we must somehow overcome this feeling and replace it by one of confidence in our intentions.

Supporting French presence does not mean blank check to French or that we should be expected to endorse all aspects of their policy in North Africa. It does mean, I believe, that we should make it clearly understood that we have confidence that French will formulate and apply programs which respond to the evolving needs of the several peoples of the area in the political as well as economic and social fields, that we believe it is in the interests of the area as well as the free world that North Africa retain its special ties with France and that we have no intention or desire to replace French in that area.

On other side of coin, we must admit that from purely practical standpoint, French progress in satisfying Nationalist aspirations has been and will continue to be limited by powerful French vested interests on spot and determined primarily by personal attitude of influential members of any French Government and by importance which they attach to this problem in relation to other temporarily pressing problems and in relation to parliamentary support they think they can count on, rather than on our efforts to expedite this progress. There is no question, however, but that full confidence of government in U.S. support of French position would assure us a more understanding and receptive audience among government leaders and add greater effectiveness to our efforts to influence French to take necessary measures to satisfy Nationalist aspirations.

In circumstances I am seeking early appointment with Faure. I expect to express regret over murder of Lemaigre-Dubreuil [3] and concern over increasingly anti-American comment in France with respect to North Africa (including July statement Embtel 5461). [4] Will draw upon appropriate portions of Deptels 4212 [5] and 4247 [6] and emphasize both basic U.S. support for French presence there and our hope that French policies can be reinvigorated to take greater account of urgent realities which must be faced if that presence is satisfactorily to be maintained.

Dillon

---

[3] Jacques Lemaigre-Dubreuil, editor of the liberal *Maroc-Presse,* was shot by French assassins on June 12.

[4] Telegram 5461 from Paris, June 13, indicated that the comments of Pierre July, French Minister for Moroccan and Tunisian Affairs, had received little notice in the press. July was apparently upset by U.S. press criticism of the transfer of French troops to Algeria and U.S. labor union condemnation of France's North African policy. (Department of State, Central Files, 671A.72/6–1355)

[5] Telegram 4212 to Paris, May 25, stated that if Faure sought U.S. support for France's North African policy, Dillon should express gratification in regard to progress on Tunisia, but concern at the inadequate measures dealing with Algeria, Libya, and Morocco. For the United States to support French efforts in those nations a policy change was required. Because of the area's importance to Western defense, the United States sought stability in North Africa. (*Ibid.,* 751S.00/5–2355)

[6] Document 58.

27. Memorandum From the Deputy Director of the Office of Western European Affairs (Tyler) to the Director of the Office (Jones) [1]

Washington, June 16, 1955.

SUBJECT

Paris Telegram No. 5487 [2] on North African Situation

It seems to me that this message confirms the dilemma in which we find ourselves with regard to United States policy toward North Africa. It fails to convince me that it is in the best interest of the United States to come out now with a ringing declaration of confidence in the purpose and progress of French policy as now observable.

One can argue, as does Paris, that we must reassure France now, encourage French progress (whatever this means), and make it clear that we consider the French presence in North Africa essential. All this in the hope that by our attitude, and political as well as material support, we will bring about not only the restoration of order but a new and permanently improved relationship between France and the North African territories. Unhappily, on the basis of the past record of the history of France's relations with her overseas territories, the above must appear to be largely based on wishful thinking. There is no new element at present discernible which justifies the expectation that the French Government, parliament and people appreciate the urgency and danger of the present situation in North Africa, or that anyone is disposed to create such an awareness. And yet this is a prerequisite to effective political action, and to the defeat of the powerful lobbies and of special interests which paralyze political action and threaten the life of any government which attempts to undertake it.

I am convinced that we must somehow succeed in bringing it home to the French that rapid and courageous and farsighted policies, adapted to the particular status and requirements of each of the three North African territories, are not merely a precondition to American support, but a precondition to the effectiveness of any American support. I think this is the vital point: I do not believe that *as things stand* there is anything that we can do to prevent the French position in North Africa from deteriorating increasingly rapidly. On this assumption, it would not only be politically inept to

[1] Source: Department of State, Central Files, 770.00/6–1655. Secret.

[2] *Supra.*

take a public position of confidence with regard to French policies in that area, but such an act could not reverse the present trend.

In my opinion, if there is to be a chance of saving North Africa, we must somehow get the French to understand not merely United States policy, but the political realities of the situation on which United States policy is based and to which the French themselves still seem to be blind (or politically impotent) in the same way as with regard to Madagascar,[3] Indochina, and North Africa itself in the past. I think that if we lose sight of this fundamental factor, we risk following a course which leads to the same frustration, failure and danger as we have experienced in Indochina.

On the basis of this analysis of the political character of the situation, I feel that the Paris analysis does not go far enough and does not draw the inevitable conclusions from its own premises, i.e.: that if we continue to admit that there must be the "other side of the coin" and that "from the purely practical standpoint" French progress will continue to be paralyzed by selfish French interests in North Africa and political cowardice at home, then any words of confidence and encouragement on our part will be a mockery and a self-deception.

In short, it seems to me that the Paris telegram sees and analyzes every aspect of the problem clearly and convincingly with the exception of the one vital element, which is: what should the United States Government do about it in order that there should be a chance of saving the situation.

I do not believe that the mere repetition to the French Government of United States hopes and exhortations will achieve the fundamental shift in French awareness of the needs of the situation. I do not know whether the possibility has been considered of bilateral talks between the President and Faure in Geneva on this subject, but it may well be that this is the only chance for the necessary measures being taken in time. Conceivably, out of such a high-level discussion could come agreement by the French to much closer consultation on North Africa with us and possibly the British than has hitherto been the case. Such consultation might find some kind of continuing formal expression, though I realize it is most unlikely that the French would ever agree to this.

[3] Madagascar experienced a nationalist revolt in March 1947.

28. Telegram From the Embassy in France to the Department of State[1]

Paris, August 4, 1955—5 p.m.

526. Embassy has concluded three-day meeting with officers from North African posts and Jernegan.[2]

There are given below conclusions and agreed recommendations following meeting. We have separated these into two parts; first covering urgent Moroccan problems, and second on aspects US policy towards North Africa over next two or three years, which we consider vital period (events during which will determine largely what will happen thereafter).

I—Morocco

Conference of Embassy and North African officers agree Morocco represents problem of high urgency for French, and particularly requires decision re throne in very near future. Concurrent conversations of Ambassador and Holmes with Faure, July, and Bourges-Maunoury, believed offer considerable reason hope for swift French action this respect (Embtel 489).[3] Dynastic problem in Morocco overshadows more important issues, such as future French relationship with Moroccans which must be negotiated, but cannot be approached until throne question solved. Conference carefully considered and accepts view of Holmes and Porter that, to be useful, any arrangement with French may bring forth must have freely-given public approval and support of Ben Youssef, especially as it pertains to possible composition of regency council if and when French decide to bring about the retirement of Sultan Ben Arafa.

If present apparent French government intentions to deal with Morocco on urgent basis bring eventual adoption of forward-looking policy such as that outlined by Grandval to Holmes (Tangier telegram 40 to Department)[4] it was agreed this would offer good

---

[1] Source: Department of State, Central Files, 7515.00/8–455. Secret. Repeated to Tangier, London, Cairo, Madrid, Casablanca, Rabat, Tunis, and Algiers.

[2] The following persons attended the meeting on North African political problems which convened in Paris August 1–3:

John D. Jernegan, Julius C. Holmes, Lewis Clark, William J. Porter, Philip A. Mangano, Robert P. Joyce, Benson E. Timmons, and, from the Embassy in Paris, Leslie S. Brady, Charles R. Moore, Robert H. McBride, and Matthew J. Looram, Jr.

The minutes of the meetings are an enclosure to despatch 314 from Paris, August 5. (*Ibid.*, 751S.00/8–555)

[3] Document 182.

[4] Telegram 40 from Tangier, July 27, summarized a conversation between Gilbert Grandval and Holmes. Grandval indicated his intention to arrive at a liberal solution of the throne problem, which involved the departure of Ben Arafa. He spoke of the opposition to his program and asked for U.S. views. Holmes responded that the

occasion for US indicate its support for French intentions. It was agreed that we should lend positive US support if a liberal policy such as that proposed by Grandval is adopted.

Should obstacles arise to prevent French Government from taking adequate and prompt action to ease Moroccan situation, conferees believed that US should make clear to French that while our desire to be helpful remains unchanged, it is unlikely we will be able to accord them same degree of support at UNGA as we have in past. This idea has already been expressed informally and personally to Faure by Ambassador (see Embtel 489). We should bear in mind that this line would imply that we would give affirmative support if France acts.

This is only specific recommendation conference makes with regard to Morocco at this time. It stems from belief that French are facing their problem which will require great political courage and wisdom to solve satisfactorily. Our role, as we see it, is not to offer specific advice in any way that can be construed as "an American plan", but to make it clear to them that their failure to act will have the most profound consequences not only for their own interests, but for those of Morocco generally, where we do not at this time see any suitable alternative to the French presence. In taking this attitude, we, of course, have in mind our own interests which are hardly likely to prosper should the French-Nationalist struggle go on to the point where both are thoroughly and permanently embittered, and in the case of Moroccans, xenophobic as well.

Though the French have to pay a high price now to obtain peace and security in Morocco, they must meet that price for it will almost inevitably become higher with passage of time. The Nationalist movement, which for the first time now has massive community support, gives signs of confidence and organization hitherto lacking, plus determination to achieve its aims. The French, it is believed, can channel these energies into a long period of Franco-Moroccan cooperation and mutual inter-dependency, but the government must move decisively and speedily to give indication that this is its aim.

II—US Policy in Next Few Years.

A. *General considerations in US policy:*

(1) US policy in North Africa in past has been governed too much by external European and Middle Eastern considerations. In future we should bear in mind more what is best for North Africa itself and free world interests there.

United States desired a sound solution along the lines of Grandval's plan. (Department of State, Central Files, 771.00/7–2755)

(2) Principal barriers to US freedom of action—pressure of Arab-Asian world on one hand and well-known French position on other—are not greatly changed and still prevent easy solutions. However, there has been recent evolution in French thinking and events in North Africa have shocked Metropolitan France from its complacency to some extent. Influence of colons in France is probably diminishing and there is indication of greater determination on part of French governmental authorities to see that policies decided upon in Paris are actually carried out in North Africa. These are important new facts in developing US policy.

(3) General US objective of promoting development North Africa peacefully as part of free world remains unchanged. Our fundamental concept of area likewise of course continues. Within this framework, however, much remains to be done.

(4) Though there seems to be less willingness in France now to "die for North Africa" than heretofore, France gives retention North Africa top political priority. As a result, France also gives North Africa top priority for military resources, almost certainly ahead even of NATO commitments.

(5) Problem is complicated by fact French have not heretofore shown political capability of solving problem. However, program which Grandval outlined to Holmes for Morocco and general approach of Faure and Mendes-France to North Africa do appear worthy of our support.

(6) Ultimate solution probably will require basic reform French Union Constitution, which is now being discussed in Assembly French Union and by other groups. We cannot, nor can French, say now precisely how this would work. Presumably end result would be some form confederation all French territories. Since French relationship as it now exists North Africa cannot be maintained indefinitely, even at prohibitive cost, this may be best solution guaranteeing permanent established bonds between Tunisia and Morocco and France. Also because of its special complexities resulting from large French colony, juridical status, etc., it may be only answer conceivable for Algeria. This is of course long-term problem.

(7) Although we do not detect serious signs Communist penetration or direction Nationalist movements so far, except to some extent Algeria, in absence of improvement, the situation may develop into opportunity Communists will exploit.

(8) There is need, as in other underdeveloped areas, for large-scale and long-range capital investment to help meet critical demographic problem throughout area.

(9) There is lack of liberal press in North Africa which would provide forum for Moslem and liberal French opinion, and we feel obvious need exists break virtual monopoly of colon press.

(10) Past US policies do not seem to have satisfied nor to have been understood by any of interested parties. We should in future endeavor to explain our policies as clearly as possible in order obtain maximum understanding and acceptance, and thus facilitate our long-range global political and strategic objectives, as well as improve our relationships in France and North Africa.

(11) In summary, basis US policy should be to support solutions which appear have some support in North Africa and appear capable being successfully implemented (e.g. Tunisian accords) even though these may not be perfect. While we should not undertake present detailed solutions to French, we should have well-developed policies as outlined for Morocco in part I which we could tie in discussions with French when opportunities occur as in recent talk with Faure (Embtel 489).

B. *Specific recommendations.*

(1) Since Franco-Tunisian conventions follow general line we have urged France follow in North Africa for several years, and were arrived at by method direct negotiations which both US and UN have consistently recommended, it is disheartening to French and confusing to Tunisians that we have not taken cognizance of conventions publicly. Therefore a public statement should be issued by Secretary when conventions take effect indicating our satisfaction. (see Deptel 411) [5] Believe this would also help Grandval in Morocco.

(2) No decision should be taken on US position re Moroccan item at UN until we see whether French act before UNGA or not. As stated in part I, we believe most strongly that if positive French action occurs, we should support French position as we have in past. If clear French will not act before UNGA we should inform them that we believe it will be impossible support them as before. We believe it is undesirable for Algeria to be opened up at all in UN framework since political as well as juridical situation is dissimilar from Morocco and Tunisia (i.e., progress as may be made in immediate future will not be in accordance with desires Moslem states though it will tend towards increasing autonomy).

(3) If French make progress in Morocco and Algeria, we should make especial efforts with Spain to obtain moderation of attacks on French policy. We should also make representations as appropriate with Egypt and other Moslem states in same sense though we realize probable ineffectiveness in latter case.

---

[5] Telegram 411, August 2, asked the Embassy for a recommendation as to the desirability of a public statement or message by the United States commenting on the ratification of the Franco-Tunisian accords. (*Ibid.*, 611.72/8–255) Dulles issued a statement on August 10. (Department of State *Bulletin*, August 22, 1955, p. 301)

(4) USIS policy in Morocco should be to continue to lie low but there is room in Tunisia and Algeria for carefully planned and supervised activity especially along lines of explaining clearly what USIA is, and what contributions it has to offer to all elements of population. If US policy should continue, as result progress in Morocco, to be continuation support French presence, USIS should play more positive role in expounding US policy and its basic concept supporting enlightened French policies. Conversely, if French do not act in Morocco and US policy becomes less favorable to France, US role would diminish even more.

(5) In France, throughout North Africa and elsewhere, our public position on North Africa should be as follows:

(a) We support continuation French presence in North Africa as in interest of the peoples of the area itself, as well as that of French, ourselves and free world generally.

(b) Twentieth century Nationalism has outdated old concepts of paternalism, etc.

(c) We give full marks to France for her remarkable material achievements in area; however, economic and social progress is no longer enough to satisfy Nationalism. In current world climate, no people will long accept second-class or inferior citizenship.

(d) Repressive policies are doomed to fail, while, on the other hand, negotiation and agreement may succeed, as has thus far been shown in Tunisia.

(e) Problem has become primarily political one and so political approach needed.

We realize line outlined above not susceptible convincing colons and extreme right-wing elements France but consider it reasonable and sound.

(6) British should be informed fully of our North African policy. It might be helpful in case of Morocco if the British could indicate support for similar ideas at an appropriate time. This might not be as helpful in cases of Algeria and Tunisia.

(7) We recommend Department give consideration to formation of task force to deal with North African problem on centralized and responsible basis. Purpose of this group would be to consider most effective way inducing France adopt and implement policies calculated protect her interests, and that of West generally, in North Africa. If such group deemed useful, it could also be charged with recommending course of action calculated best preserve US national interests in area in event French fail restore reasonably secure position.[6]

---

[6] In a letter to Holmes, August 12, Dulles indicated that the Department generally endorsed the recommendations of the Paris meeting summarized here. He requested that Holmes and Porter return to Washington for 2 or 3 weeks of consultation in September to join with others in devising a policy for Morocco and North Africa. (Department of State, Central Files, 751S.00/7–2855)

Complete minutes follow by pouch.

Dillon

29. Memorandum From the Diplomatic Agent at Tangier (Holmes) to the Secretary of State [1]

Washington, September 29, 1955.

SUBJECT

French North Africa; Recommended U.S. Actions and Attitudes

Purpose.

This paper considers the North African problem as a whole with specific and urgent attention to its Moroccan aspects in the event (a) the French Government produces an adequate plan to ease tensions in Morocco or (b) that Government fails to produce such a plan.

Recommendations.

In the past the U.S. approach to North African problems has been conditioned mainly by French considerations involving our desire not to disturb any given French parliamentary equilibrium in order to avoid endangering the attainment of important U.S. objectives, such as gaining French adherence to EDC. [2] Now, however, in the face of the riptide of nationalism in Africa and Asia and of our interests in those regions, it is believed that the U.S. should recast its thinking and it is therefore recommended that the U.S. not premise its approach to North Africa, and particularly to Morocco, on French considerations to the same degree as in the past, but instead place more emphasis on preserving the area for the West, regardless of temporary inconveniences which may arise in our relations with the French. Such an approach would have the additional benefit of tending to restore our prestige in the Afro-Asiatic world. The

---

[1] Source: Department of State, Central Files, 770.00/9–2955. Secret. Concurred in by Merchant and Jernegan. Derived from the 47-page despatch Holmes sent from Tangier July 29 embodying the findings of his investigation. (Despatch 49; *ibid.*, 751S.00/7–2955) Holmes' more abbreviated preliminary comments were incorporated in telegrams 32 and 44 from Tangier, July 24 and 29, respectively. (*Ibid.*, 751S.00/7–2455 and 751S.00/7–2955)

[2] The French rejected the EDC on August 30, 1954.

following specific line of action is therefore recommended in that context:

Morocco.

1. Until the Faure plan is implemented in Morocco, it is recommended that we take every useful opportunity to make known to the French our belief that it appears to be the best proposal so far advanced to deal with the Moroccan problem.

2. It is recommended that we endeavor to induce the British to take a similar line and, if possible, have them take the initiative in discussing it with the French.

3. It is recommended that a special effort be made to coordinate with the British an approach to the French on this subject at the Tripartite meeting in Paris in October, just prior to the NATO Council meeting which precedes the Foreign Ministers' Conference at Geneva. A suggested outline of an Anglo-American approach to the French is attached for possible use in this connection (Tab A).[3] Intervening events may of course alter the pattern of this approach.

4. It is recommended that we make known to the French that we believe it in our interest and theirs for U.S. representatives to maintain discreet contact with Moroccan nationalist leaders, as a general rule outside the French Zone of Morocco; that through such contact we can exert pressure in favor of continued moderation, and can perhaps occasionally be of direct assistance to the French themselves should they desire it.

5. If M. Faure is unable to move ahead with his plan by the time the Moroccan question is considered by the General Assembly, it is recommended that the U.S. should examine any resolutions which the Afro-Asiatic Powers may present with a view to adopting a course best calculated to induce the French to take salutary action while tending to restore and enhance U.S. prestige and influence with the Afro-Asiatic group.

6. If by January 1956 the French Government has produced no solution for the problem, and the situation in Morocco is substantially unchanged or has deteriorated, it is recommended that the U.S. invite French attention to the continuing danger to Western interests

---

[3] Not printed. British Ambassador Sir Roger Makins, in a letter to Dulles of August 8, indicated that Macmillan thought it inopportune for either of their governments to intervene with the French at that time. (Department of State, Central Files, 751U.00/8–855) On October 6, Holmes and Ambassador Winthrop W. Aldrich met with the British Prime Minister. Holmes outlined the recommendations in this memorandum. Macmillan responded that he would consult with his advisers before commenting. (Telegram 1380 from London, October 6; *ibid.*, 123–Holmes, Julius C.) Macmillan called Aldrich in on October 14 to tell him that he preferred to wait because the situation was uncertain. (Telegram 1503 from London, October 14; *ibid.*, 771A.00/10–1455)

generally, and urge the French to examine the usefulness of multilateral discussions with the Moroccan nationalists and powers most interested.[4] One result of the prospect of internationalization of the Moroccan problem might be to lessen opposition in France to liberal policies like those of M. Faure. If this step fails to produce a useful French reaction, it is recommended that consideration be given at that time to a public appeal by the Secretary that the French and the Moroccans negotiate their differences.

On the other hand, should the Faure plan for Morocco go into effect before the end of 1955, or before Morocco comes up for consideration in the UN, it is recommended that the U.S.:

1. Immediately endeavor to turn the debate on the Moroccan problem in the GA in favor of the French on the basis of favorable developments. We should concurrently express the belief that undue criticism would not be constructive during French-Moroccan negotiations.[5]
2. Give the French as much diplomatic assistance as possible in Afro-Asiatic capitals and in Madrid, with a view to ending hostile radio broadcasts and other forms of agitation as harmful to the same negotiations.
3. Make known to the nationalists our strong belief that only through negotiation can they hope to arrive at a satisfactory solution of their problems.
4. Consult with the French with a view to considering suggestions they may have as to how we can continue to be of assistance.

Algeria and Tunisia.

It does not seem advisable to make any approach to the French at this time concerning either Algeria or Tunisia. The situation in the latter country, as noted, is relatively good. As to Algeria, the complexity of the juridical and psychological factors involved make it appear probable that any approach the U.S. might make at this time would be counterproductive. However, a solution in Morocco would inevitably increase pressure for progress in Algeria, and an opportunity may thus arise later for the U.S. to use its influence in that direction.

---

[4] Dillon indicated in telegram 1632 from Paris, October 10, that he agreed with most of the points made by Holmes. In regard to recommendation 5, however, he believed that the winning of the Afro-Asiatic bloc's good will took second place to securing the best result for Morocco and North Africa generally. With respect to recommendation 6, he noted that the French were opposed to any multilateral discussion of Moroccan problems in which Spain would participate. (*Ibid.*, 771.00/10–1055)

[5] Following the restoration of Ben Youssef as Sultan, the U.N. General Assembly voted December 3 to put off further consideration of the matter. (Resolution 911 (X))

North Africa—General.

In discussions with the French on North Africa, U.S. representatives can usefully emphasize the point that continued dissension and strife there can only attract Soviet attention to an increasing degree. In that connection mention should be made of the possibility that the Soviet Government, if it considers the situation "ripe" from its viewpoint, may make such moves as taking its seat on the Committee of Control at Tangier. The establishment of a Soviet diplomatic mission at that point might well be followed by the gravest consequences throughout North Africa as a whole. The nature of Soviet overtures to Libya and to Egypt should be sufficient to convince the French that the Arab world, including North Africa, has a definite priority in Soviet plans. Such a theme could be elaborated to include a statement of our belief that France and the West generally cannot afford the soft right flank which North Africa now represents.

Should such discussions with the French occur, or become advisable, with respect to the long-range problem of French association with her protectorates and possessions, it is believed that the American approach should be to encourage France to move forward, so as to be able to control changes, rather than be forced to react to changed positions arising from violence and rebellion. She should be encouraged to revamp the concept of the French Union to include the possibility of federation with France of those countries which have already or will emerge toward the status of self-governing territories. The idea of federation of course runs counter to the traditional and historic French concept of the centralization of governing power, but something like it must emerge to counteract the attractions of Pan-Arabism and the "Brotherhood" of Islam and the pressures of extremists who will be satisfied with nothing except complete severance of all ties with France. In connection with reenforcing those ties, we shall probably be faced, sooner or later, with the question of American economic assistance to North Africa. Our primary problem will be that of deciding how to provide such assistance as we deem desirable in a manner calculated to cement rather than weaken the ties of North Africa with France and the West.

France still has the power and the wealth to turn the nationalist drive for self determination into a voluntary association of the North African peoples with her. The retention of her present status among the Powers may depend on the effectiveness with which she undertakes this task in the relatively near future.

Discussion.

North Africa—General.

The problem of North Africa is not now an African problem; it is a French one and its solution lies not in Africa but in Paris. Attention has been focused on Morocco, Algeria and Tunisia because the events creating the present situation have occurred there. Nevertheless, decisions and actions to arrest the dangerous deterioration in the French position in North Africa can only be taken in Paris.

This being so it behooves us, in assessing the problem and in arriving at a U.S. position regarding it, to understand the character and position of the French Government. It is a Government of weakness and instability and its immediate successors are not likely to be different. We are now witnessing the uninspiring spectacle of M. Faure formally announcing "unanimous" Cabinet decisions which he is powerless to carry out because those decisions have been openly opposed and sabotaged by powerful interests, including members of his own Cabinet.

Among the reasons for this extraordinary state of affairs are:

The inherent weakness in any French Government constituted under the provisions of the Fourth Republic which, to safeguard against a despotic executive, has created in effect "Government by Assembly"; the consequent inability of successive French Governments to pursue policies vigorously and consistently since their very existence depends upon constantly shifting parliamentary majorities; the lingering national psychosis of defeat in World War II expressed by hypersensitivity and often strident self assertions; the clinging to a traditional concept of greatness and glory in the face of failure to meet a changing world, without the sharp logic with which this logical people are supposed to be endowed. In spite of France's great liberal tradition, Revolution, Rights of Man, Descartes, etc., the French are essentially a conservative people; like the late George Apley, France is allergic to change.

The net effect of this state of affairs is that the French Government's ability to translate basic decisions on North Africa into action remains in grave doubt. Whatever its capacity, or incapacity, in this respect, there is no uncertainty whatever concerning the capacity and intentions of the second important element of the North African problem; i.e., North African Nationalism. It is the power and ruthlessness of that nationalism, backed by the North African communities, which brings French Governmental hesitations into bold relief. Its present attributes consist not only of the community support mentioned, but also of determined though moderate leadership with a definite program. As to the latter, the leaders at present believe in negotiation with the French, in continued association with France, and they have consistently pleaded their cause on those bases.

The continuity of this leadership is threatened by an impatient underground which, for its part, is convinced of the fruitlessness of negotiation with France and prefers to embark instead on a long-drawn struggle to gain complete independence by violence. There is no capacity here as yet to wage widespread civil war, and none to challenge the French in open combat. But current events prove that there is adequate organization, power and more than enough determination to take an increasingly heavy toll of Frenchmen and their property in North Africa. This process, unless arrested, will produce a continuing erosion of the French position in North Africa; and it may deprive the moderate nationalists of their leadership in favor of a group who would be satisfied with nothing less than the complete eviction of France from the area.

The Frenchmen of North Africa and their friends in France of similar outlook make up the third key element of the general problem. These have up to the present resisted, with considerable determination and effectiveness, French governmental steps involving concessions to nationalist aspirations. The attitude of these Frenchmen arises mainly from a desire to conserve the exceptional privileges they have enjoyed for many decades. Their strength on the one side, and that of the nationalists on the other, has caused the French Government to vacillate uncertainly while the general North African situation outside of Tunisia continues to worsen.

Tunisia.

In Tunisia, it is believed that France is on the right track as the conventions provide a working arrangement which appears satisfactory to French and Tunisians generally. Much will depend on the faithful implementation of the conventions by both sides. The prospects are good, but can be adversely affected by conditions in Algeria and Morocco and by economic difficulties. Despite the relatively good current atmosphere, much will also depend on how the French meet the almost inevitable Tunisian demands for a more rapid and eventually fuller transfer of authority than is now envisaged in the conventions.

Algeria.

Algeria is much less promising. Guerilla warfare is if anything on the increase, and the program of Governor General Soustelle is under heavy fire from vested French interests. That program, within general framework of the French Government's policy of integration, aims at a more liberal application of economic and educational benefits, but is not evoking the cooperation of the majority of Algerian Moslems. What course France will eventually take in Algeria is not clear, but her present policy of integration seems unlikely to succeed. To some, federation appears the only practical solution, but the psychological as well as practical adjustments required in reorganizing the French Union and the decentralization of administration which such a move would entail make it seem unlikely of achievement in the near future. For the present, therefore, governing Algeria will probably continue to involve a major military effort for France which, in conjunction with the similar effort in Morocco, will waste French strength with detrimental effect on France's NATO contribution.

Morocco.

In Morocco, the situation has both encouraging and discouraging aspects. It is discouraging because of the considerable tension and continuing violence in that country; on the other hand, some encouragement may be gleaned from the fact that M. Faure has been energetically, but thus far vainly, endeavoring to apply a program which will ease tensions. That program would involve the following moves:

1. Removal of the present Sultan who is not accepted by the Moroccan people.
2. Establishment of Throne Council.
3. Creation of Representative Government to negotiate reforms with the French.

The timely application of this plan would undoubtedly result in a relaxation of tension in Morocco, and would therefore be a step in the right direction. It would bring French and Moroccan nationalists together for negotiation, after which various pressures would tend to keep them at the conference table until they have developed future working arrangements.

Nationalist cooperation with the French in this plan depends on the successful achievement of the first step—the removal of Sultan Ben Arafa. Thus far, the French Government has not been able to achieve this for reasons mentioned above. Continued French inability to implement the Faure plan, or something very similar in the near future, will result in increasingly severe disturbances in French Morocco. The French can deal with these disturbances, but only at great economic and military cost which will eventually prove unbearable.

The recommendations in this paper have been reviewed in the light of NSC 5436/1 and OCB Progress Report of June 1, 1955 on

NSC 5436/1 [6] and are believed to fall within the courses of action approved therein. They have also been formulated after consideration of the opinion of the Joint Chiefs of Staff on the importance of U.S. bases in French North Africa as contained in the memorandum of September 15, 1955 from Mr. Murphy to the Secretary. [7]

[6] Document 25.

[7] The memorandum indicated that the JCS considered the North African bases essential even after the completion of the Spanish facilities. (Department of State, Central Files, 711.56371A/9–1555)

30. Department of State Position Paper [1]

Washington, January 17, 1956.

POSITION PAPER ON NORTH AFRICA

(For discussion with Mr. Evelyn Shuckburgh, of the United Kingdom, January 19, 1956)

Recommended U.S. Position

General Views on North Africa

The following points should be prefaced by an explanation that they represent our frankest view of the situation and that while our general attitude is well known to the French, we have not as yet spelled it all out in this fashion to them.

1. The United States is convinced that all parts of North Africa are moving, at varying rates of speed, toward independence. The emergence of self-governing states in the area will give rise, as in other areas, to a power vacuum, into which the Soviet Union will inevitably try to move, directly or through the intermediary of Arab states, especially Egypt which has definite ambitions for leadership of North Africa.

2. We believe that the Western powers must therefore move rapidly to counteract those influences and to fill the vacuum with Western influence. This means encouragement and backing for the moderate, pro-Western nationalist leadership in Morocco and Tuni-

[1] Source: Department of State, Central Files, 751S.00/1–1756. Secret. Drafted by Bovey as an attachment to a memorandum of conversation by Hadsel, January 17. The purpose of the meeting was to allow Ambassador Dillon and Assistant Secretary Allen to read and discuss the position paper, with which they essentially agreed.

sia. Such leadership may emerge later in Algeria when the French are ready to work out a new federal status for that country.

3. We believe that we should, principally through diplomatic means, enjoin upon the French, on every suitable occasion, the necessity for continuing liberal concessions in the direction of independence in Morocco and Tunisia in order that moderate pro-Western leadership may retain its popular following.

4. In expressing views on Algeria to the French we shall have to proceed with greater circumspection. We are convinced that the formula of integration is no longer workable and will probably have to give way to a formula for federation with France. We note that the British Government shares this view. Both governments, however, appear to recognize that exclusive responsibility for evolution of Algeria lies at present with France, whose own territory is involved. Like the British we have assisted the French in purchasing helicopters, but feel that ultimately a political rather than a military solution will be necessary in Algeria.

Concrete Proposals

5. In carrying out the above policy the United States hopes to be of assistance to the French and the peoples of North Africa in a number of concrete ways. These are listed here and discussed in greater length in the attached paper.[2] (AF believes that these points should at least be mentioned. If time does not permit further examination, we could discuss them later with the British in Washington and in London, though it should be made clear that none of them, except (1) under Morocco, has been discussed with the French.)

A. In Morocco

1. Maintain contacts with Moroccan leaders in order to offer practical advice and counsel of moderation as needed, especially during forthcoming Franco-Moroccan negotiations.

2. Develop programs for possible technical and economic assistance, subject to French sensibilities and domestic considerations in the United States on foreign aid in general.

3. Seek ways in which to make available to Morocco sound technical, economic and financial advice, perhaps from members of international organizations such as IMF, whose political motivation would be beyond question.

---

[2] Attachment omitted. [Footnote in the source text.]

4. Provide diplomatic support, as appropriate, for liberal French efforts to work out the future status of Morocco. Chief capitals would be Tripoli, Madrid, and, to the extent possible, in Cairo.

5. Stand ready to examine with other Algeciras powers [3] (exclusive of USSR) the effects on their position, and on ours, of imminent modification or abrogation of Treaty of Fez. [4] France has indicated she desires such consultations with United States and U.K. We are inclined to believe we should make no definite commitment on our Algeciras rights until the course of the Franco-Moroccan negotiations becomes clearer.

6. Examine with other powers now on Tangier Committee of Control ways of retaining international influence in the Zone when it becomes integrated into Morocco.

7. We should not raise with the British the question of terminating our extraterritorial rights in Morocco, since we have not informed the French. Should the British raise the point, we could reply that the matter was under study and that we would inform the British of any decision we might take in the matter.

B. In Tunisia

The overt split between the pro-Western Bourguiba moderates and the Cairo-oriented Salah ben Youssef extremists is disquieting. We have indicated publicly our support for the approach represented by Bourguiba and the Franco-Tunisian Conventions of 1955. The lack of direct United States interests and treaty relationships with Tunisia makes it more difficult to discover ways of being helpful than in Morocco. However, we are considering:

1. Possibility of economic assistance, subject again to French sensitivity and general United States domestic considerations.
2. Possible diplomatic opposition to Egyptian encouragement of Tunisian extremism.

C. Algeria

See above (No. 4 under general views on North Africa).

Probable British Position

It is not believed that the British will display any fundamental opposition to the views expressed above, though they may express

[3] Reference is to the European powers who together with the United States, signed the Act of Algeciras of April 7, 1906.

[4] The Treaty of Fez of March 30, 1912, established the French protectorate over Morocco. See *British and Foreign State Papers*, vol. 106, p. 1023.

some reticence as to the advisability of intervening directly with the French.[5]

N.B.: It would be inadvisable to mention US–UK discussions of French North Africa in any communiqué in connection with the Shuckburgh or Eden talks.

[5] At the January 19 meeting, Rountree presented U.S. views, adhering closely to this paper. Shuckburgh replied that his government wished France to retain as much influence in the area as possible. (Memorandum of conversation by Bovey, January 19; Department of State, WE Files: Lot 58 D 90, Middle East—1954–57)

31. Telegram From the Embassy in France to the Department of State [1]

Paris, March 2, 1956—1:38 p.m.

3992. I am impressed by the volume of reports from all parts of France indicating a dangerously sharp rise in anti-American sentiment because of what French public opinion believes our North African policy to be. Algerian crisis is largely responsible for this outburst of French feeling.

Belief that we are at heart sympathetic to total ejection of France from North Africa has gradually gained currency during last few years and is now spreading like wild fire. This feeling is being positively fanned by fact that no U.S. official either in France or in U.S. has made any major public announcement sympathizing with continuance French presence North Africa. Lack of such statements is being construed as admission of accuracy of current French thinking.

Lack of positive anti-French actions by U.S. Govt., plus support in U.N. which French unfortunately do not yet believe is entirely wholehearted, plus fact we have diverted small number of helicopters to France is unfortunately not enough to counter this rising tide of nationalistic anti-Americanism. What is needed and only thing that will be effectual is repeated public expressions of U.S. sympathy for continued French presence in North Africa which could be coupled with support of what has come to be known as "interdependence". I would of course be more than pleased to undertake

[1] Source: Department of State, Central Files, 751S.00/3–256. Top Secret; Limit Distribution.

series of such talks in France if and when Department should approve.

I have frequently pointed out over past years potential seriousness of French reaction to serious reverses in Algeria particularly when coupled with feeling that United States was standing by unsympathetically while French feel they are fighting for their very lives. I must now report that this dangerous potentiality is nearing realization. It is impossible to foretell eventual results should an explosion take place in France; but it would certainly pose most serious problems for entire Western alliance.

The danger is becoming imminent, the immediate weeks and months ahead will be crucial.

I recommend that this whole problem including repercussions on NATO and defense of Europe be given prompt consideration at the highest level so as to reach a policy decision before we are overtaken by rapidly moving events.

Dillon

---

32. Memorandum From the Deputy Under Secretary of State for Political Affairs (Murphy) to the Acting Secretary of State [1]

Washington, March 3, 1956.

Even though I was in Paris only three days, I realized that there is a curious, and from our point of view a very unhappy, French attitude developing which seeks to place the onus for the French predicament in Algeria and Morocco on the United States. This does not seem to apply, as far as I can ascertain, to Tunisia. This is a psychological phenomenon which undoubtedly results from a sense of frustration and failure to develop a constructive and sound program for the area. The French have been faced with this problem for many years and have not demonstrated the capacity to deal with it. Intelligent Frenchmen, of course, know that without American aid

[1] Source: Eisenhower Library, Whitman File, International File, Africa. Secret. Attached to a memorandum by Acting Secretary Hoover for the President, March 3. A copy of Dillon's message, *supra*, was also attached. Hoover indicated that he was requesting the OCB to set up a working group to evaluate the problem on an urgent basis. The original version of the Murphy memorandum is in Department of State, Central Files, 751S.00/3–356.

in World War II, French North Africa would have been lost to them. I think they also know that without our post-war aid, it would have been even more difficult for them to maintain their position without our practical assistance, and their current operations in French North Africa with the military equipment which we have supplied to them is of course an essential factor in their operations. Through the post-war period, we have also consistently supported them in the United Nations on many occasions when issues relating to French North Africa were involved, sometimes to our own embarrassment, because of the issue of colonialism.

I think Mr. Dillon is right and that we should act to offset what seems to be the beginning of a wave of anti-Americanism in France on this score. But it is a matter which must be handled with considerable caution and skill if it is not to be counter-productive. This French sentiment is more complex than just an attitude regarding French North Africa. It includes many other factors such as resentments over Indochina; general discomfiture over France's weakened world position; smaller items but important ones to the French, such as the Saar question; a natural human tendency to blame a benefactor; plus insidious work by the French Communist Party with Soviet support to destroy Franco-American friendship.

---

33. Telegram From the Embassy in France to the Department of State [1]

Paris, March 13, 1956—2 p.m.

4189. Following is a memorandum prepared by Ambassador Lodge of his conversation with Prime Minister Mollet on March 10:

Prime Minister Mollet began the conversation by asking whether there was some particular subject which I wanted to take up.

I explained that I had come to Paris at the end of an official trip involving United Nations technical assistance and United Nations specialized agencies and was now on my way home. I had been impressed during my stay in Paris by the amount of misunderstanding existing between certain elements in the United States and certain elements in France. In situations of this kind between two free countries with a long tradition of friendship, it was natural to start on the assumption that there was some fault on both sides and

[1] Source: Department of State, Central Files, 611.51/3–1356. Secret.

that consequently steps should be taken by both sides to correct matters.

United States policy was one of complete support of France, and there was no action which the United States had taken which could in the least way be interpreted as being hostile to French interests. For this reason we felt particularly hurt at the incident which had taken place in Tunisia yesterday.[2] All of these recent developments made it highly desirable that steps should be taken by both sides to bring about a better understanding, and I was glad to be able to tell him in that connection that President Eisenhower had authorized Ambassador Dillon to make a statement before a month would have passed showing American support of France.

Prime Minister Mollet said that he had already heard of the fact that Ambassador Dillon was planning a statement and that he was most grateful for it. He was aware of the misunderstanding which existed at the present time in Franco-American relations, and he hastened to agree with me that there was no cause for complaint over the official attitude of the United States Government and that this was well understood in French official circles. All of the French intelligence services have been unable to uncover a single particular instance which would support the charge of anti-French American actions.

When we talked about Franco-American misunderstandings, therefore, we were not talking about Governments but about unofficial elements in the two countries. It was natural and he thought healthy for the Communists to be anti-American. What was disconcerting, however, was the fact that in certain elements of the French Right this feeling existed. He felt that it was largely due to a human desire to find a scapegoat "abroad".

I interrupted to say that this feeling was then exploited both by Communist and Arab propaganda to which he agreed.

In listing other reasons for current Franco-American misunderstanding he began by saying that the group of men who were at the top in leading the United States, and thus leading the free world, were men of the highest caliber and in every way equal to their enormous responsibilities. He did feel, however, that at the "noncommissioned officer level" we were still often not well served. He was thinking of the Consul or the Embassy secretary or of the businessman—the man who travels and who still has an incomprehension of what a Latin really is, of what a European really is and who has an unquenchable desire to preach and to give unsolicited advice. He had been in Italy during the war and had seen the

[2] French mobs in Tunis seriously damaged the Consulate General and the USIS offices there.

Americans save millions of people from starving to death and then be hated in the process. As far as good will is concerned the manner of giving is more important than the gift.

Another reason for misunderstanding is the unthinkable black and white attitude of the American press which takes a blanket stand against what it calls "colonialism." He said the most hardhitting paragraphs of these uncomprehending editorials were the ones which the French newspapers printed over here.

While, of course, the Russian objective continued to be to destroy NATO, there were indications that the Russians were worried about the spread of Pan-Islamism. Recently Mollet had received Ambassador Vinogradov [3] of the Soviet Union who had said: "As regards this business of yours in Algeria, it would be bad if Islam were to sweep all over Africa."

In parts of Algeria the natives had taken over practically all of the functions of government, including judges and local political officials. In these places the world hero to whom the people look for leadership was not any Algerian leader; nor was it Colonel Nasser nor was it Khrushchev. The man they talked about was Mao Tse-tung. When I expressed surprise, he said that this was due to the fact that the backbone of the independence movement in Algeria was comprised of Algerians who were formerly in the French army. Many of them had been taken prisoner in Indochina and had been brainwashed by the Chinese Communists. They looked to Mao Tse-tung as the man who had thrown out the white man.

At the end he repeated his gratitude for the fact that Ambassador Dillon would make a statement. He said that material help was also needed. When I asked him to be definite he said that 80 helicopters would make all the difference. He said that now the United States was giving him helicopters at two a month. At this rate, he would have to wait for 40 months. He also wished 50 very slow-flying planes and said that a type existed which was obsolete and which they could buy for 1,000,000 francs each if we would let him have them.

The French Army had been built for the purpose of taking part in a defense against Russian attack. It would, therefore, have to be considerably revamped in order to meet the situation in Algeria. In Algeria, fast fighter planes or bombers or heavy armored columns were entirely out of the question. Helicopters, however, would show the civilian population that they did not need to give in to the terrorists.

He concluded by asking me to express his best wishes to President Eisenhower, to say that he was pro-NATO and that he

[3] Sergei Alexandrovich Vinogradov.

expected France to remain loyal to NATO, but that France must not feel she was standing alone. No one knew better than President Eisenhower how important North Africa was to NATO and to the defense of the free world. [4] We, therefore, should act on the basis of that realization. He felt that if there were three-power unity between the United States, the United Kingdom and France, it would make a greater impression in Cairo than any other single fact.

Dillon

[4] Two days after this conversation, General Jean Valluy presented a memorandum to the NATO Standing Group which explained the French view of the importance of North Africa to the alliance.

---

34. Operations Coordinating Board Report [1]

Washington, April 4, 1956.

PROGRESS REPORT ON UNITED STATES POLICY IN NORTH AFRICA (TUNISIA, MOROCCO AND ALGERIA) (NSC 5436/1) [2]

(Policy Approved by the President October 16, 1954)

(Period Covered: June 1, 1955 through April 4, 1956)

A. Listing of Major Developments During the Period

1. *Political*

a. *In Morocco*, after months of serious disorders and violence the Moroccans are well on their way to self-government. Mohammed ben Youssef was returned to the throne on November 16, 1955; a new Moroccan government, including representatives of the leading political groups, was installed in Rabat on December 7, 1955. On March 2 France recognized the independence of Morocco and both

[1] Source: Department of State, OCB Files: Lot 62 D 430, Horn of Africa. Secret. Enclosure to a memorandum from OCB Executive Assistant Charles E. Johnson of May 3. The OCB concurred in the report with the stipulation that it be updated to reflect developments since March 21 and that paragraph 5 be rewritten to clarify the language. At its April 26 meeting, the NSC noted the report and directed the NSC Planning Board to review the policy specified in NSC 5436/1 to take into account the new relations between France and Tunisia, Morocco, and Algeria. (Memorandum of discussion by Gleason; Eisenhower Library, Whitman File, and NSC Action No. 1543; Department of State, S/S–NSC Files: Lot 66 D 95)

[2] See footnote 3, Document 25.

countries announced the opening of negotiations to define a new relationship to replace the Protectorate. Throughout this critical and sensitive period, the U.S. encouraged France to offer more self government to the Moroccans, urged the Moroccans to act with moderation, and discussed with Spanish and Arab representatives the desirability of Franco-Moroccan rapprochement. The U.S. sent congratulations to the Sultan on November 18 and to the Moroccan and French governments on March 7.[3] These elicited cordial replies from the Sultan, in contrast to the more reserved answers he gave to Soviet congratulations in March. As a result of steps taken by the nationalists and the Sultan, military operations have been almost entirely suspended in the Rif, and terrorism has abated in the cities. There are signs, however, that Moroccan nationalists' interest in the Algerian cause continues.

On January 26, 1956, State announced publicly that the U.S. intended to relinquish its extra-territorial rights in Morocco, and to request appropriate Congressional action to this end. The announcement was well received by the Moroccans, but some opposition seems to be developing in Congress. The Senate Foreign Relations Committee is holding hearings on this matter on April 17.

b. *In the UNGA*, the U.S. voted for a resolution postponing further consideration of the Moroccan problem as a result of the rapprochement between the French and Moroccan governments. The Tunisian question was dropped from the UNGA agenda because of the signing of the Franco-Tunisian accords in August, 1955. The Algerian question was inscribed in the UN Agenda whereupon the French delegation quit the Assembly. The U.S. subsequently strongly supported a move to delete the Algerian item which was successfully carried.

c. *As to Tunisia*, despite the Franco-Tunisian Conventions ratified on August 4, 1955 granting substantial external autonomy to Tunisia, the situation subsequently deteriorated because of Morocco's more rapid progress toward independence, the Algerian struggle, a deepening economic crisis, and an open rift between pro-Western moderate nationalists and pan-Arab extremists. On February 27 new Franco-Tunisian negotiations began, and on March 20 a new agreement recognized the independence of Tunisia. As in the case of Morocco, this agreement will be followed by further negotiations leading to the establishment of a new relationship to replace that of the Protectorate. The Tunisian election of March 25 for a constituent assembly to draft a constitution, resulted in an overwhelming victory for the moderate nationalists led by Bourguiba.

[3] For text of the March 7 note to the Sultan of Morocco, see Document 187.

On March 9, the Consulate General and U.S. Information Agency offices in Tunis were raided by a mob of local Frenchmen and seriously damaged. The French government has presented apologies and offered to pay for any damage.

d. *In Algeria*, the situation deteriorated steadily during the reporting period. Disorders and violence have been increasing, with the danger of reaching widespread proportions. In his investiture speech Mollet proposed: (1) restoration of order; (2) free elections; and (3) negotiation of new Algerian status with Algerian representatives so elected. Mollet subsequently issued a warning to the Algerian rebels to lay down arms or face repression. There has been, however, no abatement of rebel activity and Parliament has now given Mollet full powers to deal with the situation. The French government accordingly decided to increase its military countermeasures to include the redeployment to Algeria of two additional divisions from its NATO commitment in Germany. This decision was given general sanction by the NAC on March 27. In addition France has again requested U.S. assistance in obtaining priority delivery on helicopters they have on order here. We have partially met this request by agreeing to give up priorities on 14 machines, while the larger request for 84 is now under review by the Paris Embassy and US CINCEUR, together with the French.

In an attempt to counter mounting anti-American sentiment in France as a result of French suspicions regarding our policy towards North Africa, Ambassador Dillon gave a speech in Paris on March 20 [4] assuring U.S. support for French "liberal and equitable" solutions in North Africa. This was well received in France.

2. *Military*

a. *U.S. Force level increases* for the Moroccan bases continued to be negotiated with the Foreign Office. The U.S. has requested an increase of 2,225 Air Force personnel to cover needs until July 1, 1957, on the basis that this proposal represents immediate pressing requirements within the overall U.S. request presented February, 1955 for an increase of 6,900 (Air Force: 7,400 to 12,206; Navy: 3,500 to 5,000).

b. *An increase in U.S. Forces rotational levels* has been obtained to the extent of a maximum of 30 F-100 fighter interceptor aircraft; these aircraft are in addition to the 2 U.S. squadrons stationed in Morocco for air defense, and the 2 Strategic Air Command Wings periodically rotated to the Moroccan bases for training purposes.

---

[4] Transmitted in telegram 4325, March 20. (Department of State, Central Files, 611.51/3–2056)

c. *Negotiations on Moroccan Status of Forces and Tax Relief Agreements* have been suspended by mutual agreement pending the outcome of the French-Moroccan negotiations.

d. *Additional base and transit rights* for Tunisia and Algeria which were requested in July, 1954 have not been pressed for in view of the unsettled conditions in the two areas at this time. However, France is pressing in the North Atlantic Treaty Organization (NATO) for allied approval of infrastructure projects in both areas.

e. *Base and supporting facilities* construction is proceeding satisfactorily. Four air bases and the Naval Air facilities at Lyautey are operational, and the supporting facilities (POL storage and pipeline, water installations, communications, etc.) are nearing completion. In September, 1955, French and U.S. military representatives reached a compromise agreement as to the gradual phase out of the Atlas Construction Co. in accordance with prior agreements.

f. The French and U.S. Air Forces have agreed to the incorporation of French personnel in the aircraft control and warning systems (AC&W) and for joint operation of the Moroccan Air Defense Control Center (ADCC).

g. At no time during the critical periods of violence have the bases in Morocco been molested.

3. *Economic*

a. *In Morocco*, the projects outlined in the basic materials loan of $7.5 million made to France in June, 1953, have been completed. These include improvement of the Port of Nemours (Algeria)—$1.43 million; a hydroelectric development and construction of a high tension transmission system—$4.5 million; and modernization of the railroad system—$1.86 million. Sultan ben Youssef and the nationalists have made it clear that an independent Morocco will expect economic and technical assistance. At present, the economic situation is developing unfavorably in Morocco.

b. *In Tunisia* as agreed in October 1954, the technical assistance ($250,000) and development assistance ($1.6 million) programs for the French project of agricultural development of the Mejerdah Valley are progressing satisfactorily. The economic situation of Tunisia continues to deteriorate.

4. *Cultural Activities*

Because of unsettled conditions in the area and the sensitivities of the French authorities regarding U.S. views on colonialism, the U.S. Information Service has concentrated chiefly on cultural activities, and avoided any actions which might be misconstrued adversely by the French or the nationalists. The U.S. Information Service has maintained contact with influential persons in both factions, and through a modest press program it has kept the French and Arab newspapers supplied with official U.S. statements and unofficial commentaries. The Exchange of Persons Program has thus far remained extremely limited pending clarification and improvement of relations between Tunisia and Morocco on the one hand, and France on the other.

B. Summary Statement of Operating Progress in Relation to Major NSC Objectives [5]

5. *Validity of the Basic Policy.*

a. French recognition of Moroccan and Tunisian independence in principle, and the continuing separate negotiations between France and representatives of these two countries toward agreement as to their future relationships with France ("interdependence"), indicate the necessity for a policy review. It is recommended that a review of the policy be initiated in the immediate future so that with the completion of the negotiations referred to above, consideration and formulation of a new basic policy for this area can be accomplished in the minimum amount of time. Specifically, it is considered that the substance of the objectives, outlined in paragraphs 10 through 14, and the courses of action set forth in paragraphs 15, 16, 17, 18, 19, 19–c (in part), 19–d and 19–e, 20 and 23 would continue to be valid for any revised policy paper; [6] however, it is noted that a policy review might take into account amplification of these paragraphs in view of new, and yet to be determined, relationships between France on the one hand and Morocco, Tunisia and Algeria on the other.

b. The following basic factors are suggested as background for the study-review:

(1) Politically, all of French North Africa has undergone an extremely accelerated and fundamental change during the last eight months. The Arab nationalists have, in effect, won or are winning a greater degree of independence from France. A new and still undetermined relationship between France and these three Arab areas is in the making, necessitating a re-alignment and re-evaluation of the respective political importance of three major elements: the French Government, the Arab nationalists and the local French population. Correspondingly, the U.S. policy and courses of action vis-à-vis the Arabs and the French will require continuing, changing and carefully planned methods of tactical application, lest the U.S. position in relation to any group be seriously weakened. The fundamental dilemma of supporting the aspirations of Arab nationalism, even in their moderate forms, without increasing French suspicions of our motives, is still unresolved.

---

[5] Latest NIE (71–55) on French North Africa is dated 11/29/55. [Footnote in the source text. This National Intelligence Estimate is not printed.]

[6] For text of these paragraphs, see *Foreign Relations*, 1952–1954, vol. XI, Part 1, pp. 173 ff.

(2) French North Africa is still strategically important to, and an integral part of, the NATO security area.

(3) The opportunity for communist exploitation exists and the danger has considerably increased as the prospect of Soviet diplomatic relations with Morocco and Tunisia draws nearer.

(4) The possibility of a pan-Arab, anti-Western movement, especially in Tunisia and Algeria, exists and should be planned for carefully.

(5) Militarily, irrespective of the U.S. base complex in Spain and the current value of the guided missile, the U.S. bases in North Africa continue to have an undiminished value.

(6) Mounting anti-Americanism in France resulting from our attitude toward North Africa has to be taken into account.

6. *Base Rights and Related Agreements.* U.S. rights in North Africa have been maintained. It may be possible to obtain in the near future an augmentation of the personnel ceilings in Morocco, our most pressing requirement. The resolution of other matters, such as the SOF and Tax Relief Agreements, must await the outcome of the French-Moroccan negotiations. While France is still unwilling to allow the U.S. peacetime rights for facilities in Algeria and Tunisia, it is probably to our best interest not to push this objective in view of the unsettled conditions in both areas and the current evolution of the political relations between France and the two countries. As to the Moroccan bases, their future status, as well as pending agreements may become an issue with the Moroccan government. That government may ultimately demand that the base agreements be renegotiated with them and that SOF and tax relief be concluded directly with them. Should it develop that the Moroccans have primary authority over these matters, the U.S. could take the position that the existing base agreements are valid and should be honored or revalidated by the Moroccan government. As the price for Moroccan cooperation, however, some kind of negotiation with the Moroccans on the base agreements will probably be necessary. In this connection, the U.S. may be faced with a request for substantial economic assistance.

7. *Moroccan Political and Economic Progress.*

a. With the installation of the new government on December 7, 1955 and the joint Franco-Moroccan declaration of March 2, 1956, a new phase of the relationship between the French and the nationalists has been reached. While to this extent the U.S. interest in progress toward more self-government for the Moroccans has been served, a critical period lies ahead. The Franco-Moroccan negotiations under way in Paris have as a principal objective the determination of the new "interdependent" relationship between the two countries to replace the relationships embodied in the Treaty of Fez. The crucial points will probably be the future role and responsibilities of France in Morocco's defense and foreign affairs; the fixing of adequate guarantees for the rights of French residents in the area; the establishment of economic ties between France and Morocco. Unless the current negotiations arrive at formulae which give concrete expression to Moroccan independence, it is reasonable to expect a rupture in present good relations and a renewal of widespread violence and disorder. It appears now that France is prepared to grant Morocco a very considerable degree of independence, even extending to the assumption by the Moroccans of greater control over foreign affairs and to the creation of an independent Moroccan army, while providing for an alliance coordinating Morocco's foreign policy with that of France and leaving the strategic defense of Morocco to the French. On these issues, it is to be expected both sides will endeavor to involve the U.S. On the general questions, the U.S. could restrict itself to urging discreetly moderation and compromise on both sides with the underlying purpose of endeavoring to strengthen the position of the moderate elements on both sides and particularly the moderate pro-Western elements in Morocco under the leadership of the Sultan.

b. With the completion of the economic aid programs for Morocco there have been no new requests from France for additional help. Although M. Mollet had indicated that France cannot ultimately carry the whole burden of economic development in North Africa, the French government has asked us not to hold out prospects of aid to the Moroccans during current negotiations. France is wary of U.S. assistance for the area; it fears the implication that France is unable to provide for the basic needs of Morocco. Considering the current negotiations, it may be that Morocco will not consent to preferential economic ties with France, or conversely, it may be that Morocco will continue to maintain the traditional pattern of economic relations with France. The United States prefers to see France and Morocco continue in a close economic relationship and to supplement French economic assistance rather than to supplant it. The possibility cannot be disregarded, however, that as French power declines in Morocco she may not have sufficient inducement to continue or expand public and private investment to take care of Morocco's growing needs, or prevent Morocco from exploiting the possibilities of USSR assistance. Moreover, the Moroccans have indicated clearly that they consider economic assistance as the natural counterpart of U.S. base rights. As a result, a unilateral U.S. review of Morocco's economic position and requirements is now under way in order that the U.S. may be in a position, if forced to discuss assistance as a quid pro quo for base rights, of doing so on the basis of economic requirements.

8. *Political and Economic Progress in Tunisia.*

a. Despite recognition of Tunisian independence on March 2, 1956 many serious problems remain to be solved, and the Tunisian Government is faced with serious constitutional questions, the danger of contagion from the Algerian struggle, an overt split in the nationalist movement between extremists and moderates, and a growing economic crisis. Where appropriate and feasible the U.S. should, in accordance with NSC policy, encourage French concessions to the moderate pro-Western elements in Tunisia. Since the U.S. has no treaty rights in Tunisia, as it does in Morocco, pursuance of U.S. objectives is more difficult. As Tunisia achieves a greater measure of self government, it may be possible to push harder for military bases and operating rights in the area, after consideration of the political situation as it evolves in that country.

b. Economically, as in Morocco, the French have shown no specific interest in any additional U.S. assistance. While the present U.S. technical and developmental assistance projects for the agricultural development of the Mejerdah Valley are progressing satisfactorily, the Tunisians are experiencing a deteriorating economic situation of considerable gravity. There is a danger of famine conditions this year, and, because of overpopulation in relation to land, of a continued inability of the Tunisians to feed themselves over a period of years. Ambassador Dillon and the U.S. Consul General in Tunis have recommended that the U.S. should be prepared to furnish economic assistance, in cooperation with France. As in the case of Morocco, a unilateral and confidential study of this question has been initiated.

9. *The Algerian Situation*

a. While Algeria is not included within the U.S. courses of action, U.S. assistance, during this reporting period, toward Franco-Algerian rapprochement was negligible and indirect, though the U.S. did oppose inscription of the Algerian item on the UNGA agenda when taken on September 30, 1955, and did support on November 25, 1955, a successful motion to remove that item from the agenda.

b. U.S. interest in the area centers on its importance to NATO security, and the possibility of anti-Western and/or a communist exploitation. While it is too early to know how French policy will evolve on this question, it does not seem likely that the Algerians will respond to Mollet's demand that they lay down their arms unless such demands are accompanied by more concrete offers of self government. Though the present government at least appears to recognize the inadequacy of integration as a solution, no satisfactory alternative has been worked out and the situation continues to deteriorate with Algerian demands increasing. It may be possible for the U.S. to give discreet encouragement and support, where possible, to French efforts to work out a political rather than a military solution and one which would be arrived at bilaterally. The U.S. cannot, however, disregard French nationalist feelings which focus more sharply on Algeria than on the two protectorates. Ambassador Dillon's speech of March 20, our partial assistance to date on the French request for priority delivery of helicopters, and our sympathetic attitude in NAC on the question of redeployment of French troops to Algeria were designed to take this situation into account. Such actions will, however, adversely affect our relations with the Arab states.

C. Major Problems or Areas of Difficulty

10. *Political*

a. The problem of encouraging France to grant greater self government for Morocco and Tunisia continues in an even more sensitive and delicate way. Direct or overt intervention or entanglement could seriously affect our relations with France, NATO solidarity and our relations with the Arab-Asian world.

b. Though U.S. actions in relation to the Algerian problem are limited to broad objectives and are not specified in courses of action, the U.S. could give discreet encouragement and support where possible to the French in their efforts to meet the Algerian demands for greater autonomy. U.S. interest centers not only on possible bases in the area, but is concerned particularly with internal security in a NATO sector and the possibility of anti-Western and/or communist exploitation (see below).

c. The danger of communist penetration will increase as North Africa moves toward independence, particularly if independence is won by force and through extremist tactics. The unsettled conditions and the political and military vacuum which is being created by the diminution of French control and the emergence of new and shaky Arab states, present an excellent opportunity for exploitation by the USSR, particularly when it becomes possible for the USSR to open direct diplomatic relations. The U.S. will have to determine how, in concert if possible with France, to deal with this vacuum.

d. In the North African nationalist movements there is a fundamental cleavage—potential in Morocco, overt in Tunisia and Algeria—between pan-Arab extremist elements who look toward Cairo and the pro-Western moderates who favor negotiated solutions, with continued French and Western influence as their objective. U.S. policy could consider encouraging the latter in every way possible and sharpening French awareness of the need to supply such men as Bourguiba and Mohammed V with concessions that permit them to retain their following.

e. The problem of formally relinquishing extra-territorial rights in Morocco, after announcement on January 26 of our intent to do so, is being pursued. A joint resolution, which would empower the President to carry out this policy, has been presented by the Department of State to appropriate Congressional Committees. However, a group of approximately 40 businessmen in Morocco have adopted a resolution which insists that their position not be inferior to that of any other foreign national in Morocco, and that U.S. extra-territorial rights should only be renounced after full sovereignty for Morocco is achieved and a new bilateral negotiated between the U.S. and Morocco. The RCA and Mackay radio companies have taken a similar position with respect to extra-territorial rights in Tangier where they maintain installations nominally commercial but of some importance to U.S. defense needs. The use of extra-territorial rights as a bargaining piece, however, does not appear desirable or possible.

Military

a. No further progress can be made on expanding the base rights, SOF and tax agreements until Morocco's new international status is defined. As soon as the French-Moroccan negotiations are completed, the U.S. must decide whether or not to conclude the U.S. agreements either with the French, the Moroccans, or both, depending on where the responsibility for foreign affairs and defense lies.

b. The U.S. must continue to endeavor to obtain immediate troop ceiling increase (without prejudice to our long standing proposal for a larger increase); additionally, the U.S. must consider urging the Moroccans to accept previous agreements as valid should Morocco succeed in gaining control of foreign affairs and defense matters as a result of the negotiations.

c. While the U.S. Armed Services still require additional rights in Tunisia and Algeria, it seems advisable in view of the unsettled conditions in both areas at this time, to await a more opportune political climate. At the same time the U.S. has the problem of encouraging the Moroccans to recognize the U.S. base agreements should they achieve full or shared control of foreign affairs with the French.

d. The problem of securing the return of large numbers of French troops and their equipment, largely MDAP financed, to the European theater is aggravated by the sending of additional French troops to Algeria.

12. *Economic*

The economic requirements of Tunisia and Morocco may turn out to be substantial at this time of heavily increasing requirements elsewhere. State and ICA plan to proceed urgently on a strictly unilateral and confidential basis, to analyze the requirements of these two countries in the light of possible continuing French contributions. This would enable early determination of the general order of magnitude and types of program that might be required. Thus before any negotiations are started, either with the French or Tunisia or Morocco, a decision could be made by the United States whether in the light of existing funds and other requirements, the United States is able or willing to start what will certainly be continuing programs in order of magnitude required.

13. *Cultural Contacts—Information Program*

Because of unsettled conditions in French North Africa, the scope and nature of this U.S. program presents a continuing problem. Until final settlements are achieved and relations between the U.S. and the French, and the U.S. and the Arab nationalists clarified, limited opportunities exist, in other than cultural and educational fields, to provide open and positive support of U.S. policy in the area. While plans are being prepared for some expansion in FY 1957, their implementation is contingent on political developments and close coordination with local chiefs of missions. Both the Tunisians and the Moroccans have indicated their desire for increased exchange of persons, and it is hoped the program may be expanded in 1957. Expansion in Algeria is premature at this time.

Attachment:

Financial Annex to the Progress Report covering period 6/1/55 through 4/4/56. [7]

[7] Not printed.

35. Memorandum of Discussion at the 298th Meeting of the National Security Council, Washington, September 27, 1956 [1]

Present at the 298th Council meeting were the President of the United States, presiding; the Secretary of State, the Acting Secretary of Defense; the Director, Office of Defense Mobilization. Also present were the Secretary of the Treasury, the Acting Attorney General (Item 1); the Special Assistant to the President for Disarmament; the Director, Bureau of the Budget; the Under Secretary of

[1] Source: Eisenhower Library, Whitman File, NSC Records, Top Secret. Drafted by Gleason on September 28.

State; the Chairman, Atomic Energy Commission (Items 1 and 4); the Director, International Cooperation Administration; the Federal Civil Defense Administrator (Item 1); Assistant Secretary of State Robert Bowie; Assistant Secretary of Defense Gordon Gray; the Director, U.S. Information Agency; the Chairman, Joint Chiefs of Staff; the Acting Director of Central Intelligence, the Assistant to the President, the Deputy Assistant to the President; Special Assistant to the President Clarence B. Randall; the White House Staff Secretary; the Executive Secretary, NSC; and the Deputy Executive Secretary, NSC.

[Here follows discussion of agenda items 1 and 2.]

3. Tunisia, Morocco, Algeria (NSC 5614;[2] NSC 5436/1;[3] Progress Report, dated April 4, 1956 by OCB on NSC 5436/1;[4] Memorandum for NSC from Executive Secretary, same subject, dated September 26, 1956;[5] NSC Action No. 1543[6])

Mr. Lay briefed the Council, pausing at Paragraph 20, to explain to the Council the split views. The majority of the NSC Planning Board wished Paragraph 20 to read:

"Be prepared to offer Morocco and Tunisia reasonable economic and technical aid when required by our direct interests in their political stability bearing in mind the importance of keeping the French informed with a view to obtaining their cooperation."[7]

Mr. Lay pointed out that the Treasury and Budget members of the NSC Planning Board proposed the deletion of the reference to economic aid in Paragraph 20. He asked Secretary Humphrey and Mr. Brundage if they wished to add anything to his own explanation of this split of views.

Secretary Humphrey stated that as Mr. Lay had just explained, the Budget Bureau believed that the grant of economic aid should be tied very directly to the maintenance of U.S. bases in Morocco rather than to more general objectives such as political stability.

---

[2] NSC 5614, September 17, was a draft statement of policy on Tunisia, Morocco, and Algeria. It was intended, if adopted, to supersede NSC 5436/1, and was transmitted to the members of the NSC on September 17 under cover of a note by James S. Lay, Jr. (Department of State, S/S–NSC Files: Lot 63 D 351, NSC 5614 Series)

[3] Dated October 18, 1954; see footnote 3, Document 25.

[4] Document 34.

[5] A covering memorandum by Lay transmitting to the NSC a memorandum of September 25 by the Joint Chiefs of Staff to the Secretary of Defense submitting JCS comments and recommendations on NSC 5614. (Department of State, S/S–NSC Files: Lot 63 D 351, NSC 5614 Series)

[6] See footnote 1, *supra.*

[7] Paragraph 20 of NSC 5614 reads as quoted here, except that the words "economic and" were enclosed in brackets. A footnote to the source text at this point indicated that "Treasury and Budget propose deletion" of the two words in brackets.

The President confessed that he was somewhat uncertain as to what specific interests the United States would have in these countries apart from our bases but the President added that these bases would not be very much good to the United States if there were no political stability in the area in which they were located. On the other hand, the President said we certainly could not propose to provide Morocco and Tunisia with economic assistance in the same amount which they had previously received from France. Turning to Admiral Radford, the President said he had a question to put. He pointed out that we had initially negotiated for bases in Morocco and the negotiations having been completed, we had proceeded to build these bases. No sooner had we done this than we had turned and negotiated for the erection of U.S. bases in Spain. Certainly, the President thought, we were more confident as to the stability of the situation in Spain. Why, therefore, could not this be an "either or" proposition. In short, why could not the Spanish bases be a substitute for the Moroccan bases?

Admiral Radford answered that if it proved necessary, we could look upon the Spanish bases as a substitute for the Moroccan bases but he pointed out that the bases in Spain had not yet been completed. Moreover, we were beginning to have certain troubles with the Spanish about our bases there. To this comment the President replied by stating that it seemed to him the more people we had to deal with in our efforts to secure bases, the more blackmail we were exposed to. On the whole it might be better to build a couple of more bases in Spain and get out of Morocco altogether.

Admiral Radford said that he personally agreed with the President's opinion and he believed that the Chiefs of Staff would also agree with it. Secretary Robertson of the Defense Department pointed out that the United States had a right, under its agreement with Spain, to build two or three additional bases if we want to.

Secretary Humphrey returned to the objection of the Treasury Department to the inclusion in Paragraph 20 of a reference to economic assistance to Morocco and Tunisia. Treasury's objection, he said, was two-fold. In the first instance, it was based on the feeling that it was idle and useless to make recommendations with respect to giving economic aid to these countries just as the Fairless Committee [8] was getting underway with its overall study of our foreign assistance programs. If the recommendation for economic assistance in Paragraph 20 was to be thought of as only a temporary recommendation, Secretary Humphrey said he had no particular objection

[8] Benjamin Fairless was the coordinator of a citizens committee appointed by the President to review foreign assistance programs. It reported on March 1, 1957.

to its inclusion. On the other hand, he did not wish to prejudge the findings of the Fairless Committee.

The President said that he had no objection to looking upon the possibility of economic aid as a temporary matter pending the findings of the Fairless Committee. Secretary Humphrey then went on to state his second objection to the provision of economic aid. He pointed out that the three paragraphs, 20, 21 [9] and 22, [10] all concerned provision of some kind of aid or other to these North African states. The Treasury was therefore afraid that we would end up by paying three times (laughter).

Mr. Brundage said that one of the difficulties which the Budget Bureau encountered in Paragraph 20 was the meaning of the phrase "reasonable economic and technical aid". Reasonable or otherwise, the curve of the amounts of assistance we were proposing to supply to Morocco and Tunisia moved steadily upward from the present year to FY 1959.

The President, consulting the Financial Appendix, agreed that the curve did mount upward and inquired why the upward curve was so sharp. Mr. Lay suggested that Mr. Hollister might be able to throw light on this problem. Mr. Hollister observed that the only explanation he could give of the amounts allocated to Morocco and Tunisia was that these were the largest amounts of U.S. assistance that Morocco and Tunisia would be able to absorb. In short, we did not believe that they could spend our money any faster. The President replied that the outlook suggested to him that we should make every effort to help France maintain a sufficient position in these newly independent countries to be able to help them meet their budgetary deficits.

---

[9] Paragraph 21 of NSC 5614 reads:

"Seek to maintain France as the source of military equipment and training assistance for Moroccan and Tunisian armed forces to the extent feasible without impairing U.S. relations with Morocco and Tunisia. [Consider providing U.S. military aid to Morocco or Tunisia only if this becomes necessary to retain the U.S. position in Morocco or Tunisia.]"

A footnote to this paragraph indicated that "Treasury and Budget propose deletion" of the portion enclosed in brackets.

[10] Paragraph 22 of NSC 5614 reads:

"Maintain U.S. base rights in Morocco by all feasible means, being prepared, if necessary, to offer reasonable quid pro quos therefor. [In any base negotiations, seek to obtain recognition of U.S. base rights, satisfaction of Moroccan sovereignty, and determination of the future status of existing French contractual rights. If formal negotiations prove necessary, express a preference for a single trilateral negotiation. If such a negotiation should not be politically feasible, be prepared to deal bilaterally with the Moroccans as the sovereign host government, recognizing in this event that any U.S. agreement with Morocco must be contingent on settlements by the U.S. and by Morocco of related base right problems with France.]"

A footnote to this paragraph indicated that "Treasury and Budget propose deletion" of the portion enclosed in brackets.

Secretary Humphrey then turned to the Financial Appendix and pointed out the "terrific jump" in the amount of U.S. resources devoted to North Africa. It was a jump, according to Secretary Humphrey, from the approximate figure of one million a year at the present time to fifty million a year in FY 1959. Secretary Humphrey said he hated to see such plans and programs because it was morally certain that if we went on with them, other countries in which we had bases would quickly turn and blackmail us into providing additional sums of money.

The President said he could not deny this possibility but that it seemed to him a very good investment of fifty million dollars if as a result of the investment we succeeded in keeping the Communists out of this vast and very important strategic area of North Africa. The trouble, said the President, was that we might not be able to stop at fifty million. The level might rise still higher. Particularly, the President said, we met difficulties in maintaining bases in newly independent countries without a corollary that these new countries become completely dependent economically upon us. On the other hand, the situation was much less difficult when we had our bases in more mature areas such as the United Kingdom. Accordingly, the President recommended that very careful study should be made of the North African area. It was certainly vital to our national safety but on the other hand, we were not yet in a position to make clear projections as to what we ought to pay in order to secure our bases in Morocco.

Secretary Dulles pointed out that as far as he had ever known, approval of a policy paper by the National Security Council did not commit the Administration to any fixed amount of military or economic assistance to be rendered the country in question. He predicted nevertheless that we should have to give some economic aid to Morocco and to Tunisia although it might actually prove better to shift to bases in Spain.

Mr. Brundage said he thought that the Secretary's point was covered by the first sentence of Paragraph 22 which indicates that we would maintain U.S. base rights in Morocco by all feasible means, being prepared if necessary to offer reasonable quid pro quos therefor. Secretary Dulles replied that it had never been the practice of the Administration to tie the maintenance of U.S. bases to any particular amount of economic assistance. In point of fact, this was something of a fiction but nevertheless a fiction that it was important to maintain.

Governor Stassen then suggested certain language revising Paragraph 20 which he believed might make the paragraph acceptable to Secretary Humphrey and to Mr. Brundage. In turn Secretary Dulles read to the Council the statement which appears at the beginning of all Financial Appendices to the effect that approval of a policy statement did not indicate approval of cost estimates in the Financial Appendix.

Secretary Humphrey stated that after all this was not such a serious matter and the President indicated that a sensible solution was to have the Record of Action indicate that decision as to the amount of assistance to be provided to Morocco and Tunisia should be determined on a case-by-case basis.

Concluding the discussion of this paragraph, Secretary Dulles warned that the United States may soon be obliged to commence negotiations with respect to the Moroccan bases and that these negotiations might drag out for a very long time.

Mr. Lay then directed the Council's attention to the split of views in Paragraph 21. He explained that the Treasury and Budget members of the NSC Planning Board were opposed to the majority view which called upon the United States to consider the provision of U.S. military aid to Morocco and Tunisia if such a course of action appeared to be the only way by which the United States could retain its position in these countries. After a short discussion, Secretary Humphrey said that he would not insist upon the Treasury position and would agree to accept Paragraph 21 as written if the phrase "if this fails" were inserted at the beginning of the second sentence of the paragraph.

Mr. Lay then explained to the Council the split view in Paragraph 22 where the Treasury and Budget objected to the lengthy statement with respect to the manner in which the United States would propose to conduct its base negotiations with the Moroccans.

The President promptly expressed his view that the details respecting the manner in which the negotiations would be conducted lay already in the domain of the State Department. Mr. Lay proceeded to point out the view of the Joint Chiefs of Staff that the United States should seek bilateral negotiations with the Moroccans rather than trilateral negotiations including the French as now provided for in Paragraph 22. The President's comment on the views of the Joint Chiefs of Staff was to indicate that we could hardly seek to exclude the French from these base negotiations and at the same time expect the French to help pay the future budget deficits of Morocco and Tunisia.

Secretary Dulles stated his belief that the language outlined in Paragraph 22 was too rigid a description of the manner in which we would conduct our forthcoming negotiations with Morocco although he added that the tactics set forth in Paragraph 22 were actually the tactics now proposed by the State Department for the conduct of the negotiations. The President then suggested that the material dealing with the tactics of the negotiations be stricken from the paragraph and that indication be made in the Record of Action or elsewhere that these tactics were in consonance with the plans currently being considered by the State Department.

Secretary Dulles then called the Council's attention to Paragraph 27 which called on the United States to

"be prepared to vote for discussion of the Algerian issue in the United Nations, if that appears to us likely to facilitate progress toward a settlement".

Secretary Dulles pointed out how highly complex was the matter of inscribing an item on the UN agenda. There were many other considerations than that of facilitating a solution which the United States would have to take account of before it carried out the course of action proposed in Paragraph 27. Accordingly, Secretary Dulles recommended deletion of the paragraph as being too narrow and as being inappropriate in a policy paper. The President agreed with Secretary Dulles.

The National Security Council: [11]

a. Discussed the draft statement of policy on the subject contained in NSC 5614 prepared by the NSC Planning Board pursuant to NSC Action No. 1543, in the light of the views of the Joint Chiefs of Staff transmitted by the memorandum of September 26, 1956. [12]

b. Adopted the statement of policy in NSC 5614 subject to the following amendments:

(1) *Page 9, paragraph 20:* Delete the brackets and the footnote thereto.

(2) *Page 9, paragraph 21:* Delete the brackets and the footnote thereto; and insert at the beginning of the second sentence the words "If this fails,".

(3) *Pages 9 and 10, paragraph 22:* Delete the entire section contained in the brackets; and the footnote thereto.

(4) *Page 10, paragraph 27:* Delete, renumbering subsequent paragraphs accordingly.

c. Noted the President's statement that the mutual security programs developed for Morocco and Tunisia, pursuant to the policy in NSC 5614 as amended would, as in the case of all other mutual

---

[11] The following paragraphs and Note constitute NSC Action No. 1610.

[12] See footnote 5 above. The Joint Chiefs indicated their concurrence in NSC 5614, but concluded that given the extensive military facilities in Morocco that technical aid might be insufficient to retain their use. Regarding paragraph 22, the Joint Chiefs suggested that it read as follows:

"Maintain U.S. base rights in Morocco by all feasible means, being prepared, if necessary, to offer reasonable quid pro quos therefor. In any base negotiations seek to deal bilaterally with the Moroccans as the sovereign host government, recognizing in this event that any U.S. agreements with Morocco must be contingent on settlements by the U.S. and by Morocco of related base rights problems with France."

security programs, be subject to the normal budgetary process in each instance and to review after receipt of the reports by the President's Citizen Advisers on the Mutual Security Program, headed by Mr. Benjamin Fairless.

d. Noted the statement by the Secretary of State that, in any negotiations regarding U.S. base rights in Morocco, it was the present plan of the Department of State to seek to obtain recognition of these base rights, satisfaction of Moroccan sovereignty, and determination of the future status of existing French contractual rights. If formal negotiations prove necessary, the U.S. would express a preference for a single trilateral negotiation. If such a negotiation should not be politically feasible, the U.S. would be prepared to deal bilaterally with the Moroccans as the sovereign host government, recognizing in this event that any U.S. agreement with Morocco must be contingent on settlements by the U.S. and by Morocco of related base right problems with France.

e. Noted the President's request that the Department of Defense study the feasibility of developing the U.S. bases in Spain as a substitute for the U.S. bases in Morocco.

Note: NSC 5614, as amended and approved by the President, subsequently circulated as NSC 5614/1 [13] for implementation by all appropriate Executive departments and agencies of the U.S. Government, and referred to the Operations Coordinating Board as the coordinating agency designated by the President.

The action in d, as approved by the President, subsequently transmitted to the Secretary of State for appropriate action.

The action in e, as approved by the President, subsequently transmitted to the Secretary of Defense for appropriate action.

[Here follows discussion of agenda items 4–6.]

S. Everett Gleason

[13] *Infra.*

36. National Security Council Report[1]

NSC 5614/1 *Washington, October 3, 1956.*

NOTE BY THE EXECUTIVE SECRETARY TO THE NATIONAL SECURITY COUNCIL ON TUNISIA, MOROCCO, ALGERIA

REFERENCES

A. NSC 5436/1[2]
B. Progress Report, dated April 4, 1956 by OCB on NSC 5436/1[3]
C. Memo for NSC from Executive Secretary, same subject, dated September 26, 1956[4]
D. NSC Actions Nos. 1543 and 1610[5]
E. NSC 5614[6]

The National Security Council, the Secretary of the Treasury, the Special Assistant to the President for Disarmament, and the Director, Bureau of the Budget, at the 298th Council meeting on September 27, 1956, adopted the statement of policy on the subject contained in NSC 5614, subject to the amendments thereto which are set forth in NSC Action No. 1610–b and in addition thereto (NSC Action No. 1610–c and d):

[Here follows text of NSC Action No. 1610–c and d; see footnote 12, *supra.*]

The President has this date approved the statement of policy in NSC 5614 as amended and adopted by the Council and enclosed herewith as NSC 5614/1; directs its implementation by all appropriate Executive departments and agencies of the U.S. Government; and designates the Operations Coordinating Board as the coordinating agency.[7]

The enclosed statement of policy, as adopted and approved, supersedes NSC 5436/1.

---

[1] Source: Department of State, S/S–NSC Files: Lot 63 D 351, NSC 5614 Series. Secret.

[2] See footnote 3, Document 25.

[3] Document 34.

[4] See footnotes 5 and 12, *supra.*

[5] See footnote 1, Document 34, and footnote 11, *supra.*

[6] See footnote 2, *supra.*

[7] A paper entitled "Operational Guidance With Respect to Tunisia, Morocco and Algeria in Implementation of NSC 5614/1," dated February 27, 1957, approved by the Operations Coordinating Board on February 20, is in Department of State, OCB Files: Lot 62 D 430, Horn of Africa.

A Financial Appendix and Staff Study[8] are also enclosed herewith for information.

James S. Lay, Jr.[9]

[Enclosure]

STATEMENT OF POLICY ON TUNISIA, MOROCCO, ALGERIA

General Considerations

1. Developments in Tunisia, Morocco and Algeria have a significant relation to U.S. security:

a. The area is strategically important, particularly because of the U.S. bases located there.
b. Expansion of Soviet or Egyptian influence in the area adversely affects U.S. interests.
c. The Algerian rebellion is a divisive factor in the non-Communist world, especially as between the Arab and anti-colonial countries on the one hand and the colonial powers on the other.
d. Events in Tunisia and Morocco, and particularly in Algeria, could provoke a most serious internal crisis in France, with unpredictable results on the future of French democracy and on France's alignment with NATO.
e. Developments in this region will have a bearing on colonial issues arising elsewhere in Africa, and will be regarded as a test of U.S. intentions and capabilities with respect to other dependent peoples.

2. The United States is directly involved in Morocco because of its military base rights, which were negotiated with France without Moroccan consent or official knowledge. The new sovereign Moroccan state is now determined to negotiate these base rights with the United States. In addition, the United States is involved in the Algerian problem inasmuch as the coastal region of Algeria is within the NATO area.

3. Tunisia and Morocco have recently achieved independence. Unfortunately, the far-reaching French concessions to the nationalists have been granted grudgingly, leaving a residue of suspicion and dislike of France which has been exacerbated by the Algerian development. A number of issues remain to be resolved between France and these new states. The French are unlikely, given their view of how best to defend their interests, to settle such issues in a manner that will gain political goodwill from Morocco and Tunisia.

---

[8] Neither printed.
[9] Printed from a copy which bears this typed signature.

4. Economically both Morocco and Tunisia remain heavily dependent upon France and the French settlers. About 60 percent of their trade is with France, under preferential tariff or quota arrangements. The European settlers have controlled most of the business activity and, with French investors, have provided the bulk of private investment. Furthermore, French Government contributions to public investment and ordinary budget deficits have been substantial in recent years. The area is deficient in the administrative and technical skills needed for efficient government and sound economic development. Both Morocco and Tunisia are less developed areas with low standards of living. Tunisia experiences chronic unemployment and frequent food shortages of near-famine proportions. Both countries look to the United States for aid in their economic development.

5. For its part, France hopes to maintain *presence* in Morocco and Tunisia. It wishes to protect French investments and the rights and well-being of the European residents. Perhaps more importantly, it wishes to continue a political and military relationship which the French consider very important to the security of the French Union and to France's influence in the world. It also is deeply concerned to prevent Morocco and Tunisia from aiding the Algerian rebels.

6. In Algeria the French have been trying since 1954 to put down a nationalist rebellion. About 400,000 French troops are engaged in the pacification effort. The number of guerrillas is probably between 20,000 and 30,000, but this number is greatly supplemented by part-time guerrillas and by many people willing to commit acts of individual terrorism against French troops or the European population.

7. The militant nationalist movement in Algeria has now expanded both in size and strength to the point where it can claim without serious contradiction to speak for the Moslems of Algeria, even though only a small number take an active part in the fighting. Morocco and Tunisia are safe havens for Algerian partisans and are sources of arms and other support. Arms also come in from and through Egypt and Libya. The Arab states back the Algerian nationalist cause and the nationalist political leaders operate from Cairo. The anti-colonial bloc of Arab and Asian states looks on Algeria as a major colonial issue and will continue to press for a UN finding against France so long as no settlement is reached.

8. The French government's announced policy is pacification accompanied by economic and social reform, to be followed by elections and negotiations. In 1956 the gross public cost of Algeria to France will be more than one billion dollars, of which the extraordinary cost of the emergency may amount to about $850 million. The French Communist party opposes the government's policy while

other parties support it with more or less enthusiasm, but none support French withdrawal from Algeria at this time.

9. The problem of a political settlement in Algeria is complicated by the presence of 1,200,000 Frenchmen, Spaniards, Italians, and Jews. They have had predominant political power and they operate the modern sector of the economy and own the best land. They are unwilling to share power with the Moslem majority, much less to allow majority self-determination. Any political and economic concessions to the nationalists will have to be imposed on the colons by French authority. Algeria is legally an integral part of France, so that concessions to native demands are politically more difficult to grant than was the case in Morocco and Tunisia.

10. It is unlikely that French opinion will support for long the costly military campaign in Algeria; consequently France will probably attempt to negotiate with the native leaders in the realization that major concessions are necessary. At a minimum, such concessions would include the grant of effective majority representation to the Moslem population in an all-Algerian legislature. Such a grant might be preceded by local disorders and if successfully carried out would probably be followed by a substantial emigration of Europeans. In any case, such a grant would not prevent a continuing drive for full Algerian independence.

11. Meanwhile, the Algerian dispute has adverse effects on our interests in Morocco and Tunisia, in France, and in the free world generally. The political leaders in Morocco and Tunisia naturally respond to pressures at home to support the Algerian rebels; this is a potential source of major friction with France and may contribute toward pushing Morocco and Tunisia into close association with Egypt. We are considered by the Moroccans and Tunisians, as well as by other Arab and Asian peoples, to be the chief outside support for French policy; it is widely believed that our influence could be decisive in changing French policy if we were willing to exercise it. The Soviet Union has taken the role of supporter of the oppressed Algerian "colonial" people and its local agents are busy in France and Algeria trying to gain a dominant voice in the Algerian nationalist movement. The Algerian rebellion drains French military forces from NATO and preoccupies French political energies without being a long-range unifying force in a country that badly needs greater unity. Partly on the basis of developments in Indochina, a number of political leaders and segments of French public opinion fear that not only is the United States failing to support its NATO ally wholeheartedly in its present difficulties, but that the United States actually intends eventually to supplant French influence in North Africa. In any event, the French will tend increasingly to blame the United States for any failures in North Africa. The development of a

more closely knit Western European community, in which France can seek reasonable security and prosperity, would contribute much to minimizing these strains in our alliance with France and to France's own adjustment to its status as a declining imperial power.

Policy Conclusions

12. Prolongation of the Algerian dispute adversely affects U.S. interests in North Africa as well as broader U.S. national interests. Therefore, it is in the U.S. interest that a settlement of this dispute be effected as soon as possible. However, France as the power directly concerned must itself find a settlement, if one is to be found. For this reason and in view of our extremely limited capabilities for effecting a peaceful solution of the problems of this area, we should, in so far as possible, keep our public involvement in the dispute to a minimum.

13. A close and amicable relationship between France and Morocco and Tunisia would, if attainable, be in the U.S. interest. The French have not yet, however, devised policies which appear to enhance such a prospect. The United States should assist France to the maximum extent possible to adjust its position to the contraction of the French Empire, but our own interests in North Africa, and the importance of a Western orientation for Morocco and Tunisia, may compel us to develop increasingly bilateral policies in this area. Moroccan and Tunisian nationalism could usefully serve U.S. interests as a counterweight to Egyptian ambitions both in North and in Tropical Africa.

Objectives

14. To gain Moroccan support for the maintenance of full U.S. access to the Moroccan military bases as long as such access is judged necessary or helpful to our security.

15. To associate the peoples of this area with the free world.

16. To stop the spread of Egyptian as well as Soviet and Communist influence in the North African area. [10]

17. To encourage progress toward stable government and economic well-being in the new states of North Africa.

---

[10] In a letter to Hoover of November 19, Dillon indicated that he considered NSC 5614/1 to be an excellent paper which presented the problem thoroughly and objectively. However, he thought there was too little mention of the problem of Communist infiltration in Algeria. On Hoover's behalf, C. Burke Elbrick replied on November 29 that Dillon was right in bringing up the matter and requested any documentation he might possess regarding Communist penetration of the FLN. (Department of State, S/S–NSC Files: Lot 63 D 351, NSC 5614 Memoranda)

18. To cooperate with France in its adjustment, politically and psychologically, to the rapid loss of its external territories.

19. To keep within bounds the damage to our standing with the Asian and Arab [nations] caused by the French-Algerian dispute.

Courses of Action

Morocco and Tunisia

20. Be prepared to offer Morocco and Tunisia reasonable economic and technical aid when required by our direct interest in their political stability, bearing in mind the importance of keeping the French informed with a view to obtaining their cooperation.

21. Seek to maintain France as the source of military equipment and training assistance for Moroccan and Tunisian armed forces to the extent feasible without impairing U.S. relations with Morocco and Tunisia. If this fails consider providing U.S. military aid to Morocco and Tunisia only if this becomes necessary to retain the U.S. position in Morocco or Tunisia.

22. Maintain U.S. base rights in Morocco by all feasible means, being prepared, if necessary, to offer reasonable quid pro quos therefor.

23. Support the admission of Morocco and Tunisia to the UN and to its associated organizations.

24. Expand cultural exchanges with Morocco and Tunisia; and modestly expand information activities in both countries.

25. Seek to have Moroccan and Tunisian influence exerted to moderate the demands of the Algerian nationalists, whenever this would appear likely to facilitate a settlement of the Algerian dispute.

Algeria

26. Be prepared to take any feasible actions that would hasten a settlement of the Algerian conflict, but attempt to keep our public involvement to a minimum.

France

27. Make clear to France our hope that France can maintain an influence in North Africa and our desire to help France to do so. At the same time encourage the French to find a workable settlement of the Algerian dispute. Encourage France to actions in Morocco and Tunisia that are likely to win political goodwill for the West.

28. Be prepared, subject to satisfactory evidence of French willingness to promote what we consider a reasonable policy in North Africa (a) to discuss with France our policies and actions in North Africa, and (b) to develop forms of cooperation in our

respective programs which will strengthen the Western position in the area.

---

37. Operations Coordinating Board Report [1]

Washington, November 13, 1957.

PROGRESS REPORT ON TUNISIA, MOROCCO AND ALGERIA
(NSC 5614/1, Approved October 3, 1956) [2]

(Period Covered: From March 28, 1957 through November 13, 1957)

A. Summary of Operating Progress in Relation to Major NSC Objectives

1. *Summary Evaluation.* Although our principal interests are still protected, progress toward policy objectives has been slowed by the deteriorating situation in Algeria, the repercussions of that situation in Morocco and Tunisia, and the continued stresses and strains, especially economic and social, which have followed independence. U.S. policy toward Tunisia, Morocco and Algeria as set forth in NSC 5614/1 has been reviewed from the standpoint of operating considerations and in light of operating experience to date and of anticipated future developments. No review of policy is recommended.

Regarding associating the peoples of this area with the free world, U.S. diplomatic relations with Morocco and Tunisia were consolidated; economic and technical aid agreements were negotiated and programs begun in both countries (approximately $20 million in Morocco and $8.5 million in Tunisia for FY 1957); base negotiations were begun directly with Morocco, with the French being kept generally informed as to the progress of the negotiations. The U.S. agreed to negotiate a new Treaty of Friendship, Commerce and Navigation with Morocco. The Richards Mission visited both Tunisia and Morocco, and the King of Morocco accepted the President's invitation to visit the U.S. in November. [3]

---

[1] Source: Department of State, OCB Files: Lot 62 D 430, Horn of Africa. Secret. Enclosure to a memorandum signed by Roy M. Melbourne for Elmer B. Staats. The Progress Report was noted by the NSC on November 22. (NSC Action No. 1819; *ibid.*, S/S–NSC Files: Lot 66 D 95, NSC Records of Action) The same OCB meeting on November 13, which forwarded this report to the NSC, also approved an Operations Plan for transmission to the Embassies in Tunis, Rabat, and Paris, and the Consulate General in Algiers. (*Ibid.*, OCB Files: Lot 62 D 430)

[2] *Supra.*

[3] See Documents 213 and 250–251. The King arrived November 25.

However, it appears that U.S. relations with Morocco and Tunisia may be entering a critical period in which U.S. friendship and support will be weighed in terms of our position on Algeria, on military assistance, economic aid, and diplomatic support vis-à-vis France.

Relations between France and her ex-Protectorates went by sharp ups and downs; though some issues were resolved between them, the Algerian conflict continued to poison the atmosphere and hold up settlement of many outstanding problems. Franco-Tunisian clashes on the Algerian border led the Tunisians to request help from the U.S. in supplying arms and to consider acquiring arms in Egypt or the Soviet bloc countries. The U.S. took a decision to furnish such arms if other Western sources had failed. In Algeria both sides approached a stalemate, with continuing violence and bloodshed, and an ever-widening gulf between the European and Moslem communities for which no adequate remedy has been worked out in France. The Soviet bloc, while not achieving any major coup, continued to spread its influence, particularly through commercial channels. Egyptian efforts to establish influence continued.

The U.S. position on the Algeria question was increasingly a sensitive point with the countries concerned, and U.S. prestige in North Africa declined from the temporary advantage gained during the Suez crisis. Impact of U.S. assistance was favorable but naturally has not yet had noticeable effect in alleviating serious economic and social problems in Morocco and Tunisia.

B. Major Operating Problems or Difficulties Facing the United States

2. *U.S. Bases in Morocco.* The dilemma of the bases remains. We have satisfied Moroccan amour-propre by sitting down to negotiate bilaterally. We still have the fundamental problem of liquidating or revising the 1950 Franco-American Agreements and harmonizing the status of our bases with Moroccan independence, without destroying Franco-American confidence and endangering U.S. interests, including base rights, in France. Three other major issues remain to be resolved before we can make real progress in the negotiations begun in May toward concluding a base agreement: (1) the Moroccan need for a "framework"—bilateral or regional—which will justify foreign troops and bases and provide a mechanism for equalizing treatment of French, Spanish and U.S. troops, (2) the nature and levels of our economic aid programs for Morocco, and their sufficiency as a quid pro quo for base rights, (3) the possibility of military assistance for Morocco. The U.S. is currently formulating its position on all these issues. We resumed negotiations in September and hope to make

some progress toward at least contingent agreement on texts of a base rights agreement before the larger issues are resolved and before King Mohammed V visits the U.S. in November when these issues will undoubtedly be discussed. Despite emerging problems with jurisdiction and reductions in local labor forces, the bases continue operational.

3. *U.S.-Moroccan Treaty Negotiations.* The negotiation of a new Friendship, Commerce and Navigation Treaty to which we have now consented will probably be long and difficult. Moreover, the promulgation of the new Moroccan tariff and the partial devaluation of the Moroccan franc have given rise to new complications with the local American trading community and new conflicts with the economic equality provisions of the Act of Algeciras of 1906, which appears increasingly outmoded. Negotiations of the treaty awaits an indication of readiness from the Moroccans, who have been given standard drafts for study.

4. *VOA Relay Base at Tangier.* A problem has existed for some time in regularizing the status of present VOA radio facilities in Tangier and proceeding with expansion plans for the installation of high-powered transmitters. Funds for expansion have been available since May 14, 1956. Negotiations on these two matters were suspended pending developments in negotiating a military base rights agreement. This delay has meant that radio facilities, with power substantially in excess of that currently employed, have not been available for getting a stronger signal behind the iron curtain. Talks with Moroccan officials have recently been resumed but prospects for progress are uncertain.

5. *Economic Problems.* Franco-Tunisian and Franco-Moroccan financial and economic relations during the period were characterized by recurrent crises. In both countries there have been a decline in private investment, flight of capital and severe unemployment. With the lack of adequate budgeting and economic planning in both countries, it is difficult to program U.S. economic aid in ways which will assist in meeting the crises and at the same time contribute to longer-range economic stability and development.

Programming U.S. economic aid is complicated by (1) the pressure to help solve present crises with solutions which are necessarily palliatives and fail to attack the underlying causes, (2) the lack of adequate economic planning and basic statistical data, and (3) the continuing uncertainty of the level of French aid. To some extent, the nature and degree of U.S. detailed control over the administration of aid programs has been an irritant to these newly-independent governments which are on the one hand unfamiliar with U.S. administrative procedure differing markedly from the French and on the other are extremely sensitive to any suspected interference with their internal operations.

Based on present indications, U.S. economic aid programs will continue to be developed and implemented in both countries, with special attention in Morocco to the related problem of the bases.

6. *Franco-U.S. Differences.* France will probably become increasingly suspicious and resentful of our intentions toward the area, as aid programs get under way and U.S. influence increases. Our remedies here are largely the colorless ones of restraint and tact. We plan, however, to pursue our present policy of exchanging information on our programs and plans with the French, encouraging continued French assistance and influence to North Africa with as few strings as possible. We should continue to urge the French to supply military assistance to Morocco and Tunisia in order that these countries' security requirements may be satisfied by French sources and thereby obviate their looking to the U.S. for military equipment. While direct U.S. assistance of this nature to Morocco or Tunisia may prove necessary to preserve the western orientation of these countries, the French may be expected to react sharply and adversely.

7. *Algeria.* At the present juncture it can be expected that hostilities in Algeria will continue. Despite the fact that the French military have had considerable success in suppressing the rebellion in certain areas, there is no evidence to date that the military potential of the rebel movement has been seriously affected. Moreover, French parliamentary and public opinion is not yet prepared to accept a formula which clearly contemplates the evolution of an Algerian state. Until a solution emerges we can expect no stability in the area, a progressive dissatisfaction with the U.S. and the West, and uncertainty at best in our military and economic relations with Morocco and Tunisia. Because any open U.S. intervention in the issue would probably be counterproductive in stiffening French attitudes, as well as seriously undermining U.S.-French relations, we are presently confining ourselves to discreet pressures on the French at suitable opportunities and to encouraging Moroccan and Tunisian efforts to bring the Algerian leaders to a more conciliatory point of view. The Algerian problem and our attitude on it remain the critical issue in U.S.-French relations and are an increasingly sensitive point in our relations with Morocco and Tunisia, because of the inevitable repercussions on area stability and on our position and interests in the two independent countries. In fact, the Algerian conflict has serious effects on the entire Western position in North Africa.

Note: National Intelligence Estimates regarding this area are: [4]

a. NIE 71.3–57, The Outlook for Tunisia, June 18, 1957.
b. NIE 71.1–57, The Outlook for Morocco, January 29, 1957.
c. NIE 22–57, The Outlook for France, August 13, 1957.

Attachments: [5]

Annex A—Additional Major Developments Not Covered in the Report.

Annex B—Sino-Soviet Bloc Trade Relations with Morocco and Tunisia.

Financial Annex and Pipeline Analysis.

---

[4] NIE 71.1–57 is Document 206. The other two NIEs are not printed.

[5] None printed.

UNITED STATES POLICY TOWARD FRENCH WEST AND EQUATORIAL AFRICA [1]

38. Despatch From the Consulate General in Dakar to the Department of State [2]

No. 43 *Dakar, September 6, 1955.*

REF

Department's CA–1535 August 23, 1955 [3]

SUBJECT

United States Policy in Africa South of the Sahara, with Particular Reference to the French Areas [4]

The Department's CA under reference invited comment by the addressee posts on an enclosed paper prepared in the Department on United States policy in Africa South of the Sahara.

This paper was circulated to all officers of the Consulate General and the following comments may be regarded as a collective point of view. In the first place, we all feel that this is a truly first class paper and one that honestly faces the realities of the situation. We were particularly pleased with the statement on page #2 that "the southern half of the continent is so diverse that policy designed to include the entire area may poorly fit the requirements of a particular locale". All too often Americans, particularly in journalistic and military circles, have insisted that our policy should be a uniform, rigid thing—a glove tailored to fit many diverse hands. We must have a "Middle Eastern Policy", a "Latin American Policy", etc., in which sweeping rules are set forth to apply to large areas regardless of the varieties of countries and

---

[1] For previous documentation on this subject, see *Foreign Relations,* 1952–1954, vol. XI, Part 1, pp. 261 ff.

[2] Source: Department of State, Central Files, 611.70/9–655. Confidential. Passed to Paris, London, Leopoldville, Accra, and Lagos.

[3] CA–1535 transmitted a copy of Tab B of Document 7 to various diplomatic and consular offices concerned with Africa. (*Ibid.*, 120.1470/8–2355)

[4] French West Africa consisted of Dahomey, Guinea, Ivory Coast, Mauritania, Niger, Senegal, Sudan, and the Upper Volta. French Equatorial Africa included Chad, Gabon, Moyen Congo, and Ubangi Shari. The French also ruled the trust territories of Cameroons and Togoland, in addition to Madagascar and Somaliland (Djibouti).

peoples contained therein. While it is true that certain general considerations can often be valid for large areas such as Africa South of the Sahara, the varieties here are so great that any rigid policy for the whole area is virtually impossible.

If we cannot, then, make too many plans for the area as a whole, the problem arises as to how properly to compartmentalize it. There is clearly no pat solution in view of the multitude of different races, tongues, economic potentials et cetera, but for the next generation at least it might be advisable to have separate but coordinated policies for each separate major political entity. In other words, a policy for the French Area, the British, the Belgian, the Portuguese and the Independents. Even these might have to be subdivided when the Metropolitan power itself follows varying policies within the area such as the British in East Africa as compared with the British in West Africa. The Department's paper recognizes the fact that the Metropolitan powers will continue to dominate the scene, this does not seem an illogical arrangement. Furthermore, it is only too likely that from time to time our policies towards the various dependent areas will have to be tailored to our overall objectives vis-à-vis the Metropolitan power concerned. This will in all probability remain true at least as long as the NATO organization exists and it appears that, where Africa is concerned, we must face up to the fact that the area is, as the Department's paper admits, of little interest to our military planners and we are not therefore always in a position to make an issue of African affairs with our NATO partners. If we cannot take a stand vis-à-vis the French in North Africa, it is not easy to see how we could take one in the areas to the south.

Granted then that our policies must to a certain extent at least be influenced by our broader policies with respect to the Metropolitan powers, in what ways can we make our influence felt without tangling with the landlord? This office can only form an opinion on the basis of French West Africa and the smaller units within its consular district. On this basis, however, two possible courses of action seem to outweigh all others. These are capital investment and educational exchange. The United States, so far as the French territories in Africa south of the Sahara are concerned, has drawn an absolute blank in both of these fields and basically for the same reason—the French are frightened of American "anti-colonialism." They fear that the introduction of American capital will mean the introduction of American ideas of too rapid self-determination. They fear American capital installed in the area will raise the standard of living for its employees to such an extent as to cause political unrest. They fear that African students educated in the United States will return ardent nationalists and point always to the Gold Coast in confirmation of this theory. Much of this is nonsense but it is sincerely believed in important circles. It appears to the Consulate General that our approach in the past has been a little too negative and at too low a level. When the French have made their several vague approaches about attracting American capital, we have been a bit severe with them saying that they must create a favorable climate but without offering them any really practical suggestions. We have put an appreciable amount of money into this area through FOA programs but only when hidden in the overall French program with the result that political benefits here have been absolutely nil. Surely, it might be better to help the French attract private capital which could have a direct impact and would cost the United States Government a great deal less. Rather than engage in elaborate Technical Assistance and other Governmental projects which might well be resented, it might be better to see if there is not some practical way in which American private industry can be introduced in the area with most of the political advantages and few of the political drawbacks that an official aid program would entail. As far as French West Africa is concerned, the Consulate General doubts that the objective set forth in Course of Action 2 (d) on page 8 of the Department's paper is attainable. While much progress has been made towards local self-government here, it has not reached the point where either the elected African legislatures or the French administrators could agree to official American economic programs independently of France. This is also admittedly true where private investment is concerned, but we believe that the obstacles are fewer.

Turning to educational exchange, this office as recently reported has made repeated efforts to arouse some interest here with a total lack of success. [5] Despite this, ignorance and misunderstanding here regarding the United States are so deep rooted that we feel a serious attempt should be made in this direction. The Consulate General doubts that anything can be done locally and believes that it should be taken up in Paris at the Government level. This misunderstanding of the United States arises from several sources, but is due primarily to our reputation, which the French do nothing to discourage in the local schools, for racial discrimination. For good measure, the aborigines in the United States are not forgotten and the comparison is drawn between "the only good Indian is a

---

[5] Despatch 40 from Dakar, August 29, reported that the French did not want any students from their colonies in Africa to be educated in the United States where they might be imbued with nationalism. (Department of State, Central Files, 511.51T3/8–2955)

dead Indian" and the enlightened policies of the French in Black Africa.

In an article entitled "Racism, Factor of Division" in the latest issue of *Traits d'Union*, the quarterly published by the Government to promote the various *Centres Culturelles* throughout French West Africa, the author, an African, has this to say about the United States:

" . . . [6] racism is also an American phenomenon. Racial segregation exists in America between the Whites and Blacks. The Blacks have not only their own quarters but also their schools, their hospitals, their churches, their cafes and restaurants and the hours during which they can enter stores."

" . . . Colonization has created a form of racism—a colonial racism. The shape of this racism is known—for example the American Indians were penned up by the Americans and destroyed."

> "Equally well known is the condition of the American Negros. The Americans wonder if they should not be sterilized or dumped en masse on some part of the African continent. In the meantime, despite a recent law, the Blacks of America are regarded as a menace to the white race. They cannot even be buried in the same cemeteries as Whites!"
>
> " . . . The *pure race* which is the basis of de Gobineau and of Hitlerism and of Americanism does not exist. . . . "

From this it can be seen that we have quite an educational job to do. We can counter this to some extent with information programs on the spot but this can never take the place of personal observation. A mere handful of African students returning from the United States could spread the word far and wide and could have much more influence in the long run than any amount of films, radio broadcasts, publications and the like.

The other side of the coin could see a marked increase in Americans visiting the area and they need not be confined to students. One very helpful program might be the sending of Negro organizations, such as musical groups, athletic teams, etc. This would not only be immensely popular but could serve to show that the American Negro is not always as downtrodden as the African in this area has been led to believe. There have been a few American scholars here on Fulbright, Ford Foundation, etc. grants but they have for the most part been specialists and have spent their time investigating such things as the life and habits of the Guinea worm and have measured heads in Upper Volta. The impact of such specialists is negligible. American students would have more long range interest [*impact*?] if their interest were more general and if they mixed more with the rank and file of the population.

---

[6] All ellipses are in the source text.

As regards some of the other courses of action recommended by the Department, we believe that most of them while useful as parts of the whole, cannot by themselves be too effective. We should definitely increase our information program, particularly films, but we should be careful not to defeat our own purposes by arousing suspicion on the part of both Africans and Europeans. If we go too far, our motives are suspect and anything that has an air of "propaganda" will rebound against us.

As regards United States representation in Africa, we cannot agree, as far as this post is concerned, with the suggestion that officer strength be increased over the course of the next five years unless, and only unless, a drastic revision in the amount of money available for local travel is made. At the moment, this office is adequately staffed for the amount of work that we can do in Dakar and any increases not only would be unwarranted but would make both French and Africans wonder exactly what we were up to. We are twice the size of the next largest Consulate General, the British, and everyone knows that we have only a limited amount of routine consular work to perform. Over and above this, the theory that American objectives are more easily obtained by sending into a given area a large number of officials whether or not they can do constructive work is questionable. This has marked much of our policy since the end of World War II and the undersigned, for one, has serious reservations about it.

More to the point, might be drastically to revise current administrative and fiscal practices so that a given Foreign Service post will not need so many officers and more can devote themselves to substantive work. The fact that this Consulate General with an authorized complement of only nine Americans and a similar number of locals has to have a full time Disbursing Officer is ridiculous but present accounting practices leave the Department no choice in the matter. The enormous amount of administrative work, much of which to us in the field seems senseless, also unnecessarily requires personnel who might be better employed elsewhere or in other fields.

One of the more serious problems with regard to official United States representation in this area is continuity. The present practice is for each officer and employee to serve here two years and then be transferred. The Dakar consular district comprises an area more than half the size of the United States and contains an interesting melange of many different peoples and political and economic interests. It is impossible, even with the best will in the world, to obtain much of an understanding of the area in two years, and, when we begin to understand the area a little, we are transferred. The process then starts all over again. Unfortunately there is no remedy at hand.

No officer or employee in Dakar in recent years, the undersigned included, has been willing to serve another tour at this post after only two months of home leave. The British Foreign Service in this area follows the practice of eighteen months duty followed by five months of leave and then another eighteen months. The policy of the French Government for its administrators here is virtually identical although the eighteen months tours can be repeated indefinitely. By this policy, the French and British both have a continuity which we lack and at the same time, are able to keep their people reasonably content by this generous leave policy. Obviously there is no legal way in which the Department could follow suit and such long leaves are contrary to American practice and tradition. It is also expensive but one wonders if it is, in the long run, much more expensive than our practice of paying differential allowances which, while attractive, do not achieve the continuity which might be obtained by a more liberal leave policy. The undersigned is inclined to question the basic soundness of the differential system and to wonder if the answer will not eventually be leave, rather than cash, benefits for hardship service.

It might be well at this point to leave the overall question of broad policies for the entire area and to examine the French territories of tropical Africa in particular and see whether or not they can be fitted into the area picture as a whole.

This office is competent to discuss only French West Africa and Togo and is without any particular knowledge of French Equatorial Africa and the Cameroons. However we understand that in general they compare sufficiently for certain patterns to be true for them all. One primary consideration must, it is believed be kept in mind. While the French are not repressing the peoples of the area who are, in fact, progressing towards some sort of self-determination, they are not going to haul down the flag in the foreseeable future. Recent disasters to one time French colonies elsewhere and the present unpleasantness in North Africa have made the French determined, that, come Hell or high water, *L'Afrique Noire Francaise* is going to remain in the French Union. Unless we are prepared for still another crisis in Franco-American relations we will have to work here in most cases through the French and in no case in opposition to them. This does not leave us much room for maneuver.

Fortunately the Consulate General believes that unless there are changes not easy to anticipate now in the broad lines of French policy, we can support the French without prejudicing our position in other areas. As far as this area is concerned, this will not, except in a few isolated areas, weaken our position vis-à-vis the Africans. Much has been said about the divergent policies followed by the

British and French in West Africa but in the final analysis they may not be so divergent after all. The British are proceeding with schemes for the virtual independence of the Gold Coast and Nigeria but presumably within the framework of the British Commonwealth. The French are increasing the powers of the various elected assemblies and envisage a still undefined system with the various territories having full local autonomy within the tighter framework of the French Union. Both are faced, however, with the complex problem of the lack of a governing class. While a few leaders exist who can hold down ministerial or semi-ministerial positions, the large rank and file necessary to carry out the routine day by day tasks of Government is lacking. Until this problem is solved real independence of the white man is unattainable despite the legal status of the territory itself.

Our point in raising this is to emphasize the fact that there seems no reason why we cannot, with perfect impunity, support both the French and British. Their approaches are admittedly different but their end objectives are similar and their problems are much the same. One point which must not be overlooked in considering the development of the various parts of Tropical Africa towards self-government is the fact that true self-determination requires the ability of an area to support itself. There seems to be a real possibility that the Gold Coast and Nigeria can do this but in the French area only the Ivory Coast and the Cameroons seem to have the remotest possibility of ever being able to live without European largesse. At the moment, except for the two trust territories, French possessions in Africa South of the Sahara are lumped together in geographical groupings that can only be described as absurd. French West Africa, for example, contains eight territories all supposedly politically equal ranging from the potentially rich Ivory Coast to the desert wastes of Mauretania. They are all handled as if they were the same and herein, we feel lies one of the great weaknesses of French policy in this part of the world and one on which we might in the course of time be able to exert a little pressure.

For reasons difficult for an American to understand, the French insist that those groupings and boundaries, which were arbitrarily put together in the European scramble for African real estate in the nineteenth century, are sacred. This obsession conceivably in the course of time can cause trouble and it represents an economic, administrative and political monstrosity. Rumblings are always being felt and a number of speakers in the course of the current session of the Territorial Assembly of the Ivory Coast, including it must be mentioned Frenchmen, have bitterly accused the Metropolitan and Federal Government of using the Ivory Coast as the "Milch Cow of the Federation". There has, admittedly, been much talk in Government circles in Paris about "decentralization" but nothing whatsoever has been done about it and we doubt that decentralization as discussed in Paris actually means very much. There are some areas within the French zone of Black Africa which are unquestionably capable of a highly advanced degree of self-government but there are others which are so totally lacking in both human and economic resources that they can never get by without the direct administration of a major power. Here again is another argument for not tying ourselves to a rigid, area wide, policy. Where possible we should encourage the continued progress of those territories capable of running their own affairs and use our influence with the French where we appropriately can not to stifle these areas by tying them to those that are economically and politically sterile. We should probably concentrate the courses of action outlined in the Department's paper in the former areas.

We realize the fact that the Department's paper was specifically designed for the area as a whole and avoided all considerations of a particular nature. Admittedly, in the immediately preceding paragraphs, the Consulate General has strayed from the terms of reference but the temptation was strong and no regional policy can, we believe, be prepared without consideration of the particular problems of its component parts. Reverting to an area-wide perspective, the Consulate General would like to make a few uncalled-for observations on the subject of colonialism.

Colonialism in the past ten years has been used to denote the political control of disconnected and often undeveloped area by a non indigenous power. It has been roundly denounced in many quarters as wrong in itself without any thoughtful consideration of the fact that it varies enormously in many parts of the world. British colonialism in India, for example, clearly was an anachronism and could not endure in the mid twentieth century. The same applies to other areas where there was some traditional concept of nationhood and where there had been substantial progress towards modern civilization. In Africa, we are faced with an almost complete historical void, with an infinite variety of totally different peoples, with civilization as we know it only in its birth pains. Some areas, as indicated above, are much nearer the point where they can manage their own affairs than are others but very few can get by without some support from the West. If we damn colonialism in the abstract without considering the actual facts of present day life in Africa, we are doing ourselves, the Africans and the colonial powers a disservice. In much of this part of the world, whether we like it or not, the people simply are not yet capable of managing their own affairs. Tribal allegiances are still too strong, education is only beginning to make itself felt, the concept of responsible Government for the good of the whole people is virtually unknown. The process can unquestionably be hastened but there is such a long way to go that it cannot be done overnight.

While the United States should, of course, continue to make known its sympathy for colonial peoples and its desire that they be led along the road of orderly development to the point where they can govern themselves, it should avoid sweeping indictments of all colonial regimes and should judge each area in the light of its particular problems and limitations. In our current distaste for colonialism in all its forms, we Americans sometimes forget that it was not so many years ago that we were singing "Beneath the Starry Flag, Civilize 'em with a Krag".

C. Vaughan Ferguson, Jr. [7]

[7] Printed from a copy that bears this typed signature.

39. Memorandum of a Conversation, Department of State, Washington, August 7, 1956, 4:42 p.m. [1]

SUBJECT

Forthcoming Vote on Resolution in Trusteeship Council with Regard to Referendum in French Togoland

PARTICIPANTS

The Secretary
Mr. Maurice Couve de Murville, French Ambassador
Mr. Jacques Vimont, Minister, French Embassy
Mr. Francis O. Wilcox, Assistant Secretary, IO
Mr. William R. Tyler, WE

The Ambassador told the Secretary that his Government attaches great importance to U.S. support in the forthcoming vote. He said that if the U.S. voted for the resolution, the Chinese Delegate and the Guatemalan Delegate would probably go along too, and that this would insure passage of the resolution. If the U.S. abstained, as the French Delegate had reason to believe it intended to do, this would probably swing the vote against the resolution. Such a result

[1] Source: Department of State, Central Files, 320.14/8–756. Confidential. Drafted by Tyler.

would be unfortunate and would create hard feelings in Paris, the Ambassador said.

Mr. Wilcox explained that the difficulty arose from the fact that the original intention of the U.S. to support the resolution was based on the belief that France had a majority of votes lined up in favor of it, whereas this had been subsequently proved not to be the case. In particular, the Indian Delegate, who had at first been favorable, had been overruled by Krishna Menon. [2] and the Chinese Delegate [3] was now also apparently resolved to vote against the resolution. It seemed that India dislikes the alternatives which the French law places before the people of Togoland, which it interprets as excluding or indefinitely postponing the prospect of independence for Togoland. It would certainly help matters if the French could propose a way of dispelling the Indian doubts so as to make the resolution acceptable to them, either by a modification of the text or by a preamble.

The Secretary said that he hoped that something mutually acceptable could be worked out as we wanted to be helpful in this matter. After this conversation, the French Ambassador told Mr. Wilcox that he was going to call the French Delegate on the Trusteeship Council and explore the possibilities of accompanying the resolution by a preamble which would revalidate previous statements by French representatives before the Trusteeship Council to the effect that local autonomy within the French Union does not foreclose further evolution toward independence.

---

[2] On July 23 and August 2, Indian Permanant Representative to the United Nations Ambassador Arthur S. Lall indicated to Mason Sears his expectation that India would support the French proposal. Later on August 2, however, the United States was informed that India would oppose the proposal as Lall had misinterpreted Menon's view. (Draft memorandum from Edward Mulcahy to Gerig, August 22; *ibid.*, IO/ODA Files: Lot 62 D 225, Togolands)

[3] Chiping H.C. Kiang.

40. Memorandum of a Conversation, Department of State, Washington, August 9, 1956[1]

SUBJECT

French request for United States support for resolution on French Togoland

PARTICIPANTS

Mr. Charles Lucet, Minister, French Embassy
Assistant Secretary Wilcox—IO
Mr. Roberts—EUR
Mr. Dumont—AF
Mr. McKay—ODA

Mr. Wilcox telephoned the French Ambassador this morning in order to give the Department's reply to the request made by the Ambassador to the Secretary on August 7th[2] for United States support for a French request to the Trusteeship Council to send observers to a forthcoming referendum in French Togoland.

Mr. Lucet, the French Minister, came to Mr. Wilcox' office shortly afterward. Mr. Wilcox handed him the attached memorandum, the underlined portions of which are to be introduced in the Trusteeship Council by the United States Delegation as amendments to the text which is being introduced by the French Delegation.[3] These amendments were previously cleared by EUR, WE, AF, and ODA.

Mr. Wilcox explained the U.S. position to Mr. Lucet in the following terms:

(1) We do not like the French text because we are afraid that it will cause future difficulties for both France and the U.S.;

(2) However, because we appreciate the importance which France attaches to the problem, as indicated by the Ambassador's call on the Secretary, we are not going to vote against the French text;

(2) We are willing either to:

(a) abstain on the present French text, or

(b) vote for it after formally introducing the attached amendments. (Mr. Wilcox explained that we felt it necessary to introduce these amendments in order to clarify our position in the TC.)

---

[1] Source: Department of State, Central Files, 350/8–956. Confidential. Drafted by McKay.

[2] See *supra.*

[3] The attachment is not printed. See U.N. doc. T/L.731 and Add.1, and Rev.1 for text of the French draft resolution and revision, together with the Secretary-General's statement with regard to the financial implications of the proposal. For the U.S. amendments to the draft resolution, see U.N. doc. T/L.732.

(4) We cannot commit ourselves regarding the position we would take on any amendments that might be proposed by other delegations; we would have to deal with any such amendments on their merits;

(5) We want to make it clear to the French Government that our vote in favor of the resolution would not in any way commit us to support France in any future UN difficulties that might arise from the present French course of action.

Mr. Wilcox added that the same amendments with the same explanation had just been handed to Mr. Bargues, the head of the French Delegation in New York, by Mr. Sears, the head of the U.S. Delegation.

In view of the fact that the Council may end its session tomorrow, the French text and the U.S. amendments might have to be introduced in the Council this afternoon in order to be reproduced by the Secretariat for the vote tomorrow.

Mr. Lucet thanked Mr. Wilcox and said that he would study the amendments and contact Mr. Bargues immediately. It was pointed out to him that in view of the urgency of the matter that it would probably be better to leave any future negotiations to Mr. Bargues and Mr. Sears in New York. [4]

---

[4] The French introduced their draft resolution in the Trusteeship Council on August 9 and the United States followed by introducing its three amendments. Lucet telephoned Wilcox on August 10 and asked the United States to substitute for the words "without endorsing the referendum terms" in its third amendment the following: "while reserving its final position as to the terms of the referendum and its stand with regard to future UN action in conformity with Article 76(b)." This was agreed to in the Council later that day. (Memorandum of conversation by McKay, August 13; Department of State, IO/ODA Files: Lot 62 D 225, Togolands) At its 744th meeting on August 14 the Council was twice deadlocked 7 to 7 on the French draft resolution, which thus was defeated. The French announced their intention of proceeding with the referendum anyway. At its 745th meeting, on the same date, the Council adopted a draft resolution introduced by Burma, Guatemala, India, and Syria by a vote of 7 to 5 (France), with 2 abstentions (New Zealand and the United States). For text of Resolution 1499 (XVIII), see *Yearbook of the United Nations 1956,* pp. 372–373, and 375.

41. Despatch From the Consulate General at Dakar to the Department of State [1]

No. 129 *Dakar, November 30, 1956.*

REF

Dept's CA–2548, September 28, 1955, [2] ConGen's Despatch No. 127, November 30, 1956 [3] and ConGen's Despatch No. 104, November 5, 1956 [4]

SUBJECT

Survey of the Changing Situation in French West Africa—Conclusions and Policy Recommendations

A. Summary Abstract of Political Survey of French West Africa (Despatch No. 127)

1. Over the past twelve months, the political evolution of French West Africa which previously ambled along at a leisurely rate, has suddenly been precipitated and is now proceeding at a rate which is not merely rapid but which is constantly accelerating.

2. Evidence has continued to accumulate during the year that the Consul General has been in Dakar that, just as events in North Africa came far sooner and moved more quickly than was anticipated, so in Africa South of the Sahara, political developments are unfolding with a rush of speed which is at once dizzying and dangerously intoxicating to these primitive African peoples, who for the most part are completely unready for the responsibilities of democratic self-government.

3. The French face in French West Africa a familiar dilemma: if they make concessions to the Africans too fast, the whole nationalist anti-colonial movement may get completely out of control; and if they apply the brakes too abruptly, they run the risk of falling into the equally dangerous trap of "too little and too late".

4. The problem is intensified and in fact dominated by two outside influences: the pressure of pan-Arabism on the predominantly Moslem populations of several Black African Territories; and the

[1] Source: Department of State, Central Files, 751T.00/11–3056. Limited Official Use. Repeated to Paris and USUN.

[2] In CA–2548, the Department requested that each of the principal officers at 19 African posts and missions provide a short despatch surveying the situation a year after their arrival at post and then a more detailed despatch prior to their departure. (*Ibid.*, 120.201/9–2855)

[3] In despatch 127, Browne expressed the view that French West Africa was moving inevitably toward self-government. He reported that nationalism south of the Sahara could still be influenced from without, but the critical question was whether the East or the West would intervene more effectively. (*Ibid.*, 751T.00/11–3056)

[4] Not printed. (*Ibid.*, 123–Martin, Doyle Vernon)

increasingly active exploitation of African anti-colonial sentiment by Communist agents operating chiefly in and through the labor unions.

5. So far, despite these external pressures, most mature African political leaders have remained mainly loyal to France. They want as much freedom and self-government as the French will continue to pay for; but they do not now ask for full independence which they know they could not afford. The present African political leaders are probably prepared to settle for the relatively modest degree of local self-government which they are about to receive under the "loi-cadre".[5] But these more mature leaders are beginning to be hard-pressed by a rising tide of younger African "évolués", mostly anti-French extremists strongly stamped with Marxism and/or Moslem Nationalism.

6. Thus in Africa South of the Sahara, the Niger of nationalism and the Congo of anti-colonialism are steadily rising and will before long be flowing in full flood. So far, the tam-tams of open revolt are silent; but they are increasingly taut in the heat of flaming conflict further North. In a very few years—perhaps even in a mere matter of months—the rapid current of events is likely to bring about a new and potentially dangerous situation in French West Africa.

B. Reassessment of United States Strategic Interest in Africa South of the Sahara

7. Thus, as a result of the changes and current developments in North Africa and the Middle East, and in view of the accelerated pace of political evolution in Tropical Africa, a reassessment of the United States' position with regard to the latter area is clearly called for. Hitherto our strategic interest in Africa South of the Sahara has been confined almost entirely to our preoccupation with access to certain strategic raw materials, such as uranium. If the present trend of events in North Africa and the Middle East continues, however, it appears likely that the primary emphasis of our strategic interest will necessarily shift, giving greater priority to two other factors, one geographic, the other politico-psychological.

8. The geographic factor resides in the fact that, if hostilities develop on a bigger scale in the Middle East or in North Africa the whole of French West Africa will immediately assume major importance as a rear staging base and line of air communications; while Dakar itself, perched on the western-most point of Africa, consti-

[5] The loi-cadre or enabling act became law on June 23. The loi-cadre, followed by specific implementing decrees in April 1957, conferred semiresponsible government on the individual African colonies. Territorial assemblies were enlarged, universal suffrage mandated, and the elected African vice-presidents of the respective assemblies became, in effect, prime ministers in waiting.

tutes the nearest African deep water port, naval base and air base to the Western hemisphere (see Despatch No. 128 [6] for specific strategic suggestions).

9. The political factor results from the fact that, faced with the threat of massive Soviet penetration in the Middle East and in Egypt, the United States will no doubt seek to revitalize the North Atlantic Alliance and particularly to improve relations with France and Britain. An important aspect of this strategic problem will be to remove the bitter resentment and suspicion which the French in particular—and to a lesser extent the British—feel toward the United States because they blame us as partly responsible for their ejection from Indo China and North Africa. Regardless of how far away from facts this French interpretation of our role in Indo China and North Africa may—or may not—be, we cannot afford to ignore the cumulative bitterness and distrust which has grown out of it. As of now the French are fearfully convinced that we the United States are preaching anti-Colonialism in tropical Africa primarily for the purpose of displacing them and replacing them as the dominant economic power in the area. Until we can at least diminish this suspicious resentment, any American effort to aid in the development of this sadly underdeveloped area will quickly arouse fresh fears and put additional strains on the North Atlantic Alliance and especially on our relations with France.

Re-Definition of American Policy Objectives in the Area

10. Outside of the strategic sphere, United States interests in Africa South of the Sahara are almost exclusively economic. We have, it is true, a very vital interest in making sure that this portion of Africa does not fall under the control or domination of Soviet Communism. Neither would we wish to see it become a sphere of influence of Asia (through an extension of the already large Indian minority in the area). But these political objectives are in fact negative aspects of our strategic objectives. They are of the greatest importance, but they are composed of what we do *not* want to have happen in Africa South of the Sahara. Thus, while one of our important political objectives is to gain the confidence of the Africans and to develop friendship and close contacts between Africans and Americans, our purpose in so doing is not to extend our hegemony or even our influence over them but to prevent them from falling under the domination of powers which would be a

[6] In despatch 128, November 30, Browne recommended that the United States proceed gradually to seek permission from France to establish a naval base in Dakar and an airbase in the Dakar area. (Department of State, Central Files, 751T.00/11–3056)

threat to their own freedom and well-being as well as to our security.

11. Our economic interest in the area, on the contrary, is positive and vigorous. It is not so much actual (except in the case of strategic raw materials already mentioned) as it is potential. We seek to share freely and fully in the future economic development of this underdeveloped area, and we are prepared to contribute to and aid in this development. But we most emphatically do not aspire to any economic pre-eminence over the Africans. Nor do we seek to displace or replace any European nation already established there. What we ask economically is simply that Africa evolve gradually but without undue delays toward an "open door" policy which would give to all countries an opportunity to trade freely and equitably.

D. Policy Recommendations

12. Against the background of the grave and growing Communist menace in the Middle East and North Africa, and in view of the increasingly rapid rate of political evolution in French West African and other Territories South of the Sahara, the following policy suggestions are submitted for possible consideration by the Department:

(1) The United States should openly favor and fearlessly—though not aggressively—advocate the early accession of all the tropical French African Territories to genuine and complete local self-government within the French Union.

(2) The United States should support, tactfully but firmly, the right of these Territories to the attainment of complete independence as soon as they have demonstrated their readiness to assume the responsibilities which complete independence necessarily entails.

(3) United States policy toward Africa South of the Sahara should be guided constantly by the long-range objective of achieving for the African continent an established order roughly comparable to that which exists in Latin America: i.e., the ultimate attainment of independent democratic statehood by each of the various units under conditions which exclude the domination of the entire continent by any one state, and more particularly, which exclude the conquest or domination of any of the areas by any foreign power not already established on the continent.

(4) In working toward this objective the primary role which in Latin America was assumed by the United States should in Africa be shouldered by Britain and France (and to a lesser extent by Belgium and Portugal). The United States would thus, in effect, be sponsoring and encouraging the proclamation and establishment of a "Eurafrican Monroe Doctrine". The United States would thereby be assuming a vital role which, in our own Monroe Doctrine, was played by England and especially by the British fleet. It was this agreement on the part of England to keep out of South America and to help the United States keep out any other foreign power, that

made the Monroe Doctrine a possibility and a success early in the 19th century.

(5) The United States should not merely reiterate its own "hands-off" policy, completely devoid of any Territorial ambition or desire for economic domination in the area; it should also pledge its support to Britain and France, Belgium and Portugal, in helping to promote the economic and financial progress and development of the peoples in the area, as well as its readiness if necessary to back up Franco-British military action designed to prevent any violation by Soviet or Asian Communism of the "Eurafrican Monroe Doctrine".

(6) The United States should require in return—and in fact should insist upon in advance as an indispensable preliminary—that the French and British, Belgians and Portuguese agree to move gradually but at a reasonably rapid pace toward the opening up to normal international trade and economic development of those areas in Tropical Africa which now remain under their control, with as our objective the achievement of "most favored nation" status in our commercial relations.

W. Mallory Browne

---

42. Telegram From the Embassy in France to the Department of State [1]

Paris, December 20, 1956—6 p.m.

3088. At his request I called on Deferre, Minister of Overseas Territories today. He discussed problem of debate on French Togoland in United Nations. He pointed out that this was very important matter for Franco-American relations and was place where France deserved full support of United States. He then said that United States had voted against French the other day in TC which had been deciding vote in sending French Togoland to 4th Committee without recommendation. [2] He said that French had desired not necessarily a

[1] Source: Department of State, Central Files, 7515.00/12–2056. Confidential. Repeated to USUN.

[2] The Statute of the autonomous Republic of Togoland was promulgated by Decree 56–847 of August 24, which became effective August 30. On September 10, Nicolas Grunitzky became Prime Minister. The Togolese who chose to vote in the October 28 referendum supported the Statute by a large margin. In a memorandum submitted to the Trusteeship Council on December 6 (U.N. doc. T/1290), the French requested that, in light of the referendum and a subsequent motion of the Togoland Legislative Assembly on November 2, the U.N. General Assembly and the Trusteeship Council should require France to terminate the Trusteeship Agreement. The sixth special session of the Council met expressly to deal with this issue. General Assembly (Continued)

positive recommendation but something stating that TC had studied the matter and felt that election had been fairly conducted, which Deferre said was an indisputable fact attested to by foreign newspaper men.

Drawing on Deptel 2341 [3] I told Deferre that our vote in TC had been purely tactical and should not be considered to prejudge United States position on substantive issues involved. I told Deferre that Embassy Paris as a result of talks with his ministry had fully explained French position to Department and had urged United States support for French position. I said that we had not yet received Department's views on substantive issues involved but we expected them shortly and when they arrived would be in touch with his office. Meanwhile, I said we had received statement which Department had authorized US rep TC to make for press following conclusion of debate in TC. I then gave Deferre copy of statement as shown in Deptel 2345. [4] Deferre was naturally very pleased with tone of this statement.

I told Deferre that if there had been any misunderstanding between French and US Dels, it may have been partly due to the fact that USDel had not been kept as fully informed by French reps as they might have been. Deferre said he was surprised to hear this but would send instructions to his rep in French Del to see that US was kept fully informed from here on out. He said he would also telephone Alphand and ask him to be sure State Department was kept fully informed. I have the feeling that some of the problems with French Embassy Washington and French Del mentioned in Deptel 2341 [5] may stem from fact that French case on Togoland is apparently being conducted entirely by Ministry of Overseas Territories, which probably has led to some crossed wires and jealousies via-à-vis Quai d'Orsay.

(Continued)
concurrence in the termination of a Trust was specified under Articles 12 of the Agreement and 85 of the Charter. On December 17, the Council adopted an oral proposal by Guatemala to transmit the question to the Fourth Committee of the General Assembly with the relevant documents, but without any recommendation. The vote was 8 to 6, with the deciding ballot cast by the United States. See *Yearbook of the United Nations 1956,* pp. 373–374. Ambassador Dillon in telegram 3015 from Paris, December 17, urged a negative vote in this matter. (Department of State, Central Files, 751T.00/12–1756)

[3] Telegram 2341, December 19, stated that the United States supported the Guatemalan initiative because of a conviction that the Fourth Committee would inevitably consider the issue and in order to preclude an adverse recommendation from the Council. (*Ibid.*, 751T.00/12–1956)

[4] Telegram 2345, December 19, transmitted a press statement in which the United States commented favorably on the constitutional advances in Togoland pointing toward self-government. (*Ibid.*)

[5] See footnote 3 above. Neither the French Embassy nor U.N. Delegation had kept the United States informed of their intentions and tactics.

Deferre said that matter would come up for debate on January 3. He said the case would be presented initially by Togolese Del headed by new Prime Minister of Togoland. Togolese would in effect ask the UN to give them their freedom which they had already been given by France. French side of case will be presented by Houphouet-Boigny, native-born African Minister in present French Government. Deferre himself will be present as senior adviser but will stay in background. Deferre said he plans to arrive in US on January 1st and would like very much to see Lodge sometime during the day of the 2nd. I would appreciate information as to whether Lodge will be available for meeting with Deferre on 2nd.

Deferre then pointed out that French case on Togoland was very good and in some ways was even better than British case on British Togoland which had been approved by TC with US support.[6] British Togoland was being annexed to Gold Coast whereas French Togoland was receiving its own independent status. Deferre said that French relations with Togolese Government were very good. They are in marked contrast with French relations in Morocco and Tunisia, in that Togolese are requesting Deferre to supply more French technicians and administrators than he wishes to let them have. He has pointed out to them that if they have too many it would cause a strain on their budget which would then necessitate a subsidy from France. This would have the effect of casting a shadow on their independence. Therefore, he is insisting on keeping the number of French administrators to a minimum.

Deferre then outlined the great importance of this vote from the point of view of Franco-American relations. He said it was obvious that Algerian problem would be difficult and that United States might not find it possible to vote with France in that case. If we give France full support on Togoland it would then be possible for United States to say that we support France when we think they are clearly in the right, which position would be well understood by France. Lack of support on Togoland issue would be interpreted by French as indicative of United States policy merely to oppose France at any and every opportunity. Deferre pointed out that he had real problem in getting a liberal Togolese constitution accepted by French Parliament and that if United States should now oppose such a liberal solution it would be very difficult if not impossible to explain American position to French public.

I asked Deferre if Togolese had been in contact with Liberian Govt. He said that they had not had such contacts as yet. I told him I thought it was important that Togolese delegates seek out Liberians

[6] Reference is to General Assembly Resolution 944(X), December 15. See Document 122.

promptly on arrival in New York and attempt to obtain their support which seemed to me to be very important psychologically. Deferre also said he hoped United States would use its influence with Latin American countries for a favorable vote, and in particular mentioned Guatemala. I replied that French should realize that Guatemala was a difficult and special case whenever a French question came up in United States as it was hard for Guatemalan Govt to forget support given by France to Communist Govt in Guatemala.

I fully agree with Deferre that in present situation Togoland problem is far more important than it otherwise would be, particularly in view of difficult upcoming Algerian debate. I feel it is important that United States find a way to fully support France on this issue.

Dillon

---

43. Telegram From the Department of State to the Embassy in France [1]

Washington, December 22, 1956—2:37 p.m.

2403. Paris 3022. [2] Suggest you approach Deferre urgently along following lines and inform Foreign Office:

French request for immediate termination Togoland trusteeship has presented US with difficult dilemma. US anxious avoid taking position adverse to French on this issue, especially in view of our conviction new Togoland statute represents valuable step forward and may provide useful pattern for evolution other African territories. If request for termination trusteeship were not involved, US would be prepared commend French action in most favorable terms. Hope France will be able reconsider pressing termination request for following reasons:

1. US support of French request would establish precedent which would tend undermine basic premises of whole trusteeship system. System is designed assure protection and support for dependent peoples until capable of self-government, either as inde-

---

[1] Source: Department of State, Central Files, 751T.00/12–2256. Confidential. Repeated to USUN.

[2] This reference is apparently in error; presumably it should be to telegram 3088, *supra.*

pendent entity or in association with others. US does not believe full independence is requirement for termination trusteeship in every case. Also recognize "self-government" is matter of degree and would not contend that trusteeship must continue until dependent territory has complete authority over all aspects of domestic and foreign affairs. However, powers reserved to France in new Togoland statute are so substantial that US would find it impossible to maintain position that objectives stated in Article 76(b) of the UN Charter have been realized.[3] Is noted that reserved powers, in addition French control of foreign affairs and defense, include French jurisdiction over administration of justice, penal and commercial code, currency and foreign exchange, customs, educational curricula, etc.

2. US does not question validity French decision reserve foregoing powers. Reservations seem altogether realistic in view present stage development political capabilities of Togolese people. But it is for this very reason that US convinced termination trusteeship premature. Support of request for immediate termination would leave US in position of advocating termination of dependent status regardless of capabilities of local population and regardless degree of evolution attained. Would have far-reaching implications for US policy on whole range of "colonial" issues and might weaken ability of US to support continuation of European administration in other areas that are not ready for responsibilities of self-government. Vital that fundamentals of US policy re these issues be consistent. Could not hope successfully to argue that external authority in one area must be maintained until capabilities of indigenous population fully developed while proposing that protection of trusteeship system be removed in another area where indigenous capabilities less advanced. In this context, US does not necessarily regard views and sentiments expressed by indigenous population as decisive. To do so would compel us to support immediate independence for any area whose people demand independence, without regard to their ability to sustain independent existence. Such a policy would be wholly unrealistic and dangerous to vital interests of European allies.

3. Even if US were able support French request for termination, we see virtually no chance approval by General Assembly. Unlike US, many governments will refuse recognize enormous advance

[3] At a meeting with representatives of the Administering Powers and the Netherlands on December 20, Bargues claimed that the choice given the populace of French Togoland was no more restrictive than that offered the people of British Togoland, who could only gain independence through union with the Gold Coast. France could concede autonomy to the Togolese but not independence, he revealed, because of the situation in Algeria. (Memorandum for the files by Bolard More, December 31; *ibid.*, IO/ODA Files: Lot 62 D 225, Togolands)

represented by new statute and will probably denounce new Togolese arrangements as "hoax". Validity of referendum itself will probably be widely challenged. Moreover, present GA offers worst possible atmosphere for consideration French request. Even if we believed extent of self-government granted Togoland were sufficiently great to permit US wage vigorous campaign on behalf of France (which we do not), we would see no prospect at 11th GA of obtaining majority approval of termination, let alone required two-thirds majority. US fears overwhelming GA defeat would have much more adverse impact on French position Togoland and other parts Africa then French decision withdraw request for termination.

In light foregoing considerations, US hopes France able defer request for termination at 11th GA. If French commitments to Togolese preclude withdrawal of request, US would be prepared (if French concur) sponsor compromise resolution which would: (1) note new statute is major step forward; (2) commend French initiative; (3) empower TC to send a special mission to Togoland to observe progress and report back to the 12th GA. Believe adoption resolution along these lines would avoid open conflict between French and US positions, avoid French defeat in GA and at same time sustain Togolese hopes for termination of trusteeship at future date, after further development Togolese capacity for self-government. If French willing proceed along these lines, US would seek work out text of compromise resolution in consultation with French, and would use all practical energy and influence to secure support from LA's and others. [4]

Dulles

---

[4] Dillon discussed the outline of a compromise resolution with Deferre on December 26. Deferre indicated that the French Cabinet would have to consider the U.S. proposal before making a definite reply. He did note, however, that France was committed to securing as early a termination of the trust as possible and had not granted full independence because the Togolese were not yet prepared for it. Any compromise, he maintained, had to signify to the Togolese that the termination of the trust had not been rejected but only delayed pending further consideration of the matter. (Telegram 3145 from Paris, December 26; *ibid.*, Central Files, 751T.00/12–2656)

44. Memorandum of a Conversation, Department of State, Washington, January 3, 1957 [1]

SUBJECT

Togoland

PARTICIPANTS

Mr. Hervé Alphand, French Ambassador
Mr. J. Vimont, Minister, French Embassy
Mr. Robert Murphy—G
Mr. William R. Tyler—WE

The French Ambassador told Mr. Murphy that the French have decided not to press for termination of the Trusteeship. They hope that a resolution will be introduced which will commend the progress achieved by France in Togoland, specifically with regard to the Referendum of October 1956 and the Statute for Togoland. The Ambassador also said that neither France nor the Togolese Government could accept the idea of sending a UN fact-finding mission to Togoland, and he asked for U.S. assistance in defeating any such proposal. [2]

Mr. Murphy said that he was glad to hear that the French had abandoned the idea of asking that the Trusteeship be terminated, and that he thought that this decision laid the basis for a cooperative effort between ourselves and the French to agree on a suitable resolution. He pointed out that we had suggested the idea of a UN mission as a possible alternative to the initial French idea of requesting termination of the Trusteeship at this time, in order to postpone the issue.

The Ambassador said he hoped our UN Delegation would be sent appropriate instructions, and that time was short since the matter was coming up before the Fourth Committee of the UN on Friday, January 4. [3]

---

[1] Source: Department of State, Central Files, 645K.51T3/1–357. Confidential. Drafted by Tyler. Alphand met with Murphy because Dulles was not available.

[2] In a conversation on January 4, however, Deferre informed the U.S. Mission at the United Nations that the Togolese would receive a factfinding mission if the President of the General Assembly requested it. (Memorandum of conversation, January 4; *ibid.*, IO/ODA Files: Lot 62 D 225, Togoland (French))

[3] On January 14, the Fourth Committee, by a vote of 52 (France, United States) to 10, with 14 abstentions, adopted a resolution which took note of the substantial referendum vote in favor of the Statute and expressed satisfaction that the Statute represented a significant step foward the realization of the objectives of the Trusteeship Agreement and Article 76. A study commission to look into the situation "resulting from the practical application of the Statute and the conditions under which it is being applied" was called for. For text of Resolution 1046 (XI), approved by the General Assembly on January 23, see U.N. doc. A/C.4/L.452 and Rev.1. Deferre informed Dillon on January 22 that the French were pleased with the result. (Telegram 3483 from Paris, January 22; Department of State, Central Files, 751T.00/1–1857)

45. Memorandum of a Conversation, Department of State, Washington, April 29, 1957 [1]

SUBJECT

US-Indian Resolution on Togoland in the Trusteeship Council

PARTICIPANTS

Ambassador Alphand, French Embassy
Minister Vimont, French Embassy
Mr. Elbrick, EUR
Mr. Wilcox, IO
Mr. McGregor, ODA
Mr. Nunley, EUR

Ambassador Alphand opened the discussion by referring to the UNGA resolution on Togoland adopted in January, 1957. [2] He said that this resolution had not been fully satisfactory to the French, but indicated that it represented a reasonable compromise under the circumstances and said that the French Government was pleased at having had US cooperation in achieving this compromise. He emphasized the importance of solidarity between the US and France, and among the other Western powers, on critical African problems. He then said that the French Government had been very surprised and disturbed that the US Representative on the Trusteeship Council joined India—a government not noted for friendship toward France—in sponsoring a resolution so critical of the French program in Togoland. [3]

Alphand observed that the proposed resolution, in addition to its critical reference to the existing Togolese territorial government and its demand for a change in the electoral system, contained a favorable reference to Mr. Olympio who is an avowed enemy of France and who represents only a small minority of the population of Togoland. [4] He said the French Government was especially surprised to see such a resolution tabled without advance consultation with the French, apparently on the sole basis of Olympio's allegations. In view of the common interests which France and the US

[1] Source: Department of State, Central Files, 751T.00/4–2957. Confidential. Drafted by W.T. Nunley.

[2] See footnote 3, *supra.*

[3] U.N. doc. T/L 754, jointly introduced by India and the United States on April 26.

[4] Olympio was an Ewe nationalist who favored the unification of the Ewe of British and French Togoland and Ghana and opposed the incorporation of French Togoland in the French Union.

have in the future of Africa, the Ambassador went on, this lack of consultation was difficult to understand.[5]

Ambassador Alphand pointed out that the present Togolese legislative assembly was approved by 72% of the local population, despite abstention of certain political elements such as Olympio's followers. He said the statute provides that the Assembly is elected for a five-year period, and added that the electoral responsibility now belongs to Togolese authorities rather than to France. He stressed the point that the new electoral law represents a very remarkable step forward and said that France stands alone in black Africa in organizing elections based upon popular vote. Why, he asked, does the United States feel compelled to enjoin France to do what France has already said it wants to do and in fact had actually done to a greater extent than anyone else?

The Ambassador said that the passage of the resolution would have psychological consequences which might jeopardize the French program throughout Africa and not merely within Togoland itself. For this reason, continued support of the resolution could not be regarded by the French Government as a friendly act. He said the French Government takes a very serious view of this situation and would like to see the resolution withdrawn or else to see the US vote against it if India persists in pressing it.

Mr. Wilcox asked whether the resolution embodies any significant new elements over and beyond the content of the UNGA resolution of January. Ambassador Alphand indicated that the only distinctly new element is the favorable reference to Olympio. However, he added, the new TC resolution is based on a paragraph to which the French objected in the original GA resolution. The French voted against this paragraph, as did the United States, but later accepted it within the context of the resolution as a whole.[6] The present problem arises from the fact that the substance of this one objectionable paragraph has been pulled out of context and made the subject of a separate resolution, and has been put forward before the other actions contemplated by the original resolution have been taken; in other words, before the visiting commission has studied the over-all situation and has reported to the TC.

Mr. Elbrick said that he is not surprised at the French reaction, particularly in view of the apparent absence of consultation, but said that he was surprised that the original reaction of the French

---

[5] The French were not given a copy of the draft resolution until the day before it was introduced.

[6] Paragraph 4 of Resolution 1046(XI) "*Recommends* that, in addition to such further reforms as the authorities concerned may deem appropriate, the Legislative Assembly of the Territory should be constituted, as soon as possible, by election on the basis of universal adult suffrage."

delegation in New York seemed to be so mild. Ambassador Alphand insisted that the French reaction in New York was not mild, and that the attitude of the French delegation had been misunderstood. He added that the French first thought that the resolution was being sponsored solely by India and therefore did not react strongly since they were not surprised at India's undertaking such an initiative.

Mr. Elbrick said he was not fully informed on all aspects of the problem, but that he was unable to see any reason why it should be necessary to act on the proposed resolution before the report of the visiting commission. He suggested that operative paragraph 5 of the original GA resolution might provide a basis for postponing the new resolution.[7]

Mr. Wilcox said that he could not say at this time what the US may be able to do about the matter. He said that he personally would probably have not taken the same position as the US Delegation in New York,[8] but that he could not criticize the action of the Delegation without studying the problem in more detail and obtaining more background information. Even if it should be determined that the proposed resolution is unwise, he indicated, there will remain a serious question as to the best method of proceeding to rectify the situation, since it is difficult for us to vote against a proposal that we ourselves have taken the initiative in raising. However, he concluded, we will begin at once to reexamine the problem and will inform the French Embassy of our decision as soon as possible.[9]

---

[7] Paragraph 5 "*Requests* the Trusteeship Council to study the question, taking into account the report of the Commission, and to transmit the results of its study to the General Assembly at its twelth session."

[8] Following the Indian approach, members of the U.S. Delegation to the Trusteeship Council discussed the draft resolution. Sears called Gerig on April 25, seeking Department instructions. Gerig was not enthusiastic about the text, but was persuaded to go along with it. (Memorandum from McGregor to Wilcox, April 29; Department of State, IO/ODA Files: Lot 62 D 225, Togoland (French))

[9] McGregor called Bargues on May 2 to indicate that the United States would propose that the election issue not be immediately discussed pending the special session of the Trusteeship Council scheduled for September to consider the report of the visiting Commission, which would soon embark for Togoland. He made it clear, however, that timing and not the substance of the draft resolution was the controlling factor. (Memorandum by McGregor, May 3; *ibid.*) On May 7, Sears, speaking in the Trusteeship Council, moved that the question be temporarily postponed. The Indian proposal was thus defeated on a tie vote. (Department of State Press Release 2677, May 22, 1957)

46. Despatch From the Consulate General at Dakar to the Department of State [1]

No. 77 *Dakar, October 1, 1957.*

REF

ConGen's Despatches No. 76, October 1, 1957, [2] No. 6, July 3, 1957, [3] No. 129, December 3 [*November 30*], 1956 [4] and CA–2548, September 28, 1955 [5]

SUBJECT

Summary of the Political Outlook in French West Africa, with Policy Recommendations

In the despatch referenced above the Consul General has discussed the principal political developments in French West Africa during the past twelve months. The present despatch summarizes briefly the political outlook in this area and submits certain policy suggestions.

For the sake of brevity, any discussion of current political problems or any detailed account of meanderings of African politics and politicians has been omitted from the summary. This despatch is an effort to look further ahead, to crystallize for the Department the pattern of the emerging French West African State of the near future. The conclusions listed below are those of the Consul General, but they are derived from discussions with many of the leading French administrators from the High Commissioner in Dakar down to District Commissioners deep in the interior, as well as from interviews with the African Premiers of seven of the eight Territories and Togo, and with other African political leaders of every party in French West Africa.

1. During the past year it has become apparent that French West Africa will before long become, like Ghana, an independent state.

2. This new status of sovereignty and independence will be achieved within 18 months at the earliest and 5 years at the latest. The most likely time is between late 1959 and early 1961.

3. The future (French) West African nation will be a federal state.

---

[1] Source: Department of State, Central Files, 751T.00/10-157. Confidential. Repeated to Paris, USUN, Abidjan, Lagos, Accra, and Yaoundé.

[2] In despatch 76, Browne reviewed political developments in French West Africa over the past year and judged the outlook for the future. (*Ibid.*)

[3] In despatch 6, Browne presented the psychological background of the existing political situation in French West Africa. (*Ibid.*, 751T.00/7–357)

[4] Document 41.

[5] See footnote 2, *ibid.*

4. It will be strongly decentralized, and will be composed of the present eight Territories and ultimately may include Togo.

5. To start with—and perhaps permanently—this new (French) West African State will remain within the French economic and cultural orbit.

6. It will become, and may possibly continue to be, a member of the proposed French "commonwealth" which is expected to be set up soon by a change in France's constitution: whatever the legal formula, in fact this commonwealth will have to be a loose confederal union if the emerging states are to remain within it.

7. Economically, the new West African State will at the beginning have to lean heavily on France.

8. Politically, on the contrary, it will not necessarily remain completely within the French orbit: it will not always follow France's foreign policy anymore than, say, India always follows Britain's.

9. The future independent state of (French) West Africa will associate itself closely with the other Territories of Black Africa which have become or are about to become independent.

10. It will take an active part in the efforts—likely to be lengthy—to form a West African federation, and ultimately a federation of all Black Africa.

11. It will be strongly influenced by Islam, but it will not be dominated—at least not at the beginning—by Arab policies.

12. It will maintain close and friendly relations with the new Arab states of North Africa and will be inclined to support the foreign policy of these North African states whenever their foreign policy does not conflict with its own economic interests or national aspirations and independence.

13. The future (French) West African State will be Socialist; but its socialism will neither be that of the Soviet Union nor that of the British labor party, nor will it be an imitation of French socialism; West Africa—and for that matter Black Africa as a whole—will develop its own form of socialism, strongly flavored by its ancient tribal traditions.

14. This socialism will not be belligerently anti-capitalist—at least not to start with; it will genuinely endeavor to encourage large scale investments by French and other foreign capital in the area.

15. It will be prepared to make business-like arrangements in order to encourage this influx of indispensable foreign capital, but it will drive hard bargains with all forms of big business: it will expect foreign business firms in particular to contribute with ever-increasing "generosity" to raising the standard of living, not only of the organized workers but of the African agricultural peasants out in the bush who constitute the great mass of Black Africa's millions.

16. The new West Africa will "play along" with the European Common Market scheme and with the Eurafrican concept just so long as it believes that this European combine will substantially increase financial grants to and other capital investment in the area; but it will not long submit to any Common Market projects intended to exploit rather than to enrich West Africa.

17. If the new state can successfully conclude profitable business deals with the Western world on this basis, it will quite sincerely wish to remain in the Western camp; but if such profitable (to the Africans) arrangements on a big enough scale are not concluded soon—or if they should break down—the new West African state would feel no compunction whatever in turning to the East and especially to Soviet Communism for economic aid and financial support.

18. The new (French) West African State will have all the stage props and elaborate trappings of modern Western democracy: universal suffrage, more-or-less-secret ballot, legislative assemblies, governments responsible—in theory at least—to these elected assemblies; but it will be at least a generation—perhaps a century—before Black Africa achieves real democracy even to the imperfect extent to which it has been attained in America and Europe.

19. The Africans in what is now French West Africa are not ready to shoulder the responsibilities and problems inevitably implied in the attempt to set up the kind of West African State described above. There is a tiny handful of well-educated, able leaders, and a very small group of half-educated "évolués"; but the illiterate millions of half-savage people who live in the desert and the jungle are still generations if not centuries away from responsible self-government.

20. Despite this unreadiness the Black Africans today are feeling the full force of the world tide of "nationalism": it could not be arrested and it is extremely doubtful whether it could even be delayed without the same tragic consequences which are now visible in Algeria; "for better for worse", therefore, the political evolution after the pattern outlined above is bound to come—and come quickly—in French West Africa, and the West will have to make up its mind to be patient with—and to help pay for—a lot of the "worse" as well as some of the "better".

Conclusion: On balance, therefore, the future (French) West African State (or states—it is probable that the same pattern will be followed with minor variations in French Equatorial Africa and the Cameroons) will from the point of view of the United States be a "policy risk" which, on a straight actuarial basis, might not be justified; but under existing world circumstances and in the face of the overriding fact that it is contrary to United States security and national interest to allow Africa to fall under the domination of the Soviet Union, the risk is one which we cannot afford not to take.

Policy Recommendations: United States policy toward this new state, both before and after its emergence into complete self-government, should be one of positive friendliness but not aggressive interference—of sympathetic helpfulness, but not sentimentality. The United States should endeavor to operate indirectly in Africa if at all possible, and should encourage the European countries—France, England, Belgium and Portugal—to move ahead rapidly towards granting self-government to the area, and to take the lead in providing financial assistance for the economic development of this African area.

While the United States should expect to share in the benefits of this economic development and should be prepared to contribute to its cost, American participation should only be secondary. We should expect and if necessary insist so far as practical that our European allies in NATO bear the bulk of the financial burden which will be involved. The United States should not refuse in advance to contribute our minor share to sound proposals of economic aid on an international basis; but we should regard any such proposals with a very realistic eye.

The basis of United States economic policy in this area should be to encourage American business firms who have the capital reserves, the technicians, and the know-how, to take part on a far-sighted but nevertheless business-like basis in the development and exploitation of the potentially rich natural resources of this African area.

A European Monroe Doctrine for Africa:

The Consul General believes that there might be very substantial psychological advantages as well as certain actual policy gains to be derived from the launching of a "European Monroe Doctrine for Africa".[6] The basis of this idea would be American recognition that Europe today should occupy the same position vis-à-vis the new emerging and independent states of Africa which the United States earlier occupied vis-à-vis the now independent countries of Latin America. The Monroe Doctrine it will be recalled, was not simply a unilateral declaration by the United States, though allowed to take that form; it was essentially a joint undertaking in which Britain and particularly the English fleet played a very major part.

---

[6] Holmes wrote Palmer on October 18 following his visit to Dakar, to praise the substance of despatch 77 except for the concept of a European Monroe Doctrine for Africa, which did not seem "very practicable." (Department of State, AF Files: Lot 64 D 358, Survey of U.S. Operations in Africa—Julius C. Holmes & Charles N. Manning 1957–58) Regarding the Holmes–Manning African trip, see footnote 1, Document 53.

Just as the basic point of the Monroe Doctrine was to prevent any European or Asiatic power not already established in Latin America from gaining a potentially dangerous foothold there, so our object in proposing and promoting a European Monroe Doctrine for Africa would be to prevent either Soviet or Asiatic Communism from gaining a dangerous or dominant position on the African continent.

Just as the United States thereby fostered and encouraged the achievement of independence and sovereignty by South American states in the last century, so Europe (under the aegis of NATO and the Common Market, etc.) would foster and encourage the emergence of independent states in Africa by undertaking to preserve the new states from domination and exploitation, directly or indirectly, by the Soviets.

Just as England in the case of the Monroe Doctrine made the success of this policy possible by agreeing to use its fleet to help us prevent any other power from intervening in Latin America, so the United States would play a similar role vis-à-vis Africa, and would stand behind Europe's promise of protection for the emerging African states.

Finally, just as the United States reaped certain indisputable economic advantages from its pre-eminent position vis-à-vis the Latin American countries, so the principal powers of Western Europe would be allowed to reap certain primary economic benefits from the responsibilities which they would undertake. But, just as Europe has shared freely and fully in trade and commerce with the Latin American countries, so the United States should expect and demand a fair share—although not a major share—in the development of international trade with the new and emerging African states.

Incorporation of these basic ideas (which in fact do not differ very radically from the Eisenhower Doctrine in the Middle East) into a "European Monroe Doctrine for Africa" would have the advantage of making it plain in dramatic and fairly easily understood form that the United States: (a) has no imperialist aims or ambitions in Africa, since it thereby excludes itself as well as Russia and Asia from future "colonization" of any kind in Africa; (b) it specifically acknowledges the natural pre-eminence *economically* of the Western European powers in the development of Africa; (c) it puts us on record as prepared to support—not the maintenance of the present colonial domination by the European countries—but the early emergence and continued independence and prosperity of the budding states of Black Africa, free from the fear of Soviet Communist imperialism.

W. Mallory Browne

47. Memorandum of a Conversation, Washington, October 23, 1957[1]

SUBJECT

Termination of Trusteeship for French Togo

PARTICIPANTS

M. Alphand, Ambassador of France
M. Lucet, Minister, French Embassy
M. de Laboulaye, Counselor, French Embassy
M. Leprette, First Secretary, French Embassy
M. Ajavon, President, Togolese Assembly
M. Apedo-Amah, Minister of Finance, French Togo
Mr. Ferguson, AFS
Mr. Ludlow, NEA
Mr. Gerig, ODA

Ambassador Alphand invited Messrs. Ferguson, Ludlow and Gerig to a small stag dinner last night to discuss informally and hear further detailed views of the two Togolese leaders regarding termination of trusteeship for French Togo.

The gist of the French and Togolese views, as explained by the Ambassador and by President Ajavon,[2] is as follows:

1. The French wish to have a resolution adopted by the present Assembly which would be based on a recognition by the Assembly that in accordance with Article 76(b) of the Charter, French Togo is in process of reaching one of the two objectives, namely, self-government, and therefore the GA should immediately provide for the termination of trusteeship.

2. The resolution which the French have in mind (which they said they have in draft and would make available to us shortly) would include the following essential points: (a) the Assembly to agree that the trusteeship should be terminated automatically when two or perhaps three conditions have been fulfilled. First, that France make a further transfer of powers to the Togolese Government which would include everything except foreign affairs, defense and currency (a French concession), and (b) that new elections on universal suffrage basis be held during 1958 to elect a new Legislative Assembly for Togo, and (c) that these elections might be observed by the UN at the invitation of the present Togolese Government (the last two are regarded as Togolese concessions because the present Legislative Assembly which was elected on a restricted suffrage basis in 1955 could still function for three more years).

[1] Source: Department of State, Central Files, 751T.00/10–2457. Confidential. Drafted by Gerig on October 24.

[2] Robert Ajavon was one of the leaders of the Parti Togolais du Progrès.

3. The Togolese leaders would explain to the GA that such a transfer of powers and such a newly elected Legislative Assembly would grant to French Togo full self-government. They would explain further that they do not wish to have independence at the present time, since they are not in a position to provide for their own defense nor to conduct their foreign affairs nor to operate their own currency system. By their own choice, therefore, they are requesting that these powers, for the time being, be exercised by the French Government, pending a possible later assumption of some or all of these powers. However, in their view, the Charter objective of self-government would be fulfilled and therefore the UNGA should not deprive them of the full exercise of their autonomy.

Ambassador Alphand went on to say that they hoped the US Delegation would appreciate the importance of these concessions by the French and the Togolese and would be able to support them and perhaps co-sponsor such a resolution. The Ambassador went on to emphasize that if greater steps toward independence were insisted upon by the GA, it would lead to chaos and would provide the minority opposition in Togo, led by Sylvanus Olympio and others, to open the way for extreme left and fellow-traveling if not communist elements to get control.

We said that we were not in a position to express any views for the Department since we did not yet have knowledge of the details of their plan and the draft resolution which they hope to have laid before the Assembly. We would, however, certainly give the most serious study to their proposal.

We pointed out, however, that such a plan which, in effect, would ask the Assembly to give a kind of blank check for a future development, would probably, in the light of our past experience, encounter a good deal of opposition. As they know, it was necessary to get a two-thirds vote, or 56 out of 82, which is extremely difficult at best. Moreover, if no provision is made in the resolution for some future assumption of independence before the trusteeship is terminated, there will likely be a number of delegations, particularly from the so-called Afro-Asian group, who would find the proposal inacceptable.

Ambassador Alphand said that they were fully aware of these difficulties, but believed that it was better to be defeated on a reasonable proposal than to pander to a number of prejudiced delegations who did not have the best interests of the Togolese people in view, nor the wider interests of West Africa.

The Ambassador was exceedingly disdainful of the large number of small countries who exercise, as he said, irresponsible views and voting powers in the GA. M. Ajavon added that if the Assembly does not accept this plan in its essentials, then the Government and people of Togo would be willing to disregard the trusteeship and might make it impossible for further reports to be made to the Trusteeship Council on matters which are wholly within the autonomous powers of Togo.

In the course of the discussion, the French and Togolese gentlemen pointed out that they could expect no support from Ghana, and therefore the UK would be somewhat embarrassed also to fully fall in behind the French and Togolese plan. Ghana, they said, has a long-range objective of assimilating French Togo as they assimilated British Togo last year. Ghana, therefore, will support a plan for immediate independence of French Togo in the hope that this would be the first step for breaking away from France and to become a part of a greater Ghana.

We asked the gentlemen whether they had been in contact with other African delegations, such as Liberia, Morocco, Tunisia, Sudan and Ethiopia. They said that they had had some preliminary conversations but nothing very decisive. We further asked if they had taken up their plan with Canada and Denmark, since those two countries had furnished members to the recent Special Commission which visited the Territory. They said they had not gone very far in this direction either, and had wished, first of all, to get US reaction, and if possible our support.

We said that we would, of course, discuss the matter urgently in the Department and would hope that our views would take shape in a relatively short time.

At the close of the discussion the Ambassador said France attached the highest importance to the question and he intended to take it up with the Secretary.[3]

[3] No record has been found to indicate that Alphand took this matter up with Dulles. On November 29, the General Assembly adopted Resolution 1182(XII) by a vote of 50 (France and the United States) to 1 (Ghana), with 29 abstentions. It provided for U.N. supervision of the prospective elections for the Legislative Assembly and requested the Trusteeship Council to report to the General Assembly at its next session so as to enable it, if so requested, to reach a decision concerning the termination of the Trusteeship Agreement.

UNITED STATES POLICY IN BRITISH EAST AFRICA[1]

48. Instruction From the Department of State to the Consulate General at Nairobi[2]

CA–7584 *Washington, May 4, 1955.*

SUBJECT

Your despatch 242 of December 7, 1954,[3] recommending a strong five-point U.S. policy for East Africa

The Department wishes to commend you and Consul Barrow on the preparation of despatch no. 242 in which you have given a penetrating analysis of conditions in East Africa, and on the basis of which you have recommended a 5-point program for a U.S. policy in this area.

The Department shares your view that from a long range point of view it is important that the African population of this area come into close association with American ideas and principles, particularly in light of the gradual achievement by the African of more and more political power. In this connection, however, the Department wonders if you may not have oversimplified the problem for all of East Africa by stating that "no delicate diplomacy is necessary in order for us to work here. The limits on the amount we can accomplish are to a large extent defined by what we ourselves *want* to accomplish." Admittedly the rapport between Britain and the U.S. is such as to constitute a fertile groundwork for implementing some or perhaps even all of the ideas you have recommended for a strong U.S. policy in East Africa; nevertheless, it appears by no means certain to the Department that what looks like an "open" terrain might not become sensibly restricted if too intensive or too rapid a dissemination of U.S. ideas is attempted. For example, it appears that the British are somewhat sensitive on the subject of the degree and

[1] For previous documentation on this subject, see *Foreign Relations,* 1952–1954, vol. XI, Part 1, pp. 346 ff.

[2] Source: Department of State, Central Files, 611.45P/5–455. Secret. Repeated to Dar es Salaam, London, USOM/London, and Salisbury.

[3] *Foreign Relations,* 1952–1954, vol. XI, Part 1, p. 375.

scope of USIS activity in Tanganyika, and the degree of association between the African population and representatives of foreign governments, whatever their nationality. Are you completely satisfied that this sensitivity does not obtain to any appreciable extent in Uganda?

With respect to the geographic concept of "East Africa", the Department feels it best to refrain from any tendency to treat East Africa as a single political entity because of its more direct responsibility for the future of the Trust Territory of Tanganyika as a Member of the Trusteeship Council, and also because of the opposition to political unity or federation which has manifested itself among nationalist forces in the territories themselves. Moreover, it is not at all clear that the four British East African Territories will all develop at the same pace.

Without qualifying to any degree the U.S.'s strong support of the principles set forth in Chapters XI and XII of the UN Charter, [4] experience demonstrates increasingly that it is unwise to indulge in generalizations as to either the future of the territories themselves or the future policies which the U.S. may be called upon to adopt with respect to each of them. The tempo of developments in each of the territories is in many respects different from that of the others. In time to come, for example, it is quite possible that world opinion expressed through the General Assembly and the Trusteeship Council, combined with the inevitable growth of the new national movement in Tanganyika, may oblige the British to allow much more rapid progress toward self-government there than they may deem advisable in Kenya or Uganda. For this reason the U.S. should retain a certain flexibility with respect to its future courses of action in East Africa.

The Department has considered the specific points you recommend for implementing a U.S. policy in East Africa and has the following observations to make regarding them:

1. Assignment of Consular Representatives in the Territories:

As you have surmised, for budgetary reasons the establishment of a Consulate at Uganda does not appear feasible during the next fiscal year. The Department is hopeful of being able to increase your staff by one officer in order that more frequent trips may be made by members of your staff to Uganda, Zanzibar, the Seychelles, and Mauritius, but budget appropriations alone will determine whether or not this is possible during the 1955-1956 fiscal year.

---

[4] Chapter XI concerned the Declaration Regarding Non-Self-Governing Territories and Chapter XII dealt with the International Trusteeship System.

2. The USIS Program:

The appreciable strengthening of the USIS program throughout the territories, according to USIA, cannot be undertaken in the immediate future because necessary funds are lacking. USIA hopes, however, that this situation will have improved within the next year. It is their thought that USIS might at this time have closer and more effective association with the African population in Uganda than in Kenya, and to that end would welcome the views of the Public Affairs Officer and the Consul General on the establishment of a sub-post at Kampala. The Department is disposed to press for the step-up in USIS activity in particular areas as local situations permit, rather than, for example, to press for an expansion of USIS activities at Dar-Es-Salaam, which might well meet with British resistance.

3. Educational Exchange with Institutions:

The prospectus of the International Educational Exchange Service for 1956, which will shortly be forwarded for your suggestions, contemplates the allocation, subject to congressional appropriations, of $20,844 to Kenya, with 3 leader grants and 3 students, as compared to $2800 and 1 student for 1955. IES is now trying to obtain funds to support 1 or 2 additional student grants in FY 1955, in view of the excellence of the panel of candidates presented by Nairobi. For all the African Trust Territories, including Tanganyika, IES is trying to obtain further funds for 1955, again because of the excellent performance in presenting the panel of candidates.

FOA's grant of approximately $800,000 to aid in building and equipping the new Royal Technical College is indicative of U.S. interest in increasing educational opportunities in Africa. Rutgers University of New Jersey will provide technical assistance to the new college in its early stages under an FOA sponsored contract. At the same time the Department is trying to increase the funds available for leader grants and exchange fellowships for this area. These are the principal fields for educational exchange, in which progress to date appears to have been reasonably satisfactory.

4. FOA Activity:

Following State–FOA talks in Washington with Minister Vasey,[5] FOA has concentrated its DOT reserves on developing and financing projects for Kenya, which have culminated in the recent

[5] Documentation on these talks and subsequent conversations in Kenya with Minister for Finance and Development Ernest A. Vasey is in Department of State, Central File 745R.5–MSP.

mission to Nairobi. As you are aware, the Department is most interested in lending its support to FOA programs that have a "visible" effect, as you put it, in reaching both African leaders as well as the general population.

5. Efforts by Private American Organizations:

The Department has conferred with Mr. French of CARE,[6] who was not particularly sanguine about CARE operations in East Africa at this time. He explained his views by saying that a substantial segment of negro feeling in the U.S. was against such activities "because they would constitute an endorsement of colonialism." Mr. French said, however, that a decision on the matter would have to await Mr. Joy's[7] return from Africa to New York. The Department will, of course, use its good offices to expedite such endeavors as the CARE program for East Africa. It is also supporting other FOA sponsored or encouraged projects involving U.S. private initiative.

In sum the Department agrees with you that the U.S. has a very real, long range political interest in East Africa, to wit: to ensure that the East Africans become and remain fully conscious of the position, the role, and the beliefs of the U.S. in the world today. The Department is convinced that a conscious and consistent effort must be made to ensure that East Africa does not come of age without having learned what the U.S. and the American people stand for, and that this effort must be so undertaken as to assure that these people will come to share the democratic concepts of the Western World. This is a long term interest that may have military (strategic) implications, as well as politico-cultural significance. From both a short and long term view the Department agrees that we must be sufficiently active in East Africa to offset any present or future insidious efforts of other countries who may be striving for objectives inimical to our own.

In giving expression to U.S. policy in East Africa the Department would like to mention a few caveats, which may have already come to your mind:

1. The U.S. must not undertake visible FOA or USIS programs with such eclat as to create the impression in East African minds that the political future of this area will be determined principally by the United States, not Britain. U.S. interest in this part of the continent is to work through and with British authority: While the United States does not intend to play down in any way the promotions of U.S. objectives or the presentation of American points of view, neither does it have any desire or intention of supplement-

[6] Paul Comly French.

[7] Charles Rhind Joy was an executive consultant for African affairs for CARE.

ing Britain by becoming, or appearing to become, an invisible or "shadow" government. To give the appearance of doing this might well result in the negation of U.S. efforts through creating embarrassment and misunderstanding with the British. It must therefore be borne in mind by all U.S. officials in East Africa that U.S. activity in this area must be carried out with tactfulness and care at all times. When any situation presents itself that reflects palpable British opposition or non-cooperation, the Department should be consulted.

The Department considers that, as concerns FOA activity, caution and prudence will be particularly necessary on the part of U.S. officials in Kenya, where the British are preoccupied with the Mau Mau problem. Our *immediate* objective as far as Mau Mau is concerned is to see that the British eliminate the causes of this malady, that they get at and treat the roots of this illness.

As a matter of fact the Department believes that in both East and Central Africa it is more than ever essential that all U.S. Government representatives be men and women of such vision and appreciation of human relationships that they comprehend the mental and spiritual processes of a people only now awakening to political consciousness. The "evolving" African is sensitive on many scores when he compares his intellectual accomplishments with those of the European. His ego and pride may be easily wounded by any untoward "display" of attainments on the part of representatives of the American people. A friend thus lost may prove an irrevocable loss. It is therefore incumbent upon U.S. representatives in Africa to lay stress on the diplomatic aspect of their activities.

The Department will communicate with your office periodically with respect to further implementation of the points recommended in your despatch.

Dulles

49. Despatch From the Consulate General at Nairobi to the Department of State[1]

No. 73 *Nairobi, September 15, 1955.*

REF

Icato A–41 July 29 to London repeated Nairobi A–Unn[2]

SUBJECT

Use of Term "Functioning Multi-racial Society" as ICA Objective in East Africa

The Consulate General would like to insert a word of caution as regards the first sentence last paragraph of the referenced ICA communication, to wit: "ICA/W believes that in view of the Congressional language quoted above[3] the USOM should direct its attention particularly to such areas of technical assistance as will support the development of West Africa towards independence, and Central and East Africa towards a functioning multi-racial society."

Whereas privately we may hope that our technical assistance programs will support the development of a "functioning multi-racial society" in East Africa, there is a danger in being too specific, especially in any public documents. The word "multi-racial" has unfortunately acquired many political connotations, making it a red flag to some groups, notably the Africans of Uganda and certain elements of the white settlers of Kenya. Though ICA/W is not referring to any specific form of government, the association of the term with the Lyttelton "multi-racial experiment" in Kenya,[4] which has both ardent supporters and bitter opponents, is very close.

A great ideological argument exists in these territories as to whether promoting "multi-racialism" or promoting the "predominant interest of the indigenous peoples" or maintaining "the British way

[1] Source: Department of State, Central Files, 845P.00–TA/9–1455. Secret.

[2] Not printed. (*Ibid.,* AID Files: Lot 57 A 248, ICATO London 7/1/55–9/30/55)

[3] The final language of the Congressional authorization reads: "It is the sense of the Congress that assistance under this Act shall be administered so as to assist other peoples in their efforts to achieve self-government or independence under circumstances which will enable them to assume an equal station among the free nations of the world, and to fulfill their responsibilities for self-government or independence." The House Committee on Foreign Affairs had earlier noted that some African territories were "in the process of developing new political and social institutions" whereas others were "in the process of developing multi-racial societies as an initial step towards increased self-government." The United States required, the Committee commented, "a high degree of political stability in Africa". (P.L. 138; 69 Stat. 283)

[4] Oliver Lyttleton was the British Colonial Secretary who devised a constitution for Kenya in 1954 calling for a multiracial Council of Ministers. Of the six unofficial ministers, three Europeans and two Asians were to be elected, while the sole African was to be nominated.

of life" (i.e. European supremacy) should be the prevailing objective of government. It would, in our view, be unwise for the United States Government to involve itself in that ideological conflict. Our real objective is to promote U.S. interests in the area regardless of which ideology prevails. Moreover, our attitude—and the British attitude as well—might vary from area to area, e.g. "multi-racialism" might be good for Kenya but bad for Uganda.

The Consulate General believes it would be preferable for ICA to leave itself somewhat more flexible in its objectives here. The proposition might be stated thusly: "ICA believes it should support the economic and social advance of all residents of East Africa as a complement to the political progress of the territories and as a factor in their political stability."

Edmund J. Dorsz

---

50. Despatch From the Consulate General at Nairobi to the Department of State [1]

No. 246 *Nairobi, December 30, 1955.*

REF

Despatch 242, December 7, 1954; [2] Department's CA–7584, May 5 [*4*], 1955; [3] Despatch 395, February 28, 1955 [4]

[Here follows discussion of African nationalism, African potential for self-government, East African unity, the respective positions of the Asians and the Europeans, racial segregation, and the Report of the Royal Commission on Land and Population 1953–1955 (*Cmd.* 9475).]

U.S. Policy

Against the picture we have drawn of the trends of the past year, we believe the reasons we set forth for our six-point program in despatch 242 have been fortified. We continue to believe the six points to be sound in theory—and what is equally important—capable of implementation in practice. We also believe the six points

[1] Source: Department of State, Central Files, 745P.00/12–3055. Confidential.
[2] See footnote 3, Document 48.
[3] Document 48.
[4] Not printed. (Department of State, Central Files, 120.303/2–2855)

are important not only for what they include, but also for what they omit.

The Department will recall that we specifically excluded from our program any involvement in the controversial political issues of this area, and in our despatch no. 1 of July 5, 1955 [5] we have elaborated extensively on that theme. The Consulate General itself has scrupulously avoided any action smacking of taking sides on local issues. Our position has been that we are friendly to European, Asian and African alike, but we are not committing ourselves to any of their political views or policies. To do so at this time would be entirely unwise in view of the extreme fluidity of the local political situation.

Unfortunately, certain speeches, statements and congressional resolutions from the United States have given the impression to many local people that we do take sides—that we stand categorically against colonialism and for self-government without much regard to the local capacity for self-government which, as we have pointed out above, is very limited. While fully recognizing that situations in other parts of the world, in the U.N. and on the U.S. domestic scene sometimes require that our representatives take a definite position with regard to colonialism, we have nevertheless felt constrained at various times during the year to take note of adverse local reaction and to plead for a better balance in such speeches and statements as are to be disseminated to this part of the world. Otherwise we fear a) that our basis of cooperation with local authorities will be prejudiced and b) that in being unable to suit our actions to our words we will produce disillusion among the Africans.

We therefore look upon the six points not only as a minimum program, but also as something of a maximum from the standpoint that it would be undesirable at the present stage for the U.S. to commit itself politically in this area. We therefore would like now to review those six points in terms of progress achieved, for we fully realize that the fullest possible implementation of this minimum (and maximum) program should be the focal point of our endeavors during the coming year.

1) *Strengthening U.S. Representation*

The situation in Uganda so obviously demands stronger U.S. representation there that we cannot overemphasize the importance of establishing some kind of a U.S. office in Kampala. We continue to believe a full-fledged consular and USIS office is desirable, but if funds are insufficient, a limited purpose post would give us at least some representation and liaison. We no longer feel that a "roving officer", stationed in Nairobi and making periodic visits to Uganda,

[5] Not printed. (*Ibid.,* 511.00/7–555)

would adequately meet the situation. However, even this would be better than nothing.

We note that the Department has included a consular office for Kampala in its over-the-ceiling budget estimates for FY 1957. In view of the factors noted above, we would strongly urge that, if possible, the Department attempt to get the Bureau of the Budget's concurrence to putting the request in the under-the-ceiling estimates.

We would prefer that a consular post be opened concurrently with a USIS office (also requested for FY 1957) as otherwise it will be difficult to maintain effective supervision and policy control from the distant point of Nairobi. If a full-fledged Consulate is established, we would have no objection to assigning an American Negro to USIS work as USIA has recently proposed. Otherwise, because of the political and social complexities of the situation in Uganda, we would have serious reservations about the practicability of such an assignment, and would want an opportunity of expressing further views if USIA should indicate a definite intention of assigning an American Negro to Uganda.

Generally increasing responsibilities, especially in connection with the technical assistance program, necessitates bolstering the administrative staff of the Nairobi Consulate General in order to free its substantive officers for more representational work, particularly in areas outside Nairobi. Adequate representation also means adequate funds for travel in the large area under our jurisdiction. We are presently so short of operating funds that we have to dip into travel funds for other administrative purposes.

We understand that ICA has established 2 U.S. national administrative posts at Nairobi. When these are filled, Nairobi's substantive personnel should be better able to devote their primary attention to the work for which they were assigned here rather than dissipating much of it in administration.

2) *Strengthening the Information Program*

From what we have said about the upsurge in African nationalism, it is imperative that our information program be shifted gradually to more emphasis on the African. This in turn may necessitate a partial shift from a limited leader-appeal program to a mass-appeal program. Such shifts should naturally occur gradually and must be carefully designed so as not to arouse concern on the part of local authorities. The USIS has been considerably strengthened recently by the assignment of a Cultural Affairs Officer to serve as deputy to the CPAO. But in order properly to design an effective African program, one or more top-notch African local employees are necessary. The CPAO continues to search for such persons, and finding them would be the first step in the shift of emphasis we recommend. Mobile units to carry films and other visual materials to outlying African areas would be another step.

The Department and USIA will of course be aware that the shift of emphasis recommended above will inevitably result in higher costs of operation, particularly since a large proportion of the materials for an African program would have to be produced locally. We believe, however, that in view of the political trends noted above this problem should be faced squarely and decided in accordance with our interests in the area.

3) *Strengthening the Exchange of Persons Program*

This year we have been able to send 8 student grantees and 1 leader grantee to the United States, whereas 3 American teachers have come to East Africa under the Fulbright program.[6] Whereas this is a good record in relation to past achievement, it obviously only scratches the surface of the potentialities.

From the standpoint of long-range benefit—and most of our objectives here are long-range—there is an obvious advantage to student grants. The problem in this regard is that for the next few years, the newly-opened Royal Technical College of East Africa is likely to skim off the cream of the available candidates. We thus believe it might be difficult to increase the level of our present student program even if funds therefor should be available. We believe, however, that when we do find outstanding candidates we should consider supporting them until they complete their academic programs rather than confine our grants to one year only. We suggest this on the theory that one good man fully trained and steeped in U.S. culture may ultimately prove more valuable to us than several half-trained individuals. After Royal Technical College begins turning out graduates we should find a larger number of outstanding candidates for higher training in specialized engineering and arts curricula for our program in future years. We also believe that Makerere College may be induced to modify somewhat its present preference for sending all of its best graduates to U.K. schools.

From a short-range standpoint, leader-grant candidates are easier to select and, as they are already highly-placed, bring back a more immediate benefit to us. The main difficulty is to insure that the candidates nominated by the present administration will have a lasting capacity for leadership.

As our policy is to encourage the use of the indigenous schools as much as possible, we are very much in favor of American teachers coming to East Africa. In addition to those presently placed in semi-professional training centers, we would very much like to

[6] 60 Stat. 754.

see Americans placed in professioral positions at both Makerere and the Royal Technical College where they could exert a very beneficial influence at the top level and help us develop a better student-exchange program.

4) *ICA Activities*

We were gratified with the results of the work of ICA missions in October 1954 and April–May 1955 which were successful in negotiating 11 projects in Kenya and 3 projects in Uganda plus a project to establish an American wing and provide other assistance to the Royal Technical College operating under the auspices of the East African High Commission. In Kenya, particularly, the reaction has been warm and enthusiastic among virtually all articulate elements of the population. We continue to believe that projects which emphasize the quality (rather than quantity) of U.S. principles and technique will be useful foci of U.S. influence in this part of the world.

We are not unmindful, however, that certain risks are involved and certain difficulties must be overcome if the program is to have the impact for which we hope. Indispensable to success is a) to provide American personnel of the highest caliber, and b) to implement the program gradually but expeditiously. In the latter connection, a difficulty that looms very large is the necessity to work through a triangular East Africa-London-Washington channel, with a considerable number of complications being inevitably introduced by the varying points of view from these three vantage points. The apparent desire of the Colonial Office not only to settle broad questions of policy, but also, from its remote location, to keep its finger on administrative details introduces a factor not commonly found in our technical assistance programs elsewhere, but which will apparently have to be "lived with" for the time being. We must therefore expect that there will be rough spots to get over before the program starts rolling.

Judging from many expressions of interest we continue to receive locally, we believe that Colonial Office reticence about future expansion of the program (Toica A–177) [7] has not yet percolated to the territorial governments, at least to Kenya. Nevertheless we would agree that the important consideration for us at the moment is to get moving on the projects already established, rather than concerning ourselves with possible new projects. We believe a "testing period" is highly advisable to see how the projects will work under the triangular system of administration mentioned above; it may be that substantial changes in present concepts will be necessary if the program is to work at all.

---

[7] Not printed.

5) *Private American Activities*

Our efforts to stimulate private American activities in this area have been somewhat disappointing. A representative of CARE spent several weeks in the area and talked with local officials in terms of a substantial aid program designed to relieve malnutrition and stimulate community development and public health. His recommendations were unfortunately rejected by his principals in the United States. A representative of the Church World Services discussed a very similar program with the same local officials. Whereas the present status of his recommendations is not known, the prospects for fulfillment do not appear favorable. Naturally these setbacks have not enhanced American prestige.

More recently, a representative of UNICEF [8] has discussed a similar program and is similarly making favorable recommendations to his principals. It is hoped that this time action will be forthcoming. Although administered by a U.N. agency, much of the impact of a UNICEF program may well be American as a result of using American materials and possibly personnel. We would therefore encourage the Department to examine the program carefully with a view to lending it strong support (despatches 183 [9] and 201 [10]).

On the brighter side, we should not fail to mention the helpful grants of the Carnegie Corporation for various research projects. Also a brief lecture seminar by three American virus specialists under the sponsorship of WHO contributed substantially to American prestige, particularly since their arrival coincided with a period of heavy publicity as regards vaccines against polio-myelitis. Their expert, on-the-spot comments were received with great eagerness by the local public.

6) *Area Specialization*

We were gratified to see during the year that the Department has established a small program designed to develop a corps of African specialists, which formed the sixth point of our program and upon which we elaborated at length in our despatch 395.

We were somewhat fearful at first that there would be insufficient, suitable candidates to establish a good program. However, since announcement of the program, two of our American staff at Nairobi—both well suited—have stated their tentative intention to apply, and we hope response has been equally good from other African posts. We believe every consideration should be given to good candidates who apply, even if it should cause considerable

[8] Charles A. Egger.

[9] Despatch 183, November 16, concerned "Voluntary Agency Assistance to Needy in Kenya." (Department of State, Central Files, 845R.49/11–1655)

[10] Despatch 201, November 29, dealt with the "Proposed UNICEF Aid Program to Kenya." (*Ibid.*, 845R.55/11–2955)

administrative inconvenience to the Department or to field posts. All too often developing the long-range utility of our employees has had to be neglected for the sake of short-term administrative expediency.

Conclusion

In preparing this despatch, the reporting officer has drawn heavily on the thoughts of all substantive officers of the Consulate General and USIS staffs, as well as Consul McKinnon at Dar es Salaam, to whom the draft was submitted for comment prior to completion in final form. In concluding, we wish to express our gratitude to the Department for the careful consideration and helpful comments made on our despatch 242 of last year, and also for the action the Department has taken to help implement some of our recommendations.

We hope that his report will merit equal consideration, and that it will be of assistance to the Department in the efforts it is making to obtain Executive and Congressional approval of some of the projects under discussion in this despatch.

Such comment as the Department may be disposed to share with us on the ideas embodied in this despatch will be appreciated.

Edmund J. Dorsz

---

51. Despatch From the Consulate at Dar es Salaam to the Department of State [1]

No. 117 *Dar es Salaam, March 12, 1957.*

SUBJECT

Achievement of Self-Government or Independence for Tanganyika

This despatch has been prepared to present as detailed a picture of the general scene in Tanganyika as possible so that the Department may have such facts as will be of assistance in dealing with the trusteeship affairs of Tanganyika in the United Nations.

It is the firm conviction of the reporting officer that Africa, including Tanganyika, is the "keystone" of the future of West versus East and that as such is an essential asset which will enable

[1] Source; Department of State, Central Files, 778.00/3–1257. Confidential. Passed to London.

the West to retain the balance of power in the ceaseless struggle between the free nations and communism.

Africa needs the West as much as the West needs Africa. Much has been written on the morality of the subject by the academicians so that little need be said in proof of this point. However, it is imperative that we realize that the ever increasing economic growth of the West and its increasing consumption of raw materials and the decreasing availability of these from present sources must force the West, and particularly the United States, to look to Africa as one of the few remaining undeveloped areas in which we can acquire the mineral resources to support our ever growing consumption to support our expanding economy. Africa must at all costs remain with the Western bloc!

Under no condition should any territory of Africa, and we shall now exclusively consider Tanganyika, be granted self-government until she is capable of entering the world of nations as a strong unit of the total and capable of contributing to the general welfare. To approach self-government without this prerequisite would eventually prove suicidal to the West. Such a catastrophe would permit a vacuum into which the influence of Asia and Russia would quickly flow. The arms build up by the Russians in Egypt is fair proof of this.

This concept, naturally, will prove offensive to the African nationalists of Tanganyika as elsewhere. The reaction to such a concept would undoubtedly be that the Africans would prefer to govern themselves poorly than be governed by non-Africans. This attitude is not only naive but dangerous.

To permit self-government before the achievement of political responsibility and the establishment of a sound economy would, in itself, be contrary to the objectives of the Trusteeship System. Such action would in all probability require that sooner or later the United States and other free nations of the world would be forced to take an active part in the internal affairs of the territory. In addition to offering a propaganda "bonus" to the communists, such action would prove more objectionable to the nationalists in the long run than should the paternalistic guidance to self-government of the Trusteeship arrangement be extended until such time as the progress and the abilities of its peoples would warrant the realization of the objective. Premature self-government would undoubtedly involve the Free World in additional police action at a later date as well as a far greater expenditure of funds to place the local government on a sound footing, capable of carrying its weight in the Western bloc. Much has been said about Colonialism. Great Britain has publicly announced its policy of helping its territories in Africa towards independence and the record in Asia is certainly an indication of their sincerity. The United States' attitude is well known. The major lack of agreement between the two countries appears to be the speed with which independence of Tanganyika will be achieved and a time-table for its fulfillment.

Russia has suggested two to three years and Julius Nyerere, President of the Tanganyika African National Union (TANU), [2] has said that ten to twelve years are required for the achievement of self-government. The first is ridiculous and the second naive and based on wishful thinking. It would appear that neither estimate would indicate a studied analyzation of an extremely difficult and involved problem.

That self-government will come to Tanganyika is a foregone conclusion. That the Africans of a country of roughly 8,000,000 Africans and 119,000 other mixed races would have a major part in its ultimate governing is also quite evident but it is an issue which is continuously raised and beclouded for reasons of political expediency.

The question then arises as to why ten to twelve years is a naive "estimate" for self-government? To answer this we must go back a few years in history.

Tanganyika came under the Mandate System by the terms of the peace treaty with Germany after the 1914–18 war. This was roughly 40 years ago. This meant that a complete change of administration, institutions and languages was required for the transition from German to British administration. This would be difficult enough for an advanced civilization but for an underdeveloped and backwards territory the problems were almost insurmountable. Naturally such a transition caused a "slow down" in the progress of the territory. When the problem was satisfactorily solved a greater one arose which was bantered about in the higher planes of world politics. Serious and continuing consideration was given to whether the territory would revert to its former status under German rule. Under these conditions investment, progress and social development naturally slowed to a virtual standstill. The world recession of the early '30s did little to improve this picture.

During the years of World War II, the life and death struggle of the world forced the administering power to guard her front door and pay little attention to Tanganyika. No other course was possible. It was therefore not until the establishment of the Trusteeship

---

[2] Nyerere became president of the Tanganyikan African Association (TAA) in 1953 following his return from Edinburgh University. Then on July 7, 1954, Nyerere founded TANU and became its president. He carried the case of Tanganyikan nationalists to the United Nations in 1955, 1956, and 1957, arguing in behalf of democratic elections, African paramountcy, and constitutional development toward independence.

System under the Charter of the United Nations that the political, economic, and social development of Tanganyika became a living, active and progressive force. This history is reasonable and it is not believed that any other nation, under the same conditions, would have done differently than the administering power.

We must now consider those essentials which are necessary for the establishment of self-government. *First*, there must be those who are capable of taking the responsibility of operating government and its supporting agencies as well as those who are able to manage and control the commerce and industries which are essential to maintain and build the economy of any country. Next there are the multitude of professionals such as doctors, lawyers, teachers, engineers and many others who are an essential in the day to day activity of any community.

Tanganyika does not have such Africans today, will not have them in three years and it is practically certain they will not have them in twelve years.

Appendix I is the official estimate of Africans with professional qualifications.[3] It covers those presently qualified and those who are expected to qualify by 1961. It has not been carried through 1969 which is the twelve year period quoted by Nyerere for self-government. Figures beyond 1961 would be pure fantasy.

Biographic data on certain of the African labor and political leaders of Tanganyika, who are among the most advanced and could be expected to take a part in government, is appended. Unfortunately, time does not permit data on all such persons. It will be forwarded at a later date but one thing is obvious—they are all of practically the same character and type. An examination of those submitted will evidence the fact that the majority are poorly educated and have developed little beyond the stage of childish animosities and personal jealousies. It is obvious that, although they are taking part in the development of unionism and political growth in Tanganyika, they are simply not capable or qualified to take part in the highly complex business of governing a country.

Much has been said by Nyerere and other critics of government regarding the lack of sufficient and adequate schooling. It is agreed that education is a basic essential upon which is built the future of the territory—both political and economic. It is also agreed that we can not consider an academic degree or standing as the criteria of ability. However, it certainly is an indication of the existing abilities of a people to take part in the governing of their country as well as the multitude of activities which go to make up the commercial and economic life of the territory.

---

[3] None of the Appendices is attached.

The question is then asked as to what government has done to develop educational facilities for the African and if it has been lacking as stated by the critics. This is best answered by referring to Section 19 of Appendix II—government's reply to Nyerere's speeches at the IV Committee of the United Nations General Assembly.[4] It might be here stated that the one great factor which is delaying the progress of Tanganyika is capital.

Secondly, the territory must have a healthy economy which will support its primary services such as education, communications, social services, medical facilities, etc., as well as its political development. Today, expansion and growth is extremely slow, geared to a slowly changing subsistence economy. Unless there is rapid and considerable investment from outside, as it appears that Great Britain is not in a position to supply it, it would appear that there will be little change in the foreseeable future. The budget is balanced but if capital does not develop, Tanganyika shall continue in its snail-like economic progress, and we can expect bigger and better strikes, riots, and all the dangers which accompany such a course. "Nationalism" has been awakened and it will not be stemmed or turned from a natural course. If the people do not achieve their natural aspirations supported by a growing and healthy economy, we shall find another festering sore which will be most susceptible to the salve of communism.

Comment:

At the earliest date Tanganyika must achieve self-government as envisaged by the United Nations and member states. It must, however, be a *responsible* self-government. This can be achieved only when her peoples and leaders develop to the stage where they are effectively able to take over the reins of government, commerce and industry. (Naturally with the assistance and guidance of the nations of the West.) The agitation of one nationalist in the IV Committee of the Trusteeship Council does not prove this to be so, regardless of how able the individual might be.

The existing economy of the territory will not support a larger educational development which is essential to supply the leaders.

[4] Nyerere addressed the Fourth Committee of the General Assembly on December 20, 1956. Education was only one of many subjects he raised. (See U.N. doc. A/C.4/SR.579, p. 150) A draft resolution introduced by Haiti (later revised) specifically noted the views of the TANU president. The British position was stated on February 16, 1957. (See U.N. doc. A/C.4/SR.639, pp. 441, 445–446) Despite British and U.S. opposition, the Fourth Committee on February 18, and then the General Assembly on February 26, drew the attention of the Trusteeship Council and the Administering Authority to Nyerere's views. (General Assembly Resolution 1065(XI), February 26, 1957)

The funds simply are not available in Tanganyika and it does not appear that the administering authority will be able to rectify the situation. The British financial position is well known to all. Considering the importance of Tanganyika in the future of Africa and its place in the world, it would appear that the member nations of United Nations have a joint responsibility beyond criticism and that is to assist in the achievement of self-government. Education must be stepped up. Cannot funds be found among the member nations to support this objective? Such action would only be a stake in the future peace of the world.

The economic development of the territory is the other major item which is thwarting a more speedy progress. Tanganyika must have a healthy and expanding economy to support her social progress.

Surveys and prospecting are progressing but until the actual communications, industries and mines are established the economy is not going to progress very far. In a territory which is considered by geologists to potentially be one of the most promising territories of Africa this lack of development is preposterous. It would appear that if proper incentives and subsidies were made they would in short order pay for themselves in addition to achieving a speed-up of the economic development. It would further appear that the administering authority would contribute to such a plan but the actual capital would have to come from outside.

The reward for such a policy would be the assurance and speed-up of the orderly development of a new nation which would join the world of nations as a responsible partner. To vacillate and continue as at present will, at a minimum, mean that Tanganyika will become an increasing problem to the United Nations and a potential or probable victory for the communists.

Robert L. Ware, Jr.

52. Despatch From the Consulate General at Nairobi to the Department of State [1]

No. 347 *Nairobi, May 27, 1957.*

REF

Confidential Letter from Asst. Secretary Rountree dated 4/10/57 [2] (received at Nairobi on 4/27/57); Nairobi's Despatch No. 344 of May 27, 1957 [3]

SUBJECT

Dominant Politico-Socio-Economic Factors Justifying Expansion of American Representation in British East Africa

On April 16, 1956 Nairobi transmitted to Assistant Secretary Allen an unclassified memorandum referring to other communications which gave information relating to politico-socio-economic developments likely to occur in this area. This unclassified communication was followed by a secret memorandum dated April 25, 1956 which was also sent to Assistant Secretary Allen under the latter date. [4] This despatch is designed to bring up to date the information previously submitted. It incorporates the concurrence and suggestions of the senior officers of the Consulate General and USIS/Nairobi and includes contributions from the Principal Officers at Dar es Salaam and Kampala as well as their concurrence.

Internal Pressures

As mentioned in earlier communications we expressed the view that constitutional developments would occur reasonably fast in the wide area of six countries and over 20,000,000 people coming under our consular jurisdiction. Like our earlier forecasts those we made last year were again on the conservative side.

The future of Kenya's multi-racial, Lyttleton Plan Government is problematical. The eight African elected members of Kenya's Legislative Council have refused to accept Ministerial posts in the

---

[1] Source: Department of State, Central Files, 745R.00/5–2757. Secret. Passed to London, USOM/London, and Mogadiscio.

[2] Not found in Department of State files. It conveyed a call for budget estimates. CA–7906, March 28, notified all NEA Fiscal Reporting Posts that they would soon receive a classified communication relative to the submission of Fiscal Year 1958 financial plans and Fiscal Year 1959 budget estimates. (*Ibid.*, 120.4/3–2857)

[3] Despatch 344 provided information concerning salaries and expense appropriations and country budget estimates for Fiscal Year 1958 and budget estimates for Fiscal Year 1959. (*Ibid.*, 122.6424/5–2757)

[4] Not found in Department of State files.

Government.[5] They contend that the Lyttleton Plan of multi-racial Government is no longer valid and demand an increase in African elected membership from eight to twenty-three. The Kenya Government strongly resists the African demands, contends that their demands are irresponsible and has just put into effect severely restrictive measures on the holding of political meetings by Africans. Further, the Government states that it will not consider suggestions by any one community for constitutional changes before 1960. All communities must mutually agree on constitutional changes before the Government is proposed to consider them. We cannot see the European community backing down from its present preferred position of controlling and guiding the country along lines favorable to the European. In this highly-charged atmosphere, we must anticipate mounting tensions between the contending forces.

In Uganda, the new Governor last February met with outcries from the public of "get out Crawford", "we don't need British rule" and similar slogans. Such demands stem chiefly from the people of Baganda numbering about one-fourth of Uganda's total African population of 6,000,000. The most literate, best-educated, and wealthiest Africans in Uganda, the Baganda seek self-government not only for themselves but a form of self-government which would put the other Africans in Uganda under Baganda hegemony. Leaders of the other African tribal groups recognize this danger and have expressed an unwillingness to see the British leave until all of the African tribal groupings mutually agree to constitutional changes with adequate safeguards for the less advanced tribes. Despite the continuing Baganda agitation for independence and "Self-Government Now" the Uganda government under instructions and guidance from London resolutely refuses to discuss with the Baganda before 1961 any constitutional changes. Negotiations over terms for 1957 elections in Buganda are currently deadlocked over the question of qualifications for suffrage. The Central Government has been unsuccessful in recent efforts to convince the political leaders of the Toro Kingdom that this is not the time for expansion of home rule and establishment of a district or provincial parliament and government along lines already existing in Buganda. Toro demands have grown stronger and more bitter with passage of time. These developments are illustrative of political ferment in Uganda which is destined to increase at a rapid rate and offer serious challenge to British authorities. Penetrating analysis of these cross-currents will be essential to development of a sound US policy for the future in this area where African aspirations and political power may threaten to get danger-

[5] The eight Africans were elected in March 1957 by an electorate which met education, loyalty, and property qualifications.

ously ahead of African capacity to assume management of their own affairs.

Tanganyika, where US capital is urgently desired, is moving forward politically. It has recently announced its intention to form a ministerial type of government next July which will include in government six locally appointed assistant ministers. To get the appointments, such assistant ministers must obviously be strong supporters of continued British rule in Tanganyika. The Tanganyika African National Union is not likely to take this supinely and can be expected to continue agitating for African *elected* as contrasted to *appointed* representation in government.

On May 28, by action of the Legislative Council all constituencies will adopt a "qualitative franchise", providing that each voter will vote in the next elections for candidates of all three racial groups in a given constituency. Although this is a controversial step it is indicative of an evolutionary trend and of an intent to bring the non-European forward. Agitation along this line, encouraged by United Nations discussions will continue to grow, requiring increased vigilance and effort in reporting changes.

Zanzibar and Mauritius have recently made important constitutional advances including the establishment of Ministerial forms of Government.

Somalia with an economy that is far from viable is by United Nations decision to become independent and self-governing in 1960.

The foregoing résumé indicates in capsule form the political situation developing in the several countries coming under our consular jurisdiction. The Africans in each of the three principal countries, namely Kenya. Tanganyika and Uganda, will continue pressing for more and more rights and privileges. While the British authorities are attempting to keep pace and where possible ahead of such demands, the Africans are not likely to agree that constitutional changes are developing rapidly enough. Hence, British authority must give way. Each concession, however, will create new problems for the other communities. Thus every constitutional action will be the subject of extremely difficult negotiations between the government and the communities involved.

The area in general is poor in economic resources. However, a good climate, good medical facilities, and greatly improved living conditions since the British came here have increased the African population several-fold. Population growth can be expected to develop at even a faster pace during the next generation, creating difficult pressures on the available economic resources.

Because of increasing internal pressures, the area for some years ahead will be in a political state of flux requiring wise and careful analysis by the American representatives assigned here.

External Pressures

Our classified references in the memorandum of April 25, 1956 indicate our concern over both neutralist and potential communist penetration in the area. Close to 152,000 Asians of Hindu background live in Kenya, Uganda and Tanganyika. Many of them look to India for political guidance. Hence, India has a ready-made apparatus for carrying out, either overtly or covertly, the neutralist policies advocated by the Indian Prime Minister. Because of population pressures on the Indian sub-continent, India will doubtless look longingly towards East Africa as a possible dumping ground for its excess population and will probe with every means East Africa's attempt to limit Asian immigration. Despite such pressures and the stresses and strains on Commonwealth ties, the three British East African Governments are going ahead with immigration policies designed to keep to a minimum the number of Asians coming into the area.

Thus far, communism in a relative sense has made little inroad into the area, but conditions for its penetration are excellent. With the opening by the Soviet and Soviet-controlled countries of Embassies, trade missions, etc. in nearby countries and expansion of communist activities in the Middle East, we should think that the communists will overlook this area. In this connection, we understand that an African Training School operates in Moscow. In their naivete and desire to get more and more rights by whatever means offered, we believe the Africans with increasingly Asian support would be vulnerable to communist penetration.

If the area should fall a victim of communist influence or develop an Afro-Asian outlook intensified by color considerations, much of Africa south of the Sahara would be endangered.

Political and Strategical Considerations

Kenya and Tanganyika border on the Indian Ocean. Mombasa, the port for Kenya and Uganda, is one of the best harbors in the world. During the last war, MacKinnon Road, 100 miles west of Mombasa, was established as a staging area for British and Allied troops. After the war, MacKinnon Road was allowed to run down to a point where it would require millions of dollars to restore.

Because of British losses in the Middle East and the prospective turnover of the naval base at Trincomalee to the Ceylonese, the British may in their revision of strategic planning decide to use Mombasa as a supply port for its forthcoming Indian Ocean naval task force, a possibility which may be advanced by the Naval Conference of Allied Powers. Further, the British are establishing a small military base about ten miles outside of Nairobi. Additionally, the Royal Air Force is currently surveying facilities in this area. These recent developments bearing on the strategic significance of British East Africa to British military planning would seem to warrant careful consideration by American policy makers.

Knowledge of Africa and Africans

Because of the magnitude of the problems in other parts of the world, Africa has had (until recently) a low priority in U.S. policy considerations. Hence, our posts in Africa have been widely separated and inadequately staffed. We on the spot have therefore not been in a position to devote the time and attention to the substantive part of our jobs. We believe, however, that we must get to know Africa and Africans in such a way that we can provide American policy makers at home with the information and analysis which they need to formulate policy towards this vast continent. High on our list is getting to know the Africans and to take action in time to help mold their attitudes towards the United States and things we firmly believe in. We therefore consider that to accomplish one of our principal, long-term objectives, we must accelerate action along the lines suggested as fast as our personnel roster will permit. In so doing because of the highly sensitive nature of our relations with the several communities emphasis must be placed on the selection of highly qualified personnel rather than upon mere numbers.

Getting to know the African for such purposes as selecting leader grantees as discussed in our despatch no. 410 of April 6, 1956 [6] is fraught with political implications. Despite the difficulties outlined in the despatch mentioned, our ranking officers have been making strenuous but circumspect efforts to cultivate Africans of the type we believe may become leaders in the next 10 to 20 years. If we pursue these efforts assiduously and can still keep to a minimum British suspicion of our motives, we should be able gradually to develop a good leader program for this area. While this does not directly apply to the selection of African students for attendance at American colleges and universities, substantial efforts have been made, with noticeable success, to interest a greater number of African students in this program.

At the same time, Africans throughout British East Africa are increasingly looking to the United States for things which cannot or will not be provided by the British—for instance increased educational benefits and training. Moreover, Muslims, both Arab and African, avidly desire United States information to which we may respond with an expectation of excellent dividends.

[6] Not printed. (*Ibid.*, 511.4553/4–656)

Successful Application of Earlier Recommendations

In an effort to carry out our responsibilities in the area we have in the year end political round-ups for 1954 and 1955 recommended an action program.

These included:

1) Strengthen United States representation;
2) Strengthen the United States Information Program;
3) Strengthen the Exchange of Persons Program;
4) Start implementing the ICA program approved in April, 1955;
5) Stimulate private American activities in the area; and
6) Develop a corps of area specialists for Africa.

We are grateful that to the extent possible the Department, USIA and ICA have given us much of the assistance requested. These include:

1) Establishment of consulates at Kampala and Mogadiscio;[7]
2) Expansion of the United States Information program at Nairobi and the establishment of a USIS Office in Kampala;
3) Expansion of the exchange of persons program has kept pace with our recommendations;
4) The ICA Program approved in April 1955 has already given substantial, effective assistance, chiefly in Kenya;
5) The Principal Officer at Dar es Salaam took a special course on African studies at Boston University, and the new Vice Consul to be assigned there has had similar training. Both therefore qualify under recommendation (6) above. Additionally, we have just learned that the Foreign Service Institute is hopeful of starting a seminar on African studies for Foreign Service personnel at Accra, Lagos or Kampala.

The one place where we have thus far been unable to get much done is in the stimulation of private American activity in the area. However, we understand that the Ford Foundation later this year will send a team to the area with a view to continuing earlier discussions about projects to be undertaken under the Foundation's sponsorship and support.

Indicative of a probable groundswell in this kind of activity are the following: The Carnegie Corporation continues to provide books to the McMillan Library and the East African Literature Bureau, and it has financed projects at Makerere College and the Royal Technical College; the Government of Kenya authorities have approached us with a view to obtaining U.S. assistance in the establishment of a Poliomyelitis Rehabilitation Center, and a New York medical authority has inquired whether the Government of Kenya would be

[7] The Consulate at Kampala was opened August 28; the one at Mogadiscio July 1.

receptive to the establishment of a surgical reconstruction center here.

Impact of American Actions in the Area

Every action taken by United States Government or its representatives in the area has its local repercussions, sometimes both good and bad depending upon which community is affected. Anything we do in behalf of the African is automatically suspect to a fairly large segment of the European community. Our policies should therefore be designed to win and keep the African in the western camp and at the same time attempt to avoid or minimize possible resentment or ill-will from the other communities. This will require great tact, much patience and careful planning. We therefore anticipate that American representatives here will encounter real difficulty in attempting to carry forward approved American policies and objectives in this area.

Summary of Fiscal Year 1958–59 Projections

If the Congress provides the funds requested in the enclosures to our despatch no. 302 [8] as supported by despatch no. 344 American representation in British East Africa should approach the requirements of the situation. It should enable us to give adequate backstopping to ourselves, the three constituent posts and the other American agencies here looking to us for such support. To give such backstopping, we need all of the personnel and supporting equipment and services requested in despatch no. 302.

Edmund J. Dorsz

[8] Despatch 302 from Nairobi, April 26, contained financial plans for Fiscal Year 1958 and budget estimates for Fiscal Year 1959. (Department of State, Central Files, 122.6424/4–2657)

53. Briefing Paper Prepared in the Consulate at Kampala [1]

Kampala, undated.

UGANDA BRIEFING FOR MR. JULIUS C. HOLMES

[Here follow questions and answers concerning the Uganda National Congress, East African federation, the Asian community, and the Kabaka of Buganda.]

13. *Question*: In the Consulate's view, what should be the general policy of the United States toward Uganda?

Answer: The total results of British administration in Uganda to date are certainly laudable. The stated aim of conducting Uganda along an orderly and well-conceived path to self-government of a "primarily African state" is fully deserving of American support. The British view that Uganda needs more than four additional years of preparation for self-government is correct. Any effort on our part to urge establishment of a target date would be unproductive and largely meaningless in the circumstances. A growing number of British officials have come to realize that African political pressure will determine the rate of advance more and more and force the final concession of self-government well in advance of fulfillment of even the minimum program of preparation considered essential by the U.K. Faced with this prospect against the background of sharply curtailed British financial resources for economic development and education, the U.K. will find it increasingly necessary to turn to the U.S. for assistance. To the extent that we are able to respond, it would seem that it is in this area that we might bring constructive influence to bear which would assist the British and at the same time win African support for American policies and for close association with the West.

With time growing short it will be necessary to single out the most urgent requirements in preparing Uganda for independence and to concentrate on them during the few remaining years. Perhaps the most serious gap to be filled is that of secondary education and training in technical, business and administrative skills. The shortages are acute and make Africanization of the Civil Service, for example, an impossible task at the moment. In many areas only one

[1] Source: Department of State, Central Files, 110.17–HO/11–2757. Confidential. Prepared for Julius C. Holmes and Charles N. Manning, who were concerned with administrative matters relating to U.S. posts in Africa. On October 6, they embarked on a 10-week tour of Africa to undertake a study for the Secretary of State. The Consul at Kampala, Peter Hooper, Jr., met with them at Nairobi on November 20. Hooper considered the briefing paper to be a useful summary of the Ugandan situation; he sent it to the Department as an enclosure to despatch 50, November 27.

The paper consists of a series of questions and answers.

child in one hundred is able to proceed from primary to secondary school. At the next level the cream is taken into Makerere College where the emphasis is on arts, pre-law and pre-medicine. The manpower essential to run the country is simply not being trained but this fact will most certainly not retard African political pressure.

Since it is in the American interest to assist in promoting the emergence of a stable and united Uganda, a good case can be made for directing all American aid, governmental and private, which might be allotted to Uganda into secondary and technical education. The British system of educating the elite might over thirty or forty years provide the spread of talent required but it is not geared to the much shorter timetable for self-government now inevitable in Uganda. In addition to providing the necessary technical and administrative skills, mass education at the secondary level would have a very beneficial effect in softening inter-tribal and inter-regional rivalry and creating national consciousness. The demand for education on the part of the African is insatiable. What can be done by the United States to assist in this—teachers, books, grants for simple school buildings—should, in the opinion of the Consulate, be a matter for most serious consideration.

UNITED STATES POLICY REGARDING THE CENTRAL AFRICAN FEDERATION [1]

54. Memorandum From the Officer in Charge of Southern Africa Affairs (Dumont) to Terence Todman of the Office of Dependent Area Affairs [2]

Washington, September 7, 1956.

SUBJECT

Mr. Mason Sears' Comments Regarding Status of Principal United States Foreign Service Representative in the Central African Federation

I want to thank you very much for passing on to me Mason Sears' comment to you by telephone regarding his views on elevating our post at Salisbury to Career Minister status. I think there is merit to Mason's criticism that some Africans, particularly those in Nyasaland, might consider this action by the United States as constituting in some way an endorsement of the Federal Party's present policy on race relations in the Federation. Let me explain herewith just what action the Department did take in this matter and why this action was taken.

Not very long ago we raised our post at Salisbury to that of Career Minister status for the sole purpose of permitting the United States consular representative there to have equal prestige status with that of any other foreign government represented at Salisbury. [3] In short, we thought it improper that France, India, or any other country should outrank the representative of the United States. As you probably know, a number of foreign consular representatives at Salisbury had Career Minister status or the equivalent; this situation represented a distinct disadvantage to the United States because it

---

[1] For previous documentation on this subject, see *Foreign Relations*, 1952–1954, vol. XI, Part 1, pp. 296 ff.

[2] Source: Department of State, Central Files, 122.824/9–756. Limited Official Use. Regarding Sears' trip to the Federation, see Document 10.

[3] Steere told Lord Malvern May 17 of the action the United States had taken to raise the status of the post. The Prime Minister replied that he had considered it anomalous that the United Kingdom and South Africa should be represented in the Federation by High Commissioners and the United States by a Consul General. (Despatch 351 from Salisbury, May 19; *ibid.*, 745C.13/5–1956)

meant that the United States representative, by lacking equal status with other foreign governments, would thereby not be able to have the same access to and thus exercise the same influence with high Federation officials as some of his colleagues.

It so happens that the present incumbent of our post at Salisbury is an FSO–1. He is not a Career Minister but it is quite possible that a Selection Board may recommend that he be promoted to such class. [4]

Now I would like to venture that there is another side to the coin that Mason has seen and I hope Mason will agree that it looks more lustrous than the side which has to date appeared to him: If the United States Government's representative at Salisbury is going to be in a position where he may, through personal contacts with high Federation officials, be able to bring to bear friendly and wise counsel and make suggestions regarding the future of the Federation, he cannot effectively do so if he is to play second fiddle, diplomatically speaking, to the representatives of other foreign countries stationed at Salisbury. I am satisfied, on the contrary, that with the Principal Officer position now being of Career Minister status, our Consul General in Salisbury may be able to exercise a more positive and constructive influence on such people as Lord Malvern, Sir Roy Welensky and Garfield Todd than he has been able to do in the past. This is by no means to depreciate what Consul General Steere has already accomplished thus far. You will be interested to learn that upon two occasions within the last year Mr. Steere delivered public addresses in which he, in effect, criticized the apparent lethargy characterizing the manner in which the Federal Government was implementing its policy of multi-racial partnership. Strictly speaking, Mr. Steere was somewhat out of order in venturing to speak publicly on a burning political issue in the Federation and Lord Malvern's Government could, from a legal point of view, quite properly have protested Mr. Steere's conduct as being outside the province of his proper consular functions. The Department did not take a strict and narrow position on Mr. Steere's conduct because it felt that a pretty liberal interpretation of the Foreign Service Regulations in this case was justified and that it had not been inappropriate for the United States representative at Salisbury to speak out rather clearly to remind the Federation Government that it had a lot to do

[4] Steere was notified on October 2 that he had been given Career Minister status for the duration of his assignment to Salisbury. On February 4, 1957, the Federation made public its intent to appoint Sir Edgar Whitehead Minister to the United States and head of a Federal Government Mission attached to the British Embassy. Whitehead, a former Minister of Finance in Southern Rhodesia who resigned because of health reasons in 1953, became the Prime Minister in 1958.

yet before Africans would begin to be impressed by its high sounding statements on racial partnership.

If you think a copy of this memo would be of interest to Mason, why don't you send one along to him? I enclosed a copy for this purpose if you so desire.

---

55. Instruction From the Department of State to the Consulate General at Salisbury [1]

CA–3526 *Washington, October 15, 1957.*

SUBJECT

Diplomatic Relations with the Federation of Rhodesia and Nyasaland

The Government of the Federation of Rhodesia and Nyasaland sent a letter on July 17 to foreign consular offices in Salisbury, including the American Consulate General, stating that the Federation Government is "now ready to consider any representations which may be made to it regarding the establishment in the Federation of a diplomatic mission in charge of a Diplomatic Agent." The letter emphasized that the Federation itself does not intend immediately to seek establishment of diplomatic missions abroad, and that the initiative for establishing Diplomatic Agencies in the Federation must come from the interested foreign governments themselves. [2]

While the Federation has not yet been granted full sovereignty or autonomy in international affairs by the United Kingdom, the Department has confirmed that the United Kingdom has no objection to the Federation's receiving Diplomatic Agents.

As far as the Department knows, no country has yet announced any plans for establishing a Diplomatic Agency in Salisbury. The

---

[1] Source: Department of State, Central Files, 601.0045C/10–1557. Confidential. Sent also to Rome, Paris, Lisbon, and London.

[2] Despatch 23 from Salisbury, July 23, transmitted the text of the July 17 letter. (*Ibid.*, 601.0045C/7–2357) Steere subsequently reported in despatch 46, August 1, that the Federation was looking to the United States to take the lead in establishing diplomatic relations. He advised that it was in U.S. interest to do so without delay and thought such a step would lay the foundation for "friendly" and "advantageous" relations on a permanent basis. He further believed that the United States could exert more influence and pressure on the Federation's racial policies by initiating full diplomatic relations rather than by withholding recognition. (*Ibid.*, 601.0045C/8–157) The Assistant Secretary of Commerce for International Affairs, Henry Kearns, seconded Steere's recommendation in an August 30 letter to William M. Rountree. (*Ibid.*, 611.45C/8–3057)

Department understands from the Italian Embassy in Washington that the Government of the Federal Republic of Germany, which has growing commercial interests in the Federation, is very favorably disposed toward the proposal. The Italian Embassy inquired regarding the intentions of the United States; it is the Department's impression that the Italian Government is also favorably interested in the proposal but that it is awaiting the course of the United States.

The Department recognizes that there are several cogent reasons for establishing diplomatic relations with the Federation. Created in 1953, the Federation already has most of the attributes of sovereignty and may well become an independent state within 3 to 5 years. In recent years its rate of economic development has been unsurpassed by any other country in the world. American private investment has reached a high level and can be expected to grow further.

The Department considers, however, that the future of this new country depends ultimately on its ability to win the loyalty and cooperation of its African inhabitants, who constitute over 95% of the population but who do not yet play any significant part in the government of the country. Most of the politically conscious Africans opposed the creation of the Federation in 1953 because they considered it to be a device for this perpetuation and extension of white minority rule in that part of Africa. Despite the great economic benefits which have resulted from federation, the opposition of the Africans has intensified; secessionist sentiment is strong in Nyasaland and Northern Rhodesia. The officially professed policy of the Federation Government is one of "racial partnership", but its implementation to date has apparently been inadequate to counter the opposition of the African nationalists. The white minority electorate which has a virtual monopoly of political power, does not appear to be willing in the near future to endorse any political concessions which would be apt to placate the African inhabitants.

The Department has therefore considered very carefully the question of whether the establishment of limited diplomatic relations might enhance the ability of the United States to influence the Federation Government to accelerate the implementation of its racial partnership policy, or, whether such recognition by the United States might be interpreted by both Africans and the governing European element as an endorsement of lip-service support to the policy of racial partnership. In view of the known position of the United States on racial and colonial questions in Africa, it would be preferable that the United States not be the first country to establish diplomatic relations with the Federation. Such an initiative and precedent on the part of the United States might be construed as a gratuitous endorsement of the racial status quo in the Federation and serve to encourage the latter country's pressures on the United Kingdom to grant full independence before the future political and social position of the Africans is adequately clarified.

If other countries plan, without reference to United States action, to establish diplomatic agencies in Salisbury, the problem of a United States initiative and precedent would no longer apply. Therefore, the Embassies at Rome, Paris and Bonn are requested to ascertain informally whether the Italian, French and German governments definitely intend to send Diplomatic Agents to Salisbury in the near future. In their informal inquiries, these Embassies may mention, but without elaboration, that the initial thinking of the United States is that its appointment of a Diplomatic Agent to Salisbury at this time would be premature.

The Embassy at Lisbon should informally ascertain the intentions of the Portuguese Government, but without indicating any United States views or intimating that a political consideration is involved.

These four missions should report by despatch the reactions of the respective governments as soon as possible.[3] Once the Department is informed regarding the thinking of the interested powers, the Consulate General at Salisbury will be instructed regarding the nature of the reply to be made to the letter of July 17 from the Federation Government.[4]

Dulles

---

[3] Despatch 758 from Bonn, October 31, reported that Germany did not wish to be first to appoint a diplomatic agent though, if the United States led the way, it might designate one. (*Ibid.*, 601.0045C/10–3157) The French were in no rush to act, thinking that it would be premature. (Despatch 594 from Paris, October 23; *ibid.*, 601.5145C/10–2357) The Italians expressed no enthusiasm for establishing diplomatic relations with the Federation and intended to say nothing for the moment. (Despatch 505 from Rome, October 22; *ibid.*, 601.6545C/10–2257) The Portuguese were studying the matter and had not yet determined their course of action. (Despatch 208 from Lisbon, October 28; *ibid.*, 601.5345C/10–2857)

[4] Telegram 81 to Salisbury, January 25, 1958, contained the points which Steere was to make orally to Welensky in response to the note of July 17. In essence, the U.S. position was that full diplomatic relations could not be established with non-sovereign states. (*Ibid.*, 120.245C/1–2558)

56. Despatch From the Consulate General at Salisbury to the Department of State [1]

No. 173 *Salisbury, November 4, 1957.*

SUBJECT

Visit of ICA Representative, Hyde Buller, to Federation

Begin Unclassified. The visit of Mr. Hyde Buller, Chief of the Central African Division of ICA, to Salisbury (October 27–29) was in the opinion of the reporting officer most useful, both from the U.S. and the Federation's point of view. As Mr. Buller will be submitting his own report to ICA, the Consulate General does not consider it necessary to report in detail on his visit; however, it may be of interest to summarize it briefly and to submit a few comments on the implications of an expansion of ICA activities on U.S. policy here.

In his day and a half here Mr. Buller had two meetings with a small group of key officials from the Ministries of External Affairs, Treasury, and Commerce and Industry, plus the Prime Minister's Senior Economic Adviser. [2] In these meetings he not only explained ICA policies and procedures but discussed in considerable detail specific problems arising from the Federation's applications for technical assistance and for loans under the Development Loan Fund. (See ConGen's Despatch 127, October 2, 1957) [3] He also spoke on ICA to a group of about 35 Federal and Southern Rhodesia officials concerned with agriculture, irrigation, mining, education, labor, and other technical fields, and it had been extremely helpful to them to receive information and clarification as to ICA programs and policies.

At the latter meeting two officials invited Mr. Buller to observe the work of their departments so that they could show him the benefits they had already derived from ICA technical assistance. As a result he visited the Federal Ministry of Agriculture, including its nearby research station at Henderson, where he was shown how the Ministry's work in soil classification and soil conservation has been completely reorganized along American lines as the result of its

[1] Source: Department of State, Central Files, 110.402–ICA/11–457. Confidential with Unclassified Section. Passed to USOM/London.

[2] Buller met with the Secretary for External Affairs, H.N. Parry; Deputy Secretary for External Affairs, J.B. Ross; Acting Secretary for Commerce and Industry, T.S. Bell; Under Secretary of the Federal Treasury, R.A. Griffith; the Prime Minister's Chief Economist, C.H. Thompson; and D.I. Smith of the Ministry of External Affairs. (Despatch 184 from Salisbury, November 18; *ibid.*, 110.402–ICA/11–1857)

[3] Despatch 127 reported that the Federal Government initiated a request for a loan of some £19 million from the Development Loan Fund through Rhodesia House and USOM in London. (*Ibid.*, 745C.5–MSP/10–2557)

officials being sent to observe similar work in the U.S. under ICA technical assistance grants. He also paid a visit to the Southern Rhodesia Commissioner of Roads and was shown how road construction methods have been improved as the result of similar grants to highway engineers.

Among the matters discussed at the two small meetings with key officials were the Federation's applications under the Development Loan Fund, the possibility of assigning an ICA Liaison Officer here, the Federation's applications for technical assistance in FY1958 (including an investment adviser), and its estimated technical assistance needs for FY1959–61. The Federation has already initiated its loan applications (See ConGen Despatch 127) and has submitted its FY1959–61 technical assistance needs through USOM, London. Other than requesting an investment adviser, it has not submitted any applications for technical assistance under the FY1958 program. Mr. Buller pointed out that, if the Federation intended to do so, it should lose no time, and the officials concerned indicated that a further submission would be made shortly. *End Unclassified.*

Begin Confidential. While in applying for technical assistance and development loans the Federation has included projects of direct benefit to Africans, Mr. Buller was impressed by the predominantly European coloration of his discussions. No African was present at any of them; nor did any of the proposed projects involve direct training of Africans by American technicians or the sending of African technicians to the United States. When once or twice he rather tentatively raised such possibilities, the reaction seemed more one of surprise than antagonism, followed by explanations concerning the lack of qualified Africans. While the Consulate General agrees that there are extremely few Africans qualified to participate in ICA technical assistance programs (probably none with the level of qualifications previously required for participants from this country), it agrees with Mr. Buller that the apparently complete lack of consideration of such possibilities by Federal officials is revealing. Not even the propaganda aspect, in the sense of evidence to the outside world of their determination to make "partnership" work, seems to have been considered.

The Consulate General understands it to be United States policy to support the increasing and more effective implementation of the Federation's stated policy of partnership. The technical assistance and development loan programs of ICA offer opportunities to further such a U.S. policy. It considers, therefore, that while the Federation's applications for technical assistance and development loans should be examined on their merits, a factor in selecting projects to be aided should be the extent to which they would be of the most direct possible benefit to the mass of the population

(96½% African), as well as the extent to which they might include African participation.

Similarly, the Consulate General understands that it is U.S. policy to support "federation". The ICA programs could exert some influence in this regard, too. In other words, in assessing applications, consideration should be given to the extent to which projects might strengthen the ties between the territories and how they might assist in demonstrating the benefits of federation to the less favored areas, notably Nyasaland.

While the reporting officer is aware of no official formulation of U.S. policy towards the Federation, he believes that in practice it is as described above. Opportunities for furthering such a policy are limited. Expansion of the ICA program in the Federation increases such opportunities somewhat. If, however, the introduction of political considerations into the program should become too evident here, the result would be to decrease U.S. influence. Thus the overall program must be balanced and pay heed to the Federation's own scale of priorities.

Curtis C. Strong

DEVELOPMENTS IN MOZAMBIQUE OF PARTICULAR CONCERN TO THE UNITED STATES

57. Editorial Note

Restrictions on Protestant missionaries in Mozambique became a matter of some concern to the United States in 1956 and 1957. The Consulate General in Lourenco Marques reported in despatch 93, January 14, 1956, that the Portuguese authorities in Mozambique had imposed new restrictions on schools maintained by foreign missions, which, the Consulate General commented in despatch 105, January 28, could have profound political repercussions. (Department of State, Central Files, 853P.413/1–1456 and 853.413/1–2856, respectively) The Department of State instructed Consul General R. Smith Simpson to discuss informally with the Governor General the difficulties experienced by the Protestant missions in Mozambique. (*Ibid.*, 253C.11/3–856) Simpson met with the Governor General on April 11; he reported in despatch 156, April 13, that the Governor General stated the government's intention to close all Protestant mission schools. (*Ibid.*, 253C.11/4–1356)

The Department observed in CA–10113 to Lisbon, May 29, 1957, that it had tried to deal with this problem at the local level, believing that informal discussions with the Portuguese authorities in Mozambique were preferable to other courses. While there had been some improvement with respect to religious freedom for Protestant missionaries, there had been no change with respect to the educational problem. It instructed the Embassy to make an informal approach to the Portuguese authorities concerning this problem but, in view of the current base negotiations with Portugal, left the timing of the approach to the Embassy. (*Ibid.*, 853C.413/5–2957) The Embassy reported on August 1 that once other matters were out of the way, it would approach the Foreign Office informally. (*Ibid.*, 853C.413/8–157) Further information on this subject is *ibid.*, in the files cited above and in files 753C.00 and 253C.00.

ALGERIA

UNITED STATES POLICY REGARDING THE SITUATION IN ALGERIA[1]

58. Telegram From the Department of State to the Embassy in France[2]

Washington, May 27, 1955—6:23 p.m.

4247. Pinay request for utilization Algeria helicopters[3] which only recently made available to them at their urgent request Indochina at sacrifice our needs other areas demonstrates French failure appreciate problem created for us by rapid deterioration situation North Africa and apparent inability French formulate and apply specific and imaginative programs to which local population will rally and which other countries can reasonably support.

We feel French Govt must be brought to realize both seriousness with which we view current situation, and difficulties it creates for us in absence French action other than traditional police type measures directed against natives. Fact that those engaged illegal terroristic activities counts for little in world opinion against moral reprobation and adverse political repercussions which anything of repressive nature inevitably arouses.

You should see Pinay and tell him following: we cannot as part present French program Algeria make available helicopters which are in very short supply. US-French agreement of last December provides that any surplus MDAP equipment Indochina will be returned US control for further disposition.[4] If helicopters surplus French authorities Indochina should notify MAAG. We acknowledge French having informed us their intention transfer additional troops Alge-

---

[1] For previous documentation, see *Foreign Relations*, 1952–1954, vol. XI, Part 1, pp. 382 ff. See also Documents 25–37.

[2] Source: Department of State, Central Files, 751S.00/5–2755. Secret; Priority.

[3] Pinay initially made this request known to Dillon on May 25. (Telegram 5152 from Paris, May 25; *ibid.*, 751S.00/5–2555) A formal aide-mémoire on this subject was presented to the Embassy in France on May 26. (Telegram 5218 from Paris, May 27; *ibid.*, 751S.00/5–2755)

[4] Generals Collins and Ely signed a minute of understanding on this matter for the United States and France, respectively, on December 1, 1954.

ria. [5] We recognize French determination proceed deal with situation and that it would not be realistic request that troops be divested of such of their equipment as was furnished under MDAP program. We feel however that we entitled to be frank and emphasize the increasingly grave political problems, both domestic and international, created by growing use of US furnished weapons and equipment North Africa. It has always been our earnest hope that France will be able to develop and carry out bold political, social and economic programs which we can fully and publicly support and through which French presence in North Africa may be maintained. Recent events have in our opinion greatly increased urgency of acts of statesmanship with regard to Algeria and Morocco in same spirit France has shown in approach to Tunisian situation.

Unless such acts accompany military attempts restore public order through efforts repress terrorist activities in which France now engaged, we foresee indefinite increase of latter with attendant increase in political repercussions.

Weakening of NATO defenses in Europe through splitting up and transfer of units is serious. We hope strength can be restored quickly. Number of divisions which qualify for MDAP equipment has been considerably reduced and questions arise regarding future supply and status of previously delivered MDAP equipment.

You should conclude by assuring Pinay that we desire continue support France in efforts restore peace and create basis for enduring cooperation with North African peoples in future. In order make it possible for us maintain such support we feel there is no time for France to lose in initiating measures with regard Algeria and Morocco to assure support of native populations. [6]

Dulles

---

[5] The Second Division then stationed at Nancy was to be transferred to Algeria.

[6] When Dillon took up these matters with Massigli on May 31, he indicated that it was not likely that the French would be permitted to transfer the helicopters to Algeria. (Telegram 5255 from Paris; Department of State, Central Files, 751S.00/5–3155) On June 3, Massigli notified Achilles that his government no longer sought such a release but would concentrate on attempting to buy helicopters for cash from the United States. (Telegram 5326 from Paris; *ibid.*, 751S.00/6–355) Then on June 11, after a decision by the Cabinet Coordinating Committee, Massigli informed Achilles that despite the initial U.S. response the request for the release of the helicopters would be pursued. (Telegram 5438 from Paris; *ibid.*, 751S.00/6–1155)

59. Telegram From the Department of State to the Embassy in France [1]

Washington, June 17, 1955—6:05 p.m.

4514. In making points Deptel 4513 [2] to Massigli, Achilles should make following observations as representing Department thinking:

1. We understand French view Algerian insurrection is threat to internal security of France and separate matter from disturbances in Morocco and Tunisia. We trust French can appreciate, however, that in American and doubtless much of world opinion Algerian problem, involving as it does franchise of indigenous population, appears as part of composite North African problem involving political aspirations of native populations that cannot be met by repressive police measures alone. We are reassured by Massigli statement French do not contemplate retaliatory measures against civil populations, which would shock world opinion. FYI. Certain intelligence reports are to effect French probably contemplate just such measures. Certain items on list requested are not reassuring. End FYI.

2. Degree to which US can implement its policy of support for French presence in North Africa, particularly in terms of providing material and public support, depends on effectiveness of French political, economic and social programs to deal with situation and not simply military measures. France appears to have taken such measures in Tunisia but we do not know enough about possible French "programs" and intentions for Algerian and Moroccan problems to have confidence in their potential effectiveness.

In your discretion, you may wish to observe that statements such as July made last weekend make it more difficult for US Govt to be forthcoming in giving support to French.

FYI. Department urged Defense on June 9 make eight helicopters available. We hope assistance on helicopters will provide evi-

[1] Source: Department of State, Central Files, 751S.00/6–1755. Secret. Repeated to Algiers and Saigon.

[2] Telegram 4513, June 17, instructed Achilles to inform Massigli that the United States supported the French presence in North Africa and considered Algeria legally part of Metropolitan France. It stipulated the conditions which would have to be satisfied before military equipment could be transferred from Indochina to Algeria. (*Ibid.*, 751S.00/6–1155)

dence to French Govt and public opinion that US willing respond to French appeals for assistance to extent possible.[3]

Hoover

[3] Achilles called on Massigli on June 20 and left a memorandum reflecting the text of telegram 4513. Massigli was disappointed because of anticipated long delays in the U.S. transfer procedure. Massigli noted he recognized the need for overall progress to win the support of the populace, but considered the suppression of terrorism more pressing. (Telegram 5570 from Paris; *ibid.*, 751S.00/6–2055)

60. Telegram From the Embassy in France to the Department of State[1]

Paris, October 4, 1955—3 p.m.

1522. At my request I was received this morning by Pinay. When I arrived I found Alphand in his office and Pinay said that as the conversation would probably cover the UN[2] he had asked Alphand to be present.

At the beginning of our conversation the atmosphere was one of heightened dignity and restraint stemming from badly hurt feelings. I asked Pinay what in his view could be done to restore the situation and his first attitude was that France had no suggestions to make and that this was a question for the UN to decide itself.

Pinay then said that as he had always been extremely frank with me he felt he must tell me that the support which he had received from the US had not been what he would have expected or hoped for. He said that it was a sharp contrast to the support which he had received from Spaak, and in contrast to the British position which he termed entirely satisfactory. As the conversation developed it became clear that this feeling of Pinay's arose from two separate sources. In the first place he said that he did not consider Lodge's speech had been as forceful as it could have been and that the American Delegation had not made any visible attempt to work on other delegations on France's behalf. Alphand interjected that Lodge

[1] Source: Department of State, Central Files, 320/10–455. Secret; Priority. Repeated to London and USUN.

[2] On September 30, the General Assembly voted 28 to 27, with 5 abstentions, to place "The question of Algeria" on the agenda. Lodge spoke in support of the General Committee's report, which recommended against inscription. For text of his comments and the roll call, see U.N. doc. A/PV.530, September 30, 1955, pp. 187 and 196.

had only arrived a few minutes before the meeting from Washington and apparently had not felt it necessary or advisable to be available for consultations with other delegations prior to the vote.

In this connection Pinay further specified that he felt the US could well have influenced the votes of such countries as Guatemala, Costa Rica and Liberia. I pointed out that contrary to what seemed to be the general impression that the US could control the Latin American bloc, such was not actually the case, that there had always been a great deal of independent action among the Latin American nations. Pinay said that he recognized this in some cases but he nevertheless reiterated he thought we could have influenced the vote of the three nations which he previously mentioned, as well as Uruguay and Iceland.

The second main reason for Pinay's hurt feelings toward the US was that he had not received any word from the Secretary or any other American representative after the vote. He pointed out that in contrast to this Macmillan had immediately called him and assured him of full British support for his action and he had also received similar expressions of support from practically all the smaller countries of Europe. This feeling on his part that he had been neglected by the US in his moment of trouble obviously was of equal importance in his mind to the supposed inadequate efforts by the American Delegation prior to the actual vote.

By this time as a result of a few minutes conversation, the atmosphere had changed considerably and became much more relaxed. I asked whether it would be any help if the GA should decide to reverse the vote on Algeria. Pinay made it very clear that this was the solution which the French desire and is the only solution which they will accept, while at the same time emphasizing they are asking for nothing and would ask for nothing. He said that an adjournment sine die of the debate would be totally unsatisfactory as the French felt that what was at stake was not the question of their actions in Algeria but the basic principle of whether or not the UN was competent to meddle in the internal affairs of any and all countries. He said that it was obviously the policy of the Soviets to stir up trouble throughout the world by maintaining this principle and felt that unless the Western powers reacted to this Soviet move the unity and vigor of the UN would be permanently lost to an alliance of the Bandung and Soviet blocs. He said that if this philosophy was accepted no country would be safe and cited as instances of questions that might be raised the situation of the Negroes in the southern part of the US, the situation in Northern Ireland, the division of Belgium between Walloons and Flemish, etc.

In passing he said that Macmillan had felt that this vote was a very dangerous precedent for Great Britain in connection with Northern Ireland.

I then asked whether there was any parliamentary method by which the situation could be retrieved and Alphand answered very promptly that if the commission to which the subject was referred so desired, it could declare itself incompetent to handle the matter and refer it back to the GA for action, at which time it would be possible for the GA again, if it so desired, to reverse its previous vote and decide that Algeria was not a proper subject for debate. Pinay was in full accord with this thesis and this obviously is the French hope.

Pinay then commented that he felt that public opinion in France had reacted with great dignity and pride and that this action had helped to unite the French people and had opened their eyes to the hollowness of the Soviet pretensions of friendship. He said there was extreme bitterness in the French Government towards the Soviets and that he had spoken very severely to Anikine, the Soviet Chargé d'Affaires, when he announced the indefinite postponement of the French visit to Moscow.

In response to a discreet question on my part regarding Alphand's status, Pinay said that he was presently on vacation in Paris. I asked if that might last for several weeks and Alphand mumbled "probably not that long", to which Pinay made no response. Alphand then said that if there should be any necessity of calling a meeting of the Security Council this month he, as President, would of course return, and Pinay confirmed this.

In closing Pinay said that he felt that the French had rung the tocsin of alarm over the tendency of the UN to interfere in the internal affairs of all countries for the purpose of stirring up trouble that could redound only to the benefit of the Soviet bloc, and he hoped that the warning would be heard and understood. He said his personal feeling was that the US had not fully recognized the dangers inherent in the fusion of the Bandung and Soviet blocs, which he considered the gravest threat to the stability of the world.

Dillon

61. Telegram From the Mission at the United Nations to the Department of State[1]

New York, October 5, 1955—11 a.m.

Delga 53. Re Algerian question. In finding best means disposing Algerian item we must first set record straight in Paris and insist French immediately desist baseless charges along lines reported Paris 1522[2] which if picked up by press could create situation in which we could not render assistance French badly need. Second, we must pin French down, in writing if possible, as to what they want. If this is unacceptable to us we should reason with them in private and only move in UN on a basis which we and they approve.

We cannot let French dictate terms on which we should assist them because this will only lead to further unjustified recriminations if we are unable carry them out.

Suggest accordingly that, after Dillon makes firm representations along lines Deptel 1287 to Paris,[3] he also inform French we cannot consider course action proposed by Pinay and Alphand as reported Paris 1522 because:

(a) We see no possibility obtaining required ⅔ majority for reversal Assembly's decision on inscription. US could not take position reversal would not require ⅔ majority since this would be evasion of clear-cut rule of procedure and would set extremely dangerous precedent. Such effort to evade rules would be contrary position we have taken when others sought nullify ⅔ requirement.

(b) Would be inconsistent traditional US position that discussion itself does not constitute intervention.

(c) Would place US in untenable position with respect to Netherlands, Australia, and South Africa all of whom have pressed US on this point.

(d) Failure bring about Assembly reversal, which we regard as almost certain, would damage US prestige with no advantage France. On contrary would create impossible situation for France in UN.

(e) Would lead to long, bitter debate which likely inflame situation in Algeria and Morocco.

For these reasons I suggest Dillon be instructed inform French US willing take lead in persuading largest possible majority adopt procedural motion stating simply that "The General Assembly decides not to consider further the Algerian question." We would press

---

[1] Source: Department of State, Central Files, 751S.00/10–555. Confidential; Priority; Limited Distribution.

[2] *Supra.*

[3] Dated October 4, telegram 1287 reported that Lodge had done all that he could have been expected to do in behalf of the French. It noted a general feeling among delegations in New York that the French had not campaigned effectively in their own behalf. (Department of State, Central Files, 320/10–455)

motion after briefest possible debate. Should be noted this would be preferable to Cyprus resolution of Ninth Session preamble of which implied future Assembly consideration. Once motion adopted this session, strong basis established for French seek outright defeat any future attempt raise Algerian question.[4]

Important we initiate necessary consultations as soon as possible to head off less desirable solutions certain be proposed here. If French agree US will seek have issue disposed of as soon as possible First Committee.

Lodge

[4] Lodge later reversed himself, recommending against seeking passage of a "not to consider" resolution and proposing to let the Arabs take the initiative in moving a resolution which could not receive a two-thirds vote. He thought it premature, however, to suggest anything to the French who had not yet revealed their intentions. (Delga 58 from New York, October 6; *ibid.*, 751S.00/10–655)

62. Telegram From the Department of State to the Embassy in France[1]

Washington, October 5, 1955—7:02 p.m.

1305. For Ambassador from Secretary. Please at your convenience and if you see no objection give following to Pinay from me.

"Dear Mr. Pinay: I continue to be deeply distressed at the action of the General Assembly with reference to the Algerian matter. I am even more distressed at the impression you perhaps have that the US Delegation did not adequately support you in this matter.

"As against a background of public opinion and Congressional opinion in this country with which you are familiar, we voted against inscription and made through Ambassador Lodge a strong statement on the subject. We also let it be known privately to other delegations what our position was and our hope that the General Assembly would support the General Committee. We do exert a certain influence and in this connection I was glad to observe that

[1] Source: Department of State, Central Files, 320/10–555. Secret. Drafted by Dulles. When Dillon delivered the message on October 6, Pinay emphasized that he harbored no ill feelings against the United States or Ambassador Lodge. He hoped the General Assembly would reverse itself and decide it was not competent to handle the matter. (Telegram 1584 from Paris, October 6; *ibid.*, 320/10–655)

even more of the Latin American countries voted as we did on this Algerian issue than on the Cyprus issue.

"I believe that your Government's reaction was dignified and understandable. As I said at my press conference yesterday, we must all work together so as to assure that this incident will in no way lose the voice of France from world discussions and debates. That would be too great a loss for the world.

"You can count on us to seek at the UN to do everything practical to try and repair the damage wrought.

"May I add that I believe that this type of action directed against France is intensified by Communist scheming, and that this whole aspect of the matter deserves most careful consideration. I hope we can talk about it when I am in Paris. I am glad that in the light of this development your Government also took the dignified action of postponing the trip to Moscow.

"I greatly enjoyed our talks together at New York and look forward to seeing you soon in Paris. Sincerely yours, John Foster Dulles"

Dulles

---

63. Letter From the Representative at the United Nations (Lodge) to the Ambassador in France (Dillon) [1]

New York, October 6, 1955.

DEAR DOUG: I believe you should have in mind the following facts concerning United States support of the French on the Algerian issue:

1. Foreign Minister Pinay did not personally speak to the representatives here. I am advised by the individuals concerned that in the case of El Salvador and Paraguay, that had he done so, both Paraguay and El Salvador would have voted with him.

2. It is not surprising that Guatemala voted against France when one considers that Ambassador Hoppenot in the June 1954 meeting

[1] Source: Department of State, Central Files, 320/10–755. Secret. Lodge addressed a similar personal letter to Secretary Dulles on October 7 in which he observed that the French had mismanaged their affairs. He noted that Alphand had made only a cursory plea for help 2 days before the vote. After the vote, he believed that the French had been more interested in finding a reason to walk out than in remaining to seek to overturn the result. (*Ibid.*)

of the Security Council supported actively the Communist Government of Guatemala.

3. As far as we know, the French never, at a high level, had a serious talk with the Philippines, whose vote might well have been obtained inasmuch as they are so anxious to get French support for their campaign for membership in the Security Council.

4. The Minister Counselor, Charles Lucet, left New York the day after Alphand arrived, which meant that Alphand had no senior man with experience. Lucet was replaced by Guiringaud who knew no more about United Nations procedure than Alphand did.

5. At no time did Alphand show me any list which indicated that he was working methodically. In fact, the French were apparently unprepared for the unfavorable vote, although it was certainly a possibility for which they should have been ready.

6. Immediately after the General Committee's recommendation against inscription was rejected by the margin of one vote, the President of the Assembly left it clearly open to the French to request a specific vote on the inscription of the item. They could have taken advantage of this to request a recess and meanwhile could have garnered enough votes against inscription to defeat it. Instead of taking advantage of this procedural opportunity, Pinay made his statement and left the Hall.

7. As the British demonstrated in the Cyprus affair, it takes at least ten days to organize a successful campaign in the United Nations. To try to work up something in a hurry at a casual meeting at a cocktail party the day before is most amateurish and foredoomed to failure. Their veiled threat to walk out if the vote went against them was ill-advised and certainly lost them support.

8. It is astonishing that Alphand should criticize me for not being present on Friday morning,[2] when I had told him definitely that Vice President Nixon had telephoned the day before to request me urgently to attend the first meeting of the Cabinet being held since the illness of President Eisenhower.

9. As far as saying goodbye is concerned, I received no word from one single French representative about the French departure. I heard on Saturday indirectly, and then only as a result of inquiries by my staff, that Alphand was leaving on Sunday and telephoned at once on Saturday in order to call that evening to say goodbye. But by that time Alphand had found a berth at the last minute and had left.

10. In this, as in all other occupations in life, the old saying that "God helps those who help themselves" is pertinent. The United States can help those who help themselves, but it cannot carry the

[2] September 30.

load all by itself and it is not fair to blame the United States for everything that goes wrong at the United Nations.

11. I did everything that the French asked me to do—and more. Pinay asked me to speak in the Plenary. I spoke in the Plenary and on my own responsibility added language to my speech in which I warned the delegates that inscription of the Algerian item would be very dangerous for the future of the Organization. The U.S. Delegation also made a canvass of all the Latin American countries and I personally reported it to Alphand. If the French had wanted me to take charge of their campaign, they should have asked me to do so.

The fact should not be forgotten that it can obviously lead to confusion, disorder and crossed wires to barge into a complicated situation without having been invited to do so by the party most concerned. This holds true today, and the French have still not given us a practicable statement of their wishes or intentions.

With kind regards,

Very sincerely yours,

Henry Cabot Lodge, Jr. [3]

[3] Printed from a copy that bears this typed signature.

64. Telegram From the Mission at the United Nations to the Department of State [1]

New York, November 1, 1955—1 p.m.

Delga 190. Re Algeria, Delga 184, October 31. [2] Alphand telephoned me at 11 a.m. today to say that, after reflection, he had decided to put off the operation in the Plenary session under Rule 22 for eight days.

[1] Source: Department of State, Central Files, 751S.00/11–155. Secret. Repeated to Paris.

[2] Delga 184 reported Alphand's opposition to a motion to adjourn since that would signify General Assembly competence to deal with the Algerian matter. He preferred that the issue be taken up in plenary under Rule 22 of the Rules of Procedure whereby a majority vote of those present and voting could delete it from the agenda. Alphand claimed to have Secretary-General Dag Hammarskjöld's support. Alphand also asked Lodge to seek the support of Bolivia, Iceland, Liberia, and Ethiopia and indicated that France would be willing, in return for a favorable vote, to support the Philippines for a seat on the Security Council. (*Ibid.*, 751S.00/10–3155)

He urged me to use my influence with Guatemala and Bolivia, in addition to Iceland, Ethiopia and Liberia. He said with a laugh that we have powerful arguments of a very practical character with both Guatemala and Bolivia which we could use if we wanted to. I said that I did not know what they were, but none of these countries were satellites, as the record amply proved.

FYI: I feel that sooner or later—and preferably sooner, we must make it clear to Alphand as we must to everyone, that while the US is powerful, it is not all-powerful and we cannot work miracles. End FYI.

I asked him who was going to be his floor manager, which had the advantage of at least making it clear that I was not going to be. He said it is someone I knew very well and who would be in touch with me later on during the day. When I expressed some surprise at this extreme secrecy, he said that the man who would be in touch with me later in the day would be President Maza.[3]

I pointed out that on October 15 I had discussed with President Maza the possibility of moving under Rule 22 and he had voiced strong objections to it at that time on the grounds that it would start an acrimonious colonial debate.[4] Alphand replied that that was all different now and that Maza was strongly in favor of it. That, of course, still does not take care of the question of who is to be the floor manager, a matter of critical importance to the success of such an undertaking.

FYI: This whole conversation inspires no confidence whatever. It is perfectly clear that the French are maintaining an impossible attitude of wanting to get a result achieved without lifting a finger to do it, which never works in any department of life. It is perfectly clear that he has not done his homework, that the texts of motions have not been drafted, that speakers have not been lined up, and that none of the essential practical steps have been taken. Nor is there sound basis for hope that they ever will be.

In all this there is one thing which the US should avoid, by every means within its power, and that is to become the so-called muscle man who is required to lead a strong fight in defense of French colonialism. I have now agreed to speak to Iceland, Liberia, Ethiopia, Guatemala and Bolivia. I will also make a brief statement in the Plenary. I feel that I have agreed to enough and that I should not be required to agree to anything more. I very much fear that Pinay will ask Secretary Dulles to direct me to organize a big fight in defense of French colonialism. I cannot find words to express how

[3] José Maza of Chile, President of the General Assembly, called on Lodge on November 2 and revealed that Francisco Urrutia of Colombia had agreed to act as floor manager. (Delga 201, November 2; *ibid.*, 751S.00/11–255)

[4] Reported in Delga 104, October 1. (*Ibid.*, 320/10–1555)

strongly I feel that this would be most harmful to the American position throughout the whole non-white world.

I took advantage of Alphand's call to give him the gist of Gadel 75.[5]

Lodge

[5] Gadel 75, November 1, warned of the consequences if the French moved prematurely and suffered another reversal. Though the timing was up to the French, Hoover wished France to be informed of U.S. trepidations. (*Ibid.*, 751S.00/10–3155)

65. Memorandum of a Conversation, Geneva, November 3, 1955[1]

SUBJECT

Algeria

PARTICIPANTS

M. de Margerie, France
M. Pink, UK
Mr. MacArthur
Mr. Wainhouse

We met last night at M. de Margerie's request to discuss the problem of Algeria in the General Assembly. Mr. MacArthur and I described what was involved in the effort to delete the Algerian item from the agenda of the General Assembly under Rule 22 of the Rules of Procedure of the GA. We conveyed to de Margerie the difficulties and the pit-falls in this project and what would be necessary in the way of the most painstaking preparation to seek to effect a successful outcome. We pointed out that the United States cannot get out "in front" on this issue. We expressed clearly that France must take the initiative and the responsibility in this undertaking, and that their people in New York must do their "homework." The US, we said, is prepared to make strong efforts behind the scenes to assure a favorable outcome.

M. de Margerie stated that this will require a decision by the Cabinet and his first task is to persuade M. Pinay who has great influence in the government. He inquired as to the best time to

[1] Source: Department of State, Secretary's Memoranda of Conversation: Lot 64 D 199. Confidential. Drafted by Wainhouse on November 4. The conversation took place during the Foreign Ministers Conference.

launch the project. We indicated that since the General Assembly will sit until December 10, it is not too soon to start now to lay the groundwork. We felt that thorough preparation would take not less than two weeks.

Mr. Pink expressed full agreement with what Mr. MacArthur and I had said and stated that the United Kingdom is prepared to assist in every way possible to effect a favorable outcome on the vote. Mr. Pink said Rule 22 was ambiguous and expressed the hope that the groundwork for overcoming this ambiguity will be thoroughly laid. The Secretary-General of the United Nations, we said, had looked into this matter and feels satisfied that Rule 22 applies to this kind of a situation.

M. de Margerie stated that he will put the case to M. Pinay in terms as follows:

1. The United States and the United Kingdom are prepared to help in every way possible.
2. Someone must be in charge of the undertaking. France cannot escape this responsibility, and France must select that person.
3. This undertaking cannot be effected in three or four days—a fortnight is necessary.
4. It must be made known that France is in favor of returning to the General Assembly; otherwise a number of states will not want to "walk the cat back."

M. de Margerie said that he fully appreciated the complicated political management involved in this . . . . He expressed deep gratitude to us for all that we were doing. [2]

[2] On November 25, the General Assembly decided in Resolution 909(X) "not to consider further the item entitled 'The question of Algeria'." France, which had absented itself from the General Assembly since October 1, returned on November 25. Documentation concerning Lodge's efforts on behalf of the French in this matter is *ibid.*, Central File 751S.00.

66. Telegram From the Department of State to the Embassy in France [1]

Washington, February 7, 1956—7:21 p.m.

2856. Embtel 3489. [2] You are authorized tell Pineau at your discretion that Mollet's efforts initiate liberal policy Algeria have support and sympathy US Govt.

While too early judge just what Mollet's full plan will be, nevertheless program thus far enunciated, i.e. abolition two college system, negotiations with Algerian leaders looking toward federal solution, represents significant step forward and in view serious situation confronting Mollet Algeria believe expression US encouragement this juncture appropriate. Although as you correctly stated any US démarche Egypt at this time of doubtful efficacy, nevertheless Dept would be willing consider suggestions as to how we might be helpful. [3]

For Cairo and Tripoli: Dept believes Mollet's efforts show reasonable hope of French Govt going far towards meeting Algerian demands and thus significant opportunity—perhaps last—for French reaching accord with moderate elements Algeria. In view violent opposition by local French elements Algeria and probable subsequent opposition rightist groups French Parliament, consider that US encouragement might be helpful contribution in persuading Mollet to carry through liberal policy. Request your comments soonest as to efficacy and appropriateness US démarches urging Egyptian and Libyan Govts not undermine Mollet's efforts Algeria.

Dulles

---

[1] Source: Department of State, Central Files, 751S.00/2–456. Secret. Sent also to Cairo and Tripoli and repeated to Algiers, Tangier, and London.

[2] Telegram 3489, February 4, reported that Pineau had requested U.S. support abroad, particularly in Cairo. He claimed that France could deal with the internal aspects of the Algerian problem provided that the rebels received no external aid and encouragement from the Islamic world. Dillon offered his sympathy and support. (*Ibid.*)

[3] Dillon replied in telegram 3582, February 9, that he preferred to wait until Mollet's return from Algeria. He feared that Mollet had backed away from his initial reform intentions after being pelted with raw vegetables and stones by the colons in Algiers because of his decision to appoint General Georges Catroux as Minister-President in Algeria. The colons blamed Catroux for negotiating the capitulation of Morocco and feared his appointment presaged a similar result in Algeria. Mollet responded by accepting Catroux's resignation in favor of Robert Lacoste and by embracing a less liberal line. (*Ibid.*, 751S.00/2–956)

67. Telegram From the Embassy in France to the Department of State[1]

Paris, March 7, 1956—noon.

4060. Eyes only for President, Hoover and Gruenther from Cabot Lodge. I believe that the President should now receive the following evaluation and recommendations. Dillon has read this wire and authorizes me to say that he is thinking along the same lines and is sending a message of his own.[2]

Evaluation:

(1) Because of our desire in past years not to offend either the colonial powers or the Afro-Asian powers, the United States is today in the position in which its policy receives the approval of neither. This is a chronic condition and calls for no quick action.

(2) In France, however, a situation has arisen in which the United States is getting much more than the usual amount of adverse criticism. Many Frenchmen who are usually pro-American are beginning to believe that the United States is not sorry to see France in its present difficulty over Algeria and that American business is getting poised to take over Algeria. The human tendency to blame someone else for one's own mistakes added to the skillful and persistent encouragement of these concepts by the Communists and the Arab bloc, have intensified this state of mind.

(3) If one thing is certain for the future, it is that France at best is going to have a very rough time over Algeria and that the demand for scapegoats will grow rather than diminish. If Algeria is totally lost, it will probably precipitate a drastic political upheaval in France.

(4) In any case we must in self-defense make a record for ourselves, providing a statement can be made which comforts France and at the same time does not offend the Arabs.

(5) Jebb, UK Ambassador in Paris, made a pro-French statement yesterday along this line saying the UK would stand by France. This makes it all the more important for the United States not to get into a position of being unfavorably compared with the UK as regards our friendship for France.

---

[1] Source: Department of State, Central Files, 751S.00/3–756. Top Secret. Niact.

[2] Dillon urged in telegram 4062, March 7, sent eyes only to Dulles in Karachi, that "some expression of US solidarity with France in her present difficulties in Algeria has become vitally necessary if we desire maintain wholehearted French support for NATO and western objectives in general." He recommended a high-level statement, preferably by the President, saying in substance "that French Government is trying work out liberal solution there and such efforts have full US support." (*Ibid.*)

(6) The excellent statements on Morocco[3] and Tunisia which the Department has issued will be compared in a derogatory manner with our silence on Algeria.

(7) An apparently off-hand statement by the President at a press conference could do good and should not in any way open the door to further French demands. If, for example, there is a further demand for indirect logistic help or diplomatic intervention in Cairo, these should be the subject of a separate negotiation very much on a quid pro quo basis.

Recommendation:

I therefore recommend that the President make the following statement at a press conference in response to this question:

"Has the President followed at all the recent developments in Algeria?"

In reply the President would say:

"I am surprised that anyone should even raise the question as to whether I am following the events in Algeria. The answer is of course that I am following them with close attention and with sympathy for the aspirations of the Moslem people for their advancement and progress; with sympathy for the large number of French settlers; and also for the French nation itself, our valued ally for so many years, to whom this whole question is desperately important. The program of restoring order, extending economic aid and then conducting an election as a result of which spokesmen will be chosen with whom new arrangements can be worked out seems constructive. The fact that in neighboring Tunisia and in neighboring Morocco there has been such a great and peaceful evolution in the very recent past gives one confidence for the future."

Dillon

[3] Document 187.

68. Telegram From the Department of State to the Embassy in France [1]

Washington, March 8, 1956—8:21 p.m.

3307. 1. We are also much concerned at mounting evidence anti-American feeling France over North African situation in general and Algerian problem in particular as set forth your recent telegrams.

2. At same time Department mindful of difficulties in appearing give France "blank check" for whatever course of action she may decide to undertake. Specifically, U.S. Government cannot put itself in position of underwriting in advance course of "restoring law and order" in Algeria which might well take form of long and sanguinary military campaign involving operations against civilian Moslem population.

3. Under circumstances Department considers no matter what we attempt to do in way of restoring climate of confidence and sympathy, U.S. unable go this direction as far as French would like without seriously impairing our relations with Arab world and African-Asian peoples and thereby ultimately mobilizing forces against West which would increase rather than diminish tension which it is our aim to lessen.

4. We agree that some corrective action to allay French doubts and suspicions concerning U.S. policy is highly desirable. Having considered various alternatives including suggestion Embtel 4060 [2] of statement by President during press conference, Department considers most effective immediate course of action is for Ambassador to make one or more speeches as suggested Embtel 3992 [3] in course of which points would be made which would reaffirm basic U.S. policy supporting continuation French presence North Africa and sympathy for French efforts achieve solution providing for relationship of interdependence on basis of mutual cooperation and confidence between France and peoples North Africa.

5. Since situation Tunisia and Morocco essentially different from that Algeria and represents far more advanced state on road toward independence, Ambassador's remarks on Algeria would presumably be largely of general nature and designed to create in French opinion sentiment that U.S. fully cognizant of complexity and delicacy

---

[1] Source: Department of State, Central Files, 751S.00/3–856. Secret; Limit Distribution.

[2] *Supra.*

[3] Dated March 2, telegram 3992 reported that French suspicions could only be allayed by repeated public expressions of sympathy, for past U.S. silence threatened a serious breach of confidence. The Ambassador feared negative repercussions on NATO and Western defense. (Department of State, Central Files, 751S.00/3–256)

problems which France now facing and sympathetic to her efforts work out equitable solution acceptable to both parties. Any implication U.S. considers Tunisian and Moroccan formulas as answer to Algerian problem would obviously be strongly resented.

6. Due recognition should be given to those aspects French policy past and present which represent progress in political, social and economic fields and which have resulted in the establishment of bonds between French and Moslem peoples which we hope will be preserved and indeed strengthened in future. Record of U.S. support of France's position in U.N. and of U.S. acceptance of fact that Algeria internal problem should be stressed.

7. Unless you believe it would be counterproductive it would seem opportune stress U.S. has no desire see France evicted from North Africa in order take her place and that on contrary we support strongly her efforts overcome her difficulties there and reach mutually acceptable solution which will ensure peaceful and prosperous future North Africa.

8. Department hopes that such pronouncements with proper publicity will do much assuage French resentment and diminish feeling that U.S. indifferent if not hostile to present French problems and struggle in North Africa. [4]

9. Obviously Department leaves to your discretion how and when foregoing views can be best expressed in order meet situation. However in view repercussions your statements may have in other parts of world including U.S., would appreciate having your views and reactions to foregoing and summary of remarks you would propose make together with any other suggestions you may have.

Hoover

---

[4] At the 279th meeting of the National Security Council on March 8, "the President commented that it would appear that the French were trying to make the United States the scapegoat for their difficulties." (Memorandum of discussion by Gleason; Eisenhower Library, Whitman File)

69. Telegram From the Supreme Allied Commander in Europe (Gruenther) to the Chairman of the Joint Chiefs of Staff (Radford) [1]

Paris, March 12, 1956—7:15 p.m.

ALO 382. Exclusive for Adm Radford eyes only. Earlier today I sent message number EC 91479 to JCS. [2] This is an amplification of that message.

On March 8 I saw Premier Mollet for 40 minutes. On March 10 I saw General Ely for an hour and a half, and later that day Defense Minister Bourges-Maunoury for 2 hours.

The one element which evolved from these meetings is that the government does not yet have a clear idea of how to solve the Algerian crisis. All 3 of these individuals are crystal clear, however, that Algeria must remain clearly French under some new formula which has not been devised.

Premier Mollet made a strong appeal for additional helicopters from the US. [3] I asked him if an official request had been made, but he didn't know. When I saw the Defense Minister Saturday he did not know that the Prime Minister had mentioned the helicopter subject to me. I asked him if an official request had been made and he replied, "No, not yet, but we expect to submit one very soon." He had just received a report from some French military official that 50 helicopters would be the equivalent of some 200,000 men. I expressed some skepticism over the validity of that formula, and he did not press the point further. Bourgès-Maunoury had a helicopter expert with him, and he told me that the French had not yet made

---

[1] Source: Eisenhower Library, Whitman File. Top Secret; Operational Immediate; Noforn. A handwritten marginal notation indicates the President noted the telegram on March 13. Gruenther was conferring with French military and civilian leaders on the impact of French withdrawal of troops from NATO to Algeria.

[2] In this telegram, General Gruenther suggested that the United States offer sympathetic support to the French, consider providing them with additional helicopters, be tolerant of their inability to maintain pledged NATO force commitments, and keep close track of the situation. (*Ibid.*, North Africa)

[3] According to an agreement reached on August 5, 1955, the United States agreed to divert 16 helicopters to France from USAF stocks with the stipulation that 8 were to be returned. Since the British were prepared to supply some medium helicopters, the United States was unwilling to agree to a request for 60 heavy and 20 medium helicopters made by the French Defense Minister on November 1. (Memorandum of conversation by Tyler, November 11, 1955; Department of State, Secretary's Memoranda of Conversation: Lot 64 D 199) A sale of 13 helicopters was approved in December 1955, but only 2 were to be turned over each month. Subsequently, on March 10, 1956, Mollet told Lodge that 80 helicopters and 50 slow-flying planes would make the difference. (Letter from Lodge to the President, March 10; Eisenhower Library, Whitman File, Administration Series, Lodge, Henry Cabot 1956)

up their minds which helicopter to ask for. But the expert said that they had to have more very soon.

I know General Valluy [4] well and I realize how strongly he feels about the subject of Algeria. He is an extremely sensitive individual, and I might add that there are many other Frenchmen who are developing that same characteristic under present conditions. In his inner heart he feels that France is slipping and slipping badly. He also is somewhat resentful—although he would deny this—over the treatment he has received in the United States. Basically he considers that no one in Washington pays much attention to him. It is possible that you and the other Chiefs might be able to rectify that impression by certain extra acts of courtesy from time to time. I am sure such actions would pay a big dividend. If you could find occasion to show a keen interest in Algerian developments that also may help.

There is a stronger anti-American feeling in France now than at any time in the last 5 years. Somehow most Frenchmen would like to blame their troubles on the United States. When you ask a responsible Frenchman—as I did Mollet and Bourges-Maunoury—what the United States has failed to do that it should do, the answer is always a vague one. For example, Mollet said, "I have no objection to the actions of US officials. However, unofficial Americans, as my friend Irving Brown, [5] cause us great trouble." Bourges-Maunoury said, "Sympathy from the United States will not be enough." I asked him specifically what he suggested but he had no answer.

All of this is by the way of illustrating that the French frame of mind is badly disorganized at this time. I will not hazard a guess as to the outcome.

---

[4] Jean Étienne Valluy was the French representative to the NATO Standing Group September 1953–October 1956. Thereafter he became Commander in Chief, Allied Forces, Central Europe.

[5] The AFL–CIO representative in Europe.

70. Telegram From the Embassy in France to the Department of State[1]

Paris, March 20, 1956—6 p.m.

4344. Re Deptel 3439, Mar 17.[2] I greatly appreciate the spirit behind reftel.

In view of fact that Mollet was dining with me at Residence last night, the 19th, I decided to send him preliminary draft of my speech late Monday afternoon[3] in the hope that I could informally cover the same ground with him that night.

The results were most useful as after dinner Mollet drew me aside and we had about a ten minute private talk. He thanked me warmly and asked me to convey his thanks to the Department for the support given to his policies in my speech.[4] He said that he most particularly appreciated one paragraph which he felt was primarily addressed to public opinion in the United States. This was the second paragraph in the portion of the speech devoted to Algeria beginning "while my government has been and is well aware of this problem . . . ".[5] Mollet said he felt it was most important that American public opinion come to realize that the French Government was not pursuing a colonialist policy in Algeria and that this problem could not be considered in the same context as other colonial problems but rather as a much more difficult problem of co-existence.

Mollet then told me that there were only two things which France asked from the United States. The first was greater comprehension on the part of American public opinion of the task facing France in Algeria and of the desire of the Mollet government to arrive at fair and liberal solutions. He said he hoped very much that American public opinion could gradually be educated as to the true facts of the Algerian situation. The second thing which France needed from the United States was assistance in the rapid procurement of helicopters.

---

[1] Source: Department of State, Central Files, 751S.00/3–2056. Secret.

[2] Telegram 3439 counseled Dillon not to expect mutual understanding and confidence in relations between the United States and France regarding North Africa. (*Ibid.*, 611.51/3–1756)

[3] March 19.

[4] A translation of the address which Dillon made in French at a luncheon of the Diplomatic Press Association of Paris on March 21 was transmitted in telegram 4325 from Paris, March 20. (Department of State, Central Files, 611.51/3–2056) Telegram 267 from Algiers, March 20, reported Lacoste's favorable comments on the speech. He hoped it would dispel some of the suspicion of the United States among the French military. (*Ibid.*, 611.51S/3–2056)

[5] Ellipsis in the source text.

As can be seen from the paragraph which Mollet picked out, I am in full agreement with his thesis that there is great danger in allowing the American public to over-simplify the Algerian problem and to consider it as merely another colonial problem. Due to the large and long established French population in Algeria the problem there is much more difficult and the differences between the French population in Algeria and the local Moslem population has more similarity to, for example, the Israeli-Arab problem than it does to such a purely colonial situation as Indochina. We will do what we can with United States correspondents here but it would be most helpful and indeed essential for Department spokesmen in giving press guidance and in making public statements to always bear this difference in mind and to avoid treating the Algerian problem as a simple problem of colonialism. I feel that the speech which I have just delivered should do good here in France where it should have considerable impact. It will, however, be necessary that it be followed up by other statements indicating sympathy for the French position in North Africa. Such statements naturally would be much more general in nature. It seems probable that Secretary or President may be questioned regarding policy outlined in my speech. I hope they will give general support to it in the same manner as Eden closing his speech in House of Commons, gave his blessing to Jebb's statement.[6]

My only other suggestion is a strong recommendation that we proceed with the greatest possible speed to give the French a favorable answer to their recent request for the diversion of 14 helicopters from United States Army orders this summer and fall. I do not see how we can avoid eventually giving approval to this French request and I hope that such approval can be given rapidly and graciously rather than having it dragged out of us by long and increasing French pressure in such a manner that we lose the greater part of the benefits of our decision.

Dillon

[6] Macmillan endorsed Jebb's statement in response to a question in Parliament on March 15. See *Parliamentary Debates*, House of Commons, vol. 550, p. 557.

71. Editorial Note

On June 13, the Representatives of Afghanistan, Egypt, Indonesia, Iran, Iraq, Jordan, Lebanon, Libya, Pakistan, Saudi Arabia, Syria, Thailand, and Yemen directed a letter to the President of the Security Council requesting that the Algerian matter be placed on the agenda. (U.N. doc. S/3609) France argued against the proposal on the grounds it was a domestic French concern. The issue was decided at the 730th meeting of the Council on June 26. Iran and the Soviet Union supported the proposal; Australia, Belgium, Cuba, France, Peru, the United Kingdom, and the United States rejected it, with China and Yugoslavia abstaining. (U.N. doc. S/PV.730) For Ambassador Lodge's statement of the United States position, see Department of State *Bulletin*, July 16, 1956, page 125.

---

72. Telegram From the Embassy in France to the Department of State [1]

Paris, July 25, 1956—7 p.m.

432. Reference: Embassy telegram 106, July 9. [2] I have just had most satisfactory interview with Lacoste. After talking with Mollet yesterday, Lacoste telephoned and asked if he might come to see me. I insisted on calling on him and saw him at his office this afternoon.

I told him that I had wanted to see him for some time because my main job in France was to maintain good relations between our two countries, not only on the governmental level but also on that of public opinion. I told him that I thought that Franco-American relations were in good shape everywhere except possibly in Algeria, where there still seemed to be a number of misunderstandings

[1] Source: Department of State, Central Files, 611.51S/7–2556. Secret. Repeated to Algiers.

[2] Telegram 106 reported on Dillon's meeting with Mollet on July 9 to discuss the unfriendliness which seemed to characterize relations between French and U.S. officials in Algeria. Mollet advised it was not a serious problem and that Lacoste considered U.S. policy fair. (*Ibid.*, 611.51S/7–956) This approach followed telegram 4 from Algiers, July 5, in which Clark complained in strong terms about the belief pervasive in Algeria that the United States sought to supplant France. He asserted that Americans were ostracized and all who associated with them were viewed with suspicion. In this message, part of which the Ambassador showed to Mollet, Clark suggested that another Dillon speech might reassure the French. (*Ibid.*, 751S.00/7–556)

regarding US objectives. I asked Lacoste if there was anything I could do to help clear up these misunderstandings.

Lacoste replied by saying he first wished to thank me for my speech of last March and also for my recent reiteration of the same principles which had come at a most useful moment. He said he also wished to thank the US for their extremely important help in making available military equipment, particularly helicopters, for the Algerian campaign. He then said that for understandable reasons the French throughout North Africa, but particularly in Algeria, have been in a very sensitive state of mind during the past months. He said there have been certain American private individuals who have expressed views or initiated action in Algeria which were very unhelpful to the French position. He said that he had reacted violently to the acts of these Americans and that he now realized that he had reacted too violently. He said that he now fully understood that there was no US Government support for the acts of any of such individuals, including those of Irving Brown. Therefore, in the future he would be very careful to make it evident that the US Government was not in any way acting contrary to French interests in Algeria. He clearly implied that this had not always been his view, that he was now convinced that he had been wrong in his previous estimate of the situation and would not his earlier anti-American statements [*sic*]. He told me that during Council of Ministers meeting this morning Pineau, knowing that Lacoste was going to see me later today, had said that US had been most helpful to France in its North Africa policy. Therefore, it is obvious that the matter was discussed this morning by the full Council of Ministers.

Finally, Lacoste said that if any question should arise in the future which gave him any concern he would bring it personally to my attention so that we could settle it between us without any public differences of opinion. Lacoste then said that he had very good relations with Clark, of whom he had a high opinion, and that he would continue maintain these good relations.

In view of fact that Mollet had discussed this matter with Lacoste, and that whole subject has been aired in full Ministerial meeting, I feel that there is reason to hope for a substantial improvement in Lacoste's attitude.

Dillon

73. Memorandum of a Conversation, Department of State, Washington, September 21, 1956[1]

SUBJECT

Inscription of Algerian Item at U.N.

PARTICIPANTS

M. Alphand, French Ambassador
M. Lucet, French Minister
The Acting Secretary
Mr. Wilcox
Mr. Elbrick

The Ambassador said that he wished to discuss tactics with respect to the Algerian problem in the forthcoming session of the General Assembly. He said that the situation will be different from that which obtained last year in that there are now more members of the United Nations and it is quite possible that the majority will vote for inscription of this item on the agenda. The French Government intends to clarify, before the meeting of the General Assembly, its proposals for a solution of the Algerian problem which he expected to be framed in the context of a French "Confederation". In contrast with last year's performance, the French Government did not wish to be unprepared this time and hoped to obtain the support of friendly nations to reduce the pressure on France. He referred particularly to the Afro-Asian group which, he understood, is considering a letter to the Secretary-General requesting the inscription of the Algerian item.[2] The French Government is hopeful of reducing the number of signatures to this letter and the Ambassador hoped that the U.S. Government would urge four of these countries (Liberia, Pakistan, the Philippines, and Thailand) not to sign the letter.[3] He said that these four had already shown some hesitancy about signing and he hoped that the U.S. would make representations to the four countries in their respective capitals.

[1] Source: Department of State, Central Files, 320/9–2156. Secret. Drafted by Elbrick.

[2] On October 25, 15 nations submitted such a request. As a countermove, the French asked that the question of Egyptian military assistance to the Algerian rebels be placed on the Security Council agenda. This followed France's interception on October 16 of the *Athos*, which had left Alexandria carrying weapons for the FLN. Though the matter was inscribed, France never requested a Council meeting to deliberate the issue.

[3] Lucet had similarly approached Wilcox on September 14 to request that the United States use its influence to get Liberia, China, and the Asian members of SEATO not to support the inscription move. (Memorandum of conversation by David Bane; Department of State, Central Files, 320/9–1456)

The Acting Secretary said that we view the French position sympathetically, as the Ambassador was aware, but that we are now giving consideration to the various ways and means by which the Algerian item might be handled and could not at this moment commit ourselves to any particular course of action. He pointed out that any country can request inscription of an item on the General Assembly agenda and that it would be hopeless to try to get all nations to vote against inscription. While the most we could hope for is to prevent some nations from voting for inscription, this also presents problems. He was glad that the Ambassador had raised this issue and was particularly glad to hear that the French Government plans to announce its intentions with respect to Algeria prior to the General Assembly meeting. He hoped that we could capitalize on this fact and that we could avoid being placed entirely on the defensive.

The Ambassador said that he could understand this point of view but he insisted that it would be beneficial also if we could announce our support of the French position "in advance". He said the fewer countries that sign a petition for inscription the better the French position will be. The French Government is most anxious for U.S. support. Mr. Hoover said that we must know where we are going before we make definite plans, and that the U.S. Government has not yet established a position with respect to the tactics to be employed. The Ambassador asked whether the U.S. would support the French Government on the question of competence if the item is inscribed on the agenda. Mr. Hoover replied that this involves the whole question of tactics which is still under review in the Department. At the appropriate time, of course, we will wish also to explore the matter with the French Government. At this time, we question whether it would be wise to waste ammunition in opposing inscription, in view of the unlikelihood of any success in this effort. The Ambassador said that he did not consider that we would be wasting ammunition in any sense and his Government would be most grateful if the United States, without prejudging the ultimate tactics to be adopted, could use its influence with the four nations in question in order that they and others would understand that the U.S. supports France on this issue. He said that it was very urgent that action be taken since the letter may be dispatched at any moment. The Acting Secretary said that we would study the matter.

74. Telegram From M'hammed Yazid of the National Liberation Front of Algeria to President Eisenhower [1]

New York, October 23, 1956—10:05 p.m.

MR. PRESIDENT: Five of my colleagues, including Mohamed Ben Bella, who fought under your command during World War II, have been arrested yesterday while they were on their way to participate with the Sultan of Morocco and the Tunisian Premier Habib Bourguiba in a conference to seek a peaceful solution for the Algerian problem. [2]

The conference was called by the sovereigns of the two States with the specific knowledge of the French Government which had itself requested the mediation of the Sultan of Morocco and Premier Bourguiba of Tunisia. This action which was described by the representatives of more than twenty five African and Asian governments to the United Nations as "shocking" and condemned throughout the entire civilized world, will only help to increase the tension and aggravate the situation in North Africa and make impossible the achievement of a peaceful settlement of the Franco-Algerian conflict.

Mr. President, on behalf of the Algerian people who are fighting for ideals of peace and liberty which you have always championed, I appeal to you as President of the great democracy which blazed the trail of freedom to intervene with the French Government in order to set free the five leaders of the Algerian people. This would enable them to proceed to the proposed Conference of Peace in Tunis. Your intervention, Mr. President, would certainly avert the tragic consequences of the extension throughout North Africa of the war currently taking place in Algeria.

M'Hammed Yazid

---

[1] Source: Department of State, Central Files, 771.00/10–2456. The source text is a commercial telegram.

[2] Mohammed Ben Bella, Mohammed Khider, Hocine Aït Ahmed, Mohammed Boudiaf, and Mustafa Lacheraf were captured when the plane on which they were passengers was intercepted. The first four were members of the original National Council of the Algerian Revolution; the last was an FLN information officer. Their plane was registered in France and had a French crew though it had been chartered by the Sultan who considered the FLN leaders to be his guests and under his protection.

75. Telegram From the Department of State to the Embassy in Libya [1]

Washington, October 26, 1956—8:03 p.m.

229. Embtel 245. [2] Position Department has taken re North African situation has been reached on basis careful consideration overall US foreign policy objectives involved. Our immediate objective is restoration peace and stability in area in which we maintain important interests. In pursuance this objective we have expressed concern to French Government over developments in North Africa resulting from plane incident. At same time we have urged moderation in both Morocco and Tunisia. This position does not imply any US responsibility for or sympathy with French action in intercepting plane and capturing Algerian leaders. Nor does it identify us with Moroccan and Tunisian demands French release Algerian leaders. Our position has been based solely on overall considerations US interests in countries affected.

In light foregoing we cannot agree public statement you suggest.

Foregoing is FYI only.

Embtel 242. [3] You should reply orally to Libyan note along following lines:

"Department understands concern Libyan Government over situation resulting from plane incident and interception Algerian leaders and is also concerned re tension in North Africa. US of course has no legal right demand release Algerians. We have however emphasized to French Government our serious concern over recent developments North Africa. We are continuing make every appropriate effort to encourage earliest restoration peace and stability in area."

Department repeating Deptels 1459 [4] and 1494 [5] to Paris and

---

[1] Source: Department of State, Central Files, 751S.00/10–2656. Secret; Priority.

[2] In telegram 245, October 26, Ambassador Tappin commented as follows on the French seizure of Algerian leaders: "had I deliberately sat down and sought to do so, I could not have dreamed up act more prejudicial to Western-Arab relations than this one." He suggested a statement deploring France's action as detrimental to peace. (*Ibid.*)

[3] Telegram 242, October 24, transmitted the text of a Libyan note calling attention to the potential consequences of the French action and asking the United States to intervene. (*Ibid.*, 751S.00/10–2456) Documentation on representations to the U.S. Government to intercede on behalf of the Algerian leaders is *ibid.*, Central Files 751S.00.

[4] Telegram 1459, October 23, expressed the Department's concern about the French action and its probable detrimental impact on Western interests throughout North Africa. The Embassy was requested to determine who was responsible for the action. (*Ibid.*, 751S.00/10–2256)

[5] Telegram 1494, October 25, instructed Dillon to express U.S. concern at the highest appropriate level. (*Ibid.*, 751S.00/10–2556)

Paris' 1932 [6] which will provide further background information this question.

Dulles

[6] Telegram 1932, October 24, reported on Dillon's conversation with Jean Basdevant, the top permanent official handling Moroccan and Tunisian affairs, who undertook to inform Pineau and Joxe of the U.S. concern. Mollet, however, was not prepared to free the captives who were wanted for "criminal" acts. (*Ibid.*, 751S.00/10–2456)

---

76. Memorandum of a Conversation, French Embassy, Washington, November 16, 1956 [1]

SUBJECT

Conversation with French Foreign Minister Pineau

PARTICIPANTS

Mr. Christian Pineau, French Foreign Minister
Mr. Hervé Alphand, French Ambassador
Mr. J. Daridan, Director of Political Affairs, Quai d'Orsay
Mr. William R. Tyler, WE

After a small dinner at the French Embassy, on the occasion of Mr. Pineau's unofficial visit to Washington, Daridan took me aside, and talked to me about Algeria. We were then joined by Pineau and Alphand.

1. *Algeria*: In the first part of the conversation, before we were joined by Pineau, Daridan said that "everyone" in Paris realized that the Government's program for Algeria would not succeed. The chances of achieving pacification were no better now than before. In fact, the arrest of the five FLN leaders had been an act of folly, which had involved Morocco more deeply in the issue. Daridan said France's long-term relations with Tunisia and Morocco could not be settled until the Algerian matter was disposed of; and yet no one in France who knew anything about the problem was optimistic that the new statute for Algeria which the Government had prepared would do the trick. Daridan said he thought the only hope lay in

[1] Source: Department of State, Central Files, 751S.00/11–1656. Secret. Drafted by Tyler. Enclosure to a memorandum from Tyler to Elbrick, November 26, indicating that because of the nature of the comments on Algeria the memorandum would not be given wide distribution and would be held for discussion with Ambassador Dillon.

U.S. initiative for a broad settlement of major issues in the Near East, of which Algeria was one. He said that unless we took this initiative, he feared the Algerian situation would deteriorate further, and that Morocco might eventually intervene openly with resulting chaos.

I said to Daridan that his idea that the U.S. should take the initiative on Algeria was unexpected, coming from a Frenchman. I reminded him that we had leaned over backward, in deference to French requests and sensitivities, in order to give France time to work out a solution herself, and by herself. I thought it would be far preferable for France herself to announce whatever measures she thought must be taken in order to bring peace to Algeria, and to form a permanent basis for friendly relations between Metropolitan France and that part of the world. I thought we would gladly support such measures if they seemed to us realistic and statesman-like. However, I said, I personally doubted whether it was a very tempting proposition for us to take the initiative and thereby expose ourselves to renewed charges of selling out France, and of trying to take over Algeria in France's place. Daridan repeated that he thought the situation would shortly require the leadership of the United States if catastrophe was to be averted in North Africa.

After Mr. Pineau had joined us, I asked him what he felt about the prospects for the Government's program for Algeria. He sounded very discouraged and said he thought the next stage must be to hold elections. When I asked whether he thought this could happen in the present climate of terrorism, he said nothing, but slowly raised his arms to an angle of about 30° from his body, and then let them fall again.

Pineau said he thought it important that a three-power conference be held before the Algerian question is debated in the General Assembly. I asked him when he thought that would be, and he said he thought some time in the first half of January. He did not mention any date in the immediate future for a conference.

Comment: From my conversation, I got the impression that (a) at least Pineau and the Foreign Office are very pessimistic about the situation in Algeria, and that they fear the worst for the future prospects of the West in Tunisia and Morocco, and (b) that the Government may now be coming around to a radical reappraisal of French national policy and goals in North Africa, which may involve us directly and at short notice.

[Here follows discussion of Egypt and Syria.]

77. Telegram From the Embassy in France to the Department of State[1]

Paris, November 21, 1956—11 a.m.

2508. Reference: Embassy telegram 2450, November 16, repeated Algiers 91, Rabat 172, Tunis 156.[2] We consider French Government's current attitude toward Algerian question, as reported by Mollet's Cabinet, reflects short-sightedness and lack of realism. Attitude is quite understandable, however, since articulate French opinion, and particularly opinion leading figures of most political parties, is so strongly and emotionally opposed to significant concessions on Algeria that any French Government finds it much easier to postpone than to act. Indeed, especially after serious setback in Egypt, bold and forward-looking proposals on Algeria at this time could arouse so much opposition in Assembly as to cause government's overthrow.

Nevertheless, it is hard to avoid conclusion that, if French do not come up with new proposals, situation is likely to be worse rather than better after UNGA debate. Tempers on both sides will be further frayed, intransigent positions will have been reiterated, and French Government is likely to feel it cannot "surrender" to public demands of Arab States or to hostile UN resolution. Hence conciliatory action after debate may appear to French even more untimely than it does now.

Yet restoration of close and friendly relations with Tunis and Morocco apparently depend on an acceptable Algerian settlement. If French do not move forward promptly on Algerian question, their whole position in North Africa may become untenable. Result would probably be US would have to fill vacuum, which would be extremely expensive and also most damaging to our relations with France. This problem has already arisen in connection with economic aid. We do not know whether settlement, short of independence but generous in autonomy, acceptable both to France and to Algeria's neighbors, can be devised. However, it is obvious serious attempt along these lines should be made.

If Cabinet re-examination Algerian question this week ends in usual blind alley, we should like to discuss problem frankly and sympathetically with high French officials, preferably Mollet himself. This would be difficult and delicate démarche but we think it is

---

[1] Source: Department of State, Central Files, 751S.00/11–2156. Confidential. Repeated to Rabat, Algiers, and Tunis.

[2] This telegram reported that the French were disposed to await the completion of the U.N. debate before deciding what reforms to offer. Dillon did not believe that this tendency augured well for the future. (*Ibid.*, 751S.00/11–1656)

probably unavoidable in any case since we must certainly explain to French in advance line we propose to take in UNGA debate. They expect us to support them unequivocally on this matter which they consider at the moment their most vital interest. Our failure to do so would be considered as further, and perhaps fatal, shock to French confidence in Atlantic alliance and NATO. Yet difficulties vis-à-vis Arab States in supporting unequivocally present frozen French position are all too obvious. It seems in every way desirable, therefore, that US formulate its own attitude on this issue promptly and communicate our views to French in time for them to be considered and take effect.

We suggest for Department's and USUN's consideration démarche to be made in Paris along following lines:

(1) We reiterate our desire to be helpful in UN debate on Algeria;
(2) We agree Algerian item be postponed to latter half GA session if possible;
(3) We fear that, in absence any further and more explicit French proposals, debate will be very rough, Morocco and Tunis will be in opposition, US and other friends of France will be seriously handicapped by lack of knowledge French intentions, and outcome will probably be adoption condemnatory resolution which will make solution much more difficult;
(4) If, however, French Government should find it possible to put forward before or during debate proposals sufficiently liberal to have broad appeal in GA, we would be prepared to give strongest possible support to these proposals and exert our influence in same sense on other delegations.

We should appreciate being informed whether Department would authorize approach to French along these lines.

Dillon

78. Telegram From the Department of State to the Embassy in France[1]

Washington, November 27, 1956.

2024. Paris 2508.[2] Agree you should at first appropriate opportunity make démarche re Algeria. It would seem preferable that démarche be made Mollet, although recognize that with Pineau's return Paris this may not be feasible. You should speak along following lines:

1. Reiterate our desire be as helpful as feasible in UN debate;
2. As we have already said, we will cooperate with French efforts get Algerian item postponed to latter half GA session. French will of course have to take initiative on this, although press of other items may automatically delay consideration Algeria;
3. While fully realizing that Algerian crisis is not susceptible of easy solution and that Mollet is confronted with very difficult Parliamentary situation this connection, we fear that in absence new concrete and far-reaching French plans that can obtain Algerian, as well as Moroccan and Tunisian, acceptance, debate will be rough and outcome uncertain irrespective US action;
4. US position not yet formulated (Paris 2486).[3] It will only be formulated prior UN debate when we know French plans and in light international developments at that time. Difficult predict what stand we would take as much depends on course of debate and type of resolutions presented, including position and tactics adopted by French. We would, however, expect exercise a moderating influence;
5. It seems to US that irrespective UN debate which may go badly despite French efforts new French policy towards Algeria now essential in effort improve French relations Tunisia and Morocco and restore stability North African region which is so important US, French and NATO security;
6. US fully recognizes that despite our interest North African stability decision on Algeria must be French one and US not desiring or in position give advice or comment re specifics French program. As Mollet must know we have always leaned over backwards in not intervening in Algerian issue which would seem frankly however no nearer settlement than it did at outset rebellion. It is still not our intention pressure French into taking steps which they may not believe to be wise but we believe it important try peaceful political

---

[1] Source: Department of State, Central Files, 751S.00/11–2156. Confidential; Priority; Limit Distribution. Repeated to Algiers, Rabat, Tunis, and USUN. The time of transmission is not legible.

[2] *Supra.*

[3] Telegram 2486, November 20, reported that when Robert Felix, the local representative of Lacoste, approached the Embassy to learn the U.S. position, he was told that it had not yet been formulated. Lacoste was said to favor a delay in the debate, though he tended increasingly to believe that significant reforms should precede the debate. (Department of State, Central Files, 751S.00/11–2056)

approach to problem and hope French will view matter in same light.

FYI Dept concurs that especially in light French requests from several quarters for our views on Algerian issue in connection UN debate, discreet and high level démarche on US part might be useful in contributing to bring about difficult decisions by French Govt re Algeria which Govt appears inclined put off as long as possible. At same time we must avoid any attempt by French Govt get US identified with any specific new French plan. US Govt can obviously not give blank check for support for new French Govt policy which may turn out to be meaningless and unrealizable formula. Accordingly we wish to avoid giving impression we attempting advise French re basic Algerian policies at this time in order avoid possibility US being used shoulder responsibility vis-à-vis French cabinet, Parliament or public opinion for unpopular steps French Govt may have to take to get out of present Algerian impasse. In light information presently available here, it frankly seems doubtful that any new French proposal short of negotiations with FLN on basis firm commitment complete autonomy Algeria now with possibility eventual independence would resolve Algerian crisis or improve French relations Morocco and Tunisia. End FYI.

Dept concurs with line you took with Joxe (Paris 2543).[4] We assume you do not consider that this conversation has overtaken your recommendation for démarche and in fact it would seem confirm desirability of approach to Mollet providing of course no new Govt plans formulated by cabinet in meantime.

Re Pineau's idea for Algerian elections with UN observers (New York Delga 175,[5] repeated info Paris 1992), difficult judge whether such proposal would markedly influence Algerian situation or what Moroccan and Tunisian reactions would be, much less Afro-Asian bloc. It is not clear to us how elections could be held under present climate terrorism or what prospects there are for obtaining cease fire prior substantive negotiations with FLN. Accordingly endeavor avoid comment this idea on basis lack of information makes it difficult for us judge how effective any such specific French plan may be.

Hoover

[4] Telegram 2543, November 22, reported Joxe's concern that the Algerian problem would damage French-U.S. relations. Dillon responded that one difficulty was the apparent French retreat from their intention to institute reforms prior to the U.N. debate. Joxe affirmed his agreement that such a course would be preferable and held out hope that this might yet be the case. (*Ibid.*, 751S.00/11–2256)

[5] Not printed. (*Ibid.*, 783A.56/11–2356) Lodge endorsed the idea as well as the démarche suggested by Dillon, but he disapproved of any advance commitment to support the French who had failed to produce acceptable proposals. (Delga 195, November 26; *ibid.*, 751S.00/11–2656)

79. Telegram From the Embassy in France to the Department of State [1]

Paris, November 29, 1956—6 p.m.

2677. Re Deptel 2024. [2] I saw Mollet this afternoon re reftel. There was no problem as far as Pineau was concerned as Algerian affairs are no concern of his and Mollet has always told me to talk to him directly on Algeria. I delivered message in reftel and Mollet assured me that he intended to make policy declaration before debate in GA. Mollet said, however, that he was afraid that any statement he would make would not be accepted by FLN leaders who now have put their faith in UN. His feeling is that the army of liberation, that is, those who are actually fighting in Algeria, are prepared to consider a cease fire after a reasonable offer from France. However, he feels that in no event will the FLN leaders outside of Algeria, i.e., those in Cairo, New York and elsewhere agree to anything which he may propose. He considers that their feeling is that Afro-Asiatic group plus Soviets now exercise clear working control of GA and therefore they will try and insist on having GA impose the terms of a settlement in Algeria. Such a settlement will of course be totally unacceptable to France.

Mollet said that his statement on Algeria will be bold, but probably not quite as bold as it would have been if he could have counted on good faith on the part of the FLN negotiators. He will stress complete liberty and equality for all individuals and all racial groupings in Algeria and will outline what he considers to be the minimum rights of French. He sees Algerian problem primarily as conflict between diverse non-European groups united in the Moslem religion and the hard core of Algerians of European descent. He feels that only metropolitan France can arbitrate between these two groups. He said that indigenous European elements whose loyalty is not to France, but rather to themselves as European Algerians are tending more and more towards attempting to achieve a solution along South African lines which would involve creation of an independent Algeria controlled by European elements. [3] He said that

[1] Source: Department of State, Central Files, 751S.00/11–2956. Confidential; Limit Distribution. Repeated to Algiers, Rabat, Tunis, and USUN.

[2] *Supra.*

[3] In telegram 3397 from Paris, January 14, 1957, Dillon expressed his concern that the European population in Algeria might attempt to take matters into its own hands to impose a solution. He was unsure how the French army might respond to such a development. (Department of State, Central Files, 751S.00/1–1457) Two days after Dillon stated his concern, an attempt was made upon the life of General Raoul Salan, the supreme military commander in Algeria.

an attempt at any such solution would of course be a tragedy and he was using his whole effort to avoid such a result.

Regarding UN debate he said that France would explain actions being taken in Algeria and then would maintain that Assembly could take no action because it was not competent to intervene in French internal affairs. In other words, France will rely once again on argument of incompetence of GA but prior to proposing such argument will be willing to explain her position and her intentions. If France should be beaten and anti-French resolutions voted Mollet said it is absolutely certain that France will leave the UN for good and all. He said that his government will not take such action but there was absolutely no doubt that in refusing to take such action his government would be overthrown and succeeding government would effectively take France out of UN.

Mollet said that the result in UN depended entirely on US. There would be at least 26 votes, i.e. Afro-Asiatic bloc and Soviet bloc against France. Therefore it would require full efforts of US to defeat such a move. Mollet said this was one of the reasons why he felt it so essential that he meet with President personally in near future so that details of a common policy could be worked out to face up to this difficult situation.

Dillon

---

80. Memorandum of a Conversation, Department of State, Washington, November 29, 1956 [1]

SUBJECT

Conversation With Algerian Leaders

[1] Source: Department of State, Central Files, 751S.00/11–2956. Confidential. Drafted by Bovey.

PARTICIPANTS

Ferhat Abbas
Abderrahman Kiwan

WE—Matthew Looram
AF/N—John Bovey
AF/N—Donald Norland

After describing his mission to South America, Mr. Abbas said he had been sent by the FLN (Front de Libération Nationale) to discuss the Algerian situation with U.S. officials.

He launched first into a long and bitter review of French activities in Algeria, the burden of which was that the Clemenceau laws of 1919 and the Statute of 1947[2] were all based on a false conception that Algerians could be somehow assimilated as French citizens. Moreover, this assimilation had never been carried through in good faith, since Algerians were in fact disenfranchised through a system of unequal representation in the municipal councils (⅖ Moslem, ⅗ French) and by assignment of equal number of seats in the French Assembly, even though the Moslem population of Algeria was eight times that of the French. Even when Paris did act in good faith, any moves to correct this situation were immediately sabotaged, Mr. Abbas said, by the colons in Algeria.

Mr. Abbas said there were four principal facts which American officials should know: (1) They must realize from their knowledge of the Indo-Chinese situation that France would never win the Algerian war. Algerians would continue to fight until the French accepted the principle of equality rather than assimilation. (2) The war would continue to cause grave repercussions in Tunisia and Morocco, whose close relation to Algeria explained French creation of the Protectorates and which was still a fundamental fact of political and strategic life. (3) The war created a danger of increasing Communist penetration of North Africa. If the liberation movement were decapitated (it had not been, Mr. Abbas hastily added, by the capture of the five FLN leaders on October 22), red maquis might well take over, although they had not done so anywhere in Algeria to date. (4) North Africa was North African and not Egyptian or Middle Eastern; it could therefore form a useful new element in the Arab world if the settlement of the Algerian conflict permitted.

Mr. Kiwan adverted to the possibility of North Africa serving as bridge between the West and the Middle East, and he emphasized

[2] The Clemenceau laws of February 4, 1919, made French citizenship more accessible to the Muslim population and increased the local government role of Muslims who were French subjects. The Statute of September 20, 1947, defined Algeria as a group of overseas departments. It recognized two separate communities forming distinct electoral colleges, each of which selected 60 members of the local Assembly and sent 15 representatives to France.

the evident U.S. interest in the stability of the area, not to mention our moral interest in settling a colonial conflict.

Mr. Abbas reviewed the successive failures of his own movement, the UDMA and the MTLD of Messali Hadj, to persuade the French to drop their unreasonable insistence that Algeria was French and that Algerians were French rather than North African. In reply to a question, he tried to straighten out the orientation of the various Algerian labor organizations. Mr. Kiwan came to his rescue and explained the significance of the different groups as follows: The UGTA (Union Générale des Travailleurs Algériens) was the true national labor front, which represented the FLN leadership. Upon its formation last year members of the Communist-dominated CGT had immediately deserted to UGTA and it had become affiliated with the ICFTU. The few remaining hard-core Communists had formed the UGSA (Union Générale des Syndicats Algériens), while the MTLD of Messali Hadj was grouped in the USTA (Union Syndicale des Travailleurs Algériens). USTA and UGSA were really paper organizations; they were analogous in the labor field to the maquis which Messali and the Communists respectively had tried to form for their own use instead of joining with the FLN.

In response to Mr. Looram's questioning, Mr. Abbas set forth four conditions which the French would have to accept before the FLN would accept a cease-fire: (1) recognition of the national existence of Algeria; (2) recognition of her right to independence; (3) a political amnesty; (4) recognition of a provisional Algerian Government, with which France would negotiate. Mr. Looram asked where elections fitted into this picture; Mr. Abbas emphasized strongly that elections could only be held after the provisional government was formed.

We pointed out that insistence on these points, and particularly the fourth, would probably result in an impasse, especially in the light of the present political situation in France and asked whether more gradual formulas, such as those which appeared to interest Mr. Bourguiba, could be found. Mr. Abbas said we should try to see the arguments on the Algerian side instead of coming to the rescue of Mr. Mollet. He was told it was not our intention to take sides, much less mediate, on the Algerian issue; what we were interested in learning, however, was whether Mr. Abbas foresaw, given the realities of the situation, any possibility for a peaceful compromise solution of this tragic conflict.

Mr. Kiwan interrupted to say that there really was no impasse as "our friend" Abbas might have led us to believe. He said that the provisional "government" would not need to have all the attributes of sovereignty and indicated it might be analogous to the type of Tunisian Government which had been set up to negotiate local autonomy in 1955. Both he and Mr. Abbas seemed to agree, however, that the right of Algeria to ultimate independence would have to be recognized before the FLN would stop fighting.

Comment: Kiwan seemed to be speaking as an authentic member of the FLN and constantly referred to Abbas as a "friend" rather than a colleague. He corrected at least twice the version of the situation presented by Abbas, who seemed less sure of himself.

Abbas' insistence that elections could be held only after the provisional government was formed might indicate a certain uneasiness as to the FLN's position in popular elections held before it was firmly entrenched.

---

81. Memorandum of a Conversation, Department of State, Washington, January 11, 1957, 3–4 p.m.[1]

SUBJECT

Algeria

PARTICIPANTS

U.S. Side	*French Side*
The Secretary of State	Mr. C. Pineau, French Foreign Minister
Assistant Secretary, C. McCardle	Mr. H. Alphand, French Ambassador
Assistant Secretary, Francis Wilcox	Mr. C. Lucet, French Minister
Acting Assistant Secretary, C. Burke Elbrick	Mr. F. de Laboulaye, Counselor of French Embassy
Mr. Fraser Wilkins	Mr. J. Beliard, Press Officer, French Foreign Office
Mr. William R. Tyler	

Mr. Pineau opened the conversation by producing a special file which he had brought with him to give to the Secretary, and which he said contained evidence of the nature and the extent of Communist intervention in Algeria.

The Secretary asked Mr. Pineau whether the documentation which had been seized in the plane together with the five Algerian nationalist leaders had contained any important material. Mr. Pineau answered that it had provided the French government with much

[1] Source: Department of State, Central Files, 751S.00/1–1157. Secret. Drafted by Tyler.

information on the organization of the revolutionary movement, including networks and methods of operation.

Mr. Pineau then handed the Secretary an English translation of Mr. Mollet's statement on Algeria of January 9th.[2] He said he wished to draw the Secretary's attention to two major errors of interpretation in the public press:

1) It had been stated that Mr. Mollet had called for an unconditional surrender by the Algerian Front of National Liberation. This was incorrect, as the French government was calling solely for a cessation of hostilities and had made no prior condition whatsoever. It was not calling for a surrender, and had stated that there would be no reprisals or any action against those who had engaged in the fighting while it lasted.

2) It had also been stated that once elections had been held, and the thirty deputies to the French National Assembly had been elected, the French government proposed to negotiate only with a group selected by it among these thirty deputies. This was untrue, said Mr. Pineau, because the French government intended to negotiate with all thirty deputies, whatever their affiliation—even if all thirty belonged to the F.L.N.

Mr. Pineau, turning to the question of procedure in the forthcoming debate on Algeria in the UN General Assembly, and stressing its importance, said that the French tactics had not yet been definitely settled. He said France felt it could count on the support of several countries, among them Iran, Brazil, and Colombia, and it planned to make a long presentation of the French case in the First Committee. France would participate in the general discussion, and answer attacks and criticisms of its policy. At the same time, it proposed to stress that it does not recognize the competence of the U.N. on Algeria, and it would not participate in the drafting of any resolution or in the voting. The French government, said Mr. Pineau, hoped that there would be no resolution on Algeria.

The Secretary said it would probably be very difficult to avoid some kind of resolution. He said that he had personally always advocated the view that it should be possible to discuss certain matters in the U.N. under Article 10 of the Charter without a resolution having in fact to be taken, and that debate should end with some such formula as that the discussion had been heard and

[2] Among other things, Mollet's plan called for a cease-fire followed after 90 days by a general election on the basis of universal suffrage and involving a single electoral college. Promising full equality, he declared his intention to discuss the future of Algeria with the chosen representatives of the people. Dulles conferred with President Eisenhower earlier in the day and stated that the French were seeking a blank check from the United States in support of their plan before providing any details. The President commented that this was not possible because the French might be encouraged to "whittle down" the proposal once they were confident of U.S. backing. (Eisenhower library, Dulles Papers, Meetings with the President)

noted, and that one could then pass on to the next item of business on the agenda.

Mr. Pineau said that a motion of this kind would be acceptable in the First Committee, after which it would be necessary to find a formula for a resolution after the debate in the General Assembly, on which France would abstain.

The Secretary said he thought we should instruct Ambassador Lodge to talk to the chief French Delegate and work out with him some sort of mutually acceptable resolution.

The Secretary asked Mr. Pineau whether the program for Algeria which France was going to propose at the U.N. would be the same as that set forth in the Mollet declaration. Mr. Pineau said it would, only it would be presented in greater detail, and that he expected the presentation of the French case would last about three hours, in two parts, so as not to tire unduly the members of the First Committee.

The Secretary asked Mr. Pineau again whether he thought it would be helpful if we instructed Ambassador Lodge to confer with the chief French Delegate in order to try to work out the text of a resolution together. Mr. Pineau answered in the affirmative. He said that the French government had purposely left somewhat vague the indication of its thinking on the character of a new Statute for Algeria, because this was a matter which would have to be negotiated with the elected representatives of Algeria, so that the French government could not at this stage say what the new Statute should be. Mr. Pineau said that his government hoped that the solution would be along the general lines of a Federation, comparable with the relationship of the U.S. Federal government to the states, or with the Swiss Cantons, with separation of the Executive, Legislative and Judiciary powers.

The Secretary asked Mr. Pineau whether the French government felt it could hope for a cease-fire in Algeria on the basis of the proposals. Mr. Pineau said his government felt that it was "not impossible" that the offer of a cease-fire would be accepted. He said that many of those fighting had been waiting, before committing themselves, for the debate in the U.N. to take place, and that the French government hoped that afterwards they would again be prepared to take up the cease-fire offer.

The Secretary asked Pineau whether the French planned early implementation of their proposals.

Mr. Pineau said that one major difficulty arose from the fact that the French population in Algeria would never accept a solution negotiated directly with the rebels, but that it would undoubtedly accept a solution negotiated with the elected Algerian representatives, even though the two solutions might be similar in the end.

With regard to the French willingness to invite observers from democratic countries to witness the election, Mr. Pineau said he hoped to have one observer from North America, one from South America, one from Europe and one from Asia. He said that Pakistan had already expressed its interest in sending an observer.

The Secretary said he had noted in Mr. Mollet's statement fairly detailed indications of the nature of the regime France had in mind for Algeria, and was curious to know whether the negotiations with the elected Algerian representatives would be limited to the ways in which what had been proposed should be implemented, or whether the Algerian Deputies would be free to make other proposals.

Mr. Pineau said that the French proposals set forth were only a point of departure. The Deputies might wish to propose something different, in which case the negotiations would seek to achieve a reconciliation of the two proposals.

The Secretary observed that this point was very important.

Mr. Pineau went on to say that his government was not attempting to work out an Algerian solution which it expected to last for a hundred years; it did not have in mind a solution for all time. It would perhaps be necessary later on to confer more powers on the Algerian regime. It was an evolutionary process, Mr. Pineau said, which must advance by stages. Mr. Pineau said that he could of course not say all this in public discussion, and he gave as a reason the precedent of which had happened in the case of Morocco: he said that as soon as France had declared her willingness that Morocco should be independent, the course of events was so precipitated as to have unfavorable political and economic repercussions.

The Secretary commented on his own feeling that the appetite for independence had sometimes become excessive, but this was a factor which had to be reckoned with.

Mr. Pineau concluded by saying that Algeria was not now in a position to govern itself. It did not have the required institutions and experienced personnel for this.

---

82. Editorial Note

Between February 4 and 13, the First Committee of the United Nations General Assembly considered three draft resolutions on Algeria. Draft resolution A/C.1/L.165, introduced by 18 Asian and African nations, supported Algerian self-determination and called for immediate French-Algerian negotiations. Draft resolution A/C.1/L.166, submitted by Japan, Thailand, and the Philippines, expressed the hope that France and the Algerian people would endeavor through negotiations to bring about a peaceful settlement. Draft resolution A/C.1/L.167, introduced by Argentina, Brazil, Cuba, the Dominican Republic, Italy, and Peru, expressed the hope that a peaceful and democratic solution would be found.

On February 13, the First Committee rejected the first two operative paragraphs of A/C.1/L.165 by a vote of 33 to 34 with 9 abstentions, the United States voting in opposition. Next, it adopted A/C.1/L.167 by a vote of 41 to 33 with 3 abstentions, the United States voting in favor. It then adopted A/C.1/L.166 by 37 votes to 27 with 13 abstentions, the United States voting in opposition. At the 645th plenary meeting of the General Assembly, it unanimously adopted a draft resolution, submitted by the sponsors of the two draft resolutions approved by the First Committee, expressing the hope that a peaceful, democratic, and just solution would be found, through appropriate means, in conformity with the United Nations Charter.

For text of Resolution 1012 (XI), the various draft resolutions, and the roll call votes, see United Nations, Official Records, General Assembly, Eleventh Session, Agenda Item 62, Annexes, pages 2–5. The texts of statements by Ambassador Lodge before the First Committee on February 6 and 12 are printed in Department of State *Bulletin*, March 11, 1957, pages 421–422. Related documentation is in Department of State, Central File 751S.00.

---

83. Telegram From the Consulate General at Algiers to the Department of State [1]

Algiers, June 4, 1957—11 a.m.

376. Before going on home leave in February I said (my telegram 278) [2] my departure justified as I could "see no early or

[1] Source: Department of State, Central Files, 751S.00/6–457. Confidential. Repeated to Paris, Rabat, Tunis, London, and Rome for John M. McSweeney, First Secretary of the Embassy and special NATO liaison officer with CINCSOUTH, and Edward P. Montgomery, Consul General at Valletta.

[2] Telegram 278 from Algiers, February 12, reported that the situation in Algeria remained largely unchanged. Clark foresaw no prospects for a cease-fire or for an early or desirable Algerian solution. (*Ibid.*, 751S.00/2–1257)

desirable solution to problem". Upon my return Algeria I find that phrase amply justified.

Efforts at military pacification continue as do those toward implementation Lacoste vast program of administrative and economic reform. At same time nationalists continue unabated their economic sabotage, their ambushes of military and other convoys and their assassinations of any one refusing them support or collaborating with the "enemy". In fact, our charts indicate monthly average terrorist acts this year appreciably higher than two preceding years. Chasm between two communities is widening, rational thinking is ruled out with emotions increasingly in control and eventual reconciliation disparate elements of country becoming less and less likely.

Algeria seems to be moving tragically towards catastrophe. If France had determination and perseverance necessary to complete military reconquest of country she could do so. On other hand it seems unlikely France can long continue the drain on her resources of wealth and manpower required for such task and even if she did her problem would not be solved. She would be right where she was on November 1, 1954, and in meantime her relations with Tunisians and Moroccans could be counted upon to have deteriorated seriously.

But can France compromise? More than year ago, I argued that if France delayed too long she would lose control of course of events in Algeria. That time may have come. Am told by source close Lacoste that he is frustrated with his failure to achieve quicker results, realizes his much vaunted program is a failure and is seeking graceful way out (shades of Soustelle).

If Lacoste departs and new approach is sought reaction of European element and army is unpredictable. Am told on all sides that we could expect European demonstration much more serious than took place on departure of Soustelle and that blood would be sure to flow. Also, there is definite unhappiness among military commanders and considerable question as to their reaction should civilian government once again as in Indo-China, Tunisia and Morocco pull the rug out from under their feet. That Algeria would be in turmoil for awhile seems certain.

Given this picture I venture to suggest that we be most cautious in pressuring France to any course of action in Algeria. Calm cannot be restored overnight and there are already signs France is looking for whipping boy. Our long-range interests may well therefore best be saved by letting Algeria fester for time being.

Clark

84. Memorandum of a Conversation, Department of State, Washington, June 14, 1957[1]

SUBJECT

United States Position on Algerian Dispute

PARTICIPANTS

Hervé Alphand, French Ambassador
M. Charles Lucet, Minister of French Embassy
Mr. Murphy—G
Mr. Gerald Smith—S/AE
Mr. J. J. Jova—WE

The French Ambassador called on Mr. Murphy at his request, saying that it was some time since they had spoken and he wished to review several new developments, particularly in light of the fact that France now had a new Government. The Ambassador reviewed the Bourges-Maunoury investiture speech and in regard to Algeria, he emphasized that the offer of free elections stands, but unfortunately the FLN does not appear to want them. Mr. Murphy asked if there was no indication at all of interest on the part of the FLN and M. Alphand said that unfortunately there was not. In Algeria, he said, the situation was different than in Morocco and Tunisia in that there is no one to negotiate or deal with. Mr. Murphy asked about Ben Bella and his four Algerian colleagues now in a French jail and the Ambassador changed the subject. He went on to say, however, that Bourges-Maunoury's speech introduced one new element in that Bourges-Maunoury proposed to hold local elections as soon as feasible and also to create, by decree, several new provinces with great local autonomy.

The Ambassador said that one of the principal purposes of his visit was to obtain an assurance that the U.S. does not intend to change its position that Algeria is purely a French problem. Mr. Murphy replied that this was, in fact, the principle on which we have been operating. Ambassador Alphand then referred to the growing anxiety which he sensed in Washington in regard to the coming UNGA session and asked whether the U.S. had determined its position on Algeria for the General Assembly. Mr. Murphy replied in the negative; pointing out that we desire to be helpful, but we don't know what to do. He agreed with the Ambassador that it was indeed a very serious problem for the U.S. The Ambassador said that the U.S. helped France greatly at the last UNGA session, particularly in the corridors and backstage. He asked if we would do

[1] Source: Department of State, Central Files, 751S.00/6–1457. Confidential. Drafted by Jova.

the same this year. Mr. Murphy replied that it depends in part on developments. It would be very difficult if we could point to nothing constructive. For this reason, the question of our tactical position has been held open in the hope that such developments might occur; more recently, however, the situation seemed to have worsened.

Ambassador Alphand inquired as to what importance the U.S. attached to Bourguiba's mediation efforts, indicating that the French were unable to take his influence seriously. Mr. Murphy replied that while it might well be that Bourguiba's influence was only local and that while he might be rather difficult on some issues, we could not forget that he was under many pressures. Algeria is Tunisia's number-one problem and he could assure M. Alphand that in previous conversations with Bourguiba, the latter had repeatedly reaffirmed his love for France and Tunisia's need for cooperation with France. The Ambassador said that this might be so but nevertheless Bourguiba welcomes and protects Algerian rebels and his public speeches are unfriendly to France.

The Ambassador said that he wished at this time to assure Mr. Murphy that regardless of French declarations to the contrary, French aid to Tunisia had never actually been cut off. In fact, every effort was made to avoid cutting off such aid as it was realized that this would present a difficult problem for the U.S. which had engaged itself to supplement rather than supplant French aid. Mr. Murphy observed that the Tunisian economy was certainly inadequate and relied heavily on French aid and that in spite of Bourguiba's recent difficult speeches, it must be acknowledged that he has resisted Soviet pressures and enticements. Undoubtedly some Tunisians would be quite prepared to throw him out and to turn to the Soviets. The Ambassador said that it was precisely for this reason that the French had not cut off their aid. He took the opportunity to point out that aid to North Africa, nevertheless, was a drain on French resources. France, he maintained, was actually doing more than even the U.S. in aid to under-developed countries. Mr. Murphy said he recognized the important role played by French capital in developing North Africa and observed that up until very recently the best investment a middle-class Frenchman could make was to buy an olive grove in Tunisia.

The Ambassador mentioned that French relations with Morocco were a bright spot in comparison with the rest of North Africa. Various agreements in regard to cultural, judicial, consular and administrative and technical matters were being satisfactorily concluded. These were particularly important as there were 40,000 French civil servants still in Morocco.

The Ambassador said that, in summary, it was his understanding from this conversation that he could tell his Government that U.S. policy on Algeria was still the same in regard to support for France, but that the U.S. wanted a plan or constructive step toward a solution. Mr. Murphy said that this was correct; that we would like something to be able to point to as an advance over last year's situation. He inquired whether the French had prepared their UN tactics. Ambassador Alphand said not yet, but that now that France has a new Government, it would be able to proceed on this planning and he could assure Mr. Murphy that the French wished to establish the closest liaison with the U.S. on this matter.

---

85. Memorandum From the Assistant Secretary of State for European Affairs (Elbrick) to the Deputy Under Secretary of State for Political Affairs (Murphy) [1]

Washington, June 14, 1957.

SUBJECT

French Invitation to Visit Melouza [2]

Discussion:

There is submitted herewith for your approval a telegram (Tab A) [3] authorizing the Consul General at Algiers to send a representative to visit Melouza. On June 6 the French Foreign Office extended an invitation to our Embassy in Paris to send a representative to visit the scene of the Melouza massacre. Other Embassies, including the U.K., Italy, Switzerland, Germany, India, Sweden, Japan, Turkey and Uruguay were given similar invitations. Both our Embassy in Paris and the Consulate General at Algiers thought that a refusal would be a psychological error and that on balance an Embassy officer and a member of the Consulate General should make the visit.

After due consideration, it was decided by the Department that it would be undesirable for either the Embassy or the Consulate General to accept and both were so informed, with the request that if overriding objections were perceived to U.S. refusal, the Depart-

---

[1] Source: Department of State, Central Files, 751S.00/6–1457. Confidential.

[2] In late May 1957, about 300 men in the village of Melouza were killed, apparently by FLN forces.

[3] Not printed.

ment should be urgently informed.[4] The Embassy has come back strongly recommending that at least the Consulate General be authorized to send a member of its staff. The Embassy believes that a refusal on our part will not indicate impartiality, but rather hostility to the French on the Algerian issue. The Embassy believes that in order to retain any influence with the French with regard to Algeria, the U.S. must continue to show willingness to hear and see their side of the case.[5]

It now appears that the program of the trip is to be the following: first day, meeting at Algiers with the Resident Minister; second day, visit to an administrative section in the Kabylie zone; third day, visit to Melouza, and possibly the fourth day, visit to oil installations. It is reported that a number of countries, including India, Japan, Sweden, Sudan, Italy, Holland and Belgium have agreed to send representatives and that the U.K. will send its Consul General in Algiers if we accept.[6]

It is strongly believed that despite the obvious disadvantages, the Consulate General should be authorized to send a representative if an invitation is extended to the Consulate, but that the Paris Embassy should decline for itself. This would seem to be the minimum that we should do to avoid a very adverse French reaction. To give a complete refusal as to U.S. representation would seem difficult to explain. For the Consulate General to participate in such a multi-purpose tour, moreover, would appear to be in keeping with his normal duties and not give rise to unduly unfavorable comments by other nations. If the Consul General must also refuse, his relations with the Minister Resident will be seriously jeopardized and his usefulness accordingly affected.

NEA does not concur in this course of action and will undoubtedly wish to submit its comments on the foregoing.[7] The previous messages on this matter are attached (Tab B).[8]

Recommendation:

It is recommended that you approve the attached message to Paris and Algiers (Tab A).

---

[4] Telegram 4948 to Paris, June 7, noted that the visit would serve no constructive purpose. The United States feared that France might use the occasion to request condemnation of the FLN. (Department of State, Central Files, 751S.00/6–757)

[5] In telegram 6302 from Paris, June 8, Ambassador Houghton replied that the representative from the Consulate General would not be a member of a commission of inquiry but rather an individual seeking information for the Department. (*Ibid.*, 751S.00/6–857)

[6] A notation on the source text indicates that the United Kingdom had agreed to accept, irrespective of the U.S. decision.

[7] See *infra.*

[8] Not printed.

86. Memorandum From the Assistant Secretary of State for Near Eastern, South Asian, and African Affairs (Rountree) to the Deputy Under Secretary of State for Political Affairs (Murphy) [1]

Washington, June 14, 1957.

SUBJECT

French Invitation to Visit Melouza

Discussion:

NEA does not feel that in the framework in which the French invitation to visit the scene of the Melouza massacre has been put, representatives of either the Embassy or the Consulate General at Algiers should accept. The terms of the French note make clear that the visit is being organized as a French "guided tour" in Algeria. However understandable the French plans may be, I feel that U.S. participation at this time would open us to charges of partiality, particularly since we would have little freedom to criticize or comment on the results of the tour.

Moreover, the eleven Arab states on May 24th [2] and again on June 11th [3] (following the Melouza massacre) requested U.S. support for an impartial international commission of inquiry to investigate not only Melouza but also all other atrocities in Algeria. This idea, which has been discussed publicly by the Syrian Ambassador in Washington and reported in the foreign press, will almost certainly encounter French opposition, particularly in view of its sponsorship, and I believe we should do everything we can to avoid getting

---

[1] Source: Department of State, Central Files, 751S.00/6–1457. Confidential.

[2] The Ambassadors of Syria, Egypt, Lebanon, Saudi Arabia, Iraq, Morocco, Tunisia, and Libya and the Chargés of Yemen, Sudan, and Jordan met with the Secretary on May 24, with Dr. Farid Zeineddine of Syria as their spokesman. Dulles, acknowledging that atrocities had occurred, maintained that all elements had been tainted by such acts which unfortunately were the inevitable consequence of the war. (Memorandum of conversation by Tyler and Palmer, May 24; *ibid.*)

[3] On this occasion, the Syrian, Moroccan, and Tunisian Ambassadors met with Rountree and Palmer to ask the United States to cooperate in an impartial international investigation of atrocities in Algeria. Rountree answered that the matter was being studied by the Department and thus he could make no final reply at that time. While repeating the Department's condemnation of atrocities, he emphasized the difficulty of apportioning blame and doubted that France would be receptive to the Arab proposal. (Memorandum of conversation by Palmer and Bovey, June 11; *ibid.*, 751S.00/6–1157) Acting Secretary Herter sent a note on June 28 to a number of concerned Embassies in the Middle East and Europe containing background material for discussions with host government and press representatives in regard to the Algerian question and two other problems. With respect to atrocities, it essentially repeated the preliminary statements of Dulles (May 24) and Rountree (June 11). (CA–11120; *ibid.*, 751S.00/6–2857)

entangled with it and to keep the initiative on it with the Arab states.

If we accept the present French invitation and refuse to support the Arab proposal, we would certainly open ourselves to charges of partiality, and our actions would cause grave doubts in the minds of the Moroccans and Tunisians, not to mention the other Arab states, as to the sincerity of our stated desire to encourage a peaceful solution in Algeria which would respect the legitimate interests of all concerned.

If it is decided to resist efforts of the Arab states to enlist our support for an international commission of inquiry, I believe we should explain our predicament to the French and tell them that our ability to be helpful regarding the Arab initiative would be seriously affected by our participating in the present exercise.

If, on the other hand, we decide to accept the French invitation, I believe we shall have to give serious consideration to any invitation of the Arab states to participate likewise in an international investigating commission.

EUR's position in this matter differs from that of NEA, and has been set forth in a separate memorandum.[4] The views of the respective Bureaus should, of course, be taken into account in deciding the Department's policy in the matter.

Recommendation:

That you approve the attached telegram to Paris, Algiers and London.[5]

---

[4] *Supra.*

[5] Not printed. On June 17, the Embassy officially declined the French invitation to visit the site of the Melouza massacre. The French were informed orally that the press description of the first contingent of visitors as an international commission precluded any U.S. participation. (Telegram 6454 from Paris, June 17; Department of State, Central Files, 751S.00/6–1757)

87. Memorandum of a Conversation, Department of State, Washington, July 1, 1957 [1]

SUBJECT

Speech by Senator John F. Kennedy on Algeria, on Tuesday, July 2, 1957 [2]

PARTICIPANTS

The Secretary
Ambassador Herve Alphand, Embassy of France
Mr. Jacques Vimont, Minister of French Embassy
Mr. William R. Tyler, WE

The French Ambassador called on the Secretary at his own request in order to inform him of his concern about the above speech, of which an advance text had already been distributed to the press.

The Ambassador said that the speech was violent and would inflame French opinion. He said that the fact that the speech called for a joint resolution, [3] which would be preceded by a debate, made the situation worse. He said that the result would be to delay a solution on the Algerian problem rather than hasten one, and that its effect would be to crystallize the French position and embitter Franco-U.S. relations. While the Ambassador was speaking, he was interrupted by a long distance call from Foreign Minister Pineau in Paris, after which he returned to the Secretary's office to say that Mr. Pineau had instructed him to make officially to the Secretary, in behalf of the French Government, the same points which he had raised on his own initiative. The Ambassador stressed that he was not addressing himself to the views expressed in the speech, nor was he questioning the right of the Senator to make the speech. He said that he must, however, draw the attention of the Secretary of State to the adverse effects which the speech, a debate and the proposed resolution would have on the prospects of improvement of the Algerian problem, and on French sentiment toward the United States.

The Secretary, after looking at the text of the speech, said that while it was evident that such a speech was likely to have the effect which the Ambassador had mentioned, he confessed he would himself be at a loss to explain convincingly French policy in Algeria,

---

[1] Source: Department of State, Central Files, 751S.00/7–157. Confidential. Drafted by Tyler.

[2] Senator Kennedy's speech was generally critical of U.S. policy toward the situation in Algeria. For text, see *Congressional Record*, vol. 103, pt. 8, 85th Congress, 1st Sess., July 2, 1957, pp. 10780–10793.

[3] Senator Kennedy submitted S. Res. 153; it was not adopted.

if he had to do so before the United Nations at this time or later this fall, should there have been no progress by then. The Secretary said that he was afraid that unless substantial progress were made by the time the next session of the General Assembly the situation might well blow up.

The Ambassador said that he thought it was important to stress that Senator Kennedy's speech, by hardening French sentiment and whipping up French resentment against the U.S., would delay the chances of progress. The Ambassador asked whether the Secretary thought that the resolution had a chance of passing, to which the Secretary answered that he thought it might. The Ambassador asked whether the Administration would be prepared to do something to mitigate the effects of the speech and not let it go by unanswered. The Secretary said he would consider what might be done, but that he was not in a position at this time to be more specific.[4]

[4] At a press conference on July 2, Dulles defended France's record and stated his opposition to U.S. involvement in the matter. (Department of State *Bulletin*, July 22, 1957, pp. 142–143) At a news conference on July 3, Eisenhower stated that U.S. policy would be impartial and helpful. (*Public Papers of the Presidents of the United States: Dwight D. Eisenhower, 1957*, pp. 515–527)

88. Memorandum of a Conversation, Department of State, Washington, July 10, 1957[1]

SUBJECT

Algeria

PARTICIPANTS

The Secretary
Mr. Louis Joxe, Secretary General, French Ministry of Foreign Affairs
Mr. Jacques Vimont, Minister, French Embassy
Mr. William R. Tyler, WE

In the course of his call on the Secretary Mr. Joxe raised the question of Algeria and outlined briefly his views on the necessity for France to find a formula for a solution which would enlist the support of Tunisia and Morocco in order to put an end to the present fighting. Mr. Joxe said, however, that it would not be

[1] Source: Department of State, Central Files, 751S.00/7–1057. Secret. Drafted by Tyler.

possible for France to grant independence to Algeria at this time. He said this would not be possible either politically or psychologically.

The Secretary said to Mr. Joxe that we view the Algerian situation with great concern. He pointed out that we had done a great deal to help France at the last meeting of the General Assembly, and that President Eisenhower and he himself had only recently made public statements which had been politically helpful to France. He said that the forthcoming session of the General Assembly would be a very difficult one, and that unless there was real progress toward a peaceful and just solution in Algeria, the United States would find itself unable to play the same role as it had in the past. The Secretary added that the continuation of the trouble in Algeria had an adverse effect on our efforts to encourage certain Arab countries to cooperate with each other and with the West, independently of Nasser.

Mr. Joxe told the Secretary that he fully understood this, and that he hoped very much that it would be possible for the French Government to make rapid headway in its relations with Tunisia and Morocco, so that these two countries, and Bourguiba in particular, would feel able to support France's efforts to find a solution which would be acceptable, and would contribute to the unity and western orientation of North Africa. Mr. Joxe said that Bourguiba was extremely able and could play a very important role in this regard. He said that unfortunately Bourguiba had not yet decided whether to press forward to help bring about a solution in cooperation with France, or to continue to call for an internationalization of the Algerian problem, which antagonizes French sentiment. Mr. Joxe said that Bourguiba would have to decide to do one or the other, and that he himself had hopes that if Franco-Tunisian relations continued to improve, much headway could be made between now and the fall, although it was out of the question that the French Government could come up with a complete new proposal by the time the UNGA reconvened.

89. Telegram From the Embassy in France to the Department of State[1]

Paris, August 10, 1957—1 p.m.

703. During past few weeks we have discussed Algeria with Bourges, Mollet, Pineau, Morice, Lacoste, Abel, Thomas, Felix of Lacoste's Cabinet, Champeix, Langlais of Foreign Office and many others. Out of these conversations and on basis our best assessment situation at present time, we present following for Department's consideration:

1. French appear more firmly resolved than ever not to offer independence or speak of independence in connection Algeria. Among reasons for this attitude are:

(a) Government believes neither it nor any other government which accepted independence now or for future could stay in office.

(b) Lacoste continues in office with apparent full support Bourges.

(c) French appear more confident in success their pacification operations including program for sealing Tunisian frontier and stepped-up military activities.

(d) French believe FLN disorganized and lacking coordination and effective leadership. They believe external representatives do not enjoy confidence leaders of rebellion and hope latter can be gradually weaned over to cooperate with French.

(e) French believe they can win Algerian support only by convincing Algerians France intends to stay and will be able to stay in Algeria.

(f) French argue real interests Moslem and Christian populations can best be served by democratic process insuring local autonomy with equality of rights all Algerians guaranteed by France and that independence would invite Communist penetration and control.

(g) Prospects for oil in Sahara provide strong economic incentive for holding Algeria.

2. French fully realize importance General Assembly consideration Algerian problem and necessity presenting most persuasive case possible. They hope loi-cadre now under preparation will be accepted by French Assembly and will subsequently enable France avoid unfavorable vote in United Nations. They realize difficulty formulating proposal which will attract support in United Nations General Assembly and at same time will not be so liberal as to fail in French Parliament. They probably prepared walk out General Assembly, but not Security Council, in case unfavorable vote. Pineau has told us France will not sever membership in United Nations.

[1] Source: Department of State, Central Files, 751S.00/8–1057. Secret. Repeated to Algiers, Rabat, and Tunis.

3. We are unable judge progress in pacification in Algeria or predict what can be achieved against rebellion in next few months. However, it appears doubtful that any decisive change in situation will be brought about before United Nations General Assembly meeting. We believe it futile to speculate on what loi-cadre will turn out to be. Reports of its provisions vary from division into three or four regions to "Swiss" system of more numerous "ethnic cantons", from little or no central executive or legislative to substantially strong head. We expect learn finally agreed details within ten days. However, from what we now know of general line governmental thinking, we feel sure loi-cadre will be unacceptable to FLN and will probably not go far enough win Moroccan and Tunisian support or even their abstention in General Assembly vote.

4. In above situation United States will face dilemma as French hope we will not only support their position but use our influence with other General Assembly members. If United States either openly opposes French position or takes neutral attitude, wave of anti-American feeling in France may well result. This will be serious should it coincide with further deterioration French financial situation. In other words, we might be confronted simultaneously with crisis in United Nations including possible French withdrawal and with financial and internal political crisis in France. This may be blackest picture but it is conceivable and many of our French friends are most pessimistic in their predictions.

5. For the immediate future:

(a) We believe French are right in their position that immediate independence for Algeria would be not only undesirable but dangerous.

(b) Efforts of France to develop Moslem participation through efforts on local scale and through promulgation loi-cadre may be too little and too late but they presumably are all which can be hoped for at this time.

(c) If rebellion should become quieter over next few months, if FLN reveals dissensions and weaknesses, and if loi-cadre appears be considerable step forward, it may be possible develop United Nations General Assembly resolution which we can support, which will win majority vote and on which French will not walk out. This would be best we could hope for and would get over immediate hump.

(e) [*sic*] However, our best estimate is that above conditions will probably not prevail at time United Nations General Assembly takes up Algerian question. On basis information now available we are not yet prepared make recommendations for United States position or for strategy and tactics to be followed in General Assembly. We should, however, like emphasize key importance positions and attitudes of Morocco and Tunisia on Algerian question.

6. For long range future, we hope French will encourage democratic evolutionary development in Algeria which over period time more and more French might support. Alternative, unless rebellion is crushed, could be return De Gaulle or coup d'état of right or military group. Evolutionary development might be brought about in several ways:

(1) First might be recognition right of self-determination and plan for independence within specified period of years or after certain conditions showing capacity self-government had been fulfilled, including guarantees for European population. French might well take leaf from history of our relations with Philippines. Development could be in context eventual North African federation tied to France, or French Commonwealth. French not prepared embark on such course now, but some future government might consider it.

(2) Second possibility might be internationalization Algerian situation in context Mediterranean security organization. This would presuppose improved relations with Morocco and Tunisia and sharp change in French attitude from that held at present. Such organization would represent clear attempt build shield against Communist penetration North Africa which some Frenchmen contend is basic problem behind Algerian situation. We note with interest Moroccan suggestion reported Rabat 131 to Department.[2]

(3) Third possibility would be attempt find "European" solution for Algeria in context six members Euratom and Common Market. Since democratic solution must be one supported by majority assembly, such majority must be found. In present make-up Assembly there does exist European majority upon which both Mollet and Bourges have depended. Conceivably statute could be evolved for Algeria guaranteed by the six. This might so far eliminate mutual distrust French and Moslems and with essential Moroccan and Tunisian support could provide framework for evolutionary development Algeria, both economic and political, permit France play role in six without drain of Algeria, yet at same time avoid both United Nations role (which French would probably never accept) and United States direct participation but not United States sympathetic support. Above would obviously require change French public opinion but this may become easier if realization comes that military measures and temporary palliatives will not bring about permanent solution.

7. We realize French Government and Parliament are in no mood at present consider courses such as those enumerated paragraph 6 above. However, we believe United States should think of alternatives for future since moment may come when it will be appropriate and important say some word to French about problem

[2] Telegram 131, August 8, noted that the Moroccans wanted the United States to suggest a regional association which would allow them to justify the continued presence of French and Spanish troops in their country. (*Ibid.*, 711.56371/8–857)

so threatening and potentially dangerous to free world as that of Algeria.

Houghton

---

90. Memorandum From the Assistant Secretary of State for Near Eastern, South Asian, and African Affairs (Rountree) to the Secretary of State[1]

Washington, August 28, 1957.

SUBJECT

Repercussions in North Africa of Prolonged Crisis in Algeria

Discussion:

I feel I must emphasize the seriousness of the situation resulting from a prolongation of the crisis in Algeria, not alone from the point of view of the problem which it presents for us in the forthcoming General Assembly, but in a much broader sense the symptomatic effect of the Algerian situation on Tunisia and Morocco.

The annual recurrence of the problem in the public forum of the General Assembly and the fiction that the matter is solely one of French domestic concern have tended to conceal a much more serious aspect, which is nothing less than the progressive deterioration of the entire Western position on one of NATO's flanks and the jeopardizing of our own strategic and political interests throughout North Africa. The promulgation of a Loi-Cadre for Algeria[2] seems unlikely to halt the Algerian conflict and it therefore appears that the present deterioration will continue over the coming months.

Aside from the two principal combatants, the sharpest effects of the struggle have fallen on Algeria's neighbors, Morocco and Tunisia. In these two countries, as in France itself, the question of Algeria is a basic issue of foreign and domestic policy. The fundamental

---

[1] Source: Department of State, Central Files, 751S.00/8–2857. Secret. Originally prepared as an attachment to briefing papers for the Secretary's September 1 conversation with Pineau. (Telegram 1009 to Paris, September 12; *ibid.*, 751S.00/9–1257)

[2] The proposed basic law proclaimed that Algeria was an integral part of France composed of federated territories each administering its own affairs. Since a single electoral college was to be instituted, Muslim local control would have been established subject to French overrule. This issue brought down the Bourgès-Maunoury government on September 30. In January 1958, however, a revised Loi-Cadre was implemented.

conflict between the French policy of refusing to consider the granting of independence to Algeria, and the Tunisian and Moroccan policies of support for Algerian independence, results in preventing a settlement between France and either of her ex-protectorates on major issues of finance and defense which have been pending ever since independence. The result is a dangerous instability in these two countries and a steady worsening of the political situation from the point of view of the West, for whose interests in the area France is progressively becoming less and less satisfactory as an intermediary. This deterioration adversely affects not only the national policies of Morocco and Tunisia but also the interests of the United States.

Political. Moroccans and Tunisians naturally associate themselves closely with the Algerian rebels whose struggle they regard as a fight for national liberation similar to their own and whose victory they believe essential to preservation of their own independence. The people of Morocco and Tunisia thus tend increasingly to judge nations on the basis of their stand on the Algerian issue.

Outspoken demands for Algerian independence from nations of the Middle East and even the illusory postures taken in this matter by members of the Soviet bloc contrast sharply with the cautious neutrality of most Western nations. Western and especially American hesitations are interpreted as approval of French policy in Algeria. French use of arms of United States origin in Algeria implicates us in a manner most offensive to the Moroccans and Tunisians and no amount of rationalization can satisfy their feelings on this score. On the single great issue of Algeria, therefore, public opinion in Morocco and Tunisia feels itself drawn closer to the Middle East and away from the West to the detriment of our attempts to maintain strong United States and Western influences in these nations. France is of course the principal target of hostility, but even though our relations with the political leaders of Tunisia and Morocco remain friendly, popular feeling, which must sooner or later be reflected in government, is growingly dissatisfied with the United States.

Popular pressure is also a constant threat to the stability of the pro-Western regimes on which our own position and our direct strategic interests so heavily depend. Pro-Westernism becomes less and less attractive so long as the West fails to produce a solution to the Algerian war. Moreover, both King Mohammed V and Bourguiba appear genuinely concerned that continued conflict may in the end produce extremist leadership in Algeria, whether nationalist or pro-Communist, which will pose a permanent threat to the stability of North Africa and to the existence of their own governments.

Economic. One of the last weapons remaining to France in her attempts to influence Moroccan and Tunisian policy has been the withholding of French credits necessary to the economic development of both countries. Thus Tunisia which was to have received French assistance amounting to $43 million in 1956 and $25 million in 1957 has not yet received all payments for 1956; in Morocco, which has received about $75 million in 1956 and for which $57 million has been appropriated for 1957, negotiation of the commercial and financial conventions has proceeded by ups and downs, and the outcome is still uncertain.

While French public opposition to financing two states sympathetic to the rebellion is understandable, the use of this weapon is not effective, since leaders in Morocco and Tunisia, when forced to choose, respond to their own public opinion and forego the needed aid rather than make concessions on policy toward Algeria. Thus the flow of essential French credits remains spasmodic and uncertain.

The inevitable result is that both Morocco and Tunisia are increasing pressure on the United States to supplant rather than merely to supplement French aid as at present. Present United States aid programs are of modest proportions in both countries (for 1957 $20 million in Morocco and $8 million in Tunisia). It is evident that these figures represent only a fraction of French assistance, and one should remember that the approximate $120 million of annual French financial aid to these two countries does not include contributions in military and civil payments, pricing subsidies, and private investment. It is thus clear that a rupture of Moroccan and Tunisian financial relations with France would confront the United States with the alternative of footing a bill for which present plans leave us entirely unprepared, or allowing the situation to deteriorate to the point where our own political and strategic interests would be threatened and even lost to hostile influences both internal and external.

The prospect of such a rupture and of such alternatives for the United States and the West increases every day the Algerian conflict continues. If Algeria is lost after a further protracted struggle and on terms which do not permit the protection of local Frenchmen and the continuation of French influence and French investment in North Africa, the United States and the West would be faced with an immensely difficult and costly task in preserving an important sector of the Mediterranean and the NATO area.

Military. Another consequence of the Algerian conflict has been the presence of French troops in Morocco and Tunisia. The mission of these forces, which includes protecting the flanks of Algeria and preventing arms from crossing the border, inevitably involves clashes with Moroccans and Tunisians. Despite temporary agreements and partial withdrawals of French troops from Morocco and Tunisia, a major source of friction persists. No real solution to this problem is possible and no definitive defense arrangements with France can be made until the Algerian conflict ends.

This situation has a direct adverse effect on the United States-operated bases in Morocco, which are still legally dependent on the French status. The chief reason that, after nearly four months of negotiation, we have made no real progress toward a base agreement is that the Moroccans are still groping for a satisfactory defense framework, acceptable to public opinion, in which United States bases and troops, as well as French and Spanish, will fit. No such framework can be devised so long as the Algerian war perpetuates the status of French troops as an occupying army.

Thus it will be seen that the political, economic, and military interests of the entire West, as well as the direct interests of the United States, are increasingly threatened throughout North Africa by the continuation of the Algerian war.

Recommendation:

That upon occasions in the future when the Algerian conflict is discussed with the French we mention appropriate aspects of the situation indicated above and make clear that we are preoccupied not only by the problems of UNGA strategy but also by the serious threat to area stability and Western interests in North Africa posed by the Algerian conflict.[3]

[3] The source text bears no indication of approval or disapproval.

91. Memorandum of a Conversation, Washington, August 31, 1957[1]

SUBJECT

Algeria

[1] Source: Department of State, Central Files, 751S.00/8–3157. Secret. Drafted by Tyler.

PARTICIPANTS

Ambassador Hervé Alphand, French Ambassador
Mr. Charles Lucet, Minister, French Embassy
Mr. William R. Tyler, WE

Ambassador Alphand asked me to lunch on his return from Paris. The only other person present was Mr. Lucet. The conversation was almost entirely about Algeria and the forthcoming UNGA session. Essentially, the Ambassador had nothing new to say. He went over the main points of the proposed "Loi-Cadre" for Algeria. He emphasized that this proposal constituted a new French liberal measure which France had decided to take, since the Nationalists had not yet accepted the Mollet proposals of January 9, 1957. In answer to a question, he said that the Mollet proposals remained valid and that France was prepared to undertake negotiations with the Nationalists at anytime on the basis of these proposals. He said that it was not possible, however, to wait indefinitely and to allow the present situation to continue, and that the French Government was therefore making an all-out effort to propose a series of measures which would be acceptable to the majority of Algerians and to world opinion, and which would confer an increasing degree of self-government on Algeria.

I pointed out to the Ambassador that if the new measures were presented as a substitute for the Mollet proposals, they might well be considered to mark a step backward rather than forward, particularly if, as had been reported to us, the preamble were to contain the assertion that Algeria was, and would remain, a part of France. The Ambassador said that every effort would be made by the French Government to make it clear that the new measures were not in conflict with the Mollet proposals, but represented a unilateral French effort in the absence of Nationalist acceptance of the Mollet proposals, which however remain open. He said that there was no doubt that there would be a substantial majority in the French National Assembly for the new proposals, with opposition coming only from the extreme left and the extreme right. This affirmation of a united French national will, he said, would emphasize the vital importance that France receive support in the United Nations.

At this point the Ambassador discussed the extremely adverse consequences not only to Franco-U.S. relations, but to France's whole attitude and role within the Western camp, if she were pilloried in the General Assembly and abandoned by her Allies, particularly the U.S. I said to the Ambassador that we certainly were aware of the difficulty of the situation in Algeria, not only with regard to the problem itself but also because of its repercussions on French domestic politics. I said we had heard reports that it was felt in some quarters in France that the "Loi-Cadre" had been prepared principally in deference to United States views, and that France in reality did not need to take any political measures in Algeria because the military situation was said to be improving rapidly. I said that if these reports were true, I thought that this was a dangerous theory. The Ambassador said this was not so at all and that the French Government believed strongly in its program. I said to the Ambassador that while I would not dispute the point that the role of the U.S. in the General Assembly was bound to be a very important one in the eyes of France, I thought it would be most unfortunate if, on the French side, people took the line that once the "Loi-Cadre" had been published it was then up to the U.S. to get others to accept it by endorsing it actively. Apart from the fact that this would hardly be consistent with the French desire to treat the Algerian question as a French problem, I thought that the determining factor in the acceptability of the "Loi-Cadre" would be the substance of what it had to offer, and not external efforts by other powers to promote it. I said to the Ambassador that I thought he was probably familiar with an American expression which could be translated into French as: "mettre le singe sur le dos de quelqu'un". I said that, speaking quite personally, I thought it would be important to avoid any implication that the French strategy in the UN could be interpreted in this manner. The Ambassador agreed and said that such reports probably emanated from circles close to Lacoste who was both impatient and optimistic, and felt that the new proposals went further than was necessary in view of what he felt to be a constant improvement in the Algerian situation.

The Ambassador said that it was important to note that the new proposals provided ultimately for negotiation between freely elected representatives of Algeria and the French Parliament on a future statute for Algeria which could lead to independence. He said, however, that this word was politically unmentionable in France at this time and that this reality must be realized.

In discussing the possibility of political support in the UN from Tunisia and Morocco, the Ambassador reflected the French Government's current distrust of Bourguiba, and said that he thought that the Moroccan Government was more likely to be effective and to play a moderating role.

In general, the Ambassador seemed to be unaware of the extent of information that has already appeared in the press about the French proposals, and sometimes emphasized to me the secrecy of various aspects of the French plan which have already been reported in American newspapers.

92. Memorandum From Matthew Looram of the Office of Western European Affairs to the Deputy Director of the Office (Torbert)[1]

Washington, September 13, 1957.

SUBJECT

Algeria

The following are a few thoughts gained from my recent trip to Algiers and Paris:

Paradoxically, the problem for France today is how to extricate herself from Algeria; for Algeria, the long-term problem is how to maintain French interest in the area. It is no longer a question of how France can permanently keep Algeria a part of the Metropole—it cannot be done. The eventual formation of an Algerian state in some form or another is inevitable. The task, therefore, confronting France today is to devise a means of liquidating and transforming her present relationship with Algeria without provoking an internal French crisis. With regard to Algeria, there is no evidence that it is yet ready for complete independence, and French financial assistance will be desperately required for a long time to come. In the long run, the greatest danger for Algeria is the possibility that, in the process of extricating herself from Algeria, France will become so disillusioned as to be unwilling to contribute further to the economic development of North Africa in general and Algeria in particular. If this should occur, a very costly and onerous responsibility would fall upon us.

As the Algiers Consulate General has often reported, the final decision on Algeria will be made in Paris, not Algiers, and probably as a result of factors, financial and other, extraneous to Algeria. The present situation in Algeria, although a temporary phase, can continue indefinitely. As long as the French are willing to station 400,000 troops in Algeria, they can probably hold on. In fact, the French military have had very considerable success in their pacification program in certain areas. At the moment the rebellion is in the doldrums—presumably preparing for greater activity at the occasion of the U.N. debate. It seems probable, however, that the military potential of the rebel forces remains intact, if not improving.

The military, psychological and economic effort now being made by the French in Algeria is nothing short of stupendous—

[1] Source: Department of State, Central Files, 751S.00/9–1357. Confidential. In a memorandum of October 14, John Wesley Jones recommended that the Secretary read this memorandum. (*Ibid.*, 751S.00/10–1457)

roads, housing and public works of every nature are currently being undertaken on a large scale. The military have restored contacts with the Moslem population in many areas, and the S.A.S. officers are doing a magnificent job.[2] However, the contacts are with rural elements and not the urban population. Moreover, irrespective of the efforts of the French military, the Moslem and French communities of Algeria are farther apart than ever. The successes obtained by the military can only be temporary and would be obliterated overnight by their departure.

In the political realm the French effort to date has been very limited indeed, and what has and is being done is probably all the traffic will bear for the time being. There is no basis, however, for believing that the loi-cadre, at least in its present form, will have any bearing on the course of the rebellion or will contribute to a solution of the Algerian problem. Basically a retreat from the Mollet program, it is unlikely that the loi-cadre will have a significant effect on the Moslem population and it is doubtful that it could ever fully be implemented. The fallacy of the loi-cadre, which I cannot help but feel is mere window-dressing for the benefit of the U.N. in general and the U.S. in particular, is that it inherently presupposes the suppression of the rebellion and the obliteration of the FLN as a military and political force in Algeria. The only possible utility of the loi-cadre—and this may be highly significant—is that it may be a necessary exercise for the French to go through before they are psychologically prepared for the important concessions that will be inevitable.

The continuation of the conflict and its present impasse with the resultant widening gulf between the two communities will probably make the final settlement more difficult, less satisfactory from the point of view of the French, and strengthen the hand of the Moslem extremist and anti-Western elements. It seems probable that in the last analysis the French will have to negotiate with the FLN. The only possible advantage to be gained for the French from the continuation of the pacification program is that if it continues to have some measure of success, the Moslem population might be more disposed to sue for peace and therefore pressure the FLN to accept a compromise settlement. There is, also, the possibility of some other native element emerging as a result of the current stalemate which would have an influence, if not directly on the settlement, at least on the future course of Algerian affairs. Similarly, the prolongation of the impasse would presumably induce the French to accept a compromise settlement. None of these, however, must necessarily follow.

[2] The Sections Administratives Specialisées was a specialized administrative unit.

Finally, one cannot reject out of hand the possibility, however remote, that by increased military effort the French might conceivably succeed in quashing the rebellion. However, even if the French should obtain such a miraculous success, which seems highly unlikely, their efforts in creating a new Moslem elite as an alternative to the FLN leadership would be inevitably rewarded by eventual demands from this very same elite much similar to those demands now being made by the FLN.

93. Telegram From the Mission at the United Nations to the Department of State [1]

New York, September 30, 1957—8 p.m.

Delga 76. Re Algeria. Yazid and Chanderli [2] of Algerian FLN told member USGADel today FLN basic strategy this session GA moderation and discussion substance Algerian problem chiefly by Tunisia and Morocco instead of attacks against France. Stressed moderation would depend on tone adopted by French. Stated proposals would be made First Committee for round table talks with French without any political precondition. US official inquired whether this meant France would not be asked recognize independence or right to independence Algeria before engaging in discussion and reply was affirmative. Yazid also said FLN would not insist attending talks as full participant if this preferred by France but would accept role observer. In reply to question whether he had any indication what French reaction likely to be to such proposal, Yazid said French Govt already aware of them and Pineau had thrown cold water on them at recent lunch Diplomatic Press Association Paris, but this not considered necessarily definitive position. Yazid stressed essential political and strategic unity Maghreb which reason why political direction Algerian nationalist cause shifting from Cairo to Tunisia and Morocco.

In course discussion US official introduced subject reports Communist infiltration FLN and question possibility FLN turning to Soviet Union for arms, munitions or "volunteers". Impossible ascertain from Yazid's reply whether he aware reason for introduction this subject into conversation. He said, apparently straightforwardly

[1] Source: Department of State, Central Files, 751S.00/9–3057. Secret.

[2] Abdel Kader Chanderli.

FLN considered Communists enemies and FLN would not be interested obtaining arms or military help from Soviet Union or Eastern European countries but rather from NATO area for reasons standardization weapons and ammunition. Yazid said would appreciate maintenance contact with USDel in future and was told this could easily be arranged.

Memorandum of conversation being pouched. [3]

Lodge

[3] Not printed.

---

94. Memorandum of a Conversation, Washington, November 19, 1957 [1]

SUBJECT

Algerian Debate in the U.N. General Assembly

PARTICIPANTS

French Foreign Minister Christian Pineau
M. Louis Joxe, Secretary General of the Ministry of Foreign Affairs
Ambassador Hervé Alphand
M. Charles Lucet, Minister of the French Embassy
M. Jean de la Grandville, Counselor of the French Embassy
M. Francois de Laboulaye, Counselor of the French Embassy
M. Francois de Rose, Chief of the Treaty Section of the French Ministry of Foreign Affairs
General André Martin, Deputy for Air to the French Chief of Staff
M. Albert du Chalet of the French Atomic Energy Commissariat

[1] Source: Department of State, Central Files, 751S.00/11–1957. Confidential. Drafted by Looram.

The Secretary of State
Mr. Adlai Stevenson
Mr. Robert Murphy, Deputy Under Secretary
Mr. G. Frederick Reinhardt, Counselor
Mr. C. Burke Elbrick, Assistant Secretary for EUR
Mr. Walter N. Walmsley, Deputy Assistant Secretary for IO
Mr. Joseph Palmer, Deputy Assistant Secretary for NEA
Mr. John N. Irwin, II, Deputy Assistant Secretary of Defense
Mr. B.E.L. Timmons, RA
Mr. John Bovey, AF/N
Mr. Matthew Looram, WE

Mr. Pineau stated that with regard to the French Government's policy on Algeria, the Gaillard Government [2] had now reintroduced the Loi-Cadre, which had been defeated last September, with two modifications to the original bill. First, in addition to the Algerian territorial assemblies which would be provided for in the bill, there would also be constituted community councils ("conseils des communautés") in each territory. The role of these councils would be solely to insure that the territorial assemblies did not vote discriminatory measures against the European community. Secondly, the electoral system for Algeria would be set forth in a separate bill linked to the Loi-Cadre. This would provide for proportional representation on a basis of universal suffrage in order to permit an equitable representation of all minorities. These two modifications would provide additional guarantees to the European population without detracting from the basic principles of the Loi-Cadre. During the imminent U.N. General Assembly debate, Mr. Pineau stated, he would set forth the policies of the French Government and the frequent efforts made by the French Government to contact the rebels. These efforts had always failed in view of FLN insistence on the prior condition of France's recognition of Algerian independence which was, of course, impossible for France to accept. He would stress the favorable evolution of the military situation in Algeria since the last debate and emphasize the fact that despite this success, France still intended to go ahead in working out the political evolution of Algeria. He would also say that the French Government continued to be ready to meet with the rebel leaders at any time and any place to discuss a cease-fire and the security guarantees which would be given the various rebel elements.

In reply to the Secretary's question as to what type of resolution the French expected to emerge from the debate, Mr. Pineau stated that the French desired a resolution which would resemble as closely as possible the resolution of last February. This was not ideal from the French point of view, but would be acceptable. In any event,

[2] The Gaillard government assumed power on November 5.

France was opposed to any resolution which set up a U.N. "good offices" body or which brought Morocco and Tunisia into the picture. Actually, the Tunisian and Moroccan viewpoints were not the same on this issue. The Tunisian Government wished to act as an intermediary between the FLN and the French Government; this would never be accepted by French public opinion.[3] Morocco, on the other hand, seemed to favor working toward a long-term arrangement establishing a French-Maghreb Federation including Algeria and possibly Spain and Italy. This latter idea was precisely his own idea, Mr. Pineau stated. However, he had told the Moroccan Foreign Minister[4] that such a concept would be jeopardized if it were linked with an immediate solution of the Algerian problem, which on the contrary, must come first. Mr. Pineau thought that it would be preferable to have direct conversations between France and the FLN.

In reply to the Secretary's question as to the French estimate regarding the support that a resolution such as Mr. Pineau hoped for might get in the General Assembly this year, Mr. Pineau stated that it was as yet difficult to judge. In this connection the Secretary recalled the very considerable personal efforts which Mr. Pineau had made last year in obtaining the support of other delegates. Mr. Pineau stated that he intended to do the same thing as soon as he returned to New York. He thought it would be most helpful if Ambassador Lodge could give him the same cooperation that he had given last February.

The Secretary said it was certainly our feeling that the Algerian situation would not be improved by an acrimonious debate or by a highly controversial solution. He felt, however, that the atmosphere in the U.N. was not as good as last February, when there were hopes that concrete progress might be made by France toward reaching a political solution of the problem. The Secretary said that he had just had a meeting with some of the Ambassadors of the Baghdad Pact countries who had told him they thought it would be good if the Algerian matter could be disposed of without a bitter debate. These countries were, however, thinking in terms of a possible intervention by Morocco and Tunisia in the matter, which would presumably be unacceptable to France.

Mr. Pineau stated that it was unrealistic to put both these countries on the same level in the eyes of the French public. Tunisia could not realistically be of help in this matter. Morocco, on the

---

[3] The United States was considering a formula involving Moroccan and Tunisian good offices. (Telegram 1776 to Paris, November 8; Department of State, Central Files, 751S.00/11–757)

[4] Ahmed Balafrej.

other hand, might eventually be able to be of assistance, but its possible usefulness would be completely jeopardized if it were endorsed by the U.N. at this juncture as an intermediary in the issue.

The Secretary stated that he fully shared Mr. Pineau's feeling that progress would not be served by a bitter debate or by the adoption of a resolution unacceptable to France. Basically, it was up to France to find the solution of the problem. The U.S. would be glad to be of help in this matter, but it was difficult to judge at this point what might be the best way of handling the debate. Last year, he stated, the resolution on Algeria had received unanimous approval, whereas it seemed unlikely from present indications of Soviet policy that the U.S.S.R. would go along with any such procedure. It seemed probable that the Soviets would take a vigorous line in championing the Arab cause.

Mr. Pineau stated that according to the French Delegation to the U.N., there was some sentiment in favor of having a short debate and then putting off the voting on any resolution. He inquired whether we had heard of this idea.

The Secretary replied that we had not had any reports of this nature, but that this would appear to be a good solution if it were feasible. There had been no resolution in the recent U.N. debate regarding the Syrian complaint against Turkey. This was the first time that such a procedure had been adopted. The Secretary had long considered that discussions per se in the General Assembly constituted a healthy process and that final resolutions were not necessarily required. He thought, however, that tactically it would be unwise for the French to put forward the idea in the first instance that there should be no resolution following the Algerian debate. It might eventually prove feasible, nevertheless, in the face of several proposed resolutions, none capable of obtaining a two-thirds majority, that the debate could be terminated without a resolution. Any realistic assessment of the situation, however, would have to await the outcome of Mr. Pineau's efforts in New York.

Mr. Pineau agreed and stated that after he had canvassed the Delegates at the U.N., he would ask Ambassador Alphand to see the Secretary and to discuss the situation as it appeared at that time. The Secretary agreed and stated that he would also be in touch with Ambassador Lodge in the meantime.

95. Telegram From the Department of State to the Mission at the United Nations [1]

Washington, November 22, 1957—7:45 p.m.

Gadel 88. Re Algeria. Taking account Pineau's comments Delga 460, [2] his conversation with Secretary (Deptel 3755 to London, [3] 461 to New York [4]), and probable developments in debate Department consulting with UK re desirability action along lines below. At appropriate stage GADel would initiate further consultations with Pineau, making following points as persuasively as possible but without giving impression US seeking to "pressure" French into any specific course:

1. As Secretary told Pineau, we wish assist French in every reasonable way. Close cooperation during course of GA debate last year resulted in satisfactory conclusion of Assembly consideration of Algerian item. Naturally if we could conclude debate without resolution this would be optimum result.

2. However, events of past year and sentiment in GA, particularly among Afro-Asians, as Pineau now appears recognize, may require resolution going somewhat beyond resolution of last February.

3. We believe that quasi-procedural approach which should draw broad support without "internationalizing" Algerian question or undermining French position on competence can work again, if necessary to forestall undesirable outcome, provided France, after stating its basic case, indicates its recognition of interests of other states in peace and tranquillity in Algeria and states French readiness to consult with other governments at appropriate stage.

4. Whether and when any resolution would be submitted would depend entirely upon development of debate, types of resolutions proposed, and extent of support indicated for various texts.

5. While we cannot be sure now a suitable compromise can be found that will draw together moderate elements in GA in sufficient number for adoption, as was case last February, we believe following

---

[1] Source: Department of State, Central Files, 751S.00/11–2257. Secret; Limit Distribution. Also sent to London.

[2] Delga 460 from USUN, November 21, reported on a meeting between Lodge and Pineau in which Pineau indicated that the most favorable outcome would be no resolution at all. He described as totally unacceptable any effort to introduce Morocco and Tunisia negotiators. He acknowledged, however, that a military solution was not possible. (*Ibid.*, 772.56/11–2157)

[3] Not printed. (*Ibid.*, 772.56/11–2057)

[4] Telegram 461 to New York, November 21, contained a summary of a memorandum of the November 19 conversation between Pineau and the Secretary. (*Ibid.*, 751S.00/11–2157)

draft resolution includes elements that should prove useful in such eventuality.

6. Following is text of resolution which if acceptable to Pineau French could make available at appropriate time in debate to some friendly delegation or delegations:

"*The General Assembly,*

Having heard the statements made during the discussion of the Algerian question,

Noting the steps taken by the Government of France in its efforts to bring about a solution,

Noting the statement of the Government of France of its willingness to consult with other governments having a primary interest in peace and tranquillity in Algeria,

Recalling its resolution 1012 (XI) of 15 February 1957, and in particular the expression of hope that, in a spirit of cooperation, a peaceful, democratic and just solution will be found, through appropriate means, in conformity with the principles of the Charter of the United Nations,

Reaffirms its hope that a peaceful, democratic and just solution will be found in conformity with the principles of the Charter of the United Nations,

Expresses its satisfaction that the Government of France has announced its intention to consult with other governments having a primary interest in peace and tranquillity in Algeria."

7. Draft resolution retains quasi-procedural character of resolution last year since it is based on concept of General Assembly taking cognizance of French initiative rather than containing substantive recommendations, judgment, or exhortation. French, with substantial justification, could defend at home adoption of such General Assembly resolution as similar to one adopted last year and which avoids "internationalizing" Algerian question or undermining French position on competence. Resolution avoids reference to "parties" or "negotiations".

8. Resolution leaves open manner in which objectives of resolution would be pursued by French. It would not be necessary, as we see it, for Pineau to state intention publicly in Committee to consult with Morocco and Tunisia. We believe it would be sufficient if Pineau could make general statement in opening general debate speech incorporating essence third preambular paragraph of above resolution. In corridors however it would probably be necessary indicate more precisely what French intentions were in this regard, and specifically in relation to Morocco and Tunisia. Other delegations would naturally also be free to place such interpretations on language as they desired.

9. We believe adoption above resolution would not in long run be harmful to basic French objectives and intentions re Algeria.

Above resolution would prevent adoption strong resolutions declaring in favor self-determination and independence for Algeria, denouncing French colonialism, or seeking establishment UN mediation machinery, all of which we assume remain entirely unacceptable to French.

10. If foregoing approach acceptable to French, US would wish consult further at appropriate time re sponsorship and timing suggested resolution. Tentative US view is that text would not be put forward until near end of debate, although would be necessary for France lay foundation in its statement to GA.

11. GADel should take no action pending further instructions to approach French.

12. Addressees will observe above approach carries forward thinking embodied Deptel 1776 to Paris, 315 to Tunis, 440 to Rabat, 3414 to London, and pouched USUN, Algiers, Rome, Cairo.[5] Contents this message should be held in strictest confidence.

Dulles

[5] See footnote 3, *supra*. In Delga 483, November 27, Lodge advised the Secretary that the best solution would be to persuade the French to accept Tunisian-Moroccan assistance. He was prepared to take up the matter with Pineau. (Department of State, Central Files, 751S.00/11–2757) However, he was instructed not to advance beyond the instructions in Gadel 88. (Gadel 92 to New York, November 29; *ibid.*)

96. Memorandum From the Secretary of State to the Vice President [1]

Washington, November 30, 1957.

SUBJECT

The Algerian Issue Before the United Nations General Assembly

You may recall my note of May 28, 1957[2] indicating my wish to confer with you again on the Algerian question when it arose in the General Assembly of the United Nations. The discussions in the

[1] Source: Department of State, Central Files, 751S.00/11–2957. Confidential. Drafted by Looram and transmitted to the Secretary by Elbrick on November 29.

[2] Following a meeting of the National Security Council on May 2, Vice President Nixon informed Robert Cutler that he would like the NSC to take up the position the United States would adopt in the United Nations on the Algerian issue prior to the next U.N. debate. (Memorandum from Cutler to Dulles, May 7; *ibid.*, 751S.00/5–2457) (Continued)

First Committee have now begun,[3] and I would, therefore, like to advise you of our thinking on this subject as it has developed thus far.

The issue obviously poses a difficult problem in our foreign relations, given the strong feelings of the French on the one hand and of the Afro-Asians on the other. I am frankly doubtful that the United Nations debate even under the most favorable circumstances can make a significant contribution to a practical Algerian settlement. Probably the most we can hope for is that United Nations consideration of the problem will not worsen the situation either by aggravating the sentiments of the French or the North Africans or by pushing them into intractable positions. In any case, it seems probable that a genuine solution of the Algerian problem will have to be found outside the United Nations context.

The French position on the matter, as you know, is that Algeria constitutes an internal French issue and that the United Nations in accordance with the Charter is thus precluded from intervening in such a matter. They have, nevertheless, agreed to set forth their views on the present situation and their basic policies with regard to Algeria. With regard to current developments, the French believe that the military situation in Algeria has greatly improved during the past months, that the Moslem masses are tiring of the rebellion and that continually more Moslems are willing to cooperate with the French in working out a new political solution. The French are adhering to their offer to the Algerian rebels of cease-fire, to be followed by elections and negotiations on a new statute for Algeria. They are unwilling to negotiate with the principal rebel organization, the Front of National Liberation, which they feel is not truly representative of the Algerian people.

In view of the refusal of the rebels to accept the French cease-fire offer, the French have developed a new political program entitled the "Loi-Cadre for Algeria." Originally defeated under the Bourgès-Maunoury Government, it was passed today with minor amendments. The Loi-Cadre provides for the division of the Algerian departments (exclusive of the Sahara) into approximately six territories along ethnic grounds which will be semi-autonomous units. The Europeans would presumably be in a majority in two of the territories. Each territory will have its own legislature elected on

(Continued)
Dulles wrote Nixon on May 28 that he would talk to him before instructing the delegation at the General Assembly, but he did not consider it useful for the NSC to take up the issue "at this time". (*Ibid.*)

[3] The Algerian question was inscribed on the General Assembly agenda and referred to the First Committee on September 20. That body considered the issue between November 27 and December 6.

a basis of universal suffrage and a responsible executive. Two years after the setting up of these semi-autonomous territories, an over-all federal government will be established in Algiers, leaving the French Government still responsible for foreign affairs, defense and other such matters. Although it does not appear that the Loi-Cadre is susceptible of creating any significant psychological effect on the Moslem population, at least in the first instance, and it will be difficult to implement, it might conceivably represent a useful step forward in providing for the beginning of a political evolution in Algeria. Probably more important, it may represent an interim measure capable of preparing French public opinion for the more substantial concessions that will be required.

The Front of National Liberation has rejected the Loi-Cadre as a basis for solving the Algerian issue. It continues to insist that it will only enter into negotiations with the French Government after the latter has recognized Algeria's right to independence. This rebel organization remains confident of final victory and wishes to emerge from the rebellion as the principal political party in Algeria. It is, moreover, understandably inhibited from making concessions, while the Moslem adherents are being urged to fight for the sake of Algerian independence.

Tunisia and Morocco are naturally sympathetic to the FLN and are accordingly supporting it. Concerned, however, by the repercussions of the present conflict in their own countries, Bourguiba and the King of Morocco would prefer an early negotiated settlement between the FLN and French, and to this end have proposed their good offices. We believe this is a meritorious initiative and that the Moroccans and Tunisians may eventually be able to play a useful role in this connection. It seems most unlikely, however, in view of the tenuous Parliamentary situation, that the French could accept such mediation at this juncture. Premier Gaillard has in fact rejected it. United Nations insistence on such a formula, moreover, might prevent the eventual fruition of such a proposal. French opinion appears to be moving gradually in favor of a negotiated settlement and this trend may be accelerated by current financial difficulties. It is important that the efforts in this sense of liberal French elements not be jeopardized by a nationalistic outcry over United Nations action.

We believe our own objectives in connection with Algeria at the present United Nations General Assembly session should be: (1) to discourage statements or actions which might adversely affect progress toward a substantive Algerian settlement, and (2) to avoid any impairment of United States relations with the parties principally concerned. The latter may be rather difficult to achieve. Our relations with France, as you know, have already been strained by our delivery of arms to Tunisia, and we might be running grave risks if we took a position directly antagonistic to the French during the Algerian debate. The fact that this debate is taking place on the eve of the NATO meeting, of course, intensified our concern. At the same time, we are naturally anxious to maintain friendly relations with Tunisia and Morocco and the other states of Africa and Asia.

We see our basic role as one of moderation. So far, no specific resolutions on the Algerian question have been introduced in the United Nations General Assembly. The United States position with respect to individual proposals will have to be developed in light of their particular contents and also in light of the practical alternatives available in New York. I anticipate there will be considerable consultation and negotiation with respect to various proposals, and that the final form of proposed resolutions, as well as our own final position thereon, will only emerge as a consequence of this process.

The French have expressed the hope that the Algerian debate can be concluded without the necessity of voting on any resolutions at all, as was the case in the Syrian item. This procedure might also be desirable in terms of our own interests. However, I think it may be too optimistic to expect this kind of result. The next best alternative, as we see it, would be the adoption of a resolution acceptable to the principally interested parties on both sides, and we intend to use our own influence to encourage the development of such a resolution. If no mutually acceptable formula can be worked out, then we may have to make a difficult choice among the proposals advanced by the contending parties.

I would appreciate any ideas or views you may have on this subject.

John Foster Dulles [4]

[4] Printed from a copy that bears this stamped signature.

97. Memorandum of a Conversation, Department of State, Washington, December 2, 1957[1]

SUBJECT

Algeria

PARTICIPANTS

Secretary of State John Foster Dulles
Hervé Alphand, French Ambassador
Charles Lucet, French Minister
Francois de Laboulaye, Counselor, French Embassy
Francis O. Wilcox, Assistant Secretary of State
C. Burke Elbrick, Assistant Secretary of State

Alphand said that Foreign Minister Pineau had asked him to see the Secretary, in accordance with an understanding he had had when he was recently in Washington, to explain Pineau's position following various consultations in New York on the Algerian question. Pineau had, among others, talked to the Moroccans and Tunisians. The French are unwilling to accept any intervention in the Algerian matter by the Tunisians, although they are more receptive to suggestions from the Moroccans. France may find it useful at some time in the future to use the good offices of the King of Morocco in this matter. They could not, however, contemplate any intervention by Bourguiba at this point. The French do not wish publicly to entertain any thought of accepting the good offices of the Moroccans, although they might find it useful to do so at a later date.

Pineau feels that resolutions on the Algerian question presumably would fall into two categories: (1) a strong resolution calling on France to enter into negotiations looking to the independence of Algeria, and (2) a resolution by friendly States along the lines of last year's resolution, but somewhat stronger than the latter. The first type of resolution, Pineau thought, would be defeated, at least in the General Assembly; if it is too strongly worded, it could be defeated in the Political Committee. The second type of resolution would also be rejected, in Pineau's opinion, since it could not command a two-thirds majority in the Assembly.

Under the circumstances, the French are exploring possible alternatives. It might be possible to end the debate on Algeria with no resolution at all. Alternatively, a compromise resolution might be possible. The French do not wish to make public at present any suggestion that they may be thinking in terms of a compromise. The Japanese have informed them that they would be glad to be helpful,

[1] Source: Department of State, Central Files, 751S.00/12–257. Secret. Drafted by Elbrick.

however, and it is possible that they could be induced to sponsor such a compromise resolution. Generally, such a resolution might express the hope that, following a cease-fire, negotiations be undertaken between the French and representatives chosen by the Algerian people. Such a recommendation could be added to last year's resolution. Alphand repeated that he did not wish this to be known publicly at this time.

Pineau feels that it is urgent that the United States take a position now and hoped that Lodge would be able to make a speech on Algeria tomorrow. The British and others have already expressed themselves and some Delegations are hesitant about making up their minds because the United States has not yet declared itself. In such a speech, Lodge might refer to Algeria as a special French responsibility, express the thought that the present situation offers more hope for a solution, refer to the evolutionary character of French legislation now under consideration, and state that interference by the United Nations at this time would not accelerate matters but would, in fact, make their solution more difficult.

The Secretary said that he felt it might be possible to respond to the French request, providing Lodge's speech is not directed to any specific resolution. For that reason, he thought, it might be wise to make the speech before any resolutions are introduced. He thought that Lodge could say that matters are evolving in the direction that would afford the people of Algeria a greater measure of representative government. [2] The Secretary thought it was up to the French to decide what to do about the Moroccan-Tunisian proposal and not for the General Assembly to dictate. The Secretary felt that the General Assembly would be going pretty far afield if it tried to pass on the juridical separation of a territory from a governing State. He said there is little doubt what the reaction of the United States would be if a resolution of this type concerning Puerto Rico, for example, were introduced into the General Assembly.

Alphand asked whether our Delegation in New York could help the French in lobbying in connection with a possible resolution. The Secretary said this might be possible later on but we could not commit ourselves until we see what kind of resolutions are introduced.

---

[2] The text of the address was given to Lodge on December 2 for delivery the next day at the 919th meeting of the First Committee. He was advised to indicate its general outline to the French, Moroccans, and Tunisians ahead of time. For text of the speech, see Department of State Press Release 2830, December 3, or telegram 2088 to Paris, December 4. (*Ibid.*, 751S.00/12–457)

98. Memorandum of a Conversation, Department of State, Washington, December 5, 1957[1]

SUBJECT

Algeria

PARTICIPANTS

Mr. Herve Alphand, Ambassador, Embassy of the French Republic
Mr. Charles Lucet, Minister, Embassy of the French Republic
Mr. Francois de Laboulaye, Counselor, Embassy of the French Republic
Mr. Francis O. Wilcox, IO
Mr. Joseph Palmer II, NEA
Mr. Joseph J. Sisco, UNP
Mr. Matthew J. Looram, WE

Ambassador Alphand called at his request and opened the conversation by saying the French were satisfied with Ambassador Lodge's speech in the Political Committee on Algeria. Alphand reported on a telephone conversation he had with Pineau late last night. He said Pineau believes the best procedure is to have an extreme Afro-Asian resolution and a friendly Latin America-Spanish resolution submitted. The French assume that neither resolution would receive the required support, though the Afro-Asian resolution might get a simple majority in the Committee. In these circumstances, the French could then consider a possible third or compromise resolution. Alphand reported that Menon wants to submit an Afro-Asian resolution which is acceptable to both sides. Alphand said that while this might be logical, it was psychologically impossible from the point of view of the French; it was easier for the French to be flexible if resolutions representing each side were first submitted. At this point, Alphand said parenthetically that the LA-Spanish draft was about to be put forward when Ambassador Lodge had said that it should not be submitted at this time. (Mr. Sisco later conveyed the substance of this to Mr. Barco. Mr. Barco said this was definitely not the case, that the United States had not taken any action to stop the submission of the LA-Spanish draft. Mr. Barco said the reason these delegations and the Japanese had been "scared off" was because of the existence of the Indian draft resolution which is considered reasonable by a good many delegations.)

Alphand went on to say that it was necessary to the French to have "apparent" assistance from the United States. He said the U.S. could make its assistance apparent in two ways: active assistance in

[1] Source: Department of State, Central Files, 751S.00/12–557. Confidential. Drafted by Wilcox.

the corridors; and "a very precise position by the United States in rejecting the Arab-Asian resolution [2] and in support of the LA-Spanish resolution."

Mr. Wilcox said that while we are not fully familiar with the details of the tactical situation and numerous consultations, the United States had supported the French position in its speech. We had refrained thus far from giving our support to the Arab-Asian resolution, even though the USUN staff estimate is that it might obtain a 2/3 majority. Mr. Wilcox also referred to the fact that if Indian sponsorship was objectionable to the French, such sponsorship could be broadened to include a number of states from other areas.

Alphand concluded by reiterating the need for close and apparent solidarity between the United States and France on Algeria. Mr. Wilcox responded that he was sure our Delegation was in close contact with the French and that he had a report before him from Ambassador Lodge indicating that there had been two discussions with Pineau yesterday. [3] In response to Mr. Wilcox' query, Alphand said he had no specific recommendations to make other than that there be close contact between the United States and the French delegations.

Mr. de Laboulaye called Mr. Sisco an hour later. He informed us that Alphand had just spoken to Pineau. De Laboulaye said Pineau does not feel that the Indian resolution can be amended "at the present time" to the degree which would be necessary in order to make it acceptable to the French. For this reason, Mr. de Laboulaye said the French are falling back to the previous procedure; namely, that two extreme resolutions be submitted in the expectation that the French could be more flexible on a third or compromise resolution. He said the French believe it is important that the United States take a position openly opposing the extreme Arab-Asian resolution and supporting the LA-Spanish draft. He urged that we call Ambassador Lodge and request him to take this line.

Francis O. Wilcox [4]

---

[2] Draft resolution A/C.1/L.194, sponsored by 17 Asian and African countries, was introduced on December 5. It declared that the principle of self-determination was applicable to the Algerian people and called for negotiations. For text, see United Nations, *Official Records*, General Assembly, Twelfth Session, Agenda Item 59, Annexes, pp. 2–3.

[3] In Delga 542 from USUN, December 5, Lodge summarized his meetings with Pineau, who indicated his government's opposition to the references to self-determination and negotiations in the draft resolution. (Department of State, Central Files, 751S.00/12–557)

[4] Printed from a copy that bears this typed signature.

99. Memorandum From the Assistant Secretary of State for International Organization Affairs (Wilcox) to the Secretary of State [1]

Washington, December 9, 1957.

SUBJECT

Alphand's Call on You to Discuss Strategy on Algerian Item

Discussion

Ambassador Alphand is calling on you, pursuant to M. Pineau's instructions, to discuss strategy on the Algerian item when the General Assembly plenary meets Tuesday morning. [2]

On Friday the Norwegian-Canadian amendments (acceptable to the French) to the 17-power Arab-Asian resolution passed in Committee by one vote, 37–36–7. (attached) [3] However, Liberia shifted from an abstention to a negative vote when the 17-power resolution, as amended, was voted upon, and it was therefore rejected 37–37–6. The Soviet and Arab-Asian blocs voted solidly against the resolution (only Turkey and the Philippines abstained and Laos voted in favor). The Latin Americans, with the exception of Haiti, Guatemala, Mexico, and Bolivia, supported the resolution, as did the Europeans including non-NATO countries such as Finland, Austria, and Sweden. The seven-power LA-Italian resolution, reflecting more closely the French position, was not pressed to a vote by the cosponsors. [4]

On Saturday morning, Alphand called on me to express his satisfaction with the outcome of the voting in the Political Committee. [5] He reiterated the French preference that General Assembly action be concluded without adoption of any resolution. At the same time, he acknowledged that this might not be possible since we can expect the reintroduction of proposals and amendments in plenary. (Iran has indicated it may reintroduce the 17-power resolution as amended.) Alphand agreed that if amendments to the 17-power resolution are not moderate it may be possible to end General Assembly action without a resolution; on the other hand, he feared that the amendments would be of a moderate character in which case there was danger of dissipating some of the support of the French position, principally among the Latin Americans.

---

[1] Source: Department of State, Central Files, 751S.00/12–957. Confidential.

[2] December 10.

[3] Not printed. The amendments were submitted by Canada, Norway, and Ireland on December 6. (U.N. doc. A/C.1/L.196)

[4] The resolution was submitted on December 5. (U.N. doc. A/C.1/L.195)

[5] A memorandum of the December 7 conversation by John P. Shaw (UNP) is in Department of State, Central Files, 751S.00/12–757.

In response to Alphand's request that the United States assist France in bringing about the completion of General Assembly consideration without the adoption of a resolution, I made several points to him. First, we appreciated the flexibility shown by the French in accepting the Canadian-Norwegian amendments. Alphand agreed that this improved the French position in the Assembly and that it was the correct decision. Secondly, the United States would be pleased if no resolution is adopted. However, in view of the probability that proposals and moderate amendments may be introduced in plenary, it may not be possible to achieve this objective. Thirdly, the United States position on any amendments or new proposals cannot be determined until such proposals and amendments are in fact submitted. We cannot at this point say whether we would oppose all amendments, whatever their character, particularly since the Arab-Asian strategy may be to submit amendments of a moderate character which might be generally acceptable to France. In these circumstances, we should try to maintain a flexible attitude. Fourth, Pineau can be assured that Ambassador Lodge will concert closely with him as he has this past week in helping to bring about a result acceptable to France.

---

100. Memorandum of a Conversation, Department of State, Washington, December 20, 1957 [1]

SUBJECT

Algeria and the NATO Meeting

PARTICIPANTS

Mr. Mongi Slim, Ambassador of Tunisia
Mr. M'hamed Essafi, Secretary of Embassy of Tunisia
Mr. Joseph Palmer 2nd, Deputy Assistant Secretary, AF
Mr. John A. Bovey, Jr., Deputy Director, AFN

Mr. Slim opened with a post-mortem on the Algerian debate at the UN and expressed his regret that he had not been able toward the end to work in entire harmony with the United States Delegation with regard to the amendments to the resolution.

[1] Source: Department of State, Central Files, 751S.00/12–2057. Secret. Drafted by Bovey.

Mr. Palmer said we understood the Tunisian viewpoint and that we of course shared the Ambassador's regrets. While the resolution [2] may have fallen short of the desires of both France and the Arabs, still we felt that a unanimous decision, in which the Moroccan and Tunisian initiative was recognized and the concern of the entire Assembly was made clear, was a considerable accomplishment. The fact that France had been brought to acquiesce in it was also a big step forward.

Mr. Slim said the sequel was more important than the language of the resolution and that if France follows it up we may move little by little toward meaningful contacts with Morocco and Tunisia and toward a solution. There were still many difficulties, and the next step was to start the conversations and to overcome the hesitations in France which was wavering between those who opposed the offer of good offices and those who really want to make use of it.

Mr. Palmer said that the edifice of a solution must be carefully built brick by brick and not flung up in haste. The matter was fraught with many inter-related complexities; for example, the success or failure of the forthcoming Franco-Tunisian conversations might well, in his opinion, leave a most significant effect on France's utilization of the good offices of Morocco and Tunisia.

Mr. Slim agreed and cited the question of French troops in Tunisia as another example of the complex inter-relation between the Algerian question and other North African problems. He then said he wished to close the Algerian parenthesis and reopen certain dossiers of United States-Tunisian interest. First of all, he wanted to express Tunisian gratification over the fact that the President had made no statements during the NATO meeting which recognized any privileged situation or sphere of influence of France in North Africa. He said that the Tunisian Government knew of the heavy pressures which had been brought to bear on the United States in Paris and which had caused the Tunisians to convey their apprehensions to us in Washington and Tunis.

Mr. Palmer said we were aware of Tunisian apprehensions and that there had indeed been requests for statements acknowledging French special interests. At no moment, however, had the United States ever contemplated taking any position inconsistent with Tunisian sovereignty. Mr. Palmer added that he thought the French had understood this and were really thinking of something which would be helpful to the preservation of their interests in the area rather than making a conscious effort to diminish Tunisia's status as an independent nation.

---

[2] Resolution 1184 (XII), adopted by the General Assembly on December 10.

Mr. Palmer then showed Mr. Slim the personal message which the Secretary had sent from Paris to Mr. Bourguiba.[3] Mr. Slim read it and expressed great gratification at this reassurance, which only confirmed what he had thought our position would be. He requested a copy, which Mr. Palmer made available on an informal basis.

---

[3] See Document 300.

BELGIAN CONGO

UNITED STATES CONCERN WITH DEVELOPMENTS IN THE BELGIAN CONGO[1]

101. Despatch From the Embassy in Belgium to the Department of State[2]

No. 1037 *Brussels, March 21, 1956.*

REF

Department's CA–6309, February 17, 1956;[3] Embassy's despatch No. 439, October 18, 1955[4]

SUBJECT

Embassy comments on paper entitled "Africa: Problems of United States Policy"

Summary

Determination of United States policy regarding dependent areas presents fewer immediate problems in the Congo than it does in such areas as North Africa, for the metropolitan government under its present policies is now giving and for some time may be capable of giving to the Congolese more than they demand. The predominant interests of the United States in its defense and economic arrangements with the Western European countries as well as its interest in seeing the dependent African peoples progress in an orderly fashion toward self-government can both be served in the Congo by acting through the metropolitan government. At least while present conditions prevail, this will not earn for the United States in the Congo the opprobrium of participation in "foreign oppression".

---

[1] For previous documentation on this subject, see *Foreign Relations*, 1952–1954, vol. XI, Part 1, pp. 406 ff.

[2] Source: Department of State, Central Files, 611.70/3–2156. Confidential. Sent also to Paris and Leopoldville.

[3] CA–6309 transmitted a paper entitled "Africa: Problems of United States Policy," to various diplomatic posts and consular offices concerned with Africa. The paper was prepared in response to Vice President Nixon's request for the Department's views on Africa. (*Ibid.*, 611.70/12–1756)

[4] Not printed. (*Ibid.*, 120.1470/10–1855)

So far as can presently be seen, the Belgian and Congo economies are capable of bearing the burden of the development of the Congo at its present pace without grant or loan aid from the United States Government. Need for United States Government assistance is for the present limited to a modest technical assistance program and encouragement of American private investment. This estimate should, however, be reviewed from time to time as the Congo is entering a period of rapid and perhaps basic change due to the recent Belgian decision to accelerate the political education of the Congolese. Belgian capabilities may not always remain adequate to complete its self assigned task of helping the Congolese to reach a status where they can participate in their own administration. In view of the importance of the Congo to the United States as a prime source of critical raw materials, United States aid, if a need for it developed, would have a fairly high priority. Any American offers of assistance which may be made should take carefully into consideration the rather unusual sensitivities of the Belgians which are motivated by fears of losing the Congo and their suspicion that anticolonialist tendencies might lead the United States to take positions undercutting them there.

As regards the activities and numbers of United States Government personnel in the Congo, the size of the staffs is not so important as a continuation of the policy of assigning persons there who are highly adaptable to the sensitivities of the political situation as well as to the living conditions. It is recommended that USIA adopt the policy of assigning its officers to Leopoldville after they have had a tour of duty in Brussels where they can learn at first hand of the Belgian attitudes towards and sensitivities regarding the colony. The role USIS is playing in the Congo would not necessarily be facilitated in the Embassy's opinion by increase in staff. Net progress cannot be achieved in the information field in the circumstances obtaining there unless the program enjoys the full confidence of the Belgian authorities and earning this confidence is necessarily a slow process. The United States should not put itself in the position of attempting a program which the Belgians might think would undermine them in the Congo. One means of avoiding such a development is to maintain close coordination with the appropriate Belgian authorities in our information program, insuring that they are kept informed of what we are trying to achieve. Congolese are not in general permitted to come to Belgian universities and for this reason the Belgians are now engaged in establishing university facilities in the Congo. For this reason, United States scholarships should not now be offered to Congolese Africans. *End Summary*

[Here follows an exposition of the points summarized above.]

Frederick M. Alger, Jr.

102. Despatch From the Embassy in Belgium to the Department of State[1]

No. 786 *Brussels, December 28, 1956.*

REF

Despatch 120, Nov. 28, 1956,[2] from the Consulate General at Leopoldville; Embassy's telegram 66 [*666*], December 14, 1956,[3] to the Department (repeated to Leopoldville as No. 4)

SUBJECT

Belgo-U.S. Relations in the Congo

I believe that the issues involved in the Kalonji visa case go far beyond the question of the issuance to a Congolese of a visa for entry into the United States and that this matter therefore merits very careful study.

The Consul General at Leopoldville in his despatch under reference states:

"The repercussions of his visit on European and African opinion in the Belgian Congo could be far-reaching. Paragraph two of Consul Murdock's letter[4] aptly states the dilemma in which the Belgians probably feel themselves; there can be no doubt of their

[1] Source: Department of State, Central Files, 032–Kalongi, Isaac/12–2856. Confidential.

[2] Despatch 120 reported that Isaac Kalonji had applied for a non-immigrant visa to visit the United States. If the visa were granted, Kalonji would be the first Congolese intellectual of potential political standing to make such a trip. He was a member of the Conseil de Gouvernement, an advisory body whose members were selected not elected, and one of perhaps 200 immatriculés at that time. (*Ibid.*)

[3] Telegram 666 from Brussels recommended that the Consulate General Leopoldville discuss the visa application with high Belgian authorities to confirm they were aware of the impending Kalonji visit so the onus would fall on them if the trip were forestalled. (*Ibid.*, 032–Kalonji, Isaac/12–1456)

[4] Paragraph 2 of Consul Thomas G. Murdock's letter to Consul General James Frederick Green of November 22 reads:

"I had previously had word from a certain local Government official who expressed some concern over the invitation, mainly that he did not think the individual was exactly the person to make this trip, although in principle he saw no

(Continued)

desire to keep Congolese away from any direct American presupposed 'anti-colonial' influence; yet the effect of denying a passport to a leading immatriculé and member of the Conseil de Gouvernement upon African évolué opinion would be doubly serious. It would not only cast suspicion in the African mind on the Government's good intentions, but would probably have the effect of enhancing the prestige of the United States among Africans. Hence, the possible frustration among Belgians that may be engendered by this situation would seem to dictate the utmost caution on the part of the United States Government in dealing with Mr. Kalonji's visit."

As indicated in my telegram under reference, I am strongly of the opinion that a matter of this nature should at the very outset have been a subject of informal discussion between the Consul General and high ranking authorities of the Congo Government. Such discussion would not be designed for the purpose of asking Belgian permission for our action nor for giving Belgian authorities a veto over normal and legitimate acts by our representatives in the Congo. It is evident, however, that in a case of this kind, if the Belgian authorities had considered Kalonji's visit to the United States sufficiently harmful to Belgian interests, they themselves would have been in a position to take action to prevent such a visit.

What I have in mind is the establishment of a basis of cooperation and understanding with the Belgian authorities in our own approach to the Congolese and with respect to important problems affecting our relations with the Congo and with Belgium which will aim toward convincing the Belgians that our purpose is to help them and not to undermine their position. If we consider as erroneous some given Belgian policy, particularly one involving a question of our own actions, we should not hesitate to inform the Belgian authorities accordingly at a high level. I do not think, however, that we should put ourselves in the position of taking actions in dealing with important and sensitive problems involving the Congolese and the Congo, however legitimate such actions may be, which would have the effect of undermining the basis of our cooperation and understanding with the Belgians without a very frank and thorough informal discussion of such problems with the responsible Belgian authorities. It must not be overlooked that Belgium, and not the United States, has direct responsibility for the Congo. Our efforts should be directed toward assisting and encouraging them in the

(Continued)
objections to such a project. His main objection seemed to be that the applicant was not sufficiently well prepared."

The full text of the letter was sent to the Department as enclosure 2 to despatch 120 cited in footnote 2 above.

direction we think they should go in their policies toward the Congo.

I recall the deep suspicion of United States aims in North Africa among the French, which at times in the past was directed against United States consular representatives in that area. I strongly recommend that we lean over backwards to avoid creating a similar situation in the Congo provided we can do so without sacrificing our own basic interests and principles. I believe we can do this. It is generally recognized that Congolese developments are approaching the stage when the pace of events will be considerably accelerated. It behooves us, therefore, at this stage to avoid, to the extent possible consistent with our own long range interests, taking actions which would increase the difficulties and problems the Belgians will inevitably face during the years ahead.

In the light of the foregoing I urge that the Department give careful consideration to the problem inherent in this situation. I strongly recommend that the Embassy and the Consulate General at Leopoldville as a matter of standard operating procedure maintain informal contact at a high level in the Belgian Government and in the Government General, respectively, for discussion on a continuing basis of important problems of mutual interest between Belgium and the United States. It would be expected that on sensitive matters, such as this visit to the United States of a Congolese, the Belgian authorities would be made fully aware of our views and intentions. I am convinced that we have little or nothing to lose by following such a procedure and much to gain through the establishment of a close working relationship along these lines with the appropriate Belgian authorities.

I submit this recommendation because of my serious concern over the possibilities inherent in situations such as the Kalonji case where it was recognized that the repercussions of his visit could be very far reaching but on which we made no effort to discuss the matter in a frank manner with the Belgians. I should appreciate receiving an expression of the Department's views on my recommendation.[5]

F.M. Alger, Jr.

---

[5] *Infra.*

103. Instruction From the Department of State to the Embassy in Belgium [1]

CA–7083 *Washington, March 5, 1957.*

SUBJECT

The Kalonji Case and its Bearing on Belgo-American Relations

REFERENCE

Brussel's Despatch No. 786 of December 28, 1956; [2] Leopoldville's Despatch No. 151 of January 9, 1957 [3]

The Department concurs with the Embassy with respect to the importance of both the Embassy and the Consulate General at Leopoldville maintaining informal contact at a high level with officials in the Belgian Government and in the Government General, respectively, for discussion on a continuing basis of important problems of mutual interest between Belgium and the United States. It notes with approval that the Consulate General at Leopoldville is in complete accord with this principle.

As a general principle, the Department also agrees with the Embassy that this Government should not put itself in the position of taking actions in dealing with important and sensitive problems involving the Congolese and the Congo which would have the effect of undermining the basis of US cooperation and understanding with Belgium without frank and thorough discussion of such problems with the responsible Belgian authorities. At the same time, the Department does not believe that acceptance of this principle requires us to look behind the official acts of the Belgian authorities themselves.

In the Kalonji case, the Consulate General was presented with a passport duly and recently validated for travel to the United States. Our authorities in the Congo know from experience that Africans are not given passports valid for travel abroad except by the Belgian authorities on the basis of very careful considerations and in full knowledge of the circumstances of use. The Belgian handling of the

---

[1] Source: Department of State, Central Files, 032–Kalonji, Isaac/3–557. Confidential. Repeated to Leopoldville.

[2] *Supra.*

[3] In despatch 151, Consul General Green related the reasons why he chose not to pursue the Kalonji visit with high government officials. He did not wish to give the impression that the United States had some ulterior motive in promoting the visit or was unduly concerned about it. Since the Belgians had renewed Kalonji's passport after his application for a U.S. visa, Green assumed they had no objection to the visit. (Department of State, Central Files, 032–Kalonji, Isaac/1–957)

case was, therefore, in accordance with its normal routine and the Consulate General similarly decided to process it normally.

The Department has been greatly encouraged at the indication of a somewhat more liberal Belgian policy inherent in the granting to Kalonji of a passport valid for travel to the United States. It believes that the best posture for the United States with respect to Congo developments is one of quietly expecting and therefore of quietly accepting forward steps by the administering authorities. To act otherwise would run the risk of conveying to the Belgians an impression of surprise at any progressive actions and of resignation to a less forward looking policy.

In view of the above considerations and in the light of the circumstances described in Leopoldville telegram No. 56 of December 17 [4] and Leopoldville despatch No. 151 of January 9, the Department believes the Embassy will agree that the Consulate General at Leopoldville acted correctly in handling this unprecedented case.

Dulles

[4] In telegram 56, Green stated the Belgian Government had handled the Kalonji visit as a routine matter. Since Belgium had indicated it wished to avoid a policy decision, Green advised against an official U.S. approach, which might embarrass Belgian administrators. (*Ibid.*, 032–Kalonji, Isaac/12–1756)

104. Despatch From the Embassy in Belgium to the Department of State [1]

No. 1238 *Brussels, March 21, 1957.*

SUBJECT

American Official Representation and USIS Activities in the Congo

Monsieur Delvaux de Fenffe, [2] Director General for Political Affairs in the Ministry of Foreign Affairs, today called in the reporting officer [3] to convey to him the Belgian Government's concern over the increase in the numbers of United States personnel being assigned to the Consulate General at Leopoldville and the

[1] Source: Department of State, Central File 122.536H3/3–2157. Confidential. Also sent to Leopoldville.

[2] Jacques Delvaux de Fenffe.

[3] Philip D. Sprouse.

expansion of USIS publications being issued by the Consulate General. A memorandum of this conversation is enclosed.[4]

Monsieur Delvaux explained that the Belgian Government had rejected French and British requests for the opening of additional consular offices in the Congo and requests by Arab Governments and the Indian Government for the stationing of consular representatives in the Congo, knowing that the Indians, Arabs and Communists were interested only in political activities. A Czech request for a visa for a second Czech consular officer was also being held up. He said that it was difficult for the Belgian Government to continue to reject such requests if at the same time other Governments could point to continued expansion of United States Government consular and informational activities in the area. He expressed the "hope" that the United States Government would understand the delicacy of the Belgian position and would take measures to avoid an increase in numbers of personnel or in USIS publications. He added that these questions had been raised with his Ministry by the Ministry of Colonies.

The reporting officer informed Monsieur Delvaux that he was confident that the Department of State would look with sympathy and understanding on the Belgian position but he was certain that the United States Government would accept with reluctance any effort to put a flat ceiling on the number of United States personnel assigned to the Congo as this hardly seemed to be in keeping with the very close and friendly relations between the two countries.

With reference to Monsieur Delvaux's statements regarding the recent increase in USIS publications, the reporting officer said that so long as the right of the Consulate General to issue any publication was not in question the number of such publications seemed unimportant. He pointed out that the Czech Consul,[5] for example, could use one such USIS publication as easily as five as a basis for a request to issue his own publications in the Congo.

The reporting officer said that the Embassy would convey to the Department Monsieur Delvaux's views and told him that the United

---

[4] Not printed. Sprouse noted that Delvaux de Fenffe had made a "veiled reference" to the possible political character of the USIS English classes for Africans. Sprouse emphasized that "the United States did not wish to interfere in relations between colonial powers and their possessions and its real concern arose when colonial powers did not satisfy or keep ahead of the aspirations of the native peoples and let situations boil up to the point that they explode in bloodshed in the faces of both the colonial powers and the possessions and vitally affected the position of the free world." Sprouse concluded that Belgium had theretofore kept in advance of African aspirations though "the real challenge would obviously come in the future."

[5] Consular relations with Czechoslovakia were established prior to the Communist accession to power in 1948.

States Government would view sympathetically the Belgian difficulties in this regard.

Monsieur Louis Scheyven, Secretary General of the Foreign Office, with whom the reporting officer subsequently discussed this matter, states that the Czech Government has recently put increased pressure on the Belgian Government, including a direct approach to Minister for Foreign Affairs Spaak,[6] for the assignment of a second consular officer in the Congo. Monsieur Scheyven says that the Belgian Government is placed in a difficult position in continuing to reject the Czech request and requests from the Indian and Arab Governments and for that reason wished the United States Government to keep in mind Belgian difficulties in connection with assignment of United States personnel and USIS information activities in the Congo.

The Embassy believes that the Belgians do have a genuine concern in this regard and wish to hold the line in order to prevent any further expansion of foreign government activity in the area which might have political overtones or cause difficulties for the Belgians. It is also likely that the Belgian attitude toward what it views as traditional American anti-colonialism, taken in conjunction with the recently achieved independence of Ghana,[7] Vice President Nixon's trip through Africa and the United States position vis-à-vis Ruanda-Urundi in the United Nations Trusteeship Council, points up at this time Belgian concern over future developments in the Congo.

The Embassy assumes that the recent increase in United States official personnel in the Congo which the Belgians have in mind represents the assignment of an Agricultural Officer and a second USIS Officer at Leopoldville. The Belgians may interpret such assignments as increased United States activity in fields other than those of normal consular functions.

In the light of the foregoing the Embassy recommends that this mission and the Consulate General in Leopoldville be authorized to convey to the Belgian authorities in Brussels and in Leopoldville an expression of the Department's views regarding the questions raised along the following general lines:

The United States Government views sympathetically the difficulties faced by the Belgian Government, as described by Monsieur Delvaux de Fenffe. It does not believe, of course, that the Belgian Government would wish to place any flat limitation as such on the numbers of personnel that the United States Government may wish to assign to its consular establishments in the Congo. The United States Government will, of course, make every effort possible to

[6] Paul-Henri Spaak.
[7] March 6, 1957.

avoid any non-essential increase in the numbers of personnel assigned to those consular offices, having in mind the problems the Belgian Government faces on this score. The Consulate General will undertake a careful review of the publications being issued by USIS and will keep in mind the Belgian Government's views with respect to the issuance of any additional publications in the future.[8]

It is believed that the Embassy has "scotched" a possible effort of the Ministry of Colonies to reduce the number of publications being issued by USIS. The Embassy suggests, however, that the Consulate General carefully review these publications with a view to determining whether all of them are sufficiently important to United States national interests in the Congo to require their continued publication and with a view to dropping any not considered essential or combining some of them in order to reduce their number.

It is believed that this situation is one which fits very logically into the framework which this Embassy proposed in its despatch No. 786 of December 28, 1956.[9] The Embassy believes that frank and friendly discussions of these problems with the Belgian authorities, by the Consulate General, as well as by the Embassy, should enable these problems to be worked out satisfactorily on a friendly basis and that discussions on a regular and continuing basis of problems of this nature might in the future prevent their becoming the subject of official representations at a high level in the Ministry of Foreign Affairs.

For the Ambassador:
Philip D. Sprouse
Counselor of Embassy

---

[8] In telegram 155 to Leopoldville, April 17, also sent to Brussels, the Department advised delay in conveying the views proposed in this paragraph. The Department recommended an informal approach by Green concerning personnel assignments and USIS publications. (Department of State, Central Files, 122.536H3/3–2157) Telegram 1232 from Brussels, April 18, advised against such an informal approach. (*Ibid.*, 122.536H3/4–1857) Telegram 1631 to Brussels, May 15, also sent to Leopoldville, instructed the Embassy to explain U.S. staffing plans and USIS programs to the Belgian Foreign Ministry. (*Ibid.*, 122.536H3/3–2157) Sprouse accordingly met with Delvaux de Fenffe on May 17 to present the Department's reply to the Belgian démarche. He emphasized U.S. recognition of the importance of Congo Government cooperation and confidence for the effective operation of an information program. (Despatch 1520, May 21; *ibid.*, 122.536H3/5–2157)

[9] Document 102.

105. Memorandum by the Vice Consul at Leopoldville (Gross) [1]

Leopoldville, undated.

MEMORANDUM ON THE VISIT OF VICE CONSUL GROSS TO ELISABETHVILLE ON MAY 15–20, 1957

[Here follows a summary of Vice Consul Gross' discussions with various white residents of Katanga.]

In summary, my impressions of the Katanga from this and the preceding five visits over the past year are as follows:

1) The Katanga is geographically, economically, politically, and socially entirely separate from the tropical rest of the Belgian Congo. The political evolution of the Congo now being initiated by Leopoldville and Brussels is and will be strongly resisted by the white population of the Katanga, which in its way of life and thinking is closer to the settler population of East Africa than to the white population of the tropical, Western part of the Congo. It is not entirely improbable that these differences may lead toward a secession of the Katanga from the Congo should the Africans take over in Leopoldville in the future, or a federation of the Katanga with Rhodesia. At present there is a quasi-organized movement among Europeans in the Katanga in this direction.

2) The political evolution of the African in the Katanga is far less advanced than in Leopoldville. The African seemed to me to be content with his economic prosperity, but several observers have told me that there is mounting tension beneath the surface.

3) The combination of economic prosperity for and political suppression of the African in the Katanga, plus the all important fact that the *future* of the region will be in the hands of the European, seems to me to provide an extremely fertile soil for outside subversion of the African. The African in Leopoldville appears to be willing to bide his time, knowing that the direction of political change is in his favor. Such assurance is lacking in the Katanga. The Europeans in the Katanga seem capable and willing to suppress any political threat by the Africans, at least for the short run.

4) Despite the racial situation, the Europeans in the Katanga appear to be less resentful and hostile toward the African policy of the United States than are the Belgians in Leopoldville. Partly this is due to the aristocratic upper-class social level of many of the Katangais. Many of them have visited the United States and are

[1] Source: Department of State, Central Files, 755A.00/5–2957. Confidential. Enclosure to despatch 262 from Leopoldville, May 29.

aware of its world position. Many of them are technically very highly trained and respect American technology. Finally, the non-Belgian white population seems little concerned with politics. The relative indifference or friendliness of many Katangais to Americans makes the job of gathering political information much easier than is the case in Leopoldville—among the Europeans.

5) There appears to be no avenue of contact with the African in Elisabethville. Immatriculés are not around town or at social occasions. Attempts to cultivate the African évolué in Elisabethville would probably not bring positive results commensurate with the suspicion that would be aroused among Europeans.

Richard L. Gross

---

106. Despatch From the Consulate General at Leopoldville to the Department of State [1]

No. 40 *Leopoldville, August 27, 1957.*

REF

Embassy Brussels D–132, August 2, 1957; [2] Deptel 27, repeated to Brussels 306 [3]

SUBJECT

Activities of the United States Government Personnel in the Congo

In the reference despatch on the above subject, Mr. Sprouse reports a conversation in which M. Jacques Delvaux de Fenffe, Director General of Political Affairs in the Belgian Ministry of Foreign Affairs, asserted that the Consulate General at Leopoldville was giving the impression of encouraging independence or liberation movements in the Congo as a result of contacts of United States Government personnel with political leaders of the three political movements known as Conscience Africaine, Abako, and Royaume

[1] Source: Department of State, Central Files, 122.536H3/8–2757. Confidential. Also sent to Brussels and repeated to Elisabethville, Luanda, and Yaoundé.

[2] Not printed. (*Ibid.*, 122.536H3/8–257)

[3] Telegram 27 requested the Consulate General's views on the Embassy's suggestions, conveyed in despatch 132 cited in footnote 2 above, that the Belgians should be told that any U.S. official who encouraged a Congolese independence movement would be recalled but that the Consulate General could not conduct its business without dealing with Congolese. (*Ibid.*)

du Congo.[4] M. Delvaux stated that these contacts between United States Government personnel and these political movements were of a nature to demonstrate a marked interest in these independence movements and represented definite encouragement thereof. M. Delvaux charged that our Public Affairs Officer, Consul Gilbert E. Bursley, had been particularly active in contacts with the leaders of these political movements and expressed the hope that he would not return to the Congo at the end of his home leave. These are serious allegations, which, if true, would reflect very adversely on the Consulate General and on me personally.

This despatch sets forth a detailed record of the post's contacts with Africans since my arrival here in late October 1956. It is hoped that this record will prove useful in further conversations to be undertaken with the Belgian Government on this subject. If the Department approves, I shall use this record in a future conversation with the Governor General or the Vice Governor General here.

So far as we are able to determine, there is no substance whatever to the allegations made by M. Delvaux. On the contrary, as the record below shows, my colleagues and I have been so conscious of Belgian sensitivities and so determined to avoid any suspicion of exactly the kind of activities described by M. Delvaux that we have refrained almost entirely from contacts with Africans, with the result that our reporting on developments in the Congo has been impaired.

[Here follows a detailed account of contacts with Africans by the Consulate General's staff.]

Conclusions

1. The foregoing record shows that American employees of the Consulate General, with the exception of Vice Consul Bearce, have had only a minimum of contacts with Africans, whether political leaders or not. It must be concluded, therefore, that this latest protest in Brussels is based on either a misunderstanding of the facts or a misinterpretation of them. On the principle that one might as well be hanged for a sheep as for a lamb, my colleagues and I are now inclined to regret that we did not do more in developing contacts with Africans!

2. The new protest obviously reflects once more the extreme sensitivity of the Belgian authorities about anything done or said by Americans with regard to the Belgian Congo and Ruanda-Urundi

[4] A second complaint made by M. Delvaux, to the effect that the Consulate General refused to comply with Belgian requirements for immatriculation of its non-officer personnel, is being treated in a separate dispatch. [Footnote in the source text. The despatch referred to is not printed.]

and, in particular, to anything done or said by the American personnel at this post. Our personnel has been urged to be even more circumspect than ever in their activities here, especially in relation to Africans, and to report to me any contacts with Africans.

3. The new protest probably reflects an increasing anxiety among Belgian officials, in both Brussels and Leopoldville, over the beginning of political activity and unrest in the Congo. After 75 years of relative tranquillity in the political sphere, the Belgian Administration is now being confronted by an ever increasing number of évolués who are conscious of events elsewhere in Africa, critical of one or more aspects of life in the Congo, and ambitious to participate in the government of their country. The Belgians are probably unhappy about these developments and anxious about the future; and, being human, they tend to blame anything unpleasant on someone else. In looking for a scapegoat, they quite naturally regard the United States as a leading candidate. As Mr. Sprouse rightly points out in his despatch, the Belgians are beginning to fall into the same state of mind as the French did concerning Morocco in the early 1950's.

4. As Mr. Sprouse suggests in his memorandum for use in a conversation with the Belgian Ambassador in Washington, one wonders whether any évolué can be said to be politically active or inactive. However, even though the Consulate General has made no special effort—as charged—to seek out the politically active évolués, the Consulate General will certainly have to make sure in the future that its contacts include Africans in all walks of life and with non-political as well as political interests. It should be noted that among the fairly large group of évolués—a term that has only economic and social connotations—there is a small group of African immatriculés who have a legal status giving them all the rights and privileges of Europeans. [5] What few contacts we have had with Africans, have been almost entirely with the immatriculés, who are legally "Europeans". It is quite clear, in connection with the present issue and with many others, that the Belgian authorities are trying to do two contradictory things at the same time—to turn the most advanced of the African évolués into Europeans but to continue to treat them as Africans.

[5] There are three terms used to describe the more advanced Africans: évolués are those who have had enough education to speak French; holders of the Carte de Merite Civile are the more advanced évolués, whose children may attend a European school; and immatriculés are those who are found, by careful examination by a committee, to dress, live, and eat like Europeans and who are legally granted the status of "Europeans". They report to the Population Blanche rather than the Population Noire on all official matters. [Footnote in the source text.]

5. The Consulate General is grateful for the response made to M. Delvaux by Mr. Sprouse and warmly endorses the memorandum proposed by Mr. Sprouse as the basis of a conversation with the Belgian Ambassador. It would suggest only one addition: the Belgian Government might be asked to be more specific and name the persons we are alleged to have seen too frequently.

6. The Consulate General suggests that the Belgian authorities be asked for specific suggestions as to how our personnel here can keep in touch with local leaders in the Congo, as do our consular offices as well as diplomatic offices elsewhere in the world, and report the views of the African leaders on political, economic, and social developments. If the Consulate General is to refrain even more than it has in the past from developing contacts with African leaders, its reporting to Washington will become even more inadequate in this regard than it is at present. It has been our hope that during the next year or so the post could submit voluntary reports on such political subjects as the implementation of the Statut des Villes [6] and the development of the advisory councils, which obviously have a direct bearing on the whole future, including the economic future, of the Belgian Congo. We also hope to report on several subjects that have political implications, such as the growth of an African middle class, the present status of African education, and a required basic report on labor. None of these reports will be complete unless the officers concerned can talk with African leaders as well as with Belgians. In fact, Vice Consul Gross proposed six months ago that he prepare a report on the African middle class; but I discouraged him because it would require too much direct contact with Africans.

7. There are two minor adjustments that might possibly be made here, quite independently of any consultation with the Belgian authorities.

First, in view of the evident sensitivity of the Belgian authorities to USIS activities, perhaps it would be wise to soft-pedal those activities somewhat for the next year or so. Rather than eliminate any single function, it might be advisable to decrease the staffing pattern from what it was earlier this year. Originally USIS had 2 officers and 1 American assistant; then, for a long period, 1 officer and 1 assistant; and more recently, beginning last February, again 2 officers and 1 assistant. With the departure of Public Affairs Officer Bursley, it is recommended that for the present the USIS staff

[6] A municipal reform effective March 26, intended to give Africans a means of taking part in urban administration. The African and European quarters of Elisabethville, Jadotville, and Leopoldville were to be integrated into a new administrative unit or ville.

consist of Consul Stephen and 1 *capable, French-speaking* assistant. Alternatively, if a second officer is to be appointed he should be a young, *French-speaking*, junior officer, preferably a trainee, without a consular title. Either arrangement would have the additional advantage of reducing our number of consular titles. Furthermore, the English classes could be continued on a more modest basis, even though there are some *350* applications pending, and with a special effort being made to include Belgians as well as Africans.

Second, the literal translation of American Information Service is Services Americains d'Information, which in French can mean American Intelligence Service. This awkward translation, which presumably has created difficulty in other French-speaking countries, probably creates some confusion in the minds of the public here and perhaps even among the officers of the Administration. (The Administration, however, uses the title Service de l'Information for its own agency.) Mr. Bursley mentioned his concern about this matter several times. After his departure for home leave, I substituted in the new Consular Corps list the phrase Rélations Publiques for Services d'Information. It might be advisable for USIS gradually and quietly to change its signs and letterheads to Rélations Publiques, and next year to make the same change in the local telephone directory.

8. In conclusion, I must say that I am surprised and disappointed that the Belgian Government should have raised this issue—as well as the immatriculation issue, discussed separately—with the Embassy in Brussels, before allowing the local Administration to discuss it with me here. When I completed my conversation with the Vice Governor General last May in response to the earlier protest of the Belgian Government about the size and activities of the post, he said that he would talk to the Governor General and communicate with me further if necessary. In the absence of any further communication, I had assumed that they were satisfied with the explanation I had made.

In accordance with the stated desire of the Belgian authorities for full and frank understanding of our common interests and problems, it would seem more appropriate for the local Administration to call me in first whenever they are dissatisfied with the activities of the post. If I cannot either remedy a particular situation or provide a satisfactory explanation of it, then they would be fully entitled to raise the matter in Brussels or Washington. In the future, I shall try to see the Governor General or the Vice Governor General more regularly, although they are both extremely busy men, and give them an opportunity to raise such matters if they wish to do so. I shall also ask them periodically about political developments, explaining that I am aware of their desire that the post not undertake too much political reporting among the Africans.

James Frederick Green

107. Telegram From the Embassy in Belgium to the Department of State[1]

Brussels, November 1, 1957—1 p.m.

646. Department's CA–3650[2] and Deptel 727.[3] Following is gist conversation I had with Foreign Minister Larock late yesterday:

1. Reference was made to complaint presented by Ambassador Delvaux to Sprouse August 2 to effect Belgian Government concerned certain individuals attached ConGen Leopoldville were encouraging incipient independence movements by seeing too much of certain Congolese identified with such movements. Bursley singled out individually.

2. Department had instructed me inform Larock that Murphy had conferred with Ambassador Silvercruys in Washington day before along following lines:

a. Careful investigation had disclosed no support for complaint. It was added if Belgian Government had any details, they would be appreciated.

b. Point emphatically made that US had no political or economic designs on any part Africa nor does it desire encourage independence movements against its European allies. At same time, it was emphasized US Government must necessarily keep abreast of developments in all parts of world and must know what is going on in order discharge its responsibilities.

c. Belief was expressed that future incidents of this kind might be avoided if Congo Governor General could work more closely with ConGen. It was indicated such collaboration would lessen misunder-

[1] Source: Department of State, Central Files, 122.536H3/11–157. Confidential. Sent also to Leopoldville.

[2] CA–3650 to Brussels, October 18, indicated that the Belgian Ambassador would soon be called in to receive the U.S. reply to Belgium's August 2 approach, reported in despatch 132 from Brussels; see *supra*. A copy of the talking points, prepared for Deputy Under Secretary Murphy, was enclosed and Ambassador Folger was told to make these same points to the Belgian Foreign Minister. (*Ibid.*, 122.536H3/10–1857)

[3] Telegram 727, October 31, summarized the meeting between Murphy and Baron Silvercruys on October 30. (*Ibid.*, 122.536H3/10–3157) A memorandum of this conversation by Sam L. Yates of the Office of Western European Affairs, October 30, is *ibid.*

standing and would give representatives our government prompt and forthright information as to attitudes Belgian Government.

3. Larock reference to conferences he had with Vice Gov. Gen. Cornelis last July. Cornelis stated several members ConGen, Bursley in particular, had been overzealous in contribution to activities regarded by Belgians as encouraging independence movements. Larock frank to say there was nothing in particular one could put his finger on but all added up to attitude which could result in unrest. Fragmentary information gained by Congolese invited to US and representations as to conditions in US (here he referred to USIS bulletins) had led to invidious comparisons. He mentioned visits to Congo of colored Americans which aroused curiosity and further comparisons. Mention was made of jazz sessions Bursley organized which were attended by politically active Congolese. He also stated ConGen had made point of meeting with leaders of Kingdom of Congo, a recurring and legendary idea "which of course represented wishful thinking." He indicated in his opinion members of ConGen were assuming Embassy role and not confining selves to consular functions, mentioning visas and encouragement of trade.

Having finished enumeration foregoing items which led to their complaint, Larock smiled and said he felt some of his people in Congo might be "overtouchy" but did have these reactions to ConGen activities and Cornelis, a sound, calm man, was the one who carried complaint from Governor General to Larock. He added that mutual confidence was contributed to by this complaint having been made and an unequivocal reply having been received. He saw no reason why situation could not be completely resolved along lines we suggested; i.e., closer cooperation between Governor General's office and ConGen. He said he would tell Governor General to act in this sense. He dwelt on Belgian desire "to move Congolese along to autonomy and self government" but emphasized that if they moved faster than their capabilities, their own interests as well as those of Belgium and free world would not be served. Developments all around Congo were having effects in Congo although there was no problem there yet. He knew US believes it must watch its future relations with new peoples, for fear they would grow to look to east. However, US might act in way which could have consequences contributing to unsettling some of these people.

4. I reiterated we had absolutely no political or economic designs upon any part of Africa nor did we desire encourage independence movements at expense our European allies. I then emphasized that representatives of Belgian Government in US were free to visit any part of country and meet and talk with any citizen. It was urged this freedom of movement and inquiry brought full

revelation of conditions and facts upon which good relations could be based.

5. At close, I stated Bursley had resigned from government service for personal reasons and before he knew anything of complaint. Larock was inclined to stick by his guns saying he thought it was better for all concerned Bursley not returning.

6. Although Larock obviously appeared to have share Colonial officials reservations concerning ConGen activities, overtone of whole conference was, I believe, satisfactory under circumstances. The air has been noticeably cleared and it is particularly hopeful that Larock believes this type problem can be avoided in future if Governor General and ConGen work more closely together. Larock stated he considered our reply both satisfactory and unequivocal.

Folger

108. Despatch From the Consulate General at Leopoldville to the Department of State [1]

No. 160 *Leopoldville, November 29, 1957.*

REF

Leopoldville D–141, November 14; [2] Department's Telegram No. 71, November 5; [3] Brussels Telegram No. 646 to Department, repeated as No. 20 [*10*] to Leopoldville, November 2 [*1*]; [4] Leopoldville Telegram No. 79, November 2, 1957; [5] and previous

[1] Source: Department of State, Central Files, 122.536H2/11–2957. Confidential. Also sent to Brussels and repeated to Elisabethville, Luanda, and Yaoundé.

[2] Despatch 141 commented on the action of the Government Press Service in Brussels in reprinting an extract from a French newspaper critical of the activities of the USIS and Consulate General in Leopoldville. (*Ibid.*, 122.536H2/11–1457)

[3] Telegram 71 suggested that Green might await a Belgian approach before seeking a meeting with Governor General Pétillon to repeat the points made earlier by Murphy and Folger. (*Ibid.*, 122.536H3/11–257)

[4] *Supra.*

[5] Telegram 79 summarized a conversation between Julius C. Holmes and Vice Governor General Cornélis on November 1 regarding the Belgian complaint about U.S. consular activities in the Congo. Holmes maintained there was no substance to the allegations and wondered why the local authorities had not discussed their concerns with Consul General Green. He emphasized that it was not U.S. policy to interfere in the colonial affairs of its allies and recommended that the Department instruct Green to respond in detail directly to the Governor General on this matter. (Department of State, Central Files, 122.536H3/11–357)

SUBJECT

Belgian Complaint against Activities of the Consulate General

In accordance with the Department's telegram No. 71, I waited for some time—four weeks, in fact—before talking with the local Administration about the recent complaint of the Belgian Government that officers of the Consulate General had been developing too many contacts with Africans, especially with African leaders of independence movements. Not having been called in to discuss the matter, I made an appointment to see the Vice Governor General this morning, as the Governor General has been in Brussels for consultations.

In the course of our conversation I followed the position taken earlier by Deputy Under Secretary Murphy and Ambassador Folger, together with a few details as reported below.

With regard to the charges made by the Belgian Government last August, I stated that I had made a very thorough investigation of the record since my arrival here in October 1956. Both the Public Affairs Officer, Consul Gilbert E. Bursley, and Vice Consul Roger M. Bearce, who probably had had most of the contacts with Africans, had departed on leave before the complaint was made. However, they had reported to me regularly about their activities and had given no indication whatever that they had developed any special contacts with leaders of independence movements. Other members of the staff had almost no contacts with Africans. I said that I myself had had almost no contacts with Africans, partly because I wanted first to develop a greater fluency in French, but largely because I had leaned over backwards to avoid giving any impression of seeking out African leaders. I said that I was aware of no improper activities of any kind in this regard, but that if the Administration had information about such activities I would appreciate having the details, so that our staff could avoid making any similar mistakes in the future. I added that I had asked our staff to be very circumspect in their relations with Africans and to keep me fully informed about any such relations.

The Vice Governor General vouchsafed no specific charges of any kind. He said that Mr. Bursley had been giving Africans the impression that he was sympathetic with their ambitions and that he would always give them a warm welcome (M. Cornelis used the French phrase "bon accueil" because he could not think of an adequate English phrase). Many Belgians here were aware that Mr. Bursley was giving this impression to the Africans and were becoming extremely concerned about it. I commented that as Mr. Bursley was a man of unusual energy, he may well have given the impression of doing much more than was actually the case. The Vice

Governor General replied that, whatever Mr. Bursley may or may not have done, it was the impression he gave that counted. Before Mr. Bursley left, M. Cornelis continued, people were referring to him as "The Quiet American"—the American spy in Graham Greene's novel about Saigon. For the past three or four months, he concluded, all this discussion had died down, so it was obvious that it was Mr. Bursley who had been stirring up all the trouble.

The Vice Governor General then went on to say that the situation was difficult because the Russians have "one eye" here—the Czechoslovakian Consul. Some time ago, he said, the Czechoslovakian Consul went too far in his contacts with Africans and "we had to clamp down". The Consul then protested, saying he was merely doing "exactly the same thing as the Americans".

I pointed out that Mr. Bursley had resigned from Government service for personal reasons before the Belgian Government had lodged its complaint against him, and for the present time he was not being replaced. His deputy, Consul Henry H. Stephen, was running the office for the moment and, being a much more quiet operator, would not cause any difficulty. The Vice Governor General said that it would be a very good idea to let things quiet down for a while and to make no changes in that office.

After explaining that the United States had no political or economic designs on any part of Africa and did not intend to encourage independence movements against its allies, I said that nevertheless our embassies and legations, like Belgian embassies and legations, had to keep informed about what was going on in the country around them. I said that, as I developed fluency in French, I hoped to talk with more and more Belgians and occasionally with Africans, just to find out what they are thinking about. I added that I thought it would be useful, for example, after the consultations on December 8 under the Statut des Villes, to talk with some of the new bourgmestres, both European and African, and perhaps with some of the members of the new Conseils. M. Cornelis nodded agreement, but commented only that Mr. Holmes had discussed this problem with him earlier.

I concluded by saying that I wanted to work very closely with the Governor General and himself, and that I hoped that if any further difficulties arose in the future he would call me in to discuss them. The Vice Governor General nodded agreement, saying that "all the trouble is over now" and that he was sure that there would be no further difficulties.

Comment

The Vice Governor General was, as usual, very warm and friendly throughout this conversation. He gave me the impression that he considers the episode is now closed. The fact that he, like the Belgian Ambassador in Washington and the Minister of Foreign Affairs in Brussels, failed to present any bill of particulars against former PAO Bursley would indicate that the Administration cannot substantiate its charges against him. M. Cornelis' lack of any substantive comment about future relations between the post and Africans would suggest that the Administration is taking a "wait and see" attitude.

In my presentation of our position, I endeavored to combine a frank statement of my efforts to avoid any improper activities and a firm statement that it is a perfectly proper activity for the post to talk with Africans as part of its routine work. The establishment of the new system of bourgmestres and Councils, under the Statut des Villes, will make contacts with leading Africans easier and more natural than in the past. Shortly after January 1, I shall call on the new Premier Bourgmestre, who by all accounts will be the present Commissaire Provincial, M. Tordeur, and, after asking about current developments under the new system, inform him that I intend to call on each of the eleven new bourgmestres in turn and to interview them on occasion concerning the working of the Statut des Villes.

James Frederick Green

ETHIOPIA

UNITED STATES RELATIONS WITH ETHIOPIA; THE QUESTION OF MILITARY ASSISTANCE; UNITED STATES INTEREST IN THE STRATEGIC SIGNIFICANCE OF ETHIOPIA [1]

109. Letter From the Counselor of the Embassy in Ethiopia (Taylor) to the Director of the Office of African Affairs (Cyr) [2]

Addis Ababa, December 9, 1955.

DEAR LEO: You will receive in this same pouch a despatch setting forth the recommendations of our Country Team on a longer range military program for Ethiopia. [3] You will remember that we have already sent the documents which were presented to General Cook during his visit here and the military comments on them by Colonel Berry, the new MAAG Chief. [4] It may be helpful to set forth a little additional background.

As you know, the military assistance program here was until recently in a very bad way. For one thing, there was no clear cut

[1] For previous documentation on this subject, see *Foreign Relations*, 1952–1954, vol. XI, Part 1, pp. 418, ff.

[2] Source: Department of State, AF/NE Files; Lot 67 D 226, Military Assistance 1955. Secret; Official–Informal.

[3] Despatch 141, December 2, recommended that Ethiopia be explicitly informed regarding previous deliveries of arms under the Mutual Defense Assistance Agreement of May 22, 1953 (5 UST 749; TIAS 2964); that a long-range aid plan be formulated; and that deliveries be more vigorously completed. It called for documentation to ascertain the truth of the Ethiopian contention that U.S. support had been pledged for four divisions. A reorganization plan calling for a small augmentation of the MAAG complement was also submitted for consideration. The retention of U.S. military bases and furtherance of U.S. political objectives was seen enhanced by a minimum annual military aid program of $5 million in addition to some reimbursable assistance. (*Ibid.*, Central Files, 775.5–MSP/12–255)

[4] Colonel Edward S. Berry arrived on October 18. General Orval R. Cook, Deputy CINCEUR, together with Major General W.M. Morgan, Major General J.A. Dabney, and Brigadier R.V. Lee (all of EUCOM), visited Ethiopia on an inspection tour November 17–19. Despatch 134, November 23, conveyed the documents under reference. The Chief of Staff of the Imperial Ethiopian Army, General Muleguetta Bulli, presented a lengthy memorandum entitled "Defense Needs of Ethiopia" to General Cook on November 18. The Ethiopians expressed a desire for firmer assurances of greater military support and dissatisfaction with the program as implemented theretofore. (*Ibid.*, 775.5–MSP/11–2355)

program envisaged; for another our deliveries of matériels already promised have been very slow and haphazard; thirdly, the relations between the military officers concerned were very inadequate; and finally the whole program, such as it was, was geared rather to American concepts of fighting units than to those which fit the situation here.

As you know, the Emperor has been making a heavy onslaught on all these points, first when the Congressmen came [5] and second when General Cook and his party came. It is fair to say that General Cook and his party were not much impressed with the needs of Ethiopia. They felt that the requests made were far too large, and they pressed us here to give some kind of estimate as to the needs.

The Emperor hit General Cook especially hard with the charge that someone had in 1953 committed the United States to support four divisions.

Since that time Colonel Berry has done some very good work, and we in the Embassy, together with him, have given thought to the position as a whole.

Colonel Berry has ascertained that the kind of military organization favored by the Ethiopians is quite different from that which the MAAG has heretofore been thinking of. It is a much lighter and smaller unit which he calls a "command". This discovery seems to put a quite different light on the whole military assistance program, since the support for one American type division would cost us as much as support for two plus of the lighter "commands". Working with these lighter type units would enable the United States to proceed with a military assistance program on approximately the same budgetary scale as heretofore by spreading its support over a larger number of units and thus come far closer to meeting the Ethiopian wishes than we had thought possible.

We are very keenly aware here, as I am sure you will be, of the political disadvantage of permitting the United States military effort here to go down the drain. We will have sunk $10,000,000 in Ethiopia when the program is completed. During this time, military relations with the Ethiopians have suffered severely because of the local military conditions. We feel that the Army has made a fine start in sending here an officer of the energy and common sense of Colonel Berry. He has already done some good. But it seems clear to us that if the military assistance program is not continued on a minimal basis, this will have a serious effect on our political relations. As you know, the Emperor has an inordinate interest in

[5] Despatch 130 from Addis Ababa, November 15, summarized the paper presented to Chairman Melvin Price and other members of the Subcommittee of the House Military Affairs Committee on November 10. (*Ibid.*, 033.1100–PR/11–1555)

military affairs, and our failure to follow through with him on some kind of a program is bound to react very seriously on his orientation to us.

We are very well aware of the problem that is likely to exist in connection with appropriations for foreign assistance this coming year. If the total program of foreign military and economic assistance is cut, as it is likely to be, any country with as low a priority as Ethiopia is likely to be cut out altogether. In past years it was only the strong pressure of the State Department for political considerations that led to any money at all being allocated to Ethiopia. We assume that the same kind of effort will probably have to be made this year by the State Department. [6]

If there is any additional material which we should provide, we will be glad to do so. For one thing we have in mind an over-all statement by the Country Team concerning the defense needs of Ethiopia.

As you see, I still haven't had a chance to sit down and write more general impressions of the country. With best regards to you and the others in AF.

Sincerely yours,

Paul

[6] Murphy wrote to Gordon Gray on February 27, 1956, to indicate the Department of State view that unless some satisfaction could be given to Ethiopia in response to the plea for additional aid then the good relationship which the United States currently enjoyed with that nation might be prejudiced. He urged the Department of Defense to take under consideration the funding of a military program for Ethiopia in fiscal year 1957. (*Ibid.*, 775.5–MSP/2–2156)

110. Letter From the Deputy Under Secretary of State for Political Affairs (Murphy) to the Assistant Secretary of Defense (Gray) [1]

Washington, July 5, 1956.

DEAR MR. GRAY: During the past year there has been a deterioration in the cordial relationship and influence the United States has enjoyed with Ethiopia. To some extent, the difficulties result from a feeling on the part of the Ethiopian Government that the United

[1] Source: Department of State, Central Files, 775.5–MSP/7–556. Secret.

States underestimates the political value of Ethiopian cooperation while engaging in a policy of seeking to secure cooperation from less friendly governments. This attitude has taken the form of rapidly growing discontent with the volume and scope of United States assistance. Pro-United States groups in Ethiopia have been weakened while the influence of the xenophobic clique which favors isolationist or neutralist policies has increased. At the same time, hostile Egyptian activities have been expanding in Ethiopia and immediately surrounding areas. The willingness of Egypt to do business with the Soviet Union and bloc countries has provided Communist forces with an ally in their own intensified efforts to establish themselves firmly in Northeast Africa.

These activities are in themselves sufficiently serious to warrant revision of our Ethiopian policy. The need for such action is even more apparent in view of the Near Eastern situation, where neutralist or outright hostile elements are making cooperation more difficult with certain Arab governments. Politically stable, geographically desirable and still friendly in attitude, Ethiopia is a country in which the United States can build a position of strength in the area. In achieving this broadly political objective, we would also be working in the direction of establishing a crescent of friendly countries south and west of Egypt. If such a grouping proves possible, we shall not only reinforce our Middle East position but provide an obstruction to the further penetration of Africa by inimical forces.

In the past we have been largely successful in obtaining our relatively modest objectives in Ethiopia because of the friendly attitude of the Ethiopian Government, particularly Emperor Haile Selassie. He has recognized the practical values to Ethiopia of close cooperation with the United States, both as a counterpoise to the foreign influences and as a means of obtaining necessary assistance in the modernization of his country. Under present circumstances, however, the courses of action we have been pursuing lack the necessary scope and magnitude. I believe that prompt action should be taken to remedy this situation.

It is recommended, therefore, that the Department of Defense approve a military aid program in FY 1957 in the magnitude of $5 million for the training and equipping of the Ethiopian army. [2] I

---

[2] On March 21, Gray informed Murphy that the Department of Defense intended to request $554,000 for Ethiopia from Congress in fiscal year 1957. He recognized the necessity for a longer-range military aid program, but noted that its content would be influenced by the ongoing reorganization of the Ethiopian Army. (*Ibid.*, AF/NE Files: Lot 67 D 226, Military Assistance Jan.–June 1956) On July 19, Gray indicated that the Department of Defense shared the Department of State's concern over the deterioration in relations with Ethiopia and recognized the political necessity of the proposed $5 million program. The Department of Defense required assurance that the funding would be provided from Section 401(b) so that other priority requirements would not

believe that there are overriding political considerations supporting such a program if we are to retain our influence in Ethiopia and move effectively towards establishing long-term strength for the American position in Northeast Africa. I understand that Ethiopian military needs have been surveyed by the MAAG in Addis Ababa and that its recommendations are already in the possession of the Defense Department. I, therefore, hope that a satisfactory aid program can be worked out while our Ambassador to Ethiopia, Mr. Simonson, and the MAAG Chief, Colonel Berry, are in Washington for consultation this month.

I am sending a copy of this letter to Mr. Hollister.

Sincerely yours,

Robert Murphy [3]

---

be affected. This section permitted expenditure of funds under the Mutual Defense Assistance Act (68 Stat. 843) in cases where the President determined it was in the security interest of the United States. (*Ibid.*, Military Assistance July–Dec. 1956)

[3] Printed from a copy that bears this typed signature.

---

111. Telegram From the Department of State to the Embassy in Ethiopia [1]

Washington, October 16, 1956—9:38 p.m.

229. Embtel 252. [2] Please deliver following personal message from me to Aklilou:

"Since our conversations in London, [3] I have had very much in mind your Government's request for military and development as-

---

[1] Source: Department of State, Central Files, 775.5–MSP/10–1356. Secret; Niact. Repeated to USCINCEUR, Asmara, Paris, and London.

[2] Telegram 252 from Addis Ababa, October 13, presented the country team assessment of the assistance requirements of Ethiopia. (*Ibid.*)

[3] Dulles met with Aklilou on August 18 and 24 and September 21, in London where they were both present for the Suez Canal Conferences. At their second meeting, Aklilou commented that the U.S. military aid program was slow to materialize. Rountree responded that he hoped a plan would soon be ready. (Memorandum of conversation prepared by the U.S. Delegation at London, August 24; *ibid.*, Conference Files: Lot 62 D 181, 760) During his visit to Ethiopia, Senator Theodore Francis Green of Rhode Island, Chairman of the Senate Foreign Relations Committee, had an audience with the Emperor September 18, and was sent an aide-mémoire by the Emperor's Private Secretary on September 21, which left him in no doubt as to Haile Selassie's dissatisfaction with the delays and limitations of the military aid program.

(Continued)

sistance from this Government. I have looked carefully into this matter in the spirit of cooperation and mutual interest which have characterized the long and happy relationship between our two governments. I am now pleased to inform you that we are willing to undertake a program which is, I believe, responsive to Ethiopia's military needs this year and will, at the same time, make significant contribution to the development of your country.

"In addition to the substantial technical assistance program already in operation, this Government is willing to provide in the current fiscal year: 1) a program of $5 million assistance for the Ethiopian Army; 2) one naval patrol craft to be delivered in Fiscal Year 1957; and 3) a program of economic assistance to be based on such soundly-conceived projects as we may mutually agree, the total costs to be under $5 million. This Government is also willing to accede to the suggestion of the Ethiopian Government for a survey of Ethiopian Air Force capabilities, with the understanding that such a survey is not to be considered as a commitment of US support to a future aid program for the air force.

"With respect to the military assistance program, while it is contemplated that the funds will be obligated in the current year, it may not be possible to complete all deliveries in that period.

"May I say again how much I enjoyed talking to you in London and how confident I am that our two countries will continue to maintain the same close relationships which have benefited us both so greatly in the past."

FYI, if the GOE raises question future program you should say it will be necessary take into account US legislative authority and availability of funds, as well as Ethiopia's own capacity to support resulting programs. [4]

Dulles

(Continued)
This anxiety was heightened by the fact that the details of the fiscal year 1957 program were not yet available. (Despatch 59 from Addis Ababa, September 24; *ibid.*, Central Files, 775.5–MSP/9–2456)

[4] Aklilou's immediate response, upon receipt of the Secretary's message on October 17, was that the military aid figures were too low. (Telegram 270 from Addis Ababa, October 18; *ibid.*, 775.5–MSP/10–1856) Aklilou's official response, given to Simonson on October 19, expressed his appreciation for the Secretary's personal interest in the matter and noted his satisfaction regarding the promised development assistance and the U.S. offer to survey Ethiopia's Air Force capabilities. Furthermore, he noted the Emperor's pleasure that military support would be "placed on basis permitting rational development according to agreed program, rather than on separate and fresh re-examination annually." (Telegram 283 from Addis Ababa, October 23; *ibid.*, 775.5–MSP/10–2356)

112. Memorandum of Discussion at the 304th Meeting of the National Security Council, Washington, November 15, 1956 [1]

Present at the 304th Council meeting were the President of the United States, presiding; the Acting Secretary of State; the Secretary of Defense; and the Director, Office of Defense Mobilization. Also present were the Secretary of the Treasury; the Attorney General (participating in Item 2); the Special Assistant to the President for Disarmament; the Director, Bureau of the Budget; the Special Assistant to the President for Atomic Energy; the Federal Civil Defense Administrator; the Director, International Cooperation Administration; the Acting Director, U.S. Information Agency; Assistant Secretary of Defense Gray; the Chairman, Joint Chiefs of Staff; the Director of Central Intelligence; The Assistant to the President; the Deputy Assistant to the President; Special Assistants to the President Jackson and Randall; the White House Staff Secretary; the Executive Secretary, NSC; and the Deputy Executive Secretary, NSC.

[Here follows discussion of items 1 and 2.]

3. U.S. Policy Toward Ethiopia (NSC 5615; [2] Memo for NSC from Executive Secretary, same subject, dated November 6, 1956 [3])

Mr. Jackson briefed the Council on the contents of the reference report, and explained the split views in paragraph 19, which read as follows:

"19. For the achievement of political objectives, provide the Ethiopian Armed Forces with limited military equipment and training of a kind suitable for maintaining internal security and offering resistance to local aggression [without establishing a U.S. requirement for the support of any particular mission for the Ethiopian Armed Forces]. [4] Make every effort to avoid a military build-up which would seriously strain the Ethiopian economy or lead to commitments for indefinite U.S. support."

He then invited Mr. Brundage to enlarge on the reasons why the Budget wished to include the bracketed language. Mr. Brundage explained that he was far from clear as to the meaning of "local

---

[1] Source: Eisenhower Library, Whitman File, NSC Records. Top Secret. Drafted by Gleason on November 16.

[2] NSC 5615, October 23, was a draft statement of policy on Ethiopia. It was transmitted to the members of the National Security Council under cover of a note by Executive Secretary James S. Lay, Jr. (Department of State, S/S–NSC Files: Lot 63 D 351, NSC 5615 Series)

[3] This memorandum by Lay transmitted to the NSC a memorandum dated October 30 by the Joint Chiefs of Staff to the Secretary of Defense submitting JCS comments and recommendations on NSC 5615. (*Ibid.*)

[4] Budget proposal. [Footnote and brackets in the source text.]

aggression", and that he hoped this would not prove to be the basis for introducing new programs of assistance to Ethiopia.

The President stated very firmly his great anxiety to be assured of the friendship of Ethiopia. This might well mean new programs, though he hoped that they would be kept as small as possible. He added that he had recently had a message from the Emperor of Ethiopia, who expressed his unhappiness over our alleged failures to keep our engagements to assist Ethiopia. [5] From other sources, said the President, had come an implied threat that Ethiopia would have to get arms "elsewhere" if the Ethiopians could not get them from the United States.

Secretary Wilson expressed some skepticism over a stepped-up military aid program for Ethiopia . . . . Mr. Jackson explained why the Planning Board had felt it desirable to define the kind of equipment that should be given to Ethiopia, even though it was agreed that this aid program was fundamentally political rather than military in purpose. . . .

The Council then engaged in a discussion of the problem, raised initially by Secretary Hoover, of providing an aircraft to be sold to Haile Selassie. [6] The President, after first stating that he disapproved of the Budget proposal for including a portion of paragraph 19, turned to the matter of the aircraft and suggested that if the Air

---

[5] Senator Green met with the President on November 12 to pass on the aide-mémoire presented to him in Ethiopia. (Memorandum from the President to Hoover, November 12; Department of State, Central Files, 775.5–MSP/11–1256)

[6] The Ethiopian Government preferred a Constellation so the Emperor could overfly neighboring countries. When Dulles and Aklilou discussed this subject in London on September 21, the Secretary remarked that the U.S. Government had only nine planes suitable for the Emperor's purpose and it was difficult to take any of them out of service. However, the President personally asked that one be made available on loan for 2 months until another plane could be converted. Aklilou asked if it would be possible to order a commercial plane and have it made over. Dulles promised to look into this matter upon his return home. (Memorandum of conversation by Tyler, September 21; *ibid.*, Secretary's Memoranda of Conversation: Lot 64 D 199) On November 12 the President told Acting Secretary Hoover that "you have your 'best drag' in that country when you do something for the Emperor." (Eisenhower Library, Whitman File, Eisenhower Diaries) The Department of Defense, subsequent to the November 15 NSC meeting, was prepared to make SACEUR'S Constellation 749 available, but it required reimbursement above the $700,000 Ethiopia could afford to pay. Since Ethiopian Air Lines arranged the purchase of two Douglas DC–6–B's for its own purposes, the Emperor asked if, instead of a Constellation, the same plane could be provided for his use. (Telegram 408 from Addis Ababa, December 10; Department of State, Central Files, 775.5622/12–1056) Hoover notified Simonson that this was not possible because the Constellation came from the U.S. Air Force inventory and could be offered at a price far below market value. (Telegram 360 to Addis Ababa, December 12; *ibid.*) On January 28, 1957, the Emperor's appreciation was conveyed to the United States for having agreed to supply him with a Constellation. He planned to finance the purchase out of the funds provided by the Export-Import Bank for civil aviation development. (Telegram 543 from Addis Ababa, January 28; *ibid.*, 775.5622/1–2857) The plane crashed and burned in late June 2 weeks after its delivery.

Force was to take one of our normal size Constellation aircraft out of MATS, how much would it cost to rehabilitate the plane and send it to the Emperor of Ethiopia? Admiral Radford said he couldn't precisely say, but the plane would probably be worth $1 million. Admiral Radford went on to say that he thought he could make a deal by which such a plane could be secured for sale at perhaps $700,000 to Haile Selassie. Secretary Hoover said he earnestly hoped that this would be the case. The President then said that we could readily reduce the special mission squadron by one aircraft. Secretary Wilson and Admiral Radford agreed to this proposal.

Mr. Allen Dulles said that he had one last suggestion to make apropos of Ethiopia, namely, that the NSC Planning Board be directed to take a look at the whole area of tropical Africa. He added that the . . . . Secretary Wilson expressed extreme skepticism about action which would lead to the United States taking on further obligations in such an area. The President, however, agreed that tropical Africa could suddenly become very important to the United States. In this view he was strongly supported by Secretary Hoover, on the ground that the Communists were very hard at work building up nationalism in Africa. The State Department was expanding its facilities in these areas and its program for training specialists in African affairs. Secretary Wilson said that he remained unconvinced. He expressed anxiety lest we proceed to kick the colonial powers out of Central Africa and then leave a power vacuum for the Soviets to fill. He said he was convinced that we had urged the British, for example, to get out of Suez much too soon. He did not wish us to repeat our error with respect to the Belgians and the Portuguese.

The National Security Council: [7]

a. Noted and discussed the draft statement of policy on the subject (NSC 5615) prepared by the NSC Planning Board, in the light of the views of the Joint Chiefs of Staff transmitted by the reference memorandum of November 6, 1956.

b. Adopted the statement of policy in NSC 5615, subject to the following amendments:

(1) *Page 1, paragraph 2, second sentence*: Revise to read as follows: "The U.S. Navy maintains a petroleum storage and a communication unit in Ethiopia and has established requirements for post-D-Day facilities."

(2) *Page 7, paragraph 19*: Delete the bracketed section and the footnote relating thereto.

c. Noted the President's directive that the Department of Defense make available promptly, from current inventory, an appropri-

[7] The following paragraphs and Note constitute NSC Action No. 1634. (*Ibid.*, S/S–NSC (Miscellaneous) Files: Lot 66 D 95)

ate aircraft for sale to the Ethiopian Government, in accordance with the Emperor's request.

Note: NSC 5615, as amended and approved by the President, subsequently circulated as NSC 5615/1 [8] for implementation by all appropriate Executive departments and agencies of the U.S. Government, and referred to the Operations Coordinating Board as the coordinating agency designated by the President.

The action in c above, as approved by the President, subsequently transmitted to the Secretary of Defense for implementation.

[Here follows discussion of items 4–6.]

S. Everett Gleason

[8] *Infra*.

---

113. National Security Council Report [1]

NSC 5615/1 *Washington, November 19, 1956.*

U.S. POLICY TOWARD ETHIOPIA

Note by the Executive Secretary to the National Security Council

REFERENCES

A. NSC 5615 [2]
B. Memo for NSC from Executive Secretary, same subject, dated November 6, 1956 [3]
C. NSC Action No. 1634 [4]

The National Security Council, the Secretary of the Treasury, the Special Assistant to the President for Disarmament, and the Director, Bureau of the Budget, at the 304th Council meeting on November 15, 1956, adopted the statement of policy on the subject contained in NSC 5615, subject to the amendments thereto which are set forth in NSC Action No. 1634–b.

[1] Source: Department of State, S/S–NSC Files: Lot 63 D 351, NSC 5615 Series. Secret. A Financial Appendix, Department of Defense Comments on Military Assistance, ICA Comments on Economic and Technical Assistance Programs, and Department of State Comments are not printed.

[2] See footnote 2, *supra*.

[3] See footnote 3, *supra*.

[4] See footnote 7, *supra*.

The President has this date approved the statement of policy in NSC 5615, as amended and adopted by the Council and enclosed herewith as NSC 5615/1; directs its implementation by all appropriate Executive departments and agencies of the U.S. Government; and designates the Operations Coordinating Board as the coordinating agency.

James S. Lay, Jr. [5]

[Enclosure]

STATEMENT OF POLICY ON ETHIOPIA

General Considerations

1. Ethiopia's importance to the United States transcends the country's limited power and somewhat isolated position. Current developments in the Near East increase the value to the United States of a friendly, stable government in this region of Africa. Moreover, the benefits of cooperation with the West are being carefully watched in the rest of Africa. Finally, Ethiopia is one of the few states in the Afro-Asian group which has given the United States valuable support on such matters as the UN action in Korea and the Suez Canal controversy. From a political point of view, it is of value to maintain close relations with an African state which has become a symbol of resistance to aggression and a champion of collective security.

2. In 1953, Ethiopia concluded a base agreement with the United States under which we maintain a U.S. Army radio station at Asmara, which is now being expanded and which forms a major link in the Army's world-wide communication system. The U.S. Navy maintains a petroleum storage and a communication unit in Ethiopia and has established requirements for post-D-Day facilities. The U.S. Air Force has a requirement for a signal communications base in Eritrea in lieu of Aden. Ethiopia could also serve as a base of operations to protect the shipping lanes to the Far East, Europe and the Middle East.

3. At present Ethiopia is oriented toward the West. Under the Emperor's guidance, Ethiopia provided a battalion of combat troops in Korea; has generally supported the U.S. position in the United Nations; has urged the expansion of U.S. military facilities in Ethiopia; has expressed willingness to join with the United States in a defensive alliance in the area; and has given support to the U.S.

[5] Printed from a copy that bears this typed signature

position in the Suez crisis. The Emperor attaches particular importance to close cooperation with the United States, as a counterpoise to unfriendly foreign influences. If Ethiopia's pro-Western attitude were to change, Western and U.S. prestige would suffer in Africa and the non-Communist world.

4. Of the major Western nations, the United States is the only country whose prestige and influence in Ethiopia remain high. The high regard in which the British were held after their liberation of Ethiopia has now been largely dissipated as a result of recurring differences with the Ethiopians over the Somali problem. The French, whose prestige has never been high, are distrusted because of their control over Ethiopia's access to the sea through Djibouti and the high freight rates on the French-owned railway. While Ethiopia maintains close relations with certain of the smaller Western European countries (particularly Sweden), only the United States is in a position to influence Ethiopia's continued Western orientation.

5. Although Communism has as yet made few inroads on the population at large, the USSR and other Communist countries have expanded and strengthened their activities in Ethiopia, thus increasing their capability for infiltration and subversion. The Soviet Legation has been elevated to Embassy status, enlarged and the caliber of its personnel improved. A trade agreement was recently signed with the Czechs, who, along with the East Germans, Bulgarians and Soviets, have also made offers for the construction of processing and semi-industrial enterprises. Yugoslavia and Ethiopia recently exchanged state visits; the Yugoslav Embassy has been strengthened, and the Yugoslavs have begun to show an interest in commercial enterprise in Ethiopia.

6. Egyptian activities hostile to Ethiopia have also increased. Egyptian officials have carried out propaganda and political action programs in Ethiopia and Eritrea designed to organize the large Moslem minorities against the ruling Christian Amharic dynasty. Egyptian officials have stated that a breakup of the Ethiopian Empire is inevitable unless these minorities are given political privileges. Other broadcasts in the hitherto-neglected Somali tongue appeal to Somali nationalism. Recent signs of Egyptian efforts to cultivate Ethiopian friendship are probably merely short-run tactics designed to weaken Ethiopian ties with the West, particularly over the Suez Canal issue, and do not forecast a basic change in Egyptian policy toward Ethiopia.

7. These external threats are aggravating the inherent weaknesses of the Ethiopian Government, which does not exercise effective control over the outlying areas and faces considerable discontent in Eritrea and other predominantly Moslem areas. Moreover, while

Ethiopia is stable under the Emperor's rule, his death might usher in a period of marked political instability, which may be accompanied by extensive disorders and civil strife.

8. The Somali problem is also likely to create instability over the next few years. Egyptian agitation of this question will increase Ethiopia's fears of the creation of a "Greater Somaliland" (including a large part of Ethiopia) and may stimulate Ethiopia's already strong expansionist aims toward this area. These Ethiopian aims could lead to friction with the UK, France, and Italy.

9. Even though Ethiopia remains oriented toward the West, it feels that the benefits of cooperation with the West have been small. Some Ethiopian leaders contend that the United States considers Ethiopia's cooperation less valuable than that of less friendly governments. This alleged U.S. indifference has increased the influence of the elements in Ethiopia which are suspicious of foreign influence and advocate isolationist or neutralist policies. Any increase in the influence of these elements, with a decrease in the influence of the pro-U.S. Emperor, will adversely affect U.S. interests in Ethiopia.

10. Ethiopia has been granted $12.4 million in technical assistance and $12 million in military assistance by the United States since 1952. The Export-Import Bank has authorized $27 million in credits to Ethiopia since 1946, $24 million of which was authorized in 1955. In addition, the United States has supported Ethiopia in the United Nations on various political issues such as its position with respect to the settlement of the Ethiopian-Somaliland boundary question.

11. Ethiopia is characterized by generally low standards of living, the under-utilization of its human and material resources and a shortage of administrative and technical skills. Nevertheless, it has maintained financial stability in recent years with a consistent balance of payments surplus and only a minor budgetary deficit. The Ethiopian Government's economic development expenditures are expected to total approximately $36 million per year over the next few years. A substantial part of these development expenditures will be financed with external credits.

Policy Conclusions

12. It is in the U.S. interest to counteract the forces that are threatening U.S. influence in Ethiopia, to strengthen the U.S. position in Northeast Africa generally, and to prevent further penetration of Africa by unfriendly forces. U.S. interests are now threatened by the expanding Soviet bloc influence in Ethiopia, Egyptian agitation in the area, and xenophobia among Ethiopian leaders.

13. It is important to the United States to provide evidence of long-term interest in a strong Ethiopia by programs of military and

economic assistance. Although there are military reasons for U.S. interest in Ethiopia, the justification for providing U.S. military equipment and training to that country continues to be primarily political. Technical assistance projects should be supplemented by selected economic development assistance projects as a contribution to the realization of Ethiopia's economic potential. U.S. economic aid will achieve its maximum effect if it is designed to help Ethiopia increase its ability to finance more of its own development. Some economic aid may, however, be required to supplement Ethiopia's capacity to support the planned reorganization of its armed forces.

14. U.S. political action should try to ease the fears and frustrations of the Ethiopians with respect to their own future and the events in nearby areas through consultation on (a) Near East and African developments, (b) international development of the Nile, and (c) the Somali problem.

Objectives

15. To strengthen Ethiopia's alignment with the United States and to maintain its support of free world collective security actions.

16. To assist Ethiopia to maintain political stability and make progress toward economic well-being, thereby helping demonstrate to the rest of Africa the benefits of friendly cooperation with the United States.

17. To assure the continued use of existing military facilities and to obtain additional military rights as required.

18. To check and reduce Communist and Egyptian influence in Ethiopia and the rest of Africa.

Courses of Action

19. For the achievement of political objectives, provide the Ethiopian Armed Forces with limited military equipment and training of a kind suitable for maintaining internal security and offering resistance to local aggression. Make every effort to avoid a military build-up which would seriously strain the Ethiopian economy or lead to commitments for indefinite U.S. support.

20. Provide assistance, as appropriate, to enable Ethiopia to strengthen its internal security forces (under the NSC Action No. 1290-d program [6]).

---

[6] Dated December 21, 1954, it "requested the Operations Coordinating Board to present to the Council a report on the status and adequacy of the current program to develop constabulary forces to maintain internal security and to destroy the effectiveness of the Communist apparatus in free world countries vulnerable to Communist subversion." (Department of State, S/S–NSC (Miscellaneous) Files: Lot 66 D 95) For text, see *Foreign Relations*, 1952–1954, vol. II, Part 1, p. 844.

21. Continue the U.S. technical assistance program.

22. Provide limited economic assistance, recognizing the desirability of concentrating on key development projects and the possible need for supplementing Ethiopia's capacity to support the planned reorganization of its armed forces.

23. Give support as appropriate to Ethiopia's requests for loans to finance economically sound projects within Ethiopia's capacity to service such financing.

24. Support Ethiopian participation in any international development of the Nile valley.

25. Arrange for a survey of the Ethiopian portion of the Blue Nile basin.

26. Encourage the carrying out of a general economic survey of Ethiopia by the IBRD.

27. Consult with Ethiopia on Middle East and African matters of concern to it.

28. Strengthen cultural and informational activities in Ethiopia.

29. Encourage visits of high-ranking U.S. officials to Ethiopia.

---

114. Aide-Mémoire From the Imperial Ethiopian Government to the Embassy in Ethiopia [1]

Addis Ababa, March 12, 1957.

Summary of the Remarks Made by His Imperial Majesty at the Audience Granted on March 12, 1957 to His Excellency the Vice President of the United States of America

1. His Imperial Majesty expressed great pleasure at the visit of the Vice President with whom, as a personal friend, He could discuss Ethiopian-American relations in complete frankness and without fear of misunderstanding.

2. He observed that Ethiopia is at the same time, an integral part of both Africa and of the Middle East, as is evidenced by the importance of Ethiopia in the question of the Nile waters, over three-fourths of which have their origins in that country, by the role played by Ethiopia in and out of the United Nations in the problem

---

[1] Source: Department of State, S/P–NSC Files: Lot 62 D 1, North Africa (Tunisia, Algeria, Morocco, NSC 5614, 5614/1). Secret. Attached as Tab D, No. 6 to Document 19.

of fostering the independence of African territories, and in the Suez question where, in the international conferences and in the Five Power Committee, Ethiopia represented the entire African continent.

3. In view of the significance of Ethiopia both in Africa and in the Middle East, the question of Ethiopian-American collaboration becomes particularly important. It was His Imperial Majesty's sincere hope that his visit to the United States three years ago[2] might lay the basis for a solid and close collaboration between the two countries and Governments. However, the period that has followed has not borne out those hopes.

4. For her part, Ethiopia, under the personal direction of His Imperial Majesty, has sought both in the political and in the military fields, to lay the basis for such a lasting collaboration. In political matters, Ethiopia, in cooperating with the United States, has run counter to the policies of the other States of the Middle East in sending troops to Korea—and in refusing to recognize Communist China. She has incurred severe criticism from her Middle Eastern friends for supporting American policies in these matters. In addition, in response to a direct appeal from the U.S. Ethiopia gave—and with considerable courage, in view of sharp opposition from her neighbor, Egypt—the support requested for the U.S. program for the Canal, even to the extent of participating in the Five Power Commission.

5. Likewise, in the military field, His Imperial Majesty personally gave orders to grant the U.S. requests for military facilities in Ethiopia although they far exceeded the original demands, have since been greatly augmented when it came to implementing the agreement, and have now been increased by yet further demands. Not only base installations, but also certain privileges over the entire territory of Ethiopia, have been accorded, quite unlike those in any other country in the Middle East. Also, at the time of His Imperial Majesty's visit to the President, He offered additional privileges as compensation for a broader basis of collaboration between the two countries.

6. However, that cooperation has apparently failed to materialize in any significant measure during the years. At the time of His visit, His Imperial Majesty had discussed with President Eisenhower the fields in which greater collaboration might be achieved, such as defense, ports, highways, aviation, social services, etc. The President personally assured His Imperial Majesty of his own direct and personal interest in seeing that more be accomplished than in the past with Ethiopia, and to that end, designated certain high officials

[2] For documentation on the Emperor's May 1954 visit, see *Foreign Relations, 1952–1954*, vol. XI, Part 1, pp. 451 ff.

of the U.S. Government for discussing these matters fully with the Foreign Minister of Ethiopia.[3] Detailed discussions were had and His Imperial Majesty even delayed His departure from the States in order to bring about some measure of success in the negotiations. Moreover, His Imperial Majesty has personally intervened on many subsequent occasions, both with His Excellency the American Ambassador and with high U.S. officials on official missions to Ethiopia in order to achieve some tangible basis of collaboration. However, the subsequent period has revealed but few elements of progress.

7. His Imperial Majesty pointed out by way of example, the program of assistance in social and economic fields. The Technical Assistance Program has been extended to all countries of Africa and the Middle East, yet the program for Ethiopia has been on a minimum basis, moreover, indeed, far less than many countries who are less favorably disposed towards American policies. The recently published report of the Chairman of the Foreign Relations Committee of the Senate,[4] indicates that this minimal program may now be further restricted. His Imperial Majesty remarked that, following conversations in London between Secretary of State Dulles and the Foreign Minister of Ethiopia, there had been talk of additional funds, but that that talk had been surrounded with so many retractions and contradictions and, indeed, conditions that acceptance of such assistance would have been difficult. He expressed the hope that, following the understandings reached between the Ethiopian Government and the Chief of the International Cooperation Administration, new difficulties might be avoided. Reference was also made to loan assistance from the Export-Import Bank. That assistance is deeply appreciated, but some further measure of support is necessary. In this connection, it was noted that, other Middle Eastern and African States appear to qualify for greater loan assistance, although their political and financial stability remains to be demonstrated.

8. As regards military assistance, His Imperial Majesty pointed to the very large area of Ethiopia, its long borders both in Africa and on the Red Sea and, in particular, to the crucial problem with which she is faced with the studied campaign pursued by hostile interests in the Middle East and in Europe for the dismemberment of Ethiopia in favor of a so-called Greater Somaliland. The extent of this terrible threat had been fully set out to Secretary of State Dulles by the Foreign Minister of Ethiopia during the recent London Conferences. Ethiopia cannot possibly remain passive in the face of this threat. A

---

[3] For documentation on the meetings between Aklilou and U.S. officials in June and July 1954, see *ibid.*, pp. 448 ff.

[4] The "Report on a Study Mission by Senator Green" on economic and technical assistance in Africa was issued on February 21.

program of armament is essential. In this connection, His Imperial Majesty remarked that outside of India, nowhere in the Middle East will be found the long traditions of standing armies and military missions that will be found in Ethiopia. The other territories have all been under colonial regimes until recent years, whereas Ethiopian forces have always fought with great distinction for preserving national independence.

9. However, notwithstanding the extreme urgency of these needs for military equipment, the response from the United States has been rather discouraging. No progress whatever was made until the moment when the United States asked for sweeping privileges in Ethiopia; privileges granted under conditions more favorable than anywhere else in the Middle East; yet once the base privileges were obtained and after an initial agreement for military assistance was reached, far from being maintained at the first year's level, the military assistance was reduced to one-tenth that amount and today, in the fifth year of a program, is still on a purely year to year basis—although U.S. privileges in Ethiopia have been granted for an extremely long period as compared with other areas in the Middle East, arms to the value of less than $8,000,000 have been actually delivered. Although the assistance from the United States has been slow in forthcoming, Ethiopia, on the contrary, is now asked to agree to additional privileges on a long-term basis, although she is still without the means for defending these installations. Moreover, these demands raise considerable political problems for Ethiopia. For example, His Imperial Majesty referred to the very recent objection by Egypt to the presence of American naval units in the Red Sea. If Ethiopia is to give privileges to the U.S. Fleet at Massawa, serious political repercussions may be expected at this time, both as regards other countries in the Middle East and public opinion in Ethiopia itself.

10. With this reference to political problems, His Imperial Majesty also remarked that in other fields, essential collaboration has been lacking. For example, although Ethiopia alone supplies more than three-fourths of the waters of the Nile, at the crucial point of discussions of this matter, His Imperial Majesty was not consulted by the United States. When, finally, the United States recognized the exceptional importance of the Ethiopian contribution to the problem, His Imperial Majesty was constrained to point out that, in contributing 85% of the waters of the Nile, Ethiopia must first reserve all necessary quantities for her own rapidly expanding needs in agriculture and industry, and that some financial assistance will be required for the completion of hydro-electric and other barrages to meet these needs.

11. Similarly, although recently in London, Secretary of State Dulles had promised full collaboration with Ethiopia in the questions concerning the British in Somaliland and the frontier problem with the Trust Territory of Somaliland, only a few days ago, on the very day of voting at the United Nations on the question of the frontier, the American Delegation informed the Ethiopian Delegation, contrary to those promises, that it was intending to introduce a resolution proposing precisely the solution to which Ethiopia was particularly opposed. It was only after massive support for the Ethiopian position by all the Middle Eastern and other States, friends of Ethiopia, and indeed, by the Soviet Bloc which took the floor to defend the Ethiopian position, that the U.S., which had never in fact, spoken in favor of the final Resolution, voted for it along with the others. [5]

12. His Imperial Majesty observed that all of these considerations point clearly to the necessity of a profound re-examination of relations between the two countries. His Imperial Majesty's personal policies and conviction are that close collaboration with the United States is not only of the utmost importance, but is entirely possible on the basis of a fresh and frank approach to the problems. It is in this sense that, relying on friendship with the Vice President, He has set out these problems in complete frankness and in the hope and conviction that the Vice President will, upon return to the United States, exert all his personal prestige to the achievement of this important objective.

---

[5] Resolution 1068(XI), which passed by a vote of 71 to 0, with 3 abstentions, February 26, recommended that the Governments of Ethiopia and Italy continue and complete their negotiations on the frontier between Somalia and Ethiopia.

115. Memorandum of a Conversation, Addis Ababa, March 12, 1957 [1]

SUBJECT

Visit of Vice President Richard M. Nixon

PARTICIPANTS

Ethiopian:

His Imperial Majesty Haile Selassie I, Emperor of Ethiopia
H.E. Tsahafe Tezaz Tafarra Worq Kidane Wolde, Private Secretary to HIM

American:

The Honorable Richard M. Nixon, Vice President of the United States.
Mr. Joseph Palmer 2nd, Deputy Assistant Secretary for African Affairs
Mr. Joseph Simonson, U.S. Ambassador to Ethiopia

After welcoming the Vice President and expressing pleasure that he had found it possible to visit Ethiopia at this time, the Emperor said that he would like to talk in a spirit of great frankness about the current state of U.S.-Ethiopian relations. He then spoke along the lines of the attached summary of remarks, [2] which was subsequently provided by the Minister of Foreign Affairs.

In replying to His Imperial Majesty, the Vice President emphasized the importance which the United States attaches to the maintenance of close relations with Ethiopia. He said that we understand and appreciate the support which Ethiopia has given to the cause of freedom. In the light of these factors, we are most anxious to remove any causes of misunderstanding which exist between the two countries.

Replying to the specific points raised by His Imperial Majesty, the Vice President spoke as follows:

1. He would report to the President the Emperor's feeling of disappointment on the question of military aid. He added that he had recently received information which indicated that the rate of deliveries of MDAP equipment had been slow and that he would look into this situation upon his return. He pointed out, in connection with Ethiopian concern about the continuity of programs, that the Executive Branch of the Government is dependent upon annual appropriations from the Congress, which makes difficult any long-range commitment.

2. With respect to the Emperor's criticism that the rate of interest by the Export-Import Bank was no more favorable than that available commercially, the Vice President pointed out that unfortu-

[1] Source: Department of State, S/P–NSC Files: Lot 62 D 1, North Africa (Tunisia, Algeria, Morocco, NSC 5614, 5614/1). Secret. No drafting information is given on the source text. Attached as Tab D, No. 2 to Document 19.

[2] *Supra*.

nately we are now in a period of rising interest rates. Moreover, Exim bank interest rates are fixed by law.

3. With respect to the development of the Nile, the Vice President reiterated the views he had expressed in his press conference at Entebbe to the effect that in his view Nile development should be approached cooperatively by the various riparian states, i.e., Egypt, the Sudan, Ethiopia, and the U.K. on behalf of Uganda.

In summing up, the Vice President said that he would draw to the attention of the President and the Secretary of State His Imperial Majesty's concern on the various matters discussed and would interest himself personally in facilitating a solution to them.

The Vice President then asked the Emperor what he conceived to be Ethiopia's most important developmental needs. The Emperor spoke of the problem caused by unemployment within the country. He said that he would like to utilize United States economic aid to help correct this situation. The highest priority items were communications (particularly roads), public health and education. He placed particular emphasis on roads, pointing out that these were necessary to open up the more inaccessible parts of the country for development.

The conversation then returned to the question of Nile development. The Emperor reviewed the history of Ethiopia's relationship with Great Britain on this subject, including the agreement which was negotiated between the U.K. and Ethiopia about fifty years ago whereby Ethiopia undertook in return for a promised payment of 10,000 pounds a year not to divert the waters of the Blue Nile. This payment has never been made by the British and consequently the agreement is no longer in effect. Ethiopia feels that in its own interests it should start to develop the Lake Tana and Blue Nile areas. He hoped the United States would consider this matter carefully.

In concluding, the Emperor reiterated the spirit of frankness and friendliness which had motivated him in raising these matters. The Vice President said that he greatly appreciated this frankness and that he would not fail to follow these matters up when he returned to Washington.

116. Memorandum of a Conversation, Addis Ababa, March 12, 1957[1]

SUBJECT

Visit of Vice President Richard M. Nixon

PARTICIPANTS

Ethiopian:

H.E. Ato Aklilou Abte Wolde, Foreign Minister of Ethiopia

H.E. Lidj Endalkatchew Makonnen, Assistant Minister of Foreign Affairs

American:

The Honorable Richard M. Nixon, Vice President of the United States

Mr. Joseph Palmer 2nd, Deputy Assistant Secretary for African Affairs

Mr. Joseph Simonson, U.S. Ambassador to Ethiopia

After welcoming the Vice President, Ato Aklilou said that he was familiar with the presentation which the Emperor had made.[2] There were certain points which he wished to elaborate.

Aklilou said that he wished first of all to emphasize the growing importance of Africa. A number of new states had recently emerged[3] and additional ones were in course of evolution toward self-government or independence. This is a development which Ethiopia has welcomed and to which it has lent its support. He spoke of Ethiopia as being both a Middle Eastern and African nation, which enhances its importance to the United States. It is, he said, the only non-NATO state in the Middle East which gave active support to the UN action in Korea. It had, moreover, given valuable support to the United States and the free world on many matters within and without the UN. In taking this position, it had often been criticized by other members of the Afro-Asian bloc as being too pro-Western. It has been willing to incur this criticism because of the considerations of principle which bind it to the United States, but it cannot ignore the fact that this position has increased its vulnerability to retaliation by the Afro-Asian bloc.

This brought Ato Aklilou to the second major point which he wished to make and which related to the problem of Greater Somaliland. He traced the history of this question, pointing out that it had originally been sponsored by the British and that even now

[1] Source: Department of State, S/P–NSC Files: Lot 62 D 1, North Africa (Tunisia, Algeria, Morocco, NSC 5614, 5614/1). Secret. No drafting information is given on the source text. Attached as Tab D, No. 3 to Document 19.

[2] See Document 114.

[3] The Sudan and Ghana.

influential colonial circles in the U.K. are pressing for a union of the Somalilands which would result in a detachment of a large portion of Ethiopian territory. He said that Ethiopia had been both surprised and disappointed at the position which the United States had taken this year at the General Assembly on the Somali border problem, where we had taken a position opposed to that of Ethiopia during the first few days of the debate, had failed to speak up in support of Ethiopia's position during the course of the debate, and had only supported Ethiopia when it came down to the final vote. He contrasted this with the position of the Afro-Asian and Soviet blocs, which had given effective support to Ethiopia.

On the future of the border negotiations, Aklilou expressed his conviction that the matter could easily be settled once Somalia has its independence. Ethiopia would be happy to federate with Somalia as with Eritrea if that were the wishes of the Somalis, but is equally prepared to accept Somali independence. However they could not accept a foreign-dominated Somalia.

Ato Aklilou then went on to express Ethiopia's concern at the activities of Egypt in attempting to stir up Ethiopia's Moslem population and bring about a dismemberment of the Empire. This also appeared to be the aim of British policy in the area. He said that at the time of Mr. Douglas Dodds-Parker's [4] visit here last year, the British had been quite frank in asking Ethiopia to give up parts of its territory to enhance the viability of a united Somaliland. Ethiopia had flatly refused to consider such a proposal.

Ato Aklilou said that he raised these matters in order to indicate that whereas Ethiopia wished to cooperate with the United States, it must nevertheless take effective steps to secure its own interests. It has looked to the United States for assistance in doing this, but the American response has been disappointing.

The Vice President expressed his appreciation for the frankness with which Ato Aklilou had set forth his concern. He repeated what he had told the Emperor, i.e., that he would report the Ethiopian views to the President and to the Secretary of State with a view toward seeing what action could be taken by the two countries to correct the misunderstandings which had arisen. He asked Mr. Palmer if he would like to comment on the questions which had been raised in connection with the Greater Somaliland problem.

Mr. Palmer said that he would like to make clear that United States has never lent its support to any project for a Greater Somaliland which would result in the detachment of Ethiopian territory. He added that, in the spirit of Ato Aklilou's conversations

---

[4] Dodds-Parker was a Parliamentary Under-Secretary of State in the British Foreign Office.

last year in London with Mr. Dulles, that he (Mr. Palmer) had about two months ago talked to the Foreign Office in London when he was there for conversations on other subjects. He said that the Foreign Office had assured him at that time that although in 1946 it had been British policy to seek a Greater Somaliland which would include the Ogaden Province of Ethiopia, this is no longer official British policy. He had been informed at that time that the British would probably have no objection to a union of Somalia and British Somaliland if that were the desire of the inhabitants, but that the British Government would not support any move to detach Ethiopian territory. Mr. Palmer suggested that it might be useful if he had a further conversation with Ato Aklilou when he had more time in order to explain the United States position on the Somaliland border problem, since the United States had certainly never envisaged taking a position which was contrary to Ethiopia's best interests.

In closing, the Vice President reiterated the importance which the United States attaches to its relationship with Ethiopia, his intention to report to the President and his conviction that any current misunderstandings could be ironed out in the continued interest of both countries.

---

117. Letter From the Vice President to the Secretary of Defense (Wilson) [1]

Washington, March 25, 1957.

DEAR MR. SECRETARY: On my recent trip to Africa, I had occasion to discuss our Military Aid Program to Ethiopia with the Minister of National Defense. [2] I believe that the resulting observa-

---

[1] Source: Department of State, AF/NE Files: Lot 67 D 226, Military Assistance 1957. Confidential. A copy was sent to the Secretary of State.

[2] Nixon met with Ethiopian Defense Minister Ras Abebe Aregai on March 12. The latter chiefly complained that much of the U.S. equipment received by Ethiopia was second-hand and data as to its exact monetary value was hard to come by. (Memorandum of conversation prepared in the Embassy in Addis Ababa, March 12; *ibid.*, S/P–NSC Files: Lot 62 D 1) The Army rejoinder was that 85.3 percent of the equipment intended for Ethiopia under the 1953–1956 MAP had been delivered as of January 31, 1957. The low maintenance aptitude of the Ethiopians was blamed for their inability to operate motor vehicles successfully. The Army also denied that used and recharged ammunition had been supplied. The Department of Defense further stipulated that it was precluded by formal regulations from disclosing the dollar value of MAP equipment. While the erratic pattern of the military aid was conceded, this was attributed to the interminable delays encountered in the program approval

tions will be of interest to you. I did not, of course, discuss the monetary value of future aid, nor did I make any commitments. The talks did disclose certain of their desires and objectives and convinced me of certain principles which we should observe in this specific case.

I believe that Ethiopia will have an increasingly important influence in African affairs and that our enlightened self-interest requires that we ensure their continued friendship and support of our policies. I further believe that the Armed Forces of Ethiopia could have an important stabilizing role in the Middle East in addition to their primary mission of internal security. For example, they might be employed as a neutral police force in appropriate situations.

For these reasons, I therefore urge that our Military Aid Program to Ethiopia be moderately expanded as previously recommended to you by the Chief of the Military Assistance Advisory Group, and that it be promptly executed.

Furthermore, in view of past misunderstandings, I strongly recommend that all commitments as to quantity, quality and time of delivery be kept meticulously. Finally, if it is possible to do so, I think that a fuller bookkeeping report of the program, submitted to the Ethiopians as the program is executed, would be productive of better understanding.

I believe that adherence to these principles will not only provide a military asset in a key area, but will promote diplomatic success and mutual confidence.

Please accept my sincere best wishes.

Sincerely,

Richard Nixon [3]

---

process. (Memorandum from McClelland to Palmer, March 22; *ibid.*, AF/NE Files: Lot 67 D 226, Military Assistance 1957)

[3] Printed from a copy that bears this typed signature.

118. Telegram From the Department of State to the Embassy in Ethiopia [1]

Washington, April 11, 1957—7:47 p.m.

681. For Embassy and Richards Mission. Embtel 721. [2] Unable concur suggestion reftel for total Richards offer in magnitude of $10 million for following reasons:

1) Purpose of Mission in offering additional aid is to give tangible evidence US willingness assist countries subscribing to American Doctrine increase their ability to resist external and internal Communist threats. Effectiveness additional aid in meeting these objectives can only be judged in terms of projects for which funds will be used. Mission not in position, whether from standpoint its objectives or available funds, to substitute for normal process of providing assistance under Mutual Security program.

2) Important factors in determining amount supplemental aid offered by Mission are proximity of country visited to source of Communist danger and degree to which it actually threatened. Remoteness of Ethiopia from source of Communist influence and lack of present danger would not justify major increase in proposed additional aid under American doctrine. Emphasis by Richards Mission on aid to area directly threatened by Communism represents important contribution to security of Ethiopia and other countries on periphery.

3) Ethiopia has already been offered approximately $13.6 million for military, economic and technical assistance for FY 57. This amount considerably larger than aid for any previous year. Recommendations made to Richards Mission will add substantial increment to funds already available. These now include increase in supplemental military assistance from $1.6 to $3 million (details cabled by Defense).

4) Re Embassy suggestion for approximate $4 million increase in supplemental economic aid we are highly doubtful in view difficulties and delays in implementation existing $5 million program, that IEG is capable making effective use of an FY 1957 program almost twice as large.

---

[1] Source: Department of State, Central Files, 120.1580/4–657. Secret.

[2] Telegram 721 from Addis Ababa, April 6, concerned the mission of Ambassador Richards, the President's Special Assistant, to Ethiopia. Regarding Richards' mission, see Document 17. The Embassy reported that Ethiopia expected to derive substantial military and economic assistance from the mission. Past Ethiopian disappointment with the level of U.S. help had led to a lessening of support for the U.S. position in the United Nations; decreased backing on the Suez question; and delayed in responding to the February 15 U.S. request for additional base facilities, which was linked to the Ethiopian plea for Air Force assistance. The Embassy concluded that the proposed aid package of $4,125,000 would lead to considerable dissatisfaction and, given the absence of Air Force assistance, would likely fail to win the desired Ethiopian concession of additional military facilities. Simonson endorsed the idea of taking some of the proposed aid items for 1958 and making them available in 1957. In any event, the Embassy did not consider a sum under $10 million to be sufficient. (*Ibid.*)

5) We cannot concur with suggestion for assistance to Ethiopian Air Force at this time. If as appears possible IEG presents request for Air Force aid suggest Ambassador Richards reply that we have already agreed to make a survey (without further commitment on our part) and suggest IEG wait until they have opportunity to study results this survey before deciding upon their needs. In this connection Department expects IEG will probably try to link question of additional military facilities to request for Air Force aid. To side-step this issue would probably arouse Ethiopian suspicions. Suggest therefore Richards take initiative in reiterating US contribution to Ethiopian security and expressing hope IEG can expedite action on new facilities. Since US requirements for additional facilities not considered by Defense of such urgency as to warrant their use by IEG as basis requests for increased military assistance no indication should be given that US envisages IEG action on this matter will be conditioned upon any quid pro quo.

If Richards Mission believes necessary Department and ICA would consider additional project proposals for relatively moderate increase roughly equivalent in magnitude to that for economic projects now authorized for presentation.

As a general proposition believe African countries in peripheral position e.g. Ethiopia Libya Tunisia and Morocco should so far as possible not be offered amounts of assistance under American Doctrine which would invite invidious comparisons.

FYI Completion bilateral economic aid agreement highly desirable as basis for implementing any Richards Mission projects.

Herter

119. Telegram From the Embassy in Ethiopia to the Department of State [1]

Addis Ababa, April 16, 1957—5 p.m.

760. From Richards. In meeting April 15 with Foreign Minister and three aides, [2] I reviewed American doctrine briefly, emphasizing its voluntary character. Foreign Minister stated no one doubted good

[1] Source: Department of State, Central Files, 120.1580/4–1657. Secret. Niact. Repeated to Cairo, Khartoum, and Jidda. Regarding the Richards Mission, see Document 17.

[2] John Spencer, Vice Minister of Foreign Affairs Ato Gashaou Zallaka, and Assistant Minister of Foreign Affairs Ato Ketema Yifru. (Memorandum of conversation by Troxel, April 15; *ibid.*, NEA Files: Lot 57 D 616, Richards Mission)

intentions of US and referred to US championing of rights of small nations. He described his own efforts bring about closer ties with US, then reviewed traditional pro-West and pro-American stand of Ethiopia. He next gave long exposition of problems faced by Ethiopia, some of which were result its pro-American posture mentioning (1) British efforts detach Ethiopian territory for Greater Somaliland, (2) hostile radio broadcasts from radios Cairo and Hargeisa, (3) opposition to Ethiopian policies by Syria, Egypt and other members of Afro-Asian group, which created serious difficulties in UN on matters vital to Ethiopia. (He claimed US itself had given insufficient support on such matters as Somalia frontiers.) Foreign Minister stressed criticism to which he was personally subjected because of his pro-Western stand at very time Ethiopia beset by difficulties with UK and France. Continuing his list of complaints, he said US had told him to go to IBRD for aid in developing Port of Assab; IBRD had asked why Ethiopia did not use French port of Djibouti—shocking matter since Ethiopia lost Italian War because of blockage imposed at Djibouti. He also referred to US announcement of aid for High Aswan Dam without consulting Ethiopia. Despite all this Foreign Minister said close political collaboration with US would continue but US aid needed. He mentioned risks to which Ethiopia subjected by presence US base without commitment of US to defend country or even base itself. Ethiopia willing negotiate new facilities requested by US but Ethiopia needs should be recognized. He asserted particularly that large amounts of aid had been promised Saudi Arabia which is comparably richer than Ethiopia and not particularly friendly. While disclaiming intention criticize US aid policy he said Ethiopia must assume that US as world leader will extend aid on basis of some "equilibrium". (Most of this presentation was simply elaboration of statements made to me by Emperor during audience earlier in day. [3])

Foreign Minister concluded by recalling memorandum given Vice President Nixon setting forth Ethiopia's military needs. He asked for consideration these requirements and following economic assistance items: (1) radio station to offset radio Cairo and other insidious propaganda, (2) helicopter, one for Emperor's own use, (3) police equipment to assure internal security, (4) ships, Ethiopia having discovered during recent Suez closure that it needs own merchant marine, and (5) cereals and seed grains needed as result crop failure anticipated by cause of unseasonable rains.

---

[3] The Emperor repeated essentially the same things he had told the Vice President the previous month. (Aide-Mémoire from the Imperial Ethiopian Government, April 15; *ibid.*, Ethiopia)

I commented that much of this discussion was outside my frame of reference but philosophized briefly on inevitability that US position in world brought with it many problems and conflicts in our attempts to be fair and even-handed. I undertook report his views concerning intra-area problems to President and Secretary. I made point of saying that Egypt fully understood during High Dam negotiations that we would insist upon request for rights of all riparian states.

I said I felt that US friendship was worth more than dangers involved in presence of its bases and doubted that these dangers were serious. I commented he might not think international Communism was now major danger to Ethiopia, but some countries behind Iron Curtain had once felt same way. Foreign Minister said he had not meant to criticize US or imply Ethiopia would be attacked because of friendship with US but was only describing political facts that create problems for Ethiopia.

Simonson

---

120. Telegram From the Embassy in Ethiopia to the Department of State [1]

Addis Ababa, April 18, 1957—noon.

767. From Richards. My comments on Ethiopia follow:

1. Country is more primitive and isolated than anticipated although I was impressed by dignity at court. Largely cut off and self-contained on plateau and surrounding deserts, people continue to follow ancient traditional pattern of life. USOM study concluded fewer than 5000 Ethiopians possess either fourth grade or semblance technical skill. Participation in government in modern sense or contact with outside world limited to small number, mainly from dominant Amharic tribe.

2. Despite grant by Emperor of some facade of parliamentary government (direct elections for one of two houses of Parliament scheduled for early autumn), ultimate power continues to rest with Emperor. Reportedly he does not exercise authority despotically but

[1] Source: Department of State, Central Files, 120.1580/4–1857. Secret. Repeated to Cairo, London, and Paris, and by pouch to Rome, New Delhi, Tel Aviv, Damascus, Kabul, Karachi, Ankara, Beirut, Tripoli, Amman, Athens, Rabat, Tunis, Baghdad, Khartoum, Tehran, and Jidda.

by working out compromises among special interest groups particularly Coptic church, nobles, land-owners, tribal elements and now younger group educated Ethiopians.

3. Sense of affiliation with and dependence on US remains, dating from time of Italian invasion and subsequent events. Determination to continue this relationship appears to stem in large degree from Emperor. Other officials, perhaps less conscious of past, appear more skeptical of value of this relationship. Foreign Minister, although strongly pro-American, seemed inclined to try compromise with Egypt. However, even Emperor read bill of grievances against US similar to that presented to Vice President. Gist was US failure accord adequate aid to Ethiopia or adequate support in political controversies, especially in UN. Foreign Minister elaborated this theme emphasizing controlling position in General Assembly now held by Afro-Asian group which Ethiopia antagonizing by support of US with resultant probable loss votes Ethiopia needs especially re Somaliland issue. My impression is US will have to be more responsive in future to Ethiopian views and requests if we expect to be able to continue count on Ethiopian support on major east-west issues.

4. Ethiopia not directly threatened by international Communism as such either by reason of geographical position or internal movement. Little awareness of Communist threat exists. Ethiopian stand on world issues against USSR appears motivated by friendship for US rather than fear of Communism.

5. However, Ethiopia is confronted by what might be labeled "neutralist imperialism" led by Egypt and directed both toward advancing Egyptian aspirations in Africa and forcing Ethiopia to join neutralist camp. This campaign certainly assists purposes of international Communism. Strong radio and word of mouth propaganda directed at Muslim Somali tribesmen. Ethiopian nervousness over these attacks explains to considerable extent their decision last fall to refrain from joining SCUA, in return for understanding with Egypt to tone down campaign. India also singled out as leader of attacks on Ethiopia.

6. In private conversation Foreign Minister left no doubt of his opposition to Egyptian policies. He described Nasser as "hooked" by USSR and in grip of pro-Soviet group of army officers led by Ali Sabri. [2] He thought Nasser had allowed his dependence on Soviets to reach point where he no longer free agent. By contrast Foreign Minister said Ethiopia's relations with Sudan were good and he making every effort work with Sudan. He had invited Sudanese

[2] Director of the Cabinet.

Prime Minister[3] visit Ethiopia next week after his tour of Arab states. Foreign Minister thought Sudan now awake to Egyptian designs and had no desire see itself swallowed up.

Problem of mission was to overcome feeling of neglect on part of US. Emperor and Foreign Minister made long presentations stressing this theme. I felt obliged to take up Foreign Minister rather firmly and he subsequently denied repeatedly any intention criticize US.

Ethiopia presented memorandum[4] listing economic needs—broadcasting, helicopters, internal security equipment, cereal seeds (it was unclear whether cereals for consumption also desired), and ships, orally adding port of Assab and roads—and complete military wants. Three of economic requests fully within scope of ME proposals objective of increasing strength against subversion.

I determined to offer following package grant as is:

1. 100 KW broadcasting station with ancillary equipment and training. Cost in magnitude of $1 million.
2. Civil police equipment—$200,000, plus training to be recommended by US police consultant. Estimated cost training under $200,000.
3. Two Bell aircraft helicopters—model 47–G—two with spares.
4. Recommended PL 480 program of cereal seeds if need established.
5. Selected military items in categories contained in OASD/ISA message Defense 921104 April[5] to include army medical equipment and naval training aids not to exceed $3 million. Chief MAAG to provide item details and is authorized make modifications within categories.

Aide-mémoire transmitted separately.[6]

During discussions I called attention to 15 day provision of joint resolution.[7]

Ethiopians appeared pleased at proposals, particularly economic assistance, which imparted sense of US recognition their problems and action to overcome them. At last meeting Foreign Minister made point of expressing appreciation adding that if discussions had been strong and frank that is way friends talk.

---

[3] Abdullah Khalil.

[4] See footnote 8 below.

[5] Dated April 12, not printed.

[6] Dated April 18, not printed (Department of State, Central Files, 120.1580/4–1857)

[7] H.J. Res. 117, as amended March 7, provided that, for certain kinds of authorizations, no money could be released until 15 days after a report indicating the recipient of the funds, the use to which it was to be put, and its source had been furnished to the appropriate House and Senate Committees. The text of the resolution is printed in Department of State *Bulletin*, March 25, 1957, p. 481.

Re economic assistance—Ethiopians hewed closely but not entirely to lines of memo submitted. They were much concerned over internal security problem and means of countering hostile propaganda. Consequently, my approval broadcasting station and civil police equipment and provision of training services well received. Have allowed up to $200,000 for training but have not informed Ethiopians estimated cost this item. (List of equipment approved by Haney being forwarded Department separately.) Ethiopians pressed hard for helicopters, one for use of Emperor and others primarily for security control remote areas as off shore islands. I agreed provide two helicopters similar one now used by USOM here and which has proved capable safe operation at this altitude. Embassy and USOM agree this provides good impact. Re cereal seeds, USOM agricultural chief wishes study further extent to which materials shortage likely develop. I therefore agreed to recommend to USG consideration of FY 58 PL 480 program if existence shortage confirmed. Ethiopians also asked for ships, help with Port Assab, and additional aid for highway expansion program. Complained IBRD interest rates too high in respect loans for highway development. I explained ships, highways and Assab outside context my mission and with respect Assab suggested they pursue discussions regarding port requirements, either Assab or Djibouti, with USOM here. At request of Foreign Minister I undertook to bring to attention of Maritime Administration Ethiopian interest in ships at same time holding out no hope we would help country acquire mercantile marine.

Re military assistance—at meeting of military representatives mission member deflated Ethiopian hopes for financing of complete range military ambitions, pointing out mission's objectives confined to combatting international Communism, and limitations on available funds. B.G. Amanuel Andom, J–3, and Assistant Defense Minister, Michael Imru, pressed hard for projects and demanded answer to memo presented originally to General Decker.[8] They were told bluntly mission would not comply. While scant military justification exists for agreement to deliver additional military items at present, I decided to approve $3 million package to obtain political impact, and since items already scheduled for eventual delivery. Greater impact might have been obtained by financing projects more attractive to Ethiopians but I concluded overall interests best served by remaining within general framework DOD revised list. Chief MAAG concurs.

Difficulties developed with respect to communiqué since Ethiopians at first flatly refused explicitly to endorse ME proposals or to

[8] General George H. Decker, Deputy Commander in Chief, U.S. European Command, was given the memorandum on January 31. (Despatch 172 from Addis Ababa, February 15; Department of State, Central Files, 775.5/2–1557)

condemn international Communism. They argued that to do so would cost them votes of Afro-Asian group in UNGA on Somaliland issue which to Ethiopians more direct and pressing problem than communism. After prolonged discussion and referral matter to Foreign Minister they finally accepted language in text, transmitted separately,[9] which I consider satisfactory.

Actions requested from Washington:

1. Quick delivery of internal security equipment and assignment of police consultant to USOM (already requested by IEG). I believe fast action will greatly enhance impact.
2. Contract for engineering survey and provision of broadcasting equipment.
3. Issuance of purchase authorizations for Bell helicopters. Speedy delivery most desirable.
4. Expeditious programming military equipment.
5. Favorable consideration of PL 480 program should shortage in cereals materialize.
6. Bring to attention of Maritime Administration Ethiopian interest in ships.

Simonson

[9] For text of the communiqué, see *American Foreign Policy: Current Documents, 1957*, p. 843.

121. Operations Coordinating Board Report[1]

Washington, December 18, 1957.

PROGRESS REPORT ON ETHIOPIA

(NSC 5615/1,[2] Approved November 19, 1956)

(Period Covered: From May 30, 1957 through December 18, 1957)

A. Summary of Operating Progress in Relation to Major NSC Objectives

1. *Summary Evaluation*. U.S. policy toward Ethiopia as set forth in NSC 5615/1 has been reviewed from the standpoint of operating

[1] Source: Department of State, S/P–NSC Files: Lot 62 D 1, Ethiopia. Secret. Enclosure to a memorandum from the Acting Executive Officer of the OCB, Roy M. Melbourne, to James S. Lay, Jr., dated December 23, indicating that the Progress Report was concurred in by the Board on December 18.

[2] Document 113.

considerations and in the light of operating experience to date and of anticipated future developments. No review of policy is recommended.

Progress has been made toward the achievement of U.S. objectives in Ethiopia and at present relations with the Ethiopian Government are good. Previous Ethiopian dissatisfaction with the magnitude of our aid programs and the delays in receiving military equipment has been overcome in some measure by the increased scope of U.S. aid in FY 1957 and by the acceleration of military equipment deliveries. Misunderstandings with respect to the procedures involved in the U.S. economic assistance program have persisted, however, and we are continuing to endeavor to clarify them. A continuing problem facing the U.S. is Ethiopia's penchant for seeking special treatment in connection with various matters, particularly those involving procedures under the mutual security program. Progress is being made in fulfilling the Richard Mission aid commitments. (See Annex A, Paragraph 1. [3])

Ethiopia has continued to play a small but important role in support of free world collective security measures. It retains a military liaison group in Korea and has voted for UN Resolutions regarding Hungary and postponing consideration of the Chinese representation issue. No particular problems have arisen in connection with the continued use of our existing military facilities in Ethiopia. It has now been determined that there is no urgent U.S. military requirements for additional facilities in that country. Accordingly, no further efforts are being made at this time to obtain the consent of the Ethiopian Government to the establishment of additional facilities.

Ethiopia's first general elections for the Lower House of Parliament were held during this period, representing initial steps in the transfer from "personalized" government to one based on democratic processes. Although this may contribute to the maintenance of political stability, the rate of development of democratic processes is expected to be very gradual.

---

[3] Not printed. It noted that the Ethiopians had accepted the U.S. view that the commitment of funds for broadcasting equipment was intended for internal coverage and not for international broadcasting facilities. In regard to other matters, it stated that consideration was being given to the Ethiopian request to substitute something else for the promised helicopters; it referred to USOM's request that no police equipment be sent until the country's principal needs were determined by a U.S. expert in the field; and it remarked finally that the pledged military aid was included in the regular military assistance program.

B. Major Operating Problems or Difficulties Facing the United States

2. *Ethiopian Expectations Regarding Air Force Aid.* Although the Ethiopian Government was informed that the U.S. survey of Ethiopian Air Force requirements involved no U.S. aid commitment, the Emperor recently stated that he attaches great importance to the development of his Air Force and anticipates receipt of U.S. aid as a result of the survey. It is the Defense view that there is no valid military requirement at this time for the establishment of force goals for the Ethiopian Air Force and that, therefore, none should be established. Our Embassy at Addis Ababa considers assistance to the Ethiopian Air Force necessary to the maintenance of a strong U.S. position in Ethiopia. This question is under active consideration by the Departments of State and Defense. It is recognized that MAP aid for the Ethiopian Air Force would increase the burden of recurring costs on Ethiopian budget and that such assistance should be held to the minimum necessary.[4]

3. *Ethiopian Request for Increase in U.S.-Supported Force Goals.* The Emperor has formally requested MAP support for an increase in the present ground force goal from three to four commands in order to provide for the extension of MAAG assistance to the Imperial Body Guard without at the same time reducing such assistance to the Army. It is not feasible to accede to this request. The Emperor has been informed, however, that MAP support can be extended to two brigades of the Imperial Body Guard within the present force goal if MAP support for the Army is correspondingly reduced.[5]

---

[4] The report of the USAF survey team which visited Ethiopia in April favored extending assistance over a period of years starting with a modest jet training program. EUCOM, however, did not support this recommendation finding no military justification for it in that Ethiopia belonged neither to NATO nor the Baghdad Pact. No valid military requirement for jet aircraft or for an Ethiopian Air Force to support current U.S. or NATO war plans was perceived. Although USCINCEUR recommended support for an Ethiopian Air Force, the Joint Chiefs of Staff informed the Secretary of Defense on August 27 that they saw "no valid military requirement" necessitating such a program. The Department of Defense concurred on October 9. (Department of State, AF/NE Files: Lot 67 D 226, Air Force Assistance, and Ethiopian Air Force)

The Emperor brought this matter to the attention of Ambassador Don C. Bliss (who had presented his credentials in June), on October 23. The latter commented that, while the Embassy and MAAG supported Ethiopia's request for Air Force assistance, nevertheless a final decision had not as yet been reached. The Emperor described the matter as important and urgent. (Despatch 143 from Addis Ababa, October 23; *ibid.*, Central Files, 775.11/10–2357)

[5] At his October 23 meeting with Bliss, the Emperor asserted his view that the Ethiopian Armed Forces should be established on the basis of four commands. (Despatch 143 from Addis Ababa, October 23; *ibid.*, 775.11/10–2357) The Department of State notified the Embassy in Ethiopia on November 5 that no justification was seen for increasing the number of commands. There was a willingness, however, to provide supplies for two Bodyguard Brigades in the hope that would accelerate their integration into the regular Army. (Telegram 294 to Addis Ababa, November 5; *ibid.*,

(Continued)

4. *Lack of Understanding Regarding Communist Threat*. Ethiopia's continued lack of real appreciation of the communist subversive threat presents an obstacle in combatting Soviet Bloc efforts to extend communist influence. Contributing to this lack of appreciation is Ethiopia's preoccupation with political agitation by Somali nationalists for a territorial expansion by Somaliland at Ethiopia's expense (Somaliland is scheduled to become independent by 1960) and Egyptian subversion and propaganda among the Moslem minorities generally. There also appears to be a continued lack of appreciation of the role played by Satellite Missions in furthering Soviet objectives.

5. *Restrictions on Use of U.S. Information Materials*. Although some editorials critical of Soviet policies and activities have appeared in the government-controlled press, the Ethiopian desire not to use USIS material which might evoke the hostility of the USSR continues to present difficulties. This problem is complicated by the lack of U.S. commercial wire service which would provide more balanced coverage from an unofficial source. Efforts to encourage such a wire service are continuing, and give promise of success. [6]

The recent assignment of a TASS representative to become the only full time permanent accredited foreign correspondent residing in the Ethiopian capital, will add to the problem of presenting American news and objectives to the Ethiopian Government and population. This move may also involve the inauguration of a TASS wire service in Addis Ababa. Presently, Reuters provides the only wire service.

Note: The latest National Intelligence Estimate is:

NIE 72–56, Conditions and Trends in Tropical Africa, August 14, 1956. [7]

Attachments: [8]

Annex A—Additional Major Developments Not Covered in the Report.

Financial Annex and Pipeline Analysis.

(Continued)
775.5–MSP/10–2057) The Embassy reported on December 20 that regardless of the fact that these brigades were receiving MAP equipment, the Emperor might nevertheless proceed to organize a third, which would be non-MAP-supported. Moreover, Ethiopia had not fully accepted the U.S. proposal to confine support to the seven intact Army brigades. (Telegram 507 from Addis Ababa, December 20; *ibid.*)

[6] At the OCB meeting on December 18, Allen Dulles commented that United Press might soon establish an Addis Ababa office. (*Ibid.*, OCB Files: Lot 62 D 430)

[7] Document 14.

[8] None printed.

GHANA

UNITED STATES POLICY REGARDING GHANA [1]

122. Editorial Note

Pursuant to General Assembly Resolution 860(IX) of December 14, 1954, and Trusteeship Council Resolution 1084(XV) of March 14, 1955, a special United Nations mission, composed of representatives from India, Australia, Syria, and the United States, was authorized to consider what arrangements the inhabitants of the Gold Coast desired with regard to their future. India, represented by V.K. Krishna Menon, at the behest of Great Britain and reflecting the friendship of Nehru and Nkrumah, took the initiative in seeking passage of a General Assembly resolution desired both by the British and by the Gold Coast nationalists. The mission's reports, submitted in October and November 1955 (U.N. docs. T/1206, T/1206/Add.1, and T/1210), recommended a plebiscite to determine the wishes of the people.

In Resolution 944(X) of December 15, 1955, Great Britain was authorized to conduct the plebiscite subject to United Nations observation and supervision. Voters were given the choice of opting for union with an independent Gold Coast or temporarily perpetuating the Trusteeship, apart from the Gold Coast, pending a later determination of their future. The voting took place on May 9, 1956, and resulted in 93,095, or 58 percent, favoring integration with the Gold Coast and 67,492 opposing. In the north, integration carried by the heavy margin of 49,119 to 12,707, but lost in the south by 54 percent, 54,785 to 43,976. With India once again taking the lead, the Trusteeship Council in Resolution 1496(XVIII) of July 31, 1956, voted 13–0–1 (Guatemala) to recommend to the General Assembly that it take appropriate steps, in consultation with Great Britain, to terminate the Trusteeship upon the independence of the Gold Coast. Information on these matters is in *Yearbook of the United Nations, 1956, 1957,* and *1958.*

---

[1] For previous documentation on this subject, see *Foreign Relations*, 1952–1954, vol. XI, Part 1, pp. 261 ff.

The Alternate United States Representative, Frank C. Nash, informed the General Assembly on December 13 that the United States would support the free choice of the population of British Togoland and vote for the termination of the trusteeship agreement and the integration of British Togoland with the soon to be independent Ghana. He urged minority opposition elements to accept democratic principles and to seek change by peaceful means. (USUN Press Release No. 2555) The General Assembly went on record in Resolution 1044(XI) of December 13 (64–0–9) as approving the union of Togoland under British administration with an independent Ghana. When this occurred on March 6, 1957, the trusteeship agreement expired.

---

123. Instruction From the Department of State to the Consulate General at Accra [1]

CA–6355 *Washington, February 20, 1956.*

SUBJECT

Department's views on prospect of USSR establishing diplomatic relations with the Gold Coast

Reference is made to CA–6087 of February 10, [2] and your despatches No. 149 [3] and 150 [4] of January 23, 1956. The Department has read with particular interest despatch 150 in which you indicate that through the efforts of Minister of State Kojo Botsio it seems

---

[1] Source: Department of State, Central Files, 645K.61/2–2056. Secret. Repeated to Moscow, Monrovia, London, Paris, and Lagos.

[2] CA–6087 indicated that the Department informed the British and the French of U.S. views regarding the possible establishment of diplomatic relations between Liberia and the Soviet Union. Both nations, particularly the French, were reported to be upset by the prospect of Soviet economic and political penetration of West Africa. (*Ibid.*, 661.76/2–1056)

[3] Despatch 149 noted the great interest of diplomatic and official circles in Accra in determining the degree of contact, if any, between the Gold Coast and Soviet delegations attending the inauguration of President Tubman of Liberia. It concluded that there probably had been no official meetings though private talks among the delegates had likely occurred. (*Ibid.*, 645K.61/1–2356)

[4] Despatch 150 reported the comment of the British Acting Secretary for Gold Coast External Affairs, Michael de N. Ensor, that the Soviets would eventually be invited to the independence ceremonies. (*Ibid.*) Despatch 161 from Accra, February 10, reported, on the basis of a conversation with the Governor's Secretary, P.H. Canham, that the Soviet Union and both Communist and Nationalist China were on the list of provisional invitees. (*Ibid.*, 745K.00/2–1056)

probable that the Soviet Union will be invited to the ceremonies celebrating the independence of the Gold Coast, which are expected to take place during the spring of 1957.

The recent and current diplomatic efforts of the Soviet Union to interest itself much more directly in the continent of Africa have given rise to concern on the part of the United States Government. These efforts have been illustrated by Soviet proposals to establish diplomatic relations with certain countries and by proffers of economic assistance. The two most recent instances of this have been the exchange of Ambassadors with Libya,[5] with the offer of economic aid to that country, and the proposal to establish diplomatic relations with, and give economic aid to Liberia. In the case of Liberia, you have been furnished copies of the exchange of selected correspondence, including a copy of the Department's secret telegram No. 106[6] transmitting a message from President Eisenhower to President Tubman. That telegram and earlier communications from the Department to Monrovia made clear the U.S. Government's view that the establishment of diplomatic relations between African states and the Soviet Union constitutes a Soviet device for communist penetration of the continent of Africa. Once a Soviet mission is established in an African state it becomes only a matter of time before Russian blandishments and enticements of economic aid and technical assistance are likely to be accepted.

Your despatch does not indicate that there is at this time any concerted effort in Gold Coast Government circles either to invite the USSR to send representatives to the independence ceremonies or to exchange diplomatic representatives with Russia following the date of independence. It is assumed that Botsio is acting alone in this matter. Nevertheless, the importance of his official position suggests that he might succeed in laying the framework for the establishment of diplomatic relations between the Gold Coast and the USSR. The Department views the realization of any such possibility with concern.[7] For your information, the British Embassy in Washington has already asked the Colonial Office to ascertain with what countries the Gold Coast plans to exchange diplomatic representatives following independence. The Embassy informed the Department on February 9 that it will now seek the Colonial Office's

[5] Nicolai Ivanovich Generalov assumed his post on January 11.

[6] Document 139.

[7] An article appearing in the London *Times* of February 2 (page 8) quotes A.P. Volkov (Chief of the Soviet Delegation to President Tubman's inaugural) as saying that, following independence, the exchange of diplomatic representatives between the USSR and the Gold Coast " . . . is not excluded, provided there is good will on the part of both sides." [Footnote and ellipsis in the source text.]

views regarding any Gold Coast plans to invite the USSR to send a delegation to the independence ceremonies.

The Department plans on continuing discussions of this matter informally with the British Embassy and will inform you of further developments. We doubt if you should raise this question with Prime Minister Nkrumah, but in your conversations with Ensor [8] and other officials in whom you have confidence you may wish, if you have not already done so, to express some of the following thoughts:

1. Apart from the USSR role in the Czech-Egyptian arms deal, there appears to be in full swing a real Soviet diplomatic offensive in Africa, as illustrated by the following events:

a. The exchange of diplomatic representatives with Libya, the arrival already at Tripoli of a Russian Ambassador and a staff of 17, and the subsequent offer of economic aid and technical assistance to that country.
b. The current tour of the Congo now being made for the first time by a Russian Ambassador to Belgium. [9]
c. The strenuous efforts made last month by the Soviet Delegation at President Tubman's inaugural to induce the Liberian Government to exchange Ambassadors and accept economic aid.

2. Future steps in this offensive could conceivably include:

a. The possibility that Russia momentarily will fill her long empty seat at Tangier and participate in that city's Committee of Control, [10] and, in any case, will expect to have diplomatic representation in Morocco when that country becomes independent.
b. The likelihood that Moscow may soon exchange Ambassadors with the Anglo-Egyptian Sudan and also offer that country economic aid.
c. The continued pressure on the Tubman Government to give legislative approval to the exchange of Ambassadors between Monrovia and Moscow.
c. The probability that Moscow will indicate at the earliest convenient moment the USSR's desire to exchange Ambassadors with an independent Gold Coast.

3. In the light of Soviet policy since the end of World War II, it can be safely assumed that Russia's primary objective in establishing diplomatic and consular offices in Africa is to undermine the fledgling political institutions of countries just emerged from colonial status to independence. The principal Soviet tool used to bring about

---

[8] Despatch 180 from Accra, March 12, summarized Consul General Lamm's conversation with Ensor. The latter stressed Botsio's key role in pushing for an invitation to the Soviet Union and suggested the likelihood of the Gold Coast upon independence following a neutralist foreign policy. (Department of State, Central Files, 645K.61/3–1256)

[9] Viktor Ivanovich Avilov.

[10] The Soviet Union did not in fact fill the seat.

the communist penetration of these countries and surrounding areas would be the offers of economic aid and technical assistance, with significant political strings attached. Another, most effective tool would be the organization and direction of cadres of Africans, already trained in Communist schools abroad, to proselytize and win over to communism the tribal peoples of the West African hinterland. The USSR has already earned world-wide notoriety in recent years by the manner in which it has subverted the use of diplomatic missions to serve as centers for propaganda and espionage activity. The classic illustrations, of course, are the activities of the Russian Embassies at Ottawa and Canberra. In Liberia and the Gold Coast, both of which are less sophisticated countries than Australia and Canada, such improper use of diplomatic missions might have disastrous political consequences.

The Department will communicate with you further on this matter. Any important developments coming to your attention should be reported by cable in view of the two-week delay involved in transmitting classified reports by pouch.

Hoover

---

124. Memorandum of a Conversation Between the Counselor of the British Embassy (de la Mare) and the Director of the Office of Chinese Affairs (McConaughy), Department of State, Washington, February 6, 1957 [1]

SUBJECT

Chinese Representation Issue at Gold Coast Independence Ceremony

Mr. de la Mare called to discuss the Chinese representation question at the Gold Coast Independence Ceremony, scheduled for early March. He said that Mr. Bottomley [2] had called that morning on an officer in the Office of Southern Africa Affairs to discuss this matter, and had been told that the matter was being handled primarily in FE.

He said the British Embassy had received a telegram from the Foreign Office referring to representations made in London by the American Embassy on this question. The Embassy had requested the British Government to advise the Gold Coast authorities to invite

---

[1] Source: Department of State, Central Files, 845K.424/2–657. Confidential. Drafted by McConaughy.

[2] James R.A. Bottomley, First Secretary of the British Embassy in Washington.

the GRC to the ceremony, and to withdraw the invitation to the Chinese Communists.[3] He said that both the Foreign Office and the British Embassy here consider this an "odd" request. The Foreign Office understood that the American Consul General in Accra had already urged the Gold Coast authorities to invite the GRC in place of the Chinese Communists, and had told the Gold Coast authorities that if they were interested in UN membership for the Gold Coast, it would be relevant to bear in mind that the GRC was one of the 5 permanent members of the Security Council.[4]

Mr. de la Mare said that the Foreign Office was not disposed to recommend the suggested action. The Foreign Office thought it would be wrong to expose the Gold Coast to the embarrassment of inviting the representatives of two rival governments claiming sovereignty over the same country. Furthermore, the British thought it would be a mistake for the Gold Coast to start its independent existence by antagonizing Communist China, which Mr. de la Mare described as "one of the great powers of the world". He said it would cause the Gold Coast Government to start off "with two strikes against it".

Mr. de la Mare said that the British Government had not tried to exert any special influence on the Gold Coast authorities in the selection of the governments to be invited. The Gold Coast had requested the advice of the British Government. The latter had provided a list of the countries with which the British maintained diplomatic relations. The Gold Coast authorities had accepted this list as the basis for their own list of invitees. The British considered this action appropriate and were pleased that their list had been used by the Gold Coast.

He said the British Government "rather hoped" that the Gold Coast would not recognize or establish diplomatic relations with the Chinese Communists. But the British Government considered the presence of the Chinese Communists at the inauguration ceremonies to be a different question. No objection was perceived to the presence of the Chinese Communists at the inauguration ceremony.

In questioning various points made by Mr. de la Mare, I observed that the presence of the Chinese Communists at Accra, and the absence of the GRC, would have very unfortunate effects from our standpoint, and we believed also from the British standpoint. It would enhance the international prestige of the Chinese Communists at the expense of the GRC; it would give the Chinese Communists a

[3] Telegram 4081 from London, February 1, reported that the Embassy had raised the subject with the Colonial Office and the Foreign Office. (Department of State, Central Files, 745K.02/2–157)

[4] Consul General Lamm's reports of his conversations on this subject in Accra are *ibid.*, 745K.02.

better entree into Central Africa and would materially improve their prospects for the establishment of a permanent diplomatic mission in Accra; it would tend to dispose other countries of Africa more favorably toward Communist China; it would increase the Chinese Communist potential for subversive activities in Africa and would add to Chinese Communist influence in the Afro-Asian bloc. I recalled that the British were cooperating with us on the Chinese Communist representation question in the UN through the "moratorium" arrangement, and expressed the hope that the same approach could be brought to the Gold Coast problem. I referred to British concurrence with us as to the desirability of denying an invitation to the Chinese Communists for the inauguration ceremonies of the new Malayan Government at Kuala Lumpur next August. I also mentioned that the Vice President was to attend the Gold Coast ceremonies and that the presence of a Chinese Communist delegation might present difficulties in that regard.

Mr. de la Mare said that the British Government went along with the UN moratorium arrangement "most reluctantly" and he did not know how much longer the arrangement could be continued. In any event the same principle could not be applied outside the UN. He said that the U.S. "should not put any additional strain on the delicate balance now existing between the U.S. and the UK" on the Chinese representation question by asking the UK's support for U.S. China policy, which he considered unrealistic and lacking international support. He said that the presence of Chinese Nationalist representatives at Accra might create almost as much embarrassment for high British representatives as the presence of Chinese Communists would for the Vice President.

In response to a query, he said that the British Embassy was not registering a complaint against past or prospective representations by the American Consul General at Accra on this subject. However, the British Government had not at any time attempted to pressure the Gold Coast in this matter and he hoped that the U.S. Government would show similar restraint. He did not think a further approach in Accra would do any good in any event. It was too late to withdraw the invitation to the Chinese Communists, and a belated invitation to the GRC (which he did not consider a government, but a mere de facto regime on Taiwan) would be a direct affront to the Chinese Communists and create unnecessary difficulties for the Gold Coast authorities. It would be tantamount to withdrawing the invitation to the Chinese Communists, since it was common knowledge that the Chinese Communists could not and would not attend if the Chinese Nationalists were to be present. He said that if the Gold Coast now complied with U.S. wishes it would be manifest to all that the Gold Coast was bowing to U.S. influence and was not being allowed to exercise its independent judgment. He thought this would be a made-to-order anti-imperialist propaganda theme for the Communists.

Mr. de la Mare said that if the Department wished to pursue the matter further, he was at our disposal, but as of now the reaction of the Foreign Office on the U.S. request was negative.

---

125. Telegram From the Consulate General at Accra to the Department of State[1]

Accra, February 12, 1957—2 p.m.

121. Re Deptel 112.[2] Question invitation GRC discussed with Chapman[3] secretary to Prime Minister and with Nkrumah himself on February 11. I emphasized dangers of Ghana appearing favor Communists over free world. Prime Minister and Chapman convinced serious nature situation. Difficulty lies in fact that foreign affairs still controlled by British. In addition to GRC no invitations sent to Egypt, Syria, Saudi Arabia. PM plans send letters these countries after March 6 explaining and expressing personal regret. However Nkrumah realizes GRC presents different problem, he asked me present case to governor[4] as seriously as to him and notify him that conversation completed. He then plans to see governor himself. Additional problem is inquiry by Communist China if GRC invited, to which government said no.

I discussed matter in same vein with governor. . . . He was apparently not fully aware seriousness American viewpoint or that Ghana and not British will have to bear onus. He is cabling UK Government reporting my representations and agreed present matter "from Ghana point of view." In view adamant position British I consider it unlikely that GRC will receive invitation.

Lamm

---

[1] Source: Department of State, Central Files, 745K.02/2–1257. Confidential; Priority. Also sent to London.

[2] Telegram 112, January 30, urged Lamm to continue his efforts to obtain an invitation for the GRC. (*Ibid.*, 745K.02/1–2857) On February 8, Lamm was urged to take up the case with Nkrumah if possible. (Telegram 134; *ibid.*, 745K.02/2–857)

[3] Daniel Chapman.

[4] Sir Charles Arden Clarke.

126. Memorandum of a Conversation, Department of State, Washington, February 14, 1957[1]

SUBJECT

Chinese Communist and Chinese Nationalist Representation at the Gold Coast Independence Ceremonies March 3–10

PARTICIPANTS

Sir Harold Caccia, K.C.M.G., British Ambassador
Mr. Robert Murphy, Deputy Under Secretary
Fred L. Hadsel—AFS

In expressing concern about the fact that the Gold Coast had invited the Chinese Communist regime but had failed to invite the Chinese Nationalist Government, Mr. Murphy pointed out, and Ambassador Caccia concurred, that any action which would enhance Communism in Africa was detrimental to the interests of both the United States and Great Britain. He recognized that the presence of the Chinese Nationalists but not the Chinese Communists would present certain problems to the British Delegation, but he noted that the presence of the Communists without the Nationalists presented equally serious problems to the United States. He knew that the Vice President was concerned about this situation, and he hoped that matters would not develop to the point that the Vice President would have to consider cancelling his plans to attend the celebrations. Since he knew that the United Kingdom and the United States were agreed on the general objective of curbing of Communist influence in Africa, he wondered if it would not be possible for the two Governments to work out a practical solution to the problem.

In response, Ambassador Caccia affirmed his complete sympathy with the general objective of preventing the expansion of Communist influence in Africa. He stated, however, that his Government had provided the Gold Coast with a list of countries with which the United Kingdom had diplomatic relations, and that it was on this basis that the Gold Coast had prepared its list of invitees. He recalled the concluding paragraph of his instructions from London on this subject which said that his Government proposed to take no further action in the situation.

It developed during the ensuing conversation that there existed a difference of information as to the exact situation. The Department understood from the messages it had received from London and Accra that the Gold Coast had initially intended to invite the Chinese Nationalist Government but that it had deferred to the

[1] Source: Department of State, Central Files, 745K.02/2–1457. Confidential. Drafted by Hadsel.

desires of the United Kingdom. Moreover, the Department had learned that the Prime Minister presently understood the complications of the present situation and was willing to extend an invitation if it were not for the position of the United Kingdom. The Ambassador, however, reported his impression that the British Government had not taken an active role in the final list of invitees but had merely provided the Gold Coast with a list of countries with which the United Kingdom had diplomatic relations.

Mr. Murphy suggested that one way out of the impasse would be for the Gold Coast to send an invitation directly to the Chinese Nationalist Government, thus avoiding any embarrassment to the United Kingdom and yet achieve the desired result. In order that this be done, however, it seemed highly desirable, or even necessary, that London make clear to its Governor in Accra its acquiescence in such a solution. The Ambassador suggested at some length that affirmative action would be very difficult for his Government and that he feared lest the reputation of the United States might suffer if such an invitation were extended and if it were known, as would inevitably be the case, that the United States had been influential in this action. Mr. Murphy felt that any such embarrassment to the United States was less significant than the complications which might ensue if the Chinese Communists alone came to Accra and had a resulting free hand for subversive activities. He indicated that while we would prefer to work through and with the British on this question and would ask the American Consul General in Accra to keep in touch with the British Governor, we felt that the suggested solution of a direct Gold Coast invitation would remain the best way out of the dilemma. When queried as to his reaction concerning a further approach in Accra on this question, the Ambassador responded that his Government would like to stay out of the matter as much as it could. Commenting upon the widespread pleasure which existed when it was announced that the Vice President would attend the ceremonies, the Ambassador now hoped that his attendance would not be made conditional upon a solution to this problem entirely to the liking of the United States. Mr. Murphy reaffirmed the Department's feeling that it would be much better to avoid participation of the Chinese Communists but that under present circumstances the best solution would be invitations to both Chinese Governments. He thought that the question of double representation in Accra could be handled both by the United Kingdom and the United States Delegations.

The Ambassador agreed to report these views to his Government. He was obviously without official knowledge as to what position his Government would take, but he continued to be of the opinion that if the present position were maintained his Government would not take any further action.

At the close of the conversation, the Ambassador handed Mr. Murphy an invitation to certain Departmental officials to join with the British Embassy in a ceremony in honor of the achievement of Gold Coast independence on March 6, 1957.

After returning to his Embassy, Ambassador Caccia telephoned Mr. Murphy to suggest that the Department of State approach his Government in London directly on this problem, and Mr. Murphy agreed to telegraph the Embassy in London. [2]

[2] Telegram 5684 to London, February 14, advised the Embassy on the approach it should take. (*Ibid.*)

127. Telegram From the Embassy in the United Kingdom to the Department of State [1]

London, February 15, 1957—8 p.m.

4339. Reference: Deptel 5684. [2] I have discussed problem Chinese representation Gold Coast celebrations with Selwyn Lloyd, who had evidently previously consulted Colonial Secretary, Lennox-Boyd. Lloyd reiterated that Brit have no objection to invitation being issued to GRC. Their preoccupation is solely with the problem whether issuance such invitation will entail similar invitations to Egypt and Syria. Brit firmly opposed to attendance of members royal family at ceremonies with reps of Egypt and Syria. For this reason they originally worked out with Gold Coast authorities invitation list based on countries with which Queen maintains diplomatic relations.

Lloyd said he appreciated American concern and is disposed to be as helpful as possible. To this end Brit will communicate with Nkrumah informing him that they have no objection to issuance invitation to GRC provided such an invitation will not entail the issuance of invitations to Egypt and Syria. In the event he takes line that he cannot invite GRC without inviting Egypt and Syria Brit will further attempt to persuade him that three need not be treated

[1] Source: Department of State, Central Files, 745K.02/2–1557. Confidential. Also sent to Accra.

[2] See footnote 2, *supra.*

similarly. They will rationalize that while member of the royal family could not attend ceremony attended by reps Egypt and Syria, who broke diplomatic relations with the UK, problem royal attendance will not arise in case GRC, with whom Brit relations, such as they are (consular), are at least cordial. This formula evolved during course my discussion and may not work. Lloyd professes not to know whether Nkrumah has committed himself with Egypt and Syria to the effect that they would be included if invitations extended beyond original list, or whether if so he will regard this rationalization as sufficient to extricate himself from any such commitment. Lloyd also apprehensive that Indians may get wind of intention to invite GRC and exert pressure on Egyptian and Syrian behalf. Pending outcome this Brit démarche Lloyd hoped that Consul General Accra would suspend further representations to Nkrumah.

Barbour

---

128. Memorandum From the Assistant Secretary of State for Congressional Relations (Hill) to the Vice President[1]

Washington, February 18, 1957.

SUBJECT

Communist Bloc Activities in West Africa

The Communist Bloc, as you know, has been displaying an increasing interest in the continent of Africa. In addition to various efforts at penetration and subversion in northern Africa, the Soviet Union and its allies have seized every opportunity to further their interests South of the Sahara. At the inauguration ceremonies for President Tubman of Liberia last year, for example, the Soviets sent a powerful delegation, sought to establish diplomatic relations, and made vague offers of economic assistance. We may expect a similar, or even greater, effort during the Gold Coast ceremonies.

Under these circumstances, I need hardly emphasize the fact that your leadership of the United States Delegation is considered by the Department of State as extremely significant in demonstrating

[1] Source: Department of State, Central Files, 645K.60/2–1857. Secret.

the American interest in Africa.[2] In order to keep you fully informed on this matter, we shall provide you with last minute information as a part of your briefing material for your trip. In addition to the oral briefing we are planning for you before your departure, we shall also be glad to arrange for a specific briefing on the Communist problem in Africa if you so desire.[3] At the present time, we thought you would wish a summary of this existing situation.

The Soviet Union, Rumania, Poland and Czechoslovakia have responded favorably to the Gold Coast invitations to attend the independence celebrations. We have as yet unverified intelligence to the effect that the Russians plan to make a major purchase of cocoa at the time of the ceremonies, thus trying to make an impression on the Africans at a time that prices are down and supplies are fairly abundant.

After the invitations were sent out, we were informed that on British advice the list included only those countries with which the United Kingdom had diplomatic relations. As a result, a certain number of countries, with which we have diplomatic relations, such as the Republic of China, Egypt, Saudi Arabia and Syria were omitted, while at least one government which we do not recognize, the Chinese Communist regime, was included. We were not consulted on the exact criterion which would be applied in this matter prior to issuance of the invitations, presumably because of the special relationship between the United Kingdom and the Gold Coast. When we learned that the Chinese Communists were included among the invitees (and the Chinese Government excluded), we brought the matter forcefully to the attention of both the British Government and the authorities in the Gold Coast. We believe that it was unwise to provide this opportunity for the expansion of

---

[2] The other members of the delegation were the Governor of the Virgin Islands, Walter A. Gordon; Representatives Frances P. Bolton (Ohio) and Charles C. Diggs, Jr. (Michigan); and Mason Sears. Nkrumah informally invited Dulles to attend on January 4, but the Secretary declined on January 24. (*Ibid.*, 745K.02/1–457) Dulles called Nixon on January 8 to ask if he were free to attend, but the Vice President was not sure he could. (Eisenhower Library, Dulles Papers, White House Telephone Conversations) In a memorandum dated January 24, Dulles informed Nixon that the emerging people of Africa would "follow with particular attention the degree of interest and sympathy which the United States accords these developments." Nixon called Dulles on January 28, and stated that if the President asked he would go. (*Ibid.*) In a memorandum for the President dated January 29, Dulles stressed the significance of the Vice President leading the prospective delegation. (Department of State, AF/AFS Files: Lot 60 D 37) Dulles spoke to the President in this regard on the same date and the latter promised to write to the Vice President to let him know that he considered it important that he go to Ghana. (Memorandum, January 30; Eisenhower Library, Dulles Papers, Meetings with the President)

[3] He was given a 2-hour briefing on February 25. (Memorandum from Palmer to Dulles, February 25; Department of State, Central Files, 745K.02/2–2557)

Communist influence in Africa and that an invitation to the Chinese Communists injected the East-West issue into the ceremonies in a manner which would not have occurred if the Russians and their European satellites alone had been invited.

Furthermore, the Chinese Communists since the Bandung Conference have made intensive efforts to develop closer relations with countries belonging to the Afro-Asian bloc and because of their Asian origin may be more effective purveyors of Communism in Africa than the Russian and other European Communists. They can be expected to utilize the Gold Coast ceremonies to extend invitations to visit Peiping, propose the development of cultural and trade relations and in other ways take advantage of this unique opportunity. We continue to believe that the attendance of the Chinese Communists is contrary to the interests of the West. Since they have been invited, our present tactic is to urge the extension of an invitation to the Republic of China. We hope that this may result in a decision of the Chinese Communists not to appear. However, if both Governments accept, or if neither accepts, the situation will be better than leaving the field to the regime at Peiping. We are naturally continuing to work for as satisfactory a solution of this matter as possible.[4]

Robert C. Hill[5]

[4] On February 19, the People's Republic of China announced that Marshal Nieh Jung-chen, one of the Deputy Premiers of the State Council, had been designated Special Envoy and sole representative at the independence ceremonies. Lamm reported thereafter that Nkrumah would not invite the Republic of China. (Telegram 166 from Accra, February 23; *ibid.*, 745K.02/2–2357)

[5] Printed from a copy that bears this typed signature.

129. Memorandum of a Conversation, Accra, March 4, 1957[1]

SUBJECT

Visit of Vice President Richard M. Nixon

[1] Source: Department of State, S/P–NSC Files: Lot 62 D 1, North Africa (Tunisia, Algeria, Morocco, NSC 5614, 5614/1). Confidential. No drafting information is given on the source text. Attached as Tab B to Document 19.

PARTICIPANTS

Ghanian:
His Excellency Dr. Kwame Nkrumah, Prime Minister of Ghana
His Excellency A.L. Adu, Secretary for External Affairs

American:
Vice President of the United States Richard M. Nixon
Joseph Palmer 2nd, Deputy Assistant Secretary for African Affairs
Donald W. Lamm, American Consul General

After welcoming the Vice President, the Prime Minister inquired about the President's health. The Vice President replied that the President happily had recovered fully and was basically in excellent health although he had recently been bothered by a cold.

The Vice President expressed his pleasure that he was able to be present at the Ghana independence ceremonies and congratulated the Prime Minister on his country's joining the family of nations. He said that he had been greatly impressed by the ovation which the Prime Minister had received when he arrived at the religious ceremonies yesterday and added smilingly that he thought the Prime Minister should have no difficulty getting himself elected to office in this country. He then asked if the Prime Minister would like to expound on the current problems which Ghana faces.

The Prime Minister thanked the Vice President for his remarks about his political popularity. He confessed to some weariness at the heavy political burdens he was carrying and said that at times he was tempted to throw it all over. Recovering his enthusiasm, he said that his main preoccupation, now that Ghana is about to attain political independence, is to assure the country's economic independence. History has shown that political and economic independence must proceed pari passu and that the former cannot be effective without the latter. He pointed out that Ghana's economy is primarily agricultural and heavily dependent on cocoa. This means that the health of its economy is directly related to the price of cocoa which has fluctuated widely. Only a year ago cocoa brought £500 per ton. Currently the price has dropped to £180. The Prime Minister said that he was concerned about the unhealthy situation created by such heavy reliance on one crop and was therefore anxious to diversify the economy both by general agricultural development and by exploiting the country's mineral resources—particularly bauxite. There were other possibilities as well. For example, a contract has recently been signed with an American company for petroleum exploration.

The Vice President said that he had encountered similar situations elsewhere in the world where countries' economies were heavily dependent on one crop. He mentioned as cases in point the heavy reliance of Cuba on sugar exports and San Salvador on coffee. He went on to express agreement with the Prime Minister's assessment of the importance of economic independence, stating that the experience of the United States has made us acutely aware of this fact. He pointed out that 180 years ago when we obtained our independence, we had about half the population of Ghana and were also primarily an agricultural nation. We had seen the necessity for diversification and had thus laid the foundations for the great expansion of our economy which subsequently took place. He felt that Ghana also had the natural wealth and human resources for a great development, but cautioned against excessive expectations from such uncertainties as oil. This should be regarded as a bonus if it materializes but should not form a basis for planning.

The Vice President's analogy about the early history of the United States seemed to catch the Prime Minister's imagination. He spoke with pleasure of his ten years in the United States and his admiration for that country. He remarked somewhat parenthetically that he would very much like to travel again but that his local political preoccupations would probably make this impossible for some time.

Reverting to the Volta River Project, he said that the Preparatory Commission's report had shown the project to be eminently sound from an engineering point of view. Unfortunately, however, there is the matter of financing. Ghana had managed to set aside about £60 millions for development. These funds are presently uncommitted and his hope was to use them as a contribution to the Volta project if the other financing problems could be solved. The Prime Minister went on to say that British and Canadian aluminum interests were also sympathetic and might participate. Finally the IBRD had surveyed the Ghana economy and the feasibility of the project and he was now awaiting their report. This project, he felt, would go far towards realizing Ghana's goal of economic independence.

The Vice President listened sympathetically to the Prime Minister's exposition. He said that this was obviously a matter for exploration with the interested British, Canadian and IBRD interests but assured the Prime Minister that the United States would continue to watch the situation carefully. The Vice President then went on to refer to the great contribution which private enterprise could make to the economic strengthening of underdeveloped countries. He explained the techniques which Puerto Rico has so successfully employed in "Operation Bootstrap".

The Prime Minister indicated awareness of the Puerto Rican experiment and said that although he had never met Governor

Munoz,[2] he has been in correspondence with him.

Dr. Nkrumah went on to say that Ghana has been aware of the desirability of attracting private investment. While the Government believes that certain economic facilities should properly be state-owned, it nevertheless has taken steps to encourage private investment through measures for tax relief, land tenure, etc. The Vice President said that he was glad to hear this.

There followed a brief discussion of U.S. plans for technical assistance (agriculture, veterinary and community development). The Vice President said that while the programs which the United States contemplate this year are modest, they can be of great assistance in training Ghanians for specific tasks. He spoke particularly of the value of pilot projects and of teaching by example, referring to the success of the village method in India. The Prime Minister indicated agreement with these statements.

The Vice President said that he had heard about some of the internal constitutional difficulties which Ghana is facing. He added that he would not presume to comment on Ghana's internal affairs but, drawing again from United States experience, he thought that he might point out that we had similarly been forced to face up to the issues of centralism versus localism in the first years of the Republic.[3] We had eventually resolved the problem in favor of the advantages of a large degree of centralism. All such basic problems have to be worked out in a spirit of compromise and he had no doubt that Ghana would resolve the matter in this same way. The Prime Minister indicated his agreement and referred in this connection to the recent constitutional discussions which would vest considerable power in the regional assemblies. He said Ghana would have to see how these compromises work out during the next few years.

The Vice President said that he had read and heard much about the foreign policy which Ghana would follow after independence. He asked whether he would be correct in describing Ghana's policy as "nationalist". He said he disliked the term "neutralist" which he did not find really descriptive of the policies of nations in Ghana's position. He thought that "nationalist" more accurately described the fact that such nations are determined to secure and defend their independence. He felt this distinction was important. The United States had shown by words and actions its devotion to the principle of independence. We believe that the best assurance we can have of

[2] Luis Munoz Marín.

[3] The Asante and the peoples of the Northern Territories were disposed to favor a federal solution.

our own independence is the independence of others. Unfortunately, other countries are not so motivated.

The Prime Minister said that the Vice President had accurately expressed Ghana's position. Ghana's policy, he said, will be one of non-involvement and non-alignment in the East-West struggle. "But", he said, "Ghana can never be neutral". It will jealously safeguard its independence and resist all efforts at domination. Mr. Adu intervened at this point to say that although no final decisions had yet been taken, Ghana might find it necessary to establish some kind of representation with the Soviet bloc. Dr. Nkrumah confirmed this, adding that the only firm decisions which had been taken were with respect to opening diplomatic missions in Washington, London, Paris and Monrovia.

The Vice President said that he presumed that Ghana would vigorously support freedom of speech, press, religion, and the other democratic traditions. Dr. Nkrumah was emphatic in his concurrence indicating that Ghana was firmly committed to parliamentary democracy and the democratic way of life.

The Vice President reiterated his pleasure at being present at this historic occasion. He emphasized the importance of the events which are taking place in Ghana to the whole future development of this part of Africa. The Prime Minister said that he agreed completely with the Vice President and similarly looked forward to a great future for this part of Africa.

---

130. Telegram From the Department of State to the Embassy in Ghana[1]

Washington, October 9, 1957—6:21 p.m.

111. Oct. 9 U.S. Press today featuring story discrimination against Gbedemah[2] and his personal secretary (Sutherland[3]) at

---

[1] Source: Department of State, Central Files, 845J.41/10–957. Official Use Only; Priority. Repeated to USUN.

[2] Gbedemah was in the United States to attend IBRD and International Monetary Fund (IMF) meetings in Washington and to lead the Ghanaian U.N. Delegation. He was particularly anxious to explore the outlook for financial aid and, if possible, to get the Volta River Project started. At an informal meeting with Assistant Secretary of Commerce Henry J. Kearns on September 25, he expressed interest in the P.L.480 surplus commodity disposal program. (Memorandum of conversation by Duggan, September 25; *ibid.*, 811.05145J/9–2557) The following day he consulted with ICA and State officials concerned with Ghanaian affairs, and stated his view that one ICA

Howard Johnson restaurant Dover, Delaware, based on Minister's statement to press in N.Y.

According Minister's statement to member USDelUN he and secretary entered restaurant for soft drinks which were packaged to take out. Upon indicating desire consume drinks on premises Gbedemah informed this not possible even after he had identified himself to manager. Whereupon he paid 60 cents, left drinks untouched and departed.

At Department's request Howard Johnson trying since last night communicate with Minister and express personal regrets. Company preparing press statement saying Johnson apologizing to Minister and declaring segregation *not* policy of company. Minister informed member USDelUN he making protest to Department. Protest not yet received.[4] Minister not departing for London today as planned in order accept invitation by President to have breakfast with him alone October 10.[5]

Request you personally communicate above to Prime Minister and express regrets U.S. Government over incident.

FYI Department confident President's intervention will serve to put incident in proper perspective in Minister's mind and do much to counteract bad press reaction abroad. Ghana Embassy officer informs Department Minister pleased and Ghanaians reassured by President's action. End FYI.

Dulles

---

representative in Accra was not enough. (Memorandum of conversation by Duggan, September 26; *ibid.*, 845J.00–TA/9–2657)

[3] Bill Sutherland was a black American from New Jersey who had previously operated a school in Tsito, Ghana. On October 7, he and two other black American college students were on their way with the Minister to Maryland State College at Princess Anne where Gbedemah had a speaking engagement. According to Philip Siekman, in an article in *Fortune* magazine in November 1961, one of the Americans suggested that though they had been served at a Howard Johnson restaurant in New Jersey, they would not be served in the franchise outside of Dover.

[4] Neither Gbedemah nor the Ghanaian Embassy lodged a formal protest. However, the Ghanaian Ministry of External Affairs sent the following note to Ambassador Flake: "While making allowances for local customs the Ministry wishes to invite the attention of the US Embassy to the incident and to request that such action as appropriate may be taken." (Telegram 145 from Accra, October 9; Department of State, Central Files, 845J.411/10–957)

[5] Gbedemah had breakfast at the White House with the President and Vice President Nixon on October 10. In a conversation that evening with George D. LaMont of USUN, he indicated that he had discussed the Volta River Project with the President. (Memorandum of conversation by LaMont, October 11; *ibid.*, IO/ODA Files: Lot 62 D 225, Ghana)

131. Telegram From the Embassy in Ghana to the Department of State [1]

Accra, October 10, 1957—4 p.m.

147. Embtel 145. [2] Keeping routine appointment made last week, I saw Prime Minister today.

Prime Minister was much annoyed with Gbedemah for creating fuss over incident. Prime Minister said he himself understood these things; that same thing had happened to member of his staff at Prime Ministers' conference in London but he thought little of it and ordered nothing said; that some day "everything will be all right in US and England" and meanwhile Africans had to be understanding; that if he had experienced same incident as Gbedemah he would have kept quiet, which Gbedemah should have done.

Prime Minister made guarded but nevertheless uncomplimentary reference to Sutherland and said Sutherland should have known better than to let Gbedemah stop at restaurant in question. He speculated on possibility that somebody had maneuvered Gbedemah into provocative situation, adding that "Gbedemah is just the kind that can be maneuvered".

Last night and this morning radio and press gave story heavy play, featuring President's invitation to breakfast and my statement (Embtel 144 [3]), with incident itself played down somewhat. Managing editor *Time* Magazine, (Alexander [4]) now visiting Accra told me today he thinks "we came out remarkably well" on radio and press coverage here.

In my presence today Prime Minister gave orders to Minister of Information [5] to kill any further publicity over radio or through any other media controlled by GOG. Also in my presence he telephoned editor of party organ *Evening News* and gave same order. He then telephoned *Daily Graphic*, asked for "cooperation" and received assurance *Graphic* will atrophy story.

While Prime Minister may be somewhat jealous of Gbedemah's White House visit, I am convinced he genuinely regrets what he

---

[1] Source: Department of State, Central Files, 845J.411/10–1057. Limited Official Use; Priority.

[2] See footnote 4, *supra.*

[3] Telegram 144 from Accra, October 9, conveyed Flake's reaction to the Reuters report of the incident. He stressed that he considered Gbedemah a personal friend and someone who was highly regarded in the United States. He expressed his regret at the incident, which he described as isolated and not representative of the true feeling of the U.S. Government and most Americans. (Department of State, Central Files, 845J.411/10–957)

[4] Roy Alexander.

[5] Kofi Baako.

regards as uncalled for fuss by Gbedemah. He asked me to inform my government that "this incident will not have the slightest effect on the happy relations between our two countries".

Quick action by Department and White House has in my opinion effectively sterilized this wound which otherwise would have had serious consequences on West Coast of Africa.[6]

Flake

[6] The President wrote a personal letter to Gbedemah to tell him that he had enjoyed having breakfast with him, but the Department of State advised that it not be sent, given Nkrumah's determination to downplay the incident. This was particularly true since it was felt that Gbedemah would publicize any communication that he might receive. (Memorandum from Howe to Goodpaster, October 15; *ibid.*, 033.45J11/10–1557) Howe wrote similarly to Goodpaster on November 8, following the President's receipt of a personal letter from Gbedemah dated October 23. Rather than ignore the letter, Howe suggested that Flake convey Eisenhower's appreciation orally. Gbedemah had written of the need for tolerance and mutual respect in race relations. (*Ibid.*, 033.45J11/11–857)

132. Telegram From the Embassy in Ghana to the Department of State[1]

Accra, November 6, 1957—4 p.m.

183. Reference Embtel 182[2] repeated London 3. Today's meeting with Prime Minister attended by me and representatives of UK, Canada, India, Liberia and France.

I had sent word through intermediary that I earnestly hoped Prime Minister would not tell group that exchange with USSR was imminent or imply he would turn to USSR if West failed to supply capital, but would keep question open until hearing views of group and especially until I could talk with him privately.

Prime Minister opened meeting with some verbal squirming which revealed his awareness of awkward problem he faced. He said he wanted make clear at start he has not yet taken final decision on actual exchange with USSR; that however USSR is pressuring

[1] Source: Department of State, Central Files, 645J.61/11–657. Secret; Priority. Repeated to London.

[2] Telegram 182 from Accra, November 4, stated that under pressure from the Soviets Nkrumah had promised, at the time of Ghana's independence, to exchange diplomatic missions and now the Soviets expected him to fulfill his pledge. Flake reported that he had confined himself to delaying the exchange as long as possible. (*Ibid.*, 645J.61/11–457)

through Ghana High Commissioner in London;[3] that he saw little way to hold USSR off much longer as Ghana will within next few days announce exchange with Egypt[4] (which must be done to satisfy Arab bloc before Ghana can open in Israel). He then inquired if governments represented at meeting would accept quantitative limitation on their staffs in Ghana so he could set limit on USSR.

UK MacLennan[5] said he would have to consult his government and all rest of us took same position. I added a catalog of US specific interest here as contrasted with none for USSR.

General discussion then followed in which Prime Minister virtually said he would prefer not have USSR here at all but saw no valid basis continue hold off. UK MacLennan suggested shortage of qualified personnel as excuse and I followed with example of Australia and Philippines expanding gradually while building up qualified diplomatic corps. I expressed view USSR could not attack this argument merely because Ghana now exchanging with Egypt; that while building up Ghanaian diplomatic corps he could expand old consular formula to cover all commonwealth countries and countries in Africa which could logically include Israel. When Prime Minister perked up at this idea, Indian said USSR could still ask for one way deal pending Ghana's ability to send mission to USSR, as exemplified by India having representatives from Chile before sending to Chile but on questioning by me he admitted Chile had Consul in India before independence.

Meeting ended by Prime Minister saying he would think it over and in meantime asked group come see him again after we consulted our governments on possible limitation of staffs.

As prearranged I stayed on for private talk with Prime Minister which went off well. He thanked me for my frank personal views supported by my observations in other parts of world that presence of USSR mission here could be highly detrimental to Ghana and rest of Middle Africa which Prime Minister wishes to encourage, and could I felt pose serious question of Prime Minister's own political future. He said he appreciated my speaking as friend without waiting for or being limited by official instructions. He thought I was right and said he would take another look at whole question on basis of suggested formula.

Prime Minister then told me he would not care what consequences might follow a rebuff to USSR if he could get economic development started. I took this as evidence supporting MacLennan's

---

[3] Edward O. Asafu-Adjaye.

[4] The first Ghanaian Ambassador to Egypt presented his credentials on May 9, 1958.

[5] Ian Morrison Ross MacLennan, British High Commissioner.

belief that Bing–Botsio group pressuring Prime Minister to exchange with USSR. That group may be arguing that it should provide strength in depth for assault on economic front and in extreme could be complete alternative if west should fail to help.

Prime Minister continued that he had written US President and Vice President (Embdes 145 [6]) about Volta and was hopeful of some favorable response. (Since Jackson's return Prime Minister seems reconciled to idea of beginning with alumina part of project which would cost fraction of complete project. ALCAN has promised consider this and report at early date. If ALCAN decides not proceed, Ghana hopes Reynolds will. Reynolds standing by at moment with its interests represented by Adlai Stevenson who is in touch with Jackson and Gbedemah).

Prime Minister added that with or without Volta he wanted get some other projects (e.g. textile mill) started. I told him we were standing at attention to consider immediately any request he might make for support of reduced Volta project and of any other reasonable project. He expressed his thanks and indicated he might be coming after us after study by his new economic adviser Lewis. [7]

Today's talk encourages me believe we might persuade Prime Minister use new formula to postpone indefinitely USSR exchange [8] if we can neutralize Bing–Botsio argument by showing there is no need have USSR in reserve for reasonable economic projects. [9] If Department concurs I shall proceed along this line without making any specific commitment.

Flake

---

[6] Despatch 145 from Accra, October 24, transmitted two volumes of the Report of the Volta River Preparatory Commission together with covering letters from Nkrumah to Eisenhower and Nixon. (Department of State, Central Files, 711.11–EI/10–2457) The President thanked the Prime Minister for his letter and wished Ghana "success in its efforts to solve its problems and to realize its aspirations for a peaceful, stable and prosperous future." (Letter from Eisenhower to Nkrumah, Nov. 8; *ibid.*, 711.11–EI/11–1557)

[7] Sir Arthur Lewis.

[8] Two officials from the Soviet Embassy in the United Kingdom arrived in Ghana in November to discuss the trade mission Ghana proposed sending to the Soviet Union the following year. Adu informed Flake, at Nkrumah's behest, that the Soviets had pressed for an exchange of diplomatic missions and that the Prime Minister had agreed to do so "in due course." (Department of State, Central Files, 445J.6141/12–457)

[9] In telegram 153 to Accra, November 7, the Department instructed Flake that he should avoid mentioning the Volta Project in informing Ghanaian officials of the U.S. willingness to consider well-conceived and reasonable projects. (*Ibid.*, 645J.61/11–657)

133. Telegram From the Embassy in Ghana to the Department of State [1]

Accra, November 15, 1957—2 p.m.

206. Reference: Department's telegram 162. [2] I have been asked to transmit letter of November 12 [3] from Prime Minister Nkrumah to President Eisenhower reading as follows:

Begin text.

"My Dear President, After very careful consideration I am writing to you about a matter which must affect profoundly the future political and economic development of my country.

"As you know, we achieved political independence on the 6th March 1957, and we were delighted to have your Vice-President with us on that historical occasion.

"I am convinced, however, against the broad background of Africa, that our political independence will mean little unless Ghana can continue to develop both politically and economically. Today our economy (which exercises such a direct effect on our political development) depends basically on a single crop—cocoa. We naturally view the current drop in prices of practically all commodities with great concern. The price of cocoa is, at the moment, quite good; but our position is fundamentally precarious and vulnerable, and we can base no real political and economic development on such an uncertain foundation.

"We have naturally considered most carefully other possibilities of broadening and strengthening the economy—*and in sufficient time and on a broad enough scale*—to preserve the present political momentum, and to satisfy the reasonable aspirations of our people who have now emerged into complete political independence after more than one hundred years of colonial government.

"We have launched a big programme to make the fullest use of our agricultural resources—by way of research, agricultural extension, farm-to-market roads, rural water supplies, and so on; but agricultural change takes time. Meanwhile, all our studies show that the most promising hope of a really big immediate economic advance lies in developing our great deposits of bauxite, which can be used to produce aluminium by developing also the hydro-electric possibilities of the Volta River, with its capacity of 633,000 Kilowatts. When my Minister of Finance took breakfast with you last month you were good enough to express an interest in the Project, and a fortnight ago I sent you a copy of Volume I of a report on the scheme, made by experts of international reputation after most

[1] Source: Department of State, Central Files, 711.11–EI/11–1557. Secret; Priority; Presidential Handling.

[2] Not printed. (*Ibid.*, 711.11–EI/11–1457)

[3] Adu and Jackson brought the letter to Flake because Nkrumah wanted to assure prompt delivery and proper attention. To forestall pressure for closer ties with the East, Nkrumah used the letter as justification to his Cabinet for doing nothing to "rock boat", pending a reply. (Telegram 201 from Accra, November 13; *ibid.*, 845J.2614/11–1357)

careful and exhaustive studies.[4]

"By any standards this a great project, and if possible we would naturally wish to tackle it in stages. However, the river can be effectively dammed only at one place and this dictates the scale of the entire scheme. It is planned therefore that the first stage of the project would produce 120,000 tons of aluminium ingot and the final stage of the project would produce about 210,000 tons. Government funds would be required to build the railways and hydro-electric sections of the scheme (we already are quite well advanced in building a new port) and the bauxite mining and aluminium smelting would be carried out by private companies (with probably Aluminum Limited of Canada playing the leading part). Some $225 millions of government funds would be required for the first stage and approximately $160 millions of private investment. At the final stage a further $15 millions and $100 millions respectively would be needed.

"I must emphasize, however, that the best British and North American engineering advice we have received indicates that seven years would be required to build the scheme so that the first stage of the project would require an annual investment from government funds of only $32 millions.

"Originally we hoped that the Governments of Ghana and the United Kingdom might provide the necessary governmental investment, and that the private sector would be covered by Aluminum Limited of Canada and British Aluminum Company. In the last 18 months, however, the picture has changed considerably. It has become apparent that the British Government, while still directly interested in the project, would now wish (because of its own economic difficulties) to invest less than had originally been contemplated. The International Bank for Reconstruction and Development has been consulted in general terms, but the many claims on that international organisation from all over the world (and other factors) have understandably made it reluctant to commit itself until it becomes clearer where the rest of the money would come from.

"The Prime Minister of Canada[5] has shown sympathy with the project (both for Commonwealth reasons and because of the position of Aluminum Limited), and in the private sector the Reynolds Aluminum Company has shown a direct interest in addition to the original companies—Aluminum Limited of Canada and the British Aluminum Company. Other American companies have kept themselves informed about the project generally.

"It is now apparent, however, that the scheme cannot be brought to life unless it receives a new and powerful stimulus. When the demand for aluminum was strong we were told that the scheme—though fundamentally an excellent one—would take too long to construct. Now that the demand for aluminum has slackened temporarily we are told that this is not the appropriate time to be starting big projects.

"I share your own strong confidence in the future expansion of the economies of the Western world, and if our government had all

[4] See footnote 6, *supra*.

[5] John G. Diefenbaker.

the necessary financial resources I would now unhesitatingly commit my country to the project in the belief that the world demand for aluminum from 1965 onwards would certainly absorb whatever we could produce in this country. By ourselves, however, it is impossible for us to give the scheme the stimulus which is essential to get it started.

"A failure to develop the project would mean our acceptance of economic stagnation and a demonstration that we are incapable of consolidating the political independence which we have just won.

"It is apparent that our failure in this respect would have profound effect on the rest of Africa.

"I therefore write to put these problems before you, which as I have said, can well have a decisive effect, for good or otherwise, on the future of Ghana. If you feel that you can help us, we feel that what would help us most would be for your Government to indicate its willingness to consider the possibility of participating in this great scheme, bearing in mind its vital importance to our political future. As a first step, perhaps consideration could be given to sending representatives of your Government to Ghana as soon as possible to discuss with us how best the project might be undertaken.

"Finally I should like to emphasize one basic factor. We are not asking for any gifts. At most we wish to borrow substantial sums of money at a reasonable rate of interest. The economic viability of the project is such that the loans and interest would be paid off on time. In this connection, we have studied with great interest the establishment by Congress of the Development Loan Fund and we wonder whether this might be one possible source of finance which would be suitable for the scheme.

"To my mind, this great project, vital as it is to us in the economic sense, has even more profound political implications for Ghana and the continent of Africa. Its successful implementation would, I am sure, do most to preserve and strengthen the political independence of this country; and if the Government of the United States could provide the stimulus and drive which could bring the scheme to life, I venture to suggest that such actions would demonstrate to the world most convincingly and dramatically the general policies towards this continent which both you and the Vice-President have expressed so clearly in your public statements.

"With warmest personal regards, I am, Mr. President, Yours sincerely, Kwame Nkrumah."

Letter pouched, due Department about November 22. [6]

Flake

---

[6] The President acknowledged the letter, received on November 15, in a brief message of November 21, promising to give the matter "prompt and careful consideration." (Memorandum from Howe to Goodpaster, November 20; Department of State, Central Files, 711.11–EI/11–2057) A full response was sent to Nkrumah on January 3, 1958. The Acting Secretary sent the text of the suggested reply to the President as an enclosure to a memorandum dated December 30. (*Ibid.*, 845J.2614/12–3057)

134. Telegram From the Embassy in Ghana to the Department of State [1]

Accra, December 4, 1957—4 p.m.

233. Re Deptel 188.[2] Busia says series developments notably passage emergency powers bill December 3 has discouraged members his party whose morale now low. Continuing repressive measures by GOG and threats by Edusei [3] causing sources party funds dry up as former donors especially chiefs grow increasingly cautious of involvement in opposition politics.

Busia wants GOG [*U.S.*?] immediately or in January to rally American public opinion and persuade minority group to pass resolutions condemning trend in Ghana towards dictatorial government and increasing signs of willingness to accept USSR collaboration in economic and cultural fields. He believes US minority group opinion is only thing that can give GOG pause in this direction.

He also wants raise 25 (not ten) thousand dollars in US purchase vehicles and hire party workers to offset "dangerous indoctrination" being given people by CPP agents who have unlimited funds. He specifically wants warn people against danger of USSR whose Professor Potekhin (Embtel 158 [4]) is he says not sparing word in CPP circles that USSR is only country genuinely desirous and able help Ghana.

Busia is intelligent and knowing. He would want our help to "condition" potential donors in US and also to transfer such funds

---

[1] Source: Department of State, Central Files, 845J.2614/12–457. Secret; Priority.

[2] Telegram 188 replied to telegram 227 from Accra, December 3, which expressed the Ambassador's desire to return to Washington to discuss the matters raised by Dr. Busia. Flake also wanted to discuss the Volta River Project in light of Nkrumah's approach (see *supra*). The Department authorized his return, but wished it to be portrayed as a routine matter. (Department of State, Central Files, 123–Flake, Wilson C.) Dr. Busia was one of the first two Africans appointed to the Gold Coast administrative service as assistant district commissioners in 1944. The other was A.L. Adu, a former leader of the Ghana Congress Party, supporter of the National Liberation Movement (NLM), and an organizer and leader of the United Party.

[3] Telegram 132 from Accra, October 14, reported that, at a September 20 rally marking Nkrumah's birthday, Interior Minister Krobo Edusei had threatened to arrest all opposition members if an attempt was made on the life of the Prime Minister or any CPP leader. (*Ibid.*, 745J.00/10–1457) Telegram 155 from Accra, November 5, noted that, at an October 25 rally, Edusei accused opposition leaders of conspiring to instigate a riot during the opening of the National Assembly on November 13. Edusei stated his intent to introduce an Emergency Powers Bill to deal with traitors. (*Ibid.*, 745J.00/11–557)

[4] Telegram 158 from Accra, October 15, reported that Professor I. Irutt Potekhin and two colleagues had arrived in Ghana to undertake a study of cultural, economic, and social life on behalf of the Moscow Institute of Ethnography. (*Ibid.*, 845J.432/10–1557)

to Ghana where he says they would appear to be proceeds of party fund raising efforts in Ghana.

I told Busia I could of course have nothing do with all this. He understood. He asked me see if Department could inspire some university invite him expense paid to US and I said I would explore possibility. [5]

Flake

[5] Telegram 208 to Accra, December 19, instructed Flake to tell Busia the Department of State could not be of assistance. If he wished to come to the United States under university sponsorship then he would have to contact educational leaders personally. (*Ibid.*, 845J.2614/12–457)

LIBERIA

UNITED STATES RELATIONS WITH LIBERIA [1]

135. Memorandum of a Conversation Between the Ambassador in Liberia (Jones) and President Tubman, Monrovia, January 5, 1956 [2]

SUBJECT

Soviet Request to Establish Diplomatic Mission in Monrovia

This meeting occurred at 10:00 a.m. on January 5, 1956 at the Executive Mansion at the request of Ambassador Jones in response to the following situation:

The President on January 2 had sent the Ambassador a note informing him that the Soviet Delegation had sent him a message in which "They also intimated that they (the Delegation) have been instructed by their Government to have a confidential talk with me on several subjects, one being the exchange of diplomatic representation between our two countries." (See attachment. [3])

The Ambassador said that he appreciated the President's gesture in calling him in on this problem, and that he interpreted the President's action as an invitation to counsel him in this matter. The President said that that was precisely why he had called upon him. The Ambassador then said that he felt that it was necessary to let the President know what his Government's position was concerning this development. He then said: 1) that the Government of the United States would be gravely concerned if the Government of Liberia accepted a diplomatic mission in Monrovia; 2) that Liberia's other friends among the Western powers would also be concerned; 3) that the entrance of such a mission in Liberia would be a heavy blow to the internal stability of Liberia, since the Soviets were not interested in Liberia's welfare but would use it to its own ends; 4) that once established in Liberia, the Soviets would have a foothold

[1] For previous documentation on Liberia, see *Foreign Relations*, 1952–1954, vol. XI, Part 1, pp. 482 ff.

[2] Source: Department of State, Central Files, 661.76/1–1156. Secret. Drafted by Simons. Enclosure to despatch 195 from Monrovia, January 11.

[3] Not printed.

in West Africa and cause trouble in these countries striving to attain freedom and independence; 5) that the presence of the Soviets in Liberia would impede foreign investments for Liberia; and 6) that the United States would find it difficult to understand such action in the light of its long history of assistance to Liberia.

The President thanked the Ambassador for his remarks and said that he was fully aware of the dangers inherent in accepting a Soviet mission in Monrovia. He said that in the past week it was evident that the USSR was exerting pressure to achieve such an end. He showed the Ambassador a cable, signed by Twe Sung, in which the Red Chinese Government congratulated him on the occasion of his third inauguration and made commendatory comments about Liberia's association with the Afro-Asian Conference at Bandung. He said that he knew that the Soviets were seeking to establish themselves in Liberia because they thought the attempted assassination last June [4] was a sign of internal weakness and that they could stir up trouble in Liberia. He said that he did not propose to let the Soviets high pressure him into a quick decision, and that he did not want them in Liberia.

He said that he was meeting them on January 6, 1956 and that he proposed to deal with them re establishment of diplomatic relations in the following manner: 1) budgetary plans are already set and do not permit opening new diplomatic missions; 2) GOL is unable to open such missions in Belgium and Holland whose people are doing much business in Liberia; and 3) whatever action is taken will have to depend on the Legislature. He assured the Ambassador that he was not going to let the Soviets come into Liberia.

With respect to economic aid, Mr. Tubman asserted that he did not want aid, and would not receive it even if they offered $100,000,000. He said that he knew that they were tricky, that they were seeing many Liberians in Monrovia, and that he was fearful of what they would do if they gained entrance to either Liberia or West Africa. He stated that he had never heard of the Soviet proposal to give economic aid until he read it in the *Liberian Age* on January 3, 1956, [5] and he did not appreciate their announcement before talking about it with him. He said that although Liberia had an open door policy, it was prepared to do business only with the democratic countries whose businessmen would have to stand on

---

[4] A former member of the Liberian National Police Force had tried to kill Tubman on June 22, 1955, at a reception. (Despatch 284 from Monrovia, June 26; Department of State, Central Files, 776.11/6–2655)

[5] During an interview, Soviet Ambassador Volkov stated that the Soviet Union sought to know more about Liberia, hoped for friendly relations, and was prepared to offer economic aid and technical know-how. (Despatch 189 from Monrovia, January 4; *ibid.*, 661.76/1–456)

their own feet without any interference from their governments. He said that he was satisfied with U.S. aid which was all Liberia wanted, and that he was not going to allow anyone to play the United States off against any other country.

He concluded with the remark that in both these matters he was prepared to rebuff the Soviets, and that he would do this by dragging out the matter for a long, long time.

136. Telegram From the Embassy in Liberia to the Department of State [1]

Monrovia, January 6, 1956—10 p.m.

108. Reference: Our 107. [2] Tubman met Soviet delegation from 1000 to 1045 hours today and at 1115 hours called Ambassador Jones for conference at once. Tubman reported his interview as follows:

(1) Volkov referred 1946 Liberian-USSR negotiations for treaty friendship which were suspended that year. He requested negotiations be reopened with view establishing diplomatic missions. Tubman replied establishment diplomatic relations must depend on legislative action re funds and existence of treaty friendship.

(2) Volkov requested Tubman prepare draft treaty as basis negotiations. Tubman agreed in principle to treaty friendship but considered proposal premature since USSR delegation lacked authority for such negotiations. Volkov said his credentials this mission carried sufficient authorization. Tubman sent for credentials and after reading disagreed with Volkov citing that credentials covered only inaugural ceremonies. Volkov inquired re possibility, as interim arrangement, of USSR appointing as its agent representative friendly country with mission in Monrovia and conversely Liberia designation mission friendly country in Moscow as Liberia's agent in USSR. Tubman, in jocular vein, asked Jones "who do you think would be Liberia's agent in Moscow?" Volkov requested use Liberian code to transmit via Liberian and Soviet Embassies London message requesting authorization for Soviet delegation open negotiations on treaty

[1] Source: Department of State, Central Files, 661.76/1–656. Secret. Niact. Also sent to London, Paris, Bonn, and Moscow.

[2] Telegram 107 from Monrovia, January 5, summarized the conversation recorded *supra*. (Department of State, Central Files, 661.76/1–556)

friendship. Tubman refused this request since he considered very improper for one country use code of another country. Tubman replying to question said he would not interpose any objection Soviet delegation sending message in clear.

(3) Volkov expressed Soviet interest economic and cultural development Liberia and stated USSR prepared offer economic aid Liberia. Tubman informed Volkov Liberia could not accept such arrangement so long as there was no treaty friendship.

(4) Tubman acceded to Volkov's request to announce at his party January 7 invitations for several Liberian Legation members visit Moscow.

(5) Tubman refused Volkov permission hold press conference to announce that negotiations for treaty friendship were underway. Tubman reminded Volkov such statement would be inaccurate because Volkov lacked authority enter such negotiations. Tubman stated that he was prepared to issue joint communiqué on points they discussed. End of report on interview with Volkov. [3]

(6) Tubman then informed Ambassador that early next week he would receive note on subject. Tubman concluded with following statement which he requested Ambassador transmit to US Government since "my code is not strong enough":

"When I meet Volkov within next few days I will tell him that the economic and other relations existing between the US and Liberia are neither for sale nor barter with any country. Liberia has all the aid it can use and if it needs more it will make its request to the US Government."

(7) Ambassador thanked Tubman for information and offered his assistance at all times.

Jones

---

[3] The Embassy reported that, at a Soviet Delegation party on January 7, Volkov stated his nation's willingness to provide economic aid and to receive Liberian legislators as visitors. At a private session with Tubman, he submitted additional credentials empowering him to negotiate a treaty of friendship. (Telegram 112 from Monrovia, January 9; *ibid.*, 661.76/1–956)

137. Telegram From the Embassy in Liberia to the Department of State [1]

Monrovia, January 9, 1956—noon.

109. Reference Deptel 89. [2] Tubman sending following message Eisenhower; letter handed special Ambassador Upton his departure January 8. [3]

Verbatim text:

Monrovia January 8, 1956

Your Excellency: It is with a deep sense of gratitude that I extend to you my personal thanks and appreciation for the honors accorded to me and the Government of Liberia by Your Excellency and the Government of the United States upon my third inauguration as President of Liberia by the accreditation of a large delegation composed of high ranking civil and military officials, citizens of your great government, as well as a US Naval vessel. [4]

I have read in newspapers and listened in to radio broadcasts several comments and speculations concerning the presence in Liberia of the Soviet delegation attending the inauguration.

This is intended to assure you that the Liberian Government and people are not vacillating nor mercenary, and that the century old friendship that has subsisted between our two countries; the assistance and cooperation accorded to us by your government through the years in times of difficulty and stress; your government's cooperation in entering into agreement with this government for economic and military aid together with the similitude between our frames and forms of government, ours patterned after yours, will not admit for any change whatever on our part at this, and I trust, at no future time.

Our patent regard for the agreement entered into between our two governments for economic assistance in our development programs cannot be bartered nor sold by any new traducing ideology and the visit of the Soviet delegation to Liberia seeking to effect arrangements for exchange of diplomatic representatives and economic assistance will have no effect on the Liberian Government's attitude and policy.

We believe in the democratic way of life, we are a peace-loving people, a peace pursuing and peace exercising government and a stable one and will remain so.

I thought it necessary to send you this personal note to reassure you that the Liberian Government and people can never be made the subject of speculative artifice.

---

[1] Source: Department of State, Central Files, 776.11/1–956. Secret. Priority.

[2] Telegram 89 to Monrovia, January 6, instructed Jones to tell Tubman that the United States was pleased that he had refused to exchange diplomatic representatives with the Soviets and appreciated his expressed satisfaction with U.S. assistance. (*Ibid.*, 661.76/1–556)

[3] Upton delivered this letter to Eisenhower on January 12.

[4] USS *N.K. Perry*.

With assurances of my highest esteem and personal best wishes, I remain

Sincerely yours, Tubman.

End verbatim text.

FYI since American delegation does not return Washington until January 12, Embassy request Department give special handling this cable until President receives message from Upton.

Jones

---

138. Telegram From the Embassy in Liberia to the Department of State [1]

Monrovia, January 24, 1956—8 p.m.

129. Reference: Embtel 125, [2] Deptel 99. [3]

(1) I saw Tubman for 35 minutes this morning on GOL–USSR relations presented following points orally:

(a) I appreciate confidence Tubman showing by discussing this problem with me, felt I would be less of friend if Tubman not informed my frank views and those my government;

(b) My Government would view establishment Soviet mission Monrovia as most unfavorable development especially in light Tubman's assurances this would not occur at this time;

(c) My Government very conscious USSR pressures obtain early acceptance Soviet mission, Soviets driving enter all countries along both sides Atlantic seaboard;

(d) My Government believes Soviets using joint communiqué January 20 bulldoze Liberia into accepting Soviet proposal;

(e) My Government knows all western nations watching President and Liberia to see if they will be pushover for USSR;

(f) In view use Soviets making of joint communiqué, I should like clarification concerning what action GOL legislature will take

---

[1] Source: Department of State, Central Files, 661.76/1–2456. Secret; Niact. Repeated to London, Paris, Madrid, Bonn, and Moscow.

[2] Dated January 23, it commented on the Soviet-Liberian communiqué of January 20, which indicated that the two countries would establish diplomatic relations and exchange embassies, provided that the Liberian legislature approved. (*Ibid.*, 661.76/1–2356) Telegram 122 from Monrovia, January 20, summarized the communiqué. (*Ibid.*, 661.76/1–2056)

[3] Telegram 99 to Monrovia, January 23, expressed concern over the apparent inconsistencies between Tubman's letters and oral assurances on the one hand and the communiqué on the other. It transmitted the text of a draft reply from Eisenhower to Tubman and requested the Ambassador's opinion. (*Ibid.*)

this session re Soviet proposal. Tubman listened attentively and without any interruptions my presentation.

(2) Tubman replied along following lines:

(a) He stands today in same place he always stood, he as afraid Soviets as US and legislature will not take favorable or any action this session on Soviet proposal;

(b) He had informed Volkov very plainly Liberia not ready consider Soviet proposal this time, that legislature has passed budget which fails provide funds for any new Liberian missions, and that it impossible reopen budget legislation this year;

(c) He refused Volkov's proposal use missions of friendly countries continue negotiations at this time since he unaware any friendly mission Monrovia which would undertake such negotiations and therefore it was impractical to pursue project this time. Tubman emphasized Volkov knows Liberia position as given above and he aware Soviet pressure to obtain its objective.

(3) Tubman informed me that at meeting Volkov prior departure latter questioned logic American newspapers making capital from USSR attempt establish mission Monrovia when US, UK and France exchanged missions with USSR. Tubman said he refused to be moved by this argument.

(4) Tubman thanked me for calling and said he wanted me come to him whenever I had problems same as he called me when he had problems.

(5) *Embassy comments:* Embassy believes Tubman will stand firm against Soviet proposal and prepared prevent legislature from taking favorable action on that proposal. Embassy further believes language joint communiqué was result naivete part Liberian drafters, lacked Tubman's hand because his preoccupation reorganization his government and did not reflect Tubman's true position which he confirmed today.

(6) Embassy believes Eisenhower letter along lines suggested reference 2 would be useful present time. Embassy respectfully suggests Eisenhower letter include additional statement along following lines would also be most useful: President gratified at Tubman's assurances to Ambassador Jones January 24 that Liberian legislature will not take favorable action on Soviet proposal this year.

Jones

139. Telegram From the Department of State to the Embassy in Liberia [1]

Washington, February 2, 1956—10:14 a.m.

106. Deptel 99.[2] Embtel 129.[3] Please deliver following personal message to Tubman from President Eisenhower (signed letter being pouched today):[4]

"January 27, 1956
"Dear Mr. President:
"Upon the return of the United States Delegation to your inaugural ceremonies, my personal representative, The Honorable Robert W. Upton, reported to me on his pleasant and profitable sojourn in your country, emphasizing the excellent impressions which he gained on Liberian progress under your wise leadership.[5]
"It is deeply gratifying to me to receive your friendly letters of January 6[6] and January 8[7] and particularly to have your assurances that the century-old ties of friendship between America and Liberia, the mutual democratic ideals for which our countries stand, and the economic program in which our Governments are engaged, are not to be bartered or sold for a new and false ideology. I am confident that, thanks to your understanding of international affairs and the motivations of certain governments, your intention to protect the Liberian people and nation from the insidious aims of Communism will enable you to remain firm in your resolve to resist the pressures to these ends now being brought to bear upon your Government.
"Please accept again my heartfelt wishes for your good health and success as you enter upon a new term of office and for the happiness and prosperity of the Liberian people.
"Sincerely, Dwight D. Eisenhower"

President has expressly avoided mention exchange diplomatic representatives Liberia and USSR because possible release any time to public of letter with this phrase could result in Soviet propaganda advantage. However when delivering message you should satisfy yourself Tubman clearly understands that matter of exchange diplomatic representatives uppermost in President's mind when he refers to

---

[1] Source: Department of State, Central Files, 776.11/1–2756. Secret. Repeated to Moscow.

[2] See footnote 3, *supra*.

[3] *Supra*.

[4] When Ambassador Jones delivered the message on February 9, Tubman said he would remain firm in resisting Soviet pressures. (Despatch 294 from Monrovia, April 3; Department of State, Central Files, 661.76/4–356)

[5] The report of the U.S. inaugural delegation, dated January 11, is not printed. (*Ibid.*, 776.11/1–1156)

[6] President Tubman's January 6 letter, delivered to the Department of State by the Liberian Chargé on January 13, conveyed assurances of Liberia's "faithful adherence to democracy" and intention not to accept Soviet economic aid. (Eisenhower Library, Whitman File, International File)

[7] See Document 137.

Tubman's resisting pressures now being brought to bear on Liberian Government. (As for other USSR pressures you will recall Tubman in January 6 letter stated unequivocally Liberian Government would "not accept economic aid of any kind from the Soviet Union.")

While letter bears no security classification, Department feels you should indicate to Tubman the President's message is of personal and confidential nature. Department assumes Tubman has no intention releasing it or his own two letters for publication.

Re last paragraph your 129 you may if you feel necessary or desirable express gratification Tubman's assurances to you Liberian Legislature will not take action this year on Soviet proposal for exchange. Department did not however believe such statement should be included in President's reply lest this encourage Tubman to conclude 1) U.S. considered Liberian-USSR diplomatic exchange as problem of short term or transitory nature, and hence 2) if Tubman succeeds in preventing present session Legislature from taking favorable action, further resistance to USSR pressure this end should not be expected of him.

Department feels, on contrary, that USSR will not be put off by hints, delays or Legislative inaction and that task ahead of Tubman in resisting USSR may well prove to be of long haul nature.

Dulles

---

140. Memorandum of a Conversation, U.S. Embassy, Monrovia, March 8, 1957 [1]

SUBJECT

Visit of Vice President Richard M. Nixon

PARTICIPANTS

Liberian:
His Excellency William V. S. Tubman, President of Liberia
His Excellency Momolu Dukuly, Secretary of State of Liberia
His Excellency George A. Padmore, Liberian Ambassador to the United States

---

[1] Source: Department of State, S/P–NSC Files: Lot 62 D 1, North Africa (Tunisia, Algeria, Morocco, NSC 5614, 5614/1). Secret. No drafting information is given on the source text. Attached as Tab C to Document 19.

American:
Vice President of the United States Richard M. Nixon
Richard Lee Jones, United States Ambassador to Liberia
Joseph Palmer 2nd, Deputy Assistant Secretary for African Affairs

After Ambassador Jones' dinner at the Embassy, the above-mentioned officials adjourned for a private discussion of matters of mutual concern to Liberia and the United States.

The Vice President asked if there were any matters which President Tubman particularly wished to draw to his attention. President Tubman replied that there were two main matters which he had on his mind:

1. *Military Assistance.*

President Tubman spoke about Liberia's vulnerability to external attack, tracing the history of British and French detachment of Liberian territory which he ascribed to the fact that Liberia has in the past been incapable of defending itself and unable to depend on other powers, particularly the United States, to protect it. He also cited, in this connection, the German submarine attack on Monrovia during World War I and the fact that it took allied vessels eight days to reach Liberian waters after the incident took place. He said that the United States and Liberia are now joined in a defense effort, since the United States retains the right to utilize Roberts Field and the Port of Monrovia in the event of war. This cooperation, he maintained, increases Liberia's vulnerability. What Liberia basically needs is the capability to hold off any enemy attack until assistance can come from the United States. He hoped that the United States could help Liberia in developing this capability. He then went on to speak about difficulties which Liberia has encountered in connection with reimbursable military assistance, mentioning that last year Liberia was granted over $200,000 in reimbursable aid. Although only about one-half of this equipment has been delivered, Liberia was asked a few months ago to pay for the entire amount. It did so, but is still awaiting the remaining deliveries. Vice President Nixon said that we would look into this matter as soon as possible with a view toward expediting delivery.

2. *Roads.*

President Tubman said that Liberia needs many things: public buildings, advice on public administration, et cetera. Many foreign interests are seeking to extend help to Liberia. For example, both Italian and German interests have expressed willingness to advance money for roads and housing construction and British interests have offered to do the same with respect to ore carrying vessels which would eventually become Liberian-owned if the Liberian Government can work out a suitable arrangement for the employment of these vessels by the Liberian Mining Company. The President said that he was reluctant to do business with these foreign interests and desired instead to look primarily to the United States. He indicated that Liberia does not desire grant assistance but is capable of proceeding on a loan basis. He went on to emphasize that Liberia's greatest need is for roads and that these are of higher priority than the other items mentioned. The United States has been helpful in this regard, the Exim Bank having extended two loans—one for $5 million and the other for $15 million.[2] He understood that the Exim Bank felt that this was all that Liberia's credit status would permit it to extend at the present time, but maintained that the Exim Bank's analysis of the Liberian financial position had been predicated on annual revenues of about $9 million a year whereas those revenues are now approximately $18 million a year. The present road program would still leave a substantial gap in what is needed to open up the country and Liberia therefore strongly hopes that an additional $10 million can be authorized to complete the road program—particularly the link from Bomi Hills to Kolahun. Mr. Palmer said that we agree with the high priority which Liberia ascribes to its road program. He thought that we should get on with the present program and see how that went and then, perhaps, we could consider whether further assistance might be required and possible. Ambassador Jones pointed out that the Raymond Concrete Pile Company would have extensive equipment and personnel here in connection with the $15 million road program which should permit it to tender a lower bid for any additional work. The Vice President confirmed United States sympathy for the Liberian road program and said that we would watch the situation carefully.[3]

The Vice President then turned to the future of West Africa. He spoke of his appraisal of recent events in Ghana and the great possibilities which they hold for encouraging political and economic evolution in this area in a peaceful and democratic way. At the same time, he expressed concern at the potential for Communist subversion which will exist in the period immediately ahead while Ghana is formulating its domestic and foreign policies. He said that he felt that Liberia as the oldest independent state in West Africa and Ghana as the newest have important and unique responsibilities in this area. The independence of Ghana has focused world attention on West Africa and the success which both Ghana and Liberia have in orderly development will have a profound effect on the future of the dependent areas of Africa South of the Sahara, on the so-called colonial powers and on the world in general. He said that he

[2] The first loan was approved on January 11, 1951; the second on January 20, 1955.

[3] Documents on this subject are in Department of State, Central File 876.2612.

thought that Liberia, and President Tubman in particular, had much experience and wisdom which could be used to good effect in Ghana. He asked President Tubman what his estimate was of Nkrumah and the Ghana Government.

President Tubman recalled various exchanges which he had had with Nkrumah in the past. He said that in the earlier days of Nkrumah's struggle for independence he had attempted to persuade Nkrumah to take a more moderate line in his relations with the British. He said that he had pointed out at that time that Ghana had profited greatly from its association with Britain and had told Nkrumah that he thought he would do well to think in terms of continuing that tie through membership in the British Commonwealth. He said that Nkrumah had taken this advice in the spirit in which it had been offered and he felt that he had considerable influence with him. He went on to say that Nkrumah has, of course, something of a Marxist background. He agreed with the Vice President's statement of the dangers of Communism in West Africa and said that he had urged Nkrumah not to permit the Communists to gain a foothold in that area. He said that Liberia would soon be opening an Embassy at Accra and that he would send a strong Ambassador there who could help in developing the sort of relations between Ghana and Liberia of which the Vice President had spoken.

The Vice President then spoke of the importance of the West Africans working out their own policies in accordance with their own requirements as independent states and not just following the Arab-Asian bloc or other interests which do not necessarily coincide with their own. He suggested that perhaps an African bloc which viewed African interests on their merits would be salutory. President Tubman signified his agreement with these thoughts.

The Vice President suggested that there was much that President Tubman could do himself. He thought that if, at an appropriate time, President Tubman could indicate to Nkrumah his desire to visit Accra, it might provide an opportunity for an exchange of views on these important subjects and that perhaps President Tubman could be influential in encouraging Nkrumah to undertake policies which would be in the interest of the Free World. He said that he did not think that he could expect Ghana to adopt the same attitudes in its foreign policy as the United States, but the important thing is that Ghana should be alive to the dangers of Communism and the importance of maintaining its independence. President Tubman said that he agreed and that he would try to find a way of paying an early visit to Accra. He mentioned, in this connection, that he was disturbed by Nkrumah's decision to retain the portfolios both of Foreign Affairs and of the Interior, which smacked to him of a dictatorship.[4]

The Vice President then asked President Tubman how he foresaw the evolution of dependent peoples of West Africa and whether he had any advice for the United States. President Tubman said that there could be no doubt that the dependent people had a right to their own independence. However, he thought that they should be conscious of the advantages which their ties with Britain and France gave them in terms of developing their economies. He said that they had an enormous advantage over Liberia in this respect, since Liberia virtually had to start from scratch and, although there had been some United States assistance in recent years, has had to do everything for itself. With respect to United States attitudes, he had nothing specific to suggest except that we might find it in our interest to extend some economic assistance at Ghana in due course.

There followed a short discussion on the role of private enterprise in developing Liberia, during the course of which President Tubman indicated his awareness of the importance of this factor in the evolution of the country. He mentioned that he was concerned at the number of irresponsible investors who are anxious to obtain a foothold in Liberia and said that he was particularly suspicious of the Germans in this respect. He said he could not forget that during the Hitler regime, Britain and France had suggested that the Germans might find satisfaction of their colonial ambitions in Liberia. He said that he was thinking of introducing new legislation which would require potential investors in Liberia to put up a deposit which would be forfeited in the event that no agreement were reached with respect to concessionary arrangements. He thought that this would serve as a deterrent to irresponsible investors.

Note: On March 9, President Tubman informed Vice President Nixon that he had had a reply from Nkrumah in response to the personal message which he had sent him through Vice President Tolbert upon the occasion of Ghana's independence.[5] In his reply, Nkrumah had indicated that he was appreciative of President Tubman's message, that he intended to follow the President's leadership on matters of policy, including that towards Communism, and that he had felt great revulsion at the events in Hungary and did not want the same thing to happen to Ghana.

---

[4] Krobo Edusei became Ghanaian Minister of the Interior.

[5] In one of the messages to Nkrumah, Tubman implored him to take all measures necessary to prevent the introduction into West Africa of any harmful ideology. (Telegram 183 from Monrovia, February 28; Department of State, Central Files, 645K.61/2–2857)

141. Memorandum of a Conversation Between President Tubman and the Ambassador in Liberia (Jones), Cape Palmas, April 7, 1956[1]

SUBJECT

Liberian Relations—USSR and Red China

The President met Ambassador Jones at the latter's request at his home in Cape Palmas, April 7, 1956, 12:00 noon to 1:15 p.m.

Four subjects were discussed: 1) Red China's admission to IPU; 2) Liberia's reaction to the proposal of Red China to establish diplomatic relations;[2] 3) Liberia's reaction to the Soviet invitations for the President, Vice-President and Speaker of the House of Representatives to visit Moscow this year;[3] and 4) the hiring of Filipino engineers for the road program in Liberia. They were discussed in the following order:

Introductory remarks included comments on the success of the American athletes in Liberia among which Ambassador thanked President for his letter to the athletes; regrets of Mr. G. Allen that he was unable to come here March 29, but said that he intended coming;[4] and presented President with *Congressional Record* containing Mrs. Bolton's[5] remarks on the President's speech of March 8 which was included in the *Record.* The President expressed his appreciation for Mr. Allen's wishes to visit Liberia and Mrs. Bolton's comments.

1. *Red China's Admission to IPU*: The Ambassador went over the U.S. position, i.e., a) Red China not in UN which has refused former admission to General Assembly or any of its affiliated agencies, b) Red China using every means possible to break solid stand against entrance through lower organs of UN, c) this question for Liberia related to establishment diplomatic relations with Red China and USSR, d) U.S. Congress will not appropriate funds for sending delegation to meetings at which Red China delegates are meeting, and e) U.S. Congress will not tolerate any weakening of position and its delegation will have to walk out if Red China is admitted. The Ambassador said that the President's good friend Senator Barkley[6] was the head of the U.S. Delegation and would be disappointed.

---

[1] Source: Department of State, Central Files, 661.76/4–1756. Secret. No drafting information is given on the source text.

[2] Telegram 168 from Monrovia, March 6, reported the Chinese proposal. (*Ibid.*, 601.9376/3–656)

[3] Telegram 186 from Monrovia, March 29, reported the Soviet invitation. (*Ibid.*, 661.76/3–2956)

[4] Allen visited Liberia May 27–30. His visit is described in despatch 369 from Monrovia, June 14. (*Ibid.*, 110.15–AL/6–1456)

[5] Representative Frances P. Bolton (Ohio).

[6] Former Vice President Alben W. Barkley of Kentucky.

The President said that he thought the U.S. was making too much over Red China whose position was enhanced by the opposition being shown. He said that no progress in the situation would occur so long as Red China was being kept out of all organizations, and that when it was in some organizations there was a chance to improve Red China. The Ambassador pointed out the U.S. efforts over a long period had been directed toward that end only to find that Red China's conduct had not improved. It was, therefore, impossible, he said, to have confidence that Red China would act any differently after it gained admission to these organizations.

When the President learned of Congress' strong stand and Senator Barkley's heading up the U.S. Delegation, the President asked if it was too late to act. When the Ambassador said the meeting was not over until April eight, the President called for his assistant and sent out two radiograms, one to his Ambassadors at Bonn, Paris and Rome requesting them to instruct the Liberian Delegation to vote against Red China's admission to IPU, and the second to the Delegation—the message to the latter saying "After further study and consideration of the issue, you are instructed to vote 'no' on the admission of Red China to IPU." This message was sent to Senator Frank Tolbert and Representative L.E. Mitchell.[7]

2. *Status of Liberia's Action on Establishment of Diplomatic Relations with Red China*: The Ambassador said that in the light of the President's March 8, 1956 speech on foreign policy many governments are watching Liberia, and especially the President, to see what he will do toward Red China. They understand, he said, that this is another form of Soviet pressure being exerted on Liberia to weaken its affinity to the West. He said that if Liberia accepted the Red China proposal it would indicate a readiness to do business with all Communist countries. Many of the President's admirers, he said, would find it difficult to reconcile his acceptance of such a proposal with his strong pronouncements of March 8, 1956.

The President said he was aware of these pressures. He also said that he did not intend to accept the proposal. He stated that he was going to use the same arguments that he used in the Soviet case in January 1956 to answer Red China, namely, lack of funds, no plans made in the past, and lack of legislative authority. In response to a question of when he intends to give a reply, he said he was waiting his time. The Ambassador said that he hoped the President would so word his reply that it would not give the Communists another diplomatic victory similar to what it obtained in the January Communiqué. When the President said he could not reject outright the

[7] He was appointed an Associate Justice of the Liberian Supreme Court in March 1957.

Red China proposal, the Ambassador said that while he understood that, yet it was important from Liberia's point of view not to give Red China or the USSR any diplomatic advantage from this situation. The President admitted that he was aware of the problem, but said that he was taking no action on this problem at this time.

3. *Soviet Invitations for Liberians to Visit Moscow*: The Ambassador asked the President what he intended to do about these invitations. The President said that he was not going to Moscow because he was going to other European capitals. He said he was going to West Germany and if he heard from Italy he would go there. No date was set for his trip to Germany, but he intended to go. He said that last Fall it was determined that he was not going to Lebanon because it did not want him to go to Israel afterward.

The President said, however, that he felt that someone ought to go from Liberia, either the Vice-President or the Speaker; that it would be discourteous if someone did not accept this invitation. The Ambassador said that while it would be an act of courtesy to accept the invitation, yet there was no compulsion making it necessary to accept. The President said that he disagreed with this view. The Ambassador pointed out that if this was true, then Liberia must accept all invitations which the Soviet Union was bound to send once a penetration had been made. The President admitted that this was probably so.

The Ambassador said that it was dangerous for Liberia's own well-being to accept this invitation for anyone and especially the Vice-President and Speaker. He suggested that if the latter went, the Soviets would attempt to create internal division in Liberia. The President responded with much conviction that he had implicit confidence in the Vice-President and Speaker, he felt that they could handle the situation, and he was not afraid that they would be subverted. Then he said, if they do come back and attempt to divide the country, he (the President) will put them out. He said he did not believe that the Vice-President and Speaker could be "touched" by the Soviets.

The President asserted that Liberia had certain rights as a sovereign nation, that as a sovereign nation it must act as such, and that it should assume its full position in international relations. By refusing to send anyone to Moscow, Liberia's position in the world would be belittled.

The Ambassador said that if any Liberian went to Moscow at this time it would be another diplomatic victory for USSR. He restated the view that such a visit to Moscow would not add to Liberia's prestige in the Western world, and certainly would not enhance the President's position. He pointed out that Liberia's position was being watched very carefully and people were gaining much respect for his stand in the past. What he was doing would have an effect not only on Liberia but on West Africa. What he is going to do will also affect Liberia's internal economic development since foreign investors will be affected by his stand, indeed, it could harm his unification and open door policy. The Ambassador said that all these efforts on the part of the Soviets were aimed at getting Liberia to establish diplomatic relations and acceptance of the invitations would only intensify Russian efforts toward that end. [8]

The President reiterated his views, given on several earlier occasions, that he was fully aware of what the Soviets were doing. However, he said, he has no fear of what they would be allowed to do in Liberia, for he did not intend to let them do as they would like. He said that he did not propose to accept them in Liberia.

[8] Telegram 207 from Monrovia, April 20, reported that the President, Vice President, and Speaker had all declined the Soviet invitation. (Department of State, Central Files, 661.76/4–2056)

142. Memorandum of a Conversation, White House, Washington, June 25, 1957 [1]

PARTICIPANTS

The President
The Vice President of Liberia, William R. Tolbert, Jr.
The Ambassador of Liberia, George A. Padmore
Acting Chief of Protocol, Victor Purse

At the request of the Liberian Ambassador to the United States, an appointment was set up for the Vice President of Liberia, William R. Tolbert, Jr., to pay a brief courtesy call on the President at 10:00 a.m., June 25. After the usual exchange of greetings, the President and Vice President Tolbert discussed the general economic situation in Liberia, including rubber development and mining. President Eisenhower had asked specific questions concerning these two industries.

After the discussion of the economic situation in Liberia, Vice President Tolbert presented the President with a letter from Presi-

[1] Source: Department of State, Central Files, 033.7611/6–2557. Secret. Drafted by Purse.

dent Tubman. The President said that he would make a personal reply to the letter.[2]

The Vice President then indicated that he had a problem which he would like to bring to the President's attention. He said that the Soviet Government has approached the Liberian Government for the purpose of establishing diplomatic relations and negotiating a trade treaty.[3] The Liberian Government has twice turned down the request.

Vice President Tolbert said that the Liberian Government would like very much to receive the United States Government's reaction to this proposal. The President suggested that Vice President Tolbert take that matter up when he meets with Secretary Dulles.[4]

The President indicated that many countries' dealings with the Soviets had not worked out too well. In many instances the Soviets had used their trade negotiations as a spearhead to accomplish their political purposes. If there were certain products that the Liberians could not market, these details should be brought to the attention of Dr. Randall's Economic Committee.[5]

The Vice President then expressed the appreciation of the Liberian Government for the cooperation of the United States in the joint economic and technical assistance program. The President inquired of the Vice President his impression of our technical assistance and aid programs, specifically as to whether we had too many people and whether they were being properly utilized. The Vice President felt that all the United States personnel were being profitably employed, particularly in the fields of education, highway development and health. The President felt it was very important to have the technical assistance program developed well in advance of the material aid program.

At the conclusion of the conversation, the President invited the photographers to come into his office and take pictures.

---

[2] Tubman's brief message dated June 4 and Eisenhower's reply of June 25 are in Eisenhower Library, Dulles Papers, White House Memoranda.

[3] At a social affair in Monrovia on April 5, Tubman revealed that the Soviets had approached Ambassador Simpson in London to request the initiation of negotiations for a treaty of friendship, commerce and navigation. (Despatch 248 from Monrovia, April 8; Department of State, Central Files, 661.76/4–857)

[4] See *infra.*

[5] Clarence H. Randall was a special consultant to the President on foreign economic policy and headed the Council on Foreign Economic Policy (CFEP).

143. Memorandum of a Conversation, Department of State, Washington, July 1, 1957 [1]

SUBJECT

Courtesy Call of Vice President of Liberia

PARTICIPANTS

Mr. William Tolbert, Vice President of Liberia
Mr. George A. Padmore, Ambassador of Liberia
Mr. John Foster Dulles, Secretary of State
Mr. Joseph Palmer 2nd, Deputy Assistant Secretary of State for African Affairs

After an exchange of courtesies, the Secretary said that he hoped that the Vice President had received good reports on his physical condition. The Vice President replied that the doctors had pronounced him in fine condition and that he was similarly delighted to see the Secretary looking so well. Mr. Tolbert went on to speak of his deep feelings of esteem and friendship for Vice President Nixon, emphasizing the success of his recent visit to Africa.

The Vice President next referred to his recent appointment with President Eisenhower. [2] He recalled that he had carried a personal message from President Tubman, requesting the views of President Eisenhower on what course of action Liberia should take with respect to recent approaches from the Soviet Union proposing the conclusion of a treaty of friendship and commerce. Vice President Tolbert recalled that Liberia had long withstood Soviet blandishments and wished to do nothing now which would prejudice the strength of the free world. It was for this reason that President Tubman was most anxious to obtain the advice of President Eisenhower as to whether Liberia should accept the Soviet offer to conclude such a treaty. Mr. Tolbert said he had been most impressed with President Eisenhower's reasons in advising against such action. The President had suggested he also raise this question with the Secretary, which he now wished to do.

The Secretary said that he felt that it would be quite inadvisable for Liberia to respond favorably to the Soviet initiative. He emphasized that in dealing with the Soviets one must constantly look behind their actions in order to determine their real motives. In a few isolated cases, it is possible that they may sincerely be interested in trade, but in most cases an analysis will reveal that their motives are political. Soviet trade treaties are usually followed by technicians,

[1] Source: Department of State, Central Files, 033.7611/7–157. Confidential. Drafted by Palmer.
[2] See *supra*.

who have been politically trained. Once they establish themselves in an area, it is almost impossible to get them out. As experience has shown, a revolution in Hungary was unsuccessful in dislodging them. In other cases, such as Greece, Iran and Guatemala, it took a revolution to expel them. Austria was the only place he knew of from which the Soviets had withdrawn voluntarily and here it had taken years of effort by the West. The Secretary said that he thought that, in the light of this record, any country should think twice before inviting the Soviets in. The Secretary went on to speak of the well-known religious convictions of the Liberian people and contrasted Western belief in the inalienable rights of man to the materialistic concepts which motivate the Communist government of the Soviet Union.

The Secretary continued by pointing to evidence that the Soviets are beginning to pay more attention to Africa. A few years ago they appeared to be concentrating on Latin America as a primary target. Their efforts had been largely nullified, however, by the action of the OAS in adopting the Caracas Resolution,[3] which authorized joint action in the event of a Communist take-over in any of the American Republics. Although not fully utilized during the course of the struggle in Guatemala, the existence of this Resolution had undoubtedly discouraged the Communist elements and contributed to their defeat. As a result of their abortive efforts in Guatemala, international Communism seems to have recognized the difficulties of penetrating Latin America and to have transferred the scene of its activities to Africa. The Secretary said that perhaps Africa could find some helpful guidance in the Latin American experience as to how it should comport itself to withstand the Soviet threat.

Vice President Tolbert expressed his appreciation of these observations. He reiterated that Liberia remains dedicated to her ties with the West and her desire to withstand the evil influences of Soviet imperialism. He recalled that during his meeting with the President, the latter had inquired as to whether there are any Liberian products for which no market can be found in the West. Mr. Tolbert said that at that time he had neglected to mention to the President the problem of palm oil, which Liberia used to sell in Western Europe but which is now being replaced by Nigerian and French West African sources. Mr Tolbert expressed the hope that the United States could look into the matter of assisting Liberia to dispose of

[3] Reference is to Resolution 93, "Declaration of Solidarity for the Preservation of the Political Integrity of the American States Against the Intervention of International Communism", passed at the Tenth Inter-American Conference at Caracas in March 1954. Documentation on this subject is in *Foreign Relations*, 1952–1954, vol. IV, pp. 264 ff.

this commodity. The Secretary said that we would be glad to look into the possibilities.

The Vice President said that there was one more matter he would like to mention. He pointed out that Liberia is a founding member of the United Nations and that it has always aspired to hold a high post in that organization. Speaking quite frankly, he thought that the United States had not given Liberia the support which the close relations between the two countries would seem to call for.[4] He mentioned somewhat vaguely an incident in which Liberia had been defeated by Italy for an important UN post. The Secretary laughingly pointed out that when Liberia took on Italy, with the great Latin American support which the latter usually enjoys, it was really tackling some stiff opposition. He said that this Government would, nevertheless, bear the Vice President's comments in mind.

Before taking his departure, Vice President Tolbert said he wished to express his gratitude for the U.S. Technical Assistance Programs in Liberia which he thought were making an excellent contribution to the development of the country. He said that his government is naturally impatient to push on with essential development. The Secretary said that he was glad to hear that our aid programs were effectively contributing to the growth of the country. He warned against proceeding too rapidly, citing Turkey as a case where the rate of development appears to have outstripped the capacity of the economy to absorb it.

In concluding the conversation, the Secretary recalled with pleasure the visit of President Tubman two years ago and asked the Vice President to relay to the President his very sincere best wishes.

Note: During the course of the foregoing conversation, the Secretary promised to send the Vice fresident copies of the Caracas Resolution and the special UN Report on Hungary. This material is being assembled for despatch through the Liberian Embassy.

[4] Liberia had been particularly anxious to gain U.S. support for its efforts to win a seat on the Trusteeship Council. Documentation is in Department of State, Central File 350.

144. Telegram From the Department of State to the Embassy in Liberia[1]

Washington, July 19, 1957—6:33 p.m.

12. Padmore discussion with Department July 18 still leaves unclear Liberian position on Soviet proposed commercial treaty and establishment relations. Padmore oral presentation and aide-mémoire left with Department differ.[2] He said Liberia planning "rebuff" Soviet overtures but aide-mémoire states LibGov will inform USSR, through London Embassy, not prepared negotiate this time but definitive answer in future, and remainder aide-mémoire leaves impression no real rebuff planned now. One passage appears to imply Liberians actively contemplate reverse of Ambassador's remarks: *Begin verbatim text* . . . .[3] the negotiation of a treaty with Russia or even the sending of Liberian officials to visit Moscow, would never change the avowed and determined opposition of the Liberian people to Communism or cause them to desist (*sic*) its infiltration into Liberia.[4] *End verbatim text*. In view of this rather confused presentation, Department would appreciate your ascertaining as precisely as possible actual position LibGov.[5]

Dulles

---

[1] Source: Department of State, Central Files, 661.76/7–1957. Confidential.

[2] Padmore and Grigsby met with Department officials led by Palmer. The aide-mémoire and the memorandum of conversation by Ross are both *ibid.*, 661.764/7–1857.

[3] Ellipsis in the source text.

[4] The actual text reads: "Therefore, the negotiation of a treaty with Russia, or even the sending of Liberian Officials to visit Moscow, would never change the avowed and determined opposition of the Liberian people to Communism or cause them not to desist its infiltration into Liberia."

[5] Jones replied in telegram 23, July 29, that the Liberian position was that stated in the aide-mémoire. Tubman told him that he hated the Soviets "like Satan disliked holy water" and did not want them in Liberia. (Department of State, Central Files, 661.76/7–2957)

145. Despatch From the Embassy in Liberia to the Department of State[1]

No. 242 *Monrovia, December 4, 1957.*

SUBJECT

Appraisal of President Tubman and Liberian Diplomatic Developments

Summary

Recent Liberian diplomatic developments are reviewed and compared with statements of President Tubman to me. I am fully aware that there is not always complete agreement between those statements and acts of the Government. An explanation for this discrepancy is given.

1. In view of Liberian diplomatic developments in recent months, I believe that it is desirable for me to give the Department the benefit of my thinking concerning President Tubman's position on these matters. But first, I would like to call attention briefly to the developments to which reference has been made.

(a) A Liberian delegation, headed by Secretary of Agriculture and Commerce John W. Cooper, visited the USSR in September 1957, as guests of the Soviets. Since his return to Liberia, the Secretary has continually lauded the material achievements of the Soviets publicly, privately, and to the press. This, plus Sputniks I and II, has set many Liberians to thinking and talking in more favorable terms concerning the USSR.

(b) The Government of Liberia (GOL) agreed to establish diplomatic relations with Israel and Nationalist China as of August 22, 1957. Israel rapidly implemented the agreement, and soon opened an Embassy in Monrovia. There have been several pro-Israel gestures on the part of the GOL during the past three months, and the Government-subsidized press has devoted considerable space to pro-Israel news stories. Nothing further has been heard with reference to Chinese recognition.

(c) The Liberian Government announced that Egypt and Liberia agreed to establish Legations in Cairo and Monrovia as of November 1. Then, without previous publicity, a 10-man Egyptian "economic" mission suddenly arrived in Monrovia November 24 as guests of the GOL. In reality, the delegation came for political and propaganda purposes and not for economic reasons. During their visit, which lasted 10 days (they are due to leave today), it was announced that the Egyptian Ambassador—not Minister—would arrive in six weeks. This meant that the missions have already been raised to the Embassy level.

(d) During an interview with President Tubman on November 28, he told me that Liberia plans to name one Ambassador to Egypt, Lebanon and Syria in February or March 1958. This was the first

[1] Source: Department of State, Central Files, 776.11/12–457. Secret.

time that the President had mentioned recognition of Syria to me. The information also indicated that Lebanon and Liberia are to raise their missions from Legations to Embassies, as in the case of Egypt and Israel.

2. Throughout my long, intimate association with President Tubman he has repeatedly told me that he dislikes communism and he will try to keep communists out of Liberia. He has continued to tell me that he does not intend to establish diplomatic relations with the USSR, although in an interview on November 28 he added "at least for the present."

The President has also expressed his antipathy for Nasser because of the latter's war-like activities in the Near East. In an interview with him this morning, he definitely implied that he is unhappy to have an Egyptian diplomatic mission established in Liberia. [2] He also brought out in our conversation that the Egyptians have pushed too hard and too fast—first, recognition; then a large "economic" delegation visiting Liberia less than a month after recognition; and now, sending their Ambassador here so quickly. I also got the impression that he is aware that Liberia may be infiltrated by communists—Egyptian, by inference—and he is concerned about it.

I am aware that the President's statements have not always coincided with expressions of his cabinet secretaries and action of the Government as a whole. I believe that he has not altered his personal position, but he has been and still is under pressure from some of his advisers and supporters to permit the Government to take the steps mentioned in part 1, above. For reasons best known to him, he has acquiesced in their proposals.

For purposes of conjecture, however, I am of the opinion that part of the explanation of the apparent discrepancy between statement and fact is to be found in Liberia's rivalry with Ghana. The GOL simply does not want to be left behind or be outstripped on the diplomatic level by her neighbor. There seems to be the basic attitude that if Ghana can deal with the Russians and Egyptians, so can Liberia. Also, in order to maintain internal political harmony, I suspect that the President has not deemed it wise to continue to force all of his personal views on his supporters. In other words, he is agreeing to diplomatic moves with which he is not necessarily in sympathy in order to strengthen his domestic political position.

I am fully cognizant of this general anomalous situation, and shall continue to analyze developments closely, particularly with

---

[2] Ambassador Jones accompanied an ICA evaluation team to an interview with Tubman. Tubman was worried that the Egyptian trade delegation's concern was with political matters. (Memorandum of conversation by Bourgerie; *ibid.*, AF/AFS Files: Lot 60 D 37)

reference to statements of the President as related to acts of the Government.

Richard L. Jones

146. Letter From the Deputy Assistant Secretary of State for African Affairs (Palmer) to the Ambassador in Liberia (Jones)[1]

Washington, December 16, 1957.

DEAR DICK: We have followed with interest and, I must admit, some concern the intrusion of the Egyptians into the Liberian picture and President Tubman's seemingly bland assumption that this poses no problems for Liberia. Frankly, we do not feel that this is the case and we have the impression that the Liberians' desire for international recognition and acceptance weighs more heavily on the President's mind than the obvious dangers of permitting Egyptian representatives in Liberia which, under the present scheme of things, is very little better than permitting the Soviets to come in. Indeed, in some aspects the Egyptians carry even greater dangers since, as plainly shown elsewhere, they make a strong attempt to disaffect a country's Moslem minority, a weapon not normally available to the Soviets.

I realize, of course, that the President announced his intentions more than a year ago of doing this and that he offered us a palliative in simultaneously announcing his intentions of exchanging diplomatic missions with the Government of the Republic of China. Still, a lot of water has gone over the dam since then and we are more than a little disappointed that such a major decision was made by the Liberian Government without informing us and giving us a chance to express our views.

It is still not clear to us the extent of the jurisdiction of the Liberian Ambassador to Cairo but we would hope that he would be accredited to all of the Arab States. Should Liberia accredit a representative to Syria at this juncture and not to countries such as Lebanon, Iraq, and Jordan, it is certain to be interpreted as a slap at

[1] Source: Department of State, AF/AFS Files: Lot 60 D 37. Secret; Official–Informal. Drafted by Ferguson.

the United States, and I cannot help but wonder if this may not be what certain elements in Monrovia may have had in mind.

We realize, of course, that our position in Liberia has altered as it was bound to when Ghana emerged and set new standards for independent action. The above developments, however, seem to us to indicate that the Liberians are carrying things somewhat too far, and we are concerned that we may find the Soviets in Monrovia hard on the heels of their Egyptian friends. I have discussed this matter as frankly as possible with Ambassador Padmore [2] as indicated in recent telegrams but knowing your close relationship with President Tubman, we believe you can be much more effective in warning him of the dangers of the course he is following. We hope also that you will find some means, consistent of course with Liberia's independence, to indicate that we wish he would take us into his confidence to a greater degree and at an earlier stage on matters of such great concern to both his country and to ours.

We would not, of course, wish to suggest that you draw these matters to Tubman's attention in precisely the foregoing terms. You will know best how to put them without giving rise to charges that we are trying to interfere in Liberia's sovereign responsibilities. We cannot, of course, undo the decisions which have been made regarding Egypt and the Afro-Asian Solidarity Conference [3] and I think it would be a mistake to try. We can, however, try to limit the damage.

With kindest regards and best wishes.

Sincerely yours,

Joseph Palmer 2nd [4]

---

[2] Palmer, Ferguson, and Ross met with Padmore on December 10. A memorandum of the conversation by Ross, December 10, is *ibid.*, Central Files, 670.901/12–1057.

[3] Telegram 118 to Monrovia, December 7, instructed Jones to discourage Liberian attendance at the Conference which was scheduled to convene in Cairo on December 26. (*Ibid.*, 670.901.12–657) On December 10, Tubman informed Jones that Liberia would not send or finance a delegate. (Telegram 207 from Monrovia, December 10; *ibid.*, 670.901/12–1057) Documentation on this subject is *ibid.*, 670.901.

[4] Printed from a copy that bears this typed signature.

LIBYA

UNITED STATES RELATIONS WITH LIBYA; THE QUESTION OF UNITED STATES ECONOMIC AND MILITARY ASSISTANCE TO LIBYA [1]

147. Letter From the Ambassador in Libya (Tappin) to the Assistant Secretary of State for Near Eastern, South Asian, and African Affairs (Allen) [2]

Tripoli, March 11, 1955.

DEAR MR. SECRETARY: I am writing to convey to you my personal impressions of certain factors having direct bearing on the validity and effectiveness of our present military and political attitudes toward Libya, in terms of its strategic importance in overall U.S. military planning for the European-Mediterranean-Near Eastern area and, more generally, of its place in U.S. foreign policy as a whole.

In the light of what I have learned during four short but very busy months here, [3] I feel that we should most definitely take a fresh look at Libya. In my opinion, it presents opportunities unequalled in the Near East and North Africa for the establishment not only of a secure bastion for defense of the area, but also of a springboard for swift and massive retaliation against any aggressor.

Among the numerous advantages we enjoy, the following are some of the more significant:

1. Libya is an independent state which has voluntarily granted military facilities to the U.S. on a long-term (20-year) basis with what clearly appears to be the full consent of its people. Even those who opposed the ratification of our Base Rights Agreement [4] did so for internal political reasons not directly related to the presence of American forces.

---

[1] For previous documentation on this subject, see *Foreign Relations*, 1952–1954, vol. XI, Part 1, pp. 538 ff.

[2] Source: Department of State, S/P–NSC Files: Lot 62 D 1. Top Secret; Official–Informal.

[3] He presented his credentials on November 16, 1954.

[4] Documentation on this agreement, which went into effect on October 30, 1954, is in *Foreign Relations*, 1952–1954, vol. XI, Part 1, pp. 538 ff. For text, see 5 UST (pt.3) 2449; TIAS 3107.

2. There is in Libya no anti-colonial, nationalist movement directed at an occupying or mandatory power, which might threaten the security of U.S. installations, as is the case in Morocco, for example. Moreover, there is no ascertainable internal opposition which views the Base Agreement as a reason for attacking the "ruling class" or for accusing it of supporting "imperialists". The only political opposition to the present Government is embodied in a group which is essentially pro-British and which, while it would probably not be as helpful to us as is the present Government, would nevertheless be relatively friendly if it came to power.

3. There is at present no active or sizeable Communist Party in Libya nor is there in fact any Communist influence. Although the economic basis for an organized Communist movement is present in the extreme poverty and backwardness of the mass of the people, continued US–UK economic assistance and support of development projects can prevent its exploitation.

4. There exists no articulate "unemployed-educated" group of intellectuals to plague the Government with destructive attacks and, since for the immediate future Libya will be able to employ all the educated or half-educated citizens it can train, this great bane of the Middle East will be slow to develop. Technical training can be exploited to the point where it becomes a desirable goal for young Libyans and can thus serve to prevent them from forming a center of dissatisfaction.

5. Our hands are, to date, completely clean in Libya. With the exception of the French forces in the Fezzan,[5] we are not directly associated with mandatory or occupying powers and have not acted like one ourselves. There is no underlying animosity against us because of troop activities during or since the war. The airmen of Wheelus Field have managed to establish a generally good "public relationship" with the local populace and we are formulating long-range plans to preserve and improve it.

6. There is no "free" press in the normal Middle Eastern sense of the word and consequently, provided we retain the friendship of the Government in power, we are not subject to irresponsible attack through that medium.

7. The present Prime Minister, Mustafa Ben Halim, is ambitious to become an "international statesman" and will do what he can to retain the support of the major powers (UK and US) who he realizes can materially assist him in attaining his goal.

8. The provincial police forces, largely British trained and commanded, are at present capable of maintaining internal order. This ability will be enhanced even further if they are centralized under Federal control. Additionally, if an expanded national army is achieved, its mission will be basically the maintenance of internal security and cohesion.

---

[5] On the basis of a treaty subsequently negotiated between France and Libya, the French withdrew their forces by the end of 1956.

. . . .

10. Libya occupies an advantageous geographical location, at the mid-point in the North African-Mediterranean coast line, directly south of Italy, Sicily and Malta. Its year-round excellent climate and vast areas of uninhabited desert wastelands make it an ideal area for Air Force operations and training, both tactical and strategic.

I have discussed the above advantages on numerous occasions with Col. Rollen H. Anthis, the Commanding Officer at Wheelus Field, and with senior Air Force commanders passing through or visiting Libya, in particular with Maj. Gen. Frederic E. Glantzberg, Commander of the Seventeenth Air Force, with Headquarters presently in Morocco.

That the Air Force already recognizes the possibilities for developing facilities here is exemplified in the construction and expansion of Wheelus Field, a $75 million project. This installation is incorporated in current military planning on the basis of the following missions; the list was prepared by Col. Anthis and has been approved by Gen. Glantzberg:

1. Present plans make Wheelus Field a vital link in SAC war plans for use as a bomber, tanker refueling and recon-fighter base. A TAC fighter squadron and an AC&W Group, plus two tanker squadrons, will form a critical link in the US Air Defense net in the entire Mediterranean area and presently augment the entire Air Defense System for Moroccan bases.

. . . .

3. Wheelus Field is presently nearing completion of extensive construction designed to provide large AvGas and jet fuel storage facilities, in addition to being programmed as a forward supply point for the entire Near Eastern area. Large ammunition stores, designed to support combat requirements in war-time operations, are currently on hand at Wheelus Field.

4. Air Resupply and SAC escape and invasion plans are based upon availability of Wheelus Field as a refueling point, since all aircraft radii of action are predicated on the fact that aircraft can use Wheelus as a refueling base.

5. Expansion and extension, now under way, of Globe Communications facilities at Wheelus Field make it an essential link in the US world-wide communications net. Wheelus Field is likewise the "gateway" to the Near and Far East for MATS transportation routes.

6. Wheelus Field plays an important role in the defense of the entire European area by providing important training areas for USAFE air power.

7. In the event that the Mediterranean becomes untenable in time of war for US Naval Forces, Wheelus Field will become the last

major US air base in support of Allied activities for an area extending as far east as India.

Parenthetically, it is possible that in the future the Southern Command of NATO may find itself in need of the real estate provided by the Libyan terrain and port potential around Tripoli, Benghazi and Tobruk. How utilization by NATO of this area outside of NATO might be brought about would depend somewhat on circumstances at the time, but we have a beginning in the existence of the US Base Agreement and UK Treaty with Libya.[6]

In the light of Libya's present role in US Air Force planning as outlined above and in view of the very considerable advantages inherent in Libya's political stability and fundamental friendship for and faith in the US, I feel the time has come for a review at the NSC level of US policy objectives and means of attainment with specific reference to Libya in the context of our entire North African-Near Eastern position.

I would appreciate your comments and those of your NE and AF staffs relative to a current review of Libya's possibilities and of US plans to exploit them advantageously. More particularly, I wonder whether the primary role given to the UK in Libya by the NSC[7] is still valid or advisable under present circumstances. The members of my staff here who are cognizant with British Embassy activities during the past few years have been impressed by the marked failure of the UK to wield any positive influence in Libya, either politically or economically. It is perhaps significant that the newly arrived British Ambassador, W.G.C. Graham, in a recent conversation with me, professed to be ignorant of any arrangement between the United States and the United Kingdom relative to "primary responsibility" and had assumed from his Foreign Office briefing that we, in fact, were expected to play the major role here. This attitude, if representative of official Foreign Office thinking, could in an emergency lead to much confusion and an "After you, Alphonse" situation which might seriously jeopardize both our positions. I feel very strongly that this point should be clarified with the British,

---

[6] The British Treaty of Friendship and Alliance with Libya, signed July 29, 1953, became effective on December 7, 1953. Its text is in *Modern Libya* by Majid Khadduri (Baltimore, The Johns Hopkins Press, 1963), pp. 363–385.

[7] The only existing NSC paper dealing with Libya was NSC 19/5, "U.S. Position on the Disposition of the Former Italian Colonies," printed in *Foreign Relations*, 1949, vol. IV, pp. 571–578.

once we ourselves have determined exactly what we want to accomplish here, both now and for the future.

Sincerely yours,

John L. Tappin [8]

[8] Printed from a copy that bears this typed signature.

---

148. Letter From the Acting Secretary of State to the Secretary of Defense (Wilson) [1]

Washington, November 12, 1955.

DEAR MR. SECRETARY: The Libyan Government has urged us for more than a year to grant Libya sufficient military aid to make possible the expansion of the Libyan Army, presently numbering about 1800, to a strength of about 5000, at a cost of approximately $6.5 million. [2] The Prime Minister, backed by the King, has appeared to make this an important test of United States friendship. Our Ambassador in Libya has emphasized strongly the need of a Libyan Army adequate to ensure internal security and cohesion, on which the continued smooth operation of our military facilities depends. [3]

Into this picture has now come the drastic new factor of Soviet penetration into the Near East and North Africa. Libya recently announced that it had agreed to exchange diplomatic missions with the USSR. [4] Libya, as an Arab State and neighbor to Egypt, is obviously susceptible to the influence of Egypt and appears to be under strong temptation to adopt Egyptian tactics in the conflict between East and West, not for any love for the Soviets but as a device to get what it wants in the way of arms and other assistance.

The Libyan Prime Minister has told the British Ambassador (realizing the Ambassador in turn would inform us) that Egypt has offered to supply Libya with its requirements for arms from the

[1] Source: Department of State, Central Files, 773.5–MSP/11–1255. Secret.

[2] The Libyans periodically renewed their requests to the United States for military aid. See CA–716, July 29, 1954, in *Foreign Relations*, 1952–1954, vol. XI, Part 1, p. 591.

[3] In telegram 386 from Tripoli, March 8, Ambassador Tappin expressed support for the Libyan National Army. (Department of State, Central Files, 773.56/3–855)

[4] On September 25.

stocks Egypt can amass.[5] If true, this means that Libya, through Egypt, would have access to Soviet bloc shipments. The Prime Minister said he was embarrassed by this offer but would have no basis for refusal before his Council of Ministers unless the United States made a counteroffer.[6] The Egyptians are pressing the Libyans for an answer to their offer. Thus the matter is of some urgency.

Despite the elements of bargaining that crop up here, I feel we should move swiftly to accommodate the Libyan arms request in order to forestall the spread of Soviet influence to Libya through the supply of arms. Such a development would involve obvious dangers to our presently safe and unhindered use of military bases there.

Our political position in Libya is basically a favorable one and I feel there is still a good chance of persuading Libya that it has more to lose than to gain in responding to Soviet advances. However, I think the balance might slip rapidly against us if we are unable to counter the prospect of Soviet arms with an attractive proposal of our own. Libya, for reasons of prestige and security, is like other Arab states in its determination to get arms without much regard to the source.

The British, who maintain a military mission in Libya have informed us that they have studied the Libyan requirements, and believe that they can be met at a considerably smaller cost than $6.5 million. The British estimate is approximately $1.12 million. The British have proposed that we join them in a joint gift to the Libyans of equipment in part of the above amount. We have had no indication as to whether the Libyans will be satisfied with the British appraisal. I believe that the United States should (1) agree immediately to the British proposal, and (2) at the same time decide in principle to supply the Libyans with further equipment up to the amount of $6.5 million should the need become apparent.[7] The latter decision should not be revealed to the Libyans but would be available as a basis for quick action if and when the need becomes apparent.

---

[5] Telegram 154 from Tripoli, October 7, reported Bin Halim's approach of that date to Ambassador Graham. Tappin believed that Bin Halim was still hoping for arms from the United States. (Department of State, Central Files, 774.56/10–755) The Czech-Egyptian arms deal was made public September 27.

[6] Tappin summarized his October 25 discussion with Bin Halim in telegram 178, October 27. Bin Halim claimed to have been rebuffed by the British and although he and the King preferred Western arms he was under pressure to accept or justify his rejection of the Egyptian offer. Tappin's feeling was that "for lack of a nail a shoe was lost, et cetera." (*Ibid.*, 773.56/10–2755)

[7] The Department of Defense agreed to the first recommendation and Tappin was instructed to join with Graham in informing the Libyans of this on November 15. (Telegram 168 to Tripoli, November 14; *ibid.*, 773.5–MSP/11–1455) As a consequence of the offer, the Egyptian offer was refused.

In view of the inroads the Soviets have made into Egypt through their arms play and other offers of assistance, I think it is particularly important to separate Libya from other Arab states which might be tempted to follow the Egyptian example. It is likewise important to place a barrier across the Soviet path into North Africa, for I am sure that any Soviet designs on Libya will be made with an eye to the larger game in French North Africa.

If you agree with me on the need and desirability of United States military assistance to Libya at this time, I would suggest that members of our staffs meet to determine the practical extent and form of military aid to Libya. I enclose for your information a memorandum prepared in the Department of State giving further facts on this matter. [8]

Sincerely yours,

Herbert Hoover, Jr. [9]

---

[8] Not printed. The Department of Defense responded on December 20 in a letter from E. Perkins McGuire, Deputy Assistant Secretary of Defense (ISA) for Mutual Defense Assistance Programs. He noted that any expenditure was impossible unless Libya signed a bilateral agreement as required by Section 142 of the Mutual Security Act of 1955 or the President specified such aid under the provisions of Section 401. He urged the Department of State to employ the second technique so that the $560,000 required in fiscal year 1956 could be made available. (*Ibid.*, 773.5–MSP/12–2055)

[9] Printed from a copy that bears this stamped signature.

---

149. Despatch From the Embassy in Libya to the Department of State [1]

No. 185 *Tripoli, November 30, 1955.*

SUBJECT

Libyan Exchange of Diplomatic Representatives with USSR and the United States Position in Libya

Summary:

The Libyan decision to exchange diplomatic representatives with the USSR was not made because of any feeling of friendship for Communism or support of the Soviets. Rather it was based on (1) a desire to refute charges that Libya is subservient to the West

---

[1] Source: Department of State, Central Files, 601.6173/11–3055. Secret.

and (2) the belief that Western aid to Libya would be increased if we felt that she might turn to the USSR for aid.

The Embassy feels that continued sporadic anti-Western acts and statements may be expected until the time comes when the Arab World as a whole has been convinced that to be anti-Western is not in itself proof of pro-Arabism. The Embassy is also of the opinion that a carefully considered and realistic analysis of our interests in Libya and the size of the investment we are willing to make to preserve them is essential. When this has been done, the Embassy recommends that we should make our assistance available slowly, using the hope of more as an incentive to keep Libya aligned with the West on major issues but not allowing ourselves to become unduly perturbed by generalized anti-Western statements.

The announcement on September 25, 1955, that the Governments of Libya and the USSR had agreed to exchange diplomatic representatives requires a review of the present trend of Libyan policy and its effect on the position of the United States in Libya. While it is probably too much to say that infiltration of Libya is, in itself, a primary target of the Soviet Union in this area, it is clear that Libya could be important as a means of extending Soviet influence westward across North Africa. Should Libya become a channel through which Communist subversion could be directed and supported in Tunisia, Algeria and Morocco and the usual nationalist and anti-imperialist slogans and agitation (as well as material assistance) used to keep the area in turmoil, NATO would, in effect, be outflanked. It is enough to recall the concern of the French Government at reports (fortunately false) that anti-French "terrorists" were being assisted from Libya to see the dangerous possibilities of the situation. This Embassy is, of course, not in a position to evaluate Soviet *intentions* with regard to Libya. However, on the assumption that the USSR desires to exploit North African unrest, it is essential to review the situation and consider counter-measures.

Obviously, if Libyan-Soviet diplomatic relations presage close and friendly ties between the two countries, the position of the United States here will be seriously undermined. It does not seem to the Embassy, however, that there is any chance that this will occur in the forseeable future. In fact, all indications are that the Libyan decision to agree to repeated Soviet suggestions that the two countries exchange diplomatic representatives was made on entirely different grounds.

In the first place, Libyan policy for the past year has become more and more openly one of maintaining a balance between the West (especially the US and UK) and the Arab League (especially Egypt). This is not a new policy, but during the first years of Libyan independence the political and economic realities made it essential that Libya's primary effort be directed toward stabilizing her relations with the US, the UK, and France and ensuring adequate foreign financial contribution to permit the country to survive economically. While not neglecting the Arab League, Libya found herself unable to take any great part in the consideration of League problems because her own immediate interests lay in negotiations with the West.

As a result of the conclusion of treaties with the UK and France and a Base Agreement with the United States, Libya thus became the target of accusations that she was a vassal of the West. Some of these accusations were based on her willingness to make concessions to the West, while others were founded on Libyan unwillingness (and inability) to do more than pay lip service to the two pet themes of Arab extremists—that Israel must be obliterated and that the French presence in North Africa must come to an end. This is one reason why Prime Minister Mustafa Bin Halim feels that he must make periodic statements (usually in Cairo) in which he plays down Libya's connections with the West and argues that Libya's interests are identical with those of the other Arab League States. In the present instance the whole Libyan Government, including the King, seems to have been under the impression that "proof" of Libya's independence of the West must be provided, and that the exchange of diplomatic representatives with the USSR would provide such "proof".

In the second place, it seems obvious that Libyan policy makers understand the fact that the West, especially the United States, tends to pay more attention to areas where there is an immediate danger of Soviet penetration. Moreover, there is a wide-spread impression that one good way to obtain assistance from the United States is to flirt with the USSR. For example, C. Pitt Hardacre, Principal Finance and Economic Adviser, has hinted slyly that Libya might have to turn to the Soviet bloc for assistance in financing the purchase and rehabilitation of the Tripoli power plant should no funds be forthcoming from Western sources. The Embassy is of the opinion that Libya expects that more attention from the United States and in all probability more assistance will be forthcoming as a result of this recent decision.

Other factors of less fundamental importance, including the King's naive explanation to Ambassador Tappin that having a Soviet Embassy would mean that the Communists would be in the open and could be watched more easily, were probably taken into consideration. Among these was the Libyan desire to obtain UN membership, previously blocked by a Soviet veto. It appears, however, that the major reasons for the Libyan decision were those described above: (1) a feeling that such an action would provide a needed "proof" of Libyan independence of the West and (2) the hope that increased assistance would accrue to Libya as a result of Western reaction to the Soviet threat. If this analysis is correct, the danger of active Libyan cooperation with the USSR is remote.

There is as yet no information available as to the form which Soviet diplomatic representation in Libya will take and the Libyan Foreign Office states that to date no request for agrément has been received. Until the size and nature of the Soviet diplomatic mission is known and it actually appears in Libya, it is impossible to evaluate the effect which Soviet activities will have. One obvious move would be the infiltration of potential saboteurs into Wheelus Field Air Force Base, and the Base Commander is already increasing security measures as a precaution.

To a very real extent, however, the long term Libyan attitude toward such operations as the USSR may attempt to initiate here will depend on the attitude and actions of the Western powers, particularly the US and UK. The Embassy is of the opinion that it is not only possible to prevent the USSR from establishing an advanced base in Libya (assuming that it desires to do so), but that it can be a relatively inexpensive operation. . . . , and a carefully considered and properly phased continuing program of military assistance to Libya should provide an effective barricade to Soviet penetration of the Libyan Army through . . . , as well as tying the Army to the West. Continued and expanded assistance to the Libyan Government in the training of police officers is another means by which direct action can be taken to forestall possible subversive activity. In the long run, economic and technical assistance on a realistic scale and an energetic information program should be adequate to prevent the growth of any large indigenous Communist movement. However, in all our thinking and planning it seems to the Embassy that we must keep in mind two important considerations: (1) The Libyan Government will continue to be influenced by criticism from the Arab League to the effect that it is subservient to the West and will take those steps it feels are necessary to refute this criticism. Recent examples of what may be expected are public statements in which Libya is pictured as having been the center of all anti-French activity in North Africa, and flurries of anti-Israeli editorial comment. In addition, we can expect some specific statements or actions tending to align Libya against the West. Until the

Arab World as a whole no longer believes that any anti-Western statement or act is of necessity pro-Arab, Libyan attempts to prove independence and "Arabism" can be expected to take this form. In the meantime, we should not be unduly alarmed by such activities so long as Libya remains a friend on the major issues.

(2) The Libyan Government will use every means in its power to persuade us to increase our assistance, whether it be technical, economic, or military. Flirtations with the USSR and confidential revelations of offers from the Soviets or their satellites or from other anti-West sources are one tactic which the Libyans will very probably use to obtain favorable action on their requests. One way to handle this type of maneuver would be to give the Libyans immediately anything and everything they request. Obviously this would be unwise, although not impossibly expensive simply because Libya's total needs plus her total desires are quite limited. A more realistic approach, and one which the Embassy endorses, requires that we first make sure in our own minds exactly how much we are willing to invest in Libya. Having done this, we should under no circumstances reveal our plans in toto to the Libyans. Rather we should move slowly but steadily, staggering our contributions over a period of time and using the hope of more as a "carrot", but not openly using the threat of reducing assistance. We can, however, tactfully point out on occasion the importance to Libya of continued cooperation with the West. The Embassy feels that this approach to our Libyan policy will produce the desired results, but the key to its success lies in constant attention to the problem of our position in Libya coupled with recognition of the fact that we must concentrate on obtaining Libyan cooperation on *major* issues.

For the Ambassador:
David G. Nes
First Secretary of Embassy

150. Telegram From the Department of State to the Embassy in Libya [1]

Washington, January 19, 1956—3:05 p.m.

280. Re your niact telegram 351 [2] and preceding telegrams on aid to Libya. [3] We have had this problem and your views under careful consideration. On specific items previously proposed (such as armored car gift, power plant assistance, $3 million MSA grant and grain relief) decision reached and separate telegram gives you details. On question of providing still further aid we will, within limits available resources and Congressional authorizations give Libyan needs appropriate attention.

However, US cannot place itself in position endeavoring compete with Soviet offers at every turn in road. For US respond as if by reflex action to such pressure would open us to endless blackmail; will eventually lose us real friendship, respect and influence; and is certainly not sound basis for US-Libyan cooperation.

We cannot invite Ben Halim to Washington at this time, since purpose his mission would inevitably be assumed to be acquisition large-scale US aid, with inescapable consequences whether we helped him or not.

We think it is now necessary for you to make clear to both King and Prime Minister exactly how the US views its cooperation with Libya. Unless, therefore, you perceive strong objection you should seek audience with King at once, with Ben Halim present if possible. If latter not feasible, you should arrange see King and Prime Minister independently. Your statement should be along following lines:

US takes its friendship with Libya seriously. Our attitude based on firm belief this fully reciprocated in Libyan attitude toward us. This reflected by policy of US, from birth of Libyan state to present, which has been based upon tenets of supporting sovereignty and independence of Libya, full respect its religion and culture, free association of Libya with West, and welfare of Libyan people. These

---

[1] Source: Department of State, Central Files, 773.5–MSP/1–1956. Secret; Niact. Also sent to Benghazi.

[2] Telegram 351, January 18, reported that Bin Halim had stated that Soviet offers of unlimited economic aid, in the absence of any concrete indication of U.S. "sympathetic consideration," were attractive to his Council of Ministers and Parliament. Tappin recommended that Bin Halim be invited to Washington so that he could mention it in his January 21 throne speech and thereby diminish criticism. (*Ibid.*, 601.6173/1–1856)

[3] In telegram 291, December 27, 1955, Tappin urgently requested positive consideration of various forms of aid to Libya. (*Ibid.*, 601.6173/12–2755)

principles have found expression in many forms including our assistance program.

By way of illustration this position, we have been considering with great care a number of specific problems which we know that Libya faces, and in which we may be able to be of assistance. We confidently expect to give the same kind of attention to other Libyan problems as they may arise. Thus we recognize the urgent need for wheat. To avoid delay, we expect 7.2 thousand metric tons to be on the way to Libya within next few weeks and we will continue review this need. We know needs with respect power plant in Tripoli, and, as an immediate measure, prepared concur use LARC[4] funds this purpose. We are also allocating the $3 million for general economic assistance this fiscal year. And, sympathizing with desire of Libya to strengthen its armed forces, we are not only joining with United Kingdom in acquisition mobile equipment but we would be willing to discuss additional military assistance in the near future. We are exploring this problem with UK.[5]

The United States has been watching pattern efforts Soviet Union undermine independent countries throughout world. Not unexpected, therefore, that once they succeed establishing diplomatic relations Libya they should arrive in large numbers, propose economic assistance, and if rumors correct raise questions of airstrips and other related matters. When one remembers that these steps under auspices of Molotov,[6] same person who proposed that Libya be assigned as trust territory to Soviet Union, eventual goals of Soviet Union self-evident.

We cannot, nor would it be our intention, to emulate Soviet Union, either in its irresponsible offers of aid or its deceptive motives. What we have done we would have done irrespective of Soviet presence. As in past, so we expect in future, to assist Libya in its various needs, and our goals will continue to be principles of Libyan independence and Libyan welfare. We have every confidence His Majesty and His Majesty's Government clearly perceive the implications of the Soviet offers and will not be misled by Soviet blandishments; that, aware of the true Soviet intentions, they will clearly discern the direction in which Libyan interests lie.

Dulles

[4] A Libyan-American Reconstruction Commission had been set up to help supervise U.S. economic assistance.

[5] British and U.S. officials discussed this matter on January 19. (Memorandum of conversation by Root, January 19; Department of State, WE Files: Lot 58 D 90, Middle East—1954–57)

[6] Soviet Foreign Minister.

151. Telegram From the Embassy in Libya to the Department of State [1]

Tripoli, January 19, 1956—4 p.m.

357. Accompanied by Colonel Cain and in presence permanent Under Secretary for Foreign Affairs Jerbi, I had one and one-half hour conversation with Prime Minister yesterday afternoon. After brief exchange amenities and discussion details concerning opening parliament, I opened substantive conversation by stating that, since arrival on local scene of Soviet diplomatic mission, rumors concerning Libyan intentions vis-à-vis Soviets were flooding Tripoli and coming to my attention and that for this reason I wished continue our past practice by having frank informal talk with him concerning US position under circumstances. Prime Minister replied by saying he welcomed opportunity and was prepared as always on basis our close personal association to talk with absolute frankness and candor.

I stated most serious rumor to reach me was that GOL might be contemplating extend Soviets right fly Libyan "air space", loans in connection with petroleum exploration concessions. Prime Minister categorically denied rumor had any foundation, adding that Soviet Ambassador had made no request for oil concessions or "air facilities" and that I could accept his "official assurance" that such privileges would not be granted even if requested. At this point on my invitation Colonel Cain gave full and precise explanation of implications of availability Libyan air space to Soviet aircraft.

In acknowledging validity Cain's position, Prime Minister added that Libya had made under his stewardship clear decision to side with West against Communist enemy and would under no circumstances compromise by any act this position.

However, Prime Minister continued, he was now in "impossible position" vis-à-vis his Council Ministers, Libyan Parliament and leaders other Arab countries because of failure US to recognize and meet Libyan requirements under "sympathetic consideration" provision. Soviets had offered both wheat and economic assistance "without strings" and in land where "one million people were destitute and balance one hundred thousand poor," he had no basis rejecting offers without clear evidence support of traditional allies.

---

[1] Source: Department of State, Central Files, 773.5–MSP/1–1956. Secret; Priority. Received at 2:32 p.m. on January 19. Repeated to London, Paris for Knight and Wallner, Rome for Maffitt, Cairo, Rabat for the 17th Air Force, Wiesbaden for Tunner, Bonn, Ankara, Baghdad, Beirut, Benghazi, Damascus, Amman, Tel Aviv, and Jidda.

At this point I interrupted with long dissertation on Soviet record over period 35 years as compared record of western powers, pointing to fact that basic question was one of fundamental intent. (And since I am probably only officer in foreign service whose father-in-law was Siberian slave camp inmate and who has spent six weeks in hospital as result direct Soviet action, I speak with a certain persuasion on this subject.) Even though Soviet offer was advertised as "without strings" and even though western democracies move somewhat ponderously, was there not moral question involved? Was it not clear that western powers sought only independence based on long range political stability and economic viability for Libya as friendly ally and was it not equally clear what Soviets always had as end with them. However political facts were political facts and he was in bad corner. Conversation then turned to more specific questions of relief wheat, economic assistance and arms assistance. Prime Minister reviewed his understanding of Washington conversation of July 1954 closing with roughly following words: "in Washington we were assured that it would not be necessary to haggle over details. In words of President Eisenhower, Libya would be new Philippines. As Libya's economic and military picture developed, sympathetic consideration would be given to her needs. If I could spend ten minutes with President Eisenhower, Mr. Dulles and Assistant Secretary Allen in Washington, I could convince them without trouble that US was failing to meet its moral commitments."

After much lengthy conversation concerning all aspects US assistance to Libya, which developed no new positions on either side, I attempted to sum up situation by asking Prime Minister if he could give me flat and unequivocal assurance which I could pass my Government that he did not contemplate and would not enter into any relationship with Soviets beyond normal diplomatic one and that he would limit activities Soviet mission to those normally performed by diplomatic missions. Specifically I asked if he would limit its size, refuse technical assistance, refuse economic assistance, refuse arms assistance, [deny?] permission to establish cultural or information center, prohibit operations of radio transmitter and strenuously resist subversive activities. Prime Minister's reply was that he would definitely limit Soviets to normal diplomatic activities with exception of economic assistance, which he might be "most reluctantly forced accept". He answered my specific points in each case in affirmative. As expected, he remarked as he had to British Ambassador that as final resort he might have to close all cultural centers.

Comment: This is necessarily sketchy account of long and often passionate conversation, but it omits no essential element. I am reporting in cable since time is of essence. Be assured that I gave full and concise explanation of US position and limitations as arsenal of and banker for free world and that my explanation of Soviet ambitions and techniques was full and persuasive. On Prime Minister's side, I am forced to conclusion that he feels he has bona fide grievance against US in terms our "failure" implement sympathetic consideration. Review Washington conversation July 1954 with Libyans makes clear that basic motivation which persuaded Libyans to sign base agreement without further bargaining was US promise on basis gentlemen's agreement give "sympathetic consideration meritorious economic needs in future years". Is it not fact that Libyans have received no assistance since then beyond that committed at time of signing? Is it not true that Libya is "show window" in which advantages of cooperation with free world can be displayed to Arab States to maximum advantage? . . . Is it not true that our honeymoon relations with Libyans have been best in entire Arab world? Can we safely contemplate throwing away all these advantages by protracted delays even though they may be attributable to essential slowness democratic processes?

Obviously, Libyans are bargaining. But can we logically expect them to do otherwise? And do they not hold strong hand? If we fail to meet their legitimate needs promptly, will we not later be faced with danger having to meet illegitimate needs on grounds international political competition? Personally I would be most reluctant to add Libya as permanent member of US list of public charges. But, if there are to be future US economic and military assistance programs, especially for Middle East, is there any state which we can more easily persuade to adhere to free world than Libya? Do you know of better bargain?

Tappin

152. Memorandum of a Conversation, Tripoli, January 22, 1956 [1]

PARTICIPANTS

Prime Minister Ben Halim, Government of the United Kingdom of Libya
Ambassador John L. Tappin, American Embassy, Tripoli
Colonel William J. Cain, Jr., Base Commander, Wheelus Field, Tripoli
David G. Nes, Deputy Chief of Mission, American Embassy, Tripoli

Following a small dinner party given at the Embassy residence in honor of the Ambassador's fiftieth birthday, Mr. Nes drew the Prime Minister aside to discuss with him the news from Washington re the release of economic aid, wheat, and perhaps arms assistance to Libya contained in Deptel 280 [2] and Icato 183. [3]

Mr. Nes asked the Prime Minister whether he was pleased with the information just received re economic, wheat and arms assistance and whether this information could not, in fact, be used to strengthen his internal political position. The Prime Minister said that he was pleased with two items—the wheat and the possibility of opening military staff talks re arms assistance. He was however disappointed by the figure of $3 Million in economic assistance which he described as constituting a failure on the part of the United States to live up to its commitment made during the Base Agreement discussions in Washington in July 1954. The Prime Minister reviewed his version of the latter discussions at some length and said that at the time Libya had been promised the $3 Million in economic aid for Fiscal 1955 but had been told that this was merely a "token" of good faith and that in future years the United States would consider sympathetically Libya's economic needs as they were substantiated in sound economic development projects. He and the Libyan delegation had thus been led to believe that future economic aid would greatly exceed the original $3 Million and had so informed Parliament at the time the Base Agreement was up for ratification. It was this assurance of "sympathetic consideration" which alone had enabled him to obtain Parliamentary ratification. Were he now to go to Parliament and say that he had obtained only $3 Million this year, he would be placed in an "impossible position".

[1] Source: Department of State, Central Files, 773.5–MSP/1–2556. Secret. Drafted by Nes. Enclosure to despatch 262, January 25. The substance of this discussion was also transmitted in telegram 368, January 24. (*Ibid.*, 773.5–MSP/1–2456)

[2] Document 150.

[3] Not printed.

Mr. Nes then said there were, however, a number of advantageous points which the Prime Minister should consider in connection with a grant of $3 Million. Briefly they were:

(1) An allocation of economic aid for Libya had been announced and released before that of any other Near Eastern country. The "special" position of Libya was thus recognized by Washington and there could be no question but that the United States considered Libya a trustworthy ally and friend and so had been able to release an aid figure prior to the termination of the present U.S.–U.K. discussions in Washington which were intended to establish a new U.S.–U.K. policy toward the Near East as a whole.

(2) The $3 Million was in effect an addition to the $4 Million committed as aid for this year during the Base Agreement negotiations, making a total of $7 Million. On a per capita basis, this amount would, Mr. Nes assured him, compare favorably with that given any other country.

(3) The $7 Million in economic aid was after all only a part of overall United States assistance to Libya which included gift wheat, technical assistance, and now arms aid, the total value of which would probably this year exceed $10 Million and thus equal the British financial contribution.

(4) Economic development projects took time to get underway and their cost was usually minimal during the first year or so. Therefore, it was doubtful whether Libya could absorb this year more than she was receiving from the U.S. and U.K.

Ben Halim said these arguments were perhaps sound in theory but that from a practical standpoint he would like to comment upon them in order.

(1) Receiving an allotment prior to the other Near Eastern countries might in reality result in a disadvantage, for once Libya had been "taken care of" the other countries would probably share in the remainder of the available funds in direct proportion to the threat of their Soviet penetration. He would therefore have preferred waiting to receive Libya's share until the allotments for the other Near Eastern countries, particularly Egypt, had been determined.

(2) During the Washington discussions a figure of $3 Million over and above the $4 Million Base "rent" had been referred to as a "minimum" and he had been assured future aid would greatly exceed this amount.

(3) He could not possibly consider gift wheat as a part of economic assistance since he had always presented it to the Libyan people as an humanitarian relief measure undertaken by the United States to alleviate famine conditions. Secondly, Libya had not yet received the few arms promised her; and finally, American technical assistance, although effective in providing jobs for Americans, had had little impact on Libya.

(4) Although it might be true that Libya could not absorb more than $7 Million this year, it was nevertheless impossible to plan economic development unless a commitment to finance an entire development plan was at hand. Libya must know what she can

count on from the U.S. before embarking upon actual projects, the cost of which will mount in future years.

At this point Ambassador Tappin and Colonel Cain joined in the conversation and Ambassador Tappin, in addition to reviewing the four points already made by Mr. Nes, stressed the fact that American legislative procedures made it virtually impossible for us to plan ahead insofar as economic development programs were concerned since aid had to be appropriated on a year-to-year basis. The Ambassador said that this entire problem was now under discussion at the highest levels in Washington with the Eisenhower Administration strongly favoring a system whereby the U.S. could make commitments for future years and thus enable their friends and allies to embark on long-range economic programs. Until this issue were settled there was nothing whatsoever that could be done about it and it was thus a question of faith and trust in the ultimate intentions of the U.S. He personally did not feel that the U.S. would ignore the economic needs of its friends in future years and although it was not possible to give any specific or firm assurances with regard to Libya, the Prime Minister would have to rely on the good intentions of the United States in the future. With respect to the Prime Minister's criticism of LARC, the Ambassador said that the purpose of LARC was to wisely allocate to projects U.S. aid funds but that, once allocations were made, it was the sole responsibility of the action agencies of the Libyan Government to execute the projects. Mr. Nes then pointed out that of the five major projects in which the Prime Minister had evidenced interest when LARC was set up, funds for two had already been transferred—namely the National Bank and Agriculture Bank, that funds for the third, the Tripoli Power Plant, were available for transfer as soon as agreement had been reached between the Libyan Government and the present ownership, and that with respect to the fourth and fifth projects—namely the Benghazi Harbor and Fezzan Road—the necessary preliminary surveys were under way and actual construction must necessarily await their completion. The Prime Minister admitted that this was true but said that in the first three cases the projects were not truly "development projects" and that all LARC had done was to "transfer funds".

Ambassador Tappin, in reiterating his thesis that Libya must choose between the U.S. and the Soviets on the basis of their respective long-range intentions toward Libya rather than on strictly money terms, said that Russian economic aid offers, although seemingly attractive and without strings, were made solely with a view to eventual subversion. After further lengthy discussion of Libyan economic requirements the Prime Minister arranged an appointment with the Ambassador for noon the next day and excused himself from the party.

Although an effort was made by both Ambassador Tappin and Mr. Nes to extract from the Prime Minister the latter's ideas as to the amount of economic aid he would consider acceptable, the latter would not commit himself on the subject but did make an indirect reference to a figure approximating the British annual contribution—i.e. $10.5 Million. It was evident he was thinking in terms of the Libyan Five Year Public Development and Stabilization Plan, whose total cost is estimated at $65 Million.

---

153. Telegram From the Department of State to the Embassy in Libya [1]

Washington, February 2, 1956—7:33 p.m.

304. Department studying problems raised your recent messages re situation Libya created by Soviet offers and apparent lack determination Libyan leaders to pursue policies affording adequate assurances continued cooperation with West and protection Libya against Soviet penetration.

As you surmised in Embtel 371 [2] permanent solution these problems must be based on long-term, area-wide policies designed to counter new Soviet threat. Our understandable unwillingness respond to intense pressure should not cause Libyans assume we do not care whether Soviet offers accepted and Russians permitted enter Libya in large numbers. On other hand because of implications going far beyond Libyan problem, we cannot afford give Libyans impression we prepared outbid Russians and that all Libya has to do is name price for its undertaking to turn down Soviet offers (which Ben Halim seems recognize would be against Libya's ultimate national interest).

In Deptel 280 [3] Department sought find acceptable course between foregoing extremes to guide you in reacting to Libyan pres-

---

[1] Source: Department of State, Central Files, 773.5–MSP/1–2656. Repeated to Benghazi and by pouch to London and Paris.

[2] Telegram 371, January 26, suggested that strategic considerations conceivably justified treating Libya as a special case. Ambassador Tappin requested permission to be more forthcoming in promising additional economic assistance to Libya. Otherwise he foresaw Libya's acceptance of the Soviet offer. (*Ibid.*)

[3] Document 150.

sures. We set forth extent to which commitments could now be given to Libyans regarding specific American aid. We had in mind putting this to Libyan leaders in such manner as to indicate neither (a) that US frantically seeking placate Libyans by offers which would not have been made in absence Soviet moves; nor (b) that offers were on take it or leave it basis. Regardless of whether US might later determine it possible and feasible increase aid to Libya, most essential element in present situation is recognition by Libyans that it would not be in their national interest or consistent with their efforts maintain Libyan independence and sovereignty if they should be misled by Soviet blandishments and fail recognize obvious purpose of Soviet move.

Department fully appreciates fact you view present situation with deep concern and are striving energetically to put forward recommendations which in your judgment might meet problem. While, as stated above, what we do in Libya must be carefully weighed in light implications elsewhere, we believe it possible, assuming some reasonableness on part of Libya, work out understanding re aid that will reassure both sides as to need, timing and effectiveness. Would be extremely helpful if you could return Washington as soon as convenient to participate discussions this matter. Travel orders being telegraphed separately.

Important that purpose your visit Washington not be taken as connoting anything more than routine consultation. Certainly Libyans should not be given basis for belief visit will produce substantial additional aid, which, when it failed materialize, would cause severe disappointment. For same reason hope you can avoid pleas for additional aid from Libyans.

Before departure you should hold discussion with King along lines Deptel 280. (To avoid any possibility confusion, you may wish have your own interpreters present.) [4]

Department will discuss with you in Washington your suggestions re US participation in joint "working party" suggested Embtel 381 [5] as well as question your attending Libyan cabinet meeting.

---

[4] Telegram 414, February 13, summarized the Ambassador's February 11 discussion with the King. Idris repeated that Libya's establishment of diplomatic ties with the Soviet Union had been designed to show the nation's independence. Tappin brought up the Soviet aid offer. The King's response was that the logical answer was sympathetic consideration by the West of Libya's needs in the form of concrete assistance. He promised to discuss the matter with the Prime Minister. (Department of State, Central Files, 123–Tappin, John L.)

[5] Telegram 381, January 30, reported the substance of a meeting between Tappin and Bin Halim. The Ambassador raised the possibility of a roundtable conference between himself, Embassy, USOM, and Wheelus Field representatives and the Libyan Prime Minister and Cabinet members. Tappin noted his disillusionment that Libya would even contemplate a flirtation with the Soviets. Bin Halim recognized the good

(Continued)

Suggest these meetings not be held at least until after your return Tripoli. Decision re your proposal Sahili visit Washington also deferred.

Dulles

(Continued)
intentions of the United States but maintained that Libya required an adequate response to present needs. Tappin recommended to the Department that Finance Minister Ali al-Sahili be invited to Washington as a first step in giving serious consideration to Libya's Five-Year Plan. (*Ibid.*, 773.5–MSP/1–3056)

154. Telegram From the Embassy in Libya to the Department of State [1]

Tripoli, February 7, 1956—2 p.m.

400. Further to Embtel 399, [2] I must emphasize that viewed from here hinge of Deptel 304 is "assumption some reasonableness on part of Libya." Issue clearly set forth paragraphs 2 and 4 reference telegram has been emphatically and repeatedly presented to Ben Halim by me in terms that leave no room for doubt concerning US position. Basic questions therefore are:

(1) What is Ben Halim's true intent?
(2) To what extent is his hand being forced by his Ministers and Parliament?
(3) To what extent is he using "opposition" as bargaining device increase amount US aid?
(4) To what extent is threat to deal with Soviets his own tactic?
(5) To what extent are his Ministers and Parliament threatening force him deal with Soviets?
(6) Does Ben Halim enjoy full support of King in contemplating deal with Russians or is King unaware extent dangerous flirtation already in process?
(7) To what extent is King in process voluntarily abdicating much of his power to central executive?

In seeking answers above questions, following background must be kept in mind:

[1] Source: Department of State, Central Files, 773.5–MSP/2–756. Secret. Repeated to London, Paris, and Benghazi.

[2] Telegram 399, February 7, expressed Tappin's agreement with the instructions contained in telegram 304, *supra*. (Department of State, Central Files, 773.5–MSP/2–756)

(1) Ben Halim in connivance with Egyptians brought about establishment diplomatic relations with Soviets concealing plans from friendly allies and planting with King transparent and invalid justifications. There no justification for Libyan-Soviet diplomatic relations beyond Soviet desire penetrate North Africa and Libyan willingness strengthen bargaining position even by dangerous move.

(2) Ben Halim maneuvered King into ridiculous marriage with Egyptian, using necessity for male heir as subterfuge. Given King's inclination towards monogamy, warm 25-year relationship between King and Queen Fatima, aging record of Queen Alya it clear that Egyptian-inspired maneuver was purely political attempt compromise King's position. King may or may not now recognize this fact. (In any event, he has ignored Alya for many months, leaving her contrary all Arab customs in Tripoli while he resides in Tobruk with Fatima.)

(3) Essential nature recent throne council law construed by qualified observers here as clear indication King prepared see Libya abandon constitutional monarchy upon his death.

(4) All diplomatic mission chiefs here with whom I can talk confidentially are convinced that Ben Halim especially since recent elections is bloated with power and possessed of insatiable appetite.

It is my personal evaluation that we are dealing in Ben Halim with something close to "split personality", dangerously intelligent, opportunistic, young, shrewd and ambitious both for political power and personal gain. . . . Yet when he states his conviction that Libyan long-range future should be tied to west, particularly to US, and begs as "champion of US position in Libya" (with considerable justification) for augmented dollar assistance as measure of "sympathetic consideration" for essential Libyan economic developmental needs, he is most persuasive. Thus it appears to me absolutely essential that we force his hand by participating in international effort survey Libya's true economic development requirements as described in closing paragraphs Embtel 381. [3]

In fact, before receipt Deptel 304, Ben Halim had already proceeded with establishment informal "working party" including representatives GOL, LPDSA, [4] UNO, LARC and Embassy. [5] Stated purpose this survey is obtain on urgent basis more accurate documentation and validation in "balance-sheet" form Libya's true economic development difficulties than currently available, for exposure all her friends. There is no real or implied commitment that US will close gap. It is solely long-needed realistic appraisal. Will of course

[3] See footnote 5, *supra.*

[4] The Libyan Public Development and Stabilization Agency was created in 1952 to supervise programs financed by British funds.

[5] Telegram 410, February 11, noted that Bin Halim had set up a working group of U.S., U.N., and Libyan officials which met for the first time on February 7. The latter indicated their requirements through 1961 came to $118 million, of which $76 million remained to be secured. (Department of State, Central Files, 773.5–MSP/2–1156)

take precaution to personally brief US representatives to make clear our "no commitment" position.

Real gains this process would be following:

(1) Get away from politically-conceived and unsubstantiable "five year plans" and loose bargaining figures picked from air like recent $5 million request; or

(2) "Corner" Prime Minister by forcing him submit Libya's developmental requirements to realistic review by international "working party";

(3) Put on paper for first time balance sheet Libya's needs in terms her absorptive capacity;

(4) Bring into being set of figures which will reveal how many of Libya's demands are economically demonstrable and how many are purely politically motivated;

(5) Force Prime Minister accept set of specific figures as true basis for discussion with own government and with US of Libya's needs, in order emerge from the present unhealthy situation in which we are in effect being told that we must for political reasons give Libya in economic assistance an amount greater than an unknown amount which the Soviets are willing to offer.

(6) Provide concrete basis for possible subsequent discussion with King specifically concerning Prime Minister's attitude toward US assistance offers in terms demonstrable Libyan needs and demonstrable US assistance.

If working party finds (as is distinctly possible) that Libya's true current developmental needs are in fact being met by contributions from several friendly foreign sources, we will have spiked Ben Halim's gun or given him ammunition with which to repel assaults from his Cabinet and Parliament. If on other hand working party finds that reasonable developmental needs are greater than total current outside assistance, Libya's Western Allies would at least have in hand vital measure of vulnerability to Soviet offers, regardless of whether or not we were able or willing close gap.

Tappin

155. Memorandum From the Representative at the United Nations (Lodge) to the Secretary of State[1]

Paris, March 5, 1956.

Here is the picture of U.S.-Libyan relations as one sees it in Libya:

1. Wheelus Base in Tripoli, Libya, is a $100 million installation which is vital to the defense of the United States. It is what Strategic Air Command calls a "post-strike" base, meaning that it is a base where the bombers would land for rest and refueling after having accomplished their mission. It is the only "big field" within a six hundred mile radius of Tripoli. It is a vital training area for gunnery and rocketry for the aviators of NATO. Its use by the United States is not only vital to our defense, but the use of the area for a similar purpose by the Soviet Union must obviously be denied.

2. The Soviets have established diplomatic relations and are making offers of technical and economic assistance, the purpose of which must be assumed to be to pry us out of North Africa.

3. The Libyan Prime Minister says the Libyan people are much attracted by these offers, that the United States has not done what it said it would do to help Libya get on its feet economically, and says in effect: "How about it?"

4. In this situation Wheelus Base is obviously the prime counter—if not the hostage.

5. The officers at the Base say that they cannot "tolerate" Soviet overflights—not because of the information which the Soviet flyers would learn, but because of the ease of their "rolling out" a bomb.

---

[1] Source: Department of State, Central Files, 711.56373/3–556. Top Secret. Enclosure to a letter from Lodge to Dulles. Lodge, who had been to Libya to inspect U.N. technical assistance activities, sent copies of this memorandum to George Allen and Francis Wilcox. Two days earlier he had addressed a letter on the same subject to the President. (*Ibid.*, 611.73/3–356) On March 5, he sent a memorandum on the subject of a "Proposed United States Reaction to New Soviet Tactics to Penetrate Africa by Technical, Economic and Political Means," advocating the necessity of occasional "flashy" projects to produce good will. Further, he insisted on the importance of speed in providing aid and thought long-term arrangements a wiser and cheaper course to follow. Although he did not expect them to concur, he suggested that the Soviets be invited to join with the United States in multilateral aid programs under U.N. auspices. (Eisenhower Library, Whitman File, Administration Series, Lodge, Henry Cabot 1956)

In a memorandum for the President from the Acting Secretary dated March 13, Lodge's suggestions were considered and substantial agreement was expressed with the points he made. The value of "impact" projects and the wisdom of long-term arrangements were recognized. The Acting Secretary promised to consider an approach to the Soviets, but also expressed interest in studying the desirability of U.S. participation in multilateral programs. (Department of State, FOA–ICA Files: Lot 61 A 32, Near East and Africa)

When I asked whether a refusal to "tolerate" meant that they would open fire on a Soviet plane, I was answered in the negative, but was told that the presence of a Soviet plane over the Base would result in American flyers being ordered up to fly alongside of it and watch it.

6. The integrity of our tenure of this Base could also be jeopardized if the community in which Wheelus Base is located became infiltrated by Soviet agents. More than 2,000 Libyans work at the Base every day. If there were Soviet agents among these employees and if Soviet planes were coming and going to neighboring parts of Libya, the security of the base would be weakened.

7. In the agreement which the United States has with the Libyan Government there is no provision that the Libyans will forbid Soviet overflights—an oversight to say the least.

8. We need such an agreement to protect Wheelus Base and, if present plans to acquire other military areas in Libya are to be carried out, there should be similar understandings. These should also be on a broader agreement covering Soviet activities in general.

9. In the early part of the century the U.S. bought the Virgin Islands from Denmark so as to deny their use to the Germans for coaling stations. While obviously we cannot buy Libya, we should make up our minds how much we are willing to pay to achieve the above vital assurances.

10. What we have obtained in Libya so far seems not to have been expensively obtained—$40 million over a twenty-year period, with an additional $3 million in development assistance and a promise to "consider sympathetically" Libya's further economic needs. The Libyans insist that they were led to believe during the negotiations that this latter phrase meant that we would stand by them until they got on their feet economically. In particular, Prime Minister Ben Halim says that President Eisenhower told him that he hoped that Libya would, as far as the United States was concerned, be in the Middle East what the Philippines were to the United States in the Far East. On two separate occasions Ben Halim made a point of this.

Aside from the installment of the $40 million and the additional $3 million mentioned above (totaling $12 million) the only aid given to Libya by the United States has been (a) 45,000 tons of famine-relief wheat, (b) technical assistance in the amount of $1.5 million a year (not in cash), (c) United States contribution to the United Nations technical assistance program. Following upon the Czech-Egyptian arms deal when the Egyptians offered arms to Libya, the United States and the United Kingdom promised equipment for an armored car squadron. The United Kingdom has delivered its share; the United States share, when delivered, will amount to about

$600,000. It should be noted that a "sympathetic consideration" offer of $3 million by the United States for development assistance in November, 1955, was not accepted by Prime Minister Ben Halim in the belief (stimulated by the apparent [2] success of Egypt's unfriendly tactics towards the United States) that he would get more by waiting.

11. Here, as in the Sudan, the Aswan High Dam Project has had a tremendous repercussion. The Libyan reaction is that if Egypt could get so much U.S. help by being nasty, maybe they (the Libyans) should start getting nasty, too.

12. We certainly cannot get into a contest to outbid the Soviet Union. There is no end to that and it would lead us to being blackmailed in other Arab countries—notably Morocco when it gets free and where there are so many U.S. bases.

13. But we should make up our minds to pay something more than we have if, by so doing, we get a settlement covering matters which are vital to the integrity of our Base. It is believed that a settlement could be obtained now which would get us what we want if:

(a) we provided additional economic assistance for the Libyan development program at a figure to be negotiated somewhere between $25 million and $50 million, being a six-year program (see Annex). [3]

(b) if we provided famine-relief wheat on a continuing basis to the extent required by circumstances.

(c) if we provided technical assistance to the extent required to support the development of the program.

(d) if we provided equipment in cooperation with the British for 5,000 men in the Libyan Army.

If oil is discovered in Libya—which many qualified persons seem to expect—it will probably be very difficult to get any kind of agreement out of the Libyan Government at all.

Here then are the questions which we face and which must be studied:

I. What is it worth to us to have the Libyans agree to forbid Soviet aviation in the area of Wheelus Base and to agree not to accept Soviet assistance or countenance general Soviet activity?

II. Should not the NSC paper of 1952 [4] giving the United Kingdom the paramount interest in Libya be restudied in view of the fact that the United States Strategic Air Force is certainly

[2] The word "apparent" was added to the source text in an unidentified handwriting.

[3] Not found attached.

[4] Not further identified. The last Progress Report on NSC 19/5 dated April 30, 1951, which called for a united Libya tied to the United Kingdom, is printed in *Foreign Relations*, 1951, vol. V, p. 1318.

paramount over British army bases in the light of the military realities of the present time?

III. Should Libya be admitted to NATO in view of its obviously vital importance for the training of all NATO aviators, and its vital role in NATO military operations—or should a West Mediterranean organization be created?

IV. Should the United States seek a *treaty* with Libya which would in effect agree to exclude the Soviet Union and its satellites in exchange for a cash grant? Exclusion of the USSR would be attractive to the Senate.

H.C. Lodge, Jr.

---

156. Letter From the Deputy Under Secretary of State for Political Affairs (Murphy) to the Ambassador to Libya (Tappin) [1]

Washington, March 13, 1956.

DEAR MR. AMBASSADOR: Upon your return to Tripoli you are instructed to inform the appropriate authorities of the Libyan Government that the United States Government has considered the Prime Minister's letter of February 17, 1956, setting forth Libya's estimate of its economic development requirements: [2]

1. That within the general framework of this estimate the United States Government is prepared to grant before July 1, 1956 economic aid to Libya in the amount of $5,000,000;
2. That the United States Government is prepared to ship to Libya before July 1, 1956, 5000 tons of relief wheat in addition to the 7200 tons now in the process of being shipped, thereby raising to 25,000 tons the amount of relief wheat furnished in the United States fiscal year 1956;
3. That the United States Government is prepared, subject to legislative action by the Congress, to make available $7,000,000 in economic aid to Libya between July 1, 1956 and June 30, 1957;
4. That the United States Government is prepared to consider in accordance with law the provision of up to 25,000 tons of relief wheat to Libya between July 1, 1956 and June 30, 1957;
5. That these actions are being considered by the United States Government in implementation of its commitment of 1954 to give

---

[1] Source: Department of State, Central Files, 773.5–MSP/3–1356. Secret. Tappin was in Washington for consultation.

[2] This was a covering letter to the list of projects devised by the working group, which had been set up earlier in the month. (Telegram 434 from Tripoli, February 18; *ibid.*, 773.5–MSP/2–1856)

sympathetic consideration to the economic needs of Libya in the light of the traditional friendship between the two Governments and in the light of the progress already made;

6. That the United States Government will continue in the future to determine under its commitment of 1954 the extent to which it can contribute to the economic development of Libya after Fiscal Year 1957 and that the actions of the Libyan Government as well as the progress achieved in economic development will continue strongly to influence the decision of the United States Government;[3]

7. That the United States Government is prepared between July 1, 1956 and June 30, 1957 to provide equipment, subject to legislative action by the Congress, to assist the Libyan Government to expand the Libyan Army to the extent of 1000 men as may be considered necessary after a United States military survey team has evaluated the requirements; and that the United States Government is sympathetic with Libya's needs in relation to internal security and will hope to continue to cooperate in this field;[4]

8. That the United States Government is in the process of determining whether it will construct a new road from Wheelus Air Force Base to Tripoli; and

9. That the United States Government will assist the Libyan Government in endeavoring to ascertain means of financing the expansion of the Tripoli power plant through loans.

You are requested also to inform the appropriate authorities of the Libyan Government, as a matter of instruction from your Government:

1. That the United States Government does not underestimate the mutual importance of the firm friendship and understanding now existing between the two Governments but needs reassurances concerning the present attitude of the Libyan Government in this regard;

2. That the true purpose of American aid to Libya is and has been to advance the day when Libya can stand on its own feet economically;

---

[3] In a memorandum to Murphy of March 12, Hollister indicated his view that paragraph 6 should be excluded, as well as the clause in the last paragraph which reads "that in subsequent years achievements and needs under the Six-Year Plan will be taken into account along with other factors in assessing Libyan requirements." According to Murphy, Hollister agreed, however, that this was a political decision resting with the Department. (*Ibid.*, 773.5–MSP/3–1256)

[4] On February 10, the President determined that U.S. security interests demanded that up to $560,000 of funds made available under Section 401 (b) of the Mutual Security Act of 1954 (P.L. 665 of August 26, 1954; 68 Stat. 832), as amended, should be utilized in accordance with Section 401 (a) of the Act to provide military aid to Libya. (Letter from Hollister to Richards, February 17; *ibid.*, 773.5–MSP/2–1756)

In a memorandum to the Secretary of Defense, March 8, the Joint Chiefs of Staff noted that, since U.S. airbases in Libya were essential for the effective implementation of U.S. war plans and operations in the Middle East and other areas, a small U.S. military survey team should be sent to Libya to study and prepare recommendations concerning the development of effective Libyan armed forces. (JCS Records, CCS.092 U.S. Assistance to Other Countries (8–22–46) (2) Sec. 25)

3. That the United States does not believe that the Government of Libya would endanger this type of friendship and continuing cooperation for the untried and unknown;

4. That decisions regarding American aid to Libya have been rendered more difficult by the Libyan Government's relating the question of additional aid to the matter of Soviet offers;

5. That the Libyan Government should understand that the position of the United States Government in this regard cannot be influenced by such considerations. The decisions of the United States Government have, however, been based on the assumption that the Libyan Government would not be willing to jeopardize its independence and collaboration with the free world by accepting such Soviet offers, which obviously have not been made to enhance the independence and integrity of the Libyan State;

6. That the United States Government, before concluding agreements concerning the foregoing, will wish to know what measures the Libyan Government plans to adopt with a view to curbing the size and activities of the Soviet diplomatic mission in Libya. For example, the United States Government will wish to know what policy the Libyan Government will follow in respect to a) offers of technical, economic and military assistance; and b) requests for permission to establish cultural centers or information offices, for permission to operate radio transmitters, and for petroleum concessions in Libya with the concomitant right to establish airstrips and operate aircraft; and

7. That the United States Government considers it necessary under paragraph 2 of Article III of the Base Rights Agreement that the Libyan Government establish a reserved air space surrounding Wheelus Air Force Base to insure the security of United States forces and property in Libya.

In the course of your discussions with the Libyan Government, you will wish to make it clear that the United States Government should not be considered as having assumed a responsibility to finance the Six-Year Plan in whole or in any assured part; that the United States Government will require further detailed information about the Six-Year Plan to determine how American aid in the Fiscal Years 1956 and 1957 can be effectively used; that in subsequent years achievements and needs under the Six-Year Plan will be taken into account along with other factors in assessing Libyan requirements; that the United States Government assumes that the Libyan Government will apply to its economic development, along with other friendly outside assistance, the grants-in-aid forthcoming under the French and Italian treaties; and that in relation to military aid it will be necessary to conclude an agreement pursuant to Section 142 of the Mutual Security Act, as amended.

Sincerely yours,

Robert Murphy[5]

[5] Printed from a copy that bears this typed signature.

157. Memorandum of a Conversation, Tripoli, March 22, 1956, 3:30 p.m.[1]

PARTICIPANTS

Mustafa Ben Halim, Prime Minister and Minister of Foreign Affairs of the United Kingdom of Libya
Suleiman Bey Jerbi, Under Secretary of Foreign Affairs of the United Kingdom of Libya
John L. Tappin, American Ambassador to Libya
David G. Nes, Counselor of Embassy, American Embassy, Tripoli

Ambassador Tappin and the Embassy's DCM, David G. Nes, met with Prime Minister Ben Halim at the latter's home shortly following a luncheon party given there in honor of the British Secretary of War, Mr. Anthony Head.

Ambassador Tappin stated that he had now received detailed instructions from Washington in response to the Prime Minister's letter of February 17, 1956 and that in accordance with them he was now prepared to discuss implementation of the formula suggested by the Prime Minister during his meeting with Mr. Nes on March 7 (Embtel 475).[2] The Ambassador then outlined the seven items of assistance which the United States Government was prepared to extend to Libya (Subject I of attached memorandum).[3] With respect to the first item, additional economic aid in the amount of $5 million for 1956, Ambassador Tappin stressed the fact that this was the figure twice suggested by the Prime Minister himself, during their

[1] Source: Department of State, Central Files, 773.5–MSP/3–2456. Secret. Drafted by Nes. Enclosure to despatch 327, March 24.

[2] Telegram 475 from Tripoli, March 29, reported Bin Halim's assurance to Nes that Libya was not trying to "blackmail" the United States. Bin Halim suggested that Ambassador Tappin should provide him with private assurance of U.S. financial support, which would enable him publicly to reject the Soviet offer. Thereafter, he would proceed to Washington to conclude the needed arms and economic accords, which he would proclaim upon his return home. (*Ibid.*, 873.00/3–856)

[3] Not printed; see Murphy's letter, *supra*.

after-dinner conversation of January 22, 1956, and at a conference in the Prime Minister's office the following day (Embtel 368 and Despatch 262),[4] as one which was economically valid and politically feasible. The Ambassador also expanded slightly on Item 7, concerning arms assistance, by stating that an increase of 1,000 men was established in light of Libya's internal budget limitations and the availability of necessary officer material.

When the Ambassador had completed his outline of the United States assistance offers, Mr. Nes said he would like to point out that according to the best calculations of the American Embassy economic staff, the additional economic assistance proposed would enable the Libyan Government to proceed with an economic development program and that, in fact, the funds available through fiscal 1957 were slightly in excess of those required during this initial period to get such a program properly under way.

Ambassador Tappin then informed the Prime Minister of the basis on which the United States was able to contemplate continued assistance to Libya, including the five points contained in Subject II of the attached memorandum.[5]

Using as an opening gambit the desire of the United States Government for reassurances concerning Libya's general attitudes towards her friendship with the United States, the Ambassador next stated that he would expect the Prime Minister to make either a public statement in Parliament answering Deputy Zugallai's question re Soviet offers or a statement to the press independent of Parliament clearly rejecting them (Subject III of the attached memorandum). This would fulfill the promise given to Mr. Nes on March 7 by the Prime Minister (Embtel 475) and would constitute the second step in the Prime Minister's formula.

The Ambassador then explained that additional United States assistance had been based on certain assumptions, namely that Libya would implement the verbal assurances given to the Ambassador and the Wheelus Air Force Base Commander, Colonel Cain, by the Prime Minister on January 18 (Embtel 357)[6] with respect to his relations with the Soviet Union. The United States Government desires that these assurances be formalized in a written exchange of letters. The seven points to be covered (Subject IV of the attached memorandum) were then explained to the Prime Minister.[7] Ambassador Tappin pointed out in addition that these assurances would

[4] See footnote 1, Document 152.
[5] See Murphy's letter, *supra*.
[6] Document 151.
[7] See Document 159.

necessarily have to apply to Soviet satellite countries as well as to the USSR itself (Subject V of the attached memorandum).

The Ambassador also said that the economic and arms assistance proposed would of course be covered by the usual agreements, as would the gift of famine relief wheat (Subject VI of the attached memorandum).

After reading Subject VII of the attached memorandum dealing with additional military facilities, Ambassador Tappin said that the decision of the United States Government, although necessarily based on budgetary and military considerations, would also be based of necessity on a confidence that Libya would provide a suitable political climate over a long-term period.

The Prime Minister, who had taken notes throughout the above presentation, stated that he would reply point by point.

Although he would necessarily require time for full consideration of everything Ambassador Tappin had said, his first reaction to the economic aid offers was that they were eminently fair and demonstrated the good will of the United States toward Libya. His own words were: "I can now stand up and defend my policy of orientation to the West, which I wish to continue". After Ambassador Tappin had expressed his satisfaction with the Prime Minister's reaction, the latter reiterated: "I like this offer." Ben Halim then went into an impassioned defense of his tactics vis-à-vis the United States and stated that he had been "gambling", not because of disillusionment with the United States failure to implement "sympathetic consideration", but because of Libya's real and urgent need for economic development funds. He had always been aware of United States good will and had never intended to threaten or blackmail the United States with Soviet offers. Neither had he ever wished to change Libya's basic policy of orientation to the West. Libya was, is, and would continue to be a loyal friend. He had never intended to accept a Russian or "any other" offer of assistance. He did not trust or like the Russians. Had the temper of Parliament been such as to have forced acceptance of the Russian offers, Ben Halim stated he would have first resigned.

The Prime Minister then discussed the nature and extent of Egyptian pressure which had been exerted on him in an attempt to force him to accept the Soviet offers. Although Egypt had not made an "official" offer of economic or arms aid, Ambassador El Faki on instructions from Nasser had recently made a verbal démarche. . . . Digressing for a moment, the Prime Minister then referred to the Arab League and said that he thought Libya had made a great mistake in entering the League without "conditions", since Libya's interests in many cases were not identical with those of the other Arab States.

Ben Halim then turned to the meeting of Parliament and said that he intended to hold a secret meeting on March 27 (since the formal opening of the National Bank would take place the 26th) at which he would answer Deputy Zugallai's question regarding Soviet offers by saying that Libya had in the past received full economic and political support from the United States and United Kingdom, that he had every reason to believe such support would continue and would satisfy Libya's needs, and that he would not therefore risk any association with the untried and unknown. Ben Halim explained that he wished to make his reply in secret session so that he could elaborate in detail on certain subversive activities in which the Soviet Embassy was already engaged and so that he could be frankly critical of the Soviet record in other areas. He would then ask for a vote of confidence, which he felt he would receive with only two or three dissenting votes. The next day the local press would announce that the Libyan Government had received a vote of confidence on its policy of rejecting the Soviet offers.[8]

With regard to written assurances on the seven points in which the United States was interested, Ben Halim said he could give his oral commitment on all of them with the exception of Point 7,[9] which seemed to limit Libya's right to accept aid from anyone (such as her sister Arab states) other than the United States and United Kingdom. Mr. Nes interrupted to say that this was not the intention and that the United States was only opposed to those offers of assistance specifically designed to compromise United States-Libyan relations. The Prime Minister then suggested that a formula might be devised which would take this factor into consideration and would emphasize that the "intent" of the offer would be the governing factor. As to putting these assurances into written form, Ben Halim pointed out that such a document would require Cabinet approval and that this might be difficult, since the Cabinet would immediately conclude that United States aid was conditional on written assurances limiting Libya's sovereignty. Ambassador Tappin interrupted at this point to say that there was certainly no intention on the part of the United States to make its aid "conditional" and that what was being discussed in effect was merely a statement of Libyan policy "as it in fact is". Such a statement would therefore be in accord with the assumptions as to that policy on which our extension of assistance was necessarily based. Mr. Nes pointed out also that, whereas the United States would never question the Prime

[8] The text of the speech he intended to deliver was transmitted in telegram 549 from Tripoli, March 24. (Department of State, Central Files, 873.00/3–2956)

[9] It reads: "That Libyan acceptance of economic, technical, and military assistance offers from other states will be limited to those which do not endanger U.S.-Libyan relations."

Minister's "oral" assurances, Prime Ministers were essentially temporary spokesmen for their governments, as Ben Halim surely recognized, and that therefore a written expression of the Libyan Government's policy was necessary from the long-range viewpoint. The Prime Minister replied by saying that he would like to have more time to consider the form of such a letter of assurances and requested that Mr. Nes meet with Under Secretary Jerbi the next week to work on a draft. [10]

Ambassador Tappin then brought the conversation to a close by saying that he was certain his Government would be very gratified by the constructive attitude of the Prime Minister. The Ambassador mentioned that he would like to go to Tobruk to pay a courtesy call upon the King as soon as convenient. It was agreed that he and the Prime Minister would fly over together within the next week or ten days.

[10] The terms of the U.S. aid offer were spelled out in a letter from Tappin to Bin Halim dated April 4. (Department of State, Central Files, 773.5–MSP/5–456)

158. Memorandum of a Conversation, Tobruk, April 5, 1956 [1]

SUBJECT

Conversation with King Idris, April 5, 1956, Part I

Accompanied by Prime Minister Mustafa Ben Halim, Ambassador Tappin called on King Idris in Tobruk on April 5, 1956, to discuss with him the program of U.S. economic assistance to Libya and Libyan policy in connection with Soviet activities within the country. Colonel William J. Cain, Jr., Commanding Officer of Wheelus Air Force Base, and First Secretary Rodger P. Davies of the Embassy's Benghazi office were present.

His Majesty, who appeared in good health, received the Ambassador warmly. After appropriate greetings, the Ambassador spoke of his recent visit to Washington and of the sympathetic interest in Libya's problems he had found among officers of his Government. The recent decision of His Majesty's Government, under its capable

[1] Source: Department of State, Central Files, 873.482/4–1082. Secret. Drafted by Davies. Enclosure 1 to despatch 346, April 10. Enclosure 2, not printed, was a memorandum of Part II of the conversation, which considered the Near Eastern and North African situations and radio communication equipment.

caretaker the Prime Minister, to recognize Soviet offers of assistance as part and parcel of an effort to undermine good relations of the countries of the Near East and Asia with the United States and to reject these offers would most certainly confirm the confidence of the United States in the sincerity of Libya's past affirmations of friendship.

The Ambassador said that Libya was the first country in the area to recognize officially the real basis of Soviet economic policies. In addition to serving as a reaffirmation of Libyan integrity and loyal support for the free world, this would also serve to make Libya better known and admired among the general public in the democratic world.

As His Majesty was aware, the Ambassador said, economic assistance offered by the United States to Libya preceded by many years the Soviet campaign and changes in the program recently discussed with His Majesty's Government were not related to Soviet offers but were a result of the agreement in Washington in 1954 to consider sympathetically forms of economic assistance which eventually would enable Libya to stand on her own feet. Libya's needs had been reviewed carefully and increased assistance seemed warranted by Libya's progress. While the Ambassador was certain that the Prime Minister had familiarized His Majesty with details of the United States offer for this and the coming year, he stood ready to answer any questions His Majesty might wish to raise about details of the program.

The Prime Minister translated this to the King and in addition gave him a run down of the new program which was as complete an inventory as if he had read from a memorandum.

The King replied that he was familiar with the program from the Prime Minister's discussions with him the previous week and it was pleasing to him. His Majesty said that Libya's rejection of Soviet offers was in no way related to the new U.S. program; that Soviet offers would have been rejected in any case because he did not trust the Russians. He had confidence in his friends in the West and he hoped that they had equal confidence in Libya. He praised the Ambassador for his assistance in interpreting Libyan policies to the U.S. Government.

The Ambassador said that members of the Prime Minister's staff and of his own staff were drawing up secret notes reaffirming the policies of the two Governments. While they would be classified, he was certain that those in both Governments who saw them would realize the strength of mutual confidence existing between the two. The Prime Minister translated this and, in addition, recalled to His

Majesty the details of the proposed notes. His Majesty replied that he was familiar with the texts and approved of them.[2]

The Ambassador then said that Mr. Davies had informed him when he boarded the plane in Benghazi of a cable from Washington which said that strategic conditions and the favorable political climate in Libya were such that the Department of Defense had requested the Department of State to enter into discussions with the Government of Libya for expanded military facilities.[3] In translating this, the Prime Minister informed the King that the Government of the United States was willing to discuss construction of a new base *in Cyrenaica*. The Ambassador continued that in expanding military facilities it would seem to be in Libya's interest to have facilities in Cyrenaica so that the economic benefits in terms of employment and increased purchases of commodities would be better balanced as between Tripoli and Cyrenaica. The Ambassador also recalled that His Majesty had several times suggested construction of facilities in Cyrenaica in discussions with such visitors as former Air Secretary Talbott[4] and General Tunner.

His Majesty seemed genuinely pleased and remarked that he had told various American officials that Cyrenaica was the logical place for construction of facilities since the danger was "from the East." He said that in addition to the economic benefits which Libya would welcome, the United States would gain strategically in that "the Russians are now almost our neighbors." (His Majesty obviously meant that the Soviets were penetrating through Egypt. His remark was accompanied by a hearty laugh). His Majesty said he accepted the principle of additional U.S. military facilities and would be pleased if they could be in Cyrenaica.

His Majesty excused himself for the mid-day prayers and then entertained the group plus Buseiri Shalhi, Nazir of the Royal Household, at luncheon. His Majesty's remarks on other subjects are summarized in a separate memorandum.

---

[2] For text of the Bin Halim note, see *infra.*

[3] Instructions on this matter were sent to the Ambassador in telegrams 433, 462, and 472, March 25, April 3 and 5, respectively. (Department of State, Central Files, 711.56373/3–2556, 4–256, and 4–456)

[4] Harold E. Talbott visited Libya in April 1955. Documentation on his trip is *ibid.*, 033.1100–TA and 711.56373.

159. Letter From Prime Minister Bin Halim to the Ambassador in Libya (Tappin)[1]

No. 334/Aleph/16 *Tripoli, April 20, 1956.*

EXCELLENCY: I have the honor to refer to your letter of April 20, 1956, in which you stated that your Government desired reassurances concerning the present attitude of the Government of the United Kingdom of Libya with regard to the firm friendship and understanding which has always existed between our two Governments.[2] You stated further that your Government's position with regard to aid to Libya could not be influenced by considerations arising from offers of aid from other sources but that your Government's decisions concerning assistance to Libya which were mentioned in the two notes which were exchanged between us April 4[3] had been based on the assumption that the Government of the United Kingdom of Libya would not be willing to place in danger its independence and collaboration with the United States by accepting offers from sources whose intent is to damage the relations between the Government of the United Kingdom of Libya and the Government of the United States of America.

The policy of my Government, as I have already informed Your Excellency on numerous occasions, most recently on January 18,[4] and March 22, 1956,[5] has been and will continue to be a policy of free voluntary and independent cooperation with the Government of the United States of America and the Free World. This has been the policy of Libya since its independence and your Government may rest assured that it will continue to be so.

In our conversation of January 18, 1956, referred to above, you inquired concerning certain aspects of the policy of the Libyan Government which are of paramount importance to the Government of the United States of America and to the preservation of the spirit and intent of the Agreement Between the Government of the United States of America and the Government of the United Kingdom of Libya, signed at Benghazi on September 9, 1954. I wish to confirm to Your Excellency my statement of the position of the Libyan Government with regard to these points in order that there may be no

[1] Source: Department of State, Central Files, 661.73/5–756. Enclosure to despatch 378, May 7.

[2] Tappin's note, which discouraged any Libyan turn to the "untried and unknown", was also an enclosure to despatch 378.

[3] Enclosures to despatch 372 from Tripoli, May 4. (Department of State, Central Files, 773.5–MSP/5–456)

[4] See Document 151.

[5] See Document 157.

possible misunderstanding of the Libyan Government's position in this regard.

The Government of the United Kingdom of Libya, when it agreed to exchange diplomatic representatives with the Union of Soviet Socialist Republics, did so in keeping with its sovereign right to conduct its foreign affairs in the manner it deems most desirable. It is my understanding that your Government in no way questions the sovereign right of the Libyan Government to take this action, but that your Government is concerned lest the Soviet Embassy undertake activities which might endanger Libyan-American relations or the security of the American military installations and operations in Libya. The Libyan Government does not propose to permit any foreign power to disrupt relations between it and the United States and you may reassure your Government as follows:

(1) The Soviet Diplomatic Mission in Libya will be required to restrict its staff to normal size and activities.

(2) The Union of Soviet Socialist Republics will not be permitted to open an information center or a cultural center in Libya.

(3) The Soviet Embassy will not be permitted to establish or operate a radio transmitter.

(4) The Libyan Government will not grant a petroleum concession in Libya to the Union of Soviet Socialist Republics.

(5) The Union of Soviet Socialist Republics will not be granted any access to Libyan air space.

Naturally the above policy will also apply to those countries which are satellites of the Union of Soviet Socialist Republics or whose policies are directed by the Union of Soviet Socialist Republics.

I wish further to inform you that the Libyan Government has rejected the offer of assistance which the Union of Soviet Socialist Republics recently offered and that the Libyan Government's policy is that acceptance of any other offers of economic, military or technical assistance will be limited to those which do not endanger Libyan-American relations.

Mustafa Ben Halim [6]

---

[6] Printed from a copy that bears this typed signature.

160. National Intelligence Estimate [1]

NIE 36.5–56 *Washington, June 19, 1956.*

THE OUTLOOK FOR US INTERESTS IN LIBYA [2]

The Problem

To estimate likely developments in Libya over the next few years and their impact on US interests, particularly base rights.

Conclusions

1. Provided the ailing 66-year-old King Idriss remains at the head of the government, Libya will probably be able to maintain a precarious political stability over the next few years. However, political immaturity, factionalism, and rivalry between the provinces will be continuing problems for the foreseeable future. The death or incapacitation of the King would remove Libya's principal unifying force and probably precipitate a complex internal struggle for power, with intensified competition for influence between Egypt, the USSR, the UK, and other foreign powers. (Paras. 12–13, 17, 19–21, 28–29)

2. Premier Ben Halim is not popular and his tenure remains largely dependent on royal favor and support. However, he will probably succeed in strengthening his political position, and if still in office on the death of the King, will seek to assume full control. (Paras. 14–15, 18–20)

3. Unless current and projected oil explorations prove extraordinarily successful, Libya will remain heavily dependent on foreign

---

[1] Source: Department of State, INR–NIE Files. Secret. Files of National Intelligence Estimates, Special Estimates, and Special National Intelligence Estimates, retained by the Directorate for Regional Research, Bureau of Intelligence and Research.

National Intelligence Estimates (NIE's) were high-level interdepartmental reports presenting authoritative appraisals of vital foreign policy problems. NIE's were drafted by officers from those agencies represented on the Intelligence Advisory Committee (IAC), discussed and revised by interdepartmental working groups coordinated by the Office of National Estimates of the Central Intelligence Agency (CIA), approved by the IAC, and circulated under the aegis of the CIA to the President, appropriate officers of cabinet level, and the National Security Council. The Department of State provided all political and some economic sections of NIE's.

According to a note on the cover sheet, "The following intelligence organizations participated in the preparation of this estimate: The Central Intelligence Agency and the intelligence organizations of the Departments of State, the Army, the Navy, the Air Force, and The Joint Staff. Concurred in by the Intelligence Advisory Committee on 19 June 1956. . . . The Atomic Energy Commission Representative to the IAC and the Assistant Director, Federal Bureau of Investigation, abstained, the subject being outside of their jurisdiction."

[2] Supersedes the Libyan section of NIE–54, "Probable Developments in North Africa," 31 August 1954. [Footnote in the source text. For text of NIE 71–54, see *Foreign Relations*, 1952–1954, vol. XI, Part 1, p. 153.]

assistance to pay for essential imports and to meet governmental expenses. (Para. 16)

4. Libya's foreign policy is likely to be ambivalent. The king tends to be pro-US, but his principal advisers and possible successors, including Ben Halim, are more opportunistic. Despite Libya's dependence on US and UK financial subsidies, it is sympathetic with the anticolonial and anti-Western feelings of the Arab world, and is subject to extensive Egyptian influence. Libyan leaders fear Egyptian domination and suspect Egyptian intentions, yet they will cooperate with Egypt in various policies, some of which are hostile to Western interests. However, at least as long as Idriss is in control, Libya is unlikely to join the ESS Arab bloc. (Paras. 12–30)

5. With respect to Soviet relations, Ben Halim has recently rejected, and has promised to reject in the future, Bloc offers of technical and economic assistance.[3] Nevertheless, he or his successors will almost certainly again use any future Bloc offers as bargaining counters to gain concessions from the US and UK. As time goes on, the Libyan government will probably be increasingly tempted to follow through with some deals with the Bloc, particularly if the principle of dealing with the Bloc becomes generally accepted in the area. Although the Libyans will probably continue to be restrained by fear of alienating the US and UK, and thus prejudicing the continued receipt of substantial Western assistance, they will probably go as far in the direction of deals with the Bloc as they think the traffic will bear. Should future US–UK aid fall substantially short of expectations, or should Idriss depart from the scene, the likelihood of Libyan deals with the Bloc would increase. (Paras. 31–34)

6. There are unlikely to be any serious moves toward the repudiation of US base rights so long as King Idriss remains in power. However, retention of US base rights in Libya is likely to become increasingly costly and troublesome. There is likely to be increasing nationalist opposition to base concessions, which might lead initially to demands for a reduction in the present degree of US control over these bases. Moreover, in the confused situation which would probably result from the king's death or retirement, while a continuation of US base rights would not be precluded, the difficulties and risks would be increased. (Paras. 38–42)

7. In view of the authoritarian character of the regime and the low level of popular political consciousness, we consider it unlikely that the local security of US bases will be seriously threatened within the next year or two at least. (Para. 40)

[Here follows the "Discussion" section of the paper.]

---

[3] See *supra*.

161. Telegram From the Embassy in Libya to the Department of State[1]

Tripoli, November 22, 1956—1 p.m.

357. Time has come when I feel you must give personal attention to recent decision of Export-Import Bank in refusing application Westinghouse International for ten million dollars credit finance dollar costs of rehabilitation of Tripoli electric power system.

I can only describe Deptel 315[2] received by me November 17 as "bombshell". I consider it abrupt and discourteous handling of one of most sensitive political issues in Libya today. Department action in forwarding this cable to me without comment is totally inadequate. Libyan Government officials, in particular Prime Minister, had every reason suppose loan would be processed favorably. Negotiations have been proceeding for many months. US funds have already been invested through Libyan-American Reconstruction Commission in acquisition of ownership of plant by GOL. Plant is living on borrowed time and could break down any day, completely crippling economic and social life of community.

Representatives of major American oil companies here have been informed of decision and are as incredulous and horrified as I am. Most unfortunately Libyan Prime Minister also learned of decision from Westinghouse vice president before I could head him off.

Although Libyan public opinion has veered towards Soviets on basis recent events, I have been able hold Libyan Government as island of pro-western sentiment on basis President's speech of October 31,[3] my personal prestige and skillful political maneuvering by staff this Embassy despite insufficient support from Department. Libyan Prime Minister delivers Throne speech at Parliament opening in presence of King Monday November 26. Soviets are making usual irresponsible offers here and I dread thought that they may learn of latest opportunity we have presented them on golden platter. As Ambassador in Libya I can tell you frankly that I would not blame Libyans one bit if they were to react to this newest example of US

---

[1] Source: Department of State, Central Files, 873.20/11–2356. Secret; Eyes Only; Niact.

[2] Telegram 315, November 16, informed the Ambassador that Westinghouse's loan application on behalf of the Libyan Government for a $10 million credit to finance the expansion of the Tripolitania Electricity Corporation had been turned down by the Export-Import Bank due to Libya's inadequate repayment ability. (*Ibid.*, 873.2614/11–1656)

[3] This was a radio and television report to the American people in which the President opposed the invasion of Egypt. See *Public Papers of the Presidents of the United States: Dwight D. Eisenhower, 1956*, pp. 1060–1066.

bumbling by encouraging or accepting Soviet offer. We would not even be entitled to view as blackmail.

I have previously and emphatically expressed my feelings this subject in Embtel 350.[4] In order protect stake of US Government and private American oil companies in Libya I urgently request, before noon November 25, authority tell Prime Minister US Government urgently considering question of power plant including possibility direct US Government loan.

I feel I must add one general comment. Our broad policies on Middle East in recent months have been good and well-expressed. However any policy can be vitiated by negativism in implementation. I realize I have stated basis my case strongly and frequently but remember Trojans ignored Cassandra and Troy fell.

Tappin

[4] Telegram 350, November 19, described the power plant as political and economic necessity for Libya and a political necessity for the United States. If the Export-Import Bank refusal was final, Tappin advocated an ICA loan. (Department of State, Central Files, 873.2614/11–1956)

162. Telegram From the Department of State to the Embassy in Libya[1]

Washington, December 17, 1956—7:27 p.m.

393. In light present situation Libya including 1) reported Soviet and Egyptian military offers and other indications interest[2] 2) criticisms US inactivity re commitments and 3) uncertainty re UK position Libya,[3] Department and Defense agreed we cannot delay implementation FY 57 MDA program for Libya until after we talk to UK. While recognizing disadvantages divided responsibility, doctrine, training and equipment for Libyan Army, State–Defense nevertheless agreed we should proceed soonest supply US equipment and furnish

[1] Source: Department of State, Central Files, 773.5–MSP/12–1756. Secret; Noforn. Drafted by Palmer, approved by Murphy, and cleared by Gray. Repeated to London and Paris for Knight and Wallner.

[2] Telegram 355 from Tripoli, November 22, reported that the head of the British military training mission had learned the Soviets had offered to equip and maintain the Libyan army at a level of 10,000 men. Previously Libya had requested that the British train an expanded Libyan military force. (*Ibid.*, 773.5–MSP/11–2256)

[3] The British involvement in the invasion of Egypt had led both the Libyans and the British to reassess the British military presence.

US training to meet US commitment re 1000 men.[4] This procedure also has advantage placing US in position assume additional responsibilities in event subsequently determined UK unwilling or unable discharge responsibilities in manner calculated assure Libya's pro-Western orientation.

We would propose inform UK our decision proceed rapidly carry out our commitment for 1000 men with US equipment and training, adding that we recognize this will create problem of divided responsibility re Libyan Army which we desire discuss with them in wider context present Libyan situation and other US and UK plans and programs. We would propose such talks be held London early January with US representation from State, Defense, Embassies Tripoli and London, Wheelus and CINCEUR.[5]

After ascertaining UK intentions Libya, we would then be in better position make our own assessment UK capabilities and decisions re whether we desire continuation situation which will then obtain of divided responsibility Libyan Army or whether US should begin progressively assume entire responsibility. Talks would also cover Air Force and Navy problems, UK-Libyan Treaty and similar related problems.

Foregoing FYI and comments only. We shall instruct soonest when Tripoli can inform GOL re approval program (Deptel 371),[6] program content and tentative shipping schedule and when London can broach UK FonOff.

Dulles

---

[4] A memorandum for the Secretary of Defense by General Maxwell Taylor, on behalf of the Joint Chiefs of Staff, dated December 4, emphasized the JCS view that dividing the training and advisory responsibilities between the United States and the United Kingdom was militarily unsound. The JCS proposed an early accord with the British which would provide for an increase of 1,035 men in the Libyan army to be trained and equipped by the United States. Furthermore, it urged that over time the United States should assume those roles for the entire army. (Department of State, AF/AFI Files: Lot 62 D 406, Miscellaneous)

[5] Telegram 4472 to London, December 28, repeated an approach by the British Ambassador to the Secretary of State on December 24 to suggest an exchange of views on Libya at the working level. The Department favored holding such informal talks in London in January. (*Ibid.*, Central Files, 773.5–MSP/12–1956) See Document 165.

[6] Telegram 371 to Tripoli, December 8, stated that on or about December 15 the Department hoped to have a picture of worldwide military aid assistance requirements for fiscal year 1957. (*Ibid.*, 773.5–MSP/12–856) Congress had cut the appropriation and thus all of the prospective programs had to be reviewed.

163. Letter From the Ambassador in Libya (Tappin) to the Deputy Assistant Secretary of State for Near Eastern, South Asian, and African Affairs (Palmer)[1]

Tripoli, January 1, 1957.

DEAR JOE: This is my New Year's present to you. It is the first really important letter that I have written you and, if you can find time to think it over carefully, you may even conclude that it is one of the most important letters that you have received in some time. It originally set out to be a cable, but it was soon obvious that it would be too long for such treatment.

For most of the slightly over two years that I have been Ambassador to Libya, I have been conscious of the fact that there were great opportunities for positive diplomacy in this country. . . . The existence of such a circumstance depended upon the overplaying of their hands by the Egyptians and Soviets. Both of them have done so and the Libyans, who are intensely realistic, have now come to realize that their interests, both ideological and material, can best be served by facing in a new direction.

This is not to say that the Libyans are prepared to abandon their fundamental Arabism; however, it is to say that they would now like to become a part of that part of the Arab World, North Africa, which seems to be progressing towards a brighter future through logical relationships with the West.

It is my impression that the greatest handicap that Libya has had to overcome, in the thought processes of officials of the United States Government, is the fact that she is a very poor country, populated by a largely illiterate people who number only 1,150,000, and having but 2% of her land arable. This has led many in Washington to suppose that Libya was not worth much time or thought. Actually, quite the contrary is the truth. The sheer fact of her pressing needs makes Libya a veritable bargain basement, where extraordinary values can be had at a very low cost.

It is my duty to make Washington see what we all see here and to find the words and methods of persuasion that will cause Washington to respond to the great opportunity presented by current Libyan developments. To accomplish this, I must count on you and so you are the first one whom I have set out to persuade.

Begin persuasion (this is where the original cable would have begun):

[1] Source: Department of State, AF/AFS Files: Lot 62 D 406, Miscellaneous. Secret; Official–Informal.

From Tripoli it is clear that the U.S. Government is moving positively in several fields to make the most of the opportunity presented by a sharp Libyan shift in a Westward direction. I am not too modest to state that this shift represents a major political triumph for this Embassy. It also represents an important achievement for overall U.S. foreign policy. It was directly caused by the soundness of the U.S. position on Middle East issues in recent weeks and by a strenuous and successful application of personal diplomacy in Tripoli. The net result is most encouraging to all of us here, but you must realize that we are figuratively as well as literally "on the spot."

The fact which disturbs us most is this: While all U.S. relations with Libya—diplomatic, military, economic and informational—are handled on a team basis and directed towards the achievement of the stated objective of enabling Arab Libya to act in its own best sovereign interests, regardless of geographic location and membership in the Arab community, we suspect that in Washington the several principal elements of Libyan-American relations are being handled to a considerable extent in separate compartments. Since the "country team" approach has proved such an effective instrument for policy formulation and implementation here, could not Washington form a similar body under your Chairmanship (as discussed with me by Deputy Under Secretary Murphy last March) to backstop the Libyan program and act on Embassy recommendations? This Embassy understands that specific elements of the U.S. program in Libya must be handled by appropriate U.S. Government agencies, but the inexperienced Government of Libya tends to view the U.S. Government as a single coordinated entity. In reorienting its national policies along lines it is confident we will approve, the Government of Libya supposes that U.S. policy for Libya in final analysis is no more nor less than the sum of its parts and that at some point that policy can be identified and effectuated as a single entity.

The following is a quick list of major items of U.S. assistance to Libya currently under consideration:

1) Assistance in the establishment of an adequate Federal Armed Force (Embtel 429); [2]

2) Assistance in eliminating Egyptians from the educational system (Embtel 444); [3]

---

[2] Telegram 429, December 21, reported that Bin Halim had recently informed Tappin that Libya would like to have the United States assume the entire arms burden for the country. (*Ibid.*, Central Files, 773.56/12–2156)

[3] Telegram 444, December 31, called for ICA financial assistance to Libya to make possible the replacement of Egyptian teachers who were viewed as a dangerous influence. (*Ibid.*, 873.43/12–3156)

3) Financing the rehabilitation of the Tripoli power system (Embtel 440); [4]
4) USOM/L staffing requirements (Embtel 426); [5]
5) The Wheelus Field–Tripoli Road (Embtel 243); [6]
6) The level of development assistance for FY 58.

Admittedly, all of the above bear dollar signs, large in Libyan terms but small in terms of positive U.S. gains possible here. In round figures, a real job can be done here for about $15.8 million this fiscal year and $23.1 million in FY 1958. The attached breakdown [7] shows roughly where the money would go and what segments of the program are already part of our firm commitments. These sums are not large even if we received in exchange only a strong position in Libya. However, I am still wed to the "show-window" concept and convinced that the benefits of an exemplary set of US-Libyan relations would spill over into North Africa on the one hand and the Arab League on the other. But the important fact, worth repetition, is that Libya in preparing to permanently orient her policies Westward must be able to depend upon sympathetic U.S. support in a material as well as a moral sense.

Another major element of U.S.-Libyan relations which must be discussed separately from the foregoing list is the expansion of U.S. military facilities in Libya. I urge strongly that the closest liaison be maintained in Washington between those responsible for establishing defense requirements and those responsible for backstopping Libyan political programs. This Embassy naturally is not in a position to evaluate the military necessity for expanded facilities here, but we can state without fear of contradiction that *if* the necessity exists and *if* the U.S. Government makes a reasonable effort to meet Libyan political reorientation halfway by providing an adequate basis for economic development, then this is the best place in this part of the world to acquire additional facilities *right now.*

Recent developments in Libyan-Tunisian relations, [8] highlighted by the forthcoming visit of the Prime Minister to Tunis, clearly

---

[4] Telegram 440, December 29, discussed the difficulties involved in trying to finance the power plant rehabilitation. (*Ibid.*, 873.2614/12–2956)

[5] Telegram 426, December 21, urged that approval be given to the request for U.S. technicians at a level higher than ICA seemed willing to fund. (*Ibid.*, 773.5-MSP/12–2156)

[6] Telegram 243, October 25, justified such a road on military, economic, political, and public relations ground and noted that it would eliminate a dangerous driving condition that often produced problems. (*Ibid.*, 711.56373/10–2556)

[7] The attachment, a table of estimated aid to Libya for fiscal years 1957 and 1958, is not printed.

[8] A friendship treaty between Libya and Tunisia was signed on January 6, 1957, and ratified on May 11. An English translation of the operative portion of the treaty was provided in despatch 245 from Tunis, January 14, 1957. (Department of State, Central Files, 672.731/1–1457)

foreshadow closer relations between Libya, Tunisia and Morocco, with Algeria obviously a fourth candidate for membership in an eventual North African "combination." This Embassy has long advocated the validity of a "Southern Tier Concept" trying together through coordinated programs the independent states of North Africa with the Sudan and Ethiopia, not as a military combination, but as a combination of countries which can be drawn into closer relationships with the United States and the West by purely economic and political tactics. The basic strategy would be to prove to the Afro-Asian world that reciprocal friendship with the United States is mutually beneficial. The above evolution has already begun and the main question is simply whether or not the U.S. will have enough imagination to assist in and benefit from the process.

In the light of all of the foregoing and of all we have been reporting from here by letter, cable and despatch for a couple of years, it is not [*now*?] abundantly clear that we have been granted a real opportunity to establish, at a very low cost, an exemplary set of relations with an Arab country, one that will assure us a great psychological victory throughout the Afro-Asian World at the same time that it assures the maintenance of our strategic military position here? Has any Arab country given a clearer or more deserving indication of its intention to cast its lot with us? Is not this opportunity great enough to warrant an extraordinary effort by Washington? Can't we get away from the pennypinching and the delays? Can't we cut the red tape? Can't we snatch a bargain when we see one? Add up the total cost of *generous self-stimulated* and *prompt* action on the various types of assistance currently under consideration for Libya and ask yourself where else you could buy similar political and military advantages for a comparable price. I just cannot bring myself to believe that Washington officialdom is so busy or so blind or that this Embassy has been so deficient in its presentation that the opportunity is not thoroughly apparent.

With kind personal regards and looking forward to seeing you in London,

Sincerely yours,

John L. Tappin [9]

P.S. By the way, all the recommendations in this letter will exacerbate Nasser.

. . . .

---

[9] Printed from a copy that bears this typed signature.

164. Letter From the Deputy Under Secretary of State for Political Affairs (Murphy) to the Assistant Secretary of Defense for International Security Affairs (Gray)[1]

Washington, January 8, 1957.

DEAR GORDON: I wish to refer to Mr. McGuire's letter of December 19, 1956 forwarding a copy of the Joint Chiefs of Staff's memorandum of December 4[2] concerning United States military assistance for Libya.

This Department has given careful attention to the recommendations of the Joint Chiefs and is concerned about the political consequences of this Government acting on the basis of recommendation 4.c. "that an early agreement be reached with the United Kingdom which would provide that . . . [3] the United States progressively relieve the United Kingdom of all responsibility for equipping and training the Libyan Army". As you know, the British make a considerable contribution to the Libyan economy and budget and extend equipment and training assistance to the Libyan Army. They also maintain a number of defense facilities within Libya and have a treaty of alliance with that country. While it is quite clear that the British position in Libya has deteriorated as a result of recent events in the Middle East, the extent of that deterioration is by no means certain and the possibility would still appear to exist that they can maintain a position of influence which will serve our interests in the area provided they pursue policies and programs designed to rehabilitate their position. From a political point of view, we continue to attach importance to the British position in Libya, both in terms of the financial and other contributions they make to that country and of the added strength which they are capable of providing the Western position in this part of the world.

In the light of these considerations, we feel that it would be politically unwise for this Government to take any initiative to assume any major British responsibilities in Libya unless it becomes clear that the British are unwilling or unable to discharge those responsibilities in a manner compatible with our own and other Western interests. The talks in London will provide us with the opportunity to ascertain British intentions and thereby place us in a position better to assess their capabilities for carrying out their policies and progress. We believe it important politically that we

---

[1] Source: Department of State, AF/AFI Files: Lot 62 D 406, Miscellaneous. Secret. Drafted by Palmer and attached to a memorandum from Rountree to Murphy dated January 5.

[2] See footnote 4, Document 162.

[3] Ellipsis in the source text.

utilize this opportunity to urge them to discharge their responsibilities. Should it develop, however, that they are either unwilling or unable to do so, we shall then face the decision as to which of their obligations and responsibilities we may have to assume, including that of the Libyan Army.

Because of these uncertainties in the British position and of the political importance of being in a position rapidly to implement our military assistance commitment to the Libyans, this Department, however, believes that we should assume a partial responsibility at this time for the Libyan Army. We therefore concur in recommendation 4.a. of the Joint Chiefs that the 1035 man increase in the Libyan Army should be equipped with U.S. material. With respect to recommendation 4.b. that the United States assume responsibility for training the 1035 men, this Department also concurs but feels that this should, at least for the present, be implemented in such a way as to minimize conflict with existing British training responsibilities. In conversations between our two Departments, we have suggested that this might be solved by the United States confining its training responsibilities to instruction in the use of U.S. equipment furnished under the program, but leaving tactical instruction of the 1035 men to the British training mission. I hope that the Department of Defense can give urgent consideration to this suggestion as a basis for reaching an understanding with the British on our respective training responsibilities.

I recognize that the foregoing views of this Department are at variance with the views of the Joint Chiefs that the establishment of a Military Assistance Program for Libya with divided training and advisory responsibilities between the U.S. and UK is unsound from a military point of view. From a political point of view, however, such an arrangement would appear as the only practical alternative.

This Department has also noted the views of the Joint Chiefs that no requirement exists at this time for a Libyan Air Force or a Libyan airborne unit. While recognizing the military judgment of the Joint Chiefs on this point and while also agreeing on the undesirability of such units from the point of view of the Libyan economy, we nevertheless wish to reserve our position on this matter in the light of a possible overriding political requirement for such assistance.

Sincerely yours,

Robert Murphy [4]

---

[4] Printed from a copy that bears this typed signature.

165. Telegram From the Embassy in the United Kingdom to the Department of State [1]

London, January 15, 1957—9 p.m.

3773. Pass ICA/W. Libyan talks opened morning January 15 with Kirkpatrick, Permanent Under Secretary Foreign Office, presenting UK position. He indicated UK reappraising foreign policy throughout the world with a view to refashioning UK commitments into pattern more consonant with current British economic and financial limitations. He spoke with particular feeling about financial and manpower burdens presently carried by UK . . . and expressed UK resentment that UK carrying heaviest burden any European power both in NATO and elsewhere. . . . In summary, UK economic survival now required realistic tailoring external commitments re resource availabilities.

Against this background Kirkpatrick turned to Libya. He indicated that from point view strictly UK defense interests, value of Libya as base diminishing steadily. As Russian influence in Egypt and Syria increases British becoming increasingly concerned with necessity securing its interests in Iraq and Persian Gulf, with Libya becoming marginal by comparison. UK appreciated, however, that West in general has important strategic and political stake in Libya which might be further secured should Ben Halim idea for North African confederation advance into reality. At same time Soviet threat to Egypt and Syria raises question re security Libya and, in UK eyes, underlines its marginal utility. UK as member of the Western community nevertheless prepared continue assist in Libya but only to extent permitted by her straitened economic and financial circumstances.

US representatives responded by politely emphasizing their assessment that Western interests in Libya of greater importance than indicated by UK. US has fixed military installation there which could not be readily duplicated elsewhere. United States has also noted with interest present trend towards development North African grouping friendly to West. We emphasized importance danger to NATO flank should Libya come under Soviet influence. United States, therefore, considers Libya highly important not only from viewpoint our installation there but also from viewpoint entire Western community. United States representatives indicated United States appreciation United Kingdom contribution to defense free world and sympathy its financial position but stressed United States

[1] Source: Department of State, Central Files, 773.5–MSP/1–1557. Secret; Priority; Noforn. Repeated to Tripoli.

also carrying heavy burdens. United States considered Wheelus Field to be vital contribution to defense of Western community. Wheelus' effectiveness depends stable Libyan Government, to which UK contribution highly important. We thought unusual opportunity exists in Libya to create show window for Middle East by developing set of exemplary relations that country. Kirkpatrick stated he too attracted by show window concept and cited West Berlin as successful example. However, problem of finances inevitably enters picture, Ben Halim pressing UK to reduce its military presence in Libya and substantially increase its contributions to Libyan revenue. British Cabinet today considering reducing present UK annual contribution of approximately 4 million pounds to new level of 1 million pounds. UK also considering possibility contributing 2.75 million pounds to equipping Libyan Army as non-recurring expenditure. This figure represents Foreign Office recommendation re application retrenchment program to Libya and Treasury eager cut even this amount. Kirkpatrick indicated that gap between UK availability and Libyan request in amount approximate 12 million pounds.

Kirkpatrick went on to say UK planning progressive withdrawal UK troops from Libya from present strength seven units (8,000 men) to four by end 1957 and two (2,000 men) by end 1958. These two units would be stationed Cyrenaica to assist maintenance law and order and assist defense against Egypt. Future these two units would be reviewed end 1958. UK would also wish retain overflight and reentry rights Libya for which it regards foregoing financial arrangements price willing pay.

We expressed deep concern at large gap which would be exposed Libyan financial situation if UK reduction implemented. We hoped UK would make every effort continue maximize its contribution. We added, we obviously could not say what action United States Government would take if confronted situation outlined above. We would, however, report UK views to Washington and try give UK at least preliminary reaction during present series talks.[2]

Aldrich

---

[2] In telegram 3774 from London, January 15, Aldrich indicated that, pending instructions, he would try to persuade the British to continue their aid at the present level. He recommended against informing the Libyans of the British intention and suggested informing the British regarding the possibility of the United States assuming responsibility for the Libyan army. (Department of State, Central Files, 773.5–MSP/1–1557) Telegram 3815 from London, January 18, reported that the United Kingdom was willing to maintain current funding levels through March 31, 1958, but no decision had been made regarding future aid. The British agreed to delay informing the Libyans until the United States had the chance to formulate its position. (*Ibid.*, 773.5–MSP/1–1857)

166. Memorandum of a Conversation, Tripoli, March 15, 1957[1]

SUBJECT

Visit of Vice President Richard M. Nixon

PARTICIPANTS

Libyan:

His Excellency Mustafa Ben Halim, Prime Minister of Libya
Dr. Wahbi Al-Buri, Under Secretary for Foreign Affairs of Libya

American:

Vice President of the United States Richard M. Nixon
Ambassador John L. Tappin
Deputy Assistant Secretary of State for African Affairs Joseph Palmer 2nd

The Prime Minister welcomed the Vice President and said that he was delighted that it had been possible to arrange to include Libya in the Vice President's tour of Africa. The Vice President said that he was most happy to be here and to have this opportunity to exchange views with the Prime Minister. He added that he was extremely disappointed that it had not been possible for him to get to Tobruk, as he had particularly wanted to pay his respect to and to talk with King Idris.

The conversation then ranged over the following subjects:

1. *Libya's Foreign Relations*

The Prime Minister said that he was most happy about the close relationship which exists between Libya and the United States. He thought that a great future was opening up for Africa in general and Northern Africa in particular. He spoke with concern about developments in the Middle East and the current situation in Egypt and Syria and said that he saw very little hope for the future with respect to those two countries. He said that Libya's foreign policy is predicated on the preservation of its independence. For this reason, he could not accept the leadership or domination of any other country. Cooperation among the Arab States, he emphasized, must be based upon the conception of "brotherhood". Such a concept does not admit of the existence of leadership, a fact which Egypt has not accepted. The Prime Minister went on to say that it is unfortunate but true that Libya has not been able to trust Nasser's word. He then reviewed the recent history of Egyptian-Libyan relations, including the activities of the Egyptian Military Attaché, the plot to assassinate Libyan Government leaders, the activities of the teachers,

[1] Source: Department of State, S/P–NSC Files: Lot 62 D 1, North Africa (Tunisia, Algeria, Morocco, NSC 5614, 5614/1). Secret. No drafting information is given on the source text. Attached as Tab F to Document 19.

assassinate Libyan Government leaders, the activities of the teachers, propaganda, etc. He went on to say that there are other like-minded states in North Africa who see the problem of relationships among the Arab States in the same way as Libya, and he thought that the great hope for the future lies in their cooperation. He mentioned specifically Morocco, Tunisia, and the Sudan and foresaw the future existence of a bloc which would include these states and Algeria, Ethiopia and possibly Saudi Arabia as well. He spoke in the highest terms of Bourguiba and the Sultan of Morocco and of the benefits to North Africa, the West and the Middle East of cooperation among them. He thought that a bloc such as he had described would prove to be a great attraction to the Lebanon, Jordan and Iraq.

The Vice President asked the Prime Minister whether Colonel Nasser is still popular among the masses in the Middle East and North Africa. The Prime Minister replied that unfortunately this is the case. He said that Nasser plays strongly on the Israel question to arouse the emotions of the Arab people and that he turns this against the US and the West. He went on to say that he does not agree with the US Israeli policy, but that he sees no point in insulting the US in this respect. The Arabs have only three places to go! The first is a close relationship with the Soviet Union, which is repugnant to Arabs on political, religious and ideological grounds and therefore can never be accepted. The second course is neutrality, which is impractical for any small state in the world today. This brings him, he said, the only possible alternative—a close relationship with the U.S., which has shown itself dedicated to the principle of the independence of small nations. The Prime Minister made it clear that in his judgment a close relationship with the U.S. was the only course of action compatible with Arab dignity and independence. He said he had often said to his friends in the other Arab states, including the Egyptians, that the most hopeful means of changing U.S. policy with respect to Israel is to form a close relationship which will permit the Arabs to reason with and to influence the U.S. on this question.

2. *Algeria*

The Prime Minister said that the Algerian situation gave him great concern. He had recently talked to several of the FLN leaders who had told him that they were most fearful that the Communists would exploit the situation in Algeria, as they in fact are already attempting to do through the French Communist Party. The Prime Minister believed that there is a real danger that the prolongation of the struggle may facilitate the Communists' seizing control of the Nationalist group in Algeria to the great detriment of North Africa and the West. He expressed the strong hope that the U.S. would find it possible to influence France in this situation in a way which would remove this cancer on the body of North Africa.

3. *The American Doctrine*

The Prime Minister said that he had read President Eisenhower's statement five times and that he did not see how any Arab states could be opposed to the principles involved which seemed to him entirely compatible with Libyan foreign policy and the demands of the Middle East situation. He stated that he intends at the state dinner this evening to make a public statement to the effect that Libya welcomes the doctrine in principle [2] and will discuss details with Ambassador Richards when he arrives here on March 17. [3] The Prime Minister confessed to great disappointment at the communiqué which had resulted from the meeting of the four Arab leaders in Cairo on the occasion of King Saud's return from the U.S. He said that when King Saud earlier visited King Idris, the Libyans had worked out a draft text of a communiqué in which both Libya and Saudi Arabia would give endorsement to the Eisenhower doctrine. This draft had been based on a formula which had been generally acceptable to King Saud but was watered down by a member of King Saud's staff when reduced to writing. The Prime Minister went on to say that there was no question about Saud's agreement with the doctrine. It was apparent, however, that when the King reached Cairo, he was unable to make his views prevail with the other three Arab leaders and therefore unfortunately compromised on equivocal language which does not correspond to his true feelings. The Prime Minister said that this is a case in point where Arab solidarity on a basis of equality would have been salutary. Had all the Arab states been at this meeting instead of just four, there would have been an overwhelming sentiment for the Eisenhower Doctrine and Egypt and Syria, instead of Saudi Arabia, would have found themselves in a position of having to compromise for the sake of unity.

The Vice President said that he was most happy to hear of Libya's endorsement of the principles of the Eisenhower Doctrine. He then went on to explain the philosophy which lay behind it. He said that he had observed in all the states he had visited in Africa a common determination on the part of those countries to maintain their independence and not to follow slavishly the lines of others through blocs, etc. He said that the Eisenhower Doctrine is intended to protect the independence of the states of the Middle East through the extension of security assurances and through the economic

---

[2] During his remarks, Bin Halim stated that he was convinced that the doctrine was designed to preserve Libya's independence in the face of any effort to undermine it. The text of his comments is *ibid.*, NEA Files: Lot 57 D 616, Libya.

[3] See *infra.*

development of the countries concerned so as to enhance their capabilities to resist subversion. He stated that the U.S. is opposed to all forms of domination and, contrary to the impression the Communists endeavor to create, has no wish itself to dominate.

The Prime Minister said that he understood this. He thought the Eisenhower Doctrine is exactly what is required in the Middle East at the present time and he was happy to give his public endorsement to it this evening.

4. *Foreign Aid*

The Prime Minister expressed his gratitude for the assistance which the U.S. has extended to Libya, which has made a very great contribution to the development of the country. The Vice President asked which the Prime Minister felt had highest priority: military or economic development assistance. The Prime Minister replied that Libya needs to develop both aspects side-by-side. The building of an army is necessary to preserve Libya's security and the strengthening of its economy is necessary to the creation of stability.

The Vice President asked whether the Prime Minister had any criticisms to make of the operation of U.S. programs. He said that he had noted a tendency elsewhere in the world to build up large staffs in capital cities which do not make the same contribution to the success of a program as do the technicians in the field. The Prime Minister replied that certain members of Parliament have been critical of the size of the USOM in Tripoli, but that he does not regard their criticisms as fair. He said that three years ago there had been many difficulties in connection with the administration of the Point IV [4] projects but that great progress had since been made and he thought the situation now was good. Ambassador Tappin explained the workings of LAJAS [5] and LARC, emphasizing the cooperative nature of both organizations. He thought that while these instruments are far from perfect, they nevertheless are doing a good job. The Prime Minister expressed his agreement and added that the major difficulty with the Point IV projects appears to arise from lack of funds. Often plans are drawn up as the result of great effort but funds are not available to implement them. The Vice President spoke of the desirability of concentrating on a few projects, rather than scattering aid with the result that no one project is successfully completed. He thought that it is a great waste to have people tied down in a capital drawing up plans which have no immediate prospect of realization. It would be much better to concentrate on a few projects which can be brought to completion.

---

[4] This involved technical assistance under a program which began in 1949.

[5] Libyan-American Joint Services was established in 1955 to offer aid in the implementation of U.S.-financed projects.

5. *Communism*

The Prime Minister said that he thought that North Africa at the present time is comparatively free of Communist influence and could, with continued progress, remain that way. He reiterated that his greatest fear in this respect arises from the danger of Communist penetration in Algeria. The Prime Minister then went on to emphasize his strong opposition to Communism. He spoke of the expanded Soviet Embassy staff in Tripoli, and said that the Government of Libya had recently requested the Soviets to reduce the size of their mission.

6. *North African University*

Mr. Palmer referred to a brief comment which the Prime Minister had made earlier about Libya's desire to build up its National University. He inquired whether Libya and the other North African states had given any thought to the possibility of pooling their resources to build a common university in North Africa which would serve the needs of all of them and which would, perhaps, enable them to build a more effective institution than their individual resources would permit. The Prime Minister said he had several discussions with Dr. Jamali [6] of Iraq about this. Dr. Jamali had told him that he had talked to the Department of State about it and had urged the Department to try to find a means of establishing an American University somewhere in North Africa. The Prime Minister said that he thought this is an excellent idea and one which he hoped the U.S. could assist with. He did not think it made any great difference where the university was established—whether in Tripoli, Tunis, or Morocco. He felt that the U.S. would derive great benefit from initiating such a project under American auspices. Although this might cause criticism in some quarters, it would be generally welcomed.

The Vice President said he thought the idea of a North African University had great merit. He suggested the possibility of combining under one university administration a number of separate institutions in various North African centers in a manner analogous to the system at the University of California. Thus Tripoli might have a medical or an engineering school, Tunis an agricultural school, etc.

At a subsequent occasion after the Prime Minister's luncheon for the Vice President, the following items were touched upon:

1. *Oil Development*

The Prime Minister explained the hopes that he had for oil discovery in Libya, mentioning the promising strikes the French had made next door in Algeria. He said, in this connection, that the best route for a pipeline from the Algerian fields would appear to be

[6] Mohamed Fadhil Jamali, former Iraqi Prime Minister and U.N. Representative.

through Tripoli. He added that he is very pleased with the large number of reputable American companies which are engaged in exploration activities in Libya and he ascribed this fact to the forward-looking oil legislation which Libya has enacted.

2. *Private Enterprise*

The Vice President said that he had noted in almost all countries he had visited in Africa that there is a growing awareness of the desirability of creating an atmosphere conducive to the attraction of private enterprise. He thought that this is a most encouraging development, since this is the greatest available source of capital for economic improvement. If countries can develop legislation which will at the same time embrace protection for themselves and extend assurances against arbitrary actions, they could benefit greatly from increased private investments. The Prime Minister expressed himself as being in entire agreement and said that Libya had already put legislation in effect which he thought would serve this purpose.

---

167. Telegram From the Embassy in Turkey to the Department of State[1]

Ankara, March 21, 1957—1 a.m.

2160. From Richards. Following are my impressions of Libya:

(1) Desert kingdom completely dependent upon outside subsidy from some source. In foreseeable future cannot hope to become viable without subsidy. Similar in many respects to Jordan before influx of Palestinians.

(2) Functioning of government actually most primitive although decked with trappings of modern parliamentary state. People have no awareness of ideologies. Government based on respect for King and on personal loyalties with Ben Halim apparently for present in control.

(3) Libya may be likened to marionette with at least three outside puppeteers (Egypt, USSR and US), pulling strings. British influence fading.

---

[1] Source: Department of State, Central Files, 120.1580/3–2157. Secret; Priority. Repeated to Tripoli, Cairo, Tehran, London, Karachi, Paris, New Delhi, Rome, Addis Ababa, Amman, Athens, Baghdad, Damascus, Kabul, Jidda, Khartoum, Rabat, Tel Aviv, Tunis, and Beirut. Regarding Richards' mission, see Document 17.

(4) Presence of Wheelus air base and possibility other facilities will be established Cyrenaica make Libya of major strategic importance to US. GOC Seventeenth Air Force whose command responsibilities extend across North Africa and Middle East saw military need for establishment of Middle East Command with headquarters in Libya, and advance base at Habbaniya, Iraq which would be used in case of limited war and where he foresaw no difficulties in obtaining required US rights. If such arrangements were for any reason infeasible he suggested that better military coordination in area be achieved in some manner, and that military guidance for area flow directly from the Joint Chiefs of Staff rather than through intervening operational commander. Wheelus base is self-contained unit capable of independent operation in time of war and (according base commander) with ability to provide its own perimeter protection in case of local disturbances. It obviously in US interest to foster political climate which will permit retention present US position. It is also in US interest to retain friendship of this Arab state, regardless of base rights, in order impede Soviet and pro-Soviet Egyptian influences from spreading throughout North Africa. Careful consideration should be given not only to immediate requirements but to long pull when from political evolution of Libya many of problems now faced in older Arab countries may be expected to emerge.

(5) Present government has committed itself firmly to west and Prime Minister has staked his political life on such course. Recent firm statements on President's Middle East proposals give him little possibility of successfully reversing attitude. Position taken places him in opposition to USSR and to Egyptian concept of "positive neutrality". Ben Halim is obviously counting on tangible assistance from US. Claims he already under strong attack from voice of Arabs and Moscow. US aid this year totals some $20 million ($14 million of economic development, technical cooperation and military assistance, $4 million special funds from Wheelus base agreement and over $2 million value of wheat shipment), in addition to contribution by Wheelus base of estimated $8 million to Libyan economy in terms of goods and services. US aid has shown steady rise and thus already provides demonstrable evidence value cooperation with US.

(6) However, we were told by Embassy most popular person in country is Nasser. His pictures appear throughout bazaar. He apparently has capability through emotional appeal to "street" to create disturbances for suppression of which government most dependent on efficient security forces.

(7) Egypt and Soviets have suffered reverse over past two years if situation is judged by position of present Libyan Government. Their efforts to satellize country have been rebuffed. However,

relatively favorable situation depends upon small group of men now heading government and is not reflection of attitude people insofar as this can be judged. Thus sudden and drastic change could occur.

Problem confronting mission was not to explain ME proposals and obtain acceptance by Libyan Government but to determine level of aid required to satisfy Ben Halim and permit him to maintain successfully that cooperation with US pays in hard cash.

Reception accorded mission most friendly throughout. No efforts spared to show determination cooperate with west. Libyans advanced shopping list of approximately $30 million consisting of broadcasting system, Tripoli power plant, telecommunications network, reconstruction Benghazi port and assistance in field of education. From preliminary talks with Embassy and Libyan technicians clear idea did not emerge of magnitude of aid which would satisfy Libyans.

I decided to offer economic assistance of $4.5 million, increase of $200,000 over proposal developed in Washington, but with composition considerably changed to include broadcasting ($2.5 million) assistance in field of education ($1.5 million) economic development survey ($300,000) and material for municipal water system ($200,000). Largest US contributions, in fields of broadcasting and education would go where greatest immediate benefits might be obtained in terms of political impact and of directly countering Soviet and Egyptian efforts. At present Libyan airwaves dominated by radio Cairo. Assistance offered would permit construction of 50 kilowatt station in Tripoli and 5 kilowatt station in Benghazi together with necessary technical and programming training and manufacture of inexpensive ($10) receivers tuned to radio Libya. Aid to education intended to accelerate program for removal of Egyptian influence (one project would lead to gradual pull out of 300 Libyan students now in Egypt and sending them elsewhere overseas for study).

Re Tripoli power plant, USOM advised that $2.5 million loaned from development funds sufficient to meet cash requirements from 12 to 18 months. Benghazi port development expensive ($14 million) long range project with little immediate economic or political benefits. Telecommunications ($9 million) also appeared too expensive. Although Libyans showed no great enthusiasm for economic survey, LARC and USOM considered it priority requirement to provide basis for future planning.

Also I proposed police survey, intended assist in important objective of increasing Libyan capability maintain internal security.

Package as whole appeared particularly suited accomplish purposes President's proposals.

No military assistance proposed. We maintained this should follow study by MAAG. Although not mentioned to Libyans, decision will also need to take account of future British role and US policy judgment on desirable tasks and capability of Libyan force. Prime Minister mentioned desire for small air force and navy of patrol type vessels. We said procedures for providing equipment for 1,000 men already agreed to were completed and that material should arrive shortly after signature MDAP agreement.

Summary of proposal conveyed orally noon March 19 and aide-mémoire transmitted Embtel 2158 [2] presented at meeting with Ben Halim afternoon same day. Deep Libyan disappointment, much greater than anticipated, quickly became apparent. British advisor Pitt-Hardacre predicted Prime Minister would be forced out. I emphasized limited availability of funds, strong sentiment in Congress against foreign aid, heavy demands elsewhere especially from countries right under Russian guns and large and increasing aid from US to Libya. After making clear mission had no authority commit funds beyond FY 1957, I endeavored to allay Libyan disappointment by expressing personal opinion Congress would eventually approve continuation of foreign aid programs and expectation that administration would seek substantial sums for Libya.

Ben Halim replied he understood position on funds. Libya firmly committed to west and question of repudiation of doctrine not involved. However $4.5 million figure bound to become public and would place him in impossible political position. Opponents would say he had sold Libya for $4.5 million. Ben Halim concluded that from Libyan domestic political point of view preferable leave matter on basis that Libya accepted doctrine with only some general statement in communiqué about future US aid. He thought such position could be defended publicly. He earnestly urged mission to postpone final decision on aid to Libya until completion of trip and return to Washington when assessment relative needs area countries would be possible. He strongly emphasized importance of missions not rewarding "bad boys". Ben Halim made clear he not rejecting aide-mémoire but only asking deferment in hopes eventually of obtaining more. He spoke with dignity and restraint despite obvious disappointment.

I put forward reasons for making decision now pointing out procedural difficulties involved in postponement, unlikelihood of increase and possibility funds would be exhausted. After prolonged discussion I agreed that mission, after completion of visits to other countries, would consider whether additional aid for Libya possible.

---

[2] Not printed. (*Ibid.*)

Agreed position reflected in joint communiqué (Embtel 2159).[3] Ben Halim accepted our original text, changing only paragraph regarding aid to be furnished.

I was profoundly impressed by Ben Halim and general Libyan attitude. There is no question of Libyan importance to west, desirability supporting present government and genuineness of Libyan needs. However in face of need and danger elsewhere, obvious impossibility of US making more than relatively small contribution to development needs so evident throughout the area, and large amount of aid already provided Libya in FY 1957, I thought it inadvisable to offer larger amount at this time. Small increase would not have met situation. Instead, increase in magnitude of $5 or more million would probably be required. However, I believe Libya has strong case and I may well make recommendations later for increase in aid level.

Hope we will have definite information on British intentions before time for final decision arrives. While most reluctant to see US assume such long-term commitment I see no alternative to picking up British subsidy if we are to achieve our objective of maintaining a Libyan entity friendly to west. British, of course, should be urged to carry part of burden. Once this matter settled we will be in better position decide upon rounded package which could satisfy present government and justify its pro-west policy.

Action requested from Washington: (1) Comments on proposed aid package (Tripoli should submit to Department soonest complete information on project); (2) expeditious delivery of equipment for 1,000 men; (3) arrangements for survey of police force. Embassy Tripoli could discuss survey with Libyans apart from aid question as whole; (4) policy determination re British subsidy and military role.

Warren

[3] Not printed. (*Ibid.*)

168. Telegram From the Embassy in Libya to the Department of State [1]

Tripoli, March 22, 1957—2 p.m.

634. Ambassador Richards visit here great personal success. Both GOL officials and Embassy staff knew immediately they were dealing with kind, just and wise man, shrewd bargainer and devoted servant of international good will. GOL subscribed without reservation to Eisenhower Doctrine both prior to and after detailed discussions economic aid segment of program. King Idris has twice in last week added final punctuation with statement to me that doctrine was "clearly well-intentioned and typical of champion of world peace, President Eisenhower." (Department has text joint communiqué, [2] which reinforced Prime Minister's policy statement in speech at dinner for Vice President.) [3]

However, GOL dismayed, disappointed and perhaps even disheartened at magnitude aid offered, especially in view fanfare which preceded Ambassador Richards' trip. This Embassy conscientiously and aggressively carried out Department's instruction in sincere effort blunt Libyan over-optimism concerning amount of aid, but unable prevent senior Libyan officials, especially Prime Minister, from avidly consuming US newspapers and periodicals. Furthermore, this Embassy completely in dark concerning aid levels until receipt basic paper marked "Libya Number One" dated January 30. [4] This paper arrived (presumably by "fast three-day pouch service") under cover March 5 letter from Jernegan to me. It reached this Embassy March 16 and my desk morning Sunday, March 17, coincident with arrival Ambassador Richards that afternoon.

In all fairness and with full awareness that we may be accused of having developed bad case "localitis", I must state that entire country team almost as surprised as Libyans. We hold grave apprehension lest dismay, disappointment and disheartenment develop into disillusionment. Arabs also have our proverb concerning "mountain that labored and brought forth mouse." To mix metaphors further, Libyans feel they have been good children and cannot understand why Santa Claus came with instruction to leave scooter when they needed and had asked for bicycle. Embassy likewise feels that Libyans relatively speaking have moved further in our direction

---

[1] Source: Department of State, Central Files, 120.1580/3–2257. Secret; Priority. Repeated to Tehran, Karachi, Wiesbaden for General Tunner, and Paris for Knight and Wallner.

[2] See footnote 3, *supra*.

[3] See footnote 2, Document 166.

[4] Not printed.

during past year than any other Arab country, in face massive, Egypto-Soviet offensive and aggressive subversion.

Prime Minister's view, magnitude aid offered presents highly explosive political issue. If acceptance revealed, he convinced (and I agree) his government, which firmly and publicly committed pro-US policy, will be accused of selling out for pittance and that internal and external propaganda machine of Soviet-Egyptian axis, which is already blasting him for speech to Nixon, will hold him up as example prize sucker whose policies clearly not in best interests Libya. Therefore, while accepting practically verbatim political portion joint communiqué as drafted by Richards mission, Prime Minister asked that language on economic aid be vague and that Richards mission consider Libyan needs and deserts again at end of trip with view possible increase aid offer.[5] Ambassador Richards agreed and both he and I were impressed with sincerity Ben Halim's attitude. Prime Minister said he believes next few months critical period his government, since fight with anti-Western clique and their Egyptian supporters clearly not yet finally won, and he can not afford give enemies new ammunition.

I agree thoroughly GOL risking collective neck. Fall Ben Halim Government after recent pro-US alignment would negate all political successes of US and this Embassy in Libya over past few years. Ben Halim has now been persuaded to go so far out on limb in our direction that I feel we may safely assume he has made basic objective decision on both material and ideological grounds to continue adhere pro-US policy as long as he retains control. His domestic enemies are prepared use any weapon undermine him and if they should be allowed ride to power on wave disillusionment with US aid, consequences for our position here would be serious indeed. At this point wish underline fact Ben Halim at no time even hinted at possibility obtaining better offer from other sources but to contrary put himself at mercy good judgment and understanding Libya's needs by US Government as personified in Ambassador Richards.

In light above, I consider $10 million or so now would do more good for US in Libya and throughout Middle East than $100 million elsewhere or here too late. Obviously, absolutely fatal blow would be offer aid of any magnitude to any country not supporting Eisenhower doctrine in practical terms as well as by lip service. As purely practical matter, substantial offer to Libya now would be real contribution to our attempts persuade GOL move toward complete

---

[5] Richards met with Bin Halim on May 4 and agreed to an increase in the aid package of $2.5 million for a total of $7.02 million. (Telegram 605 from Tunis, May 4; Department of State, Central Files, 120.1580/5–457)

elimination Soviet presence here. Libya can be put solidly in US camp now. Opportunity too good to miss.

Tappin

169. Telegram From the Department of State to the Embassy in Libya [1]

Washington, April 25, 1957—7:32 p.m.

742. Department has concluded its discussions with UK on Libya which began April 22 and ended this morning. As we were not in position give UK definite assurance US would assist Libya in new situation or assume primary responsibility for training and equipping Libyan army, no substantive decisions were taken at meeting. [2] (Instructions to Ambassador contained separate telegram.) [3]

Following is brief summary of talks relating to Libya:

British told us Selwyn Lloyd planned see Libyan Ambassador April 25 and felt obliged inform him in general terms UK plans reduce subsidy and withdraw troops. [4] Lloyd hoped be able say UK

[1] Source: Department of State, Central Files, 611.41/4–2557. Secret. Repeated to London.

[2] At the Bermuda Conference on March 25, Lloyd and Dulles had briefly discussed Libya. Lloyd described the matter as being urgent and they agreed that further talks would be necessary. (Memorandum of conversation by Wilkins, March 25; *ibid.*, Conference Files; Lot 62 D 181, CF 861, Bermuda 1957 Memos of Con. (MP)) On April 2, Lloyd informed the Libyan Ambassador to the United Kingdom of British intention to reduce its military forces there and cut down its economic subsidy. (Memorandum of conversation by Mak, April 6; *ibid.*, Central Files, 741.56373/4–657) The Libyan matter was pursued once again in Washington between April 22 and April 25. The U.S. Delegation was led by Joseph Palmer and the British contingent by Adam Watson of the Foreign Office. The British First Secretary, J.R.A. Bottomley, also took up some final details with Palmer on April 26. (Memoranda of conversation by Mak, June 17–18; *ibid.*, 773.5/4–2257)

[3] Telegram 738 to Tripoli, April 25, noted that further high-level consideration was required of the question whether the United States would assume British commitments in Libya. Tappin was told he might informally explore the matter with the Libyans. While he was not to make any pledges, he was free to emphasize the past record of U.S. assistance. (*Ibid.*, 641.73/4–2557)

[4] Lloyd handed an aide-mémoire to the Libyan Ambassador on April 25 in which he expressed the expectation that the United States would assume the responsibilities the United Kingdom was giving up and also suggested that tripartite consultations with the United States would follow. Both Palmer and Bottomley agreed that the aide-mémoire went too far insofar as the United States had not yet decided to pick up the burden. (*Ibid.*, 773.5/4–2257 and 4–2557)

had explained situation to US and was hopeful US would assist in situation which would be created. UK felt it important Libyans not be given impression UK was abandoning Libya without some assurance that West would see that Libya did not suffer. We emphasized UK could not commit us in this respect. British said they believed it no longer necessary retain large number UK troops Libya either for protection Libya or for UK strategic considerations and UK planned reduce ground forces level in Libya to 2,000 by end March 1958. Where these would be stationed depended partially on views US and Libyan Governments, altho HMG inclined prefer Tripoli area in view greater amenities with small detachment vicinity Tobruk. British confirmed that contemplated future contribution to Libya of £1.25 million could be used at least partially for budget support and UK would consider US request that all this amount go to budget support. At our suggestion, UK also agreed consider possibility UK continuing present level its subsidy through end June 1958 and would keep door open for increasing their contribution later if their circumstances should permit.

We explained US did not consider reduced level UK troops would constitute major factor in protection US facilities Libya although we thought they had deterring effect against invasion or internal insurrection. While we inclined believe advantages in concentrating remaining UK troops in Cyrenaica, we did not believe it appropriate for us to advise British in this matter. (Embassy's comments on question troop disposition would be appreciated.) British said they did not wish tell Libyans they had discussed troop level or dispositions with US as these points would be negotiated with Libyans along with level of subsidy. British stated they intend honor their commitments under Libyan treaty but feel they could do so without stationing large number troops there.

We explained US still considering possibility assuming primary responsibility for training and equipping Libyan army but we could make no commitment this regard now. If we eventually decide do so we would propose work out with UK schedule for phasing out UK training mission and allied responsibilities. We confirmed that Ambassador Richards had agreed undertake study Libya's military and police requirements.

British confirmed they willing US assume primary responsibility for Libyan army and said that UK willing retain UK training mission for reasonable period if we desired during transition. In response our inquiry, British said UK had agreed last June take note Libya's desire to expand army and UK had agreed give assistance by providing equipment for an expansion. UK hopes US would be able assume this commitment. Although level of 5000 mentioned in discussions with Libyans UK in no sense committed this figure. British said

Libyans had already recruited 600 of 1,000 man increase which US agreed equip and these were now in British uniforms and awaiting arrival US equipment. British reiterated that if US intends supply US equipment there would be period when Libyan army would be operating with two types equipment; this posed certain problems. There would also be problems operating two training missions but UK would agree continue its mission so long as US thought it useful. We told British these problems could be worked out on spot after our MAAG Mission arrived Libya. We reminded them that our MA Agreement not yet signed but expected signature near future. We thought some equipment could arrive Libya about 60 days after signature. British offered leave some Arabic speaking personnel in British training mission for reasonable time if we desired to assist in training Libyans. UK felt language problem particularly difficult and added that Iraqis serving in Libyan army are not popular with Libyans and not of much use except for translation purposes. We said MAAG Mission could best decide these questions. We added it our feeling that phase-out British mission might take 1 or 2 years.

We reiterated US does not contemplate OSP for Libyan army if US assumes primary responsibility although it might be useful do so initially.

All of foregoing conversations took place within clear context US consideration problem not completed and US representatives not authorized assume any commitments.

Dulles

---

170. Memorandum of Discussion at the 321st Meeting of the National Security Council, Washington, May 2, 1957 [1]

Present at the 321st Council meeting were the President of the United States, presiding; the Vice President of the United States; the Acting Secretary of State; the Secretary of Defense; and the Director, Office of Defense Mobilization. Also present were the Secretary of the Treasury; the Acting Secretary of the Interior (for Item 1); the Director, Bureau of the Budget; the Chairman, Atomic Energy Commission (participating in Item 2); the Acting Federal Civil Defense Administrator (for Item 2); the Director, National Science Foundation

[1] Source: Eisenhower Library, Whitman File, NSC Discussions. Top Secret; Eyes Only. Drafted by Gleason on May 2.

(for Item 1); the Director, International Cooperation Administration; General Twining for the Chairman, Joint Chiefs of Staff; the Director of Central Intelligence; The Assistant to the President; the Special Assistant to the President for National Security Affairs; Frederick M. Dearborn, White House Consultant; Clarence B. Randall, Special Assistant to the President; the White House Staff Secretary; the Executive Secretary, NSC; the Deputy Executive Secretary, NSC; the Secretary of the Air Force; and the Deputy Director, U.S. Information Agency.

[Here follows discussion of items 1 and 2.]

3. U.S. Policy Toward Libya (NSC Actions Nos. 801–d–(1),[2] 818–b–(2),[3] 827–a–(1)[4] and 1550;[5] Memos for NSC from Executive Secretary, same subject, dated April 12[6] and 26, 1957;[7] Memo for NSC from Executive Secretary, subject: "Report to the President on the Vice President's Visit to Africa", dated April 22, 1957[8])

In the course of his briefing, Mr. Cutler reminded the Council that the Planning Board had already been charged with the preparation of a policy statement on Libya for Council consideration. This

[2] For text of NSC Action No. 801, taken at the June 1, 1953, meeting of the National Security Council, see *Foreign Relations*, 1952–1954, vol. IX, Part 1, p. 386.

[3] NSC Action No. 818–b noted the President's desire that he be notified when the payment to Libya of rent for the airbase had been made. (Department of State, S/S–NSC (Miscellaneous) Files: Lot 66 D 95)

[4] NSC Action No. 827, taken June 25, 1953, noted that the Ambassador in Libya was prepared to pay the Libyan Government, upon its request, $1 million in rent for the airbase. (*Ibid.*)

[5] NSC Action No. 1550, taken May 8, 1956, stated that no promise or commitment of foreign assistance was to be made or implied unless it had been specifically determined that the payment accorded with approved policy, Congress had appropriated or authorized such funding or the President had resolved to seek same, the ability of the host country to support contemplated programs had been judged, and the time-span of the assistance had been taken into account. (*Ibid.*)

[6] The April 12 memorandum by Lay for the NSC transmitted a memorandum for the Secretary of Defense from the JCS dated April 2, 1957. In light of the increasing effort of the Communists and Egyptians to penetrate Libya, the JCS concluded it was necessary to ensure a strong U.S. military position there particularly because of the uncertain status of the Moroccan bases. The British decision to reduce their annual subsidy by $7.5 million was viewed as complicating matters. The JCS called for an approved statement of policy in regard to Libya. (*Ibid.*: Lot 63 D 351, NSC 5716 Series)

[7] On April 26, Lay conveyed a memorandum by Murphy with attachments for the consideration of the NSC at its May 2 meeting. Murphy stressed the impact of the British decision to cut economic and military assistance to Libya and emphasized that Libya would require external aid from a friendly Western source to counter Egyptian and Soviet efforts to exploit the situation. He maintained that in unfriendly hands, Libya would "open the gateway to all of North Africa and the NATO flank." Thus steps were being initiated to ensure that Libya would receive essential assistance. (*Ibid.*)

[8] Document 19. The report, dated April 5, was circulated to the NSC on April 22.

policy statement was expected to be ready by the end of the month. Meanwhile, however, the State Department had become convinced that Council action was necessary on one specific aspect of U.S. policy toward Libya. Inasmuch as the British had indicated to us that they proposed, by March 1958, to reduce drastically the annual subsidy which they had provided to Libya, the State Department wished to inform the Libyan Government promptly that it was our intention to sit down and review with the Libyans their current and prospective economic and financial situation. Such a move was necessary, according to the State Department, to forestall the possibility that the Libyans might turn to the USSR or Egypt in order to secure the assistance which the British were no longer prepared to provide. Mr. Cutler also noted that in FY 1957 the United States had programmed assistance to Libya in the amount of $24.5 million. While some of this assistance was of a "one shot", non-recurring character, Mr. Cutler estimated that the level of our future assistance to Libya (irrespective of the impact of the proposed British move) would run between $16 and $19 million annually. Finally, Mr. Cutler pointed out that the Joint Chiefs of Staff concurred in the State Department's proposal and in the State Department's proposed telegram to the U.S. Ambassador in Libya,[9] and he also referred to the recommendations of the Vice President in the report to the President on his African trip, recommending a policy of U.S. assistance to Libya. (A copy of Mr. Cutler's briefing note is filed in the Minutes of the meeting.)[10]

At the conclusion of Mr. Cutler's briefing, the President inquired as to the level of assistance which the British had up to now been providing to Libya. Mr. Cutler replied that the proposed British action, to be taken in March 1958, would deprive the Libyans of $8 million annually in the shape of a British subsidy. He then called on the Acting Secretary of State for his comments.

Secretary Herter replied that the State Department proposal should be looked upon merely as a "holding operation", so that the Libyans would not feel they had been left flat when the British withdrew the bulk of their subsidy and a considerable number of their troops. He pointed out the fact that the Libyan economy was simply not viable without outside help. Indeed, about the only hopeful prospect on the Libyan horizon was the possibility that oil might be struck in that country. Secretary Herter indicated that the State Department proposal did not involve any commitment or any mention of a specific level of U.S. assistance to Libya in the course of the forthcoming review of Libya's economic situation.

---

[9] Reference is to telegram 769, *infra*.

[10] Not printed.

The President commented that in view of its strategic location, its proximity to Egypt, and the evident weakness of its economy, Libya would have to be helped. The United States would be "in an awful fix" if we ever lost Libya.

Mr. Brundage pointed out that we were already providing annually to the Libyan Government twice the amount of assistance that the British have been giving them. Secretary Herter commented that it was not necessary that the level of U.S. aid stay at $24.5 million, the level of FY 1957. The level might go below this sum, because some of the assistance provided Libya in FY 1957 was "one shot" assistance which would not recur in subsequent years.

Secretary Wilson called for a study covering several years back as to what both the British and ourselves had been doing by way of assistance to Libya. Such a study might indicate that some of the assistance we are now giving Libya would take the place of the assistance that the British no longer felt able to provide. The President replied to Secretary Wilson that, as he understood it, the present State Department proposal only amounted to telling the Libyans that we did not propose to desert them. There was nothing more specific than this. Secretary Wilson said that he was only concerned that we should avoid building up the expectations of the Libyans and then earn their ill will by not seeming to fulfill these expectations. The President said that this was a U.S. policy which he favored everywhere in the world, and not only in Libya.

Mr. Hollister explained that his anxiety derived from the possibility that if we were not very careful the Libyans would be expecting us not only to do everything for them that we are now doing, but to add to this everything which the British have been doing for them and will not do after March 1958.

The Vice President commented that it was his experience, in talking with Libyan officials, that they do not regard wheat and other surplus agricultural products supplied to them by the United States, as "aid". This was true in other countries, which all tended to regard surplus commodities as something apart from aid. Nevertheless, the problem was that we did need Libya from the point of view of our strategic interests. Accordingly, unless the Libyans were lucky enough to strike oil, the United States would simply have to foot the bill. It was plain enough that Libya had no other resources.

. . . .

The President stated his agreement with the State Department proposal, but added that the words of caution which had been spoken in the National Security Council with respect to a program to assist Libya should be remembered and taken to heart.

The National Security Council: [11]

a. Discussed the memorandum on the subject by the Deputy Under Secretary of State, together with the attachments thereto (transmitted by the reference memorandum of April 26, 1957); in the light of the memorandum on the subject by the Secretary of Defense and the attached memorandum to the Secretary from the Joint Chiefs of Staff (transmitted by the reference memorandum of April 12, 1957), and of the Report to the President on the Vice President's Visit to Africa (transmitted by the reference memorandum of April 22, 1957).

b. Concurred in the proposed instructions contained in Tab A to the enclosure to the reference memorandum of April 26, 1957. [12]

c. Agreed that, in view of the current level of U.S. assistance to Libya ($24.5 million programmed for Fiscal Year 1957), the United States in reviewing the economic and financial situation with the Libyan Government should not imply that the United States would necessarily provide additional assistance in the amount by which the United Kingdom is reducing its annual subsidy.

Note: The actions in b and c above, as approved by the President, subsequently transmitted to the Secretary of State for implementation.

[Here follows discussion of items 4–8.]

S. Everett Gleason

---

[11] Paragraphs a–d and the Note constitute NSC Action No. 1707.

[12] Reference is to telegram 738 to Tripoli; see footnote 3, *supra*.

---

171. Telegram From the Department of State to the Embassy in Libya [1]

Washington, May 4, 1957—7:13 p.m.

769. Deptel 738, [2] London's 5835. [3] Pending more far-reaching NSC review our basic policy towards Libya in situation created by reduction UK subsidy after March 31, 1958, you may speak to Libyans along following lines. Department will leave to your discre-

---

[1] Source: Department of State, Central Files, 611.73/5–457. Confidential; Priority. Repeated to London. Drafted by Palmer.

[2] See footnote 3, Document 169.

[3] Telegram 5835, April 26, briefly discussed a meeting between Lloyd and Ambassador Muntasser on April 25. (Department of State, Central Files, 741.56373/4–2657)

tion whether there is advantage your taking initiative with Libyans or whether it preferable await Libyan approach to you. In making this decision you will wish bear in mind which procedure you believe is most likely contribute Libya's pro-Western orientation and ultimately result minimum financial demands on us. We also wish leave your discretion phraseology following general line, provided all points substantively covered:

"In recent conversations, the UK has explained to the US the changes in its strategic thinking and economic and financial adjustment which it is contemplating as the result of its world-wide commitments. The UK has pointed out that under present circumstances it has reluctantly reached the decision to reduce its present level of assistance to Libya as part of this overall review. While the US regrets the British decision in this regard, it appreciates the necessity for British efforts to strengthen their overall strategic economic and financial position. At the same time, the US recognizes that the British decision confronts the Libyan Government with a potentially difficult situation. Consonant with the spirit of mutual interest which has characterized the US-Libyan relationship in recent years, the US is prepared to review with the Libyan Government the economic and financial situation created by the impending UK action. In this connection, the US welcomes the continued willingness of the UK to continue to extend assistance to Libya and is confident that the GOL will similarly perceive the advantage of a continuation of this contribution from a friendly source which has afforded it so much assistance in the past. As the Libyan Government is aware, the US is also bearing very heavy responsibilities abroad and therefore welcomes contributions from other like-minded countries of the free world to the important task of assisting the under-developed areas. With respect to the role which the US might play in assisting Libya, the GOL is aware that the US Government is dependent upon annual appropriations from the Congress to implement its foreign aid programs. Accordingly, on the basis of the financial and economic review which would be undertaken, the US would consider Libya's needs for assistance, subject to the availability of Congressional appropriation of funds, and taking into account the contribution of the British Government."

Embassy London may inform FonOff substance this telegram.

Herter

172. Memorandum From the Assistant Secretary of State for Near Eastern, South Asian, and African Affairs (Rountree) to the Secretary of State [1]

Washington, May 28, 1957.

SUBJECT

Request for approval of language according qualified recognition to Libya's Arab League obligations to be incorporated in proposed Military Assistance Agreement between the United States and Libya

Discussion:

On December 20, 1956 the Under Secretary granted Circular 175 authorization to negotiate a Military Assistance Agreement with the Government of Libya on the basis of a draft text incorporating the statutory Mutual Security, and other provisions customarily sought in bilateral agreements of this kind.

Early in the negotiations the Libyan Government requested the inclusion of language in the Agreement recognizing that nothing in it conflicted with Libya's earlier obligations as a member of the Arab League. (Libya joined the original Pact of the League of Arab States of March 22, 1945, but is not a member of the later Joint Defense Treaty Between the States of the Arab League of June 17, 1950.)

Two factors motivated this request on the part of the Libyans: (1) their fear of, and hence desire to protect themselves against, political recriminations from the extremist wing of the Arab League, particularly from the neighboring Government of Egypt; and (2) the explicit recognition of its Arab League obligations which the Libyan Government had already obtained from the United States in the base rights agreement, covering Wheelus Field, among other facilities, which we concluded with Libya on September 9, 1954. Article XII of this Agreement reads, in pertinent part:

"Further, the two Governments declare that nothing in the present Agreement conflicts with or prejudices, or is intended to conflict with or to prejudice, international obligations assumed by either Government under any other existing international agreements, conventions or treaties, including, in the case of the United Kingdom of Libya, the Covenant of the League of Arab States."

Recognizing the validity of these points, we endeavored to satisfy the Libyans' request. Despite informal indications that all they wanted was pro forma recognition of their Arab League obligations, a protracted negotiation nevertheless ensued in an effort to

[1] Source: Department of State, Central Files, 773.5–MSP/5–2657. Confidential. Drafted by McClelland.

find language which met Libya's political needs but which, at the same time, did not override or conflict with the requirements of Mutual Security legislation which, in the absence of a Presidential determination, restricts the use of United States military assistance furnished to Near Eastern and African countries to legitimate self-defense.[2] Article VI of the March 22, 1945 Pact of the League of Arab States, on the other hand, contemplates possible collective military action in the case of conflicts between members of the League.

The following compromise language, acceptable to the Department's Legal Adviser and to the General Counsel of the Department of Defense, was eventually agreed upon:

"This Agreement shall not be interpreted as conflicting in any way with the obligations of the two Governments under the Charter of the United Nations, or as limiting action on the part of the Government of the United Kingdom of Libya in the legitimate self-defense of its independence, sovereignty, and territorial integrity *consistent with* the terms of the Pact of the League of Arab States of March 22, 1945."[3]

(In respect to the underlined[4] words "consistent with" in the last clause, this language is slightly at variance with the version approved by the Libyan Council of Ministers on May 16, which contains the words "as required by." No serious difficulty, however, is anticipated in obtaining Libyan concurrence in this minor change which the Department's Legal Adviser considers desirable).

Our Ambassador in Tripoli has now requested final authority to accept the incorporation of this language as a new article in the Agreement, and formally to sign the Agreement.

Because of the foreign policy and domestic political implications of such formal recognition, however circumscribed, in an international agreement, of the obligations of Libya's Arab League membership, I would welcome your specific approval of the inclusion of this language.

There is a precedent for United States' refusal to entertain such a proposal. In 1954 the Government of Iraq requested similar recognition of its Arab League membership in a military assistance agreement then under negotiation with the United States. We declined to do so, however, on foreign and domestic policy grounds; and the agreement was ultimately concluded (April 21, 1954), fol-

---

[2] Reference is to Section 105(b)(2) of the Mutual Security Act of 1954, as amended.

[3] This was the language incorporated in Article III of the MAAG Agreement signed June 30, 1957. (8 UST 957; TIAS 3857)

[4] Printed here in italics.

lowing Iraq's adherence to the Baghdad Pact, without any such reference.

It has also been noted that the recently signed agreement for the sale of United States military equipment to Saudi Arabia (April 2, 1957) makes no mention of this country's Arab League obligations; but I do not believe that this is relevant to the Libyan case in point. Saudi Arabia did not request such recognition, and the agreement was made pursuant to the conditions of Section 106 of the Mutual Security Act, which are less rigorous with respect to the transfer of arms than the sections governing grant assistance. Furthermore, Saudi Arabia's position in relation to the Arab League is far stronger than that of Libya.

Although it is unlikely that the Libyan Government would ultimately refuse to sign an agreement with the United States from which it stands only to gain, should we decline to accept any mention of Libya's Arab League relationship at this late stage in a negotiation which has been limited almost solely to this specific issue it would place our Ambassador in a very difficult position, with consequent effect on our relations with the new Libyan Government which is in the process of being formed and which we hope will be as cooperative and pro-Western as was the government under Ben Halim.

Recommendation:

Unless you perceive serious objections on foreign policy and domestic political grounds, that you approve the attached telegram to Tripoli [5] authorizing the inclusion of the proposed language, which is acceptable from the legal viewpoint, in the Military Assistance Agreement with Libya, and the signature of that Agreement.

---

[5] Telegram 831 to Tripoli, May 29, conveyed the suggested instructions. (Department of State, Central Files, 773.5–MSP/5–1357)

173. National Security Council Report [1]

NSC 5716/1 *Washington, June 29, 1957.*

U.S. POLICY TOWARD LIBYA

Note by the Executive Secretary to the National Security Council

REFERENCES

A. Memos for NSC from Executive Secretary, same subject, dated April 12 and 26, and May 1, 1957 [2]
B. Memo for NSC from Executive Secretary, subject: "Report to the President on the Vice President's Visit to Africa"; dated April 22, 1957
C. NSC Actions Nos. 1707 and 1740 [3]
D. SNIE 36.5–57 [4]
E. NSC 5716 [5]
F. Memo for NSC from Acting Executive Secretary, same subject, dated June 26, 1957 [6]

The National Security Council, the Under Secretary of the Treasury, and the Director, Bureau of the Budget, at the 328th Council meeting on June 26, 1957, adopted the statement of policy on the subject contained in NSC 5716, subject to the amendment thereto which is set forth in NSC Action No. 1740–c.

The President has this date approved the statement of policy in NSC 5716, as amended and adopted by the Council and enclosed herewith as NSC 5716/1; directs its implementation by all appropriate Executive departments and agencies of the U.S. Government; and designates the Operations Coordinating Board as the coordinating agency.

---

[1] Source: Department of State, S/S–NSC Files: Lot 63 D 351, NSC 5716 Series. Secret.

[2] The April 12 and 26 memoranda are not printed. The May 1 memorandum transmitted a memorandum for the Secretary of Defense from the JCS dated April 30. The JCS concluded it was in the U.S. interest to assure the Libyan Government that the United States would consider additional U.S. assistance to Libya. (*Ibid.*)

[3] Regarding NSC Action No. 1707, see footnote 11, Document 170. NSC Action No. 1740, taken at the 328th Meeting of the National Security Council, June 26, deleted paragraph 23 from NSC 5716 and approved NSC 5716 as amended. Paragraph 23, to which the Department of Defense and the Joint Chiefs of Staff objected, concerned the construction of additional U.S. military facilities in Libya. (Memorandum of discussion, June 27; Eisenhower Library, Whitman File, NSC Discussions)

[4] Dated May 7 and entitled "US Prospects in Libya Over the Next Few Years", not printed. (Department of State, INR–NIE Files)

[5] Dated June 17, not printed. (*Ibid.*, S/S–NSC Files: Lot 63 D 351, NSC 5716 Series)

[6] This memorandum from Gleason transmitted a memorandum for the Secretary of Defense from the JCS dated June 25, approving NSC 5716 provided paragraph 23 was deleted. (*Ibid.*)

A Financial Appendix and Annexes A through G are also enclosed for the information of the Council.[7]

James S. Lay, Jr.[8]

[Enclosure]

STATEMENT OF U.S. POLICY ON LIBYA

General Considerations

1. The Kingdom of Libya is of strategic value to the United States by virtue of its position athwart North Africa and Mediterranean communication lines and even more because of the important military bases and operating rights on Libyan territory. Libya is also important because of its potential effect on the stability and orientation of the rest of North Africa.

2. Our military position in Libya derives from a Base Agreement which was signed September 9, 1954, and which expires December 24, 1970 unless renewed. U.S. military facilities in Libya include Wheelus Air Force Base near Tripoli, gunnery and target ranges, and ancillary installations. There are tentative plans for additional installations in Libya, including an air base in Cyrenaica.

3. The King is the main source of power and the principal effective unifying factor in Libya. A strong-minded Prime Minister, however, has considerable latitude in exercising power and influence.[9] There are no political parties in Libya and political changes are of little interest to the Libyan public. Strong divisive tendencies exist among the three Federated Provinces[10] which could threaten the survival of a united Libya after the death of King Idris.

4. Libya's pro-Western orientation is largely the result of the present King's policy of friendship with the United Kingdom and the United States. Its pro-Western orientation is likely to continue as long as King Idris remains on the throne and as long as Libya is reasonably satisfied with Western support.

5. The U.K. has exercised considerable influence over the King and the Libyan Government, partly because of the U.K.'s willingness to meet Libya's annual budget deficit. However, U.K. influence in Libya has steadily declined over the past several years. This decline will be accelerated by the U.K. decision to reduce its annual subsidy

---

[7] None printed.

[8] Printed from a copy that bears this typed signature.

[9] On May 26, Abd al-Majid Ku'bar succeeded Bin Halim as Prime Minister. He was a former Speaker of the House, Foreign Minister, Minister of Communications, and Deputy Prime Minister.

[10] Tripolitania, Cyrenaica, and Fazzan.

to Libya after March 31, 1958 and to withdraw most of its troops from Libya.

6. U.S. influence in Libya has grown steadily since 1951, and in recent months Libya has moved closer to the United States. The Government recently gave strong public support to the American Doctrine for the Middle East. Of the Western nations, probably only the United States can provide the leadership, resources and influence to assure Libya's continued pro-Western orientation.

7. Egypt has, since 1951, continuously sought to bring Libya into the Egyptian orbit. By supplying advisers and officials to the Libyan federal and provincial Governments and teachers for the Libyan schools, and through the use of the Egyptian radio, movies and newspapers, Egypt has spread Egyptian propaganda and influence in Libya. The Egyptian Embassy has aggressively tried to extend Egyptian influence and, during the Suez crisis of late 1956, sought to foment disorders. The Libyan Government and the King have become fearful of Egyptian motives and have initiated steps to counteract Egyptian influence.

8. In 1945 the Soviet Union requested a trusteeship over Tripolitania and in 1956 a Soviet Embassy was established in Tripoli. Soviet offers of military and economic aid in 1956 were rejected by the Libyan Government after the United States extended additional aid to Libya. The Soviets collaborate closely with Egyptian Embassy officials in Libya and are reported to be assiduously cultivating junior Libyan officials. Direct Soviet influence has, however, remained slight and there is no known local Communist organization in Libya.

9. Libya has sought a closer relationship with Iraq and Turkey and has accepted modest assistance from these two countries in forming and training the Libyan Army. The Libyan Government wishes to strengthen Libya's relations with its North African neighbors and it recently reiterated its strong support of the Algerian nationalists. Libya's relations with most members of the Arab League are confined largely to contacts with them at the Arab League meetings and none except Egypt exerts much influence in Libya.

10. The Libyan Federal Army is overshadowed by the provincial police forces (which total between 5,000 and 6,000 men). The Federal Government and the King must rely primarily on these provincially-controlled police forces for the maintenance of internal security. Transformation of the provincial police forces into a Federal force is desirable but not politically feasible. The Government and the King are anxious to increase the strength of the Libyan Army from 1835 to at least 5,000 men. If such an army had a strong national loyalty, it could provide the Federal Government with effective military backing, contribute significantly to the internal

security and unity of Libya and offer some resistance to local aggression. However, some duplication in capability between the provincial and Federal forces would exist during the period of Federal force build-up and until the functions of the provincial forces are reduced.

11. Currently, the U.K. has primary responsibility for equipping and training the Libyan Army. The United States has undertaken, however, to train and equip a 1035-man augmentation of the Army and is considering assuming responsibility for training and supporting the entire Federal army.

12. Over 90 percent of Libya's territory is desert and only about two percent is arable. Most of the population is engaged in nomadic animal husbandry or agriculture, and production is subject to wide fluctuation because of variations in rainfall. Most of the population lives at the subsistence level and suffers from malnutrition and disease. Unless new resource discoveries are made, the potentiality for economic growth is exceedingly limited.

13. Extensive oil explorations are currently being undertaken in Libya by a number of U.S. and foreign oil companies. If significant quantities of oil or gas were to be found and exploited commercially, Libya's requirements for external subsidies would be reduced and a rising living standard could be financed.

14. Libya's foreign trade deficit in 1956 was more than made up through U.S. and U.K. military expenditures, private foreign investment and foreign grants, and Libya's holdings of dollars and sterling stood at $46 million at the end of 1956.

15. In Libyan FY 1956, the Libyan central and provincial governments received domestic revenues of roughly $17 million, and assistance primarily from the U.K. to meet the budget deficit totalled approximately $8 million. In addition foreign grants of $15 million were provided to Libya for development programs.

16. The U.K. has been the primary source of external support for Libya's budget. It intends, however, to reduce its assistance to Libya from $12.6 million (Libyan FY 1958) to approximately $3.5 million a year beginning April 1, 1958 and has urged the United States to undertake to fill the gap thus created. We have indicated to the Libyan Government our willingness to review with it Libya's economic and financial situation in the light of the British retrenchment and to consider Libya's needs for additional U.S. assistance subject to the availability of funds and taking into account the contribution of the British Government.

17. It is unlikely that the U.K. will agree to augment its new aid level to Libya and Libya will look to the United States to fill the gap. The Libyans will almost certainly make continuing efforts to raise the price of their cooperation with the United States. Should

U.S. aid proposals fall substantially below their expectations, they would probably seek to revive U.S. concern that Libya would turn to Egypt and the USSR, though they would probably not accept substantial assistance from these countries unless they concluded that U.S. aid would be wholly inadequate.

Objectives

18. Availability and use in Libya of such military facilities as the United States may require.

19. A stable and independent Libyan Government able to withstand the separatist tendencies of the provinces, free of anti-Western (particularly Egyptian and Soviet) influence, pro-U.S. and pro-Western in orientation, and giving support to Free World objectives.

Major Policy Guidance

20. *U.S. Assistance*. Extend U.S. assistance to Libya at a minimum level which, taking into account the contributions of other friendly nations, will provide reasonable assurance of the retention of U.S. defense facilities in Libya and of the political cooperation of the Libyan Government.

a. *Military Assistance*. Take primary responsibility for developing over a period of years a Libyan army trained and equipped to maintain internal security and to resist guerrilla raids; and provide military assistance for this program additional to that provided by other friendly nations. Such an armed force should not exceed in size a U.S. regimental combat team (approximately 4,500 men). Concurrent with the expansion of the Federal Army, encourage the Libyans, as internal political considerations permit, to reduce the size of the provincial police forces to the level required for the efficient execution of normal police duties.

b. *Economic and Technical Assistance*. Within the over-all minimum level of U.S. economic and technical assistance programs:

(1) Maintain a reasonable degree of economic stability.

(2) Contribute toward economic development.

(3) Assist in Libyan efforts to improve levels of technical competence in government, agriculture, teaching, health and other fields in order to facilitate the most effective use of Libya's human and natural resources.

(4) Facilitate, particularly through private enterprise, the exploration and exploitation of additional Libyan natural resources to lessen over time the extent of Libya's dependence on foreign subsidies.

(5) Contribute toward political unity.

21. *Relations with North Africa and the Middle East*.

a. Encourage Libya's disposition to draw more closely politically, culturally and economically to Tunisia and Morocco, even though conditions in the area do not now permit practical steps toward some form of broader North African political association.

b. At the same time, encourage Libya to strengthen its ties with pro-Western countries of the Middle East (such as Turkey, Iraq and Lebanon), to lessen its ties with anti-Western and neutralist Middle Eastern states (particularly Egypt), and to minimize its involvement in divisive Middle East problems and disputes.

22. *Survival of an Independent and Pro-Western Libya.*

a. Encourage Libya to follow such policies and take such steps as will strengthen Libya's independence, its national cohesiveness, and its cooperation with the Free World.

b. Be prepared to respond to a Libyan request for armed assistance under the American Doctrine for the Middle East and coordinate planning for such assistance with the U.K.'s plans for carrying out its obligations under the U.K.-Libyan Treaty of Alliance.

174. Telegram From the Embassy in Libya to the Department of State [1]

Tripoli, September 26, 1957—2 p.m.

203. Subsequent conversations between Gordon and Shaqluf and between Embassy officers and other Libyan officials tend confirm that situation is as presented Embtel 195 [2] rather than as in alarming version given by Pitt Hardacre reported in Embtel 197. [3]

Comment: Our best current evaluation is that any day now we will enter period of tough negotiating with Libyans. Hinge of issue is whether Libyans intend negotiate using bargaining tactics or whether they intend resort to blackmail. It is important to remember

[1] Source: Department of State, Central Files, 773.00/9–2657. Secret; Priority. Repeated to London, Paris to pass to SHAPE for Knight and West, Bonn to pass to Wiesbaden for CINCUSAFE, Cairo, and Benghazi.

[2] Telegram 195 from Tripoli, September 23, indicated that Prime Minister Ku'bar and members of his Council of Ministers were dissatisfied with the level of U.S. aid and did not wish future assistance to be tied to specific projects. Though the Soviets had made an offer of aid, which they publicized, the Libyan Government had not yet accepted it. (*Ibid.*, 773.00/9–2357)

[3] Telegram 197 from Tripoli, September 23, presented the views of Pitt-Hardacre, who had been compelled to resign his position. He predicted that the Libyan Government would tell the United States to take back its base and dollar aid. He asserted that the nation was in the hands of a clique which intended to swing Libya toward Egypt. Moreover, the Soviets had offered substantial economic and military help. Tappin held that the most positive interpretation was that Libya was using this as leverage to compel more favorable concessions out of the United States. (*Ibid.*, 711.56373/9–2357)

that difference between bargaining and blackmail is ethical question. Tactics adopted will be largely determined by composition of government at time negotiations begin. We have reason believe changes may be in offing but are withholding predictions until true situation becomes more apparent.

Massive Soviet-Egyptian presence and anti-US offensive are established facts and not possible future development. Admitting that Libyan inaction and past errors have brought about this dangerous situation, it nevertheless would be highly unreasonable to suppose that Libyans can negotiate with us at this juncture without some reference to Egypt-Soviet efforts to get them to accept aid from that source. If Libyan policy in future is dictated by anti-Western group within government who would seek align Libya with Moscow–Cairo axis or, in lesser sense, with Egyptian neutralism, then US decision will be simply whether we are prepared to buy time by submitting to blackmail or whether we are prepared to force issue now by flat refusal attempt outbid Egyptians and Soviets. If, however, Libyan policy in future is dictated by Libyan "nationalists" who seek extract best possible bargain from Libya's Western friends, then we can assume that Libyan tactical approach will resemble that of past and be roughly as follows:

First, they will point to prestige which Soviets and Egyptians have built up with mass of Libyan population. Second, they will state that they continue anxious keep Libya out of Soviet-Egyptian orbit but need time to consolidate own position and educate own people on best Libyan interests. Third, they will declare that only course open to them is to beseech US to maintain high level of economic assistance for essential development of country.

If they use this latter approach, we have very strong case demonstrating proven good will of US towards Libya and certainly have no reason apologize for level of aid to Libya in past. In other words, [we would be] negotiating from strong position.

But facts of life remain that decision will depend upon who controls Libyan policy. It seems evident that we must be prepared to act as we have in many countries throughout world in past decade to place adequate support behind elements which would tie Libya to free world and be willing to negotiate frankly with them concerning country's essential needs. Is it not clear that in Libya in 1957 threat of take-over by elements unfriendly to West, whether they represent straight Soviet Communism or Egyptian-style neutralism, is parallel to situation which existed in Germany, France and Italy in 1948? Was Marshall Plan result of blackmail or was it result of realistic fact-facing by USG?

Tappin

175. Telegram From the Department of State to the Embassy in Libya [1]

Washington, October 5, 1957—3:08 p.m.

276. Tripoli 193,[2] 195, 197 and 203.[3]

FYI. 1. Department fully concurs in emphasis in reftels re importance acting vigorously to assure continued pro-Western orientation Libyan Government. We also concur Embassy's estimate re dangers inherent in Libyan situation as result British retrenchment plans at time when Egyptian and Soviet intentions in area are becoming increasingly aggressive.

2. It was precisely in anticipation foregoing circumstances that Executive Branch of Government earlier this year reviewed on urgent basis US policy toward Libya. Resulting action by NSC,[4] of which you informed, provides far-reaching guidance and authority calculated we believe to achieve our objectives.

3. In accordance this authority, Department:

a. Authorized Embassy last May to inform GOL that we prepared review with GOL economic and financial situation created by UK cutback plans and to consider Libya's needs for assistance (Deptel 769):[5]

b. Embassy recently authorized inform GOL that US expediting equipment promised for 1000 men and is prepared assume responsibility training Libyan Army and discuss GOL army equipment needs.[6]

4. Department sure Embassy appreciates that within constitutional and budgetary limitations under which USG operates, foregoing constitutes far-reaching and flexible grant of authority. We are not yet aware that Embassy has yet found occasion to make use of this authority. Nor, indeed, do reports from Tripoli and London indicate precise extent to which Libyans have been informed of UK decisions. End FYI.

---

[1] Source: Department of State, Central Files, 773.5–MSP/9–2157. Secret. Repeated to London.

[2] Telegram 193, September 21, reported that the West could not afford the psychological effect that Libyan adherence to the Moscow–Cairo axis or Nasser-style neutralism would have on the Arab world generally and particularly the oil-rich states. Tappin urged the necessity of a coordinated U.S.-British position to thwart the Soviets. (*Ibid.*)

[3] Regarding telegrams 195 and 197, see footnotes 2 and 3 to telegram 203, *supra*.

[4] Reference is to Document 173.

[5] Document 171.

[6] Telegram 272 to Tripoli, October 4, authorized the Embassy to inform the Libyans that every effort would be made to ensure delivery of the equipment and uniforms by December 1. (Department of State, Central Files, 773.56/10–357)

5. Department has always assumed that coordination of UK and US approaches to Libyans could best be undertaken by US and UK Ambassadors Tripoli. Thus, we were under impression that at such time as UK decisions re reduction subsidy to Libya were communicated to GOL, US Ambassador would immediately reassure Libyan Government in sense Deptel 769, as was done (Tripoli's 744),[7] and would, when possible, follow up with discussions with Libyans re their FY 59 financial situation. Military assistance would similarly be handled along lines Deptel 230.[8]

6. In light foregoing, Embassy London should request FonOff concurrence in US and UK Ambassadors jointly preparing plan of coordinated action based on authorities available to them in order assure readjustments US and UK responsibilities in Libya are presented to Libyan Government in manner which will (a) best assure Libya's continued pro-Western orientation; (b) minimize possibility Libyans playing US and UK off against one another and (c) minimize financial burdens on both US and UK.

7. We believe foregoing also largely answers preoccupation reiterated London's 2187[9] insofar as Libya concerned. Embassy London should also reiterate to FonOff reasons why US cannot constitutionally commit itself at this time re future level of aid to Libya. FYI. We have repeatedly made this clear in course of numerous conversations with British and, in fact, have adduced it as major reason why in interests continuity it would be desirable for British continue meet Libyan deficit. End FYI. London should also reassure FonOff that we will, of course, do everything possible keep Libya oriented free world but that we cannot admit this as unilateral US

[7] Telegram 744, May 9, summarized Tappin's discussion with the King. The question of U.K. withdrawal was not raised. Bin Halim subsequently raised the issue, however, and remarked on the need to separate the issues of reduced subsidies and troop levels. Tappin informed him that the United States would be undertaking a financial and economic review of the situation. (*Ibid.*, 611.73/5–957)

[8] Telegram 230 to Tripoli, September 19, instructed Tappin to undertake an approach to the Libyans who would be told that the United States had learned of British intentions and was aware of the problems they posed. He was further to state that past U.S. commitments would be honored and that the United States was prepared to assume the responsibility of training the Libyan army and to consider equipment needs. The situation had been complicated by the delayed signing of the MAAG Agreement, which came too late to use the $1,575,000 programmed for 1957 thus making it necessary to wait for the 1958 appropriations. (*Ibid.*, 773.5/9–357)

[9] Telegram 2187 from London, October 1, called for an immediate and coordinated U.S.-U.K. response to the Soviet attempt to become more involved in Libyan affairs. Great Britain seemed to feel that the United States should assume a heavier financial burden. (*Ibid.*, 670.00/10–157)

responsibility and we continue look to British to share this vital task with us to maximum extent possible.[10]

Department hopes that it will be possible US and UK Ambassadors Tripoli submit proposed joint plan of action by October 15. If in meanwhile US Ambassador feels it desirable at any time make use of authority referred to in two numbered paragraphs above, he should feel free to do so.

Dulles

[10] In telegram 2307 from London, October 8, the Embassy reported that the British had presented details of the troop withdrawal to the Libyans on September 6, but awaited further discussions of the subsidy issue with the United States before taking up that question with Libya. The Libyans wanted a response by late October. The British still insisted that £1.25 million annually was all the assistance they could afford and hoped the United States would assume the deficit. (*Ibid.*, 773.5–MSP/10–857)

---

176. Telegram From the Embassy in Libya to the Department of State[1]

Tripoli, October 11, 1957—noon.

244. Deptel 276, repeated London 2571.[2] I am afraid that I have somehow failed to get across to Department principal point of recent cables from this Embassy (especially Embtel 226),[3] although upon review of all of them back as far as Embtel 518 of February 4,[4] I must frankly conclude that these have been both complete and explicit. However, danger of psychological defeat and even loss of position for US is so great over next few months as British withdraw that it essential that Department and Embassy see eye to eye on handling. Therefore this latest attempt describes situation.

[1] Source: Department of State, Central Files, 773.5–MSP/10–1157. Secret. Repeated to London and Benghazi.

[2] *Supra.*

[3] Telegram 226 from Tripoli, October 4, concluded that "dollar diplomacy" was required to buy time for the continued operation of U.S. air facilities. Tappin stressed the military, strategic, and political considerations compelling the United States to maintain its position in Libya and counter Egyptian and Soviet pressures. (Department of State, Central Files, 773.5–MSP/10–457)

[4] Telegram 518 from Tripoli, recommended that the United States press the British to finalize their plans. Tappin emphasized that the United States would inevitably have to make up the shortfall if Free World interests were to be preserved in Libya. (*Ibid.*)

Basic questions confronting Embassy are not only *when* to discuss future intentions with GOL but also *what* we say when we do discuss them. Availing myself of option offered me by Department in Deptel 769, [5] I have chosen only practicable tactic on question of "when" in interest of maintaining solid western front in Libya. I have waited for Libyans to approach me when British intentions have been revealed to them. I am sure Department appreciates that I could not and cannot as American Ambassador go to Libyans and confidentially inform them that US knows that British plan drastic withdrawal but are concealing fact from Libyans. This would be extremely damaging. Furthermore, since I have absolutely no basis or authority for assuring Libyans that US will be able cover gap created, such action would represent such real risk of causing Libyans to turn precipitously to Egyptians and Soviets that neither Embassy nor Department would be prepared accept.

I have been in constant touch with British Ambassador and members Embassy staff have been in constant touch with their opposite numbers in British Embassy. Confidentially, we find British here no happier than we are with proposed British course of action. In particular, they have been unhappy over heel-dragging on part London in revealing to Libyans British intentions reduce subsidy drastically. Personally suspect London has delayed in hopes US would break down and confirm intention underwrite gap, thus softening revelations considerable.

As for question of "what", there is nothing complicated about this part of issue. Do we intend take action that will result in maintenance preeminent US position in Libya, in accordance with NSC doctrine, Vice President's report [6] and other policy statements? Or do we intend take risk involved in sharing costs of Libya with Egypt-Soviet axis? Or are we prepared to apply real pressure at top level to get British to continue previous subsidy rate?

Personally, I feel strongly that one more strenuous effort should be made at highest possible level to change British decision. But if decision is unchangeable, hard facts of life are that present US plans for continued economic assistance to Libya (Deptel 230) [7] are inadequate and I must warn that, unless they are revised upward, US faces real likelihood of substantial loss of position here in favor of Egyptians and Soviets. There is no fancy language that I can use Libyans which will convert sympathetic consideration into sustaining diet. This is my personal and considered estimate of situation. Every

---

[5] Document 171.

[6] Document 19.

[7] See footnote 8, *supra.*

member of country team concurs in this view. Facts as viewed from ground in Libya appear incontrovertible.

In accordance with instructions contained Deptel 276 I conferred again with British Ambassador October 9. Our staffs met as working party yesterday. We are all meeting again this morning. Results these conferences will follow by cable soonest, but frankly we are miles apart on handling.

Tappin

177. Telegram From the Department of State to the Embassy in Libya[1]

Washington, October 16, 1957—12:40 p.m.

309. Following are highlights discussion FonMin Lloyd and members British Embassy with Secretary and Department representatives re Libya October 15 based on uncleared memo conversation:[2]

Secretary hoped British would not cut down financial and military responsibilities Libya to extent previously reported. Lloyd made clear UK financial position made cuts in both fields inevitable and did not see how British could go beyond one and one quarter million pounds annual financial aid for five years beginning in 1958. He expressed disappointment over US inability, evidenced Tripoli and here, to envisage definite commitment to Libyans re equipping army and re taking up slack resulting from British financial aid cut in 1958. He emphasized danger Libyans turning to Egypt. He also urged in strongest terms US and UK approach Libyans jointly on both problems to avoid being played against each other.

In addition to commitment already made re equipping 1000 men Secretary and Palmer recalled our willingness tell Libyans US would assume army training responsibilities and said we would be willing discuss equipment needs with Libyans soon as British cutback made known to them though we could not presently give specific figures. It was agreed joint US-UK approach on military matters might be feasible.

Re economic aid we carefully explained problems constitutional procedure which made impossible specific long-term US commit-

[1] Source: Department of State, Central Files, 773.5–MSP/10–1657. Secret; Priority. Also sent to London and Paris.

[2] Lloyd described the Libyan problem as "really a brute". (Memorandum of conversation by Bovey, October 15; *ibid.*, 711.56373/10–1557)

ments such as British could give even though US realized budget support was life and death matter for non-viable Libyan economy. This made it most difficult US participate effectively in joint démarches to Libyans. Best we could do was follow up on British announcement to Libyans by immediately offering discuss with GOL their economic requirements.

Secretary indicated serious problem of scale and precedent in proposing to Congress aid program of twenty million and over for country such as Libya if we undertook to take up slack created by British cutback.

After considerable discussion it was agreed we would try arrange joint US-UK approach to Libyans on military question. Re economic matters we indicated we had no objection trying work out initial joint approach on basis finally suggested by Lloyd: i.e., neither US nor UK would at outset name specific figures to Libyans for future financial aid but would both propose period of about three months during which we would conduct tripartite examination Libyan needs. This would make clear Libyans we both disposed help them on coordinated basis and would give Lloyd time to attempt secure allocation larger British funds for Libyan aid. However Lloyd did not appear sanguine over results this attempt.

Instructions will follow soonest.[3]

Dulles

[3] *Infra.*

---

178. Telegram From the Department of State to the Embassy in Libya[1]

Washington, October 18, 1957—5:45 p.m.

319. Deptel 309.[2] Tripoli's 244,[3] 247,[4] 249,[5] 255.[6] In line with

[1] Source: Department of State, Central Files, 773.5–MSP/10–1757. Secret; Priority. Repeated to London and Paris.

[2] *Supra.*

[3] Document 176.

[4] Telegram 247 from Tripoli, October 12, summarized the proposed tactics of the British Ambassador in broaching the troop withdrawal matter with the Libyans. Tappin thought the British would thereby give themselves too much credit in getting the United States to take over their responsibilities. (Department of State, Central Files, 773.5–MSP/10–1257)

understanding reached between Secretary and FonSec Lloyd October 15 you should join with your British colleague in making joint approach to Libyan Government on questions future UK and US military and economic aid to Libya. We would leave to you and Ambassador Graham to decide whether both these subjects should be raised at initial meeting with Libyans October 21 or 22.

Re military problem we understand that at initial meeting British Ambassador will inform GOL that in view reduction UK troop strength in Libya and fact that US is equipping and training additional 1,000 men for Libyan Army, HMG believes it more convenient and appropriate if US would assume training role heretofore held by British vis-à-vis Libyan Army. You would then implement instructions Deptel 230[7] and tell Libyans that provided such plan agreeable to Libyans, US Government prepared take over training responsibilities from British and that US furthermore is prepared discuss with Libyans their military equipment requirements. FYI. Although we contemplate US Government will be prepared equip as well as train over a period of years Libyan Army of approximately 4,500 we cannot commit ourselves to such program in advance Congressional appropriations. Also you should make no commitment re military academy. End FYI.

Re economic aid which we understand you and Graham prefer discuss at subsequent meeting, we anticipate that British Ambassador would explain HMG must reduce its aid level to Libya beginning next fiscal year and reiterate reasons why such reduction necessary. In light Lloyd's undertaking to Secretary to ask HMG review future aid level British Ambassador would not mention any figures. You would then explain to Libyans that US appreciates problem this presents for Libyan Government, and as you previously explained to GOL (Ben Halim) consonant with the spirit of mutual interest which has characterized US-Libyan relationship in recent years, US is prepared review with Libyan Government economic and financial situation created by impending UK action. Moreover on basis of financial and economic review which would be undertaken US would consider Libya's needs for assistance, subject Congressional appropriation of funds and taking into account contribution of

[5] Telegram 249 from Tripoli, October 12, described the intended British strategy in dealing with the Libyan Government regarding their reduction of economic assistance. Tappin considered the plan deficient in that the United States could not make any commitments as yet and particularly could not cite a specific sum. He opposed as premature a joint approach with the British. (*Ibid.*)

[6] Telegram 255 from Tripoli, October 17, reported that the British Ambassador was seeking to arrange a joint meeting with the Libyan Prime Minister on October 21 or 22 to discuss military problems. (*Ibid.*, 773.5–MSP/10–1757)

[7] See footnote 8, Document 175.

British Government (Deptel 769).[8] As mentioned Deptel 309 you and Ambassador Graham would propose to Libyans that we conduct tripartite examination Libyan needs over period next few months. FYI. Meanwhile British would reconsider their views on future level UK aid to Libya with view raising their aid level if at all possible. While we realize there inevitably some risk Libyans will threaten turn to Soviets or possibly Egyptians for aid if US fails give iron-clad assurances of long-term budgetary support, you should make every effort, using authority already available to you to deter Libyans from using such tactics. End FYI.

Appropriate portions this telegram have been conveyed to British Embassy here. It is expected that FonOff will shortly be instructing Graham along similar lines.

Dulles

[8] Document 171.

179. Editorial Note

On October 22, Ambassador Tappin and British Ambassador W.G.C. Graham called on Libyan Prime Minister Ku'bar, in accordance with Tappin's instructions in telegram 319, *supra*, to discuss future United States and British military aid to Libya. Also present were British First Secretary Patrick Desmond Stobart, who served as interpreter, and Edwin L. Smith, First Secretary at the United States Embassy office in Benghazi.

Tappin reported the conversation in telegram 76 from Benghazi, October 22. The British Ambassador began the interview with a presentation which Tappin described as follows:

"Skipping amenities, British Ambassador launched into discussions of changed British strategic position in Mediterranean and necessity for British economies in operation their armed services. Careful examination of Britain's fiscal position had convinced HMG that it would be unable continue commitments previously entered into concerning equipping and training Libyan Army. However, desiring to continue to be helpful to Libya in every way possible, HMG had consulted USG, knowing of latter's deep interest in Libya and hoping that latter would be able assume some of burden of responsibility for Libyan Army previously borne by Britain. He was glad to inform Prime Minister that USG, also in spirit of helpfulness, had agreed to give careful consideration to problem. He understood that, since HMG no longer could assume responsibility for equipping Libyan Army, USG had agreed to discuss equipment with Libyan Government. He felt that, if Libyan Army was to have US equipment, it was natural that USG should assume responsibility for training."

Tappin then invited the Prime Minister to comment. His report continues:

"As was predictable, Prime Minister immediately interposed strenuous objection to having Libya handed back and forth on basis 'invariably coordinated British-American plans'. He stated angrily that British commitments based on Anglo-Libyan treaty and that what British were proposing would be violation of treaty. Prime Minister added that Libya should have been consulted on any decision affecting so vitally her security and sovereignty."

Tappin then presented the United States position. His report of the conversation continues:

"Following exactly Department's instructions, I stated that I was authorized to say that US was prepared take over from British role of training Libyan Army. Secondly, I stated that American military experts would be prepared discuss with Libyan counterparts Libyan Army requirements for equipment. Feeling it necessary to do so, I went back to my original and consistent position of past several years that discussions should begin with attempt define mission of Libyan Army and, on basis defined and agreed mission, establishment of appropriate level and type equipment. I carefully avoided any discussion of size. Finally, I referred to equipment for 1000 men which USG was making every attempt deliver by December 1. Fortunately I had in hand material list furnished by MAAG chief and reading of this list saved day.

"Prime Minister obviously impressed and pleased with generous scale of equipment, but stated that this gift was separate consideration. Libya could not accept offhand British proposal without careful review of Anglo-Libyan commitments under treaty. He opined that it would require considerable amendment of treaty.

"Addressing himself to me, Prime Minister then inquired as to whether or not US commitments to arm Libyans would be subject to annual appropriations procedure. . . . lacking authority make any statement beyond saying that US prepared discuss problem on frank and friendly bases, I saw no possible course of action other than to confirm that US military aid commitments, like US economic aid commitments, were subject to congressional decision. Since it was obviously necessary to do so, I went into detailed explanation of US record as dependable ally. I declared that USG took seriously its commitments to assist its friends in preserving their essential sovereignty. I moralized concerning great expense of maintaining army.

"By this time Prime Minister appeared mollified and said Libya wanted a strong army and wanted it equipped and trained by the UK or US. Prime Minister said, however, he could not accept British position without its being given detailed study by appropriate Ministries. Also, he said, there obviously would have to be discussions between Libya, UK and US at technical level.

"At this point I felt it necessary emphatically disclaim any US commitment based on Anglo-Libyan agreements of June 1956 in London. Prime Minister raised question of air force and navy and British Ambassador back-pedaled rapidly. Prime Minister finally agreed no program drawn up at London talks but said there was agreement on principle of expanding army and studying possibility creating naval force. I stayed out of this phase of discussion. Since talks then appeared to be bogging down, I informed group that US MAAG chief was coming to Benghazi October 23 and would be available to begin preliminary discussions with Libyan army chiefs and British military mission."

The discussion concluded at this point in a "cordial" atmosphere, Tappin reported. He predicted, however, that the Prime Minister would "become increasingly annoyed as he reflects on conversation" and that "reactions of some members of Council of Ministers will force him adopt stiff attitude." He concluded by reiterating his earlier recommendation of a separate approach to the Libyans concerning economic aid, declaring that such an approach on military aid would have "placed US in stronger position both as individual country and as potential caretaker Western prestige in Libya." (Department of State, Central Files, 773.5/10–2257)

---

180. Telegram From the Department of State to the Embassy in the United Kingdom [1]

Washington, November 21, 1957—6:02 p.m.

3738. For Ambassador from Secretary. Deliver following message to Lloyd from me:

"November 21, 1957.

"The exemplary cooperation of our two countries on the Tunisian arms problem since our talks on October 15 [2] prompts me to return once more to the question of Libya which we discussed at that time and which is becoming increasingly urgent. As you will recall, you agreed to review again with your government the level of your future aid to Libya with a view toward ascertaining whether it could not be increased substantially above the figure of 1.25 million pounds which you mentioned at that time.

---

[1] Source: Department of State, Central Files, 773.5–MSP/11–2157. Secret; Priority. Repeated to Tripoli.

[2] See Document 177.

"As I believe you know, we have always attached the greatest importance to the maintenance of the British position in Libya. We believe that you have evolved with that country a relationship which constitutes a great asset for the West in a strategically important area. I appreciate the financial and military considerations which have led you to review your level of assistance towards that country, but I am deeply concerned, as I know you also are, at any possible weakening of the Western position in the vital North African area. It would be a great pity if the gains recently made in Tunisia were lost as the result of events in Libya.

"All our reports emphasize the fact that the Libyans will react most adversely to a substantial decrease in your aid level. Since you have much more flexibility than we in making long-term commitments, you are able to ensure a sense of certainty and continuity which we, with our annual appropriations process, find most difficult. This is particularly important in a case such as Libya where a deficit in the ordinary budget is involved. From our contacts with the Libyans on this subject, we gather that they are disturbed about this factor as well. I am requesting our Embassy in London to discuss with the Foreign Office the specific problems we face in Libya.[3]

"In the light of the foregoing factors, I would hope that you would find it possible to maintain your aid at its present level. If this is not, for any reason, possible, I would at least urge that you continue to assume responsibility for supporting the ordinary budget as in the past and we will do our best to maintain an adequate level of economic development.

"I wish also to mention the fact that our Ambassador in Tripoli has grave doubts about the wisdom of a joint approach to the Libyans on this subject, such as you and I discussed when you were here. He and his advisors strongly believe that such a joint approach would be resented by the Libyans, who would regard it as evidence that we are deciding among ourselves matters of vital interest to Libya and presenting that government with accomplished facts. In the light of these considerations, I would like to obtain your views whether coordinated separate approaches, such as we used so effectively on the Tunisian problem, might not be preferable."[4]

Dulles

---

[3] Memorandum of conversation not printed. (Department of State, Central Files, 773.5–MSP/11–1457)

[4] Lloyd responded on November 25 in favor of a joint approach. He discounted the possibility of Libyan resentment and contended that it would not lead the Libyans to believe that the United States was supplanting the United Kingdom. (*Ibid.*, 773.00/11–2557) On December 9, Dulles informed Lloyd that the United States would abide by its previous agreement to a joint approach and emphasized the need not to mention specific aid levels at any such meeting. (Telegram 4224 to London, December 9; *ibid.*, 773.5–MSP/12–957) Tappin was instructed in telegram 462, December 9, that the dangers of joint approach did not outweigh the risk of prejudicing Lloyd's ability to secure a favorable review (which Lloyd did not anticipate) of the level of British assistance. If no aid levels were mentioned, the Department concluded that its freedom of action could be maintained. (*Ibid.*)

181. Telegram From the Embassy in Libya to the Department of State [1]

Benghazi, December 29, 1957—9 p.m.

108. British and American Ambassadors yesterday discussed with Prime Minister and Foreign Minister [2] approach to problems arising from cutback British economic aid to Libya. Libyans took strong exception to US–UK suggestion that tripartite fact-finding committee determine Libya's economic needs before UK and GOL bilaterally decide future level aid under UK-Libyan treaty. After three hours thirty-five minutes discussion impasse broken by two Ambassadors' combined arguments and British Ambassador Graham's impromptu proposal that bilateral (HMG and GOL) and trilateral (HMG, GOL and USG) committees begin meeting at approximately same date but that former mark time until latter determines needs. This proposal must be approved by HMG and Libyan Council Ministers. Decision from latter expected tomorrow.

Ambassador Graham opened discussion by noting that time at hand to consult re Libya's economic needs according Anglo-Libyan treaty. Said new factor now present is US presence Libya which not nearly so important when treaty negotiated. Therefore, HMG, with concurrence USG, believes forthcoming talks determine future economic needs should include USG experts.

Prime Minster and Foreign Minister staunchly resisted from first suggestion that UK–GOL negotiations as provided by treaty should be affected in any way by results tripartite examination Libya's economic needs. Principal arguments adduced by Libyans with US–UK counter-arguments were as follows:

(1)Prime Minster contended most British aid has been applied to budget support; American aid cannot be applied to budget support. Therefore, he reasoned, two problems are separate. Graham agreed this largely true but said that, since US aid largest single factor in estimating Libya's needs, US should participate discussions. Ambassador Tappin suggested that in practice budgetary and extra-budgetary items can be interchanged, e.g. military expenditures. But Prime Minister replied that regulations make interchangeability budget items extremely difficult. Prime Minister took special exception to example of military expenditures; he said placing these expenditures under extraordinary budget with external controls this implies would infringe sovereignty. Ambassador Tappin pointed out that many countries, e.g. Turkey, maintain forces beyond their

[1] Source: Department of State, Central Files, 841.0073/12–2957. Confidential; Noforn. Sent to Tripoli and repeated to London and the Department of State, which is the source text.

[2] Wahbi al-Buri.

capacity to pay under such arrangements without suffering infringement sovereignty.

(2) Prime Minister and Foreign Minister adduced two historical arguments:

(a) When Anglo-Libyan treaty negotiated US not taken into consideration, why introduce US into Libyan-UK relations now? After protesting that this occurred before his time, Graham said Libya new in 1953 and that guesses as to level aid were approximate; now more precise examination needed.

(b) Foreign Minister referred several times to upward revision UK budget aid negotiated 1956 by Ben Halim. At that time US aid at peak according Foreign Minister, ergo there is no relation between UK and US aid levels. Graham replied that in fact UK did take US aid level into consideration; Libya's needs had simply reached peak at that time. Graham continued we now enter a new five-year period and face new situation.

(3) Repeated allusions made by Libyans to fact that Anglo-Libyan treaty bilateral and that bilateral not trilateral consultations contemplated by its provisions. Graham's reply was to repeat that any reasonable estimate Libyan needs must take American factor into account and that this best done by including US in committee to estimate needs. Ambassador Tappin assured Libyans US would not participate in tripartite discussion of purely UK–GOL matters, that tripartite discussion would be for purpose handling problem important to all, namely determination Libyan economic needs, and that it would be a fact-finding group, not prejudicial to future bilateral negotiations.

(4) In effort keep one up on British, Libyans presented repeatedly variations of two "how shabbily you treat us" arguments:

(a) Foreign Minister Buri complained Graham had misled him by optimistic generalities. (British ConGen [3] here agrees Buri's plaint justified.) Graham attempted pass this off but not very successful.

(b) British failure to reply to GOL request for year's delay in consultation on Libya's economic needs. For this Graham apologized and said that the suggestions being presented now by US–UK Governments were answer to this request. Buri not mollified.

(5)About middle of discussion sense of urgency introduced by Libyans. They said GOL budget must be presented in January, thus no time for extended tripartite examinations; UK–GOL negotiations must begin immediately, and not await tripartite examination. Ambassadors Graham and Tappin protested that no basis for UK–GOL negotiations without authoritative estimate from tripartite committee and that this estimate could be forthcoming within two to three weeks after its first meeting early January. Prime Minister's reluctance tie work of bilateral committee to trilateral committee finally

[3] Stobart was the Acting Consul General.

overcome by Graham's compromise proposal described first paragraph.[4]

At no time did Prime Minister object to tripartite examination Libya's needs; his objection (and he carried bulk of Libyan side of discussion) was linking work of committees. Brunt of Libyan reaction fell on British with whom they alternately professed shock, anger, and indignation, but with whom they were always courteous. With US they especially courteous and made special efforts several times explain they did not wish exclude us because they do not like us.

Other noteworthy points:

(1) Prime Minister said that Libya has 10,000 unemployed; GOL has plan for dealing with problem and that when American Ambassador sees plans he will "explode". Implication seems clear US will be asked provide large chunk aid for unemployment relief.

(2) After two hours forty minutes Prime Minister finally asked whether UK contemplates reducing aid level. When Graham replied in affirmative Prime Minister said he could not "accept" aid reductions decided unilaterally.

(3) In closing Prime Minister reminded Ambassadors that US and UK, in their relations with Libya, must always keep in mind activities of those intriguing against Libya.

Stackhouse

---

[4] Telegram 110 from Benghazi, December 30, indicated that the Libyans informed the British that they rejected the idea of a tripartite examination of their economic needs and that they were calling for immediate bilateral negotiations with the United Kingdom. (Department of State, Central Files, 841.0073/12–3057)

MOROCCO

UNITED STATES INTEREST IN DEVELOPMENTS IN MOROCCO; UNITED STATES RELATIONS WITH MOROCCO [1]

182. Telegram From the Embassy in France to the Department of State [2]

Paris, August 2, 1955—8 p.m.

489. At small dinner last night Holmes [3] and I had opportunity for useful talk with Faure and July.

Faure seemed genuinely to want our opinion about North Africa and especially Morocco, pressing Holmes for his frank views concerning situation there. There developed a friendly and outspoken discussion between the four of us.

The Prime Minister indicated emphatically and repeatedly that he has full confidence in Grandval, saying that the latter was his personal choice and that he will not fail in supporting his Resident General. When we spoke frankly of the rapidly deteriorating situation in Morocco and of the fact that the opposition is no longer that of a political party and a few nationalist leaders but of almost the entire native population rallying to the symbol of heroism and martyrdom of the deposed Sultan, Faure commented that Grandval's reports contained the same warning.

Faure is genuinely impressed with the seriousness of the situation and accepts the fact that positive action with respect to the dynastic question cannot be long delayed. That the necessity for such action is politically distasteful to him was apparent; he asked on three separate occasions whether we were convinced that no solution was possible which would include the retention of Ben Arafa.

---

[1] For previous documentation on this subject, see *Foreign Relations*, 1952–1954, vol. XI, Part 1, pp. 599 ff. See also Documents 25–37.

[2] Source: Department of State, Central Files, 771.00/8–255. Secret. Repeated to Tangier, Rabat, Algiers, Tunis, and Casablanca.

[3] Holmes was in Paris for a meeting on North African political problems which brought together officers from Algiers, Rabat, Tangier, Tunis, and Paris between August 1 and 3. The minutes of these meetings, except for the last, were transmitted as attachments to despatch 314 from Paris, August 5. (*Ibid.*, 751S.00/8–555)

There was discussion as to a formula to solve the throne problem and, although it is clear that Faure has made up his mind to do something about it, he has not yet fixed on a solution and probably will not do so until he has Grandval's specific recommendations. We made clear to him our view that any dynastic settlement must have the public approval freely given of Ben Youssef, if it is to have the acceptance of the Moroccans and cause cessation of terrorism. This appeared to be a new idea to him but he seemed to take it in his stride.

Both the Prime Minister and July talked a good bit about political opposition but expressed confidence that they would find necessary support for a new liberal policy. Faure said that he had examined carefully the Juin[4] theory of how to deal with Morocco and had concluded it is hopeless. He indicated that the number of others who have the same conclusion is sufficient to give him the support he needs.

To question as to whether the Government could act during the Parliamentary recess, the answer was in the affirmative. July, who had gone pretty far in his commitments to the Foreign Affairs Committee, said specifically that once the Assembly has adjourned and departed Paris the Government will be free to move.

Following an exchange about the imperativeness for prompt action required by the increasing high price which France must pay for a settlement, the longer there is delay, I reminded Faure that the General Assembly of the UN would meet in September and that we should all be placed in a difficult position in the absence of real progress in Morocco. I went on to express the personal view that the United States might find it very difficult to give France the kind of support on the Moroccan problem we have given the past two Assemblies, if the situation there has not substantially improved. I said that in my personal opinion in such circumstances pressure on US might be so strong as to cause US to abstain.

The Prime Minister flared up a bit at this but his good humor soon returned and he seemed to agree that he must move with sufficient speed to preclude such an eventuality.

The conversation was very friendly and frank, Faure saying that no one must listen to the nonsense about American or British interference or attempts to undermine that French position in North Africa. He said that it is a problem that concerns all of us and that he welcomes the advice and help of his American friends. His

[4] General Alphonse Juin, who had a long connection with North Africa including a period as Resident General of Morocco between May 14, 1947, and August 28, 1951, was a leader of the political element in France which favored Arafa and supported a repressive policy to suppress opposition to his rule.

parting words were that he and I must keep in close contact, that he hoped that Holmes would follow up the good relations he has established with Grandval.

Dillon

---

183. Memorandum From the Assistant Secretary of State for European Affairs (Merchant) to the Secretary of State [1]

Washington, September 21, 1955.

SUBJECT

Personal Approach to Pinay on Moroccan Problem

Discussion:

In his personal telegram to you of September 18 [2] Ambassador Dillon described Pinay's negative attitude and obstructive tactics in dealing with the Moroccan question. The telegram points out that Pinay, by nature and because of his political affiliations, is opposed to a liberal Moroccan policy, has reluctantly accepted the Faure Program in principle but has continued to throw road-blocks in the way of its actual implementation. The Ambassador believes Pinay is more responsible than Koenig [3] for the delays which have thus far been encountered as the latter is of relatively minor political importance. The Ambassador cites Pinay's precipitate departure for the U.N. ahead of the schedule as an indication of Pinay's desire to escape responsibility. The Ambassador sees this action as a renunciation by Pinay of responsibility for the important decisions now being taken in his absence.

The Ambassador believes that opposition by Pinay, whether open or covert, could be catastrophic and could materially affect the

---

[1] Source: Department of State, Central Files, 771A.00/9–2155. Secret. Drafted by George L. West, Jr. and Walworth Barbour of EUR and cleared in substance with Minister Holmes and in final form with John A. Bovey, Jr.

[2] In telegram 1251 from Paris, eyes only for the Secretary, Dillon reported that Pinay balked at giving full support to the restoration of Mohammed V and favored conservative efforts to compose the Throne Council in such a way as to impede the nationalists. Pinay was in a position to undermine Faure's efforts at reform. (*Ibid.*, 771.00/9–1855)

[3] General Pierre Koenig was the Minister of National Defense. As a leader of the Juin forces, he was opposed to the concession of any reforms and fought against the return of the old Sultan.

outcome of the forthcoming debate in the National Assembly. Even his lukewarm support would create difficulties.

The Ambassador points out that Pinay has great pride and stubbornness but that he is very susceptible to flattery. He believes that if Pinay felt you really respected him for favoring the Faure Program and that you considered that its implementation and the decision of the French Assembly depended on Pinay's stand, the latter might give an oral commitment to stand firm. The Ambassador further believes that Pinay would live up to such a commitment.

Recommendation:

That, as suggested by Ambassador Dillon, you talk privately with Pinay in New York early next week on this subject and make him aware of the importance which you ascribe to his position in support of his government's program for Morocco; that you emphasize the significance of his continued strong support of the program because of the great influence which he enjoys within his party and within the Assembly and that you endeavor to obtain his oral commitment to stand firm in his position against the pressures which you know will be present upon his return to France.[4]

I suggest, if the circumstances at the time warrant it, you might add the following: You understand the difficulty for the French Government of introducing reforms during a period of violence as this has been interpreted in some quarters as "making concessions in response to force." However, general order has now been maintained ever since August 20 and you feel that it is imperative to get ahead with the program for Morocco from this position of strength before another outburst of violence creates again the same embarrassment for the French Government in carrying out its present farseeing plan and thereby limits its elbow-room in negotiation.

---

[4] Dulles conferred with Pinay in New York on September 27. In his memorandum of that conversation, Dulles noted that he had indicated his pleasure that Pinay had been able to support Faure on the Moroccan issue. In reply, Pinay stated that he had done so, but only after saving Faure from committing serious political errors. Dulles was not certain what Pinay had in mind though he thought it might be a reference to the Premier's desire to bring back Mohammed V. In conclusion, he judged that his remarks might have produced the desired effect. (Department of State, Central Files, 771A.00/9–2755) Two days later Pinay told the U.N. General Assembly that "France intends to make of Morocco a modern, democratic and sovereign state, united with France by the ties of freely accepted interdependence." See *Official Records*, 10th Sess., 1955, 528th Plenary Mtg. (September 29, 1955), paragraphs 51–54.

184. Memorandum of a Conversation, Department of State, Washington, October 3, 1955[1]

SUBJECT

French North Africa

PARTICIPANTS

The Secretary
Assistant Secretary Merchant—EUR
Mr. Julius Holmes, American Minister to Tangier
William J. Porter, American Consul General at Rabat
EUR—Mr. Jones
AF—Mr. Cyr

Mr. Holmes informed the Secretary that he was submitting his recommendations concerning French North Africa. They include, he said, a recommendation that the Secretary coordinate with the British in an approach to the French on this subject at the Tripartite meeting in Paris in October, just prior to the NATO Council meeting which precedes the Foreign Ministers Conference at Geneva. Mr. Holmes recited the various considerations contained in his attached memorandum to the Secretary which had led him to make this recommendation.[2] He referred particularly to the recent evidences of Soviet interest in North Africa, i.e., sale of arms to Egypt,[3] establishment of diplomatic relations with Libya, and the possibility that the Russians could decide to take their seat on the Committee of Control in Tangier. The Secretary expressed special interest in the latter possibility and Mr. Holmes explained the procedure as governed by the 1945 Amendment to the Tangier Statute.

Mr. Merchant said that it had just occurred to him that it might be well to modify the proposed approach to the French in such a way that we would not give them the impression of having ganged up against them. Mr. Holmes agreed that it might be better for us and the British to make the same but separate approaches. In response to the Secretary's request, Mr. Holmes stated that the French Chamber will be in session tomorrow. In response to the Secretary's inquiry, Mr. Merchant indicated that he had been informed by de Margerie that Faure has cancelled his trip to Moscow.

Reverting to the local Moroccan situation, Mr. Holmes said that the renewed fighting was more serious than the press has indicated. In the last two raids small arms depots have been captured by

[1] Source: Department of State, Central Files, 751.00/10–355. Secret. Drafted by Cyr.
[2] Document 29.
[3] The arms sale was announced just a few days earlier on September 27.

Moroccan guerrillas. Mr. Holmes said he did not believe, as the French claim, that the raids are organized in the Spanish Zone, although it was probable that individuals who had fled to Spanish Morocco were now taking part in the raids. He felt that this was the beginning of fellagha-type fighting in Morocco. He pointed out that the fighting is taking place very near the Algerian border and that the French could soon find themselves engaged in frontier fighting along a 1500-mile border. Resident General Latour, he said, has asked for more troops. Mr. Holmes indicated that he did not think the current raids were a result of the Sultan's departure from Rabat, but rather related to a deadline set some time ago by El Fassi [4] for French implementation of agreements reached at Aix-les-Bains. [5] Mr. Holmes said it was too bad seeing the French destroy themselves. The Secretary agreed but said that it was not surprising since they were following the same pattern that he had tried to get them to abandon in the 1920's in relation to the Germans. The Secretary said that the French seem temperamentally unable to make changes peacefully before they are forced to do so. This procedure requires a certain strength, he said, which the French may not have.

Mr. Holmes referred to a statement made recently by Balafredj [6] to the effect that Morocco is an international problem and should be the subject of an international conference attended by France, Spain, Morocco, the United States and even the United Kingdom, if possible. According to Balafredj, Mr. Holmes said, the French are more inclined to listen to the UK than to the U.S. because they consider the UK more competent in the colonial field. The Secretary agreed that we know less about colonialism than the British. They are experienced in colonial administration, he said, while we instinctively are not sympathetic to its problems.

The Secretary observed with seriousness that French North Africa is an awful mess to get into. Mr. Holmes agreed indicating that we should nevertheless do all we can to help. He felt that by so doing, we would gain advantage with the nationalists. He mentioned our concern over the 12,000 Americans in Morocco and explained that arrangement had been made to have all dependents on base by

[4] Mohammed Allal El-Fassi was a leader of the Istiqlal Party and one of the more radical voices opposing French colonialism and in favor of the restoration of Mohammed V.

[5] The agreements reached by the French and Moroccan representatives at Aix-les-Bains between August 22 and 27 were upheld by the French National Assembly by a vote of 468 and 139 on October 9. They paved the way for Mohammed V's return and Moroccan independence. On October 1, Arafa departed Rabat for Tangier. Thereafter on November 16 Mohammed V arrived in Rabat.

[6] Ahmed Balafrej was one of the founders of and the titular Secretary General of the Istiqlal Party.

next April except those located in Rabat, Port Lyautey and in the outlying radar stations.

In response to the Secretary's request for his views, Mr. Merchant submitted that we have no choice but to get into the Moroccan problem for the reason that we want to keep France a great power and we have our bases to protect. He reiterated his view that we and the British should make the same but separate approaches to the French in this connection. The Secretary observed that our approach would be one reflecting our desire to be of assistance to the French. Mr. Holmes agreed and reviewed the arguments to be made in an approach to the French. What we want, he said, was to have the French in Morocco do what they have done in Tunisia. Faure has been on the right track but has been sabotaged by his own people. Mr. Holmes said that he did not know how much support we want to give to the Faure Government in general but that, in his opinion, we certainly should support him as far as Morocco is concerned.

After considerable reflection, the Secretary stated that this is a terrible thing to butt into when you are not invited. Mr. Holmes suggested that possibly we do have an invitation in the fact that MDAP equipment is being used in North Africa or in the fact that the French have asked us for help in relation to helicopters.[7]

The Secretary asked what the British think on this subject of French North Africa. Mr. Merchant said that he had not discussed it with the British. Mr. Holmes referred to the recent exchange between Messrs. Macmillan and Jebb on the subject of Algeria as a part of Metropolitan France.

After further consideration, the Secretary stated that he would be willing to feel out the British concerning the course of action laid out in Mr. Holmes' memorandum but that he would make no further decision at this time. The British know more about this subject than we do, he said. Mr. Merchant expressed the view that the approach to the British should take the form of having Mr. Holmes stop at London on his way back to Tangier. Mr. Holmes called attention to the fact that the British do not have to worry about bases in Morocco as we do. The Secretary said that maybe we should get out of the bases. Mr. Holmes stated that the Joint Chiefs of Staff have indicated that they consider continued use of the

---

[7] On May 25, Pinay asked for U.S. consent to transfer helicopters provided for French use in Indochina to Algeria. The French Second Division, upon moving from Nancy to Algeria, introduced MDAP equipment into the struggle against the insurgents.

Moroccan bases to be necessary from the military viewpoint.[8] In response to the Secretary's question, Mr. Holmes indicated that he would be proceeding to London this week where he will brief Ambassador Aldrich for an approach to the British on this subject. On leaving the Secretary's office, Mr. Merchant expressed the opinion that the Secretary will want to take a second look at this subject after Ambassador Aldrich and Mr. Holmes have discussed it with the British. Mr. Merchant and Mr. Holmes agreed that Mr. Holmes should see Ambassador Dillon in Paris but that the French Government should not be approached at this time.[9]

---

[8] On September 15, Murphy had conveyed the views of the Joint Chiefs of Staff as endorsed by the Department of Defense, to the Secretary. They concluded: "The present U.S. air and naval bases in French North Africa are essential for the most effective implementation of U.S. Emergency War Plans." (Department of State, Central Files, 711.56371A/9–1555)

[9] Holmes accompanied Ambassador Winthrop W. Aldrich to a meeting with Macmillan on October 6. Macmillan promised to consider the recommendation that a joint approach be made to France. (Telegram 1380 from London, October 6; *ibid.*, 123–Holmes, Julius C.) On October 14, he informed Aldrich that he preferred to wait and discuss the matter with Secretary Dulles in Paris, because the situation was so uncertain. (Telegram 1503 from London, October 14; *ibid.*, Central Files, 771A.00/10–1455) Dillon advised in telegram 1632, October 10, following his meeting with Holmes, that he favored strong but sympathetic intervention on the part of the United Kingdom and the United States. The major objective, as he saw it, was to keep the region free of Soviet influence and "available to western world." (*Ibid.*, 771.00/10–1055)

---

185. Telegram From the Embassy in France to the Department of State[1]

Paris, December 17, 1955—8 p.m.

2894. Reference Secto 15.[2] Stating that Pinay had not made French position on Moroccan bases fully clear this morning Foreign Office official permitted us to examine briefing paper from which Pinay spoke. Following is its substance:

---

[1] Source: Department of State, Central Files, 711.56371A/12–1755. Secret. Repeated to Bonn, Tangier, and the Commander in Chief, U.S. Air Force, Europe (CINCUSAFE).

[2] Secto 15 briefly summarized the substance of the discussion between Dulles and Pinay on Moroccan bases. (*Ibid.*)

1. French Government fully recognizes importance to over-all Atlantic strategy of these bases and their mission and naturally desires to facilitate its accomplishment.

2. American establishment in Morocco has through the years outgrown framework originally established (in being administrative center for air network extending as far as Pakistan).

3. Agreements of 1950 and 1951 have not been fully applied re French role in maintenance and tactical protection of bases.

4. In these circumstances French Government is prepared to have French and American experts meet at once to seek prompt agreement on arrangements relative to personnel ceilings necessary to give bases maximum effectiveness for western strategy. [3] This examination should also cover provisions which might be made to accelerate effective transfer to French forces of tasks which in principle are reserved for them in Morocco; such transfer should also reduce at least temporarily number of Americans required.

Present French Govt [4] is understandably not in position to deal with more important changes in existing agreements; that can be done only by new govt to be constituted following elections, taking account of current evolution in French-Moroccan relations.

Crouy explained that ceiling increase considered minor matter which could be settled quickly particularly since agreement already reached in principle on French participation radar and air defense. He said SOF and tax agreement more difficult since at least latter would require promulgation of Dahir by Moroccan Government. We reiterated importance of informing Moroccan Government of base problems and asked whether this had yet been done. Crouy replied that it had not and that question was delicate since point might shortly come when Moroccan Government would not be content with merely being "informed".

Embassy and EUCOM prepared proceed with expert discussions as soon as detailed breakdown of requirements received from respective headquarters.

Dillon

---

[3] On December 23, in telegram 2975, the Minister in France, Theodore C. Achilles, indicated that in response to the U.S. request made in February 1955 for an increase in ceilings the French expressed a willingness to permit only a 6-month boost in the air force contingent in Morocco. (*Ibid.*, 711.56371A/12–2355) The Embassy was instructed on January 13, 1956, in telegram 2560, to treat this concession as permanent and to seek a broader, more satisfactory arrangement. (*Ibid.*)

[4] The government of Edgar Faure was defeated on November 29. The National Assembly was dissolved on December 2 as the Faure Cabinet continued to govern pending the election of January 2, 1956. Guy Mollet formed the new government on January 31.

186. Memorandum From the Assistant Secretary of State for Near Eastern, South Asian, and African Affairs (Allen) to the Secretary of State [1]

Washington, January 5, 1956.

SUBJECT

Announcement of United States Intention to Terminate Rights of Extraterritorial Jurisdiction in Morocco

Discussion:

On December 31, 1955, in the course of a press interview, Abderrahim Bouabid, Minister of State without portfolio in the new Moroccan Cabinet [2] and leading nationalist member of the delegation which will shortly begin negotiations with the French for Moroccan independence, called for "the end of legal privileges *still enjoyed* by Americans in the Protectorate." He is reported to have said that capitulations are incompatible with Moroccan independence, and that American citizens should cease to constitute a juridical minority.

The rights of extraterritorial jurisdiction in question were given to the United States by Morocco in the Treaty of 1836 and were later expanded through the effect of other international agreements concluded by Morocco, the most-favored-nation clause and custom and usage.

The United States still exercises extraterritorial jurisdiction in Morocco, although not on a uniform basis in all zones. The British still continue to claim extraterritorial jurisdiction in the Spanish Zone of Morocco. The British are now negotiating the termination of these rights. In the French Zone and in the Tangier Zone, only the United States exercises extraterritorial jurisdiction.

Extraterritorial jurisdiction has, for a long time, been a symbol of colonialism. The United States has renounced its right of extraterritorial jurisdiction in all other countries of the world where it possessed them (China, Korea, Japan, Egypt, Turkey, et cetera).

So long as the French were in complete control of Morocco, the Moroccans supported the maintenance by the United States of its rights of extraterritorial jurisdiction. Now that Moroccans are moving rapidly toward independence and toward a greater voice in the conduct of foreign affairs, they want to get rid of the anachronism of extraterritoriality.

---

[1] Source: Department of State, AF/AFN Files: Lot 60 D 577, "Morocco" Folder 19. Confidential. Drafted by Bovey and Sweeney.

[2] The government of Prime Minister M'barek Bekkai was sworn in by the Sultan on December 7.

With the French already committed to leading Morocco to independent status, we cannot afford to lag behind by hanging onto this vestige of colonialism, which would be incompatible with our policy and which has ceased to be acceptable to the Moroccans as a counterweight to French rights. The continued exercise of this right would of course open us to being pilloried by Soviet propaganda. Above all, we must move promptly in order to avoid the appearance of surrendering this right involuntarily and under pressure from the Moroccans.

Recommendation:

Since the rights involved are, to a large extent, rights in treaties ratified with the advice and consent of the Senate, I recommend that the Department inform the Senate Foreign Relations Committee and possibly also the House Foreign Affairs Committee, through their Chairmen, of our intention to terminate the exercise of extraterritorial jurisdiction in Morocco.

Unless the Committee registers very strong objection, and if the circumstances at that time are appropriate, I recommend that the Department make a public announcement of its intention. I enclose a preliminary suggestion of such a statement, a copy of which we should furnish the French shortly before release, as a matter of courtesy. [3]

The exact procedure by which this intention should be carried out and the time at which it should be done will depend in part on the progress of the Franco-Moroccan negotiations and can be worked out in detail later.

---

[3] At a meeting on January 10, Dulles informed the President that the Department of State was considering an expression of willingness to surrender capitulations. On the understanding that only civilians would have their status changed, the President concurred. (Eisenhower Library, Dulles Papers, Meetings with the President) The Chairman of the Senate Foreign Relations Committee, Senator Walter F. George, was notified on January 24. Two days later the Department issued a statement declaring that it was U.S. policy to relinquish extraterritorial jurisdiction in Morocco at the appropriate time and that the Department would request Congressional action to that end. For text, see *American Foreign Policy: Current Documents, 1956,* pp. 707–708.

187. Editorial Note

On March 7, the Department of State released the text of a message which Holmes had delivered on that date to the Sultan of Morocco. It reads:

"I have been instructed by my Government to convey to Your Majesty and His Government and to the Moroccan people warmest congratulations on the recognition of Morocco's independence, as embodied in the Franco-Moroccan Declaration of March 2, 1956.

"My Government renews its wishes for the peace and prosperity of Morocco, and has asked me to express its gratification that Morocco has freely chosen, as a sovereign nation, to continue in the path of its traditional friendships." (Press Release No. 19)

---

188. Telegram From the Consulate General at Casablanca to the Department of State [1]

Casablanca, April 10, 1956—5 p.m.

239. The probable length of general strike on US military installations in Morocco called by UMT (our telegram 238) [2] is difficult predict. While union undoubtedly cannot provide financial support its striking workers long, near subsistence level on which most workers live coupled with menace of UMT terrorism provide compelling counterpressure. Strong-arm methods at transportation pickup points in population centers can be expected check effectively any return to work movement which UMT does not condone.

UMT has been under considerable pressure to produce wage and benefit increases for its workers on US bases. This is part of Moroccan's independence heritage and has little to do with present wages, which may or may not be higher than the "Prevailing" wage.

---

[1] Source: Department of State, Central Files, 71156371A/4–1056. Confidential. Repeated to Paris, Tangier, and Rabat.

[2] Telegram 238, April 10, indicated that the general strike directed at all U.S. military installations began on April 9 and was effective. The union was blamed for the strike and thus was expected to make the first move in reaching a settlement. (*Ibid.*) The Union Morocaine du Travail (UMT) was openly established on March 21, with Majoub ben Seddik as president and Taieb ben Bouazza as secretary-general. One of its components was the Union Syndical des Bases Americans (USBA). The governing agreement covering wages and other matters had been exclusively negotiated with France on January 22, and thus France had the responsibility for determining wage scales which the United States had the right to approve.

The conflicting reports which UMT has received and long delay in replies from US forces employing doubtful agency of French liaison mission have unquestionably antagonized UMT leaders. In addition the liberty of action which leaders give to their local organizations, in this case USBA, may have been responsible for action by USBA which was precipitate but which Seddik nevertheless felt he could not repudiate as he had in case of recent Atlas negotiations.

Calling strike at this time raises questions re role of Sultan in this matter. Following early March strike threat he had intervened with UMT to postpone action. It is unrealistic think UMT would dare seize upon Sultan's temporary absence in Spain to thwart wishes they knew he still entertained. Explanation lies perhaps in understanding nature of UMT. It is the vehicle of mass worker-peasant uprising, a political more than labor organization. Its allegiance is vital to those who would hold power here. The Istiqlal and Sultan are well aware of this.

Irresponsibility on part of leaders of this movement, while easy to charge, is not necessarily valid in view of nature of colossus they are heading. There is no doubt however that recent developments here inevitably bring up the wisdom of relying so heavily on Moroccan labor for fulfillment of mission of US bases here. US negotiating position is complicated, as before, by the uncertain loyalty of French intermediaries, but interservice cooperation, apparently forged by present strike, seems considerably improved. The next step appears, as far as can be predicted, for US forces, once UMT indicates willingness open negotiations without pressure of strike to offer union contract similar to that recently granted by Atlas. This contract now in process of formulation by three services, will be negotiated with UMT by French liaison mission with US observer present. Exceptions taken by union to contract will, theorectically, be referred by French mission to US services who will coordinate their reply. Success of this cumbersome system appears remote but could succeed in event UMT, having tripped into this situation, is anxious make concessions to re-establish friendly atmosphere. This will require understanding by US however and aid in finding union a face-saving formula.[3]

---

[3] In telegram 168 to Rabat, April 11, the Department of State indicated that the labor impasse might damage vital U.S. interests or endanger U.S. personnel at a crucial stage in Morocco's independence. Thus the Seventeenth Air Force (commanded by General Frederick Glantzberg) was given full authority to negotiate with the UMT and local labor authorities. (*Ibid.*) Representatives of all sides, including the French, USBA, and U.S. civilian and military personnel, met on April 11. Pending a permanent settlement of the issues, a temporary understanding was reached and the strike ended on April 13. (Telegram 241 from Casablanca, April 12; *ibid.*)

Also to be considered is possibility Moroccans are seeking this method to plough through French intermediary for position from which direct dealings with US re bases can be had. Recent FLM willingness compromise in its role of sole interlocutor of union could then be expected evaporate.

Lamont

---

189. Telegram From the Embassy in France to the Department of State[1]

Paris, April 12, 1956—6 p.m.

4740. Savary sent for me today and told me that the French Government was glad to give its agreement to an increase in air force ceiling in Morocco of 2,225 individuals as requested by US. He said that he had only two conditions to pose, the first was that there be no publicity about this change and the second that it be implemented in gradual enough manner so that there would be no shock to the Moroccan communities where air defense is situated. I immediately accepted both of these conditions on behalf of US Government.

Savary then said that there were two other items which were not conditions but which he would like to mention at same time. The first was that our request had stipulated that this was a provisional and temporary request that would satisfy our needs for the next 18 months. He requested that our experts talk with their opposite numbers at the Quai d'Orsay to arrive at somewhat more precise agreement on this point which would, of course, always be subject to review in the event of substantial change in the situation. I readily accepted this suggestion and Embassy will talk to Quai d'Orsay promptly to find out what they have in mind.

Second item which Savary wished to mention was the air defense of Morocco. He said that French military were very anxious to proceed steadily with increased French participation in the air defense of Morocco and he would like to have further discussions by the technical qualified experts on both sides. I told him that, of

[1] Source: Department of State, Central Files, 711.56371A/4–1256. Secret. Repeated to Tangier, Rabat, and Wiesbaden, Paris for CINCEUR, to Wiesbaden for CINCUSAFE; and to Rabat for the Seventeenth Air Force. Sent to the Department to be passed to the Department of Defense and to COMNAVACTS at Port Lyautey.

course, we had no objection to having such conversations but that our military felt strongly that until such time as the French were prepared to accept entire responsibility for the air defense of Morocco including all the fighter aircraft necessary for such defense US military felt that there must continue to be an important participation of American personnel in all phases of air defense of Morocco. I said that this was a technical matter which I was not competent to discuss but as a general principle our military were opposed to relinquishing any one facet of air defense as long as the primary responsibility for defense rested on American fighter aircraft. Savary said he well understood, and that he was not technically competent either but he merely wanted to mention that this was a subject in which French military were interested and would like to explore further. I said we would be glad to do so on a no-commitment basis. I further told Savary that I had heard from our military in Morocco that the initial phasing of French personnel into aircraft warning service in Morocco was proceeding very satisfactorily to all concerned.

In more or less of an aside, Savary, after glancing at his talking paper, said French were also interested in having the overall air defense command placed under the orders of the French Air Commander in Morocco. I made no comment whatsoever regarding this.

I then asked Savary if we were free to commence sending additional personnel to Morocco immediately under the new ceiling and he said "yes", that such action could start immediately and without waiting for any of the further discussion which he had suggested.

I want to emphasize that this increase in ceiling applies only to air force personnel in Morocco and does not apply to the naval ceiling at Port Lyautey which remains unchanged. I also urge that care be taken to comply with French request and my commitment that no publicity be given to this change in ceiling.

Dillon

190. Telegram From the Embassy in France to the Department of State [1]

Paris, April 12, 1956—7 p.m.

4744. Reference: Tangier 464 to Department. [2] After hearing Savary's favorable reply on the increased troop ceiling in Morocco I told him I had one question which I wished discuss with him. I said we felt this question to be important even though it was not the question of the moment but that it might become critical at any time. This was the question of our diplomatic relations with the new Moroccan Government. I said that we were continuing to deal only with the French and were following strictly the letter and spirit of the Franco-Moroccan agreements which left handling of diplomatic matters in hands of French for time being. I said that we were doing this despite continual, although informal, pressure from the Moroccans on our military to talk with them directly.

I pointed out to Savary that while we continued to deal solely with the French we realized that the Franco-Moroccan accords foresaw that Morocco would handle her own foreign relations. I said we felt it was important that when this time arrived the US be in a position to act very rapidly to recognize Moroccan competence in this field rather than delay so that other countries, such as the Soviet and satellite countries, might get in ahead of us. Savary agreed that this was important and said he would keep us closely informed of progress in this field. He said that this would be one of the first suggestions which would be taken up when negotiations are resumed in Paris at the end of next week.

I further mentioned to Savary that we had heard from Moroccans of the possibility that the Sultan might appoint a foreign minister without prior agreement with the French and I asked him what his views were on this subject. Savary replied that it was very possible that the Sultan would take such action. He said such an appointment had not been envisaged in the Franco-Moroccan accords but neither had it been specifically excluded. It was clear that the French would make no objection if the Sultan took such action. However, Savary pointed out that such action would not change the Franco-Moroccan agreement regarding the handling of foreign relations. He said that it was his understanding with the Moroccans that even if they should appoint a foreign minister of their own there

[1] Source: Department of State, Central Files, 771.00/4–1256. Secret. Repeated to Tangier and Rabat.

[2] Telegram 464, April 11, reported that while the French might prefer that a Moroccan foreign minister not be appointed as yet it was likely that they would either give in ahead of time or acquiesce thereafter. (*Ibid.*, 771.00/4–1156)

would be no change in the handling of foreign affairs until the matter had been discussed with the French.

I then asked Savary what the situation would be regarding our bases after Morocco assumed control of their foreign relations. Savary pointed out that this was a more complicated issue because it depended not only on Franco-Moroccan agreement regarding the conduct of foreign relations but also on Franco-Moroccan agreement regarding defense, as the bases were an integral part of the defense of the area. Therefore, after the Moroccans had assumed control of their own foreign relations, base matters would still be subject to Franco-Moroccan agreement on defense. While he could not prejudge the future he thought that any discussions to do with our bases would almost inevitably be three power discussions between France, Morocco and US.

Comment: In view of above I think key words of reference telegram are last words in first paragraph, "Moroccans have assumed control foreign relations". It is clear that mere appointment of foreign minister will not automatically mean that Moroccans have taken over control of foreign relations. We will keep in closest touch with Savary on this matter but I feel that in spite of reasons for prompt action in Morocco we should take no definitive action with Moroccans on this subject until we have had chance to discuss matter with French here in Paris. Savary has promised to see me promptly any time such an emergency arises. I feel it is also important once Moroccans have assumed control of their foreign relations that we continue to realize that base problems are a matter of the defense of Morocco which according to the Franco-Moroccan agreements interest both France and Morocco. France should in no event be cut out of any talks on bases until and if situation arises where Franco-Moroccan defense agreement gives sole control of this subject to Moroccan Government. I very much doubt that this will óccur in any near future, i.e., within the next couple of years.

Dillon

191. Telegram From the Consulate General at Rabat to the Department of State [1]

Rabat, May 2, 1956—4 p.m.

410. Balafrej angry reaction reported Tangier 499 [2] regrettable but not surprising. In Contel 396 [3] we stated his assumption of foreign affairs would mean exactly that, which remains true not withstanding any French or US reluctance to accord him prompt and full recognition. None of us who has lived in French-controlled territories for long periods is likely underestimate need for keeping on good terms with French (or difficulty of doing so), but I have grave doubts as to advisability getting off to bad start with Moroccans merely to please French on short term basis. If France could hold area for West, Moroccan displeasure with US would be of lesser consequence (except of course with respect to US interests) but I have yet to meet anyone really familiar with this situation who is sure France can do so.

Content and tone of Balafrej remarks to our Chargé d'Affaires should not be considered mere bluster. To so consider them would be great error. He is one of group of most determined nationalists who have taken everything French could throw at them (which was plenty) for at least 15 years. They are now emerging as government with generally pro-Western outlook. This outlook will either be confirmed or will be radically altered during critical months ahead depending on welcome or lack of it accorded them by Western nations, especially US.

For these reasons I hope Department will find it possible recast its approach to this problem. Otherwise, Moroccan esteem for US, carefully nurtured and rebuilt by Holmes despite most difficult

[1] Source: Department of State, Central Files, 671.00/5–256. Confidential; Priority. Also sent to Tangier and repeated to Paris, London, Casablanca, Algiers, and Tunis.

[2] As a consequence of a diplomatic convention concluded between France and Morocco on May 19, which became effective May 28, Morocco assumed control of its external affairs. However, even in advance of this concord, the Moroccan Government appointed Ahmed Balafrej to be Foreign Minister on April 26. Telegram 499 from Tangier, May 2, reported that Balafrej made his displeasure known to C. Vaughan Ferguson, Jr., the Chargé at Tangier, that the United States had not recognized his new status. Balafrej warned against U.S. delay in affording him official recognition. (*Ibid.*, 611.75/5–256)

[3] Telegram 396, April 26, concluded that Balafrej would, in fact, be in effective control of foreign affairs. He was described as a friend of the West, but someone whom it might be difficult to keep so disposed without disturbing the French. (*Ibid.*, 771.00/4–2556)

circumstances of recent past, will quickly disappear with rather obvious consequences.

Porter

192. Telegram From the Embassy in France to the Department of State [1]

Paris, May 28, 1956—1 p.m.

5604. Reference: Deptel 4429. [2] During discussion with Savary (Embtel 5499) [3] he assured me that we should draw no implications from exclusion of base agreements in diplomatic convention excepting that Moroccans desired to have opportunity to discuss this matter thoroughly and neither Moroccans nor French wished to hold up diplomatic convention for such negotiation, which will surely be difficult and may be long.

Agreements which Moroccans automatically accepted were host of run of the mill diplomatic agreements covering such things as citizenship, copyrights and various economic matters which France had concluded in the name of the Moroccan Government. Base agreements clearly did not fall in this category and I presume that United States accepted this situation with eyes open when they were concluded in 1950. At that time base agreements were concluded with France as the power having sole authority for the defense of Morocco and as such agreements were purely Franco-American agreements and were not concluded in the name of the Sherifian Empire as was the case with the automatic run of the mill diplomatic conventions.

I saw Massigli this morning and he fully confirmed fact that no implications should be read into omission of base agreements in

[1] Source: Department of State, Central Files, 651.71/5–2856. Secret. Repeated to Rabat and Tangier.

[2] In telegram 4429, May 25, the Department sought French interpretation of the exchange of letters between Morocco and France of May 20, whereby Morocco reserved its position with respect to the Franco-American Base Agreement of December 22, 1950. The apparent implications of this action disturbed the Department though, in general, it approved of Morocco's diplomatic independence. (*Ibid.*, 651.71/5–2256)

[3] In telegram 5499, Dillon reported on May 22 that Savary provided him with the text of the Franco-Moroccan diplomatic agreement plus the texts of the accompanying letters. (*Ibid.*)

diplomatic convention except obvious fact that status of bases must be negotiated with Moroccans both by France and by United States. At same time Massigli gave me an informal memo, rough translation of which follows:

. . . .

Massigli dwelt particularly on the first point in the memorandum regarding military aid to Moroccan forces. He pointed out that France had made a very considerable effort in giving the Moroccans equipment for their army and that they were prepared to continue to equip Moroccan army as necessary.

Therefore, they would find it very unpleasant if the United States should attempt to interfere in this field by offering military assistance to the Moroccans. The same considerations will also apply in the case of Tunisia.

Comment: I feel that this French point is very well taken and consider it important that all our military and diplomatic representatives who are apt to be in touch with the Moroccans on this subject be clearly instructed not to hold out any hopes to Moroccans for United States military aid. In addition to its bearing on relations with French this would seem to be most important from United States budgetary point of view.

Regarding Point 2C, I told Massigli that I was in full agreement with him as to advisability of insisting that our base negotiations with Moroccans be conducted on a tri-lateral basis. As a result of conversation here with Holmes I also told Massigli that Holmes shared the view that it would be preferable if negotiations could be kept on a trilateral basis.[4] I pointed out, however, that the recent history of Franco Moroccan negotiations had shown it was not always possible to operate in the way that would be best and that it might be that the Moroccans would create a situation which could force both US and the French into purely bilateral negotiations. In this event I said that I was sure that United States would want to keep in the closest possible touch with the French so that we would be in effect conducting the negotiations jointly. Massigli said that he fully agreed and that this was basic objective of the memorandum which he had just given me.

I asked Massigli what his ideas were on time schedule and he replied he thought that we should move rapidly on the base question and commence negotiations with the Moroccans as soon as

[4] In telegram 572 from Tangier, May 31, Holmes commented that the French effectively eliminated themselves from participation in future negotiations by agreeing to exclude the base agreements from their diplomatic convention with Morocco. (*Ibid.*, 651.71/5–3156)

possible. In response to a specific question of mine he said he did not think it necessary to tie the conclusion of an agreement regarding the bases to the completion of the overall Franco-Moroccan negotiations regarding the defense of Morocco. He felt the base question should be handled separately and on a priority basis.

Dillon

193. Memorandum From the Acting Assistant Secretary of State for European Affairs (Elbrick) to the Secretary of State [1]

Washington, May 31, 1956.

SUBJECT

Status of Moroccan Bases

Background of Air Base Agreement

In 1950 shortly after the outbreak of the Korean War, Defense established an urgent requirement for SAC bases in Morocco. The U.S. accordingly undertook negotiations for the establishment of these bases with the French Government in view of the latter's responsibilities for Moroccan foreign affairs under the Treaty of Fez.

During the negotiations, the U.S. urged the French to apprise the Sultan of Morocco thereof. The French refused to do this. In light of the pressing need for the bases at that time, the U.S. decided it had to go ahead under the circumstances and conclude an agreement with the French. Subsequent to signing of the agreement, the French were again requested by us to inform the Moroccans in general terms of the agreement. As far as is known, this was never done.

The Air Base Agreement of December 22, 1950 provided that the U.S. would expand and use already existent French facilities in Morocco. The bases were to remain French and any non-removable property would eventually revert to the French Air Force when the bases were no longer required by the U.S. Air Force. The validity of

[1] Source: Department of State, Central Files, 711.56371/5–3156. Confidential. Attached to Phleger's memorandum, *infra*. Drafted by Matthew J. Looram and sent through MacArthur to the Secretary and Murphy.

the Agreement was for the duration of the North Atlantic Treaty unless terminated earlier by mutual accord.

Actually, instead of expanding existent French bases, it was found necessary to build completely new air fields. The French Government acquired the land. The facilities have been completed: three SAC bases (Benguerir, Sidi Slimane, Boulhaut) and an Air Force supply depot (Nouasseur).

At the same time that the Air Base Agreement was negotiated, an identical agreement was made with the French for extending the U.S. Navy's use of the French naval-air facilities at Port Lyautey. The Navy had been operating out of Port Lyautey since 1947.

For the past six months, with the approach of national independence, the Moroccans have made it clear both to the French and to ourselves that they would wish to raise with the U.S. the whole question of the bases. The Sultan took the position, which has since been assumed by the Moroccan Government, that the Moroccans were officially unaware of the bases as they had never been informed of the agreements. The Moroccans indicated that they did not desire the U.S. to quit the bases, but at the same time it was made clear that they wished to negotiate about the bases directly with the U.S. and to obtain extensive financial assistance as a quid pro quo.

The French Government tried to oppose this development and in its negotiations on "interdependence" with the Moroccans, endeavored to obtain Moroccan acquiescence to France's maintaining responsibility for Moroccan defense and accordingly to the continuation of defense agreements, including the U.S. base agreements. If France could continue to act as an intermediary between the U.S. and the Moroccans, she would have a better chance of maintaining a monopoly over overall Moroccan defense. As was expected, the Moroccans refused to accept the French position and the French-Moroccan conventions just concluded specifically reserve the whole question of the U.S. base agreements. Had the U.S. insisted on the French obtaining Moroccan acceptance of the validity of the base agreements before signing the conventions, this could have long delayed conclusion of the conventions with serious repercussions on future U.S.-Moroccan relations.

Validity of Base Agreements

Whether or not the base agreements are binding on Morocco in the present circumstances is questionable. The agreements were not made in the name of the Moroccan Government. In fact Article 11 of the Air Base Agreement, which states that the French Government "will recommend that the Moroccan Government extend the benefits", clearly shows that France was not acting as an agent for the Moroccan Government. Moreover, the agreements were not to assure the internal security of Morocco; the preambles refer to respective responsibilities in defense of Western Europe under the North Atlantic Treaty. As a result, the Moroccans may well challenge the validity of these arrangements and deny their binding character with respect to Morocco today.

On the other hand, in view of the existence of the Treaty of Fez, the U.S. had no choice in 1950 as to whom it should negotiate with. It was impossible at that juncture for the U.S. to negotiate with the Sultan; we were therefore obliged to accept the best agreement that could be negotiated with the French.

Regardless of the legal arguments, however, it has been clear that with the termination of the French protectorate, the Moroccans would insist on raising the question of the base agreements with the U.S. The charges on the Moroccan Government are rising daily, and taking Libya as a model, the Moroccan Government is counting on the U.S. for future financial assistance. The bases provide them strong leverage in this connection.

Recommendations

1. It is recommended that: The Defense Department re-examine urgently the strategic importance of the Moroccan bases and advise the Department of State of the results of this study. (It is understood that Mr. Gordon Gray has now requested the Services to undertake such a study.) [2]

2. Following this study and depending on its results, the U.S. be prepared to negotiate about the bases with the Moroccan Government at an early date. This should be a package deal including the Air Base Agreement with technical annexes, the Port Lyautey Naval Base Agreement, a Status of Forces Agreement and a Tax Relief Agreement. As a practical matter these negotiations would probably have to be conducted on a trilateral basis to include the French Government in view of the tie-in of the foregoing with France's responsibilities in Morocco. This should not, however, preclude bilateral discussions with the Moroccans as may be necessary.

3. Although we should try to avoid establishing a link between maintaining the bases and economic aid, the U.S. should take under urgent consideration the feasibility of extending financial assistance to the Moroccan Government.

---

[2] A handwritten marginal note dated June 1 indicates that Gray had not yet decided to refer the matter to the Services.

194. Memorandum From the Legal Adviser of the Department of State (Phleger) to the Secretary of State [1]

Washington, June 6, 1956.

SUBJECT

Moroccan Bases

1. The attached paper [2] makes no mention about the legal rights of the U.S., if any, to these bases as against the Moroccan Government, but assumes as the basis for starting negotiations that we have no rights.

2. While such rights as the United States may have as against Morocco are unclear, it certainly seems unwise to start these negotiations without asserting and retaining any and all rights that the United States in fact may have. There is no objection to negotiating with Morocco for a readjustment of the base rights, having in mind its new sovereignty, but it would seem this should not be done on the basis that we do not have any rights vis-à-vis Morocco.

3. Some one in the United States Government made the agreement for these bases, and on the strength of this agreement the U.S. has spent more than $400 million. It can be imagined what criticism will be directed against those who made the agreement and expended these funds, if the U.S. now takes the position, or finds itself in the position, of having no rights to continue in occupation of the bases.

4. I suggest that whoever negotiated the agreement [3] should be called upon to advise forthwith as to the legal theory on which the base agreements were made and what rights it is claimed the U.S. has as against Morocco and to continue in possession. Further, that any negotiations be so conducted as not to prejudice whatever legal rights the United States has—this to be done, however, in such a manner as not to unduly excite or offend the Moroccans, or prejudice the success of the negotiations.

---

[1] Source: Department of State, Central Files, 711.56371/6–656. Confidential.

[2] *Supra.*

[3] The treaty was concluded by an Air Force negotiating team consisting of George Brownell, Kenyon C. Bolton, and Pierpont M. Hamilton.

195. Telegram From the Department of State to the Embassy in France [1]

Washington, July 10, 1956—7:14 p.m.

118. Pending Secretary's clearance and pouching of record of Pineau talks here last month [2] following excerpt re Morocco is for your background in current consideration base problem:

"Pineau opened discussion on North Africa at Secretary's invitation. Referring to Tunisia and Morocco he said that there had been some difficulties in last few weeks in matter of diplomatic representation. Situation was a delicate juridical one pending ratification of Conventions between France and these two countries. However problem had been solved with regard to exchange of ambassadors. Outlook for future negotiations was not unfavorable but there will be delicate points to be settled in bilateral relations with these countries. Pineau said he would keep us informed and he asked us not to allow Morocco and Tunisia to play us off against France. He said these two countries have budgetary deficits and will be turning to everyone to ask for aid. This meant that it was most important to coordinate our approaches.

Pineau turned to subject of US bases in Morocco. He said these could not be treated as part of Convention which had been signed with Morocco because this would have broadened its character too much. Convention had to be limited to subject of diplomatic representation in order that it should not be necessary to have it ratified by French Parliament. Problem of bases concerns both foreign affairs and defense, which have not yet been the subject of negotiation. Only aspect of defense which had been settled was that of Moroccan Army.

Pineau said that question of bases could not be settled without US participation and that talks would have to be tripartite.

He said that exchange of letters between French and Moroccan Governments, which had accompanied Convention, had no bearing on problem of bases which should be settled in a separate Convention. He said that French Government was ready to proceed with further discussions with us on this subject at our convenience.

---

[1] Source: Department of State, Central Files, 711.56371/7–1056. Secret; Limit Distribution. Also sent to Rabat. Although an ambassador had not yet been appointed, U.S. representation in Morocco was raised to the level of an embassy on June 11.

[2] Dulles and the French Minister of Foreign Affairs, Christian Pineau, and their aides discussed the Moroccan situation on June 18. (Memorandum of conversation by Tyler, June 21; *ibid.*, Secretary's Memoranda of Conversation: Lot 64 D 199)

Secretary said that US Government considers our agreement with French Government on bases in Morocco to be valid for duration of North Atlantic Treaty, and that responsibility should be assumed by Moroccan Government. He said that practically speaking it was essential to obtain agreement of Moroccan Government, which could not be ignored whatever the legal situation might be. He said that US is not disposed itself to invite any negotiation because our position is that our base agreement with French Government is still valid. We would prefer talks to be tripartite. However if Moroccans preferred to talk on a bilateral basis, we would reserve our position and inform French Government in order to consult on situation which might result.

Pineau said that this was a delicate point. If talks were bilateral it would be difficult to reconcile this with Secretary's argument that commitment made with France was for duration of North Atlantic Treaty. There was also practical aspect of the danger of Moroccans being 'rapacious' and asking more and more in return for bases, especially if talks were conducted outside of present agreement.

Secretary said he did not mean to imply that US was prepared to start bilateral talks but only that we do not wish to exclude at this time possibility of having bilateral talks. As he had told Pineau already, we would keep French Government informed.

Pineau said he wished to emphasize that Franco-US Base Agreement conferred not only certain rights but also certain obligations, which Moroccan Government is incapable of carrying out.

Secretary said he assumed French would inform us in same way that we would inform it, of any approach or discussion with Moroccans, and Mr. Pineau agreed."

Dulles

196. Telegram From the Embassy in France to the Department of State [1]

Paris, July 12, 1956—6 p.m.

195. Re Embtel 191. [2] Following is text delivered by Ambassador to Massigli July 12.

"By note dated July 7, 1956, the Moroccan Government formally requested the United States Government to make available to it the texts of the Franco-American base agreements of December 1950. [3] The United States Government considers that the French Government, rather than itself, should transmit these texts to the Moroccan Government. It is also the view of the United States Government that these texts should be delivered promptly to the Moroccan Government. As the French Government is aware, it has always been the position of the United States Government that the Moroccan Government should be informed of these agreements. Accordingly, the United States Government intends to reply to the Moroccan Government stating that the French Government will soon deliver the texts.

It is understood that the French Government plans to transmit the texts to the Moroccan Government under cover of a note along the following lines: (1) the French Government, with the agreement of the United States Government, is hereby transmitting to the Moroccan Government the texts of the December 1950 agreements on the bases in Morocco; (2) the French Government is prepared to furnish any supplementary information which the Moroccan Government may desire; and (3) the Agreements of 1950 are confidential in character. Such a covering note is acceptable to the United States Government. [4]

Regarding the matters raised in the French Government's communication of May 26, 1956, [5] the United States Government wishes to state the following:

(1) The basic United States position is that the agreements of December 1950 are valid and binding on the Government of France and Morocco.

---

[1] Source: Department of State, Central Files, 711.56371/7–1256. Secret. Repeated to Rabat.

[2] Telegram 191, July 12, reported Massigli's statement that France would not object to the United States informing Morocco that the French would soon provide them with the texts of the base agreements. (*Ibid.*)

[3] Balafrej gave Porter the note on July 8. (Telegram 22 from Rabat; *ibid.*, 711.56371/7–856)

[4] Pineau gave the Moroccan Ambassador to France the texts of the December 1950 base agreements on July 16. Balafrej, however, asked Porter for copies of the technical agreements which had not been provided. The Embassy informed the French Foreign Ministry of this approach and urged the French to comply. Dillon reported in telegram 408 from Paris, July 24, that the French would probably proceed to make the 1951 technical agreements plus annexes and perhaps the 1947 Port Lyautey agreement available to the Moroccans. (*Ibid.*, 711.56371/7–2456)

[5] See Document 192.

(2) The United States currently has no plans whatsoever to offer aid toward the organization and equipment of the Moroccan forces. Should the Moroccan Government approach the United States regarding military aid, we will inform the French Government promptly.

(3) The United States Government will not initiate negotiations with the Moroccan Government at this time concerning the base agreements. However, the United States Government desires to be informed in advance of any French-Moroccan negotiations affecting United States interests in the bases and the intended object and substance of these negotiations".

Dillon

---

197. Memorandum From the Deputy Director for Plans of the Central Intelligence Agency (Stewart) to the Secretary of State's Special Assistant for Intelligence (Armstrong) [1]

Washington, July 30, 1956.

SUBJECT

Observations of the Sultan on Political and Economic Problems in Morocco

According to a usually reliable source, the Sultan of Morocco, . . . in July 1956, made the following observations:

1. Morocco is presently in a difficult and dangerous situation, beset by both political and economic dangers from within and without. Some of these difficulties stem from those who desire to cause Morocco's downfall, and some are inherent in the economic situation.

2. The new Moroccan Army will require a great deal of financial aid and equipment and a well planned organization to effectively absorb the forty thousand men still currently active in the Liberation Army in Morocco. These forces are to be used not only to protect Moroccan territory, but, as far as possible, to support Moroccan policy toward Algeria. The Sultan said he desired to have a total of 80,000 men in the Army by 1958.

3. With regard to the United States, the Sultan said that Morocco's relations with the United States have a background of

---

[1] Source: Department of State, AF/AFN Files: Lot 63 D 250, Morocco History. Secret; Noforn; Continued Control. A copy was sent to the Director of Intelligence of the Air Force.

close friendship, including the friendly support of former President Franklin Roosevelt. "However, at the time of my deposition in August 1953", the Sultan said, "when I protested to the French that the United States would not countenance my deposition, I was shocked to hear from the mouth of the French officer who accompanied General Guillaume, that the U.S. had already agreed to the deposition.[2] Then upon my return from Madagascar,[3] I was informed that the U.S. would not effectively recognize our independence until France had agreed to it. And later still, I was told that the U.S. will ask France to be present at the discussions between the U.S. and Morocco over the Air Bases. To this, I cannot agree. The Air Base question is becoming a particularly bitter subject for us, largely because of the U.S. attempts to maintain the presence of the French during these discussions. This is solely a U.S.-Moroccan problem. Regardless of the questionable legality of the previous arrangement, the fact remains that the Bases are on Moroccan soil, that Morocco is a sovereign State, and, among other things, Morocco has superseded France in its dealing with Foreign Powers. There can be no resumption of honestly good relations between Morocco and the U.S. until the French element is removed from any discussion between the two countries. The French have not conducted themselves in a manner that would warrant our acceptance of their presence at these negotiations or that would warrant their right to be consulted in this or financial matters."

4. The Sultan also stated that it was a great mistake on the part of the West to consider Algeria as a separate question. Morocco, Algeria and Tunisia must be considered as one single question. Morocco supports Algerian independence and will assist in every possible way to help it achieve independence. No real peace is possible in North Africa until satisfaction is given Algeria's rightful claim. The Sultan said that the Algerian situation could provoke a general warfare in North Africa and no one can foresee the end.

5. In addition, the Sultan declared that both he and his Government will make every effort to regain sovereignty over previously held Moroccan territory, specifically Ifni, Rio de Oro, Melilla, Ceuta, Northern Mauretania, and to rectify the Algerian frontiers.

6. In closing, the Sultan said that the problem of French Communists, French supported Moroccan Communist efforts and other disruptive efforts by the French in Moroccan affairs, greatly concern him. He said the Moroccan Government was hampered by the inability to trust the Frenchmen who have occupied positions

[2] General Augustin Guillaume was the Resident General of Morocco between August 28, 1951 and May 20, 1954.

[3] Mohammed V was exiled to Madagascar.

without being morally fitted to do so. Some have gone so far as to remove or destroy many precious records which means, in many instances, "that we are left to grope as do the blind". However, the Sultan said he had instructed his Minister of Security, Mohamed Laghzaoui, to give these matters his closest attention and, particularly, to modify the rules governing foreign travellers in and out of Morocco. Although, he said, this modification will affect Americans in Morocco, the measure is not directed against them and will be applied to them with only a minimum of formality.

For the Deputy Director, Plans:
Thomas H. Karamessines
for Gordon M. Stewart[4]

[4] Printed from a copy that bears these stamped signatures.

198. Telegram From the Department of State to the Embassy in Morocco[1]

Washington, September 23, 1956—2:39 p.m.

108. Rabat's 142.[2] Department believes we should make all appropriate effort discourage Moroccans from establishing diplomatic relations Soviets and satellites at this time, recognizing, however, there are limits to which we can go in light over-all US relations that country. In general we leave Ambassador's discretion manner of presentation and extent to which he feels it wise press Moroccans this subject.

Department approves line suggested antepenultimate paragraph reference telegram[3] although believes we should be careful avoid any implication of threat re future US-Moroccan relations. You are

[1] Source: Department of State, Central Files, 661.71/9–2656. Secret; Priority. Drafted by Palmer. Repeated to Paris and by pouch to Tangier, London, Casablanca, Algiers, and Tunis.

[2] Telegram 142, September 22, stated that Balafrej informed Ambassador Cannon that the Soviets for the third time indicated their interest in establishing diplomatic relations and that Bulgaria and Czechoslovakia were also interested. (*Ibid.*, 661.71/9–2256)

[3] Cannon suggested that the Department of State might recommend deferring action until Morocco and the United States had resolved outstanding matters of common concern. He also raised the possibility of referring to U.S. objections to the establishment of a Soviet mission close to Western defense positions.

free make clear Moroccans would have appropriate support this Government in event decision is to reject Soviet request.

You may also point out that sudden interest Soviets and satellites in Morocco where legitimate interests are minimal after long period indifference surely reflects on their motives and must raise suspicions re real intentions. This has been familiar Soviet maneuver in newly independent areas where they have worked against established authority and national unity. At this time when no compelling reason establish diplomatic relations with Soviets, such action could needlessly complicate Morocco's internal problems and relations with West which is so sympathetic to her stable and prosperous development.

In rejecting Soviet note, Moroccans may wish make use following arguments:

1. Before extending its diplomatic establishment further GOM considers it necessary concentrate on and dispose of basic problems of transition affecting general welfare Moroccan people.
2. Thereafter GOM will be better able assess justification for assuming burden supporting additional diplomatic missions.
3. Moroccan diplomatic establishments in third countries and Delegation at UN available for conduct any essential business between two countries.

You are authorized attribute foregoing to Department in discussions with Balafrej.

Dulles

---

199. Note From the Ambassador in Morocco (Cannon) to Minister of Foreign Affairs Balafrej [1]

No. 63 *Rabat, October 6, 1956.*

EXCELLENCY: I have the honor to refer to the statement issued by the Department of State on January 26, 1956, [2] announcing the intention of the United States Government to relinquish its consular jurisdiction in Morocco at the appropriate time in keeping with the desire to modernize this aspect of the treaty relationship between Morocco and the United States.

---

[1] Source: Department of State, Central Files, 271.116/10–856. Enclosure to despatch 50 from Rabat, October 8.

[2] See footnote 3, Document 186.

It is the decision of my government to relinquish this day these consular jurisdictions which were accorded to the United States of America in a Treaty of Peace and Friendship first concluded with Morocco in 1787 and renewed in 1836 and in the Act of Algeciras signed in 1906; as well as to cease to exercise jurisdiction over subjects of Morocco or others who may be designated as protégés under the Convention of Madrid signed in 1880. It is my understanding, however, that American protégés will have access to the same local courts as American citizens in accordance with the procedures followed in the past when capitulations have been relinquished.

It affords me great satisfaction at the outset of my mission to convey to Your Excellency my Government's decision in this regard.[3]

Accept [etc.][4]

[3] P.L. 856, approved August 1, 1956, authorized the President to relinquish extraterritorial jurisdiction in Morocco. On September 12, Secretary Dulles recommended this be done coincident with the arrival in Rabat of Ambassador Cavendish Cannon. (Memorandum for the President; *ibid.*, AF/AFN Files: Lot 60 D 577) The President agreed on September 15. (*Ibid.*, Central Files, 271.116/9–1556)

[4] There is no signature on the source text.

200. Memorandum From the Deputy Assistant Secretary of State for African Affairs (Palmer) to the Under Secretary of State (Hoover)[1]

Washington, October 27, 1956.

SUBJECT

United States Participation in Signing of Tangier Declaration and Protocol[2]

Discussion:

On August 23, 1956, Mr. Murphy as the Acting Secretary, approved United States participation in the nine-power conference

[1] Source: Department of State, Central Files, 771.00/10–2756. Confidential. Drafted by Bovey.

[2] For text of the Final Declaration and Annexed Protocol signed at Tangier on October 29 by Belgium, France, Italy, Morocco, the Netherlands, Portugal, Spain, the United Kingdom, and the United States, see 7 UST, pt. 3, 3035. The text is also printed, together with information concerning the background of the international regime of the Tangier Zone, in *American Foreign Policy: Current Documents, 1956*, pp. 716–721.

which the Government of Morocco convened for the definitive settlement of the future status of Tangier. The authority for our signing the final instrument was defined in Mr. Allen's memorandum of August 21, 1956 (Tab A). [3]

The Conference has completed its work and has drawn up a Declaration and a Protocol, translations of which are attached as Tab B.

These documents modify no treaties to which the U.S. is a party and contain no treaty commitments on the part of the United States. The fact that the United States did not sign, and therefore is not agreeing to a modification of the Tangier Statute of 1923 [4] or the Franco-British Provisional Agreement of 1945 [5] is reflected in the reservation contained in the second paragraph of Article I of the Declaration.

The only Articles directly affecting United States interests are those contained in Chapter IV, [6] and especially in Chapter V, which concerns telecommunications and radio broadcasting. The drafting of Chapter V has presented some difficulty; it represents the best working arrangement which, after considerable effort, our Delegation has been able to secure from the Moroccan Government at this time, and leaves the way open to the negotiation of satisfactory bilateral arrangements covering the Voice of America relay facilities, concerning whose future the Moroccan Government has offered us private assurances, and the installations of RCA and Mackay. It has been approved by USIA and has been drafted in full consultation with representatives of the two companies, who were sent to the conference for this purpose, and who likewise have approved it.

Ambassador Cannon has requested authorization to sign the Declaration and Protocol with the representatives of the other eight Governments on October 29. I feel it most important that he receive this authorization promptly.

Recommendation:

That you authorize the signature of the attached Declaration and Protocol on October 29. [7]

---

[3] The tabs are not printed. The memorandum recommended U.S. participation in the conference, which was held October 8–29 in Fedala and Tangier. (Department of State, Central Files, 771.00/8–2156)

[4] For text of the Convention Regarding the Organization of the Statute of the Tangier Zone, signed at Paris, December 18, 1923, by Britain, France, and Spain, see Great Britain, Treaty Series No. 23 (1924), Cmd. 2203.

[5] The text of the Anglo-French Agreement for the Re-Establishment of the International Administration of Tangier, signed at Paris August 31, 1945, is in *A Decade of American Foreign Policy: Basic Documents, 1941–1949* (revised edition), pp. 610–613.

[6] Entitled "Concessions, Leases and Authorizations."

[7] Hoover initialed his approval on October 27.

201. Telegram From the Embassy in France to the Department of State [1]

Paris, November 13, 1956—10 p.m.

2356. French have recently made series of approaches, all of which are related in that they involve greater French use of or role in Moroccan bases. Among these are: (1) French proposals for use Port Lyautey as off-loading point, including construction storage sheds; [2] (2) French pressure (which continues strong) for greater participation in Moroccan air defense; [3] and (3) new French proposal to USAFE authorities for use air bases as safe havens in case emergencies. (On last, Department's attention called to USAFE to USCINCEUR E–CINC 17606 repeated information Chief of Staff USAF November 6.) [4]

Embassy believes time has come when we must have frank discussion on these matters with French at appropriately high level in Paris. Purpose would be to convince French of adverse effect on base negotiations of efforts by them to upset present status quo in their role on bases. We plan make approach along following lines. (1) We continue regard Franco-American agreements 1950 and 1951 as valid legal basis for Moroccan bases and our position on base negotiations remains as stated by Secretary to Pineau. [5] (2) From point of view of our relations with Moroccans over future base negotiations, we cannot afford at this time to agree to any significant new steps increasing French use of bases, particularly for French military purposes. Moroccans have already given indications that they are thinking in terms of a completely

[1] Source: Department of State, Central Files, 711.56371/11–1356. Secret. Repeated to Rabat and USCINCEUR.

[2] Cannon reported in telegram 252 from Rabat, November 1, that France would seek the right to off-load military cargoes from civilian and military ships within that facility. The base accord was silent on the matter of commercial ships and the U.S. expectation was that the French anticipated using military personnel to unload the ships. Cannon opposed the French plans and urged that the French be asked to change them. (*Ibid.*, 711.56371/11–156) The Department responded that the matter would best be settled locally by the respective commanders. (Telegram 230 to Rabat, November 3; *ibid.*, 711.56371/11–356) Cannon indicated in telegram 274, November 6, that the French intended to construct storage facilities within the American portion of the base because it could be defended more easily. Cannon thus renewed his plea for high-level intervention to dissuade the French Government. (*Ibid.*, 711.56371/11–656)

[3] Dillon reported in telegram 1750 from Paris, October 12, that the French had approached the Embassy with a request for greater participation in radar sites in Morocco, to which they felt entitled for having approved the increased U.S. troop ceiling. (*Ibid.*, 711.56371/10–1256) Telegram 1827 from Paris, October 19, reported French insistence on technical talks to work out the increased French role. Dillon recommended holding a planning meeting so as not to alienate the French. (*Ibid.*, 711.56371/10–1956)

[4] Not found in Department of State files.

[5] See Document 195.

bilateral arrangement with US on bases. If Moroccans gain impression that French are seeking to expand their involvement in bases used by US at this time, their position will become much more rigid. (3) In view these considerations, we would like to make certain comments on specific proposals French have recently made regarding US-used bases. As will be seen, we are by no means opposed in principle to all these proposals, but we do feel that caution must be exercised on any steps which would arouse such strong Moroccan reactions as to affect adversely our interests in base negotiations. (4) Re French proposal over using Port Lyautey as facility for off-loading supplies, we have already received démarche from Moroccans on this, indicating Sultan personally concerned.[6] Therefore, we feel there should be no steps by French to expand use of Port Lyautey, or to take similar steps for French military use of other bases by US. Would obviously be preferable make use existing French port facilities.[7] (5) Re further French participation in Moroccan air defense, we are fully prepared to study carefully this step and are prepared now hold technical level talks necessary to prepare for next steps. However, we feel that this particular moment would be inopportune from point of view our mutual interests for actually increasing number of French personnel in air defense.[8] (6) We also understand that French authorities have inquired as to availability US-used bases as safe haven for French civilians in case of local emergency Morocco. We consider that under base agreements French have full right of decision re using bases for such purpose. If US did have right of decision in this matter, it would not refuse access to bases for any persons seeking refuge in an emergency.

Dillon

[6] Balafrej called Porter to the Foreign Office on November 7 to express the Moroccan wish that the United States not permit French "military expansion" at Port Lyautey. He indicated that the Sultan opposed a larger French presence on any U.S. base. (Telegram 276 from Rabat, November 7; Department of State, Central Files, 711.56371/11–756)

[7] Cannon reported in telegram 290, November 13, that the French had moved into the U.S. sector of the base and begun construction the day before despite U.S. requests for delay while a local solution was sought. The Ambassador suggested that the United States should publicly disassociate itself from the French action. (*Ibid.*, 711.56371/11–1356)

[8] The Embassy in Morocco supported putting off any technical talks believing that the negative political repercussions of a greater French air defense role outweighed any commitments to convene such a meeting. (Telegram 194 from Rabat, October 17; *ibid.*, 711.56371/10–1756)

202. Telegram From the Department of State to the Embassy in Morocco[1]

Washington, November 19, 1956—12:05 p.m.

275. Rabat 257,[2] 270,[3] Paris 2111.[4] FYI. Department believes positive response Moroccan aid request entirely in keeping NSC directives[5] and French Government position as last explained (Paris 366, July 20).[6] Precise level aid would be worked out during negotiations in light (1) Progress on base rights problem (2) Availability funds (3) Progress Morocco in making economic arrangements with French, on whom it appears they must continue depend for bulk outside help (4) Information concerning economic conditions Morocco. Reply indicated below also goes as far as Department can to counteract Faure's apprehensions re US supplanting French in economic field. End FYI.

1. Embassy Rabat may therefore tell FonOff that in response to request conveyed through Ambassador Ben Aboud, US position is that indicated in penultimate paragraph your 257; that is, US prepared in principle extend economic and technical assistance to Morocco with extent and type such programs to be determined by on-spot studies and conversations between two Governments, and ICA prepared send survey team.[7] Rabat should make clear however

---

[1] Source: Department of State, Central Files, 771.5–MSP/11–356. Secret; Priority. Also sent to Paris and repeated to Tunis.

[2] Telegram 257, November 1, indicated that a Moroccan approach for economic aid was expected. Cannon asked for permission to respond affirmatively with the kind and extent of such aid to be left to negotiations. (*Ibid.*, 771.5–MSP/11–156)

[3] Telegram 270, November 3, reported that the Moroccan Ambassador to the United States, Dr. El-Mehdi Ben Aboud, had indicated to the Embassy on November 2 that approximately $70 million in aid would be required for each of the next 3 years. (*Ibid.*, 771.5–MSP/11–356)

[4] In telegram 2111, October 31, Dillon recommended against a commitment which would alienate the French and which might also encourage them to suspend their assistance. (*Ibid.*, 771.5–MSP/10–3156)

[5] Reference is to NSC 5614/1, Document 36.

[6] Telegram 366 reported that Savary had made it clear that France would not oppose the United States listening to and studying Moroccan aid requests, but preferred that no commitments be made until Franco-Moroccan negotiations were further advanced. (*Ibid.*, 772.5–MSP/7–2056)

[7] In a meeting with Acting Secretary Hoover in Washington on November 27, Balafrej expressed Morocco's need for economic assistance. (*Ibid.*, Secretary's Memoranda of Conversation: Lot 64 D 199) Following this conversation, Palmer assured Balafrej that an ICA Survey Mission would depart for Morocco in a day or two. (Memorandum of conversation by Palmer, November 28; *ibid.*, Central Files, 771.5–MSP/11–2856) Press reports to this effect caused the French to protest to the Embassy in Paris the onset of aid negotiations at a time when Franco-Moroccan financial conversations were suspended. (Telegram 2757 from Paris, December 3; *ibid.*, 771.5–MSP/12–356)

this in no way implies US acceptance any amount or time periods hitherto mentioned.

2. Moreover in order avoid arousing undue expectations Rabat should make clear GOM that as matter principle and owing statutory and budgetary limitations based on world-wide commitments US policy encourages other Western nations and international agencies share responsibilities economic aid. FYI. Funds already tentatively earmarked up to $30 million FY 57 for Morocco and additional funds will be sought for 1958 but US cannot undertake three-year commitment of type indicated by Ben Aboud. End FYI. Rabat should add it does not appear likely we could undertake at this time anything on order amounts previously discussed with French. Therefore GOM should also conclude such economic arrangements as they feel they can with French and should be told we are urging French expedite these arrangements.

3. Department taking same line with Moroccan Embassy Washington.

4. Upon receipt this telegram and related telegram Tunisia,[8] Embassy Paris should inform French of request conveyed through Ben Aboud and nature foregoing reply making clear we acting on Moroccan request and that our decisions in working out program will be facilitated by rapid conclusion Franco-Moroccan arrangements with which we desire coordinate our own. Believe that by responding positively to Moroccans and making clear our limitations to both them and French we will be in better position get both parties take more favorable view re conclusion economic and financial arrangements with each other. Moreover by informing Moroccans our intention tell French we acting positively on request we would hope minimize effective French exploitation such approaches as "clearance" and chronic Moroccan suspicions this regard.

5. We cannot of course neglect related problem bases. Embassy Rabat should therefore make clear GOM that continuing favorable Moroccan attitude toward matters affecting US interests in Morocco will be essential element in implementing agreed economic programs.

6. Material requested last paragraph your 257 being airpouched.[9]

Hoover

---

[8] Telegram 1891 to Paris, November 19, set forth the U.S. response to Tunisia's request for assistance. (*Ibid.*, 772.5–MSP/11–1956)

[9] Reference is to model draft bilateral aid agreements in both English and French and copies of any ICA preliminary studies that might exist.

203. Telegram From the Department of State to the Embassy in Morocco[1]

Washington, November 21, 1956—7:54 p.m.

284. Reports have reached Defense re organization public demonstrations and likelihood incidents anti American as well as anti French in connection French activities Port Lyautey.[2] Department therefore telephoned Balafrej New York stating (1) activities Port Lyautey result unilateral French decision and US not consulted (2) we are presently making efforts settle matter with French Government[3] (3) we are sure he will agree nothing should be done compromise our efforts (4) we would appreciate Balafrej communicating above his Government asking they make every effort avoid disorders.

Balafrej said he cabling his Government make every effort avoid disorders so that our efforts will not be compromised.[4]

Department today called in Lucet Chargé French Embassy and after referring Embassy Paris' démarche to Beaumarchais expressed serious concern US on grounds French action would adversely affect US and French interests and that deteriorating local situation endangering security base and US personnel. Lucet was asked request his government take measures discontinue present activities Port Lyautey.[5] Embassy Paris should take appropriate supporting action at highest levels.

For Rabat: 1. Embassy should immediately communicate GOM substance our conversation with Balafrej.

2. FYI During conversation French Chargé mentioned fact Moroccans had not approached French this question. We believe it might have salutary effect if GOM made feelings known to French

[1] Source: Department of State, Central Files, 711.56371/11–2156. Secret; Niact. Passed by Rabat to COMNAVACTS; also sent to Paris and passed to CINCEUR. Repeated to CINCNELM in London. Drafted by Bovey and cleared with WE and in substance with Gray of the Department of Defense.

[2] A French commercial vessel had started unloading military supplies at the wharf in the U.S. sector of the naval base on November 18.

[3] On November 16, the Embassy in Paris contacted Jacques Delarüe Caron de Beaumarchais of the French Foreign Ministry to request that nothing be done to threaten the status of U.S. bases in Morocco. (Telegram 2448 from Paris, November 16; Department of State, Central Files, 711.56371/11–1656)

[4] Ben Aboud called the Department of State on November 22 to report that his government would do all it could to maintain calm, but the French must cease their provocations. He was advised to take the matter up directly with the French. (Memorandum by Bovey; *ibid.*, 711.56371/11–2356)

[5] Dillon reported in telegram 2580, November 24, that the French would cease constructing a warehouse, but still intended to unload supplies. He noted the French Foreign Ministry had had no direct complaint from the Moroccan Government. (*Ibid.*, 711.56371/11–2456)

government. End FYI. Accordingly you may wish encourage Moroccans also talk directly to French.

Hoover

204. Telegram From the Department of State to the Embassy in Morocco[1]

Washington, December 6, 1956—8:10 p.m.

322. Rabat's 346.[2] Rather than reply formally Moroccan note at this time, Dept believes preferable first discuss matter with Balafrej (who may not have been consulted re decision make démarches US and France) in effort keep positions parties involved flexible pending further explorations among Governments concerned as to how best proceed regularize base agreements.[3] Accordingly suggest you talk Balafrej along following lines, use Paras 1 and 2 being discretionary depending on your judgment whether Balafrej consulted:

1. Dept surprised both content and tone of note. We had thought as result talks in Washington[4] that Moroccans thoroughly understood following re situation Port Lyautey: (a) US never consulted and bears no responsibility French actions Port Lyautey; (b) US concerned re French activity which poses real problem for US in terms local relationships; (c) In light legal position between US and France re bases, doubtful US has any basis demand French cease activities or any right expect prior consultation as note indicates. While we appreciate that Morocco reserves position re legality US-

[1] Source: Department of State, Central Files, 711.56371/12–156. Secret. Also sent to Paris and repeated to Paris and to London for CINCNELM. Drafted by Palmer and cleared with AF/N, L, RA, WE, and the Department of Defense.

[2] Telegram 346, December 1, summarized the oral remarks of the Acting Moroccan Foreign Minister Abderrahim Bouabid on November 29 when he presented a note protesting the Port Lyautey situation. (*Ibid.*)

[3] The substance of the Moroccan note was conveyed in telegram 340 from Rabat, November 30. The fact that the United States had permitted the French to use its portion of the facility was considered a grave affront to Moroccan sovereignty. The Moroccan Government asserted that the situation required a reexamination of the base agreements on a bilateral basis and U.S. action to compel the French to cease their military expansion. (*Ibid.*, 711.56371/11–3056) Cannon reported in telegram 344, December 1, that France considered the note the start of a campaign to begin bilateral base discussions. (*Ibid.*, 711.56371/12–156)

[4] In the course of Rountree's discussion with Balafrej of November 27, Balafrej made clear his government's unwillingness to discuss the bases with France. (Memorandum of conversation by Norland; *ibid.*, 771.5–MSP/11–2756)

French agreement on bases, we had thought Moroccans understood US point of view re legal considerations which constitute problem and limitation as to US freedom action; (d) notwithstanding foregoing limitations, we have in fact been making every effort remove causes misunderstanding in talks with French and have kept GOM currently informed our efforts.

2. Moroccan note November 29 now introduces new element in situation in stating requirement for US-Moroccan reexamination base question. As was made clear in conversations Washington, US recognizes fact of assumption Moroccan sovereignty creates new situation re bases which must be taken into account. At same time US cannot ignore interest of France in this question. It was for this reason that US in talks here expressed preference for trilateral discussions on base question but in light strong Moroccan reaction this suggestion, agreed consider matter further. US had not understood that Moroccans felt any immediate urgency re resolution this problem. On contrary, Crown Prince[5] clearly indicated GOM did not contemplate US-Moroccan negotiations re bases until after completion Franco-Moroccan agreement reached re cooperation on defense matters.

3. Question now arises as how we proceed in light Moroccan note. As we see problem, there are two distinct but related aspects: (a) short-term problem of situation at Port Lyautey; and (b) longer-term problem of regularizing situation US base facilities.

4. Re short term, US continuing make every effort settle this problem in manner consonant US-Moroccan and US-French relations. GOM may be assured we will not acquiesce in any resolution this problem detrimental Moroccan sovereignty. At same time GOM must understand that leaving aside legal considerations pointed out above, there are practical limitations on our ability bring about correction present situation. As long as French forces are in Morocco, they must obviously supply those forces. From practical viewpoint, US clearly not in position suggest alternative arrangement to this end. Only Moroccan and French Governments competent work out such arrangement and we therefore urge both Governments reach direct modus vivendi which will take account interests all parties involved, including proper respect Moroccan sovereignty, and at same time create favorable atmosphere resolution longer term problem. (FYI From US point of view, most satisfactory arrangement would be one permitting French resume use commercial facilities for normal military needs. End FYI)

[5] Crown Prince Moulay Hassan, during a private visit to the United States, conferred with Acting Secretary Hoover on November 29. He maintained that the bases, which had been agreed to by France without the knowledge of the Moroccan Government, would have to be given legal status.

5. Re long term, we not yet in position give definitive reply Moroccan statement its position which are studying as we promised Balafrej in talks here. As Balafrej seemed understand and accept we cannot ignore position of France with whom we must consult re future course of action. Such consultations necessary, not from point of view presenting Moroccans with joint US-French front, but in order carry forward search for practical solution of problem which will meet interests all three parties concerned and which began with valuable and amicable talks with Moroccan Foreign Minister here. We therefore prefer delay any formal reply to Moroccan note and would urge Moroccans be patient and help us avoid situation in which interested parties become frozen into formal positions which may complicate eventual resolution of problem. We would ask Foreign Minister in same spirit not meanwhile to publicize his notes to French and ourselves and intend ask French similarly postpone formal reply and avoid publicity.

For Paris:

A. Confirm to FonOff at highest available level substance our talks with Balafrej (Embtel 2756).[6]

B. At same time reiterate strong US concern re French activities Port Lyautey and emphasize our belief that all recent exceptional French activity there should cease in interests interrelationships US, France and Morocco. In this connection, Dept does not believe French position set forth Paris' 2602[7] constitutes satisfactory resolution problem. Although we recognize practical problem faced by France in supplying its forces, we believe this should be solved

---

[6] Telegram 2756, December 3, reported that the French had already been briefed by their Embassy in Washington. (Department of State, Central Files, 711.56371/12–356)

[7] In telegram 2602, November 26, Dillon indicated that the French position was that barracks for troops definitely would not be constructed, but no decision had been taken in regard to the supply shed. (*Ibid.*, 711.56371/11–2656) On December 8, Dillon once again took up this matter with the French Foreign Ministry. He outlined U.S. objections to the French position as stated in telegram 322. De Beaumarchais gave assurance that no construction was immediately contemplated, but traced the problem to the Moroccan Government's inability to compel the UMT to abide by an agreement which Rabat had concluded with France on October 18 to permit the entry of military supplies at Casablanca. (Telegram 2856 from Paris, Dec. 8; *ibid.*, 711.56371/12–356) Hoover advised the Embassy in Paris to make representations at a higher level of the Foreign Ministry and instructed the Embassy in Rabat to indicate that labor peace in Casablanca was needed to solve the problem. (Telegram 2274 to Paris, 337 to Rabat, December 14; *ibid.*, 711.56371/12–1356) Balafrej responded to Cannon's approaches by admitting the protest note was inexact and by agreeing that a formal response was unnecessary. He conceded it was unwise for his government to give the impression that it could not exercise control in Casablanca, but he blamed its difficulties upon resentment of the French military buildup at the time of Suez which, he asserted, had been intended for the occupation of Rabat and Fez. (Telegram 381 from Rabat, December 19; *ibid.*, 711.56371/12–1956)

between French and Moroccans on basis modus vivendi. In this connection, you should inform FonOff of Para 4 above.

C. Inform FonOff of substance Para 5 above and urge they not reply Moroccan note or give matter publicity pending further consultations re base negotiations problem which we hope be in position undertake soon. FYI We shall as soon as possible send Rabat and Paris for comment possible basis for approach to French on substance of problem. End FYI.

Dulles

---

205. Telegram From the Department of State to the Embassy in Morocco[1]

Washington, December 8, 1956—2:56 p.m.

329. Current events including 1) Balafrej conversations Washington 2) Port Lyautey developments 3) Moroccan note (Rabat's 340)[2] and 4) possible French approach to US during NATO Ministerial meeting necessitate review US position vis-à-vis French in connection Moroccan base negotiations using Secretary–Pineau June 1956 talks as point departure.

While in Washington Balafrej took initiative raising future of US-built bases Morocco. Department reiterated position US has valid and binding agreements governing use bases. Balafrej contested this, saying existing agreements with France which acted ultra vires in authorizing third power enter and build military bases Morocco without latter's consent. Balafrej emphasized Morocco's attitude as traditionally friendly towards US and stated Morocco wished reach bilateral settlement with US. Department explained preference trilateral discussions. Balafrej rejected this, emphasizing repugnance such approach to Moroccan sovereignty by asking dryly who third party would be. Otherwise Balafrej's attitude toward French surprisingly friendly and demonstrated keen desire get along with them as long as they respected Moroccan sovereignty. Department informed Balafrej we would take his views under advisement.

---

[1] Source: Department of State, Central Files, 711.56371/11–3056. Secret; Noforn. Also sent to Paris. Drafted by Cyr and Palmer and cleared with AF/N, WE, NEA, EUR, L, G, RA, and the Department of Defense.

[2] See footnote 3, *supra*.

Conversations with Balafrej made it obvious our base rights must be renegotiated to satisfaction of sovereign Morocco. Port Lyautey complications seen here as forerunner possible series incidents provoked by both sides and designed or adapted to creation friction involving US with French and/or Moroccans, as case may be, only certain result being that general atmosphere will worsen to point where effective enjoyment bases will be prejudiced.

In light foregoing, following considerations emerge:

1. US convinced permitting present situation to drift would have adverse effect US-Moroccan relations and prejudice security bases. (JCS has just reviewed and restated Moroccan bases essential US security.)[3]

2. Appears clear Moroccans will not agree either to tripartite discussion base question or anything other than strictly US-Moroccan arrangements re bases.

3. Therefore US immediate problem one of devising means negotiate bilaterally with minimum adverse effect US-French and French-Moroccan relations.

4. In addition substantive problems involved in preparing French for bilateral US-Moroccan relationship on bases, there are important tactical and timing difficulties. Thus, any US-Moroccan agreement prior conclusion Franco-Moroccan agreement on defense relationship would undoubtedly give rise French charges US trying replace France North Africa. Furthermore, it might well remove incentive Moroccans conclude defense agreement with France, cause them look to us for military assistance and generally seek substitute US for French responsibilities. On other hand, for US to take position it cannot negotiate with Moroccans on this subject until after successful conclusion Franco-Moroccan negotiations would put trump card in hands French who by procrastination could bring about deterioration US-Moroccan relationship.

---

[3] A memorandum from Secretary of Defense Charles E. Wilson transmitting the views of the JCS on this matter was submitted to the NSC as an enclosure to a memorandum from S. Everett Gleason, dated December 4. At its September 27 meeting, the NSC took cognizance of the President's request that the Department of Defense undertake a feasibility study to determine whether the Spanish bases might be substituted for those in Morocco. Admiral Arthur Radford conveyed the findings of the JCS to Wilson on November 21. While it was judged feasible to use the Spanish bases as substitutes for those in Morocco, a number of considerations militated against it. Most important, since the Spanish bases would not all be fully operational until 1962, the premature loss of the Moroccan bases would reduce U.S. capability to implement its war plans. The JCS reaffirmed its previous recommendation, as communicated to the Secretary of Defense on September 25, that the Moroccan bases be maintained "by all feasible means". Wilson concurred in a memorandum for the Executive Secretary of the NSC. (Department of State, S/P Files: Lot 62 D 1, North Africa)

In light foregoing, Department desires comments Embassies Paris and Rabat re US taking following line with French either through Embassy Paris or by Secretary in talks with Pineau:[4]

1. In recent talks Washington, Balafrej and Crown Prince took initiative raising base question along lines second para this telegram.

US made every effort persuade Moroccans discuss matter trilaterally in line Secretary's conversation with Pineau June 1956, but Balafrej clear and definite in his rejection, recalling he himself had already given French same answer in response similar French suggestion.

2. US firmly convinced a) any refusal or reluctance by US to negotiate bilaterally with Moroccans and b) continued inaction re Franco-Moroccan agreement on defense matters will work to detriment US, France and West in general.

3. US therefore believes that in broad Western interests, US must be in position move ahead with Moroccans to regularize arrangements re US base rights. We would strongly prefer do this in step with French if at all possible. Ideal solution problem would be if French and Moroccans could agree undertake and conclude negotiations re definitive defense arrangements as soon as possible with US and France consulting concurrently re their respective interests US-built bases. US-Moroccan negotiations might take place either at same time or immediately after conclusion Franco-Moroccan defense agreement. This procedure would probably result three simultaneous or near simultaneous bilateral negotiations instead of trilateral discussions rejected by Moroccans and effect would probably be much same as trilateral approach. We recognize that there are serious obstacles to this procedure, particularly difficulty French and Moroccans agreeing negotiate in light differences over Algeria. However, if French and Moroccans could find means overcoming these obstacles, we believe foregoing procedure has much commend it.

4. Should foregoing procedure prove impractical, US may have proceed bilateral discussions with Moroccans in any event. In such case, we would keep in close touch with French both before and during negotiations in effort assure minimum prejudice French interests and position Morocco.

Dulles

[4] Cannon replied in telegram 363 from Rabat, December 10, that he was in "complete accord" with the line the Department of State proposed to take with the French concerning the bases. (*Ibid.*, Central Files, 711.56371/12–1056) Dillon stressed the need for the conclusion of a defense arrangement between France and Morocco prior to any U.S.-Moroccan talks. (Telegram 2897 from Paris, December 11; *ibid.*, 711.56371/12–1156) Upon consideration of these communications, the Department instructed the Embassy in Morocco to encourage the Moroccans to begin defense negotiations with France. (Telegram 2392 to Paris, 351 to Rabat, December 21; *ibid.*, 711.56371/12–1956)

206. National Intelligence Estimate[1]

NIE 71.1–57 *Washington, January 29, 1957.*

THE OUTLOOK FOR MOROCCO[2]

The Problem

To assess prospects for Moroccan stability and viability; and to estimate the probable orientation and policies of an independent Morocco over the next few years.

Conclusions

1. At least for the short term, the Sultan and the Istiqlal Party are likely to cooperate, and the Moroccan government will probably maintain an essential minimum of control over the country. Although extreme elements may break away from the Istiqlal and form opposition groups, the government probably will retain the capability for keeping political extremism in check for the next year or two. Over the long run, mounting political opposition probably will compel the Sultan to cede much of his secular authority to representative political leaders. (Paras. 10, 22)

2. Morocco's economic difficulties will continue to be severe over the next few years. We estimate that Morocco now requires up to $100 million of new foreign investment annually even to maintain the present low standard of living. (Paras. 14, 16)

3. So long as Morocco remains economically dependent on France, the French will be able to retain some special privileges in Morocco. (Paras. 13, 15)

[1] Source: Department of State, INR–NIE Files. Secret. Files of National Intelligence Estimates, Special Estimates, and Special National Intelligence Estimates, retained by the Directorate for Regional Research, Bureau of Intelligence and Research.

National Intelligence Estimates (NIEs) were high-level interdepartmental reports presenting authoritative appraisals of vital foreign policy problems. NIEs were drafted by officers from those agencies represented on the Intelligence Advisory Committee (IAC), discussed and revised by interdepartmental working groups coordinated by the Office of National Estimates of the Central Intelligence Agency (CIA), approved by the IAC, and circulated under the aegis of the CIA to the President, appropriate officers of cabinet level, and the National Security Council. The Department of State provided all political and some economic sections of NIEs.

[2] According to a note on the cover sheet, "The following intelligence organizations participated in the preparation of this estimate: The Central Intelligence Agency and the intelligence organizations of the Departments of State, the Army, the Navy, the Air Force, and the Joint Staff. Concurred in by the Intelligence Advisory Committee on 29 January 1957. . . . The Atomic Energy Commission Representative to the IAC, and the Assistant Director, Federal Bureau of Investigation abstained, the subject being outside of their jurisdiction."

4. Morocco will almost certainly not reach a settlement on major issues with France as long as the Algerian conflict continues. An intensification of that conflict would lead to increasing violence against French colons and troops in Morocco, in which event, the Moroccan government might be unable to control widespread disorders. (Paras 10–12, 19)

5. Morocco will look increasingly to the US for diplomatic support and economic aid, especially if friction with France continues. Should the US fail substantially to meet Moroccan expectations, the present leadership would probably seek greater diversification of its sources of aid, turning to certain Western European nations and even to the Soviet Bloc. However, Communist Bloc countries are unlikely to develop any substantial influence in Morocco over the short term. Given US support and assistance, the Moroccans are likely to regard continuation of the US base program with favor. (Paras. 17, 21)

Discussion

6. In the little more than a year since Sultan Mohammed V regained his throne, Morocco has achieved independence and has entered the U.N.[3] However, Morocco faces critical problems in attempting to: (a) maintain internal control and achieve political integration and stability; (b) arrive at an acceptable relationship with France; (c) obtain vitally needed external aid, and (d) define its relations with the Arab world, with the West, and with the Soviet Bloc.

7. Morocco now incorporates the former French-protected zone, the Spanish northern and southern zones, and the International Zone of Tangier—with a total population of roughly 10 million. The former protectorate arrangement tended to strengthen regional divisions; for at least the short term the Sultan's continued rule therefore will be essential to the maintenance and extension of indigenous political and military authority. The Sultan, a shrewd politician, wishes to modernize Morocco under his personal guidance and authority.

8. All authority derives from the Sultan as both political and religious leader of the state. The Sultan has enhanced his strength by avoiding the struggles attending the daily operations of the government, and by committing his reputation and authority only on issues likely to magnify his prestige. He alone bridges the gulf between the modern and traditional elements of Moroccan society: between the rapidly multiplying working class, the small urban middle class, and

[3] Morocco entered the United Nations on November 12, 1956.

the semi-feudal tribal communities still found in much of the countryside. A national consultative assembly has been appointed as an ostensible start toward a constitutional monarchy, but the Sultan almost certainly will not permit any early decrease in his authority.

9. The foremost challenge to the Sultan's position will come from the strength and ambitions of the Istiqlal Party. The party faces a dilemma, since it cannot demonstrate its strength without a parliamentary regime, but must gain greater initiative in government in order to retain popular support. The Istiqlal is led by Foreign Minister Balafrej, whose views appear in harmony with those of the Sultan, and by the fiery religious scholar, Allal el Fassi, whose more extreme outlook has been shaped by years of bitter fighting against the French. Thus far there has been no open break with the Sultan nor any formal cleavage within the Istiqlal leadership on issues such as composition of the government, future constitutional reforms, and economic and social programs. However, the Istiqlal's labor federation ally, the Union Marocaine du Travail (UMT) with a dues-paying membership of about 300,000 (it claims a million members), is likely to exert increasing pressure upon the party and the government to fulfill the economic and social expectations aroused by independence. In addition, militant Istiqlal factions, as well as remnants of the largely disbanded guerrilla Liberation Army still active along Algeria's borders, will increasingly demand expulsion of French interests and profound political, economic, and social changes. Although the outlawed Moroccan Communist Party's current membership is numbered only in the hundreds, it will continue efforts to infiltrate the UMT, as well as the Istiqlal, and to drive the UMT toward a more extreme position.

10. Istiqlal leaders will be pressed to adopt policies at variance with the moderate course of the Sultan and his close supporters. For at least the next year or more, however, we believe that both sides will try to prevent any sharp break in their relations. There are likely to be numerous disputes: the Sultan may make greater efforts to organize his independent supporters politically, and will continue to insist upon a coalition government; Crown Prince Moulay Hassan's interference in political matters will be resented by the Istiqlal; the consultative assembly may seek to assume broader powers than the Sultan has intended; and more extreme Istiqlal and labor elements may attempt to form an opposition grouping. But urgent requirements for a united front against the French, for external aid, for a solution to the Algerian problem, and for extension of central administration to cope with regional and tribal particularism probably will dictate continued cooperation between the Sultan and the Istiqlal leaders. In these circumstances, the Moroccan government is likely to be able generally to maintain an essential minimum of

internal control for the next year or two, by relying on its 30,000-man army and by distracting a restive populace with such issues as withdrawal of French troops and advancement of territorial claims. The most serious danger to that control is the possibility of some Moroccan-French conflict which would set off a chain reaction of widespread disorders. Another danger is posed by tribal disturbances which could arise from the spread of political unrest to the countryside. Inability of the Moroccan government to control such disorders could lead to a breakdown of authority.

11. Since early 1956, Morocco has been trying to negotiate new ties with France, which has neither ratified relinquishment of its protectorate nor abandoned the aim of "interdependence" with Morocco. Negotiations have been greatly complicated by the presence of about 300,000 colons and 80,000 French troops (only six percent of which are African natives) in the former French zone, and by the continuing controversy over Algeria.[4] The French are inhibited by the need to safeguard their commercial interests and the lives and property of the colons. On the other hand, Morocco is restrained in dealing with France by: its need for external aid, France's control of its currency, the orientation of its trade toward France, and its dependence on the colons. During the next year or two, large-scale emigration of skilled French technical, administrative, and security personnel would seriously hamper government operations and could spell the loss of vital economic services.

12. Negotiations between France and Morocco over the status of the colons and the definition of "interdependence" are likely to be protracted. Meanwhile, the Moroccans probably will continue their attempts to diminish Morocco's reliance on France, will seek to reduce the number of French troops in Morocco, and will chip away at the privileged status of the colons. Despite the efforts of the Moroccan government to insure a peaceful transition, there may be further attacks on the colons. If the Algerian conflict is intensified, there will be a better than even chance of colon massacres. Over the long run, the general emigration of the colons, or at least the loss of their special privileges, appears inevitable.

13. Morocco must continue to rely on foreign financial assistance for its development needs. In the past France has been the principal source for both public and private investment. Morocco's trade pattern and currency arrangements within the franc area have also made it heavily dependent on France. Exports pay for only somewhat more than half of imports. The foreign exchange deficit

---

[4] Morocco has similar but much less critical problems with respect to Spain. About 40,000 Spanish troops and over 100,000 Spanish nationals remain in Northern Morocco, where Spanish currency continues in use. [Footnote in the source text.]

has been covered mainly by local expenditures on US airbases ($30–50 million a year on the bases and $20 million in local expenditures by US nationals from 1951–1954), by French civil and military expenditures in Morocco (of more than $100 million a year from 1952–1954), and by French public and private investment ($70–90 million a year from 1951–1954).

14. Morocco's economic difficulties will continue to be severe over the next few years. Political and economic uncertainty has curtailed production and trade and led the French to repatriate their capital (at a rate estimated as high as $150 million in 1956) and to delay any new investment. At the same time, the Moroccan government is faced with new and expensive responsibilities arising from its independent status. Whereas in the past revenues permitted allocations for development, they are now insufficient even to meet ordinary government expenditures. Unemployment, chronic in the past, has risen rapidly.

15. France agreed to lend Morocco $75 million for its development budget in 1956 but still withholds one-third of the amount. While the French Assembly appropriated $90 million for use in Morocco in calendar 1957, of which perhaps $70 million is planned as loans for the Moroccan development budget, France will delay release of these funds in hopes of obtaining concessions regarding a defense agreement and preservation of its other interests. At most, French economic aid will probably be no more than in the past; its precise amount will be determined by hard bargaining in which French efforts to preserve large influence over the Moroccan economy will be resisted. Morocco has already sought US aid of $70 million annually for three years, but this amount has been refused on grounds that it would supplant French aid. However, if French aid is decreased, Morocco will turn to the US and, failing that source, will probably seek assistance elsewhere (e.g., West Germany), including even the Soviet Bloc.

16. Morocco will continue to need supplementary outside assistance even when the present difficult situation is overcome. It needs up to $100 million of new investment each year just to maintain the present annual average per capita income ($125) of its population—increasing at an estimated two percent a year—and considerably more to increase that income. While its natural resources are substantial compared with those of other North African countries, private foreign capital is unlikely to be invested in amounts larger than in the past. For at least the short run, both ordinary budget deficits and a shortage of foreign exchange are likely.

17. France also has a large stake in forthcoming discussions regarding the US bases, which were originally set up without consulting Morocco. Even if Morocco continues to insist upon separate

negotiations with the US and with France, as seems probable, the question is closely tied to France's future defense responsibilities. There are some problems involving the US which may not be solved unless there is either full cooperation or a complete break between France and Morocco on defense issues. In any case, the issues are such that lengthy negotiations between the US and Morocco seem unavoidable. The Moroccans generally are likely to regard continuation of the base program with favor. However, they probably will press increasingly for larger US economic aid, and insist that a new base agreement be restricted to a set period and be subject to frequent review.

18. In their conduct of foreign relations the Sultan and his government have in general tended to regard Morocco as a bridge between the West and the Arab world, uncommitted fully to either grouping. On the other hand, Morocco will probably join the Arab League, though Moroccan leaders will continue to be wary of Egypt's drive toward hegemony in North Africa. Membership in the Arab League probably would not lead in the next few years to adoption of anti-Western or neutralist policies by Morocco.

19. The Algerian conflict is increasingly endangering the prospect of an amicable settlement between Morocco and France. Moroccan unofficial material aid and diplomatic and propaganda support for Algeria are increasing. Should France fail to reach an Algerian settlement soon, Moroccan aid to the rebels and French countermeasures probably would dispel any chance of establishing a special relationship between France and Morocco. In the event of widespread attacks on the colons resulting in conflict between Moroccan and French armed units, France might attempt at least partial re-establishment of military control in Morocco. On the other hand, if France were to propose further concessions to the Algerian nationalists, it might be able to use the Sultan's moderation and ambition to secure his intercession for an Algerian settlement. In any event, Moroccan territorial claims with respect to both Algeria and Mauritania are bound to create new friction. Morocco's relations with Spain are also likely to become embittered by controversy over North African areas remaining under Spanish sovereignty.

20. Another effect of the Algerian strife is its tendency to increase sentiments for unity between Morocco, Tunisia, Algeria, and possibly Libya. The recent amalgamation of leading Moroccan, Tunisian, and Algerian labor federations may foreshadow greater efforts toward eventual founding of some form of political federation. On the other hand, progress toward a federation is likely to be accompanied by a contest for leadership between the Sultan and Tunisian Premier Bourguiba.

21. Continued friction with France will lead Morocco to look increasingly toward the US both for diplomatic support and for aid to supplant that now received from the French. Should the US fail substantially to meet Moroccan expectations, even the present leadership may be compelled by internal pressures to adopt a less cooperative attitude. In any case Morocco is likely to establish formal diplomatic and expanded commercial relations with Communist Bloc countries within the next year or two. While those countries are unlikely to develop any substantial influence in Morocco during the next few years, they may do so beyond that period if appreciable progress is not made toward a stable and viable Moroccan regime.

22. Over the longer term, mounting political and economic grievances and Istiqlal opposition probably will erode the position of the Sultan. Much—if not all—of his secular authority is likely to be relinquished to representative political leaders, at least at the outset probably under a constitutional monarchy. Should such leaders fail to obtain essential external aid and to cope with likely disturbances, they in turn probably would be supplanted by more extreme and anti-Western regimes. Control of the Royal Moroccan Army would prove decisive in an internal contest for power.

---

207. Memorandum of a Conversation, Rabat, March 2, 1957 [1]

SUBJECT

Visit of Vice President Richard M. Nixon

PARTICIPANTS

Moroccan:
His Majesty Mohamed V, Sultan of Morocco
His Royal Highness Moulay Hassan, Crown Prince of Morocco
His Excellency Si M'Barek Bekkai, Prime Minister of Morocco
His Excellency Ahmed Balafrej, Minister of Foreign Affairs

American:
The Vice President of the United States, Richard M. Nixon
The Honorable Cavendish W. Cannon, U.S. Ambassador to Morocco

Following a luncheon given by the Sultan at the Palace, the Sultan withdrew with the Vice President for a personal conversation

[1] Source: Department of State, S/P–NSC Files: Lot 62 D 1, North Africa (Tunisia, Algeria, Morocco, NSC 5614, 5614/1). Secret. Attached to Document 19.

which lasted about an hour and a quarter. The Sultan began with a fifteen minute discussion of Morocco's problems. The first topic was the particular situation and series of problems of newly independent Morocco and the difficulties which the Government of Morocco faces in consolidating its position at a time when the general world situation is so tense. The Sultan spoke of Morocco's economic difficulties and the element of urgency in facing up to the unemployment problem as well as the necessity for general social programs in order to satisfy a people feeling its way to independent status. The Sultan referred to the particular relations between Morocco and the U.S. as being conditioned by the question of the air bases and pointed out that it was quite urgent that this matter be adjusted. The Sultan stated that he desires this to be done in a spirit of friendship and cooperation and with a realization of the common problems affecting both of our countries.

As regards the American attitude toward Morocco and toward the Arab states of the Middle East, the Sultan seemed to find great comfort in the position taken by the U.S. He referred to the recent visit of King Saud who had explained to him in full detail much of the background of the President's policy towards that area which the Sultan said he could fully endorse. He felt that the President's Doctrine, [2] and American policy in general, is such that Morocco could generally give its support because, as a result of its geographical position and previous history, Morocco is not so intricately engaged in local problems as are the countries of the Middle East.

As for Communism, the Sultan said he was not disturbed at the present time but realized it was necessary to keep up a common front against agitators who would take every advantage of stress or uncertainty in Morocco in order to promote political ends which would not be to the advantage of the Moroccan people.

Speaking of Africa generally, he observed that we must expect a great development in the next few years and expressed the hope that Morocco would be able to exert its good influences for an orderly evolution of nationalist tendencies in North Africa and, perhaps, the continent in general.

The Vice President replied on each of the topics raised by the Sultan in a frank and straightforward manner which obviously pleased both the Sultan and his Foreign Minister. The Vice President said he would report His Majesty's views directly to the President as was his custom. Concerning U.S. bases, the Vice President said that he realizes very well that conditions under which the American bases were established in Morocco have been considerably changed and it is perfectly evident that our situation should be regularized.

[2] The Eisenhower Doctrine for the Middle East was proclaimed on January 5.

The Vice President continued by saying that we wanted this done in such a way as to be fully compatible with Moroccan interests and that Moroccan interests would determine the basis on which we would maintain our establishments in Morocco. The Vice President expressed confidence that this matter could be worked out in a spirit of good will and friendship. The Vice President also pointed out that the maintenance of these bases is not only to the interest of the U.S. but very definitely in the interest of Morocco and the free world in general.

As regards economic aid, the Vice President discerned two aspects: (1) Our definite interest in the welfare and progress of Morocco, (2) The practical relationship between a sound economic situation here and our military position. The Vice President went into some detail regarding the legislative requirements of U.S. aid programs, pointing out that we are answerable to Congress, that we have programs with many countries, with Congress having control over the funds and that the President himself cannot always do as much as he would like or as quickly as he desires.

Notwithstanding this, the Vice President said that he felt sure that Moroccan requirements would receive very sympathetic consideration, adding that we should get the program into operation as soon as possible and that the various elements of the program could be worked out as time goes on. The Vice President added that we expect Morocco to take advantage of aid from other sources, including France.

The Vice President then asked the Sultan what he thought might be done about the Algerian problem, emphasizing that it would be better, in our view, to seek a peaceful and evolutionary solution rather than to allow violent events to provide the basis for the outcome. The Sultan said that Moroccans are naturally very deeply concerned about the Algerian question. They feel that the nationalist trend must be taken into account and that eventually there must be an acknowledgment of Algerian aspirations to independence. The Sultan agreed, however, that we should seek every means for a peaceful solution. He said that he had tried very hard to bring that about, but unfortunately had failed in his efforts up to now. The Sultan expressed the thought that the best procedure now would be to proceed toward elections which would be controlled by the U.N. and said he hoped this could be done in such a way that there would not be a period of violence in Algeria.

During the course of the audience, the Sultan indicated obliquely his strong desire to visit the U.S. In view of the history of this problem, including the Sultan's plans for a visit last fall,[3] and the Sultan's evident desire in the matter, the Vice President resorted to a general expression of hope that the visit could be arranged for some time in the future, adding that he hoped he would still be in the Vice Presidential office at the time and that he would consequently have the pleasure of seeing the Sultan in the U.S. Despite the efforts of the Vice President to project the visit somewhat indefinitely into the future, the reaction of the Sultan and the members of his government were such as to indicate that he would expect this matter to be followed up in the very near future.

[3] The Sultan expected to come to the United States for the admission of Morocco to the United Nations on November 12, 1956. Although this would not have been an official State visit, the Secretary had proposed to the President that he meet with the Sultan briefly on November 19. (Memorandum from Dulles to Eisenhower, September 28, 1956; Department of State, Central Files, 033.7111/9–2856) Mohammed V was unable to make the trip on that occasion.

208. Memorandum From the Assistant Secretary of State for Near Eastern, South Asian, and African Affairs (Rountree) to the Secretary of State[1]

Washington, March 31, 1957.

SUBJECT

Moroccan Bases

Discussion

You will recall that on June 18, 1956, you told Foreign Minister Pineau that the U.S. would prefer to straighten out in tripartite negotiations the status of the five bases from which the U.S. operates in Morocco under Agreements concluded in 1950–51 with the French. (The U.S. considers these Agreements to have been validly concluded by the French in the exercise of their Protectorate powers.) You added, however, that tripartite negotiations might not prove possible because of the Moroccan attitude. In that event you said we would reserve our position and consult the French government.

[1] Source: Department of State, Central Files, 711.56371/3–3157. Secret. Drafted by Bovey and concurred in by L, WE, EUR, G, OSD, and RA.

In November 1956, during conversations in Washington, the Moroccan Foreign Minister, Ahmed Balafrej, made clear that his government wished to discuss this question directly with the U.S. and that while the U.S. and France might have to settle bilateral problems arising out of French-U.S. Agreements, Morocco did not recognize the validity of the Agreements and would expect to deal with us on a strictly bilateral basis. Shortly thereafter the Moroccan government handed in a note, stating its desire that the base question be re-examined by the two governments.

In December Ambassador Dillon, on instructions from the Department, informed the Foreign Office of the Moroccan position and made clear that despite our best efforts, the Moroccan government was firm in its opposition to tripartite discussion of the base problems. The best alternative procedure, he stated, would therefore be three sets of bilateral negotiations, with the French and Moroccans leading off with a negotiated settlement of Morocco's military and defense arrangements, which would clarify France's military position and therefore the status of the bases from which we operate. The Ambassador also said, however, that should this prove impossible, we might have to discuss the bases directly with Morocco before France and Morocco negotiated.

In February the Foreign Office replied that France could make no definite settlement of her military status in Morocco without a prior solution of the Algerian problem, which was the basic factor governing the presence and status of French troops in Morocco. The Foreign Office asked that we therefore postpone any attempt at bilateral settlement with the Moroccans. [2] More recently, however, there have been indications that Franco-Moroccan military talks may begin shortly.

In the interim, the French have proposed strengthening their military position in Morocco by integrating French personnel into the AC&W [3] system presently run by the U.S. as a temporary measure under the 1951 Technical Agreement. (The French have based their proposal on a provision in the 1951 Technical Agreement which specifically recognized the then French over-all responsibility for the air defense of Morocco under the Protectorate regime.) On March 6, 1957, we informed the French that we could not, at this

[2] Charles W. Yost reported from Paris in telegram 4054, February 13, that he had met with Maurice Faure to ascertain whether there was any change in the status of defense negotiations with Morocco since he had taken up the question with Ambassador Dillon on December 26. Faure confessed that he had been overly optimistic on that occasion. (*Ibid.*, 711.56371/12–1357)

[3] Air Control and Warning system. [Footnote in the source text.]

late date, agree to any changes such as those proposed without Moroccan concurrence.[4]

On February 16, 1957, Mr. Balafrej reiterated to Ambassador Cannon the anxiety of the Moroccan government to proceed as soon as possible to negotiate with the U.S. and asked for an immediate indication of what steps we proposed to take. On March 2, the Sultan himself raised the question directly with the Vice President and made clear he considered the matter one of great urgency. The Moroccans have also asked for our comments on a proposal to impose duties and taxes on the automobiles of military personnel and in various other ways have raised the issue of the status of our forces.

On March 13 the Moroccan government informed our Embassy it would be impossible to conclude any final agreement on the status of the VOA relay base at Tangier until we indicate readiness at least to open conversations on the bases. This means that unless we respond positively, VOA operations also will remain in uncertain status and a $5 million expansion program will have to be postponed.

In the meantime the U.S. has been conducting negotiations with Morocco for a bilateral agreement under which we would furnish economic and technical aid, starting with about $20 million in FY 1957. Although NSC-approved policy avoids treating economic aid to Morocco as a direct quid pro quo for base rights, nevertheless at the time we responded favorably in principle to the Moroccan request in November, we said that our ability to implement aid programs would necessarily bear some relation to the continuing favorable attitude of the Moroccan government toward U.S. strategic and other interests in Morocco. The Embassy believes, however, that delays in concluding an economic aid agreement may have some connection with Moroccan anxiety to make progress with us on the base question.

---

[4] Yost summarized the Moroccan air defense problem in a letter to William R. Tyler on January 24. The French felt entitled to an increase in the number of their personnel on radar sites for having permitted a higher U.S. Air Force ceiling. The French refused the use of Boulhout Air Base for U.S. F-100 squadrons unless the United States agreed to changes in the 1951 Technical Agreement, changes which the Moroccans need not be told about. (Department of State, AF/AFN Files: Lot 63 D 250, Base Negotiations (1957) M-12) On March 2, in telegram 3391 to Paris, the Embassy was informed that the United States was willing to enter into technical discussions with the understanding that the Moroccan Government would be fully informed and would have to approve any changes directly affecting it. (*Ibid.*, Central Files, 711.56371/2–1857) The Embassy reported in telegram 4554, March 7, that the French Foreign Ministry expected to resume military negotiations with Morocco in the near future. France still insisted, however, upon a greater air defense role. (*Ibid.*, 711.56371/3–757)

The Moroccan attitude, while as yet basically not unfriendly, has thus hardened considerably toward American interests. It is perfectly clear that the primary reason is that after a full year of independence we have not yet taken concrete steps to sit down with the Moroccans and re-examine the bases arrangements in light of the new context of Moroccan sovereignty. It is also clear that all our interests will be seriously threatened if we do not take steps to do so at once. The Moroccan government is also undoubtedly anxious to start talks with the U.S. so as to increase its leverage on the French government in forthcoming military talks.

Embassy Paris (telegram 4845,[5] attached as Tab B) agrees with Embassy Rabat that this matter is now urgent and suggests we inform the French we cannot delay further the opening of U.S.-Moroccan talks.

While we should not, of course, try in our discussions with the Moroccans to conclude final arrangements on matters in which the French have a fundamental interest, I believe that we should try if possible to work out arrangements concerning our operations, while by-passing for the time being the fundamental question of Morocco's defense arrangements and the related question of possible French use of the bases as distinct from our use of them. A suggested approach to this problem vis-à-vis both France and Morocco is contained in the attached telegram.[6]

The important thing is that we should at least indicate to the Moroccans—and do so immediately—that we are ready to discuss the base question directly with them.

Recommendation

That you sign the attached telegram, (Tab A) authorizing Ambassador Cannon to enter into discussions with the Moroccan government regarding the bases and authorizing Embassy Paris to inform the French of our decision.

---

[5] Telegram 4845 from Paris, March 20, concluded that further delay in getting bilateral base negotiations started would be to the detriment of the West. (*Ibid.*, 711.56371/3–2057)

[6] *Infra.*

209. Telegram From the Department of State to the Embassy in France [1]

Washington, April 3, 1957—8:15 p.m.

3962. Rabat 550, 656-658, 689. Paris 4845, 4936. [2]

A) Embassy Rabat should make following oral reply GOM following our informing French as indicated B) below:

1) US prepared in principle open conversations re Moroccan base problem and suggests talks start following Ramadan (i.e. at beginning May as suggested Rabat 677). [3]

2) US would have preferred Franco-Moroccan negotiations precede US-Moroccan talks because of important bearing former may have on arrangements which may be discussed between US and Morocco.

3) US believes GOM will agree that US-Moroccan talks at this time could most profitably center on questions of particular interest to the two governments alone. In absence definitive Franco-Moroccan military arrangements we believe conversations should not be concerned with those aspects Morocco's over-all defense or foreign-base arrangements which would require French-Moroccan agreement.

4) While US considers its forces present in Morocco under legally valid agreements, at same time US recognizes changed situation created by Moroccan independence and accordingly prepared accept GOM invitation discuss means adapting thereto arrangements for US military operations Morocco. USG therefore appreciates opportunity exchange views with GOM on above.

5) USG intends keep French Government informed US-Moroccan discussions.

B) For Paris

1) Embassy should at once inform FonOff orally our decision along lines suggested Embtel 4845 with exception second sentence subparagraph one. [4] (FYI. We consider 1950–1951 Agreements validly executed by France on own behalf and on Morocco's behalf in exercise Protectorate powers.)

2) Embassy may also wish recall our previous discussions with Faure in December (following receipt notes addressed to both France and US by GOM) and again in March connection air defense and

---

[1] Source: Department of State, Central Files, 711.56371/3–2657. Secret. Passed to CINCEUR. Also sent to Rabat and repeated to CINCUSAFE in Wiesbaden and CINCNELM. Drafted by Bovey and cleared with G, NEA, WE, EUR, L/EUR, RA, OSD, and the Department of Defense.

[2] None printed. Telegrams 550, 658, 689, and 4936 are *ibid.*, Central File 711.56371. Telegrams 656 and 657 are *ibid.* 511.714. Regarding telegram 4845, see footnote 5, *supra*.

[3] Not printed. (Department of State, Central Files, 711.56371/3–2257)

[4] The sentence to be excluded reads: "Without going into historical fact that much of difficulty stems from refusal French Government at time agreements signed to inform Sultan of Morocco of base agreement, it is undeniable that Moroccans have no legal basis on which to recognize validity our presence on their soil."

Sultan's talk with Vice President, when we made clear growing difficulties US military position Morocco and said we might have proceed discuss matter with GOM before definitive Franco-Moroccan military settlement. You may emphasize our primary preoccupation is still to assure continuity of basis for US military operations Morocco which are vital to Western defense interests.

3) Embassy should give French substance our initial reply to GOM as indicated A) above.

4) Re timing we had of course planned inform French our decision this matter before entering into discussion with GOM but do not feel we could delay replying GOM until we have reached any detailed understanding with GOF re our respective positions in talks with Moroccans. We believe our initial reply to GOM sufficiently general and flexible permit talks with French as we proceed. Moreover if Moroccans accept suggestion paragraph A-1 above we should have more time discuss matter with French. FYI We would prefer avoid exchange position papers. (Paris 4936) End FYI.

Accordingly Embassy should make clear to French that while we welcome their comments and will take them into account as we proceed we must make reply indicated in A) above immediately. We would then be glad discuss matter further with French both before and after opening of talks with GOM May.

5) Inform Rabat when above approach made.

Dulles

---

210. Telegram from the Department of State to the Embassy in Morocco[1]

Washington, April 22, 1957—7:29 p.m.

749. Joint State Defense msg.

Part I. Following summarizes current thinking on US position during forthcoming bases discussions, for which detailed negotiating instructions will be forwarded soonest. In interim would appreciate Rabat and Paris comments.

Believe ultimate US objective is conclusion bilateral agreement under which US will be able carry on necessary military activities. With this goal in mind, it may be useful consider matters we will be discussing in forthcoming talks:

---

[1] Source: Department of State, Central Files, 711.56371/4–2257. Secret. Repeated to Paris; CINCNELM, London; and CINCUSAFE, Weisbaden; sent to Paris to be passed to CINCEUR. Drafted by Bovey and cleared with L, WE, RA, and the Department of Defense.

1. It should be reiterated to GOM US has no intention prejudice French rights and interests Morocco. In absence Franco-Moroccan military arrangements we believe conversations should not be concerned those aspects Morocco's over-all defense or foreign base arrangements which would require Franco-Moroccan agreement. Recognize that negotiation new military arrangements will impinge on number matters special concern to French and in certain areas US rights cannot be conclusively defined this time because of French interests. However in areas where ultimate definition US rights must await Franco-Moroccan agreement (e.g. title to land, air defense, etc.) it may prove necessary seek from GOM, at least on informal basis and with French concurrence or acquiescence, interim understandings which will ensure continuity US operations. French will be kept informed as talks proceed and consulted if conflicts with existing Agreements arise. Moroccans should be apprised our intention this regard. Moreover US interests must be taken into account in any Franco-Moroccan discussions.

2. Generally speaking, US position is that 1950–51 Agreements were concluded by France acting on own behalf and on behalf Morocco. Consequently they were and remain valid. However while maintaining this position we do not wish make it issue on which negotiations might founder. Rather, as we have already made clear to GOM, we prepared discuss those areas where readjustment present arrangements might be required in light changed situation in Morocco. However we believe we should leave it to Morocco to suggest such areas in first instance.

In addition, changed situation in Morocco may also provide basis for US to propose changes in existing arrangements as discussions progress (e.g. supplanting liaison mission by direct handling local procurement and contracts).

Specific instructions on tactics re 1950–51 Agreements will follow.

3. Tactically we feel US should not start out with detailed or concrete proposals, both so as to avoid danger widening scope of discussions beyond what Moroccans may have in mind and to establish with French that initiative for changes comes from Moroccans. On other hand in inviting Moroccan initiative in raising matters which concern them, we should make every effort avoid eliciting extensive list Moroccan complaints and detailed extravagant proposals for solution, articulation of which may unduly harden their thinking. Desirable middle course would appear be to ask Moroccans indicate what areas adjustment they wish include in discussions and then take prompt initiative in offering concrete US proposals to meet their problems and in making clear which matters cannot in our view be definitively settled bilaterally this time.

4. Generally speaking US position on such problems as may arise will probably be based on substance 1954 Libyan agreement except provision on payments for privately-owned land (Article VII) and criminal jurisdiction. On latter point our position, at least initially, must be seek exclusive criminal jurisdiction.

5. One purpose during discussions will be determine whether agreement might take form short unclassified covering agreement couched in general terms, which we would strongly prefer, plus such annexes or subsidiary technical agreements as might be necessary.

6. Re economic aid, we should continue be guided by view assistance not regarded as payment for base rights and will be geared primarily Moroccan needs and capacities in so far as US legislative and budgetary limitations permit and in light aid provided Morocco by France. Nevertheless we should again make clear as necessary our ability develop and carry out economic assistance programs will inevitably bear relation to Moroccan attitude toward our strategic interests Morocco. US economic aid plans which go beyond commitments already made should therefore be coordinated with progress base talks.

Embassy should also bear in mind current domestic and congressional attitudes re foreign aid.

7. Policy on military assistance programs has not changed, i.e. we do not intend institute such programs this time.

Part II.

Rabat 749.[2] Secretary has authorized Ambassador Cannon to negotiate with GOM. Composition negotiating team which will assist you will be cabled soonest. Meantime would appreciate Rabat view as to date GOM desires begin talks. If possible would prefer not take initiative in pressing GOM for date since would appreciate maximum time for preparation without appearing stall.

Dulles

[2] Telegram 749, April 12, proposed that the negotiating team be largely made up of civilian and military personnel on the scene with such help as required. (*Ibid.*, 711.56371/4–1257)

211. Telegram From the Embassy in France to the Department of State [1]

Paris, April 27, 1957—1 p.m.

5522. Below is text aide-mémoire [2] given Faure based on Deptel 4219. [3] Only additional points used drawn from Deptel 4092 [4] on which we had already informed French:

US has given most careful study to and has taken under full consideration views set forth French Government's memorandum of April 12, 1957 [5] concerning negotiations with GOM on US military operations in Morocco. In reply, US Government wishes reaffirm that it is its intention in forthcoming negotiations with GOM to discuss matters and to deal with problems other than those which can be settled only between France and Morocco. Our primary objective will be to reach arrangements mutually agreeable to Governments of Morocco and US on status of US military operations in Morocco. Within this context, we hope it will be possible to discuss with GOM such questions as status our forces, jurisdiction of local courts and officials, taxes, and customs. We cannot at this time be certain as to exact scope of negotiations, since much depends on what Moroccan Government will propose. In any case, the US has no intention whatsoever of assuming French defense responsibilities in Morocco or of prejudicing rights and interests of France in any way.

As French Government is aware, US Government considers Franco-American agreements of 1950 and 1951 to be valid. However it would seem likely that some modification of arrangements provided for under these agreements and other related technical agreements may be required at Moroccan request in recognition of Morocco's newly-acquired independence. Where such modifications appear necessary US Government will consult with French Government. In any event, US Government will keep French Government *fully* informed as negotiations progress.

Houghton

---

[1] Source: Department of State, Central Files, 711.56371/4–2757. Secret. Repeated to Rabat.

[2] The aide-mémoire was delivered on April 26.

[3] Telegram 4219, April 19, also advised against giving any commitments to the French which might cause later misunderstanding if the United States were unable to carry them out. (Department of State, Central Files, 711.56371/4–1657)

[4] Telegram 4092, April 11, authorized the Embassy, at its discretion, to assure the French that they would be kept informed. (*Ibid.*, 711.56371/4–957)

[5] Telegram 5726, April 12, conveyed an unofficial translation of the memorandum. It acceded to U.S. desire to start negotiations with Morocco. France insisted, however, on a prior understanding with the United States as to the scope and objectives of the negotiations. It also wanted assurances that the United States would not pledge military aid or reduce French military freedom. No agreement was to be reached which nullified French rights, vested by existing accords, without French permission. (*Ibid.*, 711.56371/4–1257)

212. Telegram From the Department of State to the Embassy in France[1]

Washington, May 2, 1957—7:31 p.m.

4408. Paris 5516,[2] 5564,[3] Rabat 805.[4] Department understands French concern for effects base negotiations their interests Morocco and believes we have given fullest possible consideration thereto in drafting general instructions for Embassy Rabat. Department cannot however accept Beaumarchais view we must submit proposals in advance to Paris as it would be impossible conduct negotiations on basis prior approval both Paris and Washington. This particularly applicable to status forces matters[5] mentioned Paris 5516 which are either inadequately covered or not covered at all by existing agreements and where we believe we are relatively free of obligation do more than keep French currently informed. Thus we do not interpret our aide-mémoire April 26 as committing us to prior French concurrence US proposals although we will of course keep French currently informed as talks proceed and will consult with them at appropriate moments wherever Moroccan viewpoint and our own appear require readjustments in those arrangements embodied 1950-51 agreements which still involve French interests. We must however be free discuss these matters freely with Moroccans and cannot undertake outline our positions on any given subject until we have exchanged views thereon with GOM and know what type arrangements we might be able reach with GOM.

We believe above should be made clear to French in order avoid misunderstandings and tie hands negotiators at Rabat, but leave handling to Embassy's discretion.

FYI. Our thinking as embodied in draft instructions[6] now en route is that negotiators will find three areas under discussion.

---

[1] Source: Department of State, Central Files, 711.56371/4–3057. Secret. Passed to CINCEUR. Also sent to Rabat. Repeated to Madrid and to CINCNELM, London. Drafted by Bovey and cleared with OSD, WE, L, and RA.

[2] Telegram 5516, April 26, noted that the French wanted prior knowledge of any changes which might affect their military presence and the right to be consulted on any modifications of the 1950–1951 agreements. (*Ibid.*, 711.56371/4–2657)

[3] Telegram 5564, April 30, stressed the need to accede to the French wishes for information. The Embassy called for a formal channel of communication in Paris and informal contacts in Rabat. (*Ibid.*, 711.56371/4–3057)

[4] Telegram 805, April 29, strongly opposed giving the French veto power over the conduct of the negotiations and rejected the idea of formal contacts in Rabat. (*Ibid.*, 711.56371/4–2957)

[5] The draft status of forces agreement which France and the United States had concluded on November 30, 1956, had not been signed.

[6] Instruction CA–9187, May 3. (Department of State, Central Files, 711.56371/5–357)

A) Areas where U.S.-Moroccan settlement must await Franco-Moroccan settlement, e.g. title to land, mutual defense Military Assistance Programs, French responsibilities on bases, joint French-US use of bases.

B) Areas of French interest where we consult with French (but not necessarily prior to discussion with GOM) with view obtaining their concurrence but where we would be prepared tell French we must conclude new arrangements, e.g. authorization use and occupy agreed areas and movements thereto and therefrom, traffic control aircraft, vessels and vehicles, pipelines and communication, intermediary functions French Liaison Mission, employment local labor.

C) Areas where French interest is marginal and where we would merely keep French currently informed, e.g. taxes and customs, criminal and civil jurisdiction, entry and departure personnel, post offices, etc. End FYI.

Herter

---

213. Telegram From the Embassy in Morocco to the Department of State [1]

Rabat, May 8, 1957—9 a.m.

844. From Richards. Report on visit to Morocco. [2]

I found Sultan, who is final authority on all matters of substance, preoccupied with negotiations re US military bases due to start immediately. He was unwilling to take any public position further committing Morocco to cooperate with US pending results base talks. Presumably he had very much in mind possible effect upon his bargaining position. However he asked me in private talk to tell President of his support for principles and moral spirit of ME proposals, his recognition of threat of international communism to all nations and his determination wipe out few seeds of communism existing in Morocco.

Moroccans made no request for aid from my mission and I made no commitment, although in preliminary discussions between experts figure of up to $5 million for agreed projects was mentioned.

---

[1] Source: Department of State, Central Files, 120.1580/5–857. Secret. Repeated to Paris, Tunis, London, Tripoli, New Delhi, Rome, Kabul, Athens, Ankara, Beirut, Cairo, Damascus, Amman, Jidda, Addis Ababa, Khartoum, Karachi, Tehran, Baghdad, and Tel Aviv.

[2] Regarding the Richards Mission, see Document 17.

Question of US military aid to Morocco not raised. Communiqué couched in general terms transmitted separately.

Only fleeting references were made by Moroccans to relations with France and question of Algeria not brought up.

Talks opened May 6 by meeting of mission with Foreign Minister Balafrej. After explaining principles of doctrine I said overt attack by international communism did not appear to be immediate danger here but that economic problems Morocco offered opportunity to international Communist subversion. I recalled that in discussions during the trip msn had stressed offer to use US Armed Forces in case of need with thought that this assurance would permit countries to concentrate on economic rather than military development. I suggested mission experts study local situation to see what economic assistance could be rendered although any aid could only be modest. I pointed out any assistance authorized would be distinct from normal aid program. Balafrej was most cordial in his remarks. He expressed thanks for offer saying that any aid no matter how modest would help. Although France had extended assistance in past year its budget situation difficult and many unresolved problems now existed between France and Morocco. He commented on difficulties of passing from colonial to free status adding that Morocco counts on help and advice from its friends during process. Balafrej recalled that Sultan and VP had discussed American doctrine and Sultan had stated his great interest in doctrine and its aim to help ME avoid subversion and revolutions. He reaffirmed great interest of GOM in doctrine. I inquired re official public attitude of Morocco towards doctrine. Balafrej replied that although it had been discussed in general terms with VP Nixon no public declaration had been made as situation not clear. He added possibly declaration could be made now. Balafrej said Cabinet meeting re doctrine scheduled begin at once. At conclusion of meeting it was agreed economic experts would commence discussions immediately.

Economic discussions held with second level Moroccan officials. Meeting was brief. Moroccans displayed singular lack enthusiasm discuss possible projects which they explained was due to shortness notice our arrival. Asked for time consider overnight. Met with same group morning May 7. Then became clear they had instructions from highest level avoid discussion any economic aid in context Richards msn. They pointed out that despite cultural ties Morocco was not clearly part of ME. Although they supported aims US ME policy they unwilling to conclude agreement with US on interim aid which might be interpreted as bringing Morocco into association with US in appreciation our ME policy. They went on to say that negotiations about to begin re base rights which they hoped would be conducted in favorable atmosphere and lead to mutually satisfactory result. In brief allusions to magnitude interim aid that might be extended if suitable project suggested we stated we might consider up to $5 million. Possible desirable projects were discussed, in secondary and tertiary road construction and possibly telecommunications. However, this part discussion was more conversational than serious.

Meeting with Sultan late morning May 7 confirmed intimation received from talks secondary level officials. His Majesty was most cordial throughout and stressed his friendship for US and desire for cooperation. He said many high American officials now passed through but only briefly. He hoped they could come, stay longer and become better acquainted with Morocco's problems. Talks re US bases were due commence shortly, he was anxious for favorable outcome and was sure US shared this view. Results of negotiations would of themselves make Moroccan position re doctrine clear. Sultan said matters raised in talks re American doctrine were weighty and should be carefully pondered. While affirming Moroccan support for doctrine as reported above he indicated clearly reluctance to take public position now. Sultan said he supported principles of doctrine because it was intended build up internal strength of area states and because it made clear US had no aspirations to establish itself in area. Sultan referred to Morocco as bridge between West and ME but did not seek to determine whether we consider country included in ME area. (Our conversation with other officials indicated they considered Morocco not part of ME.) In my remarks I apologized for short notice and briefness of mission's visit. I said I would be able present his views immediately to President and called attention to meeting May 9 with congressional leaders to discuss FY 58 program. I stressed that mission's visit just prior recommence base negotiations purely coincidental and arose from factors beyond mission's control. I called attention to desirability public statement, but I did not believe it advisable to push strongly for public stand at this time.

Afternoon May 7 further discussions held, first at secondary level and then with Prime Minister and Foreign Minister. Moroccans proposed brief general press statement substantially same as final text but completely non-committal. After considerable talk, we succeeded in getting inclusion of reference to "spirit of mutual understanding", fact that I had been "welcomed with great regard" and statement that position of Morocco remained same as time VP Nixon visit. I proposed this last sentence, after failing get clear statement of approval of doctrine, in order avoid any interpretation that Moroccans were less favorably disposed at present than they had indicated themselves to be then.

During discussion, Prime Minister repeatedly emphasized that there was no doubt where Morocco stood with regard communism and that this would be made even clearer by facts and actions following base negotiations. Reiterated Sultan's remarks to effect that Morocco's participation in doctrine would in fact develop out of those negotiations. He added that even though Morocco did not accept juridically presence of American bases, existence those bases was fact and showed where Morocco stood. Otherwise it would be demanding their immediate relinquishment.

I concurred that actions were more important than statements and said I was encouraged to hear his affirmation that Moroccans fully expected successful outcome negotiations.

I do not believe Sultan has decided alter policy of cooperation with west but anticipate he will use base negotiations to extract maximum advantage for Morocco. He is well aware military importance our installations and their importance in carrying out military assurances doctrine, and therefore unwilling jeopardize his bargaining position re bases on eve of negotiations. I think complete concentration on bases and failure discuss such matters as Algeria and relations with France is significant. I fear we must anticipate monetary cost of retaining bases will be heavy.

Cannon

---

214. Despatch From the Embassy in Morocco to the Department of State[1]

No. 30 *Rabat, July 25, 1957.*

SUBJECT

Analysis of US-Moroccan Base Negotiations to Date

It is interesting to pause at this point to assess the results to date of our negotiations with Morocco for military base rights. They tell little, in fact, about the terms Morocco may be prepared to grant. They are significant mainly for what they reveal of Morocco's concern for the overall policy which is to govern US-Moroccan relations.

The sequence of events has been as follows:

[1] Source: Department of State, Central Files, 711.56371/7–2557. Secret.

1. The negotiations were formally opened on May 8th in a plenary meeting of the two delegations. The Moroccans were led by Crown Prince Moulay Hassan and Foreign Minister Balafrej, and the U.S. delegation by the Ambassador. Following general statements by the Prince and the Ambassador (Embtel 860),[2] it was agreed that the technical experts on the two sides should meet to discuss the details of an agreement.

2. During the ensuing technical level meetings the American delegation followed the Department's instructions in setting forth U.S. requirements for a base agreement. By and large, despite occasional questions, the Moroccans gave little indication of their reaction to the American proposals. They did point out that these proposals seemed to them to deal mainly with "technicalities", which in their view were secondary in point of time and importance to the establishment of the "framework" within which the stationing of U.S. forces in Morocco would be authorized.

3. There then followed, from May 21 to July 17, a period in which no meetings were held. The reason for this hiatus was the preoccupation of the Foreign Ministry with French and Spanish negotiations in other fields and with local ceremonials, but government officials no doubt used the time to examine the American proposals.

4. Promptings from the Embassy led to the resumption of technical level negotiations on July 17, at which time the U.S. delegation elaborated on the theme that the mutuality of free world defense against Communism seemed to us to be the appropriate foundation for a base agreement. The Moroccans readily recognized the Communist threat to the free world but seized on our statement to stress the importance of economic and military assistance to free world defense. This was the Moroccan Government's first clear bid for economic and military assistance as a quid pro quo for military base rights. Negotiations are to be continued later this week against this background.

One of the most salient facts to be noted is the Moroccan Government's interest in the possibility of tying all aspects of the US-Moroccan relationship to one overall policy, perhaps but not necessarily to find its expression in a general covering accord. We for our part have been trying to get agreement on the various operating rights and privileges normally included in a base agreement. But the Moroccans continue to argue that the two governments should first define their relationship in matters of general policy and defense, after which the "details" of base operations can, they say, be worked out easily and rapidly.

It is not easy to reduce to practical terms what the Moroccans have in mind. We have advanced the view that language in our base agreement will adequately express general goals and principles, while the various separate agreements on bases, VOA, FCN, economic aid,

[2] Telegram 860, May 11, indicated the tenor of the opening remarks. (*Ibid.*, 711.56371/5–1157)

etc., will form an "ensemble" clearly describing the US-Moroccan relationship.

Probably the Moroccans do not yet know themselves precisely what they want or expect. Nevertheless, behind their polite demurs that the U.S. delegation has been dealing with technicalities and not the broader underlying principles some fairly definite objectives undoubtedly lurk. For example:

1. The Crown Prince in the opening session made a forceful statement of the Moroccan position that the 1950–51 agreements negotiated by the U.S. and France are and always have been invalid. There have been other clear signs that the Moroccans have no intention of succeeding to the whole or any part of those agreements, but wish to establish an entirely new understanding on the bases. It is quite possible, in this connection, that the Moroccan Government may wish to expunge the past with some formula as juridically neat and psychologically effective as that applied in the declarations abolishing the French and Spanish protectorates and the Tangier international regime.

2. This concern with liquidating the past is tied up with the fact that the U.S. and France still collaborate in the use of the bases. There is little chance that Morocco will leave this collaboration untouched and it may well insist on French withdrawal from the bases. While we have not yet come to grips with such questions as title to land, base security and defense and the eventual possession of fixed installations, the Embassy believes it will be difficult to persuade the Moroccan Government that these are problems for Morocco to work out with France.

3. The Moroccans have shown a great interest in the political framework into which U.S. base operations are to fit. They have not been very specific, but their concern probably revolves around such questions as whether the agreement is to be bilateral or multilateral (we have already stated that, in our view, a bilateral agreement between the U.S. and Morocco would seem to be indicated in the present circumstances), whether it is to form part of a mutual defense alliance, and whether Morocco is considered to fall within the sphere of NATO defense. A Western Mediterranean grouping, such as the Sultan himself has suggested,[3] seems to be one form of multilateral association which strikes the Moroccan fancy. Recently the Foreign Minister mentioned this possibility to the Ambassador as perhaps offering a framework for French and Spanish military interests in Morocco, as well as our own. There was no suggestion, however, of how a Western Mediterranean bloc could be organized while the conflict in Algeria continues.

4. The most recent conversations show unmistakably that Morocco is entertaining hopes of substantial U.S. economy and military

---

[3] As indicated in despatch 128, October 21, the Sultan and Balafrej seemed to desire a regional pact, but only on their own terms. (*Ibid.*, 711.5/10–2157)

assistance. [4] The Moroccan negotiators have argued that the former is necessary to persuade the Moroccan people that cooperation with the U.S. is a two-way street and that U.S. bases are not a new form of military occupation, while military aid is essential to Moroccan self-defense. It is clearly going to be difficult to avoid a substantial quid pro quo when, as it appears, Morocco knows a good deal about our arrangements in such countries as Spain and Saudi Arabia and is conscious of the help we give our friends in NATO, etc.

One final observation that is pertinent has to do with the political climate here. It is worth keeping in mind that, while the Palace and the Government have given every indication of being anxious to reach a satisfactory agreement on the U.S. bases, there is a public opinion here which neither can ignore. It is not surprising that Morocco, in these early stages of its independence, should be tempted by the attractions of neutralism and Arab solidarity. Perhaps more than most new countries, because it belongs both to the East and to the West and at the same time to neither, Morocco has a split political personality. We are fortunate to have in power a moderate and realistic Sultan and government which want close and fruitful relations with the United States, but goodwill to such a degree does not exist everywhere. There is in Morocco a detectable undercurrent of suspicion and reserve towards the United States and this is reinforced by any sign read as our unwillingness to help Morocco throw off the French yoke, as support of France against Algeria, as support of anyone against any Arabs, or as an effort to embroil Morocco in our conflict with the Communist world. This factor is bound to make its weight felt during the course of the negotiations.

Alfred T. Wellborn

---

[4] Consequent to the Economic and Technical Cooperation Agreement concluded by Morocco and the United States on April 2, 1957, the Export-Import Bank gave the Government of Morocco a $20 million line of credit on June 28, 1957. (8 UST 459; TIAS 3799) On July 13, Morocco expressed an interest in a 4-year P.L. 480 program in the sum of $114 million. (Telegram 40 from Rabat, July 13; *ibid.*, 411.7141/7–1357) Four days later, the Moroccan negotiators raised the question of both economic and military assistance with specific reference to the U.S. arms aid to Saudi Arabia. (Telegram 58 from Rabat, July 18; *ibid.*, 711.56371/7–1857)

215. Telegram From the Department of State to the Embassy in France[1]

Washington, August 17, 1957—1:16 p.m.

682. Ref: Rabat's 142[2] and 139.[3] Department greatly concerned by breakdown Franco-Moroccan negotiations and particularly by resulting suspension French aid. Wherever responsibility may lie results all too clear: i.e. constant turning on and off financial spigot both Morocco and Tunisia multiplying uncertainties re French intentions and progressively sapping strength of pro-Western regimes which are sole hope cooperation with France and on which entire Western position heavily depends.

While we can understand public and parliamentary difficulties French Government in supporting budgets countries who oppose France's Algerian policy it does not appear this difficulty has recently been acute in case Morocco nor does it explain present impasse.

Our own interest in matter dictated by effects on Western interests and specifically U.S. aid plans. Inevitably increased Moroccan demands would place US in extremely awkward position in light current domestic attitudes and budgetary difficulties as well as plans based on policy supplementing French aid. Limitations on US at this point combined with uncertainties re French intentions appear be producing situation of real danger all concerned.

We would hope financial convention might be treated separately from Convention d'Etablissement. Failing that would think common prudence would dictate at least maintaining flow French credits by making partial advances pending resumption negotiations and conventions. This would dispel doubts re French intentions and create better atmosphere for discussions.

While we do not presume set forth specific course action, believe Emb Paris should convey US concern over impasse, indicating our growing worry over mounting threats to Sultan's Government in face continued failure solve pressing social and economic problem and expressing our hope flow assistance, at least through partial advances, can be resumed soonest. Might be helpful express gratification over resumption aid Tunisia and emphasize our convic-

---

[1] Source: Department of State, Central Files, 651.719/8–1057. Confidential. Repeated to Rabat and Tunis. Drafted by Bovey and cleared with AFN, WE, E, U/MSA, and in substance with ICA.

[2] Telegram 142, August 10, reported that Franco-Moroccan negotiations on the Convention of Establishment governing property transfers and compensation had broken down. (*Ibid.*)

[3] Telegram 139, August 10, reported the opinion of Mehdi ben Barka, President of the Moroccan National Consultative Assembly, on the impasse. (*Ibid.*)

tion steady flow French aid both Morocco and Tunisia indispensable to preservation Western position North Africa.

Herter

---

216. Telegram From the Department of State to the Embassy in Morocco[1]

Washington, October 17, 1957—4:59 p.m.

368. Joint State–Defense Message. Rabat's 267[2] and 271.[3]

1. Department and Defense appreciate your efforts encourage Moroccans deal more concretely with base negotiations and believe we should endeavor make such progress as we can prior King's visit. We are not certain however that present more forthcoming Moroccan attitude represents more than temporary acquiescence to US pressure designed evoke information re aid level for FY 58 and incidentally draw us out on question of "framework", both questions on which their own ideas seem largely undeveloped.

2. It seems clear that base negotiations unlikely be sufficiently advanced by time King's visit to permit conclusion any formal, definitive agreement. Additionally as indicated earlier messages[4] we concerned at situation developing during course of King's visit where we shall be subjected considerable pressures for economic assistance under conditions in which insufficient progress made on base negotiations to give us something concrete in return with respect future tenure. We wish avoid situation in which King might wish utilize Washington visit to launch some premature plan for multilateral area pact for which we unprepared. However we view visit as opportunity agree broad principles which can be basis subsequent completion detailed negotiations.

---

[1] Source: Department of State, Central Files, 711.56371/9–1557. Secret. Repeated to Paris, CINCNELM, London, and CINCUSAFE, Wiesbaden; and by pouch to Tunis and Tripoli; sent to Paris to be passed to USCINCEUR and Knight. Drafted by Porter and cleared with ICA, E, RA, WE, AF, U/MSA, S/P, L/SFP, and the Department of Defense.

[2] In telegram 267, September 13, Cannon indicated that he had discussed the principal outstanding problems dividing Morocco and the United States with Balafrej on September 12. (*Ibid.*, 711.56371/9–1357)

[3] Telegram 271, September 15, noted that an understanding had been reached on September 12 with Balafrej's assistant, Mohammed Boucetta, to resume negotiations on the framework issue and technical provisions. (*Ibid.*, 711.56371/9–1557)

[4] As, for example, telegram 181, August 28. (*Ibid.*, 711.56371/8–1057)

3. In light foregoing circumstances desire on urgent basis your views re advisability your seeking early audience with King in which you would make following points:

a. We have been greatly interested in indications we have received in course base negotiations that Moroccans wish examine possibility fitting new arrangements re US bases (as well as French and Spanish forces) into some kind of multilateral framework.

b. As GOM knows US has many different types of agreements in various parts world covering status our forces and use of facilities on behalf free world. In some cases we have resorted bilateral agreements with countries concerned. In others there has been sufficient regional identity of interests to permit common cooperative defense undertakings among a group of states. Either or both could contribute to free world defense.

c. We are examining closely possibility multilateral framework in North African-Mediterranean area and we retain completely open mind re possibility multilateral cooperative effort within which US-Moroccan cooperation re US bases might be brought. King may have views re difficulties in securing effective area defense cooperation so long as divisive Algerian struggle continues and US also recognizes this likely have serious adverse effects on possibility West Mediterranean Pact.

d. As GOM knows we strongly hope this major obstacle to area peace and stability can be overcome. Meanwhile there would appear to be no reason why bilateral arrangements could not be worked out which could be adapted to a multilateral framework at a later date if necessary and desirable.

e. It may well be HM has thoughts on subject which have not occurred to us and which in his view make area defense cooperation immediately possible despite difficulties we foresee. If so we would welcome them and wish give them most careful consideration.

f. In any event it now appears improbable any definitive agreement can be reached on base matters in time for HM's visit and question arises what if anything should be said this subject during course King's visit. As HM knows, US ready and anxious reach mutually satisfactory agreement with Morocco re this matter. Possibility occurs to us US and Morocco might during course of visit find it mutually advantageous declare joint determination achieve detailed long-term agreement re continued US use bases in interests free world defense. Such declaration might usefully contain statement that pending conclusion formal agreement, US and GOM will continue cooperate to facilitate normal military operations and conduct such cooperative effort on basis friendly relations existing between two Governments.

4. We would also hope foregoing approach would draw King out on scope of consideration he desires be given to framework question while in US. Without discouraging King, if he desires broach it while Washington, believe you should point out dangers involved in possibility of leak before advanced diplomatic prepara-

tion with other countries, and absence of discussion with US Congressional leaders, etc.

5. Dept, Defense and ICA appreciate that such discussion may also require frankness in treatment of economic aid matters. Believed here that strains in Morocco likely increase greatly within coming year unless French-Moroccan relations take turn for better which unlikely if Algerian conflict continues. Our principal concern is maintain present moderate pro-Western outlook of King and Government by aiding them cope with rising internal social and political pressures, and thus protect our strategic interests. Limitations on our ability aid them, arising from reduced budgets however are known to Embassy. Given the scale of Moroccan needs and extent of our interests there however Dept and ICA doing utmost provide maximum help within limitations referred to above. We would prefer avoid saying anything to Moroccans on this subject as yet but, if conversation during audience makes this unavoidable, and if reaction to presentation bases problem appears to warrant, Ambassador would be authorized to indicate we prepared a) provide $20 million defense support for Morocco subject satisfactory arrangements with GOM regarding uses and compliance US legislation (this is maximum available this source in view total appropriation less than administration's request and world-wide demand far in excess availabilities), b) work with GOM in developing TC program, c) consider PL 480 sales program at level to be determined based on justification Moroccan request (Embtel 221) [5] according to established criteria, d) Morocco also eligible to submit projects to Development Loan Fund. You should emphasize need for coming up with suitable projects soonest, and e) in addition, expect continue assistance voluntary agency relief programs under Title III, PL 480, as well as fulfill commitment deliver 50,000 tons wheat under Title II by March 1958. [6]

6. Department and ICA realize DS level substantially less than FY 58 aid proposed by Embassy and USOM. Earmarking full amount DS contained illustrative program presented Congress despite reduction appropriations reflects Washington recognition importance defense support to base negotiations. (FYI only. Any additional economic aid would have to be provided from approximately $100 million special economic aid reserve set aside for meeting worldwide contingencies for which many requirements already exist.) End FYI.

---

[5] Telegram 221, September 4, reported that Morocco officially had requested $46 million in P.L. 480 assistance for fiscal year 1958. (*Ibid.*, 411.7141/9–457)

[6] Title II of P.L. 480 is "Famine Relief and Other Assistance"; Title III is "General Provisions". (68 Stat. 454)

7. We hope that aid matters in general can be handled so as to give us some leeway in dealing with Moroccan pressures during King's visit, and, subject Embassy and USOM comments, believe we should make every effort avoid discussing figures before visit.

8. In field of military assistance which is even more delicate than usual because of current Tunisian pressures, Department most desirous not get involved and for Moroccans continue to look to French. We of course bearing in mind comments Embtel 232.[7]

9. Your reply urgently needed.[8]

Dulles

---

[7] Telegram 232, September 6, reported that Morocco had previously stressed economic aid and the framework issue more than military assistance. (Department of State, Central Files, 700.5/9–657)

[8] Telegram 380 from Rabat, October 19, responded that, except for the economic section, the Ambassador had already taken up all the subjects raised in telegram 368 with Balafrej on October 15. (*Ibid.*, 711.56371/10–1957)

---

217. Message From the Ambassador in Morocco (Cannon) to Minister of Foreign Affairs Balafrej[1]

Rabat, November 5, 1957

Informal Account of Topics Raised in Audience with His Majesty on November 2, 1957

DEAR MR. BALAFREJ: At the end of my audience on November 2, at which you were unable to be present, His Majesty asked whether I would put down, in informal style for further consideration upon your return, the topics I had mentioned in the course of the audience. Here, then, is a brief outline of the points I chiefly had in mind.

Except for a reference to the United States press release to be issued on November 4, and an inquiry whether His Majesty during His visit to the United States would like to take advantage of technical facilities which can be made available for the broadcast of an address to the people of Morocco from the American continent, I did not discuss details of itinerary, program, etc. of the visit.

---

[1] Source: Department of State, Central Files, 771.11/11–557. Confidential–Informal. Enclosure to despatch 144 from Rabat, November 5.

I said, however, that it would be very useful indeed, and almost essential to the substantive success of the visit, if we could have an indication of the topics which His Majesty would like to bring into the conversations with the President. I explained that because of legislative and administrative requirements in our country, detailed "staff work" must be done and preparatory consultations take place before there can be decisive action, even on the highest Executive level. For this there remains very little time even now.

Chief among the topics to be discussed, I supposed, would be the Base negotiations. I said that we had had many useful and friendly meetings covering the whole general range, but these had been largely on the technical level and devoted thus far to the presentation and study of the American side of the case. It was my opinion that the negotiations would not be far enough advanced for any general formal agreement at the time of His Majesty's visit. If this is indeed the situation it is important that we together review how best to capitalize on the progress made thus far. I would like very much to have His Majesty's views on whether the meeting at Washington might not afford an opportunity for agreement on broad general principles as a basis for an agreement. If some preliminary work could now be undertaken it might then be possible, as a feature of His Majesty's visit, to issue something of a joint declaration to this effect.

I had not forgotten the earlier discussions in which the Moroccan position generally had been set forth, both as regards the agreements under which the bases were originally installed and as regards other factors in Morocco's international relationships, particularly with France and Spain, which make the negotiation of a new agreement with the United States a matter of some complexity. I noted that in these circumstances the Moroccan negotiators were still unsure of the "framework" within which the new agreement with the United States could be formulated, especially since there are other foreign military establishments in Moroccan territory. These circumstances had appeared to suggest some regional arrangement as an appropriate "framework."

I observed that there were of course very important differences between our installations here and other foreign military establishments, both as regards original purposes and present function and scope of military interest. It was at the Moroccan request that our present negotiations were undertaken on a bilateral Morocco-United States basis, and having made some progress we would probably prefer to continue on that basis. There is room for flexibility on this point, however, since American arrangements for facilities can be in the framework of either bilateral or regional relationships, in the latter case especially where one can establish the fact of a regional identity of interest. We might well contemplate in this instance a bilateral agreement so worked out as to be adaptable to an eventual multilateral or regional arrangement. This would take care of the risk of launching a plan for multilateral association before we had cleared away the problems of the bilateral relationship.

We would be deeply interested in His Majesty's views on this matter. It has occurred to me that the Royal visit may afford an occasion for His Majesty to take the initiative for a plan, which the United States could then endorse. For a matter of such importance it would be essential that there be preliminary discussions here at Rabat, and if the suggestion proves interesting to His Majesty's Government I should be grateful if I could learn something of the Moroccan thinking on the eventual membership, the character and scope, as well as the form and timetable for the formation of such an eventual association.

In the time graciously made available to me by His Majesty I did not make direct reference, in alluding to the time required for working out a regional relationship, to what is often considered a divisive element which might prove an obstacle to an early realization of a regional arrangement; namely, the Algerian issue. It might be useful to examine the validity of this argument, and I would welcome an opportunity to hear the views of His Majesty's Government on the matter. At all events this is one of the issues I had in mind in suggesting a bilateral arrangement capable of later extension.

As regards the "framework" in general, I referred to the "ensemble" of United States relations with Morocco over the years which we are confident will grow into a closer association in all fields. Considering our demonstrable record both as regards the establishment and consolidation of peace in the free world and as regards our friendly, active and practical interest in the welfare of newly established states coping with the many problems of securing their welfare and independence, I wondered whether such an "ensemble" justifying our activities here is not already in being. The subject of our economic relations is in active discussion with the appropriate officials. Apart from the question of present programs and current economic negotiations (which I did not discuss in this audience) I assured His Majesty that in negotiating for the continuation of United States military facilities in Morocco we fully realize the importance over the years, also for the United States, of a healthy economy and political and social stability in Morocco.

C.W. Cannon [2]

[2] Printed from a copy that bears this typed signature.

218. Memorandum From the Secretary of State to the President[1]

Washington, November 19, 1957.

SUBJECT

The King of Morocco's Visit to Washington, November 25–27, 1957

The King of Morocco's visit to the United States, and particularly your substantive discussions with him on November 26 and 27, may prove to be of crucial importance in determining the future course of his country. For your consideration, I enclose a staff study outlining the significance of and our objectives for this visit.[2]

Morocco is important to us not merely for the five major air bases and the Voice of America installations we have there, but because it is an Arab state open to healthy influences from the West. The King is an able statesman whose influence has been used consistently for moderation in his country's affairs. Although constitutionally a nearly absolute monarch, he is, in fact, subject and responsive to public pressures. His outlook is modern and he envisages democratic institutions for his country. In foreign affairs his influence might eventually be useful in any practical steps to settle the Algerian war, depending on French receptivity to third-party intervention. Moreover he represents a moderate influence in the Arab world in general. For example, Morocco has not joined the Arab League, has no relations with Communist states, and has a Jewish cabinet minister.

Accordingly, we consider our primary objective for the visit to be added stature for the King and his government at home and abroad in a context of United States-Moroccan amity. It is of equal importance to obtain from the King during his visit some form of official recognition for our military installations in Morocco, which were constructed under an agreement with France that the Moroccan Government contends is invalid.

[1] Source: Department of State, Central Files, 711.11/11–1957. Secret. Drafted by William N. Stokes, Officer in Charge of Northwest Africa Affairs.

[2] Not printed; the study is entitled "The Significance of, and United States Objectives for, the King of Morocco's Visit to Washington, November 25–27, 1957".

We hope to gain both objectives by means of a joint declaration signed by His Majesty and yourself, of the nature proposed in the enclosed staff study.[3] I recommend that you take the initiative at the outset of your conversations with the King in proposing such a declaration, both because it is the key to our desires for this visit and because the awkward subjects we expect the King to raise (such as Algeria and other difficulties with France) could thereby be confined to the reasonable period of time then remaining in your talks.

The King and his ministers, like the Moroccan people as a whole, are sensitive about their newly-won independence and are apprehensive lest they be accorded anything less than equal status, particularly as they feel that France has consistently given less than full practical recognition to Moroccan independence, despite the French financial and military aid given to Morocco in the past.

I am looking forward to my meeting with you on November 22 for a further discussion of these matters.[4]

John Foster Dulles[5]

---

[3] The draft declaration reads:

"The United States desires that the arrangements governing United States installations in Morocco accord fully and completely with Moroccan sovereignty and independence. His Majesty and the President declare the common intention of their Governments to reach a formal agreement in detail of this nature, and agree that in the meantime United States use of these installations will continue to be facilitated, through the friendly cooperation of their Governments."

[4] Dulles, Palmer, and Goodpaster discussed the Moroccan visit with the President in detail. The Secretary commented that the King's major concern would be Algeria and after that military bases and aid. (Memorandum of conference with the President by Goodpaster, November 23; Eisenhower Library, Whitman File, Eisenhower Diaries)

[5] Printed from a copy that bears this stamped signature.

219. Memorandum of a Conversation, Department of State, Washington, November 26, 1957, 9:30 a.m. [1]

SUBJECT

U.S. Bases and Economic Aid

PARTICIPANTS

U.S.
The Secretary
Mr. William M. Rountree, NEA
Mr. Joseph Palmer 2nd, AF
Mr. John A Bovey, Jr., AFN
Mr. Camille Newfel
Morocco
His Majesty Mohamed V, King of Morocco
His Excellency Ahmed Balafrej, Minister of Foreign Affairs
Dr. El-Mehdi Ben Aboud, Ambassador of Morocco
Mr. Abderrahman Neggai, Chief of the Royal Cabinet

The Secretary expressed the President's profound regret that he was unable to be present and hoped that His Majesty would feel free to speak and to discuss matters of interest just as if the President were there. [2] He asked him to pose any questions which he might have. The King replied that he hoped the President would be well soon and sent his best wishes for a speedy recovery, adding that he knew that with the Secretary there all would go well.

He said that in the last two years Morocco had recovered its independence and that certain questions which he hoped could speedily be resolved were still outstanding. Among those was the question of the American bases in Morocco. He said that the Moroccan viewpoint on this had already been made known to us and that he hoped to find a solution which would both safeguard Moroccan sovereignty and strengthen relations between our two countries.

The Secretary said that he was sure the King was well aware of the genuine friendship existing between the United States and Morocco which was more than we would normally have with another country and was based on a real sympathy which dated back to the early times to which His Majesty had referred on the previous evening. [3] He said that we had also had close relations with France throughout our history and that in fact there had been what might be called a race between Morocco and France to recognize the

---

[1] Source: Department of State, Secretary's Memoranda of Conversation: Lot 64 D 199. Secret. Drafted by Bovey.

[2] The President was unable to attend because of illness.

[3] Reference is apparently to the King's remarks at the State dinner the previous evening.

United States at the dawn of our history—a race which in the light of the communications of those days might be said to have ended in a tie. Thus we had a historic friendship for both Morocco and France, as well as for Spain and we would like to be helpful in resolving any of the outstanding questions between these countries and Morocco.

He said he thought it would be helpful if His Majesty could indicate more precisely ways in which we might be helpful in straightening out the pending questions to which he had referred. We would be especially happy to do this since we had a particular admiration for the wisdom and statesmanship of His Majesty.

The Secretary observed that the United States knows from experience that separation at the time of independence leaves many problems which require great patience for their solution. He mentioned the acute differences which we had had with Great Britain following independence and their resolution which had led to a lasting friendship. France, he said, was today in a difficult mood and he called His Majesty's attention to the violent reaction in France to our delivery of a small quantity of arms to Tunisia. He said that it would be easy for both the United States and Morocco to draw inferences from this, and that it would be bad for the future if either of us were to act hastily in the midst of France's present difficulty in adjusting to her problems and responsibilities.

Turning to the United States bases, the Secretary said that our present position in Morocco results from United States-French Agreements concerning which, unhappily, the French had perhaps failed to consult adequately with the Moroccan Government. He said that the desire of the United States was that any of our facilities in Morocco should be there under conditions which fully respected Moroccan sovereignty and independence. We hope and believe that Morocco on its side will recognize the importance of these bases to the collective defense of the Free World.

His Majesty would of course recall that the United Nations Charter is based on the principle of collective security. We had hoped that security could be achieved through renunciation of force and that the Security Council could organize its own forces to deter aggression. Unhappily, these hopes had not been realized; the Soviet Union had vetoed the idea of an international police force and did not itself observe the principles of the Charter which deal with the use of force. The Secretary cited the examples of Iran, Greece and Korea, mentioning that the attack on the Republic of Korea had been conducted with Soviet arms and Soviet guidance. Thus, the nations which were devoted to the principle of collective security had had to turn to Article 51 of the Charter which the Secretary himself had helped to draft and which consecrates the principle of individual and collective self-defense. This article had originally been written to provide for situations in which the United Nations itself could not serve as a deterrent.

The Secretary said that he wished to state most emphatically and categorically that the United States had no aggressive purpose whatever. At the end of both World Wars we could easily have taken the path of aggrandizement; instead we withdrew to our own shores as soon as possible and disarmed ourselves. Thus anyone who knows the United States knows that our people covet nothing and want only a system in which each country retains its independence. This, however, is impossible if we each stand alone. Interdependence is vital and both His Majesty's country and the country of President Eisenhower can give a fine example of interdependence for peace.

We recognize, the Secretary said, that a definitive agreement between us in regard to the bases will take some time to achieve. Our desire, if the King shares it, is to bring these negotiations to an early conclusion but we believe that we can reach an understanding during the interim which will justify our use of and expenditure for the bases.

The Secretary said he wished to add that the mutual security of which he had spoken was by no means limited to military matters. The United States recognized the economic needs of Morocco and we have acted to meet those needs at least to some extent. It will be our purpose to continue these efforts and even, if necessary, to increase our aid, although as the Moroccan Government must be aware, the Congress had put us on somewhat short rations in the matter of foreign aid.

The King thanked the Secretary for this exposition and especially for what he had said regarding economic assistance. His Majesty said he knew that we had always had the best sentiments towards Morocco and he thanked us for this. He wished to assure the Secretary that whatever misunderstanding might arise between Morocco and other nations, Morocco would always try to solve these through peaceful negotiations, but not in such a manner as to impair either the national sovereignty or the interests of foreigners in Morocco. His Majesty said that he knew that the United States was always ready to defend and preserve the independence of peaceful countries. Within this framework, Morocco, as an independent country, faced certain problems, including the presence of foreign armies and questions about her frontiers.

The King said that of course a definite base settlement would take time and that he hoped an interim settlement could be made by a Joint Commission which would examine the progress made thus far in the negotiations with a view to arriving at a provisional agreement. He said that he was anxious to avoid any final settlement which would leave room for anyone to consider it as a precedent for other nations to ask for bases in Morocco. While under the Protectorate, Morocco was not free to choose what collective formations she might wish to join, and the situation with respect to pending questions which were left over from the Protectorate still blocks Morocco from such free choice. His Majesty said he had no doubt as to the United States good intentions and hoped that we would understand Morocco's difficulties today during the transitional period.

Mr. Balafrej, after conferring briefly with His Majesty, explained that in the transitional period through which Morocco was now passing many difficulties were posed for the Government and notably the presence of French and Spanish troops. There arose therefrom the problem of equality of treatment which the Moroccan Government was anxious to solve. France and Spain were in Morocco for different purposes, which he described as colonial, from those of the United States, which was in Morocco for the purposes of collective security. A definitive base agreement at the present moment would risk creating precedents with regard to bases and troops and might thereby perpetuate the unacceptable purposes for which other nations were still present in Morocco. His Majesty asked whether the United States could aid in resolving differences between Spain and France because until this was done it was most difficult for Morocco to arrive at anything beyond provisional agreements with the United States.

He again thanked the Secretary for his assurances regarding economic aid. The French economy over the years had become deeply involved with, and dominant over that of Morocco. Morocco was now working to create an independent economy and was grateful to the United States for any assistance in this sense. The Moroccan economy, the King said, was fundamentally sound but was affected by the stresses and strains of the French economy to which it was linked. His country was therefore now negotiating to untie the Moroccan currency from that of France and he felt that this would permit a healthy economy.

Mr. Balafrej interjected that what His Majesty had suggested was a Joint Commission to watch over the base negotiations and to help them along in Rabat. He said that each side had posed many questions to the other and that certain questions put by the Moroccan Government had not yet received an answer, notably those on the security of the bases, customs and taxes, and the status of our forces.

His Majesty said that there was no objection to the principle of the United States bases. He did not, however, think it wise to prejudice the situation of Morocco with regard to France and Spain by according permanent status to the United States right now.

The Secretary said that he wished to suggest a formula on which the two Chiefs of State might agree and which would run as follows:

"With regard to the United States installations in Morocco, the United States desires that the governing arrangements accord fully and completely with Moroccan sovereignty and independence. The two Governments declare their intention to reach a formal agreement in detail to this effect and agree that in the meantime the United States use of these installations will continue to be facilitated through the friendly cooperation of their Governments. To this end, the United States will maintain qualified persons at Rabat to discuss and resolve current problems with Morocco."

The King said that he would accept this text for study and reminded us that the Moroccan Government had already submitted to our representatives the elements of a text which would serve as a preamble.

The Secretary asked whether His Majesty envisaged negotiating both a provisional and a definitive agreement at the same time.

The King replied that he envisaged negotiations now to reach a provisional settlement but that these would lead later to the achievement of a definitive settlement as well.

Mr. Balafrej explained that we could conclude a modus vivendi on the status of our forces pending a definitive agreement. The U.S.-French Agreements were no longer valid and thus a provisional agreement was necessary to replace them.

The Secretary said that we had hoped rather for a simple declaration that our forces would remain in Morocco pending a definitive agreement, with the additional stipulation that a Commission in Rabat could deal with current problems as they arose. The King said that he would study the text and it was agreed that Mr. Balafrej would get in touch later in the afternoon with Mr. Rountree. Accordingly, the text which the Secretary had suggested was handed to His Majesty.

220. Memorandum of a Conversation, Department of State, Washington, November 26, 1957, 5 p.m.[1]

SUBJECT

Provisional Agreement on Bases and Drafting of Joint United States-Moroccan Statement

PARTICIPANTS

U.S.

Mr. William M. Rountree, NEA
Mr. Joseph Palmer 2nd, AF
Mr. James Wilson, Defense
Mr. John A. Bovey, Jr., AFN

Morocco

His Excellency Ahmed Balafrej, Minister of Foreign Affairs
Mr. Mohammed Jaidi, Chief of Cabinet, Ministry of Foreign Affairs
Mr. Mohammed Laraki, President of Air Maroc

Mr. Balafrej produced a draft of a Joint Statement for the end of the King's talks in Washington, based on suggestions already made in Rabat. Mr. Rountree suggested that our job now was to revise this in the light of the conversations which had taken place earlier in the day between the King and the Secretary. He then handed Mr. Balafrej the United States proposals for a Joint Statement.

Mr. Balafrej remarked that so far as the bases were concerned, our draft was the same as that put forward to the King earlier in the day by the Secretary. He said that this would in effect leave United States bases and troops in status quo during the negotiation of the definitive agreement. That status was established by the United States-French Agreements of 1950, which had never been valid and which were not based on Moroccan sovereignty but rather on a military system of which France alone was a member. If the bases were to pursue their activities the status of our forces should be brought into conformity with the present status of Morocco, especially from the juridical and financial point of view.

Mr. Rountree said that it was certainly our desire to create a formal relationship in this matter which would take full account of Moroccan sovereignty, and that the conduct of our military activities during the interim should also be consistent with that principle and with the interests of both countries. He had thought the American draft pointed up our desire to proceed with arrangements in conformity with these principles and to exclude any idea that we wished to operate solely on the basis of earlier arrangements. The

[1] Source: Department of State, AF/AFN Files: Lot 63 D 250, Base Negotiations (1957) M–12. Secret. Drafted by Bovey.

United States would hope that the efforts of the negotiators in Rabat could be directed toward a permanent agreement rather than assuming that such an agreement was impossible. Negotiation of a short-term agreement would present the same difficulties as those of a long-term agreement, and there would be much less to show for our efforts.[2]

Mr. Balafrej said that Mr. Rountree had stated the principles involved correctly but that under our formula no practical results would be produced during the interim before a definitive agreement. He too hoped we could reach an agreement but in the meantime Morocco was occupied by France and Spain, and she needed a modus vivendi with us which would set no precedent to embarrass her in renegotiating the present status of these two countries and which would not entitle them to demand permanent bases.

Mr. Balafrej said that Moroccan opinion could no longer live with a system in which the French served as intermediary (as in the Liaison Mission) between the United States and Morocco, and the French flag continued to fly over the bases. Morocco wished us to continue our activities but to proceed immediately with a readjustment of French-United States arrangements.

Mr. Rountree said he understood the problem which Morocco had in negotiating with France and Spain but would appreciate Mr. Balafrej's explaining more fully why an interim agreement would produce less difficulty for Morocco in this respect than a definitive agreement.

Mr. Balafrej said that a provisional accord would not produce any precedent to which the French and the Spanish could appeal in making demands of a permanent character. It would merely provide interim coverage for the present negotiations. If we wished to leave things as they were during this interim, this was conceivable in many fields but changes were definitely needed now in the realm of customs, taxes, and jurisdiction. Mr. Balafrej suggested three years as a possible duration for the provisional agreement.

Mr. Rountree expressed his appreciation for the Minister's explanation and said that we would like to consider further the idea of the provisional agreement, which presented great difficulties for us. We would prefer postponing our reply until the next day. Meantime Mr. Balafrej might wish to answer certain questions: (1) Would the provisional agreement be detailed or merely state the general principles we had just discussed? (2) How did he envisage the mixed Commission which had been mentioned in this connection?

[2] On November 25, Mansfield D. Sprague, Assistant Secretary of Defense for International Security Affairs, wrote Palmer to reiterate the military's opposition to a provisional agreement. (*Ibid.*, Central Files, 711.11/11–2557)

Mr. Balafrej did not go into the second question, but merely indicated that a provisional agreement should be as supple as possible. Its primary purpose would be to link the United States and Morocco directly in the matter of our forces and installations. He did not want us to think that Moroccan reticence regarding a definitive agreement was due to mistrust or unfriendliness toward us, when it was really due to current problems with other states. Morocco perfectly realized that she needs United States help in consolidating her independence—and this despite the reticence of the United States, which only desired to play a role complementary to that of France.

He produced a rough draft of a provisional agreement which contained two articles and a list of subjects; the latter were later limited to customs, jurisdiction, and taxes. (Copy attached) [3] He also read off a suggestion for a paragraph in the final communiqué, which ran as follows:

"The Government of the United States affirms its desire to negotiate an agreement concerning the installations in Morocco in full respect for the sovereignty of that country. Pending conclusion of an Agreement, the two Governments affirm their desire to proceed to the necessary rearrangement of present conditions concerning the stationing of United States forces in Morocco."

Finally Mr. Balafrej said that since the King had brought up the Algerian question, His Majesty and he felt strongly that, for their own purposes at least, a reference to it should be included in the Joint Statement.

It was left that each side would study the other's drafts and that Mr. Balafrej and Mr. Rountree would meet again the next day before the final meeting of the King and the Secretary.

---

[3] Not printed.

221. Memorandum From the Assistant Secretary of State for Near Eastern, South Asian, and African Affairs (Rountree) to the Secretary of State [1]

Washington, November 27, 1957.

SUBJECT

U.S. and Moroccan Positions on Interim Agreement for Bases

Discussion

Late yesterday afternoon we discussed with Mr. Balafrej the text which you had given to the King for study earlier in the day. Mr. Balafrej made clear that this text did not meet the basic Moroccan objective, which was (1) to eliminate the French-United States Agreements as a basis for present arrangements for our military presence in Morocco and (2) to avoid creating precedents embodied in permanent agreements before the Moroccans had finished negotiating new military arrangements with Spain and France. A modified version of the joint declaration which made clear that pending a definite agreement, we would also resolve current problems in a manner compatible with Moroccan sovereignty did not turn the trick either; Mr. Balafrej said this still left a hangover from the Protectorate as the basis of our presence in Morocco and would lead to no practical results in the course the Moroccans desire. He spoke with some impatience of the continuing role of French intermediaries in United States operations in Morocco, and the continued French status of the bases and the French flag flying over them.

Mr. Balafrej pressed us hard to say that we would negotiate a provisional agreement. He mentioned three years as a possible period for its duration, and produced a draft which is attached. (Tab A) [2] (In connection with jurisdiction and customs and tax matters, we know from our negotiations in Rabat that the standard United States provisions on these matters are not satisfactory to the Moroccans.)

Mr. Balafrej finally produced a suggested text for the paragraph on bases in the Joint Communiqué, a translation of which is attached. (Tab B) [3]

It seems clear that we shall have to reach an understanding with the Moroccans which, while endeavoring to avoid anything which could be interpreted as a denunciation of the United States-French Agreements, will give satisfaction to Moroccan public opinion and

---

[1] Source: Department of State, AFN Files: Lot 63 D 250, Base Negotiations (1957) M–12. Secret. Drafted by Bovey.

[2] Not printed.

[3] Not printed.

open the way to a more direct Moroccan role in the base agreements. Such an understanding would have to provide in effect for interim agreements on the subjects indicated in the draft submitted by Mr. Balafrej, as well as any other which it may be in our interest to work out concretely at this time.

Mr. Balafrej's proposal to fix a limited duration (e.g., three years) for the interim agreement poses serious difficulties. It would create uncertainty for our long-term military planning and cause the greatest difficulty with F.Y. budgeting and financing when reasonable tenure is a condition precedent to approval and release of funds. Moreover, the Free World must be able to count on continued availability of important facilities necessary to our deterrent posture, whereas short-term arrangements would lead Soviet planners to discount our defensive strength. Short-term arrangements would run counter to our other agreements and create a difficult precedent for other negotiations (e.g., with the Philippines). Finally adoption of a provisional agreement of a limited short term period, besides further weakening our legal position that the 1950 Agreements with France are valid, would greatly strengthen the Moroccan bargaining position with respect to the terms of any permanent arrangements, and to economic aid.

Against this background, however, we must realize that in agreeing to work out interim arrangements we may well be putting ourselves in a position where we will have to agree ultimately to some time limit. In this connection, it cannot be forgotten that our chief asset in retaining our bases will be the strength and good will of the present Moroccan Government, whose wishes we should go as far as we can to respect.

In any event, it does appear that possibilities exist for reaching new arrangements with Morocco in the fields mentioned by Balafrej (customs, taxes, jurisdiction, entry and departure of personnel, currency) since the present French position on these matters now allows us to enter into more direct relations with the Moroccan Government without upsetting any major French interest in Morocco. On certain other subjects, however, (e.g., responsibilities for the air and ground defense of Morocco, and title to the land on which the bases are located) we cannot reach interim agreement with the Moroccans without destroying what the French regard as their vital interests. Settlement of these matters would have to await the outcome of Franco-Moroccan negotiations.

Recommendations

It is therefore recommended that we inform the King and Mr. Balafrej as follows:

a. We are prepared to undertake to negotiate interim working arrangements to include the subjects proposed yesterday:

(1) Moroccan authorization for stationing of U.S. forces and U.S. military operations.
(2) Conditions governing future entries and departures of U.S. personnel.
(3) Customs and tax provisions.
(4) Currency provisions.
(5) Jurisdiction provisions and such other details as we may agree later in Rabat to be in our mutual interest to include.

b. We would have great difficulty with a definite period of three years as has been proposed since this poses serious obstacles in terms of our own operations, planning and funding and serious problems with regard to the long-term strength of the collective security to which Morocco like the U.S. is devoted.

c. We would agree, however, to consider these interim agreements as governing until the conclusion of a definitive agreement. Moreover, we would hope that they could ultimately be embodied in the definitive agreement and would like them to be drafted with this in mind. However, the interim character of these arrangements would enable Morocco to reply to demands from Spain and France by saying that nothing definitive had been concluded with the United States.

d. We propose the attached paragraph for inclusion in the final joint communiqué. (Tab C) [4]

[4] Not printed. The final joint statement was worked out in a meeting between the King and the Secretary at 4:30 p.m. on November 27. For text, see *Public Papers of the Presidents of the United States: Dwight D. Eisenhower, 1957*, p. 827.

222. Telegram From the Department of State to the Embassy in Morocco [1]

Washington, December 2, 1957—9:21 p.m.

527. Joint State/ICA. At meeting with ICA Deputy for Operations FitzGerald on Nov 29 Minister National Economy Bouabid accompanied by Benkirane [2] requested US FY '58 economic assistance in amount of $50 million. Stated this was minimum requirement needed from US in order help finance 40 billion franc

[1] Source: Department of State, Central Files, 771.5–MSP/12–257. Secret. Repeated to Paris. Drafted by George Dolgin, Officer in Charge of Northern Africa Economic Affairs, and cleared with ICA and U/MSA.

[2] Permanent Secretary of the Economic Planning Committee.

equipment (development) budget. Because of limited absorptive capacity GOM could only take $40 million in commodity imports for generation local currency and needed balance as dollar credit.

Bouabid in explaining request stated that because of continuing financial and political crises in France he could no longer count with any certainty on assistance from French. Of 16 billion francs promised for 1957 no releases yet made altho 5 billion allotment promised before his departure for U.S. but not yet released. French assistance, he said, has been steadily decreasing and he expected this trend to continue. When asked how GOM able continue finance development program in light French withholdings, Bouabid stated this was done through treasury advances but if French releases not made soon, situation would become critical in January.

In reply FitzGerald expressed sympathetic understanding of financial problem facing GOM and willingness on part of U.S. to be helpful as possible in meeting requirements for external assistance but expressed serious doubts U.S. ability contribute amounts proposed by Bouabid. Explained serious limitations on our ability meet world-wide needs due drastic reduction funds by Congress. Stated U.S. program for FY '58 in addition to Defense Support could include PL 480 and Development Loan Fund. Urged Bouabid to prepare specific project requests rapidly for DLF financing. Pouching memo conversation.[3]

Dulles

---

[3] Not printed.

---

223. Memorandum From the Deputy Under Secretary of State for Economic Affairs (Dillon) to the Director of the International Cooperation Administration (Smith)[1]

Washington, December 24, 1957.

SUBJECT

U.S. Assistance to Morocco for Fiscal Year 1958

I have considered your views and agree it is necessary to mount and implement a program in Morocco quickly if we are to have a

---

[1] Source: Department of State, Central Files, 771.5–MSP/12–2457. Secret.

sound development program in the magnitude of $30 million. The point made in your numbered paragraph 2[2] will be borne in mind during the negotiations, and the Bureau of Near East and African Affairs will keep in close touch with your staff during the negotiations to ensure that the practical problems faced by ICA in mounting and implementing an economic development program are taken fully into account.

During the recent visit of the King of Morocco, the Secretary assured him that the U.S. desired to continue economic aid to Morocco in order to assist in the expansion of the Moroccan economy, and expressed a hope that we would be able to increase our aid level this year.

I agree with you that the first draft of the memorandum should not have discussed our bases in Morocco . . . . In view of the present importance of the bases, however, as established by the National Security Council, I feel we must allocate the additional $10 million for Morocco which the Secretary approved on October 1 as a potential requirement and I would be gratified if you would take the necessary action within ICA.

Douglas Dillon[3]

[2] Smith responded on December 13 to a memorandum by Palmer recommending an increase from $20 million to $30 million in defense support funds for Morocco. Paragraph 2 noted that such a program could be implemented if detailed planning could begin no later than February 1, 1958. If the base negotiation were protracted then he recommended that funds be pledged only as quickly as sound projects could "be agreed upon, engineered and implemented." (*Ibid.*, 771.5–MSP/12–1357)

[3] Printed from a copy that bears this typed signature

NIGERIA

THE QUESTION OF UNITED STATES ECONOMIC ASSISTANCE TO NIGERIA [1]

224. Memorandum of a Conversation, Department of State, Washington, October 8, 1957 [2]

SUBJECT

Visit to Department by Nigerian Federal Minister Ribadu

PARTICIPANTS

Alhaji The Honorable Mohammadu Ribadu, Nigerian Federal Minister of Lands, Mines, and Power
Mr. Reginald Barrett, Nigerian Liaison Officer
Mr. A. C. F. Armstrong, Permanent Secretary to the Minister
Mr. W. P. Gaskell, Nigerian Chief Inspector of Mines
Mr. M. L. Parker, Private Secretary to the Minister
AF—Mr. Joseph Palmer 2nd, Deputy Assistant Secretary for African Affairs
AFS—Mr. C. Vaughan Ferguson, Jr., Director, Office of Southern Africa Affairs
AFS—Mr. David E. Longanecker, Officer-in-Charge, Economic Affairs
AFS—Robert W. Ross, Liberian/Nigerian Desk Officer

After an exchange of courtesies, Mr. Palmer welcomed the Minister and his party and indicated the Department's appreciation for the opportunity to visit with them and to get better acquainted with such a distinguished representative of our friends in Nigeria. He said that the United States is deeply interested in events in Nigeria, and believes the smooth transition from dependent to independent status is being made with an admirable display of good will and mutual understanding on the part of the people and governments of the U.K. and Nigeria. Mr. Palmer hoped that the Minister's brief visit to this country after his participation in the Commonwealth Minerals Conference in Canada would be successful

[1] For previous documentation on this subject, see *Foreign Relations*, 1952–1954, vol. XI, Part 1, pp. 261 ff.

[2] Source: Department of State, Central Files, 033.45H11/10–857. Limited. Official Use. Drafted by Ross.

and asked that the Minister feel free to call upon the Department if it could be of assistance during his visit.

Minister Ribadu thanked Mr. Palmer for his courteous welcome and said that it was a great pleasure for him to be here on this his first visit to Washington. The Minister said that he wished to mention, briefly, points which were on his mind on the occasion of this talk with officers of the Department. He said that the Nigerians were continuing their progress toward independence and that they fully realized their limitations insofar as they apply to development of the country. It is the intention of Nigeria to achieve for its people a higher standard of living and a stable government working for peace and good relations with their friends abroad. He said that they are quite conscious of the need for capital to be used in the development of their resources and that the quantities needed are not available from their own sources. Under the circumstances, the Minister said, they must look to their friends, the U.K. and the U.S., for help. He said that any help which the U.S. could give would be received most gratefully, and he expressed appreciation for the support which had been given his country by Americans in the years past. The Minister said that it appeared that aid had often been given by the U.S. to countries where there was a Communistic menace. He said that there was no Communism in Nigeria and that it was their wish to develop a prosperous, stable country resistant to Communism and he believed this could be done. Despite the absence of such dangers in Nigeria he hoped that the U.S. would be willing to lend them financial assistance, both from private and official sources.

Mr. Palmer said that U.S. assistance to many countries throughout the world is not necessarily related to the existence of a Communist threat in the area involved. We are desirous of helping where we can for reasons of sympathy with the problems of the underdeveloped economies. He said it would not be possible at this time, of course, to give any indications as to the assistance which this country might be able to render to Nigeria but that he could be sure that any Nigerian request for help from America would be carefully considered. He expressed pleasure with the evident acceptance by the Government of Nigeria that it would be to their advantage to take the steps necessary to commence their independent life free of the dangerous influences of Communism.

The Honorable Ribadu and Mr. Gaskell then presented to the Department's officers a matter which was of considerable concern to the Nigerians. They said that while they realized the U.S. Government was not entirely to blame, serious problems had come to Nigeria as the result of termination earlier this year of the stockpile purchases by the U.S. of Nigerian columbite. It was explained that during the period in which the U.S. Government was paying a very high bonus for columbium ore Nigerian mining companies had invested significant amounts of money in capital equipment on the strength of the surge of columbite purchases by this country. At the same time, a large number of Nigerians had moved from their traditional economic pattern into employment in the columbite mines of the Plateau. Now that the heavy American columbite purchases had ceased, Nigerian mines had equipment on hand for which they have no need, and substantial numbers of Nigerians found themselves without employment. With the full realization that there was no likelihood of reinstitution of stockpiling purchases by the U.S. the Nigerians were interested in the Department's support of their efforts to apprize potential American consumers of columbium ores that a ready supply of this mineral is available. Mr. Gaskell said that during their stay in Canada they had gained the clear impression that many American companies which might have been interested in doing research leading to increased consumption of columbite believed that columbite is in short supply. During the period of heavy U.S. Government purchases, the chief inspector of mines said, there had been a suspension of research into expanded usage of columbium ores because the ore was in short supply. This lag in research plus the present mis-information about the availability of columbite had evidently inhibited what might have been a normal expansion in the American demand for the mineral. The Department was asked to do anything it could to assist in clarifying the picture as it applies to the availability of columbium ores. The Department officers indicated that this problem was clearly one of great concern to Nigeria and that the Department would follow through on the matter to ascertain what might be done. It was suggested that in the Minister's conferences with officers of the Bureau of Mines and the Department of Commerce here in Washington they might be able to gain some useful information, as these two agencies have more detailed knowledge of the factors involved in the problem. While the Department is most interested in the implications of the problem for Nigeria, the Minister was told, the specific remedies which might be available to the Nigerians would be more suitably suggested by those who have special knowledge of this subject.

225. Despatch From the Consulate General at Lagos to the Department of State [1]

No. 169 *Lagos, December 11, 1957.*

REF

ConGenDes. 122 dated October 28, 1957 [2]

SUBJECT

ICA Aid

In an interview this morning the Governor-General of the Federation (Sir James Robertson) introduced the subject of US aid to under-developed countries and the attitude of several of his ministers who felt that the US was being partial to countries threatened with communism when allocating funds. While not naming any ministers he said some were especially outspoken who felt that it should be pointed out to the US through the UK Government that Nigeria, hitherto not threatened with communism, considered that it had not been given the fullest consideration in its request for aid. The Governor-General said that he did not share the views of his ministers and had no intention of requesting the UK to discuss it in Washington, but he felt that the US should be aware of this line of thinking.

The reporting officer replied that he was aware of the feeling expressed in some quarters on this issue, but took the same stand as Mr. Julius Holmes when he discussed the subject with the Prime Minister on October 26th [3] and Deputy Assistant Secretary for AF when the issue arose in a discussion with Alhaji Mohammadu Ribadu, Federal Minister of Lagos Lands, Mines, and Power and other officials in the Department on October 8, 1957. (Department's Memorandum of Conversation [4]). The Governor-General declared he quite understood our position. Broadly speaking, this explained that the US viewed sympathetically the problems of all under-developed

---

[1] Source: Department of State, Central Files, 745H.5–MSP/12–1157. Confidential. Passed to London.

[2] Despatch 122 reported on conversations between Special Assistant to the Secretary Julius Holmes and Nigerian officials during a visit to Lagos by Holmes. (*Ibid.*, 745H.5–MSP/10–2857)

[3] Despatch #122 dated October 28, 1957. [Footnote in the source text. Despatch 122 summarized Holmes' conversation with Prime Minister Balewa as follows: "Balewa said that countries not faced with a communist threat or which had successfully introduced strong government and self-discipline and had effectively prevented communist infiltration, should not be viewed less seriously in overseas aid programs. Mr. Holmes explained that security understandably had priority in the allocation of funds but appropriate consideration was given to all needs." (*Ibid.*)]

[4] *Supra*.

countries and that Nigeria could expect every consideration in their application for assistance.

The Governor-General then commented on the decision of the appointment of an ICA Liaison Officer in Lagos and said that provided he was a well-informed officer his presence in Nigeria would be useful in advising applicants for ICA assistance, by screening out those requests that had less than a reasonable chance of succeeding and to guide others whose projects were sound but required some organization. He said that Nigeria was showing more interest in the US and that ICA and other aid groups must expect to receive an increasing number of appeals for assistance now that the country is moving towards independence.

. . . .

Ralph H. Hunt

SOMALIA

UNITED STATES INTEREST IN A PEACEFUL RESOLUTION OF THE BORDER DISPUTE BETWEEN SOMALIA AND ETHIOPIA

226. Aide-Mémoire From the Department of State to the Ethiopian Embassy [1]

Washington, November 5, 1955.

In a conversation with Mr. Allen on June 30 of this year, the Ambassador of Ethiopia said it was his Government's desire to negotiate a settlement of the disputed Ethiopia–Somalia boundary with Italy as quickly as possible. [2] The Ambassador emphasized, however, that this could not be done under the pressure of a deadline, such as that established in General Assembly Resolution 854(IX) of December 14, 1954. [3] Boundary disputes, the Ambassador observed, are complicated affairs which cannot be settled in a few weeks or a month.

The United States is by no means unsympathetic to this attitude, as demonstrated by its successful efforts at the Trusteeship Council meeting in July to prevent the adoption of a resolution calling for mediation within a specified period. [4] It should be understood, nevertheless, that the United States subscribes fully to the

---

[1] Source: Department of State, Central Files, 675.77/11–455. Leo G. Cyr handed the aide-mémoire to Berhanou Dinke, Counselor of the Ethiopian Embassy.

[2] Among the other subjects discussed by Ambassador Yilma Deressa and George V. Allen were Ethiopian requests for aviation and port development loans. (Memorandum of conversation by Cyr, June 30; *ibid.*, 775.5–MSP/6–3055)

[3] This resolution urged Ethiopia and Italy to negotiate directly a settlement of their dispute or resort to U.N. mediation as proposed in General Assembly Resolution 392(V) of December 15, 1950. Ambassador Deressa asserted on January 19 that the U.S. vote was viewed as a vote against Ethiopia. (Memorandum of conversation by Alfred Wellons, January 19; *ibid.*, 775.5–MSP/1–1955) At the urging of the United States, talks between Ethiopia and Italy began in June.

[4] Because Ethiopia agreed to resume negotiations, the United States tried to forestall the Trusteeship Council from adopting a resolution unacceptable to Ethiopia. Resolution 1257(XVI) of July 21 expressed the hope that direct negotiations would yield the results hoped for in Resolution 854(IX). It further recommended that in the event the negotiations fail, the mediation procedure contained in Resolutions 392(V) and 854(IX) be implemented. The vote was 7–0–5 (United States).

view set forth by the Ambassador that a boundary settlement should be reached as expeditiously as possible.

While sympathizing with Ethiopia's objection to the imposition of a deadline, the Department of State considers it in the general welfare that a border settlement be reached no later than the beginning of Somalia's independence in 1960. It is surely in Ethiopia's interest to dispose of an issue which could become a target for rising Somali nationalism and a source of discord with the new Somali state.

In addition, the trend of feeling in the United Nations on this matter should not be minimized. That organization has a natural desire to launch Somalia on its course of independence with as few problems as possible. There are consequently mounting pressures in the United Nations for recommending that the parties to the boundary dispute now resort to United Nations mediation, as provided for originally in General Assembly Resolution 392(V) of December 15, 1950. It obviously becomes increasingly difficult for the United States to oppose these pressures in the absence of progress in bilateral negotiations.

Ethiopia and Italy appear to have been frustrated so far in their desire to proceed with negotiations by certain procedural difficulties, in particular a difference of opinion over Somali representation in the negotiations. According to reports from our Embassy in Addis Ababa, Ethiopia holds, as a matter of principle, that it must deal primarily with Italy in the negotiations. At the same time the Department has the impression that Ethiopia would not object to a role for Somalis as experts or advisers on the Italian side of the negotiating table. The Department sees much practical merit in this means of associating individuals likely to hold authority in the future Somali nation with the boundary settlement. Such an arrangement would furthermore appear to be without prejudice to the Ethiopian contention that Ethiopia and Italy are the only legitimate spokesmen in the negotiations. As in all trusteeships, sovereignty in Somalia already resides in the people of that country and in the long run the success of any boundary settlement will depend on their acceptance of it.

In any event, the Department strongly hopes that the procedural issues can soon be disposed of and that through earnest and vigorous bilateral negotiation substantial progress can be made on the boundary problem itself so that the United States will be in a position to give the fullest possible support to Ethiopia during the forthcoming discussions of Somalia at the United Nations in opposing any move to insist on United Nations mediation at this time.

The Department would welcome such further views as the Ambassador may have on the boundary negotiations.[5]

[5] In a November 19 memorandum delivered to the Department of State November 22, Ethiopia thanked the United States for helping to put off mediation and agreed that the Somali-Ethiopian border should be expeditiously delimited, but stated Ethiopian desire that Italy accept the 1908 Convention—which the Somalis rejected—as the basis for negotiations. The United States expressed the view that Ethiopia should not insist upon this point and indicated that continued U.S. backing of the Ethiopian position against mediation was predicated on bilateral progress. (Telegram 272 to Addis Ababa, November 23; *ibid.*, 675.773/11–2355) On November 26, the Ethiopian Foreign Minister assured the U.S. Ambassador that Ethiopia would inform Italy of its willingness to engage in negotiations without insisting that it be solely on the basis of the 1908 Convention. (Telegram 353 from Addis Ababa, November 26; *ibid.*, 675.773/11–2655)

Resolution 947(X), adopted by the U.N. General Assembly on December 17, recommended that Ethiopia and Italy expedite their bilateral negotiations. It was adopted by a vote of 45 votes to 1 with 13 abstentions, the United States voting in favor.

---

227. Memorandum of a Conversation, Addis Ababa, March 12, 1957[1]

SUBJECT

Visit of Vice President Richard M. Nixon

PARTICIPANTS

Ethiopian:

H.E. Ato Aklilou Abte Wold, Foreign Minister of Ethiopia

Mr. John Spencer, American Advisor to Ethiopian Government

American:

Mr. Joseph Palmer 2nd, Deputy Assistant Secretary for African Affairs

Mr. Palmer said that he would like to clarify the position which the United States had taken in the General Assembly this year with respect to the Somali border problem.[2] He said that our analysis of the situation was as follows:

[1] Source: Department of State, S/P–NSC Files: Lot 62 D 1, North Africa (Tunisia, Algeria, Morocco, NSC 5614, 5614/1. Secret. No drafting information is given on the source text. Attached as Tab D, No. 5 to Document 19.

[2] Resolution 1068(XI) passed by a vote of 71–0–3 on February 26. It recommended that Italy and Ethiopia continue negotiations and report to the Twelfth General Assembly on their progress. If there were no substantial results by that time, they were urged to resort to mediation or arbitration.

Nationalism is rapidly growing in Somalia and the demands for a Greater Somaliland can be expected to increase. As the Foreign Minister knew, the United States has always opposed the detachment of any Ethiopian territory and this continues to be our position. We believe, however, Somalia can be expected to pursue its ambitions for a Greater Somaliland, including the Ogaden province of Ethiopia. We feel that under these circumstances it would be in Ethiopia's own interest to make every effort to find a means of settling the border problem before Somalia attains its independence. Otherwise, the unsettled border may prove a great temptation to Somali nationalism to pursue that part of its five-point program which calls for the detachment of the Ogaden province from Ethiopia. On the other hand, a settlement of this problem while the United Nations still maintains an interest in the Trust Territory would imply a UN blessing to the border arrangement and thereby place Ethiopia in the best possible position in the event an independent Somalia attempted to violate Ethiopian territory. We had also taken into account the fact that efforts at negotiations for the past several years have proven unsuccessful. We therefore believed that the introduction of a new element, such as mediation, arbitration or some similar device might be necessary in order to facilitate agreement. We had, therefore, authorized our delegation in New York to explore this possibility with the Ethiopians, the Italians, and other delegations to see whether a basis existed for some such impartial determination of the boundary problem. When we found that there was considerable support for one further effort at negotiations before resorting to a device of this kind, we supported the resolution which had been introduced to that effect. It is therefore clear that the U.S. had no thought of taking a position opposed to Ethiopia's interests but had regarded the explorations which it had undertaken as having been in the best interests of that country.

Aklilou thanked Mr. Palmer for his explanation of this problem which he said he understood. He went on to recount the history of the border problem and of the efforts to solve it by direct negotiation. He said that Ethiopia also was anxious to settle the matter before Somalia attains its independence but did not at all despair of doing so after independence if this became necessary. He said that Ethiopia must, in its own interest, stand on the 1908 Treaty and could not agree to any procedure whereby "hundreds of international secretariat people" would come into the area. Any solution to the boundary problem should be based on juridical considerations and not on ascertaining facts on the spot.

Mr. Palmer said that it was his understanding that the U.S. had always accepted the fact that the primary point of departure in any impartial mediatory or arbitration procedure would be the 1908

Convention and that the primary problem would be to interpret that Convention. He did not think that this principle should be applied rigidly; there might be an adjustment of the border which both sides could accept to their mutual advantage and he did not think this could be ruled out. He said he thought that it would be highly desirable if, in the event no progress is reached in negotiations during the course of the next year, the Ethiopian delegation to the UN could sit down with the interested Departmental officers in Washington prior to the opening of the General Assembly and have an exchange of views on this subject in order to insure as close an identity of views as possible and obviate any misunderstandings during the course of the next General Assembly. Aklilou expressed agreement with this suggestion.

---

228. Memorandum of a Conversation, Department of State, Washington, June 10, 1957 [1]

SUBJECT

Visit of Somali Minister of Economic Affairs

PARTICIPANTS

Hagi Farah Ali, Minister of Economic Affairs of Somalia
Mohammed Schek Osman, Deputy, Somalia Legislative Assembly
Omar Mohallim, Civil Servant
Mr. Witman, AFN
Mr. Dorros, AFN
Mr. Beard, AFN
Mr. Dolgin, AFN
Mr. Engle, WE
Mr. Dunn, ED
Mr. Johnson, ED

(Although the Minister speaks some English, and appears to understand it fairly well, he preferred to speak through an interpreter, Omar Mohallim, whose English is excellent.)

H.E. Hagi Farah Ali recalled that the Somali delegation which visited the Department last year had urged the United States to

[1] Source: Department of State, Central Files, 745U.00/6–1057. Confidential. Drafted by Beard.

establish a Consulate at Mogadiscio,[2] and expressed his appreciation that this had been done. He felt it was highly important that direct relations and channels of communication had been established between the two countries. Mr. Farah also expressed the appreciation of his Government for the assistance the United States has extended to Somalia.

During the course of the ensuing conversation, the Minister discussed three topics:

(1) the possibility Somalia may seek its independence before 1960;
(2) Somalia's hope for long-range economic assistance from the United States; and
(3) U.S. assistance in obtaining a solution to the Ethiopia-Somalia boundary question.

With regard to independence prior to 1960, the Minister noted that elections for a constituent Assembly will be held next year and Somalia will shortly thereafter have its Constitution and Chief of State. The powers retained by the Administering Authority from then on will be very limited and the Somali Government will, for all practical purposes, have as much authority as the government of an independent country. Under these circumstances, there appears to be no reason why Somalia should not be granted independence at a date earlier than that specified by the United Nations, i.e., 1960.

Mr. Farah then expressed the hope that his Government would receive economic assistance from the United States when it became independent. In this connection, he said he would like to leave with the Department a copy of the statement he had recently made before the Trusteeship Council during its consideration of the IBRD report on the economy of Somalia (copy attached).[3] He observed that, on the basis of developments in the past few years, the situation seemed to him more hopeful than the IBRD report indicated. He was optimistic; the Bank was pessimistic.

---

[2] Telegram 590 to Addis Ababa, June 22, 1956, indicated that a delegation led by Issa and Osman and the Deputy Chairman of the Legislative Assembly, Abdi Nur, visited the Department of State on June 20 and 21. The Somalis expressed appreciation for past technical assistance and hoped more aid would be forthcoming, requested the United States to exercise its influence to help settle the boundary problem, strongly opposed any federation of Somaliland with Ethiopia, rejected the notion of a Greater Somaliland within the Commonwealth, and stated they could not predict the Somali response to an offer from the East should the West fail them. (*Ibid.*, 120.277/6–2256) Memoranda of conversations are *ibid.*, 777.00/6–2156 and 675.773/6–2156.

[3] Not printed. U.N. docs. T/SR.797, May 22, and T/SR.803, May 31, contain Farah's statement. The IBRD Report concluded that Somalia would be faced with continuing substantial budgetary deficits after 1960 requiring outside economic and technical assistance. The report was discussed by the Trusteeship Council at its Twentieth Session, May 20–July 12. See U.N. doc. T/1296, January 30.

The Minister said that he would also like to request the United States to do what it could to bring about a settlement of the boundary problem with Ethiopia. Very little progress has been made in the seven years since the U.N. Resolution on this matter. During the negotiations of the past year, the Ethiopian delegation had remained adamant in its position and indicated that if a settlement were to be reached it would have to be done on its own terms. The Minister felt that the Ethiopians wished to delay a settlement until after Somalia's independence when his Government would be preoccupied with other matters.

In reply, Mr. Witman addressed himself first to the matter of independence prior to 1960. He noted that the U.N. decision to grant independence had provided for a certain period of transition to permit the Somalis to have as much time as possible to learn the many and varied tasks involved in the government of an independent state. He could, of course, appreciate the desire of the Somalis to receive their independence as soon as possible, but, speaking personally, felt that it would be advisable for the Somalis to take advantage of the full period specified by the U.N. Since the U.N. had decreed a ten-year period of Trusteeship, we cannot make an official statement on the matter of earlier independence unless it is raised in the U.N. Our attitude would be determined at that time. [4]

With regard to economic assistance, Mr. Witman said he also appreciated the desire of the Somalis to have an indication of the assistance they might expect to receive after independence. Because of our system of Government, however, we are not able to make any commitments regarding aid in future years. The Executive Branch of the Government has been seeking authorization from the Congress to be permitted to make such commitments, but, thus far, has not been authorized to do so. The only assurance we are able to give is that we are aware of the needs of Somalia and will continue to view the problem sympathetically.

The Minister said that he was aware of this and merely wished to record the desire of his Government to receive help from the United States.

With regard to the Minister's third point, the Ethiopia-Somalia boundary, Mr. Witman said that we concurred in the desirability of a settlement of this problem prior to Somalia's independence. In this regard, we have been supporting the utilization of the procedure which we have felt offered the most likely prospects of success (bilateral negotiations). As far as the United States is concerned,

---

[4] At the Bermuda Conference on March 23, Dulles told British Foreign Secretary Selwyn Lloyd that he considered the 1960 independence date for Italian Somaliland to be impractical. See Document 18.

however, we do not care what procedure is employed to reach a settlement so long as it is satisfactory to the parties directly involved. We share the hope that the problem will be resolved prior to 1960.

229. Telegram From the Department of State to the Embassy in Italy[1]

Washington, June 26, 1957—6:15 p.m.

5077. During recent conversation with Dept, Somalia Administrator Anzilotti mentioned possibility independence Somalia in early 1959.[2] Anzilotti indicated Italy would find it difficult refuse request for independence before 1960 in view of (a) plans for Somali Constitution and Head of State by end 1958, and (b) Somali wish to negotiate directly for foreign aid. Italian Ambassador Brosio also present suggested Italy, because of economic considerations, may not be in a position or wish to oppose Somali independence in 1959.

With respect question of economic aid, Anzilotti hopes Italian assistance will be continued until 1960. He expressed opinion that from standpoint over-all Western interests, Italy should continue to play important part after 1960. However, from Italian national viewpoint withdrawal in 1960 would be logical since Italy has no major interests to protect in area which is rapidly becoming political hotspot under influence Egyptian and Ethiopian intrigues.

Department informed Anzilotti that, while not ready to take definite position on independence before 1960, it believes there are advantages in not moving too rapidly. Somali Government will not be able to act effectively for some time and will therefore need as much guidance and assistance as possible. We also consider it highly desirable that problem of border with Ethiopia be resolved before independence. With respect to related issue of economic aid after independence, Dept will continue to keep Somalia's needs in mind in future planning without making present commitment. We hope Italy will continue play important part in Somalia after 1960 as contribution to world-wide Western position.

---

[1] Source: Department of State, Central Files, 777.000/6–457. Secret. Repeated to Addis Ababa, London, and Mogadiscio. Drafted by Dorros and approved by Witman.

[2] Enrico Anzilotti, former Italian Ambassador to Austria, met with Palmer and Rountree on June 13. (Memorandum of conversation by Dorros; *ibid.*, IO/ODA Files: Lot 62 D 225, US–UK Colonial Talks 1957)

Since FonOff has indicated Italy has no intention withdrawing from Somalia before 1960 and that it considers Somalia as one of areas where Italy can play primary role in maintaining pro-Western orientation (Embdes 1597 [3]), believe Embassy should seek opportunity to obtain clarification in view statements made by Anzilotti.

You may indicate to FonOff that:

1. While aware economic considerations involved Italian thinking, we consider it important in over-all Western interest that Italy continue its administration for full period provided by UN Trusteeship Agreement. Early Italian withdrawal, we feel would, for following reasons, adversely affect future orientation Somalia and political stability Horn of Africa:

a. Somali Government, while assuming increasing responsibility, lacks necessary experience and will need continued guidance and stabilizing influence Italian administration over next three years,

b. Unresolved status Ethiopian-Somali boundary constitutes serious threat stability of area. We consider it important that problem be resolved while Somalia still a U.N. responsibility to provide settlement with UN moral sanction. Early Italian withdrawal might jeopardize prospects of settlement under UN auspices,

c. While decision on early termination of Trusteeship is matter for UN decision, Italian initiative in this direction might afford anti-Western UN delegations an opportunity attack other Western positions in Africa.

2. With respect to post-independence period, we believe GOI should give earnest consideration to its continued participation in political and economic responsibilities carried by Western nations in various parts of the world. Since Italy has an interest in Somalia in view its historical ties with that country and its success in achieving objectives of Trusteeship, it is Western nation best qualified to assure continued stability and favorable orientation new Somali state. While we hope US will be able continue its help to Somalia and that other Western countries will also find it possible to assist, consider leading part in this country should be assumed by Italy.

Suggest Embassy emphasize foregoing points in future discussions with GOI officials re Somalia. [4]

Dulles

---

[3] Despatch 1597, June 4, noted that Dr. Piero Vinci, head of the Italian Foreign Office Middle East section, had informed the Embassy in Rome on June 3 that no withdrawal was contemplated. (*Ibid.*, Central Files, 777.00/6–457)

[4] Ambassador James D. Zellerbach, in a conversation with Italian Foreign Office officials on June 28, was told that Italy would continue economic and administrative support through 1960. However, the Italians claimed they could not restrain Somalia if its leaders demanded full independence before the end of 1960. Zellerbach emphasized the importance of an Italian presence for the duration of the trusteeship. (Telegram 5122 from Rome, June 29; *ibid.*, 777.00/6–2957)

230. Despatch From the Consulate at Mogadiscio to the Department of State[1]

No. 60 *Mogadiscio, October 18, 1957.*

SUBJECT

Visit of Ambassador Bliss

Ambassador Bliss and party arrived Mogadiscio on October 9, in the plane of the Naval Attaché at Cairo, and departed on October 11. In the course of the stay, Ambassador Bliss made calls on Ambassador Anzilotti, Aden Abdullah, President of the Legislative Assembly, and Abdullahi Issa, Prime Minister. He met, at lunch given by me, Hagi Farah, Minister of Economic Affairs and, at dinner given by me, Aden Abdullah and Abdullahi Issa.

1. Ambassador Anzilotti

Ambassador Anzilotti offered little of interest in his hour-long conversation with Ambassador Bliss. The border negotiations were discussed, but no new information offered. Mr. Anzilotti observed that they should be ending just about this time, with no results. He also observed that it is difficult, in view of the impending 1958 elections, for the Somali Government to agree to any proposals which might be used to embarrass them politically within Somalia. Asked about the probable outcome of the 1958 elections, Mr. Anzilotti said that it is still a little early to make predictions but that he did not expect any great change, unless there should come a split in the SYL. He said that such a split is possible but that he rather expects that it will be avoided and, if it is avoided, that the SYL should probably emerge again as the majority party, although perhaps with a smaller majority.

2. Hagi Farah

At the lunch with Hagi Farah were present also Dr. Gasbarri[2] and W.E. Corfitzen, ICA Representative.

Of greatest interest here were Dr. Gasbarri's defense of the future of the banana industry and Hagi Farah's interest in construction of a port at Chisimaio. The two are related. It was Dr. Gasbarri's contention that there exists a good chance of reducing the cost of Somali bananas to the competitive world level provided

[1] Source: Department of State, Central Files, 123–Bliss, Don C., Jr. Confidential. Passed to Rome and London. The Ambassador's account of his visit is in despatch 151 from Addis Ababa, October 28. (*Ibid.*, 121.752/10–2857)

[2] Dr. Luigi Gasbarri, President of Somalia's Economic Development Agency.

production is shifted to the lower Giuba and a port is constructed at Chisimaio. Dr. Gasbarri also argued that the European Common Market will help Somali bananas, since it will exclude from Europe Somalia's keenest competitors, namely, Spain and the Canaries, and Brazil. Hagi Farah intimated that he is planning to raise the question of U.S. financing for the Chisimaio port scheme when he visits the United States this fall.

3. Prime Minister and Aden Abdullah

As expected, these two gentlemen were interested mainly in four subjects, Ethiopia's aims on Somalia, the Ethiopian-Somali border, U.S. aid to Somalia and U.S. arms for Somalia.

Federation with Ethiopia. Ambassador Bliss introduced this subject, referring to Somali fears of Ethiopia and of U.S. support for Ethiopian aims. [3] The Ambassador stated that the Somalis need have no fear of U.S. intentions, that we are not backing federation with Ethiopia but are supporting, as we have already shown in many ways, a free and independent Somalia. This statement was received with much gratification by both men.

Ambassador Bliss continued to the effect that U.S. hopes are for mutually satisfactory relations between Ethiopia and Somalia, so that these countries together can work out their common problems.

Greater Somalia. Ambassador Bliss asked about Greater Somalia. The two men asserted that this is a concept which Somalis and a Somali State will always have in mind but the Prime Minister repeated his standard observation on this theme, to the effect that Somalia will never try to achieve a greater Somalia except by "legal, peaceful" means. It was observed by the writer that "legal, peaceful" means would probably never succeed in detaching the Somali occupied areas from Ethiopia and that Somali persistence in claiming those areas might be a significant factor in provoking Ethiopia to make gestures toward Somalia. The Prime Minister agreed but said again that Somalia could never abandon its claim to those areas. He added that, as a practical matter, however, Somali thinking for the near future was concentrated upon the British Protectorate and he said that he expected success in that aspiration. The writer asked if Somali thinking on this subject encompassed the idea of Commonwealth membership and if such membership was under consider-

[3] In despatch 49 from Mogadiscio, September 18, McGrath reported rumors of U.S. support of federation with Ethiopia. He urged that a prominent U.S. official indicate that the United States desired a free and independent Somalia. (Department of State, Central Files, 777.00/9–1857) The Department replied that, since U.S. support for Somali independence was a matter of public record, U.S. interest would be better served in private discussions. (Telegram 37 to Mogadiscio, September 27; *ibid.*, 123–Bliss, Don C., Jr.)

ation. To this Aden Abdullah replied, "No, not at all." The Prime Minister was not so outspoken in his denial, saying that Commonwealth membership would not be accepted as the price of union.

Somali-Ethiopian Border. Both men expressed dismay at the failure of the border negotiations and the Ambassador observed that the U.S. firmly supports the view that the border should be settled prior to independence. The two Somalis indicated their agreement, but expressed doubt that any conclusion could be reached in bilateral negotiations. They indicated that Somalia would like, as has been indicated before, to see the matter go to mediation in accordance with the UN resolution.

The writer observed that current Mogadiscio rumor credits to the Somali Government a preparedness to accept the existing provisional line as permanent but adds that the Government is unwilling, for internal political reasons, to do this in bilateral negotiations (Consulate despatch 56, October 9 [4]). The Prime Minister agreed that internal political factors did complicate the Somali position on the border but denied that the Government had ever expressed a willingness to accept the existing provisional line. He said that the Somalis were keeping the idea of greater Somalia separate from that of establishing a border and that they did not expect to achieve control of the Somali areas of Ethiopia by way of border negotiations. He added that the Somalis did hope, however, for something approaching the 1934 boundaries.

There was then discussion of the border crossing problem, with everyone agreeing that, wherever the border was fixed, it would probably still divide Somali tribes, so that border crossing arrangements would be of great importance.

U.S. Aid to Somalia. On the question of aid, both men observed that they were hoping for much from the U.S. Ambassador Bliss explained the difficulties which stand in the way of the United States' making advance commitments but he referred to the increasing U.S. interest in Africa and to the existing program of U.S. technical assistance in Somalia. The writer observed that, although we cannot make advance commitments, the existence and steady growth of the U.S. program here should be assurance of our continuing interest.

Aid and Premature Independence. The Prime Minister observed that, with regard to foreign aid, the Somali Government is becoming increasingly anxious, particularly since it understands that Italy plans from now until 1960 to cut back steadily the level of its aid to Somalia. Under these circumstances, he said, the Somali Government

---

[4] In despatch 56, McGrath indicated one of the sources of this report was Ambassador Anzilotti. (*Ibid.*, 675.773/10–957)

is very eager to come in touch with other nations, and particularly the U.S., and, in order to do so, it is planning to ask for its independence in January 1959. Ambassador Bliss said that the United States hoped that Somalia would not anticipate independence because we believed that Somalia would profit by having the full period in which to develop its technicians and to assimilate techniques of government. The Prime Minister observed that a difference of two years would make very little difference and that, to the Somali Government, it seemed more important to have control of its own foreign affairs, so that it could deal directly with foreign nations for aid and, perhaps, arms. Aden Abdullah added that if the United States or someone would increase its aid in this trusteeship period to take up the increasing slack being left by Italy, it might be possible for Somalia to wait until 1960 but that otherwise he, too, believed that independence in 1959 would probably be in Somalia's best interest. (*Writer's Note*: So far as I can establish, the reduction in Italian aid referred to by the Prime Minister is only the normal and expected "phasing out" of Italian civil servants in Somalia.)

Arms Aid to Somalia. Aden Abdullah referred to U.S. military aid to Ethiopia and asked if anything could be done for Somalia. Ambassador Bliss explained at some length that the American arms agreement with Ethiopia stipulates clearly that these arms shall be used for internal security only and not for foreign adventuring. There was then some discussion of the type of arms aid which the Somalis had in mind. This discussion did not produce any real clarification and it seemed that the Somalis have not yet thought through their requirements. The possibility of an ICA police training program was raised and the Somalis expressed interest.

Somali-Ethiopian Relations. On this subject, Ambassador Bliss, speaking generally, said that the United States hoped that Somalia and Ethiopia would make every effort to understand one another's point of view and to work toward an amicable settlement of any differences. The invitation of the Ethiopian Government to Aden Abdullah and Abdullahi Issa was then mentioned. Abdullahi Issa said that this invitation had been accepted in principle but that no date had been set. He added that he doubted very much whether it would be possible to go before February. Both of them seemed most reluctant to undertake the visit and Aden Abdullah observed that it might be a touchy project to undertake in an election year. "Besides," he added, "What will we talk about once we get there? We can't handle our own foreign relations."

Comment

It is considered that the Ambassador's visit and these conversations were well worthwhile. The two Somali leaders were particularly gratified to hear that the U.S. is not supporting federation with Ethiopia. The Ambassador's statements putting U.S. military aid to Ethiopia in its proper perspective were also most useful.

On the Somali side, of greatest significance were the statements about seeking independence in January 1959 and the inquiry about arms and/or police aid. The statement about early independence is the most unambiguous one I have yet heard from a leading Somali. It is also the first reference to arms from either the Prime Minister or the President.

On the border, I believe that the Prime Minister was being less than frank when he denied Somali willingness to accept the present provisional line as a permanent one. The report of this willingness has come from several sources and seems to me to be reasonably reliable.

John B. McGrath

231. Telegram From the Department of State to the Mission at the United Nations[1]

Washington, December 3, 1957—8:11 p.m.

483. On November 23 Ethiopian Ambassador Deressa called at Department with reference to upcoming UNGA discussion Ethiopian-Somali boundary. Deressa stated his Government favors compromise settlement this problem involving acceptance existing provisional border as permanent frontier. IEG confident strength its legal position, but willing to accept provisional line in interest of achieving rapid settlement. If compromise settlement not possible, IEG, as previously indicated, wishes submit interpretation 1908 boundary convention to arbitration. Ambassador said he instructed ascertain whether we would speak to Itals in favor Ethiopian Ital agreement on this compromise and enquired re possibility having

[1] Source: Department of State, Central Files, 675.773/12–357. Confidential. Repeated by pouch to Addis Ababa, Rome, and Mogadiscio. Drafted by Dorros and cleared by Bovey.

friendly countries sponsor Resolution recommending this solution. Department agreed to transmit its reply to him in New York.

Request you inform Deressa we have given careful consideration IEG views; fundamentally, US position is to favor early settlement boundary problem on basis mutually agreeable to parties directly concerned. We recognize that compromise envisaged by IEG would make possible quick solution if accepted by Italians and Somalis. However, since issue before GA is determination of procedure to settle differences in interpretation existing agreement defining boundary, resolution attempting to impose specific settlement appears to be outside GA competence. We not certain such a resolution would receive widespread support and foresee, even if Somalis were now to consent, possibility of future Somali protest this settlement imposed upon them in violation their legal claims. Believe, therefore, arbitration is more appropriate method of reaching settlement and hesitate to recommend to other delegations compromise solution which we feel may give rise to serious difficulties. We are, however, willing to mention to the Italian delegation the proposed compromise. In the event agreement on this solution does not appear possible, we hope Ethiopian and Italian Delegations can agree upon a resolution favoring arbitration and would be willing to render such assistance as may be deemed desirable in this connection. If all the parties concerned are agreeable, we would be glad to sponsor a resolution acceptable to them all recommending a procedure of arbitration. [2]

In playing intermediary role re Somali frontier question USDel should seek retain flexibility this stage as regards terms of possible arbitration resolution. In view Ethiopian sensitivity on subject USDel should consult with IEG Del soonest to ascertain its ideas re acceptable resolution. USDel should continue carefully to avoid identification with any draft resolution until assured it is in form acceptable to all parties. In this connection we doubt appropriateness suggesting to Ethiopians resolution containing recommendations re negotiation

---

[2] In Delga 538 from USUN, December 4, Ambassador Lodge reported that Deressa informed the British that only the 1908 Convention should be the subject of arbitration and not any references to grazing rights or the peace, order, and welfare of the population. (*Ibid.*, 675.773/12–457) These same points were reiterated by Deressa to Lodge on December 5, when he stated his nation's opposition to the interjection of political considerations into a juridical matter. The Italians informed the British on the same date that whereas the Somalis might be persuaded not to insist on references to grazing rights and border crossings they were adamant that the arbitration tribunal not confine itself to the 1908 Convention and that it consider the peace, order, and welfare of the population involved. (Delga 548 from USUN, December 5; *ibid.*, 675.773/12–557)

water and grazing rights which do not bear directly upon settlement frontier.

Dulles

232. Editorial Note

On December 12, Dr. Herman Wells, the Representative in the Fourth Committee, expressed support for Somaliland independence in 1960. He stressed, however, the importance of finding a solution to the border problem prior to that date. Since the Ethiopians were opposed to mediation, the United States believed the best procedure would be to create an arbitral tribunal to resolve "differences of interpretation" of the 1908 Convention. (USUN Press Release 2844) The United States and the United Kingdom tabled a draft resolution (A/C.4/L.529) which was unanimously approved in revised form by the Fourth Committee on December 13 and by the General Assembly the following day. The latter body inserted the words "His Majesty the King of Norway" in operative paragraph 2. In the operative portion of Resolution 1213(XII), the General Assembly recommended: "the parties to establish, if possible within three months, an arbitration tribunal—consisting of three jurists, one to be appointed by Ethiopia, one by Italy and one by agreement between the jurists so appointed or, failing agreement between them, by His Majesty the King of Norway—to delimit the frontier in accordance with the terms of reference to be agreed upon between the two Governments, with the assistance of an independent person to be appointed between them".

On December 17, Hagi Farah Ali thanked the United States for its help in bringing about a successful compromise which was more acceptable to his government than the draft resolution introduced by Ceylon, Greece, Indonesia, Liberia, and Sudan. (A/C.4/L.528) (Memorandum of conversation by Robert W. Huddleston, December 17; Department of State, IO/ODA Files: Lot 62 D 225, Somaliland)

SUDAN

UNITED STATES POLICY OBJECTIVES IN THE SUDAN

233. Instruction From the Department of State to Certain Diplomatic Missions[1]

CA–1323 *Washington, August 16, 1955.*

SUBJECT

US Policy Towards the Sudan

The Department has completed a review of the current situation in the Sudan with special attention to the following factors:

1. The probable time table for completion of the self-determination process. The Sudanese Parliament is expected to pass a resolution about August 16 asking that arrangements for self-determination be started. Within three months Egyptian and British troops should be withdrawn and in succession a draft law for election of the Constituent Assembly would be drawn up; the Assembly would be elected; the Assembly would choose between some link with Egypt or complete independence; a Constitution for the Sudan and the electoral laws for the first Parliament would be drawn up; and the Parliament would be elected. The entire procedure would be supervised by an International Commission and should be completed during he first months of 1956.

2. The preponderant strength of pro-independence sentiment in the Sudan. Intelligence Brief #1806, "Implications for Egyptian-Sudanese Relations of an Independent Sudan",[2] recently has been sent to the field. The brief concludes there is every indication the Sudan will choose independence, an assessment confirmed by reporting from USLO Khartoum.[3]

3. The legitimate Egyptian concern over Nile water. Dependent as it is upon the Nile, Egypt is naturally concerned over the security of her present supply of water and that she receive an equitable amount of water now unused. Furthermore, IBRD assistance in

---

[1] Source: Department of State, Central Files, 611.45W/8–1655. Confidential. Sent to Khartoum, Cairo, and London. Repeated to Addis Ababa, Paris, Athens, Rome, Nairobi, and Asmara.

[2] Not printed.

[3] Arthur E. Beach, Liaison Officer in Khartoum, reported in despatch 42, August 15, that a decision for independence could be anticipated. (Department of State, Central Files, 745W.00/8–1555)

financing the high dam at Aswan is contingent, among other factors, upon an Egyptian-Sudanese agreement on division of the waters of the Nile.

4. The intensified Egyptian campaign to bring about some type of link between Egypt and the Sudan. The tactics employed include efforts to bribe southern Sudanese and a strong press and radio campaign against Prime Minister Azhari who has come out in favor of independence.

5. The difficulties currently being experienced in the Anglo-Egyptian talks in Cairo over the composition and terms of reference of the International Commission to supervise the self-determination process. Saleh Salim [4] has proposed the USSR and a satellite as members of the Commission.

6. Accusations by Egypt that the United States is working in cooperation with the United Kingdom to assure a vote for independence. The Egyptian Ambassador acting on instructions has stressed to the Department Prime Minister Nasser's conviction that the United States is intervening and the Egyptian press and radio have carried articles to this effect.

7. The Egyptian request that the United States assist in improving Egyptian-Sudanese relations and in bringing about a Nile waters agreement. [5] The Secretary agreed to look into the matter and see what could be done.

8. The Sudanese requests for United States assistance of a technical nature and the desirability of providing the new country with appropriate guidance and modest assistance during its first years. [6]

The Department considers that the basic objectives of the United States are stability in the area, the orderly development of the Sudan in accordance with the wishes of its people, and the maintenance of friendly relations with the West and the Sudan's immediate neighbors. The United States at this time has no specific strategic requirements in the Sudan.

As a consequence of this review the Department has come to the conclusion that the United States should be guided in the immediate future by the policies given below:

1. During the process of self-determination the United States should scrupulously refrain from any actions which might be construed as affecting the "free and neutral atmosphere" and the choice of the Sudanese with respect to their future. To do otherwise would

---

[4] Major Salah Salem, Egyptian Minister of State for Sudanese Affairs, Minister of National Guidance, and a member of the Revolution Command Council.

[5] The Egyptian Ambassador, Dr. Ahmed Hussein, took up these matters with Secretary Dulles on July 29. The memorandum of conversation by Allen, July 29, is in Department of State, Central Files, 774.5/7–2955.

[6] The Sudanese had requested a ground water geologist and a hydroelectric expert. Due to the Egyptian-Sudanese controversy over control of the Nile waters, the latter request was turned down. Beach suggested a possible offer of technical assistance in noncontroversial fields. (Despatch 251 from Khartoum, June 20; *ibid.*, 845W.2614A/6–2055)

expose the United States to charges of interference by both sides to the detriment of its position in both Egypt and the Sudan.

2. The United States should endeavor as quickly as possible to facilitate an Egyptian-Sudanese agreement on the division of the Nile waters. The possibility of working through the IBRD should be explored and the complications which might result from direct involvement by the United States should be borne in mind. Additional instructions on this matter will be forwarded shortly.[7]

3. After self-determination the United States should encourage closer Egyptian-Sudanese relations, recognizing that the dependence of both countries on the Nile makes cooperation essential if there is to be stability.

4. The United States should not undertake a technical assistance program or an economic assistance program prior to self-determination. No decision has been made on whether such programs should be undertaken afterwards. No ICA personnel should be assigned at this time.

5. After self-determination the United States should undertake a small USIA program. No USIA personnel should be assigned prior to self-determination.

In the administrative sphere advantages are seen in retaining the small size of the office pending resolution of the self-determination issue, thus allaying suspicions of United States intervention. However, the Department is starting administrative preparations now to the extent limited funds permit for the establishment of a modest mission in Khartoum in the spring of 1956 on the assumption that the Sudan will opt for independence. FBO is being requested to begin promptly arrangements for suitable office quarters and for additional living quarters. Since the present lease expires on December 30, 1955, and the quarters are admittedly temporary, USLO Khartoum can explain plausibly, if necessary, that new quarters are necessary regardless of the outcome of self-determination. To avoid charges of pre-judging the issue, care should be exercised to prevent any public intimation of these plans.[8]

Dulles

[7] In CA–1631 to Khartoum, August 25, the Department informed the Liaison Office (and London and Cairo) of the chief obstacles to the IBRD arriving at a final decision on the Aswan Dam. It indicated that the United States, in concert with the United Kingdom, should make a strong effort to bring about an Egyptian-Sudanese Nile waters accord, thereby eliminating one of the major impediments to a resolution of the matter. (*Ibid.*, 645W.74322/8–2555)

[8] In his response to this instruction, Beach commented that paragraph 1 appeared to provide the basic key to U.S. actions. In regard to paragraph 2, he acknowledged the need for caution and noted that developments in Egypt would in part dictate the possibility of implementing paragraph 3. He saw the wisdom of not immediately initiating technical or economic assistance programs, but hoped each request would be considered on its merits. He saw paragraph 5 as presenting no problems. (Despatch 67 from Khartoum, October 7; *ibid.*, 611.45W/10–755)

234. Editorial Note

On January 1, 1956, the United Kingdom and Egypt recognized the independence of the Sudan. United States recognition was extended effective on that date, although the message extending recognition was delayed in transmission and delivered by the Liaison Officer in Khartoum, Arthur E. Beach, on January 2. For text of the message, see *American Foreign Policy: Current Documents, 1956*, page 728. The Department of State announced on February 17 that the Liaison Office in Khartoum had been elevated to embassy status as of February 15, with Beach as Chargé d'Affaires. Lowell C. Pinkerton was appointed Ambassador on April 12 and presented his credentials on May 17.

235. Instruction From the Department of State to the Embassy in the Sudan[1]

CA–8750 *Washington, May 7, 1956.*

SUBJECT

Instructions for Ambassador Lowell C. Pinkerton

These instructions for the Ambassador are based on the estimate that the Sudan as a new nation facing decisive choices is of importance to the United States.

The Sudan may have close relations with the Soviets, thus opening the African continent to further Soviet penetration, or continue close relations with the West; it may add to the accumulation of Arab extremism or exert a modifying influence in the Arab League; it may be the means of furthering Egyptian designs for domination or the means in certain cases of frustrating Egyptian plans inimical to the West. The orientation of the Sudan away from the Western World would involve a serious set back to American policy in the Near East and Africa.

The Sudan is strategically located, being a member of both the Arab World and of Africa. If we are to exert influence for the achievement of our objectives, we must be more directly concerned with the Sudan itself in view of its new independence. This is

[1] Source: Department of State, Central Files, 123–Pinkerton, Lowell C. Secret. Repeated to Addis Ababa, Cairo, and London.

especially true since Britain, which has carried nearly exclusive responsibility for the Sudan's Western orientation, no longer enjoys the status of a condominium power and has suffered several reverses in the Arab World. Egypt, a former condominium power, has not relinquished its ambition to exercise a dominating influence in the Sudan and seems bent on moving the Sudan in the direction of its own "neutralism", nationalism and cooperation with the Soviets.

Our objectives in the Sudan may be described as follows:

1. To support the maintenance of Sudan's independence.
2. To encourage stable governments friendly to the West generally and the United States in particular.
3. To prevent Soviet penetration of the Sudan and thus deny its use as a bridge to further Soviet penetration of the African continent. For this purpose, Sudan-Soviet relations must be nominal only.
4. To encourage the Sudan to cooperate with Egypt in cases where Egypt is friendly to United States objectives; to encourage the Sudan to frustrate Egypt in all cases where the Egyptians serve the Soviet purposes; to encourage friendly relations with the Sudan's other neighbors.

Accordingly, you are instructed to seek the earliest convenient opportunity following presentation of credentials to discuss the following matters with the Prime Minister, the Minister of Foreign Affairs [2] and other officials as you deem appropriate.

Political

1. You should say that the United States has had pleasure in welcoming the Sudan to the family of independent republics and in taking an initiative to propose the Sudan for membership in the United Nations. We will continue to support the Sudan for membership, will be pleased to give our support in the case of United Nations agencies which the Sudan would like to join, and will be helpful in every appropriate way. [3]

2. The United States has agreements for economic assistance with more than fifty countries and agreements for military assistance with more than forty countries. There are no strings attached to these agreements. Only provisions for mutual security are included. The Soviets may not include any provisions in extending their aid, but they proceed on the assumption of unseen subversion.

3. If the Sudanese authorities should request further information regarding agreements, you may leave the enclosed copies of agree-

[2] Mubarak Zarroug.

[3] The Sudan applied for U.N. membership on January 30. The United States placed the subject on the Security Council agenda. On February 6, the Security Council voted unanimously to recommend to the General Assembly the admission of the Sudan. The General Assembly acted favorably on November 12. (Resolution 1110(XI)) Documentation on this subject is in Department of State, Central File 310.2.

ments between the United States and various countries of the area. These include the Technical Cooperation Agreement with Egypt, the Amity and Economic Relations Treaty with Ethiopia, the Military Defense Assistance Agreement with Lebanon, and the Military Assistance Agreement with Iraq.[4] You should stress that these represent the various types of economic and military agreements in which the United States is engaged and in no sense are submitted for purposes of negotiation.

4. You should explain that the Government of the Sudan must be under no illusions regarding the relationship in which our offers of aid stand to Soviet offers. The United States has a history of economic and military assistance to friendly countries which antedates the recent Soviet entry to this field. We do not ask any country to take aid from us. We do not believe that threats to accept aid from Soviet sources are in the interest of any nation which desires aid from the United States. We are not bidding against the Soviets because we are not offering the same thing. Our aid does not have subversion as its ultimate purpose.

5. The Sudanese may be assured that the United States expects to have relationships with the Sudan based on its independence and not as an appendage of Egypt. From the first the United States has assumed the position that Egyptian-Sudan agreement on the division of Nile waters is a sine qua non of full United States participation in financing the High Aswan Dam project. We hope that the Sudan will have good relations with all its neighbors, including Egypt, but are confident in the Sudan's announcements that such good relations will be sought as an independent country.

6. You should say that the United States Government continues to hope that the Sudan will not exchange diplomatic representatives with Communist China, Communist North Korea, Communist Vietnam, or Communist East Germany. Our Chargé has made these representations formally. They continue to constitute our policy.[5]

---

[4] Except for the Ethiopian accord, Pinkerton presented copies of these agreements to the Sudanese Finance Minister, Ibrahim Ahmad. The Economic and Technical Cooperation agreement with Egypt had been concluded on May 5, 1951; the Military Assistance Agreement with Lebanon was dated March 23, 1953; the Military Assistance Agreement with Iraq was dated April 21, 1954; and the General Agreement for Technical Cooperation with Ethiopia had been signed on June 16, 1951. See, respectively, TIAS 2479, 3 UST 2960; TIAS 3147, 5 UST 2908; TIAS 3447, 6 UST 6014; and TIAS 2271, 2 UST 1227.

[5] On January 14, Beach forcefully made known to Zarroug U.S. opposition to Sudanese recognition of Communist China and North Korea. (Telegram 126 from Khartoum, January 14; Department of State, Central Files, 745W.02/1–1456) In telegram 152 to Khartoum, April 3, the Department advised Beach to renew strong representations against Sudanese recognition of Communist China, East Germany, North Korea, and North Vietnam. (*Ibid.*, 745W.62/1–2056)

Military

1. You should inquire concerning the progress in connection with the purchase of arms for the Sudan in view of the reports which have appeared in the press on this subject. If the reply suggests that Soviet arms are under consideration, you should point out:

(a) A transaction with the Soviets in arms inevitably increases the number of Soviet agents in the country and may tend to subvert Sudanese independence.

(b) Soviet exchanges of cotton for arms are politically inspired. The Soviet bloc is rapidly expanding its cotton production and will be able in the future to export cotton if it could promote its political objectives by so doing. Even after the transaction with the Soviets, Egypt is still selling two-thirds of its cotton to the Free World as against less than one-third to the Soviets who are in turn reselling some Egyptian cotton on the world market at a discount. The ultimate in this process is that all Egyptian cotton would be marketed through Soviet hands with the resultant power which this gives to the Soviets over the Egyptian economy.

2. If the Sudanese raise the question of American military assistance, you should reply that you will report the matter to your Government.

Economic

1. You should advise the Government of the Sudan that the United States is most anxious that the Sudan qualify for membership in the International Monetary Fund and the International Bank for Reconstruction and Development at an early date. If there is appropriate help we can render in this connection, we will be glad to do so.

2. You should make it clear to the Sudanese authorities that the United States has no desire to specify what assistance should be given to the Sudan. The Sudanese authorities know their situation and can be the best judges of what their economic needs and the various sources of assistance are. We desire that any United States aid programs be the outcome of discussions between representatives of the two governments concerned. For this purpose the United States is willing, should the Government of the Sudan desire, to send a technical group to Khartoum to discuss with the appropriate officials, Sudan's need for technical assistance and development assistance.

3. The Sudanese may attempt to get a specific figure from you describing the contemplated level of our aid. If so, you should reply that the amount will depend on the discussions of the Sudanese authorities and the United States technical groups. FYI. Subject to

action by Congress, plans have been made thus far on the basis of up to $5 million for Development Assistance, $1.5 million for Technical Assistance. Since the time is near when it will be too late to obligate FY 56 funds it is expected that funds or a Sudanese program would be from FY 1957 appropriations. However, if developments are unexpectedly rapid it might be possible to draw on FY 1956 funds to a limited extent, i.e., to send the survey group referred to in Paragraph 2 above. End FYI.

4. You may say that we appreciate the problems the Sudan must be facing in the organization of its fiscal system and government administration. It is possible, should the Sudan desire, that a few American experts in these fields now employed in the United States Government could be made available for service in the Sudan. It is also possible that the United States could participate in the remuneration of such experts. If the Government of the Sudan is interested along this line, you should communicate their requirements and suggested terms of employment and remuneration to the Department. FYI The United States Government could provide the entire remuneration for American experts, but would prefer Sudanese participation though only token. The International Monetary Fund is admirably suited to give financial advice and the Sudanese should not be discouraged from accepting such aid. Furthermore, we must not suggest any competition with the British civil servants already employed in the Sudan. By virtue of their historical experience, the British enjoy an unusual competence as advisers on administration in this country. End FYI.

5. You may say that the United States Government is prepared to sell surplus agricultural commodities to the Sudan under Public Law 480 if they are desired. The enclosed agreement with Egypt illustrates this type of transaction.[6] The Agricultural Attachés resident in Cairo, but also assigned to Khartoum, will be of assistance in explaining the transaction should the Sudanese express interest. A detailed instruction on the drafting of surplus commodity agreements is under preparation and will be sent to Khartoum in the near future.[7]

6. You may say that the United States is prepared to negotiate a treaty of Friendship, Commerce and Navigation if the Sudan desires. If interest is expressed, the enclosed copy of such a treaty with Greece[8] may be left with the authorities.

[6] Not printed.

[7] Not printed. (Department of State, Central Files, 120.171/5–856)

[8] Not printed. The Treaty was signed August 3, 1951, and went into effect on October 13, 1954. See TIAS 305; 5 UST 1829.

Cultural—Informational—Exchange of Persons:

As appropriate opportunity is provided, you should make the following proposals:

1. That the educational exchange program with the Sudan be expanded in the interests of furthering mutual understanding and continuing the interchange of knowledge and skills. Such opportunities can be provided under either the Fulbright Program or the program conducted within the authority of Public Law 402. [9] The United States would be willing to enter into a bilateral agreement to establish a Fulbright Program with the Sudan, provided Sudanese currency is available to the United States Government as a result of the sale of surplus United States agricultural commodities to the Sudan under Public Law 480. The United States would consider using a portion of the funds accruing to it from the sale of these commodities to finance an exchange of students, teachers, professors and research scholars between the two countries. In addition, the United States would be willing to provide opportunities for Sudanese leaders within and outside the Government to receive grants to visit the United States under the Public Law 402 educational exchange program. The enclosed pamphlets explain in further detail these programs. [10]

2. That a Sudanese art exhibit be arranged in the United States and an American art exhibit in Khartoum. [11]

Dulles

---

[9] U.S. Information and Educational Act of 1948 went into effect on January 27, 1948. (62 Stat. 6) The Fulbright Act, or P.L. 584, was approved on August 1, 1946. (60 Stat. 754)

[10] None printed.

[11] Ambassador Pinkerton reported on actions taken in despatch 188, June 27. (Department of State, Central Files, 745W.00/6–2756)

236. Memorandum of a Conversation, Khartoum, March 13, 1957[1]

SUBJECT

Visit of Vice President Richard M. Nixon

PARTICIPANTS

Sudanese:
His Excellency Abdullah Khalil, Prime Minister of The Sudan
His Excellency Muhammed Ahmad Mahjub, Foreign Minister of The Sudan

American:
Vice President of the United States Richard M. Nixon
Lowell C. Pinkerton, United States Ambassador to The Sudan
Joseph Palmer 2nd, Deputy Assistant Secretary for African Affairs

The Vice President said that he was delighted to have this opportunity of visiting the Sudan in connection with his tour of Africa. He had heard a great deal about the important progress which was being made in this country and had been most anxious to see it at first hand. He added that it was his custom in trips of this kind to learn as much as he could about conditions in and policies of the countries which he visited in order to make a report to the President and to the Secretary of State.

The Prime Minister replied that he was similarly most happy to have this opportunity to exchange views with the Vice President. He said that the Sudan found itself in agreement with most of the policies of the United States. He added that he was happy to be able to speak in complete frankness. The Sudan has adopted the attitude that it has nothing to hide and is anxious to open up its policies and attitudes for all to see.

The conversations then ranged over a wide variety of subjects, which may be summarized as follows:

1. Economic Aid.

The Foreign Minister said that the Sudan requires two types of economic development. The first relates to projects which are bankable and can therefore be financed either through private loans or by such agencies as the World Bank. He mentioned, illustratively, textile mills, papyrus processing plants, hydro-electric projects, et cetera. These types of projects present no problem, since the Sudan can plan for them as it is able and can pay for them out of its own

[1] Source: Department of State, S/P–NSC Files: Lot 62 D 1, North Africa (Tunisia, Algeria, Morocco, NSC 5614, 5614/1). Secret. Attached as Tab E to Document 19. No drafting information is given on the source text.

resources. The second category relates to projects which bring no direct financial return but are necessary to the development of the country. The Sudan's primary needs in this category are the development of water resources and roads. With respect to water, it is essential to the future economy of the country that means be found of settling the nomadic tribes in more permanent locations and water is necessary to this process. Such permanent settlement of the nomads would permit the development of certain of the Sudan's resources. For example, the production and export of gum arabic could be doubled if the nomadic tribes in the areas of production could be persuaded to remain there and assist in gathering this product. He went on to say that roads are necessary to open up new areas and to get products to market. The Sudan is unabashed at requesting assistance for such projects as these, because it knows that such aid will strengthen the Sudanese economy and create conditions which may make it possible in the future for the Sudan to assist some other less fortunate economy. He went on to say that the Sudan is determined to preserve its independence and will not accept aid from any country under conditions which might prejudice that objective. The Government has given considerable thought to U.S. assistance and is convinced that American aid is given without strings and for the sole purpose of aiding the country concerned to develop its own resources for its own good. Discussions had been held with Mr. Hollister during his recent visit to the Sudan and the Government is hopeful that the United States understands Sudanese needs as a result of these conversations. [2]

The Vice President confirmed the Foreign Minister's statement regarding the objectives of United States aid. He said that he would be happy to make clear in his press conference this evening that U.S. aid is given without conditions and for the purpose of building stability and preserving independence.

2. The Eisenhower Doctrine.

The Foreign Minister said that his Government is giving careful consideration to the Eisenhower Doctrine and is looking forward to

---

[2] The Permanent Under Secretary of the Sudanese Ministry of Finance, Hamza Mirghani, visited Washington in mid-December 1956, to meet with IBRD, Export-Import Bank, ICA, and Department of State officials. He made no specific requests. The Sudan, however, in other approaches, expressed interest in a ground water specialist and a statistician. (Telegram 429 to Khartoum, February 7; *ibid.*, Central Files, 745W.5–MSP/2–757) John B. Hollister met with the Sudanese Prime Minister and Minister of Finance on February 25. The Sudanese made no direct requests although Finance Minister Ibrahim Ahmad noted Sudan's need for a complete water survey, improved communications, and the construction of the Roseires Dam. He commented that the Sudan might request a survey mission. (Despatch 223 from Khartoum, March 8; *ibid.*, 745W.5–MSP/3–857)

hearing Ambassador Richards' further explanations with respect to it.[3] (The Prime Minister intervened to indicate that in his opinion the Sudanese Government would certainly go along with the President's program, but the Foreign Minister reiterated that no decisions had been taken.)

The Foreign Minister went on to say that he personally felt that from an American point of view the President's program would have been better understood and accepted in the Middle East if it had been generalized with respect to the problem of aggression rather than directed solely at the Communist menace. The Prime Minister intervened at this point to say that he disagreed with the Foreign Minister. He pointed out that he and his Government have taken the firm decision to combat communism and that he thought it is better to be outspoken on such matters and to identify the real nature of the threat. The Foreign Minister said that he was speaking purely from the point of view of how the United States could most effectively present the President's program.

The Vice President explained that there are two main aspects of the President's program. The first is to extend an assurance to the countries of the Middle East against communist aggression. The second is to so strengthen the countries of the area through economic assistance as to decrease and remove their susceptibility to communist infiltration and subversion. The objective of the Doctrine is to enable the countries of the area to maintain their independence. Naturally, U.S. motives in this respect are not purely philanthropic. The United States believes that the best way to preserve its own independence is to assist other countries in the maintenance of their independence. This means freedom from all types of domination from whatever sources.

3. Military Assistance.

The Vice President said that he had noted that contrary to what he had heard in other countries, neither the Prime Minister nor the Foreign Minister had made any mention of military assistance. He asked whether this reflects a judgment on their part that economic development must have priority over the building of larger armed forces. The Prime Minister confirmed the Vice President's analysis. He said that the country presently has excellent neighbors and does not feel threatened. In due course, it will want to expand and improve its armed forces, but it expects to do this from its own resources. First, however, it is anxious to develop the country and to

[3] See *infra.*

create the economic base necessary to support an expanded military establishment.

The Vice President said that this is eminently sound and that he was glad to see that this question was viewed with such good sense.

4. Foreign Trade.

The Foreign Minister stated that the Sudan is most anxious to expand its trade with the United States. At the present time, it earns only a comparatively few dollars from the export of gum arabic and hides and skins and from the operations of the U.S. diplomatic mission. He was hopeful that some means could be found of expanding the sale of Sudanese cotton in the United States. This is of the long staple variety and therefore not entirely competitive with American cotton. He mentioned, in this connection, the fact that the Sudan is losing part of its Indian market as the result of the sale of U.S. surplus cotton to that country and he had recently been forced to tell the Government of India that unless it resumes its former level of purchase of Sudanese cotton, the Sudan will be forced to cut its imports of Indian gray sheeting. The Foreign Minister went on to say that the Sudan's foreign cotton markets are generally assured because of the political situation in the Middle East. It is likely that both France and Great Britain will take little Egyptian cotton as compared to the past and that the Sudan will be able to sell more to those two countries. This, however, is only a temporary solution and the Sudan is most anxious to assure the retention of its regular markets.

The Vice President suggested that the Sudanese Government look into the possibility of increasing sales of cotton to the American market. He pointed out that we have a private enterprise economy and that the Sudan would therefore have to proceed through ordinary commercial channels. With respect to U.S. surplus disposal programs, he knew that it is the desire of the United States Government to endeavor to avoid disruption of normal commercial markets.

5. Communism.

The Prime Minister reiterated that the Government of the Sudan is strongly and openly opposed to communism. It believes that the best way to combat this menace is to give it complete freedom to operate above the surface rather than to drive it underground. Thus, there is a quasi-legal Communist Party which operates three newspapers. He did not think that communism had made very great inroads in the Sudan and seemed confident of his ability to cope with it, particularly if the economy can be strengthened and benefits demonstrated to the people. There has been some communist penetration of the University of Khartoum and estimates of the number of students who are communist-influenced run as high as fifty percent. However, it is his experience that those students usually forgot about communism once they graduate and assume their lifetime vocations. He noted, with respect to an inquiry by the Vice President, that there has also been some communist infiltration of Sudanese students at school in Egypt. In fact, the Egyptians have complained to him that the Sudanese are spreading communism in Egypt.

The Foreign Minister spoke of the success which communist propaganda is achieving in various areas of the world. He thought that in general it is more effective than American propaganda. The communists are particularly attacking U.S. aid programs, which he and his colleagues in the Sudanese Government know are without conditions, but which the communists represent as an effort at political domination by the U.S.

The Vice President asked the Prime Minister whether he foresaw any difficulty from the communists or from any of the Near Eastern states, particularly Egypt, in accepting U.S. assistance. The Prime Minister replied that he does not intend to be deterred by the communists. As far as Egypt is concerned, it is hardly in a position to criticize since it has accepted American economic assistance itself.

6. Relations with Egypt.

The Vice President asked the Prime Minister for his estimate of the situation in Egypt. The Prime Minister replied that he thought Nasser would be careful not to be taken over by the Soviets. He said that in a recent conversation with Nasser, he had asked the latter whether or not he was a communist and Nasser had replied emphatically in the negative. Nasser had added that he wished to have good relations with a foreign country called the Soviet Union but that he would not submit to the domination of any country. The Prime Minister went on to say that Nasser is a Moslem and has aspirations of leadership among the Moslem states. Most of the Moslems are aware of the menace of communism and for Nasser to embrace this heresy would be to throw away any pretensions he has to such leadership.

The Prime Minister went on to say that the Sudan does not presently feel menaced by Egypt. It is apparent from recent events in the area that Egypt does not possess the military capability for taking over any adjoining area by force. He said that the Sudan desires good relations with Egypt, but can not accept any Egyptian domination. Although Egypt earlier had aspirations to annex the

Sudan, he thought that Nasser now realized, after more mature reasoning, that this would not be in Egypt's interest.

The Vice President asked the Prime Minister if he had any suggestions to make as to what United States policy should be toward Egypt. The Prime Minister said that he thought we should not attempt to strengthen Nasser, but should help him in small ways. He thought we should be careful not to do anything which would result in a further deterioration of relations between the U.K. and Egypt. He was sure that Nasser desired to resume relations with the U.K. as soon as possible and, in fact, Nasser had told him this in so many words shortly after the Anglo-French intervention in the Canal area.

7. The Sudan and Africa.

The Vice President said that he had seemed to detect in the other African countries which he had visited a disposition to remain somewhat aloof from blocs and to act in the UN and otherwise in an independent manner. He thought that there was a growing tendency, in other words, for the states concerned to act in accordance with their own best interests, rather than to defer to the interests of others in the general area. The Prime Minister said that he thought that this was a correct interpretation. The Sudan desires close relations with countries in similar circumstances to its own, but it would, in the last analysis, act in accordance with its own best interests. He referred, in this connection, to the close relations which the Sudan is evolving with Ethiopia. He said that his country is most anxious to strengthen that relationship.

8. Nile Development.

The Vice President said that if he understood Sudan's policy correctly, it believes that the Nile should be developed on a cooperative basis by the riparian states concerned. The Foreign Minister confirmed this view, citing the importance of the river to the economies of all the states concerned.

9. Inflation.

The Vice President asked what the Prime Minister foresaw as the greatest danger to the Sudan at the present time. The Prime Minister unhesitatingly replied "inflation". He emphasized the low per capita income of the average Sudanese outside of the Gezira area and noted that inflationary trends could cause acute distress.

The Foreign Minister said that he would like to sum up the discussions by reiterating that the Sudan would give careful consideration to the Eisenhower program and would listen with attention to Ambassador Richards' further explanations. With regard to technical and developmental aid, the Government is confident that such assistance is offered by the United States without political conditions and the Sudan is therefore most desirous of receiving such aid.

237. Telegram From the Consulate at Asmara to the Department of State [1]

Asmara, April 22, 1957.

71. From Richards. Results Khartoum visit. Although our information indicates Prime Minister and majority Cabinet willing accept American Doctrine and would like obtain economic aid, it appears they were unable persuade minority to go along. They therefore, have made no request for aid and I have made no commitments. We agreed on brief communiqué (being telegraphed separately). [2] On arrival April 20 we found political atmosphere uncertain. Sudanese carrying pamphlets denouncing my Mission had just been arrested leaving Egyptian Consulate. It seemed evident Nasser agents were very active and that he making special effort forestall approval American Doctrine on his southern flank. Egyptian influence was making itself felt even inside Cabinet.

Shortly after arrival Khartoum Mission and Ambassador Pinkerton met with specially designated committee headed by Foreign Minister (Mahgoub [3]) and having as other members Deputy Prime Minister–Minister of Agriculture–Irrigation and Power (Hamza [4]), Minister of Finance (Ahmed), Minister of Public Works (Lwoki [5]), and Minister of Interior (Abdel Rahman [6]). Foreign Minister opened by reading note verbale (being pouched [7]) which took generally

[1] Source: Department of State, Central Files, 120.1580/4–2257. Secret. Also sent to Cairo, Damascus, Amman, London, Paris, Addis Ababa, and Jidda; repeated by pouch to Aden, New Delhi, Rome, Karachi, Kabul, Tripoli, Beirut, Tel Aviv, Rabat, Tunis, Athens, Ankara, Tehran, Khartoum, and Baghdad. Regarding the Richards Mission, see Document 17.

[2] Telegram 68, from Asmara, April 22, contained the text. (*Ibid.*) It is printed in Department of State *Bulletin*, May 13, 1957, p. 764.

[3] Muhammad Ahmad Mahjub.

[4] Mirghani Hamza.

[5] Benjamin Lwoki.

[6] Ali Abd al-Rahman.

[7] Despatch 282, April 21, transmitted the note verbale presented to the Mission on April 20, an informal record of the April 20 discussion, a note verbale dated April (Continued)

dubious view of American Doctrine, arguing it would stimulate unfortunate reaction by USSR, split Arab League, and establish Israel as permanent danger for Sudan. Document further criticized President's proposals as couched in excessively general terms, failing to deal with basic ME problems and omitting promise of aid against any aggression other than Communist. Note included statement that Sudan's policy is one of "positive neutrality" which was explained to me as that country takes no sides in east-west struggles so long as there is no direct threat to its independence and sovereignty.

Note concluded with following series of questions:

Verbatim text.

"(1) Are the military and economic aids suggested in the proposals intertwined, or can the two types of aid be separated?

"(2) Are the proposals basically intended to combat Communist states?

"(3) Are the proposals, whether they are looked at from their economic or military aspects, intended to defend independent states equally against the influence of Eastern or Western blocs?

"(4) Do the proposals aim at bringing pressure to bear on one Arab country or another?

"(5) Would the proposals allow us to maintain our policy of positive neutrality between the two major blocs?

"(6) Are the proposals and the mutual security aids interdependent?

"(7) Do the proposals envisage the acceptance of certain conditions such as those we propose to attach to economic aid when we take a decision?

"To illustrate our point, we think that (1) economic aid should not encroach on our sovereignty and national independence, (2) that the funds should be large enough to meet our needs on the one hand and justify participation in the scheme on the other, (3) that expenditure from the funds should be on those schemes proposed by US for the benefit of our country, (4) that no action that we may take in that respect should hurt the interests of any other Arab country, and (5) that we should have more dollars and few experts. Do you think that such conditions would be acceptable?" *End verbatim text.*

I made general statement stressing American friendship for Sudan and explaining US reason for declaring ME policy and objective toward which it was directed. Pointed out six Arab States and several others in ME have already publicly endorsed policy. Emphasized we not trying force policy on anyone and would still remain friends even if Sudan declined accept it.

(Continued)
21 from the Mission responding to the questions raised in the Sudanese note, and an informal record of the April 21 meeting. (Department of State, Central Files, 120.1580/4–2157)

I then gave oral answers to specific questions put in Sudanese note verbale. Further discussions followed during which I emphasized time and again that only condition, if it could be called that, attached to aid under American Doctrine was that country requesting it should agree with objectives of Doctrine and take such steps as it was fit to preserve its independence against threat of international Communism. Foreign Minister concluded meeting by saying he would report to Council of Ministers and let me know their attitude next day.

On following morning we met again with same group. Foreign Minister read from prepared notes statement that Cabinet had instructed him to make re his understanding of my answers to questions raised previous day, as follows:

Verbatim text.
"(1) Economic aid can be separated from military aid;
"(2) It is understood that acceptance of economic aid will not deprive US from maintaining a policy of positive neutrality;
"(3) Economic aid does not in any way hurt Arab country;
"(4) The schemes to be financed under this Doctrine are those which we would propose and which would be agreed upon by the US;
"(5) The funds to be spent by the Sudanese Government on the projects agreed upon would be placed at the disposal of the Sudanese Government;
"(6) The technical experts involved will be limited only to those required for the agreed projects;
"(7) Acceptance of economic aid does not bar us from accepting from other countries including the USSR." *End verbatim text.*

Foreign Minister concluded by reading following:

Verbatim text.
"This being our understanding of the picture, Council of Ministers prefer at the present time to refrain from taking any resolution accepting or rejecting such aid; it will continue its study of the matter and let its decision be known in due course." *End verbatim text.*

Discussion following this presentation brought out certain points: (a) Foreign Minister and negotiation committee had received definite instructions from Cabinet and were either unable or unwilling to deviate in any way from them or even to seek their modification at this time. However, Foreign Minister obviously envisaged that Cabinet might later adopt more favorable position and he suggested our respective experts might hold exploratory talks re projects. I declined this suggestion. (b) It appeared Sudanese Government thought that if it reached decision within few weeks to request aid under Doctrine it could still present its request to me. I tried to explain it would be most unlikely I could take any action to help Sudan after end my visit Khartoum. Jernegan later made this crystal clear in talk with Foreign Minister, who indicated his understanding but reiterated he could give us no more definite answer at this time than was contained in message from Cabinet which he had read to us. (c) While saying US would not close door on possibility future US-Sudan cooperation, we made plain that if Sudan failed take advantage of special aid available under American Doctrine, future aid request would have to be treated in different context and in light of circumstances which might prevail at that time. This connection, we explained greater limitations on provision aid under normal programs and uncertainties re future availability of funds. Referring repeated Sudanese references to their policy of "positive neutrality", I pointed out many countries have taken forthright stand in line with our policy of combating international Communism and that Congress might well be unfavorably disposed toward voting funds for country which insisted upon position of neutrality. (d) Foreign Minister confirmed my impression that if Sudan requested any aid at all it would only be in the economic field. In reply my question he said Sudan was not seeking military aid from any country. (e) Foreign Minister explicitly stated he was unable to say at this time whether Sudan agreed with American Doctrine or not. He could go no further than to say Cabinet had agreed to give matter further study.

We agreed some form of joint statements should be made re Mission's visit. Foreign Minister wanted to include seven points stated above as Cabinet's understanding of my answers to questions posed in note verbale. I demurred, saying in that case we would probably have to ask for inclusion various other points I had made. I got impression Foreign Minister felt seven points would facilitate acceptance of Doctrine and American aid by Sudanese public, and I expect he will use them in reply press questions or in some other public fashion.

After this second meeting adjourned, I sent Foreign Minister written note verbale replying questions he had raised and which I had answered orally on previous day. I did this in order make sure my oral answers were complete and not misinterpreted. (Copy this note verbale being pouched.)

I was disappointed at early and unsatisfactory end of discussion. However, in view of firm refusal of Sudanese representatives state their position on Doctrine or even make request for aid, there seemed nothing further to be done. I did not think it wise appear to attempt to force aid upon them or indicate that they could obtain it without at least giving some statement (private or public) of endorsement our policy objectives.

My impressions are:

(1) Country is in relatively good economic condition and consequently does not feel great pressure to obtain foreign aid.

(2) Government underestimates danger of Communist infiltration.

(3) Government fears involvement in great power politics and is also fearful of antagonizing Egypt and other Arab States.

(4) Prime Minister and majority in present coalition are friendly to US but are not prepared for show-down with coalition minority, for fear of causing fall of government. (Ambassador Pinkerton believes fall of Cabinet would be unfortunate for US.) We heard from highly reliable sources that vote in Cabinet meeting after our first session with Sudanese representatives was 11 to 3 in favor of acceptance American aid. All three opposed were members minority PDP Party.[8] All of negotiation group voted in favor except Ministry of Interior who leads PDP.

(5) Even those favoring US cooperation might shy away from clean cut public statement of support for American Doctrine or opposition to international Communism.

(6) Whole issue of acceptance Doctrine and request for American aid is far from settled within government. It is entirely possible request for aid will be made in next few weeks or months. If this occurs, it will be sign of victory pro-American majority group. (Whether we should respond affirmatively is of course another question and will depend on circumstances.) Prime Minister told Iraqi Minister to Sudan[9] last night that Sudan would certainly align itself with American Doctrine in time; "it had to ".

(7) Because of its location and its Arab and African connections, Sudan is definitely worth wooing. If I had been given opening, I would have thought it worth while to offer relatively substantial amount of aid to achieve Sudan alignment in favor American Doctrine. We should remain receptive and use all available means to keep it from falling under Egyptian domination or Communist influence, even though it will probably be impracticable utilize special authority of this mission in taking any concrete steps to this end. For present, I can only suggest policy of watchful waiting and gentle encouragement. We painstakingly attempted to leave an impression of understanding and friendship and believe we succeeded in that.[10]

---

[8] Identified as Ali Abd al-Rahman, Minister of Local Government; Mahammed Nur al-Din; and Hammad Tewfik, Minister of Commerce. (Telegram 67 to Asmara, April 23; *ibid.*, 120.1580/4–2357)

[9] Yassin Umar.

[10] There is no signature on the source text.

238. Operations Coordinating Board Report [1]

Washington, September 25, 1957.

OPERATIONS PLAN FOR THE SUDAN [2]

I. Objectives and Special Operating Guidance

A. U.S. Objectives regarding the Near East are:

1. Availability to the United States and its allies of the resources, the strategic positions, and the passage rights of the area, and the denial of such resources and strategic positions to the Soviet bloc.
2. Stable, viable, friendly governments in the area, capable of withstanding communist-inspired subversion from within, and willing to resist communist aggression.
3. Settlement of major issues between the Arab states and Israel as a foundation for establishing peace and order in the area.
4. Reversal of the anti-American trends of Arab opinion.
5. Prevention of the extension of Soviet influence in the area.
6. Wider recognition in the free world of the legitimate aspirations of the countries in the area to be recognized as, and have the status of, sovereign states; and wider recognition by such countries of their responsibility toward the area and toward the free world generally.

B. Special Operating Guidance:

In pursuing the policy objectives set forth above, U.S. actions in the Sudan should be guided by the following:

7. *Nationalism and Foreign Relations*. Because of the Sudan's geographic location and the Nile River, Egypt has always had a special position in the Sudan and is at the present time using various means to increase that influence at the expense of the Western powers. Egyptian activities have also given encouragement to the Soviet bloc and international communism to focus attention on the Sudan with a view to gaining political and economic strongholds in the newly independent state. We must encourage Sudanese independent devel-

---

[1] Source: Department of State, OCB Files: Lot 62 D 430, Near East Jan.–July 1957. Secret. Attached to a memorandum by Charles E. Johnson, Executive Assistant of the OCB, which noted that the OCB at its September 18 meeting had revised and concurred in the operations plan and had agreed that the United Kingdom should be encouraged to satisfy any future Sudanese military assistance requests. The Sudan should also be persuaded to approach the United Kingdom with their requests.

[2] This plan was devised pursuant to NSC 5428, "United States Objectives and Policies With Respect to the Near East", July 23, 1954. For text, see *Foreign Relations, 1952–1954*, vol. IX, Part 1, p. 525.

opment and support those elements which consider that continued Egyptian influence will ultimately result in undermining the Sudan's independent sovereign status. We should assist efforts of the Sudan to unify the diverse cultural and religious elements of the country and to reduce or eliminate divisive factors which facilitate Communist and/or Egyptian penetration and subversion. We should continue to impress on the Sudan that its future status as an independent and sovereign state will be in grave doubt if action is not taken to prevent the subversive activities of Egypt and international communism. We should seek a reduction in the size of Soviet bloc missions. We should foster further close ties between the Sudan and its neighbors in Africa, particularly Ethiopia, in an effort to expose more Sudanese officials to the views of Western-oriented countries. We should also encourage the Sudanese, when appropriate, to continue to look to the U.K. as a friend, and as a possible source of development capital.

8. *Economic Development*. In evaluating the Sudan's agricultural and natural resources, we should determine what diversification can be recommended to strengthen the present economy and assist in avoiding future adverse effects of over-reliance on an almost one-crop economy (cotton). We should promote the conclusion of a satisfactory agreement between the Sudan and other countries as appropriate for the sharing of the Nile waters. We should also bear in mind the need for an improved communications and transportation system, the lack of which is a limiting factor in economic development. The United States should use its technical assistance program, if initiated,[3] to promote the favorable orientation of Sudanese technicians and leaders toward the U.S. and the West, and to demonstrate progressive Western methods. Sudanese development projects should be given consideration under the proposed Development Loan Fund, or by other arrangements.

9. *Foreign Investment*. Encouragement should be given to the participation of U.S. business and industrial interests in the development of the Sudan, and at the same time Sudan should be encouraged to offer a favorable climate for private foreign investment.

10. *Military*. The military potential of the Sudan for providing base and transit facilities for possible future United States military needs should be kept under review, in the event restrictions in other more desirable Middle East areas make an alternative imperative. At the present time, Sudanese permission has been granted for MATS

[3] Telegram 374 from Khartoum, November 26, conveyed a formal Sudanese request for technical and economic aid under the Mutual Security Act of 1958. (Department of State, Central Files, 745W.5–MSP/11–2657) In response, the Embassy was instructed to indicate U.S. willingness to enter into negotiations. (Telegram 619, November 27; *ibid.*) An announcement to this effect followed shortly.

aircraft to overfly the Sudan and to make refueling stops at Khartoum.[4] Thus the Sudan constitutes an important communications link in the strategic military air line of communications around the world.

We should encourage the development of bilateral mutual defense arrangements between Ethiopia and the Sudan as a possible contribution to the elimination of Egyptian influence in Sudanese affairs.

11. *Labor.* Toward achieving the objectives of preventing the extension of Soviet influence in the area and in view of the influence of the Sudanese Communist Party and international communism in trade unions and peasant organizations, we should promote closer relationships between the free trade unions in the Sudan and American labor unions. These free trade unions need the kind of encouragement and moral support that comes from association with veteran non-Communist trade union leaders who know how a responsible movement can be built for the economic benefit of their membership and community. The significant capture of one-third of the Sudan trade unions by the Communists, their recent action in endeavoring to achieve unity between the Communist SWTUF (Sudan Workers' Trade Union Federation) and the free SGWTUF (Sudan Government Workers' Trade Union Federation), and their current bringing of the officials of those unions to the Soviet Union and to China for further indoctrination is a development which must be checked and reversed.

12. *Information and Cultural.* The United States should use its cultural exchange programs to promote the favorable orientation of Sudanese students and leaders toward the U.S. and the West. We should continue to promote close association between American universities and Khartoum University. We should urge the Sudan Government to take the necessary measures to counteract Communist and Egyptian activity and influence in educational and cultural institutions and organizations.

13. *Internal Security.* An increased capability to maintain public order and internal security is an important need of the Sudan. We should be prepared to offer advice and assistance on training and equipment for the Sudan's defense force and internal security organizations should such assistance and advice be requested.

---

[4] Cole reported that on October 5, Permanent Under Secretary in the Foreign Ministry Mohammed Osman Yassein expressed Sudanese concern in regard to the September overflights by U.S. aircraft carrying military equipment to Jordan. (Despatch 99, October 14; *ibid.*, 745W.5411/10–1457) The Embassy was instructed to convey U.S. regret and emphasize U.S. appreciation of landing and overflight rights granted to military aircraft. (Airgram 26, November 15; *ibid.*)

C. Selected U.S. Arrangements With or Pertaining to the Sudan:

14. *U.S. Involvements Which May Imply Military Security Guarantees.* The United States, by joint congressional resolution on the Middle East, signed by the President on March 9, 1957,[5] announced its determination to assist Middle East nations to maintain their independence. The resolution declared that the United States is prepared to commit its military forces, at the discretion of the President, against overt armed aggression by any nation controlled by international communism if the nation subject to that aggression requests such aid. The Richards Mission was in the Sudan from April 20 until April 22 of this year and thoroughly discussed the President's Middle East proposals with the Sudan Government. To date, however, the Sudan Government has neither rejected nor accepted participation in the program. Subsequently, an informal approach to the U.S. for technical assistance and substantial grants or loans has been made. An ICA survey group will go to the Sudan shortly to review Sudanese economic development needs and plans.

15. *U.S. Commitments for Funds, Goods or Services.* None.

16. *Other Arrangements.* In December 1956, on the basis of an ad hoc arrangement, three banking and monetary experts from the staff of the Federal Reserve Board were provided to assist the Sudan Government in drawing up a charter for a Central Bank.

[Here follows section II, "Current and Projected Programs and Courses of Action," comprising paragraphs 17 through 41.]

Note: National Intelligence Estimate regarding this area is: NIE 72.1–57, "The Outlook for the Sudan", August 6, 1957.[6]

---

[5] 71 Stat. 5.

[6] Not printed. (Department of State, INR–NIE Files)

TUNISIA

ESTABLISHMENT OF RELATIONS WITH TUNISIA; THE QUESTION OF UNITED STATES PROVISION OF ARMS TO TUNISIA [1]

239. Telegram From Embassy in France to the Department of State [2]

Paris, March 7, 1956—8 p.m.

4092. Re Tunis 101 to Department. [3] During conversation with Seydoux today I raised question of possible US grant of wheat to relieve threat of famine in Tunisia. I said that we did not want to do anything which could possibly embarrass French but that I wondered if in view of damage to 1956 French wheat crop the situation had not changed so that France would welcome an offer of wheat for Tunisia. Seydoux replied that he wished to be very frank with me. He said there was need of wheat in Tunisia and that he had felt it would be a good idea for this wheat to be supplied by US in conjunction with France. He said that on arrival in Paris he had found Savary very much opposed to any American assistance in Tunisia at this particular time. Savary felt that it would greatly weaken his position in negotiations that are presently under way in Tunis if the Tunisians felt they could get material or financial support elsewhere whenever it was required. Savary told Seydoux that this was merely a temporary position valid only during the period of the negotiations. In the long run Savary told Seydoux he fully recognized both necessity and advisability of US assistance for Tunisia.

Seydoux then admitted that French had been slow themselves in meeting the need because of the change of government [4] but he said that day before yesterday Ramadier had officially assured Tahar Ben

---

[1] For previous documentation on this subject, see *Foreign Relations*, 1952–1954, vol. XI, Part 1, pp. 665 ff. See also Documents 25–37.

[2] Source: Department of State, Central Files, 872.49/3–756. Secret. Repeated to Tunis.

[3] Telegram 101, March 6, reported that an opportunity existed for private U.S. organizations to make food grants to Tunisia in cooperation with similar French agencies. (*Ibid.*, 872.49/3–656)

[4] Mollet succeeded Faure, whose government fell January 31, 1956.

Ammar that France would supply 50,000 quintals of wheat a month for next five months for a total of 250,000 quintals.[5] Seydoux said that this met demands of Tunisian Government in full. He said that in view of this promise Tunisian Government was moving immediately to start distribution of wheat from their small remaining reserve stocks in Tunis, relying on French Government replace these stocks.

In view of above it appears there is no purpose in further pursuing the matter of US grant of wheat to Tunisia.

Dillon

[5] Paul Ramadier, French Minister of Finance and Economic Affairs. A quintal was the equivalent of a 100 kilograms.

240. Telegram From the Embassy in France to the Department of State[1]

Paris, March 10, 1956—1 p.m.

4158. When I saw Savary this morning I told him that I had come to receive further information on the serious and unfortunate incident at Tunis[2] and also to hear anything he might have to say on the subject. Savary replied by expressing his personal regrets and those of the French Government for the unpardonable acts. Savary also said that the French Government would of course pay for the entire cost of repairs to the damage that had been done.

Savary then went on to say that he had received a brief report from Seydoux and that according to this report the situation had been very serious. Apparently Seydoux had narrowly missed severe physical injury or possible death at the hands of the mob. He owed his safety to the energetic action of the police who had protected him from the mob. Savary said that this was one good piece of news in the whole affair as the French police in Tunis are recruited locally and might have been assumed to be strongly partisan to the local French population. I then told Savary that we had received word

[1] Source: Department of State, Central Files, 122.954/3–1056. Confidential; Niact. Repeated to Tunis.

[2] Telegrams 103 and 104 from Tunis, both dated March 9, reported attacks that evening by a mob of French demonstrators on the Consulate General and USIS offices. (*Ibid.*, 122.954/3–956)

from the Consulate in Tunis, that unfortunately the police had not shown the same attitude in protecting the American Consulate and the Information Center. Savary said that he had not heard of this aspect of the matter as yet but he assured me that he would order a full inquiry into the actions of the police.

Savary then told me that immediately after my departure from his office he would call in AFP and issue a statement saying that he had received me in order to express formal regrets of the French Government over this affair. [3]

Comment: I feel that this regrettable incident is an extreme manifestation of the widespread feeling that the United States has been unsympathetic to France in North Africa. I expect the French Government, which is obviously seriously disturbed by this occurrence, to give us every satisfaction possible and I would hope that we would promptly accept the French expression of regret and the offer to repay US for damages, with a view to letting the matter die as rapidly as possible.

Dillon

---

[3] Telegram 105 from Tunis, March 10, indicated that Seydoux called in Hughes to offer a similar apology. (*Ibid.*, 122.9542/3–1056)

---

241. Editorial Note

On March 20, the French and Tunisian Governments concluded a Protocol of Agreement recognizing Tunisian independence. United States recognition was extended on March 22. For text of a message of that date from Consul General Morris N. Hughes to the Bey of Tunis, see *American Foreign Policy: Current Documents, 1956*, page 726. The text of a message of the same date from Ambassador Douglas Dillon to the French Foreign Ministry is *ibid.*

242. Memorandum of a Conversation Between the Minister of the French Embassy (Vimont) and the Deputy Director of the Office of Western European Affairs (Tyler), Department of State, Washington, April 26, 1956 [1]

SUBJECT

Establishment of direct diplomatic relations with Tunisia

During a call at the Department, M. Vimont said that the French Government had felt that Premier Bourguiba had gone too far in summoning the Consuls of the various powers, after his self-appointment as Foreign Minister. [2] The French Government considered that if any foreign power were, as a result, to elevate its representation from that of a Consulate to that of a Legation or Embassy, this would constitute "a not very friendly gesture" ("un geste peu amical"). M. Vimont added that if the United States Government were apprehensive lest another power, not already represented in Tunisia, should seek to establish diplomatic relations ahead of the U.S., there would be ample time for the French Government to forewarn us through the High Commissioner in Tunis, and we could immediately take action first, since our representative is already on the spot.

I observed that events seemed to be moving fast, both in Tunisia and Morocco, in the direction of assumption of control of foreign relations by the two newly independent powers, and that I was afraid that the French position of insisting on waiting until the Parliament had ratified the abrogation of the treaties which had defined the previous relationship was difficult to sustain. M. Vimont said that he personally agreed, but repeated that this was the existing position of his Government.

---

[1] Source: Department of State, Central Files, 122.954/4–2656. Confidential. Drafted by Tyler.

[2] Bourguiba established a Neo-Destour government on April 14, taking the Defense and Foreign Affairs portfolios for himself in addition to the Premiership. France was unwilling to recognize Tunisia's right to establish embassies on its own in advance of the conclusion of a diplomatic convention between France and Tunisia.

243. Telegram From the Department of State to the Embassy in France [1]

Washington, May 8, 1956—5:19 p.m.

4167. Tunis 143. [2] Dept hopes impasse over foreign affairs and diplomatic representation both Morocco and Tunisia can be reached soon and approves Embassy's continuing press for prompt solution (Embtel 5206) [3] coordinating as appropriate with British. Embassy may reiterate our desire establish Embassy Tunis soonest before Arab states take lead and our hope we can shortly respond Bourguiba's request in manner similar we responded Balafrej May 7. As we have no diplomatic representative Tunis to cover interim, problem even more acute than Morocco.

ConGen Tunis should tell Bourguiba orally, as we have already told Khajeri, [4] that our March 22 message to Bey constituted recognition new independent status Tunisia as defined March 20 Protocol and that we look forward opening diplomatic mission Tunis and normal exchange diplomats. [5] We appreciate his desire US act this regard before any other country except France, as reported reftel. Therefore we continue hope Tunisia and France will reach agreement soon clarifying question diplomatic exchanges. [6]

Dulles

---

[1] Source: Department of State, Central Files, 772.02/5–856. Confidential; Priority. Also sent to Tunis; repeated to Algiers, Rabat, and Tangier.

[2] Dated May 8, telegram 143 reported that the Turkish Consul General transmitted a message from his government on May 8 which constituted recognition of Tunisia's independence although diplomatic exchange was not mentioned. (*Ibid.*)

[3] Not printed. (*Ibid.*, 601.0072/5–556)

[4] M.K. Hajeri, Bourguiba's representative and Secretary General in the Tunisian Foreign Office.

[5] The Consulate General in Tunis was raised to Embassy status on June 5 with Hughes as Chargé.

[6] For text of a diplomatic accord signed at Tunis on June 15 by French and Tunisian representatives on June 15, see *American Foreign Policy: Current Documents, 1956*, pp. 726–727.

244. Telegram From the Embassy in France to the Department of State [1]

Paris, July 20, 1956—8 p.m.

366. Savary sent for me today to give me French Government views on possible US economic aid programs for Tunisia and Morocco. As a result of Bourguiba's indication of possible interest in broad economic aid program which I had reported to Savary, French Government has considered this matter at government level and Savary said he was glad to report that government shared his personal views as reported in Embassy telegram 126 [2] (not repeated to Rabat). In other words, French Government has no objection to Tunisia and Morocco receiving economic aid from friendly countries other than France. However, French feel very strongly that such aid should not be accorded until the economic negotiations between French and these two countries are further advanced. I asked Savary whether this meant that French desired the US to hold up economic aid programs until such time as over-all interdependence agreements had been signed and ratified. Savary said that this was by no means what he meant as in their mutual interest France and both Tunisia and Morocco might prefer to let the question of defense agreement hang for quite some time, which would delay the ratification of the over-all interdependence agreements. Savary said that what the French Government had in mind was that if either Tunisia or Morocco approached US for a broad-scale economic aid program French Government would have no objection even today to US Government listening to request and then initiating the studies that would obviously be necessary before any aid program was finalized. They feel strongly that no indication of any figures regarding the size of a possible aid program should be given to Moroccans or Tunisians until their financial negotiations are further along and

---

[1] Source: Department of State, Central Files, 772.5–MSP/7–2056. Confidential. Repeated to Tunis and Rabat.

[2] Telegram 126, July 9, summarized Dillon's conversation with Savary on that date on the issue of aid to Tunisia. Three days earlier, Bourguiba had requested surplus wheat assistance due to crop failures. Savary noted that France had encouraged Tunisia to seek such emergency aid, but he thought it best that such an offer not be made until the conclusion of Franco-Tunisian economic discussions. (*Ibid.*, 411.7241/7–956) Tunisia, following a breakdown in negotiations with France, insisted that the United States, in order to affirm Tunisian freedom from French control, not coordinate relief efforts with the French. (Telegram 41 from Tunis, August 1; *ibid.*, 872.49/8–156) The International Cooperation Administration announced a gift of 45,000 tons of wheat to Tunisia under Title II of the Agricultural Trade Development and Assistance Act (P.L. 480) on September 19.

until we have discussed matter of friendly basis with French and obtained their over-all views.

Dillon

245. Telegram From the Department of State to the Embassy in France [1]

Washington, November 19, 1956—11:31 a.m.

1891. 1. Ambassador Slim November 8 informally gave Murphy note requesting in general terms US economic and technical aid. [2] Slim said he did not wish embarrass US or Tunisian Government by inviting refusal we might feel obliged make because of preoccupation present US relations with France. Therefore he preferred not hand in note formally unless we indicated in principle we would entertain request. He was given general indication US considers such requests on own merits but we were anxious avoid impression we could assume heavy share responsibility and thereby cause GOT burn its own bridges. Department promised Slim more definite reply and is therefore informing Tunisian Embassy today as follows:

A. US prepared in principle extend economic and technical assistance, with extent and type programs to be determined by on-spot studies and conversations between two governments, and ICA prepared send survey team.

B. GOT should understand that as matter principle and owing statutory and budgetary limitations based on world-wide commitments, US policy encourages other Western nations and international agencies share aid responsibilities. (FYI. Only $5 million tentatively earmarked from funds FY 1957. While Department will explore possibilities finding other funds and take Tunisian needs into account in making 1958 estimates, we cannot make definite commitment at this time. End FYI.) US could not hope undertake at this time anything on order 16 billion francs which has been under discussion Tunisians and French. Tunisians should therefore conclude such economic and financial arrangements with French as they

[1] Source: Department of State, Central Files, 772.5–MSP/11–1956. Secret. Also sent to Tunis; repeated by pouch to Rabat.

[2] Tunisian Ambassador Slim stated Tunisia's desire to avoid a repetition of the Egyptian experience where a U.S. offer of aid had recently been withdrawn. Murphy explained that the situations were not the same. (Memorandum of conversation by Bovey, November 8; *ibid.*, 651.72/11–856)

feel they can since such assistance will probably be necessary for some time. We also encouraging French expedite such arrangement.

C. GOT should also realize development concrete program will require time.

2. Embassy Tunis should follow similar line in discussion with FonOff.

3. Upon receipt this telegram and related telegram re Morocco [3] Embassy Paris should inform French of Tunisian request and nature foregoing reply, making clear we are acting on Tunisian request and that our decisions will be facilitated by rapid conclusion Franco-Tunisian arrangements which we desire coordinate our own. [4] (FYI We informed French Emb Wash of Tunisian request permitting them to read Tunisian memorandum).

FYI. Believe such consultation necessary despite Tunisian sensitivity and that once we have responded positively to Tunisians and made clear our limitations both to them and French, we will be in better position get both parties take more favorable view re conclusion economic and financial arrangements with each other. Moreover by informing Tunisians our intention tell French we acting positively on Tunisian request, we would hope allay Tunisian suspicion our approaches constitute "clearance" with French and minimize effective French exploitation these suspicions.

4. Above is entirely in keeping current NSC directives [5] and previously explained French Government position (Paris 366, July 20) US cannot remain deaf to Tunisian request and we feel that above makes clear we not planning supplant French aid as feared by Maurice Faure (Paris 2335). [6] Precise level aid would be determined during negotiations in light availability funds, information re economic conditions Tunisia, and progress Franco-Tunisian arrangements, since it is obvious Tunisians must continue depend on French for major part assistance. End FYI.

---

[3] Document 202.

[4] Dillon reported on his November 21 conversation with Maurice Faure on the subject of U.S. economic assistance to Morocco and Tunisia. Faure was gratified that U.S. aid would be supplementing rather than replacing French economic assistance. (Telegram 2541 from Paris, November 22; Department of State, Central Files, 771.5–MSP/11–2256)

[5] Reference is to NSC 5614/1, October 3, 1956. For text, see Document 36.

[6] In telegram 2335, Dillon summarized his conversation with Maurice Faure on November 10 which mainly dealt with U.S. economic assistance to Tunisia and Morocco. Faure preferred that the United States not proffer such assistance until France concluded arrangements with Morocco and Tunisia. Dillon agreed this would be preferable, but warned against delay. (Department of State, Central Files, 651.71/11–1056)

5. Will send further instructions when Tunisian request formalized.

Hoover

---

246. Memorandum of a Conversation, Washington, November 21, 1956, 11:45 a.m.[1]

SUBJECT

Tunisia

PARTICIPANTS

Mr. Habib Bourguiba, Tunisian Prime Minister
Mr. Mongi Slim, Ambassador of Tunisia
The President
Mr. Robert Murphy, Deputy Under Secretary of State

After an exchange of amenities during which the Prime Minister expressed his gratification over his reception by the President,[2] there was a brief discussion of prevailing conditions in Tunisia. The President, mentioning that he had been resident in Tunisia some time during World War II, inquired regarding the cleanup of the destruction in the port of Bizerte and the city and port of Tunis. The Prime Minister said that considerable progress had been made, but much remains to be done. He thanked the President for the contribution of 45,000 tons of wheat made to Tunisia.

There followed discussion of Franco-Tunisian relations with an explanation by Mr. Bourguiba of the efforts he had made during the years to achieve the independence of his country while remaining in friendly association with the French. He explained that the French in effect were victims of their own traditions in the colonial field and their prestige as a great nation. The President said he believed that French thinking had advanced considerably regarding the matter of colonies and he believed it perhaps unfair to say that the French ideas had not changed. Mr. Bourguiba agreed, but said that much remained to be done. The President inquired whether inspiration could be found in the attitude of Great Britain in respect of its

---

[1] Source: Department of State, Central Files, 772.00/11–2156. Confidential. Drafted by Murphy. The time of the meeting is from the President's diary.

[2] Bourguiba was in the United States to head his nation's delegation to the United Nations. He paid a brief courtesy visit to the President.

colonies. When Britain found that it was difficult to retain some of the colonies in their previous status, the idea of a commonwealth had been developed. This had led to independence for some of the countries who were held to Britain as voluntary associates by reason of their self-interest. Mr. Bourguiba agreed that something of a similar nature would be entirely possible in French North Africa, if the Algerian question could be settled. The President asked him whether he had ideas regarding a settlement for Algeria. Mr. Bourguiba said that his thinking ran along the lines of an agreement by the French in principle concerning Algerian independence which would than be worked out through stages over a period of time. He firmly believed that this type of settlement is possible and would produce a result which over the longer term would be beneficial to France. The fighting in Algeria presents for Tunisia a very serious problem and is holding back the economic and social progress of Tunisia. The Prime Minister desires to do everything he can to promote a happy solution of the Algerian problem and promised to work to that end.

The President said he wanted to make a point which represents part of his basic philosophy and that is that this Government stands for the proposition that there is only one rule of justice applying both to great nations and to small nations. He said he wanted the Prime Minister to believe that we do not believe in one rule for the larger powers and another rule for the smaller powers. The Prime Minister expressed his gratification and complete agreement.

The President referred to Israel, saying that he hoped that the existence of this tiny state in the Middle East would not poison American relations with the Moslem states be they the older states or the new ones like Tunisia. The Prime Minister assured him that the Tunisian attitude regarding Israel did not in any way adversely affect Tunisian relations with the United States. The President assured the Prime Minister of our sympathetic interest in and understanding of Moslem culture, religion, education, and customs. The President referred to the fact that he had lived in North Africa for several years, adding that Mr. Murphy was associated with him at that time, and had an abiding interest in the problems of North Africa.

In terminating the conversation, the President assured the Prime Minister of his continuing interest and hoped that the Tunisian Ambassador would work closely with the State Department; we desire to cooperate and be as helpful as we can in promoting the best interests of both countries.[3] The conversation concluded with an effusive thanks on the part of Mr. Bourguiba for the gracious reception which the President had accorded him.

[3] Shortly after this visit, President Eisenhower noted in his diary that in regard to Prime Minister Bourguiba, he "was struck by his sincerity, his intelligence and his friendliness." (Eisenhower Library, Whitman File, DDE Diaries) Later that day, Bourguiba met with Assistant Secretary Rountree with whom he took up the subject of economic assistance. (Memorandum of conversation by Bovey; Department of State, Central Files, 772.02/11–2056) On November 27, he met with Acting Secretary Hoover mainly to discuss Algeria. (Memorandum of conversation by Bovey; *ibid.*, 772.02/11–2756)

247. Letter From the Deputy Assistant Secretary of State for African Affairs (Palmer) to the Ambassador in Tunisia (Jones)[1]

Washington, December 18, 1956.

DEAR LEWIS: I just wanted to let you know what we all agree here that you took the right line with Ladgham on November 27 (your telegram 267)[2] regarding economic and technical aid. Without in any way giving the appearance of prior clearance with the French or that we are unmindful of Tunisian sensitivity to French financial pressures, I feel it most important to discourage illusions on the part of the Tunisians with respect to levels of economic assistance and numbers of technicians the U.S. would have available. This is very much in accord with the line we have been taking here.

With regard to military aid, we must, at least for the time being, discourage requests from the Tunisians. As NSC 5614, paragraph 21[3] (of which you should now have a copy) makes clear, we should try to avoid getting mixed up in this matter except as a last resort and

[1] Source: Department of State, NEA Files: Lot 58 D 545, Tunis–1956. Secret; Official–Informal. Drafted by Bovey.

[2] In telegram 267, November 28, Jones reported on his conversation of November 27 with Vice Premier (then Acting Premier) Bahi Ladgham. Ladgham suggested, as his personal opinion, that U.S. aid should be made available when France was unable or unwilling to contribute to a project. He also revealed his desire for U.S. military assistance to supply an army of 5,000 (later 10,000) men. Tunisia was willing to contribute to collective defense, but not exclusively through arrangements with France. Jones reminded him that U.S. assistance could only be modest and not enough to replace the French. (*Ibid.*, Central Files, 772.5–MSP/11–2856)

[3] Not printed. (*Ibid.*, S/S–NSC Files: Lot 63 D 351, NSC 5614 Series) NSC 5614/1 is Document 36.

in fact should seek to maintain France's responsibilities on this field as far as we can. It seems obvious that the success or failure of Franco-Tunisian military cooperation will ultimately be determined by their ability to reach an accommodation on the whole range of their relationship. This will not be easy in itself and will, of course, be greatly complicated if the Tunisians gain the impression that we are willing to provide easy alternatives for them.

We would be interested in knowing what other "multinational arrangements" you think Bourguiba or Ladgham may have in mind as a solution to the Bizerte problem. There has been in the past some rather casual talk in the Department about the possibility of a Western-Mediterranean grouping which might include France, as well as Spain, Morocco and Tunisia, and thus get around the difficulties which the prospect of NATO membership of the last three would probably create for certain members of the club, particularly the Northern European countries (and, I presume, also for Morocco and Tunisia themselves). This thinking has never crystallized, and I am not myself convinced of the wisdom much less the practicability, of a "pact solution" to the problems of Western political and military relationships with North Africa. However, we welcome all ideas and if you have any idea as to what the Tunisians might have in mind, we would be much interested.

With kindest personal wishes, I am,

Sincerely yours,

Joseph Palmer 2nd [4]

---

[4] Printed from a copy that bears this typed signature.

248. Memorandum of a Conversation, Tunis, March 18, 1957[1]

SUBJECT

Visit of Vice President Richard M. Nixon

PARTICIPANTS

Tunisian:

His Excellency Habib Bourguiba, Prime Minister of Tunisia
His Excellency Mongi Slim, Tunisian Ambassador to the United States
His Excellency Khemais Hajeri, Secretary General of the Tunisian Foreign Office

American:

Vice President of the United States Richard M. Nixon
Ambassador G. Lewis Jones
Deputy Assistant Secretary of State for African Affairs Joseph Palmer 2nd

The Vice President expressed his appreciation for the very warm and friendly welcome which had been accorded him upon his arrival. He said that it was evident that this greeting was intended for the United States and not for Mrs. Nixon and himself personally. He was particularly impressed because the sentiments flowed from the hearts of the people.

The Prime Minister said that this was indeed a sincere manifestation of the deep respect in which the US is held in Tunisia. The people reacted with such enthusiasm because they understand the policies of the US and feel that they correspond with their own hopes and aspirations. He went on to speak of Tunisia's wholehearted commitment to the cause of democracy, liberty and peace. He said that during the darkest days of Tunisia's struggle for liberation, he and his colleagues had never wavered in their devotion to the cause of democracy, even though they were being subjugated by a democratic power. There were many in France who had maintained that Tunisia could never maintain an independent existence. Tunisia is now completing the first year of its independence and, although there are many problems ahead, it has been demonstrated that the nation is able to exercise the responsibilities of liberty. The Prime Minister went on to say that Tunisia is fully committed to the West. It can never be neutral and it can never accept Communism, which it repudiates as contrary to its ideals and principles. This attitude accords with the will of the entire Tunisian people and is not an attitude simply laid down by himself and other leaders. It therefore represents a firm foundation for the building of the Tunisian state.

[1] Source: Department of State, S/P–NSC Files: Lot 62 D 1, North Africa (Tunisia, Algeria, Morocco, NSC 5614, 5614/1). Secret. No drafting information is given on the source text. Attached to Document 19.

The Prime Minister continued within this context by emphasizing the particular importance which Tunisia attaches to its ties with the United States, with which it feels at one on questions of principle and ideology. Generally speaking, Tunisia approves American policies, knowing they are dedicated to the concept of independence and of peace. Thus, he said, he had spoken out in support of the Eisenhower Doctrine because it seemed to him the only sensible course in the Middle East at the present time and because he knew that it would enhance the cause of independence and the requirements of stability in that vital area. The Prime Minister said that there have been other instances in which Tunisia does not see eye to eye with the US but, in such cases, he has been at pains to explain to the Tunisian people why it is that the US has felt compelled to act in a manner contrary to that which had been hoped for. As a consequence, even though the Tunisian people do not always agree with the US, they generally understand and respect our policies and actions.

The Vice President expressed his gratitude for these sentiments. He called attention to the fact that Bourguiba was the first Arab leader to speak out publicly in favor of the Eisenhower Doctrine. He emphasized that the President is aware of this fact, deeply appreciates it, and had asked the Vice President to convey his gratitude to the Prime Minister.

The Prime Minister next spoke of the importance which Tunisia assumes in the North African and Middle Eastern area. He spoke of his country as a "pilot project" for the development of stability, moderation and pro-Westernism in this part of the world. If Tunisia should fail, either because of the Algerian problem or through failure to develop economically and socially, the consequent blow to democracy and stability in these areas of the world would be very great indeed. But if Tunisia is successful, it will serve as a shining example of how democracy can be made to work. Thus, it will counter the false promises of Communism, which are devoted to objectives quite opposite from those for which the US and Tunisia stand.

The Prime Minister then turned to the Algerian question, which he characterized as fundamental to the future development and orientation of North Africa. He emphasized that he desires close relations with France because of the historic and cultural ties which bind the countries and also because of the complementary nature of their economies. He decried the fact that there are still colonial and militarist elements who are influential within France and who cannot accept the fact of Tunisian independence. These elements, he said, are responsible for the continuation of the war in Algeria. They would subjugate Algeria and then seize the opportunity to re-subjugate Tunisia and Morocco. There are, of course, elements in France who understand that France can never solve the Algerian problem by a program of force and who would therefore welcome an accommodation between France and the Algerian peoples which would accord with the legitimate aspirations of the latter. Unfortunately, these good elements are neither vocal nor influential. They are afraid to speak up in defense of their convictions, because they see the Algerian war prosecuted by a socialist government and ask themselves why they should be more liberal than the socialists in this matter.

In response to the Vice President's questions, the Prime Minister said that he thought that there is the basis for a settlement in Algeria on the basis of free elections with some type of international supervision. It is necessary, however, that these elections be conducted in such a way as to permit the Algerian people to decide freely their own future. In the absence of such a settlement, he despaired about the future of North Africa. The continuation of the war in Algeria is poisoning all of North Africa. Tunisia has 200,000 Algerian refugees within its borders which constitute a drain on its economy and a constant security problem. The prolongation of the war, moreover, gives the French pretext for deploying their forces within Tunisian territory in a manner prejudicial to the sovereignty of the nation. He said that the Tunisian people cannot understand why the French should be able to deploy their forces in friendly and independent Tunisian territory. He pointed out that the British and US Ambassadors did not have the right to conduct large-scale military ceremonies within a sovereign Tunisia and that it is difficult to explain, particularly to other Arab states, why the French should have such rights. Moreover, the continuation of the Algerian war is weakening the position of the moderate elements in the Algerian nationalist movement. At the present time, there are Algerian leaders who are anti-Communist and moderate, but there is great danger that, if the war drags on, the responsible leadership in Algeria will be forced to give way to irresponsible elements.

The Vice President then inquired about Tunisia's developmental needs. The Prime Minister replied that his country stands in great need of American assistance. He noted with pleasure that negotiations are under way, which he hoped could be speeded up and culminated just as quickly as possible. Tunisia's principal need is to develop the agricultural base of its economy and to supplement this with some industrial development. He hoped that US assistance, the program and details of which are yet to be negotiated, would be devoted to this end. He spoke particularly about the need for settling Tunisia's nomadic population on the land. He said that he has always regarded US assistance as supplementary to that of

France, but that he is becoming increasingly concerned about the situation in which Tunisia now finds itself. The question of aid to Morocco and Tunisia has become a domestic political issue in France, with the result that Tunisia's essential developmental needs have become subject to the whim of local French party politics. He pled for the US not to abandon Tunisia to France in this way. He pointed out that the Tunisian fiscal year has only a few days to run and as yet there is no agreement with France on aid programs for this year. He pled for "substantial" US assistance which would permit Tunisia to be truly independent of France.

After luncheon on March 19, the Vice President had an opportunity to talk to Deputy Prime Minister Ladgham, with Ambassador Jones, Mr. Palmer, Ambassador Slim and Secretary General Hajeri present.

The Vice President asked Mr. Ladgham for his views on the Arab-Israeli problem. Mr. Ladgham pointed out the different attitudes which prevail in Tunisia and North Africa toward the question of the Jews and the Palestine problem from those which exist in the Middle East. He indicated that Tunisia does not share the view of the Middle Eastern Arab states that Israel should be liquidated and made it clear that Tunisia does not approve of Colonel Nasser's policies on this and other Middle Eastern and African problems. He indicated his belief that there is a large element of imperialist ambition in Nasser's philosophy and actions.

The Vice President said that he had been struck in the several countries of Northern Africa which he had visited by the devotion of these nations to the cause of independence. He said he had the impression that all of these countries would vigorously oppose any effort at domination and would do their utmost to preserve their independence. Thus, he gathered that there is a growing tendency for these countries not to participate in blocs to the extent of slavishly following the dictates of any one country. Instead, they are tending more and more to view their problems on their merits and to preserve the necessary independence of action. This is not to deny that on many issues they will see as one with many of the Afro-Asian bloc, but he thought it significant and important that there is a growing tendency to deal with issues on their merits. Mr. Ladgham concurred with the Vice President's statement which he said represents the Tunisian point of view.

The Vice President went on to speak of the central importance of the Arab refugee problem in the settlement of the Arab-Israeli issue. He acknowledged that many attempts have been made to deal with this problem, but none of them have been effective so far. He felt that a new approach to this matter is of the utmost importance. Mr. Ladgham agreed completely with this viewpoint.

249. Editorial Note

An exchange of notes between Tunisia and the United States on March 26 formalized the conclusion of an economic and technical assistance program which had been the subject of negotiation since mid-February. Prior to the end of the United States fiscal year on June 30, $5.5 million would be made available to Tunisia, in addition to the earlier grant of $6.5 million in emergency wheat. Up to $5 million was to be in the form of commodity credits. Proceeds from the sale of such commodities in Tunisia would be applied toward the support of projects and activities in the Tunisian development budget. Approximately $500,000 could be utilized for individual technical cooperation projects. For texts of the notes, see 8 UST 427.

---

250. Telegram From the Consulate at Rabat to the Department of State [1]

Rabat, May 6, 1957—2 p.m.

835. From Richards. Report on visit to Tunis.

No difficulties encountered Tunis over re-endorsement ME proposals and Bourguiba welcomed my offer $3 million economic assistance on grant basis as "symbolic" of US friendship and support. However, we failed to reach agreement on projects or methods extending aid and up to time my departure no firm commitment existed. I did not evade question application doctrine to Tunisia but stated nation could count on US assistance if requested in event of attack by international Communism in same manner as other states in ME. To have attempted to draw fine distinction would have destroyed effectiveness of mission in Tunisia and in face of Bourguiba's acceptance of doctrine immediately after it was enunciated could have caused setback in Tunisian coop with West.

Bourguiba spent considerable time setting forth his position on Algeria and "colonialism" in general. He described economic misery and denial aspirations of peoples for independence as two main contributors to spread of Communism. He also made clear his wish

[1] Source: Department of State, Central Files, 120.1580/5–657. Secret. Repeated to Paris, London, Tripoli, New Delhi, Rome, Addis Ababa, Athens, Karachi, Kabul, Beirut, Ankara, Jidda, Damascus, Cairo, Baghdad, Tehran, Khartoum, Amman, and Tel Aviv. Regarding the Richards Mission, see Document 17.

to work with France and recognition Tunisian dependence on French economic assistance. Morning of May 4 prior to arrival of mission he called in French Ambassador [2] to inform him of mission's visit. Bourguiba told me he reached full understanding with Ambassador concerning Tunisian interest in my mission. I believe this was statesmanlike move helpful both to US and Tunisian relations with French. Regarding Algeria Bourguiba left no doubt of Tunisia's firm support for its independence. He argued forcibly against colonialism in general making point that Soviet bloc effectively capitalizing on issue. By failing to grant independence to colonial peoples free world opened itself to charges of hypocrisy when it dwelt upon enslavement of satellite countries by Communism and gave "microbes" of Communism opportunity for penetration. He urges us to bring friendly pressure on both France and Britain, two principal colonial powers in Western bloc, to make them realize need to grant independence. Although really sympathetic to those desiring freedom, for "official reasons," Bourguiba asserted, US continues to take positions which make it appear to strugglers for freedom that it backs "colonialism." He was careful to say however that he knew most vicious form of colonialism was behind Iron Curtain.

In reply I referred to US emergence from colonial status and long history of support for independence of peoples when they able exercise independence effectively. I called attention to fact US after two great wars had refrained from accepting any territory and on contrary had granted independence to former possessions. Because of complicated world responsibilities US unable at times to take as straight and open position on such problems as colonialism as it might really wish. US considered international Communism overriding danger to freedom independent people everywhere. Therefore it was obliged to place primary emphasis upon arrangements to contain this menace. Although all might not be perfect in administration of dependent territories by certain Western states, nevertheless there was great and continuing progress toward freedom and self-government of people under their tutelage. Same could not be said of Soviet "colonialism." In conclusion I said that I personally had good deal of sympathy for Bourguiba's viewpoint and although matter outside scope my mission I would report his views to President.

First meeting May 4 was "courtesy" call on Bourguiba. He described his policy of coop with West and said he unable understand attitude of countries which professed to be anti-Communist and yet refused coop with West. Their position made no sense. If those governments really anti-Communist they should welcome chance work with West.

---

[2] Georges Gorse.

In later plenary meeting presided over by Bourguiba and attended also by VP Lagdham and other Tunisian Cabinet members I described principal features of ME proposals. I said that if Tunisia were attacked by international Communism or country dominated by international Communism and requested US assistance it could be sure of US support. I also pointed to assistance which US prepared give against subversion by Communists at same time making clear my belief GOT in no danger from subversion at this time. I told Bourguiba mission able to provide Tunisia $3 million on grant basis in economic development assistance. Sum would be in addition to regular FY 57 program and any program undertaken in FY 58. Bourguiba while welcoming offer professed disappointment at figure. He elaborated at some length on manifold problems facing new country, maintaining that French credits and US aid sufficient to finance only small part of necessary work.

Since Bourguiba had to leave for another appointment communiqué then discussed. He accepted quickly our suggested draft asking only omission any reference economic aid. He thought that if aid linked to matter of "political ideology" it could be misconstrued as "counterpart" for Tunisian support for doctrine. I readily agreed to his suggestion. Despite failure agreed on aid projects both Director General of Foreign Office and Director Prime Minister's office confirmed May 6 intention issue communiqué. Text transmitted separately. [3]

After departure Bourguiba Vice Premier Ladgham made further plea for further economic assistance.

He said Tunisians were of course aware of figure mentioned in Joint Resolution [4] and had drawn up list of projects in magnitude of $57 million. I explained limitations of funds and heavy demands elsewhere. I pointed to large portion of US budget devoted to defense which served in terms of entire free world, increasing number of complaints from US taxpayers, and growing Congressional sentiment in favor reduction foreign aid programs. I also emphasized Congress wished future aid extended on loan basis. While making clear FY 1958 funds subject to action by Congress, I said there every reason anticipate US would continue an assistance program for Tunisia. During discussion I also called attention to 15 day requirement of Joint Resolution. We agreed that economic experts would meet morning May 5 to consider specific projects.

Question US military aid to Tunisia not raised.

---

[3] For text of the joint communiqué, dated May 6, see *American Foreign Policy: Current Documents, 1957*, p. 849.

[4] $200 million.

Regarding economic aid—after prior discussion Embassy I had decided that in view shortness of time it would be necessary immediately to give Tunisians figure on magnitude of aid. In our briefing session Ambassador Jones called attention to large foreign debt Tunisia already carrying and Washington decision regular FY 1957 program should be entirely on loan basis. He cited growing Tunisian disappointment over US aid as realization spread size interest charges compared to those asked by French. I concluded that by adding $3 million on grant basis (Deptel 445 to Tunis) [5] political effectiveness of entire US aid program would be considerably enhanced. No question exists that there is need in Tunisia for additional economic assistance. Furthermore Tunisians justifiably would be at loss to understand failure of US provide some assistance under doctrine after quick acceptance and in face of their strong support for West. Especially in view of Tunisian initiative in informing French Ambassador of mission visit I do not anticipate adverse French reactions.

In discussions with economic experts principal difficulties arose over findings suitable projects. Tunisians stated they had hoped magnitude of doctrine aid would have enabled them fund certain major projects such as capitalization development bank, some major dam construction, rural development of Gamouda plain ($9 million project), establishment of university. They refused consider partial funding any project on grounds they would not embark on any major project unless total financing in sight. Under circumstances they declared that top priority request was for vehicles and communications equipment for "internal security" forces, and 5 vessels for customs patrol. Upon examination established that equipment sought was primarily designed increase effectiveness army, including formation four mobile infantry battalions. We indicated willingness provide some vehicles and radio equipment for police but nothing for army. They would not differentiate between army and police, calling attention to need protect frontier villages from increasing number border violations. Insisted $1.5 million package deal minimum required this purpose and refused substitute any project in economic area for this request. With respect to balance $1.5 million they first asked for $600,000 to fund broadcasting station for which balance funds available through French. Later withdrew this request and asked for 3 helicopters ($170,000) for locust control, 25 tank trucks

[5] Telegram 445, April 6, authorized Richards to offer Tunisia an additional amount of economic aid, given Bourguiba's support for the Eisenhower Doctrine and Tunisia's need. The International Cooperation Administration believed such aid was not economically justifiable so soon after the conclusion of the March agreement. Richards was advised to stay within a limit of $3 million. (Department of State, Central Files, 120.1580/4–657)

to water arid central and south Tunisian regions, and balance for local currency cost of rural development in coastal Haouaria plain (includes drainage, small harbor construction, road building, electrification, reforestation, et cetera).

Insisted they would not accept counterpart generation through commodity imports—francs must be purchased through French by dollar check because of degree to which Tunisia fiscally and economically tied to French franc area. We felt dangerous precedent would be established if we complied while recognizing difficulties implicit in present nature Tunisian economy. Discussions ended in impasse, Tunisian experts insisting their instructions categoric that $1.5 million "minimum essential" for armed forces needs and dollar check indispensable for local currency purchase. Negotiations made more difficult by absence from Tunis May 5 of Bourguiba and Ladgham. Negotiators resumed night of May 5 after Bourguiba, Ladgham allegedly contacted by telephone and confirmed stand taken by economic experts. We emphasized that funds available to Richards under special authority might cease to be available to him May 8 but left small chink in door open for possibility Tunisians might decide on less obdurate line and communicate through US Embassy Tunis with us in Rabat or Department in Washington. I think it possible that on Bourguiba's return Tunis in next day or two Tunisians will adopt more flexible attitude. If so, we should be responsive.

My observations here confirm Bourguiba has decided upon policy of cooperation with West. He seems genuinely to believe this course in best interest of his country and also to hope that satisfactory arrangements may be worked out with French. He undoubtedly expects increasing US economic assistance and intends to press for start of military aid program. Big stumbling block of course is Algeria which bound continue plague relations with entire Western world and provide opponents of Bourguiba and his policy of cooperation with West popular opposition rallying point. Although Tunisia on surface appears relatively prosperous, economic problems obviously formidable and it is difficult to see how country could survive financially should France decide to withdraw large financial outlay still being made.

Cannon

251. Telegram From the Embassy in Tunisia to the Consulate at Rabat[1]

Tunis, May 7, 1957—3 p.m.

145. Rabat for Richards. I spent hour and half this morning alone with Deputy Prime Minister Ladgham since Bourguiba still absent in south. Following emerged:

1. Position GOT re $3 million aid offer is as expressed by Knani[2] except GOT now agrees use goods generate counterpart for economic development portion ($1.5 million). Ladgham said repeatedly GOT accepted $3 million but decision seek half in internal security equipment and half in economic assistance firm one taken by ministers following Bourguiba dinner for Richards and subsequently re-affirmed several times by Bourguiba. Ladgham said important GOT to present gift internal security equipment to Tunisian people as joint US-Tunisian effort reinforce Tunisian security: Reason for joint US-Tunisian activity in economic field self-evident. Ladgham said GOT felt that at this juncture equal division for two purposes reasonable and that "the two are inseparable". I told him he should not assume any part of $3 million available for Tunisia after Richards mission returns Washington. He accepted this fact but said, if Richards funds could not be equally divided in accordance cabinet decision, on political grounds GOT would prefer to forego entire grant thus preserving Tunisia immune from any shadow of doubt which might be cast in Tunisia or in Arab world upon integrity and sincerity of Tunisia's wholehearted acceptance Eisenhower Doctrine. GOT would look forward to continued close collaboration with USOM on economic assistance, but having weighed political impact advantages and disadvantages of accepting less than equal division for two purposes, GOT resolved, most regretfully, to do without Richards assistance if necessary.

2. Ladgham mentioned urgent GOT need for patrol craft for immigration, fisheries and customs controls; he said "We will have to find money to buy these. They will be used only by Ministry of National Economy. It seems to me that such small craft clearly fall within field internal security".

3. Reversal Knani's position re insistence on check for economic aid portion followed my rehearsing familiar arguments about necessity prevent inflation.

---

[1] Source: Department of State, Central Files, 120.1580/5–757. Secret; Niact. Also sent to Paris and repeated to the Department. The source text is the copy sent to Washington.

[2] Abdesselam Knani, Director of Planning.

4. Ladgham said that whether or not US rules and requirements will permit Ambassador Richards to make $3 million available to GOT on fifty–fifty basis, which is only basis acceptable politically, GOT has already derived from Richards mission two major benefits which dwarf $3 million. First is Ambassador Richards' assurance re extension benefits Eisenhower Doctrine to Tunisia against menace of international communism and second Ambassador Richards' promise to bring to attention President Eisenhower Tunisian views re situation in Algeria which is "creating major opportunity for spreading germs of communism".

5. Re "political grounds" (paragraph 1 above) I believe there is domestic political element. Ladgham told me in confidence that if GOT had known aid only $3 million, "we would have handled things very differently. We would not have called in all ministers thus raising their hopes and, instead, have worked with only a few. As it is, however, entire cabinet involved and it would be politically disadvantageous for 'us' to attempt to reverse or alter materially cabinet decision re fifty–fifty". Presumably those Tunisian ministers who do not share Bourguiba's enthusiasm for US took strong position after Richards mission left Bourguiba's residence.

6. *Embassy comment*: . . . Talk this morning cordial without hint diminished friendship. We know strict rules under which Richards mission operating and would not suggest for one moment Communist threat here so severe (Communist candidates snowed under in May 5 municipal elections) that exception rules should be sought meet GOT position. We suggest, however, that Ambassador Richards might, if he considers action indicated, have another look at internal security equipment sought by GOT to determine whether, in light of satisfactory GOT political attitude described above, a sufficient number of items of non-objectionable character could be added to police and gendarmérie equipment already approved by Ambassador Richards to bring total up to neighborhood $1.5 million. Most important aid Morocco re security equipment be consistent with such aid GOT. Inhibiting factor while Ambassador Richards here was presumed adverse French reaction US aid in security field. This probably element in Department ruling against patrol craft (Deptel 470).[3] However, quick and frank check with French, whose citizens Tunisians protecting, might reveal less objection than antici-

[3] Telegram 470, May 1, conveyed Department policy not to provide military items to Tunisia, especially patrol boats. (Department of State, Central Files, 120.1580/5–157)

pated to such items as small patrol craft, radio equipment, mine detectors, uniforms, et cetera.

Jones

252. Memorandum From the Assistant Secretary of State for Near Eastern, South Asian, and African Affairs (Rountree) to the Under Secretary of State (Herter) [1]

Washington, May 29, 1957.

SUBJECT

Your Appointment with Tunisian Ambassador Mongi Slim on May 29 at 4:15 p.m. [2]

Discussion:

The Tunisian Ambassador wishes to discuss with you the situation created by the suspension of French aid to Tunisia on May 20 and by the subsequent reaction of Prime Minister Bourguiba who has in effect called into question the entire range of economic relations between the two countries by announcing that the effect of the Franco-Tunisian Conventions of 1955 has been nullified by the French action.

We do not know how long French suspension of aid will continue, since Bourguiba has said that he will never change his attitude on the Algerian question, and probably will feel unable to discontinue assistance to the Algerians, which is the primary reason for the suspension. Nor do we know how far Bourguiba will go in breaking the economic and financial ties of Tunisia with France and the franc zone. It seems clear, however, that the structure of economic relations between the two countries has been seriously shaken, and the long-range prospects for their collaboration do not appear favorable at this juncture.

The Franco-Tunisian rift obviously poses a most difficult problem for the United States. Even if we deemed it politically desirable,

[1] Source: Department of State, Central Files, 611.72/5–2957. Secret. Drafted by Bovey and concurred in by EUR/WE. U/MSA also concurred except that Robert G. Barnes, Special Assistant for Mutual Security Affairs, disputed the use of the word "sympathetic" in recommendation 5.

[2] The memorandum of conversation by Bovey is not printed. (*Ibid.*, 851.10/5–2957)

our present budgetary limitations would not permit us to supply more than a fraction of the past French contribution, which has run to about $45 million a year. For Fiscal Year 1957 we are supplying $5 million in economic aid funds plus $3 million from Middle East funds. Proposed programs for 1958 would involve $5 million from the special economic assistance funds plus an undetermined amount, originally planned at $5 million, from the development loan fund.

This is obviously insufficient to enable us to be of much help if a real emergency develops. Thus far the Tunisians have requested only that we authorize temporary use of counterpart funds generated by the 1957 program to meet current obligations under their equipment budget and it appears likely that this can be done. It seems likely, however, that other requests will develop if the present rift continues.

Our reaction to such requests will probably have an important effect on the future course of our relations with Tunisia, as well as with France, and will be carefully watched also by the Moroccans, where the situation of the bases would make undue reticence on our part in the face of any Moroccan requests even more undesirable.

It is therefore evident that for the moment we have every interest in bringing about a Franco-Tunisian rapprochement, even though we may recognize that any modus vivendi may not prove permanent.

Recommendations:

It is therefore recommended that you make the following points to the Tunisian Ambassador:

1. The U.S. was, of course, unaware of any French plan to suspend aid to Tunisia and, in view of our own heavy commitments and our desire to see the responsibility for such aid shared by other friendly nations, we have based our plans on continuation of French aid.

2. These plans are reflected in budgetary provisions which cannot easily be revised, and quite apart from our desire for friendly relations between France and Tunisia, we feel that a sudden rupture of their long-standing economic relations would pose a most serious problem for Tunisia's stability and the welfare of her people.

3. We therefore cannot but regret both the French decision and the Tunisian response in calling into question the whole range of economic matters embodied in the 1955 Conventions. While understanding the reasons for the Tunisian reaction, we hope that the Tunisian Government does not intend to close the door on future Franco-Tunisian collaboration and will, on its part, refrain from formal abrogation of the 1955 Conventions. (In this connection it

may be helpful to remember that Ambassador Slim is proud of his role as architect and negotiator of these Conventions.)

4. We do not condone the French decision and hope that France will reconsider it and resume its aid under conditions consonant with Tunisian sovereignty and dignity. We have already made this view clear to the French. In this connection, we were gratified by reports of the conciliatory remarks made by Mr. Bourguiba to the Constituent Assembly in Tunis on May 27 and hope these will prove helpful. We believe it to be of the greatest importance that discretion and moderation be exercised by all concerned in the present difficulty. We are confident that the Tunisian Government will share this view.

5. We will of course give sympathetic consideration to Tunisia's situation but hope that Tunisia will understand our present limitations, which reflect our own global situation rather than deference to French sentiment. France is of course our ally and friend, but this in no way diminishes our friendship for Tunisia nor our interest in her independence and stability.

6. We continue to be grateful for Tunisia's support of U.S. policies and we were also interested by Mr. Bourguiba's announcement that Tunisia, Libya and Morocco were trying to persuade Algerian leaders to accept free elections in Algeria. We hope he will continue conciliatory efforts of this kind but believe that in order to be most effective this is also a matter calling for great discretion.

---

253. Memorandum of a Conversation Between the Minister of the French Embassy (Lucet) and the Deputy Director of the Office of Western European Affairs (Tyler), Department of State, Washington, June 1, 1957[1]

SUBJECT

1. U.S. Aid to Tunisia
2. Mediterranean Conference on Algeria Suggested by Bourguiba

Mr. Lucet said that he wanted to talk to me as a follow-up on Ambassador Alphand's call on the Acting Secretary the previous day (see memorandum of conversation dated May 31 1957).[2]

---

[1] Source: Department of State, Central Files, 772.5–MSP/6–157. Secret. Drafted by Tyler.

[2] Not printed. (*Ibid.*, 772.5–MSP/5–3157)

He said that the Ambassador had derived the impression that perhaps the Acting Secretary had not wanted to give too specific an answer to the two major questions which he had raised with regard to the two subjects he had brought up: U.S. aid to Tunisia, and the proposal for a Mediterranean conference on Algeria. Mr. Lucet asked me if I could tell him whether the policy of the U.S. on these two points was undergoing a change.

I commented that the Ambassador's presentation had not conveyed the impression of a direct question requiring a specific answer on either of the two points. I reminded Mr. Lucet that the Ambassador had referred to the existing U.S. policy on aid to Tunisia, and had merely stated the French point of view and the hope that this aid would not be increased during the period of suspension of French aid, pending the formation of a new French Government. [3] I recalled that the Acting Secretary had stressed the grave concern with which we viewed recent unfavorable developments in Franco-Tunisian relations, and that he had added that apart from the utilization of certain counterpart funds under existing U.S. economic aid, it was not at this time planned to increase aid to Tunisia.

With regard to the proposed Mediterranean conference on Algeria I said that we were aware of the French view that it would be unacceptable. It was our hope and our desire that a peaceful and equitable solution would be found for the Algerian problem. We did not think that in view of French opposition to the idea of a Mediterranean Conference, this would be a development likely to advance a solution of the Algerian problem, and we were not in favor of anything which might further embitter Franco-Tunisian relations. I pointed out that, in this case also, the Ambassador had not solicited a direct expression of opinion from Mr. Herter.

Mr. Lucet said that he did not wish to exaggerate the point which he had made, but that in view of the grave concern which Mr. Herter had expressed with regard to the Tunisian and Algerian problems, the Ambassador had wanted him to ascertain whether our policy in these two matters was still the same or was subject to modification.

I told Mr. Lucet that the Acting Secretary had reflected and expressed the concern which the U.S. Government feels with regard to recent events, and to the basic situation in North Africa. I pointed out that the policy of supplementary U.S. aid to that of France had been based on the premise that there would be French aid to supplement, as the French Government had informed us. I said that it was not based on the premise that a situation would long continue

[3] The Mollet government fell on May 22 and was succeeded by a Cabinet led by Maurice Bourgès-Maunoury on June 12.

in which the prospect of French aid would be used as an instrument of political pressure on Tunisia and Morocco, in such a way that the supply of aid would be turned on and off by France as a form of coercion.

I said that while it was understandable that in these difficult times French political sentiment should be both intense and subject to severe strains and pressures, I personally had grave doubts about the wisdom and the prospects of success of tactics such as these. I said I thought I could speak with Mr. Lucet frankly as an old personal friend, and as a friend of France, and that I was not asking or expecting him to agree with me. I said I understood that the majority of Frenchmen, particularly in the National Assembly, were exasperated by the painful and complicated character of the Algerian question. I said I was sure that all kinds of plausible and emotionally justifiable arguments could be advanced to support various political and military actions, particularly the latter, which were, nevertheless, incompatible with the sustaining and strengthening of normal and friendly relations between independent states. As a newly independent country it was inevitable that Tunisia should be hyper-sensitive to what she considered to be violations of her independence and sovereignty. For example, the issue of internal security was obviously one which provoked very strong feelings, since the Tunisian Government was responsible for internal security. I said I hoped that the foreseeable psychological effect of political and military actions by France would be carefully assessed before they were taken, whatever might be considered to be the immediate provocation or justification. It was perhaps because we doubted the wisdom of certain French attitudes in terms of the goal which France had proclaimed with regard to her relations with Tunisia and Morocco, that we felt an increasing concern about the evolution of the general situation in North Africa.

Mr. Lucet did not have very much to say in reply. He asked whether we supported Bourguiba's policies with regard to Algeria. I said, and he agreed, readily, that in so far as Bourguiba's political efforts were directed toward persuading the FLN to discuss with France the conditions of a cease-fire, in order to set the stage for free and internationally supervised elections, and thus to put an end to the hideous atrocities which were taking place in Algeria, we thought that this represented a constructive effort which both France and ourselves supported. I said, I thought it was unreasonable to expect that Tunisia's and Morocco's support of the Algerian Nationalist cause could be crushed, and I thought that any policy attempting to bring about such a result by means of pressure was doomed to failure, with attendant dangers and complications for the future of the whole of North Africa, and the interests of the free world in that area.

Mr. Lucet then referred briefly to Ambassador Houghton's visit to the States and asked whether it had any particular significance at this time. I told him that Ambassador Houghton was coming back for consultation in accordance with a timetable which had been established before the cancellation of President Coty's visit, and that there was no special significance to his trip.

254. Telegram From the Department of State to the Embassy in Tunisia [1]

Washington, June 12, 1957—7:41 p.m.

558. Deptel 526, [2] Tunis 687. [3] Re advice to Bourguiba:

FYI. At present we know neither how long French suspension aid may continue, particularly in light firm stand Bourguiba on Algeria and uncertainties re attitudes next French government nor how far political pressures generated by frontier incidents and other factors will carry GOT in breaking economic ties with France. Evident economic and political relations seriously shaken by recent Franco-Tunisian interchanges and long-range prospects Franco-Tunisian collaboration do not appear favorable. However for time being our own present and foreseeable budgetary limitations would permit us supply only small part normal French contribution even if it were politically desirable supply more. We must also bear in mind possible repercussions in Morocco any French or US action Tunisia, especially in light current negotiations for preservation vital strategic interests US and West. Thus we have every interest in encouraging Franco-Tunisian rapprochement even though we recognize difficulties in achieving any permanent modus vivendi. End FYI. Department therefore approves your initiative in conveying realities of economic situation to GOT and commends line you have taken. In

[1] Source: Department of State, Central Files, 872.10/6–1257. Secret. Repeated to Paris and by pouch to Rabat.

[2] Telegram 526, May 30, indicated that the Department and ICA had examined various ways to relieve Tunisia's financial difficulty and reported on one of the possibilities being considered. (*Ibid.*, 872.10/5–2457)

[3] Telegram 687, May 28, stated that French Ambassador Gorse was hopeful that Bourguiba's comments of May 27 might assure resumption of aid once a new French Government was installed. (*Ibid.*, 872.10/5–2857)

present fluid situation any advice we may render may appear hollow in light intervening events. Following is therefore intended as general guidance to be drawn upon in conversations with Bourguiba as you deem appropriate.

1) Inherent in US recognition of and support for Tunisian independence that we wish see country strong and stable economically as well as politically.

2) Tunisian economy over long period of years has developed in close relationship with that of France and now apparent that trade, balance of payments and other economic and financial patterns cannot be basically altered without danger of doing violence to Tunisia's stability and welfare.

3) Foregoing not to say we are insensitive to Tunisian concern re extent to which its economic relationships with France may in its judgment be inconsistent with Tunisia's sovereignty and independence. US has long stood for free, equal and mutually advantageous economic relationships among members of world community and certainly feel this principle applies to Tunisia as to other countries. At same time we recognize that emerging pattern within free world makes complete political or economic sovereignty impossible for anyone and opens new vistas for economic cooperation for mutual benefit. Such accommodations towards this end do not represent any diminution of sovereignty but actually constitute its effective exercise.

4) It has always been our hope and direction our policy both in France and Tunisia to see emergence of such mutually beneficial relationship between France and Tunisia. We would gather from Bourguiba's past statements that he would agree. Whatever obstacles and setbacks which may be encountered, we hope Tunisia will agree re validity of objective and will not despair of its achievement, despite current difficulties with French military which we hope are only temporary.

5) For our part, we are willing assist in every appropriate and feasible way. Bourguiba will understand that quite aside from foregoing considerations, there are problems of fund availabilities and legal restrictions, which necessarily limit what we can do. Nevertheless we have given evidence our willingness help as we can through our aid programs and such exceptional measures as that authorized by Deptel 526.

6) In long run and for reasons outlined above, however, such assistance on our part likely assume characteristics of palliatives and not be effective substitute for healthy and mutually advantageous relationship between Tunisia and France. It is in direction encouraging such relationship that we feel we can make best contribution Tunisia's future. We regret in this connection French decision sus-

pend aid and are doing what we can encourage French resume it under conditions consonant Tunisian sovereignty and dignity. We have been somewhat encouraged by French attitude toward approaches we have made on financial situation and had reason believe that French government would try find means of interim financial assistance before formation of new government and we will continue encourage new government take further remedial measures.

7) We recognize central importance Algeria to this and related problems Franco-Tunisian relationship. We have already pointed out to Bourguiba considerations which guide us in our attitudes toward that problem (Deptel 515)[4] and which we continue believe are important to interests Tunisia, North Africa and free world. In this connection we regard as definitely helpful and constructive Bourguiba's efforts persuade Algerian leaders accept free elections. We hope such efforts will continue and will do our best assure they are met with understanding on French side. Our efforts this respect will be greatly facilitated by moderate Tunisian approach to problem.

8) We have noted Bourguiba shares our horror recent massacre Melouza.[5] We have of course no way knowing all circumstances involved this matter. We must however condemn atrocities either side and hope Bourguiba will use his influence with Algerian leaders to make clear that excesses on their part can only stiffen French public opinion and render more difficult political concessions from Paris. We recognize reverse similarly true.

9) Regarding queries received by us from other countries re Mediterranean conference we do not believe US in position favor or oppose idea but have felt constrained point out it likely be tactically counterproductive so far as French concerned. We have however taken occasion underline constructive nature of Bourguiba's efforts with Algerian leaders along lines paragraph seven above.

10) We have emphasized our concern to French re recent incident involving tragic wounding Hajeri and are continuing efforts with French to do everything possible minimize possibility clashes such as those June 7. We concerned potentially explosive nature situation and count on Tunisia do everything possible keep temperature down.

---

[4] Telegram 515, May 24, reported that Vimont of the French Embassy had informed the Department on May 23 that French aid to Tunisia had been suspended and that France hoped such assistance could be reinstated once Tunisia adopted a more "natural" stance in regard to the Algerian conflict. The Department told Vimont that the French action would only complicate an already critical Tunisian economic situation. (*Ibid.*, 772.5–MSP/5–2457)

[5] This was one of the more brutal incidents in the Algerian insurgency. See Documents 85–86.

11) Whatever rights and wrongs in Algerian situation we hope Bourguiba will realize French cannot remain insensitive to arms traffic.

Dulles

255. Editorial Note

On July 25, the Tunisian Constituent Assembly voted unanimously to abolish the monarchy and proclaim the establishment of a Republic with Habib Bourguiba as Chief of State. Ambassador Slim called upon Acting Secretary Herter on July 26 to inform the United States officially of the change and to request recognition of the new regime. (Note No. 843; Department of State, Central Files, 772.02/7–2657) As a consequence, on July 30, Ambassador Jones conveyed a message to Sadok Mokkadem, Tunisian Secretary of State for Foreign Affairs, noting that the United States would recognize the new status of the Tunisian Government. (*Ibid.*)

256. Telegram From the Embassy in Tunisia to the Department of State [1]

Tunis, September 4, 1957—5 p.m.

148. 1. Foreign Secretary Mokaddem sent for me urgently this morning. When I arrived he said he had just spoken on phone with President Bourguiba in Switzerland and that communication he was about to make should be considered as coming directly from Bourguiba who had specifically charged him to see me without delay.

2. Mokaddem said incident near Haidra (Embassy telegram 144) [2] where French troops crossed into Tunisia and attacked small

[1] Source: Department of State, Central Files, 651.72/9–457. Secret; Priority. Repeated to Paris, Rome, Brussels, and London.

[2] Telegram 144, September 3, gave the details of the border incident from the Tunisian perspective. The clash, which left four Tunisians dead and two others missing and presumed dead, did not involve, Mokaddem emphasized, Algerian (Continued)

unit Tunisian army threw limelight on GOT's imperative necessity find arms equipment Tunisian army to (a) preserve internal order and (b) guard frontier. Tunisian defense near Haidra stopped when 30–40 rounds small arms ammunition carried by each man exhausted. This was all they had; similar situation prevails throughout Tunisian armed forces which for this reason cannot carry out their mission. "We have" he said, "absolute and immediate need for small arms and ammunition to use in legitimate self-defense. President Bourguiba has instructed me advise your government, through you, of situation and to request your urgent assistance."

3. Mokaddem said it logical for GOT look to France for arms aid, but it had waited and waited without results. GOT now despaired French aid being forthcoming particularly in light events September 1 when French forces from Algeria acted against uniformed Tunisians under "specious and piratical doctrine of hot pursuit." Not only did France refuse GOT arms, always linking them to Algeria, when GOT attempted buy small arms and ammunition in Italy and Belgium, GOF let governments these two countries know that France considered supply of arms to Tunisian forces as its province and that sales to GOT by Italian and Belgian firms would be considered "unfriendly" to France. Mokaddem said at time visit Richards mission GOT gained impression US not inclined help GOT's internal security forces, even to extent of non-lethal equipment, out of deference France.

4. Mokaddem said he hoped US-Tunisian understanding so close I would not take it as attempt at blackmail when he said that Tunisian needs so great that if Tunisia, which has steadfastly rejected idea seeking arms from satellite countries, cannot get arms from France or from Western suppliers, it may be forced to unpleasant necessity of going "elsewhere."

5. I referred to internal security survey requested by GOT and approved by ICA (Embassy despatch 514 of June 14 [3] and Icato 39 August 28) [4] and said I hoped survey team would arrive soon, since report by its experts would be of assistance to GOT in establishing rationally its real security needs. He said he was glad to hear survey

(Continued)
insurgents, and thus the French justification of "hot pursuit" did not apply. (*Ibid.*, 651.72/9–357) The French note to the Tunisian Government, however, on this matter insisted that the violence stemmed from an attack by Algerian rebels who retreated across the border to Tunisia. A summary of the note is attached to a memorandum from Elbrick to Dulles, September 12. (*Ibid.*, 033.5111/9–1257)

[3] Despatch 514 estimated the threat to Tunisia, the Tunisian capability to cope with the threat, the need for U.S. assistance, operational guidelines, and courses of action required to satisfy Tunisia's needs; and included the list of items the Tunisians had concluded they needed. (*Ibid.*, 772.5/6–1457)

[4] Not printed.

about begin, but GOT has practical and immediate need for small arms and small army weapons to maintain internal order and guard those border areas of Tunisia from which French forces have withdrawn recently with unforeseen speed. He said, "what President Bourguiba would value most highly is early US agreement in principle to assist GOT with its internal security needs and specifically its needs for small arms and small arms ammunition. This, in essence, is request President Bourguiba desires to put to Washington."

6. I undertook to communicate Bourguiba's message but counseled against great expectations.

7. *Comment*: By lying low and avoiding subject, Embassy has tried hard with some success to delay inevitable day when question now posed by Bourguiba would be brought up formally. For weeks and months Embassy has been reporting consistently frustrated hopes of French Embassy here that Paris would heed its recommendations provide equipment for even one battalion of Tunisian army which, although it has men in uniform, has little in way of weapons for them (Embassy telegram 132[5] and previous). Embassy has reported also confirmation GOF using its influence persuade manufacturing countries not sell arms GOT. In effect, from point of view GOT, this is another case of French granting "independence minus." For its internal security and as appurtenance of sovereignty, GOT has small army (about 4,000) which GOF for French reasons is preventing from securing small arms. Even before this approach we have known GOT resentment and anger at this treatment has been growing steadily. It is Bourguiba who, almost alone, has remained optimistic France would supply equipment. From what Mokaddem said this morning it appears that Bourguiba's hopeful attitude has now altered.

8. *Comment continued*: As has so frequently been demonstrated, nightmare of GOT is to be "left alone with France". Our economic aid program has value far beyond money involved in that it demonstrates US considers Tunisia independent sovereign state deserving US economic aid in its own right, i.e. US does not regard Tunisia as economic vassal of France. Worth special attention (paragraph 5 above) are words "agree in principle to assist GOT with its internal security needs". This sounds like Bourguiba himself. Always seeking evidence that his country is regarded by great powers as truly independent and sovereign, Bourguiba has thus posed touchstone of US faith and esteem; of US willingness recognize merits of what he

---

[5] Telegram 132, August 27, reported that Gorse informed the Embassy that Bourguiba's recent comments on Algeria had not improved the likelihood that France would provide him with additional arms. (Department of State, Central Files, 651.72/8–2757)

regards as clearly proven needs of solidly pro-West country for internal security equipment. On another plane of thought, Bourguiba probably feels that if US gives "agreement in principle" this will go far to relax attitude those Paris so opposed to giving Tunisian armed forces anything.

9. *Comment continued*: Happy partial solution problem from viewpoint US would, of course, be for GOF to do as French Embassy here has forcefully recommended—supply arms to Tunisian army without delay. *Army Fortnight* has focused attention on problem and this would be gesture of faith which Bourguiba and GOT would deeply appreciate and which would gain for France considerable kudos. If this is politically impossible, next best step would be for GOF quietly to advise Belgium and Italy that it would not object to sales GOT, thus ending informal blockade. Either course of action, however, does not avoid question of principle proposed by Bourguiba to US. In taking our decision, following, among other factors, should be weighed:

(a) Bourguiba's consistently pro-West policy and wholehearted endorsement of ME doctrine;
(b) Bourguiba's sharp reaction in Nabeul speech to refusal Richards mission supply army with trucks (Department will recall this speech evoked enough popular response along lines of big-fellow-vs-little-fellow to show what could happen here if Bourguiba deviated from his present pro-West line.);
(c) Fact arms and equipment are needed for Tunisian internal security;
(d) Tunisian army needs so desperate that in Embassy's judgment most unlikely arms supplied to GOT would disappear into Algeria;
(e) Bourguiba has present and growing domestic problem on his hands in having soldiers without arms and ammo and having no prospects for obtaining his requirements except from US or curtain countries (see paragraph 4 above).

10. *Comment continued*: I suggest reply to GOT making following points should be considered:

(a) US recognizes that Tunisia, as sovereign independent state, possesses obligations to preserve internal security and right of self defense.
(b) US does not consider France possesses, either formally or informally, exclusive rights with regard to supply of arms to Tunisia although there are military virtues to standardization of arms, equipment and training.
(c) Internal security survey team, which should arrive shortly at request of GOT, is evidence that US has already taken note of internal security problem in Tunisia and agrees in principle to Tunisia's eligibility for American internal security equipment and arms, either by sale, loan or grant, when need therefor for internal security purposes has been clearly established. In view of its many

commitments elsewhere, US prefers that, as in case of its economic aid, any US assistance to Tunisia in security field will supplement, but not supplant, that received from other sources.

11. *Comment continued*: Reply of this kind, accompanied by speed-up of arrival of internal security survey team would go far, I think, to meet present situation and would help resolve it, particularly if American Embassy Paris informs GOF in advance of our decision with explanation that we have sedulously held back (and indeed thereby have lost some ground) until last moment in hope French would set up Tunisia internal security forces as going concerns. Paris might add that if GOT forced go to curtain countries, even for small quantity arms, this act could well start process eventually disastrous to French and Western interest in all North Africa.

Jones

257. Telegram From the Department of State to the Embassy in Tunisia [1]

Washington, September 11, 1957—8:03 p.m.

140. FYI Department giving urgent attention present Tunisian situation in light considerations set forth Tunis' 148 [2] and 165. [3] As Emb will recognize, Tunisia's desire for US assistance in obtaining arms poses far-reaching problems for us which necessitate our assuring we proceed in manner which best accords our interests in both North Africa and France. We obviously prefer that any supply of arms should come from France or other Western country rather than US. While matter receives our consideration we wish make every

[1] Source: Department of State, Central Files, 651.72/9–957. Secret; Niact. Repeated to Paris and Rabat. Drafted and approved by Palmer and cleared in draft with G, EUR, and RA.

[2] *Supra.*

[3] Dated September 9; it reads in part as follows:

"Deterioration Tunisian pro-West orientation because of what Tunisians regard as Western arms blockade so rapid and marked that I no longer believe reply suggested paragraph 10 Embtel 148 would cover situation unless closely followed by delivery some US equipment."

Jones argued that if Bourguiba could announce on September 12, when he was to resume his weekly speeches to the nation, that the United States was prepared to supply Tunisia with internal security equipment including arms, it "would be impressive vindication of wisdom his pro-Western, pro-US policy." (Department of State, Central Files, 651.72/9–957)

effort prevent situation from deteriorating further. We are particularly concerned as to what Bourguiba may say in speech tomorrow night and believe it matter of utmost importance you endeavor talk to him beforehand along following lines. End FYI.

1. Department deeply concerned deterioration Franco-Tunisian relations with all that is implied for our Tunisian friends and further instability in vital North African region.

2. We recognize Tunisia's concern re safeguarding its sovereignty. We believe we have since Tunisian independence given evidence of our concern that Tunisia emerge as strong and stable state. Toward this end we have furnished considerable economic assistance and have recently agreed to survey Tunisia's internal security requirements.

3. We are giving most urgent attention present situation including Foreign Minister's desire for US assistance in obtaining arms. To our mind problem is to find solution which will best assure Tunisia's sovereign rights and responsibilities and contribute to area stability. We hope instruct you discuss this matter further with Bourguiba in very near future. We intend similarly discuss matter with French, indicating our grave concern at present situation.

4. If US is to be helpful in this situation it is of greatest importance that every effort be made prevent further deterioration in situation while we are studying matter. As indicated above we will endeavor expedite consideration just as much as possible, but meanwhile we hope Bourguiba will make every effort encourage Tunisian Government and people exercise all possible restraint. We intend speak to French in similar sense.

5. We need hardly add that we hope Bourguiba meanwhile will ponder carefully his remarks re possibility obtaining arms "elsewhere" if not available West. Even talk of this kind if publicly known can encourage Soviet interventions to detriment area stability and best interests Tunisia for which we entertain deepest solicitude.

6. We would appreciate receiving from Bourguiba further facts on this matter. While we are aware of previous explanation made by members GOT of problems encountered in effort equip Tunisian Army, it would be helpful if GOT could tell us as precisely as possible what equipment has been requested from France, what commitments or schedule of delivery if any France had agreed to, and what equipment France has delivered or withheld. Also what requests have been made in Belgium, Italy, or other Western countries and through what channels.

Dulles

258. Telegram From the Embassy in Tunisia to the Department of State[1]

Tunis, September 12, 1957—7 p.m.

183. 1. I managed to get to Bourguiba, who had Ladgham and Foreign Secretary Mokaddem with him, fifteen minutes before he was scheduled to record his weekly address. He looked grim and worried. As he listened with great care to numbered points Department niact 140,[2] he relaxed visibly. (*Note*: I felt justified in almost strong-arming my way into Bouguiba because Tom Brady of NYT, who interviewed him last night, had told me earlier this morning that he had found Bourguiba in bitter mood against US and west generally. Bourguiba told him he would say in his speech today that failure of west to respond to Tunisians' needs made his forthright support west no more than meaningless sentimental attachment. According Brady, Bourguiba planned say he had learned through his recent experience to sympathize with Syria and now he would have to tell Tunisian people he must seek arms elsewhere to preserve Tunisian territorial integrity. Brady says he filed story to that effect last night).

2. Bourguiba asked me to thank Department for its message and commented: "They say they are going to talk to the French. This is good. They must do this". Then, having arranged his thoughts; Bourguiba, with great sincerity and considerable emotion, spoke in the following sense:

3. "I understand problems of US. I understand why decision to give us arms is difficult for you. It represents a question of political choice. I can even understand US deciding for its own reasons to choose solidarity with France. But I too have to make a political choice. I have from outset chosen to be on side of west—above all on side of US. I as a politician have brought all Tunisia with me into western camp. However Tunisian people have right to ask what benefits have come for them from my policies. What answer can I give? Their economic development needs are great and are growing. Their need for arms to defend Tunisian soil is pressing, immediate and even greater. In first field, there is little to show; I can tell them only to hope. Re arms I must confess no results at all. It is not blackmail if I say we must go elsewhere for arms and other aid; it would be decision forced upon me by French behavior toward my country. I must be able to show people Tunisia is sovereign

[1] Source: Department of State, Central Files, 651.72/9–1257. Secret; Priority. Repeated to Paris and Rabat.

[2] *Supra.*

independent state which powers having capability of supplying arms regard as worthy of being helped in Tunisia's own right".

4. He went on: "I thank Department for information US studying problem but time is pressing upon me. Department should avoid getting bogged down in discussions with Quai d'Orsay whose only aim will be to gain time to propagate false story French forces are winning in Algeria. Arguments between Department and Quai d'Orsay will not help us. Tunisian people have recently noted that US mounted with great speed airlift of arms to Jordan (he mentioned this twice), which is a country lacking courage to say, as I have done that it is on side of US".

5. He continued: "France is in state of crisis and is driven by complexes. There is desire to kill, crush, stifle. French find it impossible act with good faith in their dealings with Maghreb where manifestations of France's psychological turmoil are destroying what France might well preserve. Only your country, by living up to its responsibilities and by being true to its ideals, can save situation: But it must not delay".

6. Thinking of recording machine waiting in next room, I directed his particular attention to paragraph 5 Depreftel adding thought that references to "elsewhere" created additional difficulties in dealing with US public opinion. Bourguiba took the point and remarked "I am glad you got to me before my speech. I will now speak with more serenity (sérénité). I hope to have Department's decision very soon".

7. Miscellaneous points:

a. Bourguiba very pleased Secretary [*Ambassador*?] received Mongi Slim September 11.[3] He said he had just decided Ladgham would head Tunisian UNGA delegation "since he knows your country and deserves some rest. I hope very much Mr. Dulles will have time to see him to discuss our common problems (Embtel 158)."[4] I replied along lines Depcirtel 191.[5]

b. Ladgham promised provide information requested paragraph 6 Depreftel. He said Belgian Ambassador had offered supply "NATO-type rifles" but that later, "obviously under French pressure", had withdrawn offer. He said quantity rifles needed together with ammo is 5,000. He said this not excessive figure taking into account needs of young men recently called to military service; "actually", he said, "we have about 6,000 men in barracks".

---

[3] Slim informed Ambassador Lodge at the United Nations on September 11 that Tunisia was considering bringing a complaint against France in the Security Council due to further acts of violence on September 7. (Memorandum from Rountree to Dulles, September 13; Department of State, Central Files, 611.72/9–1357)

[4] Telegram 158, September 6, reported Mokkadem's hopes that Dulles would be able to see him during the General Assembly session in New York. (*Ibid.*, 320/9–657)

[5] Circular telegram 191, August 31, advised the addressees of the Secretary's availability during and following the General Assembly meeting. (*Ibid.*, 320/8–3157)

c. Re Italy Ladgham said inquiries for pistols and submachineguns had been made through Italian Ambassador who at first said Italian firms would be glad send representative here take orders but later made excuses indicating Italy, "again under French pressure" unwilling supply.

d. Bourguiba himself brought up question arms given GOT leaking to Algeria. He said this could not happen because GOT keeps careful records arms equipment and holds each soldier fully responsible for arms issued. I said: "can you give a categoric assurance that arms given GOT would [not?] go to Algerians?" He replied, "I can and do".

e. Bourguiba and others deeply incensed by "false and ever-changing" communiqués issued from Algeria. They assert facts exactly as presented Tunisian communiqués (Embtel 175,[6] 159,[7] 144[8]) re border incidents and names kidnapped Tunisians fully known. It was evident they have no faith in sagacity, good-will or humanity French military Algeria who, Ladgham asserted, "refuse even to return Tunisian bodies because we would see how cruelly they were killed".

8. *Comment*: Deptel 140 arrived just in time. It should have effect somewhat tempering Bourguiba's speech, but I suspect from Bourguiba's mood of anger and frustration, speech will still be fairly rough. He will expect us to follow up on third sentence paragraph 2 and will, being Bourguiba, set great store by principle underlying decision (see paragraph 3 above and paragraph 5 Embtel 148).[9]

9. *Comment continued*: From start Bourguiba's concept has been "to win with the west"; this has brought him few friends in Arab and Communist-dominated world. A phase of problem perhaps more important than arms or no arms is possibility of setting up Tunisia as a martyr which neutralist and anti-western world can propagandize as proof positive of what happens to friends of west at hands of US when conflicting interests are involved.

Jones

---

[6] Telegram 175, September 11, referred to the government's communiqué regarding its protest to France of border incidents. (*Ibid.*, 651.72/9–1157)

[7] Telegram 159, September 7, dealt with press accounts of the government communiqué protesting the French military intrusion on that date. (*Ibid.*, 651.72/9–757)

[8] Telegram 144, September 3, referred to Ladgham's press conference of the previous day on the Haidra incident. (*Ibid.*, 651.72/9–357)

[9] Document 256.

259. Telegram From the Department of State to the Embassy in France [1]

Washington, September 12, 1957—8:07 p.m.

1019. Please deliver following personal message from Secretary to Pineau:

"Since our very useful conversations last weekend, [2] I have become seriously concerned at the rapid deterioration which we believe we detect in Franco-Tunisian relations. I fear that unless energetic steps are taken immediately we may be faced with a situation in Tunisia of serious danger to the interests of France, the US and the West in general. I recognize that much of the danger arises from the different interests and different attitudes of Tunisia and France toward Algeria and that perhaps full cooperation and understanding cannot be reached until that conflict is settled. Nevertheless the importance of Tunisia to the future orientation of North Africa and to the Free World is such that I feel we must take all feasible steps to assure her continued Western orientation.

"I recall the comments which you made to me with respect to Tunisian attitudes and actions regarding Algeria. [3] We have moreover studied the note which you presented to the Tunisian Government on September 11. I am thus aware of difficulties which are posed to the French Government in the present situation.

"My deep concern arises from the request which the new Tunisian Foreign Minister, on instructions from President Bourguiba, has recently made to us for assistance in obtaining small arms and ammunition to assure Tunisia's security and to fulfill its responsibilities in those border areas from which French forces have recently withdrawn. The Foreign Minister told us that it was logical for Tunisia to look to France in this matter but that Tunisia had waited in vain for help and that attempts to purchase arms in other Western countries had been frustrated because of the attitude of the French Government which had been made known to the Governments of those countries.

"The United States has also been given clearly to understand that if we could not be helpful in this respect the Tunisians would feel compelled to look to non-Western sources.

"I did not wish to proceed further in this matter without ascertaining more precisely your views and the facts as to French commitments with regard to equipping the Tunisian army as well as deliveries which have been made and the status of those which have been scheduled or requested. I think it would be helpful also if you felt you could tell us the nature of any Tunisian requests to other

---

[1] Source: Department of State, Central Files, 772.56/9–1257. Secret. Repeated to Tunis and Rabat.

[2] Their conversation of September 7 mainly dealt with the Algerian problem. (Memorandum of conversation by Witman, September 7; *ibid.*, 751S.00/9–757)

[3] In the September 7 conversation, Pineau noted the quasi-official aid given the rebels by Tunisia. As a consequence, he found it hard to justify financial assistance to Tunisia.

Western countries which may have been brought to your attention, and your views on such requests.

"In the present situation in Tunisia I do not believe that we can dismiss the very strong possibility that Tunisia would in fact obtain arms from the Soviet bloc if she were unable to obtain them anywhere in the Western world. I therefore believe that unless the West finds it possible to make available to Tunisia the arms and ammunition which are reasonably required to assure its legitimate defense, these needs will be met by the Soviets with consequences which are all too obvious and contain such danger for us all.

"I think you know that it has always been our desire to see France occupy a position in North Africa for which she is so well equipped by virtue of her interests and long history of responsibility in that region. I think you also know that our interests in North Africa relate to the West and free world. I would be most reluctant for the US to take an active role in the present situation—particularly insofar as the supply of arms is concerned. Your urgent views would be appreciated as to how this matter can best be handled in order to avoid consequences to which I earlier referred. If it were not possible for France to supply this equipment, would it not be possible for Tunisia to purchase equipment in some other Western country, preferably in Europe?

"I can readily appreciate that you would expect that any assistance rendered to Tunisia in this matter should be accompanied by guarantees from the Tunisian Government as to the destination of military equipment and the discharge of normal Tunisian responsibilities in assuring the proper use of such equipment on its own territory.

"As you will appreciate we believe that there is considerable urgency in this matter. Ambassador Houghton will inform you of the substance of the démarche which I have asked Ambassador Jones to make to President Bourguiba in an effort to induce calm while we have an opportunity to consider the problem. Obviously however time is running out and we cannot long delay a response to the Tunisian appeal."

Paris authorized convey to Pineau substance six numbered paragraphs Deptel 140 Tunis repeated 1005 Paris. [4]

Dulles

[4] Document 257.

260. Memorandum of a Conversation, Secretary Dulles' Suite, Waldorf Towers, New York, September 17, 1957, 12:30 p.m.[1]

TGA/MC/8

PARTICIPANTS

The Secretary	The Tunisian Ambassador, Mr. Mongi Slim
Mr. Rountree	Mr. Mestiri, Tunisian Delegation to the UN
Mr. Tyler	

SUBJECT

Tunisian Request for Arms

The Tunisian Ambassador told the Secretary that there had been increasing violations of the Tunisian frontier of late by French troops, and that these no longer represented isolated military incidents but a deliberate policy of premeditated and continuous acts of aggression. He said that French troops had several times bombarded Tunisian villages both from the air and by artillery on Algerian soil, and that defenseless Tunisian citizens had been killed and kidnapped by the French. The Tunisian Government now felt that it could not allow the situation to continue and that something must be done to put an end to it. If the situation were allowed to deteriorate, it would reach the point where Tunisia and France would find themselves at war with each other, which was something which Tunisia wished very much to avoid. The Ambassador then referred to the note which the Tunisian Government had presented to the US Government last week requesting arms. [2]

The Secretary said that this was a very difficult matter indeed. He said that it was known that the Tunisian Government had sympathy for the Algerian nationalists and that while the Tunisian Government was undoubtedly doing all it could to avoid incidents, perhaps some elements of the population might be doing things which provoke the French. The Secretary said he thought it was highly important that the greatest restraint be exercised on both sides in order to prevent the situation from deteriorating further.

The Tunisian Ambassador said that the Tunisian Government had exercised great restraint and would continue to do so. However, if the French policy of premeditated violation of Tunisian territory

[1] Source: Department of State, Central Files, 110.11–DU/9–1857. Secret. Drafted by Tyler.

[2] See footnote 2, Document 265.

continued, it would not be possible for the Tunisian Government to tolerate this indefinitely. He said that the French were invoking the right of pursuit, which did not exist in international law, and that when the U.S. and Mexico crossed each other's borders in 1917, this had been on the basis of pre-established agreement. The Tunisian Ambassador then asked whether the U.S. Government would soon be in a position to give a reply to its note about obtaining arms. The Secretary said that this matter was being given most careful consideration and that he was not in a position to give an answer now but hoped to be able to give a more positive reply soon.

The Tunisian Ambassador said that the Tunisian Government had been giving consideration to the possibility of appealing to the Security Council of the UN under Article IV of the Charter. The Secretary said that this was a difficult matter and that he thought the idea had grave drawbacks. He assured the Tunisian Ambassador that the US had already spoken to the French and would continue to do so to impress on them the desirability of exercising the greatest restraint. The Secretary told the Ambassador that he had recently had conversations with two prominent French political figures, neither of whom was a member of the Government, and that he had been struck by the intensity of their feelings with regard to the subject under discussion.

The Tunisian Ambassador said that his Government also held extremely strong feelings, and he referred to the fact that French troops in Algeria were using US equipment and that it might be that the bombs that were being dropped on Tunisian soil had been provided to France by the US. The Ambassador concluded by asking whether, in the event that the Tunisian Government decided to raise the question of French aggression in the Security Council, it could count on the support of the US Government.

The Secretary said that it was not possible to give a reply to such a question at this time and that he rather hoped that it would not be necessary for this step to be taken. He pointed out that, under the Charter, members are expected to exhaust all diplomatic possibilities for solving differences between them before having recourse to the UN. The Tunisian Ambassador replied that this was what his government was trying to do.

The Secretary said he wished to assure the Tunisian Ambassador of the admiration which he felt for the Tunisian nation, Government and people in the light of the role which they were playing as a member of the free world. He said he wished to assure the Tunisian Ambassador that we would give the matters that he had raised the most careful consideration and that we would do what we possibly could to help in the matter.

261. Telegram From the Department of State to the Embassy in France[1]

Washington, September 19, 1957—12:14 p.m.

1104. Please deliver following message from Secretary to Pineau:

"I wish to thank you for your prompt and comprehensive reply [2] to my message of September 13. I have studied your views on French-Tunisian relations with the closest attention and appreciate the frankness with which you have taken me into your confidence. I am encouraged to believe that, despite the specific incidents and issues which divide France and Tunisia at this juncture, there is nevertheless a sufficient community of interest to enable the two countries to reconcile their differences. In any case, I am sure you will agree that it is imperative to the interests of the West that the closest possible relations exist between France and Tunisia.

"In your reply, you have emphasized France's desire for the rigorous control over the quantity of arms to be supplied Tunisia and the use to which those arms would be put. I am fully aware of the very real problem which would be presented to the French Government if it were found that these arms were subsequently diverted to the Algerian rebels, utilized to their profit or employed against French troops in Tunisia. With this natural concern on the part of your government, I realize the courage and helpfulness you have shown in withdrawing your objections to the delivery by the Italian Government of a certain quantity of arms to Tunisia. As I feel that there are other very real limitations imposed by financial considerations, availability, etc., which will tend to limit the supply of arms to Tunisia, I would strongly urge you not to require the Italians, when discussing the matter with the Tunisians, to place fixed quantitative restrictions on the sale of arms to Tunisia for that country's internal security requirements. For your action to have the necessary psychological effect on the improvement of Tunisian relations with France and with the West, it seems to me important that Bourguiba not gain the impression that an arbitrary quantitative limitation has been placed on his procurement of equipment in Italy. I believe that your objective can best be reached if the Italians endeavor to hold the Tunisian request within reasonable bounds during subsequent negotiations. We would be glad to assist by utilizing our influence toward this end if you so desire. In any case, speed is of the essence if the delivery of even a limited supply of arms by Italy is to prevent Bourguiba from any ill-considered action in this regard.

"I would also like to touch briefly on the nature of the guarantees concerning the uses of equipment which you suggest the Tunisian Government should furnish. I can understand your natural concern on this score and should tell you that recently Bourguiba

---

[1] Source: Department of State, Central Files, 651.72/9–1957. Secret; Priority; Limit Distribution. Drafted by Porter and Palmer. Repeated to Tunis and Rome.

[2] Given to Houghton on September 16 and transmitted in telegram 1378 from Paris on that date. (*Ibid.*, 772.56/9–1657)

categorically assured us that arms given the Tunisian Government would not go to the Algerians. Hence I believe that satisfactory arrangements can be reached whereby adequate guarantees are given discreetly by Tunisia in conjunction perhaps with a more general public commitment that the equipment would be used only for purposes of legitimate self defense. (As you know, we always require that US equipment furnished to a foreign country be used only for purposes of legitimate self defense.) We feel that assurances of this nature would be more readily obtainable from Bourguiba and would be more useful on a long-range basis than one which bears only on the current and temporary difficulties between France and Tunisia.

"I hope you will give me your views on these two suggestions. I need not, I am sure, reiterate to you my conviction that if this problem can be swiftly and adequately settled we will have avoided manifold complications in a most strategic area."

Murphy

---

262. Telegram From the Embassy in France to the Department of State [1]

Paris, September 21, 1957—2 p.m.

1491. Reference Embtel 1483. [2] Pineau called me in this morning and with great gravity and emphasis protested against leak to UP on arms to Tunis. Without specifically saying so, he obviously attributed leak to Department.

He expressed particular indignation that leak concerned question which has been subject personal correspondence between Secretary and himself. He showed me sections article in this morning's Communist-front newspaper *Liberation* which reproduces and embroiders on UP report. Pineau pointed out his own personal position in this matter is extremely delicate and that Prime Minister and Defense Minister [3] are furious.

In light these developments Pineau asked the Secretary be informed he would be unable to reply immediately to Secretary's second message re arms to Tunis. He frankly did not see how he

---

[1] Source: Department of State, Central Files, 772.56/9–2157. Confidential; Priority. Repeated to Rome and Tunis.

[2] Telegram 1483, September 20, revealed French disquiet that the press had learned of the negotiations to permit Italy to furnish arms to Tunisia. (*Ibid.*, 772.56/9–2057)

[3] André Morice.

would get out of present difficulty and in any case would be unable to take further action before next Council of Ministers meeting September 25. He handed me communiqué transmitted following telegram. [4]

Pineau also made number of general comments re serious weakness Western diplomacy vis-à-vis Soviets as result constant leaks to press. He pointed out that present subject is one in which much can be accomplished privately but concerning which publicity tends to paralyze all interested parties.

In response to query, Pineau said he did not know what Italian reaction to publicity has been but Joxe is seeing Italian Ambassador today.

Comment: Pineau was . . . throughout entire interview. We suspect that he only with greatest difficulty obtained Bourges' and Morice's consent to last week's change in French policy and that they have now demanded he take no further action for time being.

I believe that only means of moving forward under present circumstances is for Secretary to send another urgent personal message expressing regret for publicity offering explanation, if possible and emphasizing vital importance of acting promptly on substantive issue. We would hope Pineau . . . . However extremely precarious state of Bourges government adds another hazard.

We would also hope that Italians may not feel as strongly as French on publicity and may still be prepared to proceed as planned.

Houghton

[4] The communiqué was transmitted in telegram 1492, September 21. (*Ibid.*, 772.56/9–2157)

---

263. Telegram From the Department of State to the Embassy in Tunisia [1]

Washington, September 22, 1957—5:12 p.m.

175. Pass following message from Secretary to Bourguiba:

"Since Mr. Mokaddem's conversation with Ambassador Jones on September 4 we have been giving the closest and most urgent

[1] Source: Department of State, Central Files, 772.5/9–2257. Secret; Priority; Limit Distribution. Repeated to Rome and Paris.

attention to your Government's request that the United States assist Tunisia with its internal security needs and, specifically, its need for small arms and ammunition.

"I know that I need hardly assure you of the sympathetic manner in which we have viewed this request. Ever since the establishment of relations between our two countries, the United States has been anxious to assist your Government, within the limits of our abilities, in its efforts to build a strong, stable and prosperous nation. In recognition of Tunisia's need for economic development, our two countries have worked out programs of economic development with funds made available by this Government. Similarly, in recognition of the importance to Tunisia of an effective system of internal security, we have agreed to send a small mission to assist the Tunisian Government to establish its internal security needs.

"In view of these developments, I can assure you that there is every disposition on the part of this Government to assist Tunisia in meeting its legitimate internal security needs. In this spirit, we have in the last two weeks had conversations with other interested Governments in an effort to facilitate Tunisian purchases of small arms and ammunition from nearby continental sources. These conversations, which Ambassador Jones will describe to you, are still going on and I am hopeful that they will soon bear fruit. If they should not, we shall have to find other means of meeting your requirements, keeping in mind the urgency which I know this problem presents you.

"In this connection, I assume that there will be no difficulty in Tunisia giving appropriate formal assurances regarding the use to which the arms would be put. For example, in instances in which we supply arms to foreign countries, we generally require assurances that the arms will be used only for purposes of legitimate self-defense and that they will not be transferred to other custody without the consent of the United States Government. I assume that there would be no problem in your giving assurances to whichever Western country supplies your needs.

"I look forward to meeting Mr. Ladgham. I know how closely and devotedly he and you have worked to associate a strong Tunisia with the free world and I am confident that you will be successful in this vital task."

For Embassy: Next immediately numbered telegram contains additional points to be communicated verbally to Bourguiba. [2]

Dulles

---

[2] Telegram 176, September 22, instructed Ambassador Jones to explain in general terms the exchanges between the United States and France and to urge Tunisia not to publicize U.S. efforts to satisfy Tunisia's internal security requirements. (*Ibid.*, 651.72/9–1157) President Bourguiba was pleased by the Secretary's message but was pessimistic regarding the likelihood of completing the Italian arms deal. (Telegram 246 from Tunis, September 24; *ibid.*, 772.56/9–2457)

264. Telegram From the Department of State to the Embassy in France [1]

Washington, September 22, 1957—5:23 p.m.

1155. Paris' 1491. Pass following from Secretary to Pineau:

"I have received your message concerning the UP article on arms for Tunisia. I understand fully the difficulties which arise from publication of such an article at this juncture, causing as it does embarrassment to both our governments. In this connection I can assure you positively that our information definitely indicates that the leak was of other than US origin.

"I hope you will agree that we should not permit such a regrettable occurrence to interrupt the development of a solution for a problem which should be solved without delay. Your contribution toward such a solution has been so constructive, indeed, decisive, that it would be a great loss to all concerned if progress were now to be jeopardized because of the unfortunate publication of that article.

"The United States, as you know, has been under considerable pressure from the Tunisian Government to supply arms. It is not, however, the pressure on us which motivates my concern, but rather our estimate of the internal pressures on President Bourguiba which will, we believe, compel him to accept arms from most undesirable sources under most undesirable conditions if he cannot obtain them from friendly Western nations. We have not replied to President Bourguiba despite mounting indications that a reply is becoming more essential each day if we are to prevent the Tunisians from taking a step which we are convinced would be greatly detrimental to their real interests and to those of the West generally. I therefore feel compelled today to reply to his direct request of September 4 by reassuring him that, in some way, his legitimate internal security needs will be met, but expressing the hope that this can be done from European sources. I am, of course, making it clear that we expect that Tunisia will give appropriate assurances with respect to the use and custody of the arms.

"I am also hoping that it will be possible for you to agree to the two suggestions contained in my second message to you. Much of the success of our effort to convince Mr. Bourguiba that restraint and patience are to his advantage depends, in my opinion, on the conditions which accompany our willingness to make arms available to him for his internal security needs."

For Embassy info: UP correspondent called Department offices September 19, indicating he had already filed story based on French and Italian Embassy sources. He sought Department confirmation, received none.

Dulles

---

[1] Source: Department of State, Central Files, 772.56/9–2157. Secret; Priority; Limit Distribution. Drafted by Porter. Repeated to Rome and Tunis.

265. Memorandum of a Conversation, Department of State, Washington, September 26, 1957[1]

SUBJECT

Tunisian Arms Request

PARTICIPANTS

H.E. Mongi Slim, Ambassador of Tunisia
Mr. Habib Bourguiba, Jr., Tunisian Ambassador-designate to Italy
Mr. Mhamed Esaafi, Secretary of the Tunisian Embassy
Joseph Palmer 2nd, Deputy Assistant Secretary for African Affairs
Arthur B. Allen, AFN
Donald R. Norland, AFN

The Ambassador called in order to be brought up to date on developments since his talk with Assistant Secretary Rountree on September 20th[2] concerning Tunisia's request for assistance in obtaining arms. Mr. Palmer asked whether the Ambassador had anything he wished to communicate to the State Department and the Ambassador replied that his comments might more usefully follow Mr. Palmer's. Mr. Palmer thereupon read to the Ambassador the Secretary's message to President Bourguiba of September 22nd (Deptel 175), explaining that as a result of communications difficulties, the message had not been delivered until September 24th.

Mr. Palmer went on to say that as a result of our conversations with the French, we have been encouraged by the understanding which they have shown regarding this problem. At the same time and without in any way minimizing the internal political problems facing President Bourguiba, we believe it important to recognize that the French also face very serious internal political difficulties. We have therefore tried to work quietly toward a solution which would meet Tunisia's needs but place the least strain on U.S. relations with France, which are of such importance to the entire free world. We hope that the Secretary's message will reassure the Government of Tunisia that we recognize the need for a rapid solution to Tunisia's problem and that it may be possible to achieve a period of quiet in which all concerned continue to work toward a solution. However, we recognize the pressures on President Bourguiba and have there-

---

[1] Source: Department of State, Central Files, 772.56/9–2657. Secret. Drafted by Norland and Allen.

[2] Ambassador Slim had been scheduled to see the Secretary on September 13 but difficulties in travel arrangements forced him to miss the appointment. In his stead, Ahmed Mastiri, Attaché of the Tunisian Embassy, conveyed the note the Ambassador had intended to deliver. When Slim met with Rountree on September 20, he indicated that his two major concerns were frontier violations and the need for arms. He also emphasized his strong wish that the United States would furnish the required arms. (Memorandum of conversation by Tyler, September 20; *ibid.*, 110.11–DU/9–1857)

fore informed him that if he feels it necessary, we would understand his making a public statement to the effect that the United States recognizes Tunisian internal security needs and is disposed to find a way of meeting them.

Mr. Palmer then referred to reports from Cairo that Tunisia had agreed to obtain arms from Egypt. He pointed out that, as Ambassador Slim would see from the above, our action had preceded and not been affected by this report. We have nevertheless been disturbed by it and would therefore appreciate any explanations which the Ambassador might wish to make.

Ambassador Slim thanked Mr. Palmer for the message, stating that it was what he had hoped for and expected, knowing the true sentiments of the American Government and people toward Tunisia. The Ambassador commented that he had feared that the United States answer would come a little too late. He went on to say he regretted only one thing; namely, that the United States was very often led into the position of being too solicitous of France in foreign policy considerations. The problem of arms to Tunisia could have been resolved at the time of the Richards Mission, when Tunisia had not asked for arms specifically but only for transportation and communications equipment. Even now, he commented, while a solution to the arms question appears to have been found, it does not yet appear certain. The Ambassador noted that the Italian Government had just made known its decision to allow Italian arms manufacturers to sell arms to Tunisia, observing however that there was always a considerable margin between intentions and realizations.

Ambassador Slim stressed the urgency of the question of arms assistance to Tunisia in view of continued aggression by the French military forces into Tunisian territory and emphasized that the current situation did not allow the Tunisian Government time to postpone its armament program nor develop it gradually and rationally over a period of years. Emphasizing the emergency nature of the situation, the Ambassador stated that a small amount of aid received quickly would be much more effective than a larger amount later.

Turning to the question of assurances as to the destinations of arms that might be provided Tunisia by Western nations, Ambassador Slim said he recognized the American "concern" and our desire for such assurances. Knowing the intentions of both the President and the Government of Tunisia, the Ambassador said he could, without specific instructions, assure the State Department that any arms provided Tunisia would be used only for purposes of internal security and legitimate self-defense. However, the Ambassador said, gesturing decisively, "if we are the object of aggression, we will fight back regardless of whether the attacking country is friendly or unfriendly. This would be in accordance with Article 51 of the United Nations Charter."[3]

On the question of arms from Egypt, Ambassador Slim reviewed the developments following the speech of President Bourguiba at Le Kef on August 8, 1957, when the "Army Fortnight" was launched. At that time, the President of Tunisia had appealed for funds and for arms assistance from "friendly and sister" nations in building the young Tunisian Army. Several days later Mr. Mokaddem, upon taking leave from his position at Cairo,[4] was informed by President Nasser that the Government of Egypt had answered President Bourguiba's appeal by offering a gift of arms. Mr. Mokaddem's response at the time had been to thank the Egyptian President and to state that he would report the offer to President Bourguiba.

When the September incidents along the Tunisian-Algerian frontier became known, and the Tunisian Government's lack of arms was noted widely in the press, Ambassador Slim continued, Egyptian newspapers recalled the previous Egyptian offer to the Tunisian Government. Two days ago the new Tunisian Ambassador to Egypt, Mr. Sahbani, after presenting his letters of credence to the Egyptian President, was confronted by the Egyptian press and badgered by them into making the statement that Tunisia accepted the Egyptian "gesture," which was interpreted by the press as meaning that Tunisia accepted Egyptian arms aid.

Pausing at this point, Ambassador Slim explained that there had been no formal acceptance of the Egyptian offer, and no agreement or mission to determine Tunisian needs or to discuss the quantities of arms. However, Ambassador Slim said that the Tunisian Government could not refuse "a free gift" from a nation with which it is on friendly terms and could not reject such a gift unless it was from an unfriendly nation or under "unfriendly circumstances." The Ambassador recalled in connection with the Egyptian offer what he had said earlier with regard to Italian aid—that there was a margin between acceptance in principle and its execution.

Reverting again to the great needs of the Tunisian military and police forces, Ambassador Slim stated that while he personally hoped that the United States would still find it possible to furnish Tunisian needs, Tunisian arms in any case should be of the same kind and not made up in part of arms from Western sources and in part from non-Western sources. He stated that Tunisia did not desire a diversity of armament, a statement he linked to a principle to which he held very firmly; namely, that Tunisia is and will be on

---

[3] Article 51 stated that nothing in the Charter precluded the right of self-defense if a nation was the victim of armed attack.

[4] Tunisian Ambassador to Egypt.

the side of the free world. Therefore, he reasoned, Tunisian armament can only come from the free world.

Mr. Palmer stated he wished to comment on the Ambassador's criticism that we are often too solicitous of France. He called particular attention to the fact that we have sought directness and equality in developing our relations with Tunisia. At the same time, our world responsibilities require that we take the widest possible view of all matters in order to minimize the effects of any given course of action on other countries of the free world. Mr. Palmer emphasized that he was not speaking of compromises on a matter of principle. In cases where principle is involved, we have differed fundamentally with our allies, as in the attack on Suez. We wish naturally, however, to avoid such splits and, while abiding by principle ourselves, to try to bring other countries to understand and act in accordance with the principle involved. In this sense we have attempted in recent discussions to be helpful also to France, and it is not, therefore, out of deference to French sensitivity but rather to achieve a wider understanding that we consult with the French.

Ambassador Slim remarked that he personally was sometimes accused of being too much influenced by the United States point of view (referring jokingly to Habib Bourguiba, Jr., at his side) and stated it was perhaps because he understood the United States Government's method of acting. He agreed that action need not be spectacular or public, it should only be effective. Ambassador Slim recalled that last year when the French had committed acts of aggression within Tunisian territory, he was able to tell his Government that although he did not know what the United States had done, he knew that the United States had acted because a change had been noted within forty-eight hours and the French actions stopped. In the present instance, the Ambassador continued, it is a question not only of arms but of aggression, noting that as late as Monday (September 23rd) there were reports of French aggression, kidnappings, et cetera. As for arms and the United States Government's desire to see Tunisia provided with light arms, the Ambassador said that although he did not see the possibility that United States arms would be provided now, he was taking a longer view of the matter. The Italian Government had stated Italian arms manufacturers could now sell arms to Tunisia. Would the United States see any objections to United States firms selling arms to Tunisia, the Ambassador asked?

Mr. Palmer replied that he would prefer to answer that question by again calling the Ambassador's attention to the text of the Secretary's message to President Bourguiba stating that if European sources failed, "other means" would be found.

Ambassador Slim acknowledged his understanding that the United States would seek other means to provide arms for Tunisia but emphasized that the Tunisian Government was pressed for time. If a result is not arrived at quickly in receiving Italian arms, could the United States delivery of arms be envisaged?

Mr. Palmer replied that he was fully aware of the urgency of the situation. He recalled, however, that the Tunisians had asked "assistance in obtaining arms" and said that we are working as hard as we can to find what sources of arms may be available.

Ambassador Slim said he had a final question concerning the possibility of ICA assistance in obtaining transportation and communications equipment. He recalled the answer previously given by the Department that such a program should be postponed until a program was developed for the new fiscal year. The Ambassador asked whether the Tunisian Government could hope for the receipt of about $1 million worth of transportation and communications equipment in the current ICA program.

Mr. Palmer replied that we have agreed to an internal security survey mission and have taken steps to expedite the arrival of the mission, which had been advanced to about October 15th. Among the matters to be studied by the mission would be transportation and communications equipment. Mr. Palmer stated that presumably the mission would consider all of Tunisia's needs and that we should await the mission's recommendation in the matter.

Mr. Palmer added an additional word on the subject of assurances by the Tunisian Government with regard to arms furnished to Tunisia, stating that the United States' "concern" did not reflect any doubt on our part as to past promises of the Tunisian Government in this matter. He emphasized that such undertakings are normal in any event and that in this particular case are of importance to French-Tunisian understanding.

Ambassador Slim concluded by reiterating his appreciation of the actions taken and by saying that he understood very well that the United States, like Tunisia, was interested only in restoring peace and harmony to the area.

266. Telegram From the Embassy in France to the Department of State[1]

Paris, September 26, 1957—8 p.m.

1593. Embassy telegram 1518.[2] In Ambassador's absence on official visit to Bordeaux, Pineau handed to Yost this afternoon letter to the Secretary on arms to Tunis, text of which is transmitted in immediately following telegram.[3] Pineau further commented along following lines.

He first requested utmost discretion handling of this message and particularly asked that neither its receipt nor its tenor be conveyed to GOT.

Second, referring to debate in Assembly yesterday (Embassy telegram 1566)[4] and to corresponding views privately expressed by such political leaders as Pleven and Soustelle, he said it had now become difficult to see how arms could be delivered to Tunisia by any ally of France without producing parliamentary explosion and seriously damaging Atlantic alliance. Continued publicity is aggravating the situation. He cited article in this evening's *Monde* from its Washington correspondent headlined "Washington tries to conciliate Bourguiba demands with the requirements of French security" and commencing "United States will aid Tunisia to procure the arms she needs".

As a result Italians are showing themselves most reluctant to proceed with supply of arms. Pineau intends to discuss question with Pella tomorrow when latter passes through Paris. Belgians and Spaniards moreover are unwilling to supply without written consent from French which Pineau feels he cannot provide.

Recognizing however danger that Bourguiba will turn to East for arms, French Government has decided to make itself final effort to come to terms with him. In order to ensure utmost discretion, Gorse has been summoned to Paris to receive his instructions in person. He arrives this evening, will presumably return to Tunis tomorrow evening and will meet Bourguiba Sunday or Monday.

---

[1] Source: Department of State, Central Files, 772.56/9–2657. Secret; Priority; Limit Distribution. Repeated to Rome and Tunis.

[2] Telegram 1518, September 23, reported that, after reading the Secretary's message of September 22, Pineau commented that he could not act without the approval of the Council of Ministers. He noted that the arms question came at a very bad time when the Loi-Cadre for Algeria was being debated. (*Ibid.*, 772.56/9–2357)

[3] Telegram 1594, September 26, transmitted Pineau's message which complained about Tunisian efforts to compel the French to evacuate their base at Gafsa. (*Ibid.*, 772.56/9–2657)

[4] Telegram 1566, September 25, reported the strong anti-Tunisian and anti-Loi-Cadre sentiments in the French Assembly. (*Ibid.*, 751.00/9–2557)

French will propose broad understanding by which they themselves will supply necessary arms to GOT in exchange for appropriate assurances concerning current matters at issue between two Governments. Pineau was reluctant to disclose to us exactly what would be accorded and asked, but he did make clear French would expect to retain troops in Tunisia at certain points which they understood had been previously agreed by GOT.

In response our query, Pineau said supply of arms to Tunisia by GOF would doubtless cause criticism in Assembly, but it would be less severe and less damaging to Atlantic alliance than if arms were supplied by one of France's allies. He also mentioned Minister of Defense saw advantage in providing GOT with French arms which could be clearly identified if they fell into hands of Algerian rebels.

Pineau expressed hope that this final French effort with Tunisia would be successful and that United States might be prepared to give its support. When we suggested Department would presumably wish to have more precise understanding of what proposals comprised, Pineau replied that it would be disadvantageous for United States to become involved in negotiation and that he merely hoped that at appropriate moment we could say to Tunisians that we understand French are making new proposals to them and that we hope these proposals will be considered seriously and sympathetically.

Comment: It seems probable that French have concluded not only that supply of arms to Tunisia by one or more of France's allies would arouse French opinion against those allies, but also that French position in Tunisia is being more and more reduced by increasing role which United States is playing there. We can certainly applaud renewed French effort to come to understanding with GOT. If it should succeed our immediate troubles there would be over. We very much fear however that position of French troops for Tunisia may prove extremely serious stumbling block since GOF obviously considers they have right to remain whereas GOT (Tunis 256 to Department)[5] just as obviously looks on 5 or 6 present bases as only transitional. Nevertheless we very much hope that it will be possible for Department and Embassy Tunis to stave off any further action on arms matter at least until Gorse has presented new proposals to Bourguiba.

Houghton

[5] Telegram 256, September 25, reported that after France had withdrawn its division in Tunisia to reinforce forces in Algeria, Bourguiba had not agreed to the retention of any bases except Bizerte. The other bases France sought to keep were: Gabes, Sfax, Remada, the El Aouina airbase and Salammbo Headquarters (both in Tunis), and Bizerte. (*Ibid.*, 651.72/9–2557)

267. Memorandum of a Conversation, Department of State, Washington, October 1, 1957 [1]

SUBJECT

The Supply of Arms to Tunisia

PARTICIPANTS

Ambassador Herve Alphand, French Ambassador
Minister Charles Lucet, French Embassy
Mr. C. Burke Elbrick, Assistant Secretary, EUR
Mr. H.G. Torbert, Jr., WE

Ambassador Alphand, who called on Mr. Elbrick at his own request, said that he had been instructed by his Foreign Office to present to the Department in the strongest possible terms the new situation faced by the French Government in view of yesterday's loss of the confidence vote in regard to the Tunisian arms question. [2] He had also been requested to ask for clarification of a reported statement on September 30 by a Department spokesman to the effect that the Department had no knowledge of a French request to the U.S. to reconsider the position on this question and that we had promised Bourguiba to make up "any deficit" if supply from other sources was not adequate.

With regard to the first part of his instructions, Ambassador Alphand held forth at some length on the exceedingly difficult situation in which the French Government found itself. He said that the publicity regarding United States pressure and French concession on the supplying of arms to Tunisia had made it a cause celebre in French politics, particularly in conservative circles. The French regarded Bourguiba as directly responsible for supporting military action in which Frenchmen were being killed and it was therefore unpopular, to say the least, to entertain the thought of France supplying these arms. He stated without equivocation that this issue alone was responsible for the adverse confidence vote of October 1, since a swing of only about 15 votes would have changed the decision and he was certain that at least 15 votes hinged on this issue.

Mr. Elbrick replied that we fully appreciated the French dilemma in this situation and the exceedingly delicate political issue which was raised. On the other hand, we were faced with the prospect as assessed by our experts on the area that if some very

---

[1] Source: Department of State, Central Files, 772.56/10–157. Secret. Drafted by Torbert.

[2] On September 30, the Bourgès-Maunoury government lost a vote of confidence on the Loi-Cadre for Algeria by 253 to 279.

prompt action was not taken the Tunisians would accept arms from Soviet or satellite sources through Egypt or by some other channel. This was a prospect which we could only regard as a disaster. While we might not disagree with the Ambassador's assessment that Bourguiba was pushing the situation for all the traffic would bear and was trying to panic us into action, nonetheless the fact remained that he could show a perfectly justifiable requirement for arms for his own internal defense. He had committed himself to the Tunisian public to procure arms from Western sources during October. We had indicated that we would assist in obtaining the arms although we had never mentioned October. Nonetheless, Bourguiba had put himself in this position and would have to do something to produce. The situation was a most unhappy one as far as we are concerned and we could only hope that the French would be able to give most urgent attention to the problem and perhaps reach some understanding with Bourguiba before some other steps had to be taken to reach a solution.

Ambassador Alphand indicated great doubt that anything could be done prior to the formation of a new government. He did concede under questioning that there was a possibility that discussions could be undertaken which might lead to an agreement which could be sponsored by the new government. He urged most strongly that the United States adopt a position with Bourguiba that he would have to understand the very difficult position in which France was placed by the cabinet crisis which had not been foreseen at the time of earlier conversations and commitments, and urge him to exercise restraint and attempt to keep the situation in Tunisia calm until a new French Government could be formed and the situation worked out. Ambassador Alphand was most pessimistic as to the situation which would result in French-American relations should we persist in providing or urging others to provide arms to Bourguiba rather than letting the French work the problem out themselves. He said he felt strongly that this would have a profound effect on relations between our two peoples and on the Western alliance which was of much greater importance than our direct relations with Bourguiba although he realized the seriousness of this problem too. He suggested that a new government could be formed in two or three weeks and that there was still a possibility that an agreement could be reached and some shipments of arms could be received in Tunisia before the end of October thus fulfilling Bourguiba's promise to his people.

Mr. Elbrick said that this was a most difficult problem for us. However, he would urge this position upon the Department and hoped that we might be able to hold this line for a while. He expressed himself as exceedingly pessimistic that this would be successful in keeping Bourguiba quiet, even on the short term, not to mention the unhappy outlook that any new agreement would have to be ratified by the French Parliament and might thus be delayed indefinitely. He indicated that we would, of course, have to go on making plans for an alternative arrangement but would attempt to be as discreet in the matter as possible.

In answer to a second part of this representation Mr. Elbrick and Mr. Torbert indicated that they were not aware of any statement made September 30 by a Department spokesman. (It later developed a statement, in answer to a question, was made by Mr. White similar to but not exactly in the terms quoted.) The Ambassador claimed to have seen the text of such a statement in his Embassy but on telephoning to the Embassy it was discovered that this was a text of a statement on September 26. Mr. Torbert stated that to the best of his recollection the Department had received a report on the 27th of a meeting between Mr. Pineau and Mr. Yost, [3] in which Mr. Yost was told that the French had reconsidered their decision agreeing to have Italy supply arms to Tunisia. They now preferred to arrange to supply the arms herself within the framework of an agreement with Tunisia on the various outstanding military questions. As nearly as could be remembered this message did not contain a definite request to the United States to reconsider its position although a message to this general effect was contained in a cable received from Paris on the morning of September 30. [4]

Throughout the conversation Ambassador Alphand indicated on several occasions that he had been totally unaware, except through press sources, of the history of our discussions with France on this matter until yesterday morning. He said that he understood there had been correspondence between the Secretary and Pineau but that he knew nothing about it. He observed that French-American relationship could be carried on better if important matters were handled both through our Ambassador in Paris and through him here in Washington. Toward the end of the meeting Mr. Torbert remarked to Mr. Lucet that we had in fact kept the Embassy advised on a

[3] See *supra*. Telegram 1630, September 27, summarized a similar discussion between Yost and the Prime Minister. (Department of State, Central Files, 772.56/9–2757)

[4] Telegram 1656, September 30, reported that in his remarks to the Assembly that day Pineau stated: "We are, of course, asking our allies that no decision be taken with regard to the possible delivery of arms" until the results of the negotiations between France and Tunisia are known. (*Ibid.*, 772.56/9–3057) This address was summarized in greater detail in telegram 1680, October 1. (*Ibid.*, 772.56/10–157) Pineau met with Ambassador Houghton on October 1 to protest the statement by Department spokesman Lincoln White on September 30. He asked that the United States make no arms commitments to Tunisia during the French Government crisis for that might prolong the present difficulty and endanger NATO solidarity. (Telegram 1692 from Paris, October 1; *ibid.*)

number of details of these developments. Mr. Lucet acknowledged this to be a fact.

268. Memorandum of a Conversation, Department of State, Washington, October 2, 1957 [1]

SUBJECT

Call on the Secretary of Bahi Ladgham, Acting Vice President and Secretary of State for Coordination and Defense of Tunisia
Tunisian-French Relations and the Tunisian Arms Problem

PARTICIPANTS

The Secretary
Bahi Ladgham, Acting Vice President and Secretary of State for Coordination and Defense of Tunisia
Mongi Slim, Tunisian Ambassador
Habib Bourguiba, Jr., Tunisian Ambassador-designate to Rome
Ambassador James P. Richards
Joseph Palmer 2nd, Deputy Assistant Secretary
William J. Porter—AFN

Mr. Ladgham began the conversation by saying he brought to President Eisenhower and to the Secretary the warm greetings of President Bourguiba of Tunisia. The Tunisian Government and people, he said, deeply appreciate the support they have received from the United States, not only in the present difficult circumstances, but since Tunisia's accession to independence. Tunisia's nationalism, Mr. Ladgham continued, is of a different order than the nationalism of some other Arab countries. Mr. Bourguiba and his Party have never lost sight of the essentially liberal character and ideals of the Western World and they have therefore fought against the extreme type of nationalism with its xenophobia and suspicion. In this context Bourguiba has always tried to convince the Tunisian people that there are valuable elements in the French presence in Tunisia. Bourguiba always wanted independent Tunisia to emerge with a simple nationalism that would be unencumbered by extreme ideologies which would prevent or make difficult cooperation with France and the West. Tunisia, however, demanded that relations with France be on a basis of equality and had been endeavoring to place

[1] Source: Department of State, Central Files, 772.00/10–257. Secret. Drafted by Porter.

their relations on such a basis ever since she acquired her independence.

The French conception of what their relations should be with Tunisia creates many difficulties for the Tunisian Government, Mr. Ladgham said, and he went on to cite economic matters as an example. Many areas of French-Tunisian relations remain unsettled simply because the French attitude was not that of one free country negotiating with another.

Turning to Algeria, Mr. Ladgham said that the Algerian problem is not ready for solution mainly because the French are not ready to accept Algerian claims. Referring to French statements as to the doubtful role of an independent Algeria, Mr. Ladgham stated that Morocco and Tunisia are independent and have conserved their relations with the Free World, and he believed an independent Algeria would follow their example. On the international plane, he said, North Africa can be an element of stability, inclined toward cooperation with the Free World, a cooperation now rejected by some Arab countries. Such North African cooperation, in close association with France, would be most desirable. When the Tunisians support the Algerians in present circumstances, Mr. Ladgham told the Secretary, it was not because they are against France, but simply because they are for Algerian freedom.

Mr. Ladgham stated that the Algerian War cannot be limited simply by controlling frontiers. The Algerian movement, not being governmental in character, has no sense of international obligation. The movement has developed sources of arms supply that spread far beyond any particular frontier, and Mr. Ladgham said he might add, in connection with France's feelings about the Tunisians supplying arms to the Algerians, that the Algerians have no need for Tunisian arms. They are in fact better supplied with arms than the Tunisians themselves. The French of course believe that the crossing of Tunisian frontiers by Algerians has a marked effect on the war in Algiera. But this is an aspect of the struggle which the Tunisians cannot prevent because if the Tunisians oppose the Algerians in that respect this would place Tunisia on the side of France in waging the Algerian war, a politically impossible position for the Tunisians or any other Arab Government. Mr. Ladgham added that he would mention, in connection with earlier French allegations that the Tunisians were providing arms to the Algerians, that Mr. Pineau himself had admitted recently that not one Tunisian rifle had been found in Algerian possession.

The Secretary inquired whether Algerian troops are disarmed or interned when they cross into Tunisia. Mr. Ladgham replied that they are not. He said that this is a delicate question, but that essentially it involved the fact that French armed forces are crossing the frontier more or less at will and the Tunisian Government would be meting out unequal treatment if it attempted to disarm or intern the Algerians. Mr. Ladgham subsequently corrected himself, in response to a comment by Ambassador Slim, and said that the Tunisian Government disarmed such Algerian groups when it could. He said that just as the French could not control the passage of arms when they held military positions on both sides of the frontier, neither can the Tunisian Government prevent such passage. He said that about 50 rifles a day are going into Algeria, this coming to a respectable total of 1500 a month. He said that as matters stand, however, most of the weapons in the possession of the Algerians have come from the French Army and that Communists in that Army have been active in the supply of arms to the Algerians. The Tunisian Government's efforts on frontier control, Mr. Ladgham said, consist of endeavoring to disband the Algerians in areas where there are Tunisian military units. The Tunisian Government has about 3,000 men along the whole frontier, but these are generally concentrated at important points and the mountain areas could not be said to be under control. Mr. Ladgham said that Algerian thinking was stimulated by the examples of independent Morocco and Tunisia, and the Algerians believe that the French will eventually accord independence to Algeria also. The danger in this, the Minister said, is that the French military are aware of Algerian thought in that connection and believe that a new occupation of Tunisia by the French Army would tend to eliminate such Algerian hopes.

The Tunisians were in the process of negotiating their future relations with France, Mr. Ladgham said, when they encountered French intentions to continue to occupy Tunisia militarily. He said that there is a very important French military organization now in Tunisia when one considers the size of the country. The French have made it clear that they wish to keep certain bases for strategic reasons connected with the defense of the Free World, but Mr. Ladgham asserted that with the exception of Bizerte the bases are not essential for that purpose. Such bases do, however, occupy an important place in French thinking on Algeria, and that Gafsa, for instance, is used for surveillance, communications and other matters connected with the war there. In the face of this French attitude, Mr. Ladgham stated, Tunisia will not be able to negotiate a common defense accord with France. French troops, he went on, are in small groups in many places in Tunisia and are kept there solely for the purpose of exercising pressure on the Tunisian Government. As this situation continues, the Tunisian Government loses prestige at home and abroad. In the meantime solicitations are received from various undesirable sources, and propaganda pours in with a view to undermining the pro-Western Government of the country. Citing the fact that a 400-man Tunisian unit near the frontier has no rifles, he said the men listen to the radio and ask questions about their Government while French grenades fall on them and while Russian, Czech and Egyptian propaganda and offers are being received. Soldiers without rifles begin to doubt, and conversation turns increasingly to the role of the Government. In such circumstances, Mr. Ladgham felt there was a great danger that the independence of Tunisia would become an object of ridicule, while her engagements with respect to the Free World are subjected to Arab and of course the Communist criticism. Increasingly, Mr. Ladgham remarked, the theme is heard that Tunisia's claim to independence does not correspond to reality.

In this context, the Vice President said, the arms problem is critical. Tunisia had approached Belgium, Italy, Spain and Switzerland. The Belgiums said at first they were disposed to send light arms, especially NATO rifles. Later they said it was not possible to do so because the French Government was afraid the arms would find their way to Algeria. The Italians officially agreed to sell arms to the Tunisian Government but later they notified the Tunisian Government that their situation had changed because of French intervention. The Swiss and Spanish had for similar reason indicated an inability to send arms to Tunisia. Mr. Ladgham said that the Tunisian Government, as a recognized sovereign state, cannot adopt procedures common to the rebels of Algeria who procure contraband arms. This would not, the Tunisians feel, be compatible with their status and so they have turned away from that possibility.

With respect to the Egyptian offer of arms, this took the form of a proposed gift by Nasser to Mr. Mokaddam, the Tunisian Ambassador to Cairo. It occurred in conjunction with a Tunisian national campaign to raise funds to buy arms, which succeeded in raising a sum equal to $2.5 million, enough to procure weapons for 500 men. At that time the Tunisian Government appealed to friendly nations to help out, looking hopefully in the direction of the Turkish Government. However, only Egypt replied and while thanks were expressed by the Tunisian Government as a matter of form, it was clearly understood that the Egyptian gesture was merely symbolic of Arab friendship and it would be dealt with as "symbolic". The Tunisian Government had made it clear that it did not intend to accept arms from Russia or Czechoslovakia and that remains its position because, in spite of all these difficulties, the Government adheres to the ideals and values of the Free World. It sees no reason, simply because of French errors, to turn against France completely or compromise its relations with the free nations.

The position of Tunisia, Mr. Ladgham said, of course is not like that of Jordan where arms had to be sent with great speed, but the position is, nevertheless, very delicate because it is a matter of making France understand that pressure on Tunisia by France is contrary to the best interests of the Free World. Essentially what Tunisia desires is that France raise the arms embargo. The Tunisian Government understands the United States is giving sympathetic study to the problem and the Tunisian Government is greatly touched by the solicitude shown by the United States Government, and believes that in this grave French-Tunisian crisis the U.S. has exercised a most helpful influence on France. Mr. Ladgham had noticed, for example, that during the period following the Tunisian appeal to the United States incidents had practically stopped on the frontier.

Returning to the French proposals to examine common problems anew, Mr. Ladgham said he regretted to say that the French were seeking a period in which to delay matters. He said Tunisia was disposed to examine all problems but was not prepared to retard purchases of arms and it was not possible to associate the need for arms with conversations on other matters. Tunisian arms needs, he said, are small and quite simple. If France didn't wish to supply them, that is for France to decide, but the French should leave Tunisia free to obtain them elsewhere.

Mr. Ladgham concluded by saying that he knew that the Secretary is confronted by many serious problems but he hoped nevertheless that it would be recognized that Tunisia is a valuable example. Tunisia's nationalism must not fail, as Mr. Bourguiba said, because it serves the common cause. However, even the prestige of Bourguiba and others cannot definitely survive pressures among those like the 400 men without arms whom he mentioned earlier in the conversation, and the many others who are asking if it is not a tragi-comedy which the Tunisian Government is playing. The United States can help very much to eliminate equivocation in this arms matter and thus stop the flow of contradictory reports which excite the Tunisian people.

The Secretary stated that the Tunisian Government was of course aware of the great sympathy with which the U.S. viewed the granting of independence to Tunisia and the start of the new national life of that country. The United States, once itself a colony, never lost sympathy for those who sought independence and who seemed qualified to exercise independence. Independence involves heavy responsibility, the Secretary said, and it is not gained and retained by a political fact alone. Discipline, self-control and educated people are needed. It must be understood that in the world today independence cannot be treated as incompatible with interdependence, though some nations feel independence must be absolute and with no interdependence. The Secretary was sure that that kind of independence would not last. He referred to a speech he made last

April in this sense, in which he said that independence without interdependence moved fast into a twilight ending with a blackout.

The United States Government, the Secretary continued, rejoiced in the fact that the Tunisian Government and its distinguished leader accepted to an unusual degree the concept of interdependence with the Free World, and particularly with France. This wise and enlightened policy had won for the Government of Tunisia great respect and admiration. The Secretary said that in his speech, a copy of which he handed to Mr. Ladgham, he had made the point that communist doctrine teaches ways to amalgamate extreme nationalism by encouraging it to cut traditional ties with the West. Once this had been done, the task of amalgamating the country concerned with the Communist World became easier. Though the Tunisian Government is a young government, its mature judgment enables it to see the danger and avoid it. Thus, the Tunisian Government won the admiration of the U.S. and others who wished to see independence achieve its full meaning for the Tunisian people.

The Secretary said that with regard to the French, we must recognize they have been facing difficulties since the First World War. Losses of that war have affected the strength and quality of French leadership ever since. Many of those who might lead France today lie in the trenches of Verdun. France was so weakened that she has never since been able or felt herself strong enough to do the wise thing if that appeared to diminish French prestige. The French tend to refuse to accept change until it is inevitable and it then usually requires more serious concessions than would have been necessary earlier. After World War I, had the French been conciliatory there would never have been a Hitler.

In Indo-China, it had been very difficult to get the French to accept independence for Laos and Cambodia. The U.S. had been able to exercise a useful influence there, and the French eventually accorded them independence although again this involved concessions which went beyond those necessary in the earlier stages of that problem.

In the cases of Morocco and Tunisia, the Secretary said, it should be recognized that the French showed considerable statesmanship. With respect to Algeria, we must also recognize that this is a difficult problem for the French to deal with and we should look with a measure of sympathy at their situation. Tunisia is a country with a promising and expanding future, but the French future appears to hold diminishing prestige and power. This need not be the case for the French, the Secretary went on, as the British example proves. There is no need for loss of greatness and authority in meeting such problems, just as the United States did not lose by granting independence to the Philippines. Only the USSR clings to the belief that something acquired must never be let go, and that country proved its lack of greatness in its failure to release Hungary.

The Secretary then discussed the problem of Tunisia's arms needs. He recalled that he had sent a message to Mr. Bourguiba on September 21 [*22*], 1957, recognizing that Tunisia as an independent country had the right to arm for its security, and assuring him that his needs would be met. The Secretary said he had expressed the assumption that arms would be used only for internal security and defense purposes and he added that he had assumed also that Tunisia would not find it difficult to agree to reasonable conditions of that kind. The Secretary assured Mr. Ladgham that his statement had been made deliberately and solemnly and that Mr. Ladgham could be confident that he would adhere to it. The Secretary said he did not wish to disguise the fact that the French are urging that we defer action until they had an opportunity to discuss with the Tunisians the possibility of the French supplying arms themselves to Tunisia. The Secretary commented that he was uncertain about the present status of the matter as the French Government did not appear now to be in a position to hold the kind of talks which it regards as necessary before it can meet the urgent desires of the Tunisian Government to obtain arms. We are therefore prepared to reexamine the problem with the Tunisians. He had talked to Mr. Pella, the Secretary continued, and Mr. Pella had then discussed the matter with Mr. Pineau, but the Secretary was not quite sure of the results. The Secretary then expressed the hope that the Tunisians would agree that the matter should not be handled either with respect to form or timing in a way which would unnecessarily injure the relations of the United States with France. There is no use in throwing U.S. influence away unnecessarily, the Secretary said. We must recognize this and avoid if possible a reaction in France. In saying this, the Secretary added, he was not offering it as a pretext for evasion or delay because the Tunisians had our promise and could count on it. It was essential to try to find a formula to meet Tunisia's needs and to avoid an open breach with the French. If we could not avoid such a breach, the Secretary said, we accept that, but we must do everything we can to minimize its effects.

The Secretary indicated that we would ascertain the Italian position. It appeared, he said, that because of the fall of the French Government there would be more of a delay than anticipated in dealing with the problem. The Secretary added that he was somewhat surprised that the Governments of Spain and Switzerland, who are not allies of France, had given the Tunisians negative replies. Mr. Ladgham said the replies were not clearly negative, but could be called so by the general attitude of the two governments.

After an inquiry from Ambassador Richards as to the type of arms the Tunisians have in mind, Mr. Ladgham said that the list had been sent to us. Mr. Palmer confirmed that we had received it and it contains items different than those mentioned to Ambassador Richards in Tunisia earlier in this year. At that time the Tunisian Government was primarily concerned with obtaining transportation communications equipment.

Mr. Ladgham said that he was sorry to tell the Secretary that incidents had started again on the frontier. In the last day or so, the Secretary remarked, since the fall of the Government, the French army may not be under as close control as usual. He said that we must all recognize the danger and he reiterated his hope that the Tunisian Government would continue to show restraint and caution. It was easy, the Secretary said, to tear something up but hard to put it together again.

In the final discussion the Secretary indicated that he thought the U.S. and Tunisian Governments should work together to solve this problem as rapidly as possible in a way which would result in Tunisia obtaining its arms requirements but avoid an open breach with the French. He suggested to Mr. Palmer that additional meetings be held with the Tunisians to work the matter out in this spirit. Mr. Palmer said that we would give further attention to the questions discussed and be in touch with our Tunisian friends in the next few days. Both Mr. Ladgham and the Ambassador said that they would be in New York for another week and would be at our disposition.

---

269. Telegram From the Department of State to the Embassy in France [1]

Washington, October 3, 1957—8:53 p.m.

1306. Separate message contains letter from Secretary to Pineau for early delivery on subject supply of arms to Tunisia. [2] As that message suggests it is hoped you will be able to have early, full and frank discussion with Pineau and other pertinent officials to explore whatever possibilities exist of a prompt solution to Tunisian arms

---

[1] Source: Department of State, Central Files, 772.56/10–357. Secret. Drafted by Torbert. Repeated to Tunis and Rome.

[2] Telegram 1304, October 3, not printed. (*Ibid.*)

crisis. Every attempt should be made stimulate positive French suggestions. These explorations should be held within framework that if other Western countries do not supply light arms for internal security to Tunisia or make firm arrangements satisfactory to Tunisians promptly US feels it is committed to assure such supply. Our strong first preference remains that French Government itself undertake supply. Second preference would be supply by Italy, Belgium, or other friendly Western European country including possibly such non-NATO countries as Sweden or Switzerland. We may instruct our Embassies in these countries to explore supply possibilities. Throughout conversations you should stress our sincere concern to find solution acceptable to France but our determination that some way must be found of supplying arms without excessive delay.

Dept convinced that to supply Tunisia with the means of fulfilling her security needs, far from aggravating present problems or increasing present tensions, would greatly contribute to a détente, relax pressures on the Tunisian Government and enable the present regime to approach the settlement of other problems strengthened by public confidence in the demonstrated fruitfulness of Tunisia's policy of collaboration with the West. Such an atmosphere would, we believe, immeasurably increase the Tunisian Government's freedom of maneuver and ability to compromise in reaching a settlement with France. We therefore believe that France and the United States and other Western countries have every interest in reaching an immediate decision on the Tunisian arms problem.

At same time you may advise GOF as you deem appropriate regarding Secretary's conversation Ladgham (Deptel 217).[3] You should mention that Ladgham and other Tunisians have indicated strong desire reach settlement outstanding questions with France but clearly stated unacceptability tying arms supply to such settlement. Within this framework we would be prepared do whatever we appropriately can to facilitate such settlement. Report developments urgently.[4]

Dulles

[3] Telegram 217, October 3, was based on the memorandum of conversation, *supra*. (Department of State, Central Files, 651.72/10–357)

[4] Ambassador Houghton reported in telegram 1173, October 5, that he had delivered the Secretary's message to Pineau. Pineau agreed that Tunisia should receive arms from the West, but urged that this not be done while France was in the midst of a government crisis. (*Ibid.*, 772.56/10–557)

270. Memorandum of a Conversation, Department of State, Washington, October 9, 1957 [1]

SUBJECT

Tunisian Arms

PARTICIPANTS

Sir Harold Caccia, British Ambassador
Viscount Hood, Minister, British Embassy
The Secretary
William M. Rountree, Assistant Secretary, NEA
Joseph Palmer 2nd, Deputy Assistant Secretary for African Affairs
Horace G. Torbert, Jr., WE

The Secretary said that he understood that the Tunisians have requested British assistance in obtaining arms and that the Foreign Office is considering the United Kingdom position in this matter. [2] He went on to say that, as the Ambassador undoubtedly was aware, we have had a similar request in response to which we have given the Tunisians assurances that we regard them as entitled to obtain arms for internal security and that we will assure that arrangements are made to supply them from the West. He said that we had been hopeful that the Italians might feel able to meet the Tunisian requirements and he had talked to Mr. Pella about this possibility. [3] Apparently the Italians are now wavering, however, and the Tunisians are becoming highly critical of what they regard as Italy's vacillating attitude. The Secretary indicated that he did not know what possibility there might be of the United Kingdom supplying arms, but that we would welcome such action if it were possible.

The Secretary continued by saying that this was a problem of considerable urgency to which we would have to face up in the next few days. He emphasized his view that it would be a scandal if Tunisia could not get arms from the West. Tunisia is a friendly nation. As a member of the United Nations, it enjoys the right of self-defense under Article 51 of the Charter, as the Secretary had observed in a recent letter to Mr. Pineau on this subject. [4] If, under these circumstances, the West denies arms to Tunisia, we would not be treating her as a sovereign state but as a dependency of France

[1] Source: Department of State, Central Files, 772.56/10–957. Secret. Drafted by Palmer.

[2] First Secretary of the British Embassy, Willie Morris, informed Bovey on October 7 that the Tunisians had requested arms on September 27. (Memorandum of conversation by Bovey, October 7; *ibid.*, 772.56/10–757)

[3] Dulles and Italian Foreign Minister Giuseppe Pella discussed this subject briefly on September 25, during a visit to Washington by Pella. (Memorandum of conversation by Torbert; *ibid.*, 772.56/9–2557)

[4] Summarized in telegram 1306, *supra*.

and Tunisia would be justified in obtaining her arms where she could. The Secretary said he felt the stakes were too high to permit this to happen. We do not want to make the French governmental crisis any more difficult than it is, but we cannot permit this consideration to dominate our policy to the extent that it might result in the loss of Tunisia and North Africa to the West. He felt perhaps it would be possible for us to defer actual delivery of arms until after a new French Government had assumed office, but that we could not delay establishing and identifying the source of arms and making the necessary arrangements for procurement and eventual delivery. The Secretary went on to say that it would be highly desirable if responsibility for the supply of arms could be shared. Sir Harold intervened to confirm the agreement of his Government with this thought.

The Secretary emphasized the great threat that would be posed to Western Europe and the West if the Soviets were to obtain a foothold in this area which enabled them to extend their domination over North Africa. He said that he had always believed that Africa is the natural hinterland of Europe. It contains the raw materials, the opportunities for investment, etc., which can keep Europe strong and vital. The loss of North Africa would not only endanger Europe in a strategic sense, but would very likely result in the loss of the whole African continent. The Secretary emphasized that Western Europe simply cannot afford to see this happen.

Sir Harold confirmed the fact that the British had been approached by the Tunisians with respect to arms. He said that he felt that the British Government saw the problem very much as we did. He said that he would draw the Secretary's views to the attention of his government and would let us have further indication of what the British feel should be done about the situation.

271. Memorandum From the Assistant Secretary of State for Near Eastern, South Asian, and African Affairs (Rountree) to the Secretary of State [1]

Washington, October 15, 1957.

SUBJECT

Status of and Program of Action on the Tunisian Arms Request

Discussion:

1. Our assessment of the Tunisian political situation indicates that the time remaining for Bourguiba to deal with the arms problem is dwindling rapidly. More than five weeks have passed since he requested United States assistance and three weeks since we assured him of our help. During this period our appeals to the French have been of no avail. Pineau has indicated that it is "out of the question" for the caretaker government to take effective action on this matter which was an issue in the debate leading up to its fall to the present caretaker government. He also warned that if the U.S. should supply arms before a new government takes office, it could have an extremely adverse effect on the internal French political scene. Meanwhile, Bourguiba and his pro-moderate colleagues find themselves increasingly subjected to the internal pressures of public opinion and the external pressures created by continuing border incidents and Egyptian propaganda. In his weekly speech of October 10, Bourguiba felt it necessary to reiterate his earlier public promise that Tunisia would have arms delivered in the country by the end of October. He added, in this connection, that Tunisian representatives had been sent to Italy, Sweden, Egypt, Belgium and the United States. It is, in fact, increasingly apparent that if we are to meet the situation in Tunisia, we must have publicly identified a source of arms and have effected at least a partial token delivery by October 30. It is, of course, possible that even this date could be made unrealistic as the result of another military incident between French and Tunisian forces.

2. Since your conversation with Ambassador Caccia on October 9, we have been in close touch with the British Embassy which has provided us with an informal summary of Mr. Selwyn Lloyd's views on this problem. This summary is attached at Tab A [2] and may be summarized as follows:

---

[1] Souce: Department of State, Central Files, 772.56/10–1557. Secret. Drafted by Palmer and Porter.

[2] Not printed.

A. Lloyd considers it a vital Western interest that Bourguiba obtain arms from the West and not from the Communists and feels Bourguiba should not be put in the position of having to choose between asking the Communists for arms and accepting French conditions.

B. Lloyd suggests the U.S. and U.K. give Tunisia a *confidential* commitment that the two countries would be prepared to *consider* a modest request for arms without any commitment as to types and delivery dates.

C. Lloyd also suggests that first the U.S. and then the U.K. inform the French of the foregoing, with every regard to French sensibilities. In view of indications from the French Foreign Office at the working level that they may wish to use the denial of arms to Tunisia as a bargaining weapon in any negotiations with that country, the British would propose to suggest to the French that actual deliveries could probably be delayed until Franco-Tunisian talks were under way. At the same time, Lloyd recognizes that the risks of making Bourguiba await the outcome of a Franco-Tunisian conference are too great.

D. Finally, Lloyd suggests parallel U.S. and U.K. approaches to the Belgian and Italian Governments to inform them of our concern in an effort to get them to help persuade the French of the need for action.

3. We have reacted to the foregoing as follows:

A. We have warmly welcomed the British interest, noting that our general assessments of the dangers in Tunisia are similar.

B. We have clarified the nature of our commitment to the Tunisians, pointing out that it is more far-reaching than that which the British contemplate and that we believe we have passed the point where confidential assurances can hold the position in Tunisia. We have added that we think that we must very shortly give Bourguiba definite assurances as to the source of his arms and delivery plans. We may, in fact, have to assure token deliveries by the end of October.

C. In light of the need for rapid action, we have put urgently to the British a list of questions calculated to ascertain their reactions to the elements of the plan of action set forth under "Recommendations" below. The list of questions is attached at Tab B.[3] We have not yet had the British replies, which will probably be communicated to you by Mr. Selwyn Lloyd.

Recommendations:

1. That you endeavor to obtain Mr. Selwyn Lloyd's urgent agreement to the following plan of action:

A. The U.S. and U.K. would immediately inform President Bourguiba that if we are not successful in finding a source of arms for him in Western Europe by October 23, the two Governments will undertake to supply the Tunisian Government's legitimate

[3] Not printed.

needs. (The date of October 23 is chosen as the day before Bourguiba's regular weekly broadcast when he will probably be under the most pressure.)

B. At about the same time as A, the U.S. and U.K. would make coordinated approaches to Sweden, Italy, Belgium and Denmark with a view towards ascertaining whether those governments would be willing to make arms available to Tunisia on an immediate basis.

C. At about the same time as A and B, the U.S. and U.K. would inform the French of the foregoing and join to make a final appeal to Mr. Pineau to find some way which would permit France to deal with Tunisian arms requirements. Thus we could reiterate our strong hope that France itself would find it possible to supply arms to Tunisia, thereby obviating the need for alternative arrangements. We could also make it clear that if Mr. Pineau does not feel France can move alone in this matter, we would be delighted to have France join our two countries in supplying the arms.

D. If the foregoing approaches should fail to produce results by October 23, the U.S. and U.K. would immediately begin talks with Tunisia to decide on types, quantities and delivery dates and would, in any event, proceed to send a token shipment of arms to Tunisia before the end of October.

2. That if the foregoing is acceptable to Mr. Lloyd as a basis for proceeding, you suggest our two staffs immediately proceed to work out the implementing details.

3. That if Mr. Lloyd does not feel the U.K. can go along with the foregoing and has no satisfactory alternative plan, you inform him that we feel we must proceed on these lines and express the hope that the U.K. will use its influence with the French to assure their understanding.

I shall accompany Mr. Selwyn Lloyd when he calls on you.

272. Memorandum of a Conversation, Department of State, Washington, October 15, 1957[1]

SUBJECT

Tunisian Arms Request

PARTICIPANTS

Selwyn Lloyd, British Foreign Secretary
Sir Harold Caccia, K.C.M.G., Ambassador of Great Britain
Lord Hood, Minister, Embassy of Great Britain
Dennis Laskey, Assistant to British Foreign Secretary
Willie Morris, First Secretary, Embassy of Great Britain
The Secretary
C. Burke Elbrick, Assistant Secretary, EUR
Joseph Palmer 2nd, Deputy Assistant Secretary, NEA
William N. Dale, BNA
John A. Bovey, Jr., AFN

The Secretary remarked that the United Kingdom and the United States seemed close to agreement on the handling of the Tunisian arms request, and that it only remained to clear up questions of timing. He explained that we had already undertaken a commitment to Bourguiba to see that Tunisia's arms needs were met.

Mr. Lloyd said that the only real point of difference the British had with our proposals for handling this matter was that they felt it essential that we both first inform the French of what we propose to do.

Mr. Palmer explained that although we had committed ourselves to see that Tunisia's needs were met, we had not as yet set any date with the Tunisians after which the United States would be prepared to act. This was a new element in the proposed joint action.

The Secretary said that we would probably not be able to find other sources of supply, and that he felt it was neither practical nor dignified to "shop around". We had taken the position that Tunisia was a sovereign and independent nation and we should therefore be prepared to make available a modest quantity of arms destined for Tunisia's own security needs and not to be transferred elsewhere. He said that he hoped the impact of joint US–UK action would provide insurance against the French reacting violently against either of us. The Secretary said it was unlikely that the Belgians or Italians would relish the prospect of doing an unpleasant job for us. Mr. Pella, for example, had seemed genuinely convinced of the need for helping out the Tunisians when he was here, but Italian relations with

[1] Source: Department of State, Central Files, 772.56/10–1557. Secret. Drafted by Bovey.

France had obviously made it necessary for him to accede to French objections in the matter.

Mr. Lloyd said that the British Ambassador in Paris [2] was unhappy over the prospect of British action in this matter but felt the situation would be somewhat improved by acting in concert with the United States. The Secretary said our Embassy naturally had misgivings too but that he thought we must move ahead.

Mr. Lloyd said that he still saw advantages in informing the Italians and the Belgians of our course even if they were unable to act in supplying arms, and Mr. Caccia added that they would be more likely to act if the United States and United Kingdom made clear that we were already committed. The Secretary said he saw no harm in approaching the Belgians and Italians providing this involved no undue delay and providing we did not create the impression we were trying to back out of our own responsibilities and to get some one else to do a disagreeable job for us. The wider the responsibilities in such an operation were spread, the better it would be for all. [3]

Mr. Lloyd made clear that the British proposals to us did not envisage any British commitment to Bourguiba at this point beyond stating that the United Kingdom was prepared to consider making available a modest amount of arms without commitment as to types or dates of delivery. They had as yet no specific request from the Tunisians. Mr. Palmer said we had as yet no commitment on dates and that the October deadline was one imposed by Mr. Bourguiba on himself in speaking to the Tunisian public. The Secretary said that the important thing was not simultaneous deliveries but rather our making it clear that the United States and the United Kingdom were acting in concert. He suggested we might divide between us responsibility for the various items on the list submitted to us by the Tunisians.

Mr. Lloyd felt that our representations to the French should be made on the basis that we were going to proceed to make arms available if the French were unable to do it. It was pointed out that the French would probably be unable to move during the present government crisis.

---

[2] Sir Hubert Miles Gladwyn Jebb.

[3] Telegrams 626 to Brussels and 1598 to Rome, both October 16, instructed the Embassies to make coordinated approaches with the British to discover whether Belgium or Italy would be willing to join in the undertaking to provide arms to Tunisia for internal security purposes. (Department of State, Central Files, 772.56/10–1657) Telegram 1449, from Rome, October 19, reported that the Italians were unwilling to make an immediate commitment due to the difficulties it might create for the French. (*Ibid.*, 772.56/10–1957) Telegram 572 from Brussels, October 19, stated that the Belgians were unwilling to act without consulting the French. (*Ibid.*)

The Secretary said that our approaches in Paris should probably be made severally but on the same day. Mr. Lloyd agreed to guide the British part of the operation from here and it was left that the Department would work out instructions in collaboration with the British Embassy here.

The Secretary said—and Mr. Lloyd indicated agreement—that it would be a tragedy if the whole Western position in Europe should be jeopardized by inaction in Tunisia and the loss of North Africa.

273. Memorandum of a Conversation, Department of State, Washington, October 17, 1957 [1]

SUBJECT

U.S.-British discussions—The Tunisian Arms Question

PARTICIPANTS

Ambassador Hervé Alphand, French Ambassador
Mr. Jean de la Grandville, Counselor, French Embassy
Mr. C. Burke Elbrick, Assistant Secretary, EUR
Mr. H.G. Torbert, Jr., WE

Ambassador Alphand called at his request and stated that his primary interest was in learning what had occurred at the discussions between the Secretary and Selwyn Lloyd. Mr. Elbrick said that he had not been present for the whole conversation and that a very large part had dealt with the Middle East. He thought that the Ambassador should talk to someone in NEA to get the report on this subject at first hand since they had the whole story.

Mr. Elbrick read Ambassador Alphand the ticker item from London regarding the visit of Prime Minister Macmillan to the United States on Tuesday and Wednesday of next week. [2] He said that we were under some apprehension that this might be interpreted as a sign that there was a more grave crisis in world affairs than perhaps actually existed. However, we hope world opinion would interpret the meeting for what it actually is, namely, an opportunity to discuss serious current problems between the Chiefs of Government of two countries with great many mutual interests.

---

[1] Source: Department of State, Central Files, 772.56/10–1757. Secret. Drafted by Torbert.

[2] October 22 and 23.

Selwyn Lloyd was already here and would remain in this country for the meetings.

[Here follows discussion of the Yugoslav-German problem.]

Mr. Elbrick then said the Secretary and Mr. Lloyd had discussed the problem of the urgent necessity of furnishing arms to the Tunisian Government. The British had indicated they shared our opinion that a positive solution of this problem cannot be longer postponed. As a result Ambassador Jebb and Ambassador Houghton both made representations to the French Foreign Office today to the effect that it was necessary to draw up an immediate plan of action and that we felt that at least token shipments of arms must be made to Tunisia during October.[3] We still hope the French will see their way clear to do this themselves or will associate themselves with our action. We are also talking to the Belgians and the Italians in the same sense. If the French find themselves unable to take any action on this matter or to associate themselves with it, the United Kingdom and the United States will feel obliged to proceed, in any event. He inquired whether Ambassador Alphand had any further word on this subject from Paris.

The Ambassador reacted strongly . . . . He said that he had understood that nothing would be done on this subject until he had a chance to talk to the Secretary about it. He had advised his Government in this sense and he was completely astounded that we were taking a position on this matter without having talked to him further. Mr. Elbrick said that he had had no such understanding. His recollection was that he had told Ambassador Alphand that if it were advantageous for him to see the Secretary, he would see that the Ambassador had an appointment to explain the French position. He had, in fact, suggested that the Ambassador do so in any case. Meanwhile we had had several further conversations in Paris and had the French Government's reactions and these were available to the Secretary. We had hoped to delay the matter and had, indeed, delayed it for a while but the situation did not develop favorably as we had hoped.

The Ambassador . . . observed that the United States was obviously taking a decision affecting France without consulting her. Mr. Elbrick pointed out that that was exactly what we were doing today and, in fact, had been doing for some time. The Ambassador said this was not consultation but an ultimatum. It was a most serious action. Perhaps it would enable us to keep Tunisia but he did not know about France. France had a caretaker government, was in a most delicate position, and it was unthinkable that we should do

[3] The substance of this démarche was spelled out in telegram 1452 to Paris, October 16. (*Ibid.*, 772.56/10–1657)

such a thing to an ally. Furthermore, the thing was being done behind his back and he felt most bitterly about it. Mr. Elbrick said it was not being done behind his back at all. We were advising him and trying to give the French every possible chance to meet a danger which we see but apparently France does not see. Ambassador Alphand said he saw no alternative but for him to see the Secretary immediately. He thought the United States policy was disastrous. He had thought so a year ago at the time of the Suez Crisis and could not understand our action then. He said he could not understand it now. We had made one mistake after another throughout the Middle East and in North Africa.

Mr. Elbrick said that he did not think the Secretary was unaware of the serious issues involved here or the French views on the matter but if the Ambassador desired he would arrange an appointment with the Secretary as soon as possible. As to our taking a decision in the last day or so behind his back, the actual decision was taken some weeks ago when we committed ourselves to Bourguiba that we would see that he received a supply of arms. The only thing that remained was the question of timing and the exact source. We had consulted France through every stage and were consulting her now, and hope that she will see her way clear to solve the problem. Meanwhile, Mr. Elbrick said he would have to protest the attitude that everything France did was right and that everything the United States did was wrong. He could point out quite a number of mistakes in French policy. As a matter of fact, French North African policy left a great deal to be desired from our point of view.

Ambassador Alphand . . . observed . . . that he saw no hope for France without the alliance but did not see how the alliance could exist when we deliberately went against the interests of an important ally in a matter vital to it. Mr. Elbrick said that it was not a new thing for allies to disagree. It was unfortunate and we tried to agree as much as possible but sometimes there came an issue over which we could not see eye to eye. Close alliances were created in order to surmount such disagreements and there was no reason why this alliance should not continue on a close and friendly basis, even if we have to split on this one point. We were exceedingly sorry about the difficulties that France was having and we particularly realize that they were in an unpleasant situation at the present on Algeria. Mr. Alphand asked whether we saw any way of keeping these arms from going to Algeria. Mr. Elbrick indicated that they were being provided for defensive purposes and that he thought the supply provided at this time would not be significant as a possible source for Algeria even should the Tunisians wish to use them for this purpose. However, as they had no arms for their own security forces, he felt this unlikely.

Ambassador Alphand commented that the Communists would use this action very effectively and he thought that it might have most serious consequences in the formation of the new French Government. Mr. Elbrick said that we realize there were these possibilities, the Communists would always take advantage of such a situation, and it was a risk that we would have to take.

Mr. Elbrick asked whether he still wanted to see the Secretary. The Ambassador said that after all there was nothing he could say now. He would have to wait for instructions. (He later requested such a meeting for October 18.)

In departing, Ambassador Alphand said that he spoke as he had only because he was a close friend of Mr. Elbrick and of America, and felt he could do so. He hoped he had not given offense or damaged the friendship. He hoped that his assessment of the bad effects of this were wrong, but he was afraid they were not.

---

274. Memorandum of a Conversation, Department of State, Washington, October 18, 1957 [1]

SUBJECT

Tunisian Arms Request

PARTICIPANTS

Mr. Herve Alphand, French Ambassador
Mr. Charles Lucet, French Minister
Mr. John Foster Dulles, Secretary of State
Mr. C. Burke Elbrick, Assistant Secretary, EUR
Mr. Joseph Palmer 2nd, Deputy Assistant Secretary, AF

Ambassador Alphand said that Mr. Pineau had received the Secretary's most recent message with respect to the Tunisian arms request and had asked him to convey certain reactions. [2] The Ambassador continued by saying that the French entirely understand

[1] Source: Department of State, Central Files, 772.56/10–1857. Secret. Drafted by Palmer.

[2] In telegram 1959 from Paris, October 17, Ambassador Houghton indicated that he had presented the Department's aide-mémoire to Pineau earlier that day. Since the French Government had officially resigned, Pineau could only offer his personal assessment that France's reaction would be most bitter if the United States went through with its intention to supply arms to Tunisia during the interregnum. Houghton urged delay until investiture of a new French Government and recommended that the United States ask Bourguiba not to publicize the U.S. assurance that he would soon be receiving arms. (*Ibid.*, 772.56/10–1757)

the United States reasoning in this matter. They appreciate that the shipment involved would be of a token nature, that the arms would be used only in Tunisia and that we are attempting to prevent the Tunisians from purchasing the arms from the Soviet bloc. Mr. Pineau wished to emphasize to the Secretary, however, that he was highly worried about the U.S. and the UK taking any action on this problem in the absence of a French Government. Particularly in light of Mr. Bourguiba's speech of yesterday in which he had expressed his pleasure at the recent improvement in French-Tunisian relations, it is impossible to believe that the United States and the United Kingdom could not postpone action on the arms request until after a new French Government has been formed. If the proposed U.S.–UK action should become publicly known in France, it would, in Mr. Pineau's opinion, be impossible to avoid a disastrous effect on French opinion. The Communists and neutrals would use this information to charge that there is no solidarity in NATO and that the British and Americans are making arms available to the Tunisians which will enable the latter to kill French soldiers. The Ambassador said that he knew, of course, that such charges would have no foundation in fact, but they would be widely believed in France. He went on to say that there was of course a particular need for close solidarity in the NATO alliance during the present world crisis. Under these circumstances, he strongly urged that the United States Government defer further action on this matter until a new French Government had been formed. He felt certain that the Tunisian problem would, in fact, be one of the first things dealt with by a new government.

The Secretary said there was no U.S. desire to do anything which would be either embarrassing to France in its present governmental crisis nor which would affect the solidarity of NATO. He added we were not going to do anything in this matter any sooner than is necessary to prevent a major disaster in North Africa. He could not say when events might require such action. We have tried our best to delay as long as possible and the more time we can gain, the better. But when the time comes when decisive action is called for, we cannot afford to wait any longer in making at least a token delivery. We do not intend to take such action one day sooner than is necessary to save the situation. At the same time, we cannot undertake to delay until after a French Government is formed. The Secretary concluded by saying that obviously the Ambassador could not give us any assurance as to when a French Government could be formed and, in those circumstances, France could not expect the whole world to stand still until the parliamentary crisis was resolved.

Ambassador Alphand reiterated his concern about exploitation by leftist elements in France and again urged that no action be taken until a French Government was formed. The Secretary reiterated the reasons why it was impossible for us to give such a commitment. The Ambassador then said that if it were possible to give such an assurance, he would be willing to give personal commitments that as soon as a new French Government were formed he would (1) recommend that it approve the proposed U.S.–UK action and (2) that France itself undertake the supply of arms. . . .

The Secretary said that he did not regard Bourguiba's appeal as blackmail. He said that no newly independent government could accept a situation in which it is denied the right to purchase arms for its legitimate self-defense requirements. If it did so, it could not then be regarded as independent. He pointed out that Tunisia has the right of self-defense under Article 51 of the Charter and that Bourguiba has no choice except to exercise that right by buying arms where he can. Otherwise, he could not survive in office. The Secretary pointed out that the Tunisian arms request is a logical consequence of the French action in having granted independence to Tunisia and that it would be nothing but a mockery if the West, under these circumstances, denied arms to Tunisia.

The French Ambassador observed that if Tunisia were in fact a truly independent state, it should behave like one by denying aid to the Algerians. The fact that it gave assistance to the Algerian cause through the arms traffic, maintenance of hospitals and training centers for the FLN, etc., indicated that it was not truly independent.

The Secretary said he could not agree with this analysis. The facts adduced by Mr. Alphand did not demonstrate that Tunisia was not independent but merely that it followed policies which were regarded by France as inimical to her.

Mr. Alphand said that he did not believe that it would be useful to pursue these arguments further. He noted that Ambassador Houghton had mentioned the date of October 23 when the United States and the UK might approach the Tunisian Government with respect to our further plans. He again pled that we postpone such action.

The Secretary reiterated that we could not allow a situation to develop which might permit the Soviets to gain control of Tunisia, Morocco and Algeria. Such action might result in the loss of Europe. We see the greatest dangers in this situation and so do the British. Since the Ambassador is prepared to recommend action to a new government, so presumably does he. In such circumstances, we cannot stand aside and allow this to happen merely because the French Government cannot act. The problem involved is primarily one of timing. If we can postpone action, we shall do so. With respect to the date of October 23, this was a possible date we had in mind to acquaint Mr. Bourguiba of our plans. Bourguiba has been promising his people that he would have arms by the end of October. If we can get him to accept the idea of prolongation, we shall do so. If, however, it appears necessary that we move ahead, we shall have to feel free to adopt that course.

275. Telegram From the Department of State to the Embassy in Tunisia [1]

Washington, November 2, 1957—4:27 p.m.

297. Deptel 295 to Tunis [2] and previous. For Tunis.

A. Department believes that view time elapsed since October 21 when Bourguiba agreed brief delay re arms delivery and growing likelihood Egyptian move, action should now be initiated with respect immediate token shipment for GOT.

British suggested today we plan inform French and Tunisians November 6 we ready commence delivery on chance new Government will have been formed previous day. [3] We informing British we believe it more advisable tell both GOF and GOT immediately date on which we propose commence deliveries unless agreement on arms meanwhile reached between GOF and GOT which obviates need for such action.

B. Therefore as soon as you ascertain your British colleague has received similar instructions you should inform Bourguiba as follows:

1. Subject to agreement on terms and conditions, US prepared facilitate purchase of arms by GOT from US Government stocks and to deliver token shipment November 12 unless GOF and GOT have meanwhile reached agreement obviating need such action.

2. US token shipment would consist of 500 rifles and 50,000 rounds ammunition at approximate total price $60,000 including handling charges.

[1] Source: Department of State, Central Files, 772.56/11–257. Secret; Niact. Drafted by Palmer and Bovey and approved by Murphy. Also sent to Paris, Tripoli, Rome, and Brussels; repeated to London.

[2] Telegram 295, November 1, stated that the British were prepared to make delivery of a 70,000-pound-sterling arms shipment as soon as final U.S. instructions to Tunis on this matter were formulated. (*Ibid.*, 772.56/11–157)

[3] Willie Morris conveyed this suggestion from Lloyd to Palmer. The British did not wish to damage Gaillard's prospects of forming a government. (Memorandum of conversation by Palmer, November 2; *ibid.*, 772.56/11–257)

3. Notes outlined Deptel 267 [4] should be exchanged forthwith.

4. Embassy should first propose cash settlement in local currency. If GOT unable undertake you should then explain following terms would apply this and any subsequent orders: repayments in equal annual installments within three year period of original dollar value of material furnished to be made in Tunisian currency unrestricted in use computed at exchange rate in effect at time of repayment provided that if Tunisia then has more than one legal rate of exchange—rate would be fixed by mutual agreement. In addition interest rate would be at 4 percent per annum. If President Bourguiba feels he cannot accept these terms you should report immediately but you may meanwhile proceed with exchange notes and arrangements for delivery.

5. UK Government is associated with US in this action and British Ambassador furnishing GOT list items they ready deliver same date and terms therefor.

C. Actual transfer to GOT token shipment will thus require 1) exchange notes and 2) agreement in principle cash settlement or terms outlined above. Further orders would include token shipment and involve Defense letter of offer and Tunisian letter acceptance containing agreement on types, quantities and prices items to be furnished, delivery dates, etc. List items available for sale in addition those included token shipment and prices forwarded separately by Pouch.

D. When exchange notes completed and sale arrangements agreed to Embassy Tunis should arrange details delivery with CO Wheelus through Embassy Tripoli so as be ready move for November 12 delivery.

For Paris.

When your British colleague similarly instructed Ambassador should inform French above decision and explain our estimate situation emphasizing growing danger Egyptian move renders further delay impractical in our opinion. Add we would hope for minimum publicity but cannot be confident this will be case. We hope French will be able associate themselves with this action before November 12. [5]

---

[4] Telegram 267, October 21, outlined the terms of the transaction as stipulated in the notes to be exchanged. (*Ibid.*, 772.56/10–2157) The text of the notes is in despatch 241 from Tunis, November 7. (*Ibid.*, 772.56/11–757.)

[5] The British and U.S. aides-mémoire were delivered separately to Jean-Henri Daridan, Director General of Political and Economic Affairs at the Foreign Ministry, on November 4. He expressed his regret that the move had not been delayed until the new French Government had the opportunity to consider the matter. (Despatch 748, November 5; *ibid.*, 772.56/11–557) In Washington, Torbert had a conversation with French Minister Charles Lucet, in which Torbert indicated the token arms delivery would be made even if the French and Tunisians came to an agreement. Lucet responded that this act would be viewed as an ultimatum to the new government. (Memorandum of conversation by Looram, November 4; *ibid.*, 772.56/11–457)

If not and we required make any public statement we will say we hope France will associate herself with it in future (Ambassador Tunis should so advise Bourguiba).

Paris may add we are moving forward in belief we have given French all reasonable time deal with it since Bourguiba's appeal to US on September 4 and are again allowing week's delay despite grave risks to Western interests Tunisia.

Paris should also inform French of composition US token shipment and nature assurances we are requesting.

For Tripoli.

You will receive separate instructions re balance Wheelus stockpile "M". Without consulting GOL at this time Embassy Tripoli requested indicate to Department what steps would be necessary effect road delivery in Tunisia by November 12.

For Rome and Brussels.

When Tunis and Paris report above approaches underway Embassies should inform their Governments US–UK action Tunis and Paris and should reiterate hope they will associate themselves with it.[6]

Addressees should emphasize to Governments to which accredited importance of secrecy until deliveries effected November 12. Tripoli should not approach GOL for time being.

Dulles

---

[6] Telegram 666 from Brussels, November 6, reported that Belgium appreciated being kept informed but would not furnish arms without French consent. (*Ibid.*, 772.56/11–657)

276. Memorandum of a Conversation, Department of State, Washington, November 5, 1957[1]

SUBJECT

Tunisian Arms Question

PARTICIPANTS

Mr. Mongi Slim, Ambassador of Tunisia
Mr. M'hamed Essafi, Counselor, Embassy of Tunisia
Joseph Palmer 2nd, Deputy Assistant Secretary, AF
William J. Porter, Director, AFN
Arthur B. Allen, AFN

Ambassador Slim had been asked to come to the Department to receive information concerning recent developments in connection with the question of arms for Tunisia. Mr. Palmer therefore began by explaining that we have been very busy working on the problem of Tunisia's request for assistance in obtaining arms and that over the past weekend we decided that, despite the great patience and understanding which have been exhibited by the Government of Tunisia and despite the fact that the French governmental crisis had not been definitely resolved, we should nevertheless proceed with definite plans to bring this problem to a conclusion. In coordination with the British we have therefore instructed our Embassies at Paris and Tunis to inform the French and Tunisian Governments that we propose to proceed with a token delivery of arms on November 12 unless the Governments of France and Tunisia meanwhile reach an agreement on arrangements for the purchase of arms by Tunisia which will make our proposed action unnecessary. Provided that agreement can be reached on the conditions and terms of sale, we are planning to deliver on November 12 500 rifles and 50,000 rounds of ammunition costing approximately $60,000. Mr. Palmer stated that the British also plan to offer a token shipment and Mr. Porter stated that the British plan to provide sub-machine guns, machine guns and ammunition for both.

Mr. Palmer explained that Ambassador Jones had already been authorized to inform President Bourguiba of our plans and that we understood that he had done so at 11:00 a.m. that day (November 5).[2] He stated that our Embassy at Paris had also informed the French Foreign Office of our plans on November 4 and that the only reason why the two approaches were not simultaneous was that

[1] Source: Department of State, Central Files, 772.56/11–557. Secret. Drafted by Allen.

[2] Ambassador Jones reported in telegram 435, November 5, that Bourguiba offered his thanks for the arms shipment, but would have been happier if the amount had been increased. (*Ibid.*)

President Bourguiba had been unable to receive Ambassador Jones earlier than November 5. He went on to emphasize our desire that our proposed action be kept secret as long as possible and our hope that even when we reach the delivery date of November 12 any announcements can be handled in such a way as to hold publicity at a minimum. Obviously, we hope that the French Government will still find it possible to move in some fashion which will permit them to identify themselves with this action. We think that this would be highly desirable in terms of U.S.-French relations, in terms of the French position in the Free World and in terms of Franco-Tunisian relations. We think that there is a good chance that the French may find it possible to do something. They are obviously in a difficult position with the United States and the United Kingdom both having told them that we plan to go ahead on November 12 and we believe that they will decide to go ahead also. We hope that if France does so the Tunisian Government will react in the same spirit.

Mr. Palmer concluded by saying that we seem to be reaching a climax in this matter. We are very encouraged by the attitude shown by the United Kingdom, and especially gratified that the United Kingdom agreed with us on the basis of the same principle. The decision has been difficult for both of us but we believe that we have acted correctly on a matter of principle.

Ambassador Slim began by thanking Mr. Palmer for the news he had just received. As he had said over a month ago, when the United States was directing its efforts toward helping Tunisia obtain arms from France, Italy or Belgium, he, himself hoped that arms might come from the United States also because of our common principles and community of outlook. He was delighted at the attitude of the United States and the United Kingdom. He was happy to detect in this attitude not only assistance to Tunisia in this specific instance but also the possibility of greater action which could prevent the occurrence of other difficulties in other states of the world. He hoped that this was the case because he has seen other states, which have no sympathy with the East, obliged to resort to the East for assistance. As Mr. Palmer was aware, for the past two months Tunisia had been the object of offers from Eastern countries which have been refused in the first place for ideological reasons and also because Tunisia did not desire to have heterogeneous arms for its army.

The Ambassador continued that the Tunisian Government greatly appreciates the action of the United States, not only because of the conclusion reached (in spite of difficulties which he fully understood), but also because now that the decision has been reached it may even help Tunisia obtain from France what it needs.

The Ambassador stated that he, personally, was not confident that France would actually deliver arms to Tunisia, but he agreed that it would now be easier for France to do so. He expressed the hope that France would be led to offer arms to Tunisia, and stated that an offer would not be refused.

Ambassador Slim then asked if the token shipment of arms would be made by the United States on November 12 even if France makes Tunisia an offer of arms. Mr. Palmer replied that we have agreed in principle that we will make the delivery unless a Franco-Tunisian agreement makes such action unnecessary. The Ambassador said that he wished to be precise. Was he to understand that if a Franco-Tunisian accord were reached before November 12, there would be no delivery of arms from the United States? Mr. Palmer stated that such an accord would obviously have to meet with the wishes of both sides.

Ambassador Slim then said that he would be very happy also if the decision in principle which the United States has reached applied to other matters as well, such as matériel for the police forces, whose requirements are now being surveyed by a United States mission. Mr. Porter commented that this would have to be considered in the light of the report which the survey mission will make, and added that we have been delighted to hear that the mission is receiving the full cooperation of the Tunisian authorities. Ambassador Slim asked if he was to understand that, now that the decision on principle has been made, the determination of what items may or may not be supplied for the police awaits the submission of the report of the survey mission. Mr. Palmer explained that the decision which has been taken by the United States relates to the list of arms which Tunisia needs as we received it from Mr. Ladgham. There is now the problem of negotiation between the Tunisian Government and the Governments of the United States and the United Kingdom concerning what specific items the Tunisian Government desires to purchase for its armed forces. He explained that the police survey should be considered as a separate matter. The survey mission was sent without any commitment as to matériel. He was sure that the Tunisian Government would wish to study the mission's report carefully and, of course, the United States would wish to do so.

Ambassador Slim explained that he completely understood that the question of arms was separate from the question of equipment for the police forces. However, his point was that, when Ambassador Richards visited Tunisia, the United States was unwilling to provide certain equipment which Tunisia desired for the police because these items were considered to be of a military nature. Now that the United States has decided to help Tunisia with arms this obstacle would appear to have been removed. Mr. Palmer stated that the principle established is that the United States agrees that Tunisia should be free to acquire the necessary means of legitimate self-defense. This holds whether the means are arms, transportation equipment or communications equipment.

Mr. Palmer said that he wished to repeat our appreciation of the understanding shown by the Government of Tunisia during this period and to assure the Ambassador that our admiration for President Bourguiba and his Government, already at a high level, has only been enhanced by the understanding, moderation and statesmanship they have shown in this matter. He felt that the Ambassador's role in helping us understand the problem had also been most helpful. The Ambassador thanked Mr. Palmer for his comments and said that the Tunisian Government has always been conscious of the role the United States has played and the position it has taken on Tunisia's problems. He has always been convinced that, because of the ideals Tunisia and the United States have in common, no other outcome was possible in spite of all the difficulties. He wished to say that he found the United States' attitude not only understandable but also logical and self-consistent. Sometimes it was possible to understand why a nation took a particular position, but impossible to agree that the position was logical. In the present instance, however, he agreed that our approach had been the logical one of first, trying to persuade France to provide arms for Tunisia, second, attempting to arrange for deliveries from friendly Western powers in order not to offend French susceptibilities, and finally, arranging to provide the arms ourselves.

After leaving Mr. Palmer's office, the Ambassador told Mr. Porter that he had forgotten to assure Mr. Palmer that Tunisia would keep the proposed arrangements secret. He would, however, send a message to Tunis at once asking that this be done.

277. Telegram From the Department of State to the Embassy in Tunisia [1]

Washington, November 9, 1957—2:17 p.m.

316. For Tunis:

After further consideration latest appeals by Mr. Pineau and Mr. Gaillard that U.S. and U.K. withhold delivery of arms to Tunisia until French Government takes action in matter on or about November 17, [2] you should see Bourguiba with view obtaining his agreement additional delay which we believe at this time would not exceed one week. You should make clear to Bourguiba our feeling that in view Pineau's statement French governmental action forthcoming, Bourguiba might not wish us to hold rigidly to November 12 date and he might feel it best to give French this further opportunity of four or five days to associate themselves with U.S.–U.K. in supplying arms to GOT.

For Paris:

Convey to French sense of representations to Bourguiba contained preceding paragraph. French should realize that whether they decide to supply arms or not, U.S. must make arms available to GOT as result commitments already given. Only conditions under which U.S. could withdraw from supply at this point would be as result indication from Bourguiba that GOT and GOF had reached completely satisfactory agreement which renders unnecessary Tunisian purchase of any arms from U.S.

For Tripoli:

Withhold all action re shipping arrangements until further instructed. Meanwhile take every possible precaution preclude any leak these arrangements through Libyan Government sources.

Herter

---

[1] Source: Department of State, Central Files, 772.56/11–957. Secret; Niact. Drafted by Porter. Also sent to Paris, London, and Tripoli.

[2] Pineau summoned Ambassador Houghton and the British Minister separately on the morning of November 6 to protest the early delivery date of arms to Tunisia. He hoped that the United States would be willing to seek Bourguiba's agreement to postpone receipt of the arms for a few days to give the French Government the opportunity to act. (Telegram 2313 from Paris, November 6; *ibid.*, 772.56/11–657) Ambassador Alphand conveyed a similar message to Murphy and Looram on November 8. (Memorandum of conversation by Looram, November 8; *ibid.*, 772.56/11–857)

278. Telegram From the Embassy in France to the Department of State[1]

Paris, November 9, 1957—7 p.m.

2360. Gaillard called me in this afternoon to make most strong and solemn plea for further two or three day delay in delivery arms to Tunisia. He made similar démarche to British Ambassador earlier today.

Speaking with utmost seriousness, Gaillard said that if US and UK were to deliver arms to GOT on November 12 before French Government had had opportunity to take decision on this matter, it would be considered "an unfriendly act". The reaction of French public opinion would be extremely sharp and bitter. This action on our part seemed particularly inopportune coming shortly before special NATO meeting designed to reinforce solidarity of Atlantic alliance. It would be moreover most disagreeable for him personally coming at very outset of his tenure of office. Therefore, he most solemnly urged us to delay few more days in order to permit his government to act.

He said that he is unable, since his ministers have dispersed for Armistice Day weekend, to hold Cabinet meeting on this subject before November 12. He will, however, hold meeting on that day and will himself urge that decision be taken at that time to supply arms to GOT. Quantity he has in mind is that for one battalion which he believes sufficient to meet immediate Tunisian needs. Since these arms are already held by French forces in Tunisia, delivery can be effected at once.

I told Gaillard that I would transmit his request to Washington immediately but added, as I had to Pineau, that I could not hold out much hope that at this late date delivery could be delayed. I described for his benefit long delay which has already occurred in response to Pineau's pleas. I indicated that I was fully aware of considerations which prompted his démarche and would recommend that, if possible, delay of two or three days after November 12 be granted.

I also mentioned further possible complication which has occurred to Embassy, i.e. that our negotiations with GOT may by this time have reached such point that US would feel obliged to deliver token quantity of arms next week even if affirmative French decision were taken. Gaillard was obviously astonished in light position US has hitherto taken on this point, at this possibility. He said that

---

[1] Source: Department of State, Central Files, 772.56/11–957. Secret; Niact. Repeated to Tunis. Received at 5:06 p.m.

he had supposed that, if French Government had decided to supply arms which Tunisia needs, it would [not?] be necessary for any other government to do so. He expressed fear Bourguiba would exploit separate deliveries by US and France as evidence of differences between them on North African policy. I replied I was merely indicating possible complication and suggested that, if it occurs, we might take joint action to minimize its ill effects. Gaillard agreed and said he would inform us of French Government's decision immediately after Tuesday Cabinet meeting. If decision is in negative, we would be free to take such action as we deem necessary. If decision is in affirmative, as he believed it will be, and if US nevertheless feels it must proceed with token delivery, we would concert together means of coordinating our action. He made it quite clear, however, that damaging repercussions are bound to occur if US delivers arms to Tunisia under present circumstances.

He closed by emphasizing again great gravity with which he regards this matter and by reiterating his earnest hope that we will in interests of Atlantic solidarity accord this further very brief delay.

Comment: I cannot too strongly stress firmness and solemnity with which Gaillard made this démarche. His use of expression "unfriendly act" was clearly deliberate and considered. Failure on our part to respond favorably would have worst possible effect on him personally and on his colleagues in government. In view role we hope Gaillard will play in providing France with stable government, I consider of particular importance maintenance of good personal relations with him.

I believe also he is entirely correct in estimating gravity of its effect on French public opinion. Coming as he points out just at time when we are about to make concerted effort to strengthen bonds of Atlantic community, such action might well have effects all out of proportion to its real significance. Even from viewpoint effective implementation of our North African policy, in which France is inevitably a major factor, I believe demonstration of consideration and good will on our part in this case will make possible much more successful US-French cooperation in support of Tunisia and Morocco than would be the case if we reject Gaillard's plea.

I, therefore, most earnestly recommend that we agree to wait two or three days, as may be necessary, after November 12 in order permit France to act. I would emphasize this new delay is for maximum of two or three days, which would not seem excessive favor for Gaillard to ask. We would hope that, in view understanding and patience Bourguiba has so far shown, he might agree to this further very brief delay for sake of common interests all four countries involved. I also hope that, if US and UK do find it necessary to deliver arms even though French also do so, these deliveries and publicity in regard thereto be carefully coordinated with view to assuring that deliveries appear to be complementary and not competitive.

Houghton

279. Telegram From the Embassy in Tunisia to the Department of State [1]

Tunis, November 11, 1957—2 p.m.

460. Mokkadem has just informed me as follows (paragraph 1 Embtel 457) [2] on direct instructions from Bourguiba:

1. In light all factors Bourguiba does not feel able agree additional delay (paragraph 1 Deptel 316) for variety reasons (see also paragraph 2 Embassy's reference telegram):

(a) On basis November 12 date fixed by US and UK, GOT has agreed arrival Egyptian arms "several days" after November 12. GOT not sure exact date but has given green light GOE.

(b) GOT does not believe GOF would or could provide GOT with arms on acceptable terms; its past experience with GOF re arms most unsatisfactory: for example, GOF withheld ammunition even for Tunisian Army training.

(c) Psychological point for GOT is that Tunisian Army is expression Tunisian sovereignty and French arms would reinforce impression GOT still under French tutelage.

(d) Final point was that of national dignity: GOT has been negotiating directly with USA and UK re arms. GOT does not particularly welcome addition France as factor these negotiations.

2. I asked whether GOT would refuse French arms if offered. Mokkadem replied: "We will study carefully any propositions which GOF may make to us".

3. I asked whether Bourguiba still contemplated maintaining secrecy until his speech November 14. Mokkadem said it was his

[1] Source: Department of State, Central Files, 772.56/11–1157. Secret; Niact. Repeated to Paris, London, and Tripoli. Received at 10:20 a.m.

[2] Telegram 457, November 11, stated that the French démarches seemed proof to the Tunisians that France wished to maintain control over arms supplies so as to retain its leverage; that the new government had done nothing to demonstrate its good will toward Tunisia; and that Tunisia insisted that the question of arms was unrelated to its negotiations with France. (*Ibid.*)

understanding that after arrival arms November 12 timing publicity up to Bourguiba.

4. In sum, Bourguiba is holding US to its promise deliver arms November 12. Embtel 455 [3] gives Tunisian view 5 a.m. November 12 as suitable arrival time.

5. *Comment*: So far as our relations with Bourguiba are concerned, only delivery as planned will mitigate adverse impression made upon him by US–UK démarche at last minute.

Jones

[3] Telegram 455, November 9, reported that Ambassador Jones informed Mokkadem on November 8 that the arms would come in by air. (*Ibid.*, 772.56/11–957)

280. Telegram From the Embassy in France to the Department of State [1]

Paris, November 11, 1957—6 p.m.

2366. Reference: Deptel 1779. [2] I informed Gaillard this afternoon along lines reference telegram, emphasizing that in response to his urgent plea, we are prepared to delay arms delivery a few days but that we have not heard whether GOT is prepared accept this delay.

Gaillard expressed deep personal appreciation that we had responded so promptly and favorably to his request. He continues to be gravely troubled, however, (1) that Bourguiba is in position to render judgment on matter of such importance France-US relations and (2) that most unfortunate competition between US and France for delivery arms to Tunis may be developing. He says he is reasonably confident decision will be taken in Cabinet tomorrow to supply to GOT arms for one battalion, which French feels is sufficient for their immediate needs. What, however, will be situation if Bourguiba demands of US larger quantities in excess of his needs, some of which might eventually go to Algerian rebels? This would, of course, have most serious effect on France-US relations.

I replied by pointing out that US always wished that France be sole supplier arms to Tunis and that present situation has arisen only

[1] Source: Department of State, Central Files, 772.56/11–1157. Secret; Priority. Repeated to Tunis. Received at 2:34 p.m.

[2] Printed as telegram 316 to Tunis, Document 277.

because of long delay caused by French ministerial crises and because of our conviction there is danger of supply arms to Tunisia by eastern countries. I emphasized we would insist arms we are supplying be accompanied by firm guarantee they are for internal use only and will not go into Algeria. I said we are not in position to give him assurances about the future but it would seem to us most desirable that French reach agreement with GOT as soon as possible to supply all of latter's legitimate armament needs. I pointed out US must take account of fact Tunisia is independent country which has right to buy arms anywhere but that we should certainly prefer that French continue to be main supplier if agreement to this effect can be worked out between two governments.

Houghton

---

281. Memorandum of a Telephone Conversation Between the President and the Secretary of State, Washington, November 11, 1957, 6:10 p.m. [1]

TELEPHONE CALL TO THE PRESIDENT

The Sec. explained the Tunisian situation and the dilemma we were in on small arms to Tunisia. The Sec. said he thought we should go through with it without further delay. The President agreed and said he thought the Secretary should call Alphand in and explain what we planned to do. The Sec. said that Murphy had talked to Alphand earlier. The Sec. discussed how critical the situation was in North Africa and how much was involved there.

The Pres. asked about Macmillan's stand on the above and the Sec. said the British were in entire agreement with us.

The Pres. and the Sec. agreed that our rifles shipment should come into Tunisia first. The Sec. thought that while the situation would be bad for a while the French would get over it since they needed our help.

---

[1] Source: Eisenhower Library, Dulles Papers, White House Telephone Conversations. Drafted by Mildred Asbjornson in the Secretary's office.

282. Memorandum of a Conversation, Department of State, Washington, November 11, 1957[1]

SUBJECT

Arms for Tunisia

PARTICIPANTS

Mr. Herve Alphand, Ambassador of France
Mr. Charles Lucet, Minister of France
Mr. Francois de Laboulaye, Counselor, French Embassy
Mr. John Foster Dulles, Secretary of State
Mr. Robert Murphy, Deputy Under Secretary of State
Mr. William M. Rountree, Assistant Secretary of State, NEA (for part of meeting)
Mr. Joseph Palmer 2nd, Deputy Assistant Secretary for AF

The French Ambassador called this evening at the Secretary's request. The Secretary opened the conversation by saying that we were greatly concerned at the situation which is developing with respect to the furnishing of arms to Tunisia. He said that we are now giving urgent study to the problem and that he wished to consult the French in this matter. The Secretary then reviewed the history of our commitment to Bourguiba, recalling his last conversation with the Ambassador on October 18. As a result of that conversation, we had been successful in obtaining Mr. Bourguiba's agreement to delay shipments until after the October 31 deadline to which we had been committed. Subsequently, we set a new date of November 12 on the assumption that a French Government would have been formed and had about a week to act on this matter before the shipments took place. Within the last few days, we had again talked to Mr. Bourguiba about the French desire for further delay, but for reasons which are surely persuasive, Mr. Bourguiba felt that he could not agree to a further postponement.

The Secretary went on to emphasize the lengths to which we have gone in this matter to accommodate the French, despite the dangers which we believe exist for Western interests in North Africa. He pointed out that all that is immediately involved is a token shipment of 500 rifles and 50,000 rounds of ammunition. The supply of these to Tunisia would be covered by the most explicit type of assurances, which we have already exacted from the Tunisian Government. The Secretary said that in the light of all these circumstances, he did not see any honorable alternative for the United States but to proceed as scheduled with the delivery of the

[1] Source: Department of State, Central Files, 772.56/11–1157. Secret. Drafted by Palmer.

token shipment on November 12. We would still strongly prefer, however, to do this in some way in concert with the French. He would therefore appreciate Mr. Alphand inquiring urgently of his government whether it would be prepared also to make at least a token shipment coincidentally with our own, or alternatively, authorize us to say that we are proceeding to make our delivery with the concurrence of the French Government.

Mr. Alphand said that he would of course put these points to his government. He emphasized that this problem presents very great dangers for any French Government for reasons arising from the Algerian rebellion, mentioning particularly the danger that the arms may wind up in Algerian hands. The Secretary intervened to say that he understood that Mr. Pineau himself had indicated before the French Assembly only a short time ago that there was no evidence whatsoever that Tunisia itself is supplying arms to the Algerians.

Ambassador Alphand acknowledged the correctness of the Secretary's statement. He went on to say that he thought the best course under the circumstances would be for his government to assume responsibility for the shipment of arms to Tunisia. He assumed that under these conditions the United States would cancel its plans for delivery of the token shipment and any further deliveries to Tunisia.

After consulting his United States colleagues, the Secretary informed Ambassador Alphand that the nature of our commitments to the Tunisians were such that he did not believe that we could withhold the token shipment at the present time. Mr. Rountree pointed out that our agreement is to make the token shipment on November 12 unless the governments of France and Tunisia have meanwhile reached an agreement obviating the need for such action. We interpret this to mean that only a comprehensive agreement by France and Tunisia relating to arms which is completely satisfactory to both parties would obviate the need for United States delivery of the token amounts.

Ambassador Alphand said that this was completely contrary to his previous understandings. He had always understood that if France stood ready to supply Tunisia, the United States would withdraw. He was sure that his government was under the same impression. He said that under these circumstances he hardly saw how he could conscientiously recommend that his government ship any arms to Tunisia.

The Secretary indicated understanding of the Ambassador's position, but emphasized our efforts to move in unison with the French and our continued desire to avoid the appearance of any split. He therefore hoped that the French Government would find it possible to associate itself in one way or another with our proposed actions. Mr. Alphand reiterated that he would inform his government immediately and try to let us have his reply by tomorrow.

283. Telegram From the Department of State to the Embassy in France [1]

Washington, November 11, 1957—9:19 p.m.

1786. Please pass following to Pineau from Secretary:

"Dear Mr. President:

I am greatly distressed at the situation we are in regarding arms to Tunisia. As you know, we have felt that Tunisia as a now independent nation, thanks to the statesmanlike policies of your government, is entitled to enjoy what the United Nations Charter calls the inherent right of self-defense. The Tunisian government has been trying to exercise that right by getting at least a limited quantity of small arms for purely defensive purposes. Such arms are readily available from non-Western sources. But President Bourguiba has preferred to initiate Tunisia's defense problem with a Western state. You will recall that early in September we advised your government of the urgent request made to us by President Bourguiba and in response we told him that we felt his request was a legitimate one and that we would see to it that he obtained a limited supply of small arms for defensive purposes in the near future. We hoped, however, that he would be able to get them from your own government so as to make it unnecessary to buy them elsewhere.

About the middle of October we told President Bourguiba that if he could not get arms elsewhere in Western Europe we would get him some by the first of November. Your government was informed accordingly.

Your Ambassador then called on me on October 18 and urged most strongly that we should not make any delivery until there was a new French Government and he said that he would personally recommend to that government as soon as it was formed that it should as its first act arrange to deliver arms to Tunisia.

While I did not give your Ambassador any assurances in this respect we did in fact communicate again with President Bourguiba and in agreement with him arrange that our shipment would not occur until November 12 and then only on the assumption that a satisfactory arrangement had not by then been arrived at between your Government and that of Tunisia.

[1] Source: Department of State, Central Files, 772.56/11–1157. Secret; Niact. Drafted and approved by Dulles. Repeated to Tunis and London.

Tomorrow is the 12th, the date when our promise to President Bourguiba becomes due and your government will have been in office then for a week which is a time within which, I had inferred, you would have been enabled to deal with the problem.

I know of the many problems that confront you and I do not raise this in any spirit of criticism but merely to indicate that we have in good faith done what seemed to be responsive to the plea for time which was made to us.

In view of your Government's desire for still further time we did take this up again with President Bourguiba yesterday, but unfortunately for reasons which are surely persuasive, and which seemed to President Bourguiba to be compelling, he feels he cannot release us from the November 12 date. Therefore, we have no honorable alternative but to proceed. You will appreciate that what is involved tomorrow is a token delivery of 500 rifles with ammunition. Obviously, this is not enough to solve the problem but it will, we hope, assure time to permit of mutually acceptable arrangements between your Government and that of Tunisia covering this problem comprehensively. Could you not perhaps yourselves make at least a token delivery coincidentally with our own and thus preserve the front of unity which we would greatly prefer? The UK might share in this procedure.

If your Government is not itself in a position to do anything so promptly may you not at least authorize us to say that what we are doing tomorrow is being done with your concurrence?

I emphasize that the action tomorrow is minimal in character and that we will have in hand explicit Tunisian assurances that these arms will only be used for defensive purposes and will not be transferred to anyone else. I believe you yourself have indicated to the Deputies that you are not aware of Tunisia being a supplier of arms to the Algerians. I think we both know the sources of such arms.

Please be assured that we have throughout tried to handle this matter in a way which would on the one hand reconcile Tunisia's genuine independence with the preoccupations of your own Government. We act as we do because after having sought and achieved delays we now have no honorable alternative but to act. We hope that we can act in accord with you."

Secretary spoke urgently to Ambassador Alphand along foregoing lines this evening. Alphand said he would endeavor ascertain GOF reactions urgently.

Dulles

284. Telegram From the Embassy in France to the Department of State [1]

Paris, November 12, 1957—2 p.m.

2371. For the Secretary. Deptel 1786. Secretary's message delivered to Pineau this morning at 11:30 Paris time.

Pineau had just come from restricted Cabinet meeting which he said had taken following decisions re Tunisia: French Government had decided that if United States delivers arms to Tunisia at this time France will not deliver arms to Tunisia. In this case, moreover, French Government will envisage ceasing all aid to Tunisia and would adopt entirely new policy. Reasoning behind this decision would be that if United States delivers arms to GOT, there would be no reason why United Kingdom, Spain and others (he said Spain had received Tunisian request for 6,000 rifles) would not deliver and total quantities would be far in excess of Tunisian needs. Under these circumstances it would be wholly impossible to obtain French Assembly approval for credits to Tunisia, part of which would be presumed as likely to be used for financing arms for Algerian rebels.

On other hand, Pineau declared, Cabinet had decided that if United States agreed not to deliver arms to Tunisia at this time, French would make such deliveries this evening November 12 from stocks now in Tunisia.

Pineau went on to explain, in his personal capacity and not as Foreign Minister, that United States decision to deliver arms to Tunisia regardless of what action French might take, had had most deplorable and dangerous effect. Some of his colleagues had urged that under these circumstances France not participate in NATO meeting next month. He himself felt that such action by United States would for second time defeat Algerian Loi-cadre in French Assembly, he being convinced that publicity on this issue had been responsible for its defeat in September. He said that he does not believe United States Government is fully aware how very grave a situation is being created by our proposed action in this case. He declared Prime Minister is drafting message to President Eisenhower which will be ready shortly and which he asked us to dispatch. He urged that in meantime I telephone Department and recommend that no further action on arms delivery be taken until this message has been received by President.

I explained again considerations which prompted our delivery of arms to GOT and particularly emphasized that it was only due to

[1] Source: Department of State, Central Files, 772.56/11–1257. Secret; Niact. Repeated to London and Tunis. Received at 10:36 a.m..

very long delay that we had felt obliged to commit ourselves to Bourguiba to deliver November 12 unless prior agreement had been reached between GOF and GOT obviating this necessity. Pineau reiterated that proposed French arms delivery this evening would in fact obviate that necessity. He insisted French had always been given to understand here and in Washington that United States would deliver arms to Tunisia only if France did not do so. I explained again that this had been the case until very recently, but that prolonged delay and imminence arrival Egyptian arms had obliged us to take firm commitment in regard this token delivery from which only GOT itself could release us.

Comment: We are transmitting separately Gaillard message to President.[2]

There can be no doubt that French are taking this matter even more seriously than we anticipated. They had supposed until my conversation with Gaillard over weekend that, if they delivered arms to Tunisia, we would not. They are therefore shocked to learn that we propose to deliver arms in any case, except in the unlikely event we are released from our commitment by Bourguiba.

While remarks about possible refusal to attend NATO meeting need not at the moment be taken too seriously, declaration of intention, in case we deliver arms, to cease aid to Tunisia and to follow "entirely new policy" should be taken very seriously. In view probable temper of French Assembly this might well be what French Government would be obliged to do whether it wishes to or not. Result would be to leave Tunisian baby entirely in our lap, as well of course as to create anti-American storm in France. Outcry would probably take line that we are "driving" French out of Tunisia and intend henceforth to help rebels drive them out of Algeria. It is difficult predict effect these emotions on Loi-cadre but Pineau's estimate is quite plausible. In any case prospects of getting French to adopt liberal line in Algeria would be greatly reduced and chance of her accepting Tunisia as intermediary reduced to nil. Of course if Algerian Loi-cadre should be defeated on confidence vote, government would be out again and it is very difficult to guess when next one would be constituted and what would be its character.

I do not wish to seem unduly alarmist but frankly I find it impossible to exaggerate possible damaging effect of this situation. I realize extent to which we are committed with Bourguiba but cannot help but feel that it is not even in his best interest to press matter to this extreme.

---

[2] Transmitted in telegram 2382, November 12, not printed. (*Ibid.*)

I hope you may be able to send me message for Pineau this afternoon.[3]

Houghton

[3] Telegram 1789 to Paris, sent at 12:48 p.m. November 12, authorized Houghton to inform Pineau that the United States was suspending its arms delivery to Tunisia on the understanding that France would provide an equivalent amount on the same conditions agreed to between the United States and Tunisia. (*Ibid.*) Secretary Dulles called Ambassador Houghton late that afternoon to convey the decision. Joxe was informed around 7:30 p.m. and he passed the word to Pineau at approximately 9 p.m. (Despatch 1069 from Paris, December 30; *ibid.*, 772.56/12–3057)

---

285. Telegram From the Department of State to the Embassy in Tunisia[1]

Washington, November 12, 1957—1:34 p.m.

325. For Ambassador from Secretary. Deliver following message to Bourguiba from me:

"I am gratified that the US willingness to deliver defensive arms to Tunisia has now borne fruit in a way which I think provides an important advantage for your Government. The delivery by the French of arms to you without conditions other than those which you and we had agreed on, namely, that they would be used only for defensive purposes and not transferred elsewhere, is an important step in the right direction. In the light of this delivery which we understand will be made today in replacement of the initial deliveries planned by the UK and ourselves we are ourselves suspending the delivery which the French delivery replaces.

We understand of course that this initial operation does not actually solve your arms problem. And of course our agreement to supply arms stands and we will respond under it in the event that satisfactory arrangements are not made elsewhere.

We continue to believe, as I think you believe, that the future of Tunisia lies in association with the West, including close ties with France on a basis of sovereign equality."

Dulles

[1] Source: Department of State, Central Files, 772.56/11–1257. Secret; Niact. Drafted and approved by Dulles. Repeated to Paris and London.

286. Telegram From the Department of State to the Embassy in Tunisia [1]

Washington, November 13, 1957—12:15 p.m.

327. You should reassure Bourguiba that US purpose in suspending delivery of token arms shipment was only on understanding that GOF would make delivery on November 12, as indicated Secretary's message yesterday. We have just learned that delivery was not in fact made but that French Ambassador is discussing matter with GOT today. [2] Bourguiba may be informed that if the French are not prepared to make immediate delivery under conditions similar to those agreed to with the US, US will proceed with token delivery tomorrow November 14. [3] Bourguiba should also understand that our basic position is that Tunisia is entitled quickly to get reasonable amount of arms for defensive and security purposes, that these arms should be obtainable from the West, preferably from France, but if not, elsewhere in the West, and US itself stands ready to supply them if need be.

Dulles

---

[1] Source: Department of State, Central Files, 772.56/11–1357. Secret; Niact. The source text bears a notation, initialed by Howe, that it was approved by the President. Repeated to London and Paris.

[2] Yost met with Joxe at 10:30 a.m. on November 13 and learned that the French had not made an arms delivery to Tunisia. Gorse was sent back to Tunisia to persuade Bourguiba to refuse the Egyptian arms shipment as a condition for receiving French arms. Houghton met with Pineau around 1 p.m., and indicated that the United States expected the French to complete the delivery without adding any new conditions. (Telegram 2401 from Paris, November 13; *ibid.*)

[3] Palmer spoke with Ambassador Jones on the phone at 10:20 a.m. Jones reported that earlier that morning Bourguiba had indicated to him that France had not delivered the promised arms. The Tunisians maintained that they could not reject the arms which came to them as a gift from Egypt. Unless he heard to the contrary, Ambassador Jones was instructed to tell Bourguiba by 8 p.m. that U.S. supplies would be sent the next morning. (Memorandum of conversation by Porter, November 13; *ibid.*)

287. Telegram From the Department of State to the Embassy in France [1]

Paris, November 13, 1957—1:49 p.m.

1812. Please deliver following from President to Prime Minister:

"November 13, 1957. My dear Mr. Prime Minister:

I received late yesterday your message [2] with respect to the furnishing of arms to Tunisia for its defensive purposes. I cannot at this time deal with all aspects of your message as I am leaving this noon for Oklahoma and the matter permits of no delay.

Secretary Dulles in his message to Foreign Minister Pineau of November 11 reviewed the history of this matter. He recalled our position that Tunisia as an independent nation was entitled to arms for security and defensive purposes and that, in order that Tunisia might not have to turn to dangerous sources to fill its needs in this respect, the US had pledged itself last September to see to it that Tunisia obtained a limited supply of small arms for defensive purposes in the near future. We had hoped that the Tunisian Government would be able to get them from the French Government as a normal source of supply.

About mid-October we had told President Bourguiba that if he could not get arms from France or elsewhere in Western Europe we would get him some by the first of November. The UK associated itself with this position. Your Government was informed accordingly.

On October 18 the French Ambassador urged that we should delay until there should be established a new French government and indicated that he personally felt that a first act of any such government would be promptly to arrange to deliver arms to Tunisia.

As the result of subsequent effort we obtained the agreement of President Bourguiba further to postpone the date of our delivery from November 1 to November 12. Your Government was informed of this on November 4. [3]

In reply to the Secretary of State's message of November 11 we received word that your Government would itself be prepared to deliver to the Government of Tunisia arms on November 12 if we did not do so.

Accordingly on November 12 the Secretary of State informed your Government and the Government of Tunisia that it would suspend the delivery of arms on that day and understood that the Government of the UK would probably do likewise on the understanding so far as the US was concerned that the French Government would itself that day be delivering to Tunisia 'an equivalent in arms and ammunition' to that which had been planned by the US and the UK with no conditions other than that the arms would be

[1] Source: Department of State, Central Files, 772.56/11–1357. Secret; Niact; Presidential Handling. Drafted and approved by Dulles. Repeated to London and Tunis.

[2] See footnote 2, Document 284.

[3] See footnote 5, Document 275.

for defensive purposes and not transferred elsewhere. It would be further understood that this initial transaction would not of itself solve the basic problem but that Tunisia would remain entitled to get further arms, preferably from France but if not elsewhere from a Western country and that the US would supply them if need be.

Our Ambassador in Paris communicated this message to Foreign Minister Pineau and understood that the terms under which we would suspend delivery were acceptable and that the French Government would itself make the equivalent delivery yesterday November 12.

I must point out that the Secretary's message above referred to was sent prior to my receipt of your message of November 12 and that there is a variance between the terms of your message to me and the Secretary's message to Foreign Minister Pineau which we understood to be acceptable to your Government. One notable difference is that you state that .... While we appreciate the traditional concern of France in the area of North Africa and while we hope that in fact France would continue to be a normal source of supply of Tunisia we could not agree that Tunisia, as an independent country, should feel constrained to accept any one country as a sole supplier of arms and thus in effect make its own defense and security requirements a subject for determination by another country and not of its own government. This, in our opinion, would be incompatible with genuine independence.

I do not at the time of writing this message to you, Mr. Prime Minister, know what may have transpired today but I greatly hope that arrangements have been concluded on the basis of what we thought was the understanding with Foreign Minister Pineau of yesterday. If unhappily this proves not to be the case then we feel in honor bound to carry out our engagement to the Government of Tunisia and will plan to make delivery to them tomorrow morning November 14, Tunisia time, of the token delivery of arms which had been planned.

I have naturally taken most serious note of your suggestions with reference to the possible impact of this action upon the enactment of the Loi-cadre for Algeria and also upon the position of the French Government in relation to the projected meeting of the NATO Heads of Government. I would assume that if the Loi-cadre is voted upon that vote will be determined by the judgment of the French Parliament upon the merits of the matter and upon whether or not it is judged that this law will in fact promote a just and peaceful settlement of the Algerian problem. As far as the NATO meeting is concerned I most earnestly hope that there will prevail the atmosphere of friendly cooperation without which the meeting would indeed be of doubtful value. If there should unhappily subsist any differences between us that would be an occasion for you and me to talk them over in an atmosphere of friendship and of earnest search for that mutual understanding which has so long characterized the relations between our two countries.

Sincerely, Dwight D. Eisenhower."

Confirm time and date of delivery.[4]

Dulles

[4] Although by the time this message arrived the French had already responded negatively, the decision was made after consultation with Washington to deliver it in the hope the French might be induced to change their course. It was handed to Gaillard's Chef de Cabinet at 11:50 p.m. (Despatch 1069; Department of State, Central Files, 772.56/12–3057)

288. Memorandum of a Telephone Conversation Between the Secretary of State and the Ambassador in France (Houghton), November 13, 1957, 4:28 p.m.[1]

TELEPHONE CALL FROM AMBASSADOR HOUGHTON (PARIS)

The Amb. read to the Sec. the attached.[2]

Houghton explained the background—Pineau was called at 9:10[3] and told precisely this: The Govt of the US has decided to postpone until ten o'clock this evening. At that time Bourguiba will be informed that unless the French Government delivers arms we shall deliver arms tomorrow morning. Ten minutes later at 9:20 Pineau telephoned back personally saying that he had sent a message. The attached communication, Houghton explained, was signed by Gaillard and delivered at the Embassy at 9:50 p.m.

The Sec. asked, "Can they only get arms from France?" Houghton stated frankly he did not know, although he said it might mean that. This was not spelled out in the attached message. They discussed the meaning—whether it meant other than France. In the broadest sense it might mean other than countries from the West. It might well mean other than from France.

The Sec. asked what about the British in this. Houghton said that Jebb was not in Paris but someone (I did not get the name)

[1] Source: Eisenhower Library, Dulles Papers, General Telephone Conversations. Drafted by Mildred Asbjornson in the Secretary's office.

[2] Not printed.

[3] Joxe telephoned Houghton shortly before 8 p.m. to request that the United States delay action until after the meeting of the Council of Ministers which was due to begin at 8 p.m. (Telegram 2125 from Paris, November 13; Department of State, Central Files, 772.56/11–1357) The Ambassador called Dulles at 2:55 p.m. Washington time to pass on this report and Dulles told him that Jones had been instructed to delay seeing Bourguiba until 10 p.m. (Memorandum of telephone conversation by Bernau; Eisenhower Library, Dulles Papers)

from the British Embassy had called Selwyn Lloyd in London to give a report on events. The Sec. said he would call Selwyn Lloyd right away. Houghton asked if the Sec. wanted him to wait at the Embassy and the Sec. to call him back. Sec. said yes. Houghton said the British do not see any point in going back to Gaillard.

Houghton said he had not yet got the Sec's message. Did the Sec. want him still to deliver the message and the Sec. said yes. [4]

The Sec. and Houghton agreed it was a tough situation.

[4] See *supra.*

289. Memorandum of a Telephone Conversation Between the Secretary of State and the Ambassador in France (Houghton), November 13, 1957, 6:26 p.m. [1]

TELEPHONE CALL TO AMB HOUGHTON

The Sec said he talked to the Pres and he sees no solution except for H to make a last effort and say to the French to deliver this small amount tomorrow and then talk about it afterwards. It is a small token amount which we are pledged to deliver if they don't and there is plenty of time to talk. L [2] got a negative reply almost the same as ours except they talked about not receiving arms from the East so it was not as categorical as ours. The British are going along with us. Their Amb will if necessary support this last-minute representation—if H can make it tonight and H said he will try. Also Lloyd suggested we should get Bourguiba in receiving these arms to state voluntarily he will expect to get arms from the West and we will send a message to our fellow urging him to urge that upon Bourguiba. H repeated his instructions and the Sec added the French can express the hope but make no conditions. H said he would go ahead with it himself (even though he said his advice was not asked

[1] Source: Eisenhower Library, Dulles Papers, General Telephone Conversations. Drafted by Phyllis D. Bernau in the Secretary's office.

[2] John Selwyn Lloyd.

for), and will call if he gets anything out of them. The Sec repeated this is the result of his talk with the Pres in Oklahoma City. H asked for a reply to the message from Gaillard. The Sec will but not tonight.

---

290. Memorandum of a Telephone Conversation Between the Secretary of State and the Ambassador in France (Houghton), November 13, 1957, 8 p.m. [1]

Ambassador Houghton called and said that the French Ambassador at Tunis was seeing Bourguiba at 10:30 and would ask Bourguiba not to accept any delivery of arms from the East, including the pending Egyptian shipment. The French urged that the US and UK should join in this demand and assure that Tunisia would not become another Arab state playing one side off against the other. The French urged very strongly that we should await the Bourguiba reply before making any delivery of arms. [2] The French had tried to see Bourguiba before but Bourguiba had been ill and this appointment for 10:30 Thursday morning, November 14, was the first that could be arranged.

I told the Ambassador that neither we nor, I thought, the British could go any further than the British position previously notified to the French, namely, that we hoped that Bourguiba would, in fact, indicate his own intention to seek arms only from the West, excluding the current "gift" shipment.

JFD

---

[1] Source: Eisenhower Library, Dulles Papers, General Telephone Conversations. Drafted in the Secretary's office.

[2] As a consequence of this call, the arms delivery was postponed until 1 p.m. Tunisian time (7 a.m. E.S.T.) on November 14. (Telegram 1828 to Paris, November 13; Department of State, Central Files, 772.56/11–1357)

291. Telegram From the Department of State to the Embassy in Tunisia [1]

Washington, November 13, 1957—8:19 p.m.

330. In event failure French to deliver arms with consequent US-UK decision proceed with delivery, it would be most desirable if Bourguiba should in statement commenting upon receipt these arms reiterate that Tunisia will look to the West as normal source of its arms supplies. Department requests you make every effort persuade him to do so. If possible we hope he will also be willing make some conciliatory statement re France, and comment again as he has in past upon limited quantity of arms required and that they will be used for purely defensive purposes.

We believe that Bourguiba should be willing assist in this regard particularly if he understands personally the great difficulty which decision to deliver arms will have for US and UK Governments, including risk that NATO itself will be put under very severe strain. Statement along lines indicated above would be invaluable to us in dealing with this problem and perhaps future related problems as they might arise. We would not expect that statement would preclude acceptance of pending delivery of Egyptian arms.

Department expects make firm decision re delivery after report from Ambassador Houghton expected within next few hours on his efforts persuade French proceed with French delivery without unacceptable conditions. We hope UK shipment would be made at about same time as US.

Dulles

---

[1] Source: Department of State, Central Files, 772.56/11–1357. Secret; Niact. Repeated to London and Paris.

292. Telegram From the Department of State to the Embassy in the United Kingdom [1]

Washington, November 13, 1957—8:32 p.m.

3505. Please deliver following from Secretary to Lloyd. [2]

"Dear Selwyn:

Subject to the unlikely contingency of a last minute French shift of position we will be delivering our shipment Thursday afternoon Tunis time. We are instructing our air crews at Wheelus Base to be prepared to leave around noon tomorrow the 14th. I hope that at least some part of your shipment can arrive at about the same time.

I want to express on behalf of the President and myself to you and Harold the profound satisfaction we feel that our two Governments are together at this critical moment. I am confident that we are doing the right thing, but if we were divided the future would indeed be ominous. As it is, I am sure we can ride it through without ultimate damage to NATO.

In accordance with your good suggestion we are urging upon Bourguiba in the strongest terms that when he acknowledges the receipt of arms from the US and UK he state that in view of this fact his Government expects to look to the West as the normal source of arms supply. This of course would not apply to the exceptional gift shipment from Egypt now in transit.

Sincerely yours, Foster."

Dulles

[1] Source: Department of State, Central Files, 772.56/11–1357. Secret; Niact.

[2] A series of telephone calls took place during the day as Dulles spoke to Macmillan and Lloyd in an effort to coordinate strategy. The memoranda of these telephone conversations, drafted by Phyllis D. Bernau, are in Eisenhower Library, Dulles Papers.

---

293. Memorandum of a Telephone Conversation Between the Secretary of State and the Ambassador in France (Houghton), November 13, 1957, 8:45 p.m. [1]

Ambassador Houghton said that he and the UK Chargé had called on Gaillard. Gaillard said he was bound by a "unanimous and spontaneous" Cabinet decision. He would, however, try again to

[1] Source: Eisenhower Library, Dulles Papers, General Telephone Conversations. Drafted in the Secretary's office.

reach President Coty and others and see whether there was any chance of obtaining a modification of the French position. I asked the Ambassador how long he felt we should try to hold the situation. He said he would like to have us try to hold it until there was time for the French Ambassador to call on Bourguiba at 10:30 this morning and get Bourguiba's reply. I said that we would try to hold the situation until about noon, Paris and Tunisia time, i.e., until about 6:00 a.m., E.S.T.

Ambassador Houghton said he would call us back as soon as he heard the outcome and try to do so before 6:00 a.m., our time.[2] He said he doubted very much that there would be any positive result because the French would insist on guarantees against Tunisia receiving arms elsewhere, and particularly the rejection of the Egyptian shipment now en route. Nevertheless he felt that it would help the situation if we gave the French time to play out their hand fully.

JFD

[2] At approximately 3:10 a.m., the French Prime Minister's office called the Embassy in Paris to report that the Council of Ministers had not changed its decision, and that France still called upon the British and U.S. Governments to support its demand that Bourguiba pledge not to accept arms from other than French sources. At the least, they were asked to delay delivery until Gorse had an opportunity to meet with Bourguiba. (Despatch 1069 from Paris, December 30; Department of State, Central Files, 772.56/12–3057)

---

294. Memorandum of a Telephone Conversation Between the Deputy Assistant Secretary of State for African Affairs (Palmer) and the Ambassador in France (Houghton), November 14, 1957, 7 a.m.[1]

SUBJECT

Tunisian Arms Problem

Ambassador Houghton said that he had just come back to the Embassy from seeing Mr. Pineau, who informed him that the French Ambassador at Tunis, Mr. Gorse, had seen Mr. Bourguiba this morning. Mr. Bourguiba had informed Mr. Gorse that he could not refuse the Egyptian arms shipment, as the French had requested, and that he must preserve his freedom of action in this matter.

[1] Source: Department of State, Central Files, 772.56/11–1457. Official Use Only. Drafted by Palmer.

Mr. Pineau told Ambassador Houghton that in the light of the foregoing, the French feel unable to deliver arms to Tunisia for the reasons set forth in Mr. Gaillard's message to the President. The United States and the UK must therefore assume responsibility for our actions. If the United States and the UK do deliver arms to Tunisia, France will make formal protests in Washington and London through normal diplomatic channels.

Ambassador Houghton went on to say that the French have issued a short statement covering what Mr. Pineau said to the Foreign Affairs Committee of the Assembly on this subject this morning to the following effect: Mr. Pineau reported that the U.S. and the UK were preparing to deliver arms to Tunisia. He expressed the government's regret at this action which he characterized as contrary to the concept of Atlantic solidarity which should govern in all parts of the world.

Ambassador Houghton said that he assumed we would do the same thing. I told him that I assumed that we would, but that in any event, I would see that his suggestions in this matter were brought to the Secretary's attention.

Ambassador Houghton asked that the Secretary also be informed that even though the problem of arms to Tunisia has turned out the way it has, he is glad for the sake of the record that we waited as we did for a new French Government.

Finally, Ambassador Houghton asked that Paris be informed of our decision in this matter and that a copy of any press release on this subject be sent to him as quickly as possible. He said that he planned to instruct the Embassy to refuse to comment at all on this matter but refer all inquiries to Washington.

---

295. Diary Entry by the President [1]

Washington, November 14, 1957—9 a.m.

For the past three days we have been in a terrible difficulty with France and Tunisia, based partially upon misunderstanding but

---

[1] Source: Eisenhower Library, Whitman File, Eisenhower Diaries. Top Secret.

mostly on what we believe to be French stupidity and refusal to face international facts as they exist.[2]

For a long time Prime Minister Bourguiba of Tunisia has been trying to obtain some arms from the West. His demands have seemed reasonable to us and he asked for the arms on the basis of purchase, not grant.

Our own hope was that because of the close ties of France with the North African area that the French would be the ones to deliver such arms and we urged them to do so. We conferred with the British who felt about the matter as we did.

While the French have nominally accorded Tunisia complete independence, they have so far retained in Tunisia five military bases (I believe all these are in addition to Bizerte which was to be retained by the French under the Independence Treaty). They have given to Tunisia no satisfactory answer as to when these bases are to be evacuated, if ever.

Apparently a few weeks ago the French told Bourguiba that they would deliver arms, but they demanded certain conditions to be agreed to in advance. The most unacceptable of these conditions was an engagement on the part of the Tunisians that they would not accept arms from any other nation—that France would be the sole source of supply of such equipment.

We have felt this condition to be unjustified and so informed the French, again urging them to attach a single condition that the arms be used only for defensive purposes.

In view of the inconclusive character of their talks with the French, Bourguiba finally grew desperate. He is, I think, our most independent and enthusiastic friend in the Arab World. But in view of the demands of his people for some military equipment, it became more and more difficult for him to maintain his position. Some weeks ago, therefore, we told Bourguiba that in the event the French did not deliver arms for internal order and minimum defense purposes we would, in combination with the British, deliver him a token shipment by November first. The idea was that a small token shipment (only five hundred rifles) would establish his right as head of an independent government to purchase arms from the West, in whatever area he could get the best treatment.

Soon thereafter the French government fell and there was only a caretaker government in Paris for a number of weeks. In view of this and on French request we postponed the delivery date of our token shipment to November twelfth.

---

[2] In a personal letter to Captain E. E. (Swede) Hazlett, USN (Ret.), dated November 18, President Eisenhower substantially repeated the essence of his diary comments on Tunisia. (*Ibid.*)

Suddenly on November 11th or 12th, the French protested that they had not heard that we had promised delivery on a specific date; that their new Premier Gaillard had not been in office long enough to pay attention to this problem and that they would regard our delivery of a token shipment to Tunisia as an unfriendly act. Their reaction was violent, so much so that they even held that they might have to withdraw from NATO, or at least not attend the December meeting of that body.

This put us in a dilemma. While NATO is the organization to which we attach a maximum importance in the attempt to maintain collective security against the Russian threat, we could not afford either to see Bourguiba begin to purchase arms from the Soviets nor could we be in the position of breaking our pledged word to Tunisia.

In early November the situation was complicated by a sudden move on the part of Nasser in Egypt to start a shipment of arms to Tunisia—as a gift. Bourguiba could not possibly afford to turn this offer down, which was apparently widely publicized in that area, and he attached the most extraordinary importance to the delivery of some Western arms in Tunisia before the Egyptian shipment could reach there, somewhere between the 15th or 16th of this month.

In the situation that has developed within the last three days, we have had numerous trans-Atlantic telephone calls with some very stiff notes passing between ourselves and the French, to urge them to get busy and deliver a token shipment of arms and without conditions other than that of using the arms merely for defense.

In spite of promising such delivery on the 12th, they failed to carry it out and spent the 13th in arguing among themselves and apparently with Bourguiba and the British and us. In these cables and telephone calls they threatened the most dire things such as a complete breakup of the Western Alliance.

Finally, we felt that we simply could not be blackmailed by the French weakness, and in two notes I definitely notified Gaillard that having put off Bourguiba for two additional days, we are going to deliver the token shipment of arms to him on the morning of November fourteenth.

So far as we can find out, the French have made no move to satisfy the situation so presumably the British-American shipment of arms was delivered to Bourguiba this morning. [3]

---

[3] Due to a series of logistical complications, the arms did not arrive in Tunisia until 6:50 p.m. on November 15. The British equipment had come in many hours earlier. (Despatch 178 from Tripoli, November 26; Department of State, Central Files, 772.56/11–2657)

So far as we can tell at this moment, the French reaction has not been as violent as they themselves said it would be, but it is certain that there will be trouble in the offing about the whole affair.

Incidentally, the French objection was based on the argument that Bourguiba was trying to arm his country for far more than defensive purposes. They said he was trying to buy arms from Spain, from Italy and from every other country in the West and would play one off against the other in the threat to purchase them, otherwise, from Russia.

We hold that Bourguiba is a true Western friend and will not take arms from Russia unless he is forced to by our own attitude and his internal pressures. If he purchases arms from the West, he can never be armed very heavily for the simple reason that he has not the money to buy arms in quantity. The only way he could begin to build up a big military machine would be to have gift arms.

This is approximately where the situation stands this morning.

D.D.E. [4]

[4] Printed from a copy that bears these typed initials.

---

296. Memorandum of a Conversation, Department of State, Washington, November 14, 1957 [1]

SUBJECT

Tunisian Arms

PARTICIPANTS

The Secretary
French Ambassador, Mr. Alphand
French Minister, Mr. Lucet
Counselor of the French Embassy, Mr. de Laboulaye
Mr. Elbrick—EUR
Mr. Porter—AFN

Mr. Alphand called at 3:30 to deliver an oral protest to the Secretary on the subject of delivery of arms by the United States and the United Kingdom to Tunisia. He said that the French Government formally protested the delivery of these arms and the

[1] Source: Department of State, Central Files, 772.56/11–1457. Secret. Drafted by Porter.

conditions surrounding the delivery, including the manner in which the decision of the U.S. Government had been communicated to the French Government. Mr. Alphand said the same protest was being made in London.

The French Government, Mr. Alphand said, cannot understand the attitude of its allies in this matter, an attitude which risked harming Atlantic solidarity and one which appeared to be based on the arguments of the adversaries of France.

The Secretary said he had just talked to the Tunisian Ambassador and had urged him in the strongest terms that Tunisia should seek to arrive at an arrangement with France covering her requirements and should of her own accord renounce the purchase of arms in the East. [2] The Ambassador had indicated his agreement and would urge his Government to follow this course.

The Secretary said he regretted very deeply the difference of opinion which had arisen between the United States and the French in the matter. He said that, as the Ambassador knew, we have gone to considerable extremes to afford the French an opportunity to work out a solution. Now that our delivery is being made we should both endeavor to minimize the consequences and regain the solidarity of which Mr. Alphand had spoken.

The Secretary said he had already endeavored in his talk with the Tunisian Ambassador to stress the importance of French-Tunisian relations and we will try in our press relations and in other ways to break down the differences of opinion. The Secretary said that we must not let the matter stand in the way of our working together in the future.

Ambassador Alphand inquired whether the delivery of U.S. arms is now a fact. The Secretary replied that he believed that they are in transit. Mr. Alphand said that he understood that their Ambassador in Tunis was unable to obtain Tunisian agreement not to accept an Egyptian delivery and he expressed doubt that there would be in fact any delivery by the Egyptians. The Secretary said he understood that the Egyptian shipment might be en route. Ambassador Alphand said that the Tunisian Ambassador in Paris had assured them that this was a fantastic story and that there was no likelihood of a delivery from that quarter. Mr. Elbrick said that he understood from Mr. Palmer that an Egyptian ship had left port for Tunisia and was expected to arrive on the 15th or 16th of the

[2] Dulles indicated to Ambassador Slim that it had required much courage on President Eisenhower's part to demonstrate fidelity to the principle of Tunisia's right as an independent nation to secure arms without restrictions. He added that France and NATO were more valuable to the United States than Tunisia, but the principle involved was overriding. (Memorandum of conversation by Bovey, November 14; *ibid.*)

month, and in reply to the Secretary's question as to whether the contents of the shipment had been identified, Mr. Elbrick replied affirmatively. The Secretary added that the Egyptian shipment would be a gift.

Ambassador Alphand said that the French had already given many military items to Tunisia and if Tunisia were to receive arms from French, United States, British, and Egyptian sources, she would have more than is necessary for her needs. That, Ambassador Alphand said, was the main reason why France stopped shipment.

The Secretary replied that only 500 rifles were involved. Ambassador Alphand said that rifles were very important from the French viewpoint as they were the principal item used against the French in Algeria. The Secretary expressed doubt that any of these rifles would get to Algeria.

Ambassador Alphand said that Mr. Gaillard would make a statement tomorrow and the Ambassador would urge that this be done as calmly as possible and in a manner not harmful to the Alliance.

In reply to Mr. Elbrick's question as to what the French would be saying to the press, it was agreed that on the French side the statements should consist of explanations as to why the French Government had not shipped arms, while on the American side our reasons for doing so might form the basis of press statements.

The interview ended with Mr. Alphand indicating that Mr. Pineau would arrive on November 18 in New York and would lunch with the Secretary at the French Embassy on November 19th.

297. Memorandum of a Conversation, Washington, November 19, 1957 [1]

SUBJECT

Arms for Tunisia

PARTICIPANTS

French Foreign Minister Christian Pineau
M. Louis Joxe, Secretary General of the Ministry of Foreign Affairs
Ambassador Hervé Alphand
M. Charles Lucet, Minister of the French Embassy
M. Jean de la Grandville, Counselor of the French Embassy
M. Francois de Laboulaye, Counselor of the French Embassy
M. Francois de Rose, Chief of the Treaty Section of the French Ministry of Foreign Affairs
General André Martin, Deputy for Air to the French Chief of Staff
M. Albert du Chalet of the French Atomic Energy Commissariat

The Secretary of State
Mr. Robert Murphy, Deputy Under Secretary
Mr. G. Frederick Reinhardt, Counselor
Mr. C. Burke Elbrick, Assistant Secretary EUR
Mr. Walter N. Walmsley, Deputy Assistant Secretary IO
Mr. Joseph Palmer, Deputy Assistant Secretary NEA
Mr. John N. Irwin, II, Deputy Assistant Secretary of Defense
Mr. B.E.L. Timmons, RA
Mr. John Bovey, AF/N
Mr. Matthew Looram, WE

Mr. Pineau said that he thought it would be useful to review briefly the background of the Tunisian arms issue, as he understood it, not so much to exacerbate a situation which is past, but rather in order to avoid similar difficulties in the future. The question of arms for Tunisia was raised with him in the first instance by a letter from the Secretary of State on September 14 in which the Secretary stated he was most anxious for France to deliver arms to Tunisia. If this were not possible, the letter stated, the U.S. would have to ask other European countries to supply the arms and failing this, the U.S. would have to deliver the arms itself in order to prevent Tunisia from obtaining arms from the East or the Middle East. Mr. Pineau stated that he had personally believed that the best solution was for France to furnish the arms itself and had accordingly tried to convince the Bourgès-Maunoury Cabinet to take this decision. The subsequent cabinet crisis played an adverse role in the whole matter, which, he said, he was the first to recognize. During this period the American Ambassador in Paris had frequent consultations with the

[1] Source: Department of State, Central Files, 772.56/11–1957. Secret. Drafted by Looram.

French Government with a view to seeing if a solution could not be found which would avoid a shipment of arms from the East. Shortly after the formation of the Gaillard Government, on November 8,[2] Mr. Pineau stated, he was informed by both the U.S. and U.K. Ambassadors that if France could not act by November 12, the U.S. and U.K. would have to proceed themselves with the deliveries. There was one point that was obscure at that juncture, namely, whether the U.S. and U.K. would still feel obliged to fulfill their commitments to Tunisia and furnish arms even if the French Government decided to deliver them or whether French action would obviate U.S. and U.K. action of this nature. The French assumed that if they acted, it would be unnecessary for the U.S. to deliver arms. In view of the absence of the President of the Republic, it was impossible to have a cabinet meeting before Tuesday, November 12. At that time the French Government took the decision to deliver arms to Tunisia. However, immediately thereafter the Government was informed that an Egyptian shipment of 2,000 rifles destined for Tunisia had just left Alexandria. This development altered the whole picture, Mr. Pineau stated, as the purpose of sending arms to Tunisia was to avoid arms coming from Egypt. Moreover, it would have been impossible to have justified before the French Parliament and French public opinion a decision by the French Government to deliver arms to Tunisia if Tunisia at the same time accepted arms from the Middle East. Mr. Pineau accordingly convoked the U.S. and U.K. Ambassadors immediately and requested them to urge their Governments to make a démarche to Bourguiba to reject the Egyptian offer. The U.S. reply was that such a démarche would not be appropriate and the U.K. said that it did not perceive objections to Egypt's sending this particular shipment of arms to Tunisia. It was then explained that the purpose of deliveries from Western sources was that they should arrive prior to the Egyptian shipment, rather than, as he had always understood, to prevent an Egyptian shipment completely. Mr. Pineau stated that this factor was a most important point and was the basic reason why France did not deliver the arms.

The Secretary stated that our stand regarding the need for the West to supply arms to Tunisia was based on the principle that Tunisia was a sovereign nation entitled to arms and that it was essential that the Tunisian Government not be given the impression that it had been deserted by the West, which might induce the Tunisians to reorient their policies toward the East. The U.S. had been aware that a small gift shipment from Egypt had been planned, and President Bourguiba had indicated that it would be impossible for him to reject it. We had thus never expected that the Egyptian

[2] Actually the date was November 4. [Footnote in the source text.]

shipment could be prevented. The U.S. basic purpose had been first to prevent the Tunisian Government from concluding that the Western powers were concerting in an effort to block it from obtaining a reasonable supply of arms from the West and second, to effect the deliveries prior to the arrival of the Egyptian shipment. The Secretary stated, there had evidently been an additional misunderstanding on our part, namely, we had been given to understand that France would definitely make the delivery of arms itself without any special conditions other than the guarantees regarding use and non-transferability, which had already been discussed with Bourguiba. So convinced had the U.S. been of this that our arms had been unloaded from the planes. When it was ascertained that the French Government would not act on the matter, we had had to reload and a further delay had ensued. Moreover, Prime Minister Gaillard's letter to the President had stated that the French Government would act only if no other powers furnished the arms rather than only if Tunisia did not accept arms from the East. This condition has seemed to the U.S. incompatible with Tunisian sovereignty. In any event, the Secretary said, it was recognized that there had been mutual misunderstandings, that the matter has created an adverse reaction in public opinion and that the important thing now was to look to the future.

Mr. Pineau stated that in this connection he had just received alarming news to the effect that the Egyptian arms had been unloaded at Tripoli and that 40 Tunisian trucks were required to transport the arms to Tunisia. It seemed to him that if 40 trucks were required, it was hardly a symbolic shipment, but involved much greater quantities than had been anticipated. He feared this would exacerbate the already strong feelings of the French public which the French Government was trying to appease rather than exploit, as had been wrongly reported in the press. The storm of protests by French public opinion resulting from the U.S.–U.K. decision had been even greater than the French Government had feared. It was essential to smooth over this matter, but frankly, Mr. Pineau said, it would take a considerable length of time for French public opinion to calm down. Moreover, he said, there were many adversaries of NATO in France who were ready to exploit such matters to our mutual disadvantage. He apologized for going into the matter of French domestic politics, but he thought he should set forth the difficulties of the present Parliamentary situation in order for the Secretary to be fully cognizant of the difficult situation in France. In the National Assembly there were 150 Communists, about 20 of the Left, such as Mendès-France, who looked for support from the Communists, about 70 nationalistic deputies on the Right and about 10 adherents of Mr. Soustelle. This made about 250 out of 596 deputies who could be counted on to exploit an issue which would weaken NATO. The principle which Mr. Mollet and he had long fought for in the Socialist Party and which had become the Party's basic principle was the Atlantic Pact. If this matter of the arms could not be resolved before the next Socialist Party Congress, there was a grave danger that there might emerge a majority in the Party which would question this principle. It was thus essential, he said, to explore every means for smoothing over this difference and to restore in the minds of the French public the importance and validity of the North Atlantic Treaty.

Mr. Pineau stated that with regard to specifics, the essential task, he thought, was to see to it that arms delivered to Tunisia would not find their way to the Algerian rebels. The first and most important thing to be done was to assure that the arms requested by Tunisia and delivered to her were in fact in consonance with the number of soldiers Tunisia had and not in excess of her basic requirements. The greatest danger was that if in fact there were more arms than soldiers, the arms would then have to be stored and as a result could easily be diverted to the Algerian rebels. Secondly, Mr. Pineau requested that the U.S. urge the Tunisian Government to keep close watch on the arms and to give absolute guarantees as to their safekeeping. In this connection it might be useful if the U.S. were to supply the French Government with the serial numbers of the U.S. rifles delivered. Thirdly, it was important for the U.S. to hold up further deliveries pending the National Assembly vote on the Loi-Cadre and give the French Government an opportunity to enter into negotiations with the Tunisian Government on all matters outstanding. Within such context the French Government might be able to come to an agreement on the matter of arms.

In response to the Secretary's question as to the French estimate of Tunisia's justifiable requirements, Mr. Pineau stated that it was difficult to judge in view of conflicting reports from Tunisia as to how many units they intended to constitute. At first they had mentioned requirements for one battalion, but more recently they indicated requirements for units amounting to about 6,000 men. Of course, what was important in this estimate of Tunisian requirements was how many units were in being and not how many were on paper. It was true that up until now the French forces had found among the Algerian rebels only one rifle out of the amount that France had provided Tunisia. However, the rebels had received a vast quantity of British arms that had been taken from the depots in Suez and it was important that a similar situation should not occur in Tunisia.

The Secretary stated that he thought Mr. Pineau would be interested in the fact that Bourguiba had rejected the Egyptian proposal for shipping the Egyptian arms to Tunisia via an Egyptian naval vessel, which would have provoked a great deal of publicity on the arrival of the arms in Tunisia. Bourguiba had insisted that they be unloaded in Tripoli and brought in inconspicuously by Tunisian trucks. The Secretary thought this indicated a highly desirable point of view of the Tunisian Government to play down the Egyptian deliveries.

The Secretary said that he had no objection in principle to Mr. Pineau's proposals. The U.S. had no desire to supply arms in excess of Tunisia's basic requirements which might thus provide an opportunity for them to be smuggled to Algeria. . . . There was no reason why a mutually satisfactory understanding could not be reached on this matter, although the U.S. could obviously not prevent the Tunisians from obtaining arms from other sources, such as Spain, Italy or Belgium. Secondly, the U.S. would be willing to urge the Tunisian Government to take all necessary measures for safeguarding the arms. The Tunisian Government had already given us a formal and satisfactory commitment in this sense, but we would be glad to follow up this point. Thirdly, the U.S. had no plans for further arms deliveries for the present and was in agreement that an opportunity should be given for the French and Tunisian Governments to enter into negotiations. It was the U.S. hope that this would result in Tunisia's looking to France for its normal source for arms. If a satisfactory arrangement could be made by Tunisia and France, the U.S. would no longer be interested in furnishing arms to Tunisia.

Mr. Pineau stated that in all this it was important to realize that the military situation in Algeria had profoundly changed during the last few months. A great many rebel units had been destroyed and more and more Moslems were coming over to the French side. The only important FLN military units now in existence were concentrated in Tunisia. Should these units, armed with weapons they had obtained surreptitiously from Tunisian depots, launch an attack on Algeria, the consequences could well be disastrous.

In response to Mr. Murphy's question as to whether the French Government considered that there was actual collaboration between the Tunisian Government and the FLN, Mr. Pineau replied that there was a very fine distinction between overt Tunisian assistance to the rebels and clandestine help. There were presently FLN training camps, hospitals, etc. in Tunisia near the Algerian border. However, until now the FLN had only obtained contraband arms through Tunisia, and none of the arms that had been provided to the Tunisian Government.

In response to the Secretary's question as to how the arms, presumably coming from Syria and Egypt, were reaching Algeria, Mr. Pineau stated that they came by many different ways, but the most important were via Libya and Tunisia and to a lesser extent through Morocco. All the arms which France had furnished Syria have since been shipped to the FLN and replaced by Soviet equipment.

In response to Mr. Pineau's request for information regarding the size of the current Egyptian shipment of arms, the Secretary stated that the U.S. would also wish to have information regarding this matter and would in due course convey its substance to the French Government. The Secretary added, however, that the U.S. had no reason to believe that President Bourguiba intended to build up a big military establishment or act as an intermediary for the Algerian rebels in obtaining arms. In fact, his intentions in this connection have appeared far more modest than those of many of the Arab leaders who seemed to think that their prestige was dependent on the amount of arms in their possession. The Secretary accordingly thought that this would not constitute a problem and that Bourguiba would keep his military establishment to a modest level. Mr. Pineau replied that he hoped the Secretary was right, although he frankly did not share the Secretary's confidence in Bourguiba. However, what he feared most was that the arms would find their way to the Algerian rebels, despite Bourguiba's best intentions rather than with his concurrence.

Mr. Pineau stated that it was important that consultations be initiated immediately with the U.S. with a view to reviewing the whole arms problem for Tunisia and whether or not the current shipments that Tunisia was receiving were in effect in accordance with her requirements or in excess of them. He thought it was essential that a procedure for such consultations be set up now. This might be done in Washington through consultations between the French Ambassador and the Secretary.

The Secretary replied that he, for his part, agreed to setting up such procedure, although it would of course be necessary first to obtain British concurrence to this arrangement in view of the U.K. interest in this matter. He also made clear that the Tunisian Government would have to be consulted and that the U.S., the U.K. and France could not set themselves up as independent judges of Tunisia's needs without creating a mutual resentment.

Although it was first agreed that a joint communiqué would be issued at the end of the meeting covering the discussion on the Tunisian arms issue, it was finally agreed, as the result of Mr. Pineau's objection to the draft prepared, that no communiqué would be issued. Mr. Pineau stated that he would tell the press following the meeting that he had set forth his Government's point of view with regard to the delivery of arms to Tunisia and that it had been agreed that a procedure would be sought to meet French preoccupations regarding the danger of diversions to the Algerian rebels. The Secretary cautioned Mr. Pineau in this connection not to say anything that might be misinterpreted and which might require U.S. clarification. An issuance of conflicting statements would only make matters worse. Mr. Pineau stated that he fully agreed.

298. Telegram From the Department of State to the Embassy in Tunisia [1]

Washington, November 26, 1957—6:42 p.m.

380. Following is for your guidance on arms for Tunisia.

(1) You should be prepared discourage any move on part of GOT which would result in reopening this explosive question (publicly or otherwise) prior to December 15 NATO meeting. Bourguiba must be fully cognizant serious strains to which Franco–US and Franco–UK relations subjected as result token delivery and threat not only to success forthcoming NATO meeting, but to future strength and effectiveness NATO inherent in failure resolve present US–UK differences with France on this problem. Since principle has now been established in dramatic fashion that GOT has access to US–UK arms if needed, it is also to interest GOT that French tempers be allowed to cool. You can reassure him that no formal consultations re fulfillment Tunisia's arms requirements will be undertaken without participation GOT and that we would prefer any such discussions be deferred until after NATO meeting. We stand firmly on principle Tunisia entitled have her legitimate arms requirements met by West and present problem is one of tactics and timing.

(2) Department's position on consultations visualized Pineau Washington talks (Deptel 368 to Tunis) [2] will be developed in light Bourguiba's reaction on returning from Morocco and results current Macmillan–Gaillard talks. [3] In general, our ideas coincide with those

[1] Source: Department of State, Central Files, 772.56/11–2657. Secret. Repeated to Paris, London, Rome, Madrid, and Algiers.

[2] Telegram 368, November 21, contained a summary of the November 19 Pineau–Dulles conversation. (*Ibid.*, 772.56/11–2157)

[3] As indicated in telegram 2707 from Paris, November 26, when Gaillard met with Macmillan on November 25 he sought concessions which would help his government survive when the Loi-Cadre came before the Assembly for a second time. Specifically, he wanted Macmillan to acknowledge that he had been mistaken in providing arms to Tunisia and to pledge not to do so again. Macmillan, however, was only willing to agree to consult with France to avoid similar difficulties. (*Ibid.*, 641.51/11–2657)

now held by UK, i.e., any consultations should be informal, secret, centered Tunis and provide appropriate Tunisian participation.

(3) Department thoroughly agrees we should not involve ourselves in reaching judgment independent of Tunisian wishes re size armed forces or amounts and types equipment Tunisia requires for legitimate internal security purposes. Would it be possible, nevertheless, for current ICA Police Survey to include estimate as to size Army required to supplement police and National Guard in internal security role? . . .

(4) FYI. Information and recommendations contained Tunis tel 527[4] (with which assume USOM agrees) are very convincing and every effort will be made work out procedures for meeting first and second phase police requirements. Even though it might prove possible we would not in line paragraph 1 above visualize any deliveries pending resumption US–UK–Tunisian–French consultations on entire internal security and arms requirements problem following December NATO meeting. End FYI.

(5) You will have noted from Deptel 369[5] that French have asked for serial numbers rifles included token delivery and that US Army has no record these numbers. We agree Tunis tel 525[6] Tunisian reaction would be extremely adverse were we to accede to French request and if you think desirable you may reveal request and our negative response adding that for Bourguiba's own protection, would be desirable for GOT maintain accurate record serial numbers all weapons received from US and UK. If you believe it can be done in context our desire protect GOT against false charges diversion these weapons to Algeria you might also ask for copy of records.

(6) Would appreciate any current information on size, composition, means and date delivery symbolic Egyptian arms shipment.

Dulles

---

[4] In telegram 527, November 23, Ambassador Jones commented on the preliminary report of the U.S. Police Survey Mission which had been in Tunisia since mid-October. The report pointed out serious deficiencies in small arms and communications and transportation gear which jeopardized Tunisia's ability to maintain internal security. An immediate grant of $139,000 was recommended with a subsequent program worth $661,000 to follow. (*Ibid.*, 772.5/11–2357) Ambassador Houghton anticipated no problem in regard to jeeps and landrovers, but in telegram 2679, November 25, offered the opinion that even 100 carbines might generate a French protest. He called for a delay or, at the least, urged that prior French concurrence be secured. (*Ibid.*, 772.56/11–2557)

[5] Not printed. (*Ibid.*, 772.56/11–2057)

[6] Telegram 525, November 22, conveyed Ambassador Jones' opinion, with which British Ambassador concurred, that the French should not be given the numbers. (*Ibid.*, 772.56/11–2257)

299. Telegram From the Delegation at the NATO Heads of Government Meeting to the Department of State [1]

Paris, December 16, 1957—11 p.m.

Secto 11. Following is summary yesterday's meeting President and Gaillard. Secretary, Pineau and Ambassador Houghton present. Full report being pouched. [2]

Meeting was devoted almost exclusively to North Africa. Gaillard referred to his letter to President in which he had predicted French public reaction to delivery arms to Tunisia would be very bad. He noted reaction had been even worse than expected and continues to be strongly felt. French public links differences over North Africa to part France plays in NATO. Algerian question so sensitive French opinion subordinates all other questions to it.

On Algeria he expressed appreciation for United States help in United Nations. He hopes for quick solution in Algeria because of success of pacification and because loi-cadre, which passed Assembly with substantial majority, provides political solution. Loi-cadre is inspired by similar law for black Africa which has worked well. In view increasing pacification GOF intends implement loi-cadre wherever possible.

Algerian problem, Gaillard declared, cannot be isolated from those of Morocco and Tunisia. France enjoys good relations with former as evidenced by Moroccan efforts and attitude in United Nations debate. Sultan has urged FLN to move toward cease-fire.

Outlook in Tunisia is less hopeful and government less stable. Algerian rebels have invaded Tunisia and established base from which they attack Algeria. Bourguiba is in awkward situation which he probably deplores. However even with Tunisia GOF hopes to negotiate all differences but must have our help. Best way for us to help is not to give Bourguiba impression differences exist between us. Otherwise Bourguiba will keep these differences alive. Gaillard hoped we would work out procedures to avoid differences.

In reply President said we can view question like this only in broad framework our relationship with whole Arab world. He said we recognize position of France in North Africa arising from history, trade and economic relations, but our establishment diplomatic relations with Tunisia and Morocco means that we must treat them as equal and sovereign. He hopes France will maintain ties with North Africa. France and North Africa need each other.

---

[1] Source: Department of State, Central Files, 751S.00/12–1657. Secret; Priority. Repeated to Algiers, Rabat, and Tunis.

[2] Not printed.

President added he wished to say with great emphasis he was shocked to hear from Secretary that French opinion might believe United States business interests influencing United States policy in direction supplanting French influence in North Africa. President said that is just not so. Discord in area is as harmful to United States as to French and North African interests. We hope France will play its part in maintaining stability. Specifically we hope French will help supply Tunisia. United States wishes to be of assistance but can do so much more effectively if France's relations with Tunisia and Morocco are better. If situation like that involving shipment of arms to Tunisia arises again, we will of course be ready to consult. President suggested Gaillard talk personally with Bourguiba about possible points of difficulty.

Pineau said there is no French disposition to ask United States to regard Tunisia and Morocco as other than sovereign states but he hopes we will not yield to blackmail. President pointed out we had refused arms to Egypt and Syria and they had turned to Soviets. If this were repeated in Tunisia Russians would have foothold in area. However we will find ways to be helpful in meeting this problem. In response inquiry from Gaillard, President reiterated that, if case similar to Tunisian arms should arise, we would consult and he hopes in plenty of time.

Gaillard thanked President for his understanding and added that, if President could only say publicly one-quarter of what he had just said on this subject, atmosphere would be much improved. President replied he would have no objection to making statement at some appropriate time that France should play important part in development of North Africa. Reverting to Tunisia, Gaillard said GOF intends to reopen negotiations within few days and it would be helpful if United States could say something publicly in support these negotiations. Secretary remarked President or himself might find occasion to do so in Washington. President said important for large countries to make gestures to small countries and hoped France would do so in Tunisia.

Meeting ended in atmosphere of great cordiality.

300. Telegram From the Delegation at the NATO Heads of Government Meeting to the Embassy in Tunisia [1]

Paris, December 19, 1957—8 p.m.

218. Please deliver following personal message from Secretary to Bourguiba: [2]

During the conversations here our French friends have brought up the question of relations between France and Tunisia, a topic of discussion both bilateral and before the NATO Council. We have consistently adhered to our position that Tunisia, as an independent state, is entitled to work out its own destiny, and that we should not and would not, in Tunisia's absence, take decisions affecting its vital interests. We hope that Tunisian destiny will be found in close and mutually advantageous relations with the west. It is furthermore our earnest hope that fruitful relations will be maintained between France and Tunisia.

---

[1] Source: Department of State, Central Files, 651.72/12–1957. Confidential. Repeated to the Department. The source text is the copy sent to Washington.

[2] In telegram 636 from Tunis, December 17, Ambassador Jones indicated that Bourguiba would appreciate a personal message of reassurance from the President or Secretary of State. The Tunisians were upset and worried by French press accounts which implied that the United States might have conceded the right to a special position in North Africa to France. (*Ibid.*, 651.72/12–1757) The Tunisian Chargé in Washington and the Tunisian Ambassador in France sought similar clarifications from the United States on December 17. Jones reported in telegram 657, December 21, that Bourguiba appreciated the Secretary's words. (*Ibid.*, 651.72/12–2157)

UNION OF SOUTH AFRICA

UNITED STATES RELATIONS WITH SOUTH AFRICA; UNITED STATES CONCERN WITH DEVELOPMENTS IN SOUTH AFRICA; THE APARTHEID AND SOUTH WEST AFRICA QUESTIONS AT THE UNITED NATIONS [1]

301. Minutes of the Tenth Meeting of the Delegation to the United Nations General Assembly, New York, October 25, 1955, 9:30 a.m. [2]

US/A/M/(SR)/38

[Here follows discussion of Administrative Tribunal judgments.]

Race Conflict in South Africa

Congressman Merrow then asked Mr. Sisco [3] to outline our position on the "Race Conflict in South Africa" item which was scheduled to come up in the Ad Hoc Committee that week.

Mr. Sisco pointed out that the South African Government had long followed a policy of segregation against 9,000,000 Negroes in the Union of South Africa as well as 1,500,000 people of mixed blood and about 350,000 Asians, mainly Indians. The National Party now in power had embarked upon a policy of discrimination manifested in the Groups Areas Act. [4] The question of Apartheid had been on the General Assembly's agenda since 1952, Mr. Sisco explained. In that year the General Assembly set up a commission of three members to keep the question under review and to make recommendations about how the situation could be improved. Each year, Mr. Sisco said, the Committee had submitted a report but no fruitful achievements had resulted. The Committee report had for this year concluded: 1) that Apartheid created hardships and tensions

[1] For previous documentation on this subject, see *Foreign Relations*, 1952–1954, vol. XI, Part 1, pp. 902 ff.

[2] Source: Department of State, IO Files. Secret. Drafted on November 29. No other drafting information is given on the source text. In the absence of Ambassador Lodge and Congressman Brooks Hays, Congressman Chester E. Merrow presided.

[3] Joseph J. Sisco, an adviser to the delegation.

[4] The Group Areas Act or Act 49 of 1950 was intended to restrict "Natives", "Coloureds", and whites to their own areas in respect to ownership, occupancy, and trading. The second group incorporated Indians, Malays, and Chinese.

and was in conflict with Articles 55 and 56 of the Charter, and 2) that while the Apartheid policy was still in force it was being implemented at a slower pace. [5] Mr. Sisco said, parenthetically, that the State Department analysis did not agree with this latter conclusion. The Commission had suggested as steps which might bring about an improvement in the situation: 1) more frequent contacts among the different races in South Africa and 2) UN technical experts who might be able to give useful advice upon the racial question.

The South African Government took the position that the UN lacked competence to discuss this question on the ground that it fell solely within the domestic jurisdiction of South Africa. Asian and African delegations felt on the contrary, that the UN was fully competent to deal with the matter. We had taken the position since 1953, Mr. Sisco explained, that the question should be approached with great caution. We had felt that the issue should be dealt with as a broad social problem and not merely as a question involving South Africa alone. Furthermore, we questioned the wisdom of continuing the life of the Commission on the grounds that it had not been effective in finding a constructive solution. We also had certain doubts as to competence. Congressman Merrow planned in the Ad Hoc Committee to make a statement affirming our opposition to racial discrimination and outlining our own failures and achievements in this field. Congressman Merrow would then make clear our willingness to support some kind of general resolution on this item. [6] The Indians had suggested that the present Commission be replaced by a rapporteur, who would be charged with reviewing developments on this question. Without taking the lead ourselves, Mr. Sisco said, we would like to see a resolution that would end the Commission on the ground that it had not been effective and which would not require that the item be placed automatically on the agenda of the eleventh General Assembly. A few Latin American Delegations, Mr. Sisco said, tended to favor the appointment of an official, possibly from the Secretariat, who would receive information but would not be required automatically to report to the next General Assembly.

Mr. Sisco noted that the South African Delegation had withdrawn from the Ad Hoc Committee yesterday but had announced that it reserved the right to be present to vote on any resolution on

---

[5] U.N. doc. A/2953 contains the Commission's third report, which covered the period from August 1954 through July 1955.

[6] Merrow's statement in the Ad Hoc Committee, October 27, is contained in USUN Press Release 2251, issued that same day. (Department of State, IO/ODA Files: Lot 62 D 228, Africa Apartheid—pre-1959)

this matter. Our position would depend primarily on the type of resolutions tabled by the Indians and the Latin Americans.

Mr. Bell[7] asked how we could reconcile our position on this question with our position on Algeria since on the face of it both involved intervention in domestic affairs. Mr. Sisco said that he had asked Mr. Meeker[8] before the meeting to prepare a legal memorandum on the question of competence, and that Mr. Meeker was prepared to address himself to this point.

Mr. Meeker explained that our position on South Africa rested on Articles 55 and 56 of the Charter, which stated as a purpose of the UN the promotion of respect for and observance of human rights and fundamental freedoms without distinction as to race, sex, language or religion, and obligated UN Members to take joint and separate action in cooperation with the Organization for the achievement of this purpose. This obligation of UN Members was a matter of international and not domestic concern. Apartheid, Mr. Meeker continued, was not an isolated episode but a whole course of policy regarding racial discrimination. Thus the issue arose as to whether South Africa was not living up to its Charter obligations; under Article 10 of the Charter "the General Assembly may discuss any questions or any matters within the scope of the present Charter . . . and . . . may make recommendations to the Members of the United Nations . . . "[9] The Algerian question differed from the South African question because the sponsors of the Algerian complaint showed that their object was a General Assembly resolution calling for a new constitutional law of the French Republic which would change the status of Algeria in relation to France. In the South African item there was no question of altering the South African constitution, but rather a complaint that South Africa was not living up to its human rights obligations under the Charter. There was thus a distinction, albeit a difficult one.

Mr. Bell asked if under the same reasoning it would not be possible for the UN to seek to interfere in US domestic policies with respect to the racial question. Mr. Meeker pointed out that the situation in the U.S. was totally different from that prevailing in South Africa. In the U.S. while progress might not be as consistent or as rapid as could be desired, it was still occurring, and the direction in the U.S. was toward meeting the obligations accepted in the Charter. The direction here was forward—not backward—Mr. Meeker said. In South Africa the opposite was true as the government there was trying to turn back the clock.

---

[7] Laird Bell, Alternate Representative.

[8] Leonard C. Meeker, senior adviser to the delegation on legal affairs.

[9] Ellipses are in the source text.

Mr. Brokenburr[10] asked whether we might not be accused of retreating on this issue if we should take the position this year that the question should no longer automatically be placed on the agenda. Mr. Brokenburr suggested that such a position might place us in an unfavorable light and leave us vulnerable to charges that we were taking the position because of racial conditions in the U.S. Mr. Brokenburr agreed with Mr. Meeker about the distinction between the situation in South Africa and the situation here but suggested that we might harm our own standing by appearing faint-hearted on this question.

Mr. Sisco agreed with Mr. Brokenburr's observation and pointed out that for those reasons in particular we did not plan to push, ourselves, for the kind of resolution outlined above but to support such a resolution if presented by others and to attempt to focus attention on the question of the usefulness of UN action in this field.

Senator Pastore[11] commented that we should beware lest our chickens come home to roost. The position proposed above, Senator Pastore suggested, seemed to be based on the idea that it was futile to consider discussing this question when little accomplishment of a concrete nature seemed to be possible. We had taken the general position, however, Senator Pastore pointed out, that the development of world opinion was one of the basic strengths of the UN and, as a corollary to this, that we should not stop talking merely because the fruits of such talk were not immediately apparent. Senator Pastore suggested that talk in itself could be extremely significant, as, for example, in keeping alive the hope of liberation among the Satellite people. This, Senator Pastore said, was an extremely delicate problem. It might also be suggested by our critics, Senator Pastore said, that we were willing to dilute a South African resolution because of our concern over South Africa's uranium deposits. If we agreed with the human rights provisions of the Charter, we should be explicit in saying so, Senator Pastore said. We should, in fact, go out of our way to emphasize these provisions since the chief violator of them was the Soviet Union who, by our silence, was "getting away with murder."

Mr. Blaustein[12] agreed that we should not retreat on this principle but that on the contrary we should reiterate our support for basic human rights. Congressman Merrow observed that more

---

[10] Robert L. Brokenburr, Alternate Representative.

[11] Senator John O. Pastore (Rhode Island).

[12] Jacob Blaustein, Alternate Representative.

attention would have to be paid to this question at another meeting since the time was growing late.[13]

[13] On November 9, the Ad Hoc Political Committee adopted a draft resolution sponsored by 17 nations (A/AC.80/L.1 and Corr. 1 and 2) by a vote of 37 to 7, with 13 abstentions. The United States abstained on the resolution as a whole while voting against the extension of the Commission. The United Kingdom, with U.S. support, took the lead in seeking to prevent the necessary two-thirds approval by the General Assembly for the continuation of the Commission. On December 6, only 33 members supported it while 17, including the United States, were opposed, and 9 abstained. Resolution 917(X) commended the Commission for its work, regretted South Africa's lack of cooperation, expressed concern that apartheid was being perpetuated, and called on the South African Government to adhere to Article 56 of the Charter. See *Yearbook of the United Nations 1955*, pp. 69–72. Documents on this subject are in Department of State, Central File 845A.411.

302. Memorandum of a Conversation, Department of State, Washington, November 10, 1955[1]

SUBJECT

Defense of Africa and Middle East

PARTICIPANTS

Mr. F.C. Erasmus, South African Defense Minister
General du Toit, Chief of Staff, South African Armed Forces
Mr. J.P. de Villiers, Secretary, South African Defense Department
Ambassador Holloway, South African Embassy
Mr. Anthony A.M. Hamilton, Counselor, South African Embassy
Mr. Elbrick, EUR
Mr. Miner, BNA

The South African Minister of Defense, Mr. F.C. Erasmus, called on Mr. Elbrick, November 10, by previous appointment. As this was his last official conversation during his current visit to the US, he thought it would be useful to review the subjects he had discussed

[1] Source: Department of State, Central Files, 745A.5/11–1055. Secret. Drafted by Miner.

with the Defense Department[2] and with Asst. Secretary Allen.[3] In these discussions he had put forward five principal points: 1) South African access to US radar information; 2) South African purchase of US military aircraft in the event of hostilities; 3) the convening of a Middle East-African defense conference; 4) the key position of Ethiopia; and 5) the possible establishment of a radar screen for South Africa.

The Defense Minister discussed each of these points in some detail. In discussing points 1 and 2, he followed the same line as in his conversation with Mr. Allen on November 9. Concerning Middle East-African defense, Mr. Erasmus particularly stressed that South Africa was an independent country and wished to be included at the outset in any planning that would involve use of South African forces in the event of war. He made clear, however, that South Africa did not wish at present to become a member of the Baghdad Pact.[4] As in his conversation with Mr. Allen, the South African Defense Minister stressed his belief that the USSR had by-passed the Northern Tier by virtue of the Soviet Bloc's armament arrangements with Egypt.[5] South Africa felt, he said, that a Southern Tier defense system should be established. This consideration led him to his fourth point: the importance of Ethiopia. With Egypt, and possibly the Sudan and the Arabian Peninsula, open to Soviet penetration, South Africa believed that Ethiopia had become of great strategic importance in the defense of eastern and southern Africa. He had been encouraged by learning during his present visit of indications of increased US interest in Ethiopia, specifically in the development of an airline and a port. He hoped that the US would activate its right to construct and maintain bases in that country. His fifth point was related to this consideration. South Africa was most interested in developing a radar screen to provide early warning for southern and eastern Africa. The Defense Minister hoped that the

---

[2] The South African Government had originally sought U.S. approval for Erasmus to come to Washington between June 15 and 18. (*Ibid.*, 033.45A11/4–2955) The visit was delayed until the period between November 6 and 16. In a memorandum to Elbrick dated November 10, Miner reported that the South African party had requested radar information and aircraft in their initial meeting with E. Perkins McGuire on November 8, after which they had a luncheon appointment with Secretary of Defense Wilson. (*Ibid.*, AF/AFE Files: Lot 62 D 417, U.S.–S.A. Defense Relations)

[3] The memorandum of conversation by Miner, November 9, is not printed. (*Ibid.*, Central Files, 745A.5/11–955)

[4] The Baghdad Pact was a treaty of mutual cooperation between Iran, Iraq, Turkey, Pakistan, and the United Kingdom. It was agreed to by the initial signatories on February 24, 1955. The first meeting of the members was not until the following November. For text of the pact, see *United Nations Treaty Series*, vol. 233, p. 199.

[5] Egypt announced the arms agreement with Czechoslovakia on September 27, 1955.

US might establish an air base in Ethiopia and the accompanying radar facilities. These facilities, he further hoped, could be tied in with a general early warning system for the area.

Mr. Elbrick explained that no definite replies to any of Mr. Erasmus' requests could be made at this time. The question of South African access to US radar information required study by various agencies of the US Government. He suggested that the most efficient and expeditious manner of dealing with this question would be for the South African Embassy to address a note to the Department containing the specific details of the South African request.[6] As for a US commitment to make available in wartime aircraft for purchase by South Africa, the South African Minister must be aware that such commitment was most difficult to undertake in view of the great uncertainties as to the circumstances that might prevail at the time. The South Africans could be assured that if they had on hand a considerable reserve of skilled and trained pilots in the event of war, their requests for aircraft would receive every consideration. No determination could be made now, however, as to the allocation of priorities if war should come. The South Africans might wish, however, to send us a note containing the specific details of their request on this matter.

The Department well understood Mr. Erasmus' argument that South Africa would wish to be consulted with regard to any Middle East defense plan involving the use of their forces in the event of war. As Mr. Allen had explained, the present was not a propitious occasion for any general Middle East defense conference. We would, of course, keep in mind the South Africans' views on the matter. We also understood and would give consideration to the views Mr. Erasmus had expressed concerning Ethiopia. So far as Mr. Elbrick was aware, there were no present plans for the construction of US bases or radar installations in that country. Mr. Elbrick emphasized that the Soviet Bloc's armaments arrangement with Egypt was indeed viewed seriously by the Department, but that we were not at all ready to concede that the Northern Tier had been by-passed.

Mr. Erasmus then brought forward a draft communiqué which he proposed to issue unilaterally upon his departure from Washington, November 13. He wished to know if we had any objections to it. Mr. Elbrick suggested some minor changes, stating that we appreciated the South African Minister's courtesy in showing his statement to us prior to its publication.

---

[6] On January 17, 1956, the South African Ambassador presented a note (No. TS/AIR/3/1) addressed to the Secretary of State requesting a five-man team of experts to survey and offer advice in regard to the early-warning radar and air defense system. (Department of State, Central Files, 745A.5/1–1756)

In departing, Mr. Erasmus expressed his appreciation for the friendly reception he had received in the United States.

303. Editorial Note

On December 3, the General Assembly adopted a series of resolutions relating to South West Africa. The United States was a cosponsor of Resolution 934(X) which accepted and endorsed the International Court of Justice advisory opinion of June 7. Resolution 940(X) reiterated previous General Assembly resolves that South West Africa should be placed under the Trusteeship System by means of an agreement conforming with the provisions of Chapter XII of the Charter. Resolution 942(X) requested the ICJ to provide an advisory opinion on the question of granting oral hearings to petitioners on matters relating to the Territory of South West Africa.

The United States voted against Resolution 940(X) on the grounds that reiteration of previous resolves, some of which the United States had supported, would serve no useful purpose. In respect to the issue addressed by Resolution 942(X), the United States initially was one of the sponsors of a draft resolution (U.N. doc. A/C.4/L.405) stating that the oral hearing of petitioners by the Committee on South West Africa was inadmissible as not in accordance with the procedure of the Mandate System. When it became apparent the draft resolution could not command a two-thirds majority, the United States backed the submission of the question to the Court so as to obtain a solution. See *Yearbook of the United Nations 1955*, pages 263–272. A summary of the action taken by the Tenth Session of the General Assembly on the question of South West Africa is in instruction 5619, January 26. (Department of State, Central Files, 320/1–2656)

304. Memorandum of a Conversation, Cape Town, May 15, 1956 [1]

PARTICIPANTS

The Honorable George V. Allen, Assistant Secretary of State for Near Eastern, South Asian and African Affairs
The Honorable F.C. Erasmus, Minister of Defense
Ambassador Edward T. Wailes
Mr. William M. Johnson

After a preliminary exchange of courtesies, Defense Minister Erasmus raised two defense matters of immediate concern: (1) his wish for an advance commitment by the United States to provide South Africa with the most modern jet fighters in the event of war; and (2) his request for a United States team of radar experts to advise South Africa in an early-warning defense system.

In raising point (1), Mr. Erasmus said that South Africa could not afford to maintain an up-to-date fleet of modern military aircraft during time of peace due to the rapid rate of obsolescence. He recalled that he had therefore asked, while in Washington, [2] that the United States consider continuing the former "Korean type of agreement" under which South Africa paid in full for all damage done to American equipment used by the South African Air Force. He added that his staff was currently working on South African requirements under such a program for submission to the American authorities. Mr. Allen indicated that the request would continue to receive careful consideration in Washington.

In raising point (2), Mr. Erasmus said that South Africa had already received the cooperation of Britain and Portugal in studying an early-warning defense system for southern Africa. He said Britain had permitted South Africa to survey sites in Bechuanaland and Swaziland and that he hoped South Africa would be allowed the same privilege in Basutoland. But he "didn't know". Portugal had sent a mission of two technicians to South Africa. Mr. Erasmus said he was anxious to carry out the plan over a five-year period. Mr. Allen replied that when he had left Washington final approval of South Africa's request for the dispatch of a five-man radar team appeared to be only two or three weeks away. [3]

---

[1] Source: Department of State, Central Files, 110.15–AL/5–2456. Secret. Enclosure to despatch 53 from Cape Town, May 24. Drafted by Wailes and Johnson.

[2] See Document 302.

[3] Allen had written to Gordon Gray on February 6 to indicate that compliance with the South African request "would be in accord with our foreign policy objectives." (Department of State, Central Files, 745A.5/1–1756)

Mr. Erasmus then discussed South Africa's general defense outlook. He said he thought the West's collective security system had its only gap in Africa, where there was no formal defense alignment. He expressed favor for South Africa's being associated in some way, if not integrally, with NATO. He stated South Africa's present activity, in conjunction with Britain, in arranging a "sea route" conference, probably to be held in Europe, and a defense conference of those countries represented at the Dakar and Nairobi discussions. [4] He mentioned South Africa's participation in joint naval maneuvers with French and British units.

Mr. Erasmus said South Africa planned to equip one armored division for use outside its borders in wartime. He outlined South Africa's eight-year naval build-up program. To Mr. Allen's question, Mr. Erasmus said South Africa had conscription, but that it still relied on volunteers for service outside the Union.

Mr. Allen spoke on United States defense interests and activities in the Near East and Africa. He said the United States had recognized the new Sudan government and was closely watching developments there. [5] He spoke of United States military bases in North Africa and gave an indication of their strength. He said he favored South Africa's display of initiative in defense planning in Africa, felt South Africa and the United States had mutual interests, and expressed his feeling that "one leak (one gap in the defense system) could sink the boat".

Mr. Allen said that Mr. Erasmus' visit to the United States last year served to increase the interest there in South Africa's position.

---

[4] The United States had had observers at both the Nairobi discussions of August 1951 and the March 1954 West African Defense Facilities Conference at Dakar. For documentation, see *Foreign Relations*, 1952–1954, vol. XI, Part 1, pp. 90 ff.

[5] The United States recognized Sudan's independence on January 2, 1956.

305. Memorandum of a Conversation, Department of State, Washington, July 5, 1956[1]

SUBJECT

Ambassador Holloway's Farewell Call on the Under Secretary

PARTICIPANTS

Ambassador Holloway of the Union of South Africa
The Under Secretary
AF—Mr. Cyr

Mr. Hoover expressed regret that the Ambassador was leaving Washington. Since this must be, Mr. Hoover added, he was pleased that Ambassador Holloway, with his understanding of our problems, would be stationed in such an important post as London. Ambassador Holloway replied that his transfer to London was the result of Secretary for External Affairs Forsythe's[2] resignation, which set in motion a chain of transfers. He concurred that London is an important post and added that the future of the world depends on continuing collaboration between the United States and Great Britain. South Africa is "small-fry" among the world powers, he said, but is at least as firm as the United States in its determination to combat communism, even in a third world war. The Communists have recognized this determination and would like to drive a wedge between us by pointing out that South Africa gets no aid from the United States while others do. But South Africa has no desire to be a burden on the American tax-payer and believes that a country with the capability should pay its own way. This South Africa intends to do.

But there was another matter which the Ambassador found more worrisome and concerning which he is thinking of making a public statement in a few days. The American press seems bent on poisoning the American public's mind on the subject of South Africa. Fifty per cent of the information which appears on the American press about South Africa is completely untrue or distorted. In answer to Mr. Hoover's question as to the reason, he blamed the liberal element in this country for the attacks on South Africa. Accounts of housing developments and other constructive programs make uninteresting reading material but the opposite is true of what are called repressive measures. For example, Alan Paton had written an article for *Coronet*. The editors made numerous unfavorable chang-

[1] Source: Department of State, Central Files, 611.45A/7–556. Official Use Only. Drafted by Cyr.
[2] Douglas D. Forsythe.

es which Mr. Paton could not accept. But the editors informed Mr. Paton that it was too late—the article had been published.[3]

South Africa believes in freedom, the Ambassador said, and it is therefore often asked why the Union does not give its natives the right to vote. The great bulk of the native population is still on the fringe of barbarism, he said, and the South African Government would not be so stupid as to give these people the right to vote. Rather, the Union is trying to raise the educational level of the natives and this is a long process. To give such people the right to vote, as is being done in Nigeria for example, is preposterous. Instead of understanding that the natives need to evolve, the American press takes the stand that the Union is against freedom. The South African Government intends to continue its present policies.

Mr. Hoover commented that to his knowledge many visitors to South Africa have been greatly impressed by what they have seen. It is often better in matters of public relations to go on the offensive rather than the defensive. . . .

Ambassador Holloway admitted that perhaps his Government had been remiss in this respect and indicated that he would give serious consideration to Mr. Hoover's ideas.

[3] The May 1956 issue of *Coronet* contained an article by Paton entitled "Tragedy of the Beloved Country".

---

306. Letter From the Acting Director of the Office of Southern Africa Affairs (Hadsel) to the Ambassador in Egypt (Byroade)[1]

Washington, August 3, 1956.

DEAR HANK: No one on God's earth could have possibly foreseen the fact that when we discussed two years ago the desirability of bringing the Union of South Africa into NEA[2] we would thereby find ourselves working on the same problems! Needless to say, I look forward to this collaboration with the greatest of pleasure and pledge you our wholehearted cooperation. Moreover, I can assure

[1] Source: Department of State, AF Files: Lot 58 D 627, Miscellaneous Letters. Confidential. Byroade was appointed Ambassador to South Africa on July 26. He left Egypt on September 10 and presented his credentials at his new post on October 9.

[2] South Africa had previously been under the jurisdiction of the Office of British Commonwealth and Northern European Affairs in the Bureau of European Affairs.

you that you will find South Africa an amazing country in many ways, for in climate it is something like out West and the people have a determined individualism which, I am sure, is both interesting and irritating. This situation is the surface on top of the Union's major problems, particularly those relating to race.

Though not widely known, South Africa has demonstrated a special talent for becoming a party to international harangues, in which we have been trying where possible to exercise mediating, or at least moderating influence. Last year South Africa walked out of the UN because of efforts there to investigate apartheid in the Union, which the Government regards as a purely domestic issue.[3] Apartheid was finally dropped from the UN agenda—action which was supported by the United States in a close vote[4]—and South Africa subsequently indicated it would return its delegation to the UN this fall. But South Africa will still have to answer for its refusal to accept UN trusteeship over the mandated territory of South-West Africa and perhaps its treatment of its Indian minority. Both items, usually introduced by India, have been on the UN agenda since 1946.

The Prime Minister, Mr. Strijdom,[5] and his Minister of External Affairs, Mr. Louw[6] returned to the Union a week ago from the Commonwealth Prime Ministers' Conference in London. It was widely repeated in Opposition circles that Mr. Strijdom, as anti-British an Afrikaner as he has long been, would come back a "Queen's man", but I doubt that such a sturdy Afrikaner Nationalist could be so quickly and easily converted. It is true, however, that Mr. Strijdom's Government has become increasingly less isolationist in the last ten months, to a large extent due to its concern over developments in the Near East, which it has come to regard as its defense frontier. It is seeking not only closer ties with Britain and the United States in such significant areas as defense, but has unveiled a new policy of friendly association with all its African neighbors, including such Black states as the Gold Coast. The effect of this new policy upon its restrictive racial program at home will be most interesting. Our policy has consistently been to persuade the Government and the White electorate to moderate its policy of *baasskup* or White supremacy, subtly because of the extreme hypersensitivity of South Africans to outside influence or "interference",

[3] The South African delegation walked out of the U.N. General Assembly on November 9, 1955.

[4] A Costa Rican amendment seeking to have the General Assembly agree to continue to take up the apartheid issue at its Eleventh Session failed to win the necessary two-thirds vote.

[5] Johannes Gerhardus Strijdom.

[6] Eric H. Louw.

but there may be a better opportunity now than before because of the Whites' re-examination of their traditional attitudes—and of their consciences.

From a practical political point of view, our relations with South Africa are very friendly and harmonious. South Africa is strongly anti-Communist and pro-West. It looks increasingly to the United States, instead of Britain as formerly, as its model, its leader, and its source of assistance and capital. There is more American capital invested in South Africa today than in any other African territory—over $300,000,000. 116 American companies are represented there, and there are several thousand Americans resident throughout the Union. South Africans of all races are so friendly and hospitable by nature that Americans find life in the Union usually congenial.

At the moment, the Embassy is working out the final details of a Cultural Agreement with the Government, and no snags are anticipated.[7] We are also in the process of working out a Nuclear Reactor Treaty with the Union, which will occupy a few months more at the least.[8] After eight years of effort, the Government was finally persuaded last month to agree to the most important provisions of a proposed Consular Convention;[9] namely, the duty-free entry of liquor, tobacco, and food for career consular officers! Finally, you will find in the country on your arrival the United States Air Force's best six-member team on early-warning radar systems, which the South African Defense Department requested to study its scheme for improving its defenses.[10]

Our program of assistance to South Africa in the extraction of uranium, of which it is nearly the world's largest producer, is going along very smoothly. It has been necessary, however, for Ambassador Gallman[11] and Ambassador Wailes before you to prod the producers of the strategic minerals of manganese and chrome to live up to their supply contracts.[12] I'm afraid this is a problem you will inherit and have to work with for some time. The main difficulty is the lack of railway cars, which the new Minister of Transport is

---

[7] Documentation on this subject is in Department of State, Central Files, 511.45A3/3–1956. No such agreement was concluded.

[8] On July 8, U.S. and South African representatives signed an agreement for cooperation concerning civil uses of atomic energy. The agreement became effective August 22. For text, see TIAS 3885; 8 UST (pt. 2) 1367.

[9] This convention was never concluded.

[10] On July 31, the South African Chargé was informed that the Departments of Defense and State approved the sending of a team of air defense experts to South Africa. (Department of State, Central Files, 745A.5/1–1756) The U.S. team was scheduled to leave for South Africa on August 12. Documentation on the team's recommendations is *ibid.*, 711.5845A.

[11] Waldemar J. Gallman, Ambassador from October 18, 1951 to August 15, 1954.

[12] Documentation on the U.S. effort to speed up the delivery of South African chrome ore is in Department of State, Central File 845A.2547.

doing his best to alleviate. But repeated pushing from our end still seems to be required.

Many African territories are less and less inclined to admit or tolerate foreign missionaries, and South Africa is in this group. The Embassy has avoided making any official representations in this matter, and we are only hoping that the Union's restrictions on American missionary activity there do not become any worse.[13]

About staffing, I believe the complement of your five offices are full, with the single exception of the Consul's position in Port Elizabeth. This should be filled in the near future. I believe your personal staff at the Embassy is an excellent one. It has certainly been doing an outstanding job.

I am enclosing a short statement of our general attitude towards the Union, outlined in the form of pros and cons close cooperation. I hope it may prove of some interest.

I know that you will find South Africa an interesting and congenial post, and I greatly look forward to learning of your reactions as time goes by.

Leo Cyr happens to be on leave at the moment. If he were here, I know he would join in best wishes to you and Mrs. Byroade.

Sincerely yours,

Fred L. Hadsel[14]

[Enclosure][15]

U.S. Policy Toward South Africa

Present U.S. policy is to maintain the friendly relations existing between this Government and the Union Government, notably because of South Africa's strategic importance and mineral production. At the same time, U.S. policy seeks to avoid giving the appearance, in any way, of endorsing or underwriting apartheid, South Africa's restrictive racial policy.

Assets of South Africa to the U.S.

1. South Africa is strongly anti-Communist, pro-West, and pro-American. South Africa is a member of the Commonwealth.

2. South Africa is astride the Cape sea route, the alternative to the Suez Canal, and has Africa's best developed ports.

---

[13] Documentation on this subject is *ibid.*, 845A.181.

[14] Printed from a copy that bears this typed signature.

[15] Confidential. Drafted by William M. Johnson on April 9.

3. South Africa is now thought to be the West's biggest supplier of uranium and is an important producer of the strategic minerals of chrome (1/4 of world's supply), manganese, amosite asbestos, and such lesser minerals as titanium, corundum, and so on.

4. South Africa is the only Westernized and industrialized nation in Africa and as such is the continent's best arsenal and repair shop in time of war.

5. Though small, South Africa's military force is Africa's most effective.

Liabilities of South Africa to the U.S.

1. South Africa is one of the West's greatest propaganda liabilities because of its restrictive racial policy directed at all non-whites. Apartheid appears as the most flagrant kind of "colonialism" throughout the non-white world. Apartheid may arouse anti-white sentiment among Africans everywhere.

The voting on South African issues [16] before the UN can cause the U.S. to be identified with colonialism and the maintenance of apartheid. Any cooperation with South Africa, in the UN or out, can be interpreted by non-whites as opposition or antipathy toward them.

Persuasion of the South African Government to moderate its racial policies is a good line, but extremely tricky and unlikely of much success. The Government is obdurate and hypersensitive to what it regards as "interference".

Encouragement of South Africa in participating in pan-African defense schemes and developing closer relations with other African territories in other ways is also a good line, but cannot be pushed too hard or too obviously and has inherent dangers. Though it is barely possible South Africa may accommodate itself somewhat to the development of more enlightened racial experiments elsewhere in Africa, a better understanding of South Africans by Africans to the north may only increase the opposition of those Africans to the Union and its domestic policies. The metropolitan Powers, with their own racial policies subject to increasing challenge by their African citizens, are themselves wary about adopting too cooperative an attitude toward South Africa.

[16] There have been three before the UN since 1946: the question of the international status of the mandate of South-West Africa, the treatment of South Africa's Indian minority, and the application of apartheid. [Footnote in the source text.]

307. Despatch From the Embassy in South Africa to the Department of State [1]

No. 38 *Pretoria, August 6, 1956.*

REF

Embassy Cape Town Despatch No. 2, January 27, 1956 [2]

SUBJECT

Assessment of Developments in South Africa, January–August, 1956

[Here follow sections 1–9, on such subjects as political parties, economic conditions, and foreign relations.]

10. United States Policy

During the recent visit of the Foreign Service Inspectors to the Embassy, they indicated that they intend to recommend that a new United States policy paper be drawn up in Washington for South Africa. Our present general policy guidance, which I have attempted to follow, is:

(1) to obtain the Union's cooperation in the supply of uranium and other strategic minerals and metals needed by the United States;
(2) to encourage the Union to remain in the Commonwealth and on the side of the Western nations; and
(3) to encourage the Union insofar as possible to moderate its policies.

The question which confronts us is how best to implement these policies in the overall interests of the United States.

On the first point I feel that little needs to be done since we have been receiving very good cooperation in the uranium program and our procurement of strategic items is in the best interests of both countries. This situation would probably continue under either the Nationalists or an alternative Government. It is also my impression that South African uranium is no longer of vital importance to the U.S. program, owing to the improvement in supplies from other sources.

On the second point, again there is little which actively can be done except to emphasize in personal contacts and conversations the

[1] Source: Department of State, Central Files, 745A.00/8–656. Secret. Also sent to Johannesburg, Cape Town, Durban, Port Elizabeth, Luanda, Lourenco Marques, Leopoldville, Salisbury, and Nairobi.

[2] Despatch 2 reported progress on the primary objectives of U.S. policy as outlined by President Eisenhower to Ambassador Wailes. These objectives were (1) increase the production and shipment of uranium; (2) keep the Union within the Commonwealth and an active member of the Western nations; and (3) counsel and influence the South Africans to follow a policy of moderation. (*Ibid.*, 745A.00/1–2756)

benefits of membership in the British Commonwealth and our feeling that South Africa can play a more important role in world affairs by being a member of the organization. We can also take advantage of the Union's fear of the U.S.S.R. to encourage continued membership in the Commonwealth by emphasizing its role and that of NATO as a bulwark against Communism. I have not talked with any responsible Government leaders who envisage the Union's leaving the Commonwealth, although all of them anticipate the eventual establishment of a republic. I assume we cannot quarrel with their decision to establish a republic so long as it remains in the Commonwealth, is friendly to the United States, and is firmly anti-Communist.

On the third point I do feel that we might take a more active role in encouraging a policy of moderation. I think we have made the United States' position clear in our attitude opposing colonialism, discrimination and Color legislation. The Afrikaner people are singularly stubborn and determined and so far they have not been deterred from any actions by the unfavorable reactions overseas. They feel so strongly on the question of non-interference in domestic affairs that they have not retreated an inch under pressure by the United Nations. Therefore I am led to the conclusion that the only change we can bring about will be by the slow process of education and encouragement to the more broadminded elements. In this regard I think the exchange of persons program is a most important and useful project, and I should like to recommend that it be enlarged. As I stated above, there has been increasing evidence of a slightly more liberal attitude among some Afrikaners, particularly within the leadership of the Dutch Reformed Churches. This group could have considerably more influence in the future, particularly if we could change the attitude of all the top DRC leaders. Sooner or later I feel the Dutch Reformed Church will be forced by its conscience and its religious tenets to break with the present policies of the Nationalist Government. I feel we should concentrate on the Dutch Reformed Church because of its influence with the Government leaders and because it has more White members than all other churches combined. We might consider doubling or tripling the number of DRC ministers given travel grants to the United States. Obviously, however, we cannot afford to leave other church groups out of consideration, for otherwise our effort would be too pointed. If we go forward with the proposed cultural agreement with the South African Government there might be provided additional revenue of $20,000–$25,000 a year from the Union to be used for cultural exchange. A second group among which we might do more is the Native and non-European, although I recognize the difficulties in the light of the policies of the present Government. Our primary interest is to orient the non-Europeans toward and make them friendly to the United States. We cannot afford to let the attitude prevail that we have no interest in them and the only friend from whom they can seek comfort is the Soviet Union. If arrangements can be made with the Union Government, we might therefore consider the advisability of travel grants to bring some non-Europeans to the United States. We might also seek approval from the Union Government which would permit us closer contacts with non-Europeans and enable us to place more USIA printed materials in their hands. A start on this has been made recently by arranging for several thousand anti-Communist booklets to be given the Natives through the Department of Native Affairs. Any mass program directed to the non-Europeans must have the consent of the Union Government; otherwise it would be counter-productive and our present contacts with the non-Europeans could be disrupted or terminated.

As I indicated in my referenced despatch, I see no prospect of success in a policy of pressure or coercion to cause the Union to modify its policies. I am, however, not unduly pessimistic about this country's future. I believe that we can have some influence by exercising reason and persuasion and that an integrated society is bound to evolve here in the long run. I am reinforced in this belief by my feeling that South Africa cannot continue to stand alone in its racial policies and eventually it will be influenced by the situation in the rest of Africa and in the world. This will take many years, however, and undoubtedly there will be much friction before that time.

With the exception of certain differences of view in respect to ways and means of bringing into power a more moderate and enlightened government, as referred to on page 14, the foregoing generally reflects the composite view of the officers at this post. The work of drafting has been shared, with the major part having been written by Mr. William L. Wight, Jr. Other officers who made substantial contributions were Mr. W.P. Maddox, Counselor of Embassy; Mr. L.M. Smith, Agricultural Attaché; Mr. Sydney L.W. Mellen, First Secretary; . . . . Factual data we believe to be correct, but the conclusions drawn I wish to have considered as solely my responsibility as time may well show that I have badly missed the mark.

Edward T. Wailes

308. Despatch From the Embassy in South Africa to the Department of State [1]

No. 104 *Pretoria, September 27, 1956.*

REF

Department's Circular Telegram 168, September 5, 1956 [2]

[Here follows an introduction.]

1. Current Program Review

As indicated, a considerable proportion of the mission's program activities consists of political and economic reporting, with the related functions of representation and negotiation. These activities were only recently given a thorough examination in conjunction with the visit of Foreign Service Inspectors and were deemed, as a result thereof, to be satisfactory and adequate. Given the complex political and racial problems which this country faces, and its progressive economic development, affording increasing opportunities for American investment and trade, the range and volume of reporting subjects which are of interest to the Department of State and other user-agencies is considerable.

This interest stems from the general requirements of America's security and of the American economy, as well as from our specific concern in (a) retaining South Africa as an associate of the Western front against Soviet Communism, preferably as a member of the British Commonwealth; (b) contributing to the long-run political and economic stability, as well as progressive development, of the country; (c) discreetly encouraging, where circumstances permit, a wiser and more constructive approach to the country's difficult racial problems, with an eye on the trend of events throughout Africa and Asia; (d) cooperating in securing the Cape of Good Hope route as an alternative to the Suez Canal; and (e) promoting the development of uranium and other strategic-mineral production, and securing appropriate shares thereof for the United States.

A substantial proportion of the Embassy's political and economic reporting is concerned, directly or indirectly, with subjects upon which our Government needs to be informed in pursuing such objectives as the above.

---

[1] Source: Department of State, Central Files, 121.45A2/9–2756. Confidential.

[2] Circular telegram 168 contained the President's instruction to Chiefs of Mission to begin a review of country programs in concert with representatives of other U.S. agencies, with the objective of ensuring that fiscal years 1957 and 1958 programs were administered to serve U.S. aims abroad "adequately, effectively and economically." (*Ibid.*, 120.201/9–556)

The Agricultural Attaché, and the Commercial Consul in Johannesburg, engage in trade promotion to varying degrees, in addition to performing their routine functions of scheduled reporting, representation, trade services, and exchange of information. As regards agriculture, there are no formal programs, existent or contemplated, in South Africa such as technical assistance or P.L. 480. However, the Attaché is alert to the possibilities of promoting agricultural exports into the Union, especially in order to relieve U.S. crop surpluses, and recently met with success with respect to obtaining duty-free entry of American tobacco. Currently an effort is being made to increase the Union's imports of American rice.

The USIS staff of two officers operates a combined informational-cultural program which includes the presentation of a balanced picture of the American scene in all its aspects, emphasizing specific phases to obtain appropriate audience-appeal, such as religious and cultural developments, our handling of the racial problem, the practical working of democracy in the United States, and our foreign policies. Other themes stressed include the nature of Soviet Communism and the challenge it presents to the free world, and the use of the atom for peace. The basic purpose is to demonstrate the essential soundness and humanity of United States objectives and policies, and the harmony thereof with the legitimate aspirations of peoples in South Africa and the rest of the world.

A high priority is presently being given the audience targets of the Dutch Reformed Church, universities, agricultural organizations and other groups which exercise considerable influence among the Afrikaner section of the population, and the dominant Nationalist Party which this section largely supports. The Afrikaner element (sixty percent of the Whites) has been cut off from the main currents of European thought for a century or so and is inclined to be nationalistic, narrow and provincial. With memories of the Boer War and long struggles against the English continuing to be systematically nurtured, it is inclined to be anti-British, as well as pro-republican. Most Afrikaners suffer from an inferiority complex and sense of isolation; they are receptive to friendly gestures from Americans and, from evidence already received through the operation of leader-grantee and other programs, some are susceptible to the influence of American ideas and values. It is believed that, through the instrumentality of all mission personnel, but especially through the USIS officers and its programs, some impact can in time be made upon the Afrikaner outlook which would materially serve United States objectives.

A second priority, more difficult to implement, is the non-European four-fifths of the population, to which attention is only newly being given. However backward the great majority may be, and devoid as they presently are of any political or industrial rights, the time will eventually come when the non-Europeans will constitute a significant, if not paramount, factor in the governance of this country. Moreover, what happens to them in the meantime may have repercussions far beyond South Africa. It is believed essential that they should develop a respect for America and American values, and an awareness of the menace of Communism. Through contacts made with some of the better educated leaders in colleges and schools, newspapers, and church missions, the USIS and the Embassy as a whole are beginning to penetrate the non-European community; follow-ups have been made through the medium of lectures, presentation of books to institutions, exhibits, publication of materials in its press, and the distribution of thousands of pamphlets and books (such as "What is Communism?") to Bantu schools.

I am convinced that the several activities outlined above, together with the emphasis and priorities which have been established, represent a coordinated program which is serving the interests and objectives of the United States in an economical and effective fashion.

[Here follows discussion of staffing and budgetary matters.]

2. Broad Program Evaluation

It should be evident from the above that the mission is satisfied as to the scope of the Embassy programs, and as to their direct relevance to the pursuance of valid United States objectives. No new program in the Union of South Africa is advocated at the moment. Moreover, it is believed that the present tempo of expansion of the educational exchange program (the only one which is increasing) is about right. It would neither be feasible, nor desirable, to step up such a program other than at a moderate and unostentatious rate. However, this program is so important that it warrants progressive increases annually for the next few years at least.

The Embassy would welcome the guidance which would be afforded by an authoritative statement of United States objectives with respect to South Africa and adjacent areas. Its files do not disclose any Country Paper for the Union. The series of five country objectives offered earlier in this despatch represent a formulation based on older directives from Washington and on my best judgment, which is concurred in generally by members of the staff. Insofar as they involve any deviation from post instructions, they constitute my recommendation as to a revised formulation.

I would, in particular, call attention to the third objective indicated above, viz., to encourage discreetly, "where circumstances permit, a wiser and more constructive approach to the country's difficult racial problems, with an eye on the trend of events throughout Africa and Asia". This involves a delicate issue. On the one hand, it is recognized that the United States Government should, in pursuance of its other objectives, seek to develop the friendship and cooperation of the South African Government, which, it seems likely, will remain under Nationalist Party control for some years. On the other hand, it is within the Nationalist hierarchy and ranks that one finds the greatest inflexibility of attitude with respect to keeping non-Europeans completely segregated and subordinated.

Certainly, the Chief of Mission and his senior staff must remain on good terms with the leaders of the party in power. While discreetly planting ideas as often as possible, they cannot afford to risk the employment of overt or obvious pressure in the direction of moderation. Experience has made clear that the Nationalist Government, and indeed some opposition leaders as well, react adversely, if not violently, to outside criticism and pressure with respect to racial problems.

Chiefly through the cultural program, and especially the educational exchange activity, the Embassy is, however, making a quiet but systematic effort to bring Afrikaner intellectual and political leaders into touch with more enlightened western ideas. It is doubted whether the Embassy can do more at this stage, but the problem remains under constant study here, and it is hoped that Washington agencies will give it similar attention. The Embassy has treated this matter more fully towards the close of its secret Despatch No. 38 to the Department.[3]

Outside of governmental channels, it is suggested that private foundations and agencies in the United States might explore ways and means of utilizing their resources, in greater measure, in attempts to affect the South African attitude of mind towards racial matters. Improved coordination of their present activities, and the establishment of means of keeping the Embassy regularly informed thereof, is also eminently desirable.

It should be emphasized again that the various activities of the Embassy and its affiliated agencies operate harmoniously under the central direction of the Chief of Mission and his Deputy. Appropriate controls are continuously maintained to the end that programs serve valid U.S. objectives, remain in balance with one another, are implemented with efficiency, and meet the over-all demands of economical operation.

William P. Maddox
Chargé d'Affaires ad interim

[3] *Supra.*

309. Telegram From the Mission at the United Nations to the Department of State [1]

New York, November 19, 1956—7 p.m.

Delga 128. Re South Africa (Gadel 20 [2]).

1. Senator Knowland [3] spoke to FonMin Louw this afternoon along lines Gadel 20, stressing importance U.S. Government and Delegation attached to continued participation Union of South Africa in UN and requesting him convey U.S. views to his government.

2. Louw stated he expecting instructions in few days but gave no indication re any recommendations he may have made and shed no light on status their thinking. He stated he had gone over general line of comments he made in Plenary with Prime Minister before departure, and had also raised question of policy if items inscribed. Prime Minister had approved his planned remarks and had suggested decision South African attitude if items inscribed be deferred until Louw's arrival New York and his assessment attitudes and situation there. (Forsyth (Australia) had previously informed USUN officer Louw had also told him he had no instructions yet on attitude toward UN participation.)

3. Louw maintained UN debates and "condemnation" South Africa before world bar were most important cause dissension of native and Indian populations in South Africa. He pointed out UN debates were reported widely in South African vernacular press as expressing world disapproval South African government. Repeated formal arguments made in Plenary that subject outside competence UN by virtue Article 2(7), in spite of Articles 55 and 56, and repeated that after 10 years' attack in UN, South Africa had about come to end of rope. He referred to Indian attitude as "vendetta", and saw situation in UN getting only worse as result enlarged Asian and Communist membership.

4. Re U.S. policies, Louw said he was officially and personally deeply disappointed. He described South Africa as bastion European civilization in Africa, referred strategic importance of control of Cape, and noted importance South Africa as U.S. customer. Said U.S. had never supported them on this question and was afraid there was

---

[1] Source: Department of State, Central Files, 845A.411/11–1956. Confidential.

[2] Dated November 17, Gadel 20 expressed concern at statements made by Louw implying that South Africa might withdraw from the General Assembly session or from the United Nations and requested that Lodge approach Louw and urge that it was in South Africa's interest to remain in the United Nations. (*Ibid.*, 845A.411/11–1756)

[3] Senator Knowland was a member of the delegation to the Eleventh Regular Session of the U.N. General Assembly.

one law for big powers and another for small. He referred to U.K.-French "aggression" in Egypt which he said was just that, and stated U.S. had only reacted mildly. Noted that South Africa had contributed to UN action in Korea although it had no Asian interests. Complained about hostility U.S. press, which he said distorted South African situation tremendously. Attacked Stevenson for his comments after nine day visit,[4] including "secret" meeting with native leaders on last day.

5. Louw defended present policies South African Government, contending native population contented except for external agitation, and that Indians were better off than in India. Stated Indian and native national congresses were Communist-dominated. Noted government efforts provide housing, medical services and other advantages to natives. Said they had given native populations certain types electoral rights but could not give them equal electoral status without turning over whole country to them with consequent departure white population.

6. Senator Knowland reiterated at several points hope South Africa would not leave, main arguments being (1) South African departure would not stop attacks and would only result in further discussions without South Africa's case being presented; (2) South Africa had been important founder and supporter UN and had valuable role to play; and (3) in time of world stress such as now, its absence as member of Commonwealth and as non-Communist country would be especially unfortunate.[5]

Lodge

---

[4] See footnote 3, Document 316.

[5] Gadel 29 to USUN, November 21, advised that approaches should be made to the Representatives of Australia, Canada, France, New Zealand, and the United Kingdom at the United Nations proposing that they contact Louw in a manner similar to the Knowland approach. (Department of State, Central Files, 845A.411/11–2156)

310. Telegram From the Embassy in South Africa to the Department of State [1]

Pretoria, November 21, 1956—1 p.m.

111. Reference Embtels 109, USIS 2, London 3. [2] Had long talk with Jooste Secretary ExtAff yesterday compliance Gadel 105. [3] In addition points made above reftel gave him argumentation that it was in Union's own interests, as well as Western world, to remain in UN. This included undesirability Union's absenting itself from forum in which it could effectively continue anti-Communist stand; weakening of UN itself in its period of greatest strains; on long-range ill effects of inevitable adverse world opinion and press treatment; effects of this on business climate and future foreign investment.

Jooste stated these points were largely those that had kept Union in UN for many years in face of what was felt most unjust treatment. Although disposed personally keep Union in UN, Jooste presented Union's case, which very familiar to Department, with considerable feeling.

Jooste spoke at length on general feeling South African people about UN and their judgment they had been treated badly after their support on Korea. He said people felt UN had caused nothing but trouble for Union. I replied that outcome of struggle for men's minds between East and West, partly based on this same issue of human rights, was of utmost importance to Union. He agreed but said governments had to be realistic and public opinion in Union was not based on such broad issues. He further asserted domestic politics was very important factor in decision to be made.

Also discussed matter informally with Strijdom last night. He advanced no new argumentation but spoke with strong feeling. While not definitely saying so, confirmed my impression he personally stood for withdrawal.

Understand cabinet discussing subject fully in sessions this week. One source told us last night cabinet was split on issue. In this situation recommendation of Foreign Minister Louw may be very important.

Within Nationalist Party walkout from UN would be popular move and Nat press has frankly discussed possibility withdrawal. If Union withdraws I gather permanent withdrawal is under study.

---

[1] Source: Department of State, Central Files, 310.2/11–2156. Confidential; Niact. Repeated to London. Passed to USUN.

[2] Telegram 109, repeated to USUN and to London, indicated that South Africa did not seem to be bluffing in its threats to withdraw from the United Nations. (*Ibid.*, 310.2/11–2056)

[3] Not printed. (*Ibid.*, 845A.411/11–1756)

Jooste feels in that case Union would remain outside UN at least until change of government which looks quite distant at this time. Am aware of course that, if decision has been reached to remain in UN, Jooste and Strijdom would not at this stage have communicated it to me as this would reduce whatever bargaining position Louw might have in New York. Nevertheless did gather from their attitudes that they were not bargaining.

In letter November 15 to Rountree Embassy submitted some thoughts on this problem.[4] In view of serious precedent which would be established, Union's strategic position, and US business interests here, we feel every effort consistent with our principles should be made to conciliate Union and forestall withdrawal.

Our principal conclusion, already conveyed to Department, is that unfortunately public pressure through UN will not succeed in effecting reform here but serve instead merely to harden attitudes. Our only hope of change seems to lie through quiet persuasion leaders this country. Viewed this light we're caught in dilemma where no actual good is being done and some damage by continued UN discussion. We hope Department will be able find some formula of bridging gap between intransigent position this government and continued fruitless discussions which may certainly sooner or later cause Union's permanent withdrawal, and quite possibly this session.[5]

Byroade

---

[4] A letter of November 15 from Byroade to Rountree enclosed a memorandum of the same date from Counselor of Embassy William P. Maddox commenting on position papers on South Africa-related issues in the U.N. General Assembly. Maddox commented that the Department seemed to be moving away from its policy of neutrality toward one of alignment against South African positions and argued that if the U.S. purpose was to influence South Africa to revise its racial attitudes and policies, such a shift would be counterproductive. (*Ibid.*, AF/AFE Files: Lot 64 D 358, United Nations—General—Union of South Africa)

[5] On November 27 Louw informed the U.N. General Assembly that until Article 2, paragraphs 1 and 7 of the Charter were adhered to, South Africa, while remaining as a member of the international body, would reduce its level of representation to a token basis. Louw told Acting Secretary Hoover on December 10 that South Africa would only play an active role when it could directly assist its own security interests and those of the Western nations. (Memorandum of conversation by Hadsel; *ibid.*, Central Files, 033.45A11/12–1056)

311. Letter From the Assistant Secretary of State for Near Eastern, South Asian, and African Affairs (Rountree) to the Ambassador in South Africa (Byroade)[1]

Washington, December 14, 1956.

DEAR HANK: I can well appreciate the interest expressed in your letter of November 15 in the Middle East situation.[2] In both Ankara and Tehran, I recall my own difficulties in following a rapidly shifting negotiation when the center of discussion was elsewhere.[3] As you know, there are a great many details in daily operations which are difficult to set down in communications. I have had all general "infotels" on the subject sent to you, in addition to the usual pouch material, and I hope this has given you the broad background.

We have been giving considerable thought to that part of your letter commenting on Bill Maddox' thoughtful and provocative review of U.S. positions on the South African UN items. Our feeling is that our attitude in this particular matter really points—and cannot help but point—to our whole policy toward South Africa. As Bill very accurately put it, our present policy has among its objectives the persuasion of White South Africans to moderate their racial attitudes and policies. And certainly harsh UN resolutions condemnatory of South Africa only make this objective more difficult of attainment. Mr. Louw's near withdrawal of South Africa from the UN is good evidence of the reaction which can be expected.

At the same time, we have to ask ourselves whether the White South Africans can modify their present racial views before the combination of world public opinion (including United States public opinion) and political forces in Africa produce a radical eruption in the Union and make it impossible for us to pursue our present course of patient persuasion. We are starting preparation of a new policy paper on South Africa, as suggested by Bill to the Inspectors last May, which will attempt to assess as accurately as possible the net value of the South African nation to the United States and the West. It will try to take a look at all possible courses of action, from supporting the Afrikaner point of view to adopting a critical attitude toward the Union.

So far as developments and forces within South Africa are concerned, I think we all agree with the statement Bill Maddox

[1] Source: Department of State, AF/AFE Files: Lot 64 D 358; United Nations—General—Union of South Africa. Confidential; Official–Informal. Drafted by William M. Johnson.

[2] See footnote 4, *supra*.

[3] Rountree had been Counselor of the Embassy in Ankara, 1952–1953, and Minister-Counselor of the Embassy in Tehran, 1953–1955.

made in his letter of November 13 to Joe Palmer [4] that "the present trend of events in South Africa, and particularly the policies and actions of the present government on racial and other controversial matters, are likely, if continued, to lead eventually to serious and possibly violent conflict in this country." The possibility of persuading White South Africans to see and act upon this possibility in time is not one of the strongest, unfortunately, although there are a few tender spots here and there in that tough South African hide.

But, on the other hand, can anything else be done? Is it possible to start building bridges to the non-White peoples on the hypothesis that they are inevitably destined to assume, or at least to share, the leadership of the country? What response, recognizable in practical terms, would there be from them now or in the next few years, even from the Xumas [5] and Morokas [6] among them? We shy from jeopardizing the real friendliness of the South African Whites by impolitic approaches to the non-Whites, and yet we don't want to lose the good will which non-Whites have at present for America.

I do not mean to imply that we are ready to shift from our present policy of trying to urge a modification of apartheid upon the White South Africans, which is just about the only feasible one at the moment, particularly since we need the cooperation of the South African Government on several well-understood counts. That the policy also has some hope of bearing fruit, however slight, makes it doubly attractive. But we will have to re-examine this approach periodically, in 1957 and 1958 and so on.

This thought quickly leads one to what attitude we might best take in the United Nations on the three South African items. It is at the United Nations, of course, that South Africa appears most clearly as a propaganda liability to the West. Even after South Africa's near withdrawal from the United Nations on November 27, the Indian delegation stated that it had no intention of easing its position on the South African items. Thus it is likely that whatever the United States does, the votes will probably continue to go against South Africa. It is also true that South Africa will continue to watch our positions on these issues carefully and that its attitude to the United States will reflect, at least partially, its reactions.

To begin with, it has long been the Department's policy to vote for inscription of almost any item on the United Nations agenda, so there has been little that could be done for South Africa on this

---

[4] Not found in Department of State files.

[5] Dr. A. B. Xuma was a physician and former President-General of the African National Congress.

[6] Dr. James S. Moroka was a surgeon who defeated Xuma in 1949, thereby succeeding him as President-General of the ANC, in which position he remained until 1952. Chief Albert J. Luthuli replaced Moroka.

count till now. At present, however, the Department is undertaking a general survey of recurrent United Nations agenda items to see what might be done about dropping or placing a moratorium on some of the less fruitful ones. It may be possible to include some South African questions in this group.

In our UN activities, we have reflected certain of our doubts about the legality of items such as the one on apartheid, because it is so largely a domestic affair, and this doubt has been shown in our opposition recently to the continuation of the Apartheid Commission. For this stand, we have had some informal expressions of appreciation from South African officials. Also, we have had the same reaction to our opposition on the Indian minority resolution to the so-called "mediator" and "guillotine" clauses. I think it would be inaccurate to say that our recent policy on these items has been tougher than formerly. In fact, our behind-the-scenes role at the United Nations has constantly been to urge moderation of the resolutions on the South African items.

Bill's memorandum mentioned the South Africans' disappointment over our having submitted a written brief to the ICJ on the question of hearing oral petitioners. Here again, we have a general Departmental policy. Briefs are normally submitted whenever solicited by the ICJ, on any subject. Similarly, the matter of our serving on the South West Africa Committee is dictated by the general policy that we never decline to serve if asked. But in this latter regard, we have been making motions to leave the Committee on the ground we have now served our stint.

Finally, the question of a compromise or a bargain with South Africa on these items is raised. The question is a different one now that South Africa will not actively participate in New York, but it seems to me that the proposal, though perhaps worth a try, would probably be unproductive anyway. Even if we were to vote against inscription of, say, the apartheid item on the ground of its being a domestic issue, the chances are only too good it would still be voted on the agenda by the growing Arab-Asian bloc. And the possibility of South Africa's agreeing to submit reports on South West Africa to the United Nations, where they would be put under a very strong light, seems a debatable one.

It seems to me that there are considerations involved in the South African problem in terms of United States policy which are similar to those that have assumed such importance in the recent Middle East crisis. The President put the problem very concisely when he said in his address to the Nation October 31 that we cannot have one set of principles governing our attitudes toward those who would be our enemies and another set of principles for our friends. To quote the President directly, "There can be no peace without law. And there can be no law if we were to invoke one code of international conduct for those who oppose us and another for our friends."[7] It is deep in our national heritage that we believe that the South Africans are morally wrong in their present racial policies and we should be stepping out of character if we were to act otherwise.

To get South Africa to resume full participation in United Nations activities is a big job, and I confess it doesn't look as though the United States alone can offer sufficient inducement.

As indicated earlier, the Bureau will be taking a more extensive look at South Africa during the coming year. Any further thoughts which you may have on these general problems will be most welcome.

Sincerely yours,

William M. Rountree[8]

[7] For text of this speech, see *Public Papers of the Presidents of the United States: Dwight D. Eisenhower, 1956*, pp. 1060–1066.

[8] Printed from a copy that bears this typed signature.

312. Editorial Note

On January 23, 1957, the General Assembly adopted Resolution 1047(XI) by a vote of 60 (including the United States) to 0, with 9 abstentions. The resolution authorized the Committee on South West Africa to grant hearings to petitioners. Resolution 1054(XI) was also adopted on February 26 by a vote of 47 (including the United States) to 0, with 16 abstentions. It approved and endorsed all the conclusions and recommendations of the "Report and observations of the Committee on South West Africa regarding conditions in the Territory of South West Africa." The United States, however, abstained on Resolution 1059(XI), adopted the same day by a vote of 40 to 11, with 19 abstentions. Operative paragraph 2 of this resolution requested the Secretary-General "to take whatever steps he shall deem necessary with a view to finding such a solution in line with the principles of the Charter of the United Nations and the advisory opinion of the International Court of Justice."

In regard to the issue of the treatment of Indians in South Africa, the United States Delegation was instructed to abstain on any resolution stronger than that passed the previous year. The delegation worked to win support for a formula satisfactory to the Indians and the Pakistanis and the South Africans. (Delga 446 from USUN, January 8, 1957; Department of State, Central Files, 845A.411/1–857) General Assembly Resolution 1015(XI) of January 30 passed by a vote of 42 to 0, with 12 abstentions.

The Special Political Committee on the Question of Race Conflict in South Africa deliberated apartheid January 11–21. The United States position was stated on January 16 by Philip W. Bonsal, Chief of Political Liaison on the Delegation and Ambassador to Colombia. He noted that there had been no improvement in the situation and that conditions might be worse. While denouncing all forms of discrimination, he expressed the United States view that "there is little more which the United Nations can constructively do than it has already done without the cooperation and good will of the government of the member country concerned." He indicated that the United States hoped that this matter would not automatically be placed on the agenda of the next Assembly. The constant attack on South Africa, he observed, had not contributed to an amelioration of the situation and had caused that nation to absent itself from full participation in the Assembly. He hoped that South Africa would return and maintained that real progress would have to be initiated from within South Africa. (USUN Press Release 2589, January 16, 1957; copy *ibid.*, IO/ODA Files: Lot 62 D 228, Africa–Apartheid pre-1959) The United States therefore abstained from voting on the resolution adopted by the Committee (U.N. doc A/3508), which was subsequently adopted by the General Assembly as Resolution 1016(XI) on January 30 by a vote of 56 to 5, with 12 abstentions. The resolution deplored South African discriminatory practices and invited the government to cooperate in a constructive approach to the question and return to the United Nations. See *Yearbook of the United Nations 1956*, pages 139–145 and 304–313.

313. Despatch From the Embassy in South Africa to the Department of State [1]

No. 291 *Pretoria, April 11, 1957.*

SUBJECT

Embassy Staff Study on the South African Race Problem I

Over the course of the past several months, a group of Embassy officers has used the medium of a series of informal evening sessions to further a systematic and intensive study of crucial aspects of South Africa's disturbing race-color situation with a view to formulating conclusions of possible value to the Embassy and to the Department. [2]

The study project was inspired by the basic premise that the United States Government, with its present world-wide interests and responsibilities, cannot but be vitally concerned in the growing racial tensions in South Africa. The reasons are well-known but warrant reiteration. Firstly, our strategic interests in the Middle East, together with political uncertainties in the Suez region, require (both for us and for our allies) that the southern sector of Africa with its excellent port facilities remain in a state of political stability and under the control of a friendly and effective government. Secondly, we have an important stake in South Africa's mineral and industrial economy, especially in its uranium production; we desire to insure not only a continuous flow of its materials to the U.S. and the West, but a denial of access thereto to unfriendly powers. And, thirdly, we must be concerned lest the explosive repercussions of a local debacle in race relations reach throughout Africa south of the Sahara and conceivably beyond. If Blacks come into bitter open conflict with Whites on a mass scale in South Africa, the potentials of far-reaching inter-color hostilities, essentially independent of but most certainly susceptible of being stimulated and maneuvered by Communists for their own purposes, could become a cardinal threat to American security.

A second premise was not initially established but came progressively sharper into focus as the weeks passed. Agreement developed that the condition of race relations in South Africa is not a

---

[1] Source: Department of State, Central Files, 745A.00/4–1157. Confidential. Also sent to Johannesburg, Durban, Leopoldville, Luanda, Nairobi, Cape Town, Port Elizabeth, Lourenco Marques, and Salisbury.

[2] Maddox convened the first meeting of those participating in this staff study on October 17, 1956. Various memoranda which served as a basis for this despatch and the despatch *infra* are *ibid.*, Pretoria Embassy Files: Lot 64 F 39, 350–Embassy Staff Study of Race Problems—1957.

remote danger to be dealt with a few years hence, but a *real and vital one today*, in that unless measures are taken *now* to check or reverse the presently accelerating trends, the forces in motion leading in the direction of crisis may soon push beyond human control.

In the same manner, a third premise evolved during the course of the study, accentuating the reasons advanced to support the first. Although the individual officers were not equipped to pass judgment on the comparative levels of Native development elsewhere in Africa, it was their belief that the educational attainments of a small number of Bantus in South Africa, coupled with the high degree of urbanization (nearly one-third of the Native population), have produced a core of relatively-sophisticated, politically-conscious, and articulate "elite"—numbering possibly a hundred thousand—whose influence is capable of extending beyond the borders of South Africa into and among the Native leadership of other African countries. Thus, it was felt (emphasizing the third reason under the first premise) that the United States Government should be actively and earnestly concerned with the disturbing trends of color-relations here, not solely because of their effects within South Africa, but because of their implications for a large part of the continent.

In consequence of these premises, it was held that the United States Government through its agencies and officers should systematically re-examine the South African race situation in the light of American interests in Africa, and seek to determine what measures, if any, could be taken to ensure the continuing protection of these interests in the coming years.

To provide a structure and direction for the Embassy staff study, we set ourselves four basic questions as follows:

A. What aspects of South African policies and attitudes with respect to non-Europeans do you think might lead to serious interracial tensions and conflict in a relatively short course of time?

B. What measures ought to be, and could be, taken by South Africans to correct these trends?

C. What can we as Americans in Pretoria—officially or personally—do to assist in such an effort?

D. In the light of all circumstances, what would you recommend that the U.S. Government do about the situation?

Officers participating in the project throughout were First Secretary Sydney L.W. Mellen, Second Secretary Edward W. Holmes, . . . Public Affairs Officer Thomas V. Graves, Cultural Affairs Officer C. K. Snyder, and the undersigned. The Ambassador and the Second Secretary William L. Wight, Jr. also took part until their departure for Cape Town early in January, and were kept advised of developments thereafter.

From the fifty pages of memoranda which individual officers prepared, either in formulation of ideas and proposals for presentation to the group, or in summaries of evening discussions which followed, there have been developed three reports, the substance of each of which has been approved by the Ambassador. The first of these, bearing on Questions A, B and C given above is submitted herewith to the Department. The second, relating chiefly to Question D, is classified secret and is being forwarded in a separate despatch to follow. (A full set of the original memoranda, seventeen in number, would be made available for the files of the Office of Southern Africa Affairs if desired.) (A third top secret report will be specially handled by the Ambassador in Washington.)[3]

In forwarding this first report to the Department, we are conscious that it embodies nothing that is not already familiar to those who have closely followed South African affairs in recent years. Indeed, in seeking mountains, we have probably produced only molehills. But in the process, numerous ideas have been suggested, discussed, amended, and accepted or rejected; every formulation has been subjected to searching criticism; and agreements have been hammered out only as a result of lengthy, and not always harmonious interchanges. Of interest is the fact that the project has been invaluable in clarifying and sharpening our individual thinking on the several questions; of even greater interest is the fact that out of initial and sometimes protracted disagreements there was eventually forged a set of ideas and recommendations concurred in by all.

All things considered, the Embassy is confident that the effort was of considerable value to its staff members, individually and collectively, and that it should in future years be repeated periodically.

The report below embodies recommendations which, having been approved by the Ambassador, will first of all serve as guidance and instruction to officers presently on duty in South Africa. They will keep in mind, and with all due discretion, advance in private discussions one or more of several ideas whenever and wherever it is deemed a useful purpose might be served in the direction of stemming the tide of deteriorating race relations in this area. Secondly, USIS Pretoria is being instructed, subject to approval by USIA Washington to develop programs pointing more sharply at the priority objectives formulated.

The second (secret) report, to be transmitted shortly, presents further considerations of a more highly classified character, including recommendations for the Department's diplomatic action.

[3] Not found in Department of State files.

As a result of these papers, and several previous despatches (e.g. Embassy Despatches 38 of August 6, 1956 and 104 of September 27, 1956),[4] the Embassy earnestly hopes that the Department will evolve a new country policy paper for South Africa which will reflect more sharply than heretofore the ominous implications of the South African race situation for the vital interest of the United States.

Summary of Conclusions of Questions A and B

(For statement of questions, see above)

In the consideration of A, our initial formulation contained a clause asking what aspects of racial policies were regarded as "objectionable". This was rejected at an early stage as being irrelevant from an official standpoint. Our concern was sociological rather than moralistic; we preferred to focus on a realistic appraisal of trends and probable consequences rather than simply to express emotional reactions.

Moreover, it was felt that out of a considerable number of pertinent suggestions offered in response to A, it was necessary to narrow them down by judicious selection and to concentrate on a few. Our motivation in this connection, it will be admitted, was pragmatic. We felt it was necessary to tie in B with A; in other words, to determine what policies and attitudes, in addition to being potentially dangerous, might have a reasonable chance in the South African culture and polity today of being given practical and sympathetic amelioration within the next few years.

We agreed that although many corrective measures ought to be taken, we could not expect to see a culture, with its deeply-ingrained outlooks and habits, revolutionized overnight. There must be a beginning and we should think in terms of steps and directions. At the outset these would have to be limited; they must grow from roots already planted here and there within the White culture, and thus have a fair degree of wider acceptability. It was recognized that such a criterion of selection might not prove sufficient if a substantial contribution were to be made to the task of averting crisis, but, aside from certain considerations to be developed in the secret despatch to follow, it was felt that the limited practical approach was preferable at the moment.

Eventually, we settled upon four main points, or categories of points, under A, with correspondencies under B. In narrowing these down to four, we were also bearing in mind the practical considera-

[4] Documents 307 and 308.

tions of C: What could we in the Embassy do to aid in the effort to check or reverse present trends?

In the interest of succinctness, these considerations have been boiled down as follows, the response to A being indicated as the "Problem", and the response to B as the "Action".

1. Inter-Racial Contacts

Problem (A): The failure, or reluctance, of the vast majority of Whites to establish inter-communication links with non-European leaders, as a necessary condition to the creation of a measure of mutual understanding, and to the development of consultations on the course of inter-racial relations.

Action (B): Upon the initiative of SABRA[5] and progressive leaders of universities and the DRC,[6] steps should be taken to develop more regular contacts with non-European leaders, together with a series of conferences, with the purpose of exchanging views, developing a greater measure of mutual confidence, and finding areas of agreement on inter-racial relations. (*Note*: Such small groups as the Liberal Party, the Institute of Race Relations and the Labor Party, which already have such contacts, should be encouraged to extend them.)

Discussion: The widening gap between the Whites and the Blacks was regarded as the most basic of all the circumstances we considered. A great many South Africans of various persuasions recognize this fact clearly yet, tragically, the present weight of political power is against them. At this very moment, new legislation, inspired by Dr. Verwoerd,[7] is in the course of being enacted which would seriously undermine the few remaining bridges left. Nevertheless, the idea will not be extinguished.

2. Safety Valves for the Elite

Problem (A): The failure to provide channels of opportunities for economic advancement, or avenues for responsible political expression, for a small but steadily increasing number of educated non-Europeans.

Action (B): Under the auspices of the White groups indicated above, and (if possible) with the collaboration of the Department of Native Affairs, facilities should be established to open up further avenues for professional employment, and other outlets for talent

[5] South African Bureau for Racial Affairs.

[6] Dutch Reformed Church.

[7] Dr. Hendrik Frensch Verwoerd, Nationalist leader in the Senate and South African Minister of Native Affairs.

and ambition, and to provide practical assistance to Natives seeking such opportunities.

Discussion: There was complete acceptance of the proposition that the "danger-spot" of the next decade lay among the urbanized masses, rather than among the larger number of Natives living in White rural areas on the one hand or in Native reserves on the other. And in the urban areas are concentrated the "educated elite", with its veneer of European culture and ideas, capable of leadership, aggressive and ambitious, psychologically susceptible to the extremes of Black Nationalism or Communism, frustrated at the limited opportunities available, and increasingly resentful of restrictions imposed by the Whites. It is exceedingly difficult to find the answer to the problem: certainly, something in the way of a "safety valve" outlet is essential. In addition, this "elite" leadership should, somehow, be won over to a policy of accommodation with the Whites.

3. Improving the Living Standards of the Urbanized Masses

Problem (A): The lack of adequate recognition of, and attention to, the fundamental economic (and social) problems arising from the mass concentration of Natives in compartmentalized locations removed from, but dependent upon, urban centers.

Action (B): The undertaking by governmental authorities and chambers of commerce and industry of systematic studies, among urban Natives, of the ratios of costs of living to family incomes, with a view to more equitable adjustments of wages and transport charges; the enlargement of opportunities for Natives to occupy semi-skilled and skilled jobs; a vigorous economic development of Native reserves, thereby enhancing their attractiveness, and hence improving the competitive position of Native workers in the urban industrial market; and a fuller recognition by Europeans of the practical economic value of promoting a sense of well-being and contentment among the large mass of Native workers and consumers.

Discussion: Providing "outlets" for the urban leaders would be insufficient; the leaders and the led react one upon the other and, indeed, are complementary. The very concentration of hundreds of thousands of Natives in urban locations provides receptive mass groups, closely inter-linked (despite tribal frictions) by residence and fate, responsive to suggestion and emotional appeals, and capable (as in the bus boycott) of resolute combined actions. Despite the infusion of many influences, including the threats and appeals of the African National Congress, into the current thought-action centers of the urban Natives, it was firmly believed by the group (as well as by many South Africans) that a vigorous program of economic amelioration of their (the Natives') lot would lessen their present susceptibility to militant demagoguery. (The Manager of the Johannesburg Non-European Affairs Department told me this week that his best estimate places the average cost of living for a Native family in the Johannesburg area at about £22 a month; only some 20%, he added, receive income of this amount.

4. Humanizing the Attitudes of the Whites

Problem (A): The entrenchment of an attitude of mind on the part of the Whites that the non-European is basically and unalterably inferior—resulting in policies and practices of "basskap" and inequitable treatment.

Action (B): A wider and more systematic development in school and college curricula of socio-cultural studies of non-European peoples; experimentation by European newspapers with a column (like Jan Burger's) by a Native on the Native outlook; similar experimentation by SABC [8] with programs by Native singers and entertainers; the broadening and strengthening of the work of SABRA and IRR, [9] etc.

Discussion: The problem is basic and any solution may take too long to be of any value. But the educational approach is essential and one grasps at straws in order to further it. An individual Black may be known and patronized by the White as an employee or servant; for the rest, they are an indistinguishable and unfathomable mass, and feared as a consequence. To learn to understand the Native as a personality, within his culture, will involve a slow and tortuous process but its essentiality is beyond question. Various isolated, but helpful, suggestions were made along this line, including one or two indicated above. Some hope was also seen in the present gropings at the University of South Africa and also at Stellenbosch University to establish an African Institute.

(*Note*: The suggested "actions" under the four points were regarded as minimal—simply as steps in the right direction to be successively followed by others. They were felt to be within the limited range of early practicality. They were not regarded, in themselves, as being sufficient to reverse the current alarming trends.)

Summary of Conclusions on Question C

It will be recalled that this question posed: What can we as Americans—officially or personally—do to assist in such an effort?

---

[8] South African Broadcasting Corporation.

[9] Institute of Race Relations.

Within the limits imposed by our official positions, and except on specific instructions from the Department, it was recognized that any contribution we could make in the direction of alleviating tensions, or towards the avoidance of ultimate conflict, could not be expected to have great impact. And yet, in keeping with our conviction that unless present trends are reversed, a stage of acute crisis may be reached before many years have passed, which could adversely affect American interests, it was felt that we must formulate a program of Embassy action, however limited it might be. We would do what we could, and if we could settle firmly upon a few things, we might do something useful.

1. *The systematic planting of the above ideas and an exertion of positive influence to gain an acceptability therefor at every opportunity.*

Every officer in the Embassy finds himself frequently a participant in private conversation with a South African, or South Africans, on the perennial subject of race relations. The American is often invited, or expected, to offer his views. Emphasizing that he is speaking only as an individual and not as an official, he will usually and almost necessarily from a social standpoint, have something to say on the subject. And because of the respect in which the average American is held in South Africa, his views will usually receive close attention.

The Ambassador has approved the study group's recommendation that all officers in South Africa be advised of the four priority categories of ideas presented above in response to Questions A and B, and that they be instructed to bear them in mind when engaged in private conversations and, with all judiciousness, introduce them whenever possible.

It is suggested that in this concentrated, but discreet, advancement of a few ideas, we should avoid adopting a superior moral attitude; rather, we should stress the danger of deteriorating race relations for South Africans, and for all of us in the West. We could remind them of the Communist menace, and also of the threat of militant Black nationalism. We could also suggest that if a few constructive things be undertaken in vigorous advancement of a given suggestion, something might be done to regain foreign (especially American) confidence and good-will.

By concentrating our attention on four areas of ideas, varying our emphasis and approach with the particular auditor, hammering the points home, expressing them with sincerity and conviction (as if, necessarily, they were our own personal ideas), defending them with vigor, and utilizing every appropriate opportunity of contact with South Africans to do so, we will be employing the device most appropriate to us as individual officers. Each officer has different contacts, high and low, Nationalist and opposition, official and non-official, covering every sort of occupation; a concentrated idea or set of ideas launched among these with sincerity and effectiveness can conceivably reach many ears.

2. *The concentration of USIS Programs on the promotion of the four objectives and utilization of all appropriate media to drive them home.*

The Leader-Grantee program is already directed, in part, towards several of them; it should be concentrated even more, and expanded to provide for a larger number of persons. A more positive approach should be made in contacts with press and radio leaders to stimulate thinking along these lines. Various materials should be stressed pointing up, in line with the four points and from U.S. experience, feasible channels of inter-racial contacts, the achievements of outstanding Negroes, the pragmatic value to society of developing adequately-paid and contented worker-consumers, and the changing human outlook of Americans towards Negroes. Materials might be used from areas of heavy Negro concentration, Puerto Rico, the Virgin Islands, the southern states, and even from the British West Indies, where the Blacks outnumber the Whites far more than in South Africa.

The group decided to recommend to the Ambassador that he instruct USIS to re-examine its programs in the light of the above in order to concentrate on the approved specific purposes and that, where necessary, it should request USIA to authorize a revision of the country objectives. The Ambassador has accepted this recommendation, and USIS will be instructed accordingly.

As indicated earlier in this despatch, a further report, of a secret classification, on the results of the Embassy staff project will follow.

William P. Maddox
Chargé d'Affaires a.i.

314. Despatch From the Embassy in South Africa to the Department of State [1]

No. 294 *Pretoria, April 12, 1957.*

REF

Embassy Despatch No. 291, April 11, 1957 [2]

SUBJECT

Embassy Staff Study on the South African Race Problem, II; Diplomatic Policy Recommendation

As indicated in reference despatch, a group of Embassy officers recently conducted over a period of some months a staff study of the problems arising from increasing racial tensions in South Africa. Herewith is the second report (see reference despatch for the first) setting forth some conclusions of the study as well as recommendations to the Department. These were approved by the Ambassador before his departure on home leave. (He will personally handle a third and final report (top secret) in Washington.) [3]

It is unnecessary to repeat here the several cogent reasons advanced in the former despatch as to why the United States Government, from the standpoint of its rapidly growing interests in the African continent, should be vitally concerned at the disturbing course of race developments in this country. Suffice it to say, the Embassy is convinced that the time is at hand when the combined constructive imagination and resourceful talents of the appropriate areas of the Department (and other agencies) and of the Embassy should be utilized to determine what ought to be, and might be, done by the U.S. Government to assist (1) in averting what could become a major and violent domestic crisis, with farflung repercussions, and (2) in charting a course of more harmonious inter-race relations in this area.

For the convenience of the Department, the four questions which served as the focus of the Embassy's staff study in a series of informal evening discussions are repeated here:

A. What aspects of South African policies and attitudes with respect to non-Europeans do you think might lead to serious inter-racial tensions and conflict in a relatively short course of time?

B. What measures ought to be, and could be, taken by South Africans to correct these trends?

---

[1] Source: Department of State, Central Files, 845A.411/4–1257. Secret. Also sent to Johannesburg, Durban, Leopoldville, Luanda, Nairobi, Cape Town, Port Elizabeth, Lourenco Marques, and Salisbury.

[2] *Supra.*

[3] See footnote 3, *supra.*

C. What can we as Americans in Pretoria—officially or personally—do to assist in such an effort?

D. In the light of all circumstances, what would you recommend that the U.S. Government do about the situation?

The first three of these questions were discussed in reference despatch and it is now proposed to consider the fourth. Amended in accordance with the group's suggestions and criticisms at an evening session, my original memorandum on the subject is reproduced here in the informal tone in which it was submitted to the Ambassador:

1. Diplomatic Policy Review and Recommendation

a. *Recent U.S. Policies*

The U.S. Government has over recent years actively concerned itself in the U.N. with South African racial policies but it is clear that adverse U.N. votes have only had the effect of stiffening the South African Government's attitude vis-à-vis the outside world, and have brought none of the changes we desire in its policies. The time has arrived when the basis of our policies, and the methods of our approach require re-examination.

As we understand it, the U.S. has tended to take a position founded on moral and humanitarian principles fortified by the contention that the Human Rights Convention [4] overrides the protection given in Article 2 of the U.N. Charter against interference in domestic affairs. Doubtless, we thought thereby to arouse world public opinion and to win the sympathy of the Afro-Asian bloc, but if another primary purpose was to achieve alterations in South African policies the result has been a failure in that respect.

b. *Basis of a New Policy*

It is suggested that in order to achieve our purpose we minimize public appeals based on morality and strive quietly to emphasize a straight pragmatic concern for our national (which tend to become our world-wide) interests. It is suggested we simply insist that since the practical consequences of South African policy have increasingly dangerous implications for the peace and orderly development of Africa as a whole, and therefore for American security, we feel compelled to make our concern known.

South Africans, and especially the Afrikaner element now in control, are absolutely convinced, not only of this legal right to establish domestic legislation as they choose, free from outside interference, but also of the moral justification of policies of apartheid. There is a certitude of conviction in the Afrikaner Nationalist that these policies are just and right by the highest Christian

[4] The U.N. General Assembly adopted the Universal Declaration on Human Rights (U.N. doc. A/811) on December 10, 1948.

standards. "In the language of South African Calvinism, God is sovereign and has delegated sovereignty to the lawful rulers of the land. For these rulers right action is self evident . . . "[5] (De Kiewiet, *The Anatomy of South African Misery*, p. 25.) We cannot expect to persuade by preaching and lecturing, as if we were on a higher moral plateau. The Afrikaner will have none of it; he strongly resents such audacity, or else, he may pity us. When you talk with Verwoerd about his policies, he is benign, patient and almost condescending; you, poor benighted heathen, belong to a lower level—you have not seen the light as only the good Calvinist can!

It seems, therefore, essential that we shift our ground to the practical realism of American interests. South Africans are aware of our growing interest in Africa as evidenced by the visits of Vice President Nixon and Congressional travelers; seriously troubled about communism themselves, they favor the extension of the new American doctrine into Africa; they respect our purpose and our power, and our need and determination to maintain them. If we will stay off pulpits and talk straight-from-the-shoulder common sense about the practical effects of the present trend of policies in South Africa, and their realistic implications for us all throughout the continent, they may not follow our advice, but at least we will have established a plane of more effective communication than we have had hitherto.

In other words, let's reveal to the South African less of our humanitarian concern for people of color; let's talk less about injustices and immorality, and more about what is happening in hard, cold terms as regards Black Nationalism and Communism, and the White man in Africa. South African Nationalists will still argue that they know best how to control such developments, but deep within, many are much less convinced of the practical benefits of their policies than they are of the high rectitude of their purpose.

c. *The Methods of Diplomacy*

In surveying the normal instruments at our disposal for the exercise of influence on a foreign country, it is clear that we have few available in respect to South Africa. We have no economic or military aid program. We need South African raw materials and we want the Cape Route open, so we need the friendly dispositions of the Government in power, *if* the price is not too high. We have tried frontal attacks (at least high-placed individuals have done so) and we have tried the U.N. Both have failed, and seem bound to fail.

Diplomacy, in its traditional sense, is not conducted in open forums but through secret and direct contacts between officials. I suggest that in our efforts to persuade the South Africans to our

[5] Ellipsis in the source text.

way of thinking we make use of unpublicized approaches through diplomatic channels.

We could, I believe, at various levels, make known to South African Embassy officials in Washington, and (on instructions to our own posts) to their representatives in certain other countries as well as to the Government in Pretoria, our deep apprehensions arising from our practical interests in the whole of Africa, and from those of friendly nations, at the portents of racial policies in South Africa. We could persistently and repeatedly plant ideas of this nature—they will be transmitted home secretly and the Opposition will be unable to capitalize on them for domestic political advantage. Our spokesmen could be armed with a list of specific harmful measures and events in South Africa; they might, if pressed, mention several of the four priority situations (which we have agreed on) and the remedies we have suggested.

Several other possible points of diplomatic departure might be considered. Are there any "carrots" which might be held out to the South African Government to induce it to heed persuasion? Or are there any threats or warnings which might be expressed under diplomatic secrecy with a view to affecting its course of action? Of course, South Africa desires an increase in the price of gold, but no "carrot" could be held out in that connection unless and until a point should be reached in the American economy where an increase in the price of gold would appear to offer some net advantage to the free world as a whole and to the United States. In connection with the existing uranium contracts South Africa will be keenly interested in renewal on favorable terms; although the present contracts still have a number of years to run, it might be worthwhile to explore the question whether statements could be made in advance indicating that renewal of the contracts would depend partly on the United States Government's being satisfied regarding the outlook for peaceful evolution in South Africa. Again, the South African Government has indicated an interest in having an assurance of U.S. military planes in the event of war. It desires a more active interest on our part in defense arrangements affecting Africa south of the Sahara. Probably in none of these respects are we in a position to bargain, but all possibilities of "carrots" and of "threats" should be thoroughly explored.

There is one possible "threat" to which consideration might be given. This has to do with American investments in South Africa. If the outlook in South Africa should continue to become more ominous a point might well be reached where the United States Government would feel that some kind of a warning to businessmen with respect to the long-term outlook for political stability was justified. It is true that the issuance of such a warning, even on a confidential and selective basis, would raise difficult questions such as the effect on *existing* American private investments in South Africa. Nevertheless, if the circumstances should be found to justify it, the issuance of a private warning to potential American investors would be a very serious matter for South Africa, owing to this country's dependence on a continued inflow of private foreign capital. From the standpoint of directly influencing the policies and actions of the South African Government, the most important and potentially useful phase of the United States Government's action would be to advise that Government in advance of our intended action, and the reasons therefor; the possibility might then arise of exerting effective diplomatic pressure.

Consideration might eventually be given to consulting other friendly governments privately and to enlisting their concurrent action. But we believe that no Government is in as strong a position as ours to exercise influence and pressure. South African officials accept us as the leading world power; they recognize our rapidly-growing concern with developments all over the continent of Africa; they understand that circumstances compel us to exercise positive and vigorous leadership; and (we believe) they will respect our efforts in that direction in matters involving their Governments' policies, if we act with appropriate diplomatic circumspection.

There is no assurance that a systematic resort to secret diplomacy in an effort to bring moderation into South African governmental policies would prove successful, or that even if it did, it would stave off some future catastrophe. But an effort to exert a positive diplomatic influence and pressure might be more effective than anything we have tried in the past, and conceivably could have beneficial results.

In considering all possibilities for action by the United States Government or its representatives in the future, there are a few other important points developed in the course of our staff study which we feel should be borne in mind.

2. Additional Considerations Bearing on All Questions

a. *A split in the Nationalist Party Government would be in the interests of the United States*

This proposition was advanced by one officer [6] who contended that if governmental power remains in the present hands, and if it continues to be exercised essentially in the same direction for another five or six years, only a miracle could prevent the outbreak of serious political and economic disturbances in South Africa. . . .

---

[6] This position was recommended by the First Secretary of the Embassy, Sydney L. W. Mellen, in a memorandum to Maddox dated March 15. See footnote 2, *supra*.

After exploring many facets of this question and weighing them against other conceivable desiderata and possibilities, all members of the group accepted the primary thesis that a split within the Nationalist Government would be in our interests, especially if it would result in the discard of Verwoerd and other doctrinaire extremists.

. . . .

In any case, while it is understood that the United States Government and its Embassy should, for practical as well as for diplomatic reasons, remain on friendly terms with the Government in power, we should not assume that its power is impregnable, or that a different constellation is impossible before 1963.

b. *Continuing integration of the Native into the White industrial economy is an inescapable fact and the full-scale vertical "apartheidism" of Verwoerd an impossible myth.*

The idealism underlying the advocacy by certain individuals of vigorous apartheid should be conceded; we should not make the mistake of condemning it in principle. Indeed, the gradual evolution of certain Native Reserves, such as the Transkei, into autonomous areas is not inconceivable and, under certain conditions, has much to be said for it. Actually, however, most of what is now being done in the name of apartheid represents a form of baaskap. But whatever might and should be done, the strong prospect remains that the masses essential to the industrial economy will never be dislodged from the urban centers. The dream of parallel societies is unachievable; a mixed economy is here, and eventually a mixed polity is inevitable.

c. *It is in the interest of the United States that White leadership should be preserved, or at least indefinitely prolonged, in South Africa.*

The group accepted this proposition. It agreed that, in this industrial-mining economy with its advanced technology requiring high levels of managerial competence and engineering skills, complete control by untrained non-Europeans in this generation would not result in a situation conducive to our interests. While seeking to promote the prolongation of White power and its peaceable transition to mixed-race power, we must be aware of the possibility that forces moving towards Black dominance could prove successful at some future time, and guide our conduct accordingly.

d. *In order to preserve, or at least to prolong indefinitely, their leadership, the Whites should start making concessions to the non-Europeans.*

In opposition to this thesis it was argued, and agreed, that resolute "baaskap", coupled with stringent police measures, could prolong White control in South Africa, despite outside pressures. But it was also agreed that such policies would make almost certain an eventual crisis accompanied by violence. It was acknowledged that, in the light of history, concessions by the Whites would not finally settle matters but would simply pave the way for further demands by the Blacks and for the next stage of tension. Nevertheless, if the entire *process* of transition could be spread over a long period, it would probably be effected peaceably.

e. *Militant Black Nationalism, independent but potentially an ally of Communism, is also a threat to our interests.*

Uncompromising militancy among certain Black leaders is a present phenomenon which should cause us as much concern as its counterpart among the Whites. We should oppose extremism and intemperateness among Black leaders and seek to develop programs designed to promote conciliatoriness on their part and to effect peaceful compromises with the Whites.

In concluding this, the second of its two reports, the Embassy trusts that its efforts might be of some assistance to the Department in the formulation of a new country policy paper for South Africa.

William P. Maddox

---

315. Memorandum for the File by the Deputy Director of the Office of Southern Africa Affairs (LaMont) [1]

Washington, May 3, 1957.

SUBJECT

Pretoria despatch No. 294, April 12, 1957—"Embassy Staff Study on the South African Race Problem, II; Diplomatic Policy Recommendation" [2]

The theme of this despatch is that if racial trouble breaks out in the Union of South Africa, there will be repercussions throughout the continent, and the implications will be dangerous for the peace and development of Africa as a whole. Pretoria believes that arguments against racial discrimination on this ground is better than on

---

[1] Source: Department of State, AF/AFS Files: Lot 60 D 37. Secret.

[2] *Supra.*

moral grounds. Arguments on the basis of injustice and immorality have been fruitless in the past and are likely to be fruitless in the future, hence this proposed new policy.

There seems to be no basis for argument regarding the inutility of protest on humanitarian grounds. The new policy proposed is undoubtedly better than nothing, but it is still rather remote from reality, as it is not easy to justify. No other territory in Africa has the same racial policy as the Union, and it does not necessarily follow that, if there is an explosion in the Union, there will be repercussions elsewhere in Africa. On this basis, i.e., something with which we are not in agreement endangers the peace and orderly development of the particular area and hence our own security, we could protest against something we do not like anywhere in the world.

A warning regarding the danger of investments seems too remote to bear serious consideration. Such a warning has never been given with respect to a friendly country. There is far more basis for such a warning in a great many countries of the world other than in the Union of South Africa.

In item c. on page 7, it is stated "It is in the interest of the United States that White leadership should be preserved, or at least indefinitely prolonged, in South Africa." There seems to be some confusion in this paragraph between public administration and private interests. The economy of the Union is essentially private enterprise. Presumably the managers of such enterprises will be the most competent leaders regardless of race and will be entirely separate from the political setup. Even with respect to political matters, I do not agree that it is in the interest of the United States that White leadership should be preserved unless it is with the concurrence of the rest of the population.

316. Memorandum of a Conversation, Department of State, Washington, May 3, 1957 [1]

SUBJECT

Interview of Ambassador of the Union of South Africa with Under Secretary Murphy

PARTICIPANTS

Mr. W. C. du Plessis, Ambassador of the Union of South Africa
Mr. Robert Murphy—G
George D. LaMont—AFS

Ambassador Du Plessis brought up the following two subjects during his interview:

First of all he mentioned the report of Senator Theodore F. Green, dated February 21, 1957, entitled "Economic Aid and Technical Assistance in Africa." [2] He had a copy of the report with him and specifically referred to a section on South Africa wherein Senator Green commented adversely on the Union's racial policy. He also mentioned the final sentence of this section wherein Senator Green stated "Faced with this unhappy dilemma, America in setting the course of its policy toward South Africa must balance, on the one hand, its desire for friendship with the Union Government and its policy of noninterference in the domestic affairs of another nation with, on the other hand, its traditional interest in the preservation of human rights and freedoms everywhere." He said that before going on his trip, the South African Embassy in Washington had been told that the Senator would be investigating the American aid program in various countries and, as there is no such program in the Union, his visit there would be a side trip. Also the South African Government had been told by our Embassy in Pretoria that in the Union the Senator would only be interested in the operations of the Embassy and Consular Offices. Hence, they were disagreeably surprised at his adverse comments on their domestic policies.

Mr. Murphy suggested to the Ambassador that any comments of Senator Green in his report were his personal opinions and not government policy. The Ambassador agreed but said the report was a government publication. Mr. Murphy pointed out that the report was similar in form to customary reports of Senators and Congressmen on field trips and, being of the Legislative Branch of the Government, we of course had no control over their statements. He

[1] Source: Department of State, Central Files, 745A.5–MSP/5–357. Confidential. Drafted by LaMont.

[2] Senator Green, Chairman of the Senate Foreign Relations Committee, visited South Africa in late September 1956. Documentation is *ibid.*, 033.1100–GR.

also asked the Ambassador whether he had mentioned this complaint to the Senator. The Ambassador replied that he had commented informally to the Senator at the reception of the British Embassy on the occasion of the Independence of Ghana but had not protested. Mr. Murphy said that he would bear this matter in mind and would consider what, if any action, we could take.

Ambassador Du Plessis next brought up the matter of the visit to the Union of South Africa in the next few weeks of Mr. Adlai Stevenson and his party. The Ambassador said that during the last visit of Mr. Stevenson to the Union, he had made certain adverse comments regarding their racial policy which received wide circulation in the press.[3] The Union Government fears that when he arrives on this occasion, he will be met at the airport by a large number of reporters and, should he again make adverse comments regarding racial policies there, it will receive widespread publicity in the opposition press causing embarrassment to the Government.

Mr. Murphy pointed out that this was a very delicate matter, that Mr. Stevenson was a prominent leader of the opposition political party and any approach to him by the Government might be counter-productive. It was furthermore pointed out to the Ambassador that there are many opponents in the United States of our policy of friendship to the Union because of its racial policies and, should they happen to learn of any such approach to Mr. Stevenson, we in this Government might receive a storm of protest. Mr. Murphy suggested that the Ambassador himself might very well bring this matter to the attention of Mr. Stevenson. Alternatively, he suggested that the Consul General of the Union in New York or their representative to the United Nations might bring this to the attention of Mr. Stevenson.

Ambassador Du Plessis said he thought the Consul General in New York lacked sufficient rank to act in such a matter and likewise the representative to the United Nations where their representation is at a minimum. He also did not wish to approach Mr. Stevenson personally and suggested that possibly some friend of Mr. Stevenson could be approached who would bring this to his attention.

Mr. Murphy said he would consider the matter.[4]

---

[3] Despatch 280 from Pretoria, May 9, reported on Stevenson's visit to South Africa in May 1955. (*Ibid.*, 032–Stevenson, Adlai/5–955)

[4] Rountree met with Stevenson's Executive Assistant, William Blair, on May 15. According to a memorandum for the record by Staff Assistant Eric Oulashin, Rountree stressed the importance of good relations with South Africa. Blair replied that Stevenson did not plan to make speeches and probably would minimize press contacts. (*Ibid.*, 611.45A/5–1557) Stevenson arrived in South Africa on June 5. Despatch 56 from Cape Town, June 18, reported that he held several press conferences and that the South African Government was displeased with his public criticism of its policies. (*Ibid.*, 032–Stevenson, Adlai/6–1857)

317. Memorandum From the Deputy Director of the Office of Southern Africa Affairs (LaMont) to the Deputy Assistant Secretary of State for African Affairs (Palmer)[1]

Washington, May 16, 1957.

SUBJECT

Embassy Pretoria Staff Studies of South Africa's Racial Problem

I. Embassy Pretoria despatch number 291 of April 11, 1957,[2] finds "that the condition of race relations in South Africa is not a remote danger to be dealt with a few years hence, but a *real and vital one today*, in that unless measures are taken *now* to check or reverse the presently accelerated trends, the forces in motion leading in the direction of crisis may soon push beyond human control".

Embassy Recommendations as to What the United States Can Do To Arrest These Trends:

1. Embassy officers are to act as individual propagandists to stress the practical "danger of detrimental race relations for South Africans" and to suggest four "constructive" approaches; viz., more inter-racial contacts, better non-White living standards, more professional and other opportunities for educated non-Whites, and the cultivation of more human attitudes toward non-Whites.
2. The exchanges program should be expanded and harmonized still more to the four approaches mentioned above. USIS should emphasize, principally from United States experience, the values of inter-racial contacts and of the other approaches mentioned above.

II. Embassy Pretoria despatch number 294 of April 12, 1957,[3] recommends that United States policy toward South Africa be based upon practical, realistic American national interests, not moral issues. "Let's reveal to the South Africans less of our humanitarian concern for people of color; let's talk less about injustice and immorality and more about what is happening in hard, cold terms as regards Black Nationalism and Communism, and the White man in Africa. South African Nationalists will still argue that they know best how to control such developments, but many are much less convinced of the practical benefits of their policies than they are of the high rectitude of their purpose."

---

[1] Source: Department of State, Central Files, 845A.411/5–1657. Secret. Drafted by William M. Johnson.

[2] Document 313.

[3] Document 314.

Embassy Recommendations:

I. "In surveying the normal instruments at our disposal for the exercising of influence on a foreign country, it is clear that we have few available in respect to South Africa . . . [4] I suggest that in our efforts to persuade the South Africans to our way of thinking we make use of unpublished approaches through diplomatic channels"; i.e., approaches to South African officials in Pretoria, Washington, and elsewhere, and possible cooperation with other Governments.

II. In considering carrot/threat gambits, the Embassy suggests the following possibilities: alteration of the gold price, non-renewal of the uranium contracts, withholding of United States defense commitments to South Africa, and advice to American investors.

AFS Comment:

1. AFS concurs in the recommendation that Embassy officers seize every worthwhile and judicious opportunity to influence South African Whites to moderate their racial views and policies. It feels that nothing less is acceptable. This practice has been in effect in the past and should be pursued as vigorously as possible without becoming counter-productive.

In 1953, Ambassador W. J. Gallman wrote about this practice as follows (Cape Town despatch number 57 of August 13, 1953 [5]): "Awareness among natives of their present mean way of life and a desire for an ampler one will, however, grow day by day, and no opportunity should be lost to encourage those who recognize the trend, in their efforts to spread the light. My staff and I are trying quietly and unobtrusively to do this." Again discussing the need for a "material amelioration in race relations in South Africa", Ambassador Gallman wrote in the same despatch:

[Here follow extracts from paragraphs 5–7 of despatch 57.]

2. AFS agrees that the exchanges program should be expanded and that USIS can afford to portray somewhat more boldly the progress of the Negro in the United States, without over-emphasizing those aspects of inter-racial association in the United States which might persuade the Union Government to curb the program.

3. AFS will give consideration to the advisability of making "approaches through diplomatic channels" on this matter to South African officials outside the Union, though it has some doubts about the efficacy of this means and wonders if the Embassy feels that a multiplication of American Ambassadors in a number of foreign posts can make the desired point better than one.

---

[4] Ellipsis in the source text.

[5] See *Foreign Relations*, 1952–1954, vol. XI, Part 2, p. 1002.

4. AFS does not feel that the position of the United States with respect to the carrots/threats mentioned above (gold price, uranium contracts, defense commitments, and advice to American investors regarding the stability of the South African situation) is strong enough to utilize with any reasonable hope of accomplishing the purpose intended.

---

318. Telegram From the Embassy in South Africa to the Department of State[1]

Pretoria, July 12, 1957—10 a.m.

11. In preparing position papers for twelfth UNGA on South African items, Department will doubtless give consideration measures US might take, without sacrifice essential principles, to encourage Union return full participation in UN. I assume Department agrees such return would be in interest US, UN and Western world. I also assume Department agrees that US past actions in UN on South African issues, however justifiable, have not produced benefits for groups subjected to Union Government's policies or any softening in government or public attitudes in Union.[2] In circumstance, problem is to encourage Union to reconsider its relations with UN, and to open door to more constructive approach to issues of Southwest Africa, Apartheid, and Indians in South Africa.

Of these issues, Southwest Africa undoubtedly attracts little or no domestic interest in United States and little public interest elsewhere. As gesture our part, could not US retire gracefully from committee on Southwest Africa on which it has served since inception in 1953?

Also, if US should seek obtain moratorium on fruitless UN discussion of other items, perhaps by accepting Union's contention as to "domestic affairs", opportunity for indirect influence by the US on Union Government might be improved. Regardless of pessimism about possibility changing direction of present government's racial policy, effecting such change should remain primary objective of US

---

[1] Source: Department of State, Central Files, 845A.411/7–1257. Confidential.

[2] Byroade met with Walter N. Walmsley in Washington on June 18. The Ambassador related the South African view that the United States had gone farther than it had to in the United Nations on the issues of apartheid and Indian settlers. (Memorandum of conversation by Walmsley; *ibid.*, IO/ODA Files: Lot 62 D 225, South Africa)

policy and thus any means that will increase this government's receptivity to US influence would seem to warrant full exploration.

If Department disposed consider possibility (1) withdrawal from SWA Committee and (2) exertion efforts for moratorium, opportunity might be provided undertake explorations with government here of possible compromises to facilitate return UN, such as submission reports SWA, etc. Instructions in some such connection would be welcome.

It is not our purpose suggest any appearance of US support for racial policies of the Union (this could of course be made clear by our delegation in agenda committee or Assembly debate) but rather that we face up to fact UN discussion these matters under present circumstances accomplishes no good (in fact some harm, in stirring resentment and inter-racial feeling here). Suggest Department explore carefully whether this loss is in fact balanced by positive gain with other nations from our continued support for inclusion items on agenda and voting position.

Byroade

---

319. Memorandum From the Counselor of the Embassy in South Africa (Maddox) to the Ambassador (Byroade) [1]

Pretoria, July 19, 1957.

SUBJECT

Conversation on U.S.-South African Relations with Dr. W.C. Naude, [2] Undersecretary for External Affairs

[1] Source: Department of State, Central Files, 111.45A/7–2557. Confidential. Enclosure to despatch 24 from Pretoria, July 25.

[2] Willem Christiana Naudé was the senior official in the South African Department of External Affairs.

OCCASIONS

(1) On July 17, in Dr. Naude's office, in the course of a courtesy call to introduce Drs. Campbell and Karis [3] of the Embassy staff, and Dr. Baum [4] of the Department of State

The following points of possible interest emerged from our conversation on the first of the two indicated occasions.

(a) On the subject of the United Nations, Naude expressed regret that South Africa's position, especially with respect to "domestic issues," was not better understood in the United States. He wondered how we would feel if the positions were reversed. I pointed out that we were generally disposed not to oppose the insertion for open discussion of an item on the agenda if it had international interest, even if we thought the UN had no powers with respect thereto. He admitted that, but thought that if the U.S. Government acquiesced in the discussion of, say, U.S. race relations, there would be a terrific hue and cry in the country (U.S.) generally. Dr. Campbell suggested that U.S. delegations had tried to steer a middle course on South African questions; if, for instance, we came out positively in support of South Africa, there would be public criticism within the U.S., and South Africa might become an issue in U.S. domestic politics, which would not be good.

I expressed the personal view that the U.S. Government would like to be helpful in getting South African delegations back into the UN, and wondered whether something could be worked out. Would South Africa, for instance, be willing to make some gesture, say, in regard to the South West Africa issue? We both recalled the negotiations of several years ago which came to nought. Would it be worth while to get our heads together informally on the South West question and see if we could come up with a solution which might be acceptable to our respective Governments. Naude seemed to like the idea and said he would like to talk about it again.

(b) Naude referred to the criticisms of South African racial policies in the United States, mentioning Mrs. Bolton [5] among others. He understood why Afro-Asiatic delegations in the UN struck out at his country but why did the United States have to do so? We in the West had to stand together. I remarked that Americans wanted to be friendly but, while trying to understand and to be sympathetic,

[3] Waldemar B. Campbell and Thomas G. Karis had recently been assigned to Pretoria as Second Secretaries.

[4] Robert D. Baum, chief of the African branch of the Division of Research for Near East, South Asia, and Africa.

[5] Representative Frances P. Bolton was the ranking minority member of the Subcommittee on the Near East and Africa of the Committee on Foreign Affairs of the House of Representatives. She had recently led a Special Study Mission to Africa. (House Report No. 307, Washington: Government Printing Office, 1957)

certain things like some of the recent legislation just rubbed the wrong way. I then suggested, half jokingly, that maybe a year ago we should have talked of a two-way moratorium; a moratorium on discriminatory native legislation, in return for a moratorium on discussions in the United Nations. Naude replied in respect to the legislation, "What you call pin-pricking".

Just before our departure, Naude referred to the esteem in which South Africans held the United States and emphasized his point by a story to the effect that once when (I don't know how recently) a senior External Affairs official wanted a decision on something we had requested, all the Cabinet Ministers were out of town. The official managed to locate one in the Free State and started to explain the matter over the phone. The Minister, he said, cut him off with, "Don't bother to explain. If the United States wants it, that's enough. We'll go along with it."

In the evening discussion referred to, Naude again raised the subject of U.S.-South African relations, stressing what he said was the unfortunate impression created among South Africans by American criticism and lack of American understanding. He then represented (very well, I thought) the orthodox historical and teleological justification for apartheid. I suggested that while there was much to be said for the strict, vertical, territorial theory of apartheid, it had very little to do with current realities of policy and practice. The Tomlinson Report,[6] which was an effort to blueprint territorial apartheid, seemed to have little chance of being implemented, and, even so, it still left 6 million non-Europeans in white areas in the year 2000. Another External Affairs officer present referred to the different social ratios in South Africa and the United States—the problems were utterly different. I mentioned that before coming to South Africa I had been in the British West Indies where the ratio was not 5 to 1 against the whites, but 10 to 1, and in some cases 20 to 1. And yet a mutual adjustment was being made, without any serious threat to Western civilization, the white community, and, except in rare cases, to "racial purity". Along with the other American officers present, I spoke of "human dignity", the desirability of establishing a different "direction" of policy, (but no one expected full equality or complete abolition of segregation) the need to grant concessions to win over the educated leaders, etc.

While our remarks were friendly, but critical, Naude seemed a little taken back. At one point he said, "If this is the way the American Embassy feels, then I can imagine the kind of report you send back to Washington." And then, reverting to the theme of the importance of friendly relations between our two countries, he

[6] See footnote 4, Document 10.

asked, "What is your Government trying to do down here? What does it want from us, what does it expect us to do?" My reply, ducking the question, was something to this effect, "Alright, let us forget about moral questions, who is right and who is wrong. As Americans, we realize the importance of western civilization, and of White leadership and control, remaining in South Africa. We sympathize with you in your problems and we want to remain friends. At the same time, we have a stake in your stability and in the spread of repercussions to other parts of Africa. To put it simply, we disagree that the measures you are taking will lead to a healthy social order. To some of us, they seem to spell trouble—and that would not be in our interest."

And then, he asked, "Have you put this to any of the Ministers this way?" I said that to some extent we had. (I might have added we hoped to do more.)

On departure, Naude's last remark was, "Now if your Government really had to choose between South Africa and India, which would it be?" My only reply was that I hoped we wouldn't have to make a choice.

William P. Maddox

---

320. Editorial Note

The Chairman of the Fourth Committee of the General Assembly submitted a draft resolution on October 8 to establish a Good Offices Committee on South West Africa (U.N. doc. A/3701). Both the United States and the United Kingdom were to be represented on the Committee with the third member to be nominated by the President of the Twelfth Session of the General Assembly. This was the basis of General Assembly Resolution 1143(XII), adopted on October 25 by a vote of 50 (including the United States) to 10, with 17 abstentions. The Committee was "to discuss with the Government of the Union of South Africa a basis for an agreement which would continue to accord to the Territory of South West Africa an international status". The Committee was requested to submit a report to the next session of the General Assembly "on its activities for examination and decision by the Assembly in accordance with the Charter of the United Nations". On November 1, Sir Leslie Munro designated the Brazilian Ambassador to Cuba, Vasco T.

Leitao da Cunha, as the third member. He joined Walter N. Walmsley of the United States and the British Governor General of Ghana, Sir Charles Noble Arden-Clarke. At first it seemed that some negotiations might be possible, but then the Second Secretary of the South African Embassy informed representatives of the Office of Southern Africa Affairs on December 10 that Louw apparently intended to "drag his feet" instead of offering firm support. (Memorandum of conversation by Richard D. Forster; Department of State, Central Files, 320.5745X/12–1057) See *Yearbook of the United Nations 1957*, pages 307–314.

---

321. Telegram From the Mission at the United Nations to the Department of State [1]

New York, November 20, 1957—4 p.m.

Delga 453. For Secretary from GADel. Re apartheid. As GA each year discusses problem racial segregation in South Africa, I find it increasingly difficult justify our position abstention. [2] Declaring as we so often do our belief in moral principles and necessity support Charter, our inability join others this issue has effect confirming suspicion many African and Asian members UN that on racial and colonial issues we have different standards in judging problems white and non-white peoples. Fortunately this year our stand could in part be mitigated by pointing to our responsibilities on South West Africa Good Offices Comite.

This question taken up by del before and after consideration in Special Political Comite, del is firmly convinced that if we mean what we say on racial segregation we should be more forthright in our stand in UN. Del recommends US revise policy on apartheid before next year with view to supporting moderate resolution critical South African policy this issue for following reasons:

(1) "Yes" vote on moderate resolution critical of apartheid is most consistent with US beliefs, traditions and law. Ethical position US before world rests on bedrock human rights and civil liberties,

---

[1] Source: Department of State, Central Files, 845A.411/11–2057. Confidential.

[2] Telegram 398 to USUN, October 31, instructed the delegation to abstain on the apartheid resolution then under consideration by the Special Political Committee on the Question of Race Conflict in South Africa. (*Ibid.*, 845A.411/10–3157) The draft resolution was adopted on November 4 by a vote of 59 to 5, with 10 abstentions.

and it is our interest maintain best possible posture on racial questions before UN.

(2) Department's policy abstaining on apartheid was set before Supreme Court's decision to effect segregation in education was necessarily discriminatory,[3] before new civil rights legislation, and before President's decision use troops to enforce decisions Federal Court in Little Rock.[4] These developments make it even more important we express ourselves positively on racial issues.

(3) Apartheid arouses strong feelings particularly among peoples of colonial backgrounds. Our abstention regarded by them in simplest terms as meaning we have one standard for white and another for colored races. It will not help us when next we seek Afro-Asian support on US-Soviet issues involving human rights and freedoms.

(4) Regardless our feelings on desirability apartheid issue being placed before UN, fact is it probably will continue to be and resolution critical of South Africa's apartheid policies will be put forward. Indians and Pakistanis themselves kept resolution remarkably moderate this year, but because of our known policy of abstention US Del was unable to exert any influence on it. We were not even shown copy until it was introduced. Ability to vote "yes" on resolution along lines of one this year would enable US Del in future to assure UN action remains moderate and in proper perspective.

View these considerations US Del urges reconsideration at high level of our present position on apartheid.[5]

Lodge

[3] Reference is to the Supreme Court's decision of May 17, 1954, in the case of *Brown v. Board of Education of Topeka.*

[4] President Eisenhower sent Federal troops to Little Rock Arkansas, in September 1957.

[5] The United States was one of 14 nations abstaining on November 26 when the General Assembly adopted Resolution 1178(XII) by a vote of 59 to 6. The General Assembly thereby appealed to the Union Government "to revise its policy in the light of" the purposes and principles "enshrined in the Charter of the United Nations" and in response to world opinion. See *Yearbook of the United Nations 1957*, pp. 98–102.

322. Memorandum From the Counselor of the Embassy in South Africa (Maddox) to the Deputy Assistant Secretary of State for African Affairs (Palmer)[1]

Washington, December 18, 1957.

SUBJECT

U.S. Position on Apartheid

REF

Delga 453, November 20, 1957[2]

I have taken the liberty of jotting down some comments on GADel's recommendation to the Secretary for a high-level reconsideration of our position in the UN on apartheid resolutions:

1. Racial segregation represents a violation of only *one* phase of "bedrock human rights and civil liberties". Obviously we must take our stand on the side of this bedrock principle, and support any reasonable resolution of general applicability. But if we start supporting resolutions directed at specific countries charging violation of this "right" or that "liberty" (in any political, religious, economic or social field), we can be drawn into endless controversies with governments failing to meet ideal standards, and these governments include some in the Afro-Asiatic bloc.

2. Even if we extract the "racial" violation from its general context of rights and liberties, it would be difficult to establish South Africa as the only country in the world where, in some form or another, or by one authority or another, segregation is sanctioned. A resolution of general applicability is certainly unobjectionable, but the singling out of one country among 80-odd is a very doubtful bit of justice.

3. In this respect, we ourselves are not without fault. For although segregation is contrary to the law and policy of our national government, we remain internationally responsible under the Human Rights Charter for the delinquencies of state and local governments.

4. Moreover, it can be argued with some cogency by South Africa that its official position is one of moving towards territorial

[1] Source: Department of State, AF/AFS Files: Lot 60 D 37. Confidential. Maddox was in Washington for consultation.

[2] *Supra*. A copy of the telegram had been sent to Ambassador Byroade on December 10. Ferguson indicated, in a covering letter, that AFS would continue to oppose a change in the U.S. voting pattern on apartheid "so long as the present apparent shift in Union policy continues to offer hope of the Union's eventual return to full participation in the UN." (Department of State, Central Files, 845A.411/11–2057)

autonomy for non-Whites. Those non-Whites who remain in White areas are officially regarded as temporary visitors, admittedly in an inferior status (what about Mexican migratory workers?), but eligible at any time to return to their respective, eventually-autonomous, native territories. While it may be argued that this policy results practically in discrimination, we might better concern ourselves in the UN with official national policies than with specific local practices, whether they be in the Transvaal or Arkansas.

5. As for the recent developments in the United States cited in (2) in reference telegram, these represent, not something new in our basic constitutional principles, but a specific interpretation by the Supreme Court, specific legislation under a constitutional authorization, and a specific action by the President. The basic principle of equal rights has been established since the Civil War. If it took us nearly a century to develop these specific interpretations and actions, we might be charitable towards a Government which has existed less than half a century, and has, therefore, had much less time to evolve policies. If we insist on immediate action, we will get nothing; if we are patient, we can envisage the possibility of a slow evolution: Note, for instance, the recent reception in South Africa of an official Ghanaian delegate.

6. If our purpose be to obtain an alteration in South African policies, I can see little prospect of this being achieved through repeated public denunciations in the UN. South African white attitudes, regardless of party, are hardened by organized outside criticism. Modification in attitudes and policies will come, if at all, through forces working from within; we can influence these through various subtle devices, but not, I believe, through associating ourselves with Afro-Asiatic censure.

7. A resolution supported only by the Afro-Asians would not be seriously resented in South Africa. They expect denunciation from these sources. But the votes of western delegations are closely scrutinized and will determine whether South Africa returns actively to the UN, or withdraws completely. See Embassy Pretoria Despatch Number 118 of October 1, 1957,[3] citing External Affairs Minister Louw's public statement on the matter. Louw was able to cite a slight improvement in western dispositions towards South Africa this year. Should the United States change from abstention to support of a resolution condemning South Africa apartheid, it would be a serious blow undercutting the trend towards full resumption and probably influencing a decision to withdraw from the UN entirely.

---

[3] Not printed. (*Ibid.*, 310.345A/10–157)

8. I wonder whether we would gain a sufficient measure of transitory advantage with the Afro-Asians to offset the complete loss of one western voice and vote in the UN.

9. In resources, industrial capacity, managerial competence and technological abilities, South Africa is the most advanced country on the African continent. It would seem desirable from the standpoint of U.S. interests that we seek to work patiently with South Africa to obtain a modification of its racial attitudes rather than to reject her too hastily. The impact of what could happen in South Africa would be felt throughout the continent and would adversely affect our position, negating any temporary advantage we might gain now from voting with the Afro-Asians.

Index